THE ANCIENT

FOUNDATIONS

*The literature of Greece and Rome. Included is a section on
the literature of the East.*

ROBERT WARNOCK   *The University of Connecticut*

GEORGE K. ANDERSON   *Brown University*

BOOK ONE *of* THE WORLD IN LITERATURE

SCOTT, FORESMAN AND COMPANY

Chicago   Atlanta   Dallas   Palo Alto   Fair Lawn, N.J.

THE ANCIENT FOUNDATIONS, *the first of a four-book series which includes* CENTURIES OF TRANSITION, TRADITION AND REVOLT, *and* OUR HUNDRED YEARS, *presents against a background of cultural history the literary masters of Greece and Rome and of the Ancient East.*

The authors wish to express their deep appreciation to the following friends for their kindness in reading this manuscript and offering valuable suggestions for improving it: for China, Professor Shau Wing Chan, of Stanford University; for India, Dr. Horace Poleman, cultural attaché of the American embassy in India; for the Hebrews, Rabbi Maurice Zigmond, of Harvard University; for Greece, Professor James Notopoulos, of Trinity College; and for Rome, Dr. Annarie Cazel, of the University of Connecticut. The authors wish also to acknowledge the courtesy of the publishers who have granted permission to reprint selections in copyright. Specific acknowledgment of these publishers is given on the pages where the selections appear.

CONTENTS

The selections listed in the table are complete except where superior letters appear: ^A indicates very long works of necessity abridged (with a preservation of the scope and continuity of the whole); ^s indicates representative selection. A few negligible deletions are indicated in the text.

CHAPTER TWO   GREECE AND THE BIRTH OF
THE WEST

900 B.C. TO 300 B.C.

CHAPTER THREE   THE WEST UNDER ROMAN SWAY

300 B.C. TO 200 A.D.

v

(The Table of Contents carries the translators' names for those longer works where the translation used is of particular significance. Footnotes within the text furnish a complete list of translators.)

List of Illustrations

THE ANCIENT FOUNDATIONS

ON *the general approach of this book*
and its beginning with

THE

ANCIENT EAST

Literature is in part an abiding source of beauty and entertainment for all civilized men, and in part a record of the ideas and customs, the special visions and feelings, of the people who have created it. We realize this especially when we turn from writers of our own time to the great books of the past, produced in cultures very different from our own. In reading them, we soon discover that we must learn about the nations and times that gave us those books if we are to respond to their appeal and grasp their full significance. Great art is timeless in the sense that it speaks to men of all times, but it is of its own time too and speaks to us fully only if we know something of the age that shaped it. It tells us about our past as it tells us about ourselves, and through a poem or an essay we live vicariously the life of another era as well as the life of another man. Art is not produced in a vacuum, but in the minds and souls of men in close touch with the ideas and habits of their day. In so far as they felt love and anger, religious sentiment and patriotic fervor, they were human beings like ourselves, speaking a universal tongue. But conflict springs from changing issues; divinity may be envisioned and worshiped in numerous ways; and love has taken many forms in different lands and eras. Only through knowing the background of a great book can we translate the emotions and ideas embodied in it into terms close to our own. Only then can it give us the full measure of that enjoyment for which the author wrote it in the first place.

So knowing and understanding the great books of all time will lead us in several directions at once— to pleasure in the experiences of minds more creative than our own, to an awareness of the objectives and forms of literary art that we can apply to other books to come, to a knowledge of the evolution of human culture as great writers have unconsciously chronicled it, to a contact with ideas of long standing that will be new to us and will help us to gain more understanding of ourselves and the world in which we live. Such contact will free us from provincialism in the realm of ideas and give us a sympathy and respect for points of view that are no less worthy for seeming at first foreign and strange. It will also help us to discover unexpected likenesses in ages far apart and give us a warm sense of the kinship of the whole human race.

Our point of view in The World in Literature is international. It breaks through the barriers of language by means of translation—an imperfect medium, it is true, but the only avenue for the average reader to literature in many tongues. Our point of view is eclectic. It seeks an unprejudiced acquaintance with the contributions of many lands and epochs to the complete picture of human culture. It might concentrate entirely on the *periods* of world literature— the total of social, intellectual, and aesthetic traits that give each age its special character. Or it might emphasize the literary *movements* in world history —the "isms" that have allied groups of writers with each other and sometimes set them apart in warring camps. It might see literature in terms of the *nations* that have produced it and the special qualities of each national culture. Or it might present the great books in terms of the great *men* whose minds created them—a parade of titans from Homer to the present day. Each of these four approaches forms part of our eclectic point of view.

More importantly, we set out with two complementary convictions in mind: Through the ages each great nation and each era has had its special role to play and has stamped its special contributions with its own idiosyncrasies. But no one nation and no one age is chiefly responsible for human culture as we know it today.

Since we begin with the most distant past and the nations most remote from us, the problem of understanding may seem very complex at the start. Yet our century has gone far to reduce the distance between the East and West. The airplane links us in a matter of hours. Modern wars have brought conflicts and alliances between the nations of Asia and the Occident; political differences between East and West fade as monarchy, democracy, and communism exist side by side in both areas. But the intellectual gulf is still wide, and the manners and customs of the East often seem bizarre to us. Oriental literature has exotic qualities that will startle the new reader but should challenge him to search out its wisdom and charm.

Civilization in the East was already old when the first Europeans rose out of barbarism. Sumeria around 4500 B.C., Egypt five hundred years later,

Babylonia and Assyria about 2100 B.C.—all reached cultural maturity centuries before the Greeks appeared as the first great civilized nation in the West. Their contributions were to converge on the rising Greeks and to become the solid foundation from which Western culture evolved. But all of those ancient nations had lost their power by the time of Christ and, except for the Egyptians, had been assimilated in later peoples.

Three other great nations of the ancient East—the Chinese, the Hindus, and the Hebrews—escaped that fate and have survived to our day with national and religious ideals substantially unchanged for twenty-five centuries. All three are now engaged in a desperate struggle for survival and adjustment to a modern age. They are the patriarchs among us, as they are also the newest children in the political family of nations.

The experiences of the Chinese and the Hindus have marked similarities, but the tragic experience of the Hebrews is unique. China and India have each known an almost changeless civilization during two thousand years, securely based on a national religion and an ethical code that reflect a national soul at peace with itself. Even the challenge of foreign religions—Buddhism in China and Mohammedanism in India—has not upset the basic pattern. Both nations have lived self-contained lives with little curiosity about the lands beyond their borders, except in commerce, but both have been exploited for the past four hundred years by more aggressive peoples from the West. Both hold immense lands which are still too small to support their vast populations. As a result both face bewildering problems of adjustment in the twentieth century.

Yet there are differences too. The Hindu is an extreme mystic, the Chinese an intensely practical thinker. The Hindu's caste system has long supported the aristocratic principle in Indian society, whereas the democratic tradition has always been strong in China, even through centuries of monarchy. Of all peoples the Hindus are most lacking in a sense of time, so that even the major events in Indian history are sometimes difficult to date. The Chinese, on the other hand, have a meticulous interest in chronology and consider history the most honorable form of literature. The greatest Indian poetry is narrative, especially epic; the Chinese poets have best expressed themselves in lyrics.

Hebrew history, too, is oriented by a national religion. It has been the one sure rock in the tempestuous chronicle of the Jews' struggle for survival. Through centuries of wandering and persecution, the Jews have clung to their faith for its golden promise of a better day. As their faith has served a different purpose in their national life, so it is different from the religions of China and India.

Whereas Confucianism and Hinduism in their loftiest development are as much philosophy as religion in their metaphysics, ethical systems, and social and political theories, Judaism is more narrowly a religion, dedicated to the worship of one God and to ordering the lives of His people with laws and prescriptions. While Confucianism and Hinduism remain essentially Eastern philosophies, the close spiritual ties between Judaism and Christianity place the Hebrews within the Western tradition. Indeed, the Hebraic tradition underlies the religion of the West, specifically in its holy books, more profoundly in its ethical outlook. The whole Biblical history of the Hebrews was grafted onto the Christian canon, to give background to the new religion and to amplify the personality of God, in his diverse moods of wrath and of love. From the Hebrews came monotheism as we know it in the West. Unlike the Chinese and the Hindus, the Jews have lived in close, indeed enforced, contact with other peoples and have been influenced by alien cultures to such an extent that today they are divided from each other by the barriers of language and custom in the many lands where they have settled. Their literature cuts into

A jade carving of Shou Lao, Chinese God of Longevity, symbolic of the antiquity of the civilization of the East. Ming dynasty sculpture.

the literary history of these many lands, and, except where it is anchored in the national religion, it is diverse and cosmopolitan.

Yet all three of these nations are dynamic forces in the world of our day; all three seem on the verge of a new life and a new influence in the world of the future. This chapter will try to show the ideals that have preserved their culture through so many centuries of the past and the literary art with which their great masters expressed those ideals.

CHINA

FOR more than two centuries we in the West have been gradually discovering the great culture and literature of China. Translation has come slowly, and her religious teachers and philosophers have reached us well before her poets. Only in our own century have the beauty and charm of her literature been revealed in English. To those who meet them for the first time, Li Po and Tu Fu in their poetry open a new world of enjoyment—a delicate, fragile world of bamboo and jade, yet inhabited by intensely human fellows and rollicking companions. As Confucius points to a sensible way of life, the two poets show us how to enjoy it with gusto. No others could represent the Chinese to us so well as these three master spirits.

The placid, cultured Chinese have inhabited for more than five thousand years a large area in eastern Asia roughly half the size of the United States. A kind of civilization flourished there at least fifteen thousand years before the Christian era, and reliable Chinese history extends back to 2200 B.C., many centuries before Europe emerged from barbarism. The great antiquity of Chinese culture, then, places it close to the very ancient civilizations of the Egyptians and Sumerians.

From early times the huge population of China, now about four times our own, has been divided into two rather distinct groups by the great Yangtze River, which flows from the rugged mountains of Tibet in the west through a fertile central plain into the East China Sea. The people to the north of the Yangtze, molded by a temperate climate, are tall, healthy children of the soil, robust in physique and mental outlook. From these hardy folk have come all the native dynasties of Chinese emperors. The people of the south, on the contrary, are physically small and soft, disposed by their warm, relaxing climate to enjoy easy comforts and artistic luxuries. Peaceful and even timid by nature, they have submitted for centuries to the rule of their northern brothers, but have excelled in their turn as shrewd merchants and traders. However, both north and south have contributed their share to the national philosophy, literature, and art, so that we are more impressed today by the homogeneity of Chinese culture in a population so vast than by the sectional differences in language and temperament.

Even more striking than this national uniformity is the remarkable stability of Chinese culture for the past two thousand years. Not only has there been no break in cultural tradition comparable to our Dark Ages, but actually no important change—no permanent revolutions in government from democracy to despotism, no great shift in social organization, no change in general philosophy from religious mysticism to scientific materialism, no wars between opposed schools of art. Struggle and change, for good or ill, are at the core of our Western tradition, but the complacent, conservative Chinese, satisfied with his pattern of life, has gone his accustomed way since the time of Confucius in the fifth century B.C. down to the Communist revolution of our day.

Of course, there have been periodic civil wars and invasions. In the third century B.C. the notorious Ch'in dynasty tried to submerge the Chinese democratic tradition in a unified state under despotic control, but after the Ch'in emperor had built the Great Wall to keep out Mongolian enemies from the north and burned the books of China to destroy intellectual enemies from within, he was paid for his ruthless efficiency by the destruction of his dynasty shortly after his death. The placid sanity of old China reasserted itself and digested this upstart as it has absorbed many a would-be conqueror in its long history. Only in our own century has the invasion of foreign ideas and political systems brought great changes in Chinese life, at first a pale imitation of Western democracy, now an Oriental version of communism. But in the long run it seems likely that the Chinese will assimilate these ideas also without losing their essential point of view.

The Chinese measure their long history by imperial dynasties, of which there were twenty-two between 2205 B.C., the dawn of authentic history, and 1911 A.D., the year in which China became a republic. For the outsider seeking to understand Chinese character and literature, two of these dynasties have a special interest. The Chou dynasty (1122–249 B.C.), the period of feudalism, saw the first flowering of Chinese culture, which reached its peak in the sixth and fifth centuries B.C., when China's two great philosophers, Lao-Tzŭ and Confucius, were establishing her rival religions. To the T'ang dynasty (618–906 A.D.), on the other hand,

"*Lao-Tzŭ Delivering the Tao Teh Ching*," *a rare example of the work of the Sung dynasty painter, Li Lung-Mien (1070–1106). The silk scroll on which it is painted also contains the whole Tao Teh Ching, copied by a famous calligrapher of the Sung period. Courtesy of Mrs. Agnes E. Meyer.*

belong China's greatest poets, Tu Fu and Li Po, and they are only the best-known names in this Golden Age. These two dynasties and these two groups of writers provide our key to the Chinese mind.

CHINESE PHILOSOPHY AND CHARACTER. The antagonism of China's two great religions, Taoism and Confucianism, is supposed to date from a meeting of their rival founders, Lao-Tzŭ and Confucius, toward the end of the sixth century B.C. According to tradition, Lao-Tzŭ rebuked Confucius for devoting himself to the mere forms and ceremonies of social life instead of concentrating on the higher meaning of the universe. False though the story may be, it suggests the essential difference between the two great schools of thought in China. Taoism represents Chinese mysticism, the search for a unifying principle in the universe beyond the diverse activities of practical life. Confucianism concentrates on everyday reality and instead of speculating about the infinite and eternal, sets as its goal a moral, well-regulated society on earth.

The holy Book of Tao (Tao Teh Ching), which was long ascribed to Lao-Tzŭ himself, teaches that man is part of a unified and harmonious universe governed by one eternal principle (or Tao). Caught up in the infinite flow of this great unity, man should not strive for position and power in the world of affairs. His happiness lies in the simple life, close to fundamental things. His behavior should be guided by the policy of *inaction*. "Do nothing, and all things will be done," said Lao-Tzŭ; and his great disciple, Chuang-Tzŭ, added: "Pay no attention to time, nor to right and wrong. Move into the absolute Tao, and find your peace there." He was indifferent to right and wrong because in the great Tao there is no difference between them. There are not two poles, positive and negative, but only one pole, the Tao—the origin and end of everything. Like a true mystic, Lao-Tzŭ scorned the idea of defining his unifying principle. "Those who know do not tell," he said, "and those who tell do not know." Since it is the one reality, it cannot by its very nature be defined in practical terms. The meaning of the great Tao has to be accepted on faith and understood only as it is felt.

Although the typical Chinese is far from a mystic at heart, he shows in his daily life and general outlook the strong influence of Taoism. He believes in the passive way of life and is amazed by the restless activity of the Westerner. He is still a farmer by occupation, leading a simple life close to the soil. He is skeptical of the machine age and its promise of a superior standard of living. He is content with what he has and is more interested in being happy than in getting ahead. Whether or not he is at one with the great Tao, the Chinese is at peace with himself, and when he is oppressed by tyranny and injustice, he submits with patience. The modern leaders of China have found this ancient lethargy one of their most baffling problems in arousing the people to national defense, material development, and social change.

Confucius, too, taught a passive philosophy in his negative version of the Golden Rule: "Do not do unto others what you would not have them do unto you." But unlike Lao-Tzŭ, he prescribed it as a code for living in society, not apart from it. Confucius had only contempt for a philosophy that turned its back on everyday reality and devoted itself to contemplating the infinite. Although he did not disbelieve in the world of spirits, he considered it beyond man's knowledge and concentrated on establishing a moral order in human society.

The Taoists believed in the immortality of man's spirit within the great Tao. Confucius taught a more tangible immortality on earth. One lives, he argued, so long as one's memory lives in the minds of men. And since the average man cannot be widely remembered as is a great emperor or philosopher or poet, it is the responsibility of his family to keep his spirit alive. For Confucius, the family was the foundation of society, and it consisted not only of its living members but also of their ancestors. This belief perpetuated the ancient ancestor worship of the Chinese, so that the Confucian temple represents neither God nor angels nor saints on its walls, but rather the names of long-departed ancestors who still care for their clans but who need in turn the endless homage of each descendant. For them he performs elaborate rituals prescribed by Confucius. The death of a relative demanded an established period of mourning —three years for a parent, one for a paternal uncle, nine months for a cousin. Many a young Chinese poet had his career interrupted by the untimely death of a father or mother.

This ritual of Confucius was as much social as religious, and Confucianism itself is more a code of social ethics than a religion. As a historian, Confucius had developed a deep respect for China's ancient feudal system. As an intensely rational thinker, he wished to reëstablish such an orderly social system, which should be held together and constantly linked to the past by an elaborate ritual of courtesy and good manners, of piety and devotion to ancestors. To this code of ritual and rational morality he gave the name *Li*. He argued that if the rulers and officials of China would live and govern by this strict ethical code, their example would inspire the common people and produce a genuinely healthy, moral society.

In his charming *Analects*, a collection of the Master's sayings reverently remembered by his disciples, Confucius defined this social code in detail, explaining the behavior of the true gentleman, whose life is governed by reason and morality. The Confucian gentleman is bound down by duty and convention; he seems old before his time, and, unlike the ambitious American, he aspires to be inconspicuous and a dutiful member of his family. Aristotle in Greece,

Horace in Rome, and the thinkers of eighteenth-century France and England who preached the Golden Mean as their way of life, would have understood the rational ethic of Confucius. And many a thoughtful American, critical of his own system, will admire the quiet good sense and clear-eyed realism of the Confucian, and envy him the peace of mind that his rigid social code can bring.

Mencius, the brilliant disciple of Confucius, extended his master's teachings to a democratic scheme of government, founded upon the belief of Confucius that all men are born equal. Although the Chinese state was a semifeudal empire from its known beginnings until 1911 A.D., the sovereign, or Son of Heaven, was supposed to reign on his Dragon Throne only so long as his rule brought peace and prosperity to the people. Parliaments were unthinkable, because they would suggest a conflict between the sovereign and the people, as if he were not devoted to their good. But if he should prove untrue to his mission, it was the duty of the people to rebel in order to reëstablish the rational order. Chinese history is punctuated by such periodic rebellions, not against the system, but against effete regimes. It becomes easy to see how the Chinese could readily throw over their decadent empire in our century and accept a democratic system without dislocating their national life. We have still to see whether the same may not be true of the Communist order.

The teachings of Confucius are the basis of Chinese character. To this day the family rather than the state is the center of national life, and the Chinese gains his gentleness and quiet conservatism from submitting to the veneration of his ancestors. His sense of social order and courtesy spring from the formal ritual of Confucianism. Essentially unreligious by nature, he is more interested in the relationship of men to each other than to God. Like the ancient Greek, he is rather indifferent to a life in heaven and concentrates on enjoying a well-ordered life on this earth. Only when his experiences are unfortunate or he fears misfortune does he take refuge in Taoist mysticism. In the words of Lin Yutang, "all Chinese are Confucianists when successful, and Taoists when they are failures."

POETRY IN CHINESE LIFE. Although the Chinese are not fundamentally religious, they are certainly poets to the core. And in a sense, their poetry, by expressing their wonderment at the beauty and immensity of the natural world, has fulfilled their need of religion. The quantity of Chinese poetry is staggering, for it had been seriously composed for centuries even before Confucius compiled *The Book of Songs* in the fifth century B.C. Other types of imaginative literature were long frowned on by the Chinese and hence developed comparatively late— the drama in the eleventh century A.D. and the novel in the fourteenth century. The drama was considered the vulgar amusement of the common people and the novel the secret entertainment of one's private hours, but poetry was the pastime of all men of culture. Gentlemen customarily met together to drink wine and compete in writing verses. And every government official had to be a professional poet to gain his office.

To maintain his rational social order, Confucius had taught the duty of public service for all gentlemen. Eventually the bureaucratic system which evolved was implemented by a system of examinations, the earliest known civil service tests, by which a candidate could qualify for four official grades, poetically named Flowering Talent, Promoted Man, Entered Scholar, and member of the Forest of Pens (the Imperial Academy). These examinations were entirely literary and required a knowledge of the ancient classics and the technique of writing poetry. So the very government of China was founded on respect for poetic skill.

After the poet had passed his examinations, he was forbidden to take office in his own province, because of the danger of political corruption, and he was usually sent to a remote post for a long term of public service. Since poets all aspired to the gay, stimulating life of the court, they looked upon this enforced exile as a great hardship and wrote melancholy poems of dejection and farewell to their friends as they obeyed the call of duty.

Hence the typical poet's career had three stages, each with its cluster of poetic themes. First, he is the carefree youth reveling in the life of the capital. He spends his time drinking wine, writing poetry, and enjoying the company of his male friends. Except in the very ancient period, love poetry from a man to a woman is almost never found. Women had generally a restricted and inferior status in Chinese society, and marriages were arranged by the elders of two families. Consequently, Chinese poets pose in their poems, not as romantic lovers, but as devoted friends whose greatest happiness lies in an intellectual camaraderie in which women play no part. Friendship, not love, is the great theme of this first stage, with the joys of wine as a convivial accompaniment.

The second stage finds the poet exiled at a provincial post, far from his friends at the capital. Economic need has forced him to accept his new office, and his poems now bemoan his isolation from the mental stimulation, good fellowship, and joys of the city. The themes of farewell and eventual loneliness dominate this stage. After years of provincial service the poet finally saves enough money to retire from office, but it is now useless to return to the capital, where new coteries dominate the intellectual life. Instead he settles down on a small estate with his family and perhaps a friend or two to share his quiet happiness. By now he is resigned to his fate, and his themes in this last stage are the delights of middle age and the memories of his happy youth.

CHARACTERISTICS OF CHINESE POETRY. Although narrative verse is not unknown in China, the great poetry is lyric; but the art of the Chinese lyric is considerably different from our own. The Western lyric, from the ancient Greeks and the medieval troubadours to modern times, has been identified with music and the intense emotion conveyed by music. Hence it has tended to express the poet's state of mind directly, and to describe natural objects around him indirectly through figures of speech. Chinese poetry, on the contrary, is more closely linked to the art of painting. Working with visual rather than with abstract material, the Chinese poet restrains the expression of his emotion and lets the concrete things that he describes reflect his state of mind. The Chinese looks directly at his object—a cloud, a bird, a rainstorm, a rich gown—and describes it matter-of-factly with little poetic metaphor. But, like a painter, he chooses the appropriate objects to fit his mood and subtly implies a parallel between the state of nature and the state of his mind.

Perhaps this pictorial expression springs from the nature of the Chinese language, which is still a picture language without an alphabet. The original pictograph characters have been modified into "ideographs," but to this day a Chinese poem makes as great an appeal to the eye as to the ear. Subtle differences in the appearance of the characters suggest shades of thought that bewilder the translator. But the reader need not explore these technical problems to appreciate the delicate imagery and evocative power of Chinese poetry in translation.

INDIA

To a Western reader Indian literature is the embodiment of a philosophy and a way of life complementary to our own, with an appeal that has captured the fancy of a host of Americans and Englishmen. Hindu mysticism first became known to the West around 1800, when translations of India's dramas and holy books profoundly influenced the German Romantic poets Herder and Goethe and the German philosophers Schelling and Schopenhauer. Emerson was fascinated by the message of

Vedanta in nineteenth-century America, and today a group of English writers—Christopher Isherwood, Aldous Huxley, John van Druten—are carrying it to its widest public in the West. Ancient India may seem very remote from modern America, and yet many among us during this age of atomic science have sought peace of mind in its sweeping explanation of life.

Indian culture rivals Chinese in its antiquity. A primitive civilization flourished in the Indus Valley of northwestern India at least three thousand years before Christ. But modern Indian culture descends, not from the people of that civilization, but from warlike tribes which poured through the mountains to the northwest sometime between 2000 and 900 B.C., overran the Ganges Valley to the northeast, and finally conquered all of central and southern India except the extreme south. These invaders spoke the oldest known language in the so-called Aryan, or Indo-European, family, to which belong also most of the languages of Europe and America. The term Aryan has fallen into disrepute because Adolf Hitler and his followers, ignoring the mongrel composition of all modern peoples, notoriously misapplied the term to a nonexistent race, or family of races, which were mistakenly supposed to correspond to the kindred languages they spoke. This Indo-European language of India indicates, however, that the ancient invaders of the land had a common cultural origin with the other Aryan groups: Persian, Greek, Latin, Germanic, Slavic, and Celtic.

Actually India has never been a nation, but an amalgamation of many races held together by a common cultural tradition. The triangular peninsula in south-central Asia which they occupy has about the area of Europe (excluding Russia) and about half the area of the United States. On this subcontinent live at least four hundred million people (roughly three times the population of the United States), to whom as many as fifty million more may

Symbolic of the influence of the Himalayas on Indian religious art is this Hindu structure, Kailasa Temple at Ellora. A monolith carved from solid rock, it was dedicated to the Himalayan paradise of the god Siva. According to the Mahâbhârata *the Vedas were taught here first. Construction of the temple was begun in the middle of the eighth century* A.D.

now be added each decade. This mass of people has long been administratively organized into numerous provinces and states, each with its own government. Unlike China, then, India has never been a political unit, and the antagonism of these separate states has made her an easy prey to conquerors, from Alexander the Great to the Britisher, Robert Clive. With the withdrawal of the British in 1948 after two centuries of rule, India became two distinct countries divided by hostile religious faiths—Hindu India with three quarters of the population and Moslem Pakistan with less than a quarter of the population spread over two separate states in east and west.

The original invaders of India developed their Indo-European tongue into a highly complex language called Sanskrit, which was spoken only by the learned Brahman class that was descended from the conquerors. Sanskrit was softened into a new tongue, Pali, during the Buddhist era (fifth century B.C.—fifth century A.D.) and eventually was split into many dialects, of which Hindustani and Bengali are today the most important. The Mohammedan population uses its own language, Urdù, which is largely Hindustani written in Persian script, and the Indians of the extreme south still speak their own non-Indo-European tongues, which remind us of their aboriginal ancestors. But Sanskrit remains the most important language for the foreign student of Indian culture, because it has continued as the special language of the Brahman caste, the priests and professional men. It came to have the same kind of status that Church Latin has in Catholic countries today. Most of the great literature of India is in a form of the Sanskrit language.

THE CASTE SYSTEM. When the invading tribes conquered the aborigines of India, they developed there a social system of caste which was to solidify as the characteristic pattern of Indian society to the present day. Instead of exterminating the conquered people, as many ancient invaders did, they devised a scheme of segregating them forever as a social class forbidden to intermarry or even fraternize with other classes of society. Originally this system recognized four castes, which were fancifully linked to four parts of the body of the creator god, Brahma: the priest (or Brahman) caste, associated with the head; the warrior caste, associated with the arms; the farmer-merchant caste, associated with the body; and the laborer-servant caste (for the aborigines), associated with the feet. Through the ages these four castes have been subdivided into hundreds of subcastes for weavers, barbers, blacksmiths, and other trades, but the Brahman caste has remained at the top. This social system of India, with its religious foundation, is called *Hinduism*.

The many castes correspond somewhat to the guilds of our Middle Ages, but the rigidity and exclusiveness of the Hindu system is unique in history. Each Hindu is born into his caste and can never change his predetermined trade and social status. A member of one caste may not marry into another, nor even eat with members of other castes. For each caste there is a prescribed *dhárma,* or rule of conduct for each period and circumstance in life, originally codified in the so-called Code of Mánu, dating from about the first century A.D. Following this code scrupulously constitutes the good or religious life. This the hero Arjuna learns in our selection from the *Bhágávad-Gita* when he asks the god Krishna whether it is right for a warrior to kill. At the bottom of the social scale for centuries were the Untouchables, whose very touch (or even shadow) brought pollution to a Brahman. These tragic people, who constitute one fifth of India's population, were doomed by an accident of birth to live apart from decent society and to perform the menial tasks of life as sweepers and scavengers. Until very recent times they were forbidden to own land or even to enter a temple. But the new government of India has finally outlawed the stigma of untouchability.

HINDU RELIGION. The caste system merely applies to society the religious principles of Hinduism, more properly called the philosophy of Vedanta. In placing the Brahman priest at the top of the scale, it recognized religion as the supreme reality, for Hinduism is man's whole way of life. India is of all countries the most religious. No other *cf p. 3* nation has ever approached her in subordinating every activity in life to the operation of the spirit. Confucianism places man and his society at the center of the universe. Hinduism mystically reduces man to a fragment of spirit at the mercy of nature and the great Spirit behind it.

The incentive to such a view of life came from nature itself. When the ancient Aryans arrived in India, they were confronted by the grandest and most terrifying forces of nature on earth. The world's highest mountains, the Himaláyas, loomed to impassable heights in the north. The great plains below them were often devastated by the floods of long, unpredictable rivers; yet for over half the year the earth was parched by drought. In central India they found impenetrable jungles, from which wild beasts still slink forth at night to attack and kill the people. Frequent earthquakes would flatten their villages and destroy their crops in an instant, and pestilences might kill many thousands in a season. They found every extreme of climate from month-long snowfall in the north to moist tropical heat in the south. Nature in India has always been fierce and tyrannical. Hence the Aryans developed a religion of nature worship to personify these deadly, irrational forces and placate them through hymn and sacrifice. This primitive religion was polytheistic, with a god for each natural force, and closely resembled the religion of the Greeks.

The earliest Indian literature consists of four collections of hymns and prayers, called Vedas, which were composed between 2000 and 800 B.C. to honor these gods of nature. Later they were thought to be divine revelations, *seen* by the holy men rather than composed by them. The most important of the four, the *Rig-Veda* (meaning Verse-Knowledge), contains 1028 religious poems to Indra, the wielder of the thunderbolt; Agni, the god of fire; Yāma, the king of the underworld; and many others. The tone of these ancient hymns is vigorous, positive, and optimistic, but this bright confidence in life was soon to disappear in the deepest pessimism that a nation ever developed. Perhaps because the Hindus despaired of ever finding a way to appease the malignant, destructive forces of nature, they came to turn their backs on human effort and material reality.

Like the later Greeks and the Romans, the Brahman Hindus grew dissatisfied with their naïve polytheism and sought a unifying force of divinity to supplant the earlier congress of gods. Gradually there emerged a single Over-Spirit, called Brahma, which was the source of gods, men, and all living things on earth. According to this view, which is still the foundation of Hindu faith, this one spirit eventually gave off the individual spirits of men, animals, insects, and plants, who were arranged in an order or rank from the Brahman caste down to the simplest plant. Men, as fragments of the Over-Spirit, are thus doomed to a sojourn in this material world, but they carry with them a longing for reabsorption in the Over-Spirit. This world through which they pass is nothing but *Maya*, or illusion, in comparison with the reality of the Over-Spirit. Man's life in this world of illusion is a kind of trial by which he is judged worthy or unworthy to move closer to final release. The worthy life is one lived in complete indifference to this material world, with complete lack of ambition and desire. The worthiest life of all is spent in ascetic meditation and inaction, free from worldly possessions and concerns.

Each individual spirit must go through a series of incarnations in *Maya*, in each of which his actions, or *karma*, will influence his next rebirth. If he performs his *dharma*, or appropriate duty, in one life, he will be reborn higher on the caste scale. If he does not and pursues selfish desire in this life, he may be born next time as a pig or a vegetable. The Brahman at the top of the caste scale is the holiest of living things, for if he performs his dharma he will be reabsorbed at death into the Over-Spirit. This final obliteration of the individual soul in the peace of the Over-Spirit is usually called by the Buddhist term, *Nirvana*. Only Nirvana can end the dismal round of reincarnations in this world of illusion.

So the Hindu ascetic lives his life in a studied contempt for life. His greatest objective is to subdue self and annihilate all human desire within himself. To be sure, this abstract philosophy of the Brahman had to be translated into concrete terms for the simpler-minded masses. The older polytheism has persevered, especially in the cults of Brahma, Vishnu, and Siva, who represent Creation, Preservation, and Destruction, the three stages in the career of an individual soul. But the Brahman sees in the stone and wooden idols of the masses only the endless representations of the Over-Spirit. Hence from the sixth century B.C. to the present there has been a cleavage in religious thought, or at least in interpretation, between the intellectual Brahman and the other castes. The religion of the masses still honors the many gods of the old Vedic hymns. The Brahman looks beyond them to the *Upanishads*, the later abstract interpretations of the Vedas.

BUDDHISM. According to Indian belief, the old religion is revitalized from time to time by a great religious teacher, or *buddha*, who might be compared with a Hebrew prophet in the Old Testament. The greatest of the *buddhas* was the Buddha Gautama (c.483–c.403 B.C.), who unintentionally founded a rival religion in attempting to rid popular Hinduism of its superstition and empty ritual. Born the son of a king, he renounced a life of luxury at twenty-nine and after six years of meditation received enlightenment under the Bo-tree at Gaya. After establishing a monastery to perpetuate his gospel, he spent the rest of his eighty years wandering in northern India and preaching to the populace. Years later he was deified by the Hindus as an incarnation of the god Vishnu.

Although Buddha left no writings of his own, his doctrine is preserved and broadly interpreted in volumes of Buddhist scripture composed long after his time. Apparently he accepted the tenets of Hinduism, that only through renouncing this world is man's spirit freed from the chain of painful reincarnation. But he emphasized the moral life for both gods and men and devised a system of rules for man's behavior that ignored the caste system. The Buddhist Five Commandments have a familiar sound: Kill no living thing. Do not take what is not given to you. Do not speak falsely. Drink no intoxicating drink. Do not be unchaste. For his monks, who had completely renounced the world, Buddha ordained five further commandments.

The cult of Buddha grew gradually after the deification of its founder and accumulated new ritual of the very kind that he had decried. Between 300

This statue of Buddha in Mathura, India, dates from c. 130–140 A.D. and shows the influence of Hellenistic art on India. The protuberance on the top of his head is one of the characteristic signs of Buddha.

B.C. and 500 A.D. it challenged orthodox Hinduism as the leading religion of India and eventually spread to Ceylon, China, Burma, Japan, and Siam. But in India it later declined and in the sixth century was permanently destroyed by a revival of Hinduism in its modern form. Today India's great religious teacher is honored chiefly outside his native land, from the island of Ceylon across eastern Asia to Japan.

SECULAR LITERATURE. The history of India and her literature is immeasurably confused by Hindu mysticism. In denying the reality of this world the Hindu disavowed any interest in its his-tory and decided that time as we know it has no meaning in comparison with the timelessness of the Over-Spirit. Authentic records of Indian history are very few and the most important events can seldom be dated even by centuries. Our most reliable information about India appears in foreign records—Greek and Roman in antiquity, Mohammedan in the Middle Ages, Portuguese, French, and British in modern times. Since these records do not mention the two great ages of secular literature, we can date them only very inexactly.

During the later period of "Aryan" invasion (c. 1400–c.800 B.C.), a magnificent epic literature developed. As in many European lands, warriors were inspired by long tales of heroes who conquered great enemies against great odds. In India the ancient epics came to embody not only the national ideals and primitive culture but also the Hindu philosophy and laws of life. These poems are of great length and include many irrelevant episodes and moral precepts that have been added to them in centuries of retelling and re-editing. The greatest of them, the *Mahâbhârata*, tells in 100,000 couplets of a war of succession between two families of the Bhârata (or Kuru) kingdom, but upon this central story is hung a host of old legends and myths. The other well-known epic, the *Râmâyana*, relates in 24,-000 couplets how King Rama recovered his wife Sita from her evil abductor, the giant Râvana, again with numerous digressions into folklore and animal fables. Impossibly tedious in their entirety, these epics reveal much fine narrative poetry when read in the condensations worked out and translated by Romesh Dutt.

During the centuries of Buddhist supremacy secular literature languished, but at the end of the era came a second great school of poetry. This school is associated with the court of a noble king, Vikramáditya, who established a powerful empire, replaced Buddhism with Hinduism, and patronized the arts and sciences. But whether he ascended the throne in 375 A.D. or in the sixth century or whether he existed at all is now not definitely known. Attached to his court there are said to have been nine writers and scholars, styled "The Nine Gems," of whom Kalidasa, India's greatest poet, was the brightest luminary. His fanciful play, *Shakuntala*, inspired other playwrights: Bâna, author of the *Ratnâvali*, in the seventh century and Bhavabhuti, author of two plays based on the *Râmâyana*. To this Golden Age belongs also the anonymous play, *The Little Clay Cart*, which has been successfully staged in Europe and America. Narrative poetry and the novel also flourished through these centuries, but in the ninth century Sanskrit literature entered a Dark Age, from which it has never really recovered. Of modern Indian writers only the mystical poet, Rabindranath

Tagore (1861–1941), who wrote in English as well as in Bengali, has been widely read in the West.

SANSKRIT DRAMA. The play *Shakuntala* takes us into a magical world of transcendent beauty, enveloped in Hindu thought and stylized according to the most rigid rules. Over five hundred Sanskrit plays survive to reveal the scope of the old drama and the conventions of its theater, but only about twenty-five of these are from the Golden Age. Written in the language of the aristocratic and learned classes, they were designed for a highly restricted and refined audience. They were presented in the palaces of the nobility without scenery and with stylized action far from the realism of today. Their appeal was to the sentiment and the intellect of their audience, and hence they are devoid of melodrama and vulgar theatricalism. But their very exclusiveness, their elevated style and atmosphere of religious serenity, deny them the vigor of a truly national drama such as that of the ancient Greeks or the Spanish and English during the Renaissance.

The supernatural honeycombs the plots of these plays and contributes to their dreamlike atmosphere. Human characters seem dwarfed by it and are often conventionalized into delicate phantoms. Their metaphorical speech, combined with musical background, further reflects the ideal realm they inhabit, where nature is rich and ever smiling and unhappiness is not for long. Violence was generally outlawed, as were even the physical aspects of everyday life, such as eating, biting, scratching, and kissing. Tragedy was forbidden, but there is abundant pathos in the separation and reunion of lovers and members of families. The humor is similarly restrained, and is embodied especially in the clown, who was still a Brahman despite his undignified role. As in Shakespeare, he is often the wisest character in the play.

THE HEBREWS

LESS ancient than the Chinese and Hindu cultures, yet older than any in the West, the culture of the Hebrews has followed a unique and unbroken tradition for over three thousand years. In 1500 B.C., when China, India, and Egypt had long enjoyed an advanced civilization, the Hebrews were still a small tribe of barbaric nomads tending their flocks in the Arabian desert. Their language allied them to a third family of nations with kindred tongues, the Semites, and they were cousins of their enemy neighbors, the Ammonites, Moabites, and Edomites, as well as of larger and more powerful Semitic peoples, the Phoenicians, Babylonians, Assyrians, and Carthaginians. All of these other Semitic tribes have since disappeared or been absorbed by later nations. But the Hebrews have managed to preserve their cultural integrity, if not their racial purity or their homeland, through centuries of unspeakable hardship and persecution.

THE PROMISED LAND OF ISRAEL. The ancient Hebrews endured a hard existence in the desert, plagued by the scorching sun and drought and the freezing winter wind. They grew up with a fear of nature that peopled their world with angry spirits. In their persistent trials they may have heard from their traditional patriarchs, Abraham, Isaac, and Jacob, of a fruitful land flowing with milk and honey—the Promised Land of Canaan (now Palestine), which was the western end of a Fertile Crescent extending eastward to the Persian Gulf. In time some Hebrew clans migrated to this land and battled with the Canaanites to settle there. Others wandered westward into Egypt, where they were overwhelmed and enslaved for the building of the pyramids.

Eventually, when the Egyptians were harassed by foreign enemies, a great leader, Moses, rose among the Hebrews and led his people through forty years of wandering in the desert to the verge of the Promised Land. It was Moses who replaced the primitive worship of the Hebrews with the new religion of Judaism, embodied in the Old Testament. According to legend, he compiled the first five books of the Bible (the so-called *Torah* of the Jews or *Pentateuch* of the Christians): *Genesis*,* containing the ancient myths of the Creation, the Flood, and the patriarchs Abraham, Isaac, Jacob, and Joseph; *Exodus*, relating the wanderings of the tribes from Egypt to Canaan under Moses; *Leviticus*, the ceremonial laws; *Numbers*, the census and further history of the Hebrew tribes; and *Deuteronomy*, the final pronouncements of Moses. Actually they were written by later scribes through many years and reveal the gradual evolution of the religion of the Israelites.

Judaism began as it has remained: a religion of one god; but in its first form the god, Yahveh (mistakenly called Jehovah), was the tribal god of the Hebrews, not the one God of all mankind. Originally thought to be the spirit of a mountain called Sinai, Yahveh had been worshiped by another tribe before Moses led his people to the foot of this mountain and made a Holy Covenant with Yahveh which dedicated the Israelites to him in return for his favor

*The books of the Old Testament are italicized in this introduction to suggest their chronology and place in Jewish history.

in their struggle for survival. Hence Yahveh began as one god among many tribal gods such as Moloch and Baal of the Canaanites, but was the one god worshiped by the Israelites. The Yahveh of Moses was a stern deity born out of the hard life of the persecuted Israelites, a god to be feared rather than loved. To implement the worship of Yahveh, Moses brought to his people from the top of Sinai the Ten Commandments engraved on tablets of stone. These symbols of the agreement were kept thereafter in an oblong chest called the Ark of the Covenant, which the Israelites carried with them everywhere.

It was *Joshua*, the fiery successor of Moses, who actually led the Israelites into the Promised Land in the twelfth century B.C. and began the conquest that was to carve out separate states for the twelve tribes. After his death, Israel was ruled by tribal priests, or *Judges*, until the greatest of them, *Samuel*, converted Israel into a kingdom and consecrated two successive kings, Saul and David. King David, famed in his youth as a singer, is traditionally supposed to have been the author of the *Psalms*, the Jewish hymnbook, but he was more certainly the warrior king who won for Israel a small empire. His son, King Solomon, whose forty-year reign in the tenth century B.C. is described in the first book of *Kings*, was renowned for his wisdom and was later credited with writing three books of the Bible: *Proverbs*, a treasure house of practical wisdom, *Ecclesiastes*, a philosophical inquiry into doubt, and *The Song of Songs*, a collection of love poems. He built a great temple for the worship of Yahveh which contained the Ark of the Covenant, but with his pomp and extravagance paved the way for a civil war in the reign of his selfish son, Rehoboam. As a result, the ten tribes of Israel in the north seceded in 931 B.C. under a new king, Jeroboam, while the two tribes of Judah in the south retained Rehoboam as king in their capital of Jerusalem. These two small kingdoms, never again united, wasted each other for two hundred years with constant warfare.

It was because of the laxity of the Israelites in their living and worship after the settlement in Canaan that the great line of Prophets arose to scourge kings, priests, and populace alike for their crimes against religion and Yahveh. Coming from all classes of society but especially from the country people in the wilderness, they sprang up like an invincible conscience out of the desert past to drive the nation back to righteousness. At a time when the Israelites were in danger of losing their national identity and were forsaking Yahveh for Moloch and Baal, the Prophets promised that a return to the rigorous traditions of their ancestors would bring a great future for Yahveh's people. Although often imprisoned and martyred, they persisted and in the end became the ethical spokesmen of the nation, who helped to maintain the Jews through the centuries as a distinct people, singular and aloof. In the recurrent periods of trial and persecution the Prophets have remained pillars of hope for eventual salvation.

The earliest Prophets flourished under the monarchy and are described in the Books of *Samuel* and *Kings*: Nathan, who denounced King David; Ahijah, who agitated for revolution against King Solomon; and Elijah, who attacked the worship of Baal in the northern kingdom of Israel. *Amos*, the first of the "literary Prophets," was a simple shepherd fired with the urge to reform a people lost in luxury. He lashed out against the emptiness of their religious ritual and insisted that righteous living was the only way for them to avoid the wrath of Yahveh. *Hosea*, who had suffered a personal tragedy because of a faithless wife, saw a similar disloyalty to Yahveh in the wanton living of Israel, yet preached for the first time the mercy and forgiveness of the god toward his erring people. Shortly after, in 722 B.C., the direst prophecies of Amos seemed to be justified. The great armies of Assyria conquered the northern kingdom of Israel and deported the ten tribes into an oblivion from which they have never returned.

The two tribes of Judah in the south continued another 135 years of independent existence and were to preserve the national identity of the Jewish people into the modern world. Again it was the Prophets—this time *Isaiah* and *Micah*—whose preaching purified the Jews of vice and assured them of their great future as the people of Yahveh. But the little kingdom of Judah was now squeezed between two powerful neighbors, Babylonia and Egypt. In 605 B.C. Nebuchadnezzar, the great king of Babylonia, began to absorb the militant little nation and in 587 B.C. destroyed the Temple of Solomon in Jerusalem and forced exile on the Jews.

Most of the Prophets down to this time had been vigorous nationalists who preached righteousness as the fulfillment of the Covenant between a tribal god and his people. Now there arose a new kind of prophet, *Jeremiah*, who was to broaden Judaism into a religion for all the world. To his own people he seemed a traitor because he sided with the Babylonians against the Egyptians and even remained in Jerusalem after the exile to act as liaison officer between the Babylonian governor and the remaining Jews. When the enraged Jews killed the governor, they took Jeremiah with them into Egypt, where he was eventually martyred.

Jeremiah was a man of peace, who was grieved by the brutality of his day and, as the "weeping prophet," is traditionally credited with the book of *Lamentations*. He reasoned that if Yahveh supported the Jews in their righteousness and abandoned them in their sin, He must help the enemies

The larger map shows the areas of the Near East covered by the Hebrews in their wanderings. At the right Palestine is shown in more detail.

The Hebrew Homelands

S. Fleishman

Kingdom of Galilee
Nazareth
Israel
Jordan R.
Joppa
Jabneh
Jerusalem
Dead Sea
Kingdom of Judah
Moab

Lebanon Mts.

Caspian Sea

Black Sea
Byzantium

Assyria
Nineveh
The Fertile Crescent
Tigris R.
Babylon
Babylonia
Euphrates R.
ROUTE ESTABLISHED BY THE...
BOUNDARY

Persian Gulf

Arabia

Phoenicia
Palestine

Mediterranean Sea

Alexandria

Mt. Sinai

Egypt
Nile R.
Thebes

Red Sea

BOUNDS DEFINED IN THE AGREEMENTS

of the Jews when the Jews were unworthy of help. Hence He was not alone the one god of the Jews but rather the one God of all mankind. With Jeremiah and his international vision, Yahveh became God and Judaism became a true monotheism. Religion ceased to be for Jeremiah a national matter, and in becoming international it became really the individual and personal matter that it is for Christians and Jews today. Hence in the truest sense Jeremiah paved the way for Jesus Christ and linked the dogma of Judaism with Christianity.

EXILE AND THE PROMISED MESSIAH. Yet later Prophets reasoned from Jeremiah's internationalism an even greater future for the Jews. If Yahveh was the one God of all men, then His people must be the Chosen People of mankind. *Ezekiel,* the "priest-prophet," projected a revival of nationalism upon the rebuilding of the Temple, while the anonymous prophet of the *Second Book of Isaiah* preached that the destiny of the Jews was to be the "suffering servant" of God, chosen to bring moral enlightenment to all mankind.

The immediate events seemed to bear out these new hopes. The hero *Daniel* had allegedly foretold to Nebuchadnezzar the imminent end of the Babylonian Empire, and in 538 B.C. the Persians under Cyrus captured Babylon and freed the Jews. Many returned to what was left of the Promised Land and under the promptings of the prophets *Haggai* and *Zechariah* rebuilt Jerusalem and the Temple of Solomon. Two stern reformers, *Nehemiah* and *Ezra,* established a new, puritanical code of laws to insure the strict integrity and separateness of the Chosen People, but the gentle humanity of two anonymous books of this period, *Ruth* and *Jonah,* assures us that the tolerant internationalism of Jeremiah was by no means dead. Although Judea (as their tiny land was now called) remained a part of the Persian Empire, it flourished for a time, and according to a Biblical tradition, a Jewess named *Esther* even became the wife of a Persian emperor named Ahasuerus.

But the Jews chafed under the yoke of Persia and grew restless for the fulfillment of their destiny. The last of the Prophets, *Malachi,* had repeated the promise that a great Messiah would someday appear to lead the Jews out of their misery and establish the rule of right throughout the world. This promise from Yahveh sustained them—the most loyal of them—through the last centuries of the ancient era, and they dreamed of the day when their nation, their leader, and their God would rule the earth.

But years passed, and the Messiah did not come. The great line of Prophets and the writing of the Old Testament ceased, and Judaism passed largely into the hands of the priests, who crushed the power of the laymen and lived in luxury and corruption. Many disillusioned Jews left the homeland and set-

tled in Babylon, or Athens during the Golden Age, or Alexandria in Egypt, or Rome with the rise of the great new empire in the West. Judaism and Jewish culture sprang up in tiny colonies throughout the civilized world. But wherever they might be, the expatriate Jews always looked back to Jerusalem as their capital and the center of their spiritual life.

Judea itself passed from one conqueror to another—the Persians, the Macedonians under Alexander, the Egyptians under Ptolemy, the Syrians, the Egyptians again, then the Syrians once more. At last a great Jewish leader, Judas Maccabeus, rose up against the Syrian vandals, purified the temple of Jerusalem in 165 B.C., and established a dynasty that ruled Judea for a century. But the growth of the Roman Empire eventually cost the Maccabees their throne, and a depraved tyrant named Herod succeeded them under the favor of the Roman Emperor, Augustus.

Then during Herod's reign was born Jesus (or Joshua) of Nazareth, who was hailed at first as the long-awaited Messiah of the Jews. His doctrine of universal love exalted the downtrodden simple folk of Judea above their learned but worldly priests, and when after three years of preaching in the northern province of Galilee he made his triumphant entry into Jerusalem, a delirious crowd greeted him as the new King of the Jews. But both the Jewish priests and the Roman authorities feared his power over the people and had him hastily tried and then turned him over to the Roman governor, Pontius Pilate, for execution. The people were disillusioned by his death, and when his Jewish disciple Paul (or Saul) proclaimed in Christianity a world religion, the Jews shrank back within their walls and awaited once more their own Messiah.

DIASPORA. But instead of deliverance came the greatest tragedy of their history. Cruel Roman governors despoiled Judea in the first century A.D. during constant conflict with the adamant Jewish nation. Finally in 66 A.D. open rebellion broke out, and the Emperor Vespasian sent his son Titus to annihilate the Jews. For months the siege of Jerusalem dragged on, and when the Roman legions finally battered down the city, they killed a million of its people and dragged off thousands more as slaves. But many managed to escape in the great *Diaspora,* or Scattering, and eventually settled in every part of the known world from Spain to India and China. One of the greatest Jewish scholars, Johanan ben Zakkai, was allowed to establish a school at Jabneh nearby, which continued the study of the traditional lore for later generations. Titus imagined that he had finally destroyed the troublesome little nation, but a people that had thrived on hardship for centuries was to maintain its national identity through nineteen centuries more of wandering in hostile lands.

The crisis of the Diaspora forced a change in the government of the Jews. The reign of the corrupt priests ended with the destruction of their temple, and their power passed to the stern party of Pharisees, led by the *rabbis,* who developed the great tradition of Jewish learning and ritual which was to preserve the separateness of their people against all the forces of assimilation. Elaborating the prescriptions of the *Torah,* or Law of Moses, they built mountains of precise instructions for the conduct of daily life, which had the effect of keeping their people forever apart from the feared Gentiles. In the second century the Rabbi Judah compiled a six-volume text of rabbinical law called the *Mishna.* To this was added before the sixth century a huge, disjointed commentary in sixty-three sections, full of lore and law. The *Mishna* and this elaboration are called the *Talmud.* The special pattern of Jewish religious and community life is embodied in the *Torah* and *Talmud.*

The later history of the Jews is concerned with individuals and schools, which were often as significant for their adopted countries as for the submerged nation to which they belonged by blood and religion. The rabbinical schools were moved to Babylonia in the third century, and with the triumph of Mohammedanism over the Near East in the seventh they enjoyed three centuries of toleration and prosperity culminating in the work of the great scholar, Saadya (892–942). A brutal revival of persecution in Babylonia shifted the center of Jewish life to Spain around 1000 A.D., where for over two centuries they flourished in close cooperation with Mohammedan rulers. This new freedom gave confidence to the people to relax their strict attention to ritual and law and explore the world outside in new terms. Poetry flourished, especially in Judah Halevi (1085–1140), and Jewish scientists were renowned throughout the Mediterranean world for their skill in medicine, mathematics, astronomy, and chemistry.

But outside Spain the Jews of Europe endured unspeakable persecution, especially during the Crusades, when the Christian knights put many Jews to the sword in preparation for their massacre of Mohammedans in the Holy Land. In 1215 the Church in Rome proclaimed the "Jew-badge" law, forbidding all Jews under penalty of death to appear outside their homes without a certain badge sewn on their clothes, which should act as a brand at all times. Denied ownership of land, they took refuge in business and finance and became the moneylenders of Europe, since the Church would not sanction Christian usurers. Eventually even this segregation of the Jews would not satisfy their overlords, and one after another the rulers of Europe expelled all Jews—from England in 1290, France in 1394, Spain in 1492, Portugal in 1497.

Some remained in Germany and Italy to be shut up in special areas of the cities known as *ghettos,* but more wandered back to the East. The Jews from Spain settled in Turkey, which was periodically hospitable, yet they continued to speak a dialect of Spanish written in Hebrew characters, which is still called *Ladino.* The Jews of Germany went to Poland and Russia, but retained their dialect of German in Hebrew characters known as Yiddish (after *Jüdisch,* the German word for Jewish). Hebrew had practically ceased to exist as a spoken language around the time of Jesus.

Only with the coming of the democratic spirit in the seventeenth century did the condition of the Jew in the West begin to improve. Roger Williams invited Jews to settle in Rhode Island after 1636, and Cromwell readmitted them to England in 1655. The liberal spirit of Holland fostered a new center of Jewish culture in Amsterdam, made memorable by the great Jewish philosopher, Spinoza. A German Jew of the eighteenth century, Moses Mendelssohn, immortalized by his friend Lessing in the play *Nathan the Wise,* campaigned successfully for a more generous treatment of Jews in Germany, and the revolutions in America and France gave them equal rights with Christians in two new democratic lands. In the nineteenth century one country in western Europe after another guaranteed religious and political equality to the Jewish people, and they soon began to figure prominently in Western cultural life—Heine, Auerbach, Pinero, Bret Harte, Brandes in literature; Mendelssohn, Meyerbeer, Offenbach, Goldmark, Mahler in music; Rosa Bonheur, Pissarro, and Modigliani in art; Disraeli in politics; Marx and Bergson in philosophy; Freud in psychology; Einstein in science. But in Russian Poland under the czars and throughout eastern Europe persecution continued in the *pogroms,* systematic massacre and pillage encouraged by the government.

In our own day the one hideous instance of Jewish persecution has been the program of cold-blooded extermination carried on by the German government under Adolf Hitler with cynical success before and during World War II. Suddenly faced with annihilation in Europe, frightened Jewish refugees resumed the weary wandering that has dogged their ancestors since the Diaspora. Filled with the same urge for security and national fulfillment that drove the original tribes under Moses to the Promised Land, many banded together in the Zionist movement to establish a permanent and politically independent homeland in Palestine. Although the Arab dwellers in the Holy Land raised strong opposition to this revival of Jewish nationalism, a militant Jewish army succeeded in establishing the democratic state of Israel in 1948. At last after a gap of twenty centuries a Jewish commonwealth has been reborn among the nations.

Confucius

551–479 B.C.

Confucius was a social historian and political adviser who taught his disciples a way of life, but who had no intention of founding a religion or claiming divinity for himself. Since he died with the conviction that his teachings had been futile, he would be amazed to know that he has been venerated throughout China since his death and is known as the Divine Sage, whose pronouncements embody infallible truth.

The life of Confucius is associated with eastern China north of the Yangtze River, where he was born in the feudal state of Lu, now part of Shantung province. His impoverished father was over seventy at the time of his son's birth. Perhaps because his elder brother was a cripple, Confucius, who was precocious and old before his time, early assumed the headship of the family. His natural seriousness was emphasized by the death of his mother when he was twenty-three and his retirement in mourning for the conventional period of three years. He had just begun his career as a scholar and as a teacher of gentlemen's sons, but he accepted this interruption of his work with pious submission because he believed conservatively that a sound social order depended on keeping alive the ancient ceremonies and the memory of one's ancestors. During his three years of retirement and meditation Confucius worked out the foundations of his philosophy, to the teaching of which he was to devote the rest of his life.

Confucius once summarized his intellectual development in the following words: "At fifteen I set my mind to learning. At thirty I had formed my character. At forty I was free from doubts. At fifty I understood the will of heaven. At sixty nothing that I heard disturbed me. At seventy I could follow my own desires without violating moral law." Thus he achieved his rational ideal of life, a balanced way of thinking founded upon the Golden Mean. Believing that this *Li*, or way of life, had once been the code of China's feudal rulers, he preached the need to return to it and optimistically proclaimed that, if he were in control of a state, he could establish this moral order in government in three years. For years Confucius traveled from state to state, preaching his doctrine of the *Li* and seeking a ruler who would let him try it out in government. But at last he sadly returned to his native state of Lu, to submerge in a life of reflection his disappointment with a corrupt and cynical world.

In his role of scholar Confucius wrote little, but devoted himself to editing the so-called Five Classics, the ancient records of China which supported his insistence on historical continuity. "I transmit," he once said; "I do not create." It was his great knowledge of Chinese history, not his philosophical teachings, that attracted three thousand pupils to him, for of this number only seventy-two became his special disciples in following the *Li*. One of the Five Classics, a historical chronicle called *Spring and Autumn,* he wrote himself, but the other four he merely edited, or "transmitted": *The Book of History, The Book of Changes, The Book of Ritual,* and *The Book of Songs.* The latter, a collection of 305 folk songs and sacred anthems, which Confucius interpreted allegorically to illustrate his teachings, is generally innocent of any religious purpose. In their remarkable variety the songs concern young people in love, old wives forsaken by their husbands, gentlemen at the hunt, soldiers at the wars, and the common people protesting the luxury of the rich. Although some of these charming songs are nearly four thousand years old, they have an astonishing freshness still.

The *Analects* of Confucius (so named by their first translator, James Legge) are a collection of the sayings of the Master, as they were remembered and eventually recorded by his disciples after his death. As with the *Little Flowers of Saint Francis,* the authenticity of these aphorisms has been questioned, but there can be no doubt that, taken as a whole, they represent accurately the sensible, humorous, but sometimes pontifical personality of the quiet Sage. Many of these conservative pronouncements suggest England's Dr. Johnson. Arranged in a haphazard way in the original, they do not read consecutively, but serve to illustrate the various precepts of Confucius.

Analects

CONFUCIUS THE MAN

Duke Yeh asked Tselu about Confucius, and Tselu did not make a reply. Confucius said, "Why didn't you tell him that I am a person who forgets to eat when he is enthusiastic about something, forgets all his worries when he is happy, and is not aware that old age is coming on?"

Confucius said, "There is pleasure in lying pillowed against a bent arm after a meal of simple vegetables with a drink of water. On the other hand, to enjoy wealth and power without coming by it through the right means is to me like so many floating clouds." 10

Confucius said, "There are three things about the superior man that I have not been able to attain. The true man has no worries; the wise man has no perplexities; and the brave man has no fear." Tsekung said, "But, Master, you are exactly describing yourself."

Confucius said, "As to being a Sage and a true man, I am not so presumptuous. I will admit, however, that I have unceasingly tried to do my best and to teach other people." 20

"The things that trouble or concern me are the following: lest I should neglect to improve my charac-

*Analects.*³ Translated by Lin Yutang. From *Wisdom of China and India* by Lin Yutang. Copyright, 1942, by Random House, Inc. Reprinted by permission of Random House, Inc.

ter, lest I should neglect my studies, and lest I should fail to move forward when I see the right course, or fail to correct myself when I see my mistake."

Confucius said, "I won't teach a man who is not anxious to learn, and will not explain to one who is not trying to make things clear to himself. And if I explain one-fourth and the man doesn't go back and reflect and think out the implications in the remaining three-fourths for himself, I won't bother to teach him again."

Confucius did not talk about monsters, physical exploits, unruly conduct, and the heavenly spirits.

Confucius was gentle but dignified, austere yet not harsh, polite and completely at ease.

When Confucius offered sacrifice to his ancestors, he felt as if his ancestors were present bodily, and when he offered sacrifice to the other gods, he felt as if the gods were present bodily. Confucius said, "If I don't offer sacrifice by being personally present, it is as if I didn't sacrifice at all."

Tsekung wanted to do away with the ceremony of sacrificing the lamb in winter. Confucius said, "Ah Sze, you love the lamb, but I love the institution."

Confucius said, "Wake yourself up with poetry, establish your character in *li* and complete your education in music."

For him rice could never be white enough and mince meat could never be chopped fine enough. When the food was mushy or the flavor had deteriorated, or when the fish had become bad or the meat was tainted, he would not eat. When its color had changed he would not eat. When the smell was bad, he would not eat. When it was not cooked right, he would not eat. When food was not in season, he would not eat. When the meat was not cut properly, he would not eat. When a food was not served with its proper sauce, he would not eat. Although there was a lot of meat on the table, he would not take it out of proportion with his rice; as for wine, he drank without any set limit, but would stop before getting drunk. Wine or shredded meat bought from the shops he would not eat. A meal without ginger on the table he would not eat. He did not overeat.

Tselu, Tseng Hsi, Jan Ch'iu, and Kunghsi Hua were sitting together one day, and Confucius said, "Do not think that I am a little bit older than you and therefore am assuming airs. You often say among yourselves that people don't know you. Suppose someone should know you, I should like to know how you would appear to that person." Tselu immediately replied, "I should like to rule over a country with a thousand carriages, situated between two powerful neighbors, involved in war and suffering from famine. I should like to take charge of such a country, and in three years the nation will become strong and orderly." Confucius smiled at this remark and said, "How about you, Ah Ch'iu?" Jan Ch'iu re-

plied, "Let me have a country sixty or seventy *li* square or perhaps only fifty or sixty *li* square. Put it in my charge, and in three years the people will have enough to eat, but as for teaching them moral order and music, I shall leave it to the superior man." (Turning to Kunghsi Hua) Confucius said, "How about you, Ah Ch'ih?" Kunghsi Hua replied, "Not that I say I can do it, but I'm willing to learn this. At the ceremonies of religious worship and at the conference of the princes, I should like to wear the ceremonial cap and gown and be a minor official assisting at the ceremony." "How about you, Ah Tien?" The latter (Tseng Hsi) was just playing on the *seh*, and with a bang he left the instrument and arose to speak. "My ambition is different from theirs." "It doesn't matter," said Confucius; "we are just trying to find out what each would like to do." Then he replied, "In late spring, when the new spring dress is made, I would like to go with five or six grownups and six or seven children to bathe in the River Yi, and after the bath go to enjoy the breeze in the Wuyu woods, and then sing on our way home." Confucius heaved a deep sigh and said, "You are the man after my own heart."

HIS CONVERSATION

Confucius said, "I have sometimes talked with Huei for a whole day, and he just sits there like a fool. But then he goes into his own room and thinks about what I have said and is able to think out some ideas of his own. He is not a fool."

Tsekung asked Confucius, "What kind of person do you think can be properly called a scholar?" Confucius replied, "A person who shows a sense of honor in his personal conduct and who can be relied upon to carry out a diplomatic mission in a foreign country with competence and dignity can be properly called a scholar." "What kind of person would come next?" "One who is known to be a good son in his family and has a reputation for humility and respect in a village." "What kind of person would come next after that?" "A person who is extremely careful of his conduct and speech and always keeps his word. That is a priggish, inferior type of person, but still he can rank below the above two types." "What do you think of the officials today?" "Oh!" said Confucius, "those rice-bags! They don't count at all."

Yuan Jang (who was reputed to sing at his mother's death) squatted in Confucius' presence and Confucius said, "As a child, you were impudent; after you are grown up, you have absolutely done nothing; and now in your old age you refuse to die! You blackguard!" And Confucius struck him in the shin with a cane.

58. *li,* here a unit of measure, roughly equal to one third of a mile.
70. *seh,* an ancient musical instrument of twenty-five strings, which is still in use in China.

Baron K'ang Chi was worried about thieves and burglars in the country and consulted Confucius about it. Confucius replied, "If you yourself don't love money the people will not steal, even though you reward the thieves."

Confucius said, "To know what you know and know what you don't know is the characteristic of one who knows."

Confucius said, "A man who has committed a mistake and doesn't correct it is committing another mistake."

Baron Wen Chi said that he always thought three times before he acted. When Confucius heard this, he remarked, "To think twice is quite enough."

Confucius said, "A man who has a beautiful soul always has some beautiful things to say, but a man who says beautiful things does not necessarily have a beautiful soul. A true man (or truly great man) will always be found to have courage, but a courageous man will not always be found to have true manhood."

Tsekung asked Confucius, "What would you say if all the people of the village like a person?" "That is not enough," replied Confucius. "What would you say if all the people of a village dislike a person?" "That is not enough," said Confucius. "It is better when the good people of the village like him, and the bad people of the village dislike him."

Confucius said, "It is easy to be rich and not haughty; it is difficult to be poor and not grumble."

Confucius said, "Can you ever imagine a petty soul serving as a minister of the state? Before he gets his post, he is anxious to get it, and after he has got it, he is anxious about losing it, and if he begins to be anxious about losing it, then there is nothing that he will not do."

Confucius said, "Do not worry about people not knowing you, but strive so that you may be worth knowing."

Confucius said, "A gentleman blames himself, while a common man blames others."

Someone said, "What do you think of repaying evil with kindness?" Confucius replied, "Then what are you going to repay kindness with? Repay kindness with kindness, but repay evil with justice (or severity)."

Confucius said, "Men are born pretty much alike, but through their habits they gradually grow further and further apart from each other."

Confucius said, "When you see a good man, try to emulate his example, and when you see a bad man, search yourself for his faults."

HIS PHILOSOPHY

Confucius said, "It is man that makes truth great, and not truth that makes man great."

Tselu asked about the worship of the celestial and earthly spirits. Confucius said, "We don't know yet how to serve men, how can we know about serving the spirits?" "What about death?" was the next question, and Confucius said, "We don't know yet about life, how can we know about death?"

Tsekung asked, "Is there one single word that can serve as a principle of conduct for life?" Confucius replied, "Perhaps the word 'reciprocity' (*shu*) will do. Do not do unto others what you do not want others to do unto you."

Yen Huei asked about true manhood, and Confucius said, "True manhood consists in realizing your true self and restoring the moral order or discipline (*li*). If a man can for just one day realize his true self, and restore complete moral discipline, the world will follow him. To be a true man depends on oneself. What has it got to do with others?"

Confucius said, "Humility is near to moral discipline (*li*); simplicity of character is near to true manhood; and loyalty is near to sincerity of heart. If a man will carefully cultivate these things in his conduct, he may still err a little, but he won't be far from the standard of true manhood. For with humility or a pious attitude, a man seldom commits errors; with sincerity of heart, a man is generally reliable; and with simplicity of character, he is usually generous. You seldom make a mistake when you start off from these points."

Confucius said, "The superior man loves his soul; the inferior man loves his property. The superior man always remembers how he was punished for his mistakes; the inferior man always remembers what presents he got."

Stages in the development of modern Chinese ideograph symbols from early pictographs.

Confucius said, "The superior man is liberal toward others' opinions, but does not completely agree with them; the inferior man completely agrees with others' opinions, but is not liberal toward them."

Confucius and his followers had to go for days without food in Ch'en, and some of his followers felt ill and were confined to bed. Tselu came to see Confucius in low spirits and asked, "Does the superior man also land in difficulties?" Confucius said, "Yes, the superior man also sometimes finds himself in difficulties, but when an inferior man finds himself in difficulties, he is likely to do anything."

Confucius said, "A gentleman is ashamed that his words are better than his deeds."

Confucius said, "A gentleman is careful about three things: In his youth, when his blood is strong, he is careful about sex. When he is grown up, and his blood is full, he is careful about getting into a fight (or struggle in general). When he is old, and his blood is getting thinner, he is careful about money." (A young man loves women; a middle-aged man loves struggle; and an old man loves money.)

Confucius said, "When a man has more solid worth than polish, he appears uncouth, and when a man has more polish than solid worth, he appears urbane. The proper combination of solid worth and polish alone makes a gentleman."

Confucius said, "I hate things that resemble the real things but are not the real things. I hate cockles because they get mixed up with the corn. I hate the ingratiating fellows, because they get mixed up with the good men. I hate the glib talkers, because they confuse us with honest people. I hate the music of Cheng, because it brings confusion into classical music. I hate the purple color, because it confuses us with the red color. I hate the goody-goodies, because they confuse us with the virtuous people." (Mencius)

Confucius said, "Women and the inferior people are most difficult to deal with. When you are familiar with them, they become cheeky, and when you ignore them, they resent it."

Confucius said, "Guide the people with governmental measures and control or regulate them by the threat of punishment, and the people will try to keep out of jail, but will have no sense of honor or shame. Guide the people by virtue and control or regulate them by *li*, and the people will have a sense of honor and respect."

Confucius said, "In presiding over lawsuits, I'm as good as any man. The thing is to aim so that there should be no lawsuits."

Baron K'ang Ch'i asked Confucius concerning government, and Confucius replied, "Government is merely setting things right. When you yourself lead them by the right example, who dares to go astray?"

Confucius said, "When the ruler himself does what is right, he will have influence over the people without giving commands, and when the ruler himself does not do what is right, all his commands will be of no avail."

Lin Fang asked concerning the foundation of *li*, and Confucius replied, "You are asking an important question! In this matter of rituals or ceremony, rather than be extravagant, be simple. In funeral ceremonies, rather than be expertly familiar, it is more important to have the real sentiment of sorrow."

Confucius said, "That type of scholarship which is bent on remembering things in order to answer people's questions does not qualify one to be a teacher."

Confucius said, "Ah Yu, have you heard of the six sayings about the six shortcomings?" "No," said Tselu. "Sit down, then, and I will tell you. If a man loves kindness, but doesn't love study, his shortcoming will be ignorance. If a man loves wisdom but does not love study, his shortcoming will be having fanciful or unsound ideas. If a man loves honesty and does not love study, his shortcoming will be a tendency to spoil or upset things. If a man loves simplicity but does not love study, his shortcoming will be sheer following of routine. If a man loves courage and does not love study, his shortcoming will be unruliness or violence. If a man loves decision of character and does not love study, his shortcoming will be self-will or headstrong belief in himself."

Confucius said, "Those who are born wise are the highest type of people; those who become wise through learning come next; those who learn by sheer diligence and industry, but with difficulty, come after that. Those who are slow to learn, but still won't learn, are the lowest type of people."

The Book of Songs

I (54)

Written in B.C. 718. It is the Chinese rendering of "the world well lost."

THE gourd has still its bitter leaves,
And deep the crossing at the ford.
   I wait my lord.

The ford is brimming to its banks;
The pheasant cries upon her mate.
   My lord is late.

The boatman still keeps beckoning,
And others reach their journey's end.
   I wait my friend.

The Book of Songs.[8] Translated by Helen Waddell (after James Legge). From *Lyrics from the Chinese* by Helen Waddell. Reprinted by permission of Constable and Company Ltd. and Henry Holt and Company, Inc.

II

Written in the twelfth century before Christ. It is possibly the oldest drinking song in the world.

The dew is heavy on the grass,
    At last the sun is set.
Fill up, fill up the cups of jade,
    The night's before us yet!

All night the dew will heavy lie   5
    Upon the grass and clover.
Too soon, too soon, the dew will dry,
    Too soon the night be over!

III

Written in the twelfth century before Christ, c. 1121.

The morning glory climbs above my head,
Pale flowers of white and purple, blue and red.
    I am disquieted.

Down in the withered grasses something stirred;
I thought it was his footfall that I heard.   5
    Then a grasshopper chirred.

I climbed the hill just as the new moon showed,
I saw him coming on the southern road.
    My heart lays down its load.

IV (36)

Written B.C. 680. The 'Little Preface': 'A man's praise of his Poor Wife.'

I went out at the Eastern Gate,
    I saw the girls in clouds,
Like clouds they were, and soft and bright,
    But in the crowds
I thought on the maid who is my light,   5
Down-drooping, soft as the grey twilight;
    She is my mate.

I went out by the Tower on the Wall,
    I saw the girls in flower,
Like flowering rushes they swayed and bent,   10
    But in that hour
I thought on the maid who is my saint,
In her thin white robe and her coloring faint;
    She is my all.

V (101)

Written 718 B.C. from the harem of the Palace of Wei.

The wind blows from the North.
    He looks and his eyes are cold.
He looks and smiles and then goes forth,
    My grief grows old.

The wind blows and the dust.   5
    To-morrow he swears he will come.
His words are kind, but he breaks his trust,
    My heart is numb.

All day the wind blew strong,
    The sun was buried deep.   10
I have thought of him so long, so long,
    I cannot sleep.

VI (60)

Written B.C. 769 by a divorced woman.

Yellow's the robe for honor,
    And green is for disgrace.
I wear the green and not the gold,
    And turn away my face.

I wear the green of scorning,   5
    Who wore the gold so long.
I think upon the Sages,
    Lest I should do them wrong.

It is for her he shames me.
    I sit and think apart.   10
I wonder if the Sages knew
    A woman's heart.

VII

Written B.C. 718.

The K'e still ripples to its banks,
    The moorfowl cry.
My hair was gathered in a knot,
    And you came by.

Selling of silk you were, a lad   5
    Not of our kin;
You passed at sunset on the road
    From far-off Ts'in.

The frogs were croaking in the dusk;
    The grass was wet.   10
We talked together, and I laughed;
    I hear it yet.

I thought that I would be your wife;
    I had your word.
And so I took the road with you,   15
    And crossed the ford.

I do not know when first it was
    Your eyes looked cold.
But all this was three years ago,
    And I am old

VIII

Written 675 B.C. "Is there anything whereof it may be said, 'See, this is new? it hath been already of old time, which was before us.' "

I would have gone to my lord in his need,
  Have galloped there all the way,
But this is a matter concerns the State,
  And I, being a woman, must stay.

I watched them leaving the palace yard,   5
  In carriage and robe of state.
I would have gone by the hills and the fords;
  I know they will come too late.

I may walk in the garden and gather
  Lilies of mother-of-pearl.   10
I had a plan would have saved the State.
  —But mine are the thoughts of a girl.

The Elder Statesmen sit on the mats,
  And wrangle through half the day;
A hundred plans they have drafted and dropped,   15
  And mine was the only way.

Li Po

701–762

The Chinese call Li Po affectionately "the Banished Angel," an immortal sent back to earth to do penance for a sin in Paradise. In reading his exuberant and exquisite poems on wine, friendship, and nature we can readily imagine in him the sublime beauty of the angels as well as the pagan's thirst for physical pleasure. His picturesque life is a series of anecdotes that all point to the romantic vagabond, steeped in wine and good fellowship, contemptuous of serious work or an official career, devoted to the open road and poetry.

The poet's mother named him Po (the White One) because on the night of his birth she dreamed of the Great White Star (Venus). But he was more aptly called by his later nickname, the Old Wine Genius, for his poetic gift and his taste for wine both appeared very early. Although he had mastered the Confucian Classics at ten, he was indifferent to study and postponed for years the examinations essential to an official career. The first of his four wives finally left him, taking their two children when he persisted in wasting his days with five cronies who formed with him the Six Idlers of the Bamboo Valley. In 738 he began his lifelong friendship with Tu Fu, his young rival, who revered him as a poet and yet shook his serious head at the romantic recklessness of Li Po.

At forty he went to Chang-An, the brilliant capital, and soon came to the attention of the Emperor through his wit and verses. Rewarded with a sinecure, he was a favorite alike at the tables of the great and the taverns of the poor. As one of the Eight Immortals of the Wine Cup, he caroused constantly, and once, when summoned by the Emperor, he was so drunk that his head had to be soused in water before he could entertain the court with poetry. Eventually he offended the Emperor's favorite, who jealously undermined his standing with the Emperor.

Li Po resumed his wanderings, visiting old friends who had been dispersed to provincial posts. Once he tried the official's life in the service of a prince, but the prince was deposed in a revolt and Li Po narrowly escaped hanging. This confirmed him in his career of idle pleasure, and, according to an old legend, he was drunk at the time of his death. It was said that he drowned one night when he fell out of a canoe while trying to kiss the reflection of the moon in the Yellow River.

Li Po represents for China the spirit of romance. The love of solitude and the mountains was as strong in him as the need for wine and convivial companions. He enjoyed life with a flourish, and part of his pleasure was a mystical communion with the great soul of nature. He never took to the conservative Confucian teaching of his childhood but was fascinated by Taoist mysticism and the simple, natural life. His poems to the lotus flower and the north wind are as typical of him as his drinking songs and his witty praise of women. In all of his many facets Li Po is always the romantic rebel.

Drinking Alone in the Moonlight

I

A POT of wine among flowers.
  I alone, drinking, without a companion.
I lift the cup and invite the bright moon.
My shadow opposite certainly makes us three.
But the moon cannot drink,   5
And my shadow follows the motions of my body in vain.
For the briefest time are the moon and my shadow my companions.
Oh, be joyful! One must make the most of Spring.
I sing—the moon walks forward rhythmically;
I dance, and my shadow shatters and becomes confused.   10
In my waking moments, we are happily blended.
When I am drunk, we are divided from one another and scattered.
For a long time I shall be obliged to wander without intention;
But we will keep our appointment by the far-off Cloudy River.

II

If Heaven did not love wine,   15
There would be no Wine Star in Heaven.

Drinking Alone. . . . Translated by Florence Ayscough and Amy Lowell. From *Fir Flower Tablets* by Florence Ayscough and Amy Lowell. Reprinted by permission of Houghton Mifflin Company.

A gallon, and one is in accord with all nature.   25
Only those in the midst of it can fully comprehend
    the joys of wine;
I do not proclaim them to the sober.

A Summer Day

Naked I lie in the green forest of summer. . . .
    Too lazy to wave my white feathered fan.
I hang my cap on a crag,
And bare my head to the wind that comes
Blowing through the pine trees.   5

The Ching-ting Mountain

Flocks of birds have flown high and away;
    A solitary drift of cloud, too, has gone, wander-
    ing on.
And I sit alone with the Ching-ting Peak, towering
    beyond.
We never grow tired of each other, the mountain
    and I.   4

Parting at a Wine-Shop in Nan-king

A wind, bringing willow-cotton, sweetens the
    shop,
And a girl from Wu, pouring wine, urges me to
    share it
With my comrades of the city who are here to see
    me off;
And as each of them drains his cup, I say to him in
    parting,
Oh, go and ask this river running to the east   5
If I can travel farther than a friend's love!

Down Chung-nan Mountain to the Kind Pillow and Bowl of Hu Ssü

Down the blue mountain in the evening,
    Moonlight was my homeward escort.
Looking back, I saw my path
Lie in levels of deep shadow . . .
I was passing the farm-house of a friend,   5
When his children called from a gate of thorn
And led me twining through jade bamboos

A Summer Day; The Ching-ting Mountain. Translated by Shige-yoshi Obata. Taken from *The Works of Li Po* by Shigeyoshi Obata, published and copyrighted by E. P. Dutton & Co., Inc., New York. 1922.
Parting at a Wine-Shop; Down Chung-nan Mountain. Translated by Witter Bynner and Kiang Kang-Hu. Reprinted from *The Jade Mountain* by Witter Bynner and Kiang Kang-Hu, by permission of Alfred A. Knopf, Inc. Copyright 1929 by Alfred A. Knopf, Inc.

The poet Li Po, by Liang K'ai, a Chinese artist of the 13th century.

If Earth did not love wine,
There should be no Wine Springs on Earth.
Why then be ashamed before Heaven to love wine.
I have heard that clear wine is like the Sages;   20
Again it is said that thick wine is like the Virtuous
    Worthies.
Wherefore it appears that we have swallowed both
    Sages and Worthies.
Why should we strive to be Gods and Immortals?
Three cups, and one can perfectly understand the
    Great Tao;

Where green vines caught and held my clothes.
And I was glad of a chance to rest　　　　9
And glad of a chance to drink with my friend. . . .
We sang to the tune of the wind in the pines;
And we finished our songs as the stars went down,
When, I being drunk and my friend more than
　　happy,
Between us we forgot the world.

In the Quiet Night

So bright a gleam on the foot of my bed—
　　Could there have been a frost already?
Lifting myself to look, I found that it was moonlight.
Sinking back again, I thought suddenly of home.　　4

Endless Yearning

I AM endlessly yearning
　　To be in Ch'ang-an.
. . . Insects hum of autumn by the gold brim of the
　　well;
A thin frost glistens like little mirrors on my cold
　　mat;
The high lantern flickers; and deeper grows my
　　longing.　　5
I lift the shade and, with many a sigh, gaze upon
　　the moon,
Single as a flower, centred from the clouds.
Above, I see the blueness and deepness of sky.
Below, I see the greenness and the restlessness of
　　water . . .
Heaven is high, earth wide; bitter between them
　　flies my sorrow.　　10
Can I dream through the gateway, over the moun-
　　tain?
Endless longing
Breaks my heart."

The Hard Road

PURE wine costs, for the golden cup, ten thousand
　　coppers a flagon,
And a jade plate of dainty food calls for a million
　　coins.
I fling aside my food-sticks and cup, I cannot eat nor
　　drink . . .
I pull out my dagger, I peer four ways in vain.
I would cross the Yellow River, but ice chokes the
　　ferry;　　5

In the Quiet Night; Endless Yearning; The Hard Road; A Song of Ch'ang-kan. Translated by Witter Bynner and Kiang Kang-Hu. Reprinted from *The Jade Mountain* by Witter Bynner and Kiang Kang-Hu, by permission of Alfred A. Knopf, Inc. Copyright 1929 by Alfred A. Knopf, Inc.

I would climb the T'ai-hang Mountains, but the sky
　　is blind with snow . . .
I would sit and poise a fishing-pole, lazy by a brook—
But I suddenly dream of riding a boat, sailing for
　　the sun . . .
Journeying is hard,
Journeying is hard.　　10
There are many turnings—
Which am I to follow? . . .
I will mount a long wind some day and break the
　　heavy waves
And set my cloudy sail straight and bridge the deep,
　　deep sea.

A Song
of Ch'ang-kan

MY hair had hardly covered my forehead.
　　I was picking flowers, playing by my door.
When you, my lover, on a bamboo horse,
Came trotting in circles and throwing green plums.
We lived near together on a lane in Ch'ang-kan,　　5
Both of us young and happy-hearted.
. . . At fourteen I became your wife,
So bashful that I dared not smile,
And I lowered my head toward a dark corner
And would not turn to your thousand calls;　　10
But at fifteen I straightened my brows and laughed,
Learning that no dust could ever seal our love,
That even unto death I would await you by my post
And would never lose heart in the tower of silent
　　watching.
. . . Then when I was sixteen, you left on a long
　　journey　　15
Through the Gorges of Ch'ŭ-t'ang, of rock and whirl-
　　ing water.
And then came the Fifth-month, more than I could
　　bear,
And I tried to hear the monkeys in your lofty far-off
　　sky.
Your footprints by our door, where I had watched
　　you go,　　19
Were hidden, every one of them, under green moss,
Hidden under moss too deep to sweep away.
And the first autumn wind added fallen leaves.
And now, in the Eighth-month, yellowing butterflies
Hover, two by two, in our west-garden grasses. . . .
And, because of all this, my heart is breaking　　25
And I fear for my bright cheeks, lest they fade.
. . . Oh, at last, when you return through the three
　　Pa districts,
Send me a message home ahead!
And I will come and meet you and will never mind
　　the distance,
All the way to Chang-fêng Sha.

Addressed Humorously to Tu Fu

HERE! is this you on the top of Fan-ko Moun-
 tain,
Wearing a huge hat in the noon-day sun?
How thin, how wretchedly thin, you have grown!
You must have been suffering from poetry again. 4

Tu Fu

713–770

Chinese scholars consider Tu Fu their greatest
poet. Certainly he is the finest in the classical
tradition, though foreign readers and the commoners of
China have preferred Li Po, his close friend. Beside the
reckless high spirits and romantic imagination of Li Po,
Tu Fu seems sedate and precise, yet more admirable for
his fine, sensitive character and carefully perfected style.

In contrast to the gay, dissipated life of Li Po, the career of Tu Fu is a record of endless misfortune and weary
wandering. Born into a poor but respectable family,
he was so precocious that at fifteen he had already a local following for his verse and essays. But when he first
went to the capital to take the official examination, he
was denied a degree because of some unorthodox opinions
of his and so was forced to wander through the provinces
in search of a place. Sixteen years later the old Emperor
relented and gave the poet a post in a great library. But
his prosperity was short-lived. A revolution turned him
out, and he was captured by bandits and all but starved
to death.

When he was eventually restored to favor, Tu Fu in his
new post of Censor soon offended the new Emperor with
attacks on his policy and was banished to a remote provincial post. Refusing to accept this dismal fate, he resigned from government service and lived the rest of his
life with his family in abject poverty and hardship. At
last on one of his many journeys he was caught by a flood
in a ruined temple. When he was finally rescued and
honored with a banquet, he died from overeating.

Despite his endless misfortunes, Tu Fu remained true
to himself and the exacting standards of his craft. His
themes, naturally enough, are serious and even melancholy, but are characterized by patient resignation, never
revolt. The beauty of his sentiments is the sad beauty of
the moon, and what humor appears is always quiet and
restrained into irony. His simple pictorial style reminds
us that he was a painter as well as a poet, but its subtlety
has discouraged much English translation of his work.

Addressed Humorously. . . . Translated by Shigeyoshi Obata.
Taken from *The Works of Li Po* by Shigeyoshi Obata, published
and copyrighted by E. P. Dutton & Co., Inc., New York. 1922.

A Visit to Fan with Li Po

MY honored friend, Li, writes excellent verses,
 That ring at times like Ying-Kao's masterly
 lines.
I, too, a sojourner of Tung Meng,
Love him as a younger brother loves the elder.
Drunk, we sleep both under one cover at night; 5
And in daytime we go together hand in hand.
Now longing for a place of quiet company,
We come to visit you on the city's northside.
Your little boy waits on us so handsomely,
Joy leaps in our hearts as we enter your gate. 10
What solitude! We hear only the chilly mallets,
And see the clouds bivouac before the old city wall.
Having always sung the ode of the sweet citron,
Who cares to seek for the soup of the water-herbs?
You desire not the debasement of official life, 15
But remain untrammeled like the blue, boundless sea.

Sent to Li Po as a Gift

AUTUMN comes,
 We meet each other.
You still whirl about as a thistledown in the wind.
Your Elixir of Immortality is not yet perfected
And, remembering Ko Hung, you are ashamed. 5
You drink a great deal,
You sing wild songs,
Your days pass in emptiness.
Your nature is a spreading fire,
It is swift and strenuous. 10
But what does all this bravery amount to?

The Thatched House Unroofed by an Autumn Gale

IT is the Eighth Month, the very height of autumn.
 The wind rages and roars.
It tears off three layers of my grass-roof.
The thatch flies—it crosses the river—it is scattered
 about in the open spaces by the river.

A Visit to Fan. . . . Translated by Shigeyoshi Obata. Taken from
The Works of Li Po by Shigeyoshi Obata, published and copyrighted
by E. P. Dutton & Co., Inc., New York. 1922.
A Visit to Fan. 3. **Tung Meng,** a district in Shantung province
where Li Po and Tu Fu lived during the early period of their
friendship.
Sent to Li Po . . . ; *The Thatched House.* . . . Translated by
Florence Ayscough and Amy Lowell. From *Fir Flower Tablets* by
Florence Ayscough and Amy Lowell. Reprinted by permission of
Houghton Mifflin Company.
Sent to Li Po . . . 5. **Ko Hung,** a Chinese official who spent his
last years trying to compound the Elixir of Immortality.

High-flying, it hangs, tangled and floating, from the
    tops of the forest trees;   5
Low-flying, it whirls—turns—and sinks into the hol-
    lows of the marsh.
The swarm of small boys from the South Village
    laugh at me because I am old and feeble.
How dare they act like thieves and robbers before
    my face,
Openly seizing my thatch and running into my bam-
    boo grove?
My lips are scorched, my mouth dry, I scream at
    them, but to no purpose.   10
I return, leaning on my staff. I sigh and breathe
    heavily.

Presently, of a sudden, the wind ceases. The clouds
    are the color of ink.
The autumn sky is endless—endless—stretching to-
    ward dusk and night.
My old cotton quilt is as cold as iron;
My restless son sleeps a troubled sleep, his moving
    foot tears the quilt.   15
Over the head of the bed is a leak. Not a place is dry.
The rain streams and stands like hemp—there is no
    break in its falling.
Since this misery and confusion, I have scarcely slept
    or dozed.
All the long night, I am soaking wet. When will the
    light begin to sift in?
If one could have a great house of one thousand, ten
    thousand rooms—   20
A great shelter where all the Empire's shivering
    scholars could have happy faces—
Not moved by wind or rain, solid as a mountain—
Alas! When shall I see that house standing before
    my eyes?
Then, although my own hut were destroyed, al-
    though I might freeze and die, I should be
    satisfied.

A Night Abroad

A LONG wind is rippling at the grassy shore. . . .
    Through the night, to my motionless tall
    mast,
The stars lean down from open space,
And the moon comes running up the river.
. . . If only my art might bring me fame   5
And free my sick old age from office!—
Flitting, flitting, what am I like
But a sand-snipe in the wide-wide world!

To My Retired Friend Wêi

I T is almost as hard for friends to meet
    As for the morning and evening stars.
Tonight then is a rare event,

Joining, in the candlelight,
Two men who were young not long ago   5
But now are turning grey at the temples.
. . . To find that half our friends are dead
Shocks us, burns our hearts with grief.
We little guessed it would be twenty years
Before I could visit you again.   10
When I went away, you were still unmarried;
But now these boys and girls in a row
Are very kind to their father's old friend.
They ask me where I have been on my journey;
And then, when we have talked awhile,   15
They bring and show me wines and dishes,
Spring chives cut in the night-rain
And brown rice cooked freshly a special way.
. . . My host proclaims it a festival,
He urges me to drink ten cups—   20
But what ten cups could make me as drunk
As I always am with your love in my heart?
. . . Tomorrow the mountains will separate us;
After tomorrow—who can say?

The Excursion

A NUMBER of young gentlemen of rank, accompanied by singing-girls, go out to enjoy the
cool of the evening. They encounter a shower of
rain.

I

How delightful, at sunset, to loosen the boat!
A light wind is slow to raise waves.
Deep in the bamboo grove, the guests linger;
The lotus-flowers are pure and bright in the cool
    evening air.
The young nobles stir the ice-water;   5
The Beautiful Ones wash the lotus-roots, whose
    fibres are like silk threads.
A layer of clouds above our heads is black.
It will certainly rain, which impels me to write this
    poem.

II

The rain comes, soaking the mats upon which we
    are sitting.
A hurrying wind strikes the bow of the boat.   10
The rose-red rouge of the ladies from Yŭeh is wet;
The Yen beauties are anxious about their kingfisher-
    eyebrows.
We throw out a rope and draw in to the sloping bank.

A Night Abroad; To My Retired Friend Wêi. Translated by Witter
Bynner and Kiang Kang-Hu. Reprinted from *The Jade Mountain* by
Witter Bynner and Kiang Kang-Hu, by permission of Alfred A.
Knopf, Inc. Copyright 1929 by Alfred A. Knopf, Inc.
The Excursion. Translated by Florence Ayscough and Amy Lowell.
From *Fir Flower Tablets* by Florence Ayscough and Amy Lowell. Re-
printed by permission of Houghton Mifflin Company.

We tie the boat to the willow-trees.
We roll up the curtains and watch the floating wave-
    flowers.   15
Our return is different from our setting out. The wind
    whistles and blows in great gusts.
By the time we reach the shore, it seems as though
    the Fifth Month were Autumn.

Alone
in Her Beauty

WHO is lovelier than she?
    Yet she lives alone in an empty valley.
She tells me she came from a good family
Which is humbled now into the dust.
. . . When trouble arose in the Kuan district,   5
Her brothers and close kin were killed.
What use was their high offices,
Not even shielding their own lives?—
The world has but scorn for adversity;
Hope goes out, like the light of a candle.   10
Her husband, with a vagrant heart,
Seeks a new face like a new piece of jade;
And when morning-glories furl at night
And mandarin-ducks lie side by side,
All he can see is the smile of the new love,   15
While the old love weeps unheard.
The brook was pure in its mountain source,
But away from the mountain its waters darken.
. . . Waiting for her maid to come from selling
    pearls
For straw to cover the roof again,   20
She picks a few flowers, no longer for her hair,
And lets pine-needles fall through her fingers,
And, forgetting her thin silk sleeve and the cold,
She leans in the sunset by a tall bamboo.

Vedic Hymns

The ancient hymns and prayers of the Vedas, composed by anonymous holy men between 2000 and 800 B.C., are the foundation of both the Hindu and the Buddhist religions and are the oldest writings in any Indo-European tongue. They remain the ultimate source of Vedanta and hence are sacred to hundreds of millions even today. Of the four great collections the *Rig-veda* (Verse-Knowledge) is the oldest and is the source of the other three. Compiled in stages over a long period,

Alone in Her Beauty. Translated by Witter Bynner and Kiang Kang-Hu. Reprinted from *The Jade Mountain* by Witter Bynner and Kiang Kang-Hu, by permission of Alfred A. Knopf, Inc. Copyright 1929 by Alfred A. Knopf, Inc.

it contains both primitive hymns to the folk gods of nature, such as Varuna (sky) and Agni (fire), and later hymns to abstract concepts such as *The Origin of All Things*, which lead into the philosophical discussions of the *Upanishads*. The language of these religious lyrics antedates classical Sanskrit, and their meter is based on an alternation of long and short syllables in lines of eight, eleven, or twelve syllables organized in quatrains. The best of them project an exalted sympathy with nature through noble imagery, vivid descriptions, simple, concrete diction, and a fine reverent tone.

Agni,
God of Fire

(RIG-VEDA V, 28)

LIGHTED Agni flames forth high,
    Flings a radiance on the sky,
And his lustre red and bright
Mingles with the morning light;
Facing east, with gifts and lays   5
Viswavara sings his praise.

First immortal of the skies,
Minister of our sacrifice,
Unto him thy gifts prolong
Who uplifts thy sacred songs,   10
Unto him thy blessings come
On whose altar is thy home!

Radiant on the altar shine,
Strength and lustre bright be thine;
Spread our riches with thy flame,   15
Quell our foeman's power and fame,
Bless our dwellings from above,
Men and women link in love!

Radiant on the altar shine,
Strength and lustre bright be thine;   20
Viswavara humbly bending
Chants thy glories never ending;
Form of splendor bright is thine,
On her altar ever shine.

Pious hands awake thy flame,   25
Pious lips repeat thy name;
Bear unto our sacrifice
Bright Immortals from the skies,
Bear unto the Gods in Heaven
Sacred offerings to thee given!   30

Agni, God of Fire. From *Lays of Ancient India* (Trubner's Oriental Series, 1894) translated by Romesh Dutt. Reprinted by permission of A. C. Dutt, executor.

Pious lips the chant uplift,
Pious hands provide the gift,
Priest of Gods, Immortal bright,
Thine is morning's sacred rite,
Messenger of Gods in heaven, 35
Take these offerings humbly given.

The Origin
of All Things
(RIG-VEDA X, 129)

THERE then was neither Naught nor Aught,
  No air, nor sky beyond.
What covered all? Where rested all?
  In watery gulf profound?

Nor death was then, nor deathlessness, 5
  Nor change of night and day.
That One breathed calmly, self-sustained;
  Naught else beyond It lay.

Gloom, hid in gloom, existed first,—
  One sea excluding view. 10
That One, a void in chaos wrapped,
  By inward fervor grew.

Within It first arose desire,
  The primal germ of mind,
Which nothing with existence links, 15
  As sages searching find.

The kindling ray that shot across
  The dark and drear abyss,—
Was it beneath? or high aloft?
  What bard can answer this? 20

There fecundating powers were found,
  And mighty forces strove,—
A self-supporting mass beneath,
  And energy above.

Who knows, who ever told, from whence 25
  This great creation rose?
No gods had then been born,—then who
  Can e'er the truth disclose?

Whence sprang this world, and whether framed
  By hand divine or no,— 30
Its lord in heaven alone can tell,—
  If even He can show.

The Origin of All Things. Translated by J. Muir.
1. Naught nor Aught; that is, neither the Non-Existent nor the Existent.

The Kena–Upanishad

In later periods a large literature of commentary on the Vedic hymns and prayers was developed by learned priests. In the *Brahmanas* these explanations concern myths and points of ritual, but in the magnificent *Upanishads* they take the more general form of philosophical speculation and embody the Brahman mysticism that is the climax of Hindu thought. They were intended to guide the meditations of the Hindu hermits on the meaning of the Over-Spirit and the way to final reunion with it.

The term *Upanishad* means "sitting close," as their wisdom was traditionally thought to be communicated by a teacher to a pious student who sat close beside him. Though the names of many teachers are associated with the *Upanishads,* nothing is definitely known about their authors. The most vigorous and original of the nearly 250 surviving belong to the eighth through sixth centuries B.C.

The *Talavakâra-Upanishad,* better known as the *Kena-Upanishad* from its first word, is one of the thirteen principal *Upanishads.* In it the teacher explains to the inquiring student in typically negative terms the indefinable nature of the great Spirit, "living in all that lives." Through mystical revelation man achieves union with the Spirit and "the conquest of death." But if man does not "find Truth," his spirit "sinks among fouler shapes" in degenerate incarnations and his illusory life is really a series of deaths. Communion with Spirit is attained through renouncing desire and embracing "austerity, self-control, and meditation" on the Vedas. In this fine specimen of the *Upanishads,* given here in its entirety, mystical speculation about the universe is characteristically presented in the metaphorical language of poetry.

At Whose Command?
(THE KENA-UPANISHAD)

I

SPEECH, eyes, ears, limbs, life, energy, come to my help. These books have Spirit for theme. I shall never deny Spirit, nor Spirit deny me. Let me be in union, communion with Spirit. When I am one with Spirit, may the laws these books proclaim live in me, may the laws live.

The enquirer asked: 'What has called my mind to the hunt? What has made my life begin? What wags in my tongue? What God has opened eye and ear?'
The teacher answered: 'It lives in all that lives,

At Whose Command? From *The Ten Principal Upanishads*, translated by Shree Purohit Swami and William Butler Yeats. By permission of The Macmillan Company, publishers.

hearing through the ear, thinking through the mind, speaking through the tongue, seeing through the eye. The wise man clings neither to this nor that, rises out of sense, attains immortal life.

'Eye, tongue, cannot approach it nor mind know; not knowing, we cannot satisfy enquiry. It lies beyond the known, beyond the unknown. We know through those who have preached it, have learnt it from tradition.

'That which makes the tongue speak, but needs no tongue to explain, that alone is Spirit; not what sets the world by the ears.

'That which makes the mind think, but needs no mind to think, that alone is Spirit; not what sets the world by the ears.

'That which makes the eye see, but needs no eye to see, that alone is Spirit; not what sets the world by the ears.

'That which makes the ear hear, but needs no ear to hear, that alone is Spirit; not what sets the world by the ears.

'That which makes life live, but needs no life to live, that alone is Spirit; not what sets the world by the ears.'

2

'If you think that you know much, you know little. If you think that you know It from study of your own mind or of nature, study again.'

The enquirer said: 'I do not think that I know much, I neither say that I know, nor say that I do not.'

The teacher answered: 'The man who claims that he knows, knows nothing; but he who claims nothing, knows.

'Who says that Spirit is not known, knows; who claims that he knows, knows nothing. The ignorant think that Spirit lies within knowledge, the wise man knows It beyond knowledge.

'Spirit is known through revelation. It leads to freedom. It leads to power. Revelation is the conquest of death.

'The living man who finds Spirit, finds Truth. But if he fail, he sinks among fouler shapes. The man who can see the same Spirit in every creature, clings neither to this nor that, attains immortal life.'

3

Once upon a time, Spirit planned that the gods might win a great victory. The gods grew boastful; though Spirit had planned their victory, they thought they had done it all.

Spirit saw their vanity and appeared. They could not understand; they said: 'Who is that mysterious Person?'

They said to Fire: 'Fire! Find out who is that mysterious Person.'

Fire ran to Spirit. Spirit asked what it was. Fire said: 'I am Fire; known to all.'

Spirit asked: 'What can you do?' Fire said: 'I can burn anything and everything in this world.'

'Burn it,' said Spirit, putting a straw on the ground. Fire threw itself upon the straw, but could not burn it. Then Fire ran to the gods in a hurry and confessed it could not find out who was that mysterious Person.

Then the gods asked Wind to find out who was that mysterious Person.

Wind ran to Spirit and Spirit asked what it was. Wind said: 'I am Wind; I am the King of the Air.'

Spirit asked: 'What can you do?' and Wind said: 'I can blow away anything and everything in this world.'

'Blow it away,' said Spirit, putting a straw on the ground. Wind threw itself upon the straw, but could not move it. Then Wind ran to the gods in a hurry and confessed it could not find out who was that mysterious Person.

Then the gods went to Light and asked it to find out who was that mysterious Person. Light ran towards Spirit, but Spirit disappeared upon the instant.

There appeared in the sky that pretty girl, the Goddess of Wisdom, snowy Himalaya's daughter. Light went to her and asked who was that mysterious Person.

4

The Goddess said: 'Spirit, through Spirit you attained your greatness. Praise the greatness of Spirit.' Then Light knew that the mysterious Person was none but Spirit.

That is how these gods—Fire, Wind, and Light—attained supremacy; they came nearest to Spirit and were the first to call that Person Spirit.

Light stands above Fire and Wind; because closer than they, it was the first to call that Person Spirit.

This is the moral of the tale. In the lightning, in the light of an eye, the light belongs to Spirit.

The power of the mind when it remembers and desires, when it thinks again and again, belongs to Spirit. Therefore let Mind meditate on Spirit.

Spirit is the good in all. It should be worshipped as the Good. He that knows it as the Good is esteemed by all.

You asked me about spiritual knowledge, I have explained it.

Austerity, self-control, meditation are the foundation of this knowledge; the Vedas are its house, truth its shrine.

He who knows this shall prevail against all evil, enjoy the Kingdom of Heaven, yes, for ever enjoy the blessed Kingdom of Heaven.

The Mahâbhârata

Dating from perhaps 1000 B.C., India's greatest folk epic, the *Mahâbhârata*, has been frequently edited and enlarged by later Brahman scholars, until it is now the longest poem in the world. Its 100,000 couplets abound in loosely connected stories and essays, such as the charming tale of Savitri, whose love for her husband was stronger than death. The central plot of the epic concerns a great struggle between two families of royal cousins for succession to the Kuru (or Bhârata) throne. Upon the death of old King Pandu his brother succeeded him, and the five sons of Pandu were driven into exile by the hundred sons of the new king. The third of Pandu's sons, Arjuna, became their leader (and the hero of the epic). When by a feat of marksmanship he won as his wife a beautiful princess, Draupadi, all five brothers married her.* After thirteen more years of banishment they returned to do battle with their usurping cousins and slew them with the aid of the god Krishna, the incarnation of Vishnu. The poem ends with their retirement into the forest as devout Hindus and their rise to heaven. Modern scholars believe that, like the Trojan War of the Greeks, this mythical struggle has some foundation in a protracted war between two rival kingdoms.

The most famous section of the *Mahâbhârata* is a philosophical dialogue between Arjuna and the god Krishna, his charioteer, which is often printed separately as "The Bhagavad-Gita," or simply "The Gita" (The Song of the Holy One). The subject of this poetic essay is the Hindu reconciliation of work and necessary activity in this world with the idea that the world is a mere illusion to be ignored. With his forces arrayed for battle, Arjuna hesitates to begin the slaughter and wonders how he can escape the stigma of worldly desire if he goes through with it. Krishna reassures him with a long discourse in eighteen cantos in which he explains that a disinterested performance of duty in this world involves no desire and hence no sin. The *dharma* of a warrior requires that he fight and kill. Only this subtle interpretation of actions in terms of attitude and intention has made the Hindu able to carry on even essential business in the material world.

The Gita

THEN beholding [the two armies,] drawn up on the battlefield, ready to begin the fight. . . . Arjuna noticed fathers, grandfathers, uncles, cousins, sons, grandsons, teachers, friends;

Fathers-in-law and benefactors, arrayed on both sides. Arjuna then gazed at all those kinsmen before him.

And his heart melted with pity and sadly he spoke: 'O my Lord! When I see all these, my own people, thirsting for battle,   10

'My limbs fail me and my throat is parched, my body trembles and my hair stands on end.

'The bow Gāndeeva slips from my hand, and my skin burns. I cannot keep quiet, for my mind is in a tumult.

'The omens are adverse; what good can come from the slaughter of my people on this battlefield?

'Ah, my Lord! I crave not for victory, nor for kingdom, nor for any pleasure. What were a kingdom or happiness or life to me,   20

'When those for whose sake I desire these things stand here about to sacrifice their property and their lives. . . .

'Although these men, blinded by greed, see no guilt in destroying their kin, or fighting against their friends,

'Should not we, whose eyes are open, who consider it to be wrong to annihilate our house, turn away from so great a crime? . . .

'If, on the contrary, [my enemies,] with weapons   30
in their hands, should slay me, unarmed and unresisting, surely that would be better for my welfare!' . . .

Thereupon the Lord, with a gracious smile, addressed him who was so much depressed in the midst between the two armies.

Lord Shri Krishna said: 'Why grieve for those for whom no grief is due, and yet profess wisdom. The wise grieve neither for the dead nor for the living.

'There was never a time when I was not, nor thou,   40
nor these princes were not; there will never be a time when we shall cease to be.

'As the soul experiences in this body, infancy, youth and old age, so finally it passes into another. The wise have no delusion about this.

'Those external relations which bring cold and heat, pain and happiness, they come and go; they are not permanent. Endure them bravely, O Prince!

'The hero whose soul is unmoved by circumstance, who accepts pleasure and pain with equanimity,   50
only he is fit for immortality.

'That which is not, shall never be; that which is, shall never cease to be. . . .

'He who knows the Spirit as Indestructible, Immortal, Unborn, Always-the-Same, how should he kill or cause to be killed?

'As a man discards his threadbare robes and puts on new, so the Spirit throws off Its worn-out bodies and takes fresh ones. . . .

'Even if thou thinkest of It as constantly being   60
born, constantly dying; even then, O Mighty Man! thou still hast no cause to grieve.

---

* Unlike polygamy, polyandry was uncommon among the ancient Hindus, but is vigorously defended in this case by the author of the epic.

*The Gita.*⁸ From *The Geeta*, translated by Shree Purohit Swami. Reprinted by permission of Faber and Faber Ltd.

'For death is as sure for that which is born, as birth is for that which is dead. Therefore grieve not for what is inevitable.

'The end and beginning of beings are unknown. We see only the intervening formations. Then what cause is there for grief? . . .

'Thou must look at thy duty. Nothing can be more welcome to a soldier than a righteous war. Therefore to waver in thy resolve is unworthy, O Arjuna!

'Blessed are the soldiers who find their opportunity. This opportunity has opened for thee the gates of heaven. . . .

'If killed, thou shalt attain Heaven; if victorious, enjoy the kingdom of earth. Therefore arise, and fight.

'Look upon pleasure and pain, victory and defeat, with an equal eye. Make ready for the combat, and thou shalt commit no sin.

'I have told thee the philosophy of Knowledge. Now listen! and I will explain the philosophy of Action, by means of which, O Arjuna, thou shalt break through the bondage of all action . . .

'Thou hast only the right to work; but none to the fruit thereof. Let not then the fruit of thy action be thy motive; nor yet be thou enamored of inaction.

'Perform all thy actions with mind concentrated on the Divine, renouncing attachment and looking upon success and failure with an equal eye. . . .

'Physical action is far inferior to an intellect concentrated on the Divine. Have recourse then to the Pure Intelligence. It is only the petty-minded who work for reward.

'When a man attains to Pure Reason, he renounces in this world the results of good and evil alike. Cling thou to Right Action. Spirituality is the real art of living.

'The sages guided by Pure Intellect renounce the fruit of action; and, freed from the chains of rebirth, they reach the highest bliss. . . .

'No man can attain freedom from activity by refraining from action; nor can he reach perfection by merely refusing to act. . . .

'Do thy duty as prescribed; for action for duty's sake is superior to inaction. Even the maintenance of the body would be impossible if man remained inactive.

'In this world people are fettered by action, unless it is performed as a sacrifice. Therefore, O Arjuna! let thy acts be done without attachment, as sacrifice only. . . .

'There is nothing in this universe, O Arjuna! that I am compelled to do; nor anything for Me to attain; yet I am persistently active.

'For were I not to act without ceasing, O Prince! people would be glad to do likewise.

'And if I were to refrain from action, the human race would be ruined; I should lead the world to chaos, and destruction would follow. . . .

'The four divisions of society (the wise, the soldier, the merchant, the laborer) were created by Me, according to the natural distribution of Qualities and instincts. I am the author of them. . . .

'In the light of this wisdom, our ancestors, who sought deliverance, performed their acts. Act thou also, as did our fathers of old. . . .

'What is action and what is inaction? . . .

'He who can see inaction in action, and action in inaction, is the wisest among men. . . .

'Having surrendered all claim to the results of his actions, always contented and independent, in reality he does nothing, even though he is apparently acting.

'Expecting nothing, his mind and personality controlled, without greed, doing bodily actions only; though he acts, yet he remains untainted.

'Content with what comes to him without effort of his own, mounting above the pairs of opposites, free from envy, his mind balanced both in success and in failure, though he act, yet the consequences do not bind him.

'He who is without attachment, free, his mind centered in wisdom, his actions, being done as a sacrifice, leave no trace behind. . . .

'He who knows and lives in the Absolute remains unmoved and unperturbed; he is not elated by pleasure, or depressed by pain.

'He finds happiness in his own Self, and enjoys eternal bliss, whose heart does not yearn for the contacts of earth, and whose Self is one with the Everlasting.

'He who is happy within his Self, and has found Its peace, and in whom the inner light shines, that sage attains Eternal Bliss and becomes the Spirit Itself. . . .

'Therefore, surrendering thy actions unto Me, thy thoughts concentrated on the Absolute, free from selfishness and without anticipation of reward, with mind devoid of excitement, begin thou to fight.'

The Tale of Savitri

IN the country of fair Madra lived a king in days
    of old,
Faithful to the holy Brahma, pure in heart and
    righteous-souled,

He was loved in town and country, in the court and
    hermit's den,
Sacrificer to the bright gods, helper to his brother
    men,

The Tale of Savitri. From *The Ramayana and the Mahabharata* translated by Romesh Dutt. (Everyman's Lib. Ed., E. P. Dutton & Co., Inc.) Reprinted by permission of A. C. Dutt, executor.

But the monarch, Aswapati, son or daughter had he
    none,   5
Old in years and sunk in anguish, and his days were
    almost done!

Vows he took and holy penance, and with pious
    rules conformed,
Spare in diet as *brahmachari* many sacred rites per-
    formed,

Sang the sacred hymn, *savitri*, to the gods oblations
    gave,
Through the lifelong day he fasted, uncomplaining,
    meek and brave!   10

Year by year he gathered virtue, rose in merit and
    in might,
Till the goddess of *savitri* smiled upon his sacred rite,

From the fire upon the altar which a holy radiance
    flung,
In the form of beauteous maiden, goddess of *savitri*
    sprung!

And she spake in gentle accents, blessed the monarch
    good and brave,   15
Blessed his rites and holy penance and a boon unto
    him gave:

"Penance and thy sacrifices can the Powers Immortal
    move,
And the pureness of thy conduct doth thy heart's
    affection prove,

Ask thy boon, king Aswapati, from creation's Ancient
    Sire,
True to virtue's sacred mandate speak thy inmost
    heart's desire."   20

"For an offspring brave and kingly," so the saintly
    king replied,
"Holy rites and sacrifices and this penance I have
    tried,

If these rites and sacrifices move thy favour and thy
    grace,
Grant me offspring, Prayer-Maiden, worthy of my
    noble race."

"Have thy object," spake the maiden, "Madra's pious-
    hearted king,   25
From Swaymbhu, Self-created, blessings unto thee
    I bring,

For He lists to mortal's prayer springing from a heart
    like thine,

8. *brahmachari*, those who have taken holy vows.

And He wills,—a noble daughter grace thy famed
    and royal line,

Aswapati, glad and grateful, take the blessing which
    I bring,
Part in joy and part in silence, bow unto Creation's
    King!"   30

Vanished then the Prayer-Maiden, and the king of
    noble fame,
Aswapati, Lord of coursers, to his royal city came,

Days of hope and nights of gladness Madra's happy
    monarch passed,
Till his queen of noble offspring gladsome promise
    gave at last!

As the moon each night increaseth chasing darksome
    nightly gloom,   35
Grew the unborn babe in splendour in its happy
    mother's womb,

And in fulness of the season came a girl with lotus-
    eye,
Father's hope and joy of mother, gift of kindly gods
    on high!

And the king performed its birth-rites with a glad
    and grateful mind,
And the people blessed the dear one with their wishes
    good and kind,   40

As *Savitri*, Prayer-Maiden, had the beauteous off-
    spring given,
Brahmans named the child *Savitri*, holy gift of boun-
    teous Heaven!

Grew the child in brighter beauty like a goddess from
    above,
And each passing season added fresher sweetness,
    deeper love,

Came with youth its lovelier graces, as the buds their
    leaves unfold,   45
Slender waist and rounded bosom, image as of bur-
    nished gold,

Deva-Kanya! born a goddess, so they said in all the
    land,
Princely suitors struck with splendour ventured not
    to seek her hand.

Once upon a time it happened on a bright and festive
    day,
Fresh from bath the beauteous maiden to the altar
    came to pray,   50

And with cakes and pure libations duly fed the
    Sacred Flame,
Then like Sri in heavenly radiance to her royal father
    came.

And she bowed to him in silence, sacred flowers be-
    side him laid,
And her hands she folded meekly, sweetly her obei-
    sance made,

With a father's pride, upon her gazed the ruler of the
    land,   55
But a strain of sadness lingered, for no suitor claimed
    her hand.

"Daughter," whispered Aswapati, "now, methinks,
    the time is come,
Thou shouldst choose a princely suitor, grace a royal
    husband's home,

Choose thyself a noble husband worthy of thy noble
    hand,
Choose a true and upright monarch, pride and glory
    of his land,   60

As thou choosest, gentle daughter, in thy loving
    heart's desire,
Blessing and his free permission will bestow thy
    happy sire.

For our sacred *sastras* sanction, holy Brahmans oft
    relate,
That the duty-loving father sees his girl in wedded
    state,

That the duty-loving husband watches o'er his con-
    sort's ways,   65
That the duty-loving offspring tends his mother's
    widowed days,

Therefore choose a loving husband, daughter of my
    house and love,
So thy father earn no censure or from men or gods
    above."

Fair Savitri bowed unto him and for parting bless-
    ings prayed,
Then she left her father's palace and in distant re-
    gions strayed,   70

With her guard and aged courtiers whom her watch-
    ful father sent,
Mounted on her golden chariot unto sylvan wood-
    lands went.

52. Sri, goddess of beauty and wealth. 63. *sastras*, scriptures.

Far in pleasant woods and jungle wandered she from
    day to day,
Unto *asrams,* hermitages, pious-hearted held her
    way,

Oft she stayed in holy *tirthas* washed by sacred
    limpid streams,   75
Food she gave unto the hungry, wealth beyond their
    fondest dreams.

Many days and months are over, and it once did so
    befall,
When the king and *rishi* Narad sat within the royal
    hall,

From her journeys near and distant and from places
    known to fame,
Fair Savitri with the courtiers to her father's palace
    came,   80

Came and saw her royal father, *rishi* Narad by his
    seat,
Bent her head in salutation, bowed unto their holy
    feet.

II. THE FATED BRIDEGROOM

"Whence comes she," so Narad questioned, "whither
    was Savitri led,
Wherefore to a happy husband hath Savitri not been
    wed?"

"Nay, to choose her lord and husband," so the vir-
    tuous monarch said,   85
"Fair Savitri long hath wandered and in holy *tirthas*
    stayed,

Maiden! speak unto the *rishi,* and thy choice and
    secret tell,"
Then a blush suffused her forehead, soft and slow her
    accents fell!

"Listen, father! Salwa's monarch was of old a king of
    might,
Righteous-hearted Dyumat-sena, feeble now and
    void of sight,   90

Foemen robbed him of his kingdom when in age he
    lost his sight,
And from town and spacious empire was the mon-
    arch forced to flight,

With his queen and with his infant did the feeble
    monarch stray,
And the jungle was his palace, darksome was his
    weary way,

75. *tirthas*, shrines. 78. *rishi*, holy man.

This Hindu-style painting of the 18th century now in the British Museum is called "Girl Walking in a Starry Night."

Holy vows assumed the monarch and in penance
    passed his life,   95
In the wild woods nursed his infant and with wild
    fruits fed his wife,

Years have gone in rigid penance, and that child is
    now a youth,
Him I choose my lord and husband, Satyavan, the
    Soul of Truth!"

Thoughtful was the *rishi* Narad, doleful were the
    words he said:
"Sad disaster waits Savitri if this royal youth she
    wed,   100

Truth-beloving is her father, truthful is the royal
    dame,
Truth and virtue rule his actions, Satyavan his sacred
    name,

Steeds he loved in days of boyhood and to paint them
    was his joy,

Hence they called him young Chitraswa, art-belov-
ing gallant boy,

But O pious-hearted monarch! fair Savitri hath in
    sooth   105
Courted Fate and sad disaster in that noble gallant
    youth!"

"Tell me," questioned Aswapati, "for I may not guess
    thy thought,
Wherefore is my daughter's action with a sad disaster
    fraught,

Is the youth of noble lustre, gifted in the gifts of art,
Blest with wisdom and with prowess, patient in his
    dauntless heart?"   110

"Surya's lustre in his shineth," so the *rishi* Narad said,
"Brihaspati's wisdom dwelleth in the youthful
    prince's head,

Like Mahendra in his prowess, and in patience like
    the Earth,
Yet O king! sad disaster marks the gentle youth from
    birth!"

"Tell me, *rishi*, then thy reason," so anxious monarch
    cried,   115
"Why to youth so great and gifted may this maid be
    not allied,

Is he princely in his bounty, gentle-hearted in his
    grace,
Duly versed in sacred knowledge, fair in mind and
    fair in face?"

"Free in gifts like Rantideva," so the holy *rishi* said,
"Versed in lore like monarch Sivi who all ancient
    monarchs led,   120

Like Yayati open-hearted and like Chandra in his
    grace,
Like the handsome heavenly Asvins fair and radiant
    in his face,

Meek and graced with patient virtue he controls his
    noble mind,
Modest in his kindly actions, true to friends and ever
    kind,

And the hermits of the forest praise him for his right-
    eous truth,   125
Nathless, king, thy daughter may not wed this noble-
    hearted youth!"

"Tell me, *rishi*," said the monarch, "for thy sense
    from me is hid,

Has this prince some fatal blemish, wherefore is this
    match forbid?"

"Fatal fault!" exclaimed the *rishi*, "fault that wipeth
    all his grace,
Fault that human power nor effort, rite nor penance
    can efface,   130

Fatal fault or destined sorrow! for it is decreed on
    high,
On this day, a twelve-month later, this ill-fated
    prince will die!"

Shook the startled king in terror and in fear and
    trembling cried:
"Unto short-lived, fated bridegroom ne'er my child
    shall be allied,

Come, Savitri, dear-loved maiden, choose another
    happier lord,   135
Rishi Narad speaketh wisdom, list unto his holy
    word!

Every grace and every virtue is effaced by cruel
    Fate,
On this day, a twelve-month later, leaves the prince
    his mortal state!"

"Father!" answered thus the maiden, soft and sad her
    accents fell,
"I have heard thy honoured mandate, holy Narad
    counsels well,   140

Pardon witless maiden's fancy, but beneath the eye
    of Heaven,
Only once a maiden chooseth, twice her troth may
    not be given,

Long his life or be it narrow, and his virtues great or
    none,
Satyavan is still my husband, he my heart and troth
    hath won,

What a maiden's heart hath chosen that a maiden's
    lips confess,   145
True to him thy poor Savitri goes into the wilder-
    ness!"

"Monarch!" uttered then the *rishi*, "fixed is she in
    mind and heart,
From her troth the true Savitri never, never will de-
    part,

More than mortal's share of virtue unto Satyavan is
    given,
Let the true maid wed her chosen, leave the rest to
    gracious Heaven!"   150

"*Rishi* and preceptor holy!" so the weeping monarch
    prayed,
"Heaven avert all future evils, and thy mandate is
    obeyed!"

Narad wished him joy and gladness, blessed the lov-
    ing youth and maid,
Forest hermits on their wedding every fervent bless-
    ing laid.

III. OVERTAKEN BY FATE

Twelve-month in the darksome forest by her true and
    chosen lord,   155
Sweet Savitri served his parents by her thought and
    deed and word,

Bark of tree supplied her garments draped upon her
    bosom fair,
Or the red cloth as in *asrams* holy women love to
    wear.

And the aged queen she tended with a fond and filial
    pride,
Served the old and sightless monarch like a daughter
    by his side,   160

And with love and gentle sweetness pleased her
    husband and her lord,
But in secret, night and morning, pondered still on
    Narad's word!

Nearer came the fatal morning by the holy Narad
    told,
Fair Savitri reckoned daily and her heart was still
    and cold,

Three short days remaining only! and she took a vow
    severe   165
Of *triratra*, three nights' penance, holy fasts and vigils
    drear.

Of Savitri's rigid penance heard the king with anxious
    woe,
Spake to her in loving accents, so the vow she might
    forgo:

"Hard the penance, gentle daughter, and thy wom-
    an's limbs are frail,
After three nights' fasts and vigils sure thy tender
    health may fail,"   170

"Be not anxious, loving father," meekly this Savitri
    prayed,
"Penance I have undertaken, will unto the gods be
    made."

Much misdoubting then the monarch gave his sad
    and slow assent,

Pale with fast and unseen tear-drops, lonesome nights
    Savitri spent.

Nearer came the fatal morning, and to-morrow he
    shall die,   175
Dark, lone hours of nightly silence! Tearless, sleepless
    is her eye!

"Dawns that dread and fated morning!" said Savitri,
    bloodless, brave,
Prayed her fervent prayers in silence, to the Fire
    oblations gave,

Bowed unto the forest Brahmans, to the parents kind
    and good,
Joined her hands in salutation and in reverent silence
    stood.   180

With the usual morning blessing, "Widow may'st
    thou never be,"
Anchorites and aged Brahmans blessed Savitri fer-
    vently,

O! that blessing fell upon her like the rain on thirsty
    air,
Struggling hope inspired her bosom as she drank
    those accents fair,

But returned the dark remembrance of the *rishi* Na-
    rad's word,   185
Pale she watched the creeping sunbeams, mused
    upon her fated lord!

"Daughter, now thy fast is over," so the loving par-
    ents said,
"Take thy diet after penance, for thy morning prayers
    are prayed,"

"Pardon, father," said Savitri, "let this other day be
    done,"
Unshed tear-drops filled her eyelids, glistened in the
    morning sun!   190

Satyavan, sedate and stately, ponderous axe on
    shoulder hung,
For the distant darksome jungle issued forth serene
    and strong,

But unto him came Savitri and in sweetest accents
    prayed,
As upon his manly bosom gently she her forehead
    laid:

"Long I wished to see the jungle where steals not
    the solar ray,   195
Take me to the darksome forest, husband, let me go
    to-day!"

"Come not, love," he sweetly answered with a loving
    husband's care,
"Thou art all unused to labour, forest paths thou
    may'st not dare,

And with recent fasts and vigils pale and bloodless
    is thy face,
And thy steps are weak and feeble, jungle paths thou
    may'st not trace."   200

"Fasts and vigils make me stronger," said the wife
    with wifely pride,
"Toil I shall not feel nor languor when my lord is by
    my side,

For I feel a woman's longing with my lord to trace
    the way,
Grant me, husband ever gracious, with thee let me go
    to-day!"

Answered then the loving husband, as his hands in
    hers he wove,   205
"Ask permission from my parents in the trackless
    woods to rove,"

Then Savitri to the monarch urged her longing
    strange request,
After duteous salutation thus her humble prayer ad-
    drest.

"To the jungle goes my husband, fuel and the fruit
    to seek,
I would follow if my mother and my loving father
    speak,   210

Twelve-month from this narrow *asram* hath Savitri
    stepped nor strayed,
In this cottage true and faithful ever hath Savitri
    stayed,

For the sacrificial fuel wends my lord his lonesome
    way,
Please my kind and loving parents, I would follow
    him to-day."

"Never since her wedding morning," so the loving
    king replied,   215
"Wish or thought Savitri whispered, for a boon or
    object sighed,

Daughter, thy request is granted, safely in the forest
    roam,
Safely with thy lord and husband seek again thy
    cottage home."

Bowing to her loving parents did the fair Savitri
    part,

Smile upon her pallid features, anguish in her inmost
    heart,   220

Round her sylvan greenwoods blossomed 'neath a
    cloudless Indian sky,
Flocks of pea-fowls gorgeous plumaged flew before
    her wondering eye,

Woodland rills and crystal nullahs gently roll'd o'er
    rocky bed,
Flower-decked hills in dewy brightness towering glit-
    tered overhead,

Birds of song and beauteous feather trilled a note in
    every grove,   225
Sweeter accents fell upon her, from her husband's
    lips of love!

Still with thoughtful eye Savitri watched her dear
    and fated lord,
Flail of grief was in her bosom but her pale lips
    shaped no word,

And she listened to her husband still on anxious
    thought intent,
Cleft in two her throbbing bosom as in silence still
    she went!   230

Gaily with the gathered wild-fruits did the prince his
    basket fill,
Hewed the interlacéd branches with his might and
    practised skill,

Till the drops stood on his forehead, weary was his
    aching head,
Faint he came unto Savitri and in faltering accents
    said:

"Cruel ache is on my forehead, fond and ever faith-
    ful wife,   235
And I feel a hundred needles pierce me and torment
    my life,

And my feeble footsteps falter and my senses seem
    to reel,
Fain would I beside thee linger for a sleep doth o'er
    me steal."

With a wild and speechless terror pale Savitri held
    her lord,
On her lap his head she rested as she laid him on the
    sward,   240

Narad's fatal words remembered as she watched her
    husband's head,
Burning lip and pallid forehead and the dark and
    creeping shade,

Clasped him in her beating bosom, kissed his lips
    with panting breath,
Darker grew the lonesome forest, and he slept the
    sleep of death!

IV. TRIUMPH OVER FATE

In the bosom of the shadows rose a Vision dark and
    dread,   245
Shape of gloom in inky garment and a crown was on
    his head,

Gleaming Form of sable splendour, blood-red was
    his sparkling eye,
And a fatal noose he carried, grim and godlike, dark
    and high!

And he stood in solemn silence, looked in silence on
    the dead,
And Savitri on the greensward gently placed her hus-
    band's head,   250

And a tremor shook Savitri, but a woman's love is
    strong,
With her hands upon her bosom thus she spake with
    quivering tongue:

"More than mortal is thy glory! If a radiant god thou
    be,
Tell me what bright name thou bearest, what thy
    message unto me."

"Know me," thus responded Yama, "mighty monarch
    of the dead,   255
Mortals leaving earthly mansion to my darksome
    realms are led,

Since with woman's full affection thou hast loved thy
    husband dear,
Hence before thee, faithful woman, Yama doth in
    form appear,

But his days and loves are ended, and he leaves his
    faithful wife,
In this noose I bind and carry spark of his immortal
    life,   260

Virtue graced his life and action, spotless was his
    princely heart,
Hence for him I came in person, princess, let thy
    husband part."

Yama from the prince's body, pale and bloodless,
    cold and dumb,
Drew the vital spark, *purusha*, smaller than the hu-
    man thumb,

In his noose the spark he fastened, silent went his
    darksome way,   265

Left the body shorn of lustre to its rigid cold decay,

Southward went the dark-hued Yama with the
youth's immortal life,
And, for woman's love abideth, followed still the
faithful wife.

"Turn, Savitri," outspake Yama, "for thy husband
loved and lost,
Do the rites due unto mortals by their Fate predes-
tined crost,   270

For thy wifely duty ceases, follow not in fruitless
woe,
And no farther living creature may with monarch
Yama go!"

"But I may not choose but follow where thou takest
my husband's life,
For Eternal Law divides not loving man and faithful
wife,

For a woman's true affection, for a woman's sacred
woe,   275
Grant me in thy godlike mercy farther still with him
I go!

Fourfold are our human duties: first to study holy
lore,
Then to live as good householders, feed the hungry
at our door,

Then to pass our days in penance, last to fix our
thoughts above,
But the final goal of virtue, it is Truth and deathless
Love!"   280

"True and holy are thy precepts," listening Yama
made reply,
"And they fill my heart with gladness and with pious
purpose high,

I would bless thee, fair Savitri, but the dead come
not to life,
Ask for other boon and blessing, faithful, true and
virtuous wife!"

"Since you so permit me, Yama," so the good Savitri
said,   285
"For my husband's banished father let my dearest
suit be made,

Sightless in the darksome forest dwells the monarch
faint and weak,
Grant him sight and grant him vigour, Yama, in thy
mercy speak!"

"Duteous daughter," Yama answered, "be thy pious
wishes given,
And his eyes shall be restoréd to the cheerful light
of heaven,   290

Turn, Savitri, faint and weary, follow not in fruitless
woe,
And no farther living creature may with monarch
Yama go!"

"Faint nor weary is Savitri," so the noble princess
said,
"Since she waits upon her husband, gracious Monarch of the dead,

What befalls the wedded husband still befalls the
faithful wife,   295
Where he leads she ever follows, be it death or be it
life!

And our sacred writ ordaineth and our pious *rishis*
sing,
Transient meeting with the holy doth its countless
blessings bring,

Longer friendship with the holy purifies the mortal
birth,
Lasting union with the holy is the bright sky on the
earth,   300

Union with the pure and holy is immortal heavenly
life,
For Eternal Law divides not loving man and faithful wife!"

"Blessed are thy words," said Yama, "blessed is thy
pious thought,
With a higher purer wisdom are thy holy lessons
fraught,

I would bless thee, fair Savitri, but the dead come
not to life,   305
Ask for other boon and blessing, faithful, true and
virtuous wife!"

"Since you so permit me, Yama," so the good Savitri
said,
"Once more for my husband's father be my supplication made,

Lost his kingdom, in the forest dwells the monarch
faint and weak,
Grant him back his wealth and kingdom, Yama, in
thy mercy speak!"   310

"Loving daughter," Yama answered, "wealth and
kingdom I bestow,

Turn, Savitri, living mortal may not with King Yama
    go!"

Still Savitri, meek and faithful, followed her de-
    parted lord,
Yama still with higher wisdom listened to her saintly
    word,

And the Sable King was vanquished, and he turned
    on her again,   315
And his words fell on Savitri like the cooling summer
    rain,

"Noble woman, speak thy wishes, name thy boon
    and purpose high,
What the pious mortal asketh gods in heaven may not
    deny!"

"Thou hast," so Savitri answered, "granted father's
    realm and might,
To his vain and sightless eyeballs hast restored their
    blesséd sight,   320

Grant him that the line of monarchs may not all un-
    timely end,
Satyavan may see his kingdom to his royal sons de-
    scend!"

"Have thy object," answered Yama, "and thy lord
    shall live again,
He shall live to be a father, and his children too shall
    reign,

For a woman's troth abideth longer than the fleeting
    breath,   325
And a woman's love abideth higher than the doom
    of Death!"

V. RETURN HOME

Vanished then the Sable Monarch, and Savitri held
    her way
Where in dense and darksome forest still her husband
    lifeless lay,

And she sat upon the greensward by the cold un-
    conscious dead,
On her lap with deeper kindness placed her consort's
    lifeless head,   330

And that touch of true affection thrilled him back to
    waking life,
As returned from distant regions gazed the prince
    upon his wife,

"Have I lain too long and slumbered, sweet Savitri,
    faithful spouse,
But I dreamt a Sable Person took me in a fatal
    noose!"

A Rajput Indian painting of two lovers on a terrace.

"Pillowed on this lap," she answered, "long upon the
    earth you lay,   335
And the Sable Person, husband, he hath come and
    passed away,

Rise and leave this darksome forest if thou feelest
    light and strong,
For the night is on the jungle and our way is dark
    and long."

Rising as from happy slumber looked the young
    prince on all around,
Saw the wide-extending jungle mantling all the dark-
    some ground,   340

"Yes," he said, "I now remember, ever loving faithful
    dame,
We in search of fruit and fuel to this lonesome forest
    came,

As I hewed the gnarléd branches, cruel anguish filled
    my brain,

And I laid me on the greensward with a throbbing
piercing pain,

Pillowed on thy gentle bosom, solaced by thy gentle
love,   345
I was soothed, and drowsy slumber fell on me from
skies above.

All was dark and then I witnessed, was it but a fleeting dream,
God or Vision, dark and dreadful, in the deepening
shadows gleam,

Was this dream my fair Savitri, dost thou of this
Vision know,
Tell me, for before my eyesight still the Vision seems
to glow!"   350

"Darkness thickens," said Savitri, "and the evening
waxeth late,
When the morrow's light returneth I shall all these
scenes narrate,

Now arise, for darkness gathers, deeper grows the
gloomy night,
And thy loving anxious parents trembling wait thy
welcome sight,

Hark the rangers of the forest! how their voices strike
the ear,   355
Prowlers of the darksome jungle! how they fill my
breast with fear!

Forest-fire is raging yonder, for I see a distant gleam,
And the rising evening breezes help the red and
radiant beam,

Let me fetch a burning faggot and prepare a friendly
light,
With these fallen withered branches chase the shadows of the night,   360

And if feeble still thy footsteps,—long and weary is
our way,—
By the fire repose, my husband, and return by light
of day."

"For my parents, fondly anxious," Satyavan thus
made reply,
"Pains my heart and yearns my bosom, let us to
their cottage hie,   364

When I tarried in the jungle or by day or dewy eve,
Searching in the hermitages often did my parents
grieve,

And with father's soft reproaches and with mother's
loving fears,

Chid me for my tardy footsteps, dewed me with their
gentle tears,

Think then of my father's sorrow, of my mother's
woeful plight,
If afar in wood and jungle pass we now the livelong
night,   370

Wife beloved, I may not fathom what mishap or load
of care,
Unknown dangers, unseen sorrows, even now my
parents share!"

Gentle drops of filial sorrow trickled down his manly
eye,
Fond Savitri sweetly speaking softly wiped the tear-
drops dry:

"Trust me, husband, if Savitri hath been faithful in
her love,   375
If she hath with pious offerings served the righteous
gods above,

If she hath a sister's kindness unto brother men performed,
If she hath in speech and action unto holy truth con-
formed,

Unknown blessings, mighty gladness, trust thy ever
faithful wife,
And not sorrows or disasters wait this eve our parents'
life!"   380

Then she rose and tied her tresses, gently helped her
lord to rise,
Walked with him the pathless jungle, looked with
love into his eyes,

On her neck his clasping left arm sweetly winds in
soft embrace,
Round his waist Savitri's right arm doth as sweetly
interlace,

Thus they walked the darksome jungle, silent stars
looked from above,   385
And the hushed and throbbing midnight watched
Savitri's deathless love.

Kalidasa

Flourished fifth or sixth century A.D.

The work of Kalidasa reminds us that all the
pessimism and asceticism in the Hindu's view
of life could not stifle his natural longing for worldly
beauty and human love. India's greatest poet wrote persistently of the happiness of love and marriage. As a de-

vout Hindu, he chose his themes from ancient religious stories and wove into them the orthodox Brahman views. But we remember from his plays and epics especially the sympathetic pictures of women in love, the tender portraits of children, the revealing descriptions of nature in its countless phases.

The life of Kalidasa is lost in legend. A picturesque tradition makes him the orphaned son of a Brahman, who was reared as a humble ox-driver. When a certain intellectual princess rejected all her suitors as unequal to herself in learning, they sought revenge by representing the intelligent ox-driver as a great scholar. The princess, discovering the deception after their marriage, was angered, but the gods miraculously gave Kalidasa both erudition and poetic skill, and he became one of "The Nine Gems" at the court of King Vikramáditya in Ujjain. Later, because of a curse, he was murdered by a woman who was jealous of his fame. But the truth is that we know nothing for sure about Kalidasa except what his work suggests, and cannot even date his life within a century.

Kalidasa, as the greatest playwright of the Orient, has often been called "the Hindu Shakespeare"; and the parallel goes far. Like Shakespeare he was equally at home in narrative, lyric, and dramatic poetry. Two of his poems, *The Dynasty of Raghu* and *The Birth of the War-God*, are long epics of art based on ancient myths from the *Râmâyana* and other sources. *The Seasons* is a cycle of six lyrics describing the sentiments aroused in two lovers by each of nature's seasons. Of his three extant plays, the earliest, *Malavika and Agnimitra*, is a light comedy of court intrigue, *Urvashi* is a poetic spectacle play, and *Shakuntala* is a romantic love story. Kalidasa did not write tragedies, because tragedy was forbidden in the Hindu theater. To the Hindu, defeat and death in this world could have no tragic meaning. In the plan of his dramas, too, Kalidasa reminds us of Shakespeare, in his combination of serious and comic elements within the same play, especially in his use of clowns, and in his frequent interpolation of lyric verse in the midst of dramatic scenes.

Since its first English translation in 1789, *Shakuntala* has been for most Westerners the door to Indian literature. Its fantastic love theme attracted the German poet Goethe, who borrowed from the play for his *Faust*. The Concord school of American writers read it along with more philosophical Hindu literature. And Goldmark's overture to *Shakuntala* has long been a standard concert selection. Western acclaim of the play supports the Hindu critics, who consider it their greatest drama.

Since the plot of *Shakuntala* was taken from the *Mahâbhârata* and was familiar to Kalidasa's audience, he disposes of a good deal of it through a series of prologues, in which minor characters prepare us, a little clumsily, for the big scenes. In thus minimizing the plot he makes the central situation of a husband's failure to recognize his wife seem less absurd to us. The situation is made more credible, too, by Kalidasa's invention of the curse of Durvasas, which freed the husband from his moral responsibility in the original tale. To the simple story from the epic, Kalidasa adds a message of his own: the physical desire in the first meeting of the lovers must be trans-

formed through separation into the higher union of souls. The purifying agent is the child, who brings his parents together in a new-found happiness on a plane of lofty detachment, symbolized by the beautiful hill of Hemakúta. The whole play is enveloped in a magical unreality which makes the air chariot in the last act seem quite plausible. The characters are romantic types of dashing prince and faithful wife, and the exquisite verse of the original stamps it as a sophisticated rendering of a folk story.

Shakuntala

DRAMATIS PERSONÆ

KING DUSHYANTA.
BHARATA, *nicknamed* All-tamer, *his son.*
MADHAVYA, *a clown, his companion.*
His charioteer.
RAIVATAKA, *a door-keeper.*
BHADRASENA, *a general.*
KARABHAKA, *a servant.*
PARVATAYANA, *a chamberlain.*
SOMARATA, *a chaplain.*

KANVA, *hermit-father*
SHARNGARAVA
SHARADVATA } *his pupils.*
HARITA
DURVASAS, *an irascible sage.*

The chief of police.
SUCHAKA
JANUKA } *policemen.*
A fisherman.

SHAKUNTALA, *foster-child of Kanva.*
ANUSUYA
PRIYAMVADA } *her friends.*
GAUTAMI, *hermit-mother.*

KASHYAPA, *father of the gods.*
ADITI, *mother of the gods.*
MATALI, *charioteer of heaven's king.*
GALAVA, *a pupil in heaven.*
MISHRAKESHI, *a heavenly nymph.*

Stage-director and actress (in the prologue), hermits and hermit-women, two court poets, palace attendants, invisible fairies.

The first four acts pass in Kanva's forest hermitage; acts five and six in the king's palace; act

Shakuntala. Taken from *Shakuntala: A Play; and Other Works,* by Kalidasa, translated by Professor A. W. Ryder, published by E. P. Dutton & Co., Inc. (Everyman's Library), New York. Reprinted by permission of E. P. Dent and Co. and J. M. Dent and Sons, Ltd.

seven on a heavenly mountain. The time is perhaps seven years.

ACT I

THE HUNT

(Enter, in a chariot, pursuing a deer, KING DU-SHYANTA, bow and arrow in hand; and a charioteer.)

CHARIOTEER.

Your Majesty,
    I see you hunt the spotted deer
      With shafts to end his race,
    As though God Shiva should appear
      In his immortal chase.

KING. Charioteer, the deer has led us a long chase. And even now

    His neck in beauty bends
    As backward looks he sends
10   At my pursuing car
    That threatens death from far.
    Fear shrinks to half the body small;
    See how he fears the arrow's fall!

    The path he takes is strewed
    With blades of grass half-chewed
    From jaws wide with the stress
    Of fevered weariness.
    He leaps so often and so high,
    He does not seem to run, but fly.

20 Pursue as I may, I can hardly keep him in sight.
CHARIOTEER. Your Majesty, I have been holding the horses back because the ground was rough. This checked us and gave the deer a lead. Now we are on level ground, and you will easily overtake him.
KING. Then let the reins hang loose.
CHARIOTEER. Yes, your Majesty. Look, your Majesty!

    The lines hang loose; the steeds unreined
      Dart forward with a will.
30   Their ears are pricked; their necks are strained
      Their plumes lie straight and still.
    They leave the rising dust behind;
    They seem to float upon the wind.

KING *(joyfully)*. See! The horses are gaining on the deer.

    As onward and onward the chariot flies,
    The small flashes large to my dizzy eyes.
    What is cleft in twain, seems to blur and mate;
    What is crooked in nature, seems to be straight.

Things at my side in an instant appear   40
Distant, and things in the distance, near.

A VOICE BEHIND THE SCENES. O King, this deer belongs to the hermitage, and must not be killed.
CHARIOTEER *(listening and looking)*. Your Majesty, here are two hermits, come to save the deer at the moment when your arrow was about to fall.
KING *(hastily)*. Stop the chariot.
CHARIOTEER. Yes, your Majesty. *(He does so. Enter a hermit with his pupil.)*
HERMIT *(lifting his hand)*. O King, this deer belongs to the hermitage.   50

    Why should his tender form expire,
      As blossoms perish in the fire?
    How could that gentle life endure
      The deadly arrow, sharp and sure?

    Restore your arrow to the quiver;
      To you were weapons lent
    The broken-hearted to deliver,
      Not strike the innocent.

KING *(bowing low)*. It is done. *(He does so.)*
HERMIT *(joyfully)*. A deed worthy of you, scion   60 of Puru's race, and shining example of kings. May you beget a son to rule earth and heaven.
KING *(bowing low)*. I am thankful for a Brahman's blessing.
THE TWO HERMITS. O King, we are on our way to gather firewood. Here, along the bank of the Malini, you may see the hermitage of Father Kanva, over which Shakuntala presides, so to speak, as guardian deity. Unless other deities prevent, pray enter here and receive a welcome. Besides,   70

    Beholding pious hermit-rites
      Preserved from fearful harm,
    Perceive the profit of the scars
      On your protecting arm.

KING. Is the hermit father there?
THE TWO HERMITS. No, he has left his daughter to welcome guests, and has just gone to Somatirtha, to avert an evil fate that threatens her.
KING. Well, I will see her. She shall feel my devotion, and report it to the sage.   80
THE TWO HERMITS. Then we will go on our way. *(Exit hermit with pupil.)*
KING. Charioteer, drive on. A sight of the pious hermitage will purify us.
CHARIOTEER. Yes, your Majesty. *(He counterfeits motion again.)*
KING *(looking about)*. One would know, without being told, that this is the precinct of a pious grove.
CHARIOTEER. How so?
KING. Do you not see? Why, here

---

4. **God Shiva,** third deity of the Hindu triad, a five-headed god of destruction sometimes shown armed with a bow.

73-74. **Perceive . . . arm.** The king received the scars from his bow, bent in protection of the hermits' rites.

Are rice-grains, dropped from bills of parrot chicks
Beneath the trees; and pounding-stones where sticks
A little almond-oil; and trustful deer
That do not run away as we draw near;
And river-paths that are besprinkled yet
From trickling hermit-garments, clean and wet.

Besides,

The roots of trees are washed by many a stream
That breezes ruffle; and the flowers' red gleam
10 Is dimmed by pious smoke; and fearless fawns
Move softly on the close-cropped forest lawns.

CHARIOTEER. It is all true.

KING (*after a little*). We must not disturb the hermitage. Stop here while I dismount.

CHARIOTEER. I am holding the reins. Dismount, your Majesty.

KING (*dismounts and looks at himself*). One should wear modest garments on entering a hermitage. Take these jewels and the bow. (*He gives
20 them to the charioteer.*) Before I return from my visit to the hermits, have the horses' backs wet down.

CHARIOTEER. Yes, your Majesty. (*Exit.*)

KING (*walking and looking about*). The hermitage! Well, I will enter. (*As he does so, he feels a throbbing in his arm.*)

A tranquil spot! Why should I thrill?
    Love cannot enter there—
Yet to inevitable things
    Doors open everywhere.

30 A VOICE BEHIND THE SCENES. This way, girls!

KING (*listening*). I think I hear some one to the right of the grove. I must find out. (*He walks and looks about.*) Ah, here are hermit-girls, with watering-pots just big enough for them to handle. They are coming in this direction to water the young trees. They are charming!

The city maids, for all their pains,
    Seem not so sweet and good;
Our garden blossoms yield to these
40   Flower-children of the wood.

I will draw back into the shade and wait for them. (*He stands, gazing toward them. Enter SHAKUNTALA, and her two friends.*)

FIRST FRIEND. It seems to me, dear, that Father Kanva cares more for the hermitage trees than he does for you. You are delicate as a jasmine blossom, yet he tells you to fill the trenches about the trees.

SHAKUNTALA. Oh, it isn't Father's bidding so much. I feel like a real sister to them. (*She waters the trees.*)

PRIYAMVADA. Shakuntala, we have watered the trees that blossom in the summer-time. Now let's
50 sprinkle those whose flowering-time is past. That

will be a better deed, because we shall not be working for a reward.

SHAKUNTALA. What a pretty idea! (*She does so.*)

KING (*to himself*). And this is Kanva's daughter, Shakuntala. (*In surprise.*) The good Father does wrong to make her wear the hermit's dress of bark.

The sage who yokes her artless charm
    With pious pain and grief,
Would try to cut the toughest vine
    With a soft, blue lotus-leaf.   60

Well, I will step behind a tree and see how she acts with her friends. (*He conceals himself.*)

SHAKUNTALA. Oh, Anusuya! Priyamvada has fastened this bark dress so tight that it hurts. Please loosen it. (*ANUSUYA does so.*)

PRIYAMVADA (*laughing*). You had better blame your own budding charms for that.

KING. She is quite right.

Beneath the barken dress
    Upon the shoulder tied,   70
In maiden loveliness
    Her young breast seems to hide,

As when a flower amid
    The leaves by autumn tossed—
Pale, withered leaves—lies hid,
    And half its grace is lost.

Yet in truth the bark dress is not an enemy to her beauty. It serves as an added ornament. For

The meanest vesture glows
    On beauty that enchants: 80
The lotus lovelier shows
    Amid dull water-plants;

The moon in added splendour
    Shines for its spot of dark;
Yet more the maiden slender
    Charms in her dress of bark.

SHAKUNTALA (*looking ahead*). Oh, girls, that mango-tree is trying to tell me something with his branches that move in the wind like fingers. I must go and see him. (*She does so.*)   90

PRIYAMVADA. There, Shakuntala, stand right where you are a minute.

SHAKUNTALA. Why?

PRIYAMVADA. When I see you there, it looks as if a vine were clinging to the mango-tree.

SHAKUNTALA. I see why they call you the flatterer.

KING. But the flattery is true.

Her arms are tender shoots; her lips
    Are blossoms red and warm;
Bewitching youth begins to flower   100
    In beauty on her form.

ANUSUYA. Oh, Shakuntala! Here is the jasmine-vine that you named Light of the Grove. She has chosen the mango-tree as her husband.

SHAKUNTALA (*approaches and looks at it, joyfully*). What a pretty pair they make. The jasmine shows her youth in her fresh flowers, and the mango-tree shows his strength in his ripening fruit. (*She stands gazing at them.*)

PRIYAMVADA (*smiling*). Anusuya, do you know why Shakuntala looks so hard at the Light of the Grove?

10 ANUSUYA. No. Why?

PRIYAMVADA. She is thinking how the Light of the Grove has found a good tree, and hoping that she will meet a fine lover.

SHAKUNTALA. That's what you want for yourself. (*She tips her watering-pot.*)

ANUSUYA. Look, Shakuntala! Here is the spring-creeper that Father Kanva tended with his own hands—just as he did you. You are forgetting her.

SHAKUNTALA. I'd forget myself sooner. (*She goes* 20 *to the creeper and looks at it, joyfully.*) Wonderful! Wonderful! Priyamvada, I have something pleasant to tell you.

PRIYAMVADA. What is it, dear?

SHAKUNTALA. It is out of season, but the spring-creeper is covered with buds down to the very root.

THE TWO FRIENDS (*running up*). Really?

SHAKUNTALA. Of course. Can't you see?

PRIYAMVADA (*looking at it joyfully*). And I have something pleasant to tell *you*. You are to be married 30 soon.

SHAKUNTALA (*snappishly*). You know that's just what you want for yourself.

PRIYAMVADA. I'm not teasing. I really heard Father Kanva say that this flowering vine was to be a symbol of your coming happiness.

ANUSUYA. Priyamvada, that is why Shakuntala waters the spring-creeper so lovingly.

SHAKUNTALA. She is my sister. Why shouldn't I give her water? (*She tips her watering-pot.*)

40 KING. May I hope that she is the hermit's daughter by a mother of a different caste? But it *must* be so.

Surely, she may become a warrior's bride;
  Else, why these longings in an honest mind?
The motions of a blameless heart decide
  Of right and wrong, when reason leaves us blind.

Yet I will learn the whole truth.

SHAKUNTALA (*excitedly*). Oh, oh! A bee has left the jasmine-vine and is flying into my face. (*She shows herself annoyed by the bee.*)

40–41. **May . . . caste;** otherwise she could not marry into the warrior caste, to which the king belongs.

KING (*ardently*).

As the bee about her flies,   50
Swiftly her bewitching eyes
  Turn to watch his flight.
She is practising to-day
Coquetry and glances' play
  Not from love, but fright.

Eager bee, you lightly skim
O'er the eyelid's trembling rim
  Toward the cheek aquiver.
Gently buzzing round her cheek,
Whispering in her ear, you seek   60
  Secrets to deliver.

While her hands that way and this
Strike at you, you steal a kiss,
  Love's all, honeymaker.
I know nothing but her name,
Not her caste, nor whence she came—
  You, my rival, take her.

SHAKUNTALA. Oh, girls! Save me from this dreadful bee!

THE TWO FRIENDS (*smiling*). Who are we, that 70 we should save you? Call upon Dushyanta. For pious groves are in the protection of the king.

KING. A good opportunity to present myself. Have no—(*He checks himself. Aside.*) No, they would see that I am the king. I prefer to appear as a guest.

SHAKUNTALA. He doesn't leave me alone! I am going to run away. (*She takes a step and looks about.*) Oh, dear! Oh, dear! He is following me. Please save me.

KING (*hastening forward*). Ah!   80

A king of Puru's mighty line
  Chastises shameless churls;
What insolent is he who baits
  These artless hermit-girls?

ANUSUYA. It is nothing very dreadful, sir. But our friend (*indicating* SHAKUNTALA) was teased and frightened by a bee.

KING (*to* SHAKUNTALA). I hope these pious days are happy ones. (SHAKUNTALA'S *eyes drop in embarrassment.*)

ANUSUYA. Yes, now that we receive such a dis- 90 tinguished guest.

PRIYAMVADA. Welcome, sir. Go to the cottage, Shakuntala, and bring fruit. This water will do to wash the feet.

KING. Your courteous words are enough to make me feel at home.

ANUSUYA. Then, sir, pray sit down and rest on this shady bench.

KING. You, too, are surely wearied by your pious task. Pray be seated a moment.

PRIYAMVADA (*aside to* SHAKUNTALA). My dear, we must be polite to our guest. Shall we sit down? (*The three girls sit.*)

SHAKUNTALA (*to herself*). Oh, why do I have such feelings when I see this man? They seem wrong in a hermitage.

KING. It is delightful to see your friendship. For you are all young and beautiful.

PRIYAMVADA (*aside to* ANUSUYA). Who is he, dear? With his mystery, and his dignity, and his courtesy? He acts like a king and a gentleman.

ANUSUYA. I am curious too. I am going to ask him. (*Aloud.*) Sir, you are so very courteous that I make bold to ask you something. What royal family do you adorn, sir? What country is grieving at your absence? Why does a gentleman so delicately bred submit to the weary journey into our pious grove?

SHAKUNTALA (*aside*). Be brave, my heart. Anusuya speaks your very thoughts.

KING (*aside*). Shall I tell at once who I am, or conceal it? (*He reflects.*) This will do. (*Aloud.*) I am a student of Scripture. It is my duty to see justice done in the cities of the king. And I have come to this hermitage on a tour of inspection.

ANUSUYA. Then we of the hermitage have some one to take care of us. (SHAKUNTALA *shows embarrassment.*)

THE TWO FRIENDS (*observing the demeanour of the pair. Aside to* SHAKUNTALA). Oh, Shakuntala! If only Father were here to-day.

SHAKUNTALA. What would he do?

THE TWO FRIENDS. He would make our distinguished guest happy, if it took his most precious treasure.

SHAKUNTALA. Go away! You mean something. I'll not listen to you.

KING. I too would like to ask a question about your friend.

THE TWO FRIENDS. Sir, your request is a favour to us.

KING. Father Kanva lives a lifelong hermit. Yet you say that your friend is his daughter. How can that be?

ANUSUYA. Listen, sir. There is a majestic royal sage named Kaushika—

KING. Ah, yes. The famous Kaushika.

ANUSUYA. Know, then, that he is the source of our friend's being. But Father Kanva is her real father, because he took care of her when she was abandoned.

KING. You waken my curiosity with the word "abandoned." May I hear the whole story?

ANUSUYA. Listen, sir. Many years ago, that royal sage was leading a life of stern austerities, and the gods, becoming strangely jealous, sent the nymph Menaka to disturb his devotions.

KING. Yes, the gods feel this jealousy toward the austerities of others. And then—

ANUSUYA. Then in the lovely spring-time he saw her intoxicating beauty— (*She stops in embarrassment.*)

KING. The rest is plain. Surely, she is the daughter of the nymph.

ANUSUYA. Yes.

KING. It is as it should be.

> To beauty such as this
> No woman could give birth;
> The quivering lightning flash
> Is not a child of earth.

(*To himself*). Ah, my wishes become hopes.

PRIYAMVADA (*looking with a smile at* SHAKUNTALA). Sir, it seems as if you had more to say.

KING. You are right. Your pious life interests me, and I have another question.

PRIYAMVADA. Do not hesitate. We hermit people stand ready to answer all demands.

KING. My question is this:

> Does she, till marriage only, keep her vow
> As hermit-maid, that shames the ways of love?
> Or must her soft eyes ever see, as now,
> Soft eyes of friendly deer in peaceful grove?

PRIYAMVADA. Sir, we are under bonds to lead a life of virtue. But it is her father's wish to give her to a suitable lover.

KING (*joyfully to himself*).

> O heart, your wish is won!
> All doubt at last is done;
> The thing you feared as fire,
> Is the jewel of your desire.

SHAKUNTALA (*pettishly*). Anusuya, I'm going.

ANUSUYA. What for?

SHAKUNTALA. I am going to tell Mother Gautami that Priyamvada is talking nonsense. (*She rises.*)

ANUSUYA. My dear, we hermit people cannot neglect to entertain a distinguished guest, and go wandering about.

KING (*aside*). She is going! (*He starts up as if to detain her, then checks his desires.*) A thought is as vivid as an act, to a lover.

> Though nurture, conquering nature, holds
> Me back, it seems
> As had I started and returned
> In waking dreams.

PRIYAMVADA (*approaching* SHAKUNTALA). You dear, peevish girl! You mustn't go.

SHAKUNTALA (*turns with a frown*). Why not?

87. **Mother Gautami,** the Mother Superior of the women's part of the hermitage.

PRIYAMVADA. You owe me the watering of two trees. You can go when you have paid your debt. (*She forces her to come back.*)

KING. It is plain that she is already wearied by watering the trees. See!

Her shoulders droop; her palms are reddened yet;
  Quick breaths are struggling in her bosom fair;
The blossom o'er her ear hangs limply wet;
  One hand restrains the loose, dishevelled hair.

I therefore remit her debt. (*He gives the two friends a ring. They take it, read the name engraved on it, and look at each other.*)

KING. Make no mistake. This is a present—from the king.

PRIYAMVADA. Then, sir, you ought not to part with it. Your word is enough to remit the debt.

ANUSUYA. Well, Shakuntala, you are set free by this kind gentleman—or rather, by the king himself. Where are you going now?

SHAKUNTALA (*to herself*). I would never leave him if I could help myself.

PRIYAMVADA. Why don't you go now?

SHAKUNTALA. I am not *your* servant any longer. I will go when I like.

KING (*looking at* SHAKUNTALA. *To himself*). Does she feel toward me as I do toward her? At least, there is ground for hope.

Although she does not speak to me,
  She listens while I speak;
Her eyes turn not to see my face,
  But nothing else they seek.

A VOICE BEHIND THE SCENES. Hermits! Hermits! Prepare to defend the creatures in our pious grove. King Dushyanta is hunting in the neighborhood.

The dust his horses' hoofs have raised,
  Red as the evening sky,
Falls like a locust-swarm on boughs
  Where hanging garments dry.

KING (*aside*). Alas! My soldiers are disturbing the pious grove in their search for me.

THE VOICE BEHIND THE SCENES. Hermits! Hermits! Here is an elephant who is terrifying old men, women, and children.

One tusk is splintered by a cruel blow
Against a blocking tree; his gait is slow,
For countless fettering vines impede and cling;
He puts the deer to flight; some evil thing
He seems, that comes our peaceful life to mar,
Fleeing in terror from the royal car.

(*The girls listen and rise anxiously.*)

KING. I have offended sadly against the hermits. I must go back.

THE TWO FRIENDS. Your Honour, we are fright-ened by this alarm of the elephant. Permit us to return to the cottage.

ANUSUYA (*to* SHAKUNTALA). Shakuntala dear, Mother Gautami will be anxious. We must hurry and find her.

SHAKUNTALA (*feigning lameness*). Oh, oh! I can hardly walk.

KING. You must go very slowly. And I will take pains that the hermitage is not disturbed.

THE TWO FRIENDS. Your honour, we feel as if we knew you very well. Pray pardon our shortcomings as hostesses. May we ask you to seek better entertainment from us another time?

KING. You are too modest. I feel honoured by the mere sight of you.

SHAKUNTALA. Anusuya, my foot is cut on a sharp blade of grass, and my dress is caught on an amaranth twig. Wait for me while I loosen it. (*She goes out with her two friends.*)

KING (*sighing*). They are gone. And I must go. The sight of Shakuntala has made me dread the return to the city. I will make my men camp at a distance from the pious grove. But I cannot turn my own thoughts from Shakuntala.

It is my body leaves my love, not I;
  My body moves away, but not my mind;
For back to her my struggling fancies fly
  Like silken banners borne against the wind.

(*Exit.*)

ACT II

THE SECRET

(*Enter the clown.*)

CLOWN (*sighing*). Damn! Damn! Damn! I'm tired of being friends with this sporting king. "There's a deer!" he shouts, "There's a boar!" And off he chases on a summer noon through woods where shade is few and far between. We drink hot, stinking water from the mountain streams, flavoured with leaves— nasty! At odd times we get a little tepid meat to eat. And the horses and the elephants make such a noise that I can't even be comfortable at night. Then the hunters and the bird-chasers—damn 'em—wake me up bright and early. They do make an ear-splitting rumpus when they start for the woods. But even that isn't the whole misery. There's a new pimple growing on the old boil. He left us behind and went hunting a deer. And there in a hermitage they say he found—oh, dear! oh, dear! he found a hermit-girl named Shakuntala. Since then he hasn't a thought of going back to town. I lay awake all night, thinking about it. What can I do? Well, I'll see my friend when he is dressed and beautified. (*He walks and looks about.*) Hello! Here he comes, with his bow in his hand, and his girl in his heart. He is wearing a wreath of wild flowers! I'll pretend to be all knocked up. Perhaps I can get a rest that way. (*He stands, leaning on his staff. Enter the king, as described.*)

KING (*to himself*).

Although my darling is not lightly won,
　She seemed to love me, and my hopes are bright;
Though love be balked ere joy be well begun,
　A common longing is itself delight.

(*Smiling.*) Thus does a lover deceive himself. He judges his love's feelings by his own desires.

Her glance was loving—but 'twas not for me;
　Her step was slow—'twas grace, not coquetry;
Her speech was short—to her detaining friend.
　In things like these love reads a selfish end!

CLOWN (*standing as before*). Well, king, I can't move my hand. I can only greet you with my voice.

KING (*looking and smiling*). What makes you lame?

CLOWN. Good! You hit a man in the eye, and then ask him why the tears come.

KING. I do not understand you. Speak plainly.

CLOWN. When a reed bends over like a hunchback, do you blame the reed or the river-current?

KING. The river-current, of course.

CLOWN. And you are to blame for my troubles.

KING. How so?

CLOWN. It's a fine thing for you to neglect your royal duties and such a sure job—to live in the woods! What's the good of talking? Here I am, a Brahman, and my joints are all shaken up by this eternal running after wild animals, so that I can't move. Please be good to me. Let us have a rest for just one day.

KING (*to himself*). He says this. And I too, when I remember Kanva's daughter, have little desire for the chase. For

The bow is strung, its arrow near;
　And yet I cannot bend
That bow against the fawns who share
　Soft glances with their friend.

CLOWN. He means more than he says. I might as well weep in the woods.

KING (*smiling*). What more could I mean? I have been thinking that I ought to take my friend's advice.

CLOWN (*cheerfully*). Long life to you, then.

KING. Wait. Hear me out.

CLOWN. Well, sir?

KING. When you are rested, you must be my companion in another task—an easy one.

CLOWN. Crushing a few sweetmeats?

KING. I will tell you presently.

CLOWN. Pray command my leisure.

KING. Who stands without? (*Enter the door-keeper.*)

DOOR-KEEPER. I await your Majesty's commands.

KING. Raivataka, summon the general.

DOOR-KEEPER. Yes, your Majesty. (*He goes out, then returns with the general.*) Follow me, sir. There is his Majesty, listening to our conversation. Draw near, sir.

GENERAL (*to himself*). Hunting is declared to be a sin, yet it brings nothing but good to the king. See!

He does not heed the cruel sting
Of his recoiling, twanging string;
The mid-day sun, the dripping sweat
Affect him not, nor make him fret;
His form, though sinewy and spare,
Is most symmetrically fair;
No mountain-elephant could be
More filled with vital strength than he.

(*He approaches.*) Victory to your Majesty! The forest is full of deer-tracks, and beasts of prey cannot be far off. What better occupation could we have?

KING. Bhadrasena, my enthusiasm is broken. Madhavya has been preaching against hunting.

GENERAL (*aside to the clown*). Stick to it, friend Madhavya. I will humour the king a moment. (*Aloud.*) Your Majesty, he is a chattering idiot. Your Majesty may judge by his own case whether hunting is an evil. Consider:

The hunter's form grows sinewy, strong, and light;
He learns, from beasts of prey, how wrath and fright
Affect the mind; his skill he loves to measure
With moving targets. 'Tis life's chiefest pleasure.

CLOWN (*angrily*). Get out! Get out with your strenuous life! The king has come to his senses. But you, you son of a slave-wench, can go chasing from forest to forest, till you fall into the jaws of some old bear that is looking for a deer or a jackal.

KING. Bhadrasena, I cannot take your advice. because I am in the vicinity of a hermitage. So for to-day

The hornèd buffalo may shake
The turbid water of the lake;
Shade-seeking deer may chew the cud,
Boars trample swamp-grass in the mud;
The bow I bend in hunting, may
Enjoy a listless holiday.

GENERAL. Yes, your Majesty.

KING. Send back the archers who have gone ahead. And forbid the soldiers to vex the hermitage, or even to approach it. Remember:

There lurks a hidden fire in each
　Religious hermit-bower;
Cool sun-stones kindle if assailed
　By any foreign power.

GENERAL. Yes, your Majesty.

CLOWN. Now will you get out with your strenuous life? (*Exit general.*)

KING (*to his attendants*). Lay aside your hunting dress. And you, Raivataka, return to your post of duty.

RAIVATAKA. Yes, your Majesty. (*Exit.*)

CLOWN. You have got rid of the vermin. Now be seated on this flat stone, over which the trees spread their canopy of shade. I can't sit down till you do.

KING. Lead the way.

CLOWN. Follow me. (*They sit down.*)

KING. Friend Madhavya, you do not know what vision is. You have not seen the fairest of all objects.

CLOWN. I see you, right in front of me.

KING. Yes, every one thinks himself beautiful. But I was speaking of Shakuntala, the ornament of the hermitage.

CLOWN (*to himself*). I mustn't add fuel to the flame. (*Aloud.*) But you can't have her because she is a hermit-girl. What is the use of seeing her?

KING. Fool!

> And is it selfish longing then,
>   That draws our souls on high
> Through eyes that have forgot to wink,
>   As the new moon climbs the sky?

Besides, Dushyanta's thoughts dwell on no forbidden object.

CLOWN. Well, tell me about her.

KING.
> Sprung from a nymph of heaven
>   Wanton and gay,
> Who spurned the blessing given,
>   Going her way;
>
> By the stern hermit taken
>   In her most need:
> So fell the blossom shaken,
>   Flower on a weed.

CLOWN (*laughing*). You are like a man who gets tired of good dates and longs for sour tamarind. All the pearls of the palace are yours, and you want this girl!

KING. My friend, you have not seen her, or you could not talk so.

CLOWN. She must be charming if she surprises *you*.

KING. Oh, my friend, she needs not many words.

> She is God's vision, of pure thought
>   Composed in His creative mind;
> His reveries of beauty wrought
>   The peerless pearl of womankind.
> So plays my fancy when I see
> How great is God, how lovely she.

CLOWN. How the women must hate her!

KING. This too is in my thought.

> She seems a flower whose fragrance none has tasted,
>   A gem uncut by workman's tool,
> A branch no desecrating hands have wasted,
>   Fresh honey, beautifully cool.
>
> No man on earth deserves to taste her beauty,
>   Her blameless loveliness and worth,
> Unless he has fulfilled man's perfect duty—
>   And is there such a one on earth?

CLOWN. Marry her quick, then, before the poor girl falls into the hands of some oily-headed hermit.

KING. She is dependent on her father, and he is not here.

CLOWN. But how does she feel toward you?

KING. My friend, hermit-girls are by their very nature timid. And yet

> When I was near, she could not look at me;
>   She smiled—but not to me—and half denied it;
> She would not show her love for modesty,
>   Yet did not try so very hard to hide it.

CLOWN. Did you want her to climb into your lap the first time she saw you?

KING. But when she went away with her friends, she almost showed that she loved me.

> When she had hardly left my side,
> "I cannot walk," the maiden cried,
> And turned her face, and feigned to free
> The dress not caught upon the tree.

CLOWN. She has given you some memories to chew on. I suppose that is why you are so in love with the pious grove.

KING. My friend, think of some pretext under which we may return to the hermitage.

CLOWN. What pretext do you need? Aren't you the king?

KING. What of that?

CLOWN. Collect the taxes on the hermit's rice.

KING. Fool! It is a very different tax which these hermits pay—one that outweighs heaps of gems.

> The wealth we take from common men,
>   Wastes while we cherish;
> These share with us such holiness
>   As ne'er can perish.

VOICES BEHIND THE SCENES. Ah, we have found him.

KING (*listening*). The voices are grave and tranquil. These must be hermits. (*Enter the door-keeper.*)

DOOR-KEEPER. Victory, O King. There are two hermit-youths at the gate.

90. **Collect . . . rice.** Since the rice eaten by the hermits was wild rather than cultivated, it was not subject to the king's tax.

KING. Bid them enter at once.

DOOR-KEEPER. Yes, your Majesty. (*He goes out, then returns with the youths.*) Follow me.

FIRST YOUTH (*looking at the king*). A majestic presence, yet it inspires confidence. Nor is this wonderful in a king who is half a saint. For to him

> The splendid palace serves as hermitage;
> His royal government, courageous, sage,
> Adds daily to his merit; it is given
> To him to win applause from choirs of heaven
> Whose anthems to his glory rise and swell,
> Proclaiming him a king, and saint as well.

SECOND YOUTH. My friend, is this Dushyanta, friend of Indra?

FIRST YOUTH. It is.

SECOND YOUTH.

> Nor is it wonderful that one whose arm
> Might bolt a city gate, should keep from harm
> The whole broad earth dark-belted by the sea;
> For when the gods in heaven with demons fight,
> Dushyanta's bow and Indra's weapon bright
> Are their reliance for the victory.

THE TWO YOUTHS (*approaching*). Victory, O King!

KING (*rising*). I salute you.

THE TWO YOUTHS. All hail! (*They offer fruit.*)

KING (*receiving it and bowing low*). May I know the reason of your coming?

THE TWO YOUTHS. The hermits have learned that you are here, and they request—

KING. They command rather.

THE TWO YOUTHS. The powers of evil disturb our pious life in the absence of the hermit-father. We therefore ask that you will remain a few nights with your charioteer to protect the hermitage.

KING. I shall be most happy to do so.

CLOWN (*to the king*). You rather seem to like being collared this way.

KING. Raivataka, tell my charioteer to drive up, and to bring the bow and arrows.

RAIVATAKA. Yes, your Majesty. (*Exit.*)

THE TWO YOUTHS.

> Thou art a worthy scion of
> The kings who ruled our nation
> And found, defending those in need,
> Their truest consecration.

KING. Pray go before. And I will follow straightway.

THE TWO YOUTHS. Victory, O King! (*Exeunt.*)

KING. Madhavya, have you no curiosity to see Shakuntala?

CLOWN. I *did* have an unending curiosity, but this talk about the powers of evil has put an end to it.

KING. Do not fear. You will be with me.

CLOWN. I'll stick close to your chariot-wheel. (*Enter the door-keeper.*)

DOOR-KEEPER. Your Majesty, the chariot is ready, and awaits your departure to victory. But one Karabhaka has come from the city, a messenger from the queen-mother.

KING (*respectfully*). Sent by my mother?

DOOR-KEEPER. Yes.

KING. Let him enter.

DOOR-KEEPER (*goes out and returns with* KARABHAKA). Karabhaka, here is his Majesty. You may draw near.

KARABHAKA (*approaching and bowing low*). Victory to your Majesty. The queen-mother sends her commands—

KING. What are her commands?

KARABHAKA. She plans to end a fasting ceremony on the fourth day from to-day. And on that occasion her dear son must not fail to wait upon her.

KING. On the one side is my duty to the hermits, on the other my mother's command. Neither may be disregarded. What is to be done?

CLOWN (*laughing*). Stay half-way between, like Trishanku.

KING. In truth, I am perplexed.

> Two inconsistent duties sever
> My mind with cruel shock,
> As when the current of a river
> Is split upon a rock.

(*He reflects.*) My friend, the queen-mother has always felt toward you as toward a son. Do you return, tell her what duty keeps me here, and yourself perform the offices of a son.

CLOWN. You don't think I am afraid of the devils?

KING (*smiling*). O mighty Brahman, who could suspect it?

CLOWN. But I want to travel like a prince.

KING. I will send all the soldiers with you, for the pious grove must not be disturbed.

CLOWN (*strutting*). Aha! Look at the heir-apparent!

KING (*to himself*). The fellow is a chatterbox. He might betray my longing to the ladies of the palace. Good, then! (*He takes the clown by the hand. Aloud.*) Friend Madhavya, my reverence for the hermits draws me to the hermitage. Do not think that I am really in love with the hermit-girl. Just think:

> A king, and a girl of the calm hermit-grove,
> Bred with the fawns, and a stranger to love!
> Then do not imagine a serious quest;
> The light words I uttered were spoken in jest.

74. Trishanku, a king in the *Ramáyana* who was hung between heaven and earth because a sage ordered him to heaven and the gods ordered him back to earth.

CLOWN. Oh, I understand that well enough.

(*Exeunt ambo.*)

ACT III

THE LOVE-MAKING

(*Enter a pupil, with sacred grass for the sacrifice.*)

PUPIL (*with meditative astonishment*). How great is the power of King Dushyanta! Since his arrival our rites have been undisturbed.

> He does not need to bend the bow;
> For every evil thing,
> Awaiting not the arrow, flees
> From the twanging of the string.

10 Well, I will take this sacred grass to the priests, to strew the altar. (*He walks and looks about, then speaks to some one not visible.*) Priyamvada, for whom are you carrying this cuscus-salve and the fibrous lotus-leaves? (*He listens.*) What do you say? That Shakuntala has become seriously ill from the heat, and that these things are to relieve her suffering? Give her the best of care, Priyamvada. She is the very life of the hermit-father. And I will give Gautami the holy water for her. (*Exit. Enter the lovelorn king.*)

KING (*with a meditative sigh*).

> I know that stern religion's power
20 > Keeps guardian watch my maiden o'er;
> Yet all my heart flows straight to her
> Like water to the valley-floor.

Oh, mighty Love, thine arrows are made of flowers. How can they be so sharp? (*He recalls something.*) Ah, I understand.

> Shiva's devouring wrath still burns in thee,
> As burns the eternal fire beneath the sea;
> Else how couldst thou, thyself long since consumed,
30 > Kindle the fire that flames so ruthlessly?

Indeed, the moon and thou inspire confidence, only to deceive the host of lovers.

> Thy shafts are blossoms; coolness streams
> From moon-rays: thus the poets sing;
> But to the lovelorn, falsehood seems
> To lurk in such imagining;
> The moon darts fire from frosty beams;
> Thy flowery arrows cut and sting.

And yet

40
> If Love will trouble her
> Whose great eyes madden me,

---

23. **Oh . . . flowers.** Each of the five arrows of Káma, god of love, was tipped with a flower and was directed at one of the five senses.

> I greet him unafraid,
> Though wounded ceaselessly.

O mighty god, wilt thou not show me mercy after such reproaches?

> With tenderness unending
> I cherished thee when small,
> In vain—thy bow is bending;
> On me thine arrows fall.
50 > My care for thee to such a plight
> Has brought me; and it serves me right.

I have driven off the powers of evil, and the hermits have dismissed me. Where shall I go now to rest from my weariness? There is no rest for me except in seeing her whom I love. She usually spends these hours of midday heat with her friends on the vine-wreathed banks of the Malini. I will go there. (*He walks and looks about.*) I believe the slender maiden has just passed through this corridor of young trees. For
60
> The stems from which she gathered flowers
> Are still unhealed;
> The sap where twigs were broken off
> Is uncongealed.

This is a pleasant spot, with the wind among the trees.

> Limbs that love's fever seizes,
> Their fervent welcome pay
> To lotus-fragrant breezes
70 > That bear the river-spray.

Ah, Shakuntala must be in this reedy bower. For

> In white sand at the door
> Fresh footprints appear,
> The toe lightly outlined,
> The heel deep and clear.

I will hide among the branches, and see what happens. Ah, my eyes have found their heaven. Here is the darling of my thoughts, lying upon a flower-strewn bench of stone, and attended by her two friends. I will hear what they say to each other. 80 (*Enter SHAKUNTALA with her two friends.*)

THE TWO FRIENDS (*fanning her*). Do you feel better, dear, when we fan you with these lotus-leaves?

SHAKUNTALA (*wearily*). Oh, are you fanning me, my dear girls? (*The two friends look sorrowfully at each other.*)

KING. She is seriously ill. (*Doubtfully.*) Is it the heat, or is it as I hope? (*Decidedly.*) It *must* be so.

> With salve upon her breast,
> With loosened lotus-chain,
> My darling, sore oppressed,
90 > Is lovely in her pain.

Though love and summer heat
May work an equal woe,
No maiden seems so sweet
When summer lays her low.

PRIYAMVADA (*aside to* ANUSUYA). Anusuya, since she first saw the good king, she has been greatly troubled. I do not believe her fever has any other cause.

ANUSUYA. I suspect you are right. I am going to ask her. My dear, I must ask you something. You are in a high fever.

KING. It is too true.

Her lotus-chains that were as white
As moonbeams shining in the night,
Betray the fever's awful pain,
And fading, show a darker stain.

SHAKUNTALA. Well, say whatever you like.

ANUSUYA. Shakuntala dear, you have not told us what is going on in your mind. But I have heard old, romantic stories, and I can't help thinking that you are in a state like that of a lady in love. Please tell us what hurts you. We have to understand the disease before we can even try to cure it.

KING. Anusuya expresses my own thoughts.

SHAKUNTALA. It hurts me terribly. I can't tell you all at once.

PRIYAMVADA. Anusuya is right, dear. Why do you hide your trouble? You are wasting away every day. You are nothing but a beautiful shadow.

KING. Priyamvada is right. See!

Her cheeks grow thin; her breast and shoulders fail;
Her waist is weary and her face is pale:
She fades for love; oh, pitifully sweet!
As vine-leaves wither in the scorching heat.

SHAKUNTALA. I could not tell any one else. But I shall be a burden to you.

THE TWO FRIENDS. That is why we insist on knowing, dear. Grief must be shared to be endured.

KING. To friends who share her joy and grief
　　　She tells what sorrow laid her here;
　　She turned to look her love again
　　　When first I saw her—yet I fear!

SHAKUNTALA. Ever since I saw the good king who protects the pious grove—

THE TWO FRIENDS. Go on, dear.

SHAKUNTALA. I love him, and it makes me feel like this.

THE TWO FRIENDS. Good, good! You have found a lover worthy of your devotion. But of course, a great river always runs into the sea.

KING (*joyfully*). I have heard what I longed to hear.

'Twas love that caused the burning pain;
'Tis love that eases it again;

As when, upon a sultry day,
Rain breaks, and washes grief away.

SHAKUNTALA. Then, if you think best, make the good king take pity upon me. If not, remember that I was.

KING. Her words end all doubt.

PRIYAMVADA (*aside to* ANUSUYA). Anusuya, she is far gone in love and cannot endure any delay.

ANUSUYA. Priyamvada, can you think of any scheme by which we could carry out her wishes quickly and secretly?

PRIYAMVADA. We must plan about the "secretly." The "quickly" is not hard.

ANUSUYA. How so?

PRIYAMVADA. Why, the good king shows his love for her in his tender glances, and he has been wasting away, as if he were losing sleep.

KING. It is quite true.

The hot tears, flowing down my cheek
　All night on my supporting arm
And on its golden bracelet, seek
　To stain the gems and do them harm.

The bracelet slipping o'er the scars
　Upon the wasted arm, that show
My deeds in hunting and in wars,
　All night is moving to and fro.

PRIYAMVADA. Well, she must write him a love-letter. And I will hide it in a bunch of flowers and see that it gets into the king's hand as if it were a relic of the sacrifice.

ANUSUYA. It is a pretty plan, dear, and it pleases me. What does Shakuntala say?

SHAKUNTALA. I suppose I must obey orders.

PRIYAMVADA. Then compose a pretty little love-song, with a hint of yourself in it.

SHAKUNTALA. I'll try. But my heart trembles, for fear he will despise me.

KING.

Here stands the eager lover, and you pale
　For fear lest he disdain a love so kind:
The seeker may find fortune, or may fail;
　But how could fortune, seeking, fail to find?

And again:

The ardent lover comes, and yet you fear
　Lest he disdain love's tribute, were it brought,
The hope of which has led his footsteps here—
　Pearls need not seek, for they themselves are
　　sought.

THE TWO FRIENDS. You are too modest about your own charms. Would anybody put up a parasol to keep off the soothing autumn moonlight?

84. relic of the sacrifice. Consecrated flowers left over from a sacrifice might be given to friends.

A Rajput Indian painting now in the British Museum.

SHAKUNTALA (*smiling*). I suppose I shall have to obey orders.

KING. It is only natural that I should forget to wink when I see my darling. For

> One clinging eyebrow lifted,
>   As fitting words she seeks,
> Her face reveals her passion
>   For me in glowing cheeks.

SHAKUNTALA. Well, I have thought out a little song. But I haven't anything to write with.

PRIYAMVADA. Here is a lotus-leaf, glossy as a parrot's breast. You can cut the letters in it with your nails.

SHAKUNTALA. Now listen, and tell me whether it makes sense.

THE TWO FRIENDS. Please.

SHAKUNTALA (*reads*).

> I know not if I read your heart aright;
>   Why, pitiless, do you distress me so?
> I only know that longing day and night
>   Tosses my restless body to and fro,
>   That yearns for you, the source of all its woe.

KING (*advancing*).

> Though Love torments you, slender maid,
>   Yet he consumes me quite,
> As daylight shuts night-blooming flowers
>   And slays the moon outright.

THE TWO FRIENDS (*perceive the king and rise joyfully*). Welcome to the wish that is fulfilled without delay. (SHAKUNTALA *tries to rise*.)

KING. Do not try to rise, beautiful Shakuntala.

> Your limbs from which the strength is fled,
> That crush the blossoms of your bed
> And bruise the lotus-leaves, may be
> Pardoned a breach of courtesy.

SHAKUNTALA (*sadly to herself*). Oh, my heart, you were so impatient, and now you find no answer to make.

ANUSUYA. Your Majesty, pray do this stone bench the honour of sitting upon it. (SHAKUNTALA *edges away*.)

KING (*seating himself*). Priyamvada, I trust your friend's illness is not dangerous.

PRIYAMVADA (*smiling*). A remedy is being applied and it will soon be better. It is plain, sir, that you and she love each other. But I love her too, and I must say something over again.

KING. Pray do not hesitate. It always causes pain in the end, to leave unsaid what one longs to say.

PRIYAMVADA. Then listen, sir.

KING. I am all attention.

PRIYAMVADA. It is the king's duty to save hermit-folk from all suffering. Is not that good Scripture?

KING. There is no text more urgent.

PRIYAMVADA. Well, our friend has been brought to this sad state by her love for you. Will you not take pity on her and save her life?

KING. We cherish the same desire. I feel it a great honour.

SHAKUNTALA (*with a jealous smile*). Oh, don't detain the good king. He is separated from the court ladies, and he is anxious to go back to them.

KING. Bewitching eyes that found my heart,
>   You surely see
> It could no longer live apart,
>   Nor faithless be.
> I bear Love's arrows as I can;
> Wound not with doubt a wounded man.

ANUSUYA. But, your Majesty, we hear that kings have many favourites. You must act in such a way that our friend may not become a cause of grief to her family.

KING. What more can I say?

> Though many queens divide my court,
>   But two support the throne;
> Your friend will find a rival in
>   The sea-girt earth alone.

THE TWO FRIENDS. We are content.

PRIYAMVADA (*aside to* ANUSUYA). Look, Anusuya! See how the dear girl's life is coming back moment by moment—just like a peahen in summer when the first rainy breezes come.

SHAKUNTALA. You must please ask the king's pardon for the rude things we said when we were talking together.

THE TWO FRIENDS (*smiling*). Anybody who says it was rude, may ask his pardon. Nobody else feels guilty.

SHAKUNTALA. Your Majesty, pray forgive what we said when we did not know that you were present. I am afraid that we say a great many things behind a person's back.

KING (*smiling*).

> Your fault is pardoned if I may
> Relieve my weariness
> By sitting on the flower-strewn couch
> Your fevered members press.

PRIYAMVADA. But that will not be enough to satisfy him.

SHAKUNTALA (*feigning anger*). Stop! You are a rude girl. You make fun of me when I am in this condition.

ANUSUYA. Priyamvada, there is a little fawn, looking all about him. He has probably lost his mother and is trying to find her. I am going to help him.

PRIYAMVADA. He is a frisky little fellow. You can't catch him alone. I'll go with you. (*They start to go.*)

SHAKUNTALA. I will not let you go and leave me alone.

THE TWO FRIENDS (*smiling*). You alone, when the king of the world is with you! (*Exeunt.*)

SHAKUNTALA. Are my friends gone?

KING. Do not be anxious, beautiful Shakuntala. Have you not a humble servant here, to take the place of your friends? Then tell me:

> Shall I employ the moistened lotus-leaf
> To fan away your weariness and grief?
> Or take your lily feet upon my knee
> And rub them till you rest more easily?

SHAKUNTALA. I will not offend against those to whom I owe honour. (*She rises weakly and starts to walk away.*)

KING (*detaining her*). The day is still hot, beautiful Shakuntala, and you are feverish.

> Leave not the blossom-dotted couch
> To wander in the midday heat,
> With lotus-petals on your breast,
> With fevered limbs and stumbling feet.
>   (*He lays his hand upon her.*)

SHAKUNTALA. Oh, don't! Don't! For I am not mistress of myself. Yet what can I do now? I had no one to help me but my friends.

KING. I am rebuked.

SHAKUNTALA. I was not thinking of your Majesty. I was accusing fate.

KING. Why accuse a fate that brings what you desire?

SHAKUNTALA. Why not accuse a fate that robs me of self-control and tempts me with the virtues of another?

KING (*to himself*).

> Though deeply longing, maids are coy
>   And bid their wooers wait;
> Though eager for united joy
>   In love, they hesitate.
>
> Love cannot torture them, nor move
>   Their hearts to sudden mating;
> Perhaps they even torture love
>   By their procrastinating.
>   (SHAKUNTALA *moves away.*)

KING. Why should I not have my way? (*He approaches and seizes her dress.*)

SHAKUNTALA. Oh, sir! Be a gentleman. There are hermits wandering about.

KING. Do not fear your family, beautiful Shakuntala. Father Kanva knows the holy law. He will not regret it.

> For many a hermit maiden who
>   By simple, voluntary rite
> Dispensed with priest and witness, yet
>   Found favour in her father's sight.

Ah, I have come into the open air.

SHAKUNTALA. O King, I cannot do as you would have me. You hardly know me after this short talk. But oh, do not forget me.

KING.

> When evening comes, the shadows of the tree
>   Is cast far forward, yet does not depart;
> Even so, belovèd, wheresoe'er you be,
>   The thought of you can never leave my heart.

SHAKUNTALA (*to herself*). Oh, oh! When I hear him speak so, my feet will not move away. I will hide in this amaranth hedge and see how long his love lasts. (*She hides and waits.*)

KING. Oh, my belovèd, my love for you is my whole life, yet you leave me and go away without a thought.

> Your body, soft as siris-flowers,
> Engages passion's utmost powers;
> How comes it that your heart is hard
> As stalks that siris-blossoms guard?

SHAKUNTALA. When I hear this, I have no power to go.

KING. What have I to do here, where she is not? Ah, I cannot go.

> The perfumed lotus-chain
>   That once was worn by her
> Fetters and keeps my heart
>   A hopeless prisoner.
>
>   (*He lifts it reverently.*)

SHAKUNTALA (*looking at her arm*). Why, I was so

weak and ill that when the lotus-bracelet fell off, I did not even notice it.

KING (*laying the lotus-bracelet on his heart*). Ah!

> Once, dear, on your sweet arm it lay,
> And on my heart shall ever stay;
> Though you disdain to give me joy,
> I find it in a lifeless toy.

SHAKUNTALA. I cannot hold back after that. I will use the bracelet as an excuse for my coming. (*She approaches.*)

KING (*seeing her*). The queen of my life! As soon as I complained, fate proved kind to me.

> No sooner did the thirsty bird
> With parching throat complain,
> Than forming clouds in heaven stirred
> And sent the streaming rain.

SHAKUNTALA (*standing before the king*). When I was going away, sir, I remembered that this lotus-bracelet had fallen from my arm, and I have come back for it. My heart seemed to tell me that you had taken it. Please give it back, or you will betray me, and yourself too, to the hermits.

KING. I will restore it on one condition.

SHAKUNTALA. What condition?

KING. That I may myself place it where it belongs.

SHAKUNTALA (*to herself*). What can I do?

KING. Let us sit on this stone bench. (*They walk to the bench and sit down.*)

KING (*taking* SHAKUNTALA's *hand*). Ah!

> When Shiva's anger burned the tree
> Of love in quenchless fire,
> Did heavenly fate preserve a shoot
> To deck my heart's desire?

SHAKUNTALA. Hasten, my dear, hasten.

KING (*to himself*). Now I am content. She speaks as a wife to her husband. (*Aloud.*) Beautiful Shakuntala, the clasp of the bracelet is not very firm. May I fasten it in another way?

SHAKUNTALA (*smiling*). If you like.

KING. See, my beautiful girl!

> The lotus-chain is dazzling white
> As is the slender moon at night.
> Perhaps it was the moon on high
> That joined her horns and left the sky,
> Believing that your lovely arm
> Would, more than heaven, enhance her charm.

SHAKUNTALA. I cannot see it. The pollen from the lotus over my ear has blown into my eye.

KING. Will you permit me to blow it away?

SHAKUNTALA. I should not like to be an object of pity. But why should I not trust you?

KING. Do not have such thoughts. A new servant does not transgress orders.

SHAKUNTALA. It is this exaggerated courtesy that frightens me.

KING (*to himself*). I shall not break the bonds of this sweet servitude. (*He starts to raise her face to his.* SHAKUNTALA *resists a little, then is passive.*)

KING. Oh, my bewitching girl, have no fear of me. (*Aside.*)

> Her sweetly trembling lip
> With virgin invitation
> Provokes my soul to sip
> Delighted fascination.

SHAKUNTALA. You seem slow, dear, in fulfilling your promise.

KING. The lotus over your ear is so near your eye, and so like it, that I was confused. (*He gently blows her eye.*)

SHAKUNTALA. Thank you. I can see quite well now. But I am ashamed not to make any return for your kindness.

KING. What more could I ask?

> It ought to be enough for me
> To hover round your fragrant face;
> Is not the lotus-haunting bee
> Content with perfume and with grace?

SHAKUNTALA. But what does he do if he is not content?

KING. This! This! (*He draws her face to his.*)

A VOICE BEHIND THE SCENES. O sheldrake bride, bid your mate farewell. The night is come.

SHAKUNTALA (*listening excitedly*). Oh, my dear, this is Mother Gautami, come to inquire about me. Please hide among the branches. (*The king conceals himself. Enter* GAUTAMI, *with a bowl in her hand.*)

GAUTAMI. Here is the holy water, my child. (*She helps her to rise.*) So ill, and all alone here with the gods?

SHAKUNTALA. It was just a moment ago that Priyamvada and Anusuya went down to the river.

GAUTAMI (*sprinkling* SHAKUNTALA *with the holy water*). May you live long and happy, my child. Has the fever gone down?

SHAKUNTALA. There is a difference, mother.

GAUTAMI. The sun is setting. Come, let us go to the cottage.

SHAKUNTALA (*to herself*). Oh, my heart, you delayed when your desire came of itself. Now see what you have done. (*Aloud.*) O bower that took away my pain, I bid you farewell until another blissful hour. (*Exeunt* SHAKUNTALA *and* GAUTAMI.)

KING (*advancing with a sigh.*) The path to happiness is strewn with obstacles.

> Her face, adorned with soft eye-lashes,
> Adorable with trembling flashes

76. **sheldrake,** a species of wild duck; here the Indian love-birds doomed by a curse to part from each other with the coming of night.

Of half-denial, in memory lingers;
  The sweet lips guarded by her fingers,
  The head that drooped upon her shoulder—
Why was I not a little bolder?

Where shall I go now? Let me stay a moment in this bower where my belovèd lay.

  The flower-strewn bed whereon her body tossed;
  The bracelet, fallen from her arm and lost;
  The dear love-missive, in the lotus-leaf
10 Cut by her nails: assuage my absent grief
  And occupy my eyes—I have no power,
  Though she is gone, to leave the reedy bower.

(*He reflects.*) Alas! I did wrong to delay when I had found my love. So now

  If she will grant me but one other meeting,
  I'll not delay; for happiness is fleeting;
  So plans my foolish, self-defeated heart;
  But when she comes, I play the coward's part.

A VOICE BEHIND THE SCENES. O King!

20 The flames rise heavenward from the evening altar;
  And round the sacrifices, blazing high,
  Flesh-eating demons stalk, like red cloud-masses,
  And cast colossal shadows on the sky.

KING. Have no fear, hermits. I am here.

                  (*Exit.*)

ACT IV

SHAKUNTALA'S DEPARTURE

SCENE I

(*Enter the two friends, gathering flowers.*)

ANUSUYA. Priyamvada, dear Shakuntala has been properly married by the voluntary ceremony and she has a husband worthy of her. And yet I am not quite satisfied.

PRIYAMVADA. Why not?

30 ANUSUYA. The sacrifice is over and the good king was dismissed to-day by the hermits. He has gone back to the city and there he is surrounded by hundreds of court ladies. I wonder whether he will remember poor Shakuntala or not.

PRIYAMVADA. You need not be anxious about that. Such handsome men are sure to be good. But there is something else to think about. I don't know what Father will have to say when he comes back from his pilgrimage and hears about it.

40 ANUSUYA. I believe that he will be pleased.

PRIYAMVADA. Why?

ANUSUYA. Why not? You know he wanted to give his daughter to a lover worthy of her. If fate brings this about of itself, why shouldn't Father be happy?

25–26. has been . . . ceremony; that is, without the usual ceremony but by the Gandharva ceremony, named after the musician-nymphs of Indra's heaven, who practiced it.

PRIYAMVADA. I suppose you are right. (*She looks at her flower-basket.*) My dear, we have gathered flowers enough for the sacrifice.

ANUSUYA. But we must make an offering to the gods that watch over Shakuntala's marriage. We had better gather more.   50

PRIYAMVADA. Very well.

A VOICE BEHIND THE SCENES. Who will bid me welcome?

ANUSUYA (*listening*). My dear, it sounds like a guest announcing himself.

PRIYAMVADA. Well, Shakuntala is near the cottage. (*Reflecting.*) Ah, but to-day her heart is far away. Come, we must do with the flowers we have. (*They start to walk away.*)

THE VOICE. Do you dare despise a guest like me?

  Because your heart, by loving fancies blinded,   60
    Has scorned a guest in pious life grown old,
  Your lover shall forget you though reminded,
    Or think of you as of a story told.

PRIYAMVADA. Oh, dear! The very thing has happened. The dear, absent-minded girl has offended some worthy man.

ANUSUYA (*looking ahead*). My dear, this is no ordinary somebody. It is the great sage Durvasas, the irascible. See how he strides away!

PRIYAMVADA. Nothing burns like fire. Run, fall at   70 his feet, bring him back, while I am getting water to wash his feet.

ANUSUYA. I will. (*Exit.*)

PRIYAMVADA (*stumbling*). There! I stumbled in my excitement, and the flower-basket fell out of my hand. (*She collects the scattered flowers.* ANUSUYA *returns.*)

ANUSUYA. My dear, he is anger incarnate. Who could appease him? But I softened him a little.

PRIYAMVADA. Even that is a good deal for him.   80 Tell me about it.

ANUSUYA. When he would not turn back, I fell at his feet and prayed to him. "Holy sir," I said, "remember her former devotion and pardon this offence. Your daughter did not recognise your great and holy power to-day."

PRIYAMVADA. And then——

ANUSUYA. Then he said: "My words must be fulfilled. But the curse shall be lifted when her lover sees a gem which he has given her for a token." And so he vanished.   90

PRIYAMVADA. We can breathe again. When the good king went away, he put a ring, engraved with his own name, on Shakuntala's finger to remember him by. That will save her.

ANUSUYA. Come, we must finish the sacrifice for her. (*They walk about.*)

PRIYAMVADA. Just look, Anusuya! There is the dear girl, with her cheek resting on her left hand.

She looks like a painted picture. She is thinking about him. How could she notice a guest when she has forgotten herself?

ANUSUYA. Priyamvada, we two must keep this thing to ourselves. We must be careful of the dear girl. You know how delicate she is.

PRIYAMVADA. Would any one sprinkle a jasmine-vine with scalding water? (*Exeunt ambo.*)

SCENE II. *Early Morning*

(*Enter a pupil of* KANVA, *just risen from sleep.*)

PUPIL. Father Kanva has returned from his pil-
10 grimage, and has bidden me find out what time it is. I will go into the open air and see how much of the night remains. (*He walks and looks about.*) See! The dawn is breaking. For already

The moon behind the western mount is sinking;
  The eastern sun is heralded by dawn;
From heaven's twin lights, their fall and glory
    linking,
  Brave lessons of submission may be drawn.

And again:

20 Night-blooming lilies, when the moon is hidden,
    Have naught but memories of beauty left.
  Hard, hard to bear! Her lot whom heaven has
      bidden
    To live alone, of love and lover reft. . . .

And yet again:

The moon that topped the loftiest mountain
      ranges,
  That slew the darkness in the midmost sky,
Is fallen from heaven, and all her glory changes:
30   So high to rise, so low at last to lie!

ANUSUYA (*entering hurriedly. To herself*). That is just what happens to the innocent. Shakuntala has been treated shamefully by the king.

PUPIL. I will tell Father Kanva that the hour of morning sacrifice is come. (*Exit.*)

ANUSUYA. The dawn is breaking. I am awake bright and early. But what shall I do now that I am awake? My hands refuse to attend to the ordinary morning tasks. Well, let love take its course. For the
40 dear, pure-minded girl trusted him—the traitor! Perhaps it is not the good king's fault. It must be the curse of Durvasas. Otherwise, how could the good king say such beautiful things, and then let all this time pass without even sending a message? (*She reflects.*) Yes, we must send him the ring he left as a token. But whom shall we ask to take it? The hermits are unsympathetic because they have never suffered. It seemed as if her friends were to blame and so, try as we might, we could not tell Father
50 Kanva that Shakuntala was married to Dushyanta and was expecting a baby. Oh, what shall we do?

(*Enter* PRIYAMVADA.)

PRIYAMVADA. Hurry, Anusuya, hurry! We are getting Shakuntala ready for her journey.

ANUSUYA (*astonished.*) What do you mean, my dear?

PRIYAMVADA. Listen. I just went to Shakuntala, to ask if she had slept well.

ANUSUYA. And then——

PRIYAMVADA. I found her hiding her face for shame, and Father Kanva was embracing her and 60 encouraging her. "My child," he said, "I bring you joy. The offering fell straight in the sacred fire, and auspicious smoke rose toward the sacrificer. My pains for you have proved like instruction given to a good student; they have brought me no regret. This very day I shall give you an escort of hermits and send you to your husband."

ANUSUYA. But, my dear, who told Father Kanva about it?

PRIYAMVADA. A voice from heaven that recited a 70 verse when he had entered the fire-sanctuary.

ANUSUYA. What did it say?

PRIYAMVADA. Listen.

Know, Brahman, that your child,
  Like the fire-pregnant tree,
Bears kingly seed that shall be born
  For earth's prosperity.

ANUSUYA. I am so glad, dear. But my joy is half sorrow when I think that Shakuntala is going to be taken away this very day. 80

PRIYAMVADA. We must hide our sorrow as best we can. The poor girl must be made happy to-day.

ANUSUYA. Well, here is a cocoa-nut casket, hanging on a branch of the mango-tree. I put flower-pollen in it for this very purpose. It keeps fresh, you know. Now you wrap it in a lotus-leaf, and I will get yellow pigment and earth from a sacred spot and blades of panic grass for the happy ceremony. (PRIYAMVADA *does so. Exit* ANUSUYA.)

A VOICE BEHIND THE SCENES. Gautami, bid the worthy Sharngarava and Sharadvata make ready to 90 escort my daughter Shakuntala.

PRIYAMVADA. Hurry, Anusuya, hurry! They are calling the hermits who are going to Hastinapura. (*Enter* ANUSUYA, *with materials for the ceremony.*)

ANUSUYA. Come, dear, let us go. (*They walk about.*)

PRIYAMVADA (*looking ahead*). There is Shakuntala. She took the ceremonial bath at sunrise, and now the hermit-women are giving her rice-cakes and wishing her happiness. Let's go to her. (*They do so. Enter* SHAKUNTALA *with attendants as described, and* GAUTAMI.)

SHAKUNTALA. Holy women, I salute you.

GAUTAMI. My child, may you receive the happy

93. **Hastinapura**, the residence of the king, now Delhi.

title "queen," showing that your husband honours you.

HERMIT-WOMEN. My dear, may you become the mother of a hero. (*Exeunt all but* GAUTAMI.)

THE TWO FRIENDS. Did you have a good bath, dear?

SHAKUNTALA. Good morning, girls. Sit here.

THE TWO FRIENDS (*seating themselves*). Now stand straight, while we go through the happy ceremony.

SHAKUNTALA. It has happened often enough, but I ought to be very grateful to-day. Shall I ever be adorned by my friends again? (*She weeps.*)

THE TWO FRIENDS. You ought not to weep, dear, at this happy time.

PRIYAMVADA. You are so beautiful, you ought to have the finest gems. It seems like an insult to give you these hermitage things. (*Enter* HARITA, *a hermit-youth, with ornaments.*)

HARITA. Here are ornaments for our lady. (*The women look at them in astonishment.*)

GAUTAMI. Harita, my son, whence come these things?

HARITA. From the holy power of Father Kanva.

GAUTAMI. A creation of his mind?

HARITA. Not quite. Listen. Father Kanva sent us to gather blossoms from the trees for Shakuntala, and then

One tree bore fruit, a silken marriage dress
That shamed the moon in its white loveliness;
Another gave us lac-dye for the feet;
From others, fairy hands extended, sweet
Like flowering twigs, as far as to the wrist,
And gave us gems, to adorn her as we list.

PRIYAMVADA (*looking at* SHAKUNTALA). A bee may be born in a hole in a tree, but she likes the honey of the lotus.

GAUTAMI. This gracious favour is a token of the queenly happiness which you are to enjoy in your husband's palace. (SHAKUNTALA *shows embarrassment.*)

HARITA. Father Kanva has gone to the bank of the Malini, to perform his ablutions. I will tell him of the favour shown us by the trees. (*Exit.*)

ANUSUYA. My dear, we poor girls never saw such ornaments. How shall we adorn you? But we have seen pictures. Perhaps we can arrange them right.

SHAKUNTALA. I know how clever you are. (*The two friends adorn her. Enter* KANVA, *returning after his ablutions.*)

KANVA.

Shakuntala must go to-day;
I miss her now at heart;
I dare not speak a loving word
Or choking tears will start.

My eyes are dim with anxious thought;
Love strikes me to the life:
And yet I strove for pious peace—
I have no child, no wife.

What must a father feel, when come
The pangs of parting from his child at home?

THE TWO FRIENDS. There, Shakuntala, we have arranged your ornaments. Now put on this beautiful silk dress. (SHAKUNTALA *rises and does so.*)

GAUTAMI. My child, here is your father. The eyes with which he seems to embrace you are overflowing with tears of joy. You must greet him properly. (SHAKUNTALA *makes a shamefaced reverence.*)

KANVA. My child,

Like Sharmishtha, Yayati's wife,
Win favour measured by your worth;
And may you bear a kingly son
Like Puru, who shall rule the earth.

GAUTAMI. My child, this is not a prayer, but a benediction.

KANVA. My daughter, walk from left to right about the fires in which the offering has just been thrown.

The holy fires around the altar kindle,
And at their margins sacred grass is piled;
Beneath their sacrificial odours dwindle
Misfortunes. May the fires protect you, child!

KANVA. Now you may start, my daughter. Where are Sharngarava and Sharadvata? (*Enter the two pupils.*)

THE TWO PUPILS. We are here, Father.

KANVA. Sharngarava, my son, lead the way for your sister.

SHARNGARAVA. Follow me.

KANVA. O trees of the pious grove, in which the fairies dwell,

She would not drink till she had wet
Your roots, a sister's duty,
Nor pluck your flowers; she loves you yet
Far more than selfish beauty.

'Twas festival in her pure life
When budding blossoms showed;
And now she leaves you as a wife—
Oh, speed her on her road!

SHARNGARAVA. Father,

The trees are answering your prayer
In cooing cuckoo-song,
Bidding Shakuntala farewell,
Their sister for so long.

63. **Like Sharmishtha, Yayati's wife.** Sharmishtha and Yayati were parents of Puru, hence ancestors of King Dushyanta.

INVISIBLE BEINGS.

May lily-dotted lakes delight your eye;
    May shade-trees bid the heat of noonday
        cease;
May soft winds blow the lotus-pollen nigh;
    May all your path be pleasantness and peace.

GAUTAMI. My child, the fairies of the pious grove bid you farewell. For they love the household. Pay reverence to the holy ones.

10 SHAKUNTALA (*Aside to* PRIYAMVADA). Priyamvada, I long to see my husband, and yet my feet will hardly move. It is hard, hard to leave the hermitage.

PRIYAMVADA. You are not the only one to feel sad at this farewell. See how the whole grove feels at parting from you.

The grass drops from the feeding doe;
    The peahen stops her dance;
Pale, trembling leaves are falling slow,
    The tears of clinging plants.

20 SHAKUNTALA. Father, I must say good-bye to the spring-creeper, my sister among the vines.

KANVA. I know your love for her. See! Here she is at your right hand.

SHAKUNTALA. Vine sister, embrace me too with your arms, these branches. I shall be far away from you after to-day. Father, you must care for her as you did for me.

KANVA. My child, you found the lover who
    Had long been sought by me;
30 No longer need I watch for you;
    I'll give the vine a lover true,
    This handsome mango-tree.

And now start on your journey.

SHAKUNTALA (*going to the two friends*). Dear girls, I leave her in your care too.

THE TWO FRIENDS. But who will care for poor us? (*They shed tears.*)

KANVA. Anusuya! Priyamvada! Do not weep. It is you who should cheer Shakuntala.

SHAKUNTALA. Father, there is the pregnant doe, 40 wandering about near the cottage. When she becomes a happy mother, you must send some one to bring me the good news. Do not forget.

KANVA. I shall not forget, my child.

SHAKUNTALA (*stumbling*). Oh, oh! Who is it that keeps pulling at my dress, as if to hinder me? (*She turns round to see.*)

KANVA. It is the fawn whose lip, when torn
    By kusha-grass, you soothed with oil;
The fawn who gladly nibbled corn
    Held in your hand; with loving toil
50 You have adopted him, and he
    Would never leave you willingly.

SHAKUNTALA. My dear, why should you follow me when I am going away from home? Your mother died when you were born and I brought you up. Now I am leaving you, and Father Kanva will take care of you. Go back, dear! Go back! (*She walks away, weeping.*)

KANVA. Do not weep, my child. Be brave. Look at the path before you.

Be brave, and check the rising tears
    That dim your lovely eyes;   60
Your feet are stumbling on the path
    That so uneven lies.

SHARNGARAVA. Holy Father, the Scripture declares that one should accompany a departing loved one only to the first water. Pray give us your commands on the bank of this pond, and then return.

KANVA. Then let us rest in the shade of this fig-tree. (*All do so.*) What commands would it be fitting for me to lay on King Dushyanta?

ANUSUYA. My dear, there is not a living thing in   70 the whole hermitage that is not grieving to-day at saying good-bye to you. Look!

The sheldrake does not heed his mate
    Who calls behind the lotus-leaf;
He drops the lily from his bill
    And turns on you a glance of grief.

KANVA. Son Sharngarava, when you present Shakuntala to the king, give him this message from me.

Remembering my religious worth,
    Your own high race, the love poured forth   80
By her, forgetful of her friends,
    Pay her what honour custom lends
To all your wives. And what fate gives
    Beyond, will please her relatives.

SHARNGARAVA. I will not forget your message, Father.

KANVA (*turning to* SHAKUNTALA). My child, I must now give you my counsel. Though I live in the forest, I have some knowledge of the world.

SHARNGARAVA. True wisdom, Father, gives insight   90 into everything.

KANVA. My child, when you have entered your husband's home,

Obey your elders; and be very kind
To rivals; never be perversely blind
And angry with your husband, even though he
Should prove less faithful than a man might be;
Be as courteous to servants as you may,
Not puffed with pride in this your happy day:
Thus does a maiden grow into a wife;   100
But self-willed women are the curse of life.

But what does Gautami say?

GAUTAMI. This is advice sufficient for a bride. You will not forget, my child.

KANVA. Come, my daughter, embrace me and your friends.

SHAKUNTALA. Oh, Father! Must my friends turn back too?

KANVA. My daughter, they too must some day be given in marriage. Therefore they may not go to court. Gautami will go with you.

SHAKUNTALA (*throwing her arms about her father*). I am torn from my father's breast like a vine stripped from a sandal-tree on the Malabar hills. How can I live in another soil?

KANVA. My daughter, why distress yourself so?

A noble husband's honourable wife,
You are to spend a busy, useful life
In the world's eye; and soon, as eastern skies
Bring forth the sun, from you there shall arise
A child, a blessing and a comfort strong—
You will not miss me, dearest daughter, long.

SHAKUNTALA. Farewell, Father.

KANVA. My daughter, may all that come to you which I desire for you.

SHAKUNTALA (*going to her two friends*). Come, girls! Embrace me, both of you together.

THE TWO FRIENDS. Dear, if the good king should perhaps be slow to recognise you, show him the ring with his own name engraved on it.

SHAKUNTALA. Your doubts make my heart beat faster.

THE TWO FRIENDS. Do not be afraid, dear. Love is timid.

SHARNGARAVA. Father, the sun is in mid-heaven. She must hasten.

SHAKUNTALA. Father, when shall I see the pious grove again?

KANVA. My daughter,

When you have shared for many years
The king's thoughts with the earth,
When to a son who knows no fears
You shall have given birth,

When, trusted to the son you love,
Your royal labours cease,
Come with your husband to the grove
And end your days in peace.

GAUTAMI. My child, the hour of your departure is slipping by. Bid your father turn back. No, she would never do that. Pray turn back, sir.

KANVA. Child, you interrupt my duties in the pious grove.

SHAKUNTALA. Yes, Father. You will be busy in the grove. You will not miss me. But oh! I miss you.

8–9. Therefore . . . court; that is, they may not go to a public place.

KANVA. How can you think me so indifferent?

My lonely sorrow will not go,
For seeds you scattered here
Before the cottage door, will grow;
And I shall see them, dear.

Go. And peace go with you. (*Exit* SHAKUNTALA, *with* GAUTAMI, SHARNGARAVA, *and* SHARADVATA.)

THE TWO FRIENDS (*gazing long after her*). Oh, oh! Shakuntala is lost among the trees.

KANVA. Anusuya! Priyamvada! Your companion is gone. Choke down your grief and follow me.

THE TWO FRIENDS. Father, the grove seems empty without Shakuntala.

KANVA. So love interprets. Ah! I have sent Shakuntala away, and now I am myself again. For

A girl is held in trust, another's treasure;
To arms of love my child to-day is given;
And now I feel a calm and sacred pleasure;
I have restored the pledge that came from heaven.

(*Exeunt omnes.*)

ACT V

SHAKUNTALA'S REJECTION

(*Enter the king and his retinue.*)

CHAMBERLAIN (*approaching*). Victory to your Majesty. Here are hermits who dwell in the forest at the foot of the Himalayas. They bring women with them, and they carry a message from Kanva. What is your pleasure with regard to them?

KING (*astonished*). Hermits? Accompanied by women? From Kanva?

CHAMBERLAIN. Yes.

KING. Request my chaplain Somarata in my name to receive these hermits in the manner prescribed by Scripture, and to conduct them himself before me. I will await them in a place fit for their reception.

CHAMBERLAIN. Yes, your Majesty. (*Exit.*)

KING (*rising*). Vetravati, conduct me to the fire-sanctuary.

PORTRESS. Follow me, your Majesty. (*She walks about.*) Your Majesty, here is the terrace of the fire-sanctuary. It is beautiful, for it has just been swept, and near at hand is the cow that yields the milk of sacrifice. Pray ascend it.

KING (*ascends and stands leaning on the shoulder of an attendant.*) Vetravati, with what purpose does Father Kanva send these hermits to me?

Do leaguèd powers of sin conspire
To balk religion's pure desire?
Has wrong been done to beasts that roam
Contented round the hermits' home?
Do plants no longer bud and flower,

To warn me of abuse of power?
These doubts and more assail my mind,
But leave me puzzled, lost, and blind.

PORTRESS. How could these things be in a hermitage that rests in the fame of the king's arm? No, I imagine they have come to pay homage to their king, and to congratulate him on his pious rule.

(*Enter the chaplain and the chamberlain, conducting the two pupils of* KANVA, *with* GAUTAMI *and* SHAKUNTALA.)

CHAMBERLAIN. Follow me, if you please.

SHARNGARAVA. Friend Sharadvata,

10 The king is noble and to virtue true;
None dwelling here commit the deed of shame;
Yet we ascetics view the worldly crew
As in a house all lapped about with flame.

SHARADVATA. Sharngarava, your emotion on entering the city is quite just. As for me,

Free from the world and all its ways,
I see them spending worldly days
As clean men view men smeared with oil,
As pure men, those whom passions soil,
20 As waking men view men asleep,
As free men, those in bondage deep.

CHAPLAIN. That is why men like you are great.

SHAKUNTALA (*observing an evil omen*). Oh, why does my right eye throb?

GAUTAMI. Heaven avert the omen, my child. May happiness wait upon you. (*They walk about.*)

CHAPLAIN. O hermits, here is he who protects those of every station and of every age. He has already risen, and awaits you. Behold him.

30 SHARNGARAVA. Yes, it is admirable, but not surprising. For

Fruit-laden trees bend down to earth;
The water-pregnant clouds hang low;
Good men are not puffed up by power—
The unselfish are by nature so.

PORTRESS. Your Majesty, the hermits seem to be happy. They give you gracious looks.

KING (*observing* SHAKUNTALA). Ah!

Who is she, shrouded in the veil
40 That dims her beauty's lustre,
Among the hermits like a flower
Round which the dead leaves cluster?

PORTRESS. Your Majesty, she is well worth looking at.

KING. Enough! I must not gaze upon another's wife.

SHAKUNTALA (*Aside*). Oh, my heart, why tremble so? Remember his constant love and be brave.

CHAPLAIN (*advancing*). Hail, your Majesty. The
50 hermits have been received as Scripture enjoins.

They have a message from their teacher. May you be pleased to hear it.

KING. I am all attention.

THE TWO PUPILS (*raising their right hands*). Victory, O King.

KING (*bowing low*). I salute you all.

THE TWO PUPILS. All hail.

KING. Does your pious life proceed without disturbance?

THE TWO PUPILS.

How could the pious duties fail   60
While you defend the right?
Or how could darkness' power prevail
O'er sunbeams shining bright?

KING (*to himself*). Indeed, my royal title is no empty one. (*Aloud.*) Is holy Kanva in health?

SHARNGARAVA. O King, those who have religious power can command health. He asks after your welfare and sends this message.

KING. What are his commands?

SHARNGARAVA. He says: "Since you have met this   70
my daughter and have married her, I give you my glad consent. For

You are the best of worthy men, they say;
And she, I know, Good Works personified;
The Creator wrought for ever and a day,
In wedding such a virtuous groom and bride.

She is with child. Take her and live with her in virtue."

GAUTAMI. Bless you, sir. I should like to say that no one invites me to speak.   80

KING. Speak, mother.

GAUTAMI.

Did she with father speak or mother?
Did you engage her friends in speech?
Your faith was plighted each to other;
Let each be faithful now to each.

SHAKUNTALA. What will my husband say?

KING (*listening with anxious suspicion*). What is this insinuation?

SHAKUNTALA (*to herself*). Oh, oh! So haughty and so slanderous!   90

SHARNGARAVA. "What is this insinuation?" What is your question? Surely you know the world's ways well enough.

Because the world suspects a wife
Who does not share her husband's lot,
Her kinsmen wish her to abide
With him, although he love her not.

KING. You cannot mean that this young woman is my wife.

SHAKUNTALA (*sadly to herself*). Oh, my heart,   100
you feared it, and now it has come.

SHARNGARAVA. O King,

> A king, and shrink when love is done,
> Turn coward's back on truth, and flee!

KING. What means this dreadful accusation?

SHARNGARAVA (*furiously*).

> O drunk with power! We might have known
> That you were steeped in treachery.

KING. A stinging rebuke!

GAUTAMI (*to* SHAKUNTALA). Forget your shame, my child. I will remove your veil. Then your husband will recognise you. (*She does so.*)

KING (*observing* SHAKUNTALA. *To himself*).

> As my heart ponders whether I could ever
> Have wed this woman that has come to me
> In tortured loveliness, as I endeavour
> To bring it back to mind, then like a bee

> That hovers round a jasmine flower at dawn,
> While frosty dews of morning still o'erweave it,
> And hesitates to sip ere they be gone,
> I cannot taste the sweet, and cannot leave it.

PORTRESS (*to herself*). What a virtuous king he is! Would any other man hesitate when he saw such a pearl of a woman coming of her own accord?

SHARNGARAVA. Have you nothing to say, O King?

KING. Hermit, I have taken thought. I cannot believe that this woman is my wife. She is plainly with child. How can I take her, confessing myself an adulterer?

SHAKUNTALA (*to herself*). Oh, oh, oh! He even casts doubt on our marriage. The vine of my hope climbed high, but it is broken now.

SHARNGARAVA. Not so.

> You scorn the sage who rendered whole
> His child befouled, and choked his grief,
> Who freely gave you what you stole
> And added honour to a thief!

SHARADVATA. Enough, Sharngarava. Shakuntala, we have said what we were sent to say. You hear his words. Answer him.

SHAKUNTALA (*to herself*). He loved me so. He is so changed. Why remind him? Ah, but I must clear my own character. Well, I will try. (*Aloud.*) My dear husband— (*She stops.*) No, he doubts my right to call him that. Your Majesty, it was pure love that opened my poor heart to you in the hermitage. Then you were kind to me and gave me your promise. Is it right for you to speak so now, and to reject me?

KING (*stopping his ears*). Peace, peace!

> A stream that eats away the bank,
> Grows foul, and undermines the tree.
> So you would stain your honour, while
> You plunge me into misery.

SHAKUNTALA. Very well. If you have acted so because you really fear to touch another man's wife, I will remove your doubts with a token you gave me.

KING. An excellent idea!

SHAKUNTALA (*touching her finger*). Oh, oh! The ring is lost. (*She looks sadly at* GAUTAMI.)

GAUTAMI. My child, you worshipped the holy Ganges at the spot where Indra descended. The ring must have fallen there.

KING. Ready wit, ready wit!

SHAKUNTALA. Fate is too strong for me there. I will tell you something else.

KING. Let me hear what you have to say.

SHAKUNTALA. One day, in the bower of reeds, you were holding a lotus-leaf cup full of water.

KING. I hear you.

SHAKUNTALA. At that moment the fawn came up, my adopted son. Then you took pity on him and coaxed him. "Let him drink first," you said. But he did not know you, and he would not come to drink water from your hand. But he liked it afterwards, when I held the very same water. Then you smiled and said: "It is true. Every one trusts his own sort. You both belong to the forest."

KING. It is just such women, selfish, sweet, false, that entice fools.

GAUTAMI. You have no right to say that. She grew up in the pious grove. She does not know how to deceive.

KING. Old hermit woman,

> The female's untaught cunning may be seen
> In beasts, far more in women selfish-wise;
> The cuckoo's eggs are left to hatch and rear
> By foster-parents, and away she flies.

SHAKUNTALA (*angrily*). Wretch! You judge all this by your own false heart. Would any other man do what you have done? To hide behind virtue, like a yawning well covered over with grass!

KING (*to himself*). But her anger is free from coquetry, because she has lived in the forest. See!

> Her glance is straight; her eyes are flashing red;
> Her speech is harsh, not drawlingly well-bred;
> Her whole lip quivers, seems to shake with cold;
> Her frown has straightened eyebrows arching bold.

No, she saw that I was doubtful, and her anger was feigned. Thus

> When I refused but now
> Hard-heartedly, to know
> Of love or secret vow,
> Her eyes grew red; and so,
> Bending her arching brow,
> She fiercely snapped Love's bow.

(*Aloud.*) My good girl, Dushyanta's conduct is known to the whole kingdom, but not this action.

SHAKUNTALA. Well, well. I had my way. I trusted a king, and put myself in his hands. He had a honey face and a heart of stone. (*She covers her face with her dress and weeps.*)

SHARNGARAVA. Thus does unbridled levity burn.

> Be slow to love, but yet more slow
>   With secret mate;
> With those whose hearts we do not know,
>   Love turns to hate.

KING. Why do you trust this girl, and accuse me
10 of an imaginary crime?

SHARNGARAVA (*disdainfully*). You have learned your wisdom upside down.

> It would be monstrous to believe
>   A girl who never lies;
> Trust those who study to deceive
>   And think it very wise.

KING. Aha, my candid friend! Suppose I were to admit that I am such a man. What would happen if I deceived the girl?

20 SHARNGARAVA. Ruin.

KING. It is unthinkable that ruin should fall on Puru's line.

SHARNGARAVA. Why bandy words? We have fulfilled our Father's bidding. We are ready to return.

> Leave her or take her, as you will;
>   She is your wife;
> Husbands have power for good or ill
>   O'er woman's life.

Gautami, lead the way. (*They start to go.*)

30 SHAKUNTALA. He has deceived me shamelessly. And will you leave me too? (*She starts to follow.*)

GAUTAMI (*turns around and sees her*). Sharngarava, my son, Shakuntala is following us, lamenting piteously. What can the poor child do with a husband base enough to reject her?

SHARNGARAVA (*turns angrily*). You self-willed girl! Do you dare show independence? (SHAKUNTALA *shrinks in fear.*) Listen.

> If you deserve such scorn and blame,
40 >   What will your father with your shame?
> But if you know your vows are pure,
>   Obey your husband and endure.

Remain. We must go.

KING. Hermit, why deceive this woman? Remember:

> Night-blossoms open to the moon,
>   Day-blossoms to the sun;
> A man of honour ever strives
>   Another's wife to shun.

18–19. **What . . . girl.** The king is not asking for information; he knows the answer to his question. This is simply his way of emphasizing the impossibility of his lying.

SHARNGARAVA. O King, suppose you had forgotten 50 your former actions in the midst of distractions. Should you now desert your wife—you who fear to fail in virtue?

KING. I ask *you* which is the heavier sin:

> Not knowing whether I be mad
>   Or falsehood be in her,
> Shall I desert a faithful wife
>   Or turn adulterer?

CHAPLAIN (*considering*). Now if this were done——
60
KING. Instruct me, my teacher.

CHAPLAIN. Let the woman remain in my house until her child is born.

KING. Why this?

CHAPLAIN. The chief astrologers have told you that your first child was destined to be an emperor. If the son of the hermit's daughter is born with the imperial birthmarks, then welcome her and introduce her into the palace. Otherwise, she must return to her father.
70
KING. It is good advice, my teacher.

CHAPLAIN (*rising*). Follow me, my daughter.

SHAKUNTALA. O mother earth, give me a grave! (*Exit weeping, with the chaplain, the hermits, and* GAUTAMI. *The king, his memory clouded by the curse, ponders on* SHAKUNTALA.)

VOICES BEHIND THE SCENES. A miracle! A miracle!

KING (*listening*). What does this mean? (*Enter the chaplain.*)

CHAPLAIN (*in amazement*). Your Majesty, a wonderful thing has happened.

KING. What?

CHAPLAIN. When Kanva's pupils had departed,

> She tossed her arms, bemoaned her plight, 80
>   Accused her crushing fate—

KING. What then?

CHAPLAIN.

> Before our eyes a heavenly light
> In woman's form, but shining bright,
>   Seized her and vanished straight.

(*All betray astonishment.*)

KING. My teacher, we have already settled the matter. Why speculate in vain? Let us seek repose.

CHAPLAIN. Victory to your Majesty. (*Exit.*)

KING. Vetravati, I am bewildered. Conduct me to my apartment. 90

PORTRESS. Follow me, your Majesty.

KING (*walks about. To himself*).

> With a hermit-wife I had no part,
>   All memories evade me;
> And yet my sad and stricken heart
>   Would more than half persuade me.

(*Exeunt omnes.*)

ACT VI

SEPARATION FROM SHAKUNTALA

SCENE I. *In the street before the Palace*

(*Enter the chief of police, two policemen, and a man with his hands bound behind his back.*)

THE TWO POLICEMEN (*striking the man*). Now, pickpocket, tell us where you found this ring. It is the king's ring, with letters engraved on it, and it has a magnificent great gem.

FISHERMAN (*showing fright*). Be merciful, kind gentlemen. I am not guilty of such a crime.

FIRST POLICEMAN. No, I suppose the king thought you were a pious Brahman, and made you a present of it.

FISHERMAN. Listen, please. I am a fisherman, and I live on the Ganges, at the spot where Indra came down.

SECOND POLICEMAN. You thief, we didn't ask for your address or your social position.

CHIEF. Let him tell a straight story, Suchaka. Don't interrupt.

THE TWO POLICEMEN. Yes, chief. Talk, man, talk.

FISHERMAN. I support my family with things you catch fish with—nets, you know, and hooks, and things.

CHIEF (*laughing*). You have a sweet trade.

FISHERMAN. Don't say that, master.

> You can't give up a lowdown trade
> That your ancestors began;
> A butcher butchers things, and yet
> He's the tenderest-hearted man.

CHIEF. Go on. Go on.

FISHERMAN. Well, one day I was cutting up a carp. In its maw I see this ring with the magnificent great gem. And then I was just trying to sell it here when you kind gentlemen grabbed me. That is the only way I got it. Now kill me, or find fault with me.

CHIEF (*smelling the ring*). There is no doubt about it, Januka. It has been in a fish's maw. It has the real perfume of raw meat. Now we have to find out how he got it. We must go to the palace.

THE TWO POLICEMEN (*to the fisherman*). Move on, you cutpurse, move on. (*They walk about.*)

CHIEF. Suchaka, wait here at the big gate until I come out of the palace. And don't get careless.

THE TWO POLICEMEN. Go in, chief. I hope the king will be nice to you.

CHIEF. Good-bye. (*Exit.*)

SUCHAKA. Januka, the chief is taking his time.

JANUKA. You can't just drop in on a king.

SUCHAKA. Januka, my fingers are itching (*indicating the fisherman*) to kill this cutpurse.

FISHERMAN. Don't kill a man without any reason, master.

JANUKA (*looking ahead*). There is the chief, with a written order from the king. (*To the fisherman.*) Now you will see your family, or else you will feed the crows and jackals. (*Enter the chief.*)

CHIEF. Quick! Quick!

FISHERMAN. Oh, oh! I'm a dead man.

CHIEF. Release him, you. Release the fishnet fellow. It is all right, his getting the ring. Our king told me so himself.

SUCHAKA. All right, chief. He is a dead man come back to life. (*He releases the fisherman.*)

FISHERMAN (*bowing low to the chief*). Master, I owe you my life. (*He falls at his feet.*)

CHIEF. Get up, get up! Here is a reward that the king was kind enough to give you. It is worth as much as the ring. Take it. (*He hands the fisherman a bracelet.*)

FISHERMAN (*joyfully taking it*). Much obliged.

JANUKA. He *is* much obliged to the king. Just as if he had been taken from the stake and put on an elephant's back.

SUCHAKA. Chief, the reward shows that the king thought a lot of the ring. The gem must be worth something.

CHIEF. No, it wasn't the fine gem that pleased the king. It was this way.

THE TWO POLICEMEN. Well?

CHIEF. I think, when the king saw it, he remembered somebody he loves. You know how dignified he is usually. But as soon as he saw it, he broke down for a moment.

SUCHAKA. You have done the king a good turn, chief.

JANUKA. All for the sake of this fish-killer, it seems to me. (*He looks enviously at the fisherman.*)

FISHERMAN. Take half of it, masters, to pay for something to drink.

JANUKA. Fisherman, you are the biggest and best friend I've got. The first thing we want, is all the brandy we can hold. Let's go where they keep it. (*Exeunt omnes.*)

SCENE II. *In the Palace Gardens*

(*Enter* MISHRAKESHI, *flying through the air.*)

MISHRAKESHI. I have taken my turn in waiting upon the nymphs. And now I will see what this good king is doing. Shakuntala is like a second self to me, because she is the daughter of Menaka. And it was she who asked me to do this. (*She looks about.*) It is the day of the spring festival. But I see no preparations for a celebration at court. I might learn the reason by my power of divination. But I must do as my friend asked me. Good! I will make myself invisible and stand near these girls who take care of the garden. I shall find out that way. (*She descends to earth. Enter a maid, gazing at a mango branch, and behind her, a second.*)

92. **Menaka,** a close friend of Mishrakeshi among the nymphs.

FIRST MAID.

> First mango-twig, so pink, so green,
>   First living breath of spring,
> You are sacrificed as soon as seen,
>   A festival offering.

SECOND MAID. What are you chirping about to yourself, little cuckoo?

FIRST MAID. Why, little bee, you know that the cuckoo goes crazy with delight when she sees the mango-blossom.

SECOND MAID. Oh, has the spring really come?

FIRST MAID. Yes, little bee. And this is the time when you too buzz about in crazy joy.

SECOND MAID. Hold me, dear, while I stand on tiptoe and offer this blossom to Love, the divine.

FIRST MAID. If I do, you must give me half the reward of the offering.

SECOND MAID. That goes without saying, dear. We two are one. (*She leans on her friend and takes the mango-blossom.*) Oh, see! The mango-blossom hasn't opened, but it has broken the sheath, so it is fragrant. (*She brings her hands together.*) I worship mighty Love.

> O mango-twig I give to Love
>   As arrow for his bow,
> Most sovereign of his arrows five,
>   Strike maiden-targets low.

(*She throws the twig. Enter the chamberlain.*)

CHAMBERLAIN (*angrily*). Stop, silly girl. The king has strictly forbidden the spring festival. Do you dare pluck the mango-blossoms?

THE TWO MAIDS (*frightened*). Forgive us, sir. We did not know.

CHAMBERLAIN. What! You have not heard the king's command, which is obeyed even by the trees of spring and the creatures that dwell in them. See!

> The mango branches are in bloom,
>   Yet pollen does not form;
> The cuckoo's song sticks in his throat,
>   Although the days are warm;
>
> The amaranth-bud is formed, and yet
>   Its power of growth is gone;
> The love-god timidly puts by
>   The arrow he has drawn.

MISHRAKESHI. There is no doubt of it. This good king has wonderful power.

FIRST MAID. A few days ago, sir, we were sent to his Majesty by his brother-in-law Mitravasu to decorate the garden. That is why we have heard nothing of this affair.

CHAMBERLAIN. You must not do so again.

THE TWO MAIDS. But we are curious. If we girls may know about it, pray tell us, sir. Why did his Majesty forbid the spring festival?

MISHRAKESHI. Kings are fond of celebrations. There must be some good reason.

CHAMBERLAIN (*to himself*). It is in everybody's mouth. Why should I not tell it? (*Aloud.*) Have you heard the gossip concerning Shakuntala's rejection?

THE TWO MAIDS. Yes, sir. The king's brother-in-law told us, up to the point where the ring was recovered.

CHAMBERLAIN. There is little more to tell. When his Majesty saw the ring, he remembered that he had indeed contracted a secret marriage with Shakuntala, and had rejected her under a delusion. And then he fell a prey to remorse.

> He hates the things he loved; he intermits
> The daily audience, nor in judgment sits;
> Spends sleepless nights in tossing on his bed;
> At times, when he by courtesy is led
> To address a lady, speaks another name,
> Then stands for minutes, sunk in helpless shame.

MISHRAKESHI. I am glad to hear it.

CHAMBERLAIN. His Majesty's sorrow has forbidden the festival.

THE TWO MAIDS. It is only right.

A VOICE BEHIND THE SCENES. Follow me.

CHAMBERLAIN. Ah, his Majesty approaches. Go, and attend to your duties. (*Exeunt the two maids. Enter the king, wearing a dress indicative of remorse; the clown, and the portress.*)

CHAMBERLAIN. A beautiful figure charms in whatever state. Thus, his Majesty is pleasing even in his sorrow. For

> All ornament is laid aside; he wears
>   One golden bracelet on his wasted arm;
> His lip is scorched by sighs; and sleepless cares
>   Redden his eyes. Yet all can work no harm
> On that magnificent beauty, wasting, but
> Gaining in brilliance, like a diamond cut.

MISHRAKESHI (*observing the king*). No wonder Shakuntala pines for him, even though he dishonoured her by his rejection of her.

KING (*walks about slowly, sunk in thought*).

> Alas! My smitten heart, that once lay sleeping,
>   Heard in its dreams my fawn-eyed love's laments,
> And wakened now, awakens but to weeping,
>   To bitter grief, and tears of penitence.

MISHRAKESHI. That is the poor girl's fate.

CLOWN (*to himself*). He has got his Shakuntala-sickness again. I wish I knew how to cure him.

CHAMBERLAIN (*advancing*). Victory to your Majesty. I have examined the garden. Your Majesty may visit its retreats.

KING. Vetravati, tell the minister Pishuna in my name that a sleepless night prevents me from mounting the throne of judgment. He is to investigate the citizens' business and send me a memorandum.

PORTRESS. Yes, your Majesty. (*Exit.*)

KING. And you, Parvatayana, return to your post of duty.

CHAMBERLAIN. Yes, your Majesty. (*Exit.*)

CLOWN. You have got rid of the vermin. Now amuse yourself in this garden. It is delightful with the passing of the cold weather.

KING (*sighing*). My friend, the proverb makes no mistake. Misfortune finds the weak spot. See!

No sooner did the darkness lift
  That clouded memory's power,
Than the god of love prepared his bow
  And shot the mango-flower.

No sooner did the ring recall
  My banished maiden dear,
No sooner do I vainly weep
  For her, than spring is here.

CLOWN. Wait a minute, man. I will destroy Love's arrow with my stick. (*He raises his stick and strikes at the mango branch.*)

KING (*smiling*). Enough! I see your pious power. My friend, where shall I sit now to comfort my eyes with the vines? They remind me somehow of her.

CLOWN. Well, you told one of the maids, the clever painter, that you would spend this hour in the bower of spring-creepers. And you asked her to bring you there the picture of the lady Shakuntala which you painted on a tablet.

KING. It is my only consolation. Lead the way to the bower of spring-creepers.

CLOWN. Follow me. (*They walk about.* MISHRAKE-SHI *follows.*) Here is the bower of spring-creepers, with its jewelled benches. Its loneliness seems to bid you a silent welcome. Let us go in and sit down. (*They do so.*)

MISHRAKESHI. I will hide among the vines and see the dear girl's picture. Then I shall be able to tell her how deep her husband's love is. (*She hides.*)

KING (*sighing*). I remember it all now, my friend. I told you how I first met Shakuntala. It is true, you were not with me when I rejected her. But I had told you of her at the first. Had you forgotten, as I did?

MISHRAKESHI. This shows that a king should not be separated a single moment from some intimate friend.

CLOWN. No, I didn't forget. But when you had told the whole story, you said it was a joke and there was nothing in it. And I was fool enough to believe you. No, this is the work of fate.

MISHRAKESHI. It must be.

KING (*after meditating a moment*). Help me, my friend. . . .

CLOWN. Don't talk that way. Why, the ring shows that incredible meetings do happen.

KING (*looking at the ring*). This ring deserves pity. It has fallen from a heaven hard to earn.

Your virtue, ring, like mine,
  Is proved to be but small;
Her pink-nailed finger sweet
  You clasped. How could you fall?

MISHRAKESHI. If it were worn on any other hand, it would deserve pity. My dear girl, you are far away. I am the only one to hear these delightful words.

CLOWN. Tell me how you put the ring on her finger.

MISHRAKESHI. He speaks as if prompted by my curiosity.

KING. Listen, my friend. When I left the pious grove for the city, my darling wept and said: "But how long will you remember us, dear?"

CLOWN. And then you said——

KING. Then I put this engraved ring on her finger, and said to her——

CLOWN. Well, what?

KING. Count every day one letter of my name;
  Before you reach the end, dear,
Will come to lead you to my palace halls
  A guide whom I shall send, dear.

Then, through my madness, it fell out cruelly.

MISHRAKESHI. It was too charming an agreement to be frustrated by fate.

CLOWN. But how did it get into a carp's mouth, as if it had been a fish-hook?

KING. While she was worshipping the Ganges at Shachitirtha, it fell.

CLOWN. I see.

MISHRAKESHI. That is why the virtuous king doubted his marriage with poor Shakuntala. Yet such love does not ask for a token. How could it have been?

KING. Well, I can only reproach this ring. . . .

CLOWN. But that is no reason why I should starve to death. . . . If you get out of the trap alive, call for me at the Cloud Balcony. (*Exit on the run.*) . . .

MISHRAKESHI. Shall I make him happy now? No, I heard the mother of the gods consoling Shakuntala. She said that the gods, impatient for the sacrifice, would soon cause him to welcome his true wife. I must delay no longer. I will comfort dear Shakuntala with my tidings. (*Exit through the air.*)

A VOICE BEHIND THE SCENES. Help, help!

KING (*comes to himself and listens*). It sounds as if Madhavya were in distress. . . .

CHAMBERLAIN. Save your friend, O King!

KING. From what?

CHAMBERLAIN. From great danger.

KING. Speak plainly, man.

CHAMBERLAIN. On the Cloud Balcony, open to the four winds of heaven——

KING. What has happened there?

CHAMBERLAIN.

> While he was resting on its height,
> Which palace peacocks in their flight
> Can hardly reach, he seemed to be
> Snatched up—by what, we could not see.

KING (*rising quickly*). My very palace is invaded by evil creatures. To be a king, is to be a disappointed man.

> The moral stumblings of mine own,
> The daily slips, are scarcely known;
> Who then that rules a kingdom, can
> Guide every deed of every man?

THE VOICE. Hurry, hurry!

KING (*hears the voice and quickens his steps*). Have no fear, my friend.

THE VOICE. Have no fear! When something has got me by the back of the neck, and is trying to break my bones like a piece of sugar-cane!

KING (*looks about*). A bow! a bow! (*Enter a Greek woman with a bow.*)

GREEK WOMAN. A bow and arrows, your Majesty. And here are the finger-guards. (*The king takes the bow and arrows.*)

ANOTHER VOICE BEHIND THE SCENES.

> Writhe, while I drink the red blood flowing clear
> And kill you, as a tiger kills a deer;
> Let King Dushyanta grasp his bow; but how
> Can all his kingly valour save you now?

KING (*angrily*). He scorns me, too! In one moment, miserable demon, you shall die. (*Stringing his bow.*) Where is the stairway, Parvatayana?

CHAMBERLAIN. Here, your Majesty. (*All make haste.*)

KING (*looking about*). There is no one here.

THE CLOWN'S VOICE. Save me, save me! I see you, if you can't see me. I am a mouse in the claws of the cat. I am done for.

KING. You are proud of your invisibility. But shall not my arrow see you? Stand still. Do not hope to escape by clinging to my friend.

> My arrow, flying when the bow is bent,
> Shall slay the wretch and spare the innocent;
> When milk is mixed with water in a cup,
> Swans leave the water, and the milk drink up.

(*He takes aim. Enter* MATALI *and the clown.*)

MATALI. O King, as Indra, king of the gods, commands,

> Seek foes among the evil powers alone;
> For them your bow should bend;

> Not cruel shafts, but glances soft and kind
> Should fall upon a friend.

KING (*hastily withdrawing the arrow*). It is Matali. Welcome to the charioteer of heaven's king.

CLOWN. Well! He came within an inch of butchering me. And you welcome him.

MATALI (*smiling*). Hear, O King, for what purpose Indra sends me to you.

KING. I am all attention.

MATALI. There is a host of demons who call themselves Invincible—the brood of Kalanemi.

KING. So Narada has told me.

MATALI.

> Heaven's king is powerless; you shall smite
> His foes in battle soon;
> Darkness that overcomes the day,
> Is scattered by the moon.

Take your bow at once, enter my heavenly chariot, and set forth for victory.

KING. I am grateful for the honour which Indra shows me. But why did you act thus toward Madhavya?

MATALI. I will tell you. I saw that you were overpowered by some inner sorrow, and acted thus to rouse you. For

> The spurnèd snake will swell his hood;
> Fire blazes when 'tis stirred;
> Brave men are roused to fighting mood
> By some insulting word.

KING. Friend Madhavya, I must obey the bidding of heaven's king. Go, acquaint the minister Pishuna with the matter, and add these words of mine:

> Your wisdom only shall control
> The kingdom for a time;
> My bow is strung; a distant goal
> Calls me, and tasks sublime.

CLOWN. Very well. (*Exit.*)

MATALI. Enter the chariot. (*The king does so. Exeunt omnes.*)

ACT VII

(*Enter, in a chariot that flies through the air, the king and* MATALI.)

KING. Matali, though I have done what Indra commanded, I think myself an unprofitable servant, when I remember his most gracious welcome.

MATALI. O King, know that each considers himself the other's debtor. For

> You count the service given
> Small by the welcome paid,
> Which to the king of heaven
> Seems mean for such brave aid.

KING. Ah, no! For the honour given me at parting went far beyond imagination. Before the gods, he seated me beside him on his throne. And then

> He smiled, because his son Jayanta's heart
> Beat quicker, by the self-same wish oppressed,
> And placed about my neck the heavenly wreath
> Still fragrant from the sandal on his breast.

MATALI. But what do you not deserve from heaven's king? Remember:

> Twice, from peace-loving Indra's sway
> The demon-thorn was plucked away:
> First, by Man-lion's crooked claws;
> Again, by your smooth shafts to-day.

KING. This merely proves Indra's majesty. Remember:

> All servants owe success in enterprise
> To honour paid before the great deed's done;
> Could dawn defeat the darkness otherwise
> Than resting on the chariot of the sun?

MATALI. The feeling becomes you. (*After a little.*) See, O King! Your glory has the happiness of being published abroad in heaven.

> With colours used by nymphs of heaven
> To make their beauty shine,
> Gods write upon the surface given
> Of many a magic vine,
> As worth their song, the simple story
> Of those brave deeds that made your glory.

KING. Matali, when I passed before, I was intent on fighting the demons, and did not observe this region. Tell me. In which path of the winds are we?
MATALI.

> It is the windpath sanctified
> By holy Vishnu's second stride;
> Which, freed from dust of passion, ever
> Upholds the threefold heavenly river;
> And, driving them with reins of light,
> Guides the stars in wheeling flight.

KING. That is why serenity pervades me, body and soul. (*He observes the path taken by the chariot.*) It seems that we have descended into the region of the clouds.
MATALI. How do you perceive it?
KING.

> Plovers that fly from mountain-caves,
> Steeds that quick-flashing lightning laves,
> And chariot-wheels that drip with spray—
> A path o'er pregnant clouds betray.

33. **Vishnu's second stride.** The god conquered the earth in three great steps or strides. 35. **the threefold heavenly river,** the sacred Ganges of heaven, earth, and underworld.

MATALI. You are right. And in a moment you will be in the world over which you bear rule.
KING (*looking down*). Matali, our quick descent gives the world of men a mysterious look. For

> The plains appear to melt and fall
> From mountain peaks that grow more tall;
> The trunks of trees no longer hide
> Nor in their leafy nests abide;
> The river network now is clear,
> For smaller streams at last appear:
> It seems as if some being threw
> The world to me, for clearer view.

MATALI. You are a good observer, O King. There is a noble loveliness in the earth.
KING. Matali, what mountain is this, its flanks sinking into the eastern and into the western sea? It drips liquid gold like a cloud at sunset.
MATALI. O King, this is Gold Peak, the mountain of the fairy centaurs. Here it is that ascetics most fully attain to magic powers. See!

> The ancient sage, Marichi's son,
> Child of the Uncreated One,
> Father of superhuman life,
> Dwells here austerely with his wife.

KING. I must not neglect the happy chance. I cannot go farther until I have walked humbly about the holy one.
MATALI. It is a worthy thought, O King. (*The chariot descends.*) We have come down to earth.
KING (*astonished*). Matali,

> The wheels are mute on whirling rim;
> Unstirred, the dust is lying there;
> We do not bump the earth, but skim:
> Still, still we seem to fly through air.

MATALI. Such is the glory of the chariot which obeys you and Indra.
KING. In which direction lies the hermitage of Marichi's son?
MATALI (*pointing*). See!

Where stands the hermit, horridly austere,
Whom clinging vines are choking, tough and sere;
Half-buried in an ant-hill that has grown
About him, standing post-like and alone;
Sun-staring with dim eyes that know no rest,
The dead skin of a serpent on his breast:
So long he stood unmoved, insensate there
That birds build nests within his mat of hair.

64. **Gold Peak, the mountain of the fairy centaurs,** a holy mountain of the Himalayas beside the paradise of Kubera, the god of riches. 67–70. **The ancient sage . . . life.** The ancient saga Kashyapa, the father of Vishnu, Indra, and many other gods, was the son of Marichi, who was in turn the son of Brahma, the Creator. Also, Kashyapa's wife, Aditi, was a granddaughter of Brahmā. The god Brahmā was created by Brahma the First Cause.

KING. All honour to one who mortifies the flesh so terribly.

MATALI. We have entered the hermitage of the ancient sage, whose wife Aditi tends the coral-trees.

KING. Here is deeper contentment than in heaven. I seem plunged in a pool of nectar.

MATALI (*stopping the chariot*). Descend, O King.

KING (*descending*). But how will you fare?

MATALI. The chariot obeys the word of command.
10 I too will descend. (*He does so.*) Before you, O King, are the groves where the holiest hermits lead their self-denying life.

KING. I look with amazement both at their simplicity and at what they might enjoy.

> Their appetites are fed with air
> Where grows whatever is most fair;
> They bathe religiously in pools
> Which golden lily-pollen cools;
> They pray within a jewelled home,
20 Are chaste where nymphs of heaven roam:
> They mortify desire and sin
> With things that others fast to win.

MATALI. The desires of the great aspire high. (*He walks about and speaks to some one not visible.*) Ancient Shakalya, how is Marichi's holy son occupied? (*He listens.*) What do you say? That he is explaining to Aditi, in answer to her question, the duties of a faithful wife? My matter must await a fitter time. (*He turns to the king.*) Wait here, O King, in the shade of the ashoka tree, till I have an-
30 nounced your coming to the sire of Indra.

KING. Very well. (*Exit* MATALI. *The king's arm throbs, a happy omen.*)

> I dare not hope for what I pray;
> Why thrill—in vain?
> For heavenly bliss once thrown away
> Turns into pain.

A VOICE BEHIND THE SCENES. Don't! You mustn't be so foolhardy. Oh, you are always the same.

KING. No naughtiness could feel at home in this spot. Who draws such a rebuke upon himself? (*He
40 looks towards the sound. In surprise.*) It is a child, but no child in strength. And two hermit-women are trying to control him.

> He drags a struggling lion cub,
> The lioness' milk half-sucked, half-missed,
> Towzles his mane, and tries to drub
> Him tame with small, imperious fist.

(*Enter a small boy, as described, and two hermit-women.*)

BOY. Open your mouth, cub. I want to count your teeth.

FIRST WOMAN. Naughty boy, why do you torment
50 our pets? They are like children to us. Your energy seems to take the form of striking something. No wonder the hermits call you All-tamer.

KING. Why should my heart go out to this boy as if he were my own son? No doubt my childless state makes me sentimental.

SECOND WOMAN. The lioness will spring at you if you don't let her baby go.

BOY (*smiling*). Oh, I'm dreadfully scared. (*He bites his lip.*)

KING (*in surprise*).

> The boy is seed of fire
> Which, when its grows, will burn; 60
> A tiny spark that soon
> To awful flame may turn.

FIRST WOMAN. Let the little lion go, dear. I will give you another plaything.

BOY. Where is it? Give it to me. (*He stretches out his hand.*)

KING (*looking at the hand.*) He has one of the imperial birthmarks! For

> Between the eager fingers grow
> The close-knit webs together drawn,
> Like some lone lily opening slow 70
> To meet the kindling blush of dawn.

SECOND WOMAN. Suvrata, we can't make him stop by talking. Go. In my cottage you will find a painted clay peacock that belongs to the hermit-boy Mankanaka. Bring him that.

FIRST WOMAN. I will. (*Exit.*)

BOY. Meanwhile I'll play with this one.

HERMIT-WOMAN (*looks and laughs*). Let him go.

KING. My heart goes out to this wilful child.

> They show their little buds of teeth 80
> In peals of causeless laughter;
> They hide their trustful heads beneath
> Your heart. And stumbling after
> Come sweet, unmeaning sounds that sing
> To you. The father warms
> And loves the very dirt they bring
> Upon their little forms.

HERMIT-WOMAN (*shaking her finger*). Won't you mind me? (*She looks about.*) Which one of the hermit-boys is here? (*She sees the king.*) Oh, sir, 90 please come here and free this lion cub. The little rascal is tormenting him, and I can't make him let go.

KING. Very well. (*He approaches, smiling.*) O little son of a great sage!

> Your conduct in this place apart,
> Is most unfit;
> 'Twould grieve your father's pious heart
> And trouble it.

> To animals he is as good 100
> As good can be;

You spoil it, like a black snake's brood
In sandal tree.

HERMIT-WOMAN. But, sir, he is not the son of a hermit.

KING. So it would seem, both from his looks and his actions. But in this spot, I had no suspicion of anything else. (*He loosens the boy's hold on the cub, and touching him, says to himself.*)

It makes me thrill to touch the boy,
The stranger's son, to me unknown;
What measureless content must fill
The man who calls the child his own!

HERMIT-WOMAN (*looking at the two*). Wonderful! wonderful!

KING. Why do you say that, mother?

HERMIT-WOMAN. I am astonished to see how much the boy looks like you, sir. You are not related. Besides, he is a perverse little creature and he does not know you. Yet he takes no dislike to you.

KING (*caressing the boy*). Mother, if he is not the son of a hermit, what is his family?

HERMIT-WOMAN. The family of Puru.

KING (*to himself*). He is of one family with me! Then could my thought be true? (*Aloud.*) But this is the custom of Puru's line:

In glittering palaces they dwell
While men, and rule the country well;
Then make the grove their home in age,
And die in austere hermitage.

But how could human beings, of their own mere motion, attain this spot?

HERMIT-WOMAN. You are quite right, sir. But the boy's mother was related to a nymph, and she bore her son in the pious grove of the father of the gods.

KING (*to himself*). Ah, a second ground for hope. (*Aloud.*) What was the name of the good king whose wife she was?

HERMIT-WOMAN. Who would speak his name? He rejected his true wife.

KING (*to himself*). This story points at me. Suppose I ask the boy for his mother's name. (*He reflects.*) No, it is wrong to concern myself with one who may be another's wife. (*Enter the first woman, with the clay peacock.*)

FIRST WOMAN. Look, All-tamer. Here is the bird, the *shakunta*. Isn't the *shakunta* lovely?

BOY (*looks about*). Where is my mamma? (*The two women burst out laughing.*)

FIRST WOMAN. It sounded like her name, and deceived him. He loves his mother.

SECOND WOMAN. She said: "See how pretty the peacock is." That is all.

KING (*to himself*). His mother's name is Shakuntala! But names are alike. I trust this hope may not prove a disappointment in the end, like a mirage.

BOY. I like this little peacock, sister. Can it fly? (*He seizes the toy.*)

FIRST WOMAN (*looks at the boy. Anxiously*). Oh, the amulet is not on his wrist.

KING. Do not be anxious, mother. It fell while he was struggling with the lion cub. (*He starts to pick it up.*)

THE TWO WOMEN. Oh, don't, don't! (*They look at him.*) He has touched it! (*Astonished, they lay their hands on their bosoms, and look at each other.*)

KING. Why did you try to prevent me?

FIRST WOMAN. Listen, your Majesty. This is a divine and most potent charm, called the Invincible. Marichi's holy son gave it to the baby when the birth-ceremony was performed. If it falls on the ground, no one may touch it except the boy's parents or the boy himself.

KING. And if another touch it?

FIRST WOMAN. It becomes a serpent and stings him.

KING. Did you ever see this happen to any one else?

BOTH WOMEN. More than once.

KING (*joyfully*). Then why may I not welcome my hopes fulfilled at last? (*He embraces the boy.*)

SECOND WOMAN. Come, Suvrata. Shakuntala is busy with her religious duties. We must go and tell her what has happened. (*Exeunt ambo.*)

BOY. Let me go. I want to see my mother.

KING. My son, you shall go with me to greet your mother.

BOY. Dushyanta is my father, not you.

KING (*smiling*). You show I am right by contradicting me. (*Enter SHAKUNTALA, wearing her hair in a single braid.*)

SHAKUNTALA (*doubtfully*). I have heard that All-tamer's amulet did not change when it should have done so. But I do not trust my own happiness. Yet perhaps it is as Mishrakeshi told me. (*She walks about.*)

KING (*looking at SHAKUNTALA. With plaintive joy*). It is she. It is Shakuntala.

The pale, worn face, the careless dress,
The single braid,
Show her still true, me pitiless,
The long vow paid.

SHAKUNTALA (*seeing the king pale with remorse. Doubtfully*). It is not my husband. Who is the man that soils my boy with his caresses? The amulet should protect him.

BOY (*running to his mother*). Mother, he is a man that belongs to other people. And he calls me his son.

KING. My darling, the cruelty I showed you has turned to happiness. Will you not recognise me?

SHAKUNTALA (*to herself*). Oh, my heart, believe

it. Fate struck hard, but its envy is gone and pity takes its place. It is my husband.

KING.

> Black madness flies;
> Comes memory;
> Before my eyes
> My love I see.
>
> Eclipse flees far;
> Light follows soon;
> The loving star
> Draws to the moon.

SHAKUNTALA. Victory, victo—— (*Tears choke her utterance.*)

KING.

> The tears would choke you, sweet, in vain;
> My soul with victory is fed,
> Because I see your face again—
> No jewels, but the lips are red.

BOY. Who is he, mother?

SHAKUNTALA. Ask fate, my child. (*She weeps.*)

KING.

> Dear, graceful wife, forget;
> Let the sin vanish;
> Strangely did madness strive
> Reason to banish.
>
> Thus blindness works in men,
> Love's joy to shake;
> Spurning a garland, lest
> It prove a snake. (*He falls at her feet.*)

SHAKUNTALA. Rise, my dear husband. Surely, it was some old sin of mine that broke my happiness—though it has turned again to happiness. Otherwise, how could you, dear, have acted so? You are so kind. (*The king rises.*) But what brought back the memory of your suffering wife?

KING. I will tell you when I have plucked out the dart of sorrow.

> 'Twas madness, sweet, that could let slip
> A tear to burden your dear lip;
> On graceful lashes seen to-day,
> I wipe it, and our grief, away. (*He does so.*)

SHAKUNTALA (*sees more clearly and discovers the ring*). My husband, it is the ring!

KING. Yes. And when a miracle recovered it, my memory returned.

SHAKUNTALA. That was why it was impossible for me to win your confidence.

KING. Then let the vine receive her flower, as earnest of her union with spring.

SHAKUNTALA. I do not trust it. I would rather you wore it. (*Enter* MATALI.)

MATALI. I congratulate you, O King, on reunion with your wife and on seeing the face of your son.

KING. My desires bear sweeter fruit because fulfilled through a friend. Matali, was not this matter known to Indra?

MATALI. What is hidden from the gods? Come. Marichi's holy son, Kashyapa, wishes to see you.

KING. My dear wife, bring our son. I could not appear without you before the holy one.

SHAKUNTALA. I am ashamed to go before such parents with my husband.

KING. It is the custom in times of festival. Come. (*They walk about.* KASHYAPA *appears seated, with* ADITI.)

KASHYAPA (*looking at the king*). Aditi,

> 'Tis King Dushyanta, he who goes before
> Your son in battle, and who rules the earth,
> Whose bow makes Indra's weapon seem no more
> Than a fine plaything, lacking sterner worth.

ADITI. His valour might be inferred from his appearance.

MATALI. O King, the parents of the gods look upon you with a glance that betrays parental fondness. Approach them.

KING. Matali,

> Sprung from the Creator's children, do I see
> Great Kashyapa and Mother Aditi? . . .

MATALI. It is indeed they.

KING (*falling before them*). Dushyanta, servant of Indra, does reverence to you both.

KASHYAPA. My son, rule the earth long.

ADITI. And be invincible. (SHAKUNTALA *and her son fall at their feet.*)

KASHYAPA. My daughter,

> Your husband equals Indra, king
> Of gods; your son is like his son;
> No further blessing need I bring:
> Win bliss such as his wife has won.

ADITI. My child, keep the favour of your husband. And may this fine boy be an honour to the families of both parents. Come, let us be seated. (*All seat themselves.*)

KASHYAPA.

> Faithful Shakuntala, the boy,
> And you, O King, I see
> A trinity to bless the world—
> Faith, Treasure, Piety.

KING. Holy one, your favour shown to us is without parallel. You granted the fulfillment of our wishes before you called us to your presence. For, holy one,

> The flower comes first, and then the fruit;
> The clouds appear before the rain;

Effect comes after cause; but you
First helped, then made your favour plain.

MATALI. O King, such is the favour shown by the parents of the world.

KING. Holy one, I married this your maid-servant by the voluntary ceremony. When after a time her relatives brought her to me, my memory failed and I rejected her. In so doing, I sinned against Kanva, who is kin to you. But afterwards, when I saw the ring, I perceived that I had married her. And this seems very wonderful to me.

Like one who doubts an elephant,
Though seeing him stride by,
And yet believes when he has seen
The footprints left; so I.

KASHYAPA. My son, do not accuse yourself of sin. Your infatuation was inevitable. Listen.

KING. I am all attention.

KASHYAPA. When the nymph Menaka descended to earth and received Shakuntala, afflicted at her rejection, she came to Aditi. Then I perceived the matter by my divine insight. I saw that the unfortunate girl had been rejected by her rightful husband because of Durvasas' curse. And that the curse would end when the ring came to light.

KING (to himself). Then I am free from blame.

SHAKUNTALA (to herself). Thank heaven! My husband did not reject me of his own accord. He really did not remember me. I suppose I did not hear the curse in my absent-minded state, for my friends warned me most earnestly to show my husband the ring.

KASHYAPA. My daughter, you know the truth. Do not now give way to anger against your rightful husband. Remember:

The curse it was that brought defeat and pain;
The darkness flies; you are his queen again.
Reflections are not seen in dusty glass,
Which, cleaned, will mirror all the things that pass.

KING. It is most true, holy one.

KASHYAPA. My son, I hope you have greeted as he deserves the son whom Shakuntala has borne you, for whom I myself have performed the birth-rite and the other ceremonies.

KING. Holy one, the hope of my race centres in him.

KASHYAPA. Know then that his courage will make him emperor.

Journeying over every sea,
His car will travel easily;
The seven islands of the earth
Will bow before his matchless worth;
Because wild beasts to him were tame,
All-tamer was his common name;

As Bharata he shall be known,
For he will bear the world alone.

KING. I anticipate everything from him, since you have performed the rites for him.

ADITI. Kanva also should be informed that his daughter's wishes are fulfilled. But Menaka is waiting upon me here and cannot be spared.

SHAKUNTALA (to herself). The holy one has expressed my own desire.

KASHYAPA. Kanva knows the whole matter through his divine insight. (He reflects.) Yet he should hear from us the pleasant tidings, how his daughter and her son have been received by her husband. Who waits without? (Enter a pupil.)

PUPIL. I am here, holy one.

KASHYAPA. Galava, fly through the air at once, carrying pleasant tidings from me to holy Kanva. Tell him how Durvasas' curse has come to an end, how Dushyanta recovered his memory, and has taken Shakuntala with her child to himself.

PUPIL. Yes, holy one. (Exit.)

KASHYAPA (to the king). My son, enter with child and wife the chariot of your friend Indra, and set out for your capital.

KING. Yes, holy one.

KASHYAPA. For now

May Indra send abundant rain,
Repaid by sacrificial gain;
With aid long mutually given,
Rule you on earth, and he in heaven.

KING. Holy one, I will do my best.

KASHYAPA. What more, my son, shall I do for you?

KING. Can there be more than this? Yet may this prayer be fulfilled.

May kingship benefit the land,
And wisdom grow in scholars' band;
May Shiva see my faith on earth
And make me free of all rebirth.
(Exeunt omnes.)

Talk by Rabbi Halpern (taped)
Hebrew = one who has passed over (from polytheism)

The Hebrew Bible

Israel - one who has fought with God

The Jews have a long literary tradition, dating from before the time of King David, in Hebrew, Aramaic, Yiddish, and other languages, and one of their books has a unique place in world culture. The Hebrew Bible, called simply "The Sacred Writings" by the Jews, was written in sections by many individuals between the tenth and fifth centuries B.C. By 400 B.C. the first five books, or *Torah*, had come to have a peculiar sacredness as the Word of God, but as late as 90 A.D. the rabbis were

Jews from Judeans

still debating whether some later sections, Esther, Ecclesiastes, and The Song of Songs, should have a place in the canon. Two other world religions, Christianity and Mohammedanism, eventually grafted their religious dogma onto the ancient writ, and the holy book of the Hebrews became sacred to half the world. It was a Christian divine, John Chrysostom, bishop of Constantinople in the fourth century A.D., who gave the name "Biblia," meaning "Books," to these holy books of the Jews.*

The name was well chosen, because the Hebrew Bible is not one book, but a library covering a wide variety of literary forms and subject matter. The thirty-nine books are divided by Jewish tradition into three sections: the *Law,* five books of folklore, national history, and religious code; the *Prophets*, consisting of twenty-one books of sermons, rhapsodies, and later history; and the *Writings,* a miscellaneous collection of thirteen books of hymns (Psalms), epigrams and adages (Proverbs), drama (Job), love poetry (The Song of Songs), short stories (Ruth, Esther, Daniel), and essays (Ecclesiastes). This arrangement emphasizes the literary classification of the books much better than the Christian arrangement.

Works of such diverse character served a variety of purposes in Hebrew national life. The *Law* was the basis of education in history and metaphysics; it was the source of authority in regulating the lives of men and punishing those who offended the code. Ezra originated the custom of public readings from the *Torah* on market days and on the Sabbath, when the reader would comment on the passages in the manner of a religious preacher in our day. Much of the *Prophets* obviously originated as sermons, delivered more often in the market place than in the temple. The Proverbs floated in the public memory and speech as ready rules of conduct. The Psalms were the group prayers of the temple and later of the synagogue, and were sometimes sung as hymns are sung in Christian churches. Thus all the major books sprang in one way or another from the core of Hebrew national life.

The Bible reflects several stages in the social development of the Hebrews. The tales of the patriarchs in Genesis picture simple shepherds living in tents and moving frequently to new grazing lands. But with the settlement in Canaan the tents gave way to huts and eventually to houses in villages as the Hebrews became largely an agricultural people. Since Moses recognized the cultivation

of the land as man's principal occupation, every family had its own estate, and the sons and daughters and their slaves went daily to tend the fields and the herds.

From the time of David, Jerusalem rose as the urban center of the Hebrew world, and commerce and craftsmanship gradually challenged sheepherding and farming as the chief occupations of the people. But the domestic life portrayed in the Bible remains essentially simple and earthy. The principal figures of speech are still those of the commoner's life and physical person, and the land, the plants, and the animals he knew. God is the good shepherd and we His sheep. "Keep me as the apple of the eye, hide me under the shadow of thy wings." (Psalm 17:8) "Speak to the earth, and it shall teach thee." (Job 12:8) "Flee as a bird to your mountain." (Psalm 11:1) "My days are swifter than a weaver's shuttle." (Job 7:6) "His heart is . . . as hard as a piece of the nether millstone." (Job 41:24)

Hardship made the Hebrew sober and earnest, little given to the public games and diversions so characteristic of the Greeks. Yet the love of music was strong in his nature and is reflected in the musical quality of language in the Psalms, The Song of Songs, and some of the prophetic writings. Stringed, wind, and percussion instruments are mentioned in the Bible, but it was the voice that gave utterance to the Hebrew's profound religious fervor. David directed a chorus of four thousand voices in the temple, singing the praises of the Lord, and under later kings music reached even greater heights. The tie between music and poetry was strong among the Hebrews as among the ancient Greeks.

Only in recent years has it become fashionable to see in the Bible a masterpiece of literary art. Yet its poetic power and beauty have been recognized by English authors for three centuries, and the distinctive phrasing of the King James Version has long been one of the fundamental styles in our language. Its primitive simplicity and nobility suggest Homer, although Hebrew poetry is innocent of the set accents and meters of classical verse. It depends for its effect on a few simple devices: repetition of phrase in refrain (Ecclesiastes 3:1–8), repetition of the same idea in different words (Psalm 19:7–9), contrast (Psalm 1), and abundant metaphor (The Song of Songs 2:2–3).

The prophetic books show a clear evolution in style. The early ones are close to primitive speech, with brief, loosely connected sentences and with the heightened rhythm of a chant. Later prophets show more polish, but are still highly direct and concrete in their imagery. Their message was to the people, and they shunned abstractions and literary decoration. Their chief device was parallel structure: "And he shall judge among the nations, and shall rebuke many people: and they shall beat their swords into ploughshares, and their spears into pruning hooks." (Isaiah 2:4) With simple literary devices such as these, the authors of the Hebrew Bible, largely anonymous, converted their religious and national fervor into glowing song and story.

The Psalms are the Hebrews' hymns of praise, the most important book in their third division of the Bible. Al-

---

* The oldest Hebrew text of the Bible dates from 916 A.D., but of equal importance in Biblical scholarship is a Greek translation called the *Septuagint*, made for the Alexandrian world in the third century B.C. and preserved in a manuscript of the eighth century. The Roman Catholic canon adds to the Hebrew Bible the fourteen books of the *Apocrypha*, but the Protestant canon follows the Jewish in outlawing these. Although the first complete translation of the Bible into English dates from the fourteenth century and John Wycliffe, the standard English version is the one authorized by King James I in 1604 and completed by a corps of forty-seven scholars in 1611. The simple dignity of this version has helped to make it a great English classic. The Catholic translation of comparable influence is popularly called the Douay Bible, after the University of Douai in northern France (originally Flanders), where exiled English Catholic scholars prepared it in its first form in the late sixteenth century. The several modern versions of the Douay Bible have been much revised.

though 73 of the 150 lyrics are ascribed to King David, nearly all of them are much later, dating from the periods immediately preceding and following the fifty-year exile of the Jews in Babylon. Some may be as late as the bloody reign of the Maccabees. In this supreme collection of hymns we find ecstatic avowals of the majesty of God (Psalm 97) and the universe that He created (Psalms 8 and 19) beside the humility of His worshipers (Psalms 23 and 90). The range of ideas is tremendous. All of nature finds its place in this impassioned tribute to God's power in the life of man.

Proverbs is a miscellaneous compilation of wise and witty epigrams, which, taken together, provide a practical code of living. Although devotion to God lies behind this sane advice, the emphasis is upon the earthly fruits of a sensible, virtuous life. Of the thirty-one chapters, 10 through 22 would seem to be the ancient core of the collection, traditionally attributed to wise King Solomon.

The ecstatic outcries of devotion found in Psalms and the *Prophets* meet a skeptical answer in the grim pessimism of Ecclesiastes. The ancient capacity of the Jew to bear suffering and even to enjoy it appears in the bitter conclusion that virtue does not lead to success in our world of chance. "The race is not to the swift, nor the battle to the strong." All is vanity in this soulless place, where men and beasts lead similar lives and come to the same end. What joy life holds lies not in the delusion of divine justice but in our enjoyment of work and simple, immediate pleasures. Later editors doctored this gloomy essay to read that worldly things are vain only in comparison with devotion to God.

If this melancholy appraisal of human aspiration had a hard time establishing itself in the holy canon, how can we account for the presence there of a collection of sensuous Oriental love lyrics called The Song of Songs? A series of wedding songs, ascribed alternately to bride and groom, have been arranged as a little dramatic dialogue, not unlike the idylls of the Greek Theocritus, with connecting refrains and speeches that suggest a chorus of bridesmaids. We need not speculate about the structure of this little play to enjoy the passionate tribute to nuptial love. Although the descriptions of love and the beloved seem earthly enough today, early religious commentaries interpreted them as a symbolic statement of the mutual love of God and Israel and hence admitted The Song of Songs to the Bible as a holy book.

The book of Jonah is more fable than prophecy, although its hero is ranked among the *Prophets*. The fine message of this enlightened tale has been popularly lost in the sensational incident of the "whale." Behind the frustrated career of a narrow-minded prophet lies the loftiest interpretation of Yahveh among the thirty-nine books. After being punished and forgiven for his foolish effort to escape his duty to God by running beyond His reach, Jonah must learn a second lesson: that God's mercy, as well as His authority, extends beyond His Chosen People to all others who deserve it. In saving the repentant sinners of Nineveh, God is seen to be universal in His power and His mercy.

Most charming of all the books is Ruth, the simple tale of a Moabite maiden who chose through love to follow her Jewish mother-in-law, Naomi, with her people and their god, and became the ancestor of King David himself. Behind its idyllic innocence lie a plea for the toleration of foreign marriages and an attack, as in the book of Jonah, on narrow nationalism.

man innately good, but he has been given a good and evil inclination and may choose between them.

Psalms

PSALM I

BLESSED is the man that walketh not in the counsel of the ungodly, nor standeth in the way of sinners, nor sitteth in the seat of the scornful.

But his delight is in the law of the Lord; and in his law doth he meditate day and night.

And he shall be like a tree planted by the rivers of water, that bringeth forth his fruit in his season; his leaf also shall not wither; and whatsoever he doeth shall prosper.

The ungodly are not so: but are like the chaff   10 which the wind driveth away.

Therefore the ungodly shall not stand in the judgment, nor sinners in the congregation of the righteous.

For the Lord knoweth the way of the righteous: but the way of the ungodly shall perish.

PSALM VIII

O Lord our Lord, how excellent is thy name in all the earth! who hast set thy glory above the heavens.

Out of the mouth of babes and sucklings hast thou ordained strength because of thine enemies, that   20 thou mightest still the enemy and the avenger.

When I consider thy heavens, the work of thy fingers, the moon and the stars, which thou hast ordained;

What is man, that thou art mindful of him? and the son of man, that thou visitest him?

For thou hast made him a little lower than the angels, and hast crowned him with glory and honour.

Thou madest him to have dominion over the works of thy hands; thou hast put all things under his feet: 30

All sheep and oxen, yea, and the beasts of the field;

The fowl of the air, and the fish of the sea, and whatsoever passeth through the paths of the seas.

O Lord our Lord, how excellent is thy name in all the earth!

PSALM XIX

The heavens declare the glory of God; and the firmament sheweth his handywork.

Day unto day uttereth speech, and night unto night sheweth knowledge.

There is no speech nor language, where their voice   40 is not heard.

Hebrews believe in salvation through works rather than through grace. Talmud - oral law - took 1000 years to be written. Two copies - one in Hebrew and one in Aramaic done in Babylon.

Their line is gone out through all the earth, and their words to the end of the world. In them hath he set a tabernacle for the sun,

Which is as a bridegroom coming out of his chamber, and rejoiceth as a strong man to run a race.

His going forth is from the end of the heaven, and his circuit unto the ends of it: and there is nothing hid from the heat thereof.

10 The law of the Lord is perfect, converting the soul: the testimony of the Lord is sure, making wise the simple.

The statutes of the Lord are right, rejoicing the heart: the commandment of the Lord is pure, enlightening the eyes.

The fear of the Lord is clean, enduring for ever: the judgments of the Lord are true and righteous altogether.

More to be desired are they than gold, yea, than much fine gold: sweeter also than honey and the 20 honeycomb.

Moreover by them is thy servant warned: and in keeping of them there is great reward.

Who can understand his errors? cleanse thou me from secret faults.

Keep back thy servant also from presumptuous sins; let them not have dominion over me: then shall I be upright, and I shall be innocent from the great transgression.

Let the words of my mouth, and the meditation 30 of my heart, be acceptable in thy sight, O Lord, my strength, and my redeemer.

PSALM XXIII

The Lord is my shepherd; I shall not want.

He maketh me to lie down in green pastures: he leadeth me beside the still waters.

He restoreth my soul: he leadeth me in the paths of righteousness for his name's sake.

Yea, though I walk through the valley of the shadow of death, I will fear no evil: for thou art with me; thy rod and thy staff they comfort me.

40 Thou preparest a table before me in the presence of mine enemies: thou anointest my head with oil; my cup runneth over.

Surely goodness and mercy shall follow me all the days of my life: and I will dwell in the house of the Lord for ever.

PSALM XC

Lord, thou hast been our dwelling place in all generations.

Before the mountains were brought forth, or ever thou hadst formed the earth and the world, even 50 from everlasting to everlasting, thou art God.

Thou turnest man to destruction; and sayest, Return, yet children of men.

For a thousand years in thy sight are but as yesterday when it is past, and as a watch in the night.

Thou carriest them away as with a flood; they are as a sleep: in the morning they are like grass which groweth up.

In the morning it flourisheth, and groweth up; in the evening it is cut down, and withereth.

60 For we are consumed by thine anger, and by thy wrath are we troubled.

Thou hast set our iniquities before thee, our secret sins in the light of thy countenance.

For all our days are passed away in thy wrath: we spend our years as a tale that is told.

The days of our years are threescore years and ten; and if by reason of strength they be fourscore years; yet is their strength labor and sorrow; for it is soon cut off, and we fly away.

70 Who knoweth the power of thine anger? even according to thy fear, so is thy wrath.

So teach us to number our days, that we may apply our hearts unto wisdom.

Return, O Lord, how long? and let it repent thee concerning thy servants.

O satisfy us early with thy mercy; that we may rejoice and be glad all our days.

Make us glad according to the days wherein thou hast afflicted us, and the years wherein we have seen 80 evil.

Let thy work appear unto thy servants, and thy glory unto their children.

And let the beauty of the Lord our God be upon us: and establish thou the work of our hands upon us; yea, the work of our hands establish thou it.

Proverbs

WISDOM crieth without; she uttereth her voice in the streets. (I)

Wisdom is the principal thing; therefore get wisdom; and with all thy getting, get understanding. (IV)

90 Go to the ant, thou sluggard; consider her ways, and be wise: which having no chief, overseer or ruler, provideth her meat in the summer, and gathereth her food in the harvest. How long wilt thou sleep, O sluggard? When wilt thou arise out of thy sleep? Yet a little sleep, a little slumber, a little folding of the hands to sleep: so shall thy poverty come as one that travelleth, and thy want as an armed man. (VI)

A soft answer turneth away wrath, but grievous words stir up anger. (XV)

100 A merry heart maketh a cheerful countenance, but by sorrow of the heart the spirit is broken. (XV)

Better is a dinner of herbs where love is, than a stalled ox and hatred therewith. (XV)

Pride goeth before destruction, and an haughty spirit before a fall. (XVI)

He that is slow to anger is better than the mighty; and he that ruleth his spirit than he that taketh a city. (XVI)

A merry heart doeth good like a medicine. (XVII)

It is better to dwell in a corner of the housetop, than with a brawling woman in a wide house. (XXI)

A good name is rather to be chosen than great riches. (XXII)

Train up a child in the way he should go: and when he is old he will not depart from it. (XXII)

Look not thou upon the wine when it is red, when it giveth its color in the cup, when it goeth down smoothly; at the last it biteth like a serpent, and stingeth like an adder. (XXIII)

He that maketh haste to be rich shall not be innocent. (XXVIII)

There be three things that are too wonderful for me, yea, four which I know not: the way of an eagle in the air; the way of a serpent upon a rock; the way of a ship in the midst of the sea; and the way of a man with a maid. (XXX)

Ecclesiastes

PROLOGUE

Vanity of vanities, saith the Preacher, vanity of vanities; all is vanity.

What profit hath a man of all his labour which he taketh under the sun?

One generation passeth away, and another generation cometh: but the earth abideth for ever.

The sun also ariseth, and the sun goeth down, and hasteth to his place where he arose.

The wind goeth toward the south, and turneth about unto the north; it whirleth about continually, and the wind returneth again according to his circuits.

All the rivers run into the sea; yet the sea is not full; unto the place from whence the rivers come, thither they return again.

All things are full of labour; man cannot utter it: the eye is not satisfied with seeing, nor the ear filled with hearing.

The thing that hath been, it is that which shall be; and that which is done is that which shall be done: and there is no new thing under the sun.

Is there any thing whereof it may be said, See, this is new? it hath been already of old time, which was before us.

There is no remembrance of former things; neither shall there be any remembrance of things that are to come with those that shall come after.

SOLOMON'S SEARCH FOR WISDOM (Coheleth)

I the Preacher was king over Israel in Jerusalem.

And I gave my heart to seek and search out by wisdom concerning all things that are done under heaven: this sore travail hath God given to the sons of man to be exercised therewith.

I have seen all the works that are done under the sun; and, behold, all is vanity and vexation of spirit.

That which is crooked cannot be made straight: and that which is wanting cannot be numbered.

I communed with mine own heart, saying, Lo, I am come to great estate, and have gotten more wisdom than all they that have been before me in Jerusalem: yea, my heart had great experience of wisdom and knowledge.

And I gave my heart to know wisdom, and to know madness and folly: I perceived that this also is vexation of spirit.

For in much wisdom is much grief: and he that increaseth knowledge increaseth sorrow.

I said in mine heart, Go to now, I will prove thee with mirth, therefore enjoy pleasure: and, behold, this also is vanity.

I said of laughter, It is mad: and of mirth, What doeth it?

I sought in mine heart to give myself unto wine, yet acquainting mine heart with wisdom; and to lay hold on folly, till I might see what was that good for the sons of men, which they should do under the heaven all the days of their life.

I made me great works; I builded me houses; I planted me vineyards:

I made me gardens and orchards, and I planted trees in them of all kind of fruits:

I made me pools of water, to water therewith the wood that bringeth forth trees:

I got me servants and maidens and had servants born in my house; also I had great possessions of great and small cattle above all that were in Jerusalem before me:

I gathered me also silver and gold, and the peculiar treasure of kings and of the provinces: I gat me men singers and women singers, and the delights of the sons of men, as musical instruments, and that of all sorts.

So I was great, and increased more than all that were before me in Jerusalem: also my wisdom remained with me.

And whatsoever mine eyes desired I kept not from them, I withheld not my heart from any joy; for my heart rejoiced in all my labour: and this was my portion of all my labour.

Then I looked on all the works that my hands had wrought, and on the labour that I had laboured to do: and, behold, all was vanity and vexation of spirit, and there was no profit under the sun.

And I turned myself to behold wisdom, and madness, and folly: for what can the man do that cometh after the king? even that which hath been already done.

Then I saw that wisdom excelleth folly, as far as light excelleth darkness.

The wise man's eyes are in his head; but the fool walketh in darkness: and I myself perceived also that one event happeneth to them all.

Then said I in my heart, As it happeneth to the fool, so it happeneth even to me; and why was I then more wise? Then I said in my heart, that this also is vanity.

For there is no remembrance of the wise more than of the fool for ever; seeing that which now is in the days to come shall all be forgotten. And how dieth the wise man? as the fool.

Therefore I hated life; because the work that is wrought under the sun is grievous unto me: for all is vanity and vexation of spirit.

Yea, I hated all my labour which I had taken under the sun: because I should leave it unto the man that shall be after me.

And who knoweth whether he shall be a wise man or a fool? yet shall he have rule over all my labour wherein I have laboured, and wherein I have shewed myself wise under the sun. This is also vanity.

Therefore I went about to cause my heart to despair of all the labour which I took under the sun.

For there is a man whose labour is in wisdom, and in knowledge, and in equity; yet to a man that hath not laboured therein shall he leave it for his portion. This also is vanity and a great evil.

For what hath man of all his labour, and of the vexation of his heart, wherein he hath laboured under the sun?

For all his days are sorrows, and his travail grief; yea, his heart taketh not rest in the night. This is also vanity. . . .

A TIME FOR EVERYTHING

To every thing there is a season, and a time to every purpose under the heaven:

A time to be born, and a time to die; a time to plant, and a time to pluck up that which is planted;

A time to kill, and a time to heal; a time to break down, and a time to build up;

A time to weep, and a time to laugh; a time to mourn, and a time to dance;

A time to cast away stones, and a time to gather stones together; a time to embrace, and a time to refrain from embracing;

A time to get, and a time to lose; a time to keep, and a time to cast away;

A time to rend, and a time to sew; a time to keep silence, and a time to speak;

A time to love, and a time to hate; a time of war, and a time of peace.

What profit hath he that worketh in that wherein he laboureth?

I have seen the travail, which God hath given to the sons of men to be exercised in it. . . .

And moreover I saw under the sun the place of judgment, that wickedness was there; and the place of righteousness, that iniquity was there.

I said in mine heart, God shall judge the righteous and the wicked: for there is a time there for every purpose and for every work.

I said in mine heart concerning the estate of the sons of men, that God might manifest them, and that they might see that they themselves are beasts.

For that which befalleth the sons of men befalleth beasts; even one thing befalleth them: as the one dieth, so dieth the other; yea, they have all one breath; so that a man hath no preeminence above a beast: for all is vanity.

All go unto one place; all are of the dust, and all turn to dust again.

Who knoweth the spirit of man that goeth upward, and the spirit of the beast that goeth downward to the earth?

Wherefore I perceive that there is nothing better, than that a man should rejoice in his own works; for that is his portion: for who shall bring him to see what shall be after him?

So I returned, and considered all the oppressions that are done under the sun: and behold the tears of such as were oppressed, and they had no comforter; and on the side of their oppressors there was power; but they had no comforter.

Wherefore I praised the dead which are already dead more than the living which are yet alive.

Yea, better is he than both they, which hath not yet been, who hath not seen the evil work that is done under the sun.

Again, I considered all travail, and every right work, that for this a man is envied of his neighbour. This is also vanity and vexation of spirit.

The fool foldeth his hands together, and eateth his own flesh.

Better is an handful with quietness, than both the hands full with travail and vexation of spirit.

Then I returned, and I saw vanity under the sun.

There is one alone, and there is not a second; yea, he hath neither child nor brother: yet is there no end of all his labour; neither is his eye satisfied with riches; neither saith he, For whom do I labour, and bereave my soul of good? This is also vanity, yea, it is a sore travail. . . .

THE VANITY OF HUMAN WISHES

He that loveth silver shall not be satisfied with silver; nor he that loveth abundance with increase: this is also vanity.

When goods increase, they are increased that eat them: and what good is there to the owners thereof, saving the beholding of them with their eyes?

The sleep of a labouring man is sweet, whether he eat little or much: but the abundance of the rich will not suffer him to sleep.

There is a sore evil which I have seen under the sun, namely, riches kept for the owners thereof to their hurt.

But those riches perish by evil travail: and he begetteth a son, and there is nothing in his hand.

As he came forth of his mother's womb, naked shall he return to go as he came, and shall take nothing of his labour, which he may carry away in his hand.

And this also is a sore evil, that in all points as he came, so shall he go: and what profit hath he that hath laboured for the wind?

All his days also he eateth in darkness, and he hath much sorrow and wrath with his sickness. . . .

There is an evil which I have seen under the sun, and it is common among men:

A man to whom God hath given riches, wealth, and honour, so that he wanteth nothing for his soul of all that he desireth, yet God giveth him not power to eat thereof, but a stranger eateth it: this is vanity, and it is an evil disease.

If a man beget an hundred children, and live many years, so that the days of his years be many, and his soul be not filled with good, and also that he have no burial; I say, that an untimely birth is better than he.

For he cometh in with vanity, and departeth in darkness, and his name shall be covered with darkness.

Moreover he hath not seen the sun, nor known any thing: this hath more rest than the other.

Yea, though he live a thousand years twice told, yet hath he seen no good: do not all go to one place?

All the labour of man is for his mouth, and yet the appetite is not filled.

For what hath the wise more than the fool? what hath the poor, that knoweth to walk before the living?

Better is the sight of the eyes than the wandering of the desire: this is also vanity and vexation of spirit.

That which hath been is named already, and it is known that it is man: neither may he contend with him that is mightier than he.

Seeing there be many things that increase vanity, what is man the better?

For who knoweth what is good for man in this life, all the days of his vain life which he spendeth as a shadow? for who can tell a man what shall be after him under the sun? . . .

Because to every purpose there is time and judg-ment, therefore the misery of man is great upon him.

For he knoweth not that which shall be: for who can tell him when it shall be?

There is no man that hath power over the spirit to retain the spirit; neither hath he power in the day of death: and there is no discharge in that war; neither shall wickedness deliver those that are given to it.

All this have I seen, and applied my heart unto every work that is done under the sun: there is a time wherein one man ruleth over another to his own hurt.

And so I saw the wicked buried, who had come and gone from the place of the holy, and they were forgotten in the city where they had so done: this is also vanity.

Because sentence against an evil work is not exe-cuted speedily, therefore the heart of the sons of men is fully set in them to do evil. . . .

There is a vanity which is done upon the earth; that there be just men, unto whom it happeneth according to the work of the wicked; again, there be wicked men, to whom it happeneth according to the work of the righteous: I said that this also is van-ity. . . .

All things come alike to all: there is one event to the righteous, and to the wicked; to the good and to the clean, and to the unclean; to him that sac-rificeth, and to him that sacrificeth not: as is the good, so is the sinner; and he that sweareth, as he that feareth an oath.

An early representation of the signs of the zodiac, com-mon in medieval Jewish art. This mosaic is from Beth Alpha Synagogue, Palestine, built fifth century A.D.

This is an evil among all things that are done under the sun, that there is one event unto all: yea, also the heart of the sons of men is full of evil, and madness is in their heart while they live, and after that they go to the dead.

For to him that is joined to all the living there is hope: for a living dog is better than a dead lion.

For the living know that they shall die: but the dead know not any thing, neither have they any
10 more a reward; for the memory of them is forgotten.

Also their love, and their hatred, and their envy, is now perished; neither have they any more a portion for ever in any thing that is done under the sun.

THE WAY OF LIFE

Go thy way, eat thy bread with joy, and drink thy wine with a merry heart; for God now accepteth thy works.

Let thy garments be always white; and let thy head lack no ointment.

20 Live joyfully with the wife whom thou lovest all the days of the life of thy vanity, which he hath given thee under the sun, all the days of thy vanity: for that is thy portion in this life, and in thy labour which thou takest under the sun.

Whatsoever thy hand findeth to do, do it with thy might; for there is no work, nor device, nor knowledge, nor wisdom, in the grave, whither thou goest.

I returned, and saw under the sun, that the race is not to the swift, nor the battle to the strong, neither
30 yet bread to the wise, nor yet riches to men of understanding, nor yet favour to men of skill; but time and chance happeneth to them all.

For man also knoweth not his time: as the fishes that are taken in an evil net, and as the birds that are caught in the snare; so are the sons of men snared in an evil time, when it falleth suddenly upon them.

This wisdom have I seen also under the sun, and it seemed great unto me:

There was a little city, and few men within it; and
40 there came a great king against it, and besieged it, and built great bulwarks against it:

Now there was found in it a poor wise man, and he by his wisdom delivered the city; yet no man remembered that same poor man.

Then said I, Wisdom is better than strength: nevertheless the poor man's wisdom is despised, and his words are not heard.

Truly the light is sweet, and a pleasant thing it is for the eyes to behold the sun:

50 But if a man live many years, and rejoice in them all; yet let him remember the days of darkness; for they shall be many. All that cometh is vanity.

Rejoice, O young man, in thy youth; and let thy heart cheer thee in the days of thy youth, and walk in the ways of thine heart, and in the sight of thine eyes: but know thou, that for all these things God will bring thee into judgment.

Therefore remove sorrow from thy heart, and put away evil from thy flesh: for childhood and youth
60 are vanity.

Remember now thy Creator in the days of thy youth, while the evil days come not, nor the years draw nigh, when thou shalt say, I have no pleasure in them;

While the sun, or the light, or the moon, or the stars, be not darkened, nor the clouds return after the rain:

In the day when the keepers of the house shall tremble, and the strong men shall bow themselves,
70 and the grinders cease because they are few, and those that look out of the windows be darkened,

And the doors shall be shut in the streets, when the sound of the grinding is low, and he shall rise up at the voice of the bird, and all the daughters of musick shall be brought low;

Also when they shall be afraid of that which is high, and fears shall be in the way, and the almond tree shall flourish, and the grasshopper shall be a burden, and desire shall fail: because man goeth to
80 his long home, and the mourners go about the streets:

Or ever the silver cord be loosed, or the golden bowl be broken, or the pitcher be broken at the fountain, or the wheel broken at the cistern.

Then shall the dust return to the earth as it was: and the spirit shall return unto God who gave it.

EPILOGUE

Vanity of vanities, saith the preacher; all is vanity.

And moreover, because the preacher was wise, he still taught the people knowledge; yea, he gave good heed, and sought out, and set in order many proverbs.

90 The preacher sought to find out acceptable words: and that which was written was upright, even words of truth.

The words of the wise are as goads, and as nails fastened by the masters of assemblies, which are given from one shepherd.

And further, by these, my son, be admonished: of making many books there is no end; and much study is a weariness of the flesh.

The Song of Songs

I dialogue - man + maid

I AM the rose of Sharon, and the lily of the valleys.

100 As the lily among thorns, so is my love among the daughters.

As the apple tree among the trees of the wood,

so is my beloved among the sons. I sat down under his shadow with great delight, and his fruit was sweet to my taste.

He brought me to the banqueting house, and his banner over me was love.

Stay me with flagons, comfort me with apples: for I am sick of love.

His left hand is under my head, and his right hand doth embrace me.

10 I charge you, O ye daughters of Jerusalem, by the roes, and by the hinds of the field, that ye stir not up, nor awake my love, till he please.

The voice of my beloved! behold, he cometh leaping upon the mountains, skipping upon the hills.

My beloved is like a roe or a young hart: behold, he standeth behind our wall, he looketh forth at the windows, shewing himself through the lattice.

My beloved spake, and said unto me, Rise up, my love, my fair one, and come away.

20 For, lo, the winter is past, the rain is over and gone;

The flowers appear on the earth; the time of the singing of birds is come, and the voice of the turtle is heard in our land;

The fig tree putteth forth her green figs, and the vines with the tender grape give a good smell. Arise, my love, my fair one, and come away.

O my dove, that art in the clefts of the rock, in the secret places of the stairs, let me see thy counte-
30 nance, let me hear thy voice; for sweet is thy voice, and thy countenance is comely.

Take us the foxes, the little foxes, that spoil the vines: for our vines have tender grapes.

My beloved is mine, and I am his: he feedeth among the lilies.

Until the day break, and the shadows flee away, turn, my beloved, and be thou like a roe or a young hart upon the mountains of Bether.

II maid

By night on my bed I sought him whom my soul 40 loveth: I sought him, but I found him not.

I will rise now, and go about the city in the streets, and in the broad ways I will seek him whom my soul loveth: I sought him, but I found him not.

The watchmen that go about the city found me: to whom I said, Saw ye him whom my soul loveth?

It was but a little that I passed from them, but I found him whom my soul loveth: I held him, and would not let him go, until I had brought him into my mother's house, and into the chamber of her 50 that conceived me.

I charge you, O ye daughters of Jerusalem, by the roes, and by the hinds of the field, that ye stir not up, nor awake my love, till he please.

III man

Behold, thou art fair, my love; behold, thou art fair; thou hast doves' eyes within thy locks: thy hair is as a flock of goats, that appear from mount Gilead.

Thy teeth are like a flock of sheep that are even shorn, which came up from the washing; whereof every one bear twins, and none is barren among them. 60

Thy lips are like a thread of scarlet, and thy speech is comely: thy temples are like a piece of a pomegranate within thy locks.

Thy neck is like the tower of David builded for an armoury, whereon there hang a thousand bucklers, all shields of mighty men.

Thy two breasts are like two young roes that are twins, which feed among the lilies.

Until the day break, and the shadows flee away, I will get me to the mountain of myrrh, and to the 70 hill of frankincense.

Thou art all fair, my love; there is no spot in thee.

IV maid

I sleep, but my heart waketh: it is the voice of my beloved that knocketh, saying, Open to me, my sister, my love, my dove, my undefiled: for my head is filled with dew, and my locks with the drops of the night.

I have put off my coat; how shall I put it on? I have washed my feet; how shall I defile them?

My beloved put in his hand by the hole of the door, and my bowels were moved for him. 80

I rose up to open to my beloved; and my hands dropped with myrrh, and my fingers with sweet smelling myrrh, upon the handles of the lock.

I opened to my beloved; but my beloved had withdrawn himself, and was gone: my soul failed when he spake: I sought him, but I could not find him; I called him, but he gave me no answer.

The watchmen that went about the city found me, they smote me, they wounded me; the keepers of the walls took away my vail from me. 90

I charge you, O daughters of Jerusalem, if ye find my beloved, that ye tell him, that I am sick of love.

V dialogue — daughters — maid

What is thy beloved more than another beloved, O thou fairest among women? what is thy beloved more than another beloved, that thou dost so charge us?

My beloved is white and ruddy, the chiefest among ten thousand.

His head is as the most fine gold, his locks are bushy, and black as a raven. 100

His eyes are as the eyes of doves by the rivers of waters, washed with milk, and fitly set.

His cheeks are as a bed of spices, as sweet flowers: his lips like lilies, dropping sweet smelling myrrh.

His hands are as gold rings set with the beryl: his belly is as bright ivory overlaid with sapphires.

His legs are as pillars of marble, set upon sockets of fine gold: his countenance is as Lebanon, excellent as the cedars.

His mouth is most sweet: yea, he is altogether lovely. This is my beloved, and this is my friend, O daughters of Jerusalem.

10 Whither is thy beloved gone, O thou fairest among women? whither is thy beloved turned aside? that we may seek him with thee.

My beloved is gone down into his garden, to the beds of spices, to feed in the gardens, and to gather lilies.

I am my beloved's, and my beloved is mine: he feedeth among the lilies. . . .

VI maid

I am my beloved's, and his desire is toward me.

Come, my beloved, let us go forth into the field; let us lodge in the villages.

20 Let us get up early to the vineyards; let us see if the vine flourish, whether the tender grape appear, and the pomegranates bud forth: there will I give thee my loves.

The mandrakes give a smell, and at our gates are all manner of pleasant fruits, new and old, which I have laid up for thee, O my beloved.

O that thou wert as my brother, that sucked the breasts of my mother! when I should find thee without, I would kiss thee; yea, I should not be despised.

30 I would lead thee, and bring thee into my mother's house, who would instruct me: I would cause thee to drink of spiced wine of the juice of my pomegranate.

His left hand should be under my head, and his right hand should embrace me.

I charge you, O daughters of Jerusalem, that ye stir not up, nor awake my love, until he please. . . .

VII maid

Set me as a seal upon thine heart, as a seal upon thine arm: for love is strong as death; jealousy is cruel as the grave: the coals thereof are coals of fire,
40 which hath a most vehement flame.

Many waters cannot quench love, neither can the floods drown it: if a man would give all the substance of his house for love, it would utterly be contemned. . . .

Thou that dwellest in the gardens, the companions hearken to thy voice: cause me to hear it.

Make haste, my beloved, and be thou like to a roe or to a young hart upon the mountains of spices.

Jonah

Now the word of the Lord came unto Jonah the son of Amittai, saying,
50
Arise, go to Nineveh, that great city, and cry against it; for their wickedness is come up before me.

But Jonah rose up to flee unto Tarshish from the presence of the Lord, and went down to Joppa; and he found a ship going to Tarshish: so he paid the fare thereof, and went down into it, to go with them unto Tarshish from the presence of the Lord.

But the Lord sent out a great wind into the sea, and there was a mighty tempest in the sea, so that the ship was like to be broken.
60
Then the mariners were afraid, and cried every man unto his god, and cast forth the wares that were in the ship into the sea, to lighten it of them. But Jonah was gone down into the sides of the ship; and he lay, and was fast asleep.

So the shipmaster came to him, and said unto him, What meanest thou, O sleeper? arise, call upon thy God, if so be that God will think upon us, that we perish not.

And they said every one to his fellow, Come, and
70
let us cast lots, that we may know for whose cause this evil is upon us. So they cast lots, and the lot fell upon Jonah.

Then said they unto him, Tell us, we pray thee, for whose cause this evil is upon us; What is thine occupation? and whence comest thou? what is thy country? and of what people art thou?

And he said unto them, I am an Hebrew; and I fear the Lord, the God of heaven, which hath made the sea and the dry land.
80
Then were the men exceedingly afraid, and said unto him, Why hast thou done this? For the men knew that he fled from the presence of the Lord, because he had told them.

Then said they unto him, What shall we do unto thee, that the sea may be calm unto us? for the sea wrought, and was tempestuous.

And he said unto them, Take me up, and cast me forth into the sea; so shall the sea be calm unto you: for I know that for my sake this great tempest is upon
90
you.

Nevertheless the men rowed hard to bring it to the land; but they could not: for the sea wrought, and was tempestuous against them.

Wherefore they cried unto the Lord, and said, We beseech thee, O Lord, we beseech thee, let us not perish for this man's life, and lay not upon us innocent blood: for thou, O Lord, hast done as it pleased thee.

So they took up Jonah, and cast him forth into the
100
sea: and the sea ceased from her raging.

Then the men feared the Lord exceedingly, and offered a sacrifice unto the Lord, and made vows.

Now the Lord had prepared a great fish to swallow up Jonah. And Jonah was in the belly of the fish three days and three nights.

Then Jonah prayed unto the Lord his God out of the fish's belly,

And said, I cried by reason of mine affliction unto the Lord, and he heard me; out of the belly of hell
10 cried I, and thou heardest my voice.

For thou hadst cast me into the deep, in the midst of the seas; and the floods compassed me about: all thy billows and thy waves passed over me.

Then I said, I am cast out of thy sight; yet I will look again toward thy holy temple.

The waters compassed me about, even to the soul: the depth closed me round about, the weeds were wrapped about my head.

I went down to the bottoms of the mountains; the
20 earth with her bars was about me for ever: yet hast thou brought up my life from corruption, O Lord my God.

When my soul fainted within me I remembered the Lord: and my prayer came in unto thee, into thine holy temple.

They that observe lying vanities forsake their own mercy.

But I will sacrifice unto thee with the voice of thanksgiving; I will pay that that I have vowed.
30 Salvation is of the Lord.

And the Lord spake unto the fish, and it vomited out Jonah upon the dry land.

And the word of the Lord came unto Jonah the second time, saying,

Arise, go unto Nineveh, that great city, and preach unto it the preaching that I bid thee.

So Jonah arose, and went unto Nineveh, according to the word of the Lord. Now Nineveh was an exceeding great city of three days' journey.

40 And Jonah began to enter into the city a day's journey, and he cried, and said, Yet forty days, and Nineveh shall be overthrown.

So the people of Nineveh believed God, and proclaimed a fast and put on sackcloth, from the greatest of them even to the least of them.

For word came unto the king of Nineveh, and he arose from his throne, and he laid his robe from him, and covered him with sackcloth, and sat in ashes.

And he caused it to be proclaimed and published
50 through Nineveh by the decree of the king and his nobles, saying, Let neither man nor beast, herd nor flock, taste any thing: let them not feed, nor drink water:

But let man and beast be covered with sackcloth, and cry mightily unto God: yea, let them turn every

A tenth-century Byzantine miniature painting which gives the full story of Jonah. Below, Jonah is being swallowed by the monster and cast up; above, he gives thanks and preaches to the Ninevites.

one from his evil way, and from the violence that is in their hands.

Who can tell if God will turn and repent, and turn away from his fierce anger, that we perish not?

And God saw their works, that they turned from 60 their evil way; and God repented of the evil, that he had said that he would do unto them; and he did it not.

But it displeased Jonah exceedingly, and he was very angry. And he prayed unto the Lord, and said, I pray thee, O Lord, was not this my saying, when I was yet in my country? Therefore I fled before unto Tarshish: for I knew that thou art a gracious God, and merciful, slow to anger, and of great kindness, and repentest thee of the evil. 70

Therefore now, O Lord, take, I beseech thee, my life from me; for it is better for me to die than to live.

Then said the Lord, Doest thou well to be angry?

So Jonah went out of the city, and sat on the east side of the city, and there made him a booth, and sat under it in the shadow, till he might see what would become of the city.

And the Lord God prepared a gourd, and made it to come up over Jonah, that it might be a shadow over his head, to deliver him from his grief. So Jonah was exceeding glad of the gourd.

But God prepared a worm when the morning rose the next day, and it smote the gourd that it withered.

And it came to pass, when the sun did arise, that God prepared a vehement east wind; and the sun beat upon the head of Jonah, that he fainted, and wished in himself to die, and said, It is better for me to die than to live.

10 And God said to Jonah, Doest thou well to be angry for the gourd? And he said, I do well to be angry, even unto death.

Then said the Lord, Thou hast had pity on the gourd, for the which thou hast not laboured, neither madest it grow; which came up in a night, and perished in a night:

And should not I spare Nineveh, that great city, wherein are more than sixscore thousand persons that cannot discern between their right hand and their
20 left hand; and also much cattle?

Ruth

Now it came to pass in the days when the judges ruled, that there was a famine in the land. And a certain man of Bethlehem-judah went to sojourn in the country of Moab, he, and his wife, and his two sons.

And the name of the man was Elimelech, and the name of his wife Naomi, and the name of his two sons Mahlon and Chilion, Ephrathites of Bethlehem-judah. And they came into the country of Moab, and
30 continued there.

And Elimelech Naomi's husband died; and she was left, and her two sons.

And they took them wives of the women of Moab; the name of the one was Orpah, and the name of the other Ruth: and they dwelled there about ten years.

And Mahlon and Chilion died also both of them; and the woman was left of her two sons and her husband.

Then she arose with her daughters-in-law, that she
40 might return from the country of Moab: for she had heard in the country of Moab how that the Lord had visited his people in giving them bread.

Wherefore she went forth out of the place where she was, and her two daughters-in-law with her; and they went on the way to return unto the land of Judah.

And Naomi said unto her two daughters-in-law, Go, return each to her mother's house: the Lord deal kindly with you, as ye have dealt with the dead, and
50 with me.

The Lord grant you that ye may find rest, each of you in the house of her husband. Then she kissed them; and they lifted up their voice, and wept.

And they said unto her, Surely we will return with thee unto thy people.

And Naomi said, Turn again, my daughters: why will ye go with me? are there yet any more sons in my womb, that they may be your husbands?

Turn again, my daughters, go your way; for I am too old to have an husband. If I should say, I have 60 hope, if I should have an husband also to night, and should also bear sons;

Would ye tarry for them till they were grown? would ye stay for them from having husbands? nay, my daughters; for it grieveth me much for your sakes that the hand of the Lord is gone out against me.

And they lifted up their voice, and wept again: and Orpah kissed her mother-in-law; but Ruth clave unto her.

And she said, Behold, thy sister-in-law is gone 70 back unto her people, and unto her gods: return thou after thy sister-in-law.

And Ruth said, Intreat me not to leave thee, or to return from following after thee: for whither thou goest, I will go; and where thou lodgest, I will lodge: thy people shall be my people, and thy God my God:

Where thou diest, will I die, and there will I be buried: the Lord do so to me, and more also, if ought but death part thee and me.

When she saw that she was stedfastly minded to 80 go with her, then she left speaking unto her.

So they two went until they came to Bethlehem. And it came to pass, when they were come to Bethlehem, that all the city was moved about them, and they said, Is this Naomi?

And she said unto them, Call me not Naomi, call me Mara: for the Almighty hath dealt very bitterly with me.

I went out full, and the Lord hath brought me home again empty: why then call ye me Naomi, see- 90 ing the Lord hath testified against me, and the Almighty hath afflicted me?

So Naomi returned, and Ruth the Moabitess, her daughter-in-law, with her, which returned out of the country of Moab: and they came to Bethlehem in the beginning of barley harvest.

And Naomi had a kinsman of her husband's, a mighty man of wealth, of the family of Elimelech; and his name was Boaz.

And Ruth the Moabitess said unto Naomi, Let me 100 now go to the field, and glean ears of corn after him in whose sight I shall find grace. And she said unto her, Go, my daughter.

And she went, and came, and gleaned in the field after the reapers: and her hap was to light on a part of the field belonging unto Boaz, who was of the kindred of Elimelech.

And, behold, Boaz came from Bethlehem, and said unto the reapers, The Lord be with you. And they answered him, The Lord bless thee.

Then said Boaz unto his servant that was set over the reapers, Whose damsel is this?

And the servant that was set over the reapers answered and said, It is the Moabitish damsel that came back with Naomi out of the country of Moab:

And she said, I pray you, let me glean and gather after the reapers among the sheaves: so she came, and hath continued even from the morning until now, that she tarried a little in the house.

Then said Boaz unto Ruth, Hearest thou not, my daughter? Go not to glean in another field, neither go from hence, but abide here fast by my maidens:

Let thine eyes be on the field that they do reap, and go thou after them: have I not charged the young men that they shall not touch thee? and when thou art athirst, go unto the vessels, and drink of that which the young men have drawn.

Then she fell on her face, and bowed herself to the ground, and said unto him, Why have I found grace in thine eyes, that thou shouldest take knowledge of me, seeing I am a stranger?

And Boaz answered and said unto her, It hath fully been shewed me, all that thou hast done unto thy mother-in-law since the death of thine husband: and how thou hast left thy father and thy mother, and the land of thy nativity, and art come unto a people which thou knewest not heretofore.

The Lord recompense thy work, and a full reward be given thee of the Lord God of Israel, under whose wings thou art come to trust.

Then she said, Let me find favour in thy sight, my lord; for that thou hast comforted me, and for that thou hast spoken friendly unto thine handmaid, though I be not like unto one of thine handmaidens.

And Boaz said unto her, At mealtime come thou hither, and eat of the bread, and dip thy morsel in the vinegar. And she sat beside the reapers: and he reached her parched corn, and she did eat, and was sufficed, and left.

And when she was risen up to glean, Boaz commanded his young men, saying, Let her glean even among the sheaves, and reproach her not:

And let fall also some of the handfuls of purpose for her, and leave them, that she may glean them, and rebuke her not.

So she gleaned in the field until even, and beat out that she had gleaned: and it was about an ephah of barley.

And she took it up, and went into the city: and her mother-in-law saw what she had gleaned: and she brought forth, and gave to her that she had reserved after she was sufficed.

And her mother-in-law said unto her, Where hast thou gleaned to day? and where wroughtest thou?

blessed be he that did take knowledge of thee. And she shewed her mother-in-law with whom she had wrought, and said, The man's name with whom I wrought to day is Boaz.

And Naomi said unto her daughter-in-law, Blessed be he of the Lord, who hath not left off his kindness to the living and to the dead. And Naomi said unto her, The man is near of kin unto us, one of our next kinsmen.

And Ruth the Moabitess said, He said unto me also, Thou shalt keep fast by my young men, until they have ended all my harvest.

And Naomi said unto Ruth her daughter-in-law, It is good, my daughter, that thou go out with his maidens, that they meet thee not in any other field.

So she kept fast by the maidens of Boaz to glean unto the end of barley harvest and of wheat harvest; and dwelt with her mother-in-law.

Then Naomi her mother-in-law said unto her, My daughter, shall I not seek rest for thee, that it may be well with thee?

And now is not Boaz of our kindred, with whose maidens thou wast? Behold, he winnoweth barley to night in the threshingfloor.

Wash thyself therefore, and anoint thee, and put thy raiment upon thee, and get thee down to the floor: but make not thyself known unto the man, until he shall have done eating and drinking.

And it shall be, when he lieth down, that thou shalt mark the place where he shall lie, and thou shalt go in, and uncover his feet, and lay thee down; and he will tell thee what thou shalt do.

And she said unto her, All that thou sayest unto me I will do.

And she went down unto the floor, and did according to all that her mother-in-law bade her.

And when Boaz had eaten and drunk, and his heart was merry, he went to lie down at the end of the heap of corn: and she came softly, and uncovered his feet, and laid her down.

And it came to pass at midnight, that the man was afraid, and turned himself: and, behold, a woman lay at his feet.

And he said, Who art thou? And she answered, I am Ruth thine handmaid: spread therefore thy skirt over thine handmaid; for thou art a near kinsman.

And he said, Blessed be thou of the Lord, my daughter: for thou hast shewed more kindness in the latter end than at the beginning, inasmuch as thou followedst not young men, whether poor or rich.

And now, my daughter, fear not; I will do to thee all that thou requirest: for all the city of my people doth know that thou art a virtuous woman.

And now it is true that I am thy near kinsman: howbeit there is a kinsman nearer than I.

Tarry this night, and it shall be in the morning,

that if he will perform unto thee the part of a kinsman, well; let him do the kinsman's part: but if he will not do the part of a kinsman to thee, then will I do the part of a kinsman to thee, as the Lord liveth: lie down until the morning.

And she lay at his feet until the morning: and she rose up before one could know another. And he said, Let it not be known that a woman came into the floor.

10 Also he said, Bring the vail that thou hast upon thee, and hold it. And when she held it, he measured six measures of barley, and laid it on her: and she went into the city.

And when she came to her mother-in-law, she said, Who art thou, my daughter? And she told her all that the man had done to her.

And she said, These six measures of barley gave he me; for he said to me, Go not empty unto thy mother-in-law.

20 Then said she, Sit still, my daughter, until thou know how the matter will fall: for the man will not be in rest, until he have finished the thing this day.

Then went Boaz up to the gate, and sat him down there: and, behold, the kinsman of whom Boaz spake came by; unto whom he said, Ho, such a one! turn aside, sit down here. And he turned aside, and sat down.

And he took ten men of the elders of the city, and said, Sit ye down here. And they sat down.

30 And he said unto the kinsman, Naomi, that is come again out of the country of Moab, selleth a parcel of land, which was our brother Elimelech's:

And I thought to advertise thee, saying, Buy it before the inhabitants, and before the elders of my people. If thou wilt redeem it, redeem it: but if thou wilt not redeem it, then tell me, that I may know: for there is none to redeem it beside thee; and I am after thee. And he said, I will redeem it.

Then said Boaz, What day thou buyest the field 40 of the hand of Naomi, thou must buy it also of Ruth the Moabitess, the wife of the dead, to raise up the name of the dead upon his inheritance.

And the kinsman said, I cannot redeem it for myself, lest I mar mine own inheritance: redeem thou my right to thyself; for I cannot redeem it.

Now this was the manner in former time in Israel concerning redeeming and concerning changing, for to confirm all things; a man plucked off his shoe, and gave it to his neighbour: and this was a testimony in Israel.   50

Therefore the kinsman said unto Boaz, Buy it for thee. So he drew off his shoe.

And Boaz said unto the elders, and unto all the people, Ye are witnesses this day, that I have bought all that was Elimelech's, and all that was Chilion's and Mahlon's, of the hand of Naomi.

Moreover Ruth the Moabitess, the wife of Mahlon, have I purchased to be my wife, to raise up the name of the dead upon his inheritance, that the name of the dead be not cut off from among his brethren,   60 and from the gate of his place: ye are witnesses this day.

And all the people that were in the gate, and the elders, said, We are witnesses. The Lord make the woman that is come into thine house like Rachel and like Leah, which two did build the house of Israel: and do thou worthily in Ephratah, and be famous in Bethlehem:

And let thy house be like the house of Pharez, whom Tamar bare unto Judah, of the seed which the   70 Lord shall give thee of this young woman.

So Boaz took Ruth, and she was his wife: and when he went in unto her, the Lord gave her conception, and she bare a son.

And the women said unto Naomi, Blessed be the Lord, which hath not left thee this day without a kinsman, that his name may be famous in Israel.

And he shall be unto thee a restorer of thy life, and a nourisher of thine old age: for thy daughter-in-law, which loveth thee, which is better to thee than seven   80 sons, hath born him.

And Naomi took the child, and laid it in her bosom, and became nurse unto it.

And the women her neighbours gave it a name, saying, There is a son born to Naomi; and they called his name Obed: he is the father of Jesse, the father of David.

GREECE
AND THE BIRTH
OF THE WEST

800 B.C. TO 300 B.C.

A stone replica of a mask of comedy, from a Greek theater of the fourth century B.C.

WESTERN civilization was born with the Greeks. These are the people to whom chance gave the opportunity to found our culture and establish our basic institutions. Democracy and civil liberties, philosophy and an elemental science, drama and every kind of poetry, architecture and sculpture in the classic style—these things that we take for granted were evolved by them as they met the challenge of human problems that still confront us today.

Greek culture has about it the hardy recklessness of youth. With almost no past authority to guide or restrict them, the Greeks speculated and experimented through a sudden awareness of the world in which they lived. Like most enthusiastic pioneers they made many mistakes, which seem naïve and obvious in the light of our greater experience; but we learn as much from their failures as from their success. Beset by the complexity of our own situation, we profit from their approach to problems as varied and immediate as our own, yet outlined on a smaller scale with the issues more clearly defined. In about three hundred years their rich experience raised most of the problems of civilized living, and their solutions come very close to ours. The final decline of Greek culture, the absorption of the Greeks and their traditions in the more pragmatic empires of Macedonia and Rome point an ominous lesson that we may still have to learn.

The achievements of the Greeks seem even more remarkable when we consider how few these people were and how small a land they occupied. Although the Greek world in its heyday spread far beyond Greece proper, its center was always that mountainous little peninsula jutting into the eastern Mediterranean, which was a mere 250 miles long and 45,000 square miles in area—roughly the size of New York State. In fact, the greatest cultural achievements of the Greeks were centered in a single city, Athens, which had in its Golden Age perhaps 200,000 inhabitants, of whom about a fifth were adult male citizens. A handful of great men living in close, free contact with each other made Athens the perennial ideal of Western culture.

Four fifths of Greece is covered with rugged mountains that only occasionally rise to peaks such as the sacred Olympus, Helicon, Parnassus, and Olympia. Since there are few passes through them, these mountains shut off the Greeks in self-contained communities and encouraged the clannish government of independent city-states rather than national unity and empire. Access to the sea was often simpler than contact with neighboring cities, and the settlement of colonies on the many islands surrounding the peninsula inspired a close bond between colonies and mother-states and a jealous suspicion of rival cities.

The bleak plateaus and barren mountains provided abundant marble for buildings and statues, rich veins of silver and copper, but little pasture land and even less soil for cultivation. Although their country was not so barren then as now after centuries of reckless deforestation and erosion, the Greeks were forced to till every precious foot of arable land for their meager crops of wheat, barley, flax, olives, and grapes. Inevitably they looked to the sea for sustenance from colonies, foreign trade, and even warfare. This was especially true of Athens, the great seafaring, trading city of the peninsula, be-

Black Sea

Bosporus

Byzantium

THRACE

Propontis

ASIA MINOR

Hellespont

Troy

Mitylene

Smyrna

Teos

Ephesus

Lesbos

Chios

Samos

Miletus

Cos

Cnidus

Rhodes

MACEDONIA

Lemnos

Aegean Sea

Andros

Delos

Naxos

Melos

Mediterranean

S. Fleishman

Mt. OLYMPUS

THESSALY

EUBOEA

Thermopylae

Delphi

Mt. Parnassus

Chaeronea

BOEOTIA

Leuctra

Thebes

Marathon

Plataea

ATTICA

Eleusis

Salamis

Athens

CRETE

Cnossus

Corinthian Gulf

Corinth

Saronic Gulf

Mycenae

Argos

Tiryns

Sparta

Dodona

Ithaca

Olympia

PELOPONNESUS

ITALY

LANDS OF THE GREEKS

I: 86   GREECE AND THE BIRTH OF THE WEST

cause her state of Attica was the least fertile of the lot. Her chief rival, Sparta, shut off in a fruitful valley, developed a more agrarian and provincial culture. It is not hard to discern one reason why, in politics and social institutions, Sparta stood for conservative discipline, while Athens symbolized the progressive spirit of free inquiry.

The ruggedness of the cliffs of the west coast first caused the Greeks to turn their eyes eastward to their ports on the Aegean Sea and the beautiful islands that provided colonial stepping stones for trade with Asia Minor. Across this hospitable sea the early Greeks went to plunder Troy, and over this sea and around it came the lumbering armies of Persia in a later age to fight a second great war of East and West. It was the sea, not the land, that formed the unifying force in the Greek world; the sea was the symbol of freedom to explore and exploit the world at will.

The Mediterranean climate of Greece was then more temperate than it is today. The lowlands enjoyed warm weather the year round, and Athens could boast of three hundred sunny days a year. The long dry season drained the few rivers, but the rainy winter brought back brief torrents to the parched river beds. Lacking rainfall and trees, Greece seemed as it does even today a land ablaze with light and open to the sky and the sea air. In such a land men lived constantly in the open, with less food, clothing, and shelter than northerners need. Life was natural, simple, and direct, and men living together out of doors enjoyed a free exchange of ideas and more leisure to create beautiful things.

THE COMING OF THE GREEKS

CIVILIZATION in the East was already old when the Greeks first settled Greece. Not simply China and India but the fertile valleys of the Euphrates and the Nile had produced great cultures as early as 3500 B.C. But Sumer and Egypt were long in decay when the hardy invaders whom we call Greeks battled their way with iron swords from the northeast into the rocky peninsula that was to become their home. Where they came from we do not know, but they brought with them an Indo-European language that links them in some way with the people of India and with others who spoke Indo-European tongues. They found an older people, the Aegeans, firmly settled in Greece, where for two thousand years they had been quietly evolving a remarkable culture. Although this prehistoric culture had important centers in Mycenae and Tiryns on the mainland, its greatest glory was in more ancient Cnossus on the island of Crete, where a legendary king Minos is supposed to have built the astounding palaces recently unearthed by archaeologists.* In his honor this whole precocious culture is now called Minoan.

The invading Greeks, who poured into the peninsula in successive waves after 2000 B.C., felt no awe of this superior Minoan culture. Cnossus was destroyed about 1400 B.C., perhaps by the Greeks, and Mycenae and Tiryns fell to them two centuries later. A dark period settled over the peninsula as the Greeks were assimilating the vanquished and absorbing the vestiges of their civilization. In some areas the Aegeans were annihilated or driven out; in others they apparently intermarried with the Greeks to form one race. In Sparta, however, the Aegeans (and even some of the early Greek settlers) were subjected to perpetual slavery by the Dorians, the last group of the Greek conquerors, so that throughout Spartan history no more than ten thousand (eventually only seven hundred) free citizens ruled at least twenty times as many slaves, or *helots*. Herein lies another explanation of the difference between democratic Athens and aristocratic Sparta.

The invasions continued for five centuries and eventually spread the Greeks over the countless islands of the Aegean and along the coast of Asia Minor. The Greeks were actually many tribes and did not think of themselves as one people. To the end of their ancient history they remained a group of distinct and self-conscious city-states, jealous of their separate traditions, often at war with each other, yet bound together informally by a common religion and cultural heritage.

Although they are conveniently called "Greeks," they cannot be properly called that until they settled Greece. That name for them actually originated in Italy a thousand years later, and was used to identify those who spoke the common language of Greek. Homer in the eighth century B.C. referred to his race with old sectional names—the *Achaians*, the *Argives*, the *Danaians*—to identify various Greek peoples temporarily bound together in war. Eventually the Greeks developed the name *Hellenes* (after *Hellas*, a Greek name for the Greek world) to distinguish themselves from all non-Greeks, contemptuously called "barbarians." The culture of Greece at its height is often called "Hellenic," and the later culture which it was to inspire after the loss of Greek independence is called "Hellenistic."

* The Greeks associated the Palace of Cnossus with the labyrinth of Crete, in which the hero Theseus killed the Minotaur.

The spread of the Hellenes beyond Greece was carried out by sea, for the sea was the natural road for the Greeks. Despite the small area of Greece, its coastline is as long as the eastern coast of America from Maine to Florida. The rugged shoreline notches the land with endless bays and harbors. And from these harbors sailed the Greeks, bent on war, trade, colonization; thus Hellenic culture was disseminated.

GREEK CULTURAL TIES: LANGUAGE AND RELIGION

DESPITE tribal differences, there were common cultural bonds that set all the Greeks apart from their "barbarian" neighbors. The most obvious of these was their *language*, destined to develop into perhaps the most beautiful of all the Aryan, or Indo-European, tongues. The Aegeans had had a language of their own and even a "Minoan" script (still undeciphered), but the Greeks submerged this tongue and later borrowed an alphabet from another source when their civilization developed a need for writing. The source of the Greek alphabet (and, through Latin, of all European alphabets) was a Semitic people, the Phoenicians, whose trading activities led them from their native Syria in the Near East throughout the Mediterranean. They founded cities in Sicily, Sardinia, and Spain, and in northern Africa built Carthage, later to become the great rival of Rome. The Greeks adapted the Phoenician script to their own spoken language, shifting some consonant symbols to vowels, for which Semitic languages have no symbols, and reversing the Oriental method of writing from right to left. But not until the fourth century B.C. was the Greek alphabet standardized for the whole Hellenic world. Local dialects of spoken Greek persisted, for language is a dynamic instrument; but the political and intellectual ascendancy of Athens in the fifth century gradually established Attic Greek as the norm.

An equally important bond among the Greeks was their common *religion*, which varied somewhat because of local deities and yet preserved a common core. It was as restless as their language and enjoyed a gradual evolution. As invaders, they brought with them a primitive polytheism, which expressed the awe of all primitive peoples for natural powers greater than themselves, powers that were their source of food and very existence, and yet made life insecure because of their unpredictable ability to bring flood, drought, failure, and death. Fear of the unknown had led the Greeks to invent personalities like themselves to represent these forces, gods in human form with whom they could deal through worship and ritual. To these gods they sang prayers before an altar, offered libations of milk or wine, and sacrificed animals as burnt offerings.

THE GODS OF THE GREEKS. Our earliest formal picture of Greek belief comes from Hesiod, the eighth-century poet who lived in a time when poets were still considered seers of the tribe. In the beginning, he tells us, there was Chaos, out of which came Earth and Heaven with Love as the ruling principle of creation. Love shaped matter into Titans, male and female, with an instinctive affinity and the power of further creation. These unruly Titans, predecessors of the gods, seem to personify the mighty convulsions of the physical world as it took shape. Kronos, the greatest of these, ruled Heaven and Earth with Rhea, his sister-queen, and had three daughters and three sons. The last of these children, Zeus (Jupiter *), eventually overthrew Kronos, imprisoned all of the Titans under the earth except his friend Prometheus, and began with his brothers and sisters the rule of the gods from their throne on Mount Olympus in northern Thessaly.

As leader of the victorious gods, Zeus became ruler of the earth. To his brother Poseidon (Neptune) he assigned the sea, and to Hades (Pluto) the underworld of departed spirits. Of his three sisters, Hestia (Vesta) became the goddess of the hearth, Demeter (Ceres), the goddess of agriculture, and Hera (Juno), the goddess of womanhood. Zeus married Hera and had by her the children Ares (Mars), god of war, and Hephaestos (Vulcan), the god of fire. But the affairs of Zeus with other ladies were notorious in the halls of Olympus and won him not simply the wrath of shrewish Hera, but also a considerable family: the twins Apollo (Apollo), eventually god of the sun and the arts, and Artemis (Diana), virgin goddess of the moon, the hunt, and maidenhood; Aphrodite (Venus), capricious goddess of love and beauty; Hermes (Mercury), the wily messenger of the gods; and Dionysus (Bacchus), the youthful god of wine and physical joy. To these was added Athena (Minerva), goddess of wisdom, who sprang fully grown from the brain of Zeus.

These were the chief gods of heaven, earth, the sea, and the underworld; but in the course of time a galaxy of lesser deities was invented: Eros (Cupid), the mischievous son of Venus; Pan, the piper-god of woods and fields; the nine Muses presiding over arts and sciences from their haunts on Mount Helicon and Mount Olympus; the four Winds; the nymphs and satyrs of the woods; the punishing Furies of the underworld; and the graceful water

* The names of the Roman deities that were later identified with the Greek are given in parentheses.

nymphs. Around these personalities grew up a host of charming myths that reveal the rich resources of Greek imagination and have inspired Western poets from their day to ours. They are as much a part of our culture as the Bible stories or the folk tales of England and France.

HESIOD'S FIVE AGES OF MAN. Hesiod divided the history of the world into five ages, which, though fanciful, are convenient for showing the relation of Greek religion to the history of Greece. In the first, the Age of Gold, Kronos ruled the world and Prometheus, the most humane of the Titans, created man in the image of the gods and brought him the gift of fire as the symbol of civilization. So the life of early man was golden, free from toil and misery. In the Age of Silver, Zeus and the gods established their rule over the Titans and divided the year into seasons, which plagued man with extreme heat and cold. As man turned more brutish and neglected the gods, Zeus considered annihilating the race and actually deprived men of the use of fire. But Prome-

theus, the champion of mankind, regained it and thereby won the terrible wrath of Zeus, his former friend, as Aeschylus tells us in *Prometheus Bound*. The Age of Bronze that followed may be conveniently linked with the Minoan culture, which actually evolved in what anthropologists know today as the Bronze Age. The men of this day were strong warriors, such as Perseus, Heracles, Theseus, and Jason, who destroyed their race by their violence. Or did the invasion of the Greeks actually destroy them to establish the Age of Heroes? In the fourth age the Greek world was supposed to have been ruled by heroic men—Agamemnon, Menelaus, Achilles, Nestor, and Ajax—who proved their worth in the war with Troy in the twelfth century B.C. and went in spirit from the battlefield or the hearth to a separate abode in the underworld of Hades. Alas, says Hesiod, the deterioration is now complete, for he lived (as we do) in the Age of Iron, when men never cease from toil and sorrow by day, nor from perishing by night.

HOMER AND THE AGE OF HEROES

IT is the Heroic Age of gods and men that Homer presents in the *Iliad* and the *Odyssey*, the two great monuments of the first period of Greek literature. These works alone give us a living picture of the Heroic Age, even though they were certainly produced at least three centuries after the events they relate and hence distort the picture with the perspective of a later time. The Heroic Age was one of incessant movement, frequent wars, and exciting personal adventure.

The hardy Greek invaders who had destroyed the rich Minoan civilization were not unlike the Teutonic barbarians who later overran a moribund Roman empire. Their "kings" were warrior-leaders who depended in crisis on personal followers, the free males within the tribe who were also called "kings," but of a lesser grade. All the kings were descended from Zeus and inherited their power to rule from him. A "king of kings," such as Agamemnon, sought advice from his lesser kings or family heads within the tribe and held his supreme authority only so long as he could enforce it on the others. Without written laws, the clan was governed by custom as the elders remembered and interpreted it. Crimes were avenged by families, and the revenge was stark and bloody.

The institutions of this aristocratic society were feudalistic even to the fortified towns and castles (which were to develop into city-states). Freemen who owed loyalty to the kings, or heroes, were assigned lands to cultivate, but much of the work was

done by serfs or slaves. The heroes followed the road of adventure, where they challenged each other in sport and song and sought battle to prove their strength and courage, their cunning and their valor. Their weapons were bronze, and their treasures were rich jewels and armor which they could carry with them. Unlike the later Greeks, they had no temples but worshiped their gods at improvised altars out of doors. They cremated their dead, and no man might deny burial even to his enemy, since this sacred rite was essential to the peace of the soul in Hades.

These lusty heroes lived a simple, physical life close to the soil. The tall, powerful men were not ashamed of work in the fields. King Odysseus boasted that he had no peer in reaping and mowing and could make chairs and beds for his house, boots and saddles for his riding. The beautiful women too had nimble hands. Queen Penelope wove cloth in her palace, Helen was proud of her needlework, and Nausicaä, a princess, washed the royal linen.

These men of action had little time for moralizing and no thought of international law. Hospitality was generous but unpredictable. When a town was captured, its riches were plundered, its buildings destroyed, its men killed or sold into slavery, its women made concubines or slaves. Treachery for a practical end was not only condoned but praised, and Odysseus was everywhere admired for his ingenious mendacity. Like all the Greeks of this uncertain, disordered age, he had only himself to rely on, and in the incessant struggle of his day he was supposed to use whatever craft and skill and strength he could muster.

THE WAR WITH TROY. The early Greeks fought many "wars," if we may dignify their pillaging expeditions with the name, but their destruction of Cnossus, Mycenae, and Tiryns was not chronicled as the siege of Troy was immortalized by Homer. Actually, the *Iliad* has no more trustworthy connection with this war than does *The Song of Roland* with the Moorish campaigns of Charlemagne. But Homer's idealized account of the heroic struggle has some basis in fact. Since the first enthusiastic excavations of Heinrich Schliemann, the German archaeologist, seventy-five years ago, we have learned that nine cities were successively built in ancient times on the traditional site of Troy in Asia Minor and that the sixth of these cities was probably the one destroyed by the Greeks around the traditional date, 1184 B.C.

The cause of this war is romantically ascribed by Homer to the rape of Helen, wife of the Greek king Menelaus, by the Trojan prince, Paris. Today we know that the war was merely one incident in the general extermination of the older kingdoms. Troy, strategically located at the entrance to the Hellespont, was a special target because it commanded the trade route between the Aegean and the Propontis (Sea of Marmora) and probably exacted an insufferable toll from Greek ships passing by. The annihilation of Troy assured Greek domination of the Aegean Sea. But it brought as well a dark period to the whole area as the barbaric invaders settled down to develop slowly a culture of their own, eventually more glorious than the one they had destroyed. These Dark Ages of Greece are usually dated from the last of the invasions (c. 1104 B.C.), which brought the coarse, warlike Dorian Greeks into the Peloponnese and founded the military caste of Sparta. The four centuries that followed are the cloudiest in Greek history, though they did produce Homer in the eighth century and Hesiod in the seventh. This was the hazy period when the Aegean world was gradually becoming Greek.

THE NATIONS OF HELLAS. Before the sixth century B.C., this process was complete. Hellenic culture as we know it was born, and the various branches of the new nation had settled, not simply their own peninsula, but the islands of the Aegean and the coast of Macedonia, Thrace, the Black Sea region, Asia Minor, Sicily, and southern Italy. All of this was Hellas, the Greek world.

Three chief branches of the Greek people can be distinguished in Hellas, stretched in horizontal bands across the Aegean Sea. In their contrasting political and social systems, in their differing literary forms, in their trade rivalry and eventual war is written

The effect of blindness is conveyed by this imaginary portrait of Homer from the Hellenistic period, 340–146 B.C.

the history of Greece in its Golden Age. Spread across the north from Thessaly and Boeotia to the island of Lesbos and the nearby Asiatic mainland, the *Aeolians* had founded the cities of Thebes, Delphi, Plataea, and Mitylene, and later formed in Asia Minor the Aeolian League of twelve cities. This fiery branch of the Greeks was to produce in the sixth century B.C., a school of passionate lyric poets of whom Sappho and Alcaeus are the best known.

In the south were the *Dorians*, with their great mainland cities of Sparta and Corinth and their colonies on the islands of Melos and Rhodes and at Cnidus on the Asiatic coast. Descendants of the last and most ruthless Greek invaders, the Dorians had preserved their military tradition and a rigidly aristocratic social and political system carried over from their enslavement of the original inhabitants of the land. Blessed with a reasonably fertile soil, they became farmers and sheep-herding mountaineers. In the arts they were sluggish, at least in the Golden Age; their chief poetry was the public ode, which expressed the staunch patriotism of a simple, stalwart people.

Wedged into the center of Hellas was the third branch of the Greeks, the bright-eyed *Ionians*, who settled the islands of Andros, Naxos, and Samos and maintained on Asia Minor the Ionian Confederacy of twelve cities, notably Ephesus and Miletus. Akin to them were the Attic Greeks of Athens, who seemed to blend Aeolian fire and imagination with Spartan stamina and seriousness. These contrasting strains were harmonized in the Attic temperament to produce the great leaders of Hellas in war, trade, the arts, philosophy, and political enlightenment.

With poor soil but many harbors, the Athenians took to the sea and explored the physical world as boldly as they were to explore the world of ideas. Athens in her Golden Age ° of the fifth century was to become the cosmopolitan spokesman for a free democracy, as Sparta, her Dorian rival, was the champion of military autocracy founded on caste and intense nationalism.

GOVERNMENT IN CITY-STATES

By 800 B.C. most of the Greeks had forsaken the open road and settled down in towns, many of which became the centers of the city-states in the Greek political system. These small units were a natural development of the feudal fortresses built by the tribes of the Heroic Age. Originally ruled by kings in the older tradition of Agamemnon and Menelaus, they gradually curtailed the monarch's power, until by 600 B.C. most of them were independent republics. The degree of actual democracy varied from state to state, but generally the system was oligarchic, with the state in the hands of the noble families, who alone could claim to be "citizens." This military aristocracy ruled the rural area of the state from its city stronghold and reduced the unarmed peasants to a humble position.

Such a repressive system flourished in Sparta, with its military caste and conservative provincialism. But in a mercantile city like Athens the rise of a powerful middle class brought a challenge to the old families and eventually produced rival political parties within a republic much closer to our understanding of the term. This did not happen immediately, because the biased law codes of the aristocratic governments did not provide for a widening of the governing class. Leaders of the upstart bourgeoisie, often renegade aristocrats eager for power, staged sudden revolutions and forced concessions from the nobles. Ruling as tyrants, they still depended upon the lower classes for continued

power, and engineered land reforms for the peasantry and political reforms for the mercantile classes. In their public works programs and their patronage of the arts these tyrants of the sixth century, especially Pisistratus of Athens, paved the way for the Golden Age of art, philosophy, and political freedom that Athens, at least, was to enjoy in the fifth.

By 500 B.C. such tyrannies had been displaced in most city-states by some form of popular government with a party system based on the conflicting interests of the aristocracy and the democratic classes. Whatever form it might take in individual states, such a republic generally provided the citizen with a voice in the government and the legal protection of the state as he pursued his work.

The demands of traders for some interstate (or "international") law and order eventually led to commercial treaties which granted outsiders legal representation in the courts and other privileges. The old piracy of the Heroic Age gave way to more civilized methods of trade, and even international arbitration of disputes was provided for and sometimes invoked. Unfortunately, the age-old rivalries among the cities kept them from moving further toward political union, and the tradition of violence bequeathed by the tyrants made intercity wrangling and warfare all too common. Only in the face of overwhelming danger from outside would the several states of the Greeks forget their differences and unite in a common cause.

THE PERSIAN WARS AND THE WARS OF THE CITY-STATES

Such a threat confronted them early in the fifth century, after five hundred years of relative peace with their neighbors. Around 550 B.C. the eastern kingdom of Lydia, resenting the Greek cities of Asia Minor which blocked her access to the Aegean, assumed control of them one by one. When soon afterwards Lydia was absorbed in turn by the greater kingdom of Persia, these Greek cities came under Persian rule for fifty years. This formidable neighbor

of Hellas to the east was an Oriental despotism which developed at about this time a remarkable dynasty of kings—among them Cambyses, Darius I, and Xerxes I—who rapidly extended their rule over the Near Eastern empires, including Egypt.

Persian rule of Asia Minor was comparatively benign, but in 499 B.C. the Ionian cities there,

* Not to be confused with Hesiod's Age of Gold, the first of his five ages of man previously discussed.

chafing under the unenlightened governorship of barbarians, dismissed the Persian satraps and proclaimed their independence. Athens sent them aid, but the revolt failed. Aroused by the impertinence of the Athenians, Darius resolved to conquer the Greek mainland in revenge. A naval expedition in 492 B.C. was wrecked before it could reach Athens, but Darius dispatched a second fleet in the following year. The arrival of an army of 200,000 men on the Euboean coast threw the Greeks into panic. But Athens sent a brave little band of 9000 men into the field, assisted by 1000 Plataeans, who came to their aid by forced marches. At Marathon the Greeks were outnumbered ten to one, but their courage and discipline carried the day. The lumbering Persian forces were utterly routed and pursued to their ships in one of the major battles in world history.

Darius died in 485 B.C., but his son Xerxes renewed the attack. For four years he slowly collected materials from all parts of the Persian empire and a mammoth polyglot army that Herodotus, the Greek historian of this war, numbered at two million. With a fleet of 1200 large ships and many smaller ones, this unwieldy host crossed the Hellespont in seven days and nights over two bridges of ships lashed together to provide a veritable road over the sea. Warned of the approach of this colossus, the Greek cities in the north surrendered without a fight, but Athens and Sparta, united by a common danger, made hasty and seemingly pathetic preparations for battle. As the Persians approached Athens, they found the narrow and treacherous pass of Thermopylae defended by 300 Spartans, under Leonidas, and several thousand allies. Xerxes lost thousands of his troops in a vain effort to overpower their defense, and succeeded only after a Greek traitor showed him an indirect route to the rear of the Greeks. The 300 Spartans allowed their allies to leave and held out with 700 Thespians until they were almost completely annihilated. Their noble defense inspired the most famous epitaph in the *Greek Anthology*:

"Go tell the Spartans, thou that passeth by,
  That here, obedient to their laws, we lie."

Themistocles, the commander of Athens, now ordered his people to flee for their lives, so that when Xerxes reached the city he found only a small garrison. These men he killed, and laid waste the city. But Themistocles had placed all his hope in a naval battle, where the seagoing Athenians might be a more even match for the Persians. The two fleets met in a narrow strait north of the Saronic Gulf, which gave Xerxes no space to maneuver his countless ships. From his seat on the Attic shore the Persian king watched his vast armada worsted in the decisive battle named Salamis after an island across the strait. With confusion and disease in the ranks of his army, he made a hasty retreat. A remnant of 300,000 men was left in Thessaly, but this last threat to Greek independence was defeated the next year in the battle of Plataea. In withstanding the Persian hordes the Greeks preserved their Western civilization from being engulfed by the ancient East and prepared the way for their Golden Age that followed.

The leadership of Athens in the Persian Wars gave her hegemony in Hellas through the remainder of the fifth century. She strengthened her position by forming the so-called Delian Confederacy, an arrangement whereby the Greek cities of Asia and the Aegean contributed a fixed sum of money to a common treasury at Delos (later moved to Athens) for defense against Persia. Her naval supremacy in the league converted it into a veritable Athenian empire and inevitably excited the envy and dissatisfaction of the other states. The brilliant but unscrupulous Themistocles was eventually succeeded as Athenian leader by the noble Pericles (c. 495–429 B.C.), who guided the democratic party to power, reformed the laws of the state in favor of the lower classes, and encouraged the flowering of Athenian art and philosophy. The greatest period of Greek culture is often called the Age of Pericles.

The political gulf between Athens and Sparta grew wider after the Persian enemy retired, as the power of Athens increased, and her democratic government threatened to affect the aristocratic states to the south. A rival confederacy to the Ionic had been organized by Sparta, and eventually led the Greek cities into new and shameful wars among themselves which were to destroy the vitality of Greek culture and lay Hellas open to conquest from without.

The so-called Peloponnesian War began in 431 B.C. when Sparta marched on Athens because of a protest from the Doric city of Corinth. During the siege of Athens, Pericles and many others died in a plague, but the demagogue Cleon persuaded the city to hold out, despite the satiric protests of the playwright Aristophanes. A technical defeat induced Sparta to offer peace, but the indecisive Peace of Nicias proved only the fruitlessness of these wars of the city-states. Soon afterwards Sparta was at odds with her former ally, Corinth, and Athens under the brilliant profligate Alcibiades dispatched a fleet against the Doric city of Syracuse in Sicily. But Alcibiades was deprived of his command on suspicion of sacrilege, so he turned traitor and engineered a crippling blow by the Spartans against his native city. The war between Athens and Sparta dragged on for several years, until with the loss of her fleet Athens fell to a siege in 404 B.C.

So the hegemony of Athens gave way to the hegemony of Sparta. The aristocratic Spartans promptly deposed the democratic party in Athens and established the atrocious rule of the Thirty Tyrants for a year. Overbearing methods soon roused enemies against Sparta in the other states just as Athenian rule had done. The intense individualism of the Greeks that made them withstand the threat of the Persian barbarian made them oppose as well any tyranny among themselves. It was Thebes that led the rebellion against Spartan hegemony, which did not end until 371 B.C., with the fall of Sparta. But the hegemony of Thebes, established in that year, was no more successful than the others, and dwindled to purely nominal leadership before the

Sacred War (355–346 B.C.) and the Locrian War (339–338 B.C.) made the Greek cities an easy prey for a foreign conqueror, Philip of Macedonia.

The period of the interstate wars is a sad one to record. Deep-seated differences between Dorians and Athenians gave them opposed political systems and prevented their thinking as one nation. The love of freedom that emancipated the Greeks intellectually led them to waste their vitality and resources in internecine strife. Intense individualism created Greek culture and destroyed it as well, for the Greeks carried it to an extreme.

THE GREEK POINT OF VIEW

HEREIN lies one key to the Greek spirit in the great age of Pericles. The Greek point of view was founded upon freedom, freedom *from* certain things and freedom *to do* certain things. Paramount was the freedom of man to explore himself and his world without the sanction of any authority, past or present, to restrict him. He demanded the right to do so because he felt an inner compulsion to do so. Freedom to act required freedom to think; and, excited by the challenge of worlds to investigate, he focused a clear and unprejudiced eye on things around him, to explain them and enjoy them in their own terms.

Like the Chinese, the Greek mind was unusually free from mysticism, while it lacked the Chinese enslavement to convention or tradition. Nowhere do we see this practical realism of the Greeks more clearly than in their religion. The ancient pantheon of the Greeks was devised over a period of centuries while they were still illiterate and yet were seeking a plausible explanation of natural phenomena. It was a naïve and primitive theology, as thoughtful Greeks of the fourth century came to realize, and yet it was eminently clear and sensible.

Unlike Taoism, Hinduism, or Christianity, it was a concrete representation of their experience of nature, largely free from abstract concepts of morality. As the prehistoric Greeks invented one god after another to personify the natural forces with which they had to deal, they gave these deities minds like their own, operating by purely human motives. The gods were superior to men, not in their ethical standards or conduct, but in the concrete qualities of power, beauty, and immortality. The sacrifices of animals and other food that the Greeks burned to these deities implied a hard-headed bargain; through a concrete gift they expected a concrete return in the form of good weather for their crops; freedom from natural disasters; or success in war, athletic competition, or even love. This legalistic view of the rela-

tions between god and man may be implied in the prayers and penances of other religious peoples, but nowhere is it more frankly confessed than in Greek ritual. It reflected the purely external nature of the Greek's relation with his gods and the sanctity of his mind from even their prying eyes. Zeus could watch him act, but he could not watch him think. The god could see him commit a crime when other men might not; but he could not see him meditate a crime. Since the Greek felt no spiritual contact with his gods, he had no sense of sin, which is an abstract and spiritual concept. Instead he had a severe notion of crime, which is a concrete and external act. Hence the Greek lacked the Christian conception of conscience, which is founded upon a sense of sin.

If evil meant for the concrete-minded Greeks evil-doing, or crime, the punishment of evil must be equally concrete. If the evil lay, not in meditating crime, but in doing it, the punishment must take place, not in the mind or "conscience" of the evil-doer, but upon his physical person. Murder called for revenge in kind, and the murdered man's kin were duty-bound to carry out the punishment, as Orestes knew when he killed his mother Clytemnestra for the murder of his father (this story is told in Aeschylus' play, *The Libation-Bearers*). Thus a chain of family crimes extending through generations in the manner of a feud was sanctioned, as in Aeschylus' account of the House of Atreus. If no kinsman remained to avenge a crime, a thoughtful transgressor who recognized his crime might punish himself, as Oedipus did in plucking out his own eyes. Otherwise the gods might send against him the dreaded Erinyes (Furies), snaky-haired women who pursued criminals guilty of offenses such as family murder. In Aeschylus' play, *The Eumenides*, we see them harrying Orestes after his murder of his mother. Although these grisly deities may be a primitive approach to the concept of conscience, the

The Discus-Thrower by the Greek sculptor Myron remains the embodiment of the Greek ideal of physical beauty.

concreteness of their personalities and their punishment suggests that they were bogey-women designed to discourage the committing of crime.

Freedom of the soul meant for the Greek freedom to explore and enjoy this world rather than freedom to choose his place in a world to come. He did believe in an after-place called Hades, and even the Elysian fields of the blessed spirits, but these gave him little comfort or satisfaction. Hades was a dark and static place which inspired the spirit of Achilles to tell Odysseus in the *Odyssey:* "I would rather be a slave on earth to a landless man without a fortune than be the king of the dead in the realm of the shadows." The Greek loved the challenge of life too much to look forward to "black Death." Happiness came, if at all, in this life; the hereafter, even though it carried no punishment, certainly entailed no reward.

The Greek love of intellectual freedom is reflected in the religious tolerance that generally prevailed among the cities. The Greeks had no bible to provide a canon of orthodox belief (though Homer was their bible in the cultural sense, their first of books, to be studied and even memorized by every schoolboy). Except at a few shrines, they had no sacerdotal class to codify holy tradition and preserve it without change, because the Greek view of the citizen demanded that every man should have open to him the experience of officiating at religious ceremonies. The laws of the states outlawed technical atheism, as we recall from the trial of Socrates, and public opinion, or simply good taste, protected the gods from such desecration as Alcibiades was once accused of perpetrating against the statues of Hermes. But otherwise free discussion of religious matters was widely tolerated, and resulted in frequent modification of general belief and gradual changes in practice. Soothsayers and the oracles at Delphi, Dodona, and elsewhere, who supposedly had the power to communicate with certain gods and foretell the future, were revered in earlier times, but in fifth-century Athens the seers had been discredited and the ambiguous pronouncements of the oracles already inspired skepticism. Euripides frequently casts aspersions on the seers.

The Greek citizen enjoyed another freedom less admirable in our eyes: freedom from menial work. From earliest times slavery had been accepted in the aristocratic society of the Greeks, as by all ancient nations from the Chinese to the Hebrews and Egyptians. Slaves were obtained especially by conquest of "barbarian" states, since the capture of a city usually sent a good share of the population into perpetual servitude. They did most of the menial tasks in Greek cities and enjoyed in return no legal rights. The master held a life-and-death power over them, though this was exercised more frequently in an aristocratic city like Sparta than in a democratic one like Athens, where slaves often held places of esteem in the family circle. A few advanced thinkers such as Euripides made guarded attacks on the institution, but the majority of citizens, including Plato and Aristotle, accepted slavery as the natural fate of more than half the population.

Lest we be too quick to condemn the Greeks for their institution of slavery, we should remember that slavery was continuously tolerated in Christian Europe for a thousand years after the decay of the Roman empire. Not until the thirteenth century A.D. did the practice of slavery decline. In comparison with the Orientals and the Romans, the Greek citizens were humane in their treatment of slaves, and accepted their freedom from toil, not as an invitation to idleness and vice, but as an opportunity to realize in themselves an ideal of human perfection.

'Know thyself" was the favorite motto of the Greeks, inscribed over the temple of Apollo at Delphi. Such a rule of life invited speculation, but not introspection in the limited sense, because the healthy-minded Greek believed that self-knowledge comes from experience in the world rather than retirement from it. To know oneself meant to the concrete-minded Greek the realization of all his powers—physical, intellectual, moral, and aesthetic—through developing and refining them to the highest possible degree. The Greek ideal of the individual was in no way limited: it demanded a rounded realization of the full personality of the citizen. As such, it has remained the cherished ideal of the humanistic thinker throughout the centuries, and was to inspire such men as Leonardo and Michelangelo of the Renaissance to unparalleled versatility.

The simple conditions of Greek life made it possible to achieve this ideal of human perfection, whereas the complexities of modern civilization work against it. Freed from manual labor, the Greek citizen still lived close enough to the earth to exult in physical living. His physical energies were devoted to athletics rather than toil, and their objective was the strengthening and beautifying of the body as a fit temple for the mind and spirit. The health and physical vigor of the Greek people is reflected in the advanced ages to which their great men lived and produced with no evidence of senility: Solon to seventy-nine, Pindar to eighty, Aeschylus to eighty-one, Euripides to seventy-four, Sophocles to eighty-nine, Plato to eighty-one, Isocrates to ninety-eight.

Yet health was no more important an objective of Greek athletics than was physical beauty. With their interpretation of the world in concrete terms, the Greeks saw physical perfection as a major phase of human goodness. "A sound mind in a sound body" is the conventional translation of a Greek motto that meant something closer to "a healthy mind in a beautiful body." The culture of the mind and the culture of the body were inseparable phases of the education of the individual toward a single ideal of goodness and beauty. Greek athletics had a moral purpose associated with the great public games which brought together the best citizen-athletes of all the Greek city-states for a religious festival of athletic competition on the templed slopes of Parnassus at Delphi or Olympia in the Peloponnese, two of the most sacred spots in Hellas. The display of physical beauty, strength, swiftness, and skill by the naked athletes confirmed their inner harmony of spirit, and when Pindar's chorus sang the praises of the victor at the evening celebration, they said as much of his mental qualities as of his physical prowess. This linking of physical goodness with mental goodness, of bodily beauty with spiritual beauty, is hard to grasp in a specialized age like ours that opposes the man of muscle to the man of brain.

The Greek citizen saw another facet of perfection in an active public life. The Greek system of government through a multiplicity of small city-states, rather than a centralized tyranny, gave each citizen a direct and intimate contact with all state decisions. The citizens were the state and must all take an active part in its civil and military functions. Each citizen served as soldier, as legislator, and potentially as judge and hierophant at religious ceremonies. Since he must attend the assembly personally to speak, decide, and vote on all public questions, political units were necessarily confined to the small city-state. The idea of representative government, by which one man could speak for a hundred or a thousand, is an abstract concept that seldom occurred to the concrete-minded Greeks.

Such a society tended to produce robust and vigorous extroverts who lived constantly in the market place, the gymnasium, and the Assembly rather than in the seclusion of their private homes. An introvert like Euripides felt out of place in such an open-air environment and suffered from the misunderstanding and taunts of his hardy associates. In a literal sense the Greek citizen knew no privacy; in Sparta he was actually taken from his mother's care at the age of seven or so, was reared under public guardians, and never again retreated into purely domestic life. The state allegiance took complete precedence over family ties, and marriage itself was thought to serve the good of the state rather than the private needs of the individual. Marriage was a means of producing children, and only healthy children were supposed to be reared at all. The sickly ones were commonly exposed within ten days after birth, to death or possible adoption—a practice that accounts for the ubiquitous character of the long-lost son or daughter who provides a happy ending for so many later Greek comedies and novels.

Since marriages were usually arranged by the children's fathers with no concern whatever for the young people's preference, romantic love as we know it was not idealized by the Greeks or even commonly thought to exist in the Golden Age. Domestic arrangements after marriage involved a strict division of labor: the wife managed the home and the husband took care of his public responsibilities. It goes without saying that woman's position in such a society was appallingly inferior to man's. It had not been so in the Heroic Age, when the Greeks fought a war for a woman and Homer exalted the conjugal devotion of Hector and Andromache in the *Iliad* and of Odysseus and Penelope in the *Odyssey*. But by the fifth century woman's position had de-

This Athenian red-figured provision jar shows Greek women c. 450 B.C. and typifies Greek vase painting of the Golden Age.

generated to that of childbearing servant to her husband and the state. A radical thinker like Euripides might offer a mild protest in *Alcestis* or *Medea,* but Pericles the statesman and Aristotle the social philosopher alike upheld the inferiority of woman as a natural and inevitable thing. This explains why literature of the Golden Age completely lacks the theme of romantic love so dominant in the fiction and poetry of our day. It is true that Plato in his *Symposium* gives an exalted tribute to Love as an inspiration of noble conduct, but what he has in mind is a passionate friendship between two men, the so-called "Greek love," which was generally accepted in his day but is peculiarly repugnant to our way of thinking.

These blemishes in the Greek view of life point up its radical differences from our own, but they should not obscure the general perfection of the Greek objective as the most exalted view of individual development in history. The facets of the ideal which we have sketched thus far were understood in all Greek cities; only in Athens, however, did the culminating objectives of artistic and intellectual development approach perfection. Athens, the most democratic of all the city-states and the leader of Greece in the fifth century, epitomizes the freedom for individual thinking and expression that lay behind the finest achievements of Greek culture. The same urge that shaped her free political life produced the bold and beautiful pronouncements of her poets and the unbiased inquiry of her historians and philosophers.

Artistic expression was natural to the Greeks, because every aspect of their lives exalted beauty, the outer and inner harmony of man, as the great objective of his development. Greek art is a reflection of Greek life; in its Golden Age it was the imaginative expression for every citizen of the harmonious ideal toward which he was striving. The "art for art's sake" doctrine of a specialized and materialistic culture like our own had no meaning for the Greeks. The artistic outlook, the thirst for beauty and harmony, enriched every phase of the citizen's life, and was in turn enriched by its close contact with this broad reality. The good life was in the highest sense the beautiful life, reflected in the inner harmony of all phases of the individual—physical, moral, and intellectual. A work of art was beautiful in part because it exalted the moral ideals of the race and beautified the everyday life that men knew.

The close tie between the aesthetic ideal and Greek religion is reflected in all the arts. Greek architecture developed in terms of temples rather than palaces. Greek sculpture gave concrete personalities to the gods, who were represented as types of physical perfection and inner serenity. The Greek epic reflected the lives of the gods as well as heroes, and Greek drama originated in the chorus of religious ritual. The oneness of the aesthetic and ethical ideals explains why the cultivation of the arts was so fundamental to the Greek view of the citizen.

As the culture of the Greeks matured and their primitive polytheism came to seem a naïve and inadequate explanation of their environment, the more thoughtful citizens began to focus rational curiosity on the world around them. Philosophy, at first suspiciously received by the conservatives, became eventually the core of Greek education. The youth of Athens sat at the feet of the Sophists, and the political leaders of Hellas went for training to her philosophers—Pericles to Anaxagoras, Alcibiades to Socrates, Dionysius to Plato, and Alexander the Great to Aristotle. In this broadest expansion of their horizon, we see the Greek view of life as an eager awareness of the world in which they lived and an enthusiastic urge to explore every phase of its perfection.

The atmosphere and attitude of freedom were essential to the Greek achievement, but just as essential, finally, was their peculiar capacity for self-restraint. It was this that directed their creative energy and prevented it from wasting itself in extravagance. "Know thyself" said the favorite Greek motto, but beside it on the temple at Delphi was inscribed a further rule of life, "Nothing to excess," to guide the free expression of the self. Herodotus saw this rational control as obedience to a superior principle: "Though free, they are not absolutely free, for they have a master over them, the law." To explore oneself was to become aware at last of one's limitations and of the value of self-restraint. The gods dislike a proud man who puffs himself up with self-importance until he excites their envy and invites their wrath. Both Aeschylus in *The Persians* and Herodotus in his *History* present Xerxes the Oriental potentate as the awful type of unrestrained mortal whom the gods delight to cut down. Not servile acceptance of tradition but a lofty self-restraint that imposes a natural check on eccentricity appealed to the Greeks and guided their creative energies into a considered perfection. This is the last great key to the Greek spirit.

THE PERIODS OF GREEK LITERATURE

THE great age of Greece fell between the defeat of Persia at Salamis (480 B.C.) and the Macedonian defeat of the Greeks at Chaeronea (338 B.C.). It began with a magnificent burst of national energy in a triumphant defense of the Western homeland against the East; it continued through a century of pathfinding and building in many directions; it ended in a shocking defeat that came close to national suicide. The general tendency of its achievements was from an imaginative interpretation of the world through the arts to a rational inquiry into the facts of the universe through philosophy and science: the fifth century was the great century of literature, architecture, and law; the fourth, the great century of philosophy; and only in the decadent third century did science come into its own among the Greeks.

Greek literature was born almost with the birth of the Greek nation, and the four periods of Greek literature bear a close and illuminating relationship to the periods of Greek history. The Epic period of Homer and Hesiod (down to 700 B.C.) portrays the ideals of the Heroic Age of invasion and colonization. The Lyric period (700–480 B.C.), associated with poets from islands in the Aegean, expresses the maturing of Hellenic culture. The Golden period (480–338 B.C.) belongs to Athens in her eighty-year hegemony of the city-states, to the Athenian playwrights Aeschylus, Sophocles, Euripides, and Aristophanes and the Athenian historians Herodotus and Thucydides. The Hellenistic period (338–146 B.C.) of Menander and Theocritus takes us from Athens to Alexandria in Egypt and reflects the sophistication and dissemination of Greek culture.

The epic tradition disappeared in Greece with the end of the Heroic Age. The epic is everywhere the song of a hero who is usually supposed to have founded a nation or at least to illustrate in his warlike deeds its ideals and ethical standards. But in the maturing of a people the simple problems of primitive life give way to the more complex concerns of civilization, and the folk epic becomes a treasured heritage from an era that survives only in memory. The Heroic Age was already past when the Homeric epics received their final form in the eighth century B.C. Hesiod (fl. c. 700 B.C.), who followed Homer, shows the new interests of a population that had forsaken wandering and piracy and settled down to till the soil and develop a more stable civilization. His *Works and Days* is a long tribute to the dignity of the farmer's life, directed to his miscreant brother who has cheated him of his inheritance in order to enjoy a life of luxury. Whereas Homer exalted the Achaean aristocracy, Hesiod praises the common man with his simple virtues and, in describing the plowing, planting, and reaping of the fields, gives a homely treatise on practical husbandry. His crude verse and humorless complaints about his lot make Hesiod dull reading, but he invented in this didactic poem of farm life a type called the "georgic" that Virgil, over seven centuries later, was to perfect into an elegant masterpiece.

After another obscure century, Greek poetry had a sudden revival that was to carry it without a break through the Hellenistic Age. The poetic form this time was lyric, and its masters belong especially to the Aeolian branch of Greeks and to the islands of the Aegean Sea. The new poetry was written to be sung and was identified with the lyre. Since the musical settings of all the famous lyrics of Greece have been lost, we have today only an imperfect impression of the original effect of the poems.

During the sixth century B.C., when the cities of the Aegean, such as Mitylene, Miletus, and Ephesus, were the most brilliant in Hellas, the passionate Aeolian Greeks produced a magnificent school of lyricists, whose works today survive only in tantalizing fragments. Fiery individualists as they were, they developed the lyric of personal emotion, sung by a single voice and expressing the poet's feelings of love, of grief, or of convivial joy. The greatest of these lyric poets, Alcaeus and the woman Sappho, are both associated with the Aegean island of Lesbos, where music and poetry flourished in this period; but the Aeolians eventually inspired an Ionian school of lyric poets on the mainland of Greece. Symbolically, Anacreon (fl. 525 B.C.) moved from the city of Teos in Asia Minor to Thrace and eventually to Athens, but wherever he went he took with him his gay spirits and his delight in wine and love.

Of quite a different kind are the choral odes of Pindar (522–442 B.C.), the leader of the Dorian school, who was born in Thebes but became the patriotic spokesman for all of Greece. The conservative nationalism of the Dorian people, best exemplified in the military tradition of Sparta, produced the Pindaric ode, a formal lyric sung by a chorus of many voices and expressing the emotion of a group audience on an occasion that inspired national pride. Written to honor an athletic hero at the national games, the ode took his victory as a text to praise the state from which he came and a virtue which his career displayed. The personal feelings of the Dorian poet were submerged in the intricate structure of his ode. Pindar himself preserved a masterful balance between the poetic and musical elements, but his successors, Pratinas and Philoxenus, emphasized the music, and lyric verse fell into decay.

GREEK DRAMA

THE decline of the lyric made way for the rise of dramatic poetry in the Golden Age and the climax of Greek literature in the masterpieces of tragedy. Drama in the West was invented by the Greeks as a natural development of their religious rituals, and throughout the great period it retained a religious meaning that shaped its special character. Although the early plays of Aeschylus show some similarity to the Pindaric odes, drama had an independent evolution in the religious festival that is strikingly paralleled by the origin of modern drama in medieval church services.

Although religious ceremonies honored many gods in different seasons and different sections of Hellas,

it was the festival of Dionysus, youthful god of wine and physical joy, that produced drama in sixth-century Athens. The exact steps by which choral songs praising the god became full-scale tragedies and comedies have been conjecturally reconstructed, but they remain obscure. We are reasonably sure that the *dithyramb* sung by the chorus in honor of Dionysus included a myth of the god (later of other gods) which provided the narrative ingredient for drama. It is easy and convenient to believe that, in order to increase the effect of this tribute to the god, the chorus eventually dressed up as satyrs, mythical companions of Dionysus, half-human, half-animal, with snub noses, pointed ears, and goats' tails. By

The technique of playing the lyre and the youth's pleasure in it are evident in this relief from the "Ludovisi throne."

thus honoring the god through representing themselves as his followers, they may have contributed the fundamental ingredient of drama, impersonation, and incidentally originated the term *tragedy* (from τράγος, *a he-goat*, and τραγῳδός, *a goat-singer*). Or it may have been the leader of the chorus who dressed up as a satyr or even as Dionysus himself. In any case, some such representation of satyrs lay behind the satyr play, one of the three types of drama recognized by the Greeks.

Dialogue, the literary ingredient of drama, was probably introduced by Thespis (fl. 534 B.C.) and at first took place between the leader of the chorus and the chorus itself; eventually a special member of the chorus, called the "answerer," emerged in the plays of Aeschylus as a second actor. But the chorus remained an integral part of Greek drama throughout the Golden Age. Serving in Aeschylus to point out the ethical significance of the action, to warn the characters bent on crime, and to express the emotions of the audience, the chorus provided the playwright with a means for direct comment on his action and a voice for normal and right thinking against which to evaluate the eccentric actions of the characters. With the emergence of the second and third actors the protagonists of the play gradually submerged the chorus, until in the plays of Euripides and Aristophanes the choral passages are mere musical interludes, though still a medium for exalted lyric verse.

As with the lyric, the script of a Greek drama

conveys only part of the impression intended by the author. To it must be added all the features of staging that contributed to a single composite art: music, declamation, costumes, dancing, and the ecstatic atmosphere of the religious occasion. The performance took place in a great open-air amphitheater, of which the familiar ruins of the fourth-century Theater of Dionysus in Athens carved out of the south cliff of the Acropolis or the Theater of Epidaurus shown on page 100 give us a clear impression. New tragedies were produced only once a year, at the March festival of the god, and comedies usually at the festival in January. Both festivals were under the protection of the state, like all religious celebrations, and one of the archons, or chief magistrates, of Athens administered them. The plays were presented through a three-day competition, in which one day was reserved for each of three competitors, who entered not one play alone but three tragedies (called a trilogy if they told one connected story) and a satyr play—all to be presented on the same day. One complete trilogy, the *Oresteia* of Aeschylus, has come down to us.

A playwright who wished to compete submitted his plays first to the archon, who, if he gave them preliminary approval, assigned the poet a wealthy patron to bear the expense of production and a chorus of twelve or fifteen men to sing his lines. The playwright himself might rehearse the chorus and even play a leading part in his plays. The central stage of the Greek theater consisted of a circular "dancing place" (Greek, *orchestra*) where the chorus grouped themselves in rows three deep and sang their lines in unison, to the accompaniment of a flute, while engaged in a simple religious dance. The actors of the dialogue eventually appeared on a raised platform behind the orchestra with a *skene*, or scene building, behind them, to which *paraskenia*, or wings, were added around 410 B.C. Scenery in the form of painted backdrops was common, as were a few properties; but the general staging of a Greek drama was much simpler than ours. There were no lighting effects to represent day and night and no curtain to bar the audience before the play. The actors recited their lines with great feeling but little or no action in the modern sense. The religious solemnity of the tragic occasion demanded of them a stately deportment. Their rich raiment was cut to give an ideally graceful and full effect, and their stature was increased by *buskins*, stout boots with thick soles to make them look big and impressive in their roles of gods and heroes. Since large masks were worn to make their roles clear to the far-flung audience and also to represent the grandeur of godly physiognomy, actors had to rely on resonant voices and dignified gestures for their effects. The masks of comedy were usually grotesque, and the

The Greeks made use of natural outdoor amphitheaters for the staging of their dramas. This large theater was built by the architect Polyclitus the Younger at Epidaurus in the fourth century B.C. Constructed of limestone, it has a radius of 210 feet, and is so arranged that a good view of the actors and chorus could be obtained from almost any seat.

buskin was here replaced by the low-heeled *sock*. Men or boys played women's parts, as later in the Elizabethan theater.

The effect of a Greek play was consequently quite different from ours. The religious character of the occasion dictated a stylized, rather than realistic, production. The absence because of convention of any extensive movement or violent action (such as murder) on the sacred stage resulted in brief, simple plays that concentrated on a few characters in a single situation. Aristotle's insistence on unity of action, or a single plot, was a natural outgrowth of the special conditions of the Greek theater. Although he did not require also unity of time (a twenty-four-hour period) and unity of place (a single locality), as is often supposed, it is clear that the physical limitations of the Greek stage, as well as artistic concentration, recommended something of the sort. Yet once we have accepted the conventions of Greek drama, the emotional impact of a Greek tragedy in an adequate production, or even in the library, is uniquely powerful. Consider the excitement and exaltation that it must have aroused in the Greeks themselves, as they saw the gods and heroes of their race brought to life in their most sacred adventures.

Although we know the names of many Greek playwrights of the Golden Age, only four of them —three tragic and one comic—have survived in complete works. Their forty-two extant plays were produced within almost exactly a century (c. 490–388 B.C.) and are tightly related within a continuous flow of artistic development and even a mesh of personal associations. The earliest play of Aeschylus (c. 525–456 B.C.), *The Suppliant Women*, reflects the transition from choral lyric to full-scale drama. The chorus in this work still dominates the play with its singing and dancing, and the two players for the three speaking parts are allowed very limited action. As a result, little seems to happen in the play, and we can only regret the loss of the remaining parts of the trilogy that would have carried the careers of the fifty women doomed to marry their fifty hated cousins to its logical conclusion in their wholesale murder of their husbands. *Prometheus Bound* brings greater emphasis on the central character, and in the *Oresteia* trilogy Aeschylus reaches at last a perfect balance between actors and chorus.

As the earliest of the dramatists, he is the most conservative in his approach to the religious stories that formed the plot material of Greek tragedy. With his interest in theological problems he made the *Oresteia* an embodiment of the traditional Greek ethic. A chain of crimes within a family illustrates the inheritance of criminal taint as each generation acts as an instrument of divine punishment. Driving them on in the background is the transcendent force of Moira, or Fate, an inescapable power above gods and men alike which had emerged as an impersonal law to unify the conglomeration of Greek gods and cults. Yet Aeschylus was concerned with mundane problems also. Speaking as a masterful general in the recent Persian Wars, he gave in his play, *The Persians,* the moral lesson that a tyrannical conqueror must inevitably fall before a free and modest people. And in his picture of the persecuted yet fighting individualist, Prometheus, he reminded the Athenians that they too had only recently won their freedom from tyranny.

But Aeschylus lived to see a development in public taste away from the traditional theology and pan-Hellenic patriotism for which he had stood. In the work of the noble Sophocles (c. 495–406 B.C.), only thirty years his junior, religious problems were gradually subordinated to the human drama, and the actors on the stage began to loom larger than the chorus below. Though the devout public of Aeschylus frowned on the appearance of more than two speaking actors at a time, Sophocles unhesitatingly experimented with three and four and thus enlarged the scope of his play considerably. Disliking the accepted trilogy form, he made each of his plays a self-contained and more ambitious unit. As a result, they come closer to our understanding of drama and are the only Greek tragedies commonly performed today. His *Oedipus the King* and *Antigone* are generally considered the high points of the ancient theater.

The tendencies of Sophocles were carried much further by Euripides (c. 480–407 B.C.), the most radical of the playwrights. Though Sophocles had shifted his dramatic emphasis from the heavens to humanity, he was no less a believer in the traditional religion than Aeschylus had been. Euripides, fifteen years younger than he, belonged to a new generation grown skeptical of the ancient cults. While he was still required to treat the traditional stories in his plays, he saw their problems in terms of a new philosophy rather than the pious theology supported by the state. In reducing the chorus to the status of musical interlude, he could concentrate on the characters in his drama and treat them all, gods and men alike, as human beings to be scrutinized and even criticized. In *Alcestis* he slyly condemns the Greek citizen's cavalier superiority to woman by his unsympathetic interpretation of a legendary hero who lets his wife die for him. In *Iphigenia at Aulis,* Agamemnon and Menelaus, the Homeric heroes, are represented as quarreling politicians. Euripides is the psychologist among the tragedians, though his approach is still ethical rather than scientific. By interpreting realistically the motives of the hallowed heroes, he reduces them to ordinary people, often quite inadmirable and sometimes downright foolish. His objective view of traditional material makes Euripides seem the most readable of all the playwrights today.

Naturally his radical outlook excited alarm and criticism among the conservatives, who still formed the backbone of the Athenian public. Aristophanes (c. 446–c. 386 B.C.), the biting comedian of the Greek theater, was spokesman for the conservatives and used all the freedom that the comic tradition allowed him to discredit Euripides.

So-called Old Comedy (from κῶμος, *revel*, and κωμωδος, *reveler*) is quite unlike comedy as we know it. The competition in comedy was originally held at the January festival to Dionysus,* when the god of wine was honored through heavy drinking and a resulting freedom from social restraints and personal inhibitions. The occasion acted as a social safety valve when everyone, citizen and slave, was liberated from conventional decorum, prisoners were freed from their cells for the duration, and carefree lovemaking was the order of the day. Old Comedy reflects this bacchanalian spirit in its grossly vulgar language and the broad satire in which it could traditionally indulge with impunity. It becomes a satiric reflection of many phases of the life of Athens, full of topical allusions and brutally funny attacks on parties and individuals of the day. The political and intellectual leaders feared and condemned the shockingly personal abuse in Old Comedy and eventually succeeded in transforming it into the milder Middle Comedy; but the best-known plays of Aristophanes are of the brazen older style.

As a conservative troubled by the decline of the old spirit of Athens at Marathon and Salamis, Aristophanes tried to laugh the new spirit of skepticism and state jingoism out of fashion. In *The Acharnians* and *The Knights* he attacked the demagogue Cleon and the suicidal Peloponnesian War that Cleon supported. In *The Clouds* he turned on the philosopher Socrates and the cynical reasoning of the Sophists. In the *Thesmophoriazusae* and *The Frogs* it was Euripides who was condemned as an atheist and bad artist. Today we can see that Aristophanes' fears were well founded, for no major tragedian followed Euripides; the health of Athenian society declined with the decline of its religious faith, and the interstate wars destroyed the morale and independence of the Greeks. But national evolution is, for good or ill, a dynamic thing, and all the efforts of an Aristophanes, however valiant, could not hold it back.

THE HISTORIANS AND PHILOSOPHERS

ANOTHER sign of the growing sophistication of Athenian society in the Golden Age was the rise of history as a critical record of the nation's past. As myth gave way to more accurate chronicling and prose replaced verse as the medium for preserving fact, the fifth-century Greeks came closer to the scientific spirit of free inquiry in modern times. In fact, the term *history* comes from the Greek word ἱστορίη, meaning *inquiry*, and originally encompassed geography and science as well.

Although we know that he had his predecessors, Herodotus (c. 485–c. 425 B.C.) is usually called the Father of Prose and the Father of History on the strength of his *History* of Persia and the Persian Wars with Greece, the earliest historical work to be preserved. Renowned for his incessant travels through the Mediterranean and Near East, he epitomized the urge to observe and to know that inspired Greek philosophy and science. He accumulated a vast store of notes in the manner of a modern scholar. Herodotus is often criticized for recording fantastic stories that are patently untrue, but these too he could set down in the objective spirit of the chronicler. A tribute to his aloofness is the fairness with which he presents the point of view and customs of the Persians. That stems in part from his deliberate desire to be accurate, in part from his natural kindliness, which beams out at us from every page of his charming work.

But it was the great Thucydides (c. 460–c. 400 B.C.) who brought Greek history to maturity in his *History of the Peloponnesian War*, which is our definitive account of the first twenty years of the tragic conflict. Dealing with more immediate and verifiable material than Herodotus, Thucydides is more scientific than his predecessor was in a position to be. He set for himself an ideal of absolute accuracy and recorded only what he was convinced was true. Yet he is not a routine chronicler of events. His magnificent art makes the facts and personalities live, as he reconstructs speeches, shows insight in selecting significant details, and crowds ideas into his compact and simple style. Not until Gibbon in our eighteenth century was the world to see again the equal of this master of historical method. In the century that followed Thucydides, Xenophon (c. 430–c. 359 B.C.) continued his history of the city-states in the *Hellenica* and wrote a popular account of an expedition of Greek mercenary troops in Asia

---

* The so-called Lenaea festival, although it was produced also at the city Dionysia in March. Comedy was officially sanctioned in 486 B.C.

The partially reconstructed Parthenon at Athens photographed from the Propylea.

Minor called the *Anabasis,* in which he himself figures very prominently. But the mediocrity of his mind and style is glaring after Thucydides.

Greek philosophy was born among the Ionians of Asia Minor in the sixth century B.C., where the broad religious freedom provided by the state invited a group of thinkers to explore the astronomical and mathematical science of the Near East. These earliest philosophers, Thales and Anaximander of Miletus, speculated on the physical composition of the universe in conflict with the naïve explanations of Hesiod. Shortly after, a competing school in southern Italy, including Pythagoras and Empedocles, gave rival explanations. But we know of these and other early philosophical writers largely through the comments of later writers, such as Plato, Xenophon, Aristotle, and Diogenes Laertius. The pioneers are remembered primarily because they established the Greek tradition of free inquiry that was to produce the great philosophers and scientists of a later day.

In a time when knowledge was not yet far advanced or departmentalized, the field of philosophy was not so clearly limited as it is today. We think of philosophy now as covering all areas where the absence of exact information makes speculation necessary. But in any age before scientific method is exactly understood, these areas are very broad indeed and cover data as well as conclusions from them. Our Greek word *philosophy* means simply "the love of wisdom." Only late in the fifth century was the field restricted to religion, ethics, political philosophy, and metaphysics, and Aristotle in the fourth century included logic, aesthetics, and "natural philosophy" (physics, biology, and psychology) in his areas of investigation.

When Greek philosophy came of age in Socrates and Plato, the emphasis shifted from the metaphysics of the pioneers, with their inquiries into the origin and composition of things, to problems of ethics and religion. Socrates (470–399 B.C.) abandoned his interest in what he called "physics" for matters of right and wrong, the ethical issues of justice and injustice that seriously troubled democratic Athens in the fifth century B.C. Unlike the Sophists, those professional philosophers who charged fees for their highly practical lectures on how to win success and happiness, Socrates prided himself on being merely the great "gadfly" of Athens, who lounged in the market place or the homes of his friends to pose questions and force his hearers to define the terms and concepts that they used as carelessly as had their parents who taught them. His real business was to make people think and to jog them out of smugness and prejudice. Like Confucius he insisted not on the approximate but on the exact definition of terms such as virtue, courage, love, temperance,

and friendship, because he believed that behind them lay absolute ideas, and the knowledge of this absolute and ultimate reality transcending material things was the key to right living. No one, he thought, is knowingly wicked; hence ignorance is the bane of the state.

In his discussions he pretended to know nothing himself but to follow the "Socratic method" of questioning others and drawing knowledge from them through subtle direction. In this pretense he was of course insincere, and the irony behind his questions made him a large number of enemies among the rival thinkers whom he sought to discredit by his ingenious questions. His scolding wife Xantippe thought her idle husband a wastrel, and the democratic statesmen of Athens came to consider his eternal questions dangerous to the tranquillity of the state. At last they condemned the seventy-year-old philosopher to death for atheism and corruption of youth, and, although he could easily have escaped, he chose to drink the hemlock and died a serene death among his friends.

Since Socrates left no writings, we know him today through the works of his disciple, Plato (c. 427–348 B.C.).* Plato was over forty years younger than his master and studied with him only during the last ten years of Socrates' life. Yet after the older man's death he dedicated himself to recording his philosophy and even his conversation in an idealized form. To suit the questioning method of Socrates he perfected the Platonic dialogue, a semidramatic form representing a concentrated discussion of an issue or idea by a group of men (including Socrates and a disciple or rival). At its best, as in the *Symposium,* the dialogue served to draw out a variety of opinions on a problem. Plato does not appear as a character in any of the dialogues, but he became himself such an independent thinker that he must have put many of his own opinions into the mouth of his teacher. The long dialogue, the *Republic,* is the crowning statement of his own philosophy. Plato's famous Academy, which he established in a grove of olive trees near Athens as a center for his teaching, continued until 529 A.D. and had Aristotle among its famous pupils.

Aristotle (384–322 B.C.) entered Plato's Academy at seventeen and studied there until Plato's death twenty years later. Thereafter he was the tutor of young Alexander of Macedonia and director of the Lyceum, a rival school to the Academy, which he founded around 336 B.C. The interests of Aristotle were broader than Plato's and centered in natural science rather than ethics. Yet in addition to his treatises on biology, physics, astronomy, and mathematics, we have the *Poetics,* the *Politics,* and the *Nicomachean Ethics* to remind us of the breadth

* As well as the *Memorabilia* of Xenophon.

of his inquiries. He was the great encyclopedist of human knowledge in his day and the last who dared presume to universal understanding. Although his science is primitive and often more speculation than exact knowledge, he paved the way for the more accurate science of the Hellenistic era which was to follow. In our own Dark Ages, when superstition choked off further investigation for a time, the great Aristotle was gradually elevated to a canon of natural knowledge as he was read in the Latin translations of Boethius and others; and the medieval philosophers, Albertus Magnus and Thomas Aquinas, made him the foundation of their orthodox systems. The broad achievements of the man and his place in the evolution of human thought can hardly be overestimated.

THE MACEDONIAN CONQUEST

THE century of interstate wars in Greece invited foreign invasion and conquest. Persia was quick to exploit the disunity of the states by playing one off against another and eventually regained all the Greek cities on the coast of Asia Minor by the disgraceful peace of Antalcidas (387 B.C.). But Persia was now too weak to renew the war for the Greek mainland. It remained for another power, younger and more vigorous than either Hellas or Persia, to add them both to a great new empire.

Macedonia to the north of Greece was a country of fighting mountaineers, related to the Greeks by race and language, yet beyond the reach of Hellenic culture. Still devoted to their clannish chieftains as the primitive Greeks had been, the Macedonians offered a ready and loyal instrument to any conqueror who might rise among them. Such a king arrived in 356 B.C., when Philip ascended the throne, a masterful spirit fired with an ambition for conquest. As he trained his armies in the phalanx system that he had learned as a student in Thebes, Philip had his eye on the decadent kingdom of Persia and thought of the Greek states as mere stepping stones to a larger objective. It was his skill in diplomacy as much as his ability as a soldier that made him take advantage of the disunity of the states to conquer them one by one. He interfered modestly at first in such typically Greek squabbles as the Sacred War and the Locrian War, so that when his designs on all of Greece at last became clear, the disorganized forces of Athens and Thebes were easily conquered at Chaeronea (338 B.C.). Philip's admiration for Greek character and art and his larger designs upon Persia made him deal mildly with the conquered states, as he posed simply as the commander in chief of their own Amphictyonic League of nations. Yet Greece actually lost her independence in that year and did not regain it for any appreciable period down to modern times.

As Philip was about to begin his conquest of Persia, he was assassinated by one of his officers. But his dashing son, Alexander, was to carry through Philip's plan with lightning speed. In the spring of 334 B.C. he crossed the Hellespont, leaving Antipater behind as governor of Macedonia and Greece, and began thirteen years of incessant campaigns that were to take him and his devoted armies eastward across the whole Persian empire into far-dis-

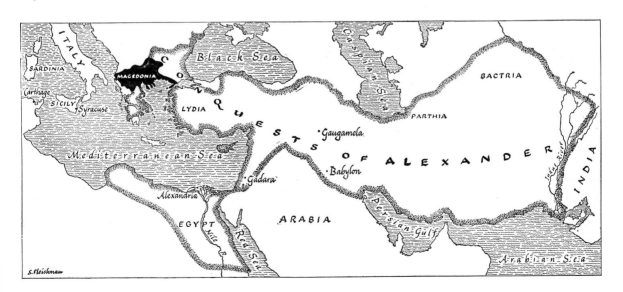

S. Fleishman

tant India. With the defeat of the Persian King Darius III at Gaugamela, Alexander set himself up in his stead as an Oriental potentate ruling one of the greatest empires in the history of the world. When he died suddenly of a fever at Babylon in 323 B.C., this thirty-three-year-old emperor had barely had time to organize his vast domain into a collection of kingdoms, which were to be ruled thereafter as separate units by his generals.

So Greece found unity at last, but in the humiliating role of vassal state to her Macedonian neighbor. Only a tiny unit in the vast empire of Alexander, she later formed part of the monarchy of Mace-donia. But wherever Alexander went, he had carried with him a love of Greek culture, imbibed from his Greek tutor, Aristotle. Remote eastern states of the old Persian empire, such as Parthia and Bactria, were Hellenized for a time, and even northwestern India received a veneer of Greek civilization. In losing the freedom of her own development Hellas had the lesser satisfaction of seeing her cultural influence spread over a vast area to which she could never have carried it herself. Alexander's successors, the Seleucids in Asia and the Ptolemies in Egypt, continued the Hellenizing process until the coming of the Roman empire in the time of Christ.

HELLENISTIC CULTURE: THE LAST CHAPTER

T HE smallest but most vigorous kingdom to be carved out of Alexander's empire was Egypt, which fell to his ablest general, Ptolemy. Here at one of the many mouths of the Nile, Alexander had projected a great new capital to be called Alexandria, the prototype of other Alexandrias that he established throughout his eastern realm. After Alexander's death Ptolemy loyally carried out his plan and made his capital the greatest city of the western world, a thriving commercial center at the juncture of several trade routes from East to West. His cultured son, Ptolemy II, invited the finest poets, philosophers, scholars, and artists of the Hellenistic world to settle in this pseudo-Greek metropolis. There resulted the curious phenomenon that the real center of Greek culture in the third century was not in Greece but in the deliberately planned Graeco-Macedonian city of Alexandria in northern Egypt.

The focal point of this activity was the great Museum of Alexandria, a kind of college for research and creative work founded by the Ptolemies to house their distinguished guests and facilitate their studies. As its name suggests, it was dedicated to the Muses and boasted the largest library in the world, a collection of half a million manuscripts (possibly 100,000 books in the modern sense). The literary scholars who gravitated to the Museum prepared our definitive texts of older Greek authors, eliminated the writers whom they considered unworthy, and generally determined what we today may know of the older literature of Greece.

Science and mathematics also made great strides at Alexandria. Euclid codified the geometrical knowledge of the Greeks in his *Elements*, which remained the standard textbook of geometry down to our own century. Archimedes (c. 287–212 B.C.), the greatest of ancient scientists, founded mechanics, statics, and dynamics, to which branches of learning no further knowledge was added until the seventeenth century. Eratosthenes (c. 276–c. 195 B.C.) first measured the circumference of the earth, assembled a source book for geography, and devised a system of historical chronology. Aristarchus of Samos in his third-century treatise *On the Sizes and Distances of the Sun and the Moon* evolved an astronomy close to our own which placed the sun, not the earth, at the center of our universe. But Hipparchus and Claudius Ptolemy, who followed him in the next century, revived the geocentric astronomy that was to be accepted by Christian theologians till Copernicus and the sixteenth century. We will find it in Dante's view of the universe.

The men of letters at Alexandria invented only one literary form, the pastoral or idyll, but it was to have a hardy development through Virgil, Spenser, Sidney, and Milton to Pope and Gay in the eighteenth century. Theocritus (third century B.C.) conceived the type as a charming picture of shepherd life in his native Sicily, often in dialogue form; and his two pupils, Bion and Moschus, developed it into the pastoral elegy that was to inspire Milton's *Lycidas,* Shelley's *Adonais,* and Arnold's *Thyrsis.* The idylls of Theocritus are as artificial as the self-conscious and sophisticated society of Alexandria that produced them. The Hellenistic civilization, for all its energy, is a pale and stereotyped reflection of the masterful genius of Hellenic culture in the Golden Age.

For nearly a hundred years, between 330 B.C. and 243 B.C., Greece made no attempt to regain her independence. Then the weakening of the Macedonian kingdom eventually inspired Sparta and some northern Greek cities to revolt in the latter year, but the two emancipated areas promptly quarreled between themselves in the familiar Greek tradition and were overwhelmed by Macedonia once more at Sellasia in 221 B.C. But Macedonia embroiled itself soon after with a new power in the West, the

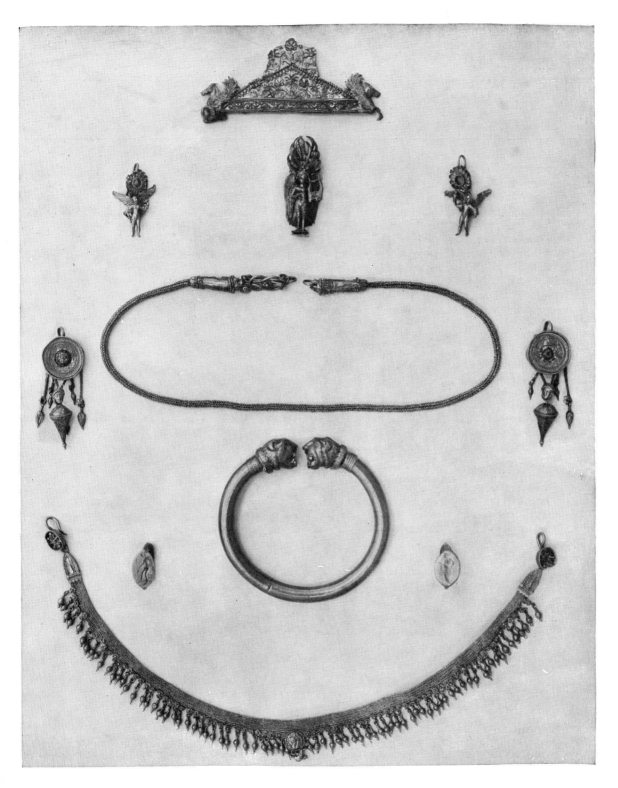

Remarkably fine workmanship in gold is displayed in this Greek jewelry of the fifth century B.C.

rising republic of Rome, by assisting the Carthaginian Hannibal in his ill-fated war with the Romans. To punish Macedonia, Rome technically freed the Greek states from her rule, but the Greeks soon found that they had merely exchanged one master for another. For a time the Romans preserved the fiction of Greek independence, but when the cities of the Achaean League openly resisted the indirect control of Rome, the Roman armies marched through them, destroyed Corinth in 146 B.C., and finally converted Greece into one province in the growing empire. This spelled the formal end of Greek independence.

Yet the prestige of Greek culture continued undimmed, as the practical Romans self-consciously borrowed the art and philosophy of Greece in its Golden and Silver Ages. Athens remained the traditional fountainhead of learning, and Plato's Academy continued to attract pupils down to the days of the emperor Justinian. Direct borrowing from Greek literature was the accepted thing in Rome, as Virgil imitated Theocritus, Hesiod, and Homer; Catullus imitated Sappho; Plautus and Terence took their plots and characters from the later comedians, Menander and Apollodorus; and Seneca borrowed from Euripides. Even the Greek language held its own as a medium of literature throughout the Roman period and especially during the so-called Greek Renaissance of the second century A.D., which was inspired by the Roman emperor Hadrian and distinguished by the Greek satires of Lucian.

But the "glory that was Greece" really died with Greek independence in the fourth century B.C. What Greece had to tell the world was complete with the last Athenian dramatists, Euripides and Aristophanes, and the last great Athenian philosophers, Plato and Aristotle. Those who followed were the scholars and the imitators, who had superior perspective but lacked the creative fire. So it is to the fifth century and the fourth that we return perennially for inspiration and wisdom. Across the centuries, those years in Athens seem more modern to us than any intervening century before the eighteenth. Her civilization, like our own, was based on experience and knowledge and the right of the individual to explore himself and his world, free from political or religious oppression. It exalted intelligence and curiosity rather than moral discipline because it believed that the ascendancy of reason over instinct could be trusted to lead to at least a pragmatic morality. The self-discipline of the Greeks had a practical end and the human perfection for which they strove had the practical goal of making man completely at home in his environment.

The success of their conquest is attested by what they handed on to Rome and even to the Asia that they Hellenized. We see it in what the Romans have handed down to us as the core of Western civilization. We should not be surprised that the Greeks did not achieve a continuing perfection or that their tragic defects—their inability to work together, their senseless wars, their subjection of women and slaves, their misuse of liberty in moral corruption and irresponsibility—eventually destroyed them altogether. No single civilization in the West has endured for long, but through the rise and decay of them all runs the enduring stream which had its source in ancient Greece.

Homer

Eighth century B.C.

The Homeric epics are the only survivals from a great school of Ionian poetry which flourished in the Greek states of Asia Minor in the eighth century B.C. The Greeks of the Golden Age knew as little about the poet Homer as we do, and many later critics have argued that "Homer" was really a group of minstrels in several generations who composed and reworked various sections of the *Iliad* and the *Odyssey*. Clearly a long oral tradition preceded these finished products, and in the *Odyssey* in particular we can see how many older stories have been grafted onto the central tale as adventures of Odysseus. But, however diverse their origin, each of the final poems must have been shaped into a consummate work of art by a single masterful hand. Perhaps both had the same arranger; perhaps both were finally composed by the traditional poet, Homer.

The century when the epic poet lived has been variously placed between the twelfth and the seventh B.C. by those who accept his existence, but the consensus of opinion links him now to the eighth. The dialect of the poems places him in Asia Minor, though whether his birthplace was Smyrna or one of the many other cities that claimed him, we cannot be sure. Tradition makes him a blind old minstrel (a favorite type in folk literature), wandering among the Ionian cities of Asia Minor.*

These speculations about the origins of the Homeric epics pale before the majesty of the works themselves. Later Greeks accepted the *Iliad* and the *Odyssey* as history, and we have seen (page 90) that the poems were probably inspired by a prehistoric war between the early invaders of Greece and the inhabitants of a strategic Aegean city in Asia Minor which Schliemann unearthed on the traditional site of Troy. The Trojan War was apparently one episode in the early Greeks' general destruction of the Minoan culture that preceded them. But to the later Greeks it took on the character of a holy war out of their Heroic Age in which the gods of Olympus fought each other in the human battles before Troy.

The war began in a contest among three goddesses, Hera, Athena, and Aphrodite, for a golden apple to be awarded to the most beautiful. Since Zeus was the husband of Hera and the father of both Athena and Aphrodite, he discreetly forced the decision on a handsome Trojan prince named Paris (or Alexandros), who was tending his flocks on Mount Ida. Hera tried to bribe Paris with the gift of an empire, and Athena with the gift of victorious war; but Aphrodite promised him the most beautiful woman in the world to be his wife, and he promptly awarded her the apple, gaining thereby the implacable hate of the other goddesses for himself and his native

Troy. Unfortunately, his prize, the paragon of loveliness, Queen Helen, was already married to Menelaus, the Greek king of Sparta, but Paris had no difficulty in carrying her away during Menelaus' absence, since Aphrodite had bewitched her with the spell of love.

Now before her marriage to Menelaus, Helen had been wooed by the principal kings of Greece, and they, to prevent bloodshed, had sworn to accept her choice and defend her husband. After the loss of Helen, Menelaus reminded the princes of their oath. All (even the reluctant Odysseus of Ithaca and Achilles, the great hero of the war) eventually joined their forces in a great Greek army to sail to Troy and recover Helen. Agamemnon of Mycenae, brother to Menelaus, who was chosen leader, was forced to sacrifice his innocent daughter, Iphigenia, at Aulis before the gods would send the Greek ships a fair wind for Troy.† When they reached Troy, the Trojans disputed their landing and shut themselves within the walls of their city, where for ten years they withstood incessant siege. Periodically King Priam of Troy would send out his armies to do battle under Hector, the mightiest of his fifty sons. Many a hero, both Greek and Trojan, fell in the fighting, but still the war dragged on.

Although the title "Iliad" is derived from *Ilios*, a Greek name for Troy, the poem does not tell the story of the whole war but rather one incident in the ninth year of the siege. Homer begins "in medias res" and leaves the reader to supply the background, which was well known to the Greek audience. The story of the *Iliad* is of the quarrel of Achilles and Agamemnon over a girl, Briseis; and of the wrath of Achilles that makes him sulk in his tent and refuse to fight, until the death of his friend Patroclus rouses him to kill his slayer, the noble Hector. The war is still in progress at the end of the *Iliad*, but we know that the Greeks won it the following year by the ruse of the Wooden Horse.

At the opening of the *Odyssey* all of the Greek princes have returned home except crafty Odysseus (Ulysses) of Ithaca. He had been doomed by the god Poseidon to wander through the Mediterranean for ten years as a punishment for blinding the god's son Polyphemus, a one-eyed Cyclops. He has already been nearly ten years on his journey when we first meet him, a forlorn fugitive bereft of his followers. The poem covers the last six weeks of his trials and shows how Odysseus is finally restored to his wife Penelope and son Telemachus and rules once more in Ithaca.

Achilles and Odysseus are the two great heroes of the Greeks, vastly different from each other, and both far removed from the Christian ideal of chivalry. In the sometimes shocking actions of these leaders we sense the realistic Greek mind at work, with its eye on the objective and its strong sense of immediate justice. Achilles is the great warrior, mighty in battle but fierce and implacable in his wrath. When Agamemnon offends him, he loses all sense of loyalty to his comrades and their cause and retires to brood over a personal grievance. His hysterical

---

* The Homeric epics were arranged in their present form in Athens around the years 537–527 B.C. The division of each epic into twenty-four books was probably made by Aristarchus, the Alexandrian scholar, in 156 B.C.

† However, the goddess Artemis substituted a deer for Iphigenia and made her a priestess in the land of the Tauri, according to the plays of Euripides.

grief for his friend Patroclus impresses us today as neurotic, and we find difficulty in rejoicing at his ferocious victory over Hector, the noble Trojan hero, so honorable in dealing even with his enemies, so devoted to his wife and little son. As Achilles in a delirium of triumph drags Hector's body at his chariot wheels, we are shocked that he should carry revenge beyond the grave.

Odysseus is the symbol of craft and guile, who fights through to victory only when he has paved the way with clever deceptions. As the princes were being rounded up for the Trojan War, he tried to escape the draft through pretending insanity. When Palamades discovered his ruse, he avenged himself by hiding gold in the tent of Palamades and falsely denouncing him as a traitor who had received a bribe of gold from Troy. It was Odysseus who led the Greek warriors in the trick of the Wooden Horse and saved his comrades from the terrible Cyclops by a series of ingenious stratagems. But the realistic Greeks justified both their heroes as resourceful men contending with a hostile world. Achilles was the pillar of strength and glorious action, Odysseus the tower of intelligence and cunning, who was wise to use his powers however he felt he had to.

Nearly as important in the epics as the human warriors are the gods above, who work out their personal grievances in the conflict of men. Aphrodite, the capricious goddess of love, intermittently supported the Trojans out of gratitude to Paris. Apollo, too, assisted the Orientals in their struggle with the Greeks from the west. But Athena, goddess of wisdom, and Hera, goddess of power, still chafing from Paris' slight to their beauty, fought a much more consistent battle on Olympus for the Greeks. Zeus, vacillating between the rival camps in his family, eventually gave in to his shrewish wife and his most terrifying daughter.

Although Homer accepted the traditional theology for poetic purposes, he represents the gods in a shocking way. Their petty squabbles and meanness, their total lack of moral principles suggest a veiled skepticism or comic intention hard to explain in so early a poet. Although the gods appear as highly concrete personalities, it is clear that he thought of them often as elaborate metaphors to represent prosaic happenings in poetic terms. Nearly every turn of the plot is initiated by a god through a human character. If we took these explanations literally, we should decide that the human actors had no power of choice whatever, that all their actions and destinies were determined by the gods and a Fate above even the gods. Actually the gods are largely convenient and poetic devices to which to attribute the inscrutable shifts of human fortune. Though the shadowy force of Fate, which grants the heroes an overwhelming foreknowledge of their own deaths, may represent an attempt to give a higher unity to the Greek pantheon, Homer usually invokes it to explain past events. The Greeks acted as we act—with at least the illusion of free will—but when their plans went conspicuously awry or conspicuously well, they set it down to Fate, just as we often do today. Later generations of Greeks took the epics as a religious textbook, but Homer was innocent of any such purpose. The frivolous

bickerings of the gods provide a refreshing foil to the deadly serious exploits of men on earth.

In the most famous essay ever written about Homer, Matthew Arnold defined his poetic qualities as rapidity, plainness and directness of diction and syntax, plainness in thought, and nobility. Although many translators of Homer have rendered some of these qualities, none (thought Arnold) has combined them all. Homer's is the "grand style," which arises "when a noble nature, poetically gifted, treats with simplicity or with severity a serious subject." And the grand style does not flourish in modern times when nobility itself is out of fashion. Several English-speaking poets—Chapman, Pope, Bryant—have tried to reproduce the majestic sweep of Homer's hexameters, but the translation of verse into verse is at best a tour de force, occasionally very successful in rendering a brief lyric but almost certain to grow pedestrian or too free in a longer work. Although a prose version, such as the Butcher-Lang Odyssey, loses the stately music of Homer's verse, it may actually communicate more faithfully the poetic qualities that Arnold found in it.

Certainly a prose version is more likely to carry the simplicity of the narrative, and Homer is to be read first as a master storyteller and creator of characters. Writing at the very dawn of literature, he tells his tale with a frank delight in action but with a primitive grandeur that makes us believe in an age of heroes and miracles. The wonderful realism in his attention to details (as in the meticulously staged meeting of Odysseus and Nausicaä), the surprisingly subtle character portrayal (as in the complex study of Agamemnon, the vacillating leader who takes refuge in the power of his office) make Homer seem more modern (or more timeless) than many a titan who followed him. Of course, "Homer nods" occasionally, as Horace first remarked in his Art of Poetry. We weary of the catalogue of the ships (Iliad, Book II), but even such passages had a special interest for his Greek audience. We quickly forget the dull stretches in the beauty and excitement of the great scenes—Hector's farewell to Andromache, Priam's visit to Achilles, Odysseus' slaughter of the suitors. The varying moods of these scenes—tender, sympathetic, and savage—suggest the great range of Homer. He is the one universal classic in Western literature.*

---

* The great national epics are classified according to the circumstances of their composition. The true folk epics, which evolved without known authorship, include the Mahâbhârata and Râmâyana (India), the Iliad and Odyssey (Greece), the Nibelungenlied (Germany), the Saga of the Volsungs (Scandinavia), Beowulf (England), The Song of Roland (France), the Poem of the Cid (Spain), and in a sense the Kalevala (Finland). The epics of art, sophisticated literary productions in imitation of folk epics (especially Homer), include the Shahnama of Firdousi (Persia), the Aeneid of Virgil (ancient Rome), and the Lusiads of Camoëns (Portugal). In addition to the true national epics, there are several special types: purely literary epics, such as the Argonautica of Apollonius of Rhodes, Orlando Furioso of Ariosto, Jerusalem Delivered of Tasso, and Spenser's Faerie Queene; religious epics, such as Dante's Commedia, Milton's Paradise Lost, and Klopstock's Messias; mock-epics, such as the ancient Greek burlesque of Homer, The Battle of the Frogs and Mice, Butler's Hudibras, Boileau's Lutrin, and Pope's Dunciad; and even beast epics, such as the medieval Reynard the Fox.

The Iliad

BOOK I

SING, goddess, the wrath of Achilles Peleus' son, the ruinous wrath that brought on the Achaians woes innumerable, and hurled down into Hades many strong souls of heroes, and gave their bodies to be a prey to dogs and all winged fowls; and so the counsel of Zeus wrought out its accomplishment from the day when first strife parted Atreides king of men and noble Achilles.

Who then among the gods set the twain at strife and variance? Even the son of Leto and of Zeus; for he in anger at the king sent a sore plague upon the host, that the folk began to perish, because Atreides had done dishonour to Chryses the priest. For he had come to the Achaians' fleet ships to win his daughter's freedom, and brought a ransom beyond telling; and bare in his hands the fillet of Apollo the Far-darter upon a golden staff; and made his prayer unto all the Achaians, and most of all to the two sons of Atreus, orderers of the host: "Ye sons of Atreus and all ye well-greaved Achaians, now may the gods that dwell in the mansions of Olympus grant you to lay waste the city of Priam, and to fare happily homeward; only set ye my dear child free, and accept the ransom in reverence to the son of Zeus, far-darting Apollo."

Then all the other Achaians cried assent, to reverence the priest and accept his goodly ransom; yet the thing pleased not the heart of Agamemnon son of Atreus, but he roughly sent him away, and laid stern charge upon him, saying: "Let me not find thee, old man, amid the hollow ships, whether tarrying now or returning again hereafter, lest the staff and fillet of the god avail thee naught. And her will I not set free; nay, ere that shall old age come on her in our house, in Argos, far from her native land, where she shall ply the loom and serve my couch. But depart, provoke me not, that thou mayest the rather go in peace."

So said he, and the old man was afraid and obeyed his word, and fared silently along the shore of the loud-sounding sea. Then went that aged man apart and prayed aloud to king Apollo, whom Leto of the fair locks bare: "Hear me, god of the silver bow, that standest over Chryse and holy Killa, and rulest Tenedos with might, O Smintheus! If ever I built a temple gracious in thine eyes, or if ever I burnt to thee fat flesh of thighs of bulls or goats, ful-

---

The Iliad. [A] Translated by Andrew Lang, Walter Leaf and Ernest Van Ness Myers. By permission of The Macmillan Company, publishers. **2–3. Achaians.** Homer calls the Greeks Achaians, Argives, or Danaans. **7. Atreides,** Agamemnon, son of Atreus. **10. son . . . Zeus,** Apollo. **15. his daughter's. . . .** Chryses' daughter was Chryseis, now the concubine of Agamemnon. **45. Smintheus,** another name for Apollo.

---

fil thou this my desire; let the Danaans pay by thine arrows for my tears."

So spake he in prayer, and Phoebus Apollo heard him, and came down from the peaks of Olympus wroth at heart, bearing on his shoulders his bow and covered quiver. And the arrows clanged upon his shoulders in his wrath, as the god moved; and he descended like to night. Then he sate him aloof from the ships, and let an arrow fly; and there was heard a dread clanging of the silver bow. First did he assail the mules and fleet dogs, but afterward, aiming at the men his piercing dart, he smote; and the pyres of the dead burnt continually in multitude.

Now for nine days ranged the god's shafts through the host; but on the tenth Achilles summoned the folk to assembly, for in his mind did goddess Hera of the white arms put the thought, because she had pity on the Danaans when she beheld them perishing. Now when they had gathered and were met in assembly, then Achilles fleet of foot stood up and spake among them: "Son of Atreus, now deem I that we shall return wandering home again—if verily we might escape death—if war at once and pestilence must indeed ravage the Achaians. But come, let us now inquire of some soothsayer or priest, yea, or an interpreter of dreams—seeing that a dream too is of Zeus—who shall say wherefore Phoebus Apollo is so wroth, whether he blame us by reason of vow or hecatomb; if perchance he would accept the savour of lambs or unblemished goats, and so would take away the pestilence from us."

So spake he and sate him down; and there stood up before them Kalchas son of Thestor, most excellent far of augurs, who knew both things that were and that should be and that had been before, and guided the ships of the Achaians to Ilios by his soothsaying that Phoebus Apollo bestowed on him. He of good intent made harangue and spake amid them: "Achilles, dear to Zeus, thou biddest me tell the wrath of Apollo, the king that smiteth afar. Therefore will I speak; but do thou make covenant with me, and swear that verily with all thy heart thou wilt aid me both by word and deed. For of a truth I deem that I shall provoke one that ruleth all the Argives with might, and whom the Achaians obey. For a king is more of might when he is wroth with a meaner man; even though for the one day he swallow his anger, yet doth he still keep his displeasure thereafter in his breast till he accomplish it. Consider thou, then, if thou wilt hold me safe."

And Achilles fleet of foot made answer and spake to him: "Yea, be of good courage, speak whatever soothsaying thou knowest; for by Apollo dear to Zeus, him by whose worship thou, O Kalchas, declarest thy soothsaying to the Danaans, no man while I live and behold light on earth shall lay violent hands upon thee amid the hollow ships; no

Apollo playing his lyre, standing between his mother, Leto, and his sister, Artemis. From a Greek amphora or jar.

man of all the Danaans, not even if thou mean Agamemnon, that now avoweth him to be greatest far of the Achaians."

Then was the noble seer of good courage, and spake: "Neither by reason of a vow is he displeased, nor for any hecatomb, but for his priest's sake to whom Agamemnon did despite, and set not his daughter free and accepted not the ransom; therefore hath the Far-darter brought woes upon us, yea, 10 and will bring. Nor will he ever remove the loathly pestilence from the Danaans till we have given the bright-eyed damsel to her father, unbought, unransomed, and carried a holy hecatomb to Chryse; then might we propitiate him to our prayer."

So said he and sate him down, and there stood up before them the hero son of Atreus, wide-ruling Agamemnon, sore displeased; and his dark heart within him was greatly filled with anger, and his eyes were like flashing fire. To Kalchas first spake he 20 with look of ill: "Thou seer of evil, never yet hast thou told me the thing that is pleasant. Evil is ever the joy of thy heart to prophesy, but never yet didst thou tell any good matter nor bring it to pass. And now with soothsaying thou makest harangue among the Danaans, how that the Far-darter bringeth woes upon them because, forsooth, I would not take the goodly ransom of the damsel Chryseis, seeing I am the rather fain to keep her own self within mine house. Yea, I prefer her before Klytaimnestra my 30 wedded wife; in no wise is she lacking beside her, neither in favour nor stature, nor wit nor skill. Yet for all this will I give her back, if that is better; rather would I see my folk whole than perishing. Only make ye me ready a prize of honour forthwith, lest I alone of all the Argives be disprized, which thing beseemeth not; for ye all behold how my prize is departing from me."

To him then made answer fleet-footed goodly Achilles: "Most noble son of Atreus, of all men most covetous, how shall the great-hearted Achaians give thee a meed of honour? We know naught of a wealth of common store, but what spoil soe'er we took from captured cities hath been apportion[ed] and it beseemeth not to beg all this back from [the] folk. Nay, yield thou the damsel to the god, and [we] Achaians will pay thee back threefold and fourfo[ld,] if ever Zeus grant us to sack some well-walled town of Troyland."

To him lord Agamemnon made answer and said: "Not in this wise, strong as thou art, O godlike 50 Achilles, beguile thou me by craft; thou shalt not outwit me nor persuade me. Dost thou wish, that thou mayest keep thy meed of honour, for me to sit idle in bereavement, and biddest me give her back? Nay, if the great-hearted Achaians will give me a meed suited to my mind, that the recompense be equal—but if they give it not, then I myself will go and take a meed of honour, thine be it or Aias', or Odysseus' that I will take unto me; wroth shall he be to whomsoever I come. But for this we will take 60 counsel hereafter; now let us launch a black ship on the great sea, and gather picked oarsmen, and set therein a hecatomb, and embark Chryseis of the fair cheeks herself, and let one of our counsellors be captain, Aias or Idomeneus or goodly Odysseus, or thou, Peleides, most redoubtable of men, to do sacrifice for us and propitiate the Far-darter."

Then Achilles fleet of foot looked at him scowling and said: "Ah me, thou clothed in shamelessness, thou of crafty mind, how shall any Achaian hearken 70 to thy bidding with all his heart, be it to go a journey or to fight the foe amain? Not by reason of the Trojan spearmen came I hither to fight, for they have not wronged me; never did they harry mine oxen nor my horses, nor ever waste my harvest in deep-soiled Phthia, the nurse of men; seeing there lieth between us long space of shadowy mountains and sounding sea; but thee, thou shameless one, followed we hither to make thee glad, by earning recompense at the Trojans' hands for Menelaos 80 and for thee, thou dog-face! All this thou reckonest not nor takest thought thereof; and now thou threatenest thyself to take my meed of honour, wherefor I travailed much, and the sons of the Achaians gave it me. Never win I meed like unto thine, when the Achaians sack any populous citadel of Trojan men; my hands bear the brunt of furious war, but when the apportioning cometh then is thy meed far ampler, and I betake me to the ships with some small thing, yet mine own, when I have fought to 90 weariness. Now will I depart to Phthia, seeing it is far better to return home on my beaked ships; nor am I minded here in dishonour to draw thee thy fill of riches and wealth."

Then Agamemnon king of men made answer to him: "Yea, flee, if thy soul be set thereon. It is not I that beseech thee to tarry for my sake; I have others by my side that shall do me honour, and above all Zeus, lord of counsel. Most hateful art thou to me of all kings, fosterlings of Zeus; thou ever lovest strife and wars and fightings. Though thou be very strong, yet that I ween is a gift to thee of God. Go home with thy ships and company and lord it among thy Myrmidons; I reck not aught of thee nor care I for thine indignation; and this shall be my threat to thee: seeing Phoebus Apollo bereaveth me of Chryseis, her with my ship and my company will I send back; and mine own self will I go to thy hut and take Briseis of the fair cheeks, even that thy meed of honour, that thou mayest well know how far greater I am than thou, and so shall another hereafter abhor to match his words with mine and rival me to my face."

So said he, and grief came upon Peleus' son, and his heart within his shaggy breast was divided in counsel, whether to draw his keen blade from his thigh and set the company aside and so slay Atreides, or to assuage his anger and curb his soul. While yet he doubted thereof in heart and soul, and was drawing his great sword from his sheath, Athene came to him from heaven, sent forth of the white-armed goddess Hera, whose heart loved both alike and had care for them. She stood behind Peleus' son and caught him by his golden hair, to him only visible, and of the rest no man beheld her. Then Achilles marvelled, and turned him about, and straightway knew Pallas Athene; and terribly shone her eyes. He spake to her winged words, and said: "Why now art thou come hither, thou daughter of aegis-bearing Zeus? Is it to behold the insolence of Agamemnon son of Atreus? Yea, I will tell thee that I deem shall even be brought to pass: by his own haughtinesses shall he soon lose his life."

Then the bright-eyed goddess Athene spake to him again: "I came from heaven to stay thine anger, if perchance thou wilt hearken to me, being sent forth of the white-armed goddess Hera, that loveth you twain alike and careth for you. Go to now, cease from strife, and let not thine hand draw the sword; yet with words indeed revile him, even as it shall come to pass. For thus will I say to thee, and so it shall be fulfilled; hereafter shall goodly gifts come to thee, yea in threefold measure, by reason of this despite; hold thou thine hand, and hearken to us."

And Achilles fleet of foot made answer and said to her: "Goddess, needs must a man observe the saying of you twain, even though he be very wroth at heart; for so is the better way. Whosoever obeyeth the gods, to him they gladly hearken."

10. **Myrmidons,** the people led by Achilles. 15. **Briseis,** the concubine of Achilles.

He said, and stayed his heavy hand on the silver hilt, and thrust the great sword back into the sheath, and was not disobedient to the saying of Athene; and she forthwith was departed to Olympus, to the other gods in the palace of aegis-bearing Zeus.

Then Peleus' son spake again with bitter words to Atreus' son, and in no wise ceased from anger: "Thou heavy with wine, thou with face of dog and heart of deer, never didst thou take courage to arm for battle among thy folk or to lay ambush with the princes of the Achaians; that to thee were even as death. Far better booteth it, forsooth, to seize for thyself the meed of honour of every man through the wide host of the Achaians that speaketh contrary to thee. Folk-devouring king! seeing thou rulest men of naught; else were this despite, thou son of Atreus, thy last. But I will speak my word to thee, and swear a mighty oath therewith: verily by this staff that shall no more put forth leaf or twig, seeing it hath for ever left its trunk among the hills, neither shall it grow green again, because the axe hath stripped it of leaves and bark; and now the sons of the Achaians that exercise judgment bear it in their hands, even they that by Zeus' command watch over the traditions—so shall this be a mighty oath in thine eyes—verily shall longing for Achilles come hereafter upon the sons of the Achaians one and all; and then wilt thou in no wise avail to save them, for all thy grief, when multitudes fall dying before manslaying Hector. Then shalt thou tear thy heart within thee for anger that thou didst in no wise honour the best of the Achaians."

So said Peleides and dashed to earth the staff studded with golden nails, and himself sat down; and over against him Atreides waxed furious. Then in their midst rose up Nestor, pleasant of speech, the clear-voiced orator of the Pylians, he from whose tongue flowed discourse sweeter than honey. Two generations of mortal men already had he seen perish, that had been of old time born and nurtured with him in goodly Pylos, and he was king among the third. He of good intent made harangue to them and said: "Alas, of a truth sore lamentation cometh upon the land of Achaia. Verily Priam would be glad and Priam's sons, and all the Trojans would have great joy of heart, were they to hear all this tale of strife between you twain that are chiefest of the Danaans in counsel and chiefest in battle. Nay, hearken to me; ye are younger both than I. Of old days held I converse with better men even than you, and never did they make light of me. Mightiest of growth were they of all men upon the earth; mightiest they were and with the mightiest fought they, even the wild tribes of the mountain caves, and destroyed them utterly. And with these held I converse, being come from Pylos, from a distant land afar; for of themselves they summoned me. So I played my part in fight; and with them could none of men that are now on earth do battle. And they laid to heart my counsels and hearkened to my voice. Even so hearken ye also, for better is it to hearken. Neither do thou, though thou art very great, seize from him his damsel, but leave her as she was given at the first by the sons of the Achaians to be a meed of honour; nor do thou, son of Peleus, think to strive with a king, might against might; seeing that no common honour pertaineth to a sceptred king to whom Zeus apportioneth glory. Though thou be strong, and a goddess mother bare thee, yet his is the greater place, for he is king over more. And thou, Atreides, abate thy fury; nay, it is even I that beseech thee to let go thine anger with Achilles, who is made unto all the Achaians a mighty bulwark of evil war."

Then lord Agamemnon answered and said: "Yea verily, old man, all this thou sayest is according unto right. But this fellow would be above all others, he would be lord of all and king among all and captain to all; wherein I deem none will hearken to him. Though the immortal gods made him a spearman, do they therefore put revilings in his mouth for him to utter?"

Then goodly Achilles brake in on him and answered: "Yea, for I should be called coward and man of naught, if I yield to thee in every matter, howsoe'er thou bid. To others give now thine orders, not to me. This, moreover, will I say to thee, and do thou lay it to thy heart. Know that not by violence will I strive for the damsel's sake, neither with thee nor any other; ye gave and ye have taken away. But of all else that is mine beside my fleet black ship, thereof shalt thou not take anything or bear it away against my will. Yea, go to now, make trial, that all these may see; forthwith thy dark blood shall gush about my spear."

Now when the twain had thus finished the battle of violent words, they stood up and dissolved the assembly beside the Achaian ships. Peleides went his way to his huts and trim ships with Menoitios' son and his company; and Atreides launched a fleet ship on the sea, and picked twenty oarsmen therefor, and embarked the hecatomb for the god, and brought Chryseis of the fair cheeks and set her therein; and Odysseus of many devices went to be their captain.

So these embarked and sailed over the wet ways; and Atreides bade the folk purify themselves. So they purified themselves, and cast the defilements into the sea and did sacrifice to Apollo, even unblemished hecatombs of bulls and goats, along the shore of the unvintaged sea; and the sweet savour arose to heaven eddying amid the smoke.

Thus were they busied throughout the host; but Agamemnon ceased not from the strife wherewith he threatened Achilles at the first; he spake to Talthybios and Eurybates that were his heralds and nimble squires: "Go ye to the tent of Achilles Peleus' son, and take Briseis of the fair cheeks by the hand and lead her hither; and if he give her not, then will I myself go, and more with me, and seize her; and that will be yet more grievous for him."

So saying he sent them forth, and laid stern charge upon them. Unwillingly went they along the beach of the unvintaged sea, and came to the huts and ships of the Myrmidons. Him found they sitting beside his hut and black ship; nor when he saw them was Achilles glad. So they in dread and reverence of the king stood, and spake to him no word, nor questioned him. But he knew in his heart, and spake to them: "All hail, ye heralds, messengers of Zeus and men, come near; ye are not guilty in my sight, but Agamemnon that sent you for the sake of the damsel Briseis. Go now, heaven-sprung Patroklos, bring forth the damsel, and give them her to lead away. Moreover, let the twain themselves be my witness before the face of the blessed gods and mortal men, yea and of him, that king untoward, against the day when there cometh need of me hereafter to save them all from shameful wreck. Of a truth he raveth with baleful mind, and hath not knowledge to look before and after, that so his Achaians might battle in safety beside their ships."

So said he, and Patroklos hearkened to his dear comrade, and led forth from the hut Briseis of the fair cheeks, and gave them her to lead away. So these twain took their way back along the Achaians' ships, and with them went the woman all unwilling. Then Achilles wept anon, and sat him down apart, aloof from his comrades on the beach of the grey sea, gazing across the boundless main; he stretched forth his hands and prayed instantly to his dear mother: "Mother, seeing thou didst of a truth bear me to so brief span of life, honour at the least ought the Olympian to have granted me, even Zeus that thundereth on high; but now doth he not honour me, no, not one whit. Verily Atreus' son, wide-ruling Agamemnon, hath done me dishonour; for he hath taken away my meed of honour and keepeth her of his own violent deed." . . .

Then Thetis weeping made answer to him: "Ah me, my child, why reared I thee, cursed in my motherhood? Would thou hadst been left tearless and griefless amid the ships, seeing thy lot is very brief and endureth no long while; but now art thou made short-lived alike and lamentable beyond all men; in an evil hour I bare thee in our halls. But I will go myself to snow-clad Olympus to tell this thy saying to Zeus, whose joy is in the thunder, if perchance he may hearken to me. But tarry thou now amid thy fleet-faring ships, and continue wroth with the Achaians, and refrain utterly from battle: for

Zeus went yesterday to Okeanos, unto the noble Ethiopians for a feast, and all the gods followed with him; but on the twelfth day will he return to Olympus, and then will I fare to Zeus' palace of the bronze threshold, and will kneel to him and think to win him."

So saying she went her way and left him there, vexed in spirit for the fair-girdled woman's sake, whom they had taken perforce despite his will: and meanwhile Odysseus came to Chryse with the holy hecatomb. When they were now entered within the deep haven, they furled their sails and laid them in the black ship, and lowered the mast by the forestays and brought it to the crutch with speed, and rowed her with oars to the anchorage. Then they cast out the mooring stones and made fast the hawsers, and so themselves went forth on to the seabeach, and forth they brought the hecatomb for the Far-darter Apollo, and forth came Chryseis withal from the seafaring ship. Then Odysseus of many counsels brought her to the altar and gave her into her father's arms, and spake unto him: "Chryses, Agamemnon king of men sent me hither to bring thee thy daughter, and to offer to Phoebus a holy hecatomb on the Danaans' behalf, wherewith to propitiate the king that hath now brought sorrow and lamentation on the Argives."

So saying he gave her to his arms, and he gladly took his dear child; and anon they set in order for the god the holy hecatomb about his well-builded altar; next washed they their hands and took up the barley meal. Then Chryses lifted up his hands and prayed aloud for them: "Hearken to me, god of the silver bow that standest over Chryse and holy Killa, and rulest Tenedos with might; even as erst thou heardest my prayer, and didst me honour, and mightily afflictedst the people of the Achaians, even so now fulfil me this my desire; remove thou from the Danaans forthwith the loathly pestilence." . . .

And when the sun went down and darkness came on them, they laid them to sleep beside the ship's hawsers; and when rosy-fingered Dawn appeared, the child of morning, then set they sail for the wide camp of the Achaians; and Apollo the Far-darter sent them a favouring gale. They set up their mast and spread the white sails forth, and the wind filled the sail's belly and the dark wave sang loud about the stem as the ship made way, and she sped across the wave, accomplishing her journey. So when they were now come to the wide camp of the Achaians, they drew up their black ship to land high upon the sands, and set in line the long props beneath her; and themselves were scattered amid their huts and ships.

But he sat by his swift-faring ships, still wroth, even the heaven-sprung son of Peleus, Achilles fleet of foot; he betook him neither to the assembly that is the hero's glory, neither to war, but consumed his heart in tarrying in his place, and yearned for the war-cry and for battle.

Now when the twelfth morn thereafter was come, then the gods that are for ever fared to Olympus all in company, led of Zeus. And Thetis forgat not her son's charge, but rose up from the sea-wave, and at early morn mounted up to great heaven and Olympus. There found she Kronos' son of the far-sounding voice sitting apart from all on the topmost peak of many-ridged Olympus. So she sat before his face and with her left hand clasped his knees, and with her right touched him beneath his chin, and spake in prayer to king Zeus son of Kronos: "Father Zeus, if ever I gave thee aid amid the immortal gods, whether by word or deed, fulfil thou this my desire: do honour to my son, that is doomed to earliest death of all men: now hath Agamemnon king of men done him dishonour, for he hath taken away his meed of honour and keepeth her of his own violent deed. But honour thou him, Zeus of Olympus, lord of counsel; grant thou victory to the Trojans the while, until the Achaians do my son honour and exalt him with recompense." . . .

Then Zeus the cloud-gatherer, sore troubled, spake to her: "Verily it is a sorry matter, if thou wilt set me at variance with Hera, whene'er she provoketh me with taunting words. Even now she upbraideth me ever amid the immortal gods, and saith that I aid the Trojans in battle. But do thou now depart again, lest Hera mark aught; and I will take thought for these things to fulfil them. Come now, I will bow my head to thee, that thou mayest be of good courage; for that, of my part, is the surest token amid the immortals; no word of mine is revocable nor false nor unfulfilled when the bowing of my head hath pledged it."

Kronion spake, and bowed his dark brow, and the ambrosial locks waved from the king's immortal head; and he made great Olympus quake.

Thus the twain took counsel and parted; she leapt therewith into the deep sea from glittering Olympus, and Zeus fared to his own palace. All the gods in company arose from their seats before their father's face; neither ventured any to await his coming, but they stood up all before him. So he sate him there upon his throne; but Hera saw, and was not ignorant how that the daughter of the Ancient of the sea, Thetis the silver-footed, had devised counsel with him. Anon with taunting words spake she to Zeus the son of Kronos: . . .

"Most dread son of Kronos, what word is this thou hast spoken? Yea, surely of old I have not asked thee nor made question, but in every quietness thou devisest all thou wilt. But now is my heart sore afraid lest thou have been won over by silver-footed Thetis, daughter of the Ancient of the sea, for she at early morn sat by thee and clasped thy knees. To her I deem thou gavest a sure pledge that thou wilt do honour to Achilles, and lay many low beside the Achaians' ships."

To her made answer Zeus the cloud-gatherer: "Lady, Good lack! ever art thou imagining, nor can I escape thee; yet shalt thou in no wise have power to fulfil, but wilt be the further from my heart; that shall be even the worse for thee. And if it be so, then such must my good pleasure be. Abide thou in silence and hearken to my bidding, lest all the gods that are in Olympus keep not off from thee my visitation, when I put forth my hands unapproachable against thee."

He said, and Hera the ox-eyed queen was afraid, and sat in silence, curbing her heart; but throughout Zeus' palace the gods of heaven were troubled. Then Hephaistos the famed craftsman began to make harangue among them, to do kindness to his dear mother, white-armed Hera: "Verily this will be a sorry matter, neither any more endurable, if ye twain thus fight for mortals' sakes, and bring wrangling among the gods; neither will there any more be joy of the goodly feast, seeing that evil triumpheth. So I give counsel to my mother, though herself is wise, to do kindness to our dear father Zeus, that our father upbraid us not again and cast the banquet in confusion. . . . Be of good courage, mother mine, and endure, though thou art vexed, lest I behold thee, that art so dear, chastised before mine eyes.". . .

He spake, and the white-armed goddess Hera smiled, and smiling took the cup at her son's hand. Then he poured wine to all the other gods from right to left, ladling the sweet nectar from the bowl. And laughter unquenchable arose amid the blessed gods to see Hephaistos bustling through the palace.

So feasted they all day till the setting of the sun; nor was their soul aught stinted of the fair banquet, nor of the beauteous lyre that Apollo held, and the Muses singing alternately with sweet voice.

Now when the bright light of the sun was set, these went each to his own house to sleep, where each one had his palace made with cunning device by famed Hephaistos the lame god; and Zeus the Olympian, the lord of lightning, departed to his couch where he was wont of old to take his rest, whenever sweet sleep visited him. There went he up and slept, and beside him was Hera of the golden throne.

BOOK II

. . . Now went the goddess Dawn to high Olympus, foretelling daylight to Zeus and all the immortals; and the king bade the clear-voiced heralds summon to the assembly the flowing-haired Achaians. So did those summon, and these gathered with speed. . . . And the kings, the fosterlings of Zeus that were about Atreus' son, eagerly marshalled them, and bright-eyed Athene in the midst, bearing the holy aegis that knoweth neither age nor death, whereon wave an hundred tassels of pure gold, all deftly woven and each one an hundred oxen worth. Therewith she passed dazzling through the Achaian folk, urging them forth; and in every man's heart she roused strength to battle without ceasing and to fight. So was war made sweeter to them than to depart in their hollow ships to their dear native land. Even as ravaging fire kindleth a boundless forest on a mountain's peaks, and the blaze is seen from afar, even so as they marched went the dazzling gleam from the innumerable bronze through the sky even unto the heavens. . . .

Now fleet Iris the wind-footed went to the Trojans, a messenger from aegis-bearing Zeus, with a grievous message. These were holding assembly at Priam's gate, being gathered all together both young men and old. And fleet-footed Iris stood hard by and spake to them; and she made her voice like to the voice of Polites son of Priam, who was the sentinel of the Trojans and was wont to sit trusting in his fleetness upon the barrow of Aisyetes of old, and on the top thereof wait the sallying of the Achaians forth from their ships. Even in his likeness did fleet-footed Iris speak to Priam: "Old man, words beyond number are still pleasant to thee as erst in the days of peace; but war without respite is upon us. Of a truth have I very oft ere now entered into battles of the warriors, yet have I never seen so goodly a host and so great; for in the very likeness of the leaves of the forest or the sands of the sea are they marching along the plain to fight against the city. But Hector, thee do I charge beyond all to do even as I shall say. Seeing that the allies are very many throughout Priam's great city, and diverse men, being scattered abroad, have diverse tongues; therefore let each one give the word to those whose chieftain he is, and them let him lead forth and have the ordering of his countrymen."

So spake she, and Hector failed not to know the voice of the goddess, and straightway dismissed the assembly, and they rushed to arms. And the gates were thrown open wide, and the host issued forth, footmen and horsemen, and mighty din arose.

BOOK III

Now when they were arrayed, each company with their captains, the Trojans marched with clamour and with shouting like unto birds, even as when there goeth up before heaven a clamour of cranes which flee from the coming of winter and sudden rain, and fly with clamour towards the streams of ocean, bearing slaughter and fate to the Pigmy men, and in early morn offer cruel battle. But on the other

side marched the Achaians in silence breathing courage, eager at heart to give succour man to man.

Even as when the south wind sheddeth mist over
the crests of a mountain, mist unwelcome to the
shepherd, but to the robber better than night, and a
man can see no further than he casteth a stone; even
so thick arose the gathering dust-clouds at their
tread as they went; and with all speed they advanced across the plain.

So when they were now come nigh in onset on
each other, godlike Alexandros played champion to
the Trojans, wearing upon his shoulders panther-skin
and curved bow and sword; and he brandished two
bronze-headed spears and challenged all the chieftains of the Argives to fight him man to man in
deadly combat. But when Menelaos dear to Ares
marked him coming in the forefront of the multitude
with long strides, then even as a lion is glad when he
lighteth upon a great carcase, a horned stag, or a
wild goat that he hath found, being an hungered;
and so he devoureth it amain, even though the fleet
hounds and lusty youths set upon him; even thus
was Menelaos glad when his eyes beheld godlike Alexandros; for he thought to take vengeance upon the
sinner. So straightway he leapt in his armour from
his chariot to the ground.

But when godlike Alexandros marked him appear
amid the champions, his heart was smitten, and he
shrank back into the host of his comrades, avoiding
death. And even as a man that hath seen a serpent
in a mountain glade starteth backward and trembling seizeth his feet beneath him, and he retreateth
back again, and paleness hath hold of his cheeks,
even so did godlike Alexandros for fear of Atreus'
son shrink back into the throng of lordly Trojans.
But Hector beheld and upbraided him with scornful
words: "Ill Paris, most fair in semblance, thou deceiver woman-mad, would thou hadst been unborn
and died unwed. Yea, that were my desire, and it
were far better than thus to be our shame and looked
at askance of all men. I ween that the flowing-haired
Achaians laugh, deeming that a prince is our champion only because a goodly favour is his; but in his
heart is there no strength nor any courage. Art thou
indeed such an one that in thy seafaring ships thou
didst sail over the deep with the company of thy
trusty comrades, and in converse with strangers
didst bring back a fair woman from a far country,
one that was by marriage daughter to warriors that
bear the spear, that she might be a sore mischief to
thy father and city and all the realm, but to our foes
a rejoicing, and to thyself a hanging of the head?
And canst thou not indeed abide Menelaos dear to
Ares? Thou mightest see what sort of warrior is he
whose lovely wife thou hast. Thy lyre will not avail
thee nor the gifts of Aphrodite, those thy locks and

11. **Alexandros, Paris.**

fair favour, when thou grovellest in the dust. But
the Trojans are very cowards: else ere this hadst
thou donned a robe of stone for all the ill thou hast
wrought."

And godlike Alexandros made answer to him
again: "Hector, since in measure thou chidest me
and not beyond measure—thy heart is ever keen,
even as an axe that pierceth a beam at the hand of a
man that shapeth a ship's timber with skill, and
thereby is the man's blow strengthened; even such is
thy heart undaunted in thy breast. Cast not in my
teeth the lovely gifts of golden Aphrodite; not to be
flung aside are the gods' glorious gifts that of their
own good will they give; for by his desire can no
man win them. But now if thou wilt have me do
battle and fight, make the other Trojans sit down and
all the Achaians, and set ye me in the midst, and
Menelaos dear to Ares, to fight for Helen and all her
wealth. And whichsoever shall vanquish and gain
the upper hand, let him take all the wealth aright,
and the woman, and bear them home. And let the
rest pledge friendship and sure oaths; so may ye
dwell in deep-soiled Troy, and let them depart to
Argos pasture-land of horses, and Achaia home of
fair women." . . .

So spake he, and they refrained from battle and
made silence speedily. And Hector spake between
the two hosts, "Hear of me, Trojans and well-
greaved Achaians, the saying of Alexandros, for
whose sake strife hath come about. He biddeth the
other Trojans and all the Achaians to lay down their
goodly armour on the bounteous earth, and himself
in the midst and Menelaos dear to Ares to fight alone
for Helen and all her wealth. And whichsoever shall
vanquish and gain the upper hand, let him take all
the wealth aright, and the woman, and bear them
home; but let all of us pledge friendship and sure
oaths."

So spake he, and they all kept silence and were
still. Then in their midst spake Menelaos of the loud
war-cry: "Hearken ye now to me, too; for into my
heart most of all is grief entered; and I deem that the
parting of Argives and Trojans hath come at last;
seeing ye have endured many ills because of my
quarrel and the first sin of Alexandros. And for
whichsoever of us death and fate are prepared, let
him lie dead: and be ye all parted with speed." . . .

So spake he, and Achaians and Trojans were glad,
deeming that they should have rest from grievous
war. So they refrained their chariots to the ranks,
and themselves alighted and doffed their arms. And
these they laid upon the earth each close to each,
and there was but small space between. . . .

Now Iris went with a message to white-armed
Helen in the likeness of her husband's sister. And in
the hall she found Helen weaving a great purple
web of double fold, and embroidering thereon many

battles of horse-taming Trojans and mail-clad Achaians, that they had endured for her sake at the hands of Ares. So fleet-footed Iris stood by her side and said: "Come hither, dear sister, that thou mayest see the wondrous doings of horse-taming Trojans and mail-clad Achaians. They that erst waged tearful war upon each other in the plain, eager for deadly battle, even they sit now in silence, and the battle is stayed, and they lean upon their shields, and the tall spears are planted by their sides. But Alexandros and Menelaos dear to Ares will fight with their tall spears for thee; and thou wilt be declared the dear wife of him that conquereth."

So spake the goddess, and put into her heart sweet longing for her former husband and her city and parents.

Forthwith she veiled her face in shining linen, and hastened from her chamber, letting fall a round tear; not unattended, for there followed with her two handmaidens. Then came she straightway to the place of the Skaian gates. And they that were with Priam and the elders of the people, sat at the Skaian gates. These had now ceased from battle for old age, yet were they right good orators, like grasshoppers that in a forest sit upon a tree and utter their lily-like voice; even so sat the elders of the Trojans upon the tower. Now when they saw Helen coming to the tower they softly spake winged words one to the other: "Small blame is it that Trojans and well-greaved Achaians should for such a woman long time suffer hardships; marvellously like is she to the immortal goddesses to look upon. Yet even so, though she be so goodly, let her go upon their ships and not stay to vex us and our children after us."

So said they, and Priam lifted up his voice and called to Helen: "Come hither, dear child, and sit before me, that thou mayest see thy former husband and thy kinsfolk and thy friends. I hold thee not to blame; nay, I hold the gods to blame who brought on me the dolorous war of the Achaians—so mayest thou now tell me who is this huge hero, this Achaian warrior so goodly and great. Of a truth there are others even taller by a head; yet did mine eyes never behold a man so beautiful nor so royal; for he is like unto one that is a king."

And Helen, fair among women, spake and answered him: "Reverend art thou to me and dread, dear father of my lord; would that sore death had been my pleasure when I followed thy son hither, and left my home and my kinsfolk and my daughter in her girlhood and the lovely company of mine age-fellows. But that was not so, wherefore I pine with weeping. Now will I tell thee that whereof thou askest me and enquirest. This is Atreides, wide-ruling Agamemnon, one that is both a goodly king and mighty spearman. And he was husband's brother to me, ah shameless me; if ever such an one there was."

And next the old man saw Odysseus, and asked: "Come now, tell me of this man too, dear child, who is he, shorter by a head than Agamemnon son of Atreus, but broader of shoulder and of chest to behold? His armour lieth upon the bounteous earth, and himself like a bell-wether rangeth the ranks of warriors. Yea, I liken him to a thick-fleeced ram ordering a great flock of white ewes."

Then Helen sprung of Zeus made answer to him: "Now this is Laertes' son, crafty Odysseus, that was reared in the realm of Ithaka, rugged though it be, and is skilled in all the ways of wile and cunning device." . . .

And thirdly the old man saw Aias, and asked: "Who then is this other Achaian warrior, goodly and great, pre-eminent among the Argives by the measure of his head and broad shoulders?"

And long-robed Helen, fair among women, answered: "This is huge Aias, bulwark of the Achaians. And on the other side amid the Cretans standeth Idomeneus like a god, and about him are gathered the captains of the Cretans. Oft did Menelaos dear to Ares entertain him in our house whene'er he came from Crete. And now behold I all the other glancing-eyed Achaians, whom well I could discern and tell their names. . . .

Meanwhile, upon his shoulders goodly Alexandros donned his beauteous armour, even he that was lord to Helen of the lovely hair. First upon his legs set he his greaves, beautiful, fastened with silver ankle-clasps; next upon his breast he donned the corslet of his brother Lykaon, and fitted it upon himself. And over his shoulders cast he his silver-studded sword of bronze, and then a shield great and sturdy. And on his mighty head he set a wrought helmet of horse-hair crest, wherever the plume nodded terribly, and he took him a strong spear fitted to his grasp. And in like wise warlike Menelaos donned his armour.

So when they had armed themselves on either side in the throng, they strode between Trojans and Achaians, fierce of aspect, and wonder came on them that beheld, both on the Trojans tamers of horses and on the well-greaved Achaians. Then took they their stand near together in the measured space, brandishing their spears in wrath each against other. First Alexandros hurled his far-shadowing spear, and smote on Atreides' round shield; but the bronze brake not through, for its point was turned in the stout shield. Next Menelaos son of Atreus lifted up his hand to cast, and made prayer to father Zeus: "King Zeus, grant me revenge on him that was first to do me wrong, even on goodly Alexandros, and subdue thou him at my hands; so that many an one of men that shall be hereafter may shudder to wrong his host that hath shown him kindness."

So said he, and poised his far-shadowing spear,

and hurled, and smote on the round shield of the son of Priam. Through the bright shield went the ponderous spear and through the inwrought breast-plate it pressed on; and straight beside his flank the spear rent the tunic, but he swerved and escaped black death. Then Atreides drew his silver-studded sword, and lifted up his hand and smote the helmet-ridge; but the sword shattered upon it unto three, yea four, and fell from his hand. Thereat Atreides looked up to the wide heaven and cried: "Father Zeus, surely none of the gods is crueller than you. Verily I thought to have gotten vengeance on Alexandros for his wickedness, but now my sword breaketh in my hand, and my spear sped from my grasp in vain, and I have not smitten him."

So saying, he leapt upon him and caught him by his horse-hair crest, and swinging him round dragged him towards the well-greaved Achaians; and he was strangled by the embroidered strap beneath his soft throat, drawn tight below his chin to hold his helm. Now would Menelaos have dragged him away and won glory unspeakable, but that Zeus' daughter Aphrodite was swift to mark, and tore asunder for him the strap of slaughtered ox's hide; so the helmet came away empty in his stalwart hand. Thereat Menelaos cast it with a swing toward the well-greaved Achaians, and his trusty comrades took it up; and himself sprang back again eager to slay him with spear of bronze. But Aphrodite snatched up Paris, very easily as a goddess may, and hid him in thick darkness, and set him down in his fragrant perfumed chamber; and herself went to summon Helen. Her she found on the high tower, and about her the Trojan women thronged. So with her hand she plucked her perfumed raiment and shook it and spake to her in the likeness of an aged dame, a wool-comber that was wont to work for her fair wool when she dwelt in Lakedaimon, whom too she greatly loved. Even in her likeness fair Aphrodite spake: "Come hither; Alexandros summoneth thee to go homeward. There is he in his chamber and inlaid bed, radiant in beauty and vesture; nor wouldst thou deem him to be come from fighting his foe, but rather to be faring to the dance, or from the dance to be just resting and set down." . . . .

So said she, and Helen sprung of Zeus was afraid, and went wrapped in her bright radiant vesture, silently, and the Trojan women marked her not; and the goddess led the way.

Now when they were come to the beautiful house of Alexandros the handmaidens turned straightway to their tasks, and the fair lady went to the high-roofed chamber; and laughter-loving Aphrodite took for her a chair and brought it, even she the goddess, and set it before the face of Paris. There Helen took her seat, the child of aegis-bearing Zeus, and with eyes turned askance spake and chode her lord:

"Thou comest back from battle; would thou hadst perished there, vanquished of that great warrior that was my former husband. Verily it was once thy boast that thou wast a better man than Menelaos dear to Ares, in the might of thine arm and thy spear. But go, now, challenge Menelaos dear to Ares to fight thee again face to face. Nay, but I, even I, bid thee refrain, nor fight a fight with golden-haired Menelaos man to man, neither attack him recklessly, lest perchance thou fall to his spear anon."

And Paris made answer to her and said: "Chide not my soul, lady, with cruel taunts. For now indeed hath Menelaos vanquished me with Athene's aid, but another day may I do so unto him; for we too have gods with us. But come now, let us have joy of love upon our couch; for never yet hath love so enwrapped my heart—not even then when first I snatched thee from lovely Lakedaimon and sailed with thee on my seafaring ships, and in the isle of Kranaë had converse with thee upon thy couch in love—as I love thee now and sweet desire taketh hold upon me." So saying he led the way to the couch, and the lady followed with him.

Thus laid they them upon their fretted couch; but Atreides the while strode through the host like to a wild beast, if anywhere he might set eyes on godlike Alexandros. But none of the Trojans or their famed allies could discover Alexandros to Menelaos dear to Ares. . . . .

BOOK VI

So was the dread fray of Trojans and Achaians left to itself, and the battle swayed oft this way and that across the plain, as they aimed against each other their bronze-shod javelins.

Now Glaukos son of Hippolochos and Tydeus' son met in the mid-space of the foes, eager to do battle. Thus when the twain were come nigh in onset on each other, to him first spake Diomedes of the loud war-cry: "Who art thou, noble sir, of mortal men? For never have I beheld thee in glorious battle ere this, yet now hast thou far outstripped all men in thy hardihood, seeing thou abidest my far-shadowing spear. Luckless are the fathers whose children face my might. If thou art some immortal come down from heaven, then will not I fight with heavenly gods. . . . But if thou art of men that eat the fruit of the field, come nigh, that anon thou mayest enter the toils of destruction."

Then Hippolochos' glorious son made answer to him: "Great-hearted Tydeides, why enquirest thou of my generation? Even as are the generations of leaves such are those likewise of men; the leaves that be the wind scattereth on the earth, and the forest buddeth and putteth forth more again, when the

91. Glaukos, leader of the Lycians, allies of Troy. Tydeus' son, Diomedes, a Greek hero.

season of spring is at hand; so of the generations of men one putteth forth and another ceaseth. Yet if thou wilt, have thine answer, that thou mayest well know our lineage, whereof many men have knowledge. There is a city Ephyre in the heart of Argos, pasture land of horses, and there dwelt noble Bellerophon. To him the gods granted beauty and lovely manhood; but Proitos in his heart devised ill for him, and being mightier far drave him from the land of the Argives, whom Zeus had made subject to his sceptre. . . . To slay him he forbare, for his soul had shame of that; but he sent him to Lykia, and gave him tokens of woe, graving in a folded tablet many deadly things, and bade him shew these to his father-in-law, the king, that he might be slain. So fared he to Lykia by the blameless convoy of the gods. Now when he came to Lykia and the stream of Xanthos, then did the king of wide Lykia honour him with all his heart; nine days he entertained him and killed nine oxen. And when on the tenth day rosy-fingered dawn appeared, then he questioned him and asked to see what token he bare from his son-in-law, even Proitos. Now when he had received of him Proitos' evil token, the king devised a cunning wile; he picked from wide Lykia the bravest men, and set an ambush. But these returned nowise home again; for noble Bellerophon slew them all. So when the king knew that he was the brave offspring of a god, he kept him there, and plighted him his daughter, and gave him the half of all the honour of his kingdom; moreover the Lykians meted him a domain pre-eminent above all, fair with vineyards and tilth to possess it. And his wife bare wise Bellerophon three children, Isandros and Hippolochos and Laodameia. . . . Hippolochos begat me, and of him do I declare me to be sprung; he sent me to Troy and bade me very instantly to be ever the best and to excel all other men, nor put to shame the lineage of my fathers that were of noblest blood in Ephyre and in wide Lykia. This is the lineage and blood whereof I avow myself to be."

So said he, and Diomedes of the loud war-cry was glad. He planted his spear in the bounteous earth and with soft words spake to the shepherd of the host: "Surely then thou art to me a guest-friend of old times through my father: for goodly Oineus of yore entertained noble Bellerophon in his halls and kept him twenty days. Moreover they gave each the other goodly gifts of friendship; Oineus gave a belt bright with purple, and Bellerophon a gold twyhandled cup, the which when I came I left in my palace. But of Tydeus I remember naught, seeing I was yet little when he left me, what time the Achaian host perished at Thebes. Therefore now am I to thee a dear guest-friend in midmost Argos, and thou in Lykia, whene'er I fare to your land. So let

8. **Proitos,** king of Argos.   46. **Oineus,** grandfather of Diomedes.

us shun each other's spears, even amid the throng; Trojans are there in multitudes and famous allies for me to slay, whoe'er it be that God vouchsafeth me and my feet overtake; and for thee are there Achaians in multitude, to slay whome'er thou canst. But let us make exchange of arms between us, that these also may know how we avow ourselves to be guest-friends by lineage."

So spake the twain, and leaping from their cars clasped each the other by his hand, and pledged their faith. . . .

Now when Hector came to the Skaian gates and to the oak-tree, there came running round about him the Trojans' wives and daughters, enquiring of sons and brethren and friends and husbands. But he bade them thereat all in turn pray to the gods; but sorrow hung over many. . . .

So were these praying to the daughter of great Zeus; and Hector was come to Alexandros' fair palace, that himself had builded with them that were most excellent carpenters then in deep-soiled Troyland. . . . There entered in Hector dear to Zeus, and his hand bare his spear, eleven cubits long: before his face glittered the bronze spear-point, and a ring of gold ran round about it. And he found Paris in his chamber busied with his beauteous arms, his shield and breastplate, and handling his curved bow; and Helen of Argos sate among her serving-women and appointed brave handiwork for her handmaidens. Then when Hector saw him he rebuked him with scornful words: "Good sir, thou dost not well to cherish this rancour in thy heart. The folk are perishing about the city and high wall in battle, and for thy sake the battle-cry is kindled and war around this city; yea thyself wouldest thou fall out with another, didst thou see him shrinking from hateful war. Up then, lest the city soon be scorched with burning fire."

And godlike Alexandros answered him: "Hector, since in measure thou chidest me and not beyond measure, therefore will I tell thee; lay thou it to thine heart and hearken to me. Not by reason so much of the Trojans, for wrath and indignation, sate I me in my chamber, but fain would I yield me to my sorrow. Even now my wife hath persuaded me with soft words, and urged me into battle; and I moreover, even I, deem that it will be better so; for victory shifteth from man to man. Go to then, tarry awhile, let me put on my armour of war; or else fare thou forth, and I will follow; and I think to overtake thee."

So said he, but Hector of the glancing helm answered him not a word. But Helen spake to him with gentle words: "My brother, even mine that am a dog, mischievous and abominable, would that on the day when my mother bare me at the first, an evil storm-wind had caught me away to a mountain or a billow of the loud-sounding sea, where the billow might have swept me away before all these things came to pass. Howbeit, seeing the gods devised all these ills in this wise, would that then I had been mated with a better man that felt dishonour and the multitude of men's reproachings. But as for him, neither hath he now sound heart, nor ever will have; thereof deem I moreover that he will reap the fruit. But now come, enter in and sit thee here upon this bench, my brother, since thy heart chiefly trouble hath encompassed, for the sake of me, that am a dog, and for Alexandros' sin; on whom Zeus bringeth evil doom, that even in days to come we may be a song in the ears of men that shall be hereafter."

Then great Hector of the glancing helm answered her: "Bid me not sit, Helen, of thy love; thou wilt not persuade me. Already my heart is set to succour the men of Troy, that have great desire for me that am not with them. But rouse thou this fellow, yea let himself make speed, to overtake me yet within the city. For I shall go into mine house to behold my housefolk and my dear wife, and infant boy; for I know not if I shall return home to them again, or if the gods will now overthrow me at the hands of the Achaians."

So spake Hector of the glancing helm and departed; and anon he came to his well-stablished house. But he found not white-armed Andromache in the halls; she with her boy and fair-robed hand-maiden had taken her stand upon the tower, weeping and wailing. And when Hector found not his noble wife within, he came and stood upon the threshold, and spake amid the serving-women: "Come tell me now true, my serving-women. Whither went white-armed Andromache forth from the hall? Hath she gone out to my sisters or unto my brothers' fair-robed wives, or to Athene's temple, where all the fair-tressed Trojan women propitiate the awful goddess?"

Then a busy housedame spake in answer to him: "Hector, seeing thou straitly chargest us tell thee true, neither hath she gone out to any of thy sisters or thy brothers' fair-robed wives, neither to Athene's temple, where all the fair-tressed Trojan women are propitiating the awful goddess; but she went to the great tower of Ilios, because she heard the Trojans were hard pressed, and great victory was for the Achaians. So hath she come in haste to the wall, like unto one frenzied; and the nurse with her beareth the child."

So spake the housedame, and Hector hastened from his house back by the same way down the well-builded streets. When he had passed through the great city and was come to the Skaian gates, whereby he was minded to issue upon the plain, then came his dear-won wife, running to meet him, even Andromache daughter of great-hearted Eëtion. . . .

So she met him now, and with her went the hand-maid bearing in her bosom the tender boy, the little child, Hector's loved son, like unto a beautiful star. . . . So now he smiled and gazed at his boy silently, and Andromache stood by his side weeping, and clasped her hand in his, and spake and called upon his name. "Dear my lord, this thy hardihood will undo thee, neither hast thou any pity for thine infant boy, nor for me forlorn that soon shall be thy widow; for soon will the Achaians all set upon thee and slay thee. But it were better for me to go down to the grave if I lose thee; for never more will any comfort be mine, when once thou, even thou, hast met thy fate, but only sorrow. Moreover I have no father nor lady mother. . . . And the seven brothers that were mine within our halls, all these on the self-same day went within the house of Hades; for fleet-footed goodly Achilles slew them all amid their kine of trailing gait and white-fleeced sheep. . . . Nay, Hector, thou art to me father and lady mother, yea and brother, even as thou art my goodly husband. Come now, have pity and abide here upon the tower, lest thou make thy child an orphan and thy wife a widow. And stay thy folk beside the fig-tree, where best the city may be scaled and the wall is assailable." . . .

Then great Hector of the glancing helm answered her: "Surely I take thought for all these things, my wife; but I have very sore shame of the Trojans and Trojan dames with trailing robes, if like a coward I shrink away from battle. Moreover mine own soul forbiddeth me, seeing I have learnt ever to be valiant and fight in the forefront of the Trojans, winning my father's great glory and mine own. Yea of a surety I know this in heart and soul; the day shall come for holy Ilios to be laid low, and Priam and the folk of Priam of the good ashen spear. Yet doth the anguish of the Trojans hereafter not so much trouble me neither Hekabe's own, neither king Priam's, neither my brethren's, the many and brave that shall fall in the dust before their foemen, as doth thine anguish in the day when some mail-clad Achaian shall lead thee weeping and rob thee of the light of freedom. So shalt thou abide in Argos and ply the loom at another woman's bidding, and bear water from fount Messeis or Hypereia, being grievously entreated, and sore constraint shall be laid upon thee. And then shall one say that beholdeth thee weep: 'This is the wife of Hector, that was foremost in battle of the horse-taming Trojans when men fought about Ilios.' Thus shall one say hereafter, and fresh grief will be thine for lack of such an husband as thou hadst to ward off the day of thraldom. But me in death may the heaped-up earth be covering, ere I hear thy crying and thy carrying into captivity."

So spake glorious Hector, and stretched out his arm to his boy. But the child shrunk crying to the bosom of his fair-girdled nurse, dismayed at his dear father's aspect, and in dread at the bronze and horse-hair crest that he beheld nodding fiercely from the helmet's top. Then his dear father laughed aloud, and his lady mother; forthwith glorious Hector took the helmet from his head, and laid it, all gleaming, upon the earth; then kissed he his dear son and dandled him in his arms, and spake in prayer to Zeus and all the gods, "O Zeus and all ye gods, vouchsafe ye that this my son may likewise prove even as I, pre-eminent amid the Trojans, and as valiant in might, and be a great king of Ilios. Then may men say of him, 'Far greater is he than his father' as he returneth home from battle; and may he bring with him blood-stained spoils from the foe-man he hath slain, and may his mother's heart be glad."

So spake he, and laid his son in his dear wife's arms; and she took him to her fragrant bosom, smil-ing tearfully. And her husband had pity to see her, and caressed her with his hand, and spake and called upon her name: "Dear one, I pray thee be not of oversorrowful heart; no man against my fate shall hurl me to Hades; only destiny, I ween, no man hath escaped, be he coward or be he valiant, when once he hath been born. But go thou to thine house and see to thine own tasks, the loom and distaff, and bid thine handmaidens ply their work; but for war shall men provide and I in chief of all men that dwell in Ilios."

So spake glorious Hector, and took up his horse-hair crested helmet; and his dear wife departed to her home oft looking back, and letting fall big tears. Anon she came to the well-stablished house of man-slaying Hector, and found therein her many hand-maidens, and stirred lamentation in them all. So be-wailed they Hector, while yet he lived, within his house: for they deemed that he would no more come back to them from battle, nor escape the fury of the hands of the Achaians.

Neither lingered Paris long in his lofty house, but clothed on him his brave armour, bedight with bronze, and hasted through the city, trusting to his nimble feet. Even as when a stalled horse, full-fed at the manger, breaketh his tether and speedeth at the gallop across the plain, being wont to bathe him in the fair-flowing stream, exultingly; and holdeth his head on high, and his mane floateth about his shoulders, and he trusteth in his glory, and nimbly his limbs bear him to the haunts and pasturage of mares; even so Priam's son Paris, glittering in his armour like the shining sun, strode down from high Pergamos laughingly, and his swift feet bare him. Forthwith he overtook his brother noble Hector, even as he was on the point to turn him away from the spot where he had dallied with his wife. To him first spake godlike Alexandros: "Sir, in good sooth I have delayed thee in thine haste by my tarrying, and came not rightly as thou badest me."

And Hector of the glancing helm answered him and said: "Good brother, no man that is right-minded could make light of thy doings in fight, see-ing thou art strong: but thou art wilfully remiss and hast no care; and for this my heart is grieved within me, that I hear shameful words concerning thee in the Trojans' mouths, who for thy sake endure much toil. But let us be going; all this will we make good hereafter, if Zeus ever vouchsafe us to set before the heavenly gods that are for everlasting the cup of deliverance in our halls, when we have chased out of Troy-land the well-greaved Achaians." . . .

BOOK VIII

Now Dawn the saffron-robed was spreading over all the earth, and Zeus whose joy is in the thunder let call an assembly of the gods upon the topmost peak of many-ridged Olympus, and himself made harangue to them and all the gods gave ear: "Hearken to me, all gods and all ye goddesses, that I may tell you that my heart within my breast com-mandeth me. One thing let none essay, be it goddess or be it god, to wit, to thwart my saying; approve ye it all together, that with all speed I may accom-plish these things. Whomsover I shall perceive minded to go, apart from the gods, to succour Tro-jans or Danaans, chastened in no seemly wise shall he return to Olympus, or I will take and cast him into misty Tartaros, right far away, where is the deepest gulf beneath the earth; there are the gate of iron and threshold of bronze, as far beneath Hades as heaven is high above the earth: then shall he know how far I am mightiest of all gods. Go to now, ye gods, make trial that ye all may know. Fasten ye a rope of gold from heaven, and all ye gods lay hold thereof and all goddesses; yet could ye not drag from heaven to earth Zeus, counsellor supreme, not though ye toiled sore. But once I likewise were minded to draw with all my heart, then should I draw you up with very earth and sea withal. There-after would I bind the rope about a pinnacle of Olympus, and so should all those things be hung in air. By so much am I beyond gods and beyond men." . . .

So saying he let harness to his chariot his bronze-shod horses, fleet of foot, with flowing manes of gold; and himself clad him with gold upon his flesh, and grasped the whip of gold, well-wrought, and mounted upon his car, and lashed the horses to start them; they nothing loth sped on between earth and starry heaven. So fared he to many-fountained Ida, mother of wild beasts, even unto Gargaros, where is his demesne and fragrant altar. There did the father of men and gods stay his horses, and unloose them from the car, and cast thick mist about them; and himself sate on the mountain-tops rejoicing in his glory, to behold the city of the Trojans and ships of the Achaians. . . .

Now while it yet was morn and the divine day waxed, so long from either side lighted the darts amain and the people fell. But when the sun bestrode mid-heaven, then did the Father balance his golden scales, and put therein two fates of death that layeth men at their length, one for horse-taming Trojans, one for mail-clad Achaians; and he took the scale-yard by the midst and lifted it, and the Achaians' day of destiny sank down. So lay the Achaians' fates on the bounteous earth, and the Trojans' fates were lifted up towards wide heaven. And the god thundered aloud from Ida, and sent his blazing flash amid the host of the Achaians; and they saw and were astonished, and pale fear gat hold upon all. . . .

And the Olympian aroused the spirit of the Trojans. So they drove the Achaians straight toward the deep fosse, and amid the foremost went Hector exulting in his strength. And even as when a hound behind wild boar or lion, with swift feet pursuing snatcheth at him, at flank or buttock, and watcheth for him as he wheeleth, so Hector pressed hard on the flowing-haired Achaians, slaying ever the hindmost, and they fled on. But when they were passed in flight through palisade and fosse, and many were fallen beneath the Trojans' hands, then halted they and tarried beside the ships, calling one upon another, and lifting up their hands to all the gods prayed each one instantly. But Hector wheeled round his beauteous-maned steeds this way and that, and his eyes were as the eyes of Gorgon or Ares bane of mortals. . . . And the sun's bright light dropped into Ocean, drawing black night across Earth the grain-giver. Against the Trojans' will daylight departed, but welcome, thrice prayed for, to the Achaians came down the murky night.

Now glorious Hector made an assembly of the Trojans, taking them apart from the ships, beside the eddying river, in an open space where was found a spot clear of dead. And they came down from their chariots to the ground to hear the word that Hector, dear unto Zeus, proclaimed. He in his hand held his spear eleven cubits long; before his face gleamed the spear-head of bronze, and a ring of gold ran round about it. Thereon he leaned and spake to the Trojans, saying: "Hearken to me, Trojans and Dardanians and allies. I thought but now to make havoc of the ships and all the Achaians and depart back again to windy Ilios; but dusk came too soon, and that in chief hath now saved the Argives and the ships beside the beach of the sea. So let us now yield to black night, and make our supper ready; unyoke ye from the chariots your fair-maned horses, and set fodder beside them. And from the city bring kine and goodly sheep with speed; and provide you with honey-hearted wine, and corn from your houses, and gather much wood withal, that all night long until early-springing dawn we may burn many fires, and the gleam may reach to heaven; lest perchance even by night the flowing-haired Achaians strive to take flight over the broad back of the sea. Verily must they not embark upon their ships unvexed, at ease; but see ye that many a one of them have a wound to nurse even at home, being stricken with arrow or keen-pointed spear as he leapeth upon his ship; that so many another man may dread to wage dolorous war on the horse-taming men of Troy. And let the heralds dear to Zeus proclaim throughout the city that young maidens and old men of hoary heads camp round the city on the battlements builded of the gods; and let the women folk burn a great fire each in her hall; and let there be a sure watch set, lest an ambush enter the city when the host is absent. Thus be it, great-hearted Trojans, as I proclaim; the counsel that now is sound, let that stand spoken; further will I proclaim at dawn amid the horse-taming men of Troy. I pray with good hope to Zeus and all the gods, to drive from hence these dogs borne onward by the fates. Howbeit for the night will we guard our own selves, and at morn by daybreak, arrayed in our armour, let us awake keen battle at the hollow ships. I will know whether Tydeus' son stalwart Diomedes shall thrust me from the ships back to the wall, or I shall lay him low with my spear and bear away his gory spoils. Tomorrow shall he prove his valour, whether he can abide the onslaught of my spear. But he amid the foremost, I ween, shall lie stricken, and many comrades round about their lord at the rising of tomorrow's sun. Would that I were immortal and ageless all my days and honoured like as Athene is honoured and Apollo, so surely as this day bringeth the Argives ill."

So Hector made harangue, and the Trojans clamoured applause. And they loosed their sweating steeds from the yoke, and tethered them with thongs, each man beside his chariot; and from the city they brought kine and goodly sheep with speed, and provided them with honey-hearted wine and corn from their houses, and gathered much wood withal; [and sacrificed to the immortals unblemished hecatombs]. And from the plain the winds bare into heaven the sweet savour. [But the blessed gods regaled not themselves nor would they aught thereof; for sore was holy Ilios hated of them, and Priam and the folk of Priam of the good ashen spear.] But these with high hopes sate them all night along the highways of the battle, and their watchfires burned in multitude. Even as when in heaven the stars about the bright moon shine clear to see, when the air is windless, and all the peaks appear and the tall headlands and glades, and from heaven breaketh open the infinite air, and all stars are seen, and the shepherd's heart is glad; even in like multitude between the ships and the streams of Xanthos appeared the watchfires that the Trojans kindled in front of Ilios. A thousand fires burned in the plain and by the side of each sate fifty in the gleam of blazing fire. And the horses champed white barley and spelt, and standing by their chariots waited for the throned Dawn.

BOOK IX

Thus kept the Trojans watch; but the Achaians were holden of heaven-sent panic, handmaid of palsying fear, and all their best were stricken to the heart with grief intolerable. Like as two winds stir up the main, the home of fishes, even the north wind and the west wind that blow from Thrace, coming suddenly; and the dark billow straightway lifteth up its crest and casteth much tangle out along the sea; even so was the Achaians' spirit troubled in their breast.

Then Atreides gathered the councillors of the Achaians, and led them to his hut, and spread before them an abundant feast. So they put forth their hands to the good cheer that lay before them. And when they had put away from them the desire of meat and drink, then the old man first began to weave his counsel, even Nestor, whose rede of old time was approved the best. He of good intent spake to them and said: "Most noble son of Atreus, Agamemnon king of men, in thy name will I end and with thy name begin, because thou art king over many hosts, and to thy hand Zeus hath entrusted sceptre and law, that thou mayest take counsel for thy folk. Thee therefore more than any it behoveth both to speak and hearken, and to accomplish what another than thou may say, when his heart biddeth him speak for profit: wheresoever thou leadest all shall turn on thee, so I will speak as meseemeth best. No other man shall have a more excellent thought than this that I bear in mind from old time even until now, since the day when thou, O heaven-sprung king, didst go and take the damsel Briseis from angry Achilles' hut by no consent of ours. Nay, I right heartily dissuaded thee; but thou yieldedst to thy proud spirit, and dishonouredest a man of valour whom even the immortals honoured; for thou didst take and keepest from him his meed of valour. Still let us even now take thought how we may appease him and persuade him with gifts of friendship and kindly words."

And Agamemnon king of men answered and said to him: "Old sir, in no false wise hast thou accused my folly. Fool was I, I myself deny it not. Worth many hosts is he whom Zeus loveth in his heart, even as now he honoureth this man and destroyeth the host of the Achaians. But seeing I was a fool in that I yielded to my sorry passion, I will make amends and give a recompense beyond telling. In the midst of you all I will name the excellent gifts; seven tripods untouched of fire, and ten talents of gold and twenty gleaming caldrons, and twelve stalwart horses, winners in the race, that have taken prizes by their speed. No lack-wealth were that man, neither undowered of precious gold, whose substance were as great as the prizes my whole-hooved steeds have borne me off. And seven women will I give, skilled in excellent handiwork, Lesbians whom I chose me from the spoils the day that he himself took stablished Lesbos, surpassing womankind in beauty." . . .

Then knightly Nestor of Gerenia answered and said: "Most noble son of Atreus, Agamemnon king of men, now are these gifts not lightly to be esteemed that thou offerest king Achilles. Come therefore, let us speed forth picked men to go with all haste to the hut of Peleus' son Achilles. Lo now, whomsoever I appoint let them consent. First let Phoinix dear to Zeus lead the way, and after him great Aias and noble Odysseus. And now bring water for our hands, and bid keep holy silence, that we may pray unto Zeus the son of Kronos, if perchance he will have mercy upon us."

So said he, and spake words that were well-pleasing unto all. Forthwith the heralds poured water on their hands, and the young men crowned the bowls with drink and gave each man his portion after they had poured the libation in the cups. And when they had made libation and drunk as their heart desired, they issued forth from the hut of Agamemnon son of Atreus. And knightly Nestor of Gerenia gave them full charge, with many a glance to each, and chiefest to Odysseus, how they should essay to prevail on Peleus' noble son.

So the twain went along the shore of the loud-sounding sea, making instant prayer to the earth-embracer, the Shaker of the Earth, that they might with ease prevail on Aiakides' great heart. So they came to the huts and ships of the Myrmidons, and found their king taking his pleasure of a loud lyre, fair, of curious work, with a silver cross-bar upon it; one that he had taken from the spoils when he laid Eëtion's city waste. Therein he was delighting his soul, and singing the glories of heroes. And over against him sate Patroklos alone in silence, watching till Aiakides should cease from singing. So the twain came forward, and noble Odysseus led the way, and they stood before his face; and Achilles sprang up amazed with the lyre in his hand, and left the seat where he was sitting, and in like manner Patroklos when he beheld the men arose. Then Achilles fleet

77. **Phoinix**, tutor of Achilles. 97. **Aiakides**, Achilles, grandson of Aeacus.

of foot greeted them and said: "Welcome; verily ye are friends that are come—sore indeed is the need—even ye that are dearest of the Achaians to me even in my wrath."

So spake noble Achilles and led them forward, and made them sit on settles and carpets of purple; and anon he spake to Patroklos being near: "Bring forth a greater bowl, thou son of Menoitios; mingle stronger drink, and prepare each man a cup, for dearest of men are these that are under my roof."

So said he, and Patroklos hearkened to his dear comrade. He cast down a great fleshing-block in the fire-light, and laid thereon a sheep's back and a fat goat's, and a great hog's chine rich with fat. Achilles carved. Then he sliced well the meat and pierced it through with spits, and Menoitios' son, that godlike hero, made the fire burn high. Then when the fire was burned down and the flame waned, he scattered the embers and laid the spits thereover, resting them on the spit-racks, when he had sprinkled them with holy salt. Then when he had roasted the meat and apportioned it in the platters, Patroklos took bread and dealt it forth on the table in fair baskets, and Achilles dealt the meat. And he sate him over against godlike Odysseus by the other wall, and bade his comrade Patroklos do sacrifice to the gods; so he cast the first-fruits into the fire. Then put they forth their hands to the good cheer lying before them. And when they had put from them the desire of meat and drink, Aias nodded to Phoinix. But noble Odysseus marked it, and filled a cup with wine and pledged Achilles: "Hail, O Achilles! The fair feast lack we not either in the hut of Agamemnon son of Atreus neither now in thine; for feasting is there abundance to our heart's desire, but our thought is not for matters of the delicious feast; nay, we behold very sore destruction, thou fosterling of Zeus, and are afraid. Now is it in doubt whether we save the benched ships or behold them perish, if thou put not on thy might. Nigh unto ships and wall have the high-hearted Trojans and famed allies pitched their camp, and kindled many fires throughout their host, and ween that they shall no more be withheld but will fall on our black ships. And Zeus son of Kronos sheweth them signs upon the right by lightning, and Hector greatly exulteth in his might and rageth furiously, trusting in Zeus, and recketh not of god nor man, for mighty madness hath possessed him. He prayeth bright Dawn to shine forth with all speed, for he hath passed his word to smite off from the ships the ensigns' tops, and to fire the hulls with devouring flame, and hard thereby to make havoc of the Achaians confounded by the smoke. Therefore am I sore afraid in my heart lest the gods fulfil his boastings, and it be fated for us to perish here in Troy-land, far from Argos pasture-land of horses. Up then! if thou art minded even at the last to save the failing sons of the Achaians from the war-din of the Trojans. Thyself shalt have grief hereafter, and when the ill is done is there no way to find a cure therefor; in good time rather take thou thought to ward the evil day from the Danaans. . . . Agamemnon offereth thee worthy gifts, so thou wilt cease from anger. . . . These will he give thee, and with them shall be she whom erst he took from thee, even the daughter of Briseus; moreover he will swear a great oath that never he went up into her bed nor had with her converse as is the wont of mankind, O king, even of men and women. All these things shall be set straightway before thee; and if hereafter the gods grant us to lay waste the great city of Priam, then enter thou in when we Achaians be dividing the spoil, and lade thy ship full of gold and bronze, and thyself choose twenty Trojan women, the fairest that there be after Helen of Argos. . . . All this will he accomplish so thou but cease from wrath. But and if Agamemnon be too hateful to thy heart, both he and his gifts, yet have thou pity on all the Achaians that faint throughout the host; these shall honour thee as a god, for verily thou wilt earn exceeding great glory at their hands. Yea now mightest thou slay Hector, for he would come very near thee in his deadly madness, because he deemeth that there is no man like unto him among the Danaans that the ships brought hither."

And Achilles fleet of foot answered and said unto him: "Heaven-sprung son of Laertes, Odysseus of many wiles, in openness must I now declare unto you my saying, even as I am minded and as the fulfilment thereof shall be, that ye may not sit before me and coax this way and that. For hateful to me even as the gates of hell is he that hideth one thing in his heart and uttereth another: but I will speak what meseemeth best. Not me, I ween, shall Agamemnon son of Atreus persuade, nor the other Danaans, seeing we were to have no thank for battling with the foemen ever without respite. He that abideth at home hath equal share with him that fighteth his best, and in like honour are held both the coward and the brave; death cometh alike to the untoiling and to him that hath toiled long. Neither have I any profit for that I endured tribulation of soul, ever staking my life in fight. Even as a hen bringeth her unfledged chickens each morsel as she winneth it, and with herself it goeth hard, even so I was wont to watch out many a sleepless night and pass through many bloody days of battle, warring with folk for their women's sake. Twelve cities of men have I laid waste from ship-board, and from land eleven, I do you to wit, throughout deep-soiled Troy-land; out of all these took I many goodly treasures and would bring and give them all to Agamemnon son of Atreus, and he staying behind amid the fleet ships would take them and portion out some few but keep the most. Now some he gave to be meeds of honour to the princes and the kings, and theirs are left untouched; only from me of all the Achaians took he my darling lady and keepeth her— let him sleep beside her and take his joy! But why must the Argives make war on the Trojans? why hath Atreides gathered his host and led them hither? is it not for lovely-haired Helen's sake? Do then the sons of Atreus alone of mortal men love their wives? surely whatsoever man is good and sound of mind loveth his own and cherisheth her, even, as I too loved mine with all my heart, though but the captive of my spear. But now that he hath taken my meed of honour from mine arms and hath deceived me, let him not tempt me that know him full well; he shall not prevail. . . . Neither will I devise counsel with him nor any enterprise, for utterly he hath deceived me and done wickedly; but never again shall he beguile me with fair speech—let this suffice him. Let him begone in peace; Zeus the lord of counsel hath taken away his wits. Hateful to me are his gifts, and I hold him at a straw's worth. Not even if he gave me ten times, yea twenty, all that now is his, and all that may come to him otherwhence, even all the revenue of Orchomenos or Egyptian Thebes where the treasure-houses are stored fullest—Thebes of the hundred gates, whence sally forth two hundred warriors through each with horses and chariots—nay, nor gifts in number as sand or dust; not even so shall Agamemnon persuade my soul till he have paid me back all the bitter despite. For thus my goddess mother telleth me, Thetis the silver-footed, that twain fates are bearing me to the issue of death. If I abide here and besiege the Trojan's city, then my returning home is taken from me, but my fame shall be imperishable; but if I go home to my dear native land, my high fame is taken from me, but my life shall endure long while, neither shall the issue of death soon reach me. Moreover I would counsel you all to set sail homeward, seeing ye shall never reach your goal of steep Ilios; of a surety far-seeing Zeus holdeth his hand over her and her folk are of good courage. So go your way and tell my answer to the princes of the Achaians, even as is the office of elders, that they may devise in their hearts some other better counsel, such as shall save them their ships and the host of the Achaians amid the hollow ships: since this counsel availeth them naught that they have now devised, by reason of my fierce wrath. . . . Go ye and declare my message; I will not take thought of bloody war until that wise Priam's son, noble Hector, come to the Myrmidons' huts and ships, slaying the Argives, and smirch the ships with fire. But about mine hut and black ship I ween that Hector, though he be very eager for battle, shall be refrained."

25. Orchomenos, a wealthy city of Boeotia.

So said he, and they took each man a two-handled cup, and made libation and went back along the line of ships; and Odysseus led the way.

BOOK XI

Now Dawn arose from her couch beside proud Tithonos, to bring light to the Immortals and to mortal men. But Zeus sent forth fierce Discord unto the fleet ships of the Achaians, and in her hands she held the signal of war. And she stood upon the huge black ship of Odysseus, that was in the midst, to make her voice heard on either side, both to the huts of Aias, son of Telamon, and to the huts of Achilles, for these twain, trusting in their valour and the might of their hands, had drawn up their trim ships at the two ends of the line. There stood the goddess and cried shrilly in a great voice and terrible, and mighty strength she set in the heart of each of the Achaians, to war and fight unceasingly. And straightway to them war grew sweeter than to depart in the hollow ships to their dear native land.

Then the son of Atreus cried aloud, and bade the Argives arm them, and himself amid them did on the flashing bronze. First he fastened fair greaves about his legs, fitted with ankle-clasps of silver; next again he did his breastplate about his breast, the breastplate that in time past Kinyras gave him for a guest-gift. For afar in Cyprus did Kinyras hear the mighty rumour how that the Achaians were about to sail forth to Troy in their ships, wherefore did Kinyras give him the breastplate, to do pleasure to the king. Now therein were ten courses of black cyanus, and twelve of gold, and twenty of tin, and dark blue snakes writhed up towards the neck, three on either side, like rainbows that the son of Kronos hath set in the clouds, a marvel of the mortal tribes of men. And round his shoulders he cast his sword, wherein shone studs of gold, but the scabbard about it was silver, fitted with golden chains. And he took the richly-dight shield of his valour that covereth all the body of a man, a fair shield, and round about it were ten circles of bronze, and thereon were twenty white bosses of tin, and one in the midst of black cyanus. And thereon was embossed the Gorgon fell of aspect glaring terribly, and about her were Dread and Terror. And from the shield was hung a baldric of silver, and thereon was curled a snake of cyanus; three heads interlaced had he, growing out of one neck. And on his head Agamemnon set a two-crested helm with fourfold plate, and plume of horse-hair, and terribly the crest nodded from above. And he grasped two strong spears, shod with bronze and keen, and far forth from him into the heaven shone the bronze; and thereat Hera and Athene thundered, honouring the king of Mykene rich in gold.

Then each man gave in charge his horses to his

charioteer, to hold them in by the fosse, well and or-derly, and themselves as heavy men at arms were hasting about, being harnessed in their gear, and unquenchable the cry arose into the Dawn. And long before the charioteers were they arrayed at the fosse, but after them a little way came up the drivers. And among them the son of Kronos aroused an evil din, and from above rained down dew dank with blood out of the upper air, for that he was about to send 10 many strong men down to Hades.

But the Trojans on the other side, on the high ground of the plain, gathered them around great Hector, and noble Polydamas, and Aineias that as a god was honoured by the people of the Trojans, and the three sons of Antenor, Polybos, and noble Age-nor, and young Akamas like unto the Immortals. And Hector in the foremost rank bare the circle of his shield. And as from amid the clouds appeareth glittering a baneful star, and then again sinketh 20 within the shadowy clouds, even so Hector would now appear among the foremost ranks, and again would be giving command in the rear, and all in bronze he shone, like the lightning of aegis-bearing father Zeus.

And even as when reapers over against each other drive their swaths through a rich man's field of wheat or barley, and thick fall the handfuls, even so the Trojans and Achaians leaped upon each other, destroying, and neither side took thought of ruinous 30 flight; and equal heads had the battle, and they rushed on like wolves. And woful Discord was glad at the sight, for she alone of the gods was with them in the war; for the other gods were not beside them, but in peace they sat within their halls, where the goodly mansion of each was builded in the folds of Olympus. And they all were blaming the son of Kronos, lord of the storm-cloud, for that he willed to give glory to the Trojans. But of them took the father no heed, but aloof from the others he sat 40 apart, glad in his glory, looking toward the city of the Trojans, and the ships of the Achaians, and the glitter of bronze, and the slayers and the slain. . . .

BOOK XIV

Now Hera of the golden throne stood on the peak of Olympus, and saw with her eyes. And she beheld Zeus sitting on the topmost crest of many-fountained Ida, and to her heart he was hateful. Then she took thought, the ox-eyed lady Hera, how she might be-guile the mind of aegis-bearing Zeus. And this seemed to her in her heart to be the best counsel, 50 namely to fare to Ida, when she had well adorned herself, if perchance he would desire to sleep beside her and embrace her body in love, and a sweet sleep and a kindly she could pour on his eyelids and his crafty wits. And she set forth to her bower, that her

dear son Hephaistos had fashioned, and therein had made fast strong doors on the pillars, with a secret bolt, that no other god might open. There did she enter in and closed the shining doors. With ambrosia first did she cleanse every stain from her winsome body, and anointed her with olive oil, ambrosial, 60 soft, and of a sweet savour; if it were but shaken, in the bronze-floored mansion of Zeus, the savour thereof went right forth to earth and heaven. There-with she anointed her fair body, and combed her hair, and with her hands plaited her shining tresses, fair and ambrosial, flowing from her immortal head. Then she clad her in her fragrant robe that Athene wrought delicately for her, and therein set many things beautifully made, and fastened it over her breast with clasps of gold. And she girdled it with a 70 girdle arrayed with a hundred tassels, and she set earrings in her pierced ears, earrings of three drops, and glistering, therefrom shone grace abundantly. And with a veil over all the peerless goddess veiled herself, a fair new veil, bright as the sun, and be-neath her shining feet she bound goodly sandals. But when she had adorned her body with all her array, she went forth from her bower, and called Aphrodite apart from the other gods, and spake to her saying: "Wilt thou obey me, dear child, in that which I shall 80 tell thee? or wilt thou refuse, with a grudge in thy heart, because I succour the Danaans, and thou the Trojans?"

Then Aphrodite the daughter of Zeus answered her: "Hera, goddess queen, daughter of mighty Kronos, say the thing that is in thy mind, my heart bids me fulfil it, if fulfil it I may, and if it may be accomplished."

Then with crafty purpose the lady Hera answered her: "Give me now Love and Desire wherewith thou 90 dost overcome all the Immortals, and mortal men. For I am going to visit the limits of the bountiful Earth, and Okeanos, father of the gods, and mother Tethys, who reared me well and nourished me in their halls. Them am I going to visit, and their end-less strife will I loose, for already this long time they hold apart from each other, apart from love and the marriage bed, since wrath had settled in their hearts. If with words I might persuade their hearts, and bring them back to love and the marriage bed, ever 100 should I be called dear to them and worshipful."

Then laughter-loving Aphrodite answered her again: "It may not be, nor seemly were it to deny that thou askest, for thou sleepest in the arms of Zeus, the chief of gods."

Therewith from her breast she loosed the broi-dered girdle, fair-wrought, wherein are all her en-chantments; therein are love, and desire, and loving converse, that steals the wits even of the wise. This girdle she laid in her hands, and spake, and said: 116 "Lo now, take this girdle and lay it up in thy bosom, this fair-wrought girdle, wherein all things are fashioned; methinks thou wilt not return with that unaccomplished, which in thy heart thou desirest."

So spake she, and the ox-eyed lady Hera smiled, and smiling laid up the zone within her breast.

Then the daughter of Zeus, Aphrodite, went to her house, and Hera, rushing down, left the peak of Olympus, and touched on Pieria and pleasant Emathia, and sped over the snowy hills of the Thracian horsemen, even over the topmost crests, nor grazed the ground with her feet, and from Athos she fared across the foaming sea, and came to Lemnos, the city of godlike Thoas. There she met Sleep, the brother of Death, and clasped her hand in his, and spake and called him by name: "Sleep, lord of all gods and of all men, if ever thou didst hear my word, obey me again even now, and I will be grateful to thee always. Lull me, I pray thee, the shining eyes of Zeus beneath his brows, so soon as I have laid me down by him in love. And gifts I will give to thee, even a fair throne, imperishable for ever, a golden throne, that Hephaistos the Lame, mine own child, shall fashion skilfully, and will set beneath it a footstool for the feet, for thee to set thy shining feet upon, when thou art at a festival."

Then sweet Sleep answered her and said: "Hera, goddess and queen, daughter of mighty Kronos, another of the eternal gods might I lightly lull to slumber, yea, were it the streams of Okeanos himself, that is the father of them all. But to Zeus the son of Kronos might I not draw near, nor lull him to slumber, unless himself commanded it. . . ."

Then the ox-eyed lady Hera answered him again: "Sleep, wherefore dost thou consider these things in thy heart? dost thou deem that Zeus of the far-borne voice will succour the Trojans even as he was wroth for the sake of Herakles, his own child? Nay come, and I will give thee one of the younger of the Graces, to wed and to be called thy wife [even Pasithea, that ever thou longest for all thy days]."

So she spake, and Sleep was glad, and answered and said: "Come now, swear to me by the inviolable water of Styx, and with one of thy hands grasp the bounteous earth, and with the other the shining sea, that all may be witnesses to us, even all the gods below that are with Kronos, that verily thou wilt give me one of the younger of the Graces, even Pasithea, that myself do long for all my days."

So spake he, nor did she disobey, the white-armed goddess Hera; she sware as he bade her, and called all the gods by name, even those below Tartaros that are called Titans. . . . But Hera swiftly drew nigh to topmost Gargaros, the highest crest of Ida, and Zeus the cloud-gatherer beheld her. And as he saw her, so love came over his deep heart, even as when first they mingled with each other in delight, and went together to the couch, their dear parents knowing it not. And he stood before her, and spoke, and said: "Hera, with what desire comest thou thus hither from Olympus, and thy horses and chariot are not here, whereon thou mightst ascend?"

Then with crafty purpose lady Hera answered him: "I am going to visit the limits of the bountiful earth, and Okeanos, father of the gods, and mother Tethys, who reared me well and cherished me in their halls. Them am I going to visit, and their endless strife will I loose, for already this long time they hold apart from each other, from love and the marriage bed, since wrath hath settled in their hearts. But my horses are standing at the foot of many-fountained Ida, my horses that shall bear me over wet and dry. And now it is because of thee that I am thus come hither, down from Olympus, lest perchance thou mightest be wroth with me hereafter, if silently I were gone to the mansion of deep-flowing Okeanos."

Then Zeus, the gatherer of the clouds, answered her and said: "Hera, thither mayst thou go on a later day. But come let us twain take pleasure in the bed of love. For never once as thus did the love of goddess or woman so mightily overflow and conquer the heart within my breast. Not when I loved the wife of Ixion, who bore Pirithoos, the peer of gods in counsel, nor when I loved Danae of the fair ankles, daughter of Akrisios, who bore Perseus, most renowned of all men, nor when I loved the famed daughter of Phoinix, who bore me Minos, and god-

Zeus pursuing a woman. From a painting on an Attic red-figured vase.

like Rhadamanthys, nay, nor even when I loved Semele, nor Alkmene in Thebes, and she bore Herakles, a child hardy of heart, but Semele bore Dionysos, a delight to mortals, nay, nor when I loved the fair-tressed queen, Demeter, nor renowned Leto, nay, nor thy very self, as now I love thee, and sweet desire possesses me."

And him the lady Hera answered with crafty purpose: "Most dread son of Kronos, what a word thou hast spoken! If now thou dost long to be couched in love on the crests of Ida, and all stands plain to view, how would it be if some one of the eternal gods should see us slumbering, and go and tell it to all the gods? It is not I that could arise from the couch and go again to thy house, nay, it would be a thing for righteous anger. But if thou wilt, and it is dear to thy heart, thou hast a chamber that thine own son Hephaistos builded, and fastened strong doors to the pillars, thither let us go and lie down, if the couch be thy desire."

Then Zeus the cloud-gatherer answered her and said: "Hera, fear not lest any god, or any man should spy the thing, so great a golden cloud will I cast all over thee. Nay, methinks not even the sun might see through it, the sun, whose light is keenest of all to behold."

So spake he, and the son of Kronos clasped his consort in his arms. And beneath them the divine earth sent forth fresh new grass, and dewy lotus, and crocus, and hyacinth, thick and soft, that raised them aloft from the ground. Therein they lay, and were clad on with a fair golden cloud, whence fell drops of glittering dew.

Thus slept the Father in quiet on the crest of Gargaros, by Sleep and love overcome, with his bedfellow in his arms. But sweet Sleep started and ran to the ships of the Achaians, to tell his tidings to the god that holdeth and shaketh the earth. And he stood near him, and spake winged words: "Eagerly now, Poseidon, do thou aid the Danaans, and give them glory for a little space, while yet Zeus sleepeth, for over him have I shed soft slumber, and Hera hath beguiled him to couch in love." . . . And Poseidon led them, the Shaker of the earth, with a dread sword of fine edge in his strong hand, like unto lightning; wherewith it is not permitted that any should mingle in woful war, but fear holds men afar therefrom. But the Trojans on the other side was renowned Hector arraying. Then did they now strain the fiercest strife of war, even dark-haired Poseidon and glorious Hector, one succouring the Trojans, the other with the Argives. And the sea washed up to the huts and ships of the Argives, and they gathered together with a mighty cry. Not so loudly bellows the wave of the sea against the land, stirred up from the deep by the harsh breath of the north wind, nor so loud is the roar of burning fire in the glades of a mountain, when it springs to burn up the forest, nor calls the wind so loudly in the high leafy tresses of the trees, when it rages and roars its loudest, as then was the cry of the Trojans and Achaians, shouting dreadfully as they rushed upon each other.

First glorious Hector cast with his spear at Aias, who was facing him full, and did not miss, striking him where two belts were stretched across his breast, the belt of his shield, and of his silver-studded sword; these guarded his tender flesh. And Hector was enraged because his swift spear had flown vainly from his hand, and he retreated into the throng of his fellows, avoiding Fate. . . . Now the Argives when they saw Hector departed rushed yet the more upon the Trojans, and were mindful of the delight of battle. . . .

Tell me now, ye Muses, that dwell in the mansions of Olympus, who was the first of the Achaians to lift the bloody spoils, when once the renowned Shaker of the earth turned the battle.

Verily it was Aias, son of Telamon, that first wounded Hyrtios, the son of Gyrtias, the leader of the Mysians strong of heart, and Antilochos stripped the spoils from Phalkes and Mermeros, and Meriones slew Morys and Hippotion, and Teukros slew Prothoon and Periphetes, and next Atreus' son wounded in the flank Hyperenor, the shepherd of the host, and the bronze point tore through and let out the entrails, and the soul through the stricken wound fled hastily, and darkness covered his eyes. But most men did Aias slay, the swift-footed son of Oileus, for there was none so speedy of foot as he, to follow when men fled, when Zeus sent terror among them.

BOOK XV

Now when they had sped in flight across the palisade and trench, and many were overcome at the hands of the Danaans, the rest were stayed, and abode beside the chariots in confusion, and pale with terror, and Zeus awoke, on the peaks of Ida, beside Hera of the golden throne. Then he leaped up, and stood, and beheld the Trojans and Achaians, those in flight, and these driving them on from the rear, even the Argives, and among them the prince Poseidon. And Hector he saw lying on the plain, and around him sat his comrades, and he was gasping with difficult breath, and his mind wandering, and was vomiting blood, for it was not the weakest of the Achaians that had smitten him. Beholding him, the father of men and gods had pity on him, and terribly he spoke to Hera, with fierce look: "O thou ill to deal with, Hera, verily it is thy crafty wile that has made noble Hector cease from the fight, and has terrified the host. Nay, but yet I know not whether thou mayst not be the first to reap the fruits of thy cruel treason, and I beat thee with stripes. Dost thou not remember, when thou wert hung from on high, and from thy feet I suspended two anvils, and round thy hands fastened a golden bond that might not be broken? And thou didst hang in the clear air and the clouds, and the gods were wroth in high Olympus, but they could not come round and unloose thee. . . . Of these things will I mind thee again, that thou mayst cease from thy wiles, that thou mayst know if it profit thee at all, the dalliance and the love, wherein thou didst lie with me, when thou hadst come from among the gods, and didst beguile me."

So spake he, and the ox-eyed lady Hera shuddered, and spake unto him winged words, saying: "Let earth now be witness hereto, and wide heaven above, and that falling water of Styx, the greatest oath and the most terrible to the blessed gods, and thine own sacred head, and our own bridal bed, whereby never would I forswear myself, that not by my will does earth-shaking Poseidon trouble the Trojans and Hector, and succour them of the other part. Nay, it is his own soul that urgeth and commandeth him, and he had pity on the Achaians, when he beheld them hard pressed beside the ships. I would even counsel him also to go even where thou, lord of the storm-cloud, mayst lead him."

So spake she, and the father of gods and men smiled, and answering her he spake winged words: "If thou, of a truth, O ox-eyed lady Hera, wouldst hereafter abide of one mind with me among the immortal gods, thereon would Poseidon, howsoever much his wish be contrariwise, quickly turn his mind otherwise, after thy heart and mine. But if indeed thou speakest the truth and soothly, go thou now among the tribes of the gods, and call Iris to come hither, and Apollo, the renowned archer, that Iris may go among the host of mail-clad Achaians and tell Poseidon the prince to cease from the war, and get him unto his own house. But let Phoebus Apollo spur Hector on to the war, and breathe strength into him again, and make him forget his anguish, that now wears down his heart, and drive the Achaians back again, when he hath stirred in them craven fear. Let them flee and fall among the many-benched ships of Achilles son of Peleus, and he shall rouse his own comrade, Patroklos; and him shall renowned Hector slay with the spear, in front of Ilios, after that he has slain many other youths. In wrath therefor shall goodly Achilles slay Hector. From that hour verily will I cause a new pursuit from the ships, that shall endure continually, even until the Achaians take steep Ilios, through the counsels of Athene. But before that hour neither do I cease in my wrath, nor will I suffer any other of the Immortals to help the Danaans there, before I accomplish that desire of the son of Peleus, as I promised him at the first, and confirmed the same

with a nod of my head, on that day when the goddess Thetis clasped my knees, imploring me to honour Achilles, the sacker of cities." . . .

Now the Argives abode them in close ranks, and shrill the cry arose on both sides, and the arrows leaped from the bow-strings, and many spears from stalwart hands, whereof some stood fast in the flesh of young men swift in fight, but many halfway, ere ever they reached the white flesh, stuck in the ground, longing to glut themselves with flesh. Now so long as Phoebus Apollo held the aegis unmoved in his hands, so long the darts smote either side amain, and the folk fell. But when he looked face to face on the Danaans of the swift steeds, and shook the aegis, and himself shouted mightily, he quelled their heart in their breast, and they forgot their impetuous valour. And as when two wild beasts drive in confusion a herd of kine, or a great flock of sheep, in the dark hour of black night, coming swiftly on them when the herdsman is not by, even so were the Achaians terror-stricken and strengthless, for Apollo sent a panic among them, but still gave renown to the Trojans and Hector. . . .

But the Trojans, when they heard the thunder of aegis-bearing Zeus, rushed yet the more eagerly upon the Argives, and were mindful of the joy of battle. And as when a great wave of the wide sea sweeps over the bulwarks of a ship, the might of the wind constraining it, which chiefly swells the waves, even so did the Trojans with a great cry bound over the wall, and drave their horses on, and at the hindmost row of the ships were fighting hand to hand with double-pointed spears, the Trojans from the chariots, but the Achaians climbing up aloft, from the black ships with long pikes that they had lying in the ships for battle at sea, jointed pikes shod at the head with bronze.

Now Patroklos, as long as the Achaians and Trojans were fighting about the wall, without the swift ships, sat in the hut of kindly Eurypylos, and was making him glad with talk, and on his cruel wound was laying herbs, to medicine his dark pain. But when he perceived the Trojans rushing over the wall, and the din and flight of the Danaans began, then did he groan, and smote his two thighs with his hands flatlings, and sorrowing he spake: "Eurypylos, no longer at all may I abide with thee here, though great thy need, for verily a great strife has arisen. But thee let thy squire comfort, while I hasten to Achilles, that I may urge him to join the battle. Who knows but with god's help I may arouse his spirit with my persuasion? and a good thing is the persuasion of a friend." . . .

BOOK XVI

So they were warring round the well-timbered ship, but Patroklos drew near Achilles, shepherd of the host, and he shed warm tears, even as a fountain of dark water that down a steep cliff pours its cloudy stream. And noble swift-footed Achilles when he beheld him was grieved for his sake, and accosted him, and spake winged words, saying: "Wherefore weepest thou, Patroklos, like a fond little maid, that runs by her mother's side, and bids her mother take her up, snatching at her gown, and hinders her in her going, and tearfully looks at her, till the mother takes her up? like her, Patroklos, dost thou let fall soft tears." . . .

But with a heavy groan didst thou speak unto him, O knight Patroklos: "O Achilles, son of Peleus, far the bravest of the Achaians, be not wroth, seeing that so great calamity has beset the Achaians. For verily all of them that aforetime were the best are lying among the ships, smitten and wounded. Smitten is the son of Tydeus, strong Diomedes, and wounded is Odysseus, spearman renowned, and Agamemnon. And about them the leeches skilled in medicines are busy, healing their wounds, but thou art hard to reconcile, Achilles. Never then may such wrath take hold of me as that thou nursest; thou brave to the hurting of others. What other man later born shall have profit of thee, if thou dost not ward off base ruin from the Argives? Pitiless that thou art, the knight Peleus was not then thy father, nor Thetis thy mother, but the grey sea bare thee, and the sheer cliffs, so untoward is thy spirit. But if in thy heart thou art shunning some oracle, and thy lady mother hath told thee somewhat from Zeus, yet me do thou send forth quickly, and make the rest of the host of the Myrmidons follow me, if yet any light may arise from me to the Danaans. And give me thy harness to buckle about my shoulders, if perchance the Trojans may take me for thee, and so abstain from battle, and the warlike sons of the Achaians may take breath, wearied as they be, for brief is the breathing in war. And lightly might we that are fresh drive men wearied with the battle back to the citadel, away from the ships and the huts."

So he spake and besought him, in his unwittingness, for truly it was to be his own evil death and fate that he prayed for. Then to him in great heaviness spake swift-footed Achilles: "Ah me, Patroklos of the seed of Zeus, what word hast thou spoken? Neither take I heed of any oracle that I wot of, nor yet has my lady mother told me somewhat from Zeus, but this dread sorrow comes upon my heart and spirit, from the hour that a man wishes to rob me who am his equal, and to take away my prize, for that he excels me in power. A dread sorrow to me is this, after all the toils that my heart hath endured. . . . But we will let bygones be bygones. No man may be angry of heart for ever, yet verily I said that I would not cease from my wrath, until

Achilles binding the wounds of his friend Patroklos.

that time when to mine own ships should come the war-cry and the battle. But do thou on thy shoulders my famous harness, and lead the war-loving Myrmidons to the fight, if indeed the dark cloud of the Trojans hath mightily surrounded the ships, and if the Argives are given back to the shore of the sea, holding but a narrow space of land, and the whole town of Troy hath come boldly against them. Yea, for they behold not the vizor of my helm shining hard at hand; swiftly would they flee, and fill the watercourses with dead, if mighty Agamemnon had been but kindly to me,—but now are they warring round the camp. For not in the hands of Diomedes, the son of Tydeus, rageth the spear, to ward off destruction from the Danaans. Neither as yet have I heard the voice of the son of Atreus, shouting out of his hated mouth, but of Hector the slayer of men doth the voice burst around me, as he calls on the Trojans, and they with their cries fill all the plain, overcoming the Achaians in the battle. But even so, Patroklos, to ward off destruction from the ships, do thou fall on mightily, lest they even burn the ships with blazing fire, and take away our desired return. But do thou obey, even as I shall put into thy mind the end of my commandment, that in my sight thou mayst win great honour and fame of all the Danaans, and they may give me back again the fairest maiden, and thereto add splendid gifts. When thou hast driven them from the ships, return, and even if the loud-thundering lord of Hera grant thee to win glory, yet long not thou apart from me to fight with the war-loving Trojans; thereby wilt thou minish mine honour. Neither do thou, exulting in war and strife, and slaying the Trojans, lead on toward Ilios, lest one of the eternal gods from Olympus come against thee; right dearly doth Apollo the Far-darter love them. Nay, return back when thou hast brought safety to the ships, and suffer the rest to fight along the plain. For would, O father Zeus, and Athene, and Apollo, would that not one of all the Trojans might escape death, nor one of the Argives, but that we twain might avoid destruction, that alone we might undo the sacred coronal of Troy." . . .

So spake he, while Patroklos was harnessing him in shining bronze. His goodly greaves, fitted with silver clasps, he first girt round his legs, and next did on around his breast the well-dight starry corslet of the swift-footed son of Aiakos. And round his shoulders he cast a sword of bronze, with studs of silver, and next took the great and mighty shield, and on his proud head set a well-wrought helm with a horsehair crest, and terribly nodded the crest from above. Then seized he two strong lances that fitted his grasp, only he took not the spear of the noble son of Aiakos, heavy, and huge, and stalwart, that none other of the Achaians could wield, but Achilles alone availed to wield it. . . .

Meanwhile Achilles went and harnessed all the Myrmidons in the huts with armour, and they gathered like ravening wolves with strength in their hearts unspeakable, that have slain a great horned stag in the hills and rend him piecemeal; and all their jaws are red with blood, and in a herd they go, to lap with their thin tongues the surface of the dark water in a dusky well, belching out the blood of the slaughter, their heart steadfast within their breasts, and their bellies swollen, even so hastened the leaders and chiefs of the Myrmidons. . . . They that were armed about the high-hearted Patroklos marched forward till they rushed in their pride on the Trojans. And straightway they poured forth like wasps that have their dwelling by the wayside, and that boys are ever wont to vex, always tormenting them in their nests beside the way in childish sport, and a common evil they make for many. And they, if ever some wayfaring man passing by stir them unwittingly, fly forth every one of them, with a heart of valour, and each defends his children; with heart and spirit like theirs the Myrmidons poured out now from the ships, and a cry arose unquenchable, and Patroklos called on his comrades, shouting aloud: "Myrmidons, ye comrades of Achilles son of Peleus, be men, my friends, and be mindful of your impetuous valour, that so we may win honour for the son of Peleus, that is far the bravest of the Argives by the ships, and whose close-fighting squires are the best. And let wide-ruling Agamemnon the son of Atreus learn his own blindness of heart, in that he nothing honoured the best of the Achaians."

So spake he, and aroused each man's heart and courage, and all in a mass they fell on the Trojans, and the ships around echoed wondrously to the cry

of the Achaians. But when the Trojans beheld the strong son of Menoitios, himself and his squire, shining in their armour, the heart was stirred in all of them, and the companies wavered, for they deemed that by the ships the swift-footed son of Peleus had cast away his wrath, and chosen reconcilement: then each man glanced round, to see where he might flee sheer destruction. . . .

And as when from Olympus a cloud fares into heaven, from the sacred air, when Zeus spreadeth forth the tempest, even so from the ships came the war-cry and the rout, nor in order due did they cross the ditch again. But his swift-footed horses bare Hector forth with his arms, and he left the host of Troy, whom the delved trench restrained against their will. And in the trench did many swift steeds that draw the car break the fore-part of the pole, and leave the chariots of their masters.

But Patroklos followed after, crying fiercely to the Danaans, and full of evil will against the Trojans, while they with cries and flight filled all the ways, for they were scattered, and on high the storm of dust was scattered below the clouds, and the whole-hooved horses strained back towards the city, away from the ships and the huts. . . . And the heart of Patroklos urged him against Hector, for he was eager to smite him, but his swift steeds bore Hector forth and away. And even as beneath a tempest the whole black earth is oppressed, on an autumn day, when Zeus pours forth rain most vehemently, being in wrath and anger against men, who judge crooked judgments forcefully in the assembly, and drive justice out, and reck not of the vengeance of the gods, and all their rivers run full, and many a scaur the torrents tear away, and down to the dark sea they rush headlong from the hills, roaring mightily, and minished are the works of men, even so mighty was the roar of the Trojan horses as they ran. . . .

Then would the sons of the Achaians have taken high-gated Troy, by the hands of Patroklos, for around and before him he raged with the spear, but that Phoebus Apollo stood on the well-builded wall, with baneful thoughts towards Patroklos, and succouring the Trojans. Thrice clomb Patroklos on the corner of the lofty wall, and thrice did Apollo force him back and smote the shining shield with his immortal hands. But when for the fourth time he came on like a god, then cried far-darting Apollo terribly, and spake winged words: "Give back, Patroklos of the seed of Zeus! Not beneath thy spear is it fated that the city of the valiant Trojans shall fall, nay nor beneath Achilles, a man far better than thou."

So spake he, and Patroklos retreated far back, avoiding the wrath of far-darting Apollo. But Hector within the Skaian gates was restraining his whole-hooved horses, pondering whether he should drive again into the din and fight, or should call unto the host to gather to the wall. While thus he was thinking, Phoebus Apollo stood by him in the guise of a young man and a strong, Asios, who was the mother's brother of horse-taming Hector, being own brother of Hekabe, and son of Dymas, who dwelt in Phrygia, on the streams of Sangarios. In his guise spake Apollo, son of Zeus, to Hector: "Hector, wherefore dost thou cease from fight? It doth not behove thee. Would that I were as much stronger than thou as I am weaker, thereon quickly shouldst thou stand aloof from war to thy hurt. But come turn against Patroklos thy strong-hooved horses, if perchance thou mayst slay him, and Apollo give thee glory."

So spake the god, and went back again into the moil of men, and sent a dread panic among the Argives, but to the Trojans and Hector gave he renown. And Hector let the other Argives be, and slew none of them, but against Patroklos he turned his strong-hooved horses, and Patroklos on the other side leaped from his chariot to the ground, with a spear in his left hand, and in his other hand grasped a shining jagged stone, that his hand covered. Firmly he planted himself and hurled it, nor long did he shrink from his foe, nor was his cast in vain, but he struck Kebriones the charioteer of Hector, on the brow with the sharp stone, as he held the reins of the horses. Both his brows the stone drave together, and his bone held not, but his eyes fell to the ground in the dust, there, in front of his feet. Then he, like a diver, fell from the well-wrought car, and his spirit left his bones. . . .

With ill design against the Trojans, Patroklos rushed upon them. Three times then rushed he on, peer of swift Ares, shouting terribly, and thrice he slew nine men. But when the fourth time he sped on like a god, thereon to thee, Patroklos, did the end of life appear, for Phoebus met thee in the strong battle, in dreadful wise. And Patroklos was not ware of him coming through the press, for hidden in thick mist did he meet him, and stood behind him, and smote his back and broad shoulders with a downstroke of his hand, and his eyes were dazed. And from his head Phoebus Apollo smote the helmet that rolled rattling away with a din beneath the hooves of the horses, the helm with upright socket, and the crests were defiled with blood and dust. Not of old was it suffered that the helm with horse-hair crest should be defiled with dust, nay, but it kept the head and beautiful face of a man divine, even of Achilles. But as then Zeus gave it to Hector, to bear on his head, yet was destruction near him. And all the long-shadowed spear was shattered in the hands of Patroklos, the spear great and heavy and strong, and sharp, while from his shoulders the tasselled shield with the baldric fell to the ground.

And the prince Apollo, son of Zeus, loosed his corslet, and blindness seized his heart and his shining limbs were unstrung, and he stood in amaze, and at close quarters from behind a Dardanian smote him on the back, between the shoulders, with a sharp spear, even Euphorbos, son of Panthoös, who excelled them of his age in casting the spear, and in horsemanship, and in speed of foot. Even thus, verily, had he cast down twenty men from their chariots, though then first had he come with his car to learn the lesson of war. He it was that first smote a dart into thee, knightly Patroklos, nor overcome thee, but ran back again and mingled with the throng, first drawing forth from the flesh his ashen spear, nor did he abide the onset of Patroklos, unarmed as he was, in the strife. But Patroklos, being overcome by the stroke of the god, and by the spear, gave ground, and retreated to the host of his comrades, avoiding Fate. But Hector, when he beheld great-hearted Patroklos give ground, being smitten with the keen bronze, came nigh unto him through the ranks, and wounded him with a spear, in the lowermost part of the belly, and drave the bronze clean through. And he fell with a crash, and sorely grieved the host of Achaians. And as when a lion hath overcome in battle an untiring boar, they twain fighting with high heart on the crests of a hill, about a little well, and both are desirous to drink, and the lion hath by force overcome the boar that draweth difficult breath; so after that he had slain many did Hector son of Priam take the life away from the strong son of Menoitios, smiting him at close quarters with the spear; and boasting over him he spake winged words: "Patroklos, surely thou saidst that thou wouldst sack my town, and from Trojan women take away the day of freedom, and bring them in ships to thine own dear country: fool! nay, in front of these were the swift horses of Hector straining their speed for the fight; and myself in wielding the spear excel among the war-loving Trojans, even I who ward from them the day of destiny: but thee shall vultures here devour. Ah, wretch, surely Achilles for all his valour, availed thee not, who straitly charged thee as thou camest, he abiding there, saying, 'Come not to me, Patroklos lord of steeds, to the hollow ships, till thou hast torn the gory doublet of man-slaying Hector about his breast;' so, surely, he spake to thee, and persuaded the wits of thee in thy witlessness."

Then faintly didst thou answer him, knightly Patroklos: "Boast greatly, as now, Hector, for to thee have Zeus, son of Kronos, and Apollo given the victory, who lightly have subdued me; for themselves stripped my harness from my shoulders. But if twenty such as thou had encountered me, here had they all perished, subdued beneath my spear. But me had ruinous Fate and the son of Leto slain, and of men Euphorbos, but thou art the third in my slaying. But another thing will I tell thee, and do thou lay it up in thy heart; verily thou thyself art not long to live, but already doth Death stand hard by thee, and strong Fate, that thou art to be subdued by the hands of noble Achilles, of the seed of Aiakos."

Even as so he spake the end of death overshadowed him. And his soul, fleeting from his limbs, went down to the house of Hades, wailing its own doom, leaving manhood and youth.

Then renowned Hector spake to him even in his death: "Patroklos, wherefore to me dost thou prophesy sheer destruction? who knows but that Achilles, the child of fair-tressed Thetis, will first be smitten by my spear, and lose his life?" . . .

BOOK XVIII

Thus fought the rest in the likeness of blazing fire, while to Achilles came Antilochos, a messenger fleet of foot. Him found he in front of his ships of upright horns, boding in his soul the things which even now were accomplished. And sore troubled he spake to his great heart: "Ay me, wherefore again are the flowing-haired Achaians flocking to the ships and flying in rout over the plain? May the gods not have wrought against me the grievous fears at my heart, even as my mother revealed and told me that while I am yet alive the best man of the Myrmidons must by deed of the men of Troy forsake the light of the sun. Surely now must Menoitios' valiant son be dead—foolhardy! surely I bade him when he should have beaten off the fire of the foe to come back to the ships nor with Hector fight amain."

While thus he held debate in his heart and soul, there drew nigh unto him noble Nestor's son, shedding hot tears, and spake his grievous tidings: "Ay me, wise Peleus' son, very bitter tidings must thou hear, such as I would had never been. Fallen is Patroklos, and they are fighting around his body, naked, for his armour is held by Hector of the glancing helm."

Thus spake he, and a black cloud of grief enwrapped Achilles, and with both hands he took dark dust and poured it over his head and defiled his comely face, and on his fragrant doublet black ashes fell. And himself in the dust lay mighty and mightily fallen, and with his own hands tore and marred his hair. And the handmaidens, whom Achilles and Patroklos took captive, cried aloud in the grief of their hearts, and ran forth around valiant Achilles, and all beat on their breasts with their hands, and the knees of each of them were unstrung. And Antilochos on the other side wailed and shed tears, holding Achilles' hands while he groaned in his noble heart, for he feared lest he should cleave his throat with the sword. Then terribly moaned Achilles; and his lady mother heard him as she sat in the depths of the sea beside her ancient sire. And thereon she uttered a cry, ". . . I will go, that I may look upon my dear child, and learn what sorrow hath come to him though he abide aloof from the war."

Thus spake she and left the cave; and the nymphs went with her weeping, and around them the surge of the sea was sundered. And when they came to deep-soiled Troy-land they went up upon the shore in order, where the ships of the Myrmidons were drawn up thickly around fleet Achilles. And as he groaned heavily his lady mother stood beside him, and with a shrill cry clasped the head of her child, and spake unto him winged words of lamentation: "My child, why weepest thou? what sorrow hath come to thy heart? Tell it forth, hide it not. One thing at least hath been accomplished of Zeus according to the prayer thou madest, holding up to him thy hands, that the sons of the Achaians should all be pent in at the ships, through lack of thee, and should suffer hateful things."

Then groaning heavily spake unto her Achilles fleet of foot: "My mother, that prayer truly hath the Olympian accomplished for me. But what delight have I therein, since my dear comrade is dead, Patroklos, whom I honoured above all my comrades as it were my very self? Him have I lost, and Hector that slew him hath stripped from him the armour great and fair, a wonder to behold, that the gods gave to Peleus a splendid gift, on the day when they laid thee in the bed of a mortal man. . . . Straightway may I die, since I might not succour my comrade at his slaying. He hath fallen afar from his country and lacked my help in his sore need. Now therefore, since I go not back to my dear native land, neither have at all been succour to Patroklos nor to all my other comrades that have been slain by noble Hector, but I sit beside my ships a profitless burden of the earth, I that in war am such an one as is none else of the mail-clad Achaians, though in council are others better—may strife perish utterly among gods and men, and wrath that stirreth even a wise man to be vexed, wrath that far sweeter than trickling honey waxeth like smoke in the breasts of men, even as I was wroth even now against Agamemnon king of men. But bygones will we let be, for all our pain, curbing the heart in our breasts under necessity. Now go I forth, that I may light on the destroyer of him I loved, on Hector; then will I accept my death whensoever Zeus willeth to accomplish it and the other immortal gods. . . . Hold not me then from the battle in thy love, for thou shalt not prevail with me."

Then Thetis the silver-footed goddess answered him saying: "Yea verily, my child, no blame is in this, that thou ward sheer destruction from thy comrades in their distress. But thy fair glittering armour of bronze is held among the Trojans. Hector of the glancing helm beareth it on his shoulders in triumph, yet not for long, I ween, shall he glory therein, for death is hard anigh him. But thou go not yet down into the mellay of war until thou see me with thine eyes come hither. In the morning will I return, at the coming up of the sun, bearing fair armour from the king Hephaistos." . . .

Thus spake she, and they forthwith went down beneath the surge of the sea. And the silver-footed goddess Thetis went on to Olympus that she might bring noble armour to her son.

So her unto Olympus her feet bore. But the Achaians with terrible cries were fleeing before man-slaying Hector till they came to the ships and to the Hellespont. Nor might the well-greaved Achaians drag the corpse of Patroklos Achilles' squire out of the darts, for now again overtook him the host and the horses of Troy, and Hector son of Priam, in might as it were a flame of fire. Thrice did glorious Hector seize him from behind by the feet, resolved to drag him away, and mightily called upon the men of Troy. . . . And now would he have won the body and gained renown unspeakable, had not fleet wind-footed Iris come speeding from Olympus with a message to the son of Peleus to array him, unknown of Zeus and the other gods, for Hera sent her. And she stood anigh and spake to him winged words: "Rouse thee, son of Peleus, of all men most redoubtable! Succour Patroklos, for whose body is terrible battle afoot before the ships. There slay they one another, these guarding the dead corpse, while the men of Troy are fierce to hale him unto windy Ilios, and chiefliest noble Hector is fain to drag him, and his heart biddeth him fix the head on the stakes of the wall when he hath sundered it from the tender neck. But arise, lie thus no longer! let awe enter thy heart to forbid that Patroklos become the sport of dogs of Troy. Thine were the shame if he go down mangled amid the dead."

And Achilles fleet of foot made answer to her and said: "And how may I go into the fray? The Trojans hold my arms; and my dear mother bade me forbear to array me until I behold her with my eyes returned, for she promised to bring fair armour from Hephaistos. Other man know I none whose noble armour I might put on, save it were the shield of Aias Telamon's son. But himself, I ween, is in the fore-front of the press, dealing death with his spear around Patroklos dead."

Then again spake unto him wind-footed fleet Iris: "Well are we also aware that thy noble armour is held from thee. But go forth unto the trench as thou art and show thyself to the men of Troy, if haply they will shrink back and refrain them from battle, and the warlike sons of the Achaians take breath [amid their toil, for small breathing-time is in the thick of fight]."

Thus spake fleet-footed Iris and went her way. But Achilles dear to Zeus arose, and around his strong shoulders Athene cast her tasselled aegis, and around his head the bright goddess set a crown of a golden cloud, and kindled therefrom a blazing flame. And as when a smoke issueth from a city and riseth up into the upper air, from an island afar off that foes beleaguer, while the others from their city fight all day in hateful war,—but with the going down of the sun blaze out the beacon-fires in line, and high aloft rusheth up the glare for dwellers round about to behold, if haply they may come with ships to help in need—thus from the head of Achilles soared that blaze toward the heavens. And he went and stood beyond the wall beside the trench, yet mingled not among the Achaians, for he minded the wise bidding of his mother. There stood he and shouted aloud, and afar off Pallas Athene uttered her voice, and spread terror unspeakable among the men of Troy. Clear as the voice of a clarion when it soundeth by reason of slaughterous foemen that beleaguer a city, so clear rang forth the voice of Aiakides. And when they heard the brazen voice of Aiakides, the souls of all of them were dismayed, and the horses of goodly manes were fain to turn the chariots backward, for they boded anguish in their hearts. And the charioteers were amazed when they saw the unwearying fire blaze fierce on the head of the great-hearted son of Peleus, for the bright-eyed goddess Athene made it blaze. Thrice from over the trench shouted mightily noble Achilles, and thrice were the men of Troy confounded and their proud allies. Yea there and then perished twelve men of their best by their own chariot wheels and spears. But the Achaians with joy drew Patroklos forth of the darts and laid him on a litter, and his dear comrades stood around lamenting him; and among them followed fleet-footed Achilles, shedding hot tears, for his true comrade he saw lying on the bier, mangled by the keen bronze. Him sent he forth with chariot and horses unto the battle, but home again welcomed never more.

Then Hera the ox-eyed queen sent down the unwearying Sun to be gone unwillingly unto the streams of Ocean. So the Sun set, and the noble Achaians made pause from the stress of battle and the hazardous war.

Now the men of Troy on their side when they were come back out of the violent fray loosed their swift horses from the chariots and gathered themselves in assembly or ever they would sup. Upon their feet they stood in the assembly, neither had any man heart to sit, for fear was fallen upon all because Achilles was come forth, after long ceasing from fell battle. Then began to speak among them wise Polydamas, son of Panthoös, for he alone saw before and after. Comrade of Hector was he, and in the same night were both born, but the one in speech was far the best, the other with the spear. So with good intent toward them he made harangue and spake: "Take good heed on both sides, O my friends; for my part I would have ye go up now to the city, nor wait for bright morning on the plain beside the ships, for we are far off from the wall. So long as this man was wroth with noble Agamemnon, so long were the Achaians easier to fight against, ay and I too rejoiced when I couched nigh their swift ships, trusting that we should seize the curved ships for a prey. But now am I sore afraid of the fleet son of Peleus; so exceeding fierce is his heart, he will not choose to abide in the plain where Trojans and Achaians both in the midst share the spirit of war, but the prize he doeth battle for will be our city and our wives. Now go we up to our fastness; hearken unto me, for thus will it be. Now hath divine night stayed the fleet son of Peleus, but if to-morrow full-armed for the onset he shall light upon us abiding here, well shall each know that it is he, for gladly will whosoever fleeth win to sacred Ilios, and many of the men of Troy shall dogs and vultures devour—far be that from my ear. But if, though loth, we hearken unto my words, this night in counsel we shall possess our strength, and the city shall be guarded of her towers and high gates and tall well-polished doors that fit thereon close-shut. But at dawn of day in armour harnessed will we take our stand along the towers. Ill will he fare if he come forth from the ships to fight with us for our wall. Back to his ships shall he betake him when in vain chase he hath given his strong-necked horses their fill of hasting every-whither beneath the town. But within it never will he have heart to force his way, nor ever lay it waste; ere then shall he be devoured of swift dogs."

Then with stern gaze spake unto him Hector of the glancing helm: "Polydamas, no longer to my liking dost thou speak now, in that thou biddest us go back and be pent within the town. Have ye not had your fill already of being pent behind the towers? Of old time all mortal men would tell of this city of Priam for the much gold and bronze thereof, but now are its goodly treasures perished out of its dwellings, and much goods are sold away to Phrygia and pleasant Maionia, since mighty Zeus dealt evilly with us. But now when the son of crooked-counselling Kronos hath given me to win glory at the ships and to pen the Achaians beside the sea, no longer, fond man, put forth such counsels among the folk. No man of Troy will hearken unto thee, I will not suffer it. But come let us all be persuaded as I shall say. Sup now in your ranks throughout the host, and keep good ward, and each watch in his place. And whoso of the Trojans is grieved beyond measure for his goods, let him gather them together and give them to the people to consume in common, for it is better they have joy thereof than the Achaians. Then at dawn of day in armour harnessed at the hollow ships we will arouse keen war. What though in very truth noble Achilles be arisen beside the ships, ill shall he fare, if he will have it so. I at least will not flee from him out of the dread-sounding war, but full facing him will I stand, to try whether he win great victory, or haply I. The war-god is alike to all and a slayer of him that would slay."

Thus Hector spake, and the men of Troy applauded with fond hearts, for Pallas Athene bereft them of their wit. And they gave assent to the ill advising of Hector, but none hearkened to Polydamas who devised good counsel. Then they supped throughout the host; but the Achaians all night made moan in lamentation for Patroklos. And first of them in the loud lamentation was the son of Peleus, laying upon the breast of his comrade his man-slaying hands and moaning very sore, even as a deep-bearded lion whose whelps some stag-hunter hath snatched away out of a deep wood. . . .

But Thetis of the silver feet came unto the house of Hephaistos, imperishable, starlike, far seen among the dwellings of Immortals, a house of bronze, wrought by the crook-footed god himself. Him found she sweating in toil and busy about his bellows. . . . The bellows he set away from the fire, and gathered all his gear wherewith he worked into a silver chest; and with a sponge he wiped his face and hands and sturdy neck and shaggy breast, and did on his doublet, and took a stout staff and went forth limping . . . and he gat him haltingly near to where Thetis was, and set him on a bright seat, and clasped her hand in his and spake and called her by her name: "Wherefore, long-robed Thetis, comest thou to our house, honoured that thou art and dear? No frequent comer art thou hitherto. Speak what thou hast at heart; my soul is fain to accomplish it, if accomplish it I can, and if it be appointed for accomplishment."

Then answered unto him Thetis shedding tears: "Hephaistos, hath there verily been any of all goddesses in Olympus that hath endured so many grievous sorrows at heart as are the woes that Kronian Zeus hath laid upon me above all others? . . . A son he gave me to bear and nourish, the chief of heroes, and he shot up like a young branch. Like a plant in a very fruitful field I reared him and sent him forth on beaked ships to Ilios to fight against the men of Troy, but never again shall I welcome him back to his home within the house of Peleus. And while he yet liveth in my sight and beholdeth the light of the sun, he sorroweth, neither can I help him any whit though I go unto him. . . . Therefore now come I a suppliant unto thy knees, if haply thou be willing to give my short-lived son shield and helmet, and goodly greaves fitted with ankle-pieces, and cuirass. For the armour that he had erst, his trusty comrade lost when he fell beneath the men of Troy; and my son lieth on the earth with anguish in his soul."

Then made answer unto her the lame god of great renown: "Be of good courage, let not these things trouble thy heart. Would that so might I avail to hide him far from dolorous death, when dread fate cometh upon him, as surely shall goodly armour be at his need, such as all men afterward shall marvel at, whosoever may behold."

Thus saying he left her there and went unto his bellows and turned them upon the fire and bade them work. And the bellows, twenty in all, blew on the crucibles, sending deft blasts on every side, now to aid his labour and now anon howsoever Hephaistos willed and the work went on. And he threw bronze that weareth not into the fire, and tin and precious gold and silver, and next he set on an anvil-stand a great anvil, and took in his hand a sturdy hammer, and in the other he took the tongs.

First fashioned he a shield great and strong, adorning it all over, and set thereto a shining rim, triple, bright-glancing, and therefrom a silver baldric. Five were the folds of the shield itself; and therein fashioned he much cunning work from his wise heart. . . .

Now when he had wrought the shield great and strong, then wrought he him a corslet brighter than a flame of fire, and he wrought him a massive helmet to fit his brows, goodly and graven, and set thereon a crest of gold, and he wrought him greaves of pliant tin.

So when the renowned lame god had finished all the armour, he took and laid it before the mother of Achilles. Then she like a falcon sprang down from snowy Olympus, bearing from Hephaistos the glittering arms.

BOOK XIX

Now Morning saffron-robed arose from the streams of Ocean to bring light to gods and men, and Thetis came to the ships, bearing his gift from the god. Her dear son she found fallen about Patroklos and uttering loud lament; and round him many of his company made moan. And the bright goddess stood beside him in their midst, and clasped her hand in his and spake and called upon his name: "My child, him who lieth here we must let be, for all our pain, for by the will of gods from the beginning was he brought low. But thou take from Hephaistos arms of pride, arms passing goodly, such as no man on his shoulders yet hath borne."

Thus spake the goddess and in front of Achilles laid the arms, and they rang all again in their glory.

And awe fell on all the Myrmidons, nor dared any to gaze thereon, for they were awe-stricken. But when Achilles looked thereon, then came fury upon him the more, and his eyes blazed terribly forth as it were a flame beneath their lids: glad was he as he held in his hands that splendid gift of a god. But when he had satisfied his soul in gazing on the glory of the arms, straightway to his mother spake he winged words: "My mother, the arms the god has given are such as it beseemeth that the work of Immortals should be, and that no mortal man should have wrought. Now therefore will I arm me in them, but I have grievous fear lest meantime on the gashed wounds of Menotios' valiant son flies light and breed worms therein, and defile his corpse—for the life is slain out of him—and so all his flesh shall rot."

Then answered him Thetis, goddess of the silver feet: "Child, have no care for this within thy mind. I will see to ward from him the cruel tribes of flies which prey on men slain in fight: for even though he lie till a whole year's course be run, yet his flesh shall be sound continually, or better even than now. But call thou the Achaian warriors to the place of assembly, and unsay thy wrath against Agamemnon shepherd of the host, and then arm swiftly for battle, and clothe thee with thy strength."

Thus saying she filled him with adventurous might, while on Patroklos she shed ambrosia and red nectar through his nostrils, that his flesh might abide the same continually.

But noble Achilles went down the beach of the sea, crying his terrible cry, and roused the Achaian warriors. . . . And last came Agamemnon king of men, with his wound upon him, for him too in the stress of battle Koön Antenor's son had wounded with his bronze-tipped spear. But when all the Achaians were gathered, then uprose fleet-footed Achilles and spake in their midst: "Son of Atreus, was this in any wise the better way for both thee and me, what time with grief at our hearts we waxed fierce in soul-devouring strife for the sake of a girl? Would that Artemis had slain her with her arrow at the ships, on the day whereon I took her to me, when I had spoiled Lyrnessos; so should not then so many Achaians have bitten the wide earth beneath their enemies' hands, by reason of my exceeding wrath. It hath been well for Hector and the Trojans, but the Achaians I think shall long remember the strife that was betwixt thee and me. But bygones will we let be, for all our pain, and curb under necessity the spirit within our breasts. I now will stay my anger: it beseems me not implacably for ever to be wroth; but come rouse speedily to the fight the flowing-haired Achaians, that I may go forth against the men of Troy and put them yet again to the proof, if they be fain to couch hard by the ships. Methinks that some among them shall be glad to rest their knees when they are fled out of the fierceness of the battle, and from before our spear."

He spake, and the well-greaved Achaians rejoiced that the great-hearted son of Peleus had made renouncement of his wrath. Then among them spake Agamemnon king of men, speaking from the place where he sat, not arisen to stand forth in their midst: "O Danaan friends and heroes, men of Ares' company, seemly is it to listen to him who standeth up to speak, nor behoveth it to break in upon his words: even toward a skilled man that were hard. For amid the uproar of many men how should one listen, or yet speak? even the clearest-voiced speech is marred. To the son of Peleus I will declare myself, but ye other Argives give heed, and each mark well my word. Oft have the Achaians spoken thus to me, and upbraided me; but it is not I who am the cause, but Zeus and Destiny and Erinys that walketh in the darkness, who put into my soul fierce madness on the day when in the assembly I, even I, bereft Achilles of his meed. What could I do? it is God who accomplisheth all. . . . But since thus blinded was I, and Zeus bereft me of my wit, fain am I to make amends, and recompense manifold for the wrong. Only arise thou to the battle and rouse the rest of the host. Gifts am I ready to offer, even all that noble Odysseus went yesterday to promise in thy hut. So, if thou wilt, stay a while, though eager, from battle, and squires shall take the gifts from my ship and carry them to thee, that thou mayest see that what I give sufficeth thee."

Then answered him Achilles swift of foot: "Most noble son of Atreus, Agamemnon king of men, for the gifts, to give them as it beseemeth, if so thou wilt, or to withhold, is in thy choice. But now let us bethink us of battle with all speed; this is no time to dally here with subtleties, for a great work is yet undone. Once more must Achilles be seen in the forefront of the battle, laying waste with his brazen spear the battalions of the men of Troy. Thereof let each of you think as he fighteth with his man.". . .

Thus he spake and dispersed the assembly with all speed. The rest were scattered each to his own ship, but the great-hearted Myrmidons took up the gifts, and bare them to the ship of godlike Achilles. And they laid them in the huts and set the women there, and gallant squires drave the horses among their troop. . . .

BOOK XX

Now for so long as gods were afar from mortal men, so long waxed the Achaians glorious, for that Achilles was come forth among them, and his long ceasing from grim battle was at an end. And the Trojans were smitten with sore trembling in the limbs of every one of them, in terror when they beheld the son of Peleus, fleet of foot, blazing in his arms, peer of man-slaying Ares. But when among the mellay of men the Olympians were come down, then leapt up in her might Strife, rouser of hosts, then sent forth Athene a cry, now standing by the hollowed trench without the wall, and now on the echoing shores she shouted aloud. And a shout uttered Ares against her, terrible as the blackness of the storm, now from the height of the city to the Trojans calling clear, or again along Simois shore over Kallikolonë he sped.

So urged the blessed gods both hosts to battle, then themselves burst into fierce war. And terribly thundered the father of gods and men from heaven above; and from beneath Poseidon made the vast earth shake and the steep mountain tops. Then trembled all the spurs of many-fountained Ida, and all her crests, and the city of the Trojans, and the ships of the Achaians. And the Lord of the Underworld, Aïdoneus, had terror in hell, and leapt from his throne in that terror and cried aloud, lest the world be cloven above him by Poseidon, Shaker of earth, and his dwelling-place be laid bare to mortals and immortals—grim halls, and vast, and lothly to the gods. So loud the roar rose of that battle of gods. For against King Poseidon stood Phoebus Apollo with his winged arrows, and against Enyalios stood Athene, bright-eyed goddess, and against Hera she of the golden shafts and echoing chase, even archer Artemis, sister of the Far-darter.

Thus gods with gods were matched. Meanwhile Achilles yearned above all to meet Hector, son of Priam, in the fray; for with that blood chiefliest his spirit bade him sate Ares, stubborn lord of war. . . .

BOOK XXII

. . . Thus toward the city he was gone in pride of heart, rushing like some victorious horse in a chariot, that runneth lightly at full speed over the plain; so swiftly plied Achilles in his feet and knees. Him the old man Priam first beheld as he sped across the plain, blazing as the star that cometh forth at harvest-time, and plain seen his rays shine forth amid the host of stars in the darkness of night, the star whose name men call Orion's Dog. Brightest of all is he, yet for an evil sign is he set, and bringeth much fever upon hapless men. Even so on Achilles' breast the bronze gleamed as he ran. And the old man cried aloud and beat upon his head with his hands, raising them on high, and with a cry called aloud beseeching his dear son; for he before the gates was standing, all hot for battle with Achilles. And the old man spake piteously unto him, stretching forth his hands: "Hector, beloved son, I pray thee await not this man alone with none beside thee, lest thou quickly meet thy doom, slain by the son of Peleus, since he is mightier far, a merciless man. Would the gods loved him even as do I! then quickly would dogs and vultures devour him on the field—thereby would cruel pain go from my heart—the man who hath bereft me of many valiant sons, slaying them and selling them captive into far-off isles. . . . Nay, come within the wall, my child, that thou preserve the men and women of Troy, neither give great triumph to the son of Peleus, and be thyself bereft of sweet life. Have compassion also on me, the helpless one, who still can feel, ill-fated; whom the father, Kronos' son, will bring to nought by a grievous doom in the path of old age, having seen full many ills, his sons perishing and his daughters carried away captive, and his chambers laid waste and infant children hurled to the ground in terrible war, and his sons' wives dragged away by the ruinous hands of the Achaians. Myself then last of all at the street door will ravening dogs tear, when some one by stroke or throw of the sharp bronze hath bereft my limbs of life—even the dogs I reared in my halls about my table and to guard my door, which then having drunk my blood, maddened at heart shall lie in the gateway. A young man all beseemeth, even to be slain in war, to be torn by the sharp bronze and lie on the field; though he be dead yet is all honourable to him, whate'er be seen: but when dogs defile the hoary head and hoary beard and the secret parts of an old man slain, this is the most piteous thing that cometh upon hapless men."

Thus spake the old man, and grasped his hoary hairs, plucking them from his head, but he persuaded not Hector's soul. Then his mother in her turn wailed tearfully, loosening the folds of her robe, while with the other hand she showed her breast; and through her tears spake to him winged words: "Hector, my child, have regard unto this bosom and pity me, if ever I gave thee consolation of my breast. Think of it, dear child, and from this side of the wall drive back the foe, nor stand in front to meet him. He is merciless; if he slay thee it will not be on a bed that I or thy wife wooed with many gifts shall bewail thee, my own dear child, but far away from us by the ships of the Argives will swift dogs devour thee."

Thus they with wailing spake to their dear son, beseeching him sore, yet they persuaded not Hector's soul, but he stood awaiting Achilles as he drew nigh in giant might. As a serpent of the mountains upon his den awaiteth a man, having fed on evil poisons, and fell wrath hath entered into him, and terribly he glareth as he coileth himself about his den, so Hector with courage unquenchable gave not back, leaning his shining shield against a jutting tower. Then sore troubled he spake to his great heart: "Ay me, if I go within the gates and walls, Polydamas will be first to bring reproach against me, since he bade me lead the Trojans to the city during this ruinous night, when noble Achilles arose. But

I regarded him not, yet surely it had been better far. And now that I have undone the host by my wantonness, I am ashamed before the men of Troy and women of trailing robes, lest at any time some worse man than I shall say: 'Hector by trusting his own might undid the host.' So will they speak; then to me would it be better far to face Achilles and either slay him and go home, or myself die gloriously before the city. Or what if I lay down my bossy shield and my stout helm, and lean my spear against the wall, and go of myself to meet noble Achilles and promise him that Helen, and with her all possessions that Alexandros brought in hollow ships to Troy, the beginning of strife, we will give to the sons of Atreus to take away, and therewithal to divide in half with the Achaians all else that this city holdeth: and if thereafter I obtain from the Trojans an oath of the Elders that they will hide nothing but divide all in twain [whatever wealth the pleasant city hold within]? But wherefore doth my heart debate thus? I might come unto him and he would not pity or regard me at all, but presently slay me unarmed as, it were but a woman, if I put off my armour. No time is it now to dally with him from oak-tree or from rock, like youth with maiden, as youth and maiden hold dalliance one with another. Better is it to join battle with all speed: let us know upon which of us twain the Olympian shall bestow renown."

Thus pondered he as he stood, but nigh on him came Achilles, brandishing from his right shoulder the Pelian ash, his terrible spear; and all around the bronze on him flashed like the gleam of blazing fire or of the Sun as he ariseth. And trembling seized Hector as he was aware of him, nor endured he to abide in his place, but left the gates behind him and fled in fear. And the son of Peleus darted after him, trusting in his swift feet. As a falcon upon the mountains, swiftest of winged things, swoopeth fleetly after a trembling dove; and she before him fleëth, while he with shrill screams hard at hand still darteth at her, for his heart urgeth him to seize her; so Achilles in hot haste flew straight for him, and Hector fled beneath the Trojans' wall, and plied swift knees. They past the watch-place and wind-waved wild fig-tree sped ever, away from under the wall, along the waggon-track, and came to the two fair-flowing springs, where two fountains rise that feed deep-eddying Skamandros. The one floweth with warm water, and smoke goeth up therefrom around as it were from a blazing fire, while the other even in summer floweth forth like cold hail or snow or ice that water formeth. And there beside the springs are broad washing-troughs hard by, fair troughs of stone, where wives and fair daughters of the men of Troy were wont to wash bright raiment, in the old time of peace, before the sons of the Achaians came. Thereby they ran, he flying, he pursuing. Valiant was the flier but far mightier he who fleetly pursued him. For not for beast of sacrifice or for an ox-hide were they striving, such as are prizes for men's speed of foot, but for the life of horse-taming Hector was their race. And as when victorious whole-hooved horses run rapidly round the turning-points, and some great prize lieth in sight, be it a tripod or a woman, in honour of a man that is dead, so thrice around Priam's city circled those twain with flying feet, and all the gods were gazing on them. Then among them spake first the father of gods and men: "Ay me, a man beloved I see pursued around the wall. My heart is woe for Hector, who hath burnt for me many thighs of oxen amid the crests of many-folded Ida, and other times on the city-height; but now is goodly Achilles pursuing him with swift feet round Priam's town. Come, give your counsel, gods, and devise whether we shall save him from death or now at last slay him, valiant though he be, by the hand of Achilles Peleus' son."

Then to him answered the bright-eyed goddess Athene: "O Father, Lord of the bright lightning and the dark cloud, what is this thou hast said? A man that is a mortal, doomed long ago by fate, wouldst thou redeem back from ill-boding death? Do it, but not all we other gods approve."

And unto her in answer spake cloud-gathering Zeus: "Be of good cheer, Trito-born, dear child: not in full earnest speak I, and I would fain be kind to thee. Do as seemeth good to thy mind, and draw not back."

Thus saying he roused Athene, that already was set thereon, and from the crests of Olympus she darted down.

But after Hector sped fleet Achilles chasing him vehemently. And as when on the mountains a hound hunteth the fawn of a deer, having started it from its covert, through glens and glades, and if it crouch to baffle him under a bush, yet scenting it out the hound runneth constantly until he find it; so Hector baffled not Peleus' fleet-footed son. Oft as he set himself to dart under the well-built walls over against the Dardanian gates, if haply from above they might succour him with darts, so oft would Achilles gain on him and turn him toward the plain, while himself he sped ever on the city-side. And as in a dream one faileth in chase of a flying man—the one faileth in his flight and the other in his chase—so failed Achilles to overtake him in the race, and Hector to escape. And thus would Hector have avoided the visitation of death, had not this time been utterly the last wherein Apollo came nigh to him, who nerved his strength and his swift knees. For to the host did noble Achilles sign with his head, and forbade them to hurl bitter darts against Hector, lest any smiting him should gain renown, and he himself come second. But when the fourth time they had reached the springs, then the Father hung his golden balances, and set therein two lots of dreary death, one of Achilles, one of horse-taming Hector, and held them by the midst and poised. Then Hector's fated day sank down, and fell to the house of Hades, and Phoebus Apollo left him. But to Peleus' son came the bright-eyed goddess Athene, and standing near spake to him winged words: "Now verily, glorious Achilles dear to Zeus, I have hope that we twain shall carry off great glory to the ships for the Achaians, having slain Hector, for all his thirst for fight. No longer is it possible for him to escape us, not even though far-darting Apollo should travail sore, grovelling before the Father, aegis-bearing Zeus. But do thou now stand and take breath, and I will go and persuade this man to confront thee in fight."

Thus spake Athene, and he obeyed, and was glad at heart, and stood leaning on his bronze-pointed ashen-spear. And she left him and came to noble Hector, like unto Deiphobos in shape and in strong voice, and standing near spake to him winged words: "Dear brother, verily fleet Achilles doth thee violence, chasing thee round Priam's town with swift feet but come let us make a stand and await him on our defence."

Then answered her great Hector of the glancing helm: "Deiphobos, verily aforetime wert thou far dearest of my brothers, whom Hekabe and Priam gendered, but now methinks I shall honour thee even more, in that thou hast dared for my sake, when thou sawest me, to come forth of the wall, while the others tarry within."

Then to him again spake the bright-eyed goddess Athene: "Dear brother, of a truth my father and lady mother and my comrades around besought me much, entreating me in turn, to tarry there, so greatly do they all tremble before him; but my heart within was sore with dismal grief. And now fight we with straight-set resolve and let there be no sparing of spears, that we may know whether Achilles is to slay us and carry our bloody spoils to the hollow ships, or whether he might be vanquished by thy spear."

Thus saying Athene in her subtlety led him on. And when they were come nigh in onset on one another, to Achilles first spake great Hector of the glancing helm: "No longer, son of Peleus, will I fly thee, as before I thrice ran round the great town of Priam, and endured not to await thy onset. Now my heart biddeth me stand up against thee; I will either slay or be slain. But come hither and let us pledge us by our gods, for they shall be best witnesses and beholders of covenants: I will entreat thee in no outrageous sort, if Zeus grant me to outstay thee, and if I take thy life, but when I have despoiled thee of thy glorious armour, O Achilles, I will give back thy dead body to the Achaians, and do thou the same."

But unto him with grim gaze spake Achilles fleet of foot: "Hector, talk not to me, thou madman, of covenants. As between men and lions there is no pledge of faith, nor wolves and sheep can be of one mind, but imagine evil continually against each other, so is it impossible for thee and me to be friends, neither shall be any pledge between us until one or other shall have fallen and glutted with blood Ares, the stubborn god of war. Bethink thee of all thy soldiership: now behoveth it thee to quit thee as a good spearman and valiant man of war. No longer is there way of escape for thee, but Pallas Athene will straightway subdue thee to my spear; and now in one hour shalt thou pay back for all my sorrows for my friends whom thou hast slain in the fury of thy spear."

He said, and poised his far-shadowing spear and hurled. And noble Hector watched the coming thereof and avoided it; for with his eye on it he crouched, and the bronze spear flew over him, and fixed itself in the earth; but Pallas Athene caught it up and gave it back to Achilles, unknown of Hector shepherd of hosts. Then Hector spake unto the noble son of Peleus: "Thou hast missed, so nowise yet, godlike Achilles, hast thou known from Zeus the hour of my doom, though thou thoughtest it. Cunning of tongue art thou and a deceiver in speech, that fearing thee I might forget my valour and strength. Not as I flee shalt thou plant thy spear in my reins, but drive it straight through my breast as I set on thee, if God hath given thee to do it. Now in thy turn avoid my spear of bronze. O that thou mightst take it all into thy flesh! Then would the war be lighter to the Trojans, if but thou wert dead, for thou art their greatest bane."

He said, and poised his long-shadowed spear and hurled it, and smote the midst of the shield of Peleus' son, and missed him not: but far from the shield the spear leapt back. And Hector was wroth that his swift weapon had left his hand in vain, and he stood downcast, for he had no second ashen spear. And he called with a loud shout to Deiphobos of the white shield, and asked of him a long spear, but he was nowise nigh. Then Hector knew the truth in his heart, and spake and said: "Ay me, now verily the gods have summoned me to death. I deemed the warrior Deiphobos was by my side, but he is within the wall, and it was Athene who played me false. Now therefore is evil death come very nigh me, not far off, nor is there way of escape. This then was from of old the pleasure of Zeus and of the far-darting son of Zeus, who yet before were fain to succour me: but now my fate hath found me. At least let me not die without a struggle or ingloriously, but in some great deed of arms whereof men yet to be born shall hear."

Thus saying he drew his sharp sword that by his flank hung great and strong, and gathered himself and swooped like a soaring eagle that darteth to the plain through the dark clouds to seize a tender lamb or crouching hare. So Hector swooped, brandishing his sharp sword. And Achilles made at him, for his heart was filled with wild fierceness, and before his breast he made a covering with his fair graven shield, and tossed his bright four-plated helm; and round it waved fair golden plumes [that Hephaistos had set thick about the crest]. As a star goeth among stars in the darkness of night, Hesperos, fairest of all stars set in heaven, so flashed there forth a light from the keen spear Achilles poised in his right hand, devising mischief against noble Hector, eyeing his fair flesh to find the fittest place. Now for the rest of him his flesh was covered by the fair bronze armour he stripped from strong Patroklos when he slew him, but there was an opening where the collar bones coming from the shoulders clasp the neck, even at the gullet, where destruction of life cometh quickliest; there, as he came on, noble Achilles drave at him with his spear, and right through the tender neck went the point. Yet the bronze-weighted ashen spear clave not the windpipe, so that he might yet speak words of answer to his foe. And he fell down in the dust, and noble Achilles spake exultingly: "Hector, thou thoughtest, whilst thou wert spoiling Patroklos, that thou wouldst be safe, and didst reck nothing of me who was afar, thou fool. But away among the hollow ships his comrade, a mightier far, even I, was left behind, who now have unstrung thy knees. Thee shall dogs and birds tear foully, but his funeral shall the Achaians make."

Then with faint breath spake unto him Hector of the glancing helm: "I pray thee by thy life and knees and parents leave me not for dogs of the Achaians to devour by the ships, but take good store of bronze and gold, gifts that my father and lady mother shall give to thee, and give them home my body back again, that the Trojans and Trojans' wives give me my due of fire after my death."

But unto him with grim gaze spake Achilles fleet of foot: "Entreat me not, dog, by knees or parents. Would that my heart's desire could so bid me myself to carve and eat raw thy flesh, for the evil thou hast wrought me, as surely is there none that shall keep the dogs from thee, not even should they bring ten or twenty fold ransom and here weigh it out, and promise even more, not even were Priam Dardanos' son to bid pay thy weight in gold, not even so shall thy lady mother lay thee on a bed to mourn her son, but dogs and birds shall devour thee utterly."

Then dying spake unto him Hector of the glancing helm: "Verily I know thee and behold thee as thou art, nor was I destined to persuade thee; truly thy heart is iron in thy breast. Take heed now lest I draw upon thee wrath of gods, in the day when Paris and

Phoebus Apollo slay thee, for all thy valour, at the Skaian gate."

He ended, and the shadow of death came down upon him, and his soul flew forth of his limbs and was gone to the house of Hades, wailing her fate, leaving her vigour and youth. Then to the dead man spake noble Achilles: "Die: for my death, I will accept it whensoever Zeus and the other immortal gods are minded to accomplish it."

10 He said, and from the corpse drew forth his bronze spear, and set it aside, and stripped the bloody armour from the shoulders. And other sons of Achaians ran up around, who gazed upon the stature and marvellous goodliness of Hector. Nor did any stand by but wounded him, and thus would many a man say looking toward his neighbour: "Go to, of a truth far easier to handle is Hector now than when he burnt the ships with blazing fire." Thus would many a man say, and wound him as he stood 20 hard by. And when fleet noble Achilles had despoiled him, he stood up among the Achaians and spake winged words: "Friends, chiefs and counsellors of the Argives, since the gods have vouchsafed us to vanquish this man who hath done us more evil than all the rest together, come let us make trial in arms round about the city, that we may know somewhat of the Trojans' purpose, whether since he hath fallen they will forsake the citadel, or whether they are minded to abide, albeit Hector is no more. But 30 wherefore doth my heart debate thus? There lieth by the ships a dead man unbewailed, unburied, Patroklos; him will I not forget, while I abide among the living and my knees can stir. Nay if even in the house of Hades the dead forget their dead, yet will I even there be mindful of my dear comrade. But come, ye sons of the Achaians, let us now, singing our song of victory, go back to the hollow ships and take with us our foe. Great glory have we won; we have slain the noble Hector, unto whom the Trojans 40 prayed throughout their city, as he had been a god."

He said, and devised foul entreatment of noble Hector. The tendons of both feet behind he slit from heel to ankle-joint, and thrust therethrough thongs of ox-hide, and bound him to his chariot, leaving his head to trail. And when he had mounted the chariot and lifted therein the famous armour, he lashed his horses to speed, and they nothing loth flew on. And dust rose around him that was dragged, and his dark 50 hair flowed loose on either side, and in the dust lay all his once fair head, for now had Zeus given him over to his foes to entreat foully in his own native land.

Thus was his head all grimed with dust. But his mother when she beheld her son, tore her hair and cast far from her her shining veil, and cried aloud with an exceeding bitter cry. And piteously moaned

his father, and around them the folk fell to crying and moaning throughout the town. Most like it seemed as though all beetling Ilios were burning 60 utterly in fire. Scarcely could the folk keep back the old man in his hot desire to get him forth of the Dardanian gates. For he besought them all, casting himself down in the mire, calling on each man by his name: "Hold, friends, and though you love me leave me to get me forth of the city alone and go unto the ships of the Achaians. Let me pray this accursed horror-working man, if haply he may feel shame before his age-fellows and pity an old man. He also hath a father such as I am, Peleus, who be- 70 gat and reared him to be a bane of Trojans—and most of all to me hath he brought woe. So many sons of mine hath he slain in their flower—yet for all my sorrow for the rest I mourn them all less than this one alone, for whom my sharp grief will bring me down to the house of Hades—even Hector. Would that he had died in my arms; then would we have wept and wailed our fill, his mother who bore him to her ill hap, and I myself."

Thus spake he wailing, and all the men of the city 80 made moan with him. And among the women of Troy, Hekabe led the wild lament: "My child, ah, woe is me! wherefore should I live in my pain, now thou art dead, who night and day wert my boast through the city, and blessing to all, both men and women of Troy throughout the town, who hailed thee as a god, for verily an exceeding glory to them wert thou in thy life:—now death and fate have overtaken thee."

Thus spake she wailing. But Hector's wife knew 90 not as yet, for no true messenger had come to tell her how her husband abode without the gates, but in an inner chamber of the lofty house she was weaving a double purple web, and broidering therein manifold flowers. Then she called to her goodly-haired handmaids through the house to set a great tripod on the fire, that Hector might have warm washing when he came home out of the battle—fond heart, and was unaware how, far from all washings, bright-eyed Athene had slain him by the hand of Achilles. 100 But she heard shrieks and groans from the battlements, and her limbs reeled, and the shuttle fell from her hands to earth. Then again among her goodly-haired maids she spake: "Come two of ye this way with me that I may see what deeds are done. It was the voice of my husband's noble mother that I heard, and in my own breast my heart leapeth to my mouth and my knees are numbed beneath me: surely some evil thing is at hand against the children of Priam. Would that such word might never reach my ear! 110 yet terribly I dread lest noble Achilles have cut off bold Hector from the city by himself and chased him to the plain and ere this ended his perilous pride that possessed him, for never would he tarry among the throng of men but ran out before them far, yielding place to no man in his hardihood."

Thus saying she sped through the chamber like one mad, with beating heart, and with her went her handmaidens. But when she came to the battlements and the throng of men, she stood still upon the wall and gazed, and beheld him dragged before the city:
—swift horses dragged him recklessly toward the hollow ships of the Achaians. Then dark night came
10 on her eyes and shrouded her, and she fell backward and gasped forth her spirit. From off her head she shook the bright attiring thereof, frontlet and net and woven band, and veil, the veil that golden Aphrodite gave her on the day when Hector of the glancing helm led her forth of the house of Eëtion, having given bride-gifts untold. And around her thronged her husband's sisters and his brothers' wives, who held her up among them, distraught even to death. But when at last she came to herself
20 and her soul returned into her breast, then wailing with deep sobs she spake among the women of Troy: "O Hector, woe is me! to one fate then were we both born, thou in Troy in the house of Priam, and I in Thebe under woody Plakos, in the house of Eëtion, who reared me from a little one—ill-fated sire of cruel-fated child. Ah, would he had begotten me not. Now thou to the house of Hades beneath the secret places of the earth departest, and me in bitter mourning thou leavest a widow in thy halls: and thy
30 son is but an infant child—son of unhappy parents, thee and me—nor shalt thou profit him, Hector, since thou art dead, neither he thee. For even if he escape the Achaians' woful war, yet shall labour and sorrow cleave unto him hereafter, for other men shall seize his lands. The day of orphanage sundereth a child from his fellows, and his head is bowed down ever, and his cheeks are wet with tears. And in his need the child seeketh his father's friends, plucking this one by cloak and that by coat, and one of them
40 that pity him holdeth his cup a little to his mouth, and moisteneth his lips, but his palate he moisteneth not. And some child unorphaned thrusteth him from the feast with blows and taunting words, 'Out with thee! no father of thine is at our board.' Then weeping to his widowed mother shall he return, even Astyanax, who erst upon his father's knee ate only marrow and fat flesh of sheep; and when sleep fell on him and he ceased from childish play, then in bed in his nurse's arms he would slumber softly
50 nested, having satisfied his heart with good things; but now that he hath lost his father he will suffer many ills, Astyanax—that name the Trojans gave him, because thou only wert the defence of their gates and their long walls. But now by the beaked ships, far from thy parents, shall coiling worms devour thee when the dogs have had their fill, as thou liest naked; yet in these halls lieth raiment of thine,

delicate and fair, wrought by the hands of women. But verily all these will I consume with burning fire
—to thee no profit, since thou wilt never lie therein, 60 yet that this be honour to thee from the men and the women of Troy."

Thus spake she wailing, and the women joined their moan.

BOOK XXIV

. . . Thus Achilles in his anger entreated noble Hector shamefully; but the blessed gods when they beheld him pitied him, and urged the clear-sighted slayer of Argus to steal the corpse away. So to all the others seemed it good, yet not to Hera or Poseidon or the bright-eyed Maiden, but they continued as 70 when at the beginning sacred Ilios became hateful to them, and Priam and his people, by reason of the sin of Alexandros in that he contemned those goddesses when they came to his steading, and preferred her who brought him deadly lustfulness. But when the twelfth morn from that day arose, then spake among the Immortals Phoebus Apollo: "Hard of heart are ye, O gods, and cruel. Hath Hector never burnt for you thigh-bones of unblemished bulls and goats? Now have ye not taken heart to 80 rescue even his corpse for his wife to look upon and his mother and his child and his father Priam and his people, who speedily would burn him in the fire and make his funeral. . . ."

Then in anger spake unto him white-armed Hera: "Even thus mightest thou speak, O Lord of the silver bow, if ye are to give equal honour to Achilles and to Hector. Hector is but a mortal and was suckled at a woman's breast, but Achilles is child of a goddess whom I myself bred up and reared and gave to 90 a man to be his wife, even to Peleus who was dearest of all men to the Immortals' heart. And all ye gods came to her bridal, and thou among them wert feasting with thy lyre, O lover of ill company, faithless ever."

Then to her in answer spake Zeus who gathereth the clouds: "Hera, be not wroth utterly with the gods: for these men's honour is not to be the same, yet Hector also was dearest to the gods of all mortals that are in Ilios. So was he to me at least, for nowise 100 failed he in the gifts I loved. . . . I were fain that some one of the gods would call Thetis to come near to me, that I may speak unto her a wise word, so that Achilles may take gifts from Priam and give Hector back."

Thus spake he, and airy-footed Iris sped forth upon the errand and between Samothrace and rocky Imbros leapt into the black sea, and the waters closed above her with a noise. And she found Thetis in a hollow cave. And standing near, fleet-footed Iris 110 spake to her: "Rise, Thetis; Zeus of immortal counsels calleth thee." . . .

And when they had come forth upon the shore they sped up to heaven, and found the far-seeing son of Kronos, and round him sat gathered all the other blessed gods that are for ever. . . . Then began speech to them the father of gods and men: ". . . Nine days hath dispute arisen among the Immortals concerning the corpse of Hector and Achilles waster of cities. Fain are they to send clear-sighted Argeïphontes to steal the body away, but now hear what glory I accord herein to Achilles, that I may keep through times to come thy honour and good will. Go with all speed to the host and bear to thy son my bidding. Say to him that the gods are displeased at him, and that I above all Immortals am wroth, because with furious heart he holdeth Hector at the beaked ships and hath not given him back, if haply he may fear me and give Hector back. But I will send Iris to great-hearted Priam to bid him go to the ships of the Achaians to ransom his dear son, and carry gifts to Achilles that may gladden his heart." Thus spake he, and Thetis the silver-footed goddess was not disobedient to his word. . . .

And airy-footed Iris sped forth upon the errand. And she came to the house of Priam, and found therein crying and moan. . . . And the messenger of Zeus stood beside Priam and spake softly unto him, and trembling came upon his limbs: "Be of good cheer in thy heart, O Priam son of Dardanos, and be not dismayed for anything, for no evil come I hither to forebode to thee, but with good will. I am the messenger of Zeus to thee, who, though he be afar off, hath great care and pity for thee. The Olympian biddeth thee ransom noble Hector and carry gifts to Achilles that may gladden his heart: go thou alone, let none other of the Trojans go with thee. . . . Let not death be in thy thought, nor any fear; such guide shall go with thee, even the slayer of Argus, who shall lead thee until his leading bring thee to Achilles. And when he shall have led thee into the hut, neither shall Achilles himself slay thee nor suffer any other herein, for not senseless is he or unforeseeing or wicked, but with all courtesy he will spare a suppliant man." . . .

Then the old man made haste to go up into his car, and drave forth from the doorway and the echoing portico. In front the mules drew the four-wheeled wain, and wise Idaios drave them; behind came the horses which the old man urged with the lash at speed along the city: and his friends all followed lamenting loud as though he were faring to his death. And when they were come down from the city and were now on the plain, then went back again to Ilios his sons and marriage kin. But the two coming forth upon the plain were not unbeheld of far-seeing Zeus. But he looked upon the old man and had compassion on him, and straightway spake

9. Argeïphontes, Hermes.

unto Hermes his dear son: "Hermes, since unto thee especially is it dear to companion men, and thou hearest whomsoever thou wilt, go forth and so guide Priam to the hollow ships of the Achaians that no man behold or be aware of him, among all the Danaans' host, until he come to the son of Peleus."

Thus spake he, and the Messenger, the slayer of Argus, was not disobedient unto his word. Straightway beneath his feet he bound on his fair sandals, golden, divine, that bare him over the wet sea and over the boundless land with the breathings of the wind. And he took up his wand wherewith he entranceth the eyes of such men as he will, and others he likewise waketh out of sleep: this did the strong slayer of Argus take in his hand, and flew. And quickly came he to Troy-land and the Hellespont, and went on his way in semblance as a young man that is a prince with the new down on his chin, as when the youth of men is the comeliest.

Now the others, when they had driven beyond the great barrow of Ilios, halted the mules and horses at the river to drink; for darkness was come down over the earth. Then the herald beheld Hermes from hard by, and marked him, and spake and said to Priam: "Consider, son of Dardanos; this is matter of prudent thought. I see a man, methinks we shall full soon be rent in pieces. Come, let us flee in our chariot, or else at least touch his knees and entreat him that he have mercy on us."

Thus spake he, and the old man was confounded, and he was dismayed exceedingly, and the hair on his pliant limbs stood up, and he stood still amazed. But the Helper came nigh of himself and took the old man's hand, and spake and questioned him: "Whither, father, dost thou thus guide these horses and mules through the divine night, when other mortals are asleep? Hadst thou no fear of the fierce-breathing Achaians, thy bitter foes that are hard anigh thee? If one of them should espy thee carrying such treasures through the swift black night, what then would be thy thought? Neither art thou young thyself, and thy companion here is old, that ye should make defence against a man that should assail thee first. But I will nowise harm thee, yea I will keep any other from thy hurt: for the similitude of my dear father I see in thee."

And to him in answer spake the old man, godlike Priam: "Even so, kind son, are all these things as thou sayest. Nevertheless hath some god stretched forth his hand even over me in that he hath sent a wayfarer such as thou to meet me, a bearer of good luck, by the nobleness of thy form and semblance; and thou art wise of heart and of blessed parents art thou sprung."

And to him again spake the Messenger, the slayer of Argus: "All this, old sire, hast thou verily spoken aright. But come say this and tell me truly whether thou art taking forth a great and goodly treasure unto alien men, where it may abide for thee in safety, or whether by this ye are all forsaking holy Ilios in fear; so far the best man among you hath perished, even thy son; for of battle with the Achaians abated he never a jot."

And to him in answer spake the old man, godlike Priam: "Who art thou, noble sir, and of whom art born? For meetly hast thou spoken of the fate of my hapless son."

And to him again spake the Messenger, the slayer of Argus: "Thou art proving me, old sire, in asking me of noble Hector. Him have I full oft seen with mine eyes in glorious battle, and when at the ships he was slaying the Argives he drave thither, piercing them with the keen bronze, and we stood still and marvelled thereat, for Achilles suffered us not to fight, being wroth against Atreus' son. His squire am I, and came in the same well-wrought ship." . . .

And the old man, godlike Priam, answered him, saying: "If verily thou art a squire of Achilles Peleus' son, come tell me all the truth, whether still my son is by the ships, or whether ere now Achilles hath riven him limb from limb and cast him to the dogs."

Then to him again spake the Messenger the slayer of Argus: "Old sire, not yet have dogs or birds devoured him, but there lieth he still by Achilles' ship, even as he fell, among the huts, and the twelfth morn now hath risen upon him, nor doth his flesh corrupt at all, neither worms consume it, such as devour men slain in war. Truly Achilles draggeth him recklessly around the barrow of his dear comrade so oft as divine day dawneth, yet marreth he him not; thou wouldst marvel if thou couldst go see thyself how dewy fresh he lieth, and is washed clean of blood, nor anywhere defiled; and all his wounds wherewith he was stricken are closed; howbeit many plunged their points in him. So careful are the blessed gods of thy son, though he be but a dead corpse, for they held him dear at heart."

Thus spake he, and the old man rejoiced, and answered him, saying: "My son, it is verily a good thing to give due offerings withal to the Immortals, for never did my child—if that child indeed I had —forget in our halls the gods who inhabit Olympus. Therefore have they remembered this for him, albeit his portion is death. But come now take from me this goodly goblet, and guard me myself and guide me, under Heaven, that I may come unto the hut of Peleus' son."

Then spake unto him again the Messenger the slayer of Argus: "Thou art proving me, old sire, who am younger than thou, but thou wilt not prevail upon me, in that thou biddest me take gifts from thee without Achilles' privity. I were afraid and shamed at heart to defraud him, lest some evil come to pass on me hereafter. But as thy guide I would

go even unto famous Argos, accompanying thee courteously in swift ship or on foot. Not from scorn of thy guide would any assail thee then."

Thus spake the Helper, and leaping on the chariot behind the horses he swiftly took lash and reins into his hands, and breathed brave spirit into horses and mules. But when they were come to the towers and trench of the ships, there were the sentinels just busying them about their supper. Then the Messenger, the slayer of Argus, shed sleep upon them all, and straightway opened the gates and thrust back the bars, and brought within Priam and the splendid gifts upon his wain. And they came to the lofty hut of the son of Peleus, which the Myrmidons made for their king and hewed therefor timber of the pine, and thatched it with downy thatching-rush that they mowed in the meadows, and around it made for him their lord a great court with close-set palisades; and the door was barred by a single bolt of pine that three Achaians wont to drive home, and three drew back that mighty bar—three of the rest, but Achilles by himself would drive it home. Then opened the Helper Hermes the door for the old man, and brought in the splendid gifts for Peleus' fleet-footed son, and descended from the chariot to the earth and spake aloud: "Old sire, I that have come to thee am an immortal god, even Hermes, for my father sent me to companion thee on thy way. But now will I depart from thee nor come within Achilles' sight; it were cause of wrath that an immortal god should thus show favour openly unto mortals. But thou go in and clasp the knees of Peleus' son and entreat him for his father's sake and his mother's of the lovely hair and for his child's sake that thou mayest move his soul."

Thus Hermes spake, and departed unto high Olympus. But Priam leapt from the car to the earth, and left Idaios in his place; he stayed to mind the horses and mules; but the old man made straight for the house where Achilles dear to Zeus was wont to sit. And therein he found the man himself, and his comrades sate apart: two only, the hero Automedon and Alkimos, of the stock of Ares, were busy in attendance; and he was lately ceased from meat, even from eating and drinking: and still the table stood beside him. But they were unaware of great Priam as he came in, and so stood he anigh and clasped in his hands the knees of Achilles, and kissed his hands, terrible, man-slaying, that slew many of Priam's sons. And as when a grievous curse cometh upon a man who in his own country hath slain another and escapeth to a land of strangers, to the house of some rich man, and wonder possesseth them that look on him—so Achilles wondered when he saw godlike Priam, and the rest wondered likewise, and looked upon one another. Then Priam spake and entreated him, saying: "Bethink thee, O Achilles like to gods, of thy father that is of like years with me, on the grievous pathway of old age. Him haply are the dwellers round about entreating evilly, nor is there any to ward from him ruin and bane. Nevertheless while he heareth of thee as yet alive he rejoiceth in his heart, and hopeth withal day after day that he shall see his dear son returning from Troy-land. But I, I am utterly unblest, since I begat sons the best men in wide Troy-land, but declare unto thee that none of them is left. Fifty I had, when the sons of the Achaians came; nineteen were born to me of one mother, and concubines bare the rest within my halls. Now of the more part had impetuous Ares unstrung the knees, and he who was yet left and guarded city and men, him slewest thou but now as he fought for his country, even Hector. For his sake come I unto the ships of the Achaians that I may win him back from thee, and I bring with me untold ransom. Yea, fear thou the gods, Achilles, and have compassion on me, even me, bethinking thee of thy father. Lo, I am yet more piteous than he, and have braved what none other man on earth hath braved before, to stretch forth my hand toward the face of the slayer of my sons."

Thus spake he, and stirred within Achilles desire to make lament for his father. And he touched the old man's hand and gently moved him back. And as they both bethought them of their dead, so Priam for man-slaying Hector wept sore as he was fallen before Achilles' feet, and Achilles wept for his own father, and now again for Patroklos, and their moan went up throughout the house. But when noble Achilles had satisfied him with lament, and the desire thereof departed from his heart and limbs, straightway he sprang from his seat and raised the old man by his hand, pitying his hoary head and hoary beard, and spake unto him winged words and said: "Ah hapless! many ill things verily thou hast endured in thy heart. How durst thou come alone to the ships of the Achaians and to meet the eyes of the man who hath slain full many of thy brave sons? of iron verily is thy heart. But come then set thee on a seat, and we will let our sorrows lie quiet in our hearts, for all our pain, for no avail cometh of chill lament. This is the lot the gods have spun for miserable men, that they should live in pain; yet themselves are sorrowless. For two urns stand upon the floor of Zeus filled with his evil gifts, and one with blessings. To whomsoever Zeus whose joy is in the lightning dealeth a mingled lot, that man chanceth now upon ill and now again on good, but to whom he giveth but of the bad kind him he bringeth to scorn, and evil famine chaseth him over the goodly earth, and he is a wanderer honoured of neither gods nor men. Even thus to Peleus gave the gods splendid gifts from his birth, for he excelled all men in good fortune and wealth, and was king of the Myrmidons,

and mortal though he was the gods gave him a goddess to be his bride. Yet even on him God brought evil, seeing that there arose to him no offspring of princely sons in his halls, save that he begat one son to an untimely death. Neither may I tend him as he groweth old, since very far from my country I am dwelling in Troy-land, to vex thee and thy children. And of thee, old sire, we have heard how of old time thou wert happy, even how of all that Lesbos, seat of Makar, boundeth to the north thereof and Phrygia farther up and the vast Hellespont—of all these folk, men say, thou wert the richest in wealth and in sons, but after that the Powers of Heaven brought this bane on thee, ever are battles and man-slayings around thy city. Keep courage, and lament not unabatingly in thy heart. For nothing wilt thou avail by grieving for thy son, neither shalt thou bring him back to life or ever some new evil come upon thee."

Then made answer unto him the old man, godlike Priam: "Bid me not to a seat, O fosterling of Zeus, so long as Hector lieth uncared for at the huts, but straightway give him back that I may behold him with mine eyes; and accept thou the great ransom that we bring. So mayest thou have pleasure thereof, and come unto thy native land, since thou hast spared me from the first."

Then fleet-footed Achilles looked sternly upon him and said: "No longer chafe me, old sire; of myself am I minded to give Hector back to thee, for there came to me a messenger from Zeus, even my mother who bare me, daughter of the Ancient One of the Sea. And I know, O Priam, in my mind, nor am unaware that some god it is that hath guided thee to the swift ships of the Achaians. For no mortal man, even though in prime of youth, would dare to come among the host, for neither could he escape the watch, nor easily thrust back the bolt of our doors. Therefore now stir my heart no more amid my troubles, lest I leave not even thee in peace, old sire, within my hut, albeit thou art my suppliant, and lest I transgress the commandment of Zeus."

Thus spake he, and the old man feared, and obeyed his word. And the son of Peleus leapt like a lion through the door of the house, not alone, for with him went two squires, the hero Automedon and Alkimos, they whom above all his comrades Achilles honoured, save only Patroklos that was dead. They then loosed from under the yoke the horses and mules, and led in the old man's crier-herald and set him on a chair, and from the wain of goodly felloes they took the countless ransom set on Hector's head. But they left two robes and a well-spun doublet, that Achilles might wrap the dead therein when he gave him to be carried home. And he called forth handmaids and bade them wash and anoint him when they had borne him apart, so that Priam should not look upon his son, lest he should not refrain the wrath at his sorrowing heart when he should look upon his son, and lest Achilles' heart be vexed thereat and he slay him and transgress the commandment of Zeus. So when the handmaids had washed the body and anointed it with oil, and had thrown over it a fair robe and a doublet, then Achilles himself lifted it and laid it on a bier, and his comrades with him lifted it onto the polished waggon. Then he groaned aloud and called on his dear comrade by his name: "Patroklos, be not vexed with me if thou hear even in the house of Hades that I have given back noble Hector unto his dear father, for not unworthy is the ransom he hath given me, whereof I will deal to thee again thy rightful share."

Thus spake noble Achilles, and went back into the hut, and sate him down on the cunningly-wrought couch whence he had arisen by the opposite wall, and spake a word to Priam: "Thy son, old sire, is given back as thou wouldest and lieth on a bier, and with the break of day thou shalt see him thyself as thou carriest him. . . . But come let us too, noble father, take thought of meat, and afterward thou shalt mourn over thy dear son as thou carriest him to Ilios; and many tears shall be his due." . . .

When they had put off the desire of meat and drink, then Priam son of Dardanos marvelled at Achilles to see how great he was and how goodly, for he was like a god to look upon. And Achilles marvelled at Priam son of Dardanos, beholding his noble aspect and hearkening to his words. But when they had gazed their fill upon one another, then first spake the old man, godlike Priam, to Achilles: "Now presently give me whereon to lie, fosterling of Zeus, that of sweet sleep also we may now take our fill at rest: for never yet have mine eyes closed beneath their lids since at thy hands my son lost his life, but I continually mourn and brood over countless griefs, grovelling in the courtyard-close amid the mire. Now at last have I tasted bread and poured bright wine down my throat, but till now I had tasted nought."

He said, and Achilles bade his comrades and handmaids to set a bedstead beneath the portico, and to cast thereon fair shining rugs and spread coverlets above and thereon to lay thick mantles to be a clothing over all. And the maids went forth from the inner hall with torches in their hands, and quickly spread two beds in haste. Then with bitter meaning said fleet-footed Achilles unto Priam: "Lie thou without, dear sire, lest there come hither one of the counsellors of the Achaians, such as ever take counsel with me by my side, as custom is. If any of such should behold thee through the swift black night, forthwith he might haply tell it to Agamemnon shepherd of the host, and thus would there be delay in giving back the dead." . . .

Thus speaking he clasped the old man's right hand at the wrist, lest he should be anywise afraid at heart. So they in the forepart of the house laid them down, Priam and the herald, with wise thoughts at their hearts, but Achilles slept in a recess of the firm-wrought hut, and beside him lay fair-cheeked Briseis.

Now all other gods and warriors lords of chariots slumbered all night, by soft sleep overcome. But not on the Helper Hermes did sleep take hold as he sought within his heart how he should guide forth king Priam from the ships unspied of the trusty sentinels. And he stood above his head and spake a word to him: "Old sire, no thought then hast thou of any evil, seeing thou yet sleepest among men that are thine enemies, for that Achilles spared thee. Truly now hast thou won back thy dear son, and at great price. But for thy life will thy sons thou hast left behind be offering threefold ransom, if but Agamemnon Atreus' son be aware of thee, and aware be all the Achaians."

Thus spake he, and the old man feared, and roused the herald. And Hermes yoked the horses and mules for them, and himself drave them lightly through the camp, and none was aware of them.

But when they came to the ford of the fair-flowing river [even eddying Xanthos, begotten of immortal Zeus,] then Hermes departed up to high Olympus, and Morning of the saffron robe spread over all the earth. And they with wail and moan drave the horses to the city, and the mules drew the dead. Nor marked them any man or fair-girdled woman until Kassandra, peer of golden Aphrodite, having gone up upon Pergamos, was aware of her dear father as he stood in the car, and the herald that was crier to the town. Then beheld she him that lay upon the bier behind the mules, and thereat she wailed and cried aloud throughout all the town: "O men and women of Troy, come ye hither and look upon Hector, if ever while he was alive ye rejoiced when he came back from battle, since great joy was he to the city and all the folk."

Thus spake she, nor was man or woman left within the city, for upon all came unendurable grief. And near the gates they met Priam bringing home the dead. First bewailed him his dear wife and lady mother, as they cast them on the fair-wheeled wain and touched his head; and around them stood the throng and wept. So all day long unto the setting of the sun they had lamented Hector in tears without the gate, had not the old man spoken from the car among the folk: "Give me place for the mules to pass through; hereafter ye shall have your fill of wailing, when I have brought him unto his home."

Thus spake he, and they parted asunder and gave place to the wain. And the others when they had brought him to the famous house, laid him on a

89. **Kassandra,** the prophetess, daughter of Priam.

fretted bed, and set beside him minstrels leaders of the dirge, who wailed a mournful lay, while the women made moan with them. And among the women white-armed Andromache led the lamentation, while in her hands she held the head of Hector slayer of men: "Husband, thou art gone young from life, and leavest me a widow in thy halls. And the child is yet but a little one, child of ill-fated parents, thee and me; nor methinks shall he grow up to man-

10 hood, for ere then shall this city be utterly destroyed. For thou art verily perished who didst watch over it, who guardedst it and keptest safe its noble wives and infant little ones. These soon shall be voyaging in the hollow ships, yea and I too with them, and thou, my child, shalt either go with me unto a place where thou shalt toil at unseemly tasks, labouring before the face of some harsh lord, or else some Achaian will take thee by the arm and hurl thee from the battlement, a grievous death, for that he is wroth

20 because Hector slew his brother or father or son, since full many of the Achaians at Hector's hands have bitten the firm earth. For no light hand had thy father in the grievous fray. Therefore the folk lament him throughout the city, and woe unspeakable and mourning hast thou left to thy parents, Hector, but with me chiefliest shall grievous pain abide. For neither didst thou stretch thy hands to me from a bed in thy death, neither didst speak to me some memorable word that I might have thought on evermore

30 as my tears fall night and day."

Thus spake she wailing, and the women joined their moan. And among them Hekabe again led the loud lament: "Hector, of all my children far dearest to my heart, verily while thou wert alive dear wert thou to the gods, and even in thy doom of death have they had care for thee. For other sons of mine whom he took captive would fleet Achilles sell beyond the unvintaged sea unto Samos and Imbros and smoking Lemnos, but when with keen-edged bronze

40 he had bereft thee of thy life he was fain to drag thee oft around the tomb of his comrade, even Patroklos whom thou slewest, yet might he not raise him up thereby. But now all dewy and fresh thou liest in our halls, like one on whom Apollo, lord of the silver bow, hath descended and slain him with his gentle darts."

Thus spake she wailing, and stirred unending moan. Then thirdly Helen led their sore lament: "Hector, of all my brethren of Troy far dearest to my

50 heart! Truly my lord is godlike Alexandros who brought me to Troy-land—would I had died ere then. For this is now the twentieth year since I went thence and am gone from my own native land, but never yet heard I evil or despiteful word from thee; nay, if any other haply upbraided me in the palace-halls, whether brother or sister of thine or brother's fair-robed wife, or thy mother—but thy father is

ever kind to me as he were my own—then wouldst thou soothe such with words and refrain them, by the gentleness of thy spirit and by thy gentle words. 60 Therefore bewail I thee with pain at heart, and my hapless self with thee, for no more is any left in wide Troy-land to be my friend and kind to me, but all men shudder at me."

Thus spake she wailing, and therewith the great multitude of the people groaned. But the old man Priam spake a word among the folk: "Bring wood, men of Troy, unto the city, and be not anywise afraid at heart of a crafty ambush of the Achaians; for this message Achilles gave me when he sent me 70 from the black ships, that they should do us no hurt until the twelfth morn arise."

Thus spake he, and they yoked oxen and mules to wains, and quickly then they flocked before the city. So nine days they gathered great store of wood. But when the tenth morn rose with light for men, then bare they forth brave Hector, weeping tears, and on a lofty pyre they laid the dead man, and thereon cast fire.

But when the daughter of Dawn, rosy-fingered 80 Morning, shone forth, then gathered the folk around glorious Hector's pyre. First quenched they with bright wine all the burning, so far as the fire's strength went, and then his brethren and comrades gathered his white bones lamenting, and big tears flowed down their cheeks. And the bones they took and laid in a golden urn, shrouding them in soft purple robes, and straightway laid the urn in a hollow grave and piled thereon great close-set stones, and heaped with speed a barrow, while watchers 90 were set everywhere around, lest the well-greaved Achaians should make onset before the time. And when they had heaped the barrow they went back, and gathered them together and feasted right well in noble feast at the palace of Priam, Zeus-fostered king.

Thus held they funeral for Hector tamer of horses.

The Odyssey

BOOK I

T ELL me, Muse, of that man, so ready at need, who wandered far and wide, after he had sacked the sacred citadel of Troy, and many were 100 the men whose towns he saw and whose mind he learnt, yea, and many the woes he suffered in his heart upon the deep, striving to win his own life and the return of his company. Nay, but even so he saved not his company, though he desired it sore. For through the blindness of their own hearts they per-

*The Odyssey.*ᴬ Translated by Samuel Butcher and Andrew Lang. By permission of The Macmillan Company, publishers.

GREEK SOLDIERS, RETURNING FROM THE WARS, BEING GREETED BY PATRIARCHS.

ished, fools, who devoured the oxen of Helios Hyperion: but the god took from them their day of returning. Of these things, goddess, daughter of Zeus, whencesoever thou hast heard thereof, declare thou even unto us.

Now all the rest, as many as fled from sheer destruction, were at home, and had escaped both war and sea, but Odysseus only, craving for his wife and for his homeward path, the lady nymph Calypso held, that fair goddess, in her hollow caves, longing to have him for her lord. But when now the year had come in the courses of the seasons, wherein the gods had ordained that he should return home to Ithaca, not even there was he quit of labours, not even among his own; but all the gods had pity on him save Poseidon, who raged continually against godlike Odysseus, till he came to his own country. Howbeit Poseidon had now departed for the distant Ethiopians, the Ethiopians that are sundered in twain, the uttermost of men, abiding some where Hyperion sinks and some where he rises. There he looked to receive his hecatomb of bulls and dams, there he made merry sitting at the feast, but the other gods were gathered in the halls of Olympian Zeus. Then among them the father of gods and men began to speak, for he bethought him in his heart of noble Aegisthus, whom the son of Agamemnon, far-famed Orestes, slew. Thinking upon him he spake out among the Immortals:

'Lo you now, how vainly mortal men do blame the gods! For of us they say comes evil, whereas they even of themselves, through the blindness of their own hearts, have sorrows beyond that which is ordained.' . . .

And the goddess, grey-eyed Athene, answered him, saying: 'My heart is rent for wise Odysseus, the hapless one, who far from his friends this long while suffereth affliction in a seagirt isle, where is the navel of the sea, a woodland isle, and therein a goddess hath her habitation, the daughter of the wizard Atlas, who knows the depths of every sea, and himself upholds the tall pillars which keep earth and sky asunder. His daughter it is that holds the hapless man in sorrow: and ever with soft and guileful tales she is wooing him to forgetfulness of Ithaca. But Odysseus yearning to see if it were but the smoke leap upwards from his own land, hath a desire to die. As for thee, thine heart regardeth it not at all, Olympian! What! did not Odysseus by the ships of the Argives make thee free offering of sacrifice in the wide Trojan land? Wherefore wast thou then so wroth with him, O Zeus?'

And Zeus the cloud-gatherer answered her, and said: 'My child, what word hath escaped the door of thy lips? Yea, how should I forget divine Odysseus, who in understanding is beyond mortals and beyond all men hath done sacrifice to the deathless gods, who keep the wide heaven? Nay, but it is Poseidon, the girdler of the earth, that hath been wroth continually with quenchless anger for the Cyclops' sake whom he blinded of his eye, even godlike Polyphemus whose power is mightiest amongst all the Cyclôpes. His mother was the nymph Thoösa, daughter of Phorcys, lord of the unharvested sea, and in the hollow caves she lay with Poseidon. From that day forth Poseidon the earth-shaker doth not indeed slay Odysseus, but driveth him wandering from his own country. But come, let us here one and all take good counsel as touching his returning, that he may be got home; so shall Poseidon let go his displeasure, for he will in no wise be able to strive alone against all, in despite of all the deathless gods.'

Then the goddess, grey-eyed Athene, answered him, and said: 'O father, our father Cronides, throned in the highest, if indeed this thing is now well pleasing to the blessed gods, that wise Odysseus

40. goddess, Calypso.

should return to his own home, let us then speed Hermes the Messenger, the slayer of Argos, to the island of Ogygia. There with all speed let him declare to the lady of the braided tresses our unerring counsel, even the return of the patient Odysseus, that so he may come to his home. But as for me I will go to Ithaca that I may rouse his son yet the more, planting might in his heart, to call an assembly of the long-haired Achaeans and speak out to all the wooers who slaughter continually the sheep of his thronging flocks, and his kine with trailing feet and shambling gait. And I will guide him to Sparta and to sandy Pylos to seek tidings of his dear father's return, if peradventure he may hear thereof and that so he may be had in good report among men.' . . .

BOOK V

. . . Nor heedless was the messenger, the slayer of Argos. Straightway he bound beneath his feet his lovely golden sandals, that wax not old, that bare him alike over the wet sea and over the limitless land, swift as the breath of the wind. And he took the wand wherewith he lulls the eyes of whomso he will, while others again he even wakes from out of sleep. With this rod in his hand flew the strong slayer of Argos. Above Pieria he passed and leapt from the upper air into the deep. Then he sped along the wave like the cormorant, that chaseth the fishes through the perilous gulfs of the unharvested sea, and wetteth his thick plumage in the brine. Such like did Hermes ride upon the press of the waves. But when he had now reached that far-off isle, he went forth from the sea of violet blue to get him up into the land, till he came to a great cave, wherein dwelt the nymph of the braided tresses: and he found her within. And on the hearth there was a great fire burning, and from afar through the isle was smelt the fragrance of cleft cedar blazing, and of sandal wood. And the nymph within was singing with a sweet voice as she fared to and fro before the loom, and wove with a shuttle of gold. And round about the cave there was a wood blossoming, alder and poplar and sweet-smelling cypress. And therein roosted birds long of wing, owls and falcons and chattering sea-crows, which have their business in the waters. And lo, there about the hollow cave trailed a gadding garden vine, all rich with clusters. And fountains four set orderly were running with clear water, hard by one another, turned each to his own course. And all around soft meadows bloomed of violets and parsley, yea, even a deathless god who came thither might wonder at the sight and be glad at heart. There the messenger, the slayer of Argos, stood and wondered. Now when he had gazed at all with wonder, anon he went into the

10. **wooers,** the wooers of Queen Penelope, who assume that her husband Odysseus is dead.

wide cave; nor did Calypso, that fair goddess, fail to know him, when she saw him face to face; for the gods use not to be strange one to another, the immortals, not though one have his habitation far away. But he found not Odysseus, the great-hearted, within the cave, who sat weeping on the shore even as aforetime, straining his soul with tears and groans and griefs, and as he wept he looked wistfully over the unharvested deep. And Calypso, that fair goddess, questioned Hermes, when she had made him sit on a bright shining seat:

'Wherefore, I pray thee, Hermes, of the golden wand, hast thou come hither, worshipful and welcome, whereas as of old thou wert not wont to visit me? Tell me all thy thought; my heart is set on fulfilling it, if fulfil it I may, and if it hath been fulfilled in the counsel of fate. But now follow me further, that I may set before thee the entertainment of strangers.'

Therewith the goddess spread a table with ambrosia and set it by him, and mixed the ruddy nectar. So the messenger, the slayer of Argos, did eat and drink. Now after he had supped and comforted his soul with food, at the last he answered, and spake to her on this wise:

'Thou makest question of me on my coming, a goddess of a god, and I will tell thee this my saying truly, at thy command. 'Twas Zeus that bade me come hither, by no will of mine; nay, who of his free will would speed over such a wondrous space of brine, whereby is no city of mortals that do sacrifice to the gods, and offer choice hecatombs? But surely it is in no wise possible for another god to go beyond or to make void the purpose of Zeus, lord of the aegis. He saith that thou hast with thee a man most wretched beyond his fellows, beyond those men that round the burg of Priam for nine years fought, and in the tenth year sacked the city and departed homeward. Yet on the way they sinned against Athene, and she raised upon them an evil blast and long waves of the sea. Then all the rest of his good company was lost, but it came to pass that the wind bare and the wave brought him hither. And now Zeus biddeth thee send him hence with what speed thou mayest, for it is not ordained that he die away from his friends, but rather it is his fate to look on them even yet, and to come to his high-roofed home and his own country.'

So spake he, and Calypso, that fair goddess, shuddered and uttered her voice, and spake unto him winged words: 'Hard are ye gods and jealous exceeding, who ever grudge goddesses openly to mate with men, if any make a mortal her dear bedfellow. . . . Him I saved as he went all alone bestriding the keel of a bark, for that Zeus had crushed and cleft his swift ship with a white bolt in the midst of the wine-dark deep. There all the rest of his good company was lost, but it came to pass that the wind bare and the wave brought him hither. And him have I loved and cherished, and I said that I would make him to know not death and age for ever. Yet forasmuch as it is in no wise possible for another god to go beyond, or make void the purpose of Zeus, lord of the aegis, let him away over the unharvested seas, if the summons and the bidding be of Zeus. But I will give him no despatch, not I, for I have no ships by me with oars, nor company to bear him on his way over the broad back of the sea. Yet will I be forward to put this in his mind, and will hide nought, that all unharmed he may come to his own country.'

Then the messenger, the slayer of Argos, answered her: 'Yea, speed him now upon his path and have regard unto the wrath of Zeus, lest haply he be angered and bear hard on thee hereafter.'

Therewith the great slayer of Argos departed, but the lady nymph went on her way to the greathearted Odysseus, when she had heard the message of Zeus. And there she found him sitting on the shore, and his eyes were never dry of tears, and his sweet life was ebbing away as he mourned for his return; for the nymph no more found favour in his sight. Howsoever by night he would sleep by her, as needs he must, in the hollow caves, unwilling lover by a willing lady. And in the day-time he would sit on the rocks and on the beach, straining his soul with tears, and groans, and griefs, and through his tears he would look wistfully over the unharvested deep. So standing near him that fair goddess spake to him:

'Hapless man, sorrow no more I pray thee in this isle, nor let thy good life waste away, for even now will I send thee hence with all my heart. Nay, arise and cut long beams, and fashion a wide raft with the axe, and lay deckings high thereupon, that it may bear thee over the misty deep. And I will place therein bread and water, and red wine to thy heart's desire, to keep hunger far away. And I will put raiment upon thee, and send a fair gale in thy wake, that so thou mayest come all unharmed to thine own country, if indeed it be the good pleasure of the gods who hold wide heaven, who are stronger than I am both to will and to do. . . . Yet didst thou know in thine heart what a measure of suffering thou art ordained to fulfil, or ever thou reach thine own country, here, even here, thou wouldst abide with me and keep this house, and wouldst never taste of death, though thou longest to see thy wife, for whom thou hast ever a desire day by day. Not in sooth that I avow me to be less noble than she in form or fashion, for it is in no wise meet that mortal women should match them with immortals, in shape and comeliness.'

And Odysseus of many counsels answered, and spake unto her: 'Be not wroth with me hereat, goddess and queen. Myself I know it well, how wise Penelope is meaner to look upon than thou, in comeliness and stature. But she is mortal and thou knowest not age nor death. Yet even so, I wish and long day by day to fare homeward and see the day of my returning. Yea, and if some god shall wreck me in the wine-dark deep, even so I will endure, with a heart within me patient of affliction. For already have I suffered full much, and much have I toiled in perils of waves and war; let this be added to the tale of those.' . . .

It was the fourth day when he had accomplished all. And, lo, on the fifth, the fair Calypso sent him on his way from the island, when she had bathed him and clad him in fragrant attire. Moreover, the goddess placed on board the ship two skins, one of dark wine, and another, a great one, of water, and corn too in a wallet, and she set therein a store of dainties to his heart's desire, and sent forth a warm and gentle wind to blow. And goodly Odysseus rejoiced as he set his sails to the breeze. So he sate and cunningly guided the craft with the helm. . . . But the East Wind and the South Wind clashed, and the stormy West, and the North, that is born in the bright air, rolling onward a great wave. Then were the knees of Odysseus loosened and his heart melted. . . . The great wave smote down upon him, driving on in terrible wise, that the raft reeled again. And far therefrom he fell, and lost the helm from his hand; and the fierce blast of the jostling winds came and brake his mast in the midst, and sail and yardarm fell afar into the deep. Long time the water kept him under, nor could he speedily rise from beneath the rush of the mighty wave. . . .

So for two nights and two days he was wandering in the swell of the sea, and much his heart boded of death. But when at last the fair-tressed Dawn brought the full light of the third day, thereafter the breeze fell, and lo, there was a breathless calm, and with a quick glance ahead (he being upborne on a great wave) he saw the land very near. And even as when most welcome to his children is the sight of a father's life, who lies in sickness and strong pains long wasting away, some angry god assailing him; and to their delight the gods have loosed him from his trouble; so welcome to Odysseus showed land and wood; and he swam onward, being eager to set foot on the strand. . . .

When he came in his swimming over against the mouth of a fair-flowing river, whereby the place seemed best in his eyes, smooth of rocks, and withal there was a covert from the wind, Odysseus felt the river running, and prayed to him in his heart:

'Hear me, O king, whosoever thou art; unto thee am I come, as to one to whom prayer is made, while I flee the rebukes of Poseidon from the deep. Yea, reverend even to the deathless gods is that man who comes as a wanderer, even as I now have come to thy stream and to thy knees after much travail. Nay pity me, O king; for I avow myself thy suppliant.'

So spake he, and the god straightway stayed his stream and withheld his waves, and made the water smooth before him, and brought him safely to the mouths of the river. And his knees bowed and his stout hands fell, for his heart was broken by the brine. And his flesh was all swollen and a great stream of sea water gushed up through his mouth and nostrils. So he lay without breath or speech, swooning, such terrible weariness came upon him. . . .

BOOK VI

So there he lay asleep, the steadfast goodly Odysseus, fordone with toil and drowsiness. Meanwhile Athene went to the land and the city of the Phaeacians, where Alcinous was reigning, with wisdom granted by the gods. To his house went the goddess, grey-eyed Athene, devising a return for the great-hearted Odysseus. She betook her to the rich-wrought bower, wherein was sleeping a maiden like to the gods in form and comeliness, Nausicaa, the daughter of Alcinous, high of heart. Beside her on either hand of the pillars of the door were two handmaids, dowered with beauty from the Graces, and the shining doors were shut.

But the goddess, fleet as the breath of the wind, swept towards the couch of the maiden, and stood above her head, and spake to her in the semblance of the daughter of a famous seafarer, Dymas, a girl of like age with Nausicaa, who had found grace in her sight. In her shape the grey-eyed Athene spake to the princess, saying:

'Nausicaa, how hath thy mother so heedless a maiden to her daughter? Lo, thou has shining raiment that lies by thee uncared for, and thy marriage-day is near at hand, when thou thyself must needs go beautifully clad, and have garments to give to them who shall lead thee to the house of the bridegroom! And, behold, these are the things whence a good report goes abroad among men, wherein a father and lady mother take delight. But come, let us arise and go a-washing with the breaking of the day, and I will follow with thee to be thy mate in the toil, that without delay thou mayst get thee ready, since truly thou art not long to be a maiden. Lo, already they are wooing thee, the noblest youths of all the Phaeacians, among that people whence thou thyself doth draw thy lineage. So come, beseech thy noble father betimes in the morning to furnish thee with mules and a wain to carry the men's raiment, and the robes, and the shining coverlets. Yea and for thyself it is seemlier far to go thus than on foot, for the places where we must wash are a great way off the town.' So spake the grey-eyed Athene, and departed to Olympus. . . .

Anon came the throned Dawn, and awakened Nausicaa of the fair robes, who straightway marvelled on the dream, and went through the halls to tell her parents, her father dear and her mother. And she found them within, her mother sitting by the hearth with the women her handmaids, spinning yarn of sea-purple stain, but her father she met as he was going forth to the renowned kings in their council, whither the noble Phaeacians called him. Standing close by her dear father she spake, saying: 'Father, dear, couldst thou not lend me a high waggon with strong wheels, that I may take the goodly raiment to the river to wash, so much as I have lying soiled? Yea and it is seemly that thou thyself, when thou art with the princes in council, shouldest have fresh raiment to wear. Also, there are five dear sons of thine in the halls, two married, but three are lusty bachelors, and these are always eager for new-washen garments wherein to go to the dances: for all these things have I taken thought.'

This she said, because she was ashamed to speak of glad marriage to her father; but he saw all and answered, saying:

'Neither the mules nor aught else do I grudge thee, my child. Go thy ways, and the thralls shall get thee ready a high waggon with good wheels, and fitted with an upper frame.'

Therewith he called to his men, and they gave ear, and without the palace they made ready the smooth-running mule-wain, and led the mules beneath the yoke, and harnessed them under the car, while the maiden brought forth from her bower the shining raiment. This she stored in the polished car, and her mother filled a basket with all manner of food to the heart's desire, dainties too she set therein, and she poured wine into a goat-skin bottle, while Nausicaa climbed into the wain. And her mother gave her soft olive oil also in a golden cruse, that she and her maidens might anoint themselves after the bath. Then Nausicaa took the whip and the shining reins, and touched the mules to start them; then there was a clatter of hoofs, and on they strained without flagging, with their load of the raiment and the maiden. Not alone did she go, for her attendants followed with her.

Now when they were come to the beautiful stream of the river, where truly were the unfailing cisterns, and bright water welled up free from beneath, and flowed past, enough to wash the foulest garments clean, there the girls unharnessed the mules from under the chariot, and turning them loose they drove them along the banks of the eddying river to graze on the honey-sweet clover. Then they took the garments from the wain, in their hands, and bore them to the black water, and briskly trod them down in the trenches, in busy rivalry. Now when they had washed and cleansed all the stains, they spread all out in order along the shore of the deep, even where the sea, in beating on the coast, washed the pebbles clean. Then having bathed and anointed them well with olive oil, they took their mid-day meal on the river's banks, waiting till the clothes should dry in the brightness of the sun. Anon, when they were satisfied with food, the maidens and the princess, they fell to playing at ball, casting away their tires, and among them Nausicaa of the white arms began the song. . . .

But when now she was about going homewards, after yoking the mules and folding up the goodly raiment, then grey-eyed Athene turned to other thoughts, that so Odysseus might awake, and see the lovely maiden, who should be his guide to the city of the Phaeacian men. So then the princess threw the ball at one of her company; she missed the girl, and cast the ball into the deep eddying current, whereat they all raised a piercing cry. Then the goodly Odysseus awoke and sat up, pondering in his heart and spirit:

'Woe is me! to what men's land am I come now? say, are they froward, and wild, and unjust, or are they hospitable, and of God-fearing mind? How shrill a cry of maidens rings round me, of the nymphs that hold the steep hill-tops, and the river-springs, and the grassy water-meadows! It must be, methinks, that I am near men of human speech. Go to, I myself will make trial and see.'

Therewith the goodly Odysseus crept out from under the coppice, having broken with his strong hand a leafy bough from the thick wood, to hold athwart his body, that it might hide his nakedness withal. And forth he sallied like a lion mountain-bred, trusting in his strength, who fares out blown and rained upon, with flaming eyes; amid the kine he goes or amid the sheep or in the track of the wild deer; yea, his belly bids him go even to the good homestead to make assay upon the flocks. Even so Odysseus was fain to draw nigh to the fair-tressed maidens, all naked as he was, such need had come upon him. But he was terrible in their eyes, being marred with the salt sea foam, and they fled cowering here and there about the jutting spits of shore. And the daughter of Alcinous alone stood firm, for Athene gave her courage of heart, and took all trembling from her limbs. So she halted and stood over against him, and Odysseus considered whether he should clasp the knees of the lovely maiden, and so make his prayer, or should stand as he was, apart, and beseech her with smooth words, if haply she might show him the town, and give him raiment. And as he thought within himself, it seemed better to stand apart, and beseech her with smooth words, lest the maiden should be angered with him if he

touched her knees: so straightway he spake a sweet and cunning word:

'I supplicate thee, O queen, whether thou art a goddess or a mortal! If indeed thou art a goddess of them that keep the wide heaven; to Artemis, then, the daughter of great Zeus, I mainly liken thee, for beauty and stature and shapeliness. But if thou art one of the daughters of men who dwell on earth, thrice blessed are thy father and thy lady mother, and thrice blessed thy brethren. Surely their souls ever glow with gladness for thy sake, each time they see thee entering the dance, so fair a flower of maidens. But he is of heart the most blessed beyond all other who shall prevail with gifts of wooing, and lead thee to his home. Never have mine eyes beheld such an one among mortals, neither man nor woman; great awe comes upon me as I look on thee. Yet in Delos once I saw as goodly a thing: a young sapling of a palm tree springing by the altar of Apollo. For thither too I went, and much people with me, on that path where my sore troubles were to be. Yea, and when I looked thereupon, long time I marvelled in spirit,—for never grew there yet so goodly a shoot from ground,—even in such wise as I wonder at thee, lady, and am astonied and do greatly fear to touch thy knees, though grievous sorrow is upon me. Yesterday, on the twentieth day, I scaped from the wine-dark deep, but all that time continually the wave bare me, and the vehement winds drave, from the isle Ogygia. And now some god has cast me on this shore, that here too, methinks, some evil may betide me; for I trow not that trouble will cease; the gods ere that time will yet bring many a thing to pass. But, queen, have pity on me, for after many trials and sore to thee first of all am I come, and of the other folk, who hold this city and land, I know no man. Nay show me the town, give me an old garment to cast about me, if thou hadst, when thou camest here, any wrap for the linen. And may the gods grant thee all thy heart's desire: a husband and a home, and a mind at one with his may they give— a good gift, for there is nothing mightier and nobler than when man and wife are of one heart and mind in a house, a grief to their foes, and to their friends great joy, but their own hearts know it best.'

Then Nausicaa of the white arms answered him, and said: 'Stranger, forasmuch as thou seemest no evil man nor foolish—and it is Olympian Zeus himself that giveth weal to men, to the good and to the evil, to each one as he will, and this thy lot doubtless is of him, and so thou must in anywise endure it: —and now, since thou hast come to our city and our land, thou shalt not lack raiment, nor aught else that is the due of a hapless suppliant, when he has met them who can befriend him. And I will show thee the town, and name the name of the people. The Phaeacians hold this city and land, and I am the daughter of Alcinous, great of heart, on whom all the might and force of the Phaeacians depend.'

Thus she spake, and called to her maidens of the fair tresses: 'Halt, my maidens, whither flee ye at the sight of a man? Ye surely do not take him for an enemy? That mortal breathes not, and never will be born, who shall come with war to the land of the Phaeacians, for they are very dear to the gods. Far apart we live in the wash of the waves, the outermost of men, and no other mortals are conversant with us. Nay, but this man is some helpless one come hither in his wanderings, whom now we must kindly entreat, for all strangers and beggars are from Zeus, and a little gift is dear. So, my maidens, give the stranger meat and drink, and bathe him in the river, where withal is a shelter from the winds.'

So she spake, but they had halted and called each to the other, and they brought Odysseus to the sheltered place, and made him sit down, as Nausicaa bade them, the daughter of Alcinous, high of heart. Beside him they laid a mantle, and a doublet for raiment, and gave him soft olive oil in the golden cruse, and bade him wash in the streams of the river. Then goodly Odysseus spake among the maidens, saying: 'I pray you stand thus apart, while I myself wash the brine from my shoulders, and anoint me with olive oil, for truly oil is long a stranger to my skin. But in your sight I will not bathe, for I am ashamed to make me naked in the company of fair-tressed maidens.'

Then they went apart and told all to their lady. But with the river water the goodly Odysseus washed from his skin the salt scurf that covered his back and broad shoulders, and from his head he wiped the crusted brine of the barren sea. But when he had washed his whole body, and anointed him with olive oil, and had clad himself in the raiment that the unwedded maiden gave him. . . .

Then to the shore of the sea went Odysseus apart, and sat down, glowing in beauty and grace, and the princess marvelled at him, and spake among her fair-tressed maidens, saying:

'Listen, my white-armed maidens, and I will say somewhat. Not without the will of all the gods who hold Olympus hath this man come among the god-like Phaeacians. Erewhile he seemed to me uncomely, but now he is like the gods that keep the wide heaven. Would that such an one might be called my husband, dwelling here, and that it might please him here to abide! But come, my maidens, give the stranger meat and drink.'

Thus she spake, and they gave ready ear and hearkened, and set beside Odysseus meat and drink, and the steadfast goodly Odysseus did eat and drink eagerly, for it was long since he had tasted food.

Now Nausicaa of the white arms had another thought. She folded the raiment and stored it in the goodly wain, and yoked the mules strong of hoof, and herself climbed into the car. Then she called on Odysseus, and spake and hailed him: 'Up now, stranger, and rouse thee to go to the city, that I may convey thee to the house of my wise father, where, I promise thee, thou shalt get knowledge of all the noblest of the Phaeacians. But do thou even as I tell thee, and thou seemest a discreet man enough. So long as we are passing along the fields and farms of men, do thou fare quickly with the maidens behind the mules and the chariot, and I will lead the way. But when we set foot within the city,—whereby goes a high wall with towers, and there is a fair haven on either side of the town, and narrow is the entrance, and curved ships are drawn up on either hand of the mole, for all the folk have stations for their vessels, each man one for himself. And there is the place of assembly about the goodly temple of Poseidon, furnished with heavy stones, deep bedded in the earth. There men look to the gear of the black ships, hawsers and sails, and there they fine down the oars. For the Phaeacians care not for bow nor quiver, but for masts, and oars of ships, and gallant barques, wherein rejoicing they cross the grey sea. Their ungracious speech it is that I would avoid, lest some man afterward rebuke me, and there are but too many insolent folk among the people. And some one of the baser sort might meet me and say: "Who is this that goes with Nausicaa, this tall and goodly stranger? Where found she him? Her husband he will be, her very own. Either she has taken in some ship-wrecked wanderer of strange men,—for no men dwell near us; or some god has come in answer to her instant prayer; from heaven has he descended, and will have her to wife for evermore. Better so, if herself she has ranged abroad and found a lord from a strange land, for verily she holds in no regard the Phaeacians here in this country, the many men and noble who are her wooers." So will they speak, and this would turn to my reproach. Yea, and I myself would think it blame of another maiden who did such things in despite of her friends, her father and mother being still alive, and was conversant with men before the day of open wedlock. But, stranger, heed well what I say, that as soon as may be thou mayest gain at my father's hands an escort and a safe return. Thou shalt find a fair grove of Athene, a poplar grove near the road, and a spring wells forth therein, and a meadow lies all around. There is my father's demesne, and his fruitful close, within the sound of a man's shout from the city. Sit thee down there and wait until such time as we may have come into the city, and reached the house of my father. But when thou deemest that we are got to the palace, then go up to the city of the Phaeacians, and ask for the house of my father

Alcinous, high of heart. It is easily known, and a young child could be thy guide, for nowise like it are builded the houses of the Phaeacians, so goodly is the palace of the hero Alcinous. But when thou art within the shadow of the halls and the court, pass quickly through the great chamber, till thou comest to my mother, who sits at the hearth in the light of the fire, weaving yarn of sea-purple stain, a wonder to behold. Her chair is leaned against a pillar, and her maidens sit behind her. And there my father's throne leans close to hers, wherein he sits and drinks his wine, like an immortal. Pass thou by him, and cast thy hands about my mother's knees, that thou mayest see quickly and with joy the day of thy returning, even if thou art from a very far country. If but her heart be kindly disposed toward thee, then is there hope that thou shalt see thy friends, and come to thy well-built house, and to thine own country.'

She spake, and smote the mules with the shining whip, and quickly they left behind them the streams of the river. . . .

BOOKS VII–VIII

. . . Odysseus went to the famous palace of Alcinous, and his heart was full of many thoughts as he stood there or ever he had reached the threshold of bronze. For there was a gleam as it were of sun or moon through the high-roofed hall of greathearted Alcinous. Brazen were the walls which ran this way and that from the threshold to the inmost chamber, and round them was a frieze of blue, and golden were the doors that closed in the good house. Silver were the door-posts that were set on the brazen threshold, and silver the lintel thereupon, and the hook of the door was of gold. And on either side stood golden hounds and silver, which Hephaestus wrought by his cunning, to guard the palace of great-hearted Alcinous, being free from death and age all their days.

There the steadfast goodly Odysseus stood and gazed. But when he had gazed at all and wondered, he passed quickly over the threshold within the house. And he found the captains and the counsellors of the Phaeacians pouring forth wine to the keen-sighted god, the slayer of Argos; for to him they poured the last cup when they were minded to take rest. Now the steadfast goodly Odysseus went through the hall, clad in a thick mist, which Athene shed around him, till he came to Arete and the king Alcinous. And Odysseus cast his hands about the knees of Arete, and then it was that the wondrous mist melted from off him, and a silence fell on them that were within the house at the sight of him, and they marvelled as they beheld him. Then Odysseus began his prayer:

'Arete, daughter of god-like Rhexenor, after many toils am I come to thy husband and to thy knees and to these guests, and may the gods vouchsafe them a happy life, and may each one leave to his children after him his substance in his halls and whatever dues of honour the people have rendered unto him. But speed, I pray you, my parting, that I may come the more quickly to mine own country, for already too long do I suffer affliction far from my friends.' . . .

Now when the mighty king Alcinous heard this saying, he took Odysseus, the wise and crafty, by the hand, and raised him from the hearth, and set him on a shining chair, whence he bade his son give place, valiant Laodamas, who sat next him and was his dearest. And a handmaid bare water for the hands in a goodly golden ewer, and poured it forth over a silver basin to wash withal, and drew to his side a polished table. And a grave dame bare wheaten bread and set it by him and laid upon the board many dainties, giving freely of such things as she had by her. . . .

. . . The heart of Odysseus melted, and the tear wet his cheeks beneath the eyelids. And as a woman throws herself wailing about her dear lord, who hath fallen before his city and the host, warding from his town and his children the pitiless day; and she beholds him dying and drawing difficult breath, and embracing his body wails aloud, while the foemen behind smite her with spears on back and shoulders and lead her up into bondage, to bear labour and trouble, and with the most pitiful grief her cheeks are wasted; even so pitifully fell the tears beneath the brows of Odysseus. Now none of all the company marked him weeping; but Alcinous alone noted it, and was aware thereof, as he sat nigh him and heard him groaning heavily. And presently he spake among the Phaeacians, masters of the oar: '. . . Say, what is the name whereby they called thee at home, even thy father and thy mother, and others thy townsmen and the dwellers round about? For there is none of all mankind nameless, neither the mean man nor yet the noble, from first hour of his birth, but parents bestow a name on every man so soon as he is born. Tell me too of thy land, thy township, and thy city, that our ships may conceive of their course to bring thee thither.' . . .

BOOK IX

And Odysseus of many counsels answered him saying: 'King Alcinous, most notable of all the people, I say that there is no more gracious or perfect delight than when a whole people makes merry, and the men sit orderly at feast in the halls and listen to the singer, and the tables by them are laden with bread and flesh, and a wine-bearer drawing the wine serves it round and pours it into the cups. This seems to me well-nigh the fairest thing in the world. But now thy heart was inclined to ask of my grievous troubles, that I may mourn for more exceeding sorrow. What then shall I tell of first, what last, for the gods of heaven have given me woes in plenty? Now, first, will I tell my name, that ye too may know it, and that I, when I have escaped the pitiless day, may yet be your host, though my home is in a far country. I am ODYSSEUS, SON OF LAERTES, who am in men's minds for all manner of wiles, and my fame reaches unto heaven. And I dwell in clear-seen Ithaca, wherein is a mountain Neriton, with trembling forest leaves, standing manifest to view, and many islands lie around, very near one to the other, Dulichium and Same, and wooded Zacynthus. Now Ithaca lies low, furthest up the sea-line toward the darkness, but those others face the dawning and the sun; a rugged isle, but a good nurse of noble youths; and for myself I can see nought beside sweeter than a man's own country. Verily Calypso, the fair goddess, would fain have kept me with her in her hollow caves, longing to have me for her lord; and likewise too, guileful Circé of Aia, would have stayed me in her halls, longing to have me for her lord. But never did they prevail upon my heart within my breast. So surely is there nought sweeter than a man's own country and his parents, even though he dwell far off in a rich home, in a strange land, away from them that begat him. But come, let me tell thee too of the troubles of my journeying, which Zeus laid on me as I came from Troy. . . . We came to the land of the Cyclôpes, a froward and a lawless folk, who trusting to the deathless gods plant not aught with their hands, neither plough; but, behold, all these things spring for them in plenty, unsown and untilled, wheat, and barley, and vines, which bear great clusters of the juice of the grape, and the rain of Zeus gives them increase. These have neither gatherings for council nor oracles of law, but they dwell in hollow caves on the crests of the high hills, and each one utters the law to his children and his wives, and they reck not one of another. . . .

'Then I commanded the rest of my well-loved company to tarry there by the ship, and to guard the ship, but I chose out twelve men, the best of my company, and sallied forth. Now I had with me a goat-skin of the dark wine and sweet. . . . With this wine I filled a great skin, and bare it with me, and corn too I put in a wallet, for my lordly spirit straightway had a boding that a man would come to me, a strange man, clothed in mighty strength, one that knew not judgment and justice.

'Soon we came to the cave, but we found him not within; he was shepherding his fat flocks in the pastures. So we went into the cave, and gazed on all that was therein. The baskets were well laden with cheeses, and the folds were thronged with lambs and kids; each kind was penned by itself, the firstlings apart, and the summer lambs apart, apart too the younglings of the flock. Now all the vessels swam with whey, the milk-pails and the bowls, the well-wrought vessels whereinto he milked. My company then spake and besought me first of all to take of the cheeses and to return, and afterwards to make haste and drive off the kids and lambs to the swift ships from out the pens, and to sail over the salt sea water. Howbeit I hearkened not (and far better would it have been), but waited to see the giant himself, and whether he would give me gifts as a stranger's due. Yet was not his coming to be with joy to my company.

'Then we kindled a fire, and made burnt-offering, and ourselves likewise took of the cheeses, and did eat, and sat waiting for him within till he came back, shepherding his flocks. And he bore a grievous weight of dry wood, against supper time. This log he cast down with a din inside the cave, and in fear we fled to the secret place of the rock. As for him, he drave his fat flocks into the wide cavern, even all that he was wont to milk; but the males both of the sheep and of the goats he left without in the deep yard. Thereafter he lifted a huge doorstone and weighty, and set it in the mouth of the cave, such an one as two and twenty good four-wheeled wains could not raise from the ground, so mighty a sheer rock did he set against the doorway. Then he sat down and milked the ewes and bleating goats all orderly, and beneath each ewe he placed her young. And anon he curdled one half of the white milk, and massed it together, and stored it in wicker-baskets, and the other half he let stand in pails, that he might have it to take and drink against supper time. Now when he had done all his work busily then he kindled the fire anew, and espied us, and made question:

' "Strangers, who are ye? Whence sail ye over the wet ways? On some trading enterprise or at adventure do ye rove, even as sea-robbers over the brine, for at hazard of their own lives they wander, bringing bale to alien men."

'So spake he, but as for us our heart within us was broken for terror of the deep voice and his own monstrous shape; yet despite all I answered and spake unto him, saying:

' "Lo, we are Achaeans, driven wandering from Troy, by all manner of winds over the great gulf of the sea; seeking our homes we fare, but another path have we come, by other ways: even such, methinks, was the will and the counsel of Zeus. And we avow us to be the men of Agamemnon, son of Atreus, whose fame is even now the mightiest under heaven, so great a city did he sack, and destroyed many people; but as for us we have lighted here, and come to these thy knees, if perchance thou wilt give us a stranger's gift, or make any present, as is the due of strangers. Nay, lord, have regard to the gods, for we are thy suppliants; and Zeus is the avenger of suppliants and sojourners, Zeus, the god of the stranger, who fareth in the company of reverend strangers."

'So I spake, and anon he answered out of his pitiless heart: "Thou art witless, my stranger, or thou hast come from afar, who biddest me either to fear or shun the gods. For the Cyclôpes pay no heed to Zeus, lord of the aegis, nor to the blessed gods, for verily we are better men than they. Nor would I, to shun the enmity of Zeus, spare either thee or thy company, unless my spirit bade me. But tell me where thou didst stay thy well-wrought ship on thy coming? Was it perchance at the far end of the island, or hard by, that I may know?"

'So he spake tempting me, but he cheated me not, who knew full much, and I answered him again with words of guile:

' "As for my ship, Poseidon, the shaker of the earth, brake it to pieces, for he cast it upon the rocks at the border of your country, and brought it nigh the headland, and a wind bare it thither from the sea. But I with these my men escaped from utter doom."

'So I spake, and out of his pitiless heart he answered me not a word, but sprang up, and laid his hands upon my fellows, and clutching two together dashed them, as they had been whelps, to the earth, and the brain flowed forth upon the ground and the earth was wet. Then cut he them up piecemeal, and made ready his supper. So he ate even as a mountain-bred lion, and ceased not, devouring entrails and flesh and bones with their marrow. And we wept and raised our hands to Zeus, beholding the cruel deeds; and we were at our wits' end. And after the Cyclops had filled his huge maw with human flesh and the milk he drank thereafter, he lay within the cave, stretched out among his sheep.

'So I took counsel in my great heart, whether I should draw near, and pluck my sharp sword from my thigh, and stab him in the breast, where the midriff holds the liver, feeling for the place with my hand. But my second thought withheld me, for so should we too have perished even there with utter doom. For we should not have prevailed to roll away with our hands from the lofty door the heavy stone which he set there. So for that time we made moan, awaiting the bright Dawn.

'Now when early Dawn shone forth, the rosy-fingered, again he kindled the fire and milked his goodly flocks all orderly, and beneath each ewe set her lamb. Anon when he had done all his work busily, again he seized yet other two men and made ready his mid-day meal. And after the meal, lightly he moved away the great door-stone, and drave his fat flocks forth from the cave, and afterwards he set it in its place again, as one might set the lid on a quiver. Then with a loud whoop, the Cyclops turned

his fat flocks towards the hills; but I was left devising evil in the deep of my heart, if in any wise I might avenge me, and Athene grant me renown.

'And this was the counsel that showed best in my sight. There lay by a sheep-fold a great club of the Cyclops, a club of olive wood, yet green, which he had cut to carry with him when it should be seasoned. Now when we saw it we likened it in size to the mast of a black ship of twenty oars, a wide merchant vessel that traverses the great sea gulf, so huge it was to view in bulk and length. I stood thereby and cut off from it a portion as it were a fathom's length, and set it by my fellows, and bade them fine it down, and they made it even, while I stood by and sharpened it to a point, and straightway I took it and hardened it in the bright fire. Then I laid it well away, and hid it beneath the dung, which was scattered in great heaps in the depths of the cave. And I bade my company cast lots among them, which of them should risk the adventure with me, and lift the bar and turn it about in his eye, when sweet sleep came upon him. And the lot fell upon those four whom I myself would have been fain to choose, and I appointed myself to be the fifth among them. In the evening he came shepherding his flocks of goodly fleece, and presently he drave his fat flocks into the cave each and all, nor left he any without in the deep court-yard, whether through some foreboding, or perchance that the god so bade him do. Thereafter he lifted the huge door-stone and set it in the mouth of the cave, and sitting down he milked the ewes and bleating goats, all orderly, and beneath each ewe he placed her young. Now when he had done all his work busily, again he seized yet other two and made ready his supper. Then I stood by the Cyclops and spake to him, holding in my hands an ivy bowl of the dark wine:

' "Cyclops, take and drink wine after thy feast of man's meat, that thou mayest know what manner of drink this was that our ship held. And lo, I was bringing it thee as a drink offering, if haply thou mayest take pity and send me on my way home, but thy mad rage is past all sufferance. O hard of heart, how may another of the many men there be come ever to thee again, seeing that thy deeds have been lawless?"

'So I spake, and he took the cup and drank it off, and found great delight in drinking the sweet draught, and asked me for it yet a second time:

' "Give it me again of thy grace, and tell me thy name straightway, that I may give thee a stranger's gift, wherein thou mayest be glad. Yea for the earth, the grain-giver, bears for the Cyclôpes the mighty clusters of the juice of the grape, and the rain of Zeus gives them increase, but this is a rill of very nectar and ambrosia."

'So he spake, and again I handed him the dark

wine. Thrice I bare and gave it him, and thrice in his folly he drank it to the lees. Now when the wine had got about the wits of the Cyclops, then did I speak to him with soft words:

' "Cyclops, thou askest me my renowned name, and I will declare it unto thee, and do thou grant me a stranger's gift, as thou didst promise. Noman is my name, and Noman they call me, my father and my mother and all my fellows."

10 'So I spake, and straightway he answered me out of his pitiless heart:

' "Noman will I eat last in the number of his fellows, and the others before him: that shall be thy gift."

'Therewith he sank backwards and fell with face upturned, and there he lay with his great neck bent round, and sleep, that conquers all men, overcame him. And the wine and the fragments of men's flesh issued forth from his mouth, and he vomited, being heavy with wine. Then I thrust in that stake under 20 the deep ashes, until it should grow hot, and I spake to my companions comfortable words, lest any should hang back from me in fear. But when that bar of olive wood was just about to catch fire in the flame, green though it was, and began to glow terribly, even then I came nigh, and drew it from the coals, and my fellows gathered about me, and some god breathed great courage into us. For their part they seized the bar of olive wood, that was sharpened at the point, and thrust it into his eye, while I 30 from my place aloft turned it about, as when a man bores a ship's beam with a drill while his fellows below spin it with a strap, which they hold at either end, and the auger runs round continually. Even so did we seize the fiery-pointed brand and whirled it round in his eye, and the blood flowed about the heated bar. And the breath of the flame singed his eyelids and brows all about, as the ball of the eye burnt away, and the roots thereof crackled in the flame. And as when a smith dips an axe or adze in 40 chill water with a great hissing, when he would temper it—for hereby anon comes the strength of iron—even so did his eye hiss round the stake of olive. And he raised a great and terrible cry, that the rock rang around, and we fled away in fear, while he plucked forth from his eye the brand bedabbled in much blood. Then maddened with pain he cast it from him with his hands, and called with a loud voice on the Cyclôpes, who dwelt about him in the caves along the windy heights. And they heard the 50 cry and flocked together from every side, and gathering round the cave asked him what ailed him:

' "What hath so distressed thee, Polyphemus, that thou criest thus aloud through the immortal night, and makest us sleepless? Surely no mortal driveth off thy flocks against thy will: surely none slayeth thyself by force or craft?"

'And the strong Polyphemus spake to them again

from out the cave: "My friends, Noman is slaying me by guile, nor at all by force."

'And they answered and spake winged words: "If 60 then no man is violently handling thee in thy solitude, it can in no wise be that thou shouldest escape the sickness sent by mighty Zeus. Nay, pray thou to thy father, the lord Poseidon."

'On this wise they spake and departed; and my heart within me laughed to see how my name and cunning counsel had beguiled them. But the Cyclops, groaning and travailing in pain, groped with his hands, and lifted away the stone from the door of the cave, and himself sat in the entry, with arms 70 outstretched to catch, if he might, any one that was going forth with his sheep, so witless, methinks, did he hope to find me. But I advised me how all might be for the very best, if perchance I might find a way of escape from death for my companions and myself, and I wove all manner of craft and counsel, as a man will for his life, seeing that great mischief was nigh. And this was the counsel that showed best in my sight. The rams of the flock were well nurtured and thick of fleece, great and goodly, with wool dark as 80 the violet. Quietly I lashed them together with twisted withies, whereon the Cyclops slept, that lawless monster. Three together I took: now the middle one of the three would bear each a man, but the other twain went on either side, saving my fellows. Thus every three sheep bare their man. But as for me I laid hold of the back of a young ram who was far the best and the goodliest of all the flock, and curled beneath his shaggy belly there I lay, and so clung face upward, grasping the wondrous fleece 90 with a steadfast heart. So for that time making moan we awaited the bright Dawn.

'So soon as early Dawn shone forth, the rosy-fingered, then did the rams of the flock hasten forth to pasture, but the ewes bleated unmilked about the pens, for their udders were swollen to bursting. Then their lord, sore stricken with pain, felt along the backs of all the sheep as they stood up before him, and guessed not in his folly how that my men were bound beneath the breasts of his thick-fleeced flocks. 100 Last of all the sheep came forth the ram, cumbered with his wool, and the weight of me and my cunning. And the strong Polyphemus laid his hands on him and spake to him, saying:

' "Dear ram, wherefore, I pray thee, art thou the last of all the flocks to go forth from the cave, who of old wast not wont to lag behind the sheep, but wert ever the foremost to pluck the tender blossom of the pasture, faring with long strides, and wert still the first to come to the streams of the rivers, and 110 first didst long to return to the homestead in the evening. But now art thou the very last. Surely thou art sorrowing for the eye of thy lord, which an evil man blinded, with his accursed fellows, when he had subdued my wits with wine, even Noman, whom I say hath not yet escaped destruction. Ah, if thou couldst feel as I, and be endued with speech, to tell me where he shifts about to shun my wrath; then should he be smitten, and his brains be dashed against the floor here and there about the cave, and my heart be lightened of the sorrows which Noman, nothing worth, hath brought me!"

'Therewith he sent the ram forth from him, and when we had gone but a little way from the cave and from the yard, first I loosed myself from under the ram and then I set my fellows free. And swiftly we drave on those stiff-shanked sheep, so rich in fat, and often turned to look about, till we came to the ship. And a glad sight to our fellows were we that had fled from death, but the others they would have bemoaned with tears; howbeit I suffered it not, but with frowning brows forbade each man to weep. Rather I bade them to cast on board the many sheep with goodly fleece, and to sail over the salt sea water. So they embarked forthwith, and sate upon the benches, and sitting orderly smote the grey sea water with their oars. But when I had not gone so far, but that a man's shout might be heard, then I spoke unto the Cyclops taunting him:

''"Cyclops, so thou wert not to eat the company of a weakling by main might in thy hollow cave! Thine evil deeds were very sure to find thee out, thou cruel man, who hadst no shame to eat thy guests within thy gates, wherefore Zeus hath requited thee, and the other gods."

'So I spake, and he was mightily angered at heart, and he brake off the peak of a great hill and threw it at us, and it fell in front of the dark-prowed ship. And the sea heaved beneath the fall of the rock, and the backward flow of the wave bare the ship quickly to the dry land, with the wash from the deep sea, and drave it to the shore. Then I caught up a long pole in my hands, and thrust the ship from off the land, and roused my company, and with a motion of the head bade them dash in with their oars, that so we might escape our evil plight. So they bent to their oars and rowed on. But when we had now made twice the distance over the brine, I would fain have spoken to the Cyclops, but my company stayed me on every side with soft words, saying:

''"Foolhardy that thou art, why wouldst thou rouse a wild man to wrath, who even now hath cast so mighty a throw towards the deep and brought our ship back to land, yea and we thought that we had perished even there? If he had heard any of us utter sound or speech he would have crushed our heads and our ship timbers with a cast of a rugged stone, so mightily he hurls."

'So spake they, but they prevailed not on my lordly spirit, and I answered him again from out an angry heart:

''"Cyclops, if any one of mortal men shall ask thee of the unsightly blinding of thine eye, say that it was Odysseus that blinded it, the waster of cities, son of Laertes, whose dwelling is in Ithaca."

'So I spake, and with a moan he answered me, saying:

''"Lo now, in very truth the ancient oracles have come upon me. There lived here a soothsayer, a noble man and a mighty, Telemus, son of Eurymus, who surpassed all men in soothsaying, and waxed old as a seer among the Cyclôpes. He told me that all these things should come to pass in the aftertime, even that I should lose my eyesight at the hand of Odysseus. But I ever looked for some tall and goodly man to come hither, clad in great might, but behold now one that is a dwarf, a man of no worth and a weakling, hath blinded me of my eye after subduing me with wine. Nay come hither, Odysseus, that I may set by thee a stranger's cheer, and speed thy parting hence, that so the Earth-shaker may vouchsafe it thee, for his son am I, and he avows him for my father. And he himself will heal me, if it be his will; and none other of the blessed gods or of mortal men."

'Even so he spake, but I answered him, and said: "Would god that I were as sure to rob thee of soul and life, and send thee within the house of Hades, as I am that not even the Earth-shaker will heal thine eye!"

'So I spake, and then he prayed to the lord Poseidon stretching forth his hands to the starry heaven: "Hear me, Poseidon, girdler of the earth, god of the dark hair, if indeed I be thine, and thou avowest thee my sire,—grant that he may never come to his home, even Odysseus, waster of cities, the son of Laertes, whose dwelling is in Ithaca; yet if he is ordained to see his friends and come unto his wellbuilt house, and his own country, late may he come in evil case, with the loss of all his company, in the ship of strangers, and find sorrows in his house."

'So he spake in prayer, and the god of the dark locks heard him. And once again he lifted a stone, far greater than the first, and with one swing he hurled it, and he put forth a measureless strength, and cast it but a little space behind the dark-prowed ship, and all but struck the end of the rudder. And the sea heaved beneath the fall of the rock, but the wave bare on the ship and drave it to the further shore.

'But when we had now reached that island, where all our other decked ships abode together, and our company were gathered sorrowing, expecting us nevermore, on our coming thither we ran our ship ashore upon the sand, and ourselves too stept forth upon the sea-beach. Next we took forth the sheep of the Cyclops from out the hollow ship, and divided them, that none through me might go lacking his proper share. But the ram for me alone my goodly-greaved company chose out, in the dividing of the sheep, and on the shore I offered him up to Zeus, even to the son of Cronos, who dwells in the dark clouds, and is lord of all, and I burnt the slices of the thighs. But he heeded not the sacrifice, but was devising how my decked ships and my dear company might perish utterly. Thus for that time we sat the livelong day, until the going down of the sun, feasting on abundant flesh and sweet wine. And when the sun had sunk and darkness had come on, then we laid us to rest upon the sea-beach. So soon as early Dawn shone forth, the rosy-fingered, I called to my company, and commanded them that they should themselves climb the ship and loose the hawsers. So they soon embarked and sat upon the benches, and sitting orderly smote the grey sea water with their oars.

'Thence we sailed onward stricken at heart, yet glad as men saved from death, albeit we had lost our dear companions.

BOOK XI

. . . 'We set in order all the gear throughout the ship and sat us down; and the wind and the helmsman guided our barque. And all day long her sails were stretched in her seafaring; and the sun sank and all the ways were darkened.

'She came to the limits of the world, to the deep flowing Oceanus. There is the land and the city of the Cimmerians, shrouded in mist and cloud, and never does the shining sun look down on them with his rays, neither when he climbs up the starry heavens, nor when again he turns earthward from the firmament, but deadly night is outspread over miserable mortals. Thither we came and ran the ship ashore and took out the sheep.

'There Perimedes and Eurylochus held the victims, but I drew my sharp sword from my thigh, and dug a pit, as it were a cubit in length and breadth, and about it poured a drink-offering to all the dead, first with mead and thereafter with sweet wine, and for the third time with water. And I sprinkled white meal thereon, and entreated with many prayers the strengthless heads of the dead, and promised that on my return to Ithaca I would offer in my halls a barren heifer, the best I had, and fill the pyre with treasure, and apart unto Teiresias alone sacrifice a black ram without spot, the fairest of my flock. But when I had besought the tribes of the dead with vows and prayers, I took the sheep and cut their throats over the trench, and the dark blood flowed forth, and lo, the spirits of the dead that be departed gathered them from out of Erebus. Brides and youths unwed, and old men of many and evil days, and tender maidens with grief yet fresh at heart;

and many there were, wounded with bronze-shod spears, men slain in fight with their bloody mail about them. And these many ghosts flocked together from every side about the trench with a wondrous cry, and pale fear gat hold on me. Then did I speak to my company and command them to flay the sheep that lay slain by the pitiless sword, and to consume them with fire, and to make prayer to the gods, to mighty Hades and to dread Persephone, and myself I drew the sharp sword from my thigh and sat there, suffering not the strengthless heads of the dead to draw nigh to the blood, ere I had word of Teiresias. . . .

'Anon came up the soul of my mother dead, Anticleia, the daughter of Autolycus the great-hearted, whom I left alive when I departed for sacred Ilios. At the sight of her I wept, and was moved with compassion, yet even so, for all my sore grief, I suffered her not to draw nigh to the blood, ere I had word of Teiresias.

'Anon came the soul of Theban Teiresias, with a golden sceptre in his hand, and he knew me and spake unto me: "Son of Laertes, of the seed of Zeus, Odysseus of many devices, what seekest thou *now*, wretched man, wherefore hast thou left the sunlight and come hither to behold the dead and a land desolate of joy? Nay, hold off from the ditch and draw back thy sharp sword, that I may drink of the blood and tell thee sooth."

'So spake he and I put up my silver-studded sword into the sheath, and when he had drunk the dark blood, even then did the noble seer speak unto me, saying: "Thou art asking of thy sweet returning, great Odysseus, but that will the god make hard for thee; for methinks thou shalt not pass unheeded by the Shaker of the Earth, who hath laid up wrath in his heart against thee, for rage at the blinding of his dear son. Yet even so, through many troubles, ye may come home, if thou wilt restrain thy spirit and the spirit of thy men so soon as thou shalt bring thy well-wrought ship nigh to the isle Thrinacia, fleeing the sea of violet blue, when ye find the herds of Helios grazing and his brave flocks, of Helios who overseeth all and overheareth all things. If thou doest these no hurt, being heedful of thy return, so may ye yet reach Ithaca, albeit in evil case. But if thou hurtest them, I foreshow ruin for thy ship and for thy men, and even though thou shalt thyself escape, late shalt thou return in evil plight, with the loss of all thy company, on board the ship of strangers, and thou shalt find sorrows in thy house, even proud men that devour thy living, while they woo thy godlike wife and offer the gifts of wooing. Yet I tell thee, on thy coming thou shalt avenge their violence. But when thou hast slain the wooers in thy halls, whether by guile, or openly with the edge of the sword, thereafter go thy way, taking with thee a shapen oar, till thou shalt come to such men as know not the sea, neither eat meat savoured with salt; yea, nor have they knowledge of ships of purple cheek, nor shapen oars which serve for wings to ships. And I will give thee a most manifest token, which cannot escape thee. In the day when another wayfarer shall meet thee and say that thou hast a winnowing fan on thy stout shoulder, even then make fast thy shapen oar in the earth and do goodly sacrifice to the lord Poseidon, even with a ram and a bull and a boar, the mate of swine, and depart for home and offer holy hecatombs to the deathless gods that keep the wide heaven, to each in order due. And from the sea shall thine own death come, the gentlest death that may be, which shall end thee foredone with smooth old age, and the folk shall dwell happily around thee. This that I say is sooth."

'So spake he, and I answered him, saying: "Teiresias, all these threads, methinks, the gods themselves have spun. But come, declare me this and plainly tell me all. I see here the spirit of my mother dead; lo, she sits in silence near the blood, nor deigns to look her son in the face nor speak to him! Tell me, prince, how may she know me again that I am he?"

'So spake I, and anon he answered me, and said: "I will tell thee an easy saying, and will put it in thy heart. Whomsoever of the dead that be departed thou shalt suffer to draw nigh to the blood, he shall tell thee sooth; but if thou shalt grudge any, that one shall go to his own place again." Therewith the spirit of the prince Teiresias went back within the house of Hades, when he had told all his oracles. But I abode there steadfastly, till my mother drew nigh and drank the dark blood; and at once she knew me, and bewailing herself spake to me winged words:

' "Dear child, how didst thou come beneath the darkness and the shadow, thou that art a living man? Grievous is the sight of these things to the living, for between us and you are great rivers and dreadful streams; first, Oceanus, which can no wise be crossed on foot, but only if one have a well-wrought ship. Art thou but now come hither with thy ship and thy company in thy long wanderings from Troy? and hast thou not yet reached Ithaca, nor seen thy wife in thy halls?"

'Even so she spake, and I answered her, and said: "O my mother, necessity was on me to come down to the house of Hades to seek to the spirit of Theban Teiresias. For not yet have I drawn near to the Achaean shore, nor yet have I set foot on mine own country, but have been wandering evermore in affliction, from the day that first I went with goodly Agamemnon to Ilios of the fair steeds, to do battle with the Trojans. But come, declare me this and plainly tell it all. What doom overcame thee of death that lays men at their length? Was it a slow disease, or did Artemis the archer slay thee with the visitation of her gentle shafts? And tell me of my father and my son, that I left behind me; doth my honour yet abide with them, or hath another already taken it, while they say that I shall come home no more? And tell me of my wedded wife, of her counsel and her purpose, doth she abide with her son and keep all secure, or hath she already wedded the best of the Achaeans?"

'Even so I spake, and anon my lady mother answered me: "Yea verily, she abideth with steadfast spirit in thy halls; and wearily for her the nights wane always and the days in shedding of tears. But the fair honour that is thine no man hath yet taken; but Telemachus sits at peace on his demesne, and feasts at equal banquets, whereof it is meet that a judge partake, for all men bid him to their house. And thy father abides there in the field, and goes not down to the town, nor lies he on bedding or rugs or shining blankets, but all the winter he sleeps, where sleep the thralls in the house, in the ashes by the fire, and is clad in sorry raiment. But when the summer comes and the rich harvest-tide, his beds of fallen leaves are strewn lowly all about the knoll of his vineyard plot. There he lies sorrowing and nurses his mighty grief, for long desire of thy return, and old age withal comes heavy upon him. Yea and even so did I too perish and meet my doom. It was not the archer goddess of the keen sight, who slew me in my halls with the visitation of her gentle shafts, nor did any sickness come upon me, such as chiefly with a sad wasting draws the spirit from the limbs; nay, it was my sore longing for thee, and for thy counsels, great Odysseus, and for thy loving-kindness, that reft me of sweet life."

'So spake she, and I mused in my heart and would fain have embraced the spirit of my mother dead. Thrice I sprang towards her, and was minded to embrace her; thrice she flitted from my hands as a shadow or even as a dream, and sharp grief arose ever at my heart. And uttering my voice I spake to her winged words:

' "Mother mine, wherefore dost thou not abide me who am eager to clasp thee, that even in Hades we twain may cast our arms each about the other, and have our fill of chill lament? Is this but a phantom that the high goddess Persephone hath sent me, to the end that I may groan for more exceeding sorrow?"

'So spake I, and my lady mother answered me anon: "Ah me, my child, of all men most ill-fated, Persephone, the daughter of Zeus, doth in no wise deceive thee, but even on this wise it is with mortals when they die. For the sinews no more bind together the flesh and the bones, but the great force of burning fire abolishes these, so soon as the life hath left the white bones, and the spirit like a dream flies forth and hovers near. But haste with all thine heart toward the sunlight, and mark all this, that even hereafter thou mayest tell it to thy wife."

Thus we twain held discourse together; and lo, the women came up, for the high goddess Persephone sent them forth, all they that had been the wives and daughters of mighty men. And they gathered and flocked about the black blood, and I took counsel how I might question them each one. And this was the counsel that showed best in my sight. I drew my long hanger from my stalwart thigh, and suffered them not all at one time to drink of the dark blood. So they drew nigh one by one, and each declared her lineage, and I made question of all.

'Now when holy Persephone had scattered this way and that the spirits of the women folk, thereafter came the soul of Agamemnon, son of Atreus, sorrowing; and round him others were gathered, the ghosts of them who had died with him in the house of Aegisthus and met their doom. And he knew me straightway when he had drunk the dark blood, yea, and he wept aloud, and shed big tears as he stretched forth his hands in his longing to reach me. But it might not be, for he had now no steadfast strength nor power at all in moving, such as was aforetime in his supple limbs.

'At the sight of him I wept and was moved with compassion, and uttering my voice, spake to him winged words: "Most renowned son of Atreus, Agamemnon, king of men, say what doom overcame thee of death that lays men at their length? Did Poseidon smite thee in thy ships, raising the dolorous blast of contrary winds, or did unfriendly men do thee hurt upon the land, whilst thou wert cutting off their oxen and fair flocks of sheep, or fighting to win a city and the women thereof?"

'So spake I, and straightway he answered, and said unto me: "Son of Laertes, of the seed of Zeus, Odysseus of many devices, it was not Poseidon that smote me in my ships, and raised the dolorous blast of contrary winds, nor did unfriendly men do me hurt upon the land, but Aegisthus it was that wrought me death and doom and slew me, with the aid of my accursed wife, as one slays an ox at the stall, after he had bidden me to his house, and entertained me at a feast. Even so I died by a death most pitiful, and round me my company likewise were slain without ceasing, like swine with glittering tusks which are slaughtered in the house of a rich and mighty man, whether at a wedding banquet or a joint-feast or a rich clan-drinking. Ere now hast thou been at the slaying of many a man, killed in single fight or in strong battle, yet thou wouldst have sorrowed the most at this sight, how we lay in the hall round the mixing-bowl and the laden boards, and the floor all ran with blood. And most pitiful of all that I heard was the voice of the daughter of Priam, of Cassandra, whom hard by me the crafty Clytem-

nestra slew. Then I strove to raise my hands as I was dying upon the sword, but to earth they fell. And that shameless one turned her back upon me, and had not the heart to draw down my eyelids with her fingers nor to close my mouth. So surely is there nought more terrible and shameless than a woman who imagines such evil in her heart, even as she too planned a foul deed, fashioning death for her wedded lord. Verily I had thought to come home most welcome to my children and my thralls; but she, out of the depth of her evil knowledge, hath shed shame on herself and on all womankind, which shall be for ever, even on the upright."

'Even so he spake, but I answered him, saying: "Lo now, in very sooth, hath Zeus of the far-borne voice wreaked wondrous hatred on the seed of Atreus through the counsels of woman from of old. For Helen's sake so many of us perished, and now Clytemnestra hath practised treason against thee, while yet thou wast afar off."

'Even so I spake, and anon he answered me, saying: "Wherefore do thou too, never henceforth be soft even to thy wife, neither show her all the counsel that thou knowest, but a part declare and let part be hid. Yet shalt not thou, Odysseus, find death at the hand of thy wife, for she is very discreet and prudent in all her ways, the wise Penelope, daughter of Icarius. Verily we left her a bride new wed when we went to the war, and a child was at her breast, who now, methinks, sits in the ranks of men, happy in his lot, for his dear father shall behold him on his company, and he shall embrace his sire as is meet. But as for my wife, she suffered me not so much as to have my fill of gazing on my son; ere that she slew me, even her lord. And yet another thing will I tell thee, and do thou ponder it in thy heart. Put thy ship to land in secret, and not openly, on the shore of thy dear country; for there is no more faith in woman. . . .

'Thus we twain stood sorrowing, holding sad discourse, while the big tears fell fast: and therewithal came the soul of Achilles, son of Peleus, and of Patroclus and of noble Antilochus and of Aias, who in face and form was goodliest of all the Danaans, after the noble son of Peleus. And the spirit of the son of Aeacus, fleet of foot, knew me again, and making lament spake to me winged words:

'"Son of Laertes, of the seed of Zeus, Odysseus of many devices, man overbold, what new deed and hardier than this wilt thou devise in thy heart? How durst thou come down to the house of Hades, where dwell the senseless dead, the phantoms of men outworn?"

'So he spake, but I answered him: "Achilles, son of Peleus, mightiest far of the Achaeans, I am come hither to seek to Teiresias, if he may tell me any counsel, how I may come to rugged Ithaca. For not yet have I come nigh the Achaean land, nor set foot on mine own soil, but am still in evil case; while as for thee, Achilles, none other than thou wast heretofore the most blessed of men, nor shall any be hereafter. For of old, in the days of thy life, we Argives gave thee one honour with the gods, and now thou art a great prince here among the dead. Wherefore let not thy death be any grief to thee, Achilles."

10 'Even so I spake, and he straightway answered me, and said: "Nay, speak not comfortably to me of death, oh great Odysseus. Rather would I live on ground as the hireling of another, with a landless man who had no great livelihood, than bear sway among all the dead that be departed. . . ."

'Therewith he departed again into the house of Hades, but I abode there still, if perchance some one of the hero folk besides might come, who died in old time. Yea and I should have seen the men of old, whom I was fain to look on, Theseus and Peirithous,
20 renowned children of the gods. But ere that might be the myriad tribes of the dead thronged up together with wondrous clamour: and pale fear gat hold of me, lest the high goddess Persephone should send me the head of the Gorgon, that dread monster, from out of Hades.

'Straightway then I went to the ship, and bade my men mount the vessel, and loose the hawsers. So speedily they went on board, and sat upon the benches. And the wave of the flood bore the barque
30 down the stream of Oceanus, we rowing first, and afterwards the fair wind was our convoy.

BOOK XII

'Now after the ship had left the stream of the river Oceanus, and was come to the wave of the wide sea . . . I saw smoke and a great wave, and heard the sea roaring. Then for very fear the oars flew from their hands, and down the stream they all splashed, and the ship was holden there, for my company no longer plied with their hands the tapering oars. But I paced the ship and cheered on my
40 men, as I stood by each one and spake smooth words: ". . . Do ye smite the deep surf of the sea with your oars, as ye sit on the benches, if peradventure Zeus may grant us to escape from and shun this death. And as for thee, helmsman, thus I charge thee, and ponder it in thine heart seeing that thou wieldest the helm of the hollow ship. Keep the ship well away from this smoke and from the wave and hug the rocks, lest the ship, ere thou art aware, start from her course to the other side, and so thou hurl us
50 into ruin." . . .

'We began to sail up the narrow strait lamenting. For on the one hand lay Scylla, and on the other mighty Charybdis in terrible wise sucked down the salt sea water. As often as she belched it forth, like a cauldron on a great fire she would seethe up

through all her troubled deeps, and overhead the spray fell on the tops of either cliff. But oft as she gulped down the salt sea water, within she was all plain to see through her troubled deeps, and the rock around roared horribly and beneath the earth was 60 manifest swart with sand, and pale fear gat hold on my men. Toward her, then, we looked fearing destruction; but Scylla meanwhile caught from out my hollow ship six of my company, the hardiest of their hands and the chief in might. And looking into the swift ship to find my men, even then I marked their feet and hands as they were lifted on high, and they cried aloud in their agony, and called me by my name for that last time of all. Even as when a fisher on some headland lets down with a long rod his baits 70 for a snare to the little fishes below, casting into the deep the horn of an ox of the homestead, and as he catches each flings it writhing ashore, so writhing were they borne upward to the cliff. And there she devoured them shrieking in her gates, they stretching forth their hands to me in the dread deathstruggle. And the most pitiful thing was this that mine eyes have seen of all my travail in searching out the paths of the sea.

'Now when we had escaped the Rocks and dread 80 Charybdis and Scylla, thereafter we soon came to the fair island of the god; where were the goodly kine, broad of brow, and the many brave flocks of Helios Hyperion. Then while as yet I was in my black ship upon the deep, I heard the lowing of the cattle being stalled and the bleating of the sheep, and on my mind there fell the saying of the blind seer, Theban Teiresias, and of Circé of Aia, who charged me very straitly to shun the isle of Helios, the gladdener of the world. 90

'Then for six days my dear company feasted on the best of the kine of Helios which they had driven off. But when Zeus, son of Cronos, had added the seventh day thereto, thereafter the wind ceased to blow with a rushing storm, and at once we climbed the ship and launched into the broad deep, when we had set up the mast and hoisted the white sails.

'But now when we left that isle nor any other land appeared, but sky and sea only, even then the son of Cronos stayed a dark cloud above the hollow 100 ship, and beneath it the deep darkened. And the ship ran on her way for no long while, for of a sudden came the shrilling West, with the rushing of a great tempest, and the blast of wind snapped the two forestays of the mast, and the mast fell backward and all the gear dropped into the bilge. And behold, on the hind part of the ship the mast struck the head of the pilot and brake all the bones of his skull together, and like a diver he dropt down from the

82–83. **goodly kine . . . flocks,** the sacred oxen of Helios, for the killing of which the companions of Odysseus and his ships are to be destroyed by Zeus.

deck, and his brave spirit left his bones. In that same hour Zeus thundered and cast his bolt upon the ship, and she reeled all over being stricken by the bolt of Zeus, and was filled with sulphur, and lo, my company fell from out the vessel. Like sea-gulls they were borne round the black ship upon the billows, and the god reft them of returning.

'But I kept pacing through my ship, till the surge loosened the sides from the keel, and the wave swept her along stript of her tackling, and brake her mast clean off at the keel. Now the backstay fashioned of an oxhide had been flung thereon; therewith I lashed together both keel and mast and sitting thereon I was borne by the ruinous winds. . . .

'Thence for nine days was I borne, and on the tenth night the gods brought me nigh to the isle of Ogygia, where dwells Calypso of the braided tresses, an awful goddess of mortal speech, who took me in and entreated me kindly. But why rehearse all this tale?' . . .

BOOK XIII

So spake he, and dead silence fell on all, and they were spell-bound throughout the shadowy halls. . . . Then the mighty Alcinous spake to the henchman: 'Pontonous, mix the bowl and serve out the wine to all in the hall, that we may pray to Father Zeus, and send the stranger on his way to his own country.'

So spake he, and Pontonous mixed the honey-hearted wine, and served it to all in turn. And they poured forth before the blessed gods that keep wide heaven, even there as they sat. . . . Now when they had come down to the ship and to the sea, straightway the good men of the escort took these things and laid them by in the hollow ship, even all the meat and drink. Then they strewed for Odysseus a rug and a sheet of linen, on the decks of the hollow ship in the hinder part thereof, that he might sleep sound. Then he too climbed aboard and laid him down in silence, while they sat upon the benches, every man in order, and unbound the hawser from the pierced stone. So soon as they leant backwards and tossed the sea water with the oar blade, a deep sleep fell upon his eyelids, a sound sleep, very sweet, and next akin to death.

So when the star came up, that is brightest of all, and goes ever heralding the light of early Dawn, even then did the sea-faring ship draw nigh the island. There is in the land of Ithaca a certain haven of Phorcys, the ancient one of the sea, and thereby are two headlands of sheer cliff, which slope to the sea on the haven's side and break the mighty wave that ill winds roll without, but within, the decked ships ride unmoored when once they have reached the place of anchorage. . . . Thither they, as having knowledge of that place, let drive their ship; and now the vessel in full course ran ashore, half her keel's length high; so well was she sped by the hands of the oarsmen. Then they alighted from the benched ship upon the land, and first they lifted Odysseus from out the hollow ship, all as he was in the sheet of linen and the bright rug, and laid him yet heavy with slumber on the sand. And they took forth the goods which the lordly Phaeacians had given him on his homeward way by grace of the great-hearted Athene. These they set in a heap by the trunk of the olive tree, a little aside from the road, lest some wayfaring man, before Odysseus awakened, should come and spoil them. Then themselves departed homeward again. . . .

[Upon awakening, Odysseus disguised himself as a beggar and learned from the faithful swineherd Eumaeus of the shocking behavior of the wooers. He revealed himself to his son Telemachus, newly returned from inquiring after his father at the court of Menelaus in Sparta, and together they planned the slaughter of the wooers. His old dog recognized his master, as did his old nurse Eurycleia while bathing his scarred legs, but Odysseus withheld his identity from his wife Penelope, who was on the point of abandoning hope of his return.]

BOOK XXI

Now the goddess, grey-eyed Athene, put it into the heart of the daughter of Icarius, wise Penelope, to set the bow and the axes of grey iron, for the wooers in the halls of Odysseus, to be the weapons of the contest, and the beginning of death. So she descended the tall staircase of her chamber, and . . . when the fair lady had come unto the wooers, she stood by the pillar of the well-builded roof, holding up her glistening tire before her face; and a faithful maiden stood on either side of her, and straightway she spake out among the wooers and declared her word, saying:

'Hear me, ye lordly wooers, who have vexed this house, that ye might eat and drink here evermore, forasmuch as the master is long gone, nor could ye find any other mark for your speech, but all your desire was to wed me and take me to wife. Nay come now, ye wooers, seeing that this is the prize that is put before you. I will set forth for you the great bow of divine Odysseus, and whoso shall most easily string the bow in his hands, and shoot through all twelve axes, with him will I go and forsake this house, this house of my wedlock, so fair and filled with all livelihood, which methinks I shall yet remember, aye, in a dream.'

So spake she, and commanded Eumaeus, the goodly swineherd, to set the bow for the wooers and the axes of grey iron. And Eumaeus took them with tears, and laid them down; and otherwhere the neatherd wept, when he beheld the bow of his lord. . . .

Therewith Telemachus cast from off his neck his cloak of scarlet, and sprang to his full height, and put away the sword from his shoulders. First he dug a good trench and set up the axes, one long trench for them all, and over it he made straight the line and round about stamped in the earth. And amazement fell on all that beheld how orderly he set the axes, though never before had he seen it so. Then he went and stood by the threshold and began to prove the bow. Thrice he made it to tremble in his great desire to draw it, and thrice he rested from his effort, though still he hoped in his heart to string the bow, and shoot through the iron. And now at last he might have strung it, mightily straining thereat for the fourth time, but Odysseus nodded frowning and stayed him, for all his eagerness.

Then first stood up Leiodes, son of Oenops, who ever sat by the fair mixing bowl at the extremity of the hall; he alone hated their infatuate deeds and was indignant with all the wooers. He now first took the bow and the swift shaft, and he went and stood by the threshold, and began to prove the bow; but he could not bend it; or ever that might be, his hands grew weary with the straining, his unworn, delicate hands. . . .

Then Antinous, son of Eupeithes, spake among them, saying: 'Up now, light a fire in the halls, Melanthius; and place a great settle by the fire and a fleece thereon, and bring forth a great ball of lard that is within, that we young men may warm and anoint the bow therewith and prove it, and make an end of the contest.'

So he spake, and Melanthius soon kindled the never-resting fire, and drew up a settle and placed it near, and put a fleece thereon, and he brought forth a great ball of lard that was within. Therewith the young men warmed the bow, and made essay, but could not string it, for they were greatly lacking of such might. . . .

Now the goodly swineherd had taken the curved bow, and was bearing it, when the wooers all cried out upon him in the halls. And thus some one of the haughty youths would speak: 'Whither now art thou bearing the curved bow, thou wretched swineherd, crazed in thy wits? Lo, soon shall the swift hounds of thine own breeding eat thee hard by thy swine, alone and away from men, if Apollo will be gracious to us and the other deathless gods.'

Even so they spake, and he took and set down the bow in that very place, being affrighted because many cried out on him in the halls. Then Telemachus from the other side spake threateningly, and called aloud:

'Father, bring hither the bow, soon shalt thou rue it that thou servest many masters. Take heed, lest I that am younger than thou pursue thee to the field, and pelt thee with stones, for in might I am the better. If only I were so much mightier in strength of arm than all the wooers that are in the halls, soon would I send many an one forth on a woeful way from out our house, for they imagine mischief against us.'

So he spake, and all the wooers laughed sweetly at him, and ceased now from their cruel anger toward Telemachus. Then the swineherd bare the bow through the hall, and went up to wise Odysseus, and set it in his hands. And he called forth the nurse Eurycleia from the chamber and spake to her:

'Wise Eurycleia, Telemachus bids thee bar the well-fitting doors of thy chamber, and if any of the women hear the sound of groaning or the din of men within our walls, let them not go forth, but abide where they are in silence at their work.'

So he spake, and wingless her speech remained, and she barred the doors of the fair-lying chambers.

Then Philoetius hasted forth silently from the house, and barred the outer gates of the fenced court. Now there lay beneath the gallery the cable of a curved ship, fashioned of the byblus plant, wherewith he made fast the gates, and then himself passed within. Then he went and sat on the settle whence he had risen, and gazed upon Odysseus. He already was handling the bow, turning it every way about, and proving it on this side and on that, lest the worms might have eaten the horns when the lord of the bow was away. And thus men spake looking each one to his neighbour:

'Verily he has a good eye, and a shrewd turn for a bow! Either, methinks, he himself has such a bow lying by at home or else he is set on making one, in such wise does he turn it hither and thither in his hands, this evil-witted beggar.'

And another again of the haughty youths would say: 'Would that the fellow may have profit thereof, just so surely as he shall ever prevail to bend this bow!'

So spake the wooers, but Odysseus of many counsels had lifted the great bow and viewed it on every side, and even as when a man that is skilled in the lyre and in minstrelsy, easily stretches a cord about a new peg, after tying at either end the twisted sheep-gut, even so Odysseus straightway bent the great bow, all without effort, and took it in his right hand and proved the bow-string, which rang sweetly at the touch, in tone like a swallow. Then great grief came upon the wooers, and the colour of their countenance was changed, and Zeus thundered loud showing forth his tokens. And the steadfast goodly Odysseus was glad thereat, in that the son of deep-counselling Cronos had sent him a sign. Then he caught up a swift arrow which lay by his table, bare, but the other shafts were stored within the hollow quiver, those whereof the Achaeans were soon to taste. He took and laid it on the bridge of the bow, and held the notch and drew the string, even from the settle whereon he sat, and with straight aim shot the shaft and missed not one of the axes, beginning from the first axe-handle, and the bronze-weighted shaft passed clean through and out at the last. Then he spake to Telemachus, saying:

'Telemachus, thy guest that sits in the halls does thee no shame. In no wise did I miss my mark, nor was I wearied with long bending of the bow. Still is
10 my might steadfast—not as the wooers say scornfully to slight me. But now is it time that supper too be got ready for the Achaeans, while it is yet light, and thereafter must we make other sport with the dance and the lyre, for these are the crown of the feast.'

Therewith he nodded with bent brows, and Telemachus, the dear son of divine Odysseus, girt his sharp sword about him and took the spear in his grasp, and stood by his high seat at his father's side, armed with the gleaming bronze.

BOOK XXII

20 Then Odysseus of many counsels stripped him of his rags and leaped on to the great threshold with his bow and quiver full of arrows, and poured forth all the swift shafts there before his feet, and spake among the wooers:

'Lo, now is this terrible trial ended at last; and now will I know of another mark, which never yet man has smitten, if perchance I may hit it and Apollo grant me renown.'

With that he pointed the bitter arrow at Antinous.
30 Now he was about raising to his lips a fair twy-eared chalice of gold, and behold, he was handling it to drink of the wine, and death was far from his thoughts. For who among men at feast would deem that one man amongst so many, how hardy soever he were, would bring on him foul death and black fate? But Odysseus aimed and smote him with the arrow in the throat, and the point passed clean out through his delicate neck, and he fell sidelong and the cup dropped from his hand as he was smitten,
40 and at once through his nostrils there came up a thick jet of slain man's blood, and quickly he spurned the table from him with his foot, and spilt the food on the ground, and the bread and the roast flesh were defiled. Then the wooers raised a clamour through the halls when they saw the man fallen, and they leaped from their high seats, as men stirred by fear, all through the hall, peering everywhere along the well-builded walls, and nowhere was there a shield or mighty spear to lay hold on. Then they re-
50 viled Odysseus with angry words:

'Stranger, thou shootest at men to thy hurt. Never again shalt thou enter other lists, now is utter doom assured thee. Yea, for now hast thou slain the man that was far the best of all the noble youths in Ithaca; wherefore vultures shall devour thee here.'

So each one spake, for indeed they thought that Odysseus had not slain him wilfully; but they knew not in their folly that on their own heads, each and all of them, the bands of death had been made fast. Then Odysseus of many counsels looked fiercely on 60 them, and spake:

'Ye dogs, ye said in your hearts that I should never more come home from the land of the Trojans, in that ye wasted my house, and lay with the maidservants by force, and traitorously wooed my wife while I was yet alive, and ye had no fear of the gods, that hold the wide heaven, nor of the indignation of men hereafter. But now the bands of death have been made fast upon you one and all.'

Even so he spake, and pale fear gat hold on the 70 limbs of all, and each man looked about, where he might shun utter doom. And Eurymachus alone answered him, and spake: 'If thou art indeed Odysseus of Ithaca, come home again, with right thou speakest thus, of all that the Achaeans have wrought, many infatuate deeds in thy halls and many in the field. Howbeit, he now lies dead that is to blame for all, Antinous; for he brought all these things upon us, not as longing very greatly for the marriage nor needing it sore, but with another purpose, that 80 Cronion has not fulfilled for him, namely, that he might himself be king over all the land of stablished Ithaca, and he was to have lain in wait for thy son and killed him. But now he is slain after his deserving, and do thou spare thy people, even thine own; and we will hereafter go about the township and yield thee amends for all that has been eaten and drunken in thy halls, each for himself bringing atonement of twenty oxen worth, and requiting thee in gold and bronze till thy heart is softened, but till 90 then none may blame thee that thou art angry.'

Then Odysseus of many counsels looked fiercely on him, and said: 'Eurymachus, not even if ye gave me all your heritage, all that ye now have, and whatsoever else ye might in any wise add thereto, not even so would I henceforth hold my hands from slaying, ere the wooers had paid for all their transgressions. And now the choice lies before you, whether to fight in fair battle or to fly, if any may avoid death and the fates. But there be some, me- 100 thinks, that shall not escape from utter doom.'

He spake, and their knees were straightway loosened and their hearts melted within them. And Eurymachus spake among them yet again:

'Friends, it is plain that this man will not hold his unconquerable hands, but now that he has caught up the polished bow and quiver, he will shoot from the smooth threshold, till he has slain us all; wherefore let us take thought for the delight of battle. Draw your blades, and hold up the tables to ward 110 off the arrows of swift death, and let us all have at him with one accord, and drive him, if it may be, from the threshold and the doorway and then go through the city, and quickly would the cry be raised. Thereby should this man soon have shot his latest bolt.'

Therewith he drew his sharp two-edged sword of bronze, and leapt on Odysseus with a terrible cry, but in the same moment goodly Odysseus shot the arrow forth and struck him on the breast by the pap, and drave the swift shaft into his liver. So he let the sword fall from his hand, and grovelling over the table he bowed and fell, and spilt the food and the two-handled cup on the floor. And in his agony he smote the ground with his brow, and spurning with both his feet he overthrew the high seat, and the mist of death was shed upon his eyes.

Then Amphinomus made at renowned Odysseus, setting straight at him, and drew his sharp sword, if perchance he might make him give ground from the door. But Telemachus was beforehand with him, and cast and smote him from behind with a bronze-shod spear between the shoulders, and drave it out through the breast, and he fell with a crash and struck the ground full with his forehead. Then Telemachus sprang away, leaving the long spear fixed in Amphinomus, for he greatly dreaded lest one of the Achaeans might run upon him with his blade, and stab him as he drew forth the spear, or smite him with a down stroke of the sword. So he started and ran and came quickly to his father, and stood by him, and spake winged words:

'Father, lo, now I will bring thee a shield and two spears and a helmet all of bronze, close fitting on the temples, and when I return I will arm myself, and likewise give arms to the swineherd and to the neatherd yonder: for it is better to be clad in full armour.'

And Odysseus of many counsels answered him saying: 'Run and bring them while I have arrows to defend me, lest they thrust me from the doorway, one man against them all.'

So he spake, and Telemachus obeyed his dear father, and went forth to the chamber, where his famous weapons were lying. Thence he took out four shields and eight spears, and four helmets of bronze, with thick plumes of horse hair, and he started to bring them and came quickly to his father. Now he girded the gear of bronze about his own body first, and in like manner the two thralls did on the goodly armour, and stood beside the wise and crafty Odysseus. Now he, so long as he had arrows to defend him, kept aiming and smote the wooers one by one in his house, and they fell thick one upon another. But when the arrows failed the prince in his archery, he leaned his bow against the doorpost of the stablished hall, against the shining faces of the entrance. As for him he girt his fourfold shield about his shoulders and bound on his mighty

head a well-wrought helmet, with horse hair crest, and terribly the plume waved aloft. And he grasped two mighty spears tipped with bronze. . . .

Then Athene, daughter of Zeus, drew nigh, like Mentor in fashion and in voice, and Odysseus was glad when he saw her and spake, saying:

'Mentor, ward from us hurt, and remember me thy dear companion, that befriended thee often, and thou art of like age with me.'

So he spake, deeming the while that it was Athene, summoner of the host. But the wooers on the other side shouted in the halls, and first Agelaus son of Damastor rebuked Athene, saying:

'Mentor, let not the speech of Odysseus beguile thee to fight against the wooers, and to succour him. For methinks that on this wise we shall work our will. When we shall have slain these men, father and son, thereafter shalt thou perish with them, such deeds thou art set on doing in these halls; nay, with thine own head shalt thou pay the price. But when with the sword we shall have overcome your violence, we will mingle all thy possessions, all that thou hast at home or in the field, with the wealth of Odysseus, and we will not suffer thy sons nor thy daughters to dwell in the halls, nor thy good wife to gad about in the town of Ithaca.'

So spake he, and Athene was mightily angered at heart, and chid Odysseus in wrathful words: 'Odysseus, thou hast no more steadfast might nor any prowess, as when for nine whole years continually thou didst battle with the Trojans for high born Helen, of the white arms, and many men thou slewest in terrible warfare, and by thy device the wide-wayed city of Priam was taken. How then, now that thou art come to thy house and thine own possessions, dost thou bewail thee and art of feeble courage to stand before the wooers? Nay, come hither, friend, and stand by me, and I will show thee a thing, that thou mayest know what manner of man is Mentor, son of Alcimus, to repay good deeds in the ranks of foemen.'

She spake, and gave him not yet clear victory in full, but still for a while made trial of the might and prowess of Odysseus and his renowned son. As for her she flew up to the roof timber of the murky hall, in such fashion as a swallow flies, and there sat down. . . .

Then once more the wooers threw their sharp spears eagerly; but behold, Athene so wrought that many of them were in vain. One man smote the doorpost of the stablished hall, and another the well-fastened door, and the ashen spear of another wooer, heavy with bronze, stuck in the wall. Yet Amphimedon hit Telemachus on the hand by the wrist lightly, and the shaft of bronze wounded the surface of the skin. . . . Then again Odysseus, the wise and crafty, he and his men cast their swift spears into the press of the wooers, and now once more Odysseus, waster of cities, smote Eurydamas, and Telemachus Amphimedon, and the swineherd slew Polybus, and last, the neatherd struck Ctesippus in the breast and boasted over him. Then Athene held up her destroying aegis on high from the roof, and their minds were scared, and they fled through the hall, like a drove of kine that the flitting gadfly falls upon and scatters hither and thither in spring time, when the long days begin. But the others set on like vultures of crooked claws and curved beak, that come forth from the mountains and dash upon smaller birds, and these scour low in the plain, stooping in terror from the clouds, while the vultures pounce on them and slay them, and there is no help nor way of flight, and men are glad at the sport; even so did the company of Odysseus set upon the wooers and smite them right and left through the hall; and there rose a hideous moaning as their heads were smitten, and the floor all ran with blood.

But the son of Terpes, the minstrel, still sought how he might shun black fate, Phemius, who sang among the wooers of necessity. He stood with the loud lyre in his hand hard by the postern gate, and his heart was divided within him, whether he should slip forth from the hall and sit down by the well-wrought altar of great Zeus of the household court, whereon Laertes and Odysseus had burnt many pieces of the thighs of oxen, or should spring forward and beseech Odysseus by his knees. And as he thought thereupon this seemed to him the better way, to embrace the knees of Odysseus, son of Laertes. So he laid the hollow lyre on the ground between the mixing-bowl and the high seat inlaid with silver, and himself sprang forward and seized Odysseus by the knees, and besought him and spake winged words:

'I entreat thee by thy knees, Odysseus, and do thou show mercy on me and have pity. It will be a sorrow to thyself in the aftertime if thou slayest me who am a minstrel, and sing before gods and men. Yea none has taught me but myself, and the god has put into my heart all manner of lays, and methinks I sing to thee as to a god, wherefore be not eager to cut off my head. And Telemachus will testify of this, thine own dear son, that not by mine own will or desire did I resort to thy house to sing to the wooers at their feasts; but being so many and stronger than I they led me by constraint.'

So he spake, and the mighty prince Telemachus heard him and quickly spake to his father at his side: 'Hold thy hand, and wound not this blameless man with the sword; and let us save also the henchman Medon, that ever had charge of me in our house when I was a child, unless perchance Philoetius or the swineherd have already slain him, or he hath met thee in thy raging through the house.'

So he spake, and Medon, wise of heart, heard him. For he lay crouching beneath a high seat, clad about in the new-flayed hide of an ox and shunned black fate. So he rose up quickly from under the seat, and cast off the oxhide, and sprang forth and caught Telemachus by the knees, and besought him and spake winged words:

'Friend, here am I; prithee stay thy hand and speak to thy father, lest he harm me with the sharp sword in the greatness of his strength, out of his anger for the wooers that wasted his possessions in the halls, and in their folly held thee in no honour.'

And Odysseus of many counsels smiled on him and said: 'Take courage, for lo, he has saved thee and delivered thee, that thou mayst know in thy heart, and tell it even to another, how far more excellent are good deeds than evil. But go forth from the halls and sit down in the court apart from the slaughter, thou and the full-voiced minstrel, till I have accomplished all that I must needs do in the house.'

Therewith the two went forth and gat them from the hall. So they sat down by the altar of great Zeus, peering about on every side, still expecting death. And Odysseus peered all through the house, to see if any man was yet alive and hiding away to shun black fate. But he found all the sort of them fallen in their blood in the dust, like fishes that the fishermen have drawn forth in the meshes of the net into a hollow of the beach from out the grey sea, and all the fish, sore longing for the salt sea waves, are heaped upon the sand, and the sun shines forth and takes their life away; so now the wooers lay heaped upon each other. Then Odysseus of many counsels spake to Telemachus:

'Telemachus, go, call me the nurse Eurycleia, that I may tell her a word that is on my mind.'

So he spake, and Telemachus obeyed his dear father, and smote at the door, and spake to the nurse Eurycleia: 'Up now, aged wife, that overlookest all the women servants in our halls, come hither, my father calls thee and has somewhat to say to thee.'

Even so he spake, and wingless her speech remained, and she opened the doors of the fair-lying halls, and came forth, and Telemachus led the way before her. So she found Odysseus among the bodies of the dead, stained with blood and soil of battle, like a lion that has eaten of an ox of the homestead and goes on his way, and all his breast and his cheeks on either side are flecked with blood, and he is terrible to behold; even so was Odysseus stained, both hands and feet. Now the nurse, when she saw the bodies of the dead and the great gore of blood, made ready to cry aloud for joy, beholding so great an adventure. But Odysseus checked and held her in her eagerness, and uttering his voice spake to her winged words:

'Within thine own heart rejoice, old nurse, and be still, and cry not aloud; for it is an unholy thing to boast over slain men. Now these hath the destiny of the gods overcome, and their own cruel deeds, for they honoured none of earthly men, neither the bad nor yet the good, that came among them. Wherefore they have met a shameful death through their own infatuate deeds. But come, tell me the tale of the women in my halls, which of them dishonour me, and which be guiltless.'

Then the good nurse Eurycleia answered him: 'Yea now, my child, I will tell thee all the truth. Thou hast fifty women-servants in thy halls, that we have taught the ways of housewifery, how to card wool and to bear bondage. Of these twelve in all have gone the way of shame, and honour not me, nor their lady Penelope. And Telemachus hath but newly come to his strength, and his mother suffered him not to take command over the women in this house. But now, let me go aloft to the shining upper chamber, and tell all to thy wife, on whom some god hath sent a sleep.'

And Odysseus of many counsels answered her, saying: 'Wake her not yet, but bid the women come hither, who in time past behaved themselves unseemly.'

So he spake, and the old wife passed through the hall, to tell the women and to hasten their coming. Then Odysseus called to him Telemachus, and the neatherd, and the swineherd, and spake to them winged words:

'Begin ye now to carry out the dead, and bid the women help you, and thereafter cleanse the fair high seats and the tables with water and porous sponges. And when ye have set all the house in order, lead the maidens without the stablished hall, between the vaulted room and the goodly fence of the court, and there slay them with your long blades, till they shall have all given up the ghost and forgotten the love that of old they had at the bidding of the wooers, in secret dalliance.'

Even so he spake, and the women came all in a crowd together, making a terrible lament and shedding big tears. So first they carried forth the bodies of the slain, and set them beneath the gallery of the fenced court, and propped them one on another; and Odysseus himself hasted the women and directed them, and they carried forth the dead perforce. Thereafter they cleansed the fair high seats and the tables with water and porous sponges. And Telemachus, and the neatherd, and the swineherd, scraped with spades the floor of the well-builded house, and, behold, the maidens carried all forth and laid it without the doors.

Now when they had made an end of setting the hall in order, they led the maidens forth from the stablished hall, and drove them up in a narrow space between the vaulted room and the goodly fence of the court, whence none might avoid; and wise Telemachus began to speak to his fellows, saying: 60

'God forbid that I should take these women's lives by a clean death, these that have poured dishonour on my head and on my mother, and have lain with the wooers.'

With that word he tied the cable of a dark-prowed ship to a great pillar and flung it round the vaulted room, and fastened it aloft, that none might touch the ground with her feet. And even as when thrushes, long of wing, or doves fall into a net that is set in a thicket, as they seek to their roosting-place, 70 and a loathly bed harbours them, even so the women held their heads all in a row, and about all their necks nooses were cast, that they might die by the most pitiful death. And they writhed with their feet for a little space, but for no long while. . . .

BOOK XXIII

Then the ancient woman went up into the upper chamber laughing aloud, to tell her mistress how her dear lord was within, and her knees moved fast for joy, and her feet stumbled one over the other; and she stood above the lady's head and spake to her, 80 saying:

'Awake, Penelope, dear child, that thou mayest see with thine own eyes that which thou desirest day by day. Odysseus hath come, and hath got him to his own house, though late hath he come, and hath slain the proud wooers that troubled his house, and devoured his substance and oppressed his child.'

Then wise Penelope answered her: 'Dear nurse, the gods have made thee distraught, the gods that can make foolish even the wisdom of the wise, and 90 that stablish the simple in understanding. They it is that have marred thy reason, though heretofore thou hadst a prudent heart. Why dost thou mock me, who have a spirit full of sorrow, to speak these wild words, and rousest me out of sweet slumber, that had bound me and overshadowed mine eyelids? Never yet have I slept so sound since the day that Odysseus went forth to see that evil Ilios, never to be named. Go to now, get thee down and back to the women's chamber, for if any other of the maids 100 of my house had come and brought me such tidings, and wakened me from sleep, straightway would I have sent her back woefully to return within the women's chamber; but this time thine old age shall stand thee in good stead.'

Then the good nurse Eurycleia answered her: 'I mock thee not, dear child, but in very deed Odysseus is here, and hath come home, even as I tell thee. But long ago Telemachus was ware of him, that he was within the house, yet in his prudence he hid the 110 counsels of his father, that he might take vengeance on the violence of the haughty wooers.'

Thus she spake, and then was Penelope glad, and leaping from her bed she fell on the old woman's neck, and let fall the tears from her eyelids. . . . She went down from the upper chamber, and much her heart debated, whether she should stand apart, and question her dear lord or draw nigh, and clasp and kiss his head and hands. But when she had come within and had crossed the threshold of stone, she sat down over against Odysseus, in the light of the fire, by the further wall. Now he was sitting by the tall pillar, looking down and waiting to know if perchance his noble wife would speak to him, when her eyes beheld him. But she sat long in silence, and amazement came upon her soul, and now she would look upon him steadfastly with her eyes, and now again she knew him not, for that he was clad in vile raiment. And Telemachus rebuked her, and spake and hailed her:

'Mother mine, ill mother, of an ungentle heart, why turnest thou thus away from my father, and dost not sit by him and question him and ask him all? No other woman in the world would harden her heart to stand thus aloof from her lord, who after much travail and sore had come to her in the twentieth year to his own country. But thy heart is ever harder than stone.'

Then wise Penelope answered him, saying: 'Child, my mind is amazed within me, and I have no strength to speak, nor to ask him aught, nay nor to look on him face to face. But if in truth this be Odysseus, and he hath indeed come home, verily we shall be ware of each other the more surely, for we have tokens that we twain know, even we, secret from all others.' . . . Meanwhile, the house-dame Eurynome had bathed the great-hearted Odysseus

On his way back to Greece, Odysseus forced his sailors to tie him to the mast of his ship in order to succeed in passing the land of the Sirens. From a Greek vase painting.

within his house, and anointed him with olive-oil, and cast about him a goodly mantle and a doublet. Moreover, Athene shed great beauty from his head downwards, and made him greater and more mighty to behold, and from his head caused deep curling locks to flow, like the hyacinth flower. And as when some skilful man overlays gold upon silver, one that Hephaestus and Pallas Athene have taught all manner of craft, and full of grace is his handiwork, even so did Athene shed grace about his head and shoulders, and forth from the bath he came, in form like to the Immortals. Then he sat down again on the high seat, whence he had arisen, over against his wife, and spake to her, saying:

'Strange lady, surely to thee above all womankind the Olympians have given a heart that cannot be softened. No other woman in the world would harden her heart to stand thus aloof from her husband, who after much travail and sore had come to her, in the twentieth year, to his own country. Nay come, nurse, strew a bed for me to lie all alone, for assuredly her spirit within her is as iron.'

Then wise Penelope answered him again: 'Strange man, I have no proud thoughts nor do I think scorn of thee, nor am I too greatly astonied, but I know right well what manner of man thou wert, when thou wentest forth out of Ithaca, on the long-oared galley. But come, Eurycleia, spread for him the good bed-stead outside the established bridal chamber that he built himself. Thither bring ye forth the good bed-stead and cast bedding thereon, even fleeces and rugs and shining blankets.'

So she spake and made trial of her lord, but Odysseus in sore displeasure spake to his true wife, saying: 'Verily a bitter word is this, lady, that thou hast spoken. Who has set my bed otherwhere? Hard it would be for one, how skilled soever, unless a god were to come that might easily set it in another place, if so he would. But of men there is none living, howsoever strong in his youth, that could lightly up-heave it, for a great token is wrought in the fashioning of the bed, and it was I that made it and none other. There was growing a bush of olive, long of leaf, and most goodly of growth, within the inner court, and the stem as large as a pillar. Round about this I built the chamber, till I had finished it, with stones close set, and I roofed it over well and added thereto compacted doors fitting well. Next I sheared off all the light wood of the long-leaved olive, and rough-hewed the trunk upwards from the root, and smoothed it around with the adze, well and skilfully, and made straight the line thereto and so fashioned it into the bed-post, and I bored it all with the auger. Beginning from this bed-post, I wrought at the bedstead till I had finished it, and made it fair with inlaid work of gold and of silver and of ivory.

Then I made fast therein a bright purple band of oxhide. Even so I declare to thee this token, and I know not, lady, if the bedstead be yet fast in his place, or if some man has cut away the stem of the olive tree, and set the bedstead otherwhere.'

So he spake, and at once her knees were loosened, and her heart melted within her, as she knew the sure tokens that Odysseus showed her. Then she fell a weeping, and ran straight toward him and cast her hands about his neck, and kissed his head and spake, saying:

'Be not angry with me, Odysseus, for thou wert ever at other times the wisest of men. It is the gods that gave us sorrow, the gods who begrudged us that we should abide together and have joy of our youth, and come to the threshold of old age. So now be not wroth with me hereat nor full of indignation, because at the first, when I saw thee, I did not welcome thee straightway. For always my heart within my breast shuddered, for fear lest some man should come and deceive me with his words, for many they be that devise gainful schemes and evil. Nay even Argive Helen, daughter of Zeus, would not have lain with a stranger, and taken him for a lover, had she known that the warlike sons of the Achaeans would bring her home again to her own dear country. Howsoever, it was the god that set her upon this shameful deed; nor ever, ere that, did she lay up in her heart the thought of this folly, a bitter folly, whence on us too first came sorrow. But now that thou hast told all the sure tokens of our bed, which never was seen by mortal man, save by thee and me and one maiden only, the daughter of Actor, that my father gave me ere yet I had come hither, she who kept the doors of our strong bridal chamber, even now dost thou bend my soul, all ungentle as it is.'

Thus she spake, and in his heart she stirred yet a greater longing to lament, and he wept as he embraced his beloved wife and true. And even as when the sight of land is welcome to swimmers, whose well-wrought ship Poseidon hath smitten on the deep, all driven with the wind and swelling waves, and but a remnant hath escaped the grey sea-water and swum to the shore, and their bodies are all crusted with the brine, and gladly have they set foot on land and escaped an evil end; so welcome to her was the sight of her lord, and her white arms she would never quite let go from his neck. And now would the rosy-fingered Dawn have risen upon their weeping, but the goddess, grey-eyed Athene, had other thoughts. The night she held long in the utmost West, and on the other side she stayed the golden throned Dawn by the stream Oceanus, and suffered her not to harness the swift-footed steeds that bear light to men, Lampus and Phaethon, the steeds ever young, that bring the morning.

Aeschylus

525–456 B.C.

Aeschylus was born during the lifetime of Thespis, the "inventor" of tragedy. To the single actor that Thespis had drawn from the older chorus Aeschylus added a second, which at last made possible mature dramatic dialogue. The seven extant plays of Aeschylus, the oldest preserved of Greek dramas, reveal in themselves an extraordinary development from the choral lyrics of *The Suppliant Women* (c. 490 B.C.) to the full-scale tragedy of *Agamemnon* (458 B.C.).

Yet the man who brought Western drama to maturity was more than a playwright. Born into an ancient noble family in Eleusis, a religious center of Attica, Aeschylus fought at Marathon and Salamis and prided himself on his prowess as a soldier. In the theater he directed and acted in his own plays, and is said to have written as many as seventy tragedies and numerous satyr plays. He first won the prize for tragedy in the contest of 484 B.C. and gained it, in all, thirteen times. His epitaph, however, preserved his military rather than his literary reputation: "Here lies the Athenian Aeschylus, son of Euphorion, who died in grain-growing Gela. The plain of Marathon could tell his great courage, and the long-haired Mede who discovered it there."

The world of Aeschylus was democratic, vigorous Athens rising to hegemony over the Greek states. As he was growing up, Attica rid herself of the last of her tyrants and established a democratic constitution that Aeschylus supports by implication. *Prometheus Bound* (c. 479 B.C.) studies the conflict between brute power and human rights, between the authoritarian rule of Zeus and the courageous independence of the last of the Titans. *The Persians* (472 B.C.) not only glorifies the victory of the Greeks over their Eastern enemies but warns against the evils of Oriental despotism. As a member of a conservative old family in a town sacred to the earth-goddess, Demeter, Aeschylus reveals the conventional religious views of the older generation, and his plays usually turn on moral or theological issues—the right of sanctuary in *The Suppliant Women*, the punishment of pride in *The Persians*, the inheritance of crime in the *Oresteia*, and the power of Fate everywhere.

His dramatic technique is old-fashioned, though he made great strides beyond his predecessors. In his plays the chorus, though reduced, is still an organic element, advising the characters, interpreting their actions, and drawing moral lessons. His limitation to two actors, though they might represent more than two characters, restricted the scope of his action. Any one play, confined by these conventions, had to have a very simple plot; but Aeschylus developed the scheme of presenting a more extended story through a trilogy, or series of three related plays (of which the *Oresteia* is our only extant example). Violent action and any considerable movement were still outlawed as sacrilegious, but he compensated for the restriction by using spectacular stage effects and rich costumes. Although his plays are more dignified than those of Euripides, his is a theatrical dignity. It reposes in the grand style of his lines, sometimes close to bombast, but more often animated by a cosmic vision and lofty poetic inspiration. The titanic majesty of his themes and his verse revives an age in which men were not afraid to be noble.

Agamemnon, the masterpiece of Aeschylus, is the first play in the *Oresteia* trilogy, which relates a grim tale of vengeful crimes within one famous family. As the responsibility for avenging crime passes through the generations of the ill-fated House of Atreus, we see in operation the Greek doctrine of punishment in kind. Atreus, King of Mycenae, had committed an initial crime when, finding that his brother Thyestes had seduced Aethra, his wife, he served him a dish containing the flesh of Thyestes' own children. Placing a curse on the House of Atreus, Thyestes dedicated his only surviving son, Aegisthus, to revenge on his brother and his brother's sons, Agamemnon and Menelaus.

Agamemnon of Mycenae married the charming Clytemnestra, half-sister of Helen of Troy, who bore him two daughters, Electra and Iphigenia, and a son, Orestes. When Helen was snatched from her husband, Menelaus, by the Trojan prince Paris, Menelaus induced his brother Agamemnon to recruit the Greek princes for the expedition against Troy. But the Greek ships lay becalmed at Aulis because the goddess Artemis demanded the sacrifice of a princess before they might sail. Agamemnon, the leader of the host, lured his daughter Iphigenia to Aulis and offered her as sacrifice, although, unknown to anyone, Artemis rescued her at the last moment and made her a priestess among the savage Tauri. Agamemnon's act sped the Greek ships to Troy, but it won him the undying hatred of his wife Clytemnestra, who made common cause with the vengeful Aegisthus and plotted her husband's murder as they waited out the long years of the war. The play *Agamemnon* portrays the return of the triumphant king with his captive prize, the Trojan princess Cassandra, and Clytemnestra's savage murder of them both.

But the vengeful crimes continue in the next generation. Electra had saved her young brother from her mother, who feared his revenge. While he was being reared by his uncle in a nearby kingdom, Electra frequently reminded him by letter of his duty to avenge his father's death. When the Delphic oracle confirmed this duty, Orestes returned to Mycenae and, egged on by the bloodthirsty Electra, murdered his mother and Aegisthus. At last the family crimes were ended, but for a time the divine punishers, the Furies, pursued the haggard Orestes—even to the land of the savage Tauri, where he rescued his sister, Iphigenia the priestess. Only a formal trial before Athena freed Orestes from his punishment, when it was established that he had acted in obedience to the Delphic oracle. So peace finally came to the House of Atreus.

As *Agamemnon* tells of the murder of the king, the

second play in the trilogy, *The Libation-Bearers* (*Choephoroe*), relates Orestes' murder of Clytemnestra and Aegisthus, and the third, *The Furies* (*Eumenides*), completes the story with the punishment and trial of Orestes. Although each of the *Oresteia* plays rises to its own climax, the three form a tightly knit unit, so that the dramatic resolution of the hateful conflict does not come until the end of the third play. Taken together, they are somewhat like a modern play in three acts. As the general title suggests, Orestes is the leading character in this drama, even though he does not appear in the first play. Like Siegfried in Wagner's *Ring* operas, he gradually emerges in the cycle and eventually carries the whole action to its peaceful resolution.

The *Oresteia* is the supreme achievement of Aeschylus. Though the dramatic conventions of his day required a simpler plot and less action than appear in the later plays of Sophocles, he makes use of the trilogy scheme to give a magnificent and terrifying spectacle of human hate and suffering and the inexorable operation of divine law in the affairs of men. His favorite theme—pride goeth before a fall—is grimly illustrated in the career of Agamemnon. Although the style is sometimes inflated, the effect is generally lofty and poetic. A testimony to the enduring influence of this masterpiece is Eugene O'Neill's psychoanalytic interpretation of the same characters and plot in his modern version of the trilogy, *Mourning Becomes Electra*.

Agamemnon

CHARACTERS IN THE PLAY

A WATCHMAN
CHORUS OF ARGIVE ELDERS
CLYTEMNESTRA, *wife of* AGAMEMNON
A HERALD
AGAMEMNON, *King of Argos*
CASSANDRA, *daughter of Priam, and slave of* AGAMEMNON
AEGISTHUS, *son of Thyestes, cousin of* AGAMEMNON

(SCENE: *Before the palace of* AGAMEMNON *in Argos. In front of the palace stand statues of the gods, and altars prepared for sacrifice. It is night. On the roof of the palace appears a* WATCHMAN.)

WATCHMAN.

I PRAY the gods to quit me of my toils,
　To close the watch I keep, this livelong year;
For as a watch-dog lying, not at rest,
Propped on one arm, upon the palace-roof
Of Atreus' race, too long, too well I know   5
The starry conclave of the midnight sky,
Too well, the splendours of the firmament,
The lords of light, whose kingly aspect shows—

Agamemnon. Translated by E. D. A. Morshead. From the *House of Atreus . . .*, by Aeschylus. By permission of The Macmillan Company, publishers.

What time they set or climb the sky in turn—
The year's divisions, bringing frost or fire. 10

And now, as ever, am I set to mark
When shall stream up the glow of signal-flame,
The bale-fire bright, and tell its Trojan tale—
Troy town is ta'en: such issue holds in hope
She in whose woman's breast beats heart of man. 15

Thus upon mine unrestful couch I lie,
Bathed with the dews of night, unvisited
By dreams—ah me!—for in the place of sleep
Stands Fear as my familiar, and repels
The soft repose that would mine eyelids seal. 20

And if at whiles, for the lost balm of sleep,
I medicine my soul with melody
Of trill or song—anon to tears I turn,
Wailing the woe that broods upon this home,
Not now by honour guided as of old. 25

But now at last fair fall the welcome hour
That sets me free, whene'er the thick night glow
With beacon-fire of hope deferred no more.
All hail!
     (*A beacon-light is seen reddening the distant sky.*)
Fire of the night, that brings my spirit day, 30
Shedding on Argos light, and dance, and song,
Greetings to fortune, hail!

Let my loud summons ring within the ears
Of Agamemnon's queen, that she anon
Start from her couch and with a shrill voice cry 35

12. **signal-flame,** the last in the series of signal fires, lighted in succession to announce the victory. 15. **She . . . heart of man.** Clytemnestra.

A joyous welcome to the beacon-blaze,
For Ilion's fall; such fiery message gleams
From yon high flame; and I, before the rest,
Will foot the lightsome measure of our joy;
For I can say, *My master's dice fell fair—* 40
Behold! the triple sice, the lucky flame!
Now be my lot to clasp, in loyal love,
The hand of him restored, who rules our home:
Home—but I say no more: upon my tongue
Treads hard the ox o' the adage.
                              Had it voice, 45
The home itself might soothliest tell its tale;
I, of set will, speak words the wise may learn,
To others, nought remember nor discern.   (*Exit.*)
     (*The* CHORUS OF ARGIVE ELDERS *enters, each lean-
ing on a staff. During their song* CLYTEMNESTRA *ap-
pears in the background, kindling the altars.*)

CHORUS.   *Parodos*
Ten livelong years have rolled away,
Since the twin lords of sceptred sway, 50
By Zeus endowed with pride of place,
The doughty chiefs of Atreus' race,
     Went forth of yore,
To plead with Priam, face to face,
     Before the judgment-seat of War! 55

A thousand ships from Argive land
Put forth to bear the martial band,
That with a spirit stern and strong
Went out to right the kingdom's wrong—
Pealed, as they went, the battle-song, 60
     Wild as the vultures' cry;

45. **Treads . . . ox o' the adage.** The ox signified silence in an old Greek proverb. 50. **twin lords,** Agamemnon and Menelaus.

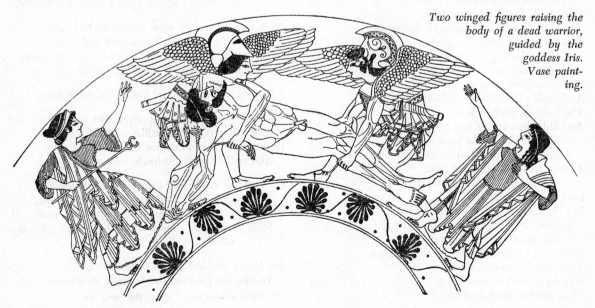

*Two winged figures raising the
body of a dead warrior,
guided by the
goddess Iris.
Vase paint-
ing.*

When o'er the eyrie, soaring high,
In wild bereavèd agony,
Around, around, in airy rings,
They wheel with oarage of their wings, 65
But not the eyas-brood behold,
That called them to the nest of old;
But let Apollo from the sky,
Or Pan, or Zeus, but hear the cry,
The exile cry, the wail forlorn, 70
Of birds from whom their home is torn—
On those who wrought the rapine fell,
Heaven sends the vengeful fiends of hell.

Even so doth Zeus, the jealous lord
And guardian of the hearth and board, 75
Speed Atreus' sons, in vengeful ire,
'Gainst Paris—sends them forth on fire,
Her to buy back, in war and blood,
Whom one did wed but many woo'd!
And many, many, by his will, 80
The last embrace of foes shall feel,
And many a knee in dust be bowed,
And splintered spears on shields ring loud,
Of Trojan and of Greek, before
That iron bridal-feast be o'er! 85
But as he willed 'tis ordered all,
And woes, by heaven ordained, must fall—
Unsoothed by tears or spilth of wine
Poured forth too late, the wrath divine
Glares vengeance on the flameless shrine. 90

And we in grey dishonoured eld,
Feeble of frame, unfit were held
To join the warrior array
That then went forth unto the fray:
And here at home we tarry, fain 95
Our feeble footsteps to sustain,
Each on his staff—so strength doth wane,
And turns to childishness again.
For while the sap of youth is green,
And, yet unripened, leaps within, 100
The young are weakly as the old,
And each alike unmeet to hold
The vantage post of war!
And ah! when flower and fruit are o'er,
And on life's tree the leaves are sere, 105
Age wendeth propped its journey drear,
As forceless as a child, as light
And fleeting as a dream of night
Lost in the garish day!
But thou, O child of Tyndareus, 110
Queen Clytemnestra, speak! and say
What messenger of joy to-day
Hath won thine ear? what welcome news,
That thus in sacrificial wise
E'en to the city's boundaries 115
Thou biddest altar-fires arise?

Each god who doth our city guard,
And keeps o'er Argos watch and ward
From heaven above, from earth below—
The mighty lords who rule the skies, 120
The market's lesser deities,
To each and all the altars glow,
Piled for the sacrifice!
And here and there, anear, afar,
Streams skyward many a beacon-star, 125
Conjur'd and charm'd and kindled well
By pure oil's soft and guileless spell,
Hid now no more
Within the palace' secret store.

O queen, we pray thee, whatsoe'er, 130
Known unto thee, were well revealed,
That thou wilt trust it to our ear,
And bid our anxious heart be healed!
That waneth now unto despair—
Now, waxing to a presage fair, 135
Dawns, from the altar, Hope—to scare
From our rent hearts the vulture Care.

List! for the power is mine, to chant on high
The chiefs' emprise, the strength that omens gave!
List! on my soul breathes yet a harmony, 140
From realms of ageless powers, and strong to save!

How brother kings, twin lords of one command,
Led forth the youth of Hellas in their flower,
Urged on their way, with vengeful spear and brand,
By warrior-birds, that watched the parting hour.

Go forth to Troy, the eagles seemed to cry— 146
And the sea-kings obeyed the sky-kings' word,
When on the right they soared across the sky,
And one was black, one bore a white tail barred.

High o'er the palace were they seen to soar, 150
Then lit in sight of all, and rent and tare,
Far from the fields that she should range no more,
Big with her unborn brood, a mother-hare.

(Ah woe and well-a-day! but be the issue fair!)

And one beheld, the soldier-prophet true, 155
And the two chiefs, unlike of soul and will,
In the twy-coloured eagles straight he knew,
And spake the omen forth, for good and ill.

Go forth, he cried, *and Priam's town shall fall.*
Yet long the time shall be; and flock and herd, 160
The people's wealth, that roam before the wall,
Shall force hew down, when Fate shall give the
word.

But O beware! lest wrath in Heaven abide,
To dim the glowing battle-forge once more,
155. soldier-prophet true, Calchas, the Greek seer.

And mar the mighty curb of Trojan pride,   165
   The steel of vengeance, welded as for war!

For virgin Artemis bears jealous hate
   Against the royal house, the eagle-pair,
Who rend the unborn brood, insatiate—   169
   Yea, loathes their banquet on the quivering hare.

(Ah woe and well-a-day! but be the issue fair!)

For well she loves—the goddess kind and mild—
   The tender new-born cubs of lions bold,
Too weak to range—and well the sucking child
   Of every beast that roams by wood and wold.   175

So to the Lord of Heaven she prayeth still,
   "Nay, if it must be, be the omen true!
Yet do the visioned eagles presage ill;
   The end be well, but crossed with evil too!"

Healer Apollo! be her wrath controll'd,   180
   Nor weave the long delay of thwarting gales,
To war against the Danaans and withhold
   From the free ocean-waves their eager sails!

She craves, alas! to see a second life
   Shed forth, a curst unhallowed sacrifice—   185
'Twixt wedded souls, artificer of strife,
   And hate that knows not fear, and fell device.

At home there tarries like a lurking snake,
   Biding its time, a wrath unreconciled,
A wily watcher, passionate to slake,   190
   In blood, resentment for a murdered child.

Such was the mighty warning, pealed of yore—
   Amid good tidings, such the word of fear,
What time the fateful eagles hovered o'er
   The kings, and Calchas read the omen clear.   195

(In strains like his, once more,
Sing woe and well-a-day! but be the issue fair!)

   Zeus—if to The Unknown
      That name of many names seem good—
   Zeus, upon Thee I call.   200
      Thro' the mind's every road
   I passed, but vain are all,
Save that which names thee Zeus, the Highest
      One,
   Were it but mine to cast away the load,
The weary load, that weighs my spirit down.   205

170. *Yea, loathes . . . hare.* As goddess of childbirth, Artemis pities the mother hare, slain by the eagles as she is about to give birth to her young.   180. **Healer Apollo,** brother of Artemis.   184. **a second life;** the first was Iphigenia, the "murdered child."   198–199. **Zeus . . . seem good.** Aeschylus spiritualizes Zeus into a concept of divinity broader than the Zeus of Homer.

   He that was Lord of old,
In full-blown pride of place and valour bold,
   Hath fallen and is gone, even as an old tale told!
   And he that next held sway,
   By stronger grasp o'erthrown   210
   Hath pass'd away!
And whoso now shall bid the triumph-chant arise
   To Zeus, and Zeus alone,
He shall be found the truly wise.

'Tis Zeus alone who shows the perfect way   215
   Of knowledge: He hath ruled,
Men shall learn wisdom, by affliction schooled.

   In visions of the night, like dropping rain,
   Descend the many memories of pain
Before the spirit's sight: through tears and dole   220
   Comes wisdom o'er the unwilling soul—
   A boon, I wot, of all Divinity,
That holds its sacred throne in strength, above the
   sky!

And then the elder chief, at whose command
   The fleet of Greece was manned,   225
      Cast on the seer no word of hate,
      But veered before the sudden breath of Fate—

      Ah, weary while! for, ere they put forth sail,
      Did every store, each minish'd vessel, fail,
      While all the Achaean host   230
        At Aulis anchored lay,
      Looking across to Chalcis and the coast
      Where refluent waters welter, rock, and sway;

      And rife with ill delay
   From northern Strymon blew the thwarting
      blast—   235
      Mother of famine fell,
      That holds men wand'ring still
Far from the haven where they fain would be!—
   And pitiless did waste
Each ship and cable, rotting on the sea,   240
   And, doubling with delay each weary hour,
Withered with hope deferred th' Achaeans' warlike
   flower.

      But when, for bitter storm, a deadlier relief,
      And heavier with ill to either chief,
Pleading the ire of Artemis, the seer avowed,   245
      The two Atreidae smote their sceptres on the
      plain,
      And, striving hard, could not their tears re-
      strain!

206–211. **He that . . . Hath pass'd away.** Zeus had been preceded as ruler of all by Uranus and Cronus, each deposed by force.   226. **Cast . . . hate.** Agamemnon did not blame Calchas, the seer, for his hateful prophecy.   235. **Strymon,** a river in Macedonia.

And then the elder monarch spake aloud—
Ill lot were mine, to disobey!
And ill, to smite my child, my household's love
and pride! 250
To stain with virgin blood a father's hands, and
slay
My daughter, by the altar's side!
'Twixt woe and woe I dwell—
I dare not like a recreant fly, 254
And leave the league of ships, and fail each true ally;
For rightfully they crave, with eager fiery mind,
The virgin's blood, shed forth to lull the adverse
wind—
God send the deed be well!

Thus on his neck he took
Fate's hard compelling yoke; 260
Then, in the counter-gale of will abhorr'd, accursed,
To recklessness his shifting spirit veer'd—
Alas! that Frenzy, first of ills and worst,
With evil craft men's souls to sin hath ever stirred!

And so he steeled his heart—ah, well-a-day—
Aiding a war for one false woman's sake, 266
His child to slay,
And with her spilt blood make
An offering, to speed the ships upon their way!

Lusting for war, the bloody arbiters 270
Closed heart and ears, and would nor hear nor heed
The girl-voice plead,
Pity me, Father! nor her prayers,
Nor tender, virgin years.

So, when the chant of sacrifice was done, 275
Her father bade the youthful priestly train
Raise her, like some poor kid, above the altar-stone,
From where amid her robes she lay
Sunk all in swoon away—
Bade them, as with the bit that mutely tames the
steed, 280
Her fair lips' speech refrain,
Lest she should speak a curse on Atreus' home and
seed,

So, trailing on the earth her robe of saffron dye,
With one last piteous dart from her beseeching eye
Those that should smite she smote— 285
Fair, silent, as a pictur'd form, but fain
To plead, *Is all forgot?*
How oft those halls of old,
Wherein my sire high feast did hold,
Rang to the virginal soft strain, 290
When I, a stainless child,
Sang from pure lips and undefiled,
Sang of my sire, and all
His honoured life, and how on him should fall
Heaven's highest gift and gain! 295

And then—but I beheld not, nor can tell,
What further fate befel:
But this is sure, that Calchas' boding strain
Can ne'er be void or vain. 299
This wage from Justice' hand do sufferers earn,
The future to discern:
And yet—farewell, O secret of To-morrow!
Fore-knowledge is fore-sorrow.
Clear with the clear beams of the morrow's sun,
The future presseth on. 305
Now, let the house's tale, how dark soe'er,
Find yet an issue fair!—
So prays the loyal, solitary band
That guards the Apian land.
(*They turn to* CLYTEMNESTRA, *who leaves the al-*
tars and comes forward.)

LEADER OF THE CHORUS. Episode
O queen, I come in reverence of thy sway— 310
For, while the ruler's kingly seat is void,
The loyal heart before his consort bends.
Now—be it sure and certain news of good,
Or the fair tidings of a flatt'ring hope, 314
That bids thee spread the light from shrine to shrine,
I, fain to hear, yet grudge not if thou hide.
CLYTEMNESTRA.
As saith the adage, *From the womb of Night*
Spring forth, with promise fair, the young child
Light.
Ay—fairer even than all hope my news—
By Grecian hands is Priam's city ta'en! 320
LEADER.
What say'st thou? doubtful heart makes treach'rous
ear.
CLYTEMNESTRA.
Hear then again, and plainly—Troy is ours!
LEADER.
Thrills thro' my heart such joy as wakens tears.
CLYTEMNESTRA.
Ay, thro' those tears thine eye looks loyalty.
LEADER.
But hast thou proof, to make assurance sure? 325
CLYTEMNESTRA.
Go to; I have—unless the god has lied.
LEADER.
Hath some night-vision won thee to belief?
CLYTEMNESTRA.
Out on all presage of a slumb'rous soul!
LEADER.
But wert thou cheered by Rumour's wingless word?
CLYTEMNESTRA.
Peace—thou dost chide me as a credulous girl. 330
LEADER.
Say then, how long ago the city fell?
CLYTEMNESTRA.
Even in this night that now brings forth the dawn.

309. **Apian land,** Argos, over which King Apis once ruled.

LEADER.

Yet who so swift could speed the message here?

CLYTEMNESTRA.

From Ida's top Hephaestus, lord of fire,
Sent forth his sign; and on, and ever on, 335
Beacon to beacon sped the courier-flame.
From Ida to the crag, that Hermes loves,
Of Lemnos; thence unto the steep sublime
Of Athos, throne of Zeus, the broad blaze flared.
Thence, raised aloft to shoot across the sea, 340
The moving light, rejoicing in its strength,
Sped from the pyre of pine, and urged its way,
In golden glory, like some strange new sun,
Onward, and reached Macistus' watching heights.
There, with no dull delay nor heedless sleep, 345
The watcher sped the tidings on in turn,
Until the guard upon Messapius' peak
Saw the far flame gleam on Euripus' tide,
And from the high-piled heap of withered furze
Lit the new sign and bade the message on. 350
Then the strong light, far-flown and yet undimmed,
Shot thro' the sky above Asopus' plain,
Bright as the moon, and on Cithaeron's crag
Aroused another watch of flying fire.
And there the sentinels no whit disowned, 355
But sent redoubled on, the hest of flame—
Swift shot the light, above Gorgopis' bay,
To Aegiplanctus' mount, and bade the peak
Fail not the onward ordinance of fire.
And like a long beard streaming in the wind, 360
Full-fed with fuel, roared and rose the blaze,
And onward flaring, gleamed above the cape,
Beneath which shimmers the Saronic bay,
And thence leapt light unto Arachne's peak,
The mountain watch that looks upon our town. 365
Thence to th' Atreides' roof—in lineage fair,
A bright posterity of Ida's fire.
So sped from stage to stage, fulfilled in turn,
Flame after flame, along the course ordained,
And lo! the last to speed upon its way 370
Sights the end first, and glows unto the goal.
And Troy is ta'en, and by this sign my lord
Tells me the tale, and ye have learned my word.

LEADER.

To heaven, O queen, will I upraise new song: 374
But, wouldst thou speak once more, I fain would hear
From first to last the marvel of the tale.

CLYTEMNESTRA.

Think you—this very morn—the Greeks in Troy,
And loud therein the voice of utter wail!
Within one cup pour vinegar and oil,
And look! unblent, unreconciled, they war. 380
So in the twofold issue of the strife
Mingle the victor's shout, the captives' moan.
For all the conquered whom the sword has spared
Cling weeping—some unto a brother slain,
Some childlike to a nursing father's form, 385

And wail the loved and lost, the while their neck
Bows down already 'neath the captive's chain.
And lo! the victors, now the fight is done,
Goaded by restless hunger, far and wide
Range all disordered thro' the town, to snatch 390
Such victual and such rest as chance may give
Within the captive halls that once were Troy—
Joyful to rid them of the frost and dew,
Wherein they couched upon the plain of old—
Joyful to sleep the gracious night all through, 395
Unsummoned of the watching sentinel.
Yet let them reverence well the city's gods,
The lords of Troy, tho' fallen, and her shrines;
So shall the spoilers not in turn be spoiled.
Yea, let no craving for forbidden gain 400
Bid conquerors yield before the darts of greed.
For we need yet, before the race be won,
Homewards, unharmed, to round the course once
    more.
For should the host wax wanton ere it come,
Then, tho' the sudden blow of fate be spared, 405
Yet in the sight of gods shall rise once more
The great wrong of the slain, to claim revenge.
Now, hearing from this woman's mouth of mine,
The tale and eke its warning, pray with me,
Luck sway the scale, with no uncertain poise, 410
For my fair hopes are changed to fairer joys.

LEADER.

A gracious word thy woman's lips have told,
Worthy a wise man's utterance, O my queen;
Now with clear trust in thy convincing tale
I set me to salute the gods with song, 415
Who bring us bliss to counterpoise our pain.

(CLYTEMNESTRA *goes into the palace.*)

CHORUS.

Zeus, Lord of heaven! and welcome night
Of victory, that hast our might
    With all the glories crowned!
On towers of Ilion, free no more, 420
Hast flung the mighty mesh of war,
    And closely girt them round,
Till neither warrior may 'scape,
Nor stripling lightly overleap
The trammels as they close, and close, 425
Till with the grip of doom our foes
    In slavery's coil are bound!

Zeus, Lord of hospitality,
In grateful awe I bend to thee—
    'Tis thou hast struck the blow!
    At Alexander, long ago, 430
We marked thee bend thy vengeful bow,
But long and warily withhold
The eager shaft, which, uncontrolled
And loosed too soon or launched too high, 435
Had wandered bloodless through the sky.

431. **Alexander**, Paris, whose sin went unpunished until the fall of Troy.

Zeus, the high God!—whate'er be dim in doubt,
This can our thought track out—
The blow that fells the sinner is of God,
And as he wills, the rod   440
Of vengeance smiteth sore. One said of old,
The gods list not to hold
A reckoning with him whose feet oppress
The grace of holiness—
An impious word! for whenso'er the sire   445

Breathed forth rebellious fire—
What time his household overflowed the measure
Of bliss and health and treasure—
His children's children read the reckoning plain,
At last, in tears and pain.   450
On me let weal that brings no woe be sent,
And therewithal, content!
Who spurns the shrine of Right, nor wealth nor
power
Shall be to him a tower,
To guard him from the gulf: there lies his lot,   455
Where all things are forgot.

Lust drives him on—lust, desperate and wild,
Fate's sin-contriving child—
And cure is none; beyond concealment clear,
Kindles sin's baleful glare.   460
As an ill coin beneath the wearing touch
Betrays by stain and smutch
Its metal false—such is the sinful wight.
Before, on pinions light,
Fair Pleasure flits, and lures him childlike on, 465
While home and kin make moan
Beneath the grinding burden of his crime;
Till, in the end of time,
Cast down of heaven, he pours forth fruitless prayer
To powers that will not hear.   470
And such did Paris come
Unto Atreides' home,
And thence, with sin and shame his welcome to re-
pay,
Ravished the wife away—

And she, unto her country and her kin   475
Leaving the clash of shields and spears and arming
ships,
And bearing unto Troy destruction for a dower,
And overbold in sin,
Went fleetly thro' the gates, at midnight hour.
Oft from the prophets' lips   480
Moaned out the warning and the wail—Ah woe!
Woe for the home, the home! and for the chieftains,
woe!
Woe for the bride-bed, warm
Yet from the lovely limbs, the impress of the form
Of her who loved her lord, awhile ago!   485

472. **Atreides**, Menelaus, son of Atreus.

And woe! for him who stands
Shamed, silent, unreproachful, stretching hands
That find her not, and sees, yet will not see,
That she is far away!
And his sad fancy, yearning o'er the sea,   490
Shall summon and recall
Her wraith, once more to queen it in his hall.
And sad with many memories,
The fair cold beauty of each sculptured face—
And all to hatefulness is turned their grace,   495
Seen blankly by forlorn and hungering eyes!

And when the night is deep,
Come visions, sweet and sad, and bearing pain
Of hopings vain—
Void, void and vain, for scarce the sleeping sight 500
Has seen its old delight,
When thro' the grasps of love that bid it stay
It vanishes away
On silent wings that roam adown the ways of sleep.

Such are the sights, the sorrows fell,   505
About our hearth—and worse, whereof I may not
tell.
But, all the wide town o'er,
Each home that sent its master far away
From Hellas' shore,   509
Feels the keen thrill of heart, the pang of loss, to-day.
For, truth to say,
The touch of bitter death is manifold!
Familiar was each face, and dear as life,
That went unto the war,
But thither, whence a warrior went of old,   515
Doth nought return—
Only a spear and sword, and ashes in an urn!

For Ares, lord of strife,
Who doth the swaying scales of battle hold,
War's money-changer, giving dust for gold,   520
Sends back, to hearts that held them dear,
Scant ash of warriors, wept with many a tear,
Light to the hand, but heavy to the soul;
Yea, fills the light urn full
With what survived the flame—   525
Death's dusty measure of a hero's frame!
Alas! one cries, and yet alas again!
Our chief is gone, the hero of the spear,
And hath not left his peer!
Ah woe! another moans—*my spouse is slain,*   530
The death of honour, rolled in dust and blood,
Slain for a woman's sin, a false wife's shame!
Such muttered words of bitter mood
Rise against those who went forth to reclaim;
Yea, jealous wrath creeps on against th' Atreides'
name.   535

And others, far beneath the Ilian wall,
Sleep their last sleep—the goodly chiefs and tall,

Couched in the foeman's land, whereon they gave
Their breath, and lords of Troy, each in his Trojan
    grave.

Therefore for each and all the city's breast   540
  Is heavy with a wrath supprest,
As deeply and deadly as a curse more loud
  Flung by the common crowd:
And, brooding deeply, doth my soul await
  Tidings of coming fate,   545
Buried as yet in darkness' womb.
For not forgetful is the high gods' doom
  Against the sons of carnage: all too long
Seems the unjust to prosper and be strong,
  Till the dark Furies come,   550
And smite with stern reversal all his home,
  Down into dim obstruction—he is gone,
And help and hope, among the lost, is none!

O'er him who vaunteth an exceeding fame,
  Impends a woe condign;   555
The vengeful bolt upon his eyes doth flame,
  Sped from the hand divine.
This bliss be mine, ungrudged of God, to feel—
  To tread no city to the dust,
  Nor see my own life thrust   560
Down to a slave's estate beneath another's heel!

Behold, throughout the city wide
Have the swift feet of Rumour hied,
  Roused by the joyful flame:
But is the news they scatter, sooth?   565
Or haply do they give for truth
  Some cheat which heaven doth frame?
A child were he and all unwise,
  Who let his heart with joy be stirred.
To see the beacon-fires arise,   570
  And then, beneath some thwarting word,
  Sicken anon with hope deferred.
  The edge of woman's insight still
  Good news from true divideth ill;
Light rumours leap within the bound   575
Then fences female credence round,
But, lightly born, as lightly dies
The tale that springs of her surmise.
  (*Several days elapse.*)
LEADER OF THE CHORUS.
Soon shall we know whereof the bale-fires tell,
The beacons, kindled with transmitted flame;   580
Whether, as well I deem, their tale is true,
Or whether like some dream delusive came
The welcome blaze but to befool our soul.
For lo! I see a herald from the shore
Draw hither, shadowed with the olive-wreath—   585
And thirsty dust, twin-brother of the clay,
Speaks plain of travel far and truthful news—
No dumb surmise, nor tongue of flame in smoke,

Fitfully kindled from the mountain pyre;
But plainlier shall his voice say, *All is well,*   590
Or—but away, forebodings adverse, now,
And on fair promise fair fulfilment come!
And whoso for the state prays otherwise,
Himself reap harvest of his ill desire!
    (A HERALD *enters.*)
HERALD.
O land of Argos, fatherland of mine!   595
To thee at last, beneath the tenth year's sun,
My feet return; the bark of my emprise,
Tho' one by one hope's anchors broke away,
Held by the last, and now rides safely here.
Long, long my soul despaired to win, in death,   600
Its longed-for rest within our Argive land:
And now all hail, O earth, and hail to thee,
New-risen sun! and hail our country's God,
High-ruling Zeus, and thou, the Pythian lord,   604
Whose arrows smote us once—smite thou no more!
Was not thy wrath wreaked full upon our heads,
O king Apollo, by Scamander's side?
Turn thou, be turned, be saviour, healer, now!
And hail, all gods who rule the street and mart
And Hermes hail! my patron and my pride,   610
Herald of heaven, and lord of heralds here!
And Heroes, ye who sped us on our way—
To one and all I cry, *Receive again*
With grace such Argives as the spear has spared.

Ah, home of royalty, belovèd halls,   615
And solemn shrines, and gods that front the morn!
Benign as erst, with sun-flushed aspect greet
The king returning after many days.
For as from night flash out the beams of day,
So out of darkness dawns a light, a king,   620
On you, on Argos—Agamemnon comes.
Then hail and greet him well! such meed befits
Him whose right hand hewed down the towers of
    Troy
With the great axe of Zeus who righteth wrong—
And smote the plain, smote down to nothingness   625
Each altar, every shrine; and far and wide
Dies from the whole land's face its offspring fair.
Such mighty yoke of fate he set on Troy—
Our lord and monarch, Atreus' elder son,
And comes at last with blissful honour home;   630
Highest of all who walk on earth to-day—
Not Paris nor the city's self that paid
Sin's price with him, can boast, *Whate'er befall,*
The guerdon we have won outweighs it all.
But at Fate's judgment-seat the robber stands   635
Condemned of rapine, and his prey is torn
Forth from his hands, and by his deed is reaped
A bloody harvest of his home and land
Gone down to death, and for his guilt and lust
His father's race pays double in the dust.   640

607. **Scamander,** a river flowing beside Troy.

LEADER.

Hail, herald of the Greeks, new-come from war.

HERALD.

All hail! not death itself can fright me now.

LEADER.

Was thine heart wrung with longing for thy land?

HERALD.

So that this joy doth brim mine eyes with tears.

LEADER.

On you too then this sweet distress did fall— 645

HERALD.

How say'st thou? make me master of thy word.

LEADER.

You longed for us who pined for you again.

HERALD.

Craved the land us who craved it, love for love?

LEADER.

Yea, till my brooding heart moaned out with pain.

HERALD.

Whence thy despair, that mars the army's joy? 650

LEADER.

Sole cure of wrong is silence, saith the saw.

HERALD.

Thy kings afar, couldst thou fear other men?

LEADER.

Death had been sweet, as thou didst say but now.

HERALD.

'Tis true; Fate smiles at last. Throughout our toil,
These many years, some chances issued fair, 655
And some, I wot, were chequered with a curse.
But who, on earth, hath won the bliss of heaven,
Thro' time's whole tenor an unbroken weal?
I could a tale unfold of toiling oars,
Ill rest, scant landings on a shore rock-strewn, 660
All pains, all sorrows, for our daily doom.
And worse and hatefuller our woes on land;
For where we couched, close by the foeman's wall,
The river-plain was ever dank with dews,
Dropped from the sky, exuded from the earth, 665
A curse that clung unto our sodden garb,
And hair as horrent as a wild beast's fell.
Why tell the woes of winter, when the birds
Lay stark and stiff, so stern was Ida's snow?
Or summer's scorch, what time the stirless wave 670
Sank to its sleep beneath the noon-day sun?
Why mourn old woes? their pain has passed away;
And passed away, from those who fell, all care,
For evermore, to rise and live again.
Why sum the count of death, and render thanks 675
For life by moaning over fate malign?
Farewell, a long farewell to all our woes!
To us, the remnant of the host of Greece,
Comes weal beyond all counterpoise of woe;
Thus boast we rightfully to yonder sun, 680
Like him far-fleeted over sea and land.
The Argive host prevailed to conquer Troy,

669. **Ida,** a mountain range near Troy.

And in the temples of the gods of Greece
Hung up these spoils, a shining sign to Time.
Let those who learn this legend bless aright 685
The city and its chieftains, and repay
The meed of gratitude to Zeus who willed
And wrought the deed. So stands the tale fulfilled.

LEADER.

Thy words o'erbear my doubt: for news of good,
The ear of age hath ever youth enow: 690
But those within and Clytemnestra's self
Would fain hear all; glad thou their ears and mine.

(CLYTEMNESTRA *enters.*)

CLYTEMNESTRA.

That night, when first the fiery courier came,
In sign that Troy is ta'en and razed to earth,
So wild a cry of joy my lips gave out, 695
That I was chidden—*Hath the beacon watch*
Made sure unto thy soul the sack of Troy?
A very woman thou, whose heart leaps light
At wandering rumours!—and with words like these
They showed me how I strayed, misled of hope. 700
Yet on each shrine I set the sacrifice,
And, in the strain they held for feminine,
Went heralds thro' the city, to and fro,
With voice of loud proclaim, announcing joy; 704
And in each fane they lit and quenched with wine
The spicy perfumes fading in the flame.
All is fulfilled: I spare your longer tale—
The king himself anon shall tell me all.
Remains to think what honour best may greet
My lord, the majesty of Argos, home. 710
What day beams fairer on a woman's eyes
Than this, whereon she flings the portal wide,
To hail her lord, heaven-shielded, home from war?
This to my husband, that he tarry not,
But turn the city's longing into joy! 715
Yea, let him come, and coming may he find
A wife no other than he left her, true
And faithful as a watch-dog to his home,
His foemen's foe, in all her duties leal,
Trusty to keep for ten long years unmarred 720
The store whereon he set his master-seal.
Be steel deep-dyed, before ye look to see
Ill joy, ill fame, from other wight, in me!

HERALD.

'Tis fairly said: thus speaks a noble dame,
Nor speaks amiss, when truth informs the boast. 725

(CLYTEMNESTRA *returns into the palace.*)

LEADER.

So has she spoken—be it yours to learn
By clear interpreters her specious word.
Turn to me, herald—tell me if anon
The second well-loved lord of Argos comes?
Hath Menelaus safely sped with you? 730

HERALD.

Alas—brief boon unto my friends it were,
To flatter them, for truth, with falsehoods fair!

LEADER.
Speak joy, if truth be joy, but truth, at worst—
Too plainly, truth and joy are here divorced.

HERALD.
The hero and his bark were rapt away   735
Far from the Grecian fleet; 'tis truth I say.

LEADER.
Whether in all men's sight from Ilion borne,
Or from the fleet by stress of weather torn?

HERALD.
Full on the mark thy shaft of speech doth light,
And one short word hath told long woes aright.   740

LEADER.
But say, what now of him each comrade saith?
What their forebodings, of his life or death?

HERALD.
Ask me no more: the truth is known to none,
Save the earth-fostering, all-surveying Sun.   744

LEADER.
Say, by what doom the fleet of Greece was driven?
How rose, how sank the storm, the wrath of heaven?

HERALD.
Nay, ill it were to mar with sorrow's tale
The day of blissful news. The gods demand
Thanksgiving sundered from solicitude.
If one as herald came with rueful face   750
To say, *The curse has fallen, and the host*
Gone down to death; and one wide wound has
      reached
The city's heart, and out of many homes
Many are cast and consecrate to death,
Beneath the double scourge, that Ares loves,   755
The bloody pair, the fire and sword of doom—
If such sore burden weighed upon my tongue,
'Twere fit to speak such words as gladden fiends.
But—coming as he comes who bringeth news
Of safe return from toil, and issues fair,   760
To men rejoicing in a weal restored—
Dare I to dash good words with ill, and say
How the gods' anger smote the Greeks in storm?
For fire and sea, that erst held bitter feud,
Now swore conspiracy and pledged their faith,   765
Wasting the Argives worn with toil and war.
Night and great horror of the rising wave
Came o'er us, and the blasts that blow from Thrace
Clashed ship with ship, and some with plunging
      prow
Thro' scudding drifts of spray and raving storm   770
Vanished, as strays by some ill shepherd driven.
And when at length the sun rose bright, we saw
Th' Aegaean sea-field flecked with flowers of death,
Corpses of Grecian men and shattered hulls.
For us indeed, some god, as well I deem,   775
No human power, laid hand upon our helm,
Snatched us or prayed us from the powers of air,
And brought our bark thro' all, unharmed in hull:
And saving Fortune sat and steered us fair,

So that no surge should gulf us deep in brine,   780
Nor grind our keel upon a rocky shore.

So 'scaped we death that lurks beneath the sea,
But, under day's white light, mistrustful all
Of fortune's smile, we sat and brooded deep,   784
Shepherds forlorn of thoughts that wandered wild
O'er this new woe; for smitten was our host,
And lost as ashes scattered from the pyre.
Of whom if any draw his life-breath yet,
Be well assured, he deems of us as dead,
As we of him no other fate forebode.   790
But heaven save all! If Menelaus live,
He will not tarry, but will surely come:
Therefore if anywhere the high sun's ray
Descries him upon earth, preserved by Zeus,
Who wills not yet to wipe his race away,   795
Hope still there is that homeward he may wend.
Enough—thou hast the truth unto the end.   (*Exit.*)

CHORUS.
Say, from whose lips the presage fell?
Who read the future all too well,
      And named her, in her natal hour,   800
      Helen, the bride with war for dower?
'Twas one of the Invisible,
      Guiding his tongue with prescient power.
On fleet, and host, and citadel,
      War, sprung from her, and death did lour,   805
When from the bride-bed's fine-spun veil
She to the Zephyr spread her sail.
Strong blew the breeze—the surge closed o'er
The cloven track of keel and oar,
      But while she fled, there drove along,   810
      Fast in her wake, a mighty throng—
Athirst for blood, athirst for war,
      Forward in fell pursuit they sprung,
Then leapt on Simois' bank ashore,
      The leafy coppices among—   815
No rangers, they, of wood and field,
But huntsmen of the sword and shield.

Heaven's jealousy, that works its will,
Sped thus on Troy its destined ill,
      Well named, at once, the Bride and Bane;   820
      And loud rang out the bridal strain;
But they to whom that song befell
      Did turn anon to tears again;
Zeus tarries, but avenges still
      The husband's wrong, the household's stain!   825
He, the hearth's lord, brooks not to see
Its outraged hospitality.

Even now, and in far other tone,
Troy chants her dirge of mighty moan,
      Woe upon Paris, woe and hate!   830
      Who wooed his country's doom for mate—

814. **Simois**, a river near Troy.

This is the burthen of the groan,
  Wherewith she wails disconsolate
The blood, so many of her own
  Have poured in vain, to fend her fate;   835
Troy! thou hast fed and freed to roam
A lion-cub within thy home!

A suckling creature, newly ta'en   *(Helen)*
From mother's teat, still fully fain
    Of nursing care; and oft caressed,   840
    Within the arms, upon the breast,
  Even as an infant, has it lain;
    Or fawns and licks, by hunger pressed,
  The hand that will assuage its pain;
    In life's young dawn, a well-loved guest,   845
A fondling for the children's play,
A joy unto the old and grey.

But waxing time and growth betrays
The blood-thirst of the lion-race,
    And, for the house's fostering care,   850
    Unbidden all, it revels there,
And bloody recompense repays—
    Rent flesh of kine, its talons tare:
  A mighty beast, that slays, and slays,
    And mars with blood the household fair,   855
A God-sent pest invincible,
A minister of fate and hell.

Even so to Ilion's city came by stealth
    A spirit as of windless seas and skies,
A gentle phantom-form of joy and wealth,   860
    With love's soft arrows speeding from its eyes—
Love's rose, whose thorn doth pierce the soul in sub-
    tle wise.

Ah, well-a-day! the bitter bridal-bed,
    When the fair mischief lay by Paris' side!
What curse on palace and on people sped   865
    With her, the Fury sent on Priam's pride,
By angered Zeus! what tears of many a widowed
    bride!

Long, long ago to mortals this was told,
  How sweet security and blissful state
Have curses for their children—so men hold—   870
    And for the man of all-too prosperous fate
Springs from a bitter seed some woe insatiate.

Theme {
Alone, alone, I deem far otherwise:
  Not bliss nor wealth it is, but impious deed,
From which that after-growth of ill doth rise!   875
  Woe springs from wrong, the plant is like the
    seed—
While Right, in honour's house, doth its own likeness
    breed.

Some past impiety, some grey old crime,
  Breeds the young curse, that wantons in our ill,
Early or late, when haps th' appointed time—   880
  And out of light brings power of darkness still,
A master-fiend, a foe, unseen, invincible;

A pride accursed, that broods upon the race   883
  And home in which dark Atè holds her sway—
Sin's child and Woe's, that wears its parents' face;

While Right in smoky cribs shines clear as day,
And decks with weal his life, who walks the righteous
    way.

From gilded halls, that hands polluted raise,
  Right turns away with proud averted eyes,
And of the wealth, men stamp amiss with praise,
  Heedless, to poorer, holier temples hies,   891
And to Fate's goal guides all, in its appointed wise.
  (AGAMEMNON *enters in a chariot, accompanied by*
CASSANDRA.)
  (*The* CHORUS *sings its welcome.*)
Hail to thee, chief of Atreus' race,
Returning proud from Troy subdued!
How shall I greet thy conquering face?   895
How nor a fulsome praise obtrude,
Nor stint the meed of gratitude?
For mortal men who fall to ill
Take little heed of open truth,
But seek unto its semblance still: 900
The show of weeping and of ruth
To the forlorn will all men pay,
But, of the grief their eyes display,
Nought to the heart doth pierce its way.
And, with the joyous, they beguile   905
Their lips unto a feignèd smile,
And force a joy, unfelt the while;
But he who as a shepherd wise
  Doth know his flock, can ne'er misread
Truth in the falsehood of his eyes,   910
Who veils beneath a kindly guise
  A lukewarm love in deed.
And thou, our leader—when of yore
Thou badest Greece go forth to war
For Helen's sake—I dare avow   915
That then I held thee not as now;
That to my vision thou didst seem
Dyed in the hues of disesteem.
I held thee for a pilot ill,
And reckless, of thy proper will,   920
Endowing others doomed to die
With vain and forced audacity!
Now from my heart, ungrudgingly,
To those that wrought, this word be said—
Well fall the labour ye have sped—   925
Let time and search, O king, declare
884. Atè, goddess of guilt and revenge.

What men within thy city's bound
Were loyal to the kingdom's care,
And who were faithless found.

AGAMEMNON.

First, as is meet, a king's All-hail be said   930
To Argos, and the gods that guard the land—
Gods who with me availed to speed us home,
With me availed to wring from Priam's town
The due of justice. In the court of heaven
The gods in conclave sat and judged the cause,   935
Not from a pleader's tongue, and at the close,
Unanimous into the urn of doom
This sentence gave, *On Ilion and her men*,
Death: and where hope drew nigh to pardon's urn
No hand there was to cast a vote therein.   940
And still the smoke of fallen Ilion
Rises in sight of all men, and the flame
Of Atè's hecatomb is living yet,
And where the towers in dusty ashes sink,
Rise the rich fumes of pomp and wealth consumed
For this must all men pay unto the gods   946
The meed of mindful hearts and gratitude:
For by our hands the meshes of revenge
Closed on the prey, and for one woman's sake
Troy trodden by the Argive monster lies—   950
The foal, the shielded band that leapt the wall,
What time with autumn sank the Pleiades.
Yea, o'er the fencing wall a lion sprang
Ravening, and lapped his fill of blood of kings.

Such prelude spoken to the gods in full,   955
To you I turn, and to the hidden thing
Whereof ye spake but now: and in that thought
I am as you, and what ye say, say I.
For few are they who have such inborn grace,
As to look up with love, and envy not,   960
When stands another on the height of weal.
Deep in his heart, whom jealousy hath seized,
Her poison lurking doth enhance his load;
For now beneath his proper woes he chafes,
And sighs withal to see another's weal.   965

I speak not idly, but from knowledge sure—
There be who vaunt an utter loyalty,
That is but as the ghost of friendship dead,
A shadow in a glass, of faith gone by.
One only—he who went reluctant forth   970
Across the seas with me—Odysseus—he
Was loyal unto me with strength and will,
A trusty trace-horse bound unto my car.
Thus—be he yet beneath the light of day,
Or dead, as well I fear—I speak his praise.   975

Lastly, whate'er be due to men or gods,
With joint debate, in public council held,
We will decide, and warily contrive
That all which now is well may so abide:

For that which haply needs the healer's art,   980
That will we medicine, discerning well
If cautery or knife befit the time.

Now, to my palace and the shrines of home,
I will pass in, and greet you first and fair,
Ye gods, who bade me forth, and home again—   985
And long may Victory tarry in my train!

(CLYTEMNESTRA *enters, followed by maidens bearing crimson robes.*)

CLYTEMNESTRA.

Old men of Argos, lieges of our realm,
Shame shall not bid me shrink lest ye should see
The love I bear my lord. Such blushing fear
Dies at the last from hearts of human kind.   990
From mine own soul and from no alien lips,
I know and will reveal the life I bore,
Reluctant, through the lingering livelong years,
The while my lord beleaguered Ilion's wall.

First, that a wife sat sundered from her lord,   995
In widowed solitude, was utter woe—
And woe, to hear how rumour's many tongues
All boded evil—woe, when he who came
And he who followed spake of ill on ill,
Keening *Lost, lost, all lost!* thro' hall and bower.   1000
Had this my husband met so many wounds,
As by a thousand channels rumour told,
No network e'er was full of holes as he.
Had he been slain, as oft as tidings came
That he was dead, he well might boast him now   1005
A second Geryon of triple frame,
With triple robe of earth above him laid—
For that below, no matter—triply dead,
Dead by one death for every form he bore.
And thus distraught by news of wrath and woe,   1010
Oft for self-slaughter had I slung the noose,
But others wrenched it from my neck away.
Hence haps it that Orestes, thine and mine,
The pledge and symbol of our wedded troth,
Stands not beside us now, as he should stand.   1015
Nor marvel thou at this: he dwells with one
Who guards him loyally; 'tis Phocis' king,
Strophius, who warned me erst, *Bethink thee, queen,*
What woes of doubtful issue well may fall!
Thy lord in daily jeopardy at Troy,   1020
While here a populace uncurbed may cry,
"Down with the council, down!" bethink thee too,
'Tis the world's way to set a harder heel
On fallen power.
                    For thy child's absence then
Such mine excuse, no wily afterthought.   1025
For me, long since the gushing fount of tears
Is wept away; no drop is left to shed.
Dim are the eyes that ever watched till dawn,
Weeping, the bale-fires, piled for thy return,
Night after night unkindled. If I slept,   1030

Each sound—the tiny humming of a gnat,
Roused me again, again, from fitful dreams
Wherein I felt thee smitten, saw thee slain,
Thrice for each moment of mine hour of sleep.

All this I bore, and now, released from woe,   1035
I hail my lord as watch-dog of a fold,
As saving stay-rope of a storm-tossed ship,
As column stout that holds the roof aloft,
As only child unto a sire bereaved,
As land beheld, past hope, by crews forlorn,   1040
As sunshine fair when tempest's wrath is past,
As gushing spring to thirsty wayfarer,
So sweet it is to 'scape the press of pain.
With such salute I bid my husband hail!   1044
Nor heaven be wroth therewith! for long and hard
I bore that ire of old.   Sweet lord, step forth,
Step from thy car, I pray—nay, not on earth
Plant the proud foot, O king, that trod down Troy!
Women! why tarry ye, whose task it is
To spread your monarch's path with tapestry?   1050
Swift, swift, with purple strew his passage fair,
That justice lead him to a home, at last,
He scarcely looked to see.
   (*The attendant women spread the tapestry.*)
                     For what remains,
Zeal unsubdued by sleep shall nerve my hand
To work as right and as the gods command.   1055
   AGAMEMNON (*still in the chariot*).
Daughter of Leda, watcher o'er my home,
Thy greeting well befits mine absence long,
For late and hardly has it reached its end.
Know, that the praise which honour bids us crave,
Must come from others' lips, not from our own: 1060
See too that not in fashion feminine
Thou make a warrior's pathway delicate;
Not unto me, as to some Eastern lord,
Bowing thyself to earth, make homage loud.
Strew not this purple that shall make each step   1065
An arrogance; such pomp beseems the gods,
Not me. A mortal man to set his foot
On these rich dyes? I hold such pride in fear,
And bid thee honour me as man, not god.
Fear not—such footcloths and all gauds apart,   1070
Loud from the trump of Fame my name is blown;
Best gift of heaven it is, in glory's hour,
To think thereon with soberness: and thou—
Bethink thee of the adage, *Call none blest*
Till peaceful death have crowned a life of weal.   1075
'Tis said: I fain would fare unvexed by fear.
   CLYTEMNESTRA.
Nay, but unsay it—thwart not thou my will!
   AGAMEMNON.
Know, I have said, and will not mar my word.
   CLYTEMNESTRA.
Was it fear made this meekness to the gods?

   AGAMEMNON.
If cause be cause, 'tis mine for this resolve.   1080
   CLYTEMNESTRA.
What, think'st thou, in thy place had Priam done?
   AGAMEMNON.
He surely would have walked on broidered robes.
   CLYTEMNESTRA.
Then fear not thou the voice of human blame.
   AGAMEMNON.
Yet mighty is the murmur of a crowd.
   CLYTEMNESTRA.
Shrink not from envy, appanage of bliss.   1085
   AGAMEMNON.
War is not woman's part, nor war of words.
   CLYTEMNESTRA.
Yet happy victors well may yield therein.
   AGAMEMNON.
Dost crave for triumph in this petty strife?
   CLYTEMNESTRA.
Yield; of thy grace permit me to prevail!
   AGAMEMNON.
Then, if thou wilt, let some one stoop to loose   1090
Swiftly these sandals, slaves beneath my foot;
And stepping thus upon the sea's rich dye,
I pray, *Let none among the gods look down*
With jealous eye on me—reluctant all,
To trample thus and mar a thing of price,   1095
Wasting the wealth of garments silver-worth.
Enough hereof: and, for the stranger maid,
Lead her within, but gently: God on high
Looks graciously on him whom triumph's hour
Has made not pitiless. None willingly   1100
Wear the slave's yoke—and she, the prize and flower
Of all we won, comes hither in my train,
Gift of the army to its chief and lord.
—Now, since in this my will bows down to thine,
I will pass in on purples to my home.   1105
   (*He descends from the chariot, and walks on the*
tapestry *to the palace.*)
   CLYTEMNESTRA.
A Sea there is—and who shall stay its springs?
And deep within its breast, a mighty store,
Precious as silver, of the purple dye,
Whereby the dipped robe doth its tint renew.
Enough of such, O king, within thy halls   1110
There lies, a store that cannot fail; but I—
I would have gladly vowed unto the gods
Cost of a thousand garments trodden thus,
(Had once the oracle such gift required)
Contriving ransom for thy life preserved.   1115
For while the stock is firm the foliage climbs,
Spreading a shade, what time the dog-star glows;
And thou, returning to thine hearth and home,
Art as a genial warmth in winter hours,
Or as a coolness, when the lord of heaven   1120
Mellows the juice within the bitter grape.
Such boons and more doth bring into a home

The present footstep of its proper lord.
Zeus, Zeus, Fulfilment's lord! my vows fulfil,
And whatsoe'er it be, work forth thy will! 1125
     (*She follows* AGAMEMNON *into the palace.*)

CHORUS.
Wherefore for ever on the wings of fear
    Hovers a vision drear
Before my boding heart? a strain,
Unbidden and unwelcome, thrills mine ear,
    Oracular of pain. 1130
Not as of old upon my bosom's throne
    Sits Confidence, to spurn
Such fears, like dreams we know not to discern.
Old, old and grey long since the time has grown,
    Which saw the linkèd cables moor 1135
The fleet, when erst it came to Ilion's sandy shore;

    And now mine eyes and not another's see
      Their safe return.

    Yet none the less in me
The inner spirit sings a boding song, 1140
    Self-prompted, sings the Furies' strain—
      And seeks, and seeks in vain,
      To hope and to be strong!

Ah! to some end of Fate, unseen, unguessed,
    Are these wild throbbings of my heart and
      breast— 1145
      Yea, of some doom they tell—
        Each pulse, a knell.
    Lief, lief I were, that all
To unfulfilment's hidden realm might fall.

    Too far, too far our mortal spirits strive, 1150
      Grasping at utter weal, unsatisfied—
Till the fell curse, that dwelleth hard beside,
Thrust down the sundering wall. Too fair they
      blow,
    The gales that waft our bark on Fortune's
      tide!
    Swiftly we sail, the sooner all to drive 1155
    Upon the hidden rock, the reef of woe.
Then if the hand of caution warily
    Sling forth into the sea 1158
Part of the freight, lest all should sink below,
From the deep death it saves the bark: even so,
    Doom-laden though it be, once more may rise
    His household, who is timely wise.

    How oft the famine-stricken field
Is saved by God's large gift, the new year's yield!

    But blood of man once spilled, 1165
Once at his feet shed forth, and darkening the
     plain,—
    Nor chant nor charm can call it back again.

So Zeus hath willed:
Else had he spared the leech Asclepius, skilled 1169
    To bring man from the dead: the hand divine
Did smite himself with death—a warning and a
    sign—

    Ah me! if Fate, ordained of old,
Held not the will of gods constrained, controlled,
    Helpless to us-ward, and apart—
    Swifter than speech my heart 1175
Had poured its presage out!
Now, fretting, chafing in the dark of doubt,
    'Tis hopeless to unfold
Truth, from fear's tangled skein; and, yearning to
    proclaim
    Its thought, my soul is prophecy and flame. 1180
      (*Re-enter* CLYTEMNESTRA.)

CLYTEMNESTRA.
Get thee within thou too, Cassandra, go!
For Zeus to thee in gracious mercy grants
To share the sprinklings of the lustral bowl,
Beside the altar of his guardianship,
Slave among many slaves. What, haughty still? 1185
Step from the car; Alcmena's son, 'tis said,
Was sold perforce and bore the yoke of old.
Ay, hard it is, but, if such fate befall,
'Tis a fair chance to serve within a home
Of ancient wealth and power. An upstart lord, 1190
To whom wealth's harvest came beyond his hope,
Is as a lion to his slaves, in all
Exceeding fierce, immoderate in sway.
Pass in: thou hearest what our ways will be.

LEADER OF THE CHORUS.
Clear unto thee, O maid, is her command, 1195
But thou—within the toils of Fate thou art—
If such thy will, I urge thee to obey;
Yet I misdoubt thou dost nor hear nor heed.

CLYTEMNESTRA.
I wot—unless like swallows she doth use
Some strange barbarian tongue from oversea— 1200
My words must speak persuasion to her soul.

LEADER.
Obey: there is no gentler way than this.
Step from the car's high seat and follow her.

CLYTEMNESTRA.
Truce to this bootless waiting here without!
I will not stay: beside the central shrine 1205
The victims stand, prepared for knife and fire—
Offerings from hearts beyond all hope made glad.
Thou—if thou reckest aught of my command,
'Twere well done soon: but if thy sense be shut
From these my words, let thy barbarian hand 1210
Fulfil by gesture the default of speech.

LEADER.
No native is she, thus to read thy words

1183. *sprinklings of the lustral bowl*, the holy waters of purification.
1186. **Alcmena's son**, Hercules.

Unaided: like some wild thing of the wood,
New-trapped, behold! she shrinks and glares on thee.
CLYTEMNESTRA.
'Tis madness and the rule of mind distraught,   1215
Since she beheld her city sink in fire,
And hither comes, nor brooks the bit, until
In foam and blood her wrath be champed away.
See ye to her; unqueenly 'tis for me,
Unheeded thus to cast away my words.   1220
(*Exit* CLYTEMNESTRA.)
LEADER.
But with me pity sits in anger's place.
Poor maiden, come thou from the car; no way
There is but this—take up thy servitude.
CASSANDRA (*chanting*).
Woe, woe, alas! Earth, Mother Earth! and thou
Apollo, Apollo!   1225
LEADER.
Peace! shriek not to the bright prophetic god,
Who will not brook the suppliance of woe.
CASSANDRA.
Woe, woe, alas! Earth, Mother Earth! and thou
Apollo, Apollo!
LEADER.
Hark, with wild curse she calls anew on him,   1230
Who stands far off and loathes the voice of wail.
CASSANDRA.
Apollo, Apollo!
God of all ways, but only Death's to me,
Once and again, O thou, Destroyer named,
Thou hast destroyed me, thou, my love of old!   1235
LEADER.
She grows presageful of her woes to come,
Slave tho' she be, instinct with prophecy.
CASSANDRA.
Apollo, Apollo!
God of all ways, but only Death's to me,
O thou Apollo, thou Destroyer named!   1240
What way hast led me, to what evil home?
LEADER.
Know'st thou it not? The home of Atreus' race:
Take these my words for sooth and ask no more.
CASSANDRA.
Home cursed of God! Bear witness unto me,
Ye visioned woes within—   1245
The blood-stained hands of them that smite their
kin—
The strangling noose, and, spattered o'er
With human blood, the reeking floor!
LEADER.
How like a sleuth-hound questing on the track,
Keen-scented unto blood and death she hies!   1250
CASSANDRA.
Ah! can the ghostly guidance fail,
Whereby my prophet-soul is onwards led?

1224.(*chanting*). Cassandra is in the trance of prophecy.

Look! for their flesh the spectre-children wail,
Their sodden limbs on which their father fed!
LEADER.
Long since we knew of thy prophetic fame,—   1255
But for those deeds we seek no prophet's tongue.
CASSANDRA.
God! 'tis another crime—
Worse than the storied woe of olden time,
Cureless, abhorred, that one is plotting here—
A shaming death, for those that should be dear!   1260
Alas! and far away, in foreign land,
He that should help doth stand!
LEADER.
I knew th' old tales, the city rings withal—
But now thy speech is dark, beyond my ken.
CASSANDRA.
O wretch, O purpose fell!   1265
Thou for thy wedded lord
The cleansing wave hast poured—
A treacherous welcome!
How the sequel tell?
Too soon 'twill come, too soon, for now, even now,
She smites him, blow on blow!   1270
LEADER.
Riddles beyond my rede—I peer in vain
Thro' the dim films that screen the prophecy.
CASSANDRA.
God! a new sight! a net, a snare of hell,
Set by her hand—herself a snare more fell!
A wedded wife, she slays her lord,   1275
Helped by another hand!
Ye powers, whose hate
Of Atreus' home no blood can satiate,
Raise the wild cry above the sacrifice abhorred!
CHORUS.
Why biddest thou some fiend, I know not whom,
Shriek o'er the house? Thine is no cheering word.
Back to my heart in frozen fear I feel   1281
My wanning life-blood run—
The blood that round the wounding steel
Ebbs slow, as sinks life's parting sun—   1284
Swift, swift and sure, some woe comes pressing on!
CASSANDRA.
Away, away—keep him away—
The monarch of the herd, the pasture's pride,
Far from his mate! In treach'rous wrath,
Muffling his swarthy horns, with secret scathe
She gores his fenceless side!   1290
Hark! in the brimming bath,
The heavy plash—the dying cry—
Hark—in the laver—hark, he falls by treachery!
CHORUS.
I read amiss dark sayings such as thine,
Yet something warns me that they tell of ill.   1295
O dark prophetic speech,
Ill tidings dost thou teach
Ever, to mortals here below!

Ever some tale of awe and woe
Thro' all thy windings manifold   1300
Do we unriddle and unfold!

CASSANDRA.
Ah well-a-day! the cup of agony,
Whereof I chant, foams with a draught for me.
Ah lord, ah leader, thou hast led me here—   1304
Was't but to die with thee whose doom is near?

CHORUS.
Distraught thou art, divinely stirred,
And wailest for thyself a tuneless lay,
As piteous as the ceaseless tale
Wherewith the brown melodious bird
Doth ever Itys! Itys! wail,   1310
Deep-bowered in sorrow, all its little life-time's day!

CASSANDRA.
Ah for thy fate, O shrill-voiced nightingale!
Some solace for thy woes did Heaven afford,
Clothed thee with soft brown plumes, and life
          apart from wail—
But for my death is edged the double-biting
          sword!   1315

CHORUS.
What pangs are these, what fruitless pain,
  Sent on thee from on high?
Thou chantest terror's frantic strain,
Yet in shrill measured melody.
How thus unerring canst thou sweep along   1320
The prophet's path of boding song?

CASSANDRA.
Woe, Paris, woe on thee! thy bridal joy
Was death and fire upon thy race and Troy!
  And woe for thee, Scamander's flood!
  Beside thy banks, O river fair,   1325
  I grew in tender nursing care
From childhood unto maidenhood!
Now not by thine, but by Cocytus' stream
And Acheron's banks shall ring my boding scream.

CHORUS.
  Too plain is all, too plain!   1330
A child might read aright thy fateful strain.
  Deep in my heart their piercing fang
  Terror and sorrow set, the while I heard
  That piteous, low, tender word,
Yet to mine ear and heart a crushing pang.   1335

CASSANDRA.
  Woe for my city, woe for Ilion's fall!
  Father, how oft with sanguine stain
  Streamed on thine altar-stone the blood of cattle,
          slain
    That heaven might guard our wall!
    But all was shed in vain.   1340
  Low lie the shattered towers whereas they fell,
  And I—ah burning heart!—shall soon lie low
          as well.

1308–1310. **As . . . wail.** Procné, transformed into a nightingale, mourned for her son Itys, whom she had killed and served as a dish to her husband in revenge for his infidelity.

CHORUS.
  Of sorrow is thy song, of sorrow still!
    Alas, what power of ill
    Sits heavy on thy heart and bids thee tell   1345
    In tears of perfect moan thy deadly tale?
Some woe—I know not what—must close thy pious
          wail.

CASSANDRA.
List! for no more the presage of my soul,
Bride-like, shall peer from its secluding veil;
But as the morning wind blows clear the east,   1350
More bright shall blow the wind of prophecy,
And as against the low bright line of dawn
Heaves high and higher yet the rolling wave,
So in the clearing skies of prescience
Dawns on my soul a further, deadlier woe,   1355
And I will speak, but in dark speech no more.
Bear witness, ye, and follow at my side—
I scent the trail of blood, shed long ago.
Within this house a choir abidingly
Chants in harsh unison the chant of ill;   1360
Yea, and they drink, for more enhardened joy,
Man's blood for wine, and revel in the halls,
Departing never, Furies of the home.
They sit within, they chant the primal curse,
Each spitting hatred on that crime of old,   1365
The brother's couch, the love incestuous
That brought forth hatred to the ravisher.
Say, is my speech or wild and erring now,
Or doth its arrow cleave the mark indeed?
They called me once, *The prophetess of lies,*   1370
The wandering hag, the pest of every door—
Attest ye now, *She knows in very sooth*
The house's curse, the storied infamy.

LEADER OF THE CHORUS.
Yet how should oath—how loyally soe'er
I swear it—aught avail thee? In good sooth,   1375
My wonder meets thy claim: I stand amazed
That thou, a maiden born beyond the seas,
Dost as a native know and tell aright
Tales of a city of an alien tongue.

CASSANDRA.
That is my power—a boon Apollo gave.   1380

LEADER.
God though he were, yearning for mortal maid?

CASSANDRA.
Ay! what seemed shame of old is shame no more.

LEADER.
Such finer sense suits not with slavery.

CASSANDRA.
He strove to win me, panting for my love.

LEADER.
Came ye by compact unto bridal joys?   1385

CASSANDRA.
Nay—for I plighted troth, then foiled the god.

LEADER.
Wert thou already dowered with prescience?

CASSANDRA.
Yea—prophetess to Troy of all her doom.
    LEADER.
How left thee then Apollo's wrath unscathed?
    CASSANDRA.
I, false to him, seemed prophet false to all.   1390
    LEADER.
Not so—to us at least thy words seem sooth.
    CASSANDRA.
Woe for me, woe! Again the agony—
Dread pain that sees the future all too well
With ghastly preludes whirls and racks my soul.
Behold ye—yonder on the palace roof   1395
The spectre-children sitting—look, such things
As dreams are made on, phantoms as of babes,
Horrible shadows, that a kinsman's hand
Hath marked with murder, and their arms are full—
A rueful burden—see, they hold them up,   1400
The entrails upon which their father fed!

For this, for this, I say there plots revenge
A coward lion, couching in the lair—
Guarding the gate against my master's foot—
My master—mine—I bear the slave's yoke now,   1405
And he, the lord of ships, who trod down Troy,
Knows not the fawning treachery of tongue
Of this thing false and dog-like—how her speech
Glozes and sleeks her purpose, till she win
By ill fate's favour the desirèd chance,   1410
Moving like Atè to a secret end.
O aweless soul! the woman slays her lord—
Woman? what loathsome monster of the earth
Were fit comparison? The double snake—
Or Scylla, where she dwells, the seaman's bane,   1415
Girt round about with rocks? some hag of hell,
Raving a truceless curse upon her kin?
Hark—even now she cries exultingly
The vengeful cry that tells of battle turned—
How fain, forsooth, to greet her chief restored!   1420
Nay then, believe me not: what skills belief
Or disbelief? Fate works its will—and thou
Wilt see and say in ruth, *Her tale was true.*
    LEADER.
Ah—'tis Thyestes' feast on kindred flesh—
I guess her meaning and with horror thrill,   1425
Hearing no shadow'd hint of th' o'er-true tale,
But its full hatefulness: yet, for the rest,
Far from the track I roam, and know no more.
    CASSANDRA.
'Tis Agamemnon's doom thou shalt behold.
    LEADER.
Peace, hapless woman, to thy boding words!   1430
    CASSANDRA.
Far from my speech stands he who sains and saves.

1401. The entrails . . . fed. Thyestes unknowingly ate his sons'
flesh, served to him by his brother Atreus.

    LEADER.
Ay—were such doom at hand—which God forbid!
    CASSANDRA.
Thou prayest idly—these move swift to slay.
    LEADER.
What man prepares a deed of such despite?
    CASSANDRA.
Fool! thus to read amiss mine oracles.   1435
    LEADER.
Deviser and device are dark to me.
    CASSANDRA.
Dark! all too well I speak the Grecian tongue.
    LEADER.
Ay—but in thine, as in Apollo's strains,
Familiar is the tongue, but dark the thought.
    CASSANDRA.
Ah, ah the fire! it waxes, nears me now—   1440
Woe, woe for me, Apollo of the dawn!

Lo, how the woman-thing, the lioness
Couched with the wolf—her noble mate afar—
Will slay me, slave forlorn! Yea, like some witch,
She drugs the cup of wrath, that slays her lord,   1445
With double death—his recompense for me!
Ay, 'tis for me, the prey he bore from Troy,
That she hath sworn his death, and edged the steel!
Ye wands, ye wreaths that cling around my neck,
Ye showed me prophetess yet scorned of all—   1450
I stamp you into death, or e'er I die—
Down, to destruction!

              Thus I stand revenged—
Go, crown some other with a prophet's woe.
Look! it is he, it is Apollo's self
Rending from me the prophet-robe he gave.   1455
God! while I wore it yet, thou saw'st me mocked
There at my home by each malicious mouth—
To all and each, an undivided scorn.
The name alike and fate of witch and cheat—
Woe, poverty, and famine—all I bore;   1460
And at this last the god hath brought me here
Into death's toils, and what his love had made,
His hate unmakes me now: and I shall stand
Not now before the altar of my home,
But me a slaughter-house and block of blood   1465
Shall see hewn down, a reeking sacrifice.
Yet shall the gods have heed of me who die,
For by their will shall one requite my doom.
He, to avenge his father's blood outpoured,
Shall smite and slay with matricidal hand.   1470
Ay, he shall come—tho' far away he roam,
A banished wanderer in a stranger's land—
To crown his kindred's edifice of ill,
Called home to vengeance by his father's fall:
Thus have the high gods sworn, and shall fulfil.   1475
And now why mourn I, tarrying on earth,

1443. wolf, Aegisthus. 1469. He, Orestes.

Since first mine Ilion has found its fate
And I beheld, and those who won the wall
Pass to such issue as the gods ordain?
I too will pass and like them dare to die!   1480
  (*She turns and looks upon the palace door.*)
Portal of Hades, thus I bid thee hail!
Grant me one boon—a swift and mortal stroke,
That all unwrung by pain, with ebbing blood
Shed forth in quiet death, I close mine eyes.

  LEADER.
Maid of mysterious woes, mysterious lore,   1485
Long was thy prophecy: but if aright
Thou readest all thy fate, how, thus unscared,
Dost thou approach the altar of thy doom,
As fronts the knife some victim, heaven-controlled?
  CASSANDRA.
Friends, there is no avoidance in delay.   1490
  LEADER.
Yet who delays the longest, his the gain.
  CASSANDRA.
The day is come—flight were small gain to me!
  LEADER.
O brave endurance of a soul resolved!
  CASSANDRA.
That were ill praise, for those of happier doom.
  LEADER.
All fame is happy, even famous death.   1495
  CASSANDRA.
Ah sire, ah brethren, famous once were ye!
  (*She moves to enter the house, then starts back.*)
  LEADER.
What fear is this that scares thee from the house?
  CASSANDRA.
Pah!
  LEADER.
What is this cry? some dark despair of soul?   1499
  CASSANDRA.
Pah! the house fumes with stench and spilth of blood.
  LEADER.
How? 'tis the smell of household offerings.
  CASSANDRA.
'Tis rank as charnel-scent from open graves.
  LEADER.
Thou canst not mean this scented Syrian nard?
  CASSANDRA.
Nay, let me pass within to cry aloud
The monarch's fate and mine—enough of life.   1505
Ah friends!
Bear to me witness, since I fall in death,
That not as birds that shun the bush and scream
I moan in idle terror. This attest
When for my death's revenge another dies,   1510
A woman for a woman, and a man
Falls, for a man ill-wedded to his curse.
Grant me this boon—the last before I die.
  LEADER.
Brave to the last! I mourn thy doom foreseen.

  CASSANDRA.
Once more one utterance, but not of wail,   1515
Though for my death—and then I speak no more.

Sun! thou whose beam I shall not see again,
To thee I cry, Let those whom vengeance calls
To slay their kindred's slayers, quit withal
The death of me, the slave, the fenceless prey.   1520

Ah state of mortal man! in time of weal,
A line, a shadow! and if ill fate fall,
One wet sponge-sweep wipes all our trace away—
And this I deem less piteous, of the twain.
  (*Exit into the palace.*)
  CHORUS (*singing*).
Too true it is! our mortal state   1525
With bliss is never satiate,
And none, before the palace high
And stately of prosperity,
Cries to us with a voice of fear,
Away! 'tis ill to enter here!   1530

Lo! this our lord hath trodden down,
By grace of heaven, old Priam's town,
  And praised as god he stands once more
  On Argos' shore!
Yet now—if blood shed long ago   1535
Cries out that other blood shall flow—
His life-blood, his, to pay again
The stern requital of the slain—
Peace to that braggart's vaunting vain,
  Who, having heard the chieftain's tale,   1540
  Yet boasts of bliss untouched by bale!
  (*A loud cry from within.*)
  VOICE OF AGAMEMNON.
O I am sped—a deep, a mortal blow.
  LEADER OF THE CHORUS.
Listen, listen! who is screaming as in mortal agony?
  VOICE OF AGAMEMNON.
O! O! again, another, another blow!
  LEADER.
The bloody act is over—I have heard the monarch's
  cry—   1545
Let us swiftly take some counsel, lest we too be
  doomed to die.
  ONE OF THE CHORUS.
'Tis best, I judge, aloud for aid to call,
"Ho! loyal Argives! to the palace, all!"
  ANOTHER.
Better, I deem, ourselves to bear the aid,   1549
And drag the deed to light, while drips the blade.
  ANOTHER.
Such will is mine, and what thou say'st I say:
Swiftly to act! the time brooks no delay.
  ANOTHER.
Ay, for 'tis plain, this prelude of their song
Foretells its close in tyranny and wrong.

ANOTHER.

Behold, we tarry—but thy name, Delay,   1555
They spurn, and press with sleepless hand to slay.
ANOTHER.

I know not what 'twere well to counsel now—
Who wills to act, 'tis his to counsel how.
ANOTHER.

Thy doubt is mine: for when a man is slain,
I have no words to bring his life again.   1560
ANOTHER.

What? e'en for life's sake, bow us to obey
These house-defilers and their tyrant sway?
ANOTHER.

Unmanly doom! 'twere better far to die—
Death is a gentler lord than tyranny.
ANOTHER.

Think well—must cry or sign of woe or pain   1565
Fix our conclusion that the chief is slain?
ANOTHER.

Such talk befits us when the deed we see—
Conjecture dwells afar from certainty.
LEADER OF THE CHORUS.

I read one will from many a diverse word,
To know aright, how stands it with our lord!   1570
(*The central doors of the palace open, disclosing*
CLYTEMNESTRA, *who comes forward. The body of*
AGAMEMNON *lies, muffled in a long robe, within a*
silver-sided laver; the corpse of CASSANDRA *is laid be-*
side him.)
CLYTEMNESTRA.

Ho, ye who heard me speak so long and oft
The glozing word that led me to my will—
Hear how I shrink not to unsay it all!
How else should one who willeth to requite
Evil for evil to an enemy   1575
Disguised as friend, weave the mesh straitly round
      him,
Not to be overleaped, a net of doom?
This is the sum and issue of old strife,
Of me deep-pondered and at length fulfilled.
All is avowed, and as I smote I stand   1580
With foot set firm upon a finished thing!
I turn not to denial: thus I wrought
So that he could nor flee nor ward his doom.
Even as the trammel hems the scaly shoal,
I trapped him with inextricable toils,   1585
The ill abundance of a baffling robe;
Then smote him, once, again—and at each wound
He cried aloud, then as in death relaxed
Each limb and sank to earth; and as he lay,   1589
Once more I smote him, with the last third blow,
Sacred to Hades, saviour of the dead.
And thus he fell, and as he passed away,
Spirit with body chafed; each dying breath
Flung from his breast swift bubbling jets of gore,
And the dark sprinklings of the rain of blood   1595

1584. as the trammel . . . shoal, as the net catches a shoal of fish.

Fell upon me; and I was fain to feel
That dew—not sweeter is the rain of heaven
To cornland, when the green sheath teems with
      grain.
Elders of Argos—since the thing stands so,
I bid you to rejoice, if such your will: 1600
Rejoice or not, I vaunt and praise the deed,
And well I ween, if seemly it could be,
'Twere not ill done to pour libations here,
Justly—ay, more than justly—on his corpse
Who filled his home with curses as with wine,   1605
And thus returned to drain the cup he filled.
LEADER.

I marvel at thy tongue's audacity,
To vaunt thus loudly o'er a husband slain.
CLYTEMNESTRA.

Ye hold me as a woman, weak of will,
And strive to sway me: but my heart is stout,   1610
Nor fears to speak its uttermost to you,
Albeit ye know its message. Praise or blame,
Even as ye list,—I reck not of your words.
Lo! at my feet lies Agamemnon slain,
My husband once—and him this hand of mine,   1615
A right contriver, fashioned for his death.
Behold the deed!
CHORUS (*chanting*).

      Woman, what deadly birth,
What venomed essence of the earth
      Or dark distilment of the wave,   1620
            To thee such passion gave,
      Nerving thine hand
      To set upon thy brow this burning crown,
            The curses of thy land?
Our king by thee cut off, hewn down!   1625
      Go forth—they cry—accursèd and forlorn,
            To hate and scorn!
CLYTEMNESTRA.

O ye just men, who speak my sentence now,
The city's hate, the ban of all my realm!
Ye had no voice of old to launch such doom   1630
On him, my husband, when he held as light
My daughter's life as that of sheep or goat,
One victim from the thronging fleecy fold!
Yea, slew in sacrifice his child and mine,
The well-loved issue of my travail-pangs,   1635
To lull and lay the gales that blew from Thrace.
That deed of his, I say, that stain and shame,
Had rightly been atoned by banishment;
But ye, who then were dumb, are stern to judge
This deed of mine that doth affront your ears.   1640
Storm out your threats, yet knowing this for sooth,
That I am ready, if your hand prevail
As mine now doth, to bow beneath your sway:
If God say nay, it shall be yours to learn
By chastisement a late humility.   1645
CHORUS (*chanting*).

      Bold is thy craft, and proud

Thy confidence, thy vaunting loud;
Thy soul, that chose a murd'ress' fate,
  Is all with blood elate—
    Maddened to know   1650
The blood not yet avenged, the damnèd spot
  Crimson upon thy brow.
But Fate prepares for thee thy lot—
Smitten as thou didst smite, without a friend,
    To meet thine end!   1655

CLYTEMNESTRA.

Hear then the sanction of the oath I swear—
By the great vengeance for my murdered child,
By Atè, by the Fury unto whom
This man lies sacrificed by hand of mine,
I do not look to tread the hall of Fear,   1660
While in this hearth and home of mine there burns
The light of love—Aegisthus—as of old
Loyal, a stalwart shield of confidence—
As true to me as this slain man was false,
Wronging his wife with paramours at Troy, 1665
Fresh from the kiss of each Chryseis there!
Behold him dead—behold his captive prize,
Seeress and harlot—comfort of his bed,
True prophetess, true paramour—I wot
The sea-bench was not closer to the flesh, 1670
Full oft, of every rower, than was she.
See, ill they did, and ill requites them now.
His death ye know: she as a dying swan
Sang her last dirge, and lies, as erst she lay,
Close to his side, and to my couch has left 1675
A sweet new taste of joys that know no fear.

CHORUS.

Ah woe and well-a-day! I would that Fate—
  Not bearing agony too great,
Nor stretching me too long on couch of pain—
  Would bid mine eyelids keep   1680
The morningless and unawakening sleep!
    For life is weary, now my lord is slain,
      The gracious among kings!
Hard fate of old he bore and many grievous things,
    And for a woman's sake, on Ilian land— 1685
Now is his life hewn down, and by a woman's hand.

      O Helen, O infatuate soul,
      Who bad'st the tides of battle roll,
      O'erwhelming thousands, life on life,
      'Neath Ilion's wall!   1690
  And now lies dead the lord of all.
    The blossom of thy storied sin
    Bears blood's inexpiable stain,
    O thou that erst, these halls within,
    Wert unto all a rock of strife,   1695
      A husband's bane!

CLYTEMNESTRA.

Peace! pray not thou for death as though
Thine heart was whelmed beneath this woe,
Nor turn thy wrath aside to ban

The name of Helen, nor recall   1700
How she, one bane of many a man,
Sent down to death the Danaan lords,
To sleep at Troy the sleep of swords,
And wrought the woe that shattered all.

CHORUS.

Fiend of the race! that swoopest fell   1705
  Upon the double stock of Tantalus,
Lording it o'er me by a woman's will,
  Stern, manful, and imperious—
    A bitter sway to me!
    Thy very form I see,   1710
  Like some grim raven, perched upon the slain,
Exulting o'er the crime, aloud, in tuneless strain!

CLYTEMNESTRA.

Right was that word—thou namest well
The brooding race-fiend, triply fell!
From him it is that murder's thirst,   1715
Blood-lapping, inwardly is nursed—
Ere time the ancient scar can sain,
New blood comes welling forth again.

CHORUS.

Grim is his wrath and heavy on our home,
  That fiend of whom thy voice has cried, 1720
Alas, an omened cry of woe unsatisfied,
  An all-devouring doom!

Ah woe, ah Zeus! from Zeus all things befall—
  Zeus the high cause and finisher of all!—
Lord of our mortal state, by him are willed 1725
  All things, by him fulfilled!
Yet ah my king, my king no more!
What words to say, what tears to pour
  Can tell my love for thee?
The spider-web of treachery   1730
She wove and wound, thy life around,
  And lo! I see thee lie,
And thro' a coward, impious wound
  Pant forth thy life and die!
A death of shame—ah woe on woe!   1735
A treach'rous hand, a cleaving blow!

CLYTEMNESTRA.

My guilt thou harpest, o'er and o'er!
I bid thee reckon me no more
  As Agamemnon's spouse.
The old Avenger, stern of mood   1740
For Atreus and his feast of blood,
    Hath struck the lord of Atreus' house,
And in the semblance of his wife
    The king hath slain.—
Yea, for the murdered children's life,   1745
  A chieftain's in requital ta'en.

1705. **Fiend . . . race**, The evil genius in the race of Tantalus, the grandfather of Atreus, which was ultimately responsible for placing the fate of the race in the hands of women, Helen and Clytemnestra.

CHORUS.

Thou guiltless of this murder, thou!
  Who dares such thought avow?
  Yet it may be, wroth for the parent's deed,
  The fiend hath holpen thee to slay the son.   1750
    Dark Ares, god of death, is pressing on
    Thro' streams of blood by kindred shed,
    Exacting the accompt for children dead,
  For clotted blood, for flesh on which their sire did
    feed.

    Yet ah my king, my king no more!   1755
    What words to say, what tears to pour
      Can tell my love for thee?
    The spider-web of treachery
    She wove and wound, thy life around,
      And lo! I see thee lie,   1760
    And thro' a coward, impious wound
      Pant forth thy life and die!
    A death of shame—ah woe on woe!
    A treach'rous hand, a cleaving blow!

CLYTEMNESTRA.

I deem not that the death he died   1765
  Had overmuch of shame:
For this was he who did provide
  Foul wrong unto his house and name:
His daughter, blossom of my womb,
He gave unto a deadly doom,   1770
  Iphigenia, child of tears!
And as he wrought, even so he fares.
Nor be his vaunt too loud in hell;
For by the sword his sin he wrought,
And by the sword himself is brought   1775
  Among the dead to dwell.

CHORUS.

    Ah whither shall I fly?
For all in ruin sinks the kingly hall;
Nor swift device nor shift of thought have I,
  To 'scape its fall.   1780
A little while the gentler rain-drops fail;
I stand distraught—a ghastly interval,
Till on the roof-tree rings the bursting hail
  Of blood and doom. Even now fate whets the
    steel   1784
On whetstones new and deadlier than of old,
The steel that smites, in Justice' hold,
  Another death to deal.
O Earth! that I had lain at rest
    And lapped for ever in thy breast,
    Ere I had seen my chieftain fall
    Within the laver's silver wall,
    Low-lying on dishonoured bier!
    And who shall give him sepulchre,
    And who the wail of sorrow pour?
    Woman, 'tis thine no more!
    A graceless gift unto his shade

From a Greek mask. Such tribute, by his murd'ress paid!

Strive not thus wrongly to atone
The impious deed thy hand hath done.
Ah who above the god-like chief   1800
Shall weep the tears of loyal grief?
Who speak above his lowly grave
The last sad praises of the brave?

CLYTEMNESTRA.

Peace! for such task is none of thine.
  By me he fell, by me he died,   1805
And now his burial rites be mine!
Yet from these halls no mourners' train
  Shall celebrate his obsequies;
Only by Acheron's rolling tide
His child shall spring unto his side,   1810
  And in a daughter's loving wise
Shall clasp and kiss him once again!

CHORUS.

Lo! sin by sin and sorrow dogg'd by sorrow—
  And who the end can know?
The slayer of to-day shall die to-morrow—   1815
  The wage of wrong is woe.
While Time shall be, while Zeus in heaven is lord,
  His law is fixed and stern;
On him that wrought shall vengeance be outpoured—
  The tides of doom return.   1820
The children of the curse abide within
  These halls of high estate—
And none can wrench from off the home of sin
  The clinging grasp of fate.

CLYTEMNESTRA.

Now walks thy word aright, to tell   1825
This ancient truth of oracle;
But I with vows of sooth will pray
To him, the power that holdeth sway
  O'er all the race of Pleisthenes—
Tho' dark the deed and deep the guilt,   1830
With this last blood, my hands have spilt,
  I pray thee let thine anger cease!
I pray thee pass from us away
  To some new race in other lands,
There, if thou wilt, to wrong and slay   1835
  The lives of men by kindred hands.

For me 'tis all sufficient meed,
Tho' little wealth or power were won,
So I can say, *'Tis past and done.*
The bloody lust and murderous,   1840
The inborn frenzy of our house,
  Is ended, by my deed!
        (*Enter* AEGISTHUS.)

AEGISTHUS.

Dawn of the day of rightful vengeance, hail!
I dare at length aver that gods above
Have care of men and heed of earthly wrongs.   1845
I, I who stand and thus exult to see

1829. all . . . Pleisthenes, the house of Atreus. Pleisthenes may have
been the actual father of Agamemnon and son of Atreus.

This man lie wound in robes the Furies wove,
Slain in the requital of his father's craft.
Take ye the truth, that Atreus, this man's sire,
The lord and monarch of this land of old, 1850
Held with my sire Thyestes deep dispute,
Brother with brother, for the prize of sway,
And drave him from his home to banishment.
Thereafter, the lorn exile homeward stole
And clung a suppliant to the hearth divine, 1855
And for himself won this immunity—
Not with his own blood to defile the land
That gave him birth. But Atreus, godless sire
Of him who here lies dead, this welcome planned—
With zeal that was not love he feigned to hold 1860
In loyal joy a day of festal cheer,
And bade my father to his board, and set
Before him flesh that was his children once.
First, sitting at the upper board alone,
He hid the fingers and the feet, but gave 1865
The rest—and readily Thyestes took
What to his ignorance no semblance wore
Of human flesh, and ate: behold what curse
That eating brought upon our race and name!
For when he knew what all unhallowed thing 1870
He thus had wrought, with horror's bitter cry
Back-starting, spewing forth the fragments foul,
On Pelops' house a deadly curse he spake—
As darkly as I spurn this damnèd food,
So perish all the race of Pleisthenes! 1875
Thus by that curse fell he whom here ye see,
And I—who else?—this murder wove and planned;
For me, an infant yet in swaddling bands,
Of the three children youngest, Atreus sent
To banishment by my sad father's side: 1880
But Justice brought me home once more, grown now
To manhood's years; and stranger tho' I was,
My right hand reached unto the chieftain's life,
Plotting and planning all that malice bade.
And death itself were honour now to me, 1885
Beholding him in Justice' ambush ta'en.

LEADER OF THE CHORUS.

Aegisthus, for this insolence of thine
That vaunts itself in evil, take my scorn.
Of thine own will, thou sayest, thou hast slain
The chieftain, by thine own unaided plot 1890
Devised the piteous death: I rede thee well,
Think not thy head shall 'scape, when right prevails,
The people's ban, the stones of death and doom.

AEGISTHUS.

This word from thee, this word from one who rows
Low at the oars beneath, what time we rule, 1895
We of the upper tier? Thou'lt know anon,
'Tis bitter to be taught again in age,
By one so young, submission at the word.
But iron of the chain and hunger's throes
Can minister unto an o'erswoln pride 1900
Marvellous well, ay, even in the old.

Hast eyes, and seest not this? Peace—kick not thus
Against the pricks, unto thy proper pain!

LEADER.

Thou womanish man, waiting till war did cease,
Home-watcher and defiler of the couch, 1905
And arch-deviser of the chieftain's doom!

AEGISTHUS.

Bold words again! but they shall end in tears.
The very converse, thine, of Orpheus' tongue:
He roused and led in ecstasy of joy
All things that heard his voice melodious; 1910
But thou as with the futile cry of curs
Wilt draw men wrathfully upon thee. Peace!
Or strong subjection soon shall tame thy tongue.

LEADER.

Ay, thou art one to hold an Argive down—
Thou, skilled to plan the murder of the king, 1915
But not with thine own hand to smite the blow!

AEGISTHUS.

That fraudful force was woman's very part,
Not mine, whom deep suspicion from of old
Would have debarred. Now by his treasure's aid
My purpose holds to rule the citizens. 1920
But whoso will not bear my guiding hand,
Him for his corn-fed mettle I will drive
Not as a trace-horse, light-caparisoned,
But to the shafts with heaviest harness bound.
Famine, the grim mate of the dungeon dark, 1925
Shall look on him and shall behold him tame.

LEADER.

Thou losel soul, was then thy strength too slight
To deal in murder, while a woman's hand,
Staining and shaming Argos and its gods,
Availed to slay him? Ho, if anywhere 1930
The light of life smite on Orestes' eyes,
Let him, returning by some guardian fate,
Hew down with force her paramour and her!

AEGISTHUS.

How thy word and act shall issue, thou shalt shortly
understand.

LEADER.

Up to action, O my comrades! for the fight is hard at
hand. 1935
Swift, your right hands to the sword hilt! bare the
weapon as for strife—

AEGISTHUS.

Lo! I too am standing ready, hand on hilt for death
or life.

LEADER.

'Twas thy word and we accept it: onward to the
chance of war!

CLYTEMNESTRA.

Nay, enough, enough, my champion! we will smite
and slay no more.
Already have we reaped enough the harvest-field of
guilt: 1940

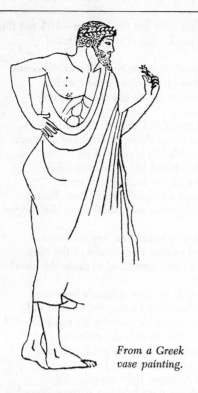

*From a Greek
vase painting.*

Enough of wrong and murder, let no other blood be
    spilt.
Peace, old men! and pass away unto the homes by
    Fate decreed,
Lest ill valour meet our vengeance—'twas a neces-
    sary deed.
But enough of toils and troubles—be the end, if ever,
    now,   1944
Ere thy talon, O Avenger, deal another deadly blow.
'Tis a woman's word of warning, and let who will
    list thereto.

AEGISTHUS.
But that these should loose and lavish reckless blos-
    soms of the tongue,
And in hazard of their fortune cast upon me words
    of wrong,
And forget the law of subjects, and revile their ruler's
    word—

LEADER.
Ruler? but 'tis not for Argives, thus to own a dastard
    lord!   1950

AEGISTHUS.
I will follow to chastise thee in my coming days of
    sway.

LEADER.
Not if Fortune guide Orestes safely on his home-
    ward way.

AEGISTHUS.
Ah, well I know how exiles feed on hopes of their
    return.

LEADER.
Fare and batten on pollution of the right, while 'tis
    thy turn.

AEGISTHUS.
Thou shalt pay, be well assurèd, heavy quittance for
    thy pride.   1955

LEADER.
Crow and strut, with her to watch thee, like a cock,
    his mate beside!

CLYTEMNESTRA.
Heed not thou too highly of them—let the cur-pack
    growl and yell:
I and thou will rule the palace and will order all
    things well.   (*Exeunt.*)

Sophocles

c. 495–406 B.C.

Sophocles belonged to Athens at the zenith of
her political power and cultural splendor, and
even in such a day he seemed the supreme embodiment of
noble character and versatile genius. To the Athenians he
was the favorite of the gods. He had been born into a
wealthy and socially prominent family.* He grew up as
the model citizen, handsome and sweet-natured, sociable
and temperate, pious and intellectual. About 440 B.C. he
was elected one of the ten generals of Athens—the highest elective office of the state. His piety and conservative
religious views won him priesthoods in several cults. His
serenity endeared him to such friends as Herodotus the
historian and youthful Aristophanes, who expressed his
admiration in his comedy *The Frogs.* He preserved his
intellectual powers to the age of ninety, composing one
of his masterpieces, *Oedipus at Colonus,* shortly before his
death. Phrynichus, his contemporary in comedy, voiced a
universal tribute in the words: "Blessed is Sophocles, a
happy and fortunate man who died after a long life. Author of many beautiful tragedies, he came to a beautiful
end and lived to see no evil day."

Sophocles was much less interested in religious problems than Aeschylus or in social criticism than Euripides.
Although as conservative as Aeschylus, he belonged to a
new generation, no longer troubled by matters of state
important during the Persian Wars. And while he lived
the robust life of the typical Greek citizen, he divorced
his plays from contemporary issues and concentrated on
the timeless problems of well-intentioned men and women
striving for happy and honest lives against the odds of
fortune. Instead of the theological issues that concerned
Aeschylus he emphasizes the human meaning in the tragic

* It is convenient to remember that in the year of Salamis (480 B.C.)
Aeschylus, a man of forty-five, fought in the battle; Sophocles, a
youth of fifteen, was chosen to lead a boys' chorus celebrating the
return of the victors; and Euripides was born.

operation of eternal laws. To this sympathetic vision of the plight of mankind he brings the technique of a master artist. Turning away from the trilogy scheme of Aeschylus, he gives more plot and action to the single play and freely uses three or four actors at once. A better craftsman than Euripides, he molds his material into a harmonious work of art, with a careful, inevitable construction and a simple, yet noble style that is free from the grandiloquence of Aeschylus.

Although Sophocles wrote at least 120 plays and won the first prize twenty-four times (more than any other playwright), the Alexandrine scholars preserved only seven of his tragedies, of which the three greatest treat one connected story. Though written at different periods of his career and in no sense a trilogy, *Oedipus the King*, *Oedipus at Colonus*, and *Antigone* give three incidents in the tragic history of the house of Laius, King of Thebes. Laius, married to Jocasta, had been warned by an oracle of Apollo that his newborn son would kill him if he lived to manhood. So the king exposed the baby to death in a barren place, but a kindly shepherd took him to the childless king and queen of Corinth, who named him Oedipus and reared him as their son. Grown to manhood, Oedipus was shocked by a prophecy of the oracle that he would kill his father and marry his mother. Not knowing that the king and queen were his adopted parents, in horror he left Corinth to seek his fortune elsewhere. On the road to Thebes "at a place where three roads met," Oedipus unknowingly encountered his own father, Laius, driving with an attendant. A dispute arose about the right of the road, and when the attendant killed one of Oedipus' horses, the enraged Oedipus killed the two men, thus fulfilling the first of the prophecies.

At Thebes he found the populace harassed by a monster called the Sphinx, who killed every traveler to the city who could not answer the riddle, "What is it that goes on four feet in the morning, on two at noon, and on three in the evening?" The vacant throne of Laius and the hand of his queen were offered by the desperate people to any man who could solve the riddle. The guess of Oedipus was "man, who creeps on all fours as a child, who walks erect as a man, and who leans on a staff in his old age." The mortified Sphinx killed herself, and the grateful Thebans accepted Oedipus as their king and the husband of Queen Jocasta. So the second prophecy was fulfilled.

In the happy years that followed, Oedipus had two sons, Eteocles and Polynices, and two daughters, Antigone and Ismene, by his wife-mother. Then at last Thebes was afflicted by a great plague, and the earnest king asked the oracle to reveal the cause of the gods' displeasure. In *Oedipus the King* we learn how he was ordered to find the slayer of Laius and how his vigorous pursuit of the criminal gradually proved that he himself was the man. In horror Jocasta killed herself and Oedipus tore out his eyes and banished himself to a life of wandering. In *Oedipus at Colonus* we see the melancholy end of the haggard king. Accompanied by his daughters, he finally reached the spot where the oracle had prophesied that he would die. Learning that his sons were fighting

each other for the throne of Thebes, he indignantly laid upon them the curse that they would kill each other. Then as a clap of thunder announced his end, Oedipus blessed his daughters and found peace at last.

The curse of Oedipus upon his sons was fulfilled. Since it was Polynices who had challenged the rule of Eteocles and attacked the city, Creon, the brother of Jocasta, who succeeded to the throne, decreed that the body of Polynices should not be buried. This act was peculiarly shocking to the Greeks, since burial was essential for admission to Hades. In the *Antigone*, the faithful sister, Antigone, defied the decree of Creon and secretly performed a token rite of burial over the corpse of Polynices. The angry Creon, sensitive to any rebellion against his guilty rule, ordered Antigone to be buried alive, even though she was betrothed to his own son. Soon after, he suffered a change of heart and countermanded his order, but too late, for Antigone, his son, and his wife had all committed suicide. With this grim warning against abuse of power in the desolate figure of Creon, Sophocles brings the tragic tale of Thebes to an end.

Oedipus the King, the most famous of Greek plays and the one chosen by Aristotle in his *Poetics* as the model of tragedy, won only the second prize in its competition, behind a now-forgotten work by a nephew of Aeschylus. The date of the competition is unknown. Despite its fame the play is hardly so typical of Greek tragedies as several others, though it is one of the best constructed and most gripping. The relentless prosecution of a single dramatic motif, the gradual discovery of the identity and hence the crimes of Oedipus, makes for complete unity. But the final downfall of the hero for crimes committed before the opening of the play is distinctly unusual. Aristotle's description of a tragic hero as an essentially worthy man with one tragic flaw of character that leads him into error is hard for us to apply to this well-intentioned king, who is doomed to disaster before his birth and commits his crimes without knowing that he is doing so. Yet the Greeks' more practical and unquestioning interpretation of divine law found no obstacle here. Man is subject to the whims of Fate, and with a sublime show of irony Fate placed a mark of impurity upon this man from birth which was as inescapable a flaw as pride or obstinacy. In addition, one of the crimes of Oedipus, the murder of Laius, was an impetuous one, which might reflect a further tragic flaw of insolence and hot temper. In any case, the workings of Fate are inscrutable to man, and as the concluding chorus reminds us: "Count no man happy until you witness his final day."

The sardonic operation of fate is reflected in the *dramatic irony* of the play whereby the audience knows at the start the secret that Oedipus is trying to find and follows with terrified fascination his gradual discovery. Not simply the situation but many of the speeches are profoundly ironic as we see in them double meanings that the hero is in no position to grasp. When he vows to track down and punish the slayer of Laius as he would his own father's assassin, we know that it *is* his own father and that *he* is the assassin. Such speeches as these contribute a great deal to our sympathy for the pathetic human being who finds himself so innocently the sport of the gods. Although many playwrights have treated the tragic tale of Oedipus—Aeschylus and Euripides in lost plays, Seneca, Corneille, Dryden, and Voltaire in later imitations—none of the others comes close to the majesty and humanity of Sophocles.

Oedipus the King

CHARACTERS IN THE PLAY

OEDIPUS, *King of Thebes*
PRIEST OF ZEUS
CREON, *brother of* JOCASTA
TEIRESIAS, *the blind prophet*
JOCASTA
FIRST MESSENGER, *a shepherd from Corinth*
A SHEPHERD, *formerly in the service of Laius*
SECOND MESSENGER, *from the house*
CHORUS OF THEBAN ELDERS
The children ANTIGONE *and* ISMENE, *daughters of*
OEDIPUS *and* JOCASTA

(SCENE: *Before the palace of Oedipus at Thebes. In front of the large central doors there is an altar; a smaller altar stands also near each of the two side-doors. Suppliants—old men, youths, and young children—are seated on the steps of the altars. They are dressed in white tunics and cloaks,—their hair bound with white fillets. On the altars they have laid down olive-branches wreathed with fillets of wool. The* PRIEST OF ZEUS, *a venerable man, is alone standing, facing the central doors of the palace. These are now thrown open. Followed by two attendants, who place themselves on either side of the doors,* OEDIPUS *enters, in the robes of a king. For a moment he gazes silently on the groups at the altars, and then speaks.*)

OEDIPUS.

My children, latest-born to Cadmus who was of old, why are ye set before me thus with wreathed branches of suppliants, while the city reeks with incense, rings with prayers for health and cries of woe? I deemed it unmeet, my children, to hear these things at the mouth of others, and have come hither myself, I, Oedipus renowned of all.

Tell me, then, thou venerable man—since it is thy natural part to speak for these—in what mood are ye 10 placed here, with what dread or what desire? Be sure that I would gladly give all aid; hard of heart were I, did I not pity such suppliants as these.

Oedipus the King. Translated by R. C. Jebb. From *The Tragedies of Sophocles* by R. C. Jebb. By permission of The Macmillan Company, publishers.

PRIEST OF ZEUS. Nay, Oedipus, ruler of my land, thou seest of what years we are who beset thy altars,—some, nestlings still too tender for far flights,—some, bowed with age, priests, as I of Zeus,—and these, the chosen youth; while the rest of the folk sit with wreathed branches in the market-places, and before the two shrines of Pallas, and where Ismenus gives answer by fire. 20

For the city, as thou thyself seest, is now too sorely vexed, and can no more lift her head from beneath the angry waves of death; a blight is on her in the fruitful blossoms of the land, in the herds among the pastures, in the barren pangs of women; and withal the flaming god, the malign plague, hath swooped on us, and ravages the town; by whom the house of Cadmus is made waste, but dark Hades rich in groans and tears.

It is not as deeming thee ranked with gods that I 30 and these children are suppliants at thy hearth, but as deeming thee first of men, both in life's common chances, and when mortals have to do with more than man: seeing that thou camest to the town of Cadmus, and didst quit us of the tax that we rendered to the hard songstress; and this, though thou knewest nothing from us that could avail thee, nor hadst been schooled; no, by a god's aid, 'tis said and believed, didst thou uplift our life.

And now, Oedipus, king glorious in all eyes, we 40 beseech thee, all we suppliants, to find for us some succour, whether by the whisper of a god thou knowest it, or haply as in the power of man; for I see that, when men have been proved in deeds past, the issues of their counsels, too, most often have effect.

On, best of mortals, again uplift our State! On, guard thy fame,—since now this land calls thee savior for thy former zeal; and never be it our memory of thy reign that we were first restored and afterward cast down: nay, lift up this State in such wise 50 that it fall no more!

With good omen didst thou give us that past happiness; now also show thyself the same. For if thou art to rule this land, even as thou art now its lord, 'tis better to be lord of men than of a waste: since neither walled town nor ship is anything, if it is void and no men dwell with thee therein.

OEDIPUS. O, my piteous children, known, well known to me are the desires wherewith ye have come: well wot I that ye suffer all; yet, sufferers as ye 60 are, there is not one of you whose suffering is as mine. Your pain comes on each one of you for himself alone, and for no other; but my soul mourns at once for the city, and for myself, and for thee.

So that ye rouse me not, truly, as one sunk in sleep: no, be sure that I have wept full many tears,

19-20. where Ismenus . . . answer; the altar for burnt offerings in the temple of Apollo. 36. hard songstress. The Sphinx destroyed those who could not answer her riddle.

gone many ways in wanderings of thought. And the sole remedy which, well pondering, I could find, this I have put into act. I have sent the son of Menoeceus, Creon, mine own wife's brother, to the Pythian house of Phoebus, to learn by what deed or word I might deliver this town. And already, when the lapse of days is reckoned, it troubles me what he doth; for he tarries strangely, beyond the fitting space. But when he comes, then shall I be no true man if I do not all that the god shows.

PRIEST. Nay, in season hast thou spoken; at this moment these sign to me that Creon draws near.

OEDIPUS. O king Apollo, may he come to us in the brightness of saving fortune, even as his face is bright!

PRIEST. Nay, to all seeming, he brings comfort; else would he not be coming crowned thus thickly with berry-laden bay.

OEDIPUS. We shall know soon: he is at range to hear.—(*Enter* CREON.) Prince, my kinsman, son of Menoeceus, what news hast thou brought us from the god?

CREON. Good news: I tell thee that even troubles hard to bear,—if haply they find the right issue,—will end in perfect peace.

OEDIPUS. But what is the oracle? So far, thy words make me neither bold nor yet afraid.

CREON. If thou wouldest hear while these are nigh, I am ready to speak; or else to go within.

OEDIPUS. Speak before all: the sorrow which I bear is for these more than for mine own life.

CREON. With thy leave, I will tell what I heard from the god. Phoebus our lord bids us plainly to drive out a defiling thing, which (he saith) hath been harboured in this land, and not to harbour it, so that it cannot be healed.

OEDIPUS. By what rite shall we cleanse us? What is the manner of the misfortune?

CREON. By banishing a man, or by bloodshed in quittance of bloodshed, since it is that blood which brings the tempest on our city.

OEDIPUS. And who is the man whose fate he thus reveals?

CREON. Laius, king, was lord of our land before thou wast pilot of this State.

OEDIPUS. I know it well—by hearsay, for I saw him never.

CREON. He was slain; and the god now bids us plainly to wreak vengeance on his murderers—whosoever they be.

OEDIPUS. And where are they upon the earth? Where shall the dim track of this old crime be found?

CREON. In this land,—said the god. What is sought for can be caught; only that which is not watched escapes.

OEDIPUS. And was it in the house, or in the field, or on strange soil that Laius met this bloody end?

CREON. 'Twas on a visit to Delphi, as he said, that he had left our land; and he came home no more, after he had once set forth.

OEDIPUS. And was there none to tell? Was there no comrade of his journey who saw the deed, from whom tidings might have been gained, and used?

CREON. All perished, save one who fled in fear, and could tell for certain but one thing of all that he saw.

OEDIPUS. And what was that? One thing might show the clue to many, could we get but a small beginning for hope.

CREON. He said that robbers met and fell on them, not in one man's might, but with full many hands.

OEDIPUS. How, then, unless there was some trafficking in bribes from here, should the robber have dared thus far?

CREON. Such things were surmised; but, Laius once slain, amid our troubles no avenger arose.

OEDIPUS. But, when royalty had fallen thus, what trouble in your path can have hindered a full search?

CREON. The riddling Sphinx had made us let dark things go, and was inviting us to think of what lay at our doors.

OEDIPUS. Nay, I will start afresh, and once more make dark things plain. Right worthily hath Phoebus, and worthily hast thou, bestowed this care on the cause of the dead; and so, as is meet, ye shall find me too leagued with you in seeking vengeance for this land, and for the god besides. On behalf of no far-off friend, no, but in mine own cause, shall I dispel this taint. For whoever was the slayer of Laius might wish to take vengeance on me also with a hand as fierce. Therefore, in doing right to Laius, I serve myself.

Come, haste ye, my children, rise from the altar-steps, and lift these suppliant boughs; and let some other summon hither the folk of Cadmus, warned that I mean to leave nought untried; for our health (with the god's help) shall be made certain—or our ruin.

PRIEST. My children, let us rise; we came at first to seek what this man promises of himself. And may Phoebus, who sent these oracles, come to us therewith, our saviour and deliverer from the pest.

(*Exeunt* OEDIPUS *and* PRIEST. *Enter* CHORUS OF THEBAN ELDERS.)

CHORUS. O sweetly-speaking message of Zeus, in what spirit hast thou come from golden Pytho unto glorious Thebes? I am on the rack, terror shakes my soul, O thou Delian healer to whom wild cries rise, in holy fear of thee, what thing thou wilt work for me, perchance unknown before, perchance renewed with the revolving years: tell me, thou immortal Voice, born of Golden Hope!

4–5. **Pythian . . . Phoebus,** the Delphic oracle.

104. **Delian healer.** Apollo was born on the island of Delos.

First call I on thee, daughter of Zeus, divine Athena, and on thy sister, guardian of our land, Artemis, who sits on her throne of fame, above the circle of our Agora, and on Phoebus the far-darter: O shine forth on me, my three-fold help against death! If ever aforetime, in arrest of ruin hurrying on the city, ye drove a fiery pest beyond our borders, come now also!

10 Woe is me, countless are the sorrows that I bear; a plague is on all our host, and thought can find no weapon for defence. The fruits of the glorious earth grow not; by no birth of children do women surmount the pangs in which they shriek; and life on life mayest thou see sped, like bird on nimble wing, aye, swifter than resistless fire, to the shore of the western god.

By such deaths, past numbering, the city perishes: unpitied, her children lie on the ground, spreading pestilence, with none to mourn: and meanwhile 20 young wives, and grey-haired mothers with them, uplift a wail at the steps of the altars, some here, some there, entreating for their weary woes. The prayer to the Healer rings clear, and, blent therewith, the voice of lamentation: for these things, golden daughter of Zeus, send us the bright face of comfort.

And grant that the fierce god of death, who now with no brazen shields, yet amid cries as of battle, wraps me in the flame of his onset, may turn his back in speedy flight from our land, borne by a fair wind 30 to the great deep of Amphitrite, or to those waters in which none find haven, even to the Thracian wave; for if night leave aught undone, day follows to accomplish this. O thou who wieldest the powers of the fire-fraught lightning, O Zeus our father, slay him beneath thy thunderbolt! (*Enter* OEDIPUS.)

Lycean King, fain were I that thy shafts also, from thy bent bow's string of woven gold, should go abroad in their might, our champions in the face of the foe; yea, and the flashing fires of Artemis where-40 with she glances through the Lycian hills. And I call him whose locks are bound with gold, who is named with the name of this land, ruddy Bacchus to whom Bacchants cry, the comrade of the Maenads, to draw near with the blaze of his blithe torch, our ally against the god unhonoured among gods.

OEDIPUS. Thou prayest: and in answer to thy prayer,—if thou wilt give a loyal welcome to my words and minister to thine own disease,—thou mayest hope to find succour and relief from woes. These 50 words will I speak publicly, as one who has been a stranger to this report, a stranger to the deed; for I

should not be far on the track, if I were tracing it alone, without a clue. But as it is,—since it was only after the time of the deed that I was numbered a Theban among Thebans,—to you, the Cadmeans all, I do thus proclaim.

Whosoever of you knows by whom Laius son of Labdacus was slain, I bid him to declare all to me. And if he is afraid, I tell him to remove the danger of the charge from his path by denouncing himself; 60 for he shall suffer nothing else unlovely, but only leave the land, unhurt. Or if any one knows an alien, from another land, as the assassin, let him not keep silence; for I will pay his guerdon, and my thanks shall rest with him besides.

But if ye keep silence—if any one, through fear, shall seek to screen friend or self from my behest— hear ye what I then shall do. I charge you that no one of this land, whereof I hold the empire and the throne, give shelter or speak word unto that mur-70 derer, whosoever he be,—make him partner of his prayer or sacrifice, or serve him with the lustral rite; but that all ban him their homes, knowing that *this* is our defiling thing, as the oracle of the Pythian god hath newly shown me. I then am on this wise the ally of the god and of the slain. And I pray solemnly that the slayer, whoso he be, whether his hidden guilt is lonely or hath partners, evilly, as he is evil, may wear out his unblest life. And for myself I pray that if, with my privity, he should become an inmate of my 80 house, I may suffer the same things which even now I called down upon others. And on you I lay it to make all these words good, for my sake, and for the sake of the god, and for our land's, thus blasted with barrenness by angry heaven.

For even if the matter had not been urged on us by a god, it was not meet that ye should leave the guilt thus unpurged, when one so noble, and he your king, had perished; rather were ye bound to search it out. And now, since 'tis I who hold the powers which once 90 he held, who possess his bed and the wife who bare seed to him; and since, had his hope of issue not been frustrate, children born of one mother would have made ties betwixt him and me—but, as it was, fate swooped upon his head; by reason of these things will I uphold this cause, even as the cause of mine own sire, and will leave nought untried in seeking to find him whose hand shed that blood, for the honour of the son of Labdacus and of Polydorus and elder Cadmus and Agenor who was of old. 100

And for those who obey me not, I pray that the gods send them neither harvest of the earth nor fruit of the womb, but that they be wasted by their lot that now is, or by one yet more dire. But for all you, the loyal folk of Cadmus to whom these things seem good, may Justice, our ally, and all the gods be with you graciously for ever.

30. **Amphitrite,** mother of Poseidon; here, the Atlantic Ocean. 31. **Thracian wave,** the Black Sea. 36. **Lycean King,** Apollo, god of light; from Lyceus, a surname of Apollo. 43. **Maenads,** frenzied worshipers of Bacchus.

99–100. **Labdacus . . . old,** the full ancestry of Laius.

LEADER OF THE CHORUS. As thou hast put me on my oath, on my oath, O king, I will speak. I am not the slayer, nor can I point to him who slew. As for the question, it was for Phoebus, who sent it, to tell us this thing—who can have wrought the deed.

OEDIPUS. Justly said; but no man on the earth can force the gods to what they will not.

LEADER. I would fain say what seems to me next best after this.

OEDIPUS. If there is yet a third course, spare not to show it.

LEADER. I know that our lord Teiresias is the seer most like to our lord Phoebus; from whom, O king, a searcher of these things might learn them most clearly.

OEDIPUS. Not even this have I left out of my cares. On the hint of Creon, I have twice sent a man to bring him; and this long while I marvel why he is not here.

LEADER. Indeed (his skill apart) the rumours are but faint and old.

OEDIPUS. What rumours are they? I look to every story.

LEADER. Certain wayfarers were said to have killed him.

OEDIPUS. I, too, have heard it, but none sees him who saw it.

LEADER. Nay, if he knows what fear is, he will not stay when he hears thy curses, so dire as they are.

OEDIPUS. When a man shrinks not from a deed, neither is he scared by a word.

LEADER. But there is one to convict him. For here they bring at last the godlike prophet, in whom alone of men doth live the truth.

(*Enter* TEIRESIAS, *led by a boy.*)

OEDIPUS. Teiresias, whose soul grasps all things, the lore that may be told and the unspeakable, the secrets of heaven and the low things of earth,—thou feelest, though thou canst not see, what a plague doth haunt our State,—from which, great prophet, we find in thee our protector and only savior. Now, Phoebus —if indeed thou knowest it not from the messengers —sent answer to our question that the only riddance from this pest which could come was if we should learn aright the slayers of Laius, and slay them, or send them into exile from our land. Do thou, then, grudge neither voice of birds nor any other way of seer-lore that thou hast, but rescue thyself and the State, rescue me, rescue all that is defiled by the dead. For we are in thy hand; and man's noblest task is to help others by his best means and powers.

TEIRESIAS. Alas, how dreadful to have wisdom where it profits not the wise! Aye, I knew this well, but let it slip out of mind; else would I never have come here.

OEDIPUS. What now? How sad thou hast come in!

TEIRESIAS. Let me go home; most easily wilt thou bear thine own burden to the end, and I mine, if thou wilt consent.

OEDIPUS. Thy words are strange, nor kindly to this State which nurtured thee, when thou withholdest this response.

TEIRESIAS. Nay, I see that thou, on thy part, openest not thy lips in season: therefore I speak not, that neither may I have thy mishap.

OEDIPUS. For the love of the gods, turn not away, if thou hast knowledge: all we suppliants implore thee on our knees.

TEIRESIAS. Aye, for ye are all without knowledge; but never will I reveal my griefs—that I say not thine.

OEDIPUS. How sayest thou? Thou knowest the secret, and wilt not tell it, but art minded to betray us and to destroy the State?

TEIRESIAS. I will pain neither myself nor thee. Why vainly ask these things? Thou wilt not learn them from me.

OEDIPUS. What, basest of the base,—for thou wouldest anger a very stone,—wilt thou never speak out? Can nothing touch thee? Wilt thou never make an end?

TEIRESIAS. Thou blamest my temper, but seest not that to which thou thyself art wedded: no, thou findest fault with me.

OEDIPUS. And who would not be angry to hear the words with which thou now dost slight this city?

TEIRESIAS. The future will come of itself, though I shroud it in silence.

OEDIPUS. Then, seeing that it must come, thou on thy part shouldst tell me thereof.

TEIRESIAS. I will speak no further; rage, then, if thou wilt, with the fiercest wrath thy heart doth know.

OEDIPUS. Aye, verily, I will not spare—so wroth I am—to speak all my thought. Know that thou seemest to me e'en to have helped in plotting the deed, and to have done it, short of slaying with thy hands. Hadst thou eyesight, I would have said that the doing, also, of this thing was thine alone.

TEIRESIAS. In sooth?—I charge thee that thou abide by the decree of thine own mouth, and from this day speak neither to these nor to me: *thou art* the accursed defiler of this land.

OEDIPUS. So brazen with thy blustering taunt? And wherein dost thou trust to escape thy due?

TEIRESIAS. I have escaped: in my truth is my strength.

OEDIPUS. Who taught thee this? It was not, at least, thine art.

TEIRESIAS. Thou: for thou didst spur me into speech against my will.

OEDIPUS. What speech? Speak again that I may learn it better.

TEIRESIAS. Didst thou not take my sense before? Or art thou tempting me in talk?

OEDIPUS. No, I took it not so that I can call it known:—speak again.

TEIRESIAS. I say that thou art the slayer of the man whose slayer thou seekest.

OEDIPUS. Now thou shalt rue that thou hast twice said words so dire.

TEIRESIAS. Wouldst thou have me say more, that thou mayest be more wroth?

OEDIPUS. What thou wilt; it will be said in vain.

10 TEIRESIAS. I say that thou hast been living in unguessed shame with thy nearest kin, and seest not to what woe thou hast come.

OEDIPUS. Dost thou indeed think that thou shalt always speak thus without smarting?

TEIRESIAS. Yes, if there is any strength in truth.

OEDIPUS. Nay, there is,—for all save thee; for thee that strength is not, since thou art maimed in ear, and in wit, and in eye.

TEIRESIAS. Aye, and thou art a poor wretch to utter 20 taunts which every man here will soon hurl at thee.

OEDIPUS. Night, endless night hath thee in her keeping, so that thou canst never hurt me, or any man who sees the sun.

TEIRESIAS. No, thy doom is not to fall by *me*: Apollo is enough, whose care it is to work that out.

OEDIPUS. Are these Creon's devices, or thine?

TEIRESIAS. Nay, Creon is no plague to thee; thou art thine own.

OEDIPUS. O wealth, and empire, and skill surpass-30 ing skill in life's keen rivalries, how great is the envy that cleaves to you, if for the sake, yea, of this power which the city hath put into my hands, a gift unsought, Creon the trusty, Creon mine old friend, hath crept on me by stealth, yearning to thrust me out of it, and hath suborned such a scheming juggler as this, a tricky quack, who hath eyes only for his gains, but in his art is blind!

Come, now, tell me, where hast thou proved thyself a seer? Why, when the Watcher was here who 40 wove dark song, didst thou say nothing that could free this folk? Yet the riddle, at least, was not for the first comer to read; there was need of a seer's skill; and none such thou wast found to have either by help of birds, or as known from any god: no, I came, I, Oedipus the ignorant, and made her mute, when I had seized the answer by my wit, untaught of birds. And it is I whom thou art trying to oust, thinking to stand close to Creon's throne. Methinks thou and the plotter of these things will rue your zeal to purge the 50 land. Nay, didst thou not seem to be an old man, thou shouldst have learned to thy cost how bold thou art.

LEADER. To our thinking, both this man's words and thine, Oedipus, have been said in anger. Not for such words is our need, but to seek how we shall best discharge the mandates of the god.

TEIRESIAS. King though thou art, the right of reply, at least, must be deemed the same for both; of that I too am lord. Not to thee do I live servant, but to Loxias; and so I shall not stand enrolled under Creon 60 for my patron. And I tell thee—since thou hast taunted me even with blindness—that thou hast sight, yet seest not in what misery thou art, nor where thou dwellest, nor with whom. Dost thou know of what stock thou art? And thou hast been an unwitting foe to thine own kin, in the shades, and on the earth above; and the double lash of thy mother's and thy father's curse shall one day drive thee from this land in dreadful haste, with darkness then on the eyes that now see true. 70

And what place shall not be harbour to thy shriek, what of all Cithaeron shall not ring with it soon, when thou hast learnt the meaning of the nuptials in which, within that house, thou didst find a fatal haven, after a voyage so fair? And a throng of other ills thou guessest not, which shall make thee level with thy true self and with thine own brood.

Therefore heap thy scorns on Creon and on my message: for no one among men shall ever be crushed more miserably than thou. 80

OEDIPUS. Are these taunts to be indeed borne from *him*?—Hence, ruin take thee! Hence, this instant! Back!—away!—avaunt thee from these doors!

TEIRESIAS. I had never come, not I, hadst thou not called me.

OEDIPUS. I knew not that thou wast about to speak folly, or it had been long ere I had sent for thee to my house.

TEIRESIAS. Such am I,—as thou thinkest, a fool; but for the parents who begat thee, sane. 90

OEDIPUS. What parents? Stay . . . and who of men is my sire?

TEIRESIAS. This day shall show thy birth and shall bring thy ruin.

OEDIPUS. What riddles, what dark words thou always speakest!

TEIRESIAS. Nay, art not thou most skilled to unravel dark speech?

OEDIPUS. Make that my reproach in which thou shalt find me great. 100

TEIRESIAS. Yet 'twas just that fortune that undid thee.

OEDIPUS. Nay, if I delivered this town, I care not.

TEIRESIAS. Then I will go: so do thou, boy, take me hence.

OEDIPUS. Aye, let him take thee: while here, thou art a hindrance, thou, a trouble: when thou hast vanished, thou wilt not vex me more.

TEIRESIAS. I will go when I have done mine errand, fearless of thy frown: for thou canst never destroy 110 me. And I tell thee—the man of whom thou hast this long while been in quest, uttering threats, and proclaiming a search into the murder of Laius—that

60. **Loxias,** Apollo as the god of oracles.

man is here,—in seeming, an alien sojourner, but anon he shall be found a native Theban, and shall not be glad of his fortune. A blind man, he who now hath sight, a beggar, who now is rich, he shall make his way to a strange land, feeling the ground before him with his staff. And he shall be found at once brother and father of the children with whom he consorts; son and husband of the woman who bore him; heir to his father's bed, shedder of his father's blood.

So go thou in and think on that; and if thou find that I have been at fault, say thenceforth that I have no wit in prophecy.

(TEIRESIAS *is led out by the boy.* OEDIPUS *enters the palace.*)

CHORUS. Who is he of whom the divine voice from the Delphian rock hath spoken, as having wrought with red hands horrors that no tongue can tell?

It is time that he ply in flight a foot stronger than the feet of stormswift steeds: for the son of Zeus is springing on him, all armed with fiery lightnings, and with him come the dread, unerring Fates.

Yea, newly given from snowy Parnassus, the message hath flashed forth to make all search for the unknown man. Into the wild wood's covert, among caves and rocks he is roaming, fierce as a bull, wretched and forlorn on his joyless path, still seeking to put from him the doom spoken at Earth's central shrine: but that doom ever lives, ever flits around him.

Dreadly, in sooth, dreadly doth the wise augur move me, who approve not, nor am able to deny. How to speak, I know not; I am fluttered with forebodings; neither in the present have I clear vision, nor of the future. Never in past days, nor in these, have I heard how the house of Labdacus or the son of Polybus had, either against other, any grief that I could bring as proof in assailing the public fame of Oedipus, and seeking to avenge the line of Labdacus for the undiscovered murder.

Nay, Zeus indeed and Apollo are keen of thought, and know the things of earth; but that mortal seer wins knowledge above mine, of this there can be no sure test; though man may surpass man in lore. Yet, until I see the word made good, never will I assent when men blame Oedipus. Before all eyes, the winged maiden came against him of old, and he was seen to be wise; he bore the test, in welcome service to our State; never, therefore, by the verdict of my heart shall he be adjudged guilty of crime.

(*Enter* CREON.)

CREON. Fellow-citizens, having learned that Oedipus the king lays dire charges against me, I am here,

34–35. **son of Polybus,** Oedipus.

indignant. If, in the present troubles, he thinks that he has suffered from *me,* by word or deed, aught that tends to harm, in truth I crave not my full term of years, when I must bear such blame as this. The wrong of this rumour touches me not in one point alone, but has the largest scope, if I am to be called a traitor in the city, a traitor too by thee and by my friends.

LEADER OF THE CHORUS. Nay, but this taunt came under stress, perchance, of anger, rather than from the purpose of the heart.

CREON. And the saying was uttered, that *my* counsels won the seer to utter his falsehoods?

LEADER. Such things were said—I know not with what meaning.

CREON. And was this charge laid against me with steady eyes and steady mind?

LEADER. I know not; I see not what my masters do: but here comes our lord forth from the house.

(*Enter* OEDIPUS.)

OEDIPUS. Sirrah, how camest thou here? Hast thou a front so bold that thou hast come to my house, who art the proved assassin of its master,—the palpable robber of my crown? Come, tell me, in the name of the gods, was it cowardice or folly that thou sawest in me, that thou didst plot to do this thing? Didst thou think that I would not note this deed of thine creeping on me by stealth, or, aware, would not ward it off? Now is not thine attempt foolish,—to seek, without followers or friends, a throne,—a prize which followers and wealth must win?

CREON. Mark me now,—in answer to thy words, hear a fair reply, and then judge for thyself on knowledge.

OEDIPUS. Thou art apt in speech, but I have a poor wit for thy lessons, since I have found thee my malignant foe.

CREON. Now first hear how I will explain this very thing—

OEDIPUS. Explain me not one thing—that thou art not false.

CREON. If thou deemest that stubbornness without sense is a good gift, thou art not wise.

OEDIPUS. If thou deemest that thou canst wrong a kinsman and escape the penalty, thou art not sane.

CREON. Justly said, I grant thee: but tell me what is the wrong that thou sayest thou hast suffered from me.

OEDIPUS. Didst thou advise, or didst thou not, that I should send for that reverend seer?

CREON. And now I am still of the same mind.

OEDIPUS. How long is it, then, since Laius—

CREON. Since Laius . . . ? I take not thy drift . . .

OEDIPUS. —was swept from men's sight by a deadly violence?

CREON. The count of years would run far into the past.

OEDIPUS. Was this seer, then, of the craft in those days?

CREON. Yea, skilled as now, and in equal honour.

OEDIPUS. Made he, then, any mention of me at that time?

10 CREON. Never, certainly, when I was within hearing.

OEDIPUS. But held ye not a search touching the murder?

CREON. Due search we held, of course—and learned nothing.

OEDIPUS. And how was it that this sage did not tell his story *then*?

CREON. I know not; where I lack light, 'tis my wont to be silent.

20 OEDIPUS. Thus much, at least, thou knowest, and couldst declare with light enough.

CREON. What is that? If I know it, I will not deny.

OEDIPUS. That, if he had not conferred with thee, he would never have named *my* slaying of Laius.

CREON. If so he speaks, thou best knowest; but I claim to learn from thee as much as thou hast now from me.

OEDIPUS. Learn thy fill: I shall never be found guilty of the blood.

30 CREON. Say, then—thou hast married my sister?

OEDIPUS. The question allows not of denial.

CREON. And thou rulest the land as she doth, with like sway?

OEDIPUS. She obtains from me all her desire.

CREON. And rank not I as a third peer of you twain?

OEDIPUS. Aye, 'tis just therein that thou art seen a false friend.

CREON. Not so, if thou wouldst reason with thine
40 own heart as I with mine. And first weigh this,— whether thou thinkest that any one would choose to rule amid terrors rather than in unruffled peace,— granting that he is to have the same powers. Now I, for one, have no yearning in my nature to be a king rather than to do kingly deeds, no, nor hath any man who knows how to keep a sober mind. For now I win all boons from thee without fear; but, were I ruler myself, I should be doing much e'en against mine own pleasure.

50 How, then, could royalty be sweeter for me to have than painless rule and influence? Not yet am I so misguided as to desire other honours than those which profit. Now, all wish me joy; now, every man has a greeting for me; now, those who have a suit to thee crave speech with me, since therein is all their hope of success. Then why should I resign these things, and take those? No mind will become false,

while it is wise. Nay, I am no lover of such policy, and, if another put it into deed, never could I bear to act with him. 60

And, in proof of this, first, go to Pytho, and ask if I brought thee true word of the oracle; then next, if thou find that I have planned aught in concert with the soothsayer, take and slay me, by the sentence not of one mouth, but of twain—by mine own, no less than thine. But make me not guilty in a corner, on unproved surmise. It is not right to adjudge bad men good at random, or good men bad. I count it a like thing for a man to cast off a true friend as to cast away the life in his own bosom, which most he loves. 70 Nay, thou wilt learn these things with sureness in time, for time alone shows a just man; but thou couldst discern a knave even in one day.

LEADER. Well hath he spoken, O king, for one who giveth heed not to fall: the quick in counsel are not sure.

OEDIPUS. When the stealthy plotter is moving on me in quick sort, I, too, must be quick with my counterplot. If I await him in repose, his ends will have been gained, and mine missed. 80

CREON. What wouldst thou, then? Cast me out of the land?

OEDIPUS. Not so: I desire thy death—not thy banishment—that thou mayest show forth what manner of thing is envy.

CREON. Thou speakest as resolved not to yield or to believe?

OEDIPUS. No; for thou persuadest me not that thou art worthy of belief.

CREON. No, for I find thee not sane. 90

OEDIPUS. Sane, at least, in mine own interest.

CREON. Nay, thou shouldst be so in mine also.

OEDIPUS. Nay, thou art false.

CREON. But if thou understandest nought?

OEDIPUS. Yet must I rule.

CREON. Not if thou rule ill.

OEDIPUS. Hear him, O Thebes!

CREON. Thebes is for me also—not for thee alone.

(JOCASTA *enters.*)

LEADER. Cease, princes; and in good time for you I see Jocasta coming yonder from the house, with 100 whose help ye should compose your present feud.

JOCASTA. Misguided men, why have ye raised such foolish strife of tongues? Are ye not ashamed, while the land is thus sick, to stir up troubles of your own? Come, go thou into the house,—and thou, Creon, to thy home,—and forbear to make much of a petty grief.

CREON. Kinswoman, Oedipus thy lord claims to do dread things unto me, even one or other of two ills, —to thrust me from the land of my fathers, or to slay 110 me amain.

88–89. No; for . . . belief. This line was added by the translator.

OEDIPUS. Yea; for I have caught him, lady, working evil, by ill arts, against my person.

CREON. Now may I see no good, but perish accursed, if I have done aught to thee of that wherewith thou chargest me!

JOCASTA. O, for the gods' love, believe it, Oedipus—first, for the awful sake of this oath unto the gods,—then for my sake and for theirs who stand before thee!

CHORUS. Consent, reflect, hearken, O my king, I pray thee!

OEDIPUS. What grace, then wouldest thou have me grant thee?

CHORUS. Respect him who aforetime was not foolish, and who now is strong in his oath.

OEDIPUS. Now dost thou know what thou cravest?

CHORUS. Yea.

OEDIPUS. Declare, then, what thou meanest.

CHORUS. That thou shouldest never use an unproved rumour to cast a dishonouring charge on the friend who has bound himself with a curse.

OEDIPUS. Then be very sure that, when thou seekest this, for me thou art seeking destruction, or exile from this land.

CHORUS. No, by him who stands in the front of all the heavenly host, no, by the Sun! Unblest unfriended, may I die by the uttermost doom, if I have that thought! But my unhappy soul is worn by the withering of the land, and again by the thought that our old sorrows should be crowned by sorrows springing from you twain.

OEDIPUS. Then let him go, though I am surely doomed to death, or to be thrust dishonoured from the land. Thy lips, not his, move my compassion by their plaint; but he, where'er he be, shall be hated.

CREON. Sullen in yielding art thou seen, even as vehement in the excesses of thy wrath; but such natures are justly sorest for themselves to bear.

OEDIPUS. Then wilt thou not leave me in peace, and get thee gone?

CREON. I will go my way; I have found thee undiscerning, but in the sight of these I am just.

(*Exit* CREON.)

CHORUS. Lady, why dost thou delay to take yon man into the house?

JOCASTA. I will do so, when I have learned what hath chanced.

CHORUS. Blind suspicion, bred of talk, arose; and, on the other part, injustice wounds.

JOCASTA. It was on both sides?

CHORUS. Aye.

JOCASTA. And what was the story?

CHORUS. Enough, methinks, enough—when our land is already vexed—that the matter should rest where it ceased.

OEDIPUS. Seest thou to what thou hast come, for all

thy honest purpose, in seeking to slack and blunt my zeal?

CHORUS. King, I have said it not once alone—be sure that I should have been shown a madman, bankrupt in sane counsel, if I put thee away—thee, who gavest a true course to my beloved country when distraught by troubles—thee, who now also art like to prove our prospering guide.

JOCASTA. In the name of the gods, tell me also, O king, on what account thou hast conceived this steadfast wrath.

OEDIPUS. That will I; for I honour thee, lady, above yonder men:—the cause is Creon, and the plots that he hath laid against me.

JOCASTA. Speak on—if thou canst tell clearly how the feud began.

OEDIPUS. He says that I stand guilty of the blood of Laius.

JOCASTA. As on his own knowledge? Or on hearsay from another?

OEDIPUS. Nay, he hath made a rascal seer his mouthpiece; as for himself, he keeps his lips wholly pure.

JOCASTA. Then absolve thyself of the things whereof thou speakest; hearken to me, and learn for thy comfort that nought of mortal birth is a sharer in the science of the seer. I will give thee pithy proof of that.

An oracle came to Laius once—I will not say from Phoebus himself, but from his ministers—that the doom should overtake him to die by the hand of his child, who should spring from him and me.

Now Laius,—as, at least, the rumour saith,—was murdered one day by foreign robbers at a place where three highways meet. And the child's birth was not three days past, when Laius pinned its ankles together, and had it thrown, by others' hands, on a trackless mountain.

So, in that case, Apollo brought it not to pass that the babe should become the slayer of his sire, or that Laius should die—the dread thing which he feared—by his child's hand. Thus did the messages of seercraft map out the future. Regard them, thou, not at all. Whatsoever needful things the god seeks, he himself will easily bring to light.

OEDIPUS. What restlessness of soul, lady, what tumult of the mind hath just come upon me since I heard thee speak!

JOCASTA. What anxiety hath startled thee, that thou sayest this?

OEDIPUS. Methought I heard this from thee,—that Laius was slain where three highways meet.

JOCASTA. Yea, that was the story; nor hath it ceased yet.

OEDIPUS. And where is the place where this befell?

JOCASTA. The land is called Phocis; and branching roads lead to the same spot from Delphi and from Daulia.

OEDIPUS. And what is the time that hath passed since these things were?

JOCASTA. The news was published to the town shortly before thou wast first seen in power over this land.

OEDIPUS. O Zeus, what hast thou decreed to do unto me?

JOCASTA. And wherefore, Oedipus, doth this thing weigh upon thy soul?

OEDIPUS. Ask me not yet; but say what was the stature of Laius, and how ripe his manhood.

JOCASTA. He was tall,—the silver just lightly strewn among his hair; and his form was not greatly unlike to thine.

OEDIPUS. Unhappy that I am! Methinks I have been laying myself even now under a dread curse, and knew it not.

JOCASTA. How sayest thou? I tremble when I look on thee, my king.

OEDIPUS. Dread misgivings have I that the seer can see. But thou wilt show better if thou wilt tell me one thing more.

JOCASTA. Indeed—though I tremble—I will answer all thou askest, when I hear it.

OEDIPUS. Went he in small force, or with many armed followers, like a chieftain?

JOCASTA. Five they were in all,—a herald one of them; and there was one carriage, which bore Laius.

OEDIPUS. Alas! 'Tis now clear indeed.—Who was he who gave you these tidings, lady?

JOCASTA. A servant—the sole survivor who came home.

OEDIPUS. Is he haply at hand in the house now?

JOCASTA. No, truly; so soon as he came thence, and found thee reigning in the stead of Laius, he supplicated me, with hand laid on mine, that I would send him to the fields, to the pastures of the flocks, that he might be far from the sight of this town. And I sent him; he was worthy, for a slave, to win e'en a larger boon than that.

OEDIPUS. Would, then, that he could return to us without delay!

JOCASTA. It is easy: but wherefore dost thou enjoin this?

OEDIPUS. I fear, lady, that mine own lips have been unguarded; and therefore am I fain to behold him.

JOCASTA. Nay, he shall come. But I too, methinks, have a claim to learn what lies heavy on thy heart, my king.

OEDIPUS. Yea, and it shall not be kept from thee, now that my forebodings have advanced so far. Who, indeed, is more to me than thou, to whom I should speak in passing through such a fortune as this?

My father was Polybus of Corinth,—my mother, the Dorian Merope; and I was held the first of all the folk in that town, until a chance befell me, worthy, indeed, of wonder, though not worthy of mine own heat concerning it. At a banquet, a man full of wine cast it at me in his cups that I was not the true son of my sire. And I, vexed, restrained myself for that day as best I might; but on the next I went to my mother and father, and questioned them; and they were wroth for the taunt with him who had let that word fly. So on their part I had comfort; yet was this thing ever rankling in my heart; for it still crept abroad with strong rumour. And, unknown to mother or father, I went to Delphi; and Phoebus sent me forth disappointed of that knowledge for which I came, but in his response set forth other things, full of sorrow and terror and woe; even that I was fated to defile my mother's bed; and that I should show unto men a brood which they could not endure to behold; and that I should be the slayer of the sire who begat me.

And I, when I had listened to this, turned to flight from the land of Corinth, thenceforth wotting of its region by the stars alone, to some spot where I should never see fulfilment of the infamies foretold in mine evil doom. And on my way I came to the regions in which thou sayest that this prince perished. Now, Lady, I will tell thee the truth. When in my journey I was near to those three roads, there met me a herald, and a man seated in a carriage drawn by colts, as thou hast described; and he who was in front, and the old man himself, were for thrusting me rudely from the path. Then, in anger, I struck him who pushed me aside—the driver; and the old man, seeing it, watched the moment when I was passing, and, from the carriage, brought his goad with two teeth down full upon my head. Yet was he paid with interest; by one swift blow from the staff in this hand he was rolled right out of the carriage, on his back; and I slew every man of them.

But if this stranger had any tie of kinship with Laius, who is now more wretched than the man before thee? What mortal could prove more hated of heaven? Whom no stranger, no citizen, is allowed to receive in his house; whom it is unlawful that any one accost; whom all must repel from their homes! And this—this curse—was laid on me by no mouth but mine own! And I pollute the bed of the slain man with the hands by which he perished. Say, am I vile? Oh, am I not utterly unclean?—seeing that I must be banished, and in banishment see not mine own people, nor set foot in mine own land, or else be joined in wedlock to my mother, and slay my sire, even Polybus, who begat and reared me.

Then would not he speak aright of Oedipus, who judged these things sent by some cruel power above man? Forbid, forbid, ye pure and awful gods, that I should see that day! No, may I be swept from among men, ere I behold myself visited with the brand of such a doom!

LEADER OF THE CHORUS. To us, indeed, these

things, O king, are fraught with fear; yet have hope, until at least thou hast gained full knowledge from him who saw the deed.

OEDIPUS. Hope, in truth, rests with me thus far alone; I can await the man summoned from the pastures.

JOCASTA. And when he has appeared—what wouldst thou have of him?

OEDIPUS. I will tell thee. If his story be found to tally with thine, I, at least, shall stand clear of disaster.

JOCASTA. And what of special note didst thou hear from me?

OEDIPUS. Thou wast saying that he spoke of Laius as slain by robbers. If, then, he still speaks, as before, of several, I was not the slayer: a solitary man could not be held the same with that band. But if he names one lonely wayfarer, then beyond doubt this guilt leans to me.

JOCASTA. Nay, be assured that thus, at least, the tale was first told; he cannot revoke that, for the city heard it, not I alone. But even if he should diverge somewhat from his former story, never, king, can he show that the murder of Laius, at least, is truly square to prophecy; of whom Loxias plainly said that he must die by the hand of my child. Howbeit that poor innocent never slew him, but perished first itself. So henceforth, for what touches divination, I would not look to my right hand or my left.

OEDIPUS. Thou judgest well. But nevertheless send some one to fetch the peasant, and neglect not this matter.

JOCASTA. I will send without delay. But let us come into the house: nothing will I do save at thy good pleasure.

(OEDIPUS and JOCASTA go into the palace.)

CHORUS. May destiny still find me winning the praise of reverent purity in all words and deeds sanctioned by those laws of range sublime, called into life throughout the high clear heaven, whose father is Olympus alone; their parent was no race of mortal men, no, nor shall oblivion ever lay them to sleep; the god is mighty in them, and he grows not old.

Insolence breeds the tyrant; Insolence, once vainly surfeited on wealth that is not meet nor good for it, when it hath scaled the topmost ramparts, is hurled to a dire doom, wherein no service of the feet can serve. But I pray that the god never quell such rivalry as benefits the State; the god will I ever hold for our protector.

But if any man walks haughtily in deed or word, with no fear of Justice, no reverence for the images of gods, may an evil doom seize him for his ill-starred pride, if he will not win his vantage fairly, nor keep him from unholy deeds, but must lay profaning hands on sanctities.

Where such things are, what mortal shall boast any more that he can ward the arrows of the gods from his life? Nay, if such deeds are in honour, wherefore should we join in the sacred dance?

No more will I go reverently to earth's central and inviolate shrine, no more to Abae's temple or Olympia, if these oracles fit not the issue, so that all men shall point at them with the finger. Nay, king,— if thou art rightly called,—Zeus all-ruling, may it not escape thee and thine ever-deathless power!

The old prophecies concerning Laius are fading; already men are setting them at nought, and nowhere is Apollo glorified with honours; the worship of the gods is perishing.

(JOCASTA comes forth, bearing a branch, wreathed with festoons of wool, which, as a suppliant, she is about to lay on the altar of the household god, Lycean Apollo, in front of the palace.)

JOCASTA. Princes of the land, the thought has come to me to visit the shrines of the gods, with this wreathed branch in my hands, and these gifts of incense. For Oedipus excites his soul overmuch with all manner of alarms, nor, like a man of sense, judges the new things by the old, but is at the will of the speaker, if he speak terrors.

Since, then, by counsel I can do no good, to thee, Lycean Apollo, for thou art nearest, I have come, a suppliant with these symbols of prayer, that thou mayest find us some riddance from uncleanness. For now we are all afraid, seeing *him* affrighted, even as they who see fear in the helmsman of their ship.

(While JOCASTA is offering her prayers to the god, a MESSENGER, evidently a stranger, enters and addresses the Elders of the CHORUS.)

MESSENGER. Might I learn from you, strangers, where is the house of the king Oedipus? Or, better still, tell me where he himself is—if ye know.

LEADER OF THE CHORUS. This is his dwelling, and he himself, stranger, is within; and this lady is the mother of his children.

MESSENGER. Then may she be ever happy in a happy home, since she is his heaven-blest queen.

JOCASTA. Happiness to thee also, stranger! 'tis the due of thy fair greeting.—But say what thou hast come to seek or to tell.

MESSENGER. Good tidings, lady, for thy house and for thy husband.

JOCASTA. What are they? And from whom hast thou come?

MESSENGER. From Corinth: and at the message which I will speak anon thou wilt rejoice—doubtless; yet haply grieve.

JOCASTA. And what is it? How hath it thus a double potency?

MESSENGER. The people will make him king of the Isthmian land, as 'twas said there.

JOCASTA. How then? Is the aged Polybus no more in power?

MESSENGER. No, verily: for death holds him in the tomb.

JOCASTA. How sayest thou? Is Polybus dead, old man?

MESSENGER. If I speak not the truth, I am content to die.

JOCASTA. O handmaid, away with all speed, and tell this to thy master! O ye oracles of the gods, where stand ye now! This is the man whom Oedipus long feared and shunned, lest he should slay him; and now this man hath died in the course of destiny, not by his hand.

(OEDIPUS *enters.*)

OEDIPUS. Jocasta, dearest wife, why hast thou summoned me forth from these doors?

JOCASTA. Hear this man, and judge, as thou listenest, to what the awful oracles of the gods have come.

OEDIPUS. And he—who may he be, and what news hath he for me?

JOCASTA. He is from Corinth, to tell that thy father Polybus lives no longer, but hath perished.

OEDIPUS. How, stranger? Let me have it from thine own mouth.

MESSENGER. If I must first make these tidings plain, know indeed that he is dead and gone.

OEDIPUS. By treachery, or by visit of disease?

MESSENGER. A light thing in the scale brings the aged to their rest.

OEDIPUS. Ah, he died, it seems, of sickness?

MESSENGER. Yea, and of the long years that he had told.

OEDIPUS. Alas, alas! Why, indeed, my wife, should one look to the hearth of the Pythian seer, or to the birds that scream above our heads, on whose showing I was doomed to slay my sire? But he is dead, and hid already beneath the earth; and here am I, who have not put hand to spear.—Unless, perchance, he was killed by longing for me: thus, indeed, I should be the cause of his death. But the oracles as they stand, at least, Polybus hath swept with him to his rest in Hades: they are worth nought.

JOCASTA. Nay, did I not so foretell to thee long since?

OEDIPUS. Thou didst: but I was misled by my fear.

JOCASTA. Now no more lay aught of those things to heart.

OEDIPUS. But surely I must needs fear my mother's bed?

JOCASTA. Nay, what should mortal fear, for whom the decrees of Fortune are supreme, and who hath clear foresight of nothing? 'Tis best to live at random, as one may. But fear not thou touching wedlock with thy mother. Many men ere now have so fared in dreams also: but he to whom these things are as nought bears his life most easily.

OEDIPUS. All these bold words of thine would have been well, were not my mother living; but as it is, since she lives, I must needs fear—though thou sayest well.

JOCASTA. Howbeit thy father's death is a great sign to cheer us.

OEDIPUS. Great, I know; but my fear is of her who lives.

MESSENGER. And who is the woman about whom ye fear?

OEDIPUS. Merope, old man, the consort of Polybus.

MESSENGER. And what is it in her that moves your fear?

OEDIPUS. A heaven-sent oracle of dread import, stranger.

MESSENGER. Lawful, or unlawful, for another to know?

OEDIPUS. Lawful, surely. Loxias once said that I was doomed to espouse mine own mother, and to shed with mine own hands my father's blood. Wherefore my home in Corinth was long kept by me afar; with happy event, indeed,—yet still 'tis sweet to see the face of parents.

MESSENGER. Was it indeed for fear of this that thou wast an exile from that city?

OEDIPUS. And because I wished not, old man, to be the slayer of my sire.

MESSENGER. Then why have I not freed thee, king, from this fear, seeing that I came with friendly purpose?

OEDIPUS. Indeed thou shouldst have guerdon due from me.

MESSENGER. Indeed 'twas chiefly for this that I came—that, on thy return home, I might reap some good.

OEDIPUS. Nay, I will never go near my parents.

MESSENGER. Ah my son, 'tis plain enough that thou knowest not what thou doest.

OEDIPUS. How, old man? For the gods' love, tell me.

MESSENGER. If for these reasons thou shrinkest from going home.

OEDIPUS. Aye, I dread lest Phoebus prove himself true for me.

MESSENGER. Thou dreadest to be stained with guilt through thy parents?

OEDIPUS. Even so, old man—this it is that ever affrights me.

MESSENGER. Dost thou know, then, that thy fears are wholly vain?

OEDIPUS. How so, if I was born of those parents?

MESSENGER. Because Polybus was nothing to thee in blood.

OEDIPUS. What sayest thou? Was Polybus not my sire?

MESSENGER. No more than he who speaks to thee, but just so much.

OEDIPUS. And how can my sire be level with him who is as nought to me?

MESSENGER. Nay, he begat thee not, any more than I.

OEDIPUS. Nay, wherefore, then, called he me his son?

MESSENGER. Know that he had received thee as a gift from my hands of yore.

OEDIPUS. And yet he loved me so dearly, who came from another's hand?

MESSENGER. Yea, his former childlessness won him thereto.

OEDIPUS. And thou—hadst thou bought me or found me by chance, when thou gavest me to him?

MESSENGER. Found thee in Cithaeron's winding glens.

OEDIPUS. And wherefore wast thou roaming in those regions?

MESSENGER. I was there in charge of mountain flocks.

OEDIPUS. What, thou wast a shepherd—a vagrant hireling?

MESSENGER. But thy preserver, my son, in that hour.

OEDIPUS. And what pain was mine when thou didst take me in thine arms?

MESSENGER. The ankles of thy feet might witness.

OEDIPUS. Ah me, why dost thou speak of that old trouble?

MESSENGER. I freed thee when thou hadst thine ankles pinned together.

OEDIPUS. Aye, 'twas a dread brand of shame that I took from my cradle.

MESSENGER. Such, that from that fortune thou wast called by the name which still is thine.

OEDIPUS. Oh, for the gods' love—was the deed my mother's or father's? Speak!

MESSENGER. I know not; he who gave thee to me wots better of that than I.

OEDIPUS. What, thou hadst me from another? Thou didst not light on me thyself?

MESSENGER. No: another shepherd gave thee up to me.

OEDIPUS. Who was he? Art thou in case to tell clearly?

MESSENGER. I think he was called one of the household of Laius.

OEDIPUS. The king who ruled this country long ago?

MESSENGER. The same: 'twas in his service that the man was a herd.

OEDIPUS. Is he still alive, that I might see him?

MESSENGER. Nay, ye folk of the country should know best.

OEDIPUS. Is there any of you here present that knows the herd of whom he speaks—that hath seen him in the pastures or the town? Answer! The hour hath come that these things should be finally revealed.

LEADER OF THE CHORUS. Methinks he speaks of no other than the peasant whom thou wast already fain to see; but our lady Jocasta might best tell that.

OEDIPUS. Lady, wottest thou of him whom we lately summoned? Is it of him that this man speaks?

JOCASTA. Why ask of whom he spoke? Regard it not . . . waste not a thought on what he said . . . 'twere idle.

OEDIPUS. It must not be that, with such clues in my grasp, I should fail to bring my birth to light.

JOCASTA. For the gods' sake, if thou hast any care for thine own life, forbear this search! My anguish is enough.

OEDIPUS. Be of good courage; though I be found the son of servile mother,—aye, a slave by three descents,—*thou* wilt not be proved base-born.

JOCASTA. Yet hear me, I implore thee: do not thus.

OEDIPUS. I must not hear of not discovering the whole truth.

JOCASTA. Yet I wish thee well—I counsel thee for the best.

OEDIPUS. These best counsels, then, vex my patience.

JOCASTA. Ill-fated one! Mayst thou never come to know who thou art!

OEDIPUS. Go, some one, fetch me the herdsman hither,—and leave yon woman to glory in her princely stock.

JOCASTA. Alas, alas, miserable!—that word alone can I say unto thee, and no other word henceforth for ever.

(*She rushes into the palace.*)

LEADER. Why hath the lady gone, Oedipus, in a transport of wild grief? I misdoubt, a storm of sorrow will break forth from this silence.

OEDIPUS. Break forth what will! Be my race never so lowly, I must crave to learn it. Yon woman, perchance,—for she is proud with more than a woman's pride—thinks shame of my base source. But I, who hold myself son of Fortune that gives good, will not be dishonoured. She is the mother from whom I spring; and the months, my kinsmen, have marked me sometimes lowly, sometimes great. Such being my lineage, never more can I prove false to it, or spare to search out the secret of my birth.

CHORUS (*singing*). If I am a seer or wise of heart, O Cithaeron, thou shalt not fail—by yon heaven, thou shalt not!—to know at tomorrow's full moon that Oedipus honours thee as native to him, as his nurse, and his mother, and that thou art celebrated in our dance and song, because thou art well-pleasing to our prince. O Phoebus to whom we cry, may these things find favour in thy sight!

---

35. name . . . thine; Oedipus means "swollen foot."

Who was it, my son, who of the race whose years are many that bore thee in wedlock with Pan, the mountain-roaming father? Or was it a bride of Loxias that bore thee? For dear to him are all the upland pastures. Or perchance 'twas Cyllene's lord, or the Bacchants' god, dweller on the hill-tops, that received thee, a new-born joy, from one of the Nymphs of Helicon, with whom he most doth sport.

OEDIPUS. Elders, if 'tis for me to guess, who have never met with him, I think I see the herdsman of whom we have long been in quest; for in his venerable age he tallies with yon stranger's years, and withal I know those who bring him, methinks, as servants of mine own. But perchance thou mayest have the advantage of me in knowledge, if thou hast seen the herdsman before.

LEADER. Aye, I know him, be sure; he was in the service of Laius—trusty as any man, in his shepherd's place.

(The HERDSMAN *is brought in.)*

OEDIPUS. I ask thee first, Corinthian stranger, is this he whom thou meanest?

MESSENGER. This man whom thou beholdest.

OEDIPUS. Ho thou, old man—I would have thee look this way, and answer all that I ask thee. Thou wast once in the service of Laius?

HERDSMAN. I was—a slave not bought, but reared in his house.

OEDIPUS. Employed in what labour, or what way of life?

HERDSMAN. For the best part of my life I tended flocks.

OEDIPUS. And what the regions that thou didst chiefly haunt?

HERDSMAN. Sometimes it was Cithaeron, sometimes the neighbouring ground.

OEDIPUS. Then wottest thou of having noted yon man in these parts—

HERDSMAN. Doing what? . . . What man dost thou mean? . . .

OEDIPUS. This man here—or of having ever met him before?

HERDSMAN. Not so that I could speak at once from memory.

MESSENGER. And no wonder, master. But I will bring clear recollection to his ignorance. I am sure that he well wots of the time when we abode in the region of Cithaeron,—he with two flocks, I, his comrade, with one,—three full half-years, from spring to Arcturus; and then for the winter I used to drive my flock to mine own fold, and he took his to the fold of Laius. Did aught of this happen as I tell, or did it not?

HERDSMAN. Thou speakest the truth—though 'tis long ago.

5. **Cyllene's lord,** Hermes.

MESSENGER. Come, tell me now—wottest thou of having given me a boy in those days, to be reared as mine own foster-son?

HERDSMAN. What now? Why dost thou ask the question?

MESSENGER. Yonder man, my friend, is he who then was young.

HERDSMAN. Plague seize thee—be silent once for all!

OEDIPUS. Ha! chide him not, old man—thy words need chiding more than his.

HERDSMAN. And wherein, most noble master, do I offend?

OEDIPUS. In not telling of the boy concerning whom he asks.

HERDSMAN. He speaks without knowledge—he is busy to no purpose.

OEDIPUS. Thou wilt not speak with a good grace, but thou shalt on pain.

HERDSMAN. Nay, for the gods' love, misuse not an old man!

OEDIPUS. Ho, some one—pinion him this instant!

HERDSMAN. Alas, wherefore? what more wouldst thou learn?

OEDIPUS. Didst thou give this man the child of whom he asks?

HERDSMAN. I did,—and would I had perished that day!

OEDIPUS. Well, thou wilt come to that, unless thou tell the honest truth.

HERDSMAN. Nay, much more am I lost, if I speak.

OEDIPUS. The fellow is bent, methinks, on more delays . . .

HERDSMAN. No, no!—I said before that I gave it to him.

OEDIPUS. Whence hadst thou got it? In thine own house, or from another?

HERDSMAN. Mine own it was not—I had received it from a man.

OEDIPUS. From whom of the citizens here? from what home?

HERDSMAN. Forbear, for the gods' love, master, forbear to ask more!

OEDIPUS. Thou art lost if I have to question thee again.

HERDSMAN. It was a child, then, of the house of Laius.

OEDIPUS. A slave? or one born of his own race?

HERDSMAN. Ah me—I am on the dreaded brink of speech.

OEDIPUS. And I of hearing; yet must I hear.

HERDSMAN. Thou must know, then, that 'twas said to be his own child—but thy lady within could best say how these things are.

OEDIPUS. How? She gave it to thee?

HERDSMAN. Yea, O king.

OEDIPUS. For what end?

HERDSMAN. That I should make away with it.

OEDIPUS. Her own child, the wretch?

HERDSMAN. Aye, from fear of evil prophecies.

OEDIPUS. What were they?

HERDSMAN. The tale ran that he must slay his sire.

OEDIPUS. Why, then, didst thou give him up to this old man?

HERDSMAN. Through pity, master, as deeming that he would bear him away to another land, whence he himself came; but he saved him for the direst woe. For if thou art what this man saith, know that thou wast born to misery.

OEDIPUS. Oh, oh! All brought to pass—all true! Thou light, may I now look my last on thee—I who have been found accursed in birth, accursed in wedlock, accursed in the shedding of blood!

(He rushes into the palace.)

CHORUS. Alas, ye generations of men, how mere a shadow do I count your life! Where, where is the mortal who wins more of happiness than just the seeming, and, after the semblance, a falling away? Thine is a fate that warns me,—thine, thine, unhappy Oedipus—to call no earthly creature blest.

For he, O Zeus, sped his shaft with peerless skill, and won the prize of an all-prosperous fortune; he slew the maiden with crooked talons who sang darkly; he arose for our land as a tower against death. And from that time, Oedipus, thou hast been called our king, and hast been honoured supremely, bearing sway in great Thebes.

But now whose story is more grievous in men's ears? Who is a more wretched captive to fierce plagues and troubles, with all his life reversed?

Alas, renowned Oedipus! The same bounteous place of rest sufficed thee, as child and as sire also, that thou shouldst make thereon thy nuptial couch. Oh, how can the soil wherein thy father sowed, unhappy one, have suffered thee in silence so long?

Time the all-seeing hath found thee out in thy despite: he judgeth the monstrous marriage wherein begetter and begotten have long been one.

Alas, thou child of Laius, would, would that I had never seen thee! I wail as one who pours a dirge from his lips; sooth to speak, 'twas thou that gavest me new life, and through thee darkness hath fallen upon mine eyes.

(Enter SECOND MESSENGER *from the palace.)*

SECOND MESSENGER. Ye who are ever most honoured in this land, what deeds shall ye hear, what deeds behold, what burden of sorrow shall be yours, if, true to your race, ye still care for the house of Labdacus! For I ween that not Ister nor Phasis could wash this house clean, so many are the ills that it

50. **Ister nor Phasis**, two rivers.

shrouds, or will soon bring to light,—ills wrought not unwittingly, but of purpose. And those griefs smart most which are seen to be of our own choice.

LEADER. Indeed those which we knew before fall not short of claiming sore lamentation: besides them, what dost thou announce?

SECOND MESSENGER. This is the shortest tale to tell and to hear: our royal lady Jocasta is dead.

LEADER. Alas, hapless one! From what cause?

SECOND MESSENGER. By her own hand. The worst pain in what hath chanced is not for you, for yours it is not to behold. Nevertheless, so far as mine own memory serves, ye shall learn that unhappy woman's fate.

When, frantic, she had passed within the vestibule, she rushed straight towards her nuptial couch, clutching her hair with the fingers of both hands; once within the chamber, she dashed the doors together at her back; then called on the name of Laius, long since a corpse, mindful of that son, begotten long ago, by whom the sire was slain, leaving the mother to breed accursed offspring with his own.

And she bewailed the wedlock wherein, wretched, she had borne a two-fold brood, husband by husband, children by her child. And how thereafter she perished, is more than I know. For with a shriek Oedipus burst in, and suffered us not to watch her woe unto the end; on him, as he rushed around, our eyes were set. To and fro he went, asking us to give him a sword,—asking where he should find the wife who was no wife, but a mother whose womb had borne alike himself and his children. And, in his frenzy, a power above man was his guide; for 'twas none of us mortals who were nigh. And with a dread shriek, as though some one beckoned him on, he sprang at the double doors, and from their sockets forced the bending bolts, and rushed into the room.

There beheld we the woman hanging by the neck in a twisted noose of swinging cords. But he, when he saw her, with a dread, deep cry of misery, loosed the halter whereby she hung. And when the hapless woman was stretched upon the ground, then was the sequel dread to see. For he tore from her raiment the golden brooches wherewith she was decked, and lifted them, and smote full on his own eye-balls, uttering words like these: "No more shall ye behold such horrors as I was suffering and working! long enough have ye looked on those whom ye ought never to have seen, failed in knowledge of those whom I yearned to know—henceforth ye shall be dark!"

To such dire refrain, not once alone but oft struck he his eyes with lifted hand; and at each blow the ensanguined eye-balls bedewed his beard, nor sent forth sluggish drops of gore, but all at once a dark shower of blood came down like hail.

From the deeds of twain such ills have broken

forth, not on one alone, but with mingled woe for man and wife. The old happiness of their ancestral fortune was aforetime happiness indeed; but to-day —lamentation, ruin, death, shame, all earthly ills that can be named—all, all are theirs.

LEADER. And hath the sufferer now any respite from pain?

SECOND MESSENGER. He cries for some one to unbar the gates and show to all the Cadmeans his father's slayer, his mother's—the unholy word must not pass my lips,—as purposing to cast himself out of the land, and abide no more, to make the house accursed under his own curse. Howbeit he lacks the strength, and one to guide his steps; for the anguish is more than man may bear. And he will show this to thee also; for lo, the bars of the gates are withdrawn, and soon thou shalt behold a sight which even he who abhors it must pity.

(*The central door of the palace is now opened.* OEDIPUS *comes forth, leaning on attendants; the bloody stains are still upon his face.*)

CHORUS. O dread fate for men to see, O most dreadful of all that have met mine eyes! Unhappy one, what madness hath come on thee? Who is the unearthly foe that, with a bound of more than mortal range, hath made thine ill-starred life his prey?

Alas, alas, thou hapless one! Nay, I cannot e'en look on thee, though there is much that I would fain ask, fain learn, much that draws my wistful gaze,— with such a shuddering dost thou fill me!

OEDIPUS. Woe is me! Alas, alas, wretched that I am! Whither, whither am I borne in my misery? How is my voice swept abroad on the wings of the air? Oh my Fate, how far hast thou sprung!

CHORUS. To a dread place, dire in men's ears, dire in their sight.

OEDIPUS. O thou horror of darkness that enfoldest me, visitant unspeakable, resistless, sped by a wind too fair!

Ay me! and once again, ay me!

How is my soul pierced by the stab of these goads, and withal by the memory of sorrows!

CHORUS. Yea, amid woes so many a twofold pain may well be thine to mourn and to bear.

OEDIPUS. Ah, friend, thou still art steadfast in thy tendance of me,—thou still hast patience to care for the blind man! Ah me! Thy presence is not hid from me—no, dark though I am, yet know I thy voice full well.

CHORUS. Man of dread deeds, how couldst thou in such wise quench thy vision? What more than human power urged thee?

OEDIPUS. Apollo, friends, Apollo was he that brought these my woes to pass, these my sore, sore woes: but the hand that struck the eyes was none save mine, wretched that I am! Why was I to see, when sight could show me nothing sweet?

CHORUS. These things were even as thou sayest.

OEDIPUS. Say, friends, what can I more behold, what can I love, what greeting can touch mine ear with joy? Haste, lead me from the land, friends, lead me hence, the utterly lost, the thrice accursed, yea, the mortal most abhorred of heaven!

CHORUS. Wretched alike for thy fortune and for thy sense thereof, would that I had never so much as known thee!

OEDIPUS. Perish the man, whoe'er he was, that freed me in the pastures from the cruel shackle on my feet, and saved me from death, and gave me back to life,—a thankless deed! Had I died then, to my friends and to thine own soul I had not been so sore a grief.

CHORUS. I also would have had it thus.

OEDIPUS. So had I not come to shed my father's blood, nor been called among men the spouse of her from whom I sprang: but now am I forsaken of the gods, son of a defiled mother, successor to his bed who gave me mine own wretched being: and if there be yet a woe surpassing woes, it hath become the portion of Oedipus.

CHORUS. I know not how I can say that thou hast counselled well: for thou wert better dead than living and blind.

OEDIPUS. Show me not at large that these things are not best done thus: give me counsel no more. For, had I sight, I know not with what eyes I could e'en have looked on my father, when I came to the place of the dead, aye, or on my miserable mother, since against both I have sinned such sins as strangling could not punish. But deem ye that the sight of children, born as mine were born, was lovely for me to look upon? No, no, not lovely to mine eyes for ever! No, nor was this town with its towered walls, nor the sacred statues of the gods, since I, thrice wretched that I am,—I, noblest of the sons of Thebes, —have doomed myself to know these no more, by mine own command that all should thrust away the impious one,—even him whom gods have shown to be unholy—and of the race of Laius!

After bearing such a stain upon me, was I to look with steady eyes on this folk? No, verily: no, were there yet a way to choke the fount of hearing, I had not spared to make a fast prison of this wretched frame, that so I should have known nor sight nor sound; for 'tis sweet that our thought should dwell beyond the sphere of griefs.

Alas, Cithaeron, why hadst thou a shelter for me? When I was given to thee, why didst thou not slay me straightway, that so I might never have revealed my source to men? Ah, Polybus,—ah, Corinth, and thou that wast called the ancient house of my fathers, how seeming-fair was I your nursling, and what ills were festering beneath! For now I am found evil, and of evil birth. O ye three roads, and thou secret glen,—thou coppice, and narrow way where three paths met—ye who drank from my hands that father's blood which was mine own,—remember ye, perchance, what deeds I wrought for you to see,—and then, when I came hither, what fresh deeds I went on to do?

O marriage-rites, ye gave me birth, and when ye had brought me forth, again ye bore children to your child, ye created an incestuous kinship of fathers, brothers, sons,—brides, wives, mothers,—yea, all the foulest shame that is wrought among men! Nay, but 'tis unmeet to name what 'tis unmeet to do:—haste ye, for the gods' love, hide me somewhere beyond the land, or slay me, or cast me into the sea, where ye shall never behold me more! Approach,—deign to lay your hands on a wretched man;—hearken, fear not,—my plague can rest on no mortal beside.

(*Enter* CREON.)

LEADER. Nay, here is Creon, in meet season for thy requests, crave they act or counsel; for he alone is left to guard the land in thy stead.

OEDIPUS. Ah me, how indeed shall I accost him? What claim to credence can be shown on my part? For in the past I have been found wholly false to him.

CREON. I have not come in mockery, Oedipus, nor to reproach thee with any bygone fault. (*To the attendants.*) But ye, if ye respect the children of men no more, revere at least the all-nurturing flame of our lord the Sun,—spare to show thus nakedly a pollution such as this,—one which neither earth can welcome, nor the holy rain, nor the light. Nay, take him into the house as quickly as ye may; for it best accords with piety that kinsfolk alone should see and hear a kinsman's woes.

OEDIPUS. For the gods' love—since thou hast done a gentle violence to my presage, who hast come in a spirit so noble to me, a man most vile—grant me a boon:—for thy good I will speak, not for mine own.

CREON. And what wish art thou so fain to have of me?

OEDIPUS. Cast me out of this land with all speed, to a place where no mortal shall be found to greet me more.

CREON. This would I have done, be thou sure, but that I craved first to learn all my duty from the god.

OEDIPUS. Nay, his behest hath been set forth in full,—to let me perish, the parricide, the unholy one, that I am.

CREON. Such was the purport; yet, seeing to what a pass we have come, 'tis better to learn clearly what should be done.

OEDIPUS. Will ye, then, seek a response on behalf of such a wretch as I am?

CREON. Aye, for thou thyself wilt now surely put faith in the god.

OEDIPUS. Yea; and on thee lay I this charge, to thee will I make this entreaty:—give to her who is within such burial as thou thyself wouldest; for thou wilt meetly render the last rites to thine own. But for me—never let this city of my sire be condemned to have me dwelling therein, while I live: no, suffer me to abide on the hills, where yonder is Cithaeron, famed as mine,—which my mother and sire, while they lived, set for my appointed tomb,—that so I may die by their decree who sought to slay me. Howbeit of thus much am I sure,—that neither sickness nor aught else can destroy me; for never had I been snatched from death, but in reserve for some strange doom.

Nay, let *my* fate go whither it will: but as touching my children,—I pray thee, Creon, take no care on thee for my sons; they are men, so that, be they where they may, they can never lack the means to live. But my two girls, poor hapless ones,—who never knew my table spread apart, or lacked their father's presence, but ever in all things shared my daily bread,—I pray thee, care for *them;* and—if thou canst—suffer me to touch them with my hands, and to indulge my grief. Grant it, prince, grant it, thou noble heart! Ah, could I but once touch them with my hands, I should think that they were with me, even as when I had sight . . .

(CREON's *attendants lead in the children* ANTIGONE *and* ISMENE.)

Ha? O ye gods, can it be my loved ones that I hear sobbing,—can Creon have taken pity on me and sent me my children—my darlings? Am I right?

CREON. Yea: 'tis of my contriving, for I knew thy joy in them of old,—the joy that now is thine.

OEDIPUS. Then blessed be thou, and, for guerdon of this errand, may heaven prove to thee a kinder guardian than it hath to me! My children, where are ye? Come hither,—hither to the hands of him whose mother was your own, the hands whose offices have wrought that your sire's once bright eyes should be such orbs as these,—his, who seeing nought, knowing nought, became your father by her from whom he sprang! For you also do I weep—behold you I cannot—when I think of the bitter life in days to come which men will make you live. To what company of the citizens will ye go, to what festival, from which ye shall not return home in tears, instead of

From a Greek mask.

sharing in the holiday? But when ye are now come to years ripe for marriage, who shall he be, who shall be the man, my daughters, that will hazard taking unto him such reproaches as must be baneful alike to my offspring and to yours? For what misery is wanting? Your sire slew his sire, he had seed of her who bare him, and begat you at the sources of his own being! Such are the taunts that will be cast at you; and who then will wed? The man lives not, no, it cannot be, my children, but ye must wither in barren maidenhood.

Ah, son of Menoeceus, hear me—since thou art the only father left to them, for we, their parents, are lost, both of us,—allow them not to wander poor and unwed, who are thy kinswomen, nor abase them to the level of my woes. Nay, pity them, when thou seest them at this tender age so utterly forlorn, save for thee. Signify thy promise, generous man, by the touch of thy hand! To you, my children, I would have given much counsel, were your minds mature; but now I would have this to be your prayer—that ye live where occasion suffers, and that the life which is your portion may be happier than your sire's.

CREON. Thy grief hath had large scope enough: nay, pass into the house.

OEDIPUS. I must obey, though 'tis in no wise sweet.

CREON. Yea: for it is in season that all things are good.

OEDIPUS. Knowest thou, then, on what conditions I will go?

CREON. Thou shalt name them; so shall I know them when I hear.

OEDIPUS. See that thou send me to dwell beyond this land.

CREON. Thou askest me for what the god must give.

OEDIPUS. Nay, to the gods I have become most hateful.

CREON. Then shalt thou have thy wish anon.

OEDIPUS. So thou consentest?

CREON. 'Tis not my wont to speak idly what I do not mean.

OEDIPUS. Then 'tis time to lead me hence.

CREON. Come, then,—but let thy children go.

OEDIPUS. Nay, take not these from me!

CREON. Crave not to be master in all things: for the mastery which thou didst win hath not followed thee through life.

CHORUS. Dwellers in our native Thebes, behold, this is Oedipus, who knew the famed riddle, and was a man most mighty; on whose fortunes what citizen did not gaze with envy? Behold into what a stormy sea of dread trouble he hath come!

Therefore, while our eyes wait to see the destined final day, we must call no one happy who is of mortal race, until he hath crossed life's border, free from pain.

Euripides
c. 480–c. 407 B.C.

Although Sophocles is generally considered the greatest Greek tragedian, Euripides has long been the most popular and is certainly the most modern and arresting in point of view. A poorer artist and a more revolutionary thinker than Sophocles or Aeschylus, he was suspiciously received in his day and won the first prize only five times in an active career of nearly fifty years, during which he wrote some ninety plays. But his free-thinking spirit was in tune with a new generation which was philosophically minded rather than religious, and decadent in its radicalism, so that after his death he quickly outdistanced his predecessors in popular esteem. As many as eighteen of his plays have survived, in comparison with seven each of his predecessors. His popularity in the declining years of Greece was due to his veiled but exciting iconoclasm and to the theatrical devices which his predecessors had scorned, as much as to the humanness of his characters and his warm poetic style.

Sometimes called the psychologist among the Greek playwrights, Euripides was himself a challenging subject for a psychologist. Born probably in 480 B.C., the year of Salamis, he was even in childhood an aloof and grim-faced introvert. Although his father trained him as a professional boxer and wrestler, he came to loathe athletics and turned instead to painting, music, and playwriting. His introspective nature often led him to retirement among his many books or in a cave on Salamis, where he is said to have written his plays. He performed his military service, but later took no interest in the army, the Assembly, the religious festivals, or other concerns of the well-rounded Greek citizen. His wife found him a cold, difficult man, but the many searching and sometimes unflattering pictures of women in his tragedies reveal less of a sour attitude toward them than his characteristic urge to analyze personality and to project the pathetic qualities in human life.

As a dispassionate observer of his contemporaries, he won their distrust and hostility by his social criticism and disrespect for tradition. Aristophanes voiced the conservatives' alarm at his brutal satire of Euripides in the *Thesmophoriazusae* and *The Frogs*. But he was enthusiastically accepted in the radical circles of Anaxagoras, Protagoras, and Socrates, the philosophers, and outside Athens he had many admirers. In Sicily, where his works were especially popular, some Athenian prisoners once won freedom because they could recite speeches from his plays. At last the sensitive poet grew weary of censure and misunderstanding at home and accepted the invitation of the King of Macedonia to settle in his northern kingdom, where he probably wrote his final masterpieces, the *Bacchae* and *Iphigenia at Aulis*. After his death in his seventies one of his sons produced his last plays at

Athens and won him a posthumous first prize. Sophocles, who outlived him, made his chorus wear mourning that year in Euripides' honor.

Although Euripides presents the time-honored myths that were still considered the only suitable subjects for a religious theater, he was far from a religious man, if not actually an atheist. He was interested in the old tales, not as holy legends, but as vehicles of character study and social comment. His heroes and heroines, regardless of their traditional sanctity, emerge as strikingly human creations, sympathetically but objectively studied for their weaknesses and even morbid traits. Although he is a moralistic pyschologist rather than a scientific one, his moral outlook was closer to the radical views of Socrates than to the conventional theology of Aeschylus and Sophocles. He took a realistic view of mankind but implied a conception of justice superior to the pragmatic ethics of Homer. As he could reduce an ancient hero like Agamemnon to the level of a vacillating politician, so he could give a sympathetic picture of a traditional villainess, like Phaedra, the faithless wife, or Medea, the murderer of her own children. Like Dante in his *Commedia,* he detested the smug self-satisfaction of an Admetus (in *Alcestis*) or Pentheus (in *Bacchae*) but was lenient toward those who committed crimes while overcome by passion.

Interested primarily in character, Euripides often seemed to consider plot no more than a necessary nuisance and developed theatrical devices to dispose of it and to allow himself freedom to concentrate on his men and women. He frequently used a monologue-prologue to give a rapid review of the background of the plot, and popularized a spectacular device for bringing a quick and usually happy end to the story, called the *deus ex machina,* whereby a god not previously involved in the action would suddenly descend in a magic car (for which actual machinery was provided) to rescue an innocent Iphigenia from slaughter or arrange a marriage for a guilty Medea. To a modern reader this melodramatic device often does violence to the logic of the plot, but for the Greeks it placed a seal of divine approval on the solution. Occasionally it was used to solve an otherwise unsolvable situation, but more often to foretell the future of the characters, as only a god was in a position to do. Again, to concentrate on his central characters, Euripides reduced the status of the traditional chorus to brief interludes between the scenes and predicted the disappearance of the chorus entirely in the centuries to follow. This was in line with the increased realism that he introduced into the conception, dialogue, and staging of his dramas.

Although several other plays challenge its place, the masterpiece of Euripides is probably *Hippolytus.* Even the Athenians recognized its worth by giving it one of his few first prizes in 428 B.C. No other of his works has a better constructed plot or a fuller study of character, and the scenes of Phaedra's confession of love for her stepson and of the final reconciliation of father and son are among the most appealing in Greek tragedy. The same poignant domestic tale was to inspire the later French master, Racine, to write his best play; and both Sophocles and

Seneca produced plays of that name. The parallel with the tale of Joseph and Potiphar's wife in Genesis is obvious.

Hippolytus was a startling novelty on the Athenian stage because it was the first work to present sexual passion freely as a source of tragedy. The old legend had long intrigued Euripides, and he had written an earlier play on the same subject, now lost, which apparently concentrated on the illicit desires of Phaedra, as Racine's play was to do. But Hippolytus is the central character of the extant play, and Euripides has given a masterful study of a young man's misguided attempt at sexual adjustment.

Barely out of adolescence, Hippolytus has an exaggerated sense of chastity and has joined the monkish Orphic brotherhood, which leads him to despise women and Aphrodite, the goddess of love, who represents them in his eyes. This fatal show of pride in his purity attracts the malevolence of the goddess, who bewitches Phaedra as an instrument of his undoing. There is no perversion implied in the nature of Hippolytus. He is a rugged youth, devoted to athletics and the hunt (symbolized by Artemis, the virgin goddess of the chase), who errs in being excessively idealistic and prudish. His self-righteousness leads him to be insolent toward a goddess—an unforgivable act in Greek eyes. Only this condones the shabbiness of Aphrodite in making this otherwise innocent youth the victim of a vicious plot. But even after Theseus confronts him with his accusation, Hippolytus maintains his supercilious attitude and seems to justify his father's attack, if not his suspicions. In accepting banishment and death he seems to feel more pity for his misguided father than for himself.

Phaedra is one of the famous women characters of Euripides. As with Medea in his play of that name, her crime is unflinchingly declared, and yet somewhat excused on the ground that she was simply an instrument of divine justice. Born into a family that had suffered much for love, Phaedra fights her passion for her stepson, but its intensity is too great for her. Her situation inspires our sympathy for a decent and modest woman who is wracked against her will by illicit desires. The picture of a woman in love is painted with realistic detail—her irresponsibility, her vanity, her humiliating frustration and hateful accusation after the sting of Hippolytus' rebuff. Though her career in the play is shocking, Euripides convinces us that she, like the others, is merely a fallible human being. In many respects she is more admirable than the loyal but hard-headed nurse who advises her.

This play illustrates the frequent tendency of Greek authors from Homer down to use the gods as mere abstractions, poetic devices, or metaphors to represent human experience. Aphrodite and Artemis symbolize opposite poles of behavior—wanton sex gratification and asceticism, both of which violated the Greek ideal of "nothing to excess." Like the *Bacchae, Hippolytus* teaches that no man should inhibit the instinctive urges in his nature. The natural life, led with moderation, is the ideal one.

Hippolytus

CHARACTERS IN THE PLAY

APHRODITE
HIPPOLYTUS, *son of* THESEUS
ATTENDANTS OF HIPPOLYTUS
CHORUS OF TROEZENIAN WOMEN
NURSE OF PHAEDRA
PHAEDRA, *wife of* THESEUS
THESEUS
MESSENGER
ARTEMIS

(SCENE: *Before the royal palace at Troezen. The goddess* APHRODITE *appears.*)

APHRODITE.

WIDE o'er man my realm extends, and proud the name that I, the goddess Cypris, bear, both in heaven's courts and 'mongst all those who dwell within the limits of the sea and the bounds of Atlas, beholding the sungod's light; those that respect my power I advance to honour, but bring to ruin all who vaunt themselves at me. For even in the race of gods this feeling finds a home, even pleasure at the honour men pay them. And the truth of this I soon will show; for that son of Theseus, born of the Amazon, Hippolytus, whom holy Pittheus taught, alone of all the dwellers in this land of Troezen, calls me vilest of the deities. Love he scorns, and, as for marriage, will none of it; but Artemis, daughter of Zeus, sister of Phoebus, he doth honour, counting her the chief of goddesses, and ever through the greenwood, attendant on his virgin goddess, he clears the earth of wild beasts with his fleet hounds, enjoying the comradeship of one too high for mortal ken. 'Tis not this I grudge him, no! why should I? But for his sins against me, I will this very day take vengeance on Hippolytus; for long ago I cleared the ground of many obstacles, so it needs but trifling toil. For as he came one day from the home of Pittheus to witness the solemn mystic rites and be initiated therein in Pandion's land, Phaedra, his father's noble wife, caught sight of him, and by my designs she found her heart was seized with wild desire. And ere she came to this Troezenian realm, a temple did she rear to Cypris hard by the rock of Pallas where it o'erlooks this country, for love of the youth in another land; and to win his love in days to come she called after his name the temple she had founded for the goddess. Now, when Theseus left the land of Cecrops, flying the pollution of the blood of Pallas' sons, and with his wife sailed to this shore, content to suffer exile for a year, then began the wretched wife to pine away in silence, moaning 'neath love's cruel scourge, and none of her servants knows what ails her. But this passion of hers must not fail thus. No, I will discover the matter to Theseus, and all shall be laid bare. Then will the father slay his child, my bitter foe, by curses, for the lord Poseidon granted this boon to Theseus; three wishes of the god to ask, nor ever ask in vain. So Phaedra is to die, an honoured death 'tis true, but still to die; for I will not let her suffering outweigh the payment of such forfeit by my foes as shall satisfy my honour. But lo! I see the son of Theseus coming hither—Hippolytus, fresh from the labours of the chase. I will get me hence. At his back follows a long train of retainers, in joyous cries of revelry uniting hymns of praise to Artemis, his goddess; for little he recks that Death hath oped his gates for him, and that this is his last look upon the light.

(APHRODITE *vanishes.* HIPPOLYTUS *and his retinue of hunting* ATTENDANTS *enter, singing. They move to worship at an altar of* ARTEMIS *on one side of the stage.*)

HIPPOLYTUS. Come follow, friends, singing to Artemis, daughter of Zeus, throned in the sky, whose votaries we are.

ATTENDANTS. Lady goddess, awful queen, daughter of Zeus, all hail! hail! child of Latona and of Zeus, peerless mid the virgin choir, who hast thy dwelling in heaven's wide mansions at thy noble father's court, in the golden house of Zeus. All hail! most beauteous Artemis, lovelier far than all the daughters of Olympus!

HIPPOLYTUS. For thee, O mistress mine, I bring this woven wreath, culled from a virgin meadow, where nor shepherd dares to herd his flock nor ever scythe hath mown, but o'er the mead unshorn the bee doth wing its way in spring; and with the dew from rivers drawn purity that garden tends. Such as know no cunning lore, yet in whose nature self-control, made perfect, hath a home, these may pluck the flowers, but not the wicked world. Accept, I pray, dear mistress, mine this chaplet from my holy hand to crown thy locks of gold; for I, and none other of mortals, have this high guerdon, to be with thee, with thee converse, hearing thy voice, though not thy face beholding. So be it mine to end my life as I began.

LEADER OF THE ATTENDANTS. My prince! we needs must call upon the gods, our lords, so wilt thou listen to a friendly word from me?

Hippolytus. Translated by E. P. Coleridge. Reprinted by permission of G. Bell and Sons, Ltd.

11. **Pittheus,** grandfather of Theseus and mentor of Hippolytus.

26. **Pandion's land,** Athens, of which Pandion had been king.

34–35. **Now, when . . . sons.** Theseus fled from Athens after killing the sons of Pallas, son of Pandion, for attempting to regain the Athenian throne.

HIPPOLYTUS. Why, that will I! else were I proved a fool.

LEADER. Dost know, then, the way of the world?

HIPPOLYTUS. Not I; but wherefore such a question?

LEADER. It hates reserve which careth not for all men's love.

HIPPOLYTUS. And rightly too; reserve in man is ever galling.

LEADER. But there's a charm in courteous affability?

10 HIPPOLYTUS. The greatest surely; aye, and profit, too, at trifling cost.

LEADER. Dost think the same law holds in heaven as well?

HIPPOLYTUS. I trow it doth, since all our laws we men from heaven draw.

LEADER. Why, then, dost thou neglect to greet an august goddess?

HIPPOLYTUS. Whom speak'st thou of? Keep watch 20 upon thy tongue lest it some mischief cause.

LEADER. Cypris I mean, whose image is stationed o'er thy gate.

HIPPOLYTUS. I greet her from afar, preserving still my chastity.

LEADER. Yet is she an august goddess, far renowned on earth.

HIPPOLYTUS. 'Mongst gods as well as men we have our several preferences.

LEADER. I wish thee luck, and wisdom too, so far 30 as thou dost need it.

HIPPOLYTUS. No god, whose worship craves the night, hath charms for me.

LEADER. My son, we should avail us of the gifts that gods confer.

HIPPOLYTUS. Go in, my faithful followers, and make ready food within the house; a well-filled board hath charms after the chase is o'er. Rub down my steeds ye must, that when I have had my fill I may yoke them to the chariot and give them proper 40 exercise. As for thy Queen of Love, a long farewell to her.

(HIPPOLYTUS *goes into the palace, followed by all the* ATTENDANTS *except the* LEADER, *who prays before a statue of* APHRODITE *on the other side of the stage.*)

LEADER. Meantime I with sober mind, for I must not copy my young master, do offer up my prayer to thy image, lady Cypris, in such words as it becomes a slave to use. But thou should'st pardon all, who, in youth's impetuous heat, speak idle words of thee; make as though thou hearest not, for gods must needs be wiser than the sons of men.

(*The* LEADER *goes into the palace. The* CHORUS OF TROEZENIAN WOMEN *enters.*)

CHORUS. A rock there is, where, as they say, the 50 ocean dew distils, and from its beetling brow it pours a copious stream for pitchers to be dipped therein;

'twas here I had a friend washing robes of purple in the trickling stream, and she was spreading them out on the face of a warm sunny rock; from her I had the tidings, first of all, that my mistress—

Was wasting on the bed of sickness, pent within her house, a thin veil o'ershadowing her head of golden hair. And this is the third day I hear that she hath closed her lovely lips and denied her chaste body all sustenance, eager to hide her suffering and reach 60 death's cheerless bourn.

Maiden, thou must be possessed, by Pan made frantic or by Hecate, or by the Corybantes dread, and Cybele the mountain mother. Or maybe thou hast sinned against Dictynna, huntress-queen, and art wasting for thy guilt in sacrifice unoffered. For she doth range o'er lakes' expanse and past the bounds of earth upon the ocean's tossing billows.

Or doth some rival in thy house beguile thy lord, the captain of Erechtheus' sons, that hero nobly born, 70 to secret amours hid from thee? Or hath some mariner sailing hither from Crete reached this port that sailors love, with evil tidings for our queen, and she with sorrow for her grievous fate is to her bed confined?

Yea, and oft o'er woman's wayward nature settles a feeling of miserable helplessness, arising from labor-pains or passionate desire. I, too, have felt at times this sharp thrill shoot through me, but I would cry to Artemis, queen of archery, who comes from heaven to aid us in our travail, and thanks to heaven's 80 grace she ever comes at my call with welcome help. Look! where the aged nurse is bringing her forth from the house before the door, while on her brow the cloud of gloom is deepening. My soul longs to learn what is her grief, the canker that is wasting our queen's fading charms.

(PHAEDRA *is led out and placed upon a couch by the* NURSE *and attendants.*)

NURSE. O, the ills of mortal men! the cruel diseases they endure! What can I do for thee? from what refrain? Here is the bright sun-light, here the azure sky; lo! we have brought thee on thy bed of sickness 90 without the palace; for all thy talk was of coming hither, but soon back to thy chamber wilt thou hurry. Disappointment follows fast with thee, thou hast no joy in aught for long; the present has no power to please; on something absent next thy heart is set. Better be sick than tend the sick; the first is but a single ill, the last unites mental grief with manual toil. Man's whole life is full of anguish; no respite from his woes he finds; but if there is aught to love beyond this life, night's dark pall doth wrap it round.

62–64. **Maiden . . . mother,** all religious explanations of insanity.
70. **Erechtheus' sons,** the Athenians, after a mythical king of Athens.

And so we show our mad love of this life because its light is shed on earth, and because we know no other, and have naught revealed to us of all our earth may hide; and trusting to fables we drift at random.

PHAEDRA. Lift my body, raise my head! My limbs are all unstrung, kind friends. O handmaids, lift my arms, my shapely arms.
10 The tire on my head is too heavy for me to wear; away with it, and let my tresses o'er my shoulders fall.

NURSE. Be of good heart, dear child; toss not so wildly to and fro. Lie still, be brave, so wilt thou find thy sickness easier to bear; suffering for mortals is nature's iron law.

PHAEDRA. Ah! would I could draw a draught of water pure from some dew-fed spring, and lay me down to rest in the grassy meadow 'neath the poplar's
20 shade!

NURSE. My child, what wild speech is this? O say not such things in public, wild whirling words of frenzy bred!

PHAEDRA. Away to the mountain take me! to the wood, to the pine-trees I will go, where hounds pursue the prey, hard on the scent of dappled fawns. Ye gods! what joy to hark them on, to grasp the barbed dart, to poise Thessalian hunting-spears close to my golden hair, then let them fly.
30 NURSE. Why, why, my child, these anxious cares? What hast thou to do with the chase? Why so eager for the flowing spring, when hard by these towers stands a hill well watered, whence thou may'st freely draw?

PHAEDRA. O Artemis, who watchest o'er sea-beat Limna and the race-course thundering to the horse's hoofs, would I were upon thy plains curbing Venetian steeds!

NURSE. Why betray thy frenzy in these wild whirl-
40 ing words? Now thou wert for hasting hence to the hills away to hunt wild beasts, and now thy yearning is to drive the steed over the waveless sands. This needs a cunning seer to say what god it is that reins thee from the course, distracting thy senses, child.

PHAEDRA. Ah me! alas! what have I done? Whither have I strayed, my senses leaving? Mad, mad! stricken by some demon's curse! Woe is me! Cover my head again, nurse. Shame fills me for the words I have spoken. Hide me then; from my eyes the tear-
50 drops stream, and for very shame I turn them away. 'Tis painful coming to one's senses again, and madness, evil though it be, has this advantage, that one has no knowledge of reason's overthrow.

NURSE. There then I cover thee; but when will death hide my body in the grave? Many a lesson length of days is teaching me. Yea, mortal men should pledge themselves to moderate friendships only, not to such as reach the very heart's core; affec-
60 tion's ties should be light upon them to let them slip or draw them tight. For one poor heart to grieve for twain, as I do for my mistress, is a burden sore to bear. Men say that too engrossing pursuits in life more oft cause disappointment than pleasure, and too oft are foes to health. Wherefore I do not praise excess so much as moderation, and with me wise men will agree.   (PHAEDRA lies back on the couch.)

LEADER OF THE CHORUS. O aged dame, faithful nurse of Phaedra, our queen, we see her sorry plight; but what it is that ails her we cannot discern, so fain
70 would learn of thee and hear thy opinion.

NURSE. I question her, but am no wiser, for she will not answer.

LEADER. Nor tell what source these sorrows have?

NURSE. The same answer thou must take, for she is dumb on every point.

LEADER. How weak and wasted is her body!

NURSE. What marvel? 'tis three days now since she has tasted food.

LEADER. Is this infatuation, or an attempt to die?

NURSE. 'Tis death she courts; such fasting aims at
80 ending life.

LEADER. A strange story! Is her husband satisfied?

NURSE. She hides from him her sorrow, and vows she is not ill.

LEADER. Can he not guess it from her face?

NURSE. He is not now in his own country.

LEADER. But dost not thou insist in thy endeavour to find out her complaint, her crazy mind?

NURSE. I have tried every plan, and all in vain; yet not even now will I relax my zeal, that thou too,
90 if thou stayest, mayst witness my devotion to my unhappy mistress. Come, come, my darling child, let us forget, the twain of us, our former words; be thou more mild, smoothing that sullen brow and changing the current of thy thought, and I, if in aught before I failed in humouring thee, will let that be and find some better course. If thou art sick with ills thou canst not name, there be women here to help to set thee right; but if thy trouble can to men's ears be divulged, speak, that physicians may pronounce on
100 it. Come, then, why so dumb? Thou shouldst not so remain, my child, but scold me if I speak amiss, or, if I give good counsel, yield assent. One word, one look this way! Ah me! Friends, we waste our toil to no purpose; we are as far away as ever; she would not relent to my arguments then, nor is she yielding now. Well, grow more stubborn than the sea, yet be assured of this, that if thou diest thou art a traitress to thy children, for they will ne'er inherit their father's halls, nay, by that knightly queen the Amazon
110 who bore a son to lord it over thine, a bastard born but not a bastard bred, whom well thou knowest, e'en Hippolytus—

PHAEDRA (aroused by his name). Oh! oh!

NURSE. Ha! doth that touch the quick?

PHAEDRA. Thou hast undone me, nurse; I do adjure by the gods, mention that man no more.

NURSE. There now! thou art thyself again, but e'en yet refusest to aid thy children and preserve thy life.

PHAEDRA. My babes I love, but there is another storm that buffets me.

NURSE. Daughter, are thy hands from bloodshed pure?

10 PHAEDRA. My hands are pure, but on my soul there rests a stain.

NURSE. The issue of some enemy's secret witchery?

PHAEDRA. A friend is my destroyer, one unwilling as myself.

NURSE. Hath Theseus wronged thee in any wise?

PHAEDRA. Never may I prove untrue to him!

NURSE. Then what strange mystery is there that drives thee on to die?

PHAEDRA. O, let my sin and me alone! 'tis not 20 'gainst thee I sin.

NURSE. Never willingly! and, if I fail, 'twill rest at thy door.

PHAEDRA. How now? Thou usest force in clinging to my hand.

NURSE. Yea, and I will never loose my hold upon thy knees.

PHAEDRA. Alas for thee! my sorrows, shouldst thou learn them, would recoil on thee.

NURSE. What keener grief for me than failing to 30 win thee?

PHAEDRA. 'Twill be death to thee; though to me that brings renown.

NURSE. And dost thou then conceal this boon despite my prayers?

PHAEDRA. I do, for 'tis out of shame I am planning an honourable escape.

NURSE. Tell it, and thine honour shall the brighter shine.

PHAEDRA. Away, I do conjure thee; loose my hand.

40 NURSE. I will not, for the boon thou shouldst have granted me is denied.

PHAEDRA. I will grant it out of reverence for thy holy suppliant touch.

NURSE. Henceforth I hold my peace; 'tis thine to speak from now.

PHAEDRA. Ah! hapless mother, what a love was thine!

NURSE. Her love for the bull? daughter, or what meanest thou?

PHAEDRA. And woe to thee! my sister, bride of 50 Dionysus.

NURSE. What ails thee, child? speaking ill of kith and kin.

PHAEDRA. Myself the third to suffer! how am I undone!

47. **Her love . . . bull.** To punish Minos, the father of Phaedra, Poseidon inspired her mother, Pasiphaë, with passion for a bull, by whom she bore the Minotaur.   49–50. **bride of Dionysus,** Ariadne.

NURSE. Thou strik'st me dumb! Where will this history end?

PHAEDRA. That "love" has been our curse from time long past.

NURSE. I know no more of what I fain would learn.

PHAEDRA. Ah! would thou couldst say for me what 60 I have to tell.

NURSE. I am no prophetess to unriddle secrets.

PHAEDRA. What is it they mean when they talk of people being in "love"?

NURSE. At once the sweetest and the bitterest thing, my child.

PHAEDRA. I shall only find the latter half.

NURSE. Ha! my child, art thou in love?

PHAEDRA. The Amazon's son, whoever he may 70 be—

NURSE. Mean'st thou Hippolytus?

PHAEDRA. 'Twas thou, not I, that spoke his name.

NURSE. O heavens! what is this, my child? Thou hast ruined me. Outrageous! friends; I will not live and bear it; hateful is life, hateful to mine eyes the light. This body I resign, will cast it off, and rid me of existence by my death. Farewell, my life is o'er. Yea, for the chaste have wicked passions, 'gainst their will maybe, but still they have. Cypris, it seems, is not a goddess after all, but something greater far, 80 for she hath been the ruin of my lady and of me and our whole family.

CHORUS. O, too clearly didst thou hear our queen uplift her voice to tell her startling tale of piteous suffering. Come death ere I reach thy state of feeling, loved mistress. O horrible! woe, for these miseries! woe, for the sorrows on which mortals feed! Thou art undone! thou hast disclosed thy sin to heaven's light. What hath each passing day and every hour in store for thee? Some strange event will come to 90 pass in this house. For it is no longer uncertain where the star of thy love is setting, thou hapless daughter of Crete.

PHAEDRA. Women of Troezen, who dwell here upon the frontier edge of Pelops' land, oft ere now in heedless mood through the long hours of night have I wondered why man's life is spoiled; and it seems to me their evil case is not due to any natural fault of judgment, for there be many dowered with sense, but we must view the matter in this light: by 100 teaching and experience we learn the right but neglect it in practice, some from sloth, others from preferring pleasure of some kind or other to duty. Now life has many pleasures, protracted talk, and leisure, that seductive evil; likewise there is shame which is of two kinds, one a noble quality, the other a curse to families; but if for each its proper time were clearly known, these twain could not have had the selfsame letters to denote them. So then since I had made up my mind on these points, 'twas not likely 110 any drug would alter it and make me think the contrary. And I will tell thee too the way my judgment went. When love wounded me, I bethought me how I best might bear the smart. So from that day forth I began to hide in silence what I suffered. For I put no faith in counsellors, who know well to lecture others for presumption, yet themselves have countless troubles of their own. Next I did devise noble endurance of these wanton thoughts, striving by continence for victory. And last when I could not succeed in mastering love hereby, methought it best to die; and none can gainsay my purpose. For fain I would my virtue should to all appear, my shame have few to witness it. I knew my sickly passion now; to yield to it I saw how infamous; and more, I learnt to know so well that I was but a woman, a thing the world detests. Curses, hideous curses on that wife who first did shame her marriage-vow for lovers other than her lord! 'Twas from noble families this curse began to spread among our sex. For when the noble countenance disgrace, poor folk of course will think that it is right. Those too I hate who make profession of purity, though in secret reckless sinners. How can these, queen Cypris, ocean's child, e'er look their husbands in the face? do they never feel one guilty thrill that their accomplice, night, or the chambers of their house will find a voice and speak? This it is that calls on me to die, kind friends, that so I may ne'er be found to have disgraced my lord, or the children I have borne; no! may they grow up and dwell in glorious Athens, free to speak and act, heirs to such fair fame as a mother can bequeath. For to know that father or mother has sinned doth turn the stoutest heart to slavishness. This alone, men say, can stand the buffets of life's battle, a just and virtuous soul in whomsoever found. For time unmasks the villain soon or late, holding up to them a mirror as to some blooming maid. 'Mongst such may I be never seen!

LEADER OF THE CHORUS. Now look! how fair is chastity however viewed, whose fruit is good repute amongst men.

NURSE. My queen, 'tis true thy tale of woe, but lately told, did for the moment strike me with wild alarm, but now I do reflect upon my foolishness; second thoughts are often best even with men. Thy fate is no uncommon one nor past one's calculations; thou art stricken by the passion Cypris sends. Thou art in love; what wonder? so are many more. Wilt thou, because thou lov'st, destroy thyself? 'Tis little gain, I trow, for those who love or yet may love their fellows, if death must be their end; for though the Love-Queen's onset in her might is more than man can bear, yet doth she gently visit yielding hearts, and only when she finds a proud unnatural spirit, doth she take and mock it past belief. Her path is in the sky, and mid the ocean's surge she rides; from her all nature springs; she sows the seeds of love, inspires the warm desire to which we sons of earth all owe our being. They who have aught to do with books of ancient scribes, or themselves engage in studious pursuits, know how Zeus of Semele was enamoured, how the bright-eyed goddess of the Dawn once stole Cephalus to dwell in heaven for the love she bore him; yet these in heaven abide nor shun the gods' approach, content, I trow, to yield to their misfortune. Wilt thou refuse to yield? thy sire, it seems, should have begotten thee on special terms or with different gods for masters, if in these laws thou wilt not acquiesce. How many, prithee, men of sterling sense, when they see their wives unfaithful, make as though they saw it not? How many fathers, when their sons have gone astray, assist them in their amours? 'Tis part of human wisdom to conceal the deed of shame. Nor should man aim at excessive refinement in his life; for they cannot with exactness finish e'en the roof that covers in a house; and how dost thou, after falling into so deep a pit, think to escape? Nay, if thou hast more of good than bad, thou wilt fare exceeding well, thy human nature considered. O cease, my darling child, from evil thoughts, let wanton pride be gone, for this is naught else, this wish to rival gods in perfectness. Face thy love; 'tis heaven's will thou shouldst. Sick thou art, yet turn thy sickness to some happy issue. For there are charms and spells to soothe the soul; surely some cure for thy disease will be found. Men, no doubt, might seek it long and late if our women's minds no scheme devise.

LEADER. Although she gives thee at thy present need the wiser counsel, Phaedra, yet do I praise thee. Still my praise may sound more harsh and jar more cruelly on thy ear than her advice.

PHAEDRA. 'Tis even this, too plausible a tongue, that overthrows good governments and homes of men. We should not speak to please the ear but point the path that leads to noble fame.

NURSE. What means this solemn speech? No need of rounded phrases,—but a man. Straightway must we move to tell him frankly how it is with thee. Had not thy life to such a crisis come, or wert thou with self-control endowed, ne'er would I to gratify thy passions have urged thee to this course; but now 'tis a struggle fierce to save thy life, and therefore less to blame.

PHAEDRA. Accursed proposal! peace, woman! never utter those shameful words again!

NURSE. Shameful, maybe, yet for thee better than honour's code. Better this deed, if it shall save thy life, than that name thy pride will kill thee to retain.

PHAEDRA. I conjure thee, go no further! for thy words are plausible but infamous; for though as yet love has not undermined my soul, yet, if in specious words thou dress thy foul suggestion, I shall be beguiled into the snare from which I am now escaping.

NURSE. If thou art of this mind, 'twere well thou

ne'er hadst sinned; but as it is, hear me; for that is the next best course; I in my house have charms to soothe thy love,—'twas but now I thought of them;— these shall cure thee of thy sickness on no disgraceful terms, thy mind unhurt, if thou wilt be but brave. But from him thou lovest we must get some token, a word or fragment of his robe, and thereby unite in one love's twofold stream.

PHAEDRA. Is thy drug a salve or potion?

NURSE. I cannot tell; be content, my child, to profit by it and ask no questions.

PHAEDRA. I fear me thou wilt prove too wise for me.

NURSE. If thou fear this, confess thyself afraid of all; but why thy terror?

PHAEDRA. Lest thou shouldst breathe a word of this to Theseus' son.

NURSE. Peace, my child! I will do all things well; only be thou, queen Cypris, ocean's child, my partner in the work! And for the rest of my purpose, it will be enough for me to tell it to our friends within the house. (*Exit* NURSE.)

CHORUS (*singing*). O Love, Love, that from the eyes diffusest soft desire, bringing on the souls of those, whom thou dost camp against, sweet grace, O never in evil mood appear to me, nor out of time and tune approach! Nor fire nor meteor hurls a mightier bolt than Aphrodite's shaft shot by the hands of Love, the child of Zeus.

Idly, idly by the streams of Alpheus and in the Pythian shrines of Phoebus, Hellas heaps the slaughtered steers; while Love we worship not, Love, the king of men, who holds the key to Aphrodite's sweetest bower,—worship not him who, when he comes, lays waste and marks his path to mortal hearts by wide-spread woe.

There was that maiden in Oechalia, a girl unwed, that knew no wooer yet nor married joys; her did the Queen of Love snatch from her home across the sea and gave unto Alcmena's son, mid blood and smoke and murderous marriage-hymns, to be to him a frantic fiend of hell; woe! woe for his wooing!

Ah! holy walls of Thebes, ah! fount of Dirce, ye could testify what course the love-queen follows. For with the blazing levin-bolt did she cut short the fatal marriage of Semele, mother of Zeus-born Bacchus. All things she doth inspire, dread goddess, winging her flight hither and thither like a bee.

PHAEDRA. Peace, oh women, peace! I am undone.

LEADER OF THE CHORUS. What, Phaedra, is this dread event within thy house?

29. **Alpheus,** the major river of southern Greece. 36. **maiden,** Iolé, carried away by Hercales. 42. **Dirce,** who mistreated her husband's former wife and was thrown into the fountain in punishment. 43–45. **For with . . . Bacchus.** The lightning of Zeus killed Semele as she gave birth to Dionysus.

PHAEDRA. Hush! let me hear what those within are saying.

LEADER. I am silent; this is surely the prelude to evil.

PHAEDRA. Great gods! how awful are my sufferings!

CHORUS. What a cry was there! what loud alarm! say what sudden terror, lady, doth thy soul dismay.

PHAEDRA. I am undone. Stand here at the door and hear the noise arising in the house.

CHORUS. Thou art already by the bolted door; 'tis for thee to note the sounds that issue from within. And tell me, O tell me what evil can be on foot.

PHAEDRA. 'Tis the son of the horse-loving Amazon who calls, Hippolytus, uttering foul curses on my servant.

CHORUS. I hear a noise, but cannot clearly tell which way it comes. Ah! 'tis through the door the sound reached thee.

PHAEDRA. Yes, yes, he is calling her plainly enough a go-between in vice, traitress to her master's honour.

CHORUS. Woe, woe is me! thou art betrayed, dear mistress! What counsel shall I give thee? thy secret is out; thou art utterly undone.

PHAEDRA. Ah me! ah me!

CHORUS. Betrayed by friends!

PHAEDRA. She hath ruined me by speaking of my misfortune; 'twas kindly meant, but an ill way to cure my malady.

LEADER OF THE CHORUS. O what wilt thou do now in thy cruel dilemma?

PHAEDRA. I only know one way, one cure for these my woes, and that is instant death.

(HIPPOLYTUS *rushes out of the palace, followed by the* NURSE.)

HIPPOLYTUS. O mother earth! O sun's unclouded orb! What words, unfit for any lips, have reached my ears!

NURSE. Peace, my son, lest some one hear thy outcry.

HIPPOLYTUS. I cannot hear such awful words and hold my peace.

NURSE. I do implore thee by thy fair right hand.

HIPPOLYTUS. Let go my hand, touch not my robe.

NURSE. O by thy knees I pray, destroy me not utterly.

HIPPOLYTUS. Why say this, if, as thou pretendest, thy lips are free from blame?

NURSE. My son, this is no story to be noised abroad.

HIPPOLYTUS. A virtuous tale grows fairer told to many.

NURSE. Never dishonour thy oath, my son.

HIPPOLYTUS. My tongue an oath did take, but not my heart.

NURSE. My son, what wilt thou do? destroy thy friends?

HIPPOLYTUS. Friends indeed! the wicked are no friends of mine.

NURSE. O pardon me; to err is only human, child.

HIPPOLYTUS. Great Zeus, why didst thou, to man's sorrow, put woman, evil counterfeit, to dwell where shines the sun? If thou wert minded that the human race should multiply, it was not from women they should have drawn their stock, but in thy temples they should have paid gold or iron or ponderous
10 bronze and bought a family, each man proportioned to his offering, and so in independence dwelt, from women free. But now as soon as ever we would bring this plague into our home we bring its fortune to the ground. 'Tis clear from this how great a curse a woman is; the very father, that begot and nurtured her, to rid him of the mischief, gives her a dower and packs her off; while the husband, who takes the noxious weed into his home, fondly decks his sorry idol in fine raiment and tricks her out in robes, squan-
20 dering by degrees, unhappy wight! his house's wealth. For he is in this dilemma; say his marriage has brought him good connections, he is glad then to keep the wife he loathes; or, if he gets a good wife but useless relations, he tries to stifle the bad luck with the good. But it is easiest for him who has settled in his house as wife a mere cipher, incapable from simplicity. I hate a clever woman; never may she set foot in *my* house who aims at knowing more than women need; for in these clever women Cypris
30 implants a larger story of villainy, while the artless woman is by her shallow wit from levity debarred. No servant should ever have had access to a wife, but men should put to live with them beasts, which bite, not talk, in which case they could not speak to any one nor be answered back by them. But, as it is, the wicked in their chambers plot wickedness, and their servants carry it abroad. Even thus, vile wretch, thou cam'st to make me partner in an outrage on my father's honour; wherefore I must wash that stain
40 away in running streams, dashing the water into my ears. How could I commit so foul a crime when by the very mention of it I feel myself polluted? Be well assured, woman, 'tis only my religious scruple saves thee. For had not I unawares been caught by an oath, 'fore heaven! I would not have refrained from telling all unto my father. But now I will from the house away, so long as Theseus is abroad, and will maintain strict silence. But, when my father comes, I will return and see how thou and thy mis-
50 tress face him, and so shall I learn by experience the extent of thy audacity. Perdition seize you both! I can never satisfy my hate for women, no! not even though some say this is ever my theme, for of a truth they always are evil. So either let some one prove them chaste, or let me still trample on them for ever. (*Exit* HIPPOLYTUS.)

CHORUS. O the cruel, unhappy fate of women!

What arts, what arguments have we, once we have made a slip, to loose by craft the tight-drawn knot?

PHAEDRA. I have met my deserts. O earth, O light 60 of day! How can I escape the stroke of fate? How my pangs conceal, kind friends? What god will appear to help me, what mortal to take my part or help me in unrighteousness? The present calamity of my life admits of no escape. Most hapless I of all my sex!

LEADER OF THE CHORUS. Alas, alas! the deed is done, thy servant's schemes have gone awry, my queen, and all is lost.

PHAEDRA (*to the* NURSE). Accursed woman! traitress to thy friends! How hast thou ruined me! May 70 Zeus, my ancestor, smite thee with his fiery bolt and uproot thee from thy place. Did I not foresee thy purpose, did I not bid thee keep silence on the very matter which is now my shame? But thou wouldst not be still; wherefore my fair name will not go with me to the tomb. But now I must another scheme devise. Yon youth, in the keenness of his fury, will tell his father of my sin, and the aged Pittheus of my state, and fill the world with stories to my shame. Perdition seize thee and every meddling fool who 80 by dishonest means would serve unwilling friends!

NURSE. Mistress, thou may'st condemn the mischief I have done, for sorrow's sting o'ermasters thy judgment; yet can I answer thee in face of this, if thou wilt hear. 'Twas I who nurtured thee; I love thee still; but in my search for medicine to cure thy sickness I found what least I sought. Had I but succeeded, I had been counted wise, for the credit we get for wisdom is measured by our success.

PHAEDRA. Is it just, is it any satisfaction to me, that 90 thou shouldst wound me first, then bandy words with me?

NURSE. We dwell on this too long; I was not wise, I own; but there are yet ways of escape from the trouble, my child.

PHAEDRA. Be dumb henceforth; evil was thy first advice to me, evil too thy attempted scheme. Begone and leave me, look to thyself; I will my own fortunes for the best arrange. (*Exit* NURSE.)

Ye noble daughters of Troezen, grant me the only 100 boon I crave; in silence bury what ye here have heard.

LEADER. By majestic Artemis, child of Zeus, I swear I will never divulge aught of thy sorrows.

PHAEDRA. 'Tis well. But I, with all my thought, can but one way discover out of this calamity, that so I may secure my children's honour, and find myself some help as matters stand. For never, never will I bring shame upon my Cretan home, nor will I, to save one poor life, face Theseus after my disgrace. 110

LEADER. Art thou bent then on some cureless woe?

PHAEDRA. On death; the means thereto must I devise myself.

LEADER. Hush!

PHAEDRA. Do thou at least advise me well. For this very day shall I gladden Cypris, my destroyer, by yielding up my life, and shall own myself vanquished by cruel love. Yet shall my dying be another's curse, that he may learn not to exult at my misfortunes; but when he comes to share the self-same plague with me, he will take a lesson in wisdom. (*Exit* PHAEDRA.)

CHORUS. O to be nestling 'neath some pathless cavern, there by god's creating hand to grow into a bird amid the wingèd tribes! Away would I soar to Adria's wave-beat shore and to the waters of Eridanus; where a father's hapless daughters in their grief for Phaethon distil into the glooming flood the amber brilliance of their tears.

And to the apple-bearing strand of those minstrels in the west I then would come, where ocean's lord no more to sailors grants a passage o'er the deep dark main, finding there the heaven's holy bound, upheld by Atlas, where water from ambrosial founts wells up beside the couch of Zeus inside his halls, and holy earth, the bounteous mother, causes joy to spring in heavenly breasts.

O white-winged bark, that o'er the booming ocean-wave didst bring my royal mistress from her happy home, to crown her queen 'mongst sorrow's brides! Surely evil omens from either port, at least from Crete, were with that ship, what time to glorious Athens it sped its way, and the crew made fast its twisted cable-ends upon the beach of Munychus, and on the land stept out.

Whence comes it that her heart is crushed, cruelly afflicted by Aphrodite with unholy love; so she by bitter grief o'erwhelmed will tie a noose within her bridal bower to fit it to her fair white neck, too modest for this hateful lot in life, prizing o'er all her name and fame, and striving thus to rid her soul of passion's sting.

(*The* NURSE *rushes out of the palace.*)

NURSE. Help! ho! To the rescue all who near the palace stand! She hath hung herself, our queen, the wife of Theseus.

LEADER OF THE CHORUS. Woe worth the day! the deed is done; our royal mistress is no more, dead she hangs in the dangling noose.

NURSE. Haste! some one bring a two-edged knife wherewith to cut the knot about her neck.

FIRST SEMI-CHORUS. Friends, what shall we do? think you we should enter the house, and loose the queen from the tight-drawn noose?

SECOND SEMI-CHORUS. Why should *we*? Are there not young servants here? To do too much is not a safe course in life.

NURSE. Lay out the hapless corpse, straighten the limbs. This was a bitter way to sit at home and keep my master's house! (*Exit* NURSE.)

LEADER OF THE CHORUS. She is dead, poor lady; so I hear. Already are they laying out the corpse.

(THESEUS *and his retinue have entered.*)

THESEUS. Women, can ye tell me what the uproar in the palace means? There came the sound of servants weeping bitterly to mine ear. None of my household deign to open wide the gates and give me glad welcome as a traveller from prophetic shrines. Hath aught befallen old Pittheus? No. Though he be well advanced in years, yet should I mourn, were he to quit this house.

LEADER. 'Tis not against the old, Theseus, that fate, to strike thee, aims this blow; prepare thy sorrow for a younger corpse.

THESEUS. Woe is me! is it a child's life death robs me of?

LEADER. They live; but, cruellest news of all for thee, their mother is no more.

THESEUS. What! my wife dead? By what cruel mischance?

LEADER. About her neck she tied the hangman's knot.

THESEUS. Had grief so chilled her blood? or what had befallen her?

LEADER. I know but this, for I am myself but now arrived at the house to mourn thy sorrows, O Theseus.

THESEUS. Woe is me! why have I crowned my head with woven garlands, when misfortune greets my embassage? Unbolt the doors, servants, loose their fastenings, that I may see the piteous sight, my wife, whose death is death to me.

(*The central doors of the palace open, disclosing the corpse.*)

CHORUS. Woe! woe is thee for thy piteous lot! thou hast done thyself a hurt deep enough to overthrow this family. Ah! ah! the daring of it! done to death by violence and unnatural means, the desperate effort of thy own poor hand! Who cast the shadow o'er thy life, poor lady?

THESEUS. Ah me, my cruel lot! sorrow hath done her worst on me. O fortune, how heavily hast thou set thy foot on me and on my house, by fiendish hands inflicting an unexpected stain? Nay, 'tis complete effacement of my life, making it impossible; for I see, alas! so wide an ocean of grief that I can never swim to shore again, nor breast the tide of this calamity. How shall I speak of thee, my poor wife, what tale of direst suffering tell? Thou art vanished like a bird from the covert of my hand, taking one headlong leap from me to Hades' halls. Alas, and woe! this is a bitter, bitter sight! This must be a judgment

13–15. **where . . . tears.** The sisters of Phaethon mourned his death after his ill-fated attempt to drive the chariot of the sun. Their tears turned to amber. 30. **Munychus,** the port of Athens.

sent by God for the sins of an ancestor, which from some far source I am bringing on myself.

LEADER OF THE CHORUS. My prince, 'tis not to thee alone such sorrows come; thou hast lost a noble wife, but so have many others.

THESEUS. Fain would I go hide me 'neath earth's blackest depth, to dwell in darkness with the dead in misery, now that I am reft of thy dear presence! for thou hast slain me than thyself e'en more. Who 10 can tell me what caused the fatal stroke that reached thy heart, dear wife? Will no one tell me what befell? doth my palace all in vain give shelter to a herd of menials? Woe, woe for thee, my wife! sorrows past speech, past bearing, I behold within my house; myself a ruined man, my home a solitude, my children orphans!

CHORUS. Gone and left us hast thou, fondest wife and noblest of all women 'neath the sun's bright eye or night's star-lit radiance. Poor house, what sorrows 20 are thy portion now! My eyes are wet with streams of tears to see thy fate; but the sequel to this tragedy has long with terror filled me.

THESEUS. Ha! what means this letter? clasped in her dear hand it hath some strange tale to tell. Hath she, poor lady, as a last request, written her bidding as to my marriage and her children? Take heart, poor ghost; no wife henceforth shall wed thy Theseus or invade his house. Ah! how yon seal of my dead wife stamped with her golden ring affects my sight! Come, 30 I will unfold the sealed packet and read her letter's message to me.

CHORUS. Woe unto us! Here is yet another evil in the train by heaven sent. Looking to what has happened, I should count my lot in life no longer worth one's while to gain. My master's house, alas! is ruined, brought to naught, I say. Spare it, O Heaven, if it may be. Hearken to my prayer, for I see, as with prophetic eye, an omen boding ill.

THESEUS. O horror! woe on woe! and still they 40 come, too deep for words, too heavy to bear. Ah me!

LEADER OF THE CHORUS. What is it? speak, if I may share in it.

THESEUS. This letter loudly tells a hideous tale! where can I escape my load of woe? For I am ruined and undone, so awful are the words I find here written clear as if she cried them to me; woe is me!

LEADER. Alas! thy words declare themselves the harbingers of woe.

THESEUS. I can no longer keep the cursed tale 50 within the portal of my lips, cruel though its utterance be. Ah me! Hippolytus hath dared by brutal force to violate my honour, recking naught of Zeus, whose awful eye is over all. O father Poseidon, once didst thou promise to fulfil three prayers of mine; answer one of these and slay my son, let him not escape this single day, if the prayers thou gavest me were indeed with issue fraught.

LEADER. O king, I do conjure thee, call back that prayer; hereafter thou wilt know thy error. Hear, I pray.

THESEUS. Impossible! moreover I will banish him from this land, and by one of two fates shall he be struck down; either Poseidon, out of respect to my prayer, will cast his dead body into the house of Hades; or exiled from this land, a wanderer to some foreign shore, shall he eke out a life of misery.

LEADER. Lo! where himself doth come, thy son Hippolytus, in good time; dismiss thy hurtful rage, King Theseus, and bethink thee what is best for thy family.

(HIPPOLYTUS enters.)

HIPPOLYTUS. I heard thy voice, father, and hasted to come hither; yet know I not the cause of thy present sorrow, but would fain learn of thee.

(He sees PHAEDRA's body.)

Ha! what is this? thy wife is dead? 'Tis very strange; it was but now I left her; a moment since she looked upon the light. How came she thus? the manner of her death? this would I learn of thee, father. Art dumb? silence availeth not in trouble; nay, for the heart that fain would know all must show its curiosity even in sorrow's hour. Be sure it is not right, father, to hide misfortunes from those who love, ay, more than love thee.

THESEUS. O ye sons of men, victims of a thousand idle errors, why teach your countless crafts, why scheme and seek to find a way for everything, while one thing ye know not nor ever yet have made your prize, a way to teach them wisdom whose souls are void of sense?

HIPPOLYTUS. A very master in his craft the man, who can force fools to be wise! But these ill-timed subtleties of thine, father, make me fear thy tongue is running wild through trouble.

THESEUS. Fie upon thee! man needs should have some certain test set up to try his friends, some touchstone of their hearts, to know each friend whether he be true or false; all men should have two voices, one the voice of honesty, expediency's the other, so would honesty confute its knavish opposite, and then we could not be deceived.

HIPPOLYTUS. Say, hath some friend been slandering me and hath he still thine ear? and I, though guiltless, banned? I am amazed; thy random, frantic words fill me with wild alarm.

THESEUS. O the mind of mortal man! to what lengths will it proceed? What limit will its bold assurance have? for if it goes on growing as man's life advances, and each successor outdo the man before him in villainy, the gods will have to add another sphere unto the world, which shall take in the knaves and villains. Behold this man; he, my own son, hath outraged mine honour, his guilt most clearly proved by my dead wife. Now, since thou hast dared this loathly crime, come, look thy father in the face. Art thou the man who dost with gods consort, as one above the vulgar herd? art thou the chaste and sinless saint? Thy boasts will never persuade me to be guilty of attributing ignorance to gods. Go then, vaunt thyself, and drive thy petty trade in viands formed of lifeless food; take Orpheus for thy chief and go a-revelling, with all honour for the vapourings of many a written scroll, seeing thou now art caught. Let all beware, I say, of such hypocrites! who hunt their prey with fine words, and all the while are scheming villainy. She is dead; dost think that this will save thee? Why this convicts thee more than all, abandoned wretch! What oaths, what pleas can outweigh this letter, so that thou shouldst 'scape thy doom? Thou wilt assert she hated thee, that 'twixt the bastard and the true-born child nature has herself put war; it seems then by thy showing she made a sorry bargain with her life, if to gratify her hate of thee she lost what most she prized. 'Tis said, no doubt, that frailty finds no place in man but is innate in woman; my experience is, young men are no more secure than women, whenso the Queen of Love excites a youthful breast; although their sex comes in to help them. Yet why do I thus bandy words with thee, when before me lies the corpse, to be the clearest witness? Begone at once, an exile from this land, and ne'er set foot again in god-built Athens nor in the confines of my dominion. For if I am tamely to submit to this treatment from such as thee, no more will Sinis, robber of the Isthmus, bear me witness how I slew him, but say my boasts are idle, nor will those rocks Scironian, that fringe the sea, call me the miscreants' scourge.

LEADER. I know not how to call happy any child of man; for that which was first has turned and now is last.

HIPPOLYTUS. Father, thy wrath and the tension of thy mind are terrible; yet this charge, specious though its arguments appear, becomes a calumny, if one lay it bare. Small skill have I in speaking to a crowd, but have a readier wit for comrades of mine own age and small companies. Yea, and this is as it should be; for they, whom the wise despise, are better qualified to speak before a mob. Yet am I constrained under the present circumstances to break silence. And at the outset will I take the point which formed the basis of thy stealthy attack on me, designed to put me out of court unheard; dost see yon sun, this earth? These do not contain, for all thou dost deny it, chastity surpassing mine. To reverence God I count the highest knowledge, and to adopt as friends not those who attempt injustice, but such as

would blush to propose to their companions aught disgraceful or pleasure them by shameful services; to mock at friends is not my way, father, but I am still the same behind their backs as to their face. The very crime thou thinkest to catch me in, is just the one I am untainted with, for to this day have I kept me pure from women. Nor know I aught thereof, save what I hear or see in pictures, for I have no wish to look even on these, so pure my virgin soul. I grant my claim to chastity may not convince thee; well, 'tis then for thee to show the way I was corrupted. Did this woman exceed in beauty all her sex? Did I aspire to fill the husband's place after thee and succeed to thy house? That surely would have made me out a fool, a creature void of sense. Thou wilt say, "Your chaste man loves to lord it." No, no! say I, sovereignty pleases only those whose hearts are quite corrupt. Now, I would be the first and best at all the games in Hellas, but second in the state, for ever happy thus with the noblest for my friends. For there one may be happy, and the absence of danger gives a charm beyond all princely joys. One thing I have not said, the rest thou hast. Had I a witness to attest my purity, and were I pitted 'gainst her still alive, facts would show thee on enquiry who the culprit was. Now by Zeus, the god of oaths, and by the earth, whereon we stand, I swear to thee I never did lay hand upon thy wife nor would have wished to, or have harboured such a thought. Slay me, ye gods! rob me of name and honour, from home and city cast me forth, a wandering exile o'er the earth! nor sea nor land receive my bones when I am dead, if I am such a miscreant! I cannot say if she through fear destroyed herself, for more than this am I forbid. With her discretion took the place of chastity, while I, though chaste, was not discreet in using this virtue.

LEADER. Thy oath by heaven, strong security, sufficiently refutes the charge.

THESEUS. A wizard or magician must the fellow be, to think he can first flout me, his father, then by coolness master my resolve.

HIPPOLYTUS. Father, thy part in this doth fill me with amaze; wert thou my son and I thy sire, by heaven! I would have slain, not let thee off with banishment, hadst thou presumed to violate my honour.

THESEUS. A just remark! yet shalt thou not die by the sentence thine own lips pronounce upon thyself; for death, that cometh in a moment, is an easy end for wretchedness. Nay, thou shalt be exiled from thy fatherland, and wandering to a foreign shore drag out a life of misery; for such are the wages of sin.

HIPPOLYTUS. Oh! what wilt thou do? Wilt thou banish me, without so much as waiting for Time's evidence on my case?

THESEUS. Ay, beyond the sea, beyond the bounds of Atlas, if I could, so deeply do I hate thee.

HIPPOLYTUS. What! banish me untried, without

60

70

80

90

100

7-10. **take Orpheus . . . caught.** Hippolytus was apparently associated with the Orphic brotherhood, a kind of monastic order. 32-34. **nor . . . scourge.** A second robber, Sciron, kicked his victims from a rock into the sea. He too was killed by Theseus.

even testing my oath, the pledge I offer, or the voice of seers?

THESEUS. This letter here, though it bears no seers' signs, arraigns thy pledges; as for birds that fly o'er our heads, a long farewell to them.

HIPPOLYTUS (*aside*). Great gods! why do I not unlock my lips, seeing that I am ruined by you, the objects of my reverence? No, I will not; I should nowise persuade those whom I ought to, and in vain should break the oath I swore.

THESEUS. Fie upon thee! that solemn air of thine is more than I can bear. Begone from thy native land forthwith!

HIPPOLYTUS. Whither shall I turn? Ah me! whose friendly house will take me in, an exile on so grave a charge?

THESEUS. Seek one who loves to entertain as guests and partners in his crimes corrupters of men's wives.

HIPPOLYTUS. Ah me! this wounds my heart and brings me nigh to tears to think that I should appear so vile, and thou believe me so.

THESEUS. Thy tears and forethought had been more in season when thou didst presume to outrage thy father's wife.

HIPPOLYTUS. O house, I would thou couldst speak for me and witness if I am so vile!

THESEUS. Dost fly to speechless witnesses? This deed, though it speaketh not, proves thy guilt clearly.

HIPPOLYTUS. Alas! Would I could stand and face myself, so should I weep to see the sorrows I endure.

THESEUS. Ay, 'tis thy character to honour thyself far more than reverence thy parents, as thou shouldst.

HIPPOLYTUS. Unhappy mother! son of sorrow! Heaven keep all friends of mine from bastard birth!

THESEUS. Ho! servants, drag me hence! You heard my proclamation long ago condemning him to exile.

HIPPOLYTUS. Whoso of them doth lay a hand on me shall rue it; thyself expel me, if thy spirit move thee, from the land.

THESEUS. I will, unless my word thou straight obey; no pity for thy exile steals into my heart.

(THESEUS *goes in. The central doors of the palace are closed.*)

HIPPOLYTUS. The sentence then, it seems, is passed. Ah, misery! How well I know the truth herein, but know no way to tell it! O daughter of Latona, dearest to me of all deities, partner, comrade in the chase, far from glorious Athens must I fly. Farewell, city and land of Erechtheus; farewell, Troezen, most joyous home wherein to pass the spring of life; 'tis my last sight of thee, farewell! Come, my comrades in this land, young like me, greet me kindly and escort me forth, for never will ye behold a purer soul, for all my father's doubts.

(*Exit* HIPPOLYTUS.)

CHORUS. In very deed the thoughts I have about the gods, whenso they come into my mind, do much to soothe its grief, but though I cherish secret hopes of some great guiding will, yet am I at fault when I survey the fate and doings of the sons of men; change succeeds to change, and man's life veers and shifts in endless restlessness.

Fortune grant me this, I pray, at heaven's hand,— a happy lot in life and a soul from sorrow free; opinions let me hold not too precise nor yet too hollow; but, lightly changing my habits to each morrow as it comes, may I thus attain a life of bliss!

For now no more is my mind free from doubts, unlooked-for sights greet my vision; for lo! I see the morning star of Athens, eye of Hellas, driven by his father's fury to another land. Mourn, ye sands of my native shores, ye oak-groves on the hills, where with his fleet hounds he would hunt the quarry to the death, attending on Dictynna, awful queen.

No more will he mount his car drawn by Venetian steeds, filling the course round Limna with the prancing of his trained horses. Nevermore in his father's house shall he wake the Muse that never slept beneath his lute-strings; no hand will crown the spots where rests the maiden Latona 'mid the boskage deep; nor ever more shall our virgins vie to win thy love, now thou art banished.

While I with tears at thy unhappy fate shall endure a lot all undeserved. Ah! hapless mother, in vain didst thou bring forth, it seems. I am angered with the gods; out upon them! O ye linkèd Graces, why are ye sending from his native land this poor youth, a guiltless sufferer, far from his home?

LEADER OF THE CHORUS. But lo! I see a servant of Hippolytus hasting with troubled looks towards the palace.

(A MESSENGER *enters.*)

MESSENGER. Ladies, where may I find Theseus, king of the country? pray, tell me if ye know; is he within the palace here?

LEADER. Lo! himself approaches from the palace.

(THESEUS *enters.*)

MESSENGER. Theseus, I am the bearer of troublous tidings to thee and all citizens who dwell in Athens or the bounds of Troezen.

THESEUS. How now? hath some strange calamity o'ertaken these two neighbouring cities?

MESSENGER. In one brief word, Hippolytus is dead. 'Tis true one slender thread still links him to the light of life.

THESEUS. Who slew him? Did some husband come to blows with him, one whose wife, like mine, had suffered brutal violence?

MESSENGER. He perished through those steeds that

drew his chariot, and through the curses thou didst utter, praying to thy sire, the ocean-king, to slay thy son.

THESUS. Ye gods and king Poseidon, thou hast proved my parentage by hearkening to my prayer! Say how he perished; how fell the uplifted hand of Justice to smite the villain who dishonoured me?

MESSENGER. Hard by the wave-beat shore were we combing out his horses' manes, weeping the while, for one had come to say that Hippolytus was harshly exiled by thee and nevermore would return to set foot in this land. Then came he, telling the same doleful tale to us upon the beach, and with him was a countless throng of friends who followed after. At length he stayed his lamentation and spake: "Why weakly rave on this wise? My father's commands must be obeyed. Ho! servants, harness my horses to the chariot; this is no longer now city of mine." Thereupon each one of us bestirred himself, and, ere a man could say 'twas done, we had the horses standing ready at our master's side. Then he caught up the reins from the chariot-rail, first fitting his feet exactly in the hollows made for them. But first with outspread palms he called upon the gods, "O Zeus, now strike me dead, if I have sinned, and let my father learn how he is wronging me, in death at least, if not in life." Therewith he seized the whip and lashed each horse in turn; while we, close by his chariot, near the reins, kept up with him along the road that leads direct to Argos and Epidaurus. And just as we were coming to a desert spot, a strip of sand beyond the borders of this country, sloping right to the Saronic gulf, there issued thence a deep rumbling sound, as it were an earthquake, a fearsome noise, and the horses reared their heads and pricked their ears, while we were filled with wild alarm to know whence came the sound; when, as we gazed toward the wave-beat shore, a wave tremendous we beheld towering to the skies, so that from our view the cliffs of Sciron vanished, for it hid the isthmus and the rock of Asclepius; then swelling and frothing with a crest of foam, the sea discharged it toward the beach where stood the harnessed car, and in the moment that it broke, that mighty wall of waters, there issued from the wave a monstrous bull, whose bellowing filled the land with fearsome echoes, a sight too awful as it seemed to us who witnessed it. A panic seized the horses there and then, but our master, to horses' ways quite used, gripped in both hands his reins, and tying them to his body pulled them backward as the sailor pulls his oar; but the horses gnashed the forged bits between their teeth and bore him wildly on, regardless of their master's guiding hand or rein or jointed car. And oft as he would take the guiding rein and steer for softer ground, showed that bull in front to turn him back again, maddening his team with terror; but if in their frantic career they ran towards the rocks, he would draw nigh the chariot-rail, keeping up with them, until, suddenly dashing the wheel against a stone, he upset and wrecked the car; then was dire confusion, axle-boxes and linchpins springing into the air. While he, poor youth, entangled in the reins was dragged along, bound by a stubborn knot, his poor head dashed against the rocks, his flesh all torn, the while he cried out piteously, "Stay, stay, my horses whom my own hand hath fed at the manger, destroy me not utterly. O luckless curse of a father! Will no one come and save me for all my virtue?" Now we, though much we longed to help, were left far behind. At last, I know not how, he broke loose from the shapely reins that bound him, a faint breath of life still in him; but the horses disappeared, and that portentous bull, among the rocky ground, I know not where. I am but a slave in thy house, 'tis true, O king, yet will I never believe so monstrous a charge against thy son's character, no! not though the whole race of womankind should hang itself, or one should fill with writing every pine-tree tablet grown on Ida, sure as I am of his uprightness.

LEADER. Alas! new troubles come to plague us, nor is there any escape from fate and necessity.

THESEUS. My hatred for him who hath thus suffered made me glad at thy tidings, yet from regard for the gods and him, because he is my son, I feel neither joy nor sorrow at his sufferings.

MESSENGER. But say, are we to bring the victim hither, or how are we to fulfil thy wishes? Bethink thee; if by me thou wilt be schooled, thou wilt not harshly treat thy son in his sad plight.

THESEUS. Bring him hither, that when I see him face to face, who hath denied having polluted my wife's honour, I may by words and heaven's visitation convict him.   (*Exit* MESSENGER.)

CHORUS. Ah! Cypris, thine the hand that guides the stubborn hearts of gods and men; thine, and that attendant boy's, who, with painted plumage gay, flutters round his victims on lightning wing. O'er the land and booming deep on golden pinion borne flits the god of Love, maddening the heart and beguiling the senses of all whom he attacks, savage whelps on mountains bred, ocean's monsters, creatures of this sun-warmed earth, and man; thine, O Cypris, thine alone the sovereign power to rule them all.

(ARTEMIS *appears above.*)

ARTEMIS. Hearken, I bid thee, noble son of Aegeus: lo! 'tis I, Latona's child, that speak, I, Artemis. Why, Theseus, to thy sorrow dost thou rejoice at these tidings, seeing that thou hast slain thy son most impiously, listening to a charge not clearly proved, but falsely sworn to by thy wife? though clearly has the curse therefrom upon thee fallen. Why dost thou not

GREECE AND THE BIRTH OF THE WEST

for very shame hide beneath the dark places of the earth, or change thy human life and soar on wings to escape this tribulation? 'Mongst men of honour thou hast now no share in life.

Hearken, Theseus; I will put thy wretched case. Yet will it naught avail thee, if I do, but vex thy heart; still with this intent I came, to show thy son's pure heart,—that he may die with honour,—as well the frenzy and, in a sense, the nobleness of thy wife; for she was cruelly stung with a passion for thy son by that goddess whom all we, that joy in virgin purity, detest. And though she strove to conquer love by resolution, yet by no fault of hers she fell, thanks to her nurse's strategy, who did reveal her malady unto thy son under oath. But he would none of her counsels, as indeed was right, nor yet, when thou didst revile him, would he break the oath he swore, from piety. She meantime, fearful of being found out, wrote a lying letter, destroying by guile thy son, but yet persuading thee.

THESEUS. Woe is me!

ARTEMIS. Doth my story wound thee, Theseus? Be still awhile; hear what follows, so wilt thou have more cause to groan. Dost remember those three prayers thy father granted thee, fraught with certain issue? 'Tis one of these thou hast misused, unnatural wretch, against thy son, instead of aiming it at an enemy. Thy sea-god sire, 'tis true, for all his kind intent, hath granted that boon he was compelled, by reason of his promise, to grant. But thou alike in his eyes and in mine hast shewn thy evil heart, in that thou hast forestalled all proof or voice prophetic, hast made no inquiry, nor taken time for consideration, but with undue haste cursed thy son even to the death.

THESEUS. Perdition seize me! Queen revered!

ARTEMIS. An awful deed was thine, but still even for this thou mayest obtain pardon; for it was Cypris that would have it so, sating the fury of her soul. For this is law amongst us gods; none of us will thwart his neighbour's will, but ever we stand aloof. For be well assured, did I not fear Zeus, never would I have incurred the bitter shame of handing over to death a man of all his kind to me most dear. As for thy sin, first thy ignorance absolves thee from its villainy, next thy wife, who is dead, was lavish in her use of convincing arguments to influence thy mind. On thee in chief this storm of woe hath burst, yet is it some grief to me as well; for when the righteous die, there is no joy in heaven, albeit we try to destroy the wicked, house and home.

CHORUS. Lo! where he comes, this hapless youth, his fair young flesh and auburn locks most shamefully handled. Unhappy house! what twofold sorrow doth o'ertake its halls, through heaven's ordinance!

(HIPPOLYTUS enters, assisted by his attendants.)

HIPPOLYTUS. Ah! ah! woe is me! foully undone by an impious father's impious imprecation! Undone, undone! woe is me! Through my head shoot fearful pains; my brain throbs convulsively. Stop, let me rest my worn-out frame. Oh, oh! Accursed steeds, that mine own hand did feed, ye have been my ruin and my death. O by the gods, good sirs, I beseech ye, softly touch my wounded limbs. Who stands there at my right side? Lift me tenderly; with slow and even step conduct a poor wretch cursed by his mistaken sire. Great Zeus, dost thou see this? Me thy reverent worshipper, me who left all men behind in purity, plunged thus into yawning Hades 'neath the earth, reft of life; in vain the toils I have endured through my piety towards mankind. Ah me! ah me! O the thrill of anguish shooting through me! Set me down, poor wretch I am; come Death to set me free! Kill me, end my sufferings. O for a sword two-edged to hack my flesh, and close this mortal life! Ill-fated curse of my father! the crimes of bloody kinsmen, ancestors of old, now pass their boundaries and tarry not, and upon me are they come all guiltless as I am; ah! why? Alas, alas! what can I say? How from my life get rid of this relentless agony? O that the stern Death-god, night's black visitant, would give my sufferings rest!

ARTEMIS. Poor sufferer! cruel the fate that links thee to it! Thy noble soul hath been thy ruin.

HIPPOLYTUS. Ah! the fragrance from my goddess wafted! Even in my agony I feel thee near and find relief; she is here in this very place, my goddess Artemis.

ARTEMIS. She is, poor sufferer! the goddess thou hast loved the best.

HIPPOLYTUS. Dost see me, mistress mine? dost see my present suffering?

ARTEMIS. I see thee, but mine eyes no tear may weep.

HIPPOLYTUS. Thou hast none now to lead the hunt or tend thy fane.

ARTEMIS. None now; yet e'en in death I love thee still.

HIPPOLYTUS. None to groom thy steeds, or guard thy shrines.

ARTEMIS. 'Twas Cypris, mistress of iniquity, devised this evil.

HIPPOLYTUS. Ah me! now know I the goddess who destroyed me.

ARTEMIS. She was jealous of her slighted honour, vexed at thy chaste life.

HIPPOLYTUS. Ah! then I see her single hand hath struck down three of us.

ARTEMIS. Thy sire and thee, and last thy father's wife.

HIPPOLYTUS. My sire's ill-luck as well as mine I mourn.

ARTEMIS. He was deceived by a goddess's design.

HIPPOLYTUS. Woe is thee, my father, in this sad mischance!

THESEUS. My son, I am a ruined man; life has no joys for me.

HIPPOLYTUS. For this mistake I mourn thee rather than myself.

THESEUS. O that I had died for thee, my son!

HIPPOLYTUS. Ah! those fatal gifts thy sire Poseidon gave.

THESEUS. Would God these lips had never uttered that prayer!

HIPPOLYTUS. Why not? thou wouldst in any case have slain me in thy fury then.

THESEUS. Yes; Heaven had perverted my power to think.

HIPPOLYTUS. O that the race of men could bring a curse upon the gods!

ARTEMIS. Enough! for though thou pass to gloom beneath the earth, the wrath of Cypris shall not, at her will, fall on thee unrequited, because thou hadst a noble righteous soul. For I with mine own hand will with these unerring shafts avenge me on another, who is her votary, dearest to her of all the sons of men. And to thee, poor sufferer, for thy anguish now will I grant high honours in the city of Troezen; for thee shall maids unwed before their marriage cut off their hair, thy harvest through the long roll of time of countless bitter tears. Yea, and for ever shall the virgin choir hymn thy sad memory, nor shall Phaedra's love for thee fall into oblivion and pass away unnoticed. But thou, O son of old Aegeus, take thy son in thine arms, draw him close to thee, for unwittingly thou slewest him, and men may well commit an error when gods put it in their way. And thee Hippolytus, I admonish; hate not thy sire, for in this death thou dost but meet thy destined fate. And now farewell! 'tis not for me to gaze upon the dead, or pollute my sight with death-scenes, and e'en now I see thee nigh that evil.

(ARTEMIS *vanishes.*)

HIPPOLYTUS. Farewell, blest virgin queen! leave me now! How easily thou resignest our long friendship! I am reconciled with my father at thy desire, yea, for ever before I would obey thy bidding. Ah me! the darkness is settling even now upon my eyes. Take me, father, in thy arms, lift me up.

THESEUS. Woe is me, my son! what art thou doing to me thy hapless sire!

HIPPOLYTUS. I am a broken man; yes, I see the gates that close upon the dead.

THESEUS. Canst leave me thus with murder on my soul!

HIPPOLYTUS. No, no; I set thee free from this bloodguiltiness.

21–22. **For I . . . another.** Artemis will have a boar give a fatal wound to Adonis, beloved of Aphrodite, in revenge for the death of Hippolytus.

THESEUS. What sayest thou? dost absolve me from bloodshed?

HIPPOLYTUS. Artemis, the archer-queen, is my witness that I do.

THESEUS. My own dear child, how generous dost thou show thyself to thy father!

HIPPOLYTUS. Farewell, dear father! a long farewell to thee! 60

THESEUS. O that holy, noble soul of thine!

HIPPOLYTUS. Pray to have children such as me born in lawful wedlock.

THESEUS. O leave me not, my son; endure awhile.

HIPPOLYTUS. 'Tis finished, my endurance; I die, father; quickly cover my face with a mantle.

THESEUS. O glorious Athens, realm of Pallas, what a splendid hero ye have lost! Ah me, ah me! How 70 oft shall I remember thy evil works, O Cypris!

CHORUS. On all our citizens hath come this universal sorrow, unforeseen. Now shall the copious tear gush forth, for sad news about great men takes more than usual hold upon the heart.

Aristophanes

c. 446–c. 386 B.C.

The social, political, and intellectual changes that beset Athens in the later fifth century were variously received by her citizens. The Sophist philosophers and Cleon, the democratic politician, saw practical advantages in the new liberalism. Euripides and Socrates, though critical of the old tradition, sought a new morality more acceptable to their generation. Thucydides, the detached historian of his day, was caught up in the new intellectual currents and yet was grimly pessimistic about the future of a state that had chosen this very path. It remained for Aristophanes, the archconservative, to voice the militant alarm of the landed aristocracy in an era of atheism, radical democracy, and costly war. It is a tribute to the political freedom of his time that this raucous spokesman for the tory minority was allowed with almost complete impunity to pour abuse on his contemporaries in play after play.

Just why Aristophanes embraced the cause of the conservatives so passionately is hard to determine on the basis of the scanty records of his life. Although his family owned a tract of land in Aegina, he was apparently not of Athenian stock and for a time had to produce his comedies under the names of others. Cleon, the demagogue who succeeded Pericles, tried to prosecute his persistent foe on the technicality of his alien birth, but the great popularity of Aristophanes in Athens guaranteed his immunity. His conservatism was probably an ingrained bias.

Goldwater

He was not a profound thinker and had no positive program of reform. He followed the negative policy of condemning change regardless of its merits and demanding a return to the old merely because it recalled security and happier times.

The Old Comedy tradition of Athens offered Aristophanes an ideal instrument for his attack. Still preserving the reckless abandon of Dionysian revelry, the comic festival sanctioned all manner of rough-and-tumble farce, indecent dialogue, and shocking personal satire. Though the sober bigwigs grew uneasy at its moral license and outrageous pasquinade, the populace favored the ancient institution as a social safety valve not unlike the Mardi Gras of New Orleans and carnivals throughout the world. The comedies of Aristophanes shamelessly introduce Socrates, Euripides, and other butts of his ridicule in their own guise and involve them in low comedy situations in which they are discredited by fictitious characters embodying his own common sense. Even the gods, such as Dionysus in *The Frogs*, may be honored as buffoons in this perverse kind of drama, which tries at every point to be the complete antithesis of lofty tragedy. And yet imbedded in the topsy-turvy antics are earnest ideas and some of the most exquisite lyrics in Greek literature. As if anything can be expected here but the expected, Aristophanes sandwiches cheek-and-jowl hilarious farce, serious satire, and the most exalted choral poetry.

Growing up in the early years of the Peloponnesian War, Aristophanes became convinced that this fruitless struggle was bringing ruin to all of Greece. Although begun under the enlightened Pericles, the war was now protracted by Cleon, a democratic imperialist, with his ruthless insistence on total victory. Aristophanes opened his career with a series of comedies satirizing the war and especially Cleon, whom he held responsible for it. *The Babylonians* (426 B.C.), now lost, condemned the cruelty of Athenian rule of lesser states, and *The Acharnians* showed the amusing advantages enjoyed by one Athenian citizen who made a private peace with Sparta. In *The Knights,* the first play produced under the playwright's own name, Cleon—a leather-seller by trade—finds his political chicanery excelled by a sausage-seller, who thereby wins the government. An armistice the next year and the death of Cleon a year later ended this series. In 416 B.C. the government forbade the lampooning of living politicians on the stage.

Aristophanes assumed a milder manner, but in *The Birds* and *Lysistrata* he continued through fantasy and bawdy farce his plea for peace. Eventually he turned his conservative disapproval on yet another intellectual, Euripides, whose sacrilegious versions of hallowed myths he condemned as bad art and a dangerous undermining of the traditions of the state. In *The Frogs* (405 B.C.), written a year after the death of Euripides, the god Dionysus journeys to Hades to bring back a worthy playwright to relight the fires of tragedy. After listening to a debate between Aeschylus and Euripides in which sharp criticism is exchanged, he chooses Aeschylus over the bumptious, opinionated Euripides. Although *The Frogs* competes with *The Clouds* as Aristophanes' masterpiece, it depends for its delightful effect on literary points difficult for the layman to interpret. The later plays of Aristophanes, such as *Plutus* (388 B.C.), are playful satires on society as a whole, that look toward the inoffensive school of Middle Comedy, divorced from personal satire and brash vulgarity. The New Comedy of Menander in the fourth century completes the transition to an urbane comedy of manners close to our own in spirit.

The Clouds is probably the masterpiece of Aristophanes and certainly his most influential work. Although it was awarded only a third prize in its original version (423 B.C.), he rewrote it into something like its present form, and as such it was his own favorite among his comedies. The reasons are easy to find. It is the most intellectual of his plays, the most divorced from buffoonery, and it attacks what he thought to be the root of social decay in his time: an educational system that was leading to slick cynicism rather than to reform of morals at home and abroad. Socrates was the most conspicuous and most colorful of the teachers of Athens, and Aristophanes chose him as a symbol of the new-style education and philosophy. Actually he was far from being a spokesman for the Sophistic teachings credited to him in this play. The ideas travestied in the dialogue were derived from other, more strictly pragmatic philosophers; and of course Socrates never kept a school and prided himself on never teaching for pay.

Borrowing Socrates' famous name, Aristophanes made him a composite figure, with the master's personal traits for humor but with the ideas and practices of the whole group, most of whom Socrates disliked as heartily as did Aristophanes. Indeed, Plato's *Symposium* indicates that the two men were good friends, and the earlier version of *The Clouds* was certainly more friendly to Socrates than is the present one. The blight of this play on Socrates' reputation was severe and permanent, and at his trial for his life a quarter of a century later Plato reports that Socrates defended himself against this gross misrepresentation of what he stood for.

It is illuminating to place side by side Plato's idealized portrait of his master and Aristophanes' caricature. Somewhere between the two must have lain the real Socrates, who unfortunately left no writing to speak for him directly. Since later generations have followed Plato in sentimentalizing him as the symbol of man's free search for truth, it does no harm to be reminded of a counterview.

Aristophanes' play is shot through with prejudice and pettiness. His attack on the scientific explanation of natural phenomena in the school scene seems embarrassingly unenlightened today, and attributing to Socrates Protagoras' boast to make the unjust argument sound better than the just is a rank libel. But the conservative social critic was right in deciding that the era of speculation was destroying the moral stamina of the Greek people, and Socrates was certainly a leader in the whole movement. Regardless of its fairness or lack of it, this skit is one of the greatest personal satires in literature.

The Clouds

CHARACTERS IN THE PLAY

STREPSIADES
PHEIDIPPIDES, *his son*
SERVANT OF STREPSIADES
SOCRATES
DISCIPLES OF SOCRATES
RIGHT LOGIC
WRONG LOGIC
PASIAS, *a money-lender*
AMYNIAS, *another money-lender*
CHORUS OF CLOUDS

SCENE: *A street in Athens with two houses, that of* STREPSIADES *and that of* SOCRATES. *A room in the former is open to view, revealing two beds occupied by* STREPSIADES *and* PHEIDIPPIDES.

STREPSIADES.

O DEAR! O dear!
   O Lord! O Zeus! these nights, how long they are.
Will they ne'er pass? will the day never come?
Surely I heard the cock crow, hours ago.
Yet still my servants snore. These are new customs. 5
O 'ware of war for many various reasons;
One fears in war even to flog one's servants.
And here's this hopeful son of mine wrapped up
Snoring and sweating under five thick blankets.
Come, we'll wrap up and snore in opposition. 10
                (*Tries to sleep*)
But I can't sleep a wink, devoured and bitten
By ticks, and bugbears, duns, and race-horses,
All through this son of mine. *He* curls his hair,
And sports his thoroughbreds, and drives his tandem;
Even in dreams he rides: while I—I'm ruined, 15
Now that the Moon has reached her twentieths,
And paying-time comes on. Boy! light a lamp,
And fetch my ledger: now I'll reckon up
Who are my creditors, and what I owe them.
Come, let me see then. *Fifty pounds to Pasias!* 20
Why fifty pounds to Pasias? what were they for?
O, for the hack from Corinth. O dear! O dear!
I wish my eye had been hacked out before—
   PHEIDIPPIDES (*in his sleep*). You are cheating,
     Philon; keep to your own side.

STREPSIADES. Ah! there it is! that's what has ruined
   me! 25
Even in his very sleep he thinks of horses.
   PHEIDIPPIDES (*in his sleep*). How many heats do
     the war-chariots run?
   STREPSIADES. A pretty many heats you have run
     your father.
Now then, what debt assails me after Pasias?
A curricle and wheels. Twelve pounds. Amynias. 30
   PHEIDIPPIDES (*in his sleep*). Here, give the horse
     a roll, and take him home.
   STREPSIADES. You have rolled me *out* of house and
     home, my boy,
Cast in some suits already, while some swear
They'll seize my goods for payment.
   PHEIDIPPIDES.   Good, my father,
What makes you toss so restless all night long? 35
   STREPSIADES. There's a bumbailiff from the mattress bites me.
   PHEIDIPPIDES. Come now, I prithee, let me sleep
     in peace.
   STREPSIADES. Well then, you sleep; only be sure of
     this,
These debts will fall on your own head at last.
Alas, alas! 40
For ever cursed be that same match-maker,
Who stirred me up to marry your poor mother.
Mine in the country was the pleasantest life,
Untidy, easy-going, unrestrained,
Brimming with olives, sheepfolds, honey-bees. 45
Ah! then I married—I a rustic—her
A fine town-lady, niece of Megacles.
A regular, proud, luxurious, Coesyra.
This wife I married, and we came together, 49
I rank with wine-lees, fig-boards, greasy woolpacks;
She all with scents, and saffron, and tongue-kissings,
Feasting, expense, and lordly modes of loving.
She was not idle though, she was too fast.
I used to tell her, holding out my cloak, 54
Threadbare and worn; *Wife, you're too fast by half.*
   SERVANT-BOY. Here's no more oil remaining in the
     lamp.
   STREPSIADES. O me! what made you light the tippling lamp?
Come and be whipp'd.
   SERVANT-BOY.   Why, what would you whip me
     for?
   STREPSIADES. Why did you put one of those thick
     wicks in?
Well, when at last to me and my good woman 60
This hopeful son was born, our son and heir,
Why then we took to wrangle on the name.

The Clouds. Translated by B. Bickley Rogers. Reprinted by permission of G. Bell and Sons, Ltd.
17. **And paying-time comes on.** Interest on debts had to be paid on the first of the month. 22. **hack,** horse.

47–48. **A . . . Coesyra.** The aristocratic Megacleid family included Pericles and Alcibiades and was descended from Coesyra, distinguished for her pride and love of luxury. 50. **fig-boards,** boards for drying figs in the sun.

She was for giving him some knightly name,
"Callippides," "Xanthippus," or "Charippus":
I wished "Pheidonides," his grandsire's name. 65
Thus for some time we argued: till at last
We compromised it in Pheidippides.
This boy she took, and used to spoil him, saying,
Oh! when you are driving to the Acropolis, clad
Like Megacles, in your purple; whilst I said 70
Oh! when the goats you are driving from the fells,
Clad like your father, in your sheepskin coat.
Well, he cared nought for my advice, but soon
A galloping consumption caught my fortunes.
Now cogitating all night long, I've found 75
One way, one marvellous transcendent way,
Which if he'll follow, we may yet be saved.
So,—but, however, I must rouse him first;
But how to rouse him kindliest? that's the rub.
Pheidippides, my sweet one.

PHEIDIPPIDES.   Well, my father. 80

STREPSIADES. Shake hands, Pheidippides, shake
hands and kiss me.

PHEIDIPPIDES. There; what's the matter?

STREPSIADES.   Dost thou love me, boy?

PHEIDIPPIDES. Ay! by Poseidon there, the God of
horses.

STREPSIADES. No, no, not that: miss out the God
of horses,
That God's the origin of all my evils. 85
But if you love me from your heart and soul,
My son, obey me.

PHEIDIPPIDES.   Very well: what in?

STREPSIADES. Strip with all speed, strip off your
present habits,
And go and learn what I'll advise you to.

PHEIDIPPIDES. Name your commands.

STREPSIADES.   Will you obey?

PHEIDIPPIDES.   I will, by Dionysus! 90

STREPSIADES. Well then, look this way.
See you that wicket and the lodge beyond?

PHEIDIPPIDES. I see: and prithee what is that, my
father?

STREPSIADES. That is the thinking-house of sapient
souls.
There dwell the men who teach—aye, who persuade
us, 95
That Heaven is one vast fire-extinguisher
Placed round about us, and that we're the cinders.
Aye, and they'll teach (only they'll want some
money),
How one may speak and conquer, right or wrong.

PHEIDIPPIDES. Come, tell their names.

STREPSIADES.   Well, I can't
quite remember, 100
But they're deep thinkers, and true gentlemen.

PHEIDIPPIDES. Out on the rogues! I know them.
Those rank pedants,
Those palefaced, barefoot vagabonds you mean:
That Socrates, poor wretch, and Chaerephon.

STREPSIADES. Oh! Oh! hush! hush! don't use those
foolish words; 105
But if the sorrows of my barley touch you,
Enter their Schools and cut the Turf for ever.

PHEIDIPPIDES. I wouldn't go, so help me Dionysus,
For all Leogoras's breed of Phasians!

STREPSIADES. Go, I beseech you, dearest, dearest
son, 110
Go and be taught.

PHEIDIPPIDES. And what would you have me learn?

STREPSIADES. 'Tis known that in their Schools they
keep two Logics,
The Worse, Zeus save the mark, the Worse and
Better.
This Second Logic then, I mean the Worse one,
They teach to talk unjustly and—prevail. 115
Think then, you only learn that Unjust Logic,
And all the debts, which I have incurred through
you,—
I'll never pay, no, not one farthing of them.

PHEIDIPPIDES. I will not go. How could I face the
knights
With all my colour worn and torn away! 120

STREPSIADES. O! then, by Earth, you have eat your
last of mine,
You, and your coach-horse, and your sigma-brand:
Out with you! Go to the crows, for all I care.

PHEIDIPPIDES. But uncle Megacles won't leave me
long
Without a horse: I'll go to him: good-bye. 125
                    (*He leaves.*)

STREPSIADES. I'm thrown, by Zeus, but I won't
long lie prostrate.
I'll pray the Gods and send myself to school:
I'll go at once and try their thinking-house.
Stay: how can I, forgetful, slow, old fool,
Learn the nice hair-splittings of subtle Logic? 130
Well, go I must. 'Twont do to linger here.
Come on, I'll knock the door. Boy! Ho there, boy!
    (STREPSIADES *goes to the house of* SOCRATES.)

STUDENT (*within*). O, hang it all! who's knocking
at the door?

STREPSIADES. Me! Pheidon's son: Strepsiades of
Cicynna.

STUDENT. Why, what a clown you are! to kick our
door, 135
In such a thoughtless, inconsiderate way!
You've made my cogitation to miscarry.

65. **Pheidonides,** which means "son of thrift." 67. **Pheidippides.**
The composite name ludicrously combined the grandfather's thrift
and the mother's aristocratic squandering.

104. **Chaerephon,** companion of Socrates for many years. 106. **sorrows of my barley;** as a rustic, Strepsiades thinks of his property in
terms of grain. 109. **Leogoras's breed of Phasians,** pheasants bred
by the luxurious idler, Leogoras. 119–120. **How . . . away!** He
means facing his aristocratic friends with his complexion ruined by
study.

STREPSIADES. Forgive me: I'm an awkward country fool.
But tell me, what was that I made miscarry?
  STUDENT. 'Tis not allowed: Students alone may hear. 140
  STREPSIADES. O that's all ~ ': you may tell *me*:
    I'm come
To be a student in ~ _king-house.
  STUDENT. Co~ . But they're high mysteries,
    reme~
'Twas S~ was asking Chaerephon,
How ~ eet of its own a flea could jump. 145
For o~ first bit the brow of Chaerephon,
Then bounded off to Socrates's head.
  STREPSIADES. How did he measure this?
  STUDENT.   Most cleverly.
He warmed some wax, and then he caught the flea,
And dipped its feet into the wax he'd melted: 150
Then let it cool, and there were Persian slippers!
These he took off, and so he found the distance.
  STREPSIADES. O Zeus and king, what subtle intellects!
  STUDENT. What would you say then if you heard another,
Our Master's own?
  STREPSIADES.   O come, do tell me that. 155
  STUDENT. Why, Chaerephon was asking him in turn,
Which theory did he sanction; that the gnats
Hummed through their mouth, or backwards, through the tail?
  STREPSIADES. Aye, and what said your Master of the gnat?
  STUDENT. He answered thus: the entrail of the gnat 160
Is small: and through this narrow pipe the wind
Rushes with violence straight towards the tail;
There, close against the pipe, the hollow rump
Receives the wind, and whistles to the blast.
  STREPSIADES. So then the rump is trumpet to the gnats! 165
O happy, happy in your entrail-learning!
Full surely need he fear nor debts nor duns,
Who knows about the entrails of the gnats.
  STUDENT. And yet last night a mighty thought we lost
Through a green lizard.
  STREPSIADES.   Tell me, how was that? 170
  STUDENT. Why, as Himself, with eyes and mouth wide open,
Mused on the moon, her paths and revolutions,
A lizard from the roof squirted full on him.
  STREPSIADES. He, he, he, he. I like the lizard's spattering Socrates.
  STUDENT. Then yesterday, poor we, we'd got no dinner. 175

152. **found,** measured.

STREPSIADES. Hah! what did he devise to do for barley?
  STUDENT. He sprinkled on the table—some fine ash—
He bent a spit—he grasped it compass-wise—
And—filched a mantle from the Wrestling School.
  STREPSIADES. Good heavens! Why Thales was a fool to this! 180
O open, open, wide the study door,
And show me, show me, show me Socrates.
I die to be a student. Open, open!
(*The interior of Socrates' house is opened to view.*)
O Heracles, what kind of beasts are these!
  STUDENT. Why, what's the matter? what do you think they're like? 185
  STREPSIADES. Like? why those Spartans whom we brought from Pylus:
What makes them fix their eyes so on the ground?
  STUDENT. They seek things underground.
  STREPSIADES.   O! to be sure,
Truffles! You there, don't trouble about that!
I'll tell you where the best and finest grow. 190
Look! why do those stoop down so very much?
  STUDENT. They're diving deep into the deepest secrets.
  STREPSIADES. Then why's their rump turned up towards the sky?
  STUDENT. It's taking private lessons on the stars.
                  (*To the other Students*)
Come, come: get in: HE'll catch us presently. 195
  STREPSIADES. Not yet! not yet! just let them stop one moment,
While I impart a little matter to them.
  STUDENT. No, no: they must go in: 'twould never do
To expose themselves too long to the open air.
  STREPSIADES. O! by the Gods, now, what are these? do tell me. 200
  STUDENT. This is Astronomy.
  STREPSIADES.   And what is this?
  STUDENT. Geometry.
  STREPSIADES.   Well, what's the use of that?
  STUDENT. To mete out lands.
  STREPSIADES.   What, for allotment grounds?
  STUDENT. No, but all lands.
  STREPSIADES.   A choice idea, truly.
Then every man may take his choice, you mean. 205
  STUDENT. Look; here's a chart of the whole world.
    Do you see?
This city's Athens.

179. **And . . . Wrestling School.** Apparently the supercilious student is mystifying the rustic Strepsiades with nonsense. 180. **Thales,** the philosopher, here symbolizing wisdom. 186–187. **those Spartans . . . Pylus,** war-prisoners. 203. **allotment grounds,** conquered lands allotted to Athenian citizens.

STREPSIADES. Athens? I like that.
I see no dicasts sitting. That's not Athens.

STUDENT. In very truth, this is the Attic ground.

STREPSIADES. And where then are my townsmen of
Cicynna? 210

STUDENT. Why, thereabouts; and here, you see,
Euboea:
Here, reaching out a long way by the shore.

STREPSIADES. Yes, overreached by us and Pericles.
But now, where's Sparta?

STUDENT. Let me see: O, here.

STREPSIADES. Heavens! how near us. O do please
manage this, 215
To shove her off from us, a long way further.

STUDENT. We can't do that, by Zeus.

STREPSIADES. The worse for
you.
Hallo! who's that? that fellow in the basket?

STUDENT. That's he.

STREPSIADES. Who's HE?

STUDENT. Socrates.

STREPSIADES. Socrates!
You sir, call out to him as loud as you can. 220

STUDENT. Call him yourself: I have not leisure
now.

STREPSIADES. Socrates! Socrates!
Sweet Socrates!

SOCRATES. Mortal! why call'st thou me?

STREPSIADES. O, first of all, please tell me what
you are doing.

SOCRATES. I walk on air, and contem-plate the
Sun. 225

STREPSIADES. O then from a basket you contemn
the Gods,
And not from the earth, at any rate?

SOCRATES. Most true.
I could not have searched out celestial matters
Without suspending judgement, and infusing
My subtle spirit with the kindred air. 230
If from the ground I were to seek these things,
I could not find: so surely doth the earth
Draw to herself the essence of our thought.
The same too is the case with water-cress.

STREPSIADES. Hillo! what's that? 235
Thought draws the essence into water-cress?
Come down, sweet Socrates, more near my level,
And teach the lessons which I come to learn.

SOCRATES. And wherefore art thou come?

STREPSIADES. To learn to speak.
For owing to my horrid debts and duns, 240
My goods are seized, I'm robbed, and mobbed, and
plundered.

SOCRATES. How did you get involved with your
eyes open?

STREPSIADES. A galloping consumption seized my
money.
Come now: do let me learn the unjust Logic
That can shirk debts: now do just let me learn it.
Name your own price, by all the Gods I'll pay it. 246

SOCRATES. The Gods! why you must know the
Gods with us
Don't pass for current coin.

STREPSIADES. Eh? what do you use then?
Have you got iron, as the Byzantines have?

SOCRATES. Come, would you like to learn celestial
matters. 250
How their truth stands?

STREPSIADES. Yes, if there's any truth.

SOCRATES. And to hold intercourse with yon bright
Clouds,
Our virgin Goddesses?

STREPSIADES. Yes, that I should.

SOCRATES. Then sit you down upon that sacred
bed.

STREPSIADES. Well, I am sitting.

SOCRATES. Here then, take
this chaplet. 255

STREPSIADES. Chaplet? why? why? now, never,
Socrates:
Don't sacrifice poor me, like Athamas.

SOCRATES. Fear not: our entrance-services require
All to do this.

STREPSIADES. But what am I to gain?

SOCRATES. You'll be the flower of talkers, prattlers,
gossips: 260
Only keep quiet.

STREPSIADES. Zeus! your words come true!
I shall be flour indeed with all this peppering.

SOCRATES. Old man sit you still, and attend to my
will,
and hearken in peace to my prayer,
O Master and King, holding earth in your swing, 265
O measureless infinite Air;
And thou glowing Ether, and Clouds who enwreathe
her
with thunder, and lightning, and storms,
Arise ye and shine, bright Ladies Divine,
to your student in bodily forms. 270

STREPSIADES. No, but stay, no, but stay, just one
moment I pray,
while my cloak round my temples I wrap.
To think that I've come, stupid fool, from my home,
with never a waterproof cap!

SOCRATES. Come forth, come forth, dread Clouds,
and to earth 275
your glorious majesty show;

208. **I see no dicasts sitting.** It was notorious that a good share of
the Athenian citizenry was constantly doing judicial duty. 213.
overreached, exhausted of tribute by the conquering Athenians.

249. **Have . . . have?** They lacked silver for coins. 257. **Don't
. . . Athamas.** He mistakes the chaplet of initiation for the chaplet
of sacrifice which he has seen on a character in a play by Sophocles.
262. **peppering;** with ceremonial flour.

Whether lightly ye rest on the time-honoured crest
   of Olympus environed in snow,
Or tread the soft dance 'mid the stately expanse
   of Ocean, the nymphs to beguile, 280
Or stoop to enfold with your pitchers of gold,
   the mystical waves of the Nile,
Or around the white foam of Maeotis ye roam,
   or Mimas all wintry and bare,
O hear while we pray, and turn not away 285
  from the rites which your servants prepare.

 CHORUS.   Clouds of all hue,
Rise we aloft with our garments of dew.
Come from old Ocean's unchangeable bed, 289
Come, till the mountain's green summits we tread,
Come to the peaks with their landscapes untold,
Gaze on the Earth with her harvests of gold,
 Gaze on the rivers in majesty streaming,
 Gaze on the lordly, invincible Sea,
Come, for the Eye of the Ether is beaming, 295
 Come, for all Nature is flashing and free.
 Let us shake off this close-clinging dew
 From our members eternally new,
 And sail upwards the wide world to view.
   Come away! Come away! 300

 SOCRATES. O Goddesses mine, great Clouds and
  divine,
   ye have heeded and answered my prayer.
Heard ye their sound, and the thunder around,
   as it thrilled through the tremulous air?
 STREPSIADES. Yes, by Zeus, and I shake, and I'm
  all of a quake, 305
   and I fear I must sound a reply,
Their thunders have made my soul so afraid,
   and those terrible voices so nigh:
So if lawful or not, I must run to a pot,
   by Zeus, if I stop I shall die. 310
 SOCRATES. Don't act in our schools like those Com-
  edy-fools
   with their scurrilous scandalous ways.
Deep silence be thine: while this Cluster divine
   their soul-stirring melody raise.

 CHORUS.   Come then with me, 315
Daughters of Mist, to the land of the free.
Come to the people whom Pallas hath blest,
Come to the soil where the Mysteries rest;
Come, where the glorified Temple invites
The pure to partake of its mystical rites: 320
Holy the gifts that are brought to the Gods,
 Shrines with festoons and with garlands are
  crowned,
Pilgrims resort to the sacred abodes,
 Gorgeous the festivals all the year round.

283, 284. **Maeotis, Mimas,** a remote sea and mountain.

And the Bromian rejoicings in Spring, 325
When the flutes with their deep music ring,
And the sweetly-toned Choruses sing
   Come away! Come away!

 STREPSIADES. O Socrates pray, by all the Gods,
  say,
   for I earnestly long to be told, 330
Who are these that recite with such grandeur and
  might?
   are they glorified mortals of old?
 SOCRATES. No mortals are there, but Clouds of the
  air,
   great Gods who the indolent fill:
These grant us discourse, and logical force, 335
   and the art of persuasion instil,
And periphrasis strange, and a power to arrange,
   and a marvellous judgement and skill.
 STREPSIADES. So then when I heard their omnipotent word,
   my spirit felt all of a flutter, 340
And it yearns to begin subtle cobwebs to spin
   and about metaphysics to stutter,
And together to glue an idea or two,
   and battle away in replies:
So if it's not wrong, I earnestly long 345
   to behold them myself with my eyes.
 SOCRATES. Look up in the air, towards Parnes out
  there,
   for I see they will pitch before long
These regions about.
 STREPSIADES.   Where? point me them out.
 SOCRATES. They are drifting, an infinite throng,
And their long shadows quake over valley and
  brake. 351
 STREPSIADES. Why, whatever's the matter to-day?
I can't see, I declare.
 SOCRATES.   By the Entrance; look there!
 STREPSIADES. Ah, I just got a glimpse, by the way.
 SOCRATES. There, now you must see how resplend-
  ent they be, 355
   or your eyes must be pumpkins, I vow.
 STREPSIADES. Ah! I see them proceed; I should
  think so indeed:
   great powers! they fill everything now.
 SOCRATES. So then till this day that celestials were
  they,
   you never imagined or knew? 360
 STREPSIADES. Why, no, on my word, for I always
  had heard
   they were nothing but vapour and dew.
 SOCRATES. O, then I declare, you can't be aware
   that 'tis these who the sophists protect,

325. **Bromian rejoicings in Spring,** the spring festival of Dionysus.
347. **Parnes out there,** an Attic mountain, visible to the theater
audience. 353. **Entrance,** opening which admitted the chorus to the
orchestra.

Prophets sent beyond sea, quacks of every degree,
        fops signet-and-jewel-bedecked, 366
Astrological knaves, and fools who their staves
        of dithyrambs proudly rehearse—
'Tis the Clouds who all these support at their ease,
        because they exalt them in verse. 370
STREPSIADES. 'Tis for this then they write of "the
    on-rushin' might
        o' the light-stappin' rain-drappin' Cloud,"
And the "thousand black curls whilk the Tempest-
    lord whirls,"
        and the "thunder-blast stormy an' loud,"
And "birds o' the sky floatin' upwards on high," 375
        and "air-water leddies" which "droon
Wi' their saft falling dew the gran' Ether sae blue,"
        and then in return they gulp doon
Huge gobbets o' fishes an' bountifu' dishes
        o' mavises prime in their season. 380
SOCRATES. And is it not right such praise to re-
    quite?
STREPSIADES.   Ah, but tell me then what
    is the reason
That if, as you say, they are Clouds, they to-day
        as women appear to our view?
For the ones in the air are not women, I swear. 385
SOCRATES.   Why, what do they seem
    then to you?
STREPSIADES. I can't say very well, but they strag-
    gle and swell
        like fleeces spread out in the air;
Not like women they flit, no, by Zeus, not a bit,
        but these have got noses to wear. 390
SOCRATES. Well, now then, attend to this question,
    my friend.
STREPSIADES.   Look sharp, and propound
    it to me.
SOCRATES. Didst thou never espy a Cloud in the
    sky,
        which a centaur or leopard might be,
Or a wolf, or a cow?
STREPSIADES.   Very often, I vow: 395
        and show me the cause, I entreat.
SOCRATES. Why, I tell you that these become just
    what they please,
        and whenever they happen to meet
One shaggy and wild, like the tangle-haired child
    of old Xenophantes, their rule 400
Is at once to appear like Centaurs, to jeer
        the ridiculous look of the fool.
STREPSIADES. What then do they do if Simon they
    view,
        that fraudulent harpy to shame?
SOCRATES. Why, his nature to show to us mortals
    below, 405
        a wolfish appearance they frame.

399. **tangle-haired child of old Xenophantes,** Hieronymus, a dithyrambic poet. 403. **Simon,** probably a minor Sophist.

STREPSIADES. O, they then I ween having yester-
    day seen
        Cleonymus quaking with fear,
(Him who threw off his shield as he fled from the
    field),
        metamorphosed themselves into deer. 410
SOCRATES. Yes, and now they espy soft Cleisthenes
    nigh,
        and therefore as women appear.
STREPSIADES. O then without fail, All hail! and
    All hail!
        my welcome receive; and reply
With your voices so fine, so grand and divine, 415
        majestical Queens of the Sky!
CHORUS. Our welcome to thee, old man, who
    wouldst see
        the marvels that science can show:
And thou, the high-priest of this subtlety feast,
    say what would you have us bestow? 420
Since there is not a sage for whom we'd engage
        our wonders more freely to do,
Except, it may be, for Prodicus; he
    for his knowledge may claim them, but you,
For that sideways you throw your eyes as you go,
        and are all affectation and fuss; 426
No shoes will you wear, but assume the grand air
    on the strength of your dealings with us.
STREPSIADES. O Earth! what a sound, how august
    and profound!
        it fills me with wonder and awe. 430
SOCRATES. These, these then alone, for true Dei-
    ties own,
        the rest are all Godships of straw.
STREPSIADES. Let Zeus be left out: He's a God
    beyond doubt:
        come, that you can scarcely deny.
SOCRATES. Zeus, indeed! there's no Zeus: don't
    you be so obtuse. 435
STREPSIADES.   No Zeus up aloft in the sky!
Then, you first must explain, who it is sends the
    rain;
        or I really must think you are wrong.
SOCRATES. Well then, be it known, these send it
    alone:
        I can prove it by arguments strong. 440
Was there ever a shower seen to fall in an hour
        when the sky was all cloudless and blue?
Yet on a fine day, when the Clouds are away,
        he might send one, according to you.
STREPSIADES. Well, it must be confessed, that
    chimes in with the rest: 445
        your words I am forced to believe.
Yet before, I had dreamed that the rain-water
    streamed
        from Zeus and his chamber-pot sieve.

411. **soft Cleisthenes,** an effeminate debauchee, probably in the
theater at the time. 423. **Prodicus,** the best of the Sophists.

But whence then, my friend, does the thunder descend?
        that does make me quake with affright!
SOCRATES. Why 'tis they, I declare, as they roll through the air.   451
STREPSIADES.   What the Clouds? did I hear you aright?
SOCRATES. Ay: for when to the brim filled with water they swim,
        by Necessity carried along,
They are hung up on high in the vault of the sky,
        and so by Necessity strong   456
In the midst of their course, they clash with great force,
        and thunder away without end.
STREPSIADES. But is it not He who compels this to be?
        does not Zeus this Necessity send?   460
SOCRATES. No Zeus have we there, but a Vortex of air.
STREPSIADES.   What! Vortex? that's something, I own.
I knew not before, that Zeus was no more,
        but Vortex was placed on his throne!
But I have not yet heard to what cause you referred   465
        the thunder's majestical roar.
SOCRATES. Yes, 'tis they, when on high full of water they fly,
        and then, as I told you before,
By Compression impelled, as they clash, are compelled
        a terrible clatter to make.   470
STREPSIADES. Come, how can that be? I really don't see.
SOCRATES.   Yourself as my proof I will take.
Have you never then eat the broth-puddings you get
        when the Panathenaea comes round,
And felt with what might your bowels all night   475
        in turbulent tumult resound?
STREPSIADES. By Apollo, 'tis true, there's a mighty to-do,
        and my belly keeps rumbling about;
And the puddings begin to clatter within
        and kick up a wonderful rout: 480
Quite gently at first, papapax, papapax,
        but soon pappapappax away,
Till at last, I'll be bound, I can thunder as loud,
        papapappappapappax, as They.
SOCRATES. Shalt thou then a sound so loud and profound   485
        from thy belly diminutive send,
And shall not the high and the infinite Sky
        go thundering on without end?

For both, you will find, on an impulse of wind
        and similar causes depend.   490
STREPSIADES. Well, but tell me from Whom comes the bolt through the gloom,
        with its awful and terrible flashes;
And wherever it turns, some it singes and burns,
        and some it reduces to ashes!
For this 'tis quite plain, let who will send the rain,
        that Zeus against perjurers dashes.   496
SOCRATES. And how, you old fool of a dark-ages school,
        and an antediluvian wit,
If the perjured they strike, and not all men alike,
        have they never Cleonymus hit?   500
Then of Simon again, and Theorus explain:
        known perjurers, yet they escape.
But he smites his own shrine with his arrows divine,
        and Sunium, Attica's cape,
And the ancient gnarled oaks: now what prompted those strokes?   505
        They never forswore I should say.
STREPSIADES. Can't say that they do: your words appear true.
        Whence comes then the thunderbolt, pray?
SOCRATES. When a wind that is dry, being lifted on high,
        is suddenly pent into these,   510
It swells up their skin, like a bladder, within,
        by Necessity's changeless decrees:
Till, compressed very tight, it bursts them outright,
        and away with an impulse so strong,
That at last by the force and the swing of its course,
        it takes fire as it whizzes along.   516
STREPSIADES. That's exactly the thing that I suffered one Spring,
        at the great feast of Zeus, I admit:
I'd a paunch in the pot, but I wholly forgot
        about making the safety-valve slit.   520
So it spluttered and swelled, while the saucepan I held,
        till at last with a vengeance it flew:
Took me quite by surprise, dung-bespattered my eyes,
        and scalded my face black and blue!
CHORUS. O thou who wouldst fain great wisdom attain,   525
        and comest to us in thy need,
All Hellas around shall thy glory resound,
        such a prosperous life thou shalt lead:
So thou art but endued with a memory good,
        and accustomed profoundly to think,   530
And thy soul wilt inure all wants to endure,
        and from no undertaking to shrink,
And art hardy and bold, to bear up against cold,
        and with patience a supper thou losest:

---

474. **Panathenaea,** festival at which oxen were sacrificed.

504. **Sunium, Attica's cape,** a promontory in southern Attica.

Nor too much dost incline to gymnastics and wine,
      but all lusts of the body refusest: 536
And esteemest it best, what is always the test
      of a truly intelligent brain,
To prevail and succeed whensoever you plead,
      and hosts of tongue-conquests to gain.
STREPSIADES. But as far as a sturdy soul is con-
    cerned   541
      and a horrible restless care,
And a belly that pines and wears away
      on the wretchedest, frugalest fare,
You may hammer and strike as long as you like;   545
      I am quite invincible there.
SOCRATES. Now then you agree in rejecting
    with me
      the Gods you believed in when young,
And *my* creed you'll embrace "*I believe in wide
space,
      in the Clouds, in the eloquent Tongue.*"
STREPSIADES. If I happened to meet other Gods
    in the street,   551
      I'd show the cold shoulder, I vow.
No libation I'll pour: not one victim more
      on their altars I'll sacrifice now.
CHORUS. Now be honest and true, and say what
    we shall do: 555
      since you never shall fail of our aid,
If you hold us most dear in devotion and fear,
      and will ply the philosopher's trade.
STREPSIADES. O Ladies Divine, small ambition is
    mine:
      I only most modestly seek,   560
Out and out for the rest of my life to be best
      of the children of Hellas to speak.
CHORUS. Say no more of your care, we have
    granted your prayer:
      and know from this moment, that none
More acts shall pass through in the People than
    you: 565
      such favour from us you have won.
STREPSIADES. Not acts, if you please: I want noth-
    ing of these:
      this gift you may quickly withdraw;
But I wish to succeed, just enough for my need,
      and to slip through the clutches of law.
CHORUS. This then you shall do, for your wishes
    are few: 571
      not many nor great your demands,
So away with all care from henceforth, and prepare
      to be placed in our votaries' hands.
STREPSIADES. This then will I do, confiding in you,
    for Necessity presses me sore,   576
And so sad is my life, 'twixt my cobs and my wife,
      that I cannot put up with it more.
So now, at your word, I give and afford
My body to these, to treat as they please,   580
To have and to hold, in squalor, in cold,

In hunger and thirst, yea by Zeus, at the worst,
To be flayed out of shape from my heels to my nape
So along with my hide from my duns I escape,
And to men may appear without conscience or fear,
Bold, hasty, and wise, a concocter of lies,   586
A rattler to speak, a dodger, a sneak,
A regular claw of the tables of law,
A shuffler complete, well worn in deceit,
A supple, unprincipled, troublesome cheat;   590
A hang-dog accurst, a bore with the worst,
In the tricks of the jury-courts thoroughly versed.
If all that I meet this praise shall repeat,
Work away as you choose, I will nothing refuse,
Without any reserve, from my head to my shoes.
You shan't see me wince though my gutlets you
    mince,   596
And these entrails of mine for a sausage combine,
Served up for the gentlemen students to dine.
CHORUS. Here's a spirit bold and high
Ready-armed for any strife.   600
                  (*To* STREPSIADES)
If you learn what I can teach
      Of the mysteries of speech,
Your glory soon shall reach
      To the summit of the sky.
STREPSIADES. And what am I to gain?
CHORUS.   With the Clouds you will obtain
The most happy, the most enviable life.
STREPSIADES. Is it possible for me Such felicity
    to see?   605
CHORUS. Yes, and men shall come and wait
      In their thousands at your gate,
Desiring consultations and advice
On an action or a pleading
      From the man of light and leading,
And you'll pocket many talents in a trice.
                  (*To* SOCRATES)
Here, take the old man, and do all that you can,
    your new-fashioned thoughts to instil,   611
And stir up his mind with your notions refined,
    and test him with judgement and skill.
SOCRATES. Come now, you tell me something of
    your habits:
For if I don't know them, I can't determine   615
What engines I must bring to bear upon you.
STREPSIADES. Eh! what? Not going to storm me,
    by the Gods?
SOCRATES. No, no: I want to ask you a few ques-
    tions.
First: is your memory good?
STREPSIADES.   Two ways, by Zeus:
If I'm owed anything, I'm mindful, very: 620
But if I owe, (Oh, dear!) forgetful, very.
SOCRATES. Well then: have you the gift of speak-
    ing in you?
STREPSIADES. The gift of speaking, no: of cheat-
    ing, yes.

SOCRATES. No? how then can you learn?
STREPSIADES.   Oh, well enough.
SOCRATES. Then when I throw you out some
  clever notion   625
About the laws of nature, you must catch it.
STREPSIADES. What! must I snap up sapience, in
  dog-fashion?
SOCRATES. Oh! why the man's an ignorant old
  savage:
I fear, my friend, that you'll require the whip.
Come, if one strikes you, what do you do?
STREPSIADES.   I'm struck: 630
Then in a little while I call my witness:
Then in another little while I summon him.
SOCRATES. Put off your cloak.
STREPSIADES.   Why, what have I done wrong?
SOCRATES. O, nothing, nothing: all go in here
  naked.
STREPSIADES. Well, but I have not come with a
  search-warrant.   635
SOCRATES. Fool! throw it off.
STREPSIADES.   Well, tell me this one thing;
If I'm extremely careful and attentive,
Which of your students shall I most resemble?
SOCRATES. Why, Chaerephon. You'll be his very
  image.
STREPSIADES. What! I shall be half-dead! O luck-
  less me!   640
SOCRATES. Don't chatter there, but come and fol-
  low me;
Make haste now, quicker, here.
STREPSIADES.   Oh, but do first
Give me a honied cake: Zeus! how I tremble,
To go down there, as if to see Trophonius.
SOCRATES. Go on! why keep you pottering round
  the door?   645

CHORUS. Yes! go, and farewell; as your courage is
  great,
    So bright be your fate.
  May all good fortune his steps pursue,
    Who now, in his life's dim twilight haze,
  Is game such venturesome things to do,   650
  To steep his mind in discoveries new,
    To walk, a novice, in wisdom's ways. . . .
                                          (Later)
SOCRATES. Never by Chaos, Air, and Respiration,
Never, no never have I seen a clown
So helpless, and forgetful, and absurd!   655
Why if he learns a quirk or two he clean
Forgets them ere he has learnt them: all the same,
I'll call him out of doors here to the light.
Take up your bed, Strepsiades, and come!

644. **Trophonius,** the oracle of Trophonius situated in a subterranean
cave whose entryway was lined with demons who could be placated
with cakes. 653. **Chaos, Air, and Respiration,** the new gods of Socrates.

STREPSIADES. By Zeus, I can't: the bugs make such
  resistance.   660
SOCRATES. Make haste. There, throw it down, and
  listen.
STREPSIADES.   Well!
SOCRATES. Attend to me: what shall I teach you
  first
That you've not learnt before? Which will you have,
Measures or rhythms or the right use of words?
STREPSIADES. Oh! measures to be sure: for very
  lately   665
A grocer swindled me of full three pints.
SOCRATES. I don't mean that: but which do you
  like the best
Of all the measures; six feet, or eight feet?
STREPSIADES. Well, I like nothing better than the
  yard.
SOCRATES. Fool! don't talk nonsense.
STREPSIADES.   What will you bet me now   670
That two yards don't exactly make six feet?
SOCRATES. Consume you! what an ignorant clown
  you are!
Still, perhaps you can learn tunes more easily.
STREPSIADES. But will tunes help me to repair my
  fortunes?
SOCRATES. They'll help you to behave in com-
  pany: 675
If you can tell which kind of tune is best
For the sword-dance, and which for finger music.
STREPSIADES. For fingers! aye, but I know that.
SOCRATES.   Say on, then.
STREPSIADES. What is it but this finger? though
  before,
Ere this was grown, I used to play with that.   680
SOCRATES. Insufferable dolt!
STREPSIADES.   Well but, you goose,
I don't want to learn this.
SOCRATES.   What *do* you want then?
STREPSIADES. Teach me the Logic! teach me the
  unjust Logic!
SOCRATES. But you must learn some other matters
  first:
As, what are males among the quadrupeds.   685
STREPSIADES. I should be mad indeed not to know
  that.
The Ram, the Bull, the Goat, the Dog, the Fowl.
SOCRATES. Ah! there you are! there's a mistake at
  once!
You call the male and female fowl the same.
STREPSIADES. How! tell me how.
SOCRATES.   Why fowl and fowl of course.   690
STREPSIADES. That's true though! what then shall
  I say in future?
SOCRATES. Call one a fowless and the other a fowl.
STREPSIADES. A fowless? Good! Bravo! Bravo! by
  Air.

677. **finger music,** the dactyl.

Now for that one bright piece of information
I'll give you a barley bumper in your trough.　695
  SOCRATES. Look there, a fresh mistake; you called
    it trough,
Masculine, when it's feminine.
  STREPSIADES.　　　　　　　　How, pray?
How did I make it masculine?
  SOCRATES.　　　　　　　Why "trough,"
Just like "Cleonymus."
  STREPSIADES.　　　　　I don't quite catch it.
  SOCRATES. Why "trough," "Cleonymus," both mas-
    culine.　700
  STREPSIADES. Ah, but Cleonymus has got no
    trough,
His bread is kneaded in a rounded mortar:
Still, what must I say in future?
  SOCRATES.　　　　　　　What! why call it
A "troughless," female, just as one says "an actress."
  STREPSIADES. A "troughess," female?
  SOCRATES.　　　That's the way to call it.　705
  STREPSIADES. O "troughess" then and Miss Cleon-
    ymus.
  SOCRATES. Still you must learn some more about
    these names;
Which are the names of men and women.
  STREPSIADES. Oh, I know which are women.
  SOCRATES.　　　　　　　Well, repeat some.
  STREPSIADES. Demetria, Cleitagora, Philinna.　710
  SOCRATES. Now tell me some men's names.
  STREPSIADES.　　　　　O yes, ten thousand.
Philon, Melesias, Amynias.
  SOCRATES. Hold! I said men's names: these are
    women's names.
  STREPSIADES. No, no, they're men's.
  SOCRATES.　　　　They are *not* men's, for how
Would you address Amynias if you met him?　715
  STREPSIADES. How? somehow thus: "Here, here,
    Amynia!"
  SOCRATES. Amynia! a woman's name, you see.
  STREPSIADES. And rightly too; a sneak who shirks
    all service!
But all know this: let's pass to something else.
  SOCRATES. Well, then, you get into the bed.
  STREPSIADES.　　　　　　And then?　720
  SOCRATES. Excogitate about your own affairs.
  STREPSIADES. Not there: I do beseech, not there:
    at least
Let me excogitate on the bare ground.
  SOCRATES. There is no way but this.
  STREPSIADES.　　　　　　O luckless me!
How I shall suffer from the bugs to-day.　725

697. **Masculine, when it's feminine.** The mixing of genders satirizes
the grammatical subtleties of the sophists.　702. **His . . . mortar.**
The meaning of this passage is obscure.　716. **Amynia.** The vocative
of Amynias is feminine in form, and Amynias was notoriously effeminate.

  SOCRATES. Now then survey in every way,
    with airy judgement sharp and quick:
Wrapping thoughts around you thick:
And if so be in one you stick,
Never stop to toil and bother,　730
Lightly, lightly, lightly leap,
To another, to another;
Far away be balmy sleep.
  STREPSIADES. Ugh! Ugh! Ugh! Ugh! Ugh!
  CHORUS. What's the matter? where's the pain?　735
  STREPSIADES. Friends! I'm dying. From the bed
Out creep bugbears scantly fed,
And my ribs they bite in twain,
And my life-blood out they suck,
And my manhood off they pluck,　740
And my loins they dig and drain,
And I'm dying, once again.
  CHORUS. O take not the smart so deeply to heart.
  STREPSIADES.　　　　　Why, what can I do?
Vanished my skin so ruddy of hue,　745
Vanished my life-blood, vanished my shoe,
Vanished my purse, and what is still worse
As I hummed an old tune till my watch should
    be past,
I had very near vanished myself at the last.

  SOCRATES. Hallo there, are you pondering?
  STREPSIADES.　　　　　Eh! what? I?　750
Yes to be sure.
  SOCRATES.　　　And what have your ponderings
    come to?
  STREPSIADES. Whether these bugs will leave a bit
    of me.
  SOCRATES. Consume you, wretch!
  STREPSIADES.　　　Faith, I'm consumed already.
  SOCRATES. Come, come, don't flinch: pull up the
    clothes again:
Search out and catch some very subtle dodge　755
To fleece your creditors.
  STREPSIADES.　　　　　O me, how can I
Fleece any one with all these fleeces on me?
    (*Puts his head under the clothes.*)
  SOCRATES. Come, let me peep a moment what he's
    doing.
Hey! he's asleep!
  STREPSIADES.　No, no! no fear of that!
  SOCRATES. Caught anything?
  STREPSIADES.　　　　　No, nothing.
  SOCRATES.　　　　Surely, something.　760
  STREPSIADES. Well, I had something in my hand,
    I'll own.
  SOCRATES. Pull up the clothes again, and go on
    pondering.
  STREPSIADES. On what? now do please tell me,
    Socrates.
  SOCRATES. What is it that you want? first tell me
    that.

STREPSIADES. You have heard a million times what
    'tis I want: 765
My debts! my debts! I want to shirk my debts.
    SOCRATES. Come, come, pull up the clothes: refine
      your thoughts
With subtle wit: look at the case on all sides:
Mind you divide correctly.
    STREPSIADES.   Ugh! O me.
    SOCRATES. Hush: if you meet with any diffi-
      culty   770
Leave it a moment: then return again
To the same thought: then lift and weigh it well.
    STREPSIADES. Oh, here, dear Socrates!
    SOCRATES.   Well, my old friend.
    STREPSIADES. I've found a notion how to shirk my
      debts.
    SOCRATES. Well then, propound it.
    STREPSIADES.   What do you think of this? 775
Suppose I hire some grand Thessalian witch
To conjure down the Moon, and then I take it
And clap it into some round helmet-box,
And keep it fast there, like a looking-glass,—
    SOCRATES. But what's the use of that?
    STREPSIADES.   The use, quotha: 780
Why if the Moon should never rise again,
I'd never pay one farthing.
    SOCRATES.   No! why not?
    STREPSIADES. Why, don't we pay our interest by
      the month?
    SOCRATES. Good! now I'll proffer you another
      problem.
Suppose an action: damages, five talents: 785
Now tell me how you can evade that same.
    STREPSIADES. How! how! can't say at all: but I'll
      go seek.
    SOCRATES. Don't wrap your mind for ever round
      yourself,
But let your thoughts range freely through the air,
Like chafers with a thread about their feet. 790
    STREPSIADES. I've found a bright evasion of the
      action:
Confess yourself, 'tis glorious.
    SOCRATES.   But what is it?
    STREPSIADES. I say, haven't you seen in druggists'
      shops
That stone, that splendidly transparent stone,
By which they kindle fire?
    SOCRATES.   The burning-glass? 795
    STREPSIADES. That's it: well then, I'd get me one
      of these,
And as the clerk was entering down my case,
I'd stand, like this, some distance towards the sun,
And burn out every line.

769. **Mind you divide correctly.** This refers to the division of genus
into species in logic. 790. **Like chafers . . . feet.** The thread was
tied by boys to tantalize the insects.

    SOCRATES.   By the Three Graces,
A clever dodge!
    STREPSIADES.   O me, how pleased I am 800
To have a debt like that clean blotted out.
    SOCRATES. Come, then, make haste and snap up
      this.
    STREPSIADES.   Well, what?
    SOCRATES. How to prevent an adversary's suit
Supposing you were sure to lose it; tell me.
    STREPSIADES. O, nothing easier.
    SOCRATES.   How, pray?
    STREPSIADES.   Why thus, 805
While there was yet one trial intervening,
Ere mine was cited, I'd go hang myself.
    SOCRATES. Absurd!

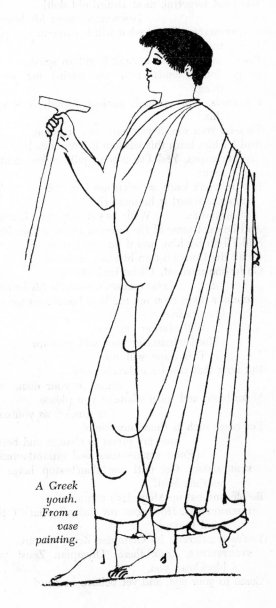

*A Greek
youth.
From a
vase
painting.*

STREPSIADES. No, by the Gods, it isn't though:
They could not prosecute me were I dead.

SOCRATES. Nonsense! Be off: I'll try no more to
teach you. 810

STREPSIADES. Why not? do, please: now, please
do, Socrates.

SOCRATES. Why you forgot all that you learn, directly.
Come, say what you learnt first: there's a chance for
you.

STREPSIADES. Ah! what was first?—Dear me: what-
ever was it?—
Whatever's that we knead the barley in?— 815
Bless us, what was it?

SOCRATES. Be off, and feed the crows,
You most forgetful, most absurd old dolt!
                    (SOCRATES *enters his house.*)

STREPSIADES. O me! what will become of me, poor
wretch!
I'm clean undone: I haven't learnt to speak.—
O gracious Clouds, now do advise me something. 820

CHORUS. Our counsel, ancient friend, is simply
this,
To send your son, if you have one at home,
And let him learn this wisdom in your stead.

STREPSIADES. Yes! I've a son, quite a fine gentleman:
But he won't learn, so what am I to do? 825

CHORUS. What! is he master?

STREPSIADES. Well: he's strong and vigorous,
And he's got some of the Coesyra blood within him:
Still I'll go for him, and if he won't come
By all the Gods I'll turn him out of doors.
Go in one moment, I'll be back directly. 830
                    (STREPSIADES *returns to his house.*)

CHORUS. Dost thou not see how bounteous we our
favours free
        Will shower on you,
    Since whatsoe'er your will prepare
        This dupe will do.
But now that you have dazzled and
                    elated so your man, 835
Make haste and seize whate'er you please
                    as quickly as you can,
For cases such as these, my friend,
                    are very prone to change and bend.
            (*Enter* STREPSIADES *and* PHEIDIPPIDES.)

STREPSIADES. Get out! you shan't stop here: so
help me Mist!
Be off, and eat up Megacles's columns.

PHEIDIPPIDES. How now, my father? what's i' the
wind to-day? 840
You're wandering; by Olympian Zeus, you are.

STREPSIADES. Look there! Olympian Zeus! you
blockhead you,
Come to *your* age, and yet believe in Zeus!

PHEIDIPPIDES. Why prithee, what's the joke?

STREPSIADES. 'Tis so preposterous
When babes like you hold antiquated notions. 845
But come and I'll impart a thing or two,
A wrinkle, making you a man indeed.
But, mind: don't whisper this to any one.

PHEIDIPPIDES. Well, what's the matter?

STREPSIADES. Didn't you swear by Zeus?

PHEIDIPPIDES. I did.

STREPSIADES. See now, how good a thing is
learning. 850
There is no Zeus, Pheidippides.

PHEIDIPPIDES. Who then?

STREPSIADES. Why Vortex reigns, and he has
turned out Zeus.

PHEIDIPPIDES. Oh me, what stuff.

STREPSIADES. Be sure that this is so.

PHEIDIPPIDES. Who says so, pray?

STREPSIADES. The Melian—Socrates,
And Chaerephon, who knows about the flea-
tracks. 855

PHEIDIPPIDES. And are you come to such a pitch of
madness
As to put faith in brain-struck men?

STREPSIADES. O hush!
And don't blaspheme such very dexterous men
And sapient too: men of such frugal habits
They never shave, nor use your precious ointment,
Nor go to baths to clean themselves: but you 861
Have taken *me* for a corpse and cleaned me out.
Come, come, make haste, do go and learn for me.

PHEIDIPPIDES. What can one learn from them that
is worth knowing?

STREPSIADES. Learn! why, whatever's clever in the
world: 865
And you shall learn how gross and dense you are.
But stop one moment: I'll be back directly.

PHEIDIPPIDES. O me! what must I do with my mad
father?
Shall I indict him for his lunacy,
Or tell the undertakers of his symptoms? 870

STREPSIADES. Now then! you see this, don't you?
what do you call it?

PHEIDIPPIDES. That? why a fowl.

STREPSIADES. Good! now then, what is this?

PHEIDIPPIDES. That's a fowl too.

STREPSIADES. What both! Ridiculous!
Never say that again, but mind you always
Call this a fowless and the other a fowl. 875

PHEIDIPPIDES. A fowless! These then are the
mighty secrets
You have picked up amongst those earth-born fellows.

STREPSIADES. And lots besides: but everything I
learn
I straight forget: I am so old and stupid.

854. **The Melian,** that is, an atheist, like Diagoras of Melos.

PHEIDIPPIDES. And this is what you have lost your
    mantle for? 880

STREPSIADES. It's very absent sometimes: 'tisn't lost.

PHEIDIPPIDES. And what have you done with your
    shoes, you dotard you?

STREPSIADES. Like Pericles, all for the best, I've
    lost them.
Come, come; go with me: humour me in this,
And then do what you like. Ah! I remember 885
How I to humour you, a coaxing baby,
With the first obol which my judgeship fetched me
Bought you a go-cart at the great Diasia.

PHEIDIPPIDES. The time will come when you'll re-
    pent of this.

STREPSIADES. Good boy to obey me. (*They go to
    the house of* SOCRATES.) Hallo! Socrates. 890
Come here; come here; I've brought this son of
mine.
Trouble enough, I'll warrant you. (*Enter* SOCRATES.)

SOCRATES.   Poor infant,
Not yet aware of my suspension-wonders.

PHEIDIPPIDES. You'd make a wondrous piece of
    ware, suspended.

STREPSIADES. Hey! Hang the lad! Do you abuse
    the Master? 895

SOCRATES. And look, "suthspended!" In what fool-
    ish fashion
He mouthed the word with pouting lips agape.
How can *he* learn evasion of a suit,
Timely citation, damaging replies?
Hyperbolus, though, learnt them for a talent. 900

STREPSIADES. O never fear! he's very sharp, by
    nature.
For when he was a little chap, *so* high,
He used to build small baby-houses, boats,
Go-carts of leather, darling little frogs
Carved from pomegranates, you can't think how
    nicely! 905
So now, I prithee, teach him both your Logics,
The Better, as you call it, and the Worse
Which with the worse cause can defeat the Better;
Or if not both, at all events the Worse.

SOCRATES. Aye, with his own ears he shall hear
    them argue. 910
I shan't be there.

STREPSIADES. But please remember this,
Give him the knack of reasoning down all Justice.
(RIGHT LOGIC *and* WRONG LOGIC *enter, quarreling
violently.*)

RIGHT LOGIC. Come show yourself now
                with your confident brow.
    —To the stage, if you dare!

WRONG LOGIC. Lead on where you please:
          I shall smash you with ease, 915
    If an audience be there.

883. **Like Pericles . . . best;** so Pericles accounted for money spent
on bribing the enemy.

RIGHT LOGIC. *You'll* smash me, you say! And who
    are *you*, pray?

WRONG LOGIC. A Logic, like you.

RIGHT LOGIC.   But the Worst of the two.

WRONG LOGIC. Yet you I can drub whom my Bet-
    ter they dub.

RIGHT LOGIC. By what artifice taught?

WRONG LOGIC.   By original thought. 920

RIGHT LOGIC. Aye, truly your trade so successful
    is made.
By means of these noodles of ours, I'm afraid.

WRONG LOGIC. Not noodles, but wise.

RIGHT LOGIC.   I'll smash you and your lies!

WRONG LOGIC. By what method, forsooth?

RIGHT LOGIC.   By speaking the Truth.

WRONG LOGIC. Your words I will meet, and en-
    tirely defeat: 925
There never *was* Justice or Truth, I repeat.

RIGHT LOGIC. No Justice! you say?

WRONG LOGIC.   Well, where does it stay?

RIGHT LOGIC. With the Gods in the air.

WRONG LOGIC.   If Justice be there,
How comes it that Zeus could his father reduce,
Yet live with their Godships unpunished and loose?

RIGHT LOGIC. Ugh! Ugh! These evils come thick,
                I feel awfully sick, 931
A basin, quick, quick!

WRONG LOGIC. You're a useless old drone with one
    foot in the grave!

RIGHT LOGIC. You're a shameless, unprincipled,
    dissolute knave!

WRONG LOGIC. Hey! a rosy festoon.

RIGHT LOGIC.   And a vulgar
    buffoon! 935

WRONG LOGIC. What! Lilies from *you?*

RIGHT LOGIC.   And a par-
    ricide too!

WRONG LOGIC. 'Tis with gold (you don't know it)
    you sprinkle my head.

RIGHT LOGIC. O gold is it now? but it used to be
    lead!

WRONG LOGIC. But now it's a grace and a glory in-
    stead.

RIGHT LOGIC. You're a little too bold.

WRONG LOGIC.   You're a good
    deal too old. 940

RIGHT LOGIC. 'Tis through you I well know not a
    stripling will go
To attend to the rules which are taught in the
    Schools;
But Athens one day shall be up to the fools.

WRONG LOGIC. How squalid your dress!

RIGHT LOGIC.   Yours is fine,
    I confess.
Yet of old, I declare, but a pauper you were; 945
And passed yourself off, our compassion to draw
    As a Telephus, (Euripidéan)

Well pleased from a beggarly wallet to gnaw
At inanities Pandeletéan.

WRONG LOGIC. O me! for the wisdom you've mentioned in jest!   950

RIGHT LOGIC. O me! for the folly of you, and the
rest

Who you to destroy their children employ!

WRONG LOGIC. *Him* you never shall teach: you are
quite out of date.

RIGHT LOGIC. If not, he'll be lost, as he'll find to
his cost:

Taught nothing by you but to chatter and prate.

WRONG LOGIC. He raves, as you see: let him be, let
him be.   956

RIGHT LOGIC. Touch him if you dare! I bid you beware.

CHORUS. Forbear, forbear to wrangle and scold!
Each of you show

You what you taught their fathers of old,   960
You let us know

Your system untried, that hearing each side
From the lips of the Rivals the youth may decide
To which of your schools he will go.

RIGHT LOGIC. This then will I do.   964

WRONG LOGIC.   And so will I too.

CHORUS. And who will put in his claim to begin?

WRONG LOGIC. If *he* wishes, he may: I kindly give
way:

And out of his argument quickly will I
Draw facts and devices to fledge the reply
Wherewith I will shoot him and smite and refute
him.   970

And at last if a word from his mouth shall be heard
My sayings like fierce savage hornets shall pierce
His forehead and eyes,

Till in fear and distraction he yields and he—dies!

CHORUS. With thoughts and words and maxims
pondered well   975

Now then in confidence let both begin:
Try which his rival can in speech excel:
Try which this perilous wordy war can win,
Which all my votaries' hopes are fondly centred
in.

O Thou who wert born our sires to adorn   980
with characters blameless and fair,

Say on what you please, say on and to these
your glorious Nature declare.

RIGHT LOGIC. To hear then prepare of the Discipline rare

which flourished in Athens of yore   985

When Honour and Truth were in fashion with youth
and Sobriety bloomed on our shore;

First of all the old rule was preserved in our school
that "boys should be seen and not heard:"

And then to the home of the Harpist would come
decorous in action and word   991

All the lads of one town, though the snow peppered
down,

in spite of all wind and all weather:

And they sang an old song as they paced it along,
not shambling with thighs glued together:

"O the dread shout of War how it peals from afar,"
or *"Pallas the Stormer adore,"*   997

To some manly old air all simple and bare
which their fathers had chanted before.

And should anyone dare the tune to impair   1000
and with intricate twistings to fill,

Such as Phrynis is fain, and his long-winded train,
perversely to quaver and trill,

Many stripes would he feel in return for his zeal,
as to genuine Music a foe.   1005

And every one's thigh was forward and high
as they sat to be drilled in a row,

So that nothing the while indecent or vile
the eye of a stranger might meet;

And then with their hand they would smooth down
the sand   1010

whenever they rose from their seat,

To leave not a trace of themselves in the place
for a vigilant lover to view.

They never would soil their persons with oil
but were inartificial and true.   1015

Nor tempered their throat to a soft mincing note
and sighs to their lovers addressed:

Nor laid themselves out, as they strutted about,
to the wanton desires of the rest:

Nor would anyone dare such stimulant fare   1020
as the head of the radish to wish:

Nor to make over bold with the food of the old,
the anise, and parsley, and fish:

Nor dainties to quaff, nor giggle and laugh,
nor foot within foot to enfold.   1025

WRONG LOGIC. Faugh! this smells very strong of
some musty old song,

and Chirrupers mounted in gold;

And Slaughter of beasts, and old-fashioned feasts.

RIGHT LOGIC.   Yet these are the precepts
which taught

The heroes of old to be hardy and bold,   1030
and the Men who at Marathon fought!

But now must the lad from his boyhood be clad
in a Man's all-enveloping cloak:

So that, oft as the Panathenaea returns,
I feel myself ready to choke

948-949. **Well . . . Pandeletéan.** Telephus, wounded by Achilles,
sought a cure from him in the disguise of a beggar. In Euripides' lost
play on the subject, Aristophanes detected ideas of the Sophist Pan-
deletus in the beggar's speech.

990. **And . . . come.** Music was a major branch of ancient Greek
education.   1002. **Phrynis,** native of Mitylene and leader of a revolutionary school of contemporary music.   1027. **Chirrupers mounted
in gold.** Athenians of ancient families wore golden grasshoppers as
tokens of their lineage.

When the dancers go by with their shields to their
    thigh, 1036
                not caring for Pallas a jot.
You therefore, young man, choose me while you can;
            cast in with my Method your lot;
And then you shall learn the forum to spurn, 1040
        and from dissolute baths to abstain,
And fashions impure and shameful abjure,
        and scorners repel with disdain:
And rise from your chair if an elder be there,
        and respectfully give him your place, 1045
And with love and with fear your parents revere,
        and shrink from the brand of Disgrace,
And deep in your breast be the Image impressed
        of Modesty, simple and true,
Nor resort any more to a dancing-girl's door, 1050
        nor glance at the harlotry crew,
Lest at length by the blow of the Apple they throw
        from the hopes of your Manhood you fall.
Nor dare to reply when your Father is nigh,
        nor "musty old Japhet" to call 1055
In your malice and rage that Sacred Old Age
        which lovingly cherished your youth.
WRONG LOGIC. Yes, yes, my young friend, if to
    him you attend,
        by Bacchus I swear of a truth
You will scarce with the sty of Hippocrates vie, 1060
        as a mammy-suck known even there!
RIGHT LOGIC. But then you'll excel in the games
    you love well,
        all blooming, athletic and fair:
Not learning to prate as your idlers debate
        with marvellous prickly dispute, 1065
Nor dragged into Court day by day to make sport
        in some small disagreeable suit:
But you will below to the Academe go,
        and under the olives contend
With your chaplet of reed, in a contest of speed
        with some excellent rival and friend: 1071
All fragrant with woodbine and peaceful content,
        and the leaf which the lime blossoms fling,
When the plane whispers love to the elm in the
    grove
        in the beautiful season of Spring. 1075
If then you'll obey and do what I say,
And follow with me the more excellent way,
Your chest shall be white, your skin shall be
    bright,
Your arms shall be tight, your tongue shall be
    slight,
And everything else shall be proper and right.
But if you pursue what men nowadays do, 1081

You will have, to begin, a cold pallid skin,
Arms small and chest weak, tongue practised to
    speak,
Special laws very long, and the symptoms all
    strong
Which show that your life is licentious and
    wrong. 1085
And your mind he'll prepare so that foul to be
    fair
And fair to be foul you shall always declare;
And you'll find yourself soon, if you listen to him,
With the filth of Antimachus filled to the brim!

CHORUS. O glorious Sage! with loveliest Wisdom
    teeming! 1090
    Sweet on thy words does ancient Virtue rest!
Thrice happy they who watched thy Youth's
    bright beaming!
    Thou of the vaunted genius, do thy best;
This man has gained applause: His Wisdom
    stands confessed.
And you with clever words and thoughts must needs
    your case adorn 1095
Else he will surely win the day, and you retreat
    with scorn.

WRONG LOGIC. Aye, say you so? why I have been
            half-burst; I do so long
To overthrow his arguments
          with arguments more strong. 1100
I am the Lesser Logic? True:
          these Schoolmen call me so,
Simply because I was the first
          of all mankind to show
How old established rules and laws 1105
          might contradicted be:
And this, as you may guess, is worth
          a thousand pounds to me,
To take the feebler cause, and yet
          to win the disputation. 1110
And mark me now, how I'll confute
          his boasted Education!
You said that always from warm baths
          the stripling must abstain:
Why must he? on what grounds do you 1115
          of these warm baths complain?
RIGHT LOGIC. Why, it's the worst thing possible,
          it quite unstrings a man.
WRONG LOGIC. Hold there: I've got you round the
    waist:
          escape me if you can. 1120
And first: of all the sons of Zeus
          which think you was the best?
Which was the manliest? which endured
          more toils than all the rest?

1036–37. **When . . . jot.** In the war-dance the young men show disrespect for Athena by letting their shields hang down listlessly. 1052. **the Apple they throw**; as an invitation to love. 1055. **musty old Japhet**, one of the old Titans, and hence an old fogy. 1060. **sty of Hippocrates**; the sons of Hippocrates were notoriously piggish and stupid.

1089. **Antimachus,** unknown.

RIGHT LOGIC. Well, I suppose that Heracles   1125
            was bravest and most bold.
WRONG LOGIC. And are the baths of Heracles
            so wonderfully cold?
Aha! you blame warm baths, I think.
  RIGHT LOGIC.   This, this is what they say: 1130
This is the stuff our precious youths
            are chattering all the day!
This is what makes them haunt the baths,
            and shun the manlier Games!
WRONG LOGIC. Well then, we'll take the Forum
    next: 1135
            I praise it, and he blames.
But if it *was* so bad, do you think
            old Homer would have made
Nestor and all his worthies ply
            a real forensic trade?   1140
Well: then he says a stripling's tongue
            should always idle be:
I say it should be used of course:
            so there we disagree.
And next he says you must be chaste.   1145
            A most preposterous plan!
Come, tell me did you ever know
            one single blessed man
Gain the least good by chastity?
         come, prove I'm wrong: make haste.   1150
RIGHT LOGIC. Yes, many, many! Peleus gained
            a sword by being chaste.
WRONG LOGIC. A sword indeed! a wondrous meed
            the unlucky fool obtained.
Hyperbolus the Lamp-maker   1155
            hath many a talent gained
By knavish tricks which I have taught:
            but not a sword, no, no!
RIGHT LOGIC. Then Peleus did to his chaste life
            the bed of Thetis owe.   1160
WRONG LOGIC. And then she cut and ran away!
            for nothing so engages
A woman's heart as forward warmth,
            old shred of those dark Ages!
For take this chastity, young man: 1165
            sift it inside and out:
Count all the pleasures, all the joys,
            it bids you live without:
No kind of dames, no kind of games,
          no laughing, feasting, drinking,—   1170
Why, life itself is little worth
            without these joys, I'm thinking.
Well, I must notice now the wants
            by Nature's self implanted;

You love, seduce, you can't help that,   1175
            you're caught, convicted. Granted.
You're done for; you can't say one word:
            while if you follow me
Indulge your genius, laugh and quaff,
            hold nothing base to be.   1180
Why if you're in adultery caught,
            your pleas will still be ample:
You've done no wrong, you'll say, and then
            bring Zeus as your example.
He fell before the wondrous powers   1185
            by Love and Beauty wielded:
And how can you, the Mortal, stand,
            where He, the Immortal, yielded?
RIGHT LOGIC. Aye, but suppose in spite of all,
            he must be wedged and sanded.   1190
Won't he be probed, or else can you
            prevent it? now be candid.
WRONG LOGIC. And what's the damage if it should
    be so?
RIGHT LOGIC. What greater damage can the young
    man know?
WRONG LOGIC. What will you do, if this dispute
    I win?   1195
RIGHT LOGIC. I'll be for ever silent.
WRONG LOGIC.   Good, begin.
The Counsellor: from whence comes he?
RIGHT LOGIC. From probed adulterers.
WRONG LOGIC.   I agree.
The Tragic Poets: whence are they?
RIGHT LOGIC. From probed adulterers.
WRONG LOGIC.   So I say.   1200
The Orators: what class of men?
RIGHT LOGIC. All probed adulterers.
WRONG LOGIC.   Right again.
You feel your error, I'll engage,
But look once more around the stage,
Survey the audience, which they be,   1205
Probed or not Probed.
RIGHT LOGIC.   I see, I see.
WRONG LOGIC. Well, give your verdict.
RIGHT LOGIC.   It must go
For probed adulterers: him I know,
And him, and him: the Probed are most.
WRONG LOGIC. How stand we then?
RIGHT LOGIC.   I own, I've lost.   1210
O Cinaeds, Cinaeds, take my robe!
Your words have won, to you I run
To live and die with glorious Probe!
      (*They go into the house of* SOCRATES.)

SOCRATES. Well, what do you want? to take away
    your son
At once, or shall I teach him how to speak?   1215

1127–28. And . . . cold? Warm springs were called "springs of Hercales" after some given him by Athena for refreshment.   1151–52.
Peleus . . . chaste. For repulsing the advances of another's wife
the gods rewarded Peleus with a sword. Later he married Thetis,
who deserted him after the birth of Achilles.

1191. **probed.** This refers to a physical punishment for adultery.
1211. **Cinaeds,** debauchees.

STREPSIADES. Teach him, and flog him, and be
    sure you well
Sharpen his mother wit, grind the one edge
Fit for my little law-suits, and the other,
Why, make that serve for more important matters.
    SOCRATES. Oh, never fear! He'll make a splendid
    sophist.   1220
    STREPSIADES. Well, well, I hope he'll be a poor
    pale rascal.

(SOCRATES *retires with* PHEIDIPPIDES *into his
house, and* STREPSIADES *into his.*)

CHORUS. Go: but in us the thought is strong,
           you will repent of this ere long.
Now we wish to tell the Judges
           all the blessings they shall gain   1225
If, as Justice plainly warrants,
           we the worthy prize obtain.
First, whenever in the Season
           ye would fain your fields renew,
All the world shall wait expectant   1230
           till we've poured our rain on you:
Then of all your crops and vineyards
           we will take the utmost care
So that neither drought oppress them,
           nor the heavy rain impair.   1235
But if anyone amongst you
           dare to treat our claims with scorn,
Mortal he, the Clouds immortal,
           better had he ne'er been born!
He from his estates shall gather   1240
           neither corn, nor oil, nor wine,
For whenever blossoms sparkle
           on the olive or the vine
They shall all at once be blighted:
           we will ply our slings so true.   1245
And if ever we behold him
           building up his mansions new,
With our tight and nipping hailstones
           we will all his tiles destroy.
But if he, his friends or kinsfolk,   1250
           would a marriage-feast enjoy,
All night long we'll pour in torrents:
           so perchance he'll rather pray
To endure the drought of Egypt,
           than decide amiss to-day!   1255

(*Enter* STREPSIADES.)

STREPSIADES. The fifth, the fourth, the third, and
    then the second,
And then that day which more than all the rest
I loathe and shrink from and abominate,
Then comes at once that hateful Old-and-New day.

And every single blessed dun has sworn   1260
He'll stake his gage, and ruin and destroy me.
And when I make a modest small request,
"O my good friend, part don't exact at present,
And part defer, and part remit," they swear
So they shall never touch it, and abuse me   1265
As a rank swindler, threatening me with actions.
Now let them bring their actions! Who's afraid?
Not I: if these have taught my son to speak.
But here's the door: I'll knock and soon find out.
Boy! Ho there, boy! (*Enter* SOCRATES.)
    SOCRATES.   I clasp Strepsiades.   1270
    STREPSIADES. And I clasp you: but take this meal-
    bag first.
'Tis meet and right to glorify one's Tutors.
But tell me, tell me, has my son yet learnt
That Second Logic which he saw just now?
    SOCRATES. He hath.
    STREPSIADES.   Hurrah! great Sovereign Knav-
    ery!   1275
    SOCRATES. You may escape whatever suit you
    please.
    STREPSIADES. What, if I borrowed before wit-
    nesses?
    SOCRATES. Before a thousand, and the more the
    merrier.
    STREPSIADES. Then shall my song be loud and
    deep.
Weep, obol-weighers, weep, weep, weep,   1280
Ye, and your principals, and compound interests,
For ye shall never pester me again.
    Such a son have I bred,
    (He is within this door),
Born to inspire my foemen with dread,   1285
Born his old father's house to restore:
Keen and polished of tongue is he,
He my Champion and Guard shall be,
He will set his old father free,
Run you, and call him forth to me.   1290
"O my child! O my sweet! come out, I entreat;
    'Tis the voice" of your sire. (*Enter* PHEIDIPPIDES)
    SOCRATES. Here's the man you require.
    STREPSIADES. Joy, joy of my heart!
    SOCRATES. Take your son and depart.   1295
    STREPSIADES. O come, O come, my son, my son,
O dear! O dear!
O joy, to see your beautiful complexion!
Aye now you have an aspect Negative
And Disputative, and our native query   1300
Shines forth there: "What d'ye say?" You've the
    true face
Which rogues put on, of injured innocence.

1222-23. **Go . . . long.** The chorus now turns to the audience for a
second parabasis.   1256. **The fifth . . . second.** The days of the last
third of the Attic month were reckoned backwards.   1259. **Old-and-
New day,** the day when the moon was old for part of the day and new
for part.

1261. **stake his gage,** deposit the cost of legal procedure in summoning
the debtor to court.   1271. **meal-bag,** the reward he had promised.
1291-92. **"O . . . voice."** These and other lines in this scene parody
passages from Euripides.   1301. **"What d'ye say?"** This is an impudent question to intimidate an opponent.

You have the regular Attic look about you.
So now, you save me, for 'twas you undid me.

PHEIDIPPIDES. What is it ails you?

STREPSIADES.   Why the Old-and-
New day.   1305

PHEIDIPPIDES. And is there such a day as Old-
and-New?

STREPSIADES. Yes: that's the day they mean to
stake their gages.

PHEIDIPPIDES. They'll lose them if they stake
them. What! do you think
That one day can be two days, both together?

STREPSIADES. Why, can't it be so?

PHEIDIPPIDES.   Surely not; or else   1310
A woman might at once be old and young.

STREPSIADES. Still, the law says so.

PHEIDIPPIDES.   True: but I believe
They don't quite understand it.

STREPSIADES.   You explain it.

PHEIDIPPIDES. Old Solon had a democratic turn.

STREPSIADES. Well, but that's nothing to the Old-
and-New.   1315

PHEIDIPPIDES. Hence then he fixed that sum-
monses be issued
For these two days, the old one and the new one,
So that the gage be staked on the New-month.

STREPSIADES. What made him add "the old" then?

PHEIDIPPIDES.   I will tell you.
He wished the litigants to meet on *that* day   1320
And compromise their quarrels: if they could not,
Then let them fight it out on the New-month.

STREPSIADES. Why then do Magistrates receive
the stakes
On the Old-and-New instead of the New-month?

PHEIDIPPIDES. Well, I believe they act like the
Foretasters.   1325
They wish to bag the gage as soon as possible,
And thus they gain a whole day's foretaste of it.

STREPSIADES. Aha! poor dupes, why sit ye moon-
ing there,
Game for us Artful Dodgers, you dull stones,
You ciphers, lambkins, butts piled up together!   1330
Oh! my success inspires me, and I'll sing
Glad eulogies on me and thee, my son.

    "*Man, most blessed, most divine,*
    What a wondrous wit is thine,
    What a son to grace thy line,"   1335
    Friends and neighbours day by day
        Thus will say,
When with envious eyes my suits they see you win;
But first I'll feast you, so come in, my son, come in.

(*They retire into the house. Enter* PASIAS *and a*
witness.)

PASIAS. What! must a man lose his own property!

1314. Old Solon . . . turn. Solon had named the "Old-and-New
day." 1325. Foretasters, those appointed to taste beforehand food
served at a public banquet.

No: never, never. Better have refused   1341
With a bold face, than be so plagued as this.
See! to get paid my own just debts, I'm forced
To drag you to bear witness, and what's worse
I needs must quarrel with my townsman here.   1345
Well, I won't shame my country, while I live,
I'll go to law, I'll summon him . . .

(*Enter* STREPSIADES.)

STREPSIADES.   Hallo!

PASIAS. To the next Old-and-New.

STREPSIADES.   Bear witness, all!
He named two days. You'll summon me; what for?

PASIAS. The fifty pounds I lent you when you
bought   1350
That iron-grey.

STREPSIADES. Just listen to the fellow!
The whole world knows that I detest all horses.

PASIAS. I swear you swore by all the Gods to
pay me.

STREPSIADES. Well, now I swear I won't: Pheidippides
Has learnt since then the unanswerable Logic.   1355

PASIAS. And will you therefore shirk my just demand?

STREPSIADES. Of course I will: else why should he
have learnt it?

PASIAS. And will you dare forswear it by the
Gods?

STREPSIADES. The Gods indeed! What Gods?

PASIAS. Poseidon, Hermes, Zeus.

STREPSIADES.   By Zeus I would,   1360
Though I gave twopence halfpenny for the privilege.

PASIAS. O then confound you for a shameless
rogue!

STREPSIADES. Hallo! this butt should be rubbed
down with salt.

PASIAS. Zounds! you deride me!

STREPSIADES.   Why 'twill hold four gallons.

PASIAS. You 'scape me not, by Mighty Zeus, and
all   1365
The Gods!

STREPSIADES. I wonderfully like the Gods;
An oath by Zeus is sport to knowing ones.

PASIAS. Sooner or later you'll repent of this.
Come do you mean to pay your debts or don't you?
Tell me, and I'll be off.

STREPSIADES.   Now do have patience;   1370
I'll give you a clear answer in one moment.

(*He fetches a kneading-trough from his house.*)

PASIAS. What do you think he'll do?

WITNESS.   I think he'll pay you.

STREPSIADES. Where is that horrid dun? O here:
now tell me
What you call this.

PASIAS.   What I call that? a trough.

1363. Hallo . . . salt. Thus were the insane treated. Strepsiades
likens Pasias to a wine-skin.

STREPSIADES. Heavens! what a fool: and do *you*
    want your money? 1375
I'd never pay one penny to a fellow
Who calls my troughess, trough. So there's your
    answer.
PASIAS. Then you won't pay me?
STREPSIADES.   No, not if I know it.
Come put your best foot forward, and be off:
March off, I say, this instant!
PASIAS.   May I die 1380
If I don't go at once and stake my gage!
           (*Exit* PASIAS *and witness.*)
STREPSIADES. No don't: the fifty pounds are loss
    enough:
And really on my word I would not wish you
To lose this too just for one silly blunder.
           (*Enter* AMYNIAS.)

AMYNIAS. Ah me! Oh! Oh! Oh! 1385
STREPSIADES. Hallo! who's that making that hor-
    rible noise?
Not one of Carcinus's snivelling Gods?
AMYNIAS. Who cares to know what I am? what
    imports it?
An ill-starred man.
STREPSIADES.   Then keep it to yourself.
AMYNIAS. "O heavy fate!" "O Fortune, thou hast
    broken 1390
My chariot wheels!" "Thou hast undone me,
    Pallas!"
STREPSIADES. How! has Tlepolemus been at you,
    man?
AMYNIAS. Jeer me not, friend, but tell your worthy
    son
To pay me back the money which I lent him:
I'm in a bad way and the times are pressing. 1395
STREPSIADES. What money do you mean?
AMYNIAS.   Why, what he borrowed.
STREPSIADES. You *are* in a bad way, I really think.
AMYNIAS. Driving my four-wheel out I fell, by
    Zeus.
STREPSIADES. You rave as if you'd fall'n times
    out-of-mind. 1399
AMYNIAS. I rave? how so? I only claim my own.
STREPSIADES. You can't be quite right, surely.
AMYNIAS.   Why, what mean you?
STREPSIADES. I shrewdly guess your brain's re-
    ceived a shake.
AMYNIAS. I shrewdly guess that you'll receive a
    summons
If you don't pay my money.
STREPSIADES.   Well then, tell me,
Which theory do you side with, that the rain 1405

1387. **Carcinus's snivelling Gods,** characters in the lost tragedies of
Carcinus. 1390–91. "O . . . Pallas!" These lines are from a play
about Licymnius and Tlepolemus by a son of Carcinus.

Falls fresh each time, or that the Sun draws back
The same old rain, and sends it down again?
AMYNIAS. I'm very sure I neither know nor care.
STREPSIADES. Not care! good heavens! And do *you*
    claim your money,
So unenlightened in the Laws of Nature? 1410
AMYNIAS. If you're hard up then, pay me back the
    Interest
At least.
STREPSIADES. Int-er-est? what kind of a beast is
    that?
AMYNIAS. What else than day by day and month
    by month
Larger and larger still the silver grows
As time sweeps by?
STREPSIADES.   Finely and nobly said. 1415
What then! think you the Sea is larger now
Than 'twas last year?
AMYNIAS.   No surely, 'tis no larger:
It is not right it should be.
STREPSIADES.   And do you then,
Insatiable grasper! when the Sea,
Receiving all these Rivers, grows no larger, 1420
Do you desire your silver to grow larger?
Come now, you prosecute your journey off!
Here, fetch the whip.
AMYNIAS.   Bear witness, I appeal.
STREPSIADES. Be off! what, won't you? Gee up,
    sigma-brand! 1424
AMYNIAS. I say! a clear assault!
STREPSIADES.   You won't be off?
I'll stimulate you; Zeus! I'll goad your haunches.
Aha! you run: I thought I'd stir you up
You and your phaetons, and wheels, and all!
(AMYNIAS *runs off.* STREPSIADES *enters his house.*)

CHORUS. What a thing it is to long for matters
    which are wrong!
    For you see how this old man 1430
    Is seeking, if he can
    His creditors trepan:
    And I confidently say
    That he will this very day
        Such a blow 1435
Amid his prosperous cheats receive,
        that he will deeply grieve.

For I think that he has won what he wanted for his
    son,
    And the lad has learned the way
    All justice to gainsay, 1440
    Be it what or where it may:
    That he'll trump up any tale,
    Right or wrong, and so prevail.
    This I know.
Yea! and perchance the time will come 1445
    when he shall wish his son were dumb.

(STREPSIADES *rushes onstage, followed by* PHEIDIP-
PIDES.)

STREPSIADES.   Oh! Oh!
Help! Murder! Help! O neighbours, kinsfolk,
    townsmen,
Help, one and all, against this base assault,
Ah! Ah! my cheek! my head! O luckless me!   1450
Wretch! do you strike your father?

PHEIDIPPIDES.   Yes, Papa.

STREPSIADES. See! See! he owns he struck me.

PHEIDIPPIDES.   To be sure.

STREPSIADES. Scoundrel! and parricide! and house-
    breaker!

PHEIDIPPIDES. Thank you: go on, go on: do please
    go on.
am quite delighted to be called such names!   1455

STREPSIADES. O probed Adulterer.

PHEIDIPPIDES.   Roses from your lips.

STREPSIADES. Strike you your father?

PHEIDIPPIDES.   O dear yes; what's more,
I'll prove I struck you justly.

STREPSIADES.   Struck me justly!
Villain! how can you strike a father justly?

PHEIDIPPIDES. Yes, and I'll demonstrate it, if you
    please.   1460

STREPSIADES. Demonstrate this?

PHEIDIPPIDES.   O yes, quite easily.
Come, take your choice, which Logic do you choose?

STREPSIADES. Which what?

PHEIDIPPIDES.   Logic: the Better or the Worse?

STREPSIADES. Ah, then, in very truth I've had you
    taught
To reason down all Justice, if you think   1465
You can prove this, that it is just and right
That fathers should be beaten by their sons!

PHEIDIPPIDES. Well, well, I think I'll prove it, if
    you'll listen,
So that even you won't have one word to answer.

STREPSIADES. Come, I should like to hear what
    you've to say.   1470

CHORUS. 'Tis yours, old man, some method to con-
    trive
    This fight to win:
He would not without arms wherewith to strive
    So bold have been.
He knows, be sure, whereon to trust.   1475
His eager bearing proves he must.
So come and tell us from what cause
                this sad dispute began;
Come, tell us how it first arose:
                do tell us if you can.   1480

STREPSIADES. Well from the very first I will
                the whole contention show:
'Twas when I went into the house
                to feast him, as you know,
I bade him bring his lyre and sing,   1485
                the supper to adorn,

Some lay of old Simonides,
                as, how the Ram was shorn:
But he replied, to sing at meals
                was coarse and obsolete;   1490
Like some old beldame humming airs
                the while she grinds her wheat.

PHEIDIPPIDES. And should you not be thrashed
    who told   your son, from food abstaining
To SING! as though you were, forsooth   1495
                cicalas entertaining.

STREPSIADES. You hear him! so he said just now
                or e'er high words began:
And next he called Simonides
                a very sorry man.   1500
And when I heard him, I could scarce
                my rising wrath command;
Yet so I did, and him I bid
                take myrtle in his hand
And chant some lines from Aeschylus,   1505
                but he replied with ire,
"Believe me, I'm not one of those
                who Aeschylus admire,
That rough, unpolished, turgid bard,
                that mouther of bombast!"   1510
When he said this, my heart began
                to heave extremely fast;
Yet still I kept my passion down,
                and said, "Then prithee you,
Sing one of those new-fangled songs   1515
                which modern striplings do."
And he began the shameful tale
                Euripides has told
How a brother and a sister lived
                incestuous lives of old.   1520
Then, then I could no more restrain,
                but first I must confess
With strong abuse I loaded him,
                and so, as you may guess,
We stormed and bandied threat for threat: 1525
                till out at last he flew,
And smashed and thrashed and thumped and
    bumped
                and bruised me black and blue.

PHEIDIPPIDES. And rightly too, who coolly dared
                Euripides to blame,   1530
Most sapient bard.

STREPSIADES.   Most sapient bard!
                you, what's your fitting name?
Ah! but he'll pummel me again.

PHEIDIPPIDES.   He will: and justly too.

STREPSIADES. What! justly, heartless villain! when
                'twas I who nurtured you.   1536
I knew your little lisping ways,
                how soon, you'd hardly think,

1496. cicalas entertaining; they supposedly lived on dew. 1519–20.
How . . . old. This refers to Macareus and Canache in the lost
play, *Aeolus*.

If you cried "bree!" I guessed your wants,
   and used to give you drink: 1540
If you said "mamm!" I fetched you bread
   with fond discernment true,
And you could hardly say "Cacca!"
   when through the door I flew
And held you out a full arm's length 1545
   your little needs to do:
But now when I was crying
 That I with pain was dying,
 You brute! you would not tarry
 Me out of doors to carry, 1550
 But choking with despair
 I've been and done it there.

CHORUS. Sure all young hearts are palpitating now
   To hear him plead,
 Since if those lips with artful words avow
   The daring deed, 1556
 And once a favouring verdict win,
 A fig for every old man's skin.

O thou! who rakest up new thoughts
   with daring hands profane. 1560
Try all you can, ingenious man,
   that verdict to obtain.

PHEIDIPPIDES. How sweet it is these novel arts,
   these clever words to know
And have the power established rules 1565
   and laws to overthrow.
Why in old times when horses were
   my sole delight, 'twas wonder
If I could say a dozen words
   without some awful blunder! 1570
But now that he has made me quit
   that reckless mode of living,
And I have been to subtle thoughts
   my whole attention giving,
I hope to prove by logic strict 1575
   'tis right to beat my father.

STREPSIADES. O! buy your horses back, by Zeus,
   since I would ten times rather
Have to support a four-in-hand,
   so I be struck no more. 1580

PHEIDIPPIDES. Peace. I will now resume the thread
   where I broke off before.
And first I ask: when I was young,
   did you not strike me then?

STREPSIADES. Yea: for I loved and cherished you.

PHEIDIPPIDES. Well, solve me this again, 1586
Is it not just that I your son
   should cherish you alike,
And strike you, since, as you observe,
   to cherish means to strike? 1590
What! must my body needs be scourged
   and pounded black and blue

And yours be scathless? was not I
   as much freeborn as you?
"Children are whipped, and shall not sires be
   whipped?" 1595
Perhaps you'll urge that children's minds
   alone are taught by blows:—
Well: Age is Second Childhood then:
   that everybody knows.
And as by old experience Age 1600
   should guide its steps more clearly,
So when they err, they surely should
   be punished more severely.

STREPSIADES. But Law goes everywhere for me:
   deny it, if you can. 1605

PHEIDIPPIDES. Well was not he who made the law,
   a man, a mortal man,
As you or I, who in old times
   talked over all the crowd?
And think you that to you or me 1610
   the same is not allowed,
To change it, so that sons by blows
   should keep their fathers steady?
Still, we'll be liberal, and blows
   which we've received already 1615
We will forget, we'll have no ex-
   post-facto legislation.
—Look at the game-cocks, look at all
   the animal creation,
Do not *they* beat their parents? Aye: 1620
   I say then, that in fact
They are as we, except that they
   no special laws enact.

STREPSIADES. Why don't you then, if always where
   the game-cock leads you follow, 1625
Ascend your perch to roost at night,
   and dirt and ordure swallow?

PHEIDIPPIDES. The case is different there, old man,
   as Socrates would see.

STREPSIADES. Well then you'll blame yourself at
   last, 1630
   if you keep striking me.

PHEIDIPPIDES. How so?

STREPSIADES. Why, if it's right for me to
   punish you my son,
You can, if you have got one, yours.

PHEIDIPPIDES. Aye, but suppose I've none.
Then having gulled me you will die, 1635
   while I've been flogged in vain.

STREPSIADES. Good friends! I really think he has
   some reason to complain.
I must concede he has put the case
   in quite a novel light: 1640
I really think we should be flogged
   unless we act aright!

PHEIDIPPIDES. Look to a fresh idea then.

1595. "Children . . . whipped?" The line is quoted from the *Alcestis* of Euripides.

1539. **bree,** a baby word for drink.

STREPSIADES. He'll be my death I vow.

PHEIDIPPIDES. Yet then perhaps you will not grudge 1645

ev'n what you suffer now.

STREPSIADES. How! will you make me like the blows

which I've received to-day?

PHEIDIPPIDES. Yes, for I'll beat my mother too.

STREPSIADES. What! What is that you say! 1650

Why, this is worse than all.

PHEIDIPPIDES. But what, if as I proved the other,

By the same Logic I can prove

'tis right to beat my mother?

STREPSIADES. Aye! what indeed! if this you plead,

If this you think to win, 1656

Why then, for all I care, you may

To the Accursed Pit convey

Yourself with all your learning new,

Your master, and your Logic too, 1660

And tumble headlong in.

O Clouds! O Clouds! I owe all this to you!

Why did I let you manage my affairs!

CHORUS. Nay, nay, old man, you owe it to yourself.

Why didst thou turn to wicked practices? 1665

STREPSIADES. Ah, but ye should have asked me that before,

And not have spurred a poor old fool to evil.

CHORUS. Such is our plan. We find a man

On evil thoughts intent,

Guide him along to shame and wrong,

Then leave him to repent. 1671

STREPSIADES. Hard words, alas! yet not more hard than just.

It was not right unfairly to keep back

The money that I borrowed. Come, my darling,

Come and destroy that filthy Chaerephon 1675

And Socrates; for they've deceived us both!

PHEIDIPPIDES. No. I will lift no hand against my Tutors.

STREPSIADES. Yes do, come, reverence Paternal Zeus.

PHEIDIPPIDES. Look there! Paternal Zeus! what an old fool.

Is there a Zeus?

STREPSIADES. There is.

PHEIDIPPIDES. There is *no* Zeus. 1680

Young Vortex reigns, and he has turned out Zeus.

1658. **Accursed Pit**, the Barathrum, a thirty-foot pit into which criminals or their remains were sometimes cast.

STREPSIADES. No Vortex reigns. That was my foolish thought

All through this vortex here. Fool that I was,

To think a piece of earthenware a God.

PHEIDIPPIDES. Well, rave away, talk nonsense to yourself. 1685

(*He returns into the house of* STREPSIADES.)

STREPSIADES. Oh! fool, fool, fool, how mad I must have been

To cast away the Gods, for Socrates.

Yet Hermes, gracious Hermes, be not angry

Nor crush me utterly, but look with mercy

On faults to which his idle talk hath led me. 1690

And lend thy counsel; tell me, had I better

Plague them with lawsuits, or how else annoy them

(*Affects to listen.*)

Good: your advice is good: I'll have no lawsuits,

I'll go at once and set their house on fire,

The prating rascals. Here, here, Xanthias, 1695

Quick, quick here, bring your ladder and your pitchfork,

Climb to the roof of their vile thinking-house,

Dig at their tiles, dig stoutly, an' thou lovest me,

Tumble the very house about their ears.

And someone fetch me here a lighted torch, 1700

And I'll soon see if, boasters as they are,

They won't repent of what they've done to me.

(*He sets fire to the house of* SOCRATES.)

STUDENT 1 (*from within*). O dear! O dear!

STREPSIADES. Now, now, my torch, send out a lusty flame.

STUDENT 1. Man! what are you at there?

STREPSIADES. What am I at? I'll tell you. 1705

I'm splitting straws with your house-rafters here.

STUDENT 2. Oh me! who's been and set our house on fire?

STREPSIADES. Who was it, think you, that you stole the cloak from?

STUDENT 3. O Murder! Murder!

STREPSIADES. That's the very thing,

Unless this pick prove traitor to my hopes, 1710

Or I fall down, and break my blessed neck.

SOCRATES. Hallo! what are you at, up on our roof?

STREPSIADES. I walk on air, and contemplate the Sun.

SOCRATES. O! I shall suffocate. O dear! O dear!

CHAEREPHON. And I, poor devil, shall be burnt to death. 1715

STREPSIADES. For with what aim did ye insult the Gods,

And pry around the dwellings of the Moon?

Strike, smite them, spare them not, for many reasons,

BUT MOST BECAUSE THEY HAVE BLASPHEMED THE GODS!

CHORUS. Lead out of the way: for I think we may say 1720

We have acted our part very fairly to-day.

Thucydides

c. 460–c. 400 B.C.

The Greeks considered history a fine art, as worthy in its way as epic and tragedy, and dedicated one of their nine Muses, Clio, to its care. Certainly few modern historians combine the objective inquiry into fact and the imaginative re-creation of the past that distinguish Thucydides, their greatest master. He had predecessors, of course, who gradually shaped this ideal through their own experiments, but even the *History* of Herodotus (c. 484–c. 425 B.C.) seems primitive and naïve when compared with Thucydides' *History of the Peloponnesian War*.

Yet Thucydides was not so much a research historian as a chronicler of contemporary events, in some of which he took an active part. He lived in the discouraging days of city-state wars when the national unity and democratic ideals that had inspired Herodotus were disintegrating and the decline of faith in tradition and of hope for the future was undermining the Greek way of life. Stoically he watched this beginning of Greek suicide and set down the facts about the ruinous wars for later generations to read.

He was born into a rich Athenian family, and, narrowly escaping death in the great plague of 429 B.C. that killed Pericles, lived to assume command of an Athenian naval expedition to Thrace in 425. The failure of his efforts there to prevent the Spartans from capturing an Athenian city led him into voluntary exile, since he suspected that the democratic leader in Athens, Cleon, would victimize him as an aristocrat. During the twenty years of war that followed, he traveled widely, especially in the realm of the Spartans and their allies, who welcomed him because of his exile and gave him a knowledge of their activities that contributed to the impartiality of his later history. With the end of the war in 404 B.C., victorious Sparta deposed the democratic party in Athens and Thucydides returned under the hateful rule of the Thirty Tyrants. From the very start of the war he had been keeping his records of events, but not until the end of it, apparently, did he set about his *History* in earnest. He was still engaged on it when he died (or was murdered) around 400 B.C.

The incomplete *History* carries the story of the war from 431 B.C. to the Revolution of the Four Hundred in 411 B.C. It is preceded by a sketch of Greek military history from Minoan times, obviously much less trustworthy than the chronicle Thucydides recorded at first hand, though his method even here invites our confidence. With great pride in his undertaking he makes a stern promise of accuracy and sets forth the first real historical method in Western literature. The hearsay and miracles that had charmed Herodotus are severely ruled out. His silence about the gods and his cynical mention of oracles assure us that Thucydides belonged to the new philosophical order; for him the age of faith and the old religion was a thing of the past.

Yet the most famous episodes in the *History* are the very ones where, as he explains, he has taken liberty with his text—namely, the speeches of statesmen and emissaries on great occasions. No text existed for the Funeral Oration of Pericles, but Thucydides has re-created it as he actually heard it spoken. He explained his procedure as follows: "As to the words spoken by orators it was hard for me and for others from whom I received them at secondhand to remember the exact words that were spoken. But I have made each orator speak as befitted the occasion and as I thought he would have spoken, keeping nevertheless as closely as possible to the general sense of what was really spoken." If the speech of Pericles sounds more finished and rhetorical than the homely utterances of a straightforward man of affairs, we must still be grateful to the artist in Thucydides that preserved his noble sentiments on that occasion in such vivid and tangible form.

In the grim sequence of martial events that form the *History* it is refreshing to come upon two of the great political documents of Greece, which give us our most direct insight into the meaning of Greek democracy to the Greeks themselves. The Funeral Oration of Pericles, which is the Greek counterpart of Lincoln's Gettysburg Address, was delivered at a celebration for the Athenians who had died in the first year of war. It is not a militant address, but a magnificent tribute to the democratic Athens that had been Pericles' ideal. It is an inspirational talk that proudly reviews the free institutions and enlightened culture for which the Athenians were fighting. This enkindling speech, which remains alive for democratic people everywhere, takes on a melancholy cast when we realize that the very features of Athenian culture honored here were to suffer a mortal blow in the long war that lay ahead.

The Melian Dialogue, associated with a political incident fifteen years later (416 B.C.), gives a much less flattering view of the Athenians. Far from tolerant abroad, they had sent envoys supported by troops to demand that the Spartan colony of Melos surrender and join the Athenian confederacy. Although in a hopeless military position, the Melians pleaded for political justice and civic honor, since they desired only to remain neutral in the war. The cynical, or realistic, Athenians argued that the Melians' honor would be more disgraced by the fall of their city than by renunciation of their tie with Sparta. But the Melians chose the road of principle, dismissed the Athenian envoys, and were soon annihilated. Thucydides does not represent them as foolish, however. In our century more than one nation has had to choose whether to live in slavery or die for freedom and honor. Thucydides was gravely concerned about the decline of political morality in his day. Without swerving from his objective approach to his material, he has made the Melian Dialogue a noble plea for justice among nations, regardless of their strength. This is only one of many passages in his *History* that rise to the heights of inspiration and art.

Funeral Speech
of Pericles

DURING the same winter, in accordance with an old national custom, the funeral of those who first fell in this war was celebrated by the Athenians at the public charge. The ceremony is as follows: Three days before the celebration they erect a tent in which the bones of the dead are laid out, and every one brings to his own dead any offering which he pleases. At the time of the funeral the bones are placed in chests of cypress wood, which are conveyed on hearses; there is one chest for each tribe. They also carry a single empty litter decked with a pall for all whose bodies are missing, and cannot be recovered after the battle. The procession is accompanied by anyone who chooses, whether citizen or stranger, and the female relatives of the deceased are present at the place of interment and make lamentation. The public sepulchre is situated in the most beautiful spot outside the walls; there they always bury those who fall in war; only after the battle of Marathon the dead, in recognition of their pre-eminent valor, were interred on the field. When the remains have been laid in the earth, some man of known ability and high reputation, chosen by the city, delivers a suitable oration over them; after which the people depart. Such is the manner of interment; and the ceremony was repeated from time to time throughout the war. Over those who were the first buried Pericles was chosen to speak. At the fitting moment he advanced from the sepulchre to a lofty stage, which had been erected in order that he might be heard as far as possible by the multitude, and spoke as follows:—

"Most of those who have spoken here before me have commended the lawgiver who added this oration to our other funeral customs; it seemed to them a worthy thing that such an honor should be given at their burial to the dead who have fallen on the field of battle. But I should have preferred that, when men's deeds have been brave, they should be honored in deed only, and with such an honor as this public funeral, which you are now witnessing. Then the reputation of many would not have been imperilled on the eloquence or want of eloquence of one, and their virtues believed or not as he spoke well or ill. For it is difficult to say neither too little nor too much; and even moderation is apt not to give the impression of truthfulness. The friend of the dead who knows the facts is likely to think that the words of the speaker fall short of his knowledge and of his wishes; another who is not so well-informed, when he hears of anything which surpasses his own powers, will be envious and will suspect exaggeration. Mankind are tolerant of the praises of others so long as each hearer thinks that he can do as well or nearly as well himself, but, when the speaker rises above him, jealousy is aroused and he begins to be incredulous. However, since our ancestors have set the seal of their approval upon the practice, I must obey, and to the utmost of my power shall endeavor to satisfy the wishes and beliefs of all who hear me.

"I will speak first of our ancestors, for it is right and seemly that now, when we are lamenting the dead, a tribute should be paid to their memory. There has never been a time when they did not inhabit this land, which by their valor they have handed down from generation to generation, and we have received from them a free state. But if they were worthy of praise, still more were our fathers, who added to their inheritance, and after many a struggle transmitted to us their sons this great empire. And we ourselves assembled here today, who are still most of us in the vigor of life, have carried the work of improvement further, and have richly endowed our city with all things, so that she is sufficient for herself both in peace and war. Of the military exploits by which our various possessions were acquired, or of the energy with which we or our fathers drove back the tide of war, Hellenic or Barbarian, I will not speak; for the tale would be long and is familiar to you. But before I praise the dead, I should like to point out by what principles of action we rose to power, and under what institutions and through what manner of life our empire became great. For I conceive that such thoughts are not unsuited to the occasion, and that this numerous assembly of citizens and strangers may profitably listen to them.

"Our form of government does not enter into rivalry with the institutions of others. We do not copy our neighbors, but are an example to them. It is true that we are called a democracy, for the administration is in the hands of the many and not of the few. But while the law secures equal justice to all alike in their private disputes, the claim of excellence is also recognized; and when a citizen is in any way distinguished, he is preferred to the public service, not as a matter of privilege, but as the reward of merit. Neither is poverty a bar, but a man may benefit his country whatever be the obscurity of his condition. There is no exclusiveness in our public life, and in our private intercourse we are not suspicious of one another, nor angry with our neighbor if he does what he likes; we do not put on sour looks at him which, though harmless, are not pleas-

---

Funeral . . . Pericles. Translated by Benjamin Jowett. Published by The Clarendon Press, Oxford.
3. **war,** the Peloponnesian War, a 27-year-old struggle between Athens and Sparta and their respective allies.

ant. While we are thus unconstrained in our private intercourse, a spirit of reverence pervades our public acts; we are prevented from doing wrong by respect for the authorities and for the laws, having an especial regard to those which are ordained for the protection of the injured as well as to those unwritten laws which bring upon the transgressor of them the reprobation of the general sentiment.

"And we have not forgotten to provide for our weary spirits many relaxations from toil; we have regular games and sacrifices throughout the year; our homes are beautiful and elegant; and the delight which we daily feel in all these things helps to banish melancholy. Because of the greatness of our city the fruits of the whole earth flow in upon us; so that we enjoy the goods of other countries as freely as of our own.

"Then, again, our military training is in many respects superior to that of our adversaries. Our city is thrown open to the world, and we never expel a foreigner or prevent him from seeing or learning anything of which the secret if revealed to an enemy might profit him. We rely not upon management or trickery, but upon our own hearts and hands. And in the matter of education, whereas they from early youth are always undergoing laborious exercises which are to make them brave, we live at ease, and yet are equally ready to face the perils which they face. And here is the proof. The Lacedaemonians come into Attica not by themselves, but with their whole confederacy following; we go alone into a neighbor's country; and although our opponents are fighting for their homes and we on a foreign soil, we have seldom any difficulty in overcoming them. Our enemies have never yet felt our united strength; the care of a navy divides our attention, and on land we are obliged to send our own citizens everywhere. But they, if they meet and defeat a part of our army, are as proud as if they had routed us all, and when defeated they pretend to have been vanquished by us all.

"If then we prefer to meet danger with a light heart but without laborious training, and with a courage which is gained by habit and not enforced by law, are we not greatly the gainers? Since we do not anticipate the pain, although, when the hour comes, we can be as brave as those who never allow themselves to rest; and thus too our city is equally admirable in peace and in war. For we are lovers of the beautiful, yet simple in our tastes, and we cultivate the mind without loss of manliness. Wealth we employ, not for talk and ostentation, but when there is a real use for it. To avow poverty with us is no disgrace; the true disgrace is in doing nothing to avoid it. An Athenian citizen does not neglect the state because he takes care of his own household; and even those of us who are engaged in business have a very fair idea of politics. We alone regard a man who takes no interest in public affairs, not as a harmless, but as a useless character; and if few of us are originators, we are all sound judges of a policy. The great impediment to action is, in our opinion, not discussion, but the want of that knowledge which is gained by discussion preparatory to action. For we have a peculiar power of thinking before we act and of acting too, whereas other men are courageous from ignorance, but hesitate upon reflection. And they are surely to be esteemed the bravest spirits who, having the clearest sense both of the pains and pleasures of life, do not on that account shrink from danger. In doing good, again, we are unlike others; we make our friends by conferring, not by receiving favors. Now he who confers a favor is the firmer friend, because he would fain by kindness keep alive the memory of an obligation; but the recipient is colder in his feelings, because he knows that in requiting another's generosity he will not be winning gratitude but only paying a debt. We alone do good to our neighbors not upon a calculation of interest, but in the confidence of freedom and in a frank and fearless spirit. To sum up: I say that Athens is the school of Hellas, and that the individual Athenian in his own person seems to have the power of adapting himself to the most varied forms of action with the utmost versatility and grace. This is no passing and idle word, but truth and fact; and the assertion is verified by the position to which these qualities have raised the state. For in the hour of trial Athens alone among her contemporaries is superior to the report of her. No enemy who comes against her is indignant at the reverses which he sustains at the hands of such a city; no subject complains that his masters are unworthy of him. And we shall assuredly not be without witnesses; there are mighty monuments of our power which will make us the wonder of this and of succeeding ages; we shall not need the praises of Homer or of any other panegyrist whose poetry may please for the moment, although his representation of the facts will not bear the light of day. For we have compelled every land and every sea to open a path for our valor, and have everywhere planted eternal memorials of our friendship and of our enmity. Such is the city for whose sake these men nobly fought and died; they could not bear the thought that she might be taken from them; and every one of us who survive should gladly toil on her behalf.

"I have dwelt upon the greatness of Athens because I want to show you that we are contending for a higher prize than those who enjoy none of these privileges, and to establish by manifest proof the merit of these men whom I am now commem-

29. **Lacedaemonians**, the Spartans.

orating. Their loftiest praise has been already spoken. For in magnifying the city I have magnified them, and men like them whose virtues made her glorious. And of how few Hellenes can it be said as of them, that their deeds when weighed in the balance have been found equal to their fame! Methinks that a death such as theirs has been gives the true measure of a man's worth; it may be the first revelation of his virtues, but is at any rate their final seal. For even those who come short in other ways may justly plead the valor with which they have fought for their country; they have blotted out the evil with the good, and have benefited the state more by their public services than they have injured her by their private actions. None of these men were enervated by wealth or hesitated to resign the pleasures of life; none of them put off the evil day in the hope, natural to poverty, that a man, though poor, may one day become rich. But, deeming that the punishment of their enemies was sweeter than any of these things, and that they could fall in no nobler cause, they determined at the hazard of their lives to be honorably avenged, and to leave the rest. They resigned to hope their unknown chance of happiness; but in the face of death they resolved to rely upon themselves alone. And when the moment came they were minded to resist and suffer, rather than to fly and save their lives; they ran away from the word of dishonor, but on the battle-field their feet stood fast, and in an instant, at the height of their fortune, they passed away from the scene, not of their fear, but of their glory.

"Such was the end of these men; they were worthy of Athens, and the living need not desire to have a more heroic spirit, although they may pray for a less fatal issue. The value of such a spirit is not to be expressed in words. Anyone can discourse to you forever about the advantages of a brave defence, which you know already. But instead of listening to him I would have you day by day fix your eyes upon the greatness of Athens, until you become filled with the love of her; and when you are impressed by the spectacle of her glory, reflect that this empire has been acquired by men who knew their duty and had the courage to do it, who in the hour of conflict had the fear of dishonor always present to them, and who, if ever they failed in an enterprise, would not allow their virtues to be lost to their country, but freely gave their lives to her as the fairest offering which they could present at her feast. The sacrifice which they collectively made was individually repaid to them; for they received again each one for himself a praise which grows not old, and the noblest of all sepulchres—I speak not of that in which their remains are laid, but of that in which their glory survives, and is proclaimed always and on every fitting occasion both in word and deed. For the whole earth is the sepulchre of famous men; not only are they commemorated by columns and inscriptions in their own country, but in foreign lands there dwells also an unwritten memorial of them, graven not on stone but in the hearts of men. Make them your examples, and, esteeming courage to be freedom and freedom to be happiness, do not weigh too nicely the perils of war. The unfortunate who has no hope of a change for the better has less reason to throw away his life than the prosperous who, if he survive, is always liable to a change for the worse, and to whom any accidental fall makes the most serious difference. To a man of spirit, cowardice and disaster coming together are far more bitter than death striking him unperceived at a time when he is full of courage and animated by the general hope.

"Wherefore I do not now commiserate the parents of the dead who stand here; I would rather comfort them. You know that your life has been passed amid manifold vicissitudes; and that they may be deemed fortunate who have gained most honor, whether an honorable death like theirs, or an honorable sorrow like yours, and whose days have been so ordered that the term of their happiness is likewise the term of their life. I know how hard it is to make you feel this, when the good fortune of others will too often remind you of the gladness which once lightened your hearts. And sorrow is felt at the want of those blessings, not which a man never knew, but which were a part of his life before they were taken from him. Some of you are of an age at which they may hope to have other children, and they ought to bear their sorrow better; not only will the children who may hereafter be born make them forget their own lost ones, but the city will be doubly a gainer. She will not be left desolate, and she will be safer. For a man's counsel cannot have equal weight or worth, when he alone has no children to risk in the general danger. To those of you who have passed their prime, I say: 'Congratulate yourselves that you have been happy during the greater part of your days; remember that your life of sorrow will not last long, and be comforted by the glory of those who are gone. For the love of honor alone is ever young, and not riches, as some say, but honor is the delight of men when they are old and useless.'

"To you who are the sons and brothers of the departed, I see that the struggle to emulate them will be an arduous one. For all men praise the dead, and, however pre-eminent your virtue may be, hardly will you be thought, I do not say to equal, but even to approach them. The living have their rivals and detractors, but when a man is out of the way, the honor and good-will which he receives is unalloyed. And, if I am to speak of womanly virtues to those of you who will henceforth be widows, let me sum them up in one short admonition: To a woman not to show more weakness than is natural to her sex is a great glory, and not to be talked about for good or for evil among men.

"I have paid the required tribute, in obedience to the law, making use of such fitting words as I had. The tribute of deeds has been paid in part; for the dead have been honorably interred, and it remains only that their children should be maintained at the public charge until they are grown up: this is the solid prize with which, as with a garland, Athens crowns her sons living and dead, after a struggle like theirs. For where the rewards of virtue are greatest, there the noblest citizens are enlisted in the service of the state. And now, when you have duly lamented, every one his own dead, you may depart."

Such was the order of the funeral celebrated in this winter, with the end of which ended the first year of the Peloponnesian War.

The Melian Dialogue

THE Athenians next made an expedition against the island of Melos with thirty ships of their own, six Chian, and two Lesbian, twelve hundred hoplites and three hundred archers besides twenty mounted archers of their own, and about fifteen hundred hoplites furnished by their allies in the islands. The Melians are colonists of the Lacedaemonians who would not submit to Athens like the other islanders. At first they were neutral and took no part. But when the Athenians tried to coerce them by ravaging their lands, they were driven into open hostilities. The generals, Cleomedes the son of Lycomedes and Tisias the son of Tisimachus, encamped with the Athenian forces on the land. But before they did the country any harm they sent envoys to negotiate with the Melians. Instead of bringing these envoys before the people, the Melians desired them to explain their errand to the magistrates and to the dominant class. They spoke as follows:—

"Since we are not allowed to speak to the people, lest, forsooth, a multitude should be deceived by seductive and unanswerable arguments which they would hear set forth in a single uninterrupted oration (for we are perfectly aware that this is what you mean in bringing us before a select few), you who are sitting here may as well make assurance yet surer. Let us have no set speeches at all, but do you reply to each several statement of which you disapprove, and criticize it at once. Say first of all how you like this mode of proceeding."

The Melian representatives answered:—"The quiet

The Melian Dialogue. Translated by Benjamin Jowett. Published by The Clarendon Press, Oxford.

interchange of explanations is a reasonable thing, and we do not object to that. But your warlike movements, which are present not only to our fears but to our eyes, seem to belie your words. We see that, although you may reason with us, you mean to be our judges; and that at the end of the discussion, if the justice of our cause prevail and we therefore refuse to yield, we may expect war; if we are convinced by you, slavery."

ATHENIANS. "Nay, but if you are only going to argue from fancies about the future, or if you meet us with any other purpose than that of looking your circumstances in the face and saving your city, we have done; but if this is your intention we will proceed."

MELIANS. "It is an excusable and natural thing that men in our position should neglect no argument and no view which may avail. But we admit that this conference has met to consider the question of our preservation; and therefore let the argument proceed in the manner which you propose."

ATHENIANS. "Well, then, we Athenians will use no fine words; we will not go out of our way to prove at length that we have a right to rule, because we overthrew the Persians; or that we attack you now because we are suffering any injury at your hands. We should not convince you if we did; nor must you expect to convince us by arguing that, although a colony of the Lacedaemonians, you have taken no part in their expeditions, or that you have never done us any wrong. But you and we should say what we really think, and aim only at what is possible, for we both alike know that into the discussion of human affairs the question of justice only enters where there is equal power to enforce it, and that the powerful exact what they can, and the weak grant what they must."

MELIANS. "Well, then, since you set aside justice and invite us to speak of expediency, in our judgment it is certainly expedient that you should respect a principle which is for the common good; that to every man when in peril a reasonable claim should be accounted a claim of right, and that any plea which he is disposed to urge, even if failing of the point a little, should help his cause. Your interest in this principle is quite as great as ours, inasmuch as you, if you fall, will incur the heaviest vengeance, and will be the most terrible example to mankind."

ATHENIANS. "The fall of our empire, if it should fall, is not an event to which we look forward with dismay; for ruling states such as Lacedaemon are not cruel to their vanquished enemies. With the Lacedaemonians, however, we are not now contending; the real danger is from our many subject states, who may of their own motion rise up and overcome their masters. But this is a danger which you may leave to us. And we will now endeavor to show that we have come in the interests of our empire, and that in what we are about to say we are only seeking the preservation of your city. For we want to make you ours with the least trouble to ourselves, and it is for the interests of us both that you should not be destroyed."

MELIANS. "It may be your interest to be our masters, but how can it be ours to be your slaves?"

10 ATHENIANS. "To you the gain will be that by submission you will avert the worst; and we shall be all the richer for your preservation."

MELIANS. "But must we be your enemies? Will you not receive us as friends if we are neutral and remain at peace with you?"

ATHENIANS. "No, your enmity is not half so mischievous to us as your friendship; for the one is in the eyes of our subjects an argument of our power, the other of our weakness."

20 MELIANS. "But are your subjects really unable to distinguish between states in which you have no concern, and those which are chiefly your own colonies, and in some cases have revolted and been subdued by you?"

ATHENIANS. "Why, they do not doubt that both of them have a good deal to say for themselves on the score of justice, but they think that states like yours are left free because they are able to defend themselves, and that we do not attack them because we 30 dare not. So that your subjection will give us an increase of security, as well as an extension of empire. For we are masters of the sea, and you who are islanders, and insignificant islanders too, must not be allowed to escape us."

MELIANS. "But do you not recognize another danger? For, once more, since you drive us from the plea of justice and press upon us your doctrine of expediency, we must show you what is for our interest, and, if it be for yours also, may hope to con- 40 vince you:—Will you not be making enemies of all who are now neutrals? When they see how you are treating us they will expect you some day to turn against them; and if so, are you not strengthening the enemies whom you already have, and bringing upon you others who, if they could help, would never dream of being your enemies at all?"

ATHENIANS. "We do not consider our really dangerous enemies to be any of the peoples inhabiting the mainland who, secure in their freedom, may 50 defer indefinitely any measures of precaution which they take against us, but islanders who, like you, happen to be under no control, and all who may be already irritated by the necessity of submission to our empire—these are our real enemies, for they are the most reckless and most likely to bring themselves as well as us into a danger which they cannot but foresee."

MELIANS. "Surely then, if you and your subjects will brave all this risk, you to preserve your empire and they to be quit of it, how base and cowardly 6 would it be in us, who retain our freedom, not to do and suffer anything rather than be your slaves."

ATHENIANS. "Not so, if you calmly reflect: for you are not fighting against equals to whom you cannot yield without disgrace, but you are taking counsel whether or no you shall resist an overwhelming force. The question is not one of honor but of prudence."

MELIANS. "But we know that the fortune of war is sometimes impartial, and not always on the side of 7 numbers. If we yield now, all is over; but if we fight, there is yet a hope that we may stand upright."

ATHENIANS. "Hope is a good comforter in the hour of danger, and when men have something else to depend upon, although hurtful, she is not ruinous. But when her spendthrift nature has induced them to stake their all, they see her as she is in the moment of their fall, and not till then. While the knowledge of her might enable them to be wary of her, 8 she never fails. You are weak and a single turn of the scale might be your ruin. Do not you be thus deluded; avoid the error of which so many are guilty, who, although they might still be saved if they would take the natural means, when visible grounds of confidence forsake them, have recourse to the invisible, to prophecies and oracles and the like, which ruin men by the hopes which they inspire in them."

MELIANS. "We know only too well how hard the 9 struggle must be against your power, and against fortune, if she does not mean to be impartial. Nevertheless we do not despair of fortune; for we hope to stand as high as you in the favor of heaven, because we are righteous, and you against whom we contend are unrighteous; and we are satisfied that our deficiency in power will be compensated by the aid of our allies the Lacedaemonians; they cannot refuse to help us, if only because we are their kinsmen, and for the sake of their own honor. And therefore 10 our confidence is not so utterly blind as you suppose."

ATHENIANS. "As for the Gods, we expect to have quite as much of their favor as you: for we are not doing or claiming anything which goes beyond common opinion about divine or men's desires about human things. For of the Gods we believe, and of men we know, that by a law of their nature wherever they can rule they will. This law was not made by us, and we are not the first who have acted upon it; 11 we did but inherit it, and shall bequeath it to all time, and we know that you and all mankind, if you were as strong as we are, would do as we do. So much for the Gods; we have told you why we expect to stand as high in their good opinion as you. And then as to the Lacedaemonians—when you imagine that out of very shame they will assist, we admire the innocence of your idea, but we do not envy you the folly of it. The Lacedaemonians are exceedingly virtuous among themselves and according to their national standard of morality. But, in respect of their dealings with others, although many things might be said, they can be described in a few words—of all men whom we know they are the most notorious for identifying what is pleasant with what is honorable, and what is expedient with what is just. But how inconsistent is such a character with your present blind hope of deliverance!"

MELIANS. "That is the very reason why we trust them; they will look to their interest, and therefore will not be willing to betray the Melians, who are their own colonists, lest they should be distrusted by their friends in Hellas and play into the hands of their enemies."

ATHENIANS. "But do you not see that the path of expediency is safe, whereas justice and honor involve danger in practice, and such dangers the Lacedaemonians seldom care to face?"

MELIANS. "On the other hand, we think that whatever perils there may be, they will be ready to face them for our sakes, and will consider danger less dangerous where we are concerned. For if they need our aid we are close at hand, and they can better trust our loyal feeling because we are their kinsmen."

ATHENIANS. "Yes, but what encourages men who are invited to join in a conflict is clearly not the goodwill of those who summon them to their side, but a decided superiority in real power. To this no men look more keenly than the Lacedaemonians; so little confidence have they in their own resources, that they only attack their neighbors when they have numerous allies, and therefore they are not likely to find their way by themselves to an island, when we are masters of the sea."

MELIANS. "But they may send their allies: the Cretan sea is a large place; and the masters of the sea will have more difficulty in overtaking vessels which want to escape than the pursued in escaping. If the attempt should fail they may invade Attica itself, and find their way to allies of yours whom Brasidas did not reach; and then you will have to fight, not for the conquest of a land in which you have no concern, but nearer home, for the preservation of your confederacy and of your own territory."

ATHENIANS. "Help may come from Lacedaemon to you as it has come to others, and should you ever have actual experience of it, then you will know that never once have the Athenians retired from a siege through fear of a foe elsewhere. You told us that the safety of your city would be your first care, but we remark that, in this long discussion, not a word has been uttered by you which would give a reasonable man expectation of deliverance. Your strongest grounds are hopes deferred, and what power you have is not to be compared with that which is already arrayed against you. Unless after we have withdrawn you mean to come, as even now you may, to a wiser conclusion, you are showing a great want of sense. For surely you cannot dream of flying to that false sense of honor which has been the ruin of so many when danger and dishonor were staring them in the face. Many men with their eyes still open to the consequences have found the word 'honor' too much for them, and have suffered a mere name to lure them on, until it has drawn down upon them real and irretrievable calamities; through their own folly they have incurred a worse dishonor than fortune would have inflicted upon them. If you are wise you will not run this risk; you ought to see that there can be no disgrace in yielding to a great city which invites you to become her ally on reasonable terms, keeping your own land, and merely paying tribute; and that you will certainly gain no honor if, having to choose between two alternatives, safety and war, you obstinately prefer the worse. To maintain our rights against equals, to be politic with superiors, and to be moderate toward inferiors is the path of safety. Reflect once more when we have withdrawn, and say to yourselves over and over again that you are deliberating about your one and only country, which may be saved or may be destroyed by a single decision."

The Athenians left the conference: the Melians, after consulting among themselves, resolved to persevere in their refusal, and made answer as follows: —"Men of Athens, our resolution is unchanged; and we will not in a moment surrender that liberty which our city, founded seven hundred years ago, still enjoys; we will trust to the good fortune which, by the favor of the Gods, has hitherto preserved us, and for human help to the Lacedaemonians, and endeavor to save ourselves. We are ready however to be your friends, and the enemies neither of you nor of the Lacedaemonians, and we ask you to leave our country when you have made such a peace as may appear to be in the interest of both parties."

Such was the answer of the Melians; the Athenians, as they quitted the conference, spoke as follows:—"Well, we must say, judging from the decision at which you have arrived, that you are the only men who deem the future to be more certain than the present, and regard things unseen as already realized in your fond anticipation, and that the more you cast yourselves upon the Lacedaemonians and fortune and hope, and trust them, the more complete will be your ruin."

Plato

c. 427–348 B.C.

If the portrait of Socrates in *The Clouds* is ridiculously unfair, the counterpicture in Plato's dialogues sometimes comes close to idolatry. Socrates numbered among his followers some of the best and most diverse minds of the new generation—Antisthenes the Cynic, Aristippus the Cyrenaic, Eucleides the Skeptic, Alcibiades the reckless politician. But only two set themselves the grateful task of recording their master's words and personality for future ages. Xenophon was more a man of action than a philosopher, and his *Memorabilia* of Socrates are superficial, though reverent and honest. It remained for Plato, the greatest of the disciples, to create our traditional portrait of the Great Gadfly.

Socrates was already in his sixties when Aristocles (later called Plato) came to him for instruction as an earnest youth not yet twenty. The slovenly person of Socrates was often seen at rich men's tables and he drew most of his followers from the aristocratic youth of the day. Plato was no exception, for his family was one of the most ancient and distinguished in Athens. In his youth he approached, like Sophocles, the Greek ideal—handsome, skilled in athletics, brave in battle, and talented in mathematics, politics, music, poetry, and drama. Although the influence of Socrates led him to renounce the theater for philosophy, the dramatic form of the dialogue that he chose to convey his ideas gave him a happy opportunity to express his dramatic talent.

For ten formative years he absorbed the teachings of Socrates. Then in rapid succession came the collapse of Athens in the Peloponnesian War, the year's rule of the Thirty Tyrants, the restoration of the democratic party, and the trial and execution of Socrates. Completely disillusioned with politics and the democratic system of Athens, Plato left to travel for over ten years in Egypt, Italy, and Sicily. In 387 B.C. he returned to Athens and with the financial help of his friends founded his Academy in an olive grove sacred to the hero Academus, not the first of ancient universities, but the most famous and enduring. The Academy charged no tuition fee, but was supported by the donations of wealthy patrons, and attracted some of the greatest minds of the next generation—Aristotle, Demosthenes, Xenocrates. Although the lectures and discussions at the Academy included such technical subjects as mathematics, astronomy, and music, Plato's personal interests were in ethics, politics, and law—in general, the subjects of his dialogues.

Following the bent of Socrates more closely than any other of the disciples, Plato perfected his theory of Ideas as the ultimate reality underlying individual things. The material objects that we perceive by the senses are perpetually changing and eventually disappear. Only the generalized images, or ideas of these things, which are made by divinity, can be perceived in the mind, remain constant, and constitute the true reality. Knowledge lies in grasping these ideas rather than in knowing specific things. The highest of all the ideas is goodness, the moving principle of the world and hence undistinguishable from divinity itself. All education, then, is ultimately ethical in design, aspiring to the knowledge of goodness; and Plato represents Socrates, the great teacher, as drawing out of his disciples by questions the true definition of such moral ideas as temperance, courage, beauty, and love. Through understanding these ideas they are led to virtue.

It can readily be seen that Plato's ethics was the core of his philosophy; and even his metaphysics was a kind of ethical idealism. We should not be surprised that in aesthetics too, he should tolerate only that art and literature that lead to an understanding of goodness. In the last excerpt from the *Republic* given here he illustrates his general theory of Ideas by opposing the objects called bed and table to the ideas of bed and table—the ultimate reality in this instance. But he proceeds to a third possibility in the artist's depiction, or imitation, of the bed or table, and draws his famous conclusion that all art is imitation of reality. As such it provides deception rather than knowledge and must be ruled out of the philosopher's education. It can be tolerated at all only when it concentrates on ethical objectives and inspires men to that search for knowledge which is goodness. This theory of art as the servant of the philosopher's state leads to a propagandistic view of art and is opposed to the doctrine of "art for art's sake."

Yet Plato was as much artist as philosopher and, in his only known writings, chose one of the most charming of literary forms to expound and popularize his ideas. He did not invent the philosophical dialogue, but in perfecting it he made it his own. It appealed to him originally as the ideal medium for representing the question-and-answer teaching of Socrates, and later, as in the *Symposium*, it could embody the round-table discussion of an idea in the search for truth. In the most artistic of the dialogues there is genuine give-and-take, and the speakers are adroitly differentiated like character creations in drama. In the later dialogues, when the artist in Plato succumbs to the philosopher, the dialogue is sheer pretense, and the lesser characters are allowed to interpolate mere yes and no in the monologues of Socrates (become himself a thin disguise for Plato). Of course the conversations are intended to be idealized versions of reality, synthesized in the early period from recollections or written notes, but eventually quite fictitious. The philosophers whom he presented expressed amazement at the words Plato put into their mouths. But he remains true to the spirit of his personalities and, like Thucydides in his speeches, represents what they at least might have said. And the details of setting and stage business give a dramatic reality to the best of the dialogues, a reality which is heightened by the rambling turns of the discussions and the inconclusive ends of many of them.

The dialogues of Plato are conventionally grouped by the three periods in which they are supposed to have been written. Shortly after the death of Socrates, before Plato had reached a secure philosophy of his own, he completed eight or nine short dialogues to record the personality, method, and characteristic ideas of his master. These are the most dramatic and popular of all and apparently the most faithful to the person and philosophy of Socrates. The best known are the three in which Plato recounts the actual trial and death of Socrates in an effort to vindicate him before the Athenian public. Of these, the *Apology* is not a dialogue but the substance of a speech made by Socrates at his trial. The bravery and independence of the man, as well as his jocularity and insolence, are masterfully conveyed in the artistic prose of Plato. The *Crito* reveals the efforts of his friends to save Socrates from execution and his insistence on living and dying by the laws of the state.

In middle life Plato composed about a dozen dialogues still built around the personality of his teacher but certainly embodying much more of his own thinking. Both the art and the philosophy of the man reach their zenith here. The *Phaedo* returns to the scene of his master's death and reveals him discoursing on the immortality of the soul just before he heroically drinks the hemlock. The *Phaedrus* and the *Symposium* discuss the controversial subject of Platonic love. But it is the monumental *Republic* that is best remembered from his entire career. He returned to writing late in life with a half-dozen dialogues, notably the *Parmenides* and *Laws*, but his art had declined and his philosophy was settling into an authoritarianism that completely repudiated Athenian democracy.

Actually this was not new with Plato. His aristocratic background and training were early reflected in his theory of Ideas, which subordinated the world of beds and tables so important to the democratic merchant class to those virtues—temperance, courage, wisdom, and justice—that belonged to the aristocratic ideal of the Greeks. In the *Republic* he defined an aristocratic utopia in which ideal goodness is achieved by paternalistic rule over the unenlightened working classes by a cultured minority, carefully chosen and educated, and living according to a Spartan communism. Indeed, the Spartan state came closest to the ideal of Plato, and his own effort to persuade Dionysius I and II, tyrants of Syracuse, to bring his ideal state to reality produced less of it than had the code of Lycurgus in Sparta. Clearly Plato is not a reassuring thinker for a democratic state as we know it, but his art and his idealism have made him an enduring force in Western thought. His Academy survived till the sixth century A.D., and through the Neoplatonists of the third century A.D. he helped to shape the ethics of Christianity.

Apology

How you, O Athenians, have been affected by my accusers, I cannot tell; but I know that they almost made me forget who I was—so persuasively did they speak; and yet they have hardly uttered a word of truth. But of the many falsehoods

Apology. Translated by Benjamin Jowett. Published by The Clarendon Press, Oxford. Plato's version of Socrates' speech of defense at his trial in 399 B.C. is much idealized.

told by them, there was one which quite amazed me; —I mean when they said that you should be upon your guard and not allow yourselves to be deceived by the force of my eloquence. To say this, when they were certain to be detected as soon as I opened [10] my lips and proved myself to be anything but a great speaker, did indeed appear to me most shameless—unless by the force of eloquence they mean the force of truth; for if such is their meaning, I admit that I am eloquent. But in how different a way from theirs! Well, as I was saying, they have scarcely spoken the truth at all; but from me you shall hear the whole truth: not, however, delivered after their manner in a set oration duly ornamented with words and phrases. No, by heaven! but I shall use the [20] words and arguments which occur to me at the moment; for I am confident in the justice of my cause: at my time of life I ought not to be appearing before you, O men of Athens, in the character of a juvenile orator—let no one expect it of me. And I must beg of you to grant me a favour:—If I defend myself in my accustomed manner, and you hear me using the words which I have been in the habit of using in the agora, at the tables of the money-changers, or anywhere else, I would ask you [30] not to be surprised, and not to interrupt me on this account. For I am more than seventy years of age, and appearing now for the first time in a court of law, I am quite a stranger to the language of the place; and therefore I would have you regard me as if I were really a stranger, whom you would excuse if he spoke in his native tongue, and after the fashion of his country:—Am I making an unfair request of you? Never mind the manner, which may or may not be good; but think only of the truth of [40] my words, and give heed to that: let the speaker speak truly and the judge decide justly.

And first, I have to reply to the older charges and to my first accusers, and then I will go on to the later ones. For of old I have had many accusers, who have accused me falsely to you during many years; and I am more afraid of them than of Anytus and his associates, who are dangerous, too, in their own way. But far more dangerous are the others, who began when you were children, and took pos- [50] session of your minds with their falsehoods, telling of one Socrates, a wise man, who speculated about the heaven above, and searched into the earth beneath, and made the worse appear the better cause. The disseminators of this tale are the accusers whom I dread; for their hearers are apt to fancy that such enquirers do not believe in the existence of the gods. And they are many, and their charges against me are of ancient date, and they were made by them in the days when you were more impressible than you [60] are now—in childhood, or it may have been in

47. **Anytus,** a wealthy politician and chief prosecutor of Socrates.

youth—and the cause when heard went by default, for there was none to answer. And hardest of all, I do not know and cannot tell the names of my accusers; unless in the chance case of a comic poet. All who from envy and malice have persuaded you—some of them having first convinced themselves—all this class of men are most difficult to deal with; for I cannot have them up here, and cross-examine them, and therefore I must simply fight with shadows in my own defence, and argue when there is no one who answers. I will ask you then to assume with me, as I was saying, that my opponents are of two kinds; one recent, the other ancient: and I hope that you will see the propriety of my answering the latter first, for these accusations you heard long before the others, and much oftener.

Well, then, I must make my defence, and endeavour to clear away in a short time, a slander which has lasted a long time. May I succeed, if to succeed be for my good and yours, or likely to avail me in my cause! The task is not an easy one; I quite understand the nature of it. And so leaving the event with God, in obedience to the law I will now make my defence.

I will begin at the beginning, and ask what is the accusation which has given rise to the slander of me, and in fact has encouraged Meletus to prefer this charge against me. Well, what do the slanderers say? They shall be my prosecutors, and I will sum up their words in an affidavit: "Socrates is an evil-doer, and a curious person, who searches into things under the earth and in heaven, and he makes the worse appear the better cause; and he teaches the aforesaid doctrines to others." Such is the nature of the accusation: it is just what you have yourselves seen in the comedy of Aristophanes, who has introduced a man whom he calls Socrates, going about and saying that he walks in air, and talking a deal of nonsense concerning matters of which I do not pretend to know either much or little—not that I mean to speak disparagingly of any one who is a student of natural philosophy. I should be very sorry if Meletus could bring so grave a charge against me. But the simple truth is, O Athenians, that I have nothing to do with physical speculations. Very many of those here present are witnesses to the truth of this, and to them I appeal. Speak then, you who have heard me, and tell your neighbours whether any of you have ever known me hold forth in few words or in many upon such matters. . . . You hear their answer. And from what they say of this part of the charge you will be able to judge of the truth of the rest.

As little foundation is there for the report that I am a teacher and take money; this accusation has

4. a comic poet; an allusion to *The Clouds* of Aristophanes.
27. Meletus, a minor tragic poet.

no more truth in it than the other. Although, if a man were really able to instruct mankind, to receive money for giving instruction would, in my opinion, be an honour to him. There is Gorgias of Leontium, and Prodicus of Ceos, and Hippias of Elis, who go the round of the cities, and are able to persuade the young men to leave their own citizens by whom they might be taught for nothing, and come to them whom they not only pay, but are thankful if they may be allowed to pay them. There is at this time a Parian philosopher residing in Athens, of whom I have heard; and I came to hear of him in this way: —I came across a man who has spent a world of money on the Sophists, Callias, the son of Hipponicus, and knowing that he had sons, I asked him: "Callias," I said, "if your two sons were foals or calves, there would be no difficulty in finding some one to put over them; we should hire a trainer of horses, or a farmer, probably, who would improve and perfect them in their own proper virtue and excellence; but as they are human beings, whom are you thinking of placing over them? Is there any one who understands human and political virtue? You must have thought about the matter, for you have sons; is there any one?" "There is," he said. "Who is he?" said I; "and of what country? and what does he charge?" "Evenus the Parian," he replied; "he is the man, and his charge is five minae." Happy is Evenus, I said to myself, if he really has this wisdom, and teaches at such a moderate charge. Had I the same, I should have been very proud and conceited; but the truth is that I have no knowledge of the kind.

I dare say, Athenians, that some one among you will reply, "Yes, Socrates, but what is the origin of these accusations which are brought against you; there must have been something strange which you have been doing? All these rumours and this talk about you would never have arisen if you had been like other men: tell us, then, what is the cause of them, for we should be sorry to judge hastily of you." Now, I regard this as a fair challenge, and I will endeavour to explain to you the reason why I am called wise and have such an evil fame. Please to attend then. And although some of you may think that I am joking, I declare that I will tell you the entire truth. Men of Athens, this reputation of mine has come of a certain sort of wisdom which I possess. If you ask me what kind of wisdom, I reply, wisdom such as may perhaps be attained by man, for to that extent I am inclined to believe that I am wise; whereas the persons of whom I was speaking have a superhuman wisdom, which I may fail to describe, because I have it not myself; and he who says that I have, speaks falsely, and is taking away my character. And here, O men of Athens, I must beg you not to interrupt me, even if I seem to say something extravagant. For the word which I will speak is not mine. I will refer you to a witness who is worthy of credit; that witness shall be the god of Delphi—he will tell you about my wisdom, if I have any, and of what sort it is. You must have known Chaerephon; he was early a friend of mine, and also a friend of yours, for he shared in the recent exile of the people, and returned with you. Well, Chaerephon, as you know, was very impetuous in all his doings, and he went to Delphi and boldly asked the oracle to tell him whether—as I was saying, I must beg you not to interrupt—he asked the oracle to tell him whether any one was wiser than I was, and the Pythian prophetess answered, that there was no man wiser. Chaerephon is dead himself; but his brother, who is in court, will confirm the truth of what I am saying.

Why do I mention this? Because I am going to explain to you why I have such an evil name. When I heard the answer, I said to myself, What can the god mean? and what is the interpretation of his riddle? for I know that I have no wisdom, small or great. What then can he mean when he says that I am the wisest of men? And yet he is a god, and cannot lie; that would be against his nature. After long consideration, I thought of a method of trying the question. I reflected that if I could only find a man wiser than myself, then I might go to the god with a refutation in my hand. I should say to him, "Here is a man who is wiser than I am; but you said that I was the wisest." Accordingly I went to one who had the reputation of wisdom, and observed him— his name I need not mention; he was a politician whom I selected for examination—and the result was as follows: When I began to talk with him, I could not help thinking that he was not really wise, although he was thought wise by many, and still wiser by himself; and thereupon I tried to explain to him that he thought himself wise, but was not really wise, and the consequence was that he hated me, and his enmity was shared by several who were present and heard me. So I left him, saying to myself, as I went away: Well, although I do not suppose that either of us knows anything really beautiful and good, I am better off than he is,—for he knows nothing, and thinks that he knows; I neither know nor think that I know. In this latter particular, then, I seem to have slightly the advantage of him. Then I went to another who had still higher pretensions to wisdom, and my conclusion was exactly the same. Whereupon I made another enemy of him, and of many others besides him.

Then I went to one man after another, being not unconscious of the enmity which I provoked, and I lamented and feared this: but necessity was laid upon me,—the word of God, I thought, ought to be considered first. And I said to myself, Go I must to all who appear to know, and find out the meaning of the oracle. And I swear to you, Athenians, by the dog I swear!—for I must tell you the truth—the result of my mission was just this: I found that the men most in repute were all but the most foolish; and that others less esteemed were really wiser and better. I will tell you the tale of my wanderings and of the "Herculean" labours, as I may call them, which I endured only to find at last the oracle irrefutable. After the politicians, I went to the poets; tragic, dithyrambic, and all sorts. And there, I said to myself, you will be instantly detected; now you will find out that you are more ignorant than they are. Accordingly I took them some of the most elaborate passages in their own writings, and asked what was the meaning of them—thinking that they would teach me something. Will you believe me? I am almost ashamed to confess the truth, but I must say that there is hardly a person present who would not have talked better about their poetry than they did themselves. Then I knew that not by wisdom do poets write poetry, but by a sort of genius and inspiration, they are like diviners or soothsayers who also say many fine things, but do not understand the meaning of them. The poets appeared to me to be much in the same case; and I further observed that upon the strength of their poetry they believed themselves to be the wisest of men in other things in which they were not wise. So I departed, conceiving myself to be superior to them for the same reason that I was superior to the politicians.

At last I went to the artisans. I was conscious that I knew nothing at all, as I may say, and I was sure that they knew many fine things; and here I was not mistaken, for they did know many things of which I was ignorant, and in this they certainly were wiser than I was. But I observed that even the good artisans fell into the same error as the poets; —because they were good workmen they thought that they also knew all sorts of high matters, and this defect in them overshadowed their wisdom; and therefore I asked myself on behalf of the oracle, whether I would like to be as I was, neither having their knowledge nor their ignorance, or like them in both; and I made answer to myself and to the oracle that I was better off as I was.

This inquisition has led to my having many enemies of the worst and most dangerous kind, and has given occasion also to many calumnies. And I am called wise, for my hearers always imagine that I myself possess the wisdom which I find wanting in others: but the truth is, O men of Athens, that God only is wise; and by his answer he intends to show that the wisdom of men is worth little or nothing; he is not speaking of Socrates, he is only using my name by way of illustration, as if he said, He, O men, is the wisest, who, like Socrates, knows that his wisdom is in truth worth nothing. And so I go about the world obedient to the god, and search and make enquiry into the wisdom of any one, whether citizen or stranger, who appears to be wise; and if he is not wise, then in vindication of the oracle I show him that he is not wise; and my occupation quite absorbs me, and I have no time to give either to any public matter of interest or to any concern of my own, but I am in utter poverty by reason of my devotion to the god.

There is another thing:—young men of the richer classes, who have not much to do, come about me of their own accord; they like to hear the pretenders examined, and they often imitate me, and proceed to examine others; there are plenty of persons, as they quickly discover, who think that they know something, but really know little or nothing; and then those who are examined by them instead of being angry with themselves are angry with me: This confounded Socrates, they say; this villainous misleader of youth!—and then if somebody asks them, Why, what evil does he practise or teach? they do not know, and cannot tell; but in order that they may not appear to be at a loss, they repeat the ready-made charges which are used against all philosophers about teaching things up in the clouds and under the earth, and having no gods, and making the worse appear the better cause; for they do not like to confess that their pretence of knowledge has been detected—which is the truth; and as they are numerous and ambitious and energetic, and are drawn up in battle array and have persuasive tongues, they have filled your ears with their loud and inveterate calumnies. And this is the reason why my three accusers, Meletus and Anytus and Lycon, have set upon me; Meletus, who has a quarrel with me on behalf of the poets; Anytus, on behalf of the craftsmen and politicians; Lycon, on behalf of the rhetoricians: and, as I said at the beginning, I cannot expect to get rid of such a mass of calumny all in a moment. And this, O men of Athens, is the truth and the whole truth; I have concealed nothing, I have dissembled nothing. And yet, I know that my plainness of speech makes them hate me, and what is their hatred but a proof that I am speaking the truth? Hence has arisen the prejudice against me; and this is the reason of it, as you will find out either in this or in any future enquiry.

I have said enough in my defence against the first class of my accusers; I turn to the second class. They are headed by Meletus, that good man and true lover of his country as he calls himself. Against these, too, I must try to make a defence:—Let their affidavit be read: it contains something of this kind: It says that Socrates is a doer of evil, who corrupts the youth; and who does not believe in the gods of the State, but has other new divinities of his own. Such is the charge; and now let us examine the par-

ticular counts. He says that I am a doer of evil, and corrupt the youth; but I say, O men of Athens, that Meletus is a doer of evil, in that he pretends to be in earnest when he is only in jest, and is so eager to bring men to trial from a pretended zeal and interest about matters in which he really never had the smallest interest. And the truth of this I will endeavour to prove to you.

Come hither, Meletus, and let me ask a question of you. You think a great deal about the improvement of youth?

Yes, I do.

Tell the judges, then, who is their improver; for you must know, as you have taken the pains to discover their corrupter, and are citing and accusing me before them. Speak, then, and tell the judges who their improver is.—Observe, Meletus, that you are silent, and have nothing to say. But is not this rather disgraceful, and a very considerable proof of what I was saying, that you have no interest in the matter? Speak up, friend, and tell us who their improver is.

The laws.

But that, my good sir, is not my meaning. I want to know who the person is, who, in the first place, knows the laws.

The judges, Socrates, who are present in court.

What, do you mean to say, Meletus, that they are able to instruct and improve youth?

Certainly they are.

What, all of them, or some only and not others?

All of them.

By the goddess Here, that is good news! There are plenty of improvers, then. And what do you say of the audience,—do they improve them?

Yes, they do.

And the senators?

Yes, the senators improve them.

But perhaps the members of the assembly corrupt them?—or do they improve them?

They improve them.

Then every Athenian improves and elevates them; all with the exception of myself; and I alone am their corrupter? Is that what you affirm?

That is what I stoutly affirm.

I am very unfortunate if you are right. But suppose I ask you a question: How about horses? Does one man do them harm and all the world good? Is not the exact opposite the truth? One man is able to do them good, or at least not many;—the trainer of horses, that is to say, does them good, and others who have to do with them rather injure them? Is not that true, Meletus, of horses, or of any other animals? Most assuredly it is; whether you and Anytus say yes or no. Happy indeed would be the condition of youth if they had one corrupter only, and all the rest of the world were their improvers.

But you, Meletus, have sufficiently shown that you never had a thought about the young: your carelessness is seen in your not caring about the very things which you bring against me.

And now, Meletus, I will ask you another question—by Zeus I will: Which is better, to live among bad citizens, or among good ones? Answer, friend, I say; the question is one which may be easily answered. Do not the good do their neighbours good, and the bad do them evil?

Certainly.

And is there any one who would rather be injured than benefited by those who live with him? Answer, my good friend, the law requires you to answer—does any one like to be injured?

Certainly not.

And when you accuse me of corrupting and deteriorating the youth, do you allege that I corrupt them intentionally or unintentionally?

Intentionally, I say.

But you have just admitted that the good do their neighbours good, and the evil do them evil. Now, is that a truth which your superior wisdom has recognized thus early in life, and am I, at my age, in such darkness and ignorance as not to know that if a man with whom I have to live is corrupted by me, I am very likely to be harmed by him; and yet I corrupt him, and intentionally, too—so you say, although neither I nor any other human being is ever likely to be convinced by you. But either I do not corrupt them, or I corrupt them unintentionally; and on either view of the case you lie. If my offence is unintentional, the law has no cognizance of unintentional offences: you ought to have taken me privately, and warned and admonished me; for if I had been better advised, I should have left off doing what I only did unintentionally—no doubt I should, but you would have nothing to say to me and refused to teach me. And now you bring me up in this court, which is a place not of instruction, but of punishment.

It will be very clear to you, Athenians, as I was saying, that Meletus has no care at all, great or small, about the matter. But still I should like to know, Meletus, in what I am affirmed to corrupt the young. I suppose you mean, as I infer from your indictment, that I teach them not to acknowledge the gods which the State acknowledges, but some other new divinities or spiritual agencies in their stead. These are the lessons by which I corrupt the youth, as you say.

Yes, that I say emphatically.

Then, by the gods, Meletus, of whom we are speaking, tell me and the court, in somewhat plainer terms, what you mean! For I do not as yet understand whether you affirm that I teach other men to acknowledge some gods, and therefore that I do believe in gods, and am not an entire atheist—this you do not lay to my charge,—but only you say

that they are not the same gods which the city recognizes—the charge is that they are different gods. Or, do you mean that I am an atheist simply, and a teacher of atheism?

I mean the latter—that you are a complete atheist.

What an extraordinary statement! Why do you think so, Meletus? Do you mean that I do not believe in the godhead of the sun, or moon, like other men?

I assure you, judges, that he does not: for he says that the sun is stone, and the moon earth.

Friend Meletus, you think that you are accusing Anaxagoras: and you have but a bad opinion of the judges, if you fancy them illiterate to such a degree as not to know that these doctrines are found in the books of Anaxagoras the Clazomenian, which are full of them. And so, forsooth, the youth are said to be taught them by Socrates, when there are not infrequently exhibitions of them at the theatre (price of admission one drachma at the most); and they might pay their money, and laugh at Socrates if he pretends to father these extraordinary views. And so, Meletus, you really think that I do not believe in any god?

I swear by Zeus that you believe absolutely in none at all.

Nobody will believe you, Meletus, and I am pretty sure that you do not believe yourself. I cannot help thinking, men of Athens, that Meletus is reckless and impudent, and that he has written this indictment in a spirit of mere wantonness and youthful bravado. Has he not compounded a riddle, thinking to try me? He said to himself:—I shall see whether the wise Socrates will discover my facetious contradiction, or whether I shall be able to deceive him and the rest of them. For he certainly does appear to me to contradict himself in the indictment as much as if he said that Socrates is guilty of not believing in the gods, and yet of believing in them—but this is not like a person who is in earnest.

I should like you, O men of Athens, to join me in examining what I conceive to be his inconsistency; and do you, Meletus, answer. And I must remind the audience of my request that they would not make a disturbance if I speak in my accustomed manner:

Did ever man, Meletus, believe in the existence of human things, and not of human beings? . . . I wish, men of Athens, that he would answer, and not be always trying to get up an interruption. Did ever any man believe in horsemanship, and not in horses? or in flute-playing, and not in flute-players? No, my

71. **Anaxagoras**, an Ionian philosopher, the first to propose the atomic theory of matter, and to suggest that the sun and moon were not gods but matter. Expelled from Athens 450 B.C. 77. **exhibitions . . . theatre.** Euripides and others incorporated the ideas of Anaxagoras in their plays.

friend; I will answer to you and to the court, as you refuse to answer for yourself. There is no man who ever did. But now please to answer the next question: Can a man believe in spiritual and divine agencies, and not in spirits or demigods?

He cannot.

How lucky I am to have extracted that answer, by the assistance of the court! But then you swear in the indictment that I teach and believe in divine 10 or spiritual agencies (new or old, no matter for that); at any rate, I believe in spiritual agencies,— so you say and swear in the affidavit; and yet if I believe in divine beings, how can I help believing in spirits or demigods;—must I not? To be sure I must; and therefore I may assume that your silence gives consent. Now what are spirits or demigods? are they not either gods or the sons of gods?

Certainly they are.

But this is what I call the facetious riddle in-20 vented by you: the demigods or spirits are gods, and you say first that I do not believe in gods, and then again that I do believe in gods; that is, if I believe in demigods. For if the demigods are the illegitimate sons of gods, whether by the nymphs or by any other mothers, of whom they are said to be the sons— what human being will ever believe that there are no gods if they are the sons of gods? You might as well affirm the existence of mules, and deny that of horses and asses. Such nonsense, Meletus, could 30 only have been intended by you to make trial of me. You have put this into the indictment because you had nothing real of which to accuse me. But no one who has a particle of understanding will ever be convinced by you that the same men can believe in divine and superhuman things, and yet not believe that there are gods and demigods and heroes.

I have said enough in answer to the charge of Meletus: any elaborate defence is unnecessary; but I know only too well how many are the enmities 40 which I have incurred, and this is what will be my destruction if I am destroyed;—not Meletus, nor yet Anytus, but the envy and detraction of the world, which has been the death of many good men, and will probably be the death of many more; there is no danger of my being the last of them.

Some one will say: And are you not ashamed, Socrates, of a course of life which is likely to bring you to an untimely end? To him I may fairly answer: There you are mistaken: a man who is good for any-50 thing ought not to calculate the chance of living or dying; he ought only to consider whether in doing anything he is doing right or wrong—acting the part of a good man or of a bad. Whereas, upon your view, the heroes who fell at Troy were not good for much, and the son of Thetis above all, who altogether despised danger in comparison with dis-

55. son of Thetis, Achilles.

grace; and when he was so eager to slay Hector, his goddess mother said to him, that if he avenged his companion Patroclus, and slew Hector, he would die himself—"Fate," she said, in these or the like words, 60 "waits for you next after Hector"; he, receiving this warning, utterly despised danger and death, and instead of fearing them, feared rather to live in dishonour, and not to avenge his friend. "Let me die forthwith," he replies, "and be avenged of my enemy, rather than abide here by the beaked ships, a laughing stock and a burden of the earth." Had Achilles any thought of death and danger? For wherever a man's place is, whether the place which he has chosen or that in which he has been placed 70 by a commander, there he ought to remain in the hour of danger; he should not think of death or of anything but of disgrace. And this, O men of Athens, is a true saying.

Strange, indeed, would be my conduct, O men of Athens, if I, who, when I was ordered by the generals whom you chose to command me at Potidaea and Amphipolis and Delium, remained where they placed me, like any other man, facing death—if now, when, as I conceive and imagine, God orders me to 80 fulfil the philosopher's mission of searching into myself and other men, I were to desert my post through fear of death, or any other fear; that would indeed be strange, and I might justly be arraigned in court for denying the existence of the gods, if I disobeyed the oracle because I was afraid of death, fancying that I was wise when I was not wise. For the fear of death is indeed the pretence of wisdom, and not real wisdom, being a pretence of knowing the unknown; and no one knows whether death, which men 90 in their fear apprehended to be the greatest evil, may not be the greatest good. Is not this ignorance of a disgraceful sort, the ignorance which is the conceit that a man knows what he does not know? And in this respect only I believe myself to differ from men in general, and may perhaps claim to be wiser than they are:—that whereas I know but little of the world below, I do not suppose that I know: but I do know that injustice and disobedience to a better, whether God or man, is evil and dishonourable, and 100 I will never fear or avoid a possible good rather than a certain evil. And therefore if you let me go now, and are not convinced by Anytus, who said that since I had been prosecuted I must be put to death; (or if not that I ought never to have been prosecuted at all); and that if I escape now, your sons will all be utterly ruined by listening to my words—if you say to me, Socrates, this time we will not mind Anytus, and you shall be let off, but upon one condition, that you are not to enquire and speculate in this 110 way any more, and that if you are caught doing so again you shall die;—if this was the condition on which you let me go, I should reply: Men of Athens,

I honour and love you; but I shall obey God rather than you, and while I have life and strength I shall never cease from the practice and teaching of philosophy, exhorting any one whom I meet and saying to him after my manner: You, my friend,—a citizen of the great and mighty and wise city of Athens,— are you not ashamed of heaping up the greatest amount of money and honour and reputation, and caring so little about wisdom and truth and the greatest improvement of the soul, which you never regard or heed at all? And if the person with whom I am arguing, says: Yes, but I do care; then I do not leave him or let him go at once; but I proceed to interrogate and examine and cross-examine him, and if I think that he has no virtue in him, but only says that he has, I reproach him with undervaluing the greater, and overvaluing the less. And I shall repeat the same words to every one whom I meet, young and old, citizen and alien, but especially to the citizens, inasmuch as they are my brethren. For know that this is the command of God; and I believe that no greater good has ever happened in the State than my service to the God. For I do nothing but go about persuading you all, old and young alike, not to take thought for your persons or your properties, but first and chiefly to care about the greatest improvement of the soul. I tell you that virtue is not given by money, but that from virtue comes money and every other good of man, public as well as private. This is my teaching, and if this is the doctrine which corrupts the youth, I am a mischievous person. But if any one says that this is not my teaching, he is speaking an untruth. Wherefore, O men of Athens, I say to you, do as Anytus bids or not as Anytus bids, and either acquit me or not; but whichever you do, understand that I shall never alter my ways, not even if I have to die many times.

Men of Athens, do not interrupt, but hear me; there was an understanding between us that you should hear me to the end: I have something more to say, at which you may be inclined to cry out; but I believe that to hear me will be good for you, and therefore I beg that you will not cry out. I would have you know, that if you kill such an one as I am, you will injure yourselves more than you will injure me. Nothing will injure me, not Meletus nor yet Anytus—they cannot, for a bad man is not permitted to injure a better than himself. I do not deny that Anytus may, perhaps, kill him, or drive him into exile, or deprive him of civil rights; and he may imagine, and others may imagine, that he is inflicting a great injury upon him: but there I do not agree. For the evil of doing as he is doing—the evil of unjustly taking away the life of another—is greater far.

And now, Athenians, I am not going to argue for my own sake, as you may think, but for yours, that you may not sin against the God by condemning me, who am his gift to you. For if you kill me you will not easily find a successor to me, who, if I may use such a ludicrous figure of speech, am a sort of gadfly, given to the State by God; and the State is a great and noble steed who is tardy in his motions owing to his very size, and requires to be stirred into life. I am that gadfly which God has attached to the State, and all day long and in all places am always fastening upon you, arousing and persuading and reproaching you. You will not easily find another like me, and therefore I would advise you to spare me. I dare say that you may feel out of temper (like a person who is suddenly awakened from sleep), and you think that you might easily strike me dead as Anytus advises, and then you would sleep on for the remainder of your lives, unless God in his care of you sent you another gadfly. When I say that I am given to you by God, the proof of my mission is this:—if I had been like other men, I should not have neglected all my own concerns or patiently seen the neglect of them during all these years, and have been doing yours, coming to you individually like a father or elder brother, exhorting you to regard virtue; such conduct, I say, would be unlike human nature. If I had gained anything, or if my exhortations had been paid, there would have been some sense in my doing so; but now, as you will perceive, not even the impudence of my accusers dares to say that I have ever exacted or sought pay of any one; of that they have no witness. And I have a sufficient witness to the truth of what I say—my poverty.

Some one may wonder why I go about in private giving advice and busying myself with the concerns of others, but do not venture to come forward in public and advise the State. I will tell you why. You have heard me speak at sundry times and in divers places of an oracle or sign which comes to me, and is the divinity which Meletus ridicules in the indictment. This sign, which is a kind of voice, first began to come to me when I was a child; it always forbids but never commands me to do anything which I am going to do. This is what deters me from being a politician. And rightly, as I think. For I am certain, O men of Athens, that if I had engaged in politics, I should have perished long ago, and done no good either to you or to myself. And do not be offended at my telling you the truth: for the truth is, that no man who goes to war with you or any other multitude, honestly striving against the many lawless and unrighteous deeds which are done in a State, will save his life; he who will fight for the right, if he would live even for a brief space, must have a private station and not a public one.

I can give you convincing evidence of what I say, not words only, but what you value far more—actions. Let me relate to you a passage of my own life which will prove to you that I should never have yielded to injustice from any fear of death and that "as I should have refused to yield" I must have died at once. I will tell you a tale of the courts, not very interesting perhaps, but nevertheless true. The only office of State which I ever held, O men of Athens, was that of senator: the tribe Antiochis, which is my tribe, had the presidency at the trial of the generals who had not taken up the bodies of the slain after the battle of Arginusae, and you proposed to try them in a body, contrary to law, as you all thought afterwards; but at the time I was the only one of the Prytanes who was opposed to the illegality, and I gave my vote against you; and when the orators threatened to impeach and arrest me, and you called and shouted, I made up my mind that I would run the risk, having law and justice with me, rather than take part in your injustice because I feared imprisonment and death. This happened in the days of the democracy. But when the oligarchy of the Thirty was in power, they sent for me and four others into the rotunda, and bade us bring Leon the Salaminian from Salamis, as they wanted to put him to death. This was a specimen of the sort of commands which they were always giving with the view of implicating as many as possible in their crimes; and then I showed, not in word only but in deed, that, if I may be allowed to use such an expression, I cared not a straw for death, and that my great and only care was lest I should do an unrighteous or unholy thing. For the strong arm of that oppressive power did not frighten me into doing wrong; and when we came out of the rotunda the other four went to Salamis and fetched Leon, but I went quietly home. For which I might have lost my life, had not the power of the Thirty shortly afterwards come to an end. And many will witness to my words.

Now, do you really imagine that I could have survived all these years, if I had led a public life, supposing that like a good man I had always maintained the right and had made justice, as I ought, the first thing? No, indeed, men of Athens, neither I nor any other man. But I have been always the same in all my actions, public as well as private, and never have I yielded any base compliance to those who are slanderously termed my disciples, or to any other. Not that I have any regular disciples. But if any one likes to come and hear me while I am pursuing my mission, whether he be young or old, he is not excluded. Nor do I converse only with those who pay; but any one, whether he be rich or poor, may ask and answer me and listen to my words; and whether he turns out to be a bad man or a good one, neither result can be justly imputed to me; for I never taught or professed to teach him anything. And if any one

14. **Prytanes,** a committee on public affairs.

says that he has ever learned or heard anything from me in private which all the world has not heard, let me tell you that he is lying.

But I shall be asked, Why do people delight in continually conversing with you? I have told you already, Athenians, the whole truth about this matter: they like to hear the cross-examination of the pretenders to wisdom; there is amusement in it. Now, this duty of cross-examining other men has been imposed upon me by God; and has been signified to me by oracles, visions, and in every way in which the will of divine power was ever intimated to any one. This is true, O Athenians; or, if not true, would be soon refuted. If I am or have been corrupting the youth, those of them who are now grown up and have become sensible that I gave them bad advice in the days of their youth should come forward as accusers, and take their revenge; or if they do not like to come themselves, some of their relatives, fathers, brothers, or other kinsmen, should say what evil their families have suffered at my hands. Now is their time. Many of them I see in the court. There is Crito, who is of the same age and of the same deme with myself, and there is Critobulus his son, whom I also see. Then again there is Lysanias of Sphettus, who is the father of Aeschines—he is present; and also there is Antiphon of Cephisus, who is the father of Epigenes; and there are the brothers of several who have associated with me. There is Nicostratus the son of Theosdotides, and the brother of Theodotus (now Theodotus himself is dead, and therefore he, at any rate, will not seek to stop him); and there is Paralus the son of Demodocus, who had a brother Theages; and Adeimantus the son of Ariston, whose brother Plato is present; and Aeantodorus, who is the brother of Apollodorus, whom I also see. I might mention a great many others, some of whom Meletus should have produced as witnesses in the course of his speech; and let him still produce them, if he has forgotten—I will make way for him. And let him say, if he has any testimony of the sort which he can produce. Nay, Athenians, the very opposite is the truth. For all these are ready to witness on behalf of the corrupter, of the injurer of their kindred, as Meletus and Anytus call me; not the corrupted youth only—there might have been a motive for that—but their uncorrupted elder relatives. Why should they too support me with their testimony? Why, indeed, except for the sake of truth and justice, and because they know that I am speaking the truth, and that Meletus is a liar.

Well, Athenians, this and the like of this is all the defence which I have to offer. Yet a word more. Perhaps there may be some one who is offended at me, when he calls to mind how he himself on a similar, or even a less serious occasion, prayed and entreated

91. **Plato;** one of Plato's very few allusions to himself in his works.

the judges with many tears, and how he produced his children in court, which was a moving spectacle, together with a host of relations and friends; whereas I, who am probably in danger of my life, will do none of these things. The contrast may occur to his mind, and he may be set against me, and vote in anger because he is displeased at me on this account. Now, if there be such a person among you,—mind, I do not say that there is,—to him I may fairly reply: My friend, I am a man, and like other men, a creature of flesh and blood, and not "of wood or stone," as Homer says; and I have a family, yes, and sons, O Athenians, three in number, one almost a man, and two others who are still young; and yet I will not bring any of them hither in order to petition you for an acquittal. And why not? Not from any self-assertion or want of respect for you. Whether I am or am not afraid of death is another question, of which I will not now speak. But, having regard to public opinion, I feel that such conduct would be discreditable to myself, and to you, and to the whole State. One who has reached my years, and who has a name for wisdom, ought not to demean himself. Whether this opinion of me be deserved or not, at any rate the world has decided that Socrates is in some way superior to other men. And if those among you who are said to be superior in wisdom and courage, and any other virtue, demean themselves in this way, how shameful is their conduct! I have seen men of reputation, when they have been condemned, behaving in the strangest manner: they seemed to fancy that they were going to suffer something dreadful if they died, and that they could be immortal if you only allowed them to live; and I think that such are a dishonour to the State, and that any stranger coming in would have said of them that the most eminent men of Athens, to whom the Athenians themselves give honour and command, are no better than women. And I say that these things ought not to be done by those of us who have a reputation; and if they are done, you ought not to permit them; you ought rather to show that you are far more disposed to condemn the man who gets up a doleful scene and makes the city ridiculous, than him who holds his peace.

But, setting aside the question of public opinion, there seems to be something wrong in asking a favour of a judge, and thus procuring an acquittal, instead of informing and convincing him. For his duty is, not to make a present of justice, but to give judgment; and he has sworn that he will judge according to the laws, and not according to his own good pleasure; and we ought not to encourage you, nor should you allow yourselves to be encouraged, in this habit of perjury—there can be no piety in that. Do not then require me to do what I consider dishonourable and impious and wrong, especially now, when I am being tried for impiety on the indictment of Meletus. For if, O men of Athens, by force of persuasion and entreaty I could overpower your oaths, then I should be teaching you to believe that there are no gods, and in defending should simply convict myself of the charge of not believing in them. But that is not so—far otherwise. For I do believe that there are gods, and in a sense higher than that in which any of my accusers believe in them. And to you and to God I commit my cause, to be determined by you as is best for you and me.

———

There are many reasons why I am not grieved, O men of Athens, at the vote of condemnation. I expected it, and am only surprised that the votes are so nearly equal; for I had thought that the majority against me would have been far larger; but now, had thirty votes gone over to the other side, I should have been acquitted. And I may say, I think, that I have escaped Meletus. I may say more; for without the assistance of Anytus and Lycon, any one may see that he would not have had a fifth part of the votes, as the law requires, in which case he would have incurred a fine of a thousand drachmae.

And so he proposes death as the penalty. And what shall I propose on my part, O men of Athens? Clearly that which is my due. And what is my due? What returns shall be made to the man who has never had the wit to be idle during his whole life; but has been careless of what the many care for—wealth, and family interests, and military offices, and speaking in the assembly, and magistracies, and plots, and parties. Reflecting that I was really too honest a man to be a politician and live, I did not go where I could do no good to you or to myself; but where I could do the greatest good privately to every one of you, thither I went, and sought to persuade every man among you that he must look to himself, and seek virtue and wisdom before he looks to his private interests, and look to the State before he looks to the interests of the State; and that this should be the order which he observes in all his actions. What shall be done to such an one? Doubtless some good thing, O men of Athens, if he has his reward; and the good should be of a kind suitable to him. What would be a reward suitable to a poor man who is your benefactor, and who desires leisure that he may instruct you? There can be no reward so fitting as maintenance in the Prytaneum, O men of Athens, a reward which he deserves far more than the citizen who has won the prize at Olympia in the horse or chariot race, whether the chariots were

67–68. . . . is best for you and me. A vote was taken at this point and Socrates was condemned by a small majority. He was then asked to propose his own penalty. 105. as maintenance . . . Prytaneum; that is, at public expense in the council hall.

drawn by two horses or by many. For I am in want, and he has enough; and he only gives you the appearance of happiness, and I give you the reality. And if I am to estimate the penalty fairly, I should say that maintenance in the Prytaneum is the just return.

Perhaps you think that I am braving you in what I am saying now, as in what I said before about the tears and prayers. But this is not so. I speak rather because I am convinced that I never intentionally wronged any one, although I cannot convince you —the time has been too short; if there were a law at Athens, as there is in other cities, that a capital cause should not be decided in one day, then I believe that I should have convinced you. But I cannot in a moment refute great slanders; and, as I am convinced that I never wronged another, I will assuredly not wrong myself. I will not say of myself that I deserve any evil, or propose any penalty. Why should I? Because I am afraid of the penalty of death which Meletus proposes? When I do not know whether death is a good or an evil, why should I propose a penalty which would certainly be an evil? Shall I say imprisonment? And why should I live in prison, and be the slave of the magistrate of the year —of the Eleven? Or shall the penalty be a fine, and imprisonment until the fine is paid? There is the same objection. I should have to lie in prison, for money I have none, and cannot pay. And if I say exile (and this may possibly be the penalty which you will affix), I must indeed be blinded by the love of life if I am so irrational as to expect that when you, who are my own citizens, cannot endure my discourses and words, and have found them so grievous and odious that you will have no more of them, others are likely to endure me. No, indeed, men of Athens, that is not very likely. And what a life should I lead, at my age, wandering from city to city, ever changing my place of exile, and always being driven out! For I am quite sure that wherever I go, there, as here, the young men will flock to me; and if I drive them away, their elders will drive me out at their request; and if I let them come, their fathers and friends will drive me out for their sakes.

Some one will say: Yes, Socrates, but cannot you hold your tongue, and then you may go into a foreign city, and no one will interfere with you? Now, I have great difficulty in making you understand my answer to this. For if I tell you that to do as you say would be a disobedience to the God, and therefore that I cannot hold my tongue, you will not believe that I am serious; and if I say again that daily to discourse about virtue, and of those other things about which you hear me examining myself and others, is the greatest good of man, and that the unexamined life is not worth living, you are still less likely to believe me. Yet I say what is true, although a

thing of which it is hard for me to persuade you. Also, I have never been accustomed to think that I deserve to suffer any harm. Had I money I might have estimated the offence at what I was able to pay, and not have been much the worse. But I have none, and therefore I must ask you to proportion the fine to my means. Well, perhaps I could afford a mina, and therefore I propose that penalty: Plato, Crito, Critobulus, and Apollodorus, my friends here, bid me say thirty minae, and they will be the sureties. Let thirty minae be the penalty; for which sum they will be ample security to you.

Not much time will be gained, O Athenians, in return for the evil name which you will get from the detractors of the city, who will say that you killed Socrates, a wise man; for they will call me wise, even although I am not wise, when they want to reproach you. If you had waited a little while, your desire would have been fulfilled in the course of nature. For I am far advanced in years, as you may perceive, and not far from death. I am speaking now not to all of you, but only to those who have condemned me to death. And I have another thing to say to them: You think that I was convicted because I had no words of the sort which would have procured my acquittal—I mean, if I had thought fit to leave nothing undone or unsaid. Not so; the deficiency which led to my conviction was not of words—certainly not. But I had not the boldness or impudence or inclination to address you as you would have liked me to do, weeping and wailing and lamenting, and saying and doing many things which you have been accustomed to hear from others, and which, as I maintain, are unworthy of me. I thought at the time that I ought not to do anything common or mean when in danger: nor do I now repent of the style of my defence; I would rather die having spoken after my manner, than speak in your manner and live. For neither in war nor yet at law ought I or any man to use every way of escaping death. Often in battle there can be no doubt that if a man will throw away his arms, and fall on his knees before his pursuers, he may escape death; and in other dangers there are other ways of escaping death, if a man is willing to say and do anything. The difficulty, my friends, is not to avoid death, but to avoid unrighteousness; for that runs faster than death. I am old and move slowly, and the slower runner has overtaken me, and my accusers are keen and quick, and the faster runner, who is unrighteousness, has overtaken them. And now I depart hence condemned by you to suffer the penalty of death,—they too go their ways condemned by the truth to suffer the penalty of vil-

69. . . . **ample security to you.** The insolence of this speech led the judges to condemn Socrates to death.

lainy and wrong; and I must abide by my award—let them abide by theirs. I suppose that these things may be regarded as fated,—and I think that they are well.

And now, O men who have condemned me, I would fain prophesy to you; for I am about to die, and in the hour of death men are gifted with prophetic power. And I prophesy to you who are my murderers, that immediately after my departure punishment far heavier than you have inflicted on me will surely await you. Me you have killed because you wanted to escape the accuser, and not to give an account of your lives. But that will not be as you suppose: far otherwise. For I say that there will be more accusers of you than there are now; accusers whom hitherto I have restrained: and as they are younger they will be more inconsiderate with you, and you will be more offended at them. If you think that by killing men you can prevent some one from censuring your evil lives, you are mistaken; that is not a way of escape which is either possible or honourable; the easiest and the noblest way is not to be disabling others, but to be improving yourselves. This is the prophecy which I utter before my departure to the judges who have condemned me.

Friends, who would have acquitted me, I would like also to talk with you about the thing which has come to pass, while the magistrates are busy, and before I go to the place at which I must die. Stay then a little, for we may as well talk with one another while there is time. You are my friends, and I should like to show you the meaning of this event which has happened to me. O my judges—for you I may truly call judges—I should like to tell you of a wonderful circumstance. Hitherto the divine faculty of which the internal oracle is the source has constantly been in the habit of opposing me even about trifles, if I was going to make a slip or error in any matter; and now as you see there has come upon me that which may be thought, and is generally believed to be, the last and worst evil. But the **oracle made no sign of opposition, either when I was** leaving my house in the morning, or when I was on my way to the court, or while I was speaking, at anything which I was going to say; and yet I have often been stopped in the middle of a speech, but now in nothing I either said or did touching the matter in hand has the oracle opposed me. What do I take to be the explanation of this silence? I will tell you. It is an intimation that what has happened to me is a good, and that those of us who think that death is an evil are in error. For the customary sign would surely have opposed me had I been going to evil and not to good.

Let us reflect in another way, and we shall see that there is great reason to hope that death is a good; for one of two things—either death is a state of nothingness and utter unconsciousness, or, as men say, there is a change and migration of the soul from this world to another. Now, if you suppose that there is no consciousness, but a sleep like the sleep of him who is undisturbed even by dreams, death will be an unspeakable gain. For if a person were to select the night in which his sleep was undisturbed even by dreams, and were to compare with this the other days and nights of his life, and then were to tell us how many days and nights he had passed in the course of his life better and more pleasantly than this one, I think that any man, I will not say a private man, but even the great king will not find many such days or nights, when compared with the others. Now, if death be of such a nature, I say that to die is gain; for eternity is then only a single night. But if death is the journey to another place, and there, as men say, all the dead abide, what good, O my friends and judges, can be greater than this? If, indeed, when the pilgrim arrives in the world below, he is delivered from the professors of justice in this world, and finds the true judges who are said to give judgment there, Minos and Rhadamanthus and Aeacus and Triptolemus, and other sons of God who were righteous in their own life, that pilgrimage will be worth making. What would not a man give if he might converse with Orpheus and Musaeus and Hesiod and Homer? Nay, if this be true, let me die again and again. I myself, too, shall have a wonderful interest in there meeting and conversing with Palamedes, and Ajax the son of Telamon, and any other ancient hero who has suffered death through an unjust judgment; and there will be no small pleasure, as I think, in comparing my own sufferings with theirs. Above all, I shall then be able to continue my search into true and false knowledge; as in this world, so also in the next; and I shall find out who is wise, and who pretends to be wise, and is not. What would not a man give, O judges, to be able to examine the leader of the great Trojan expedition; or Odysseus or Sisyphus, or numberless others, men and women too! What infinite delight would there be in conversing with them and asking them questions! In another world they do not put a man to death for asking questions: assuredly not. For besides being happier than we are, they will be immortal, if what is said is true.

Wherefore, O judges, be of good cheer about death, and know of a certainty, that no evil can happen to a good man, either in life or after death. He and his are not neglected by the gods; nor has my own approaching end happened by mere chance. But I see clearly that the time had arrived when it was better for me to die and be released from trouble: wherefore the oracle gave no sign. For which reason, also, I am not angry with my condemners, or with my accusers; they have done me no harm, although they did not mean to do me any good; and for this I may gently blame them.

Still, I have a favour to ask of them. When my sons are grown up, I would ask you, O my friends, to punish them; and I would have you trouble them, as I have troubled you, if they seem to care about riches, or anything, more than about virtue; or if they pretend to be something when they are really nothing,—then reprove them, as I have reproved you, for not caring about that for which they ought to care, and thinking that they are something when they are really nothing. And if you do this, both I and my sons will have received justice at your hands.

The hour of departure has arrived, and we go our ways—I to die, and you to live. Which is better God only knows.

Crito

PERSONS OF THE DIALOGUE:
SOCRATES *and* CRITO

SCENE: *The Prison of Socrates.*

SOCRATES.

WHY have you come at this hour, Crito? it must be quite early?

CRITO. Yes, certainly.

SOCRATES. What is the exact time?

CRITO. The dawn is breaking.

SOCRATES. I wonder that the keeper of the prisoner would let you in.

CRITO. He knows me, because I often come, Socrates; moreover, I have done him a kindness.

SOCRATES. And are you only just arrived?

CRITO. No, I came some time ago.

SOCRATES. Then why did you sit and say nothing, instead of at once awakening me?

CRITO. I should not have liked myself, Socrates, to be in such great trouble and unrest as you are—indeed I should not: I have been watching with amazement your peaceful slumbers; and for that reason I did not awake you, because I wished to minimize the pain. I have always thought you to be of a happy disposition; but never did I see anything like the easy, tranquil manner in which you bear this calamity.

SOCRATES. Why, Crito, when a man has reached my age he ought not to be repining at the approach of death.

CRITO. And yet other old men find themselves in similar misfortunes, and age does not prevent them from repining.

Crito. Translated by Benjamin Jowett. Published by The Clarendon Press, Oxford. Crito is a faithful follower of Socrates, who here receives his master's instructions on the duty of obedience to the laws.

SOCRATES. That is true. But you have not told me why you come at this early hour.

CRITO. I come to bring you a message which is sad and painful; not, as I believe, to yourself, but to all of us who are your friends, and saddest of all to me.

SOCRATES. What? Has the ship come from Delos, on the arrival of which I am to die?

CRITO. No, the ship has not actually arrived, but she will probably be here to-day, as persons who have come from Sunium tell me that they left her there; and therefore to-morrow, Socrates, will be the last day of your life.

SOCRATES. Very well, Crito; if such is the will of God, I am willing; but my belief is that there will be a delay of a day.

CRITO. Why do you think so?

SOCRATES. I will tell you. I am to die on the day after the arrival of the ship.

CRITO. Yes; that is what the authorities say.

SOCRATES. But I do not think that the ship will be here until to-morrow; this I infer from a vision which I had last night, or rather only just now, when you fortunately allowed me to sleep.

CRITO. And what was the nature of the vision?

SOCRATES. There appeared to me the likeness of a woman, fair and comely, clothed in bright raiment, who called to me and said: O Socrates,

"The third day hence to fertile Phthia shalt thou go."

CRITO. What a singular dream, Socrates!

SOCRATES. There can be no doubt about the meaning, Crito, I think.

CRITO. Yes; the meaning is only too clear. But, oh! my beloved Socrates, let me entreat you once more to take my advice and escape. For if you die I shall not only lose a friend who can never be replaced, but there is another evil: people who do not know you and me will believe that I might have saved you if I had been willing to give money, but that I did not care. Now, can there be a worse disgrace than this—that I should be thought to value money more than the life of friend? For the many will not be persuaded that I wanted you to escape, and that you refused.

SOCRATES. But why, my dear Crito, should we care about the opinion of the many? Good men, and they are the only persons who are worth considering, will think of these things truly as they occurred.

CRITO. But you see, Socrates, that the opinion of the many must be regarded, for what is now happening shows that they can do the greatest evil to any one who has lost their good opinion.

SOCRATES. I only wish it were so, Crito; and that

50–51. **Has the ship . . . die.** Every year a sacred embassy was sent to the island of Delos. From the time this ship left Athens until it returned, the city was in a state of purification, and no public execution could take place. Since the embassy departed during Socrates' trial, his death had to be delayed until its return.

the many could do the greatest evil; for then they would also be able to do the greatest good—and what a fine thing this would be! But in reality they can do neither; for they cannot make a man either wise or foolish; and whatever they do is the result of chance.

CRITO. Well, I will not dispute with you; but please to tell me, Socrates, whether you are not act-ing out of regard to me and your other friends: are you not afraid that if you escape from prison we may get into trouble with the informers for having stolen you away, and lose either the whole or a great part of our property; or that even a worse evil may hap-pen to us? Now, if you fear on our account, be at ease; for in order to save you, we ought surely to run this, or even a greater risk; be persuaded, then, and do as I say.

SOCRATES. Yes, Crito, that is one fear which you mention, but by no means the only one.

CRITO. Fear not—there are persons who are will-ing to get you out of prison at no great cost; and as for the informers, they are far from being exorbitant in their demands—a little money will satisfy them. My means, which are certainly ample, are at your service, and if you have a scruple about spending all mine, here are strangers who will give you the use of theirs; and one of them, Simmias the Theban, has brought a large sum of money for this very pur-pose; and Cebes and many others are prepared to spend their money in helping you to escape. I say, therefore, do not hesitate on our account, and do not say, as you did in the court, that you will have a difficulty in knowing what to do with yourself anywhere else. For men will love you in other places to which you may go, and not in Athens only; there are friends of mine in Thessaly, if you like to go to them, who will value and protect you, and no Thes-salian will give you any trouble. Nor can I think that you are at all justified, Socrates, in betraying your own life when you might be saved; in acting thus you are playing into the hands of your enemies, who are hurrying on your destruction. And further I should say that you are deserting your own children; for you might bring them up and educate them; in-stead of which you go away and leave them, and they will have to take their chance; and if they do not meet with the usual fate of orphans, there will be small thanks to you. No man should bring chil-dren into the world who is unwilling to persevere to the end in their nurture and education. But you ap-pear to be choosing the easier part, not the better and manlier, which would have been more becoming in one who professes to care for virtue in all his actions, like yourself. And, indeed, I am ashamed not only of you, but of us who are your friends, when I reflect that the whole business will be attributed entirely to our want of courage. The trial need never

have come on, or might have been managed differ-ently; and this last act, or crowning folly, will seem to have occurred through our negligence and cow-ardice, who might have saved you, if we had been good for anything; and you might have saved your-self, for there was no difficulty at all. See now, Soc-rates, how sad and discreditable are the conse-quences, both to us and you. Make up your mind, then, or rather have your mind already made up, for the time of deliberation is over, and there is only one thing to be done, which must be done this very night, and if we delay at all will be no longer practi-cable or possible; I beseech you therefore, Socrates, be persuaded by me, and do as I say.

SOCRATES. Dear Crito, your zeal is invaluable, if a right one; but if wrong, the greater the zeal the greater the danger; and therefore we ought to con-sider whether I shall or shall not do as you say. For I am and always have been one of those natures who must be guided by reason, whatever the reason may be which upon reflection appears to me to be the best; and now that this chance has befallen me, I cannot repudiate my own words: the principles which I have hitherto honoured and revered I still honour, and unless we can at once find other and better principles, I am certain not to agree with you; no, not even if the power of the multitude could in-flict many more imprisonments, confiscations, deaths, frightening us like children with hobgoblin terrors. What will be the fairest way of considering the ques-tion? Shall I return to your old argument about the opinions of men?—we were saying that some of them are to be regarded, and others not. Now, were we right in maintaining this before I was con-demned? And has the argument which was once good now proved to be talk for the sake of talking— mere childish nonsense? That is what I want to con-sider with your help, Crito:—whether, under my present circumstances, the argument appears to be in any way different or not; and is to be allowed by me or disallowed. That argument, which, as I be-lieve, is maintained by many persons of authority, was to the effect, as I was saying, that the opinions of some men are to be regarded, and of other men not to be regarded. Now you, Crito, are not going to die to-morrow—at least, there is no human proba-bility of this—and therefore you are disinterested and not liable to be deceived by the circumstances in which you are placed. Tell me, then, whether I am right in saying that some opinions, and the opin-ions of some men only, are to be valued, and that other opinions, and the opinions of other men, are not to be valued. I ask you whether I was right in maintaining this?

CRITO. Certainly.

SOCRATES. The good are to be regarded, and not the bad?

CRITO. Yes.

SOCRATES. And the opinions of the wise are good, and the opinions of the unwise are evil?

CRITO. Certainly.

SOCRATES. And what was said about another matter? Is the pupil who devotes himself to the practice of gymnastics supposed to attend to the praise and blame and opinion of every man, or of one man only —his physician or trainer, whoever he may be?

CRITO. Of one man only.

SOCRATES. And he ought to fear the censure and welcome the praise of that one only, and not of the many?

CRITO. Clearly so.

SOCRATES. And he ought to act and train, and eat and drink in the way which seems good to his single master who has understanding, rather than according to the opinion of all other men put together?

CRITO. True.

SOCRATES. And if he disobeys and disregards the opinion and approval of the one, and regards the opinion of the many who have no understanding, will he not suffer?

CRITO. Certainly he will.

SOCRATES. And what will the evil be, whither tending and what affecting, in the disobedient person?

CRITO. Clearly, affecting the body; that is what is destroyed by the evil.

SOCRATES. Very good; and is not this true, Crito, of other things which we need not separately enumerate? In questions of just and unjust, fair and foul, good and evil, which are the subjects of our present consultation, ought we to follow the opinion of the many and to fear them; or the opinion of the one man who has understanding? ought we not to fear and reverence him more than all the rest of the world: and if we desert him shall we not destroy and injure that principle in us which may be assumed to be improved by justice and deteriorated by injustice; —there is such a principle?

CRITO. Certainly there is, Socrates.

SOCRATES. Take a parallel instance:—if, acting under the advice of those who have no understanding, we destroy that which is improved by health and is deteriorated by disease, would life be worth having? And that which has been destroyed is—the body?

CRITO. Yes.

SOCRATES. Could we live, having an evil and corrupted body?

CRITO. Certainly not.

SOCRATES. And will life be worth having, if that higher part of man be destroyed, which is improved by justice and depraved by injustice? Do we suppose that principle, whatever it may be in man, which has to do with justice and injustice, to be inferior to the body?

CRITO. Certainly not.

SOCRATES. More honourable than the body?

CRITO. Far more.

SOCRATES. Then, my friend, we must not regard what the many say of us: but what he, the one man who has understanding of just and unjust, will say. and what the truth will say. And therefore you begin in error when you advise that we should regard the opinion of the many about just and unjust, good and evil, honourable and dishonourable.—"Well," some one will say, "but the many can kill us."

CRITO. Yes, Socrates; that will clearly be the answer.

SOCRATES. And it is true: but still I find with surprise that the old argument is unshaken as ever. And I should like to know whether I may say the same of another proposition—that not life, but a good life, is to be chiefly valued?

CRITO. Yes, that also remains unshaken.

SOCRATES. And a good life is equivalent to a just and honourable one—that holds also?

CRITO. Yes, it does.

SOCRATES. From these premises I proceed to argue the question whether I ought or ought not to try to escape without the consent of the Athenians: and if I am clearly right in escaping, then I will make the attempt; but if not, I will abstain. The other considerations which you mention, of money and loss of character and the duty of educating one's children, are, I fear, only the doctrines of the multitude, who would be as ready to restore people to life, if they were able, as they are to put them to death— and with as little reason. But now, since the argument has thus far prevailed, the only question which remains to be considered is, whether we shall do rightly either in escaping or in suffering others to aid in our escape and paying them in money and thanks, or whether in reality we shall not do rightly; and if the latter, then death or any other calamity which may ensue on my remaining here must not be allowed to enter into the calculation.

CRITO. I think that you are right, Socrates; how then shall we proceed?

SOCRATES. Let us consider the matter together, and do you either refute me if you can, and I will be convinced; or else cease, my dear friend, from repeating to me that I ought to escape against the wishes of the Athenians: for I highly value your attempts to persuade me to do so, but I may not be persuaded against my own better judgment. And now please to consider my first position, and try how you can best answer me.

CRITO. I will.

SOCRATES. Are we to say that we are never intentionally to do wrong, or that in one way we ought and in another way we ought not to do wrong, or is doing wrong always evil and dishonourable, as I was

just now saying, and as has been already acknowledged by us? Are all our former admissions which
were made within a few days to be thrown away?
And have we, at our age, been earnestly discoursing
with one another all our life long only to discover
that we are no better than children? Or, in spite of
the opinion of the many, and in spite of consequences whether better or worse, shall we insist on
the truth of what was then said, that injustice is
always an evil and dishonour to him who acts unjustly? Shall we say so or not?

CRITO. Yes.

SOCRATES. Then we must do no wrong?

CRITO. Certainly not.

SOCRATES. Nor when injured injure in return, as
the many imagine; for we must injure no one at all?

CRITO. Clearly not.

SOCRATES. Again, Crito, may we do evil?

CRITO. Surely not, Socrates.

SOCRATES. And what of doing evil in return for
evil, which is the morality of the many—is that just
or not?

CRITO. Not just.

SOCRATES. For doing evil to another is the same as
injuring him?

CRITO. Very true.

SOCRATES. Then we ought not to retaliate or render evil for evil to any one, whatever evil we may
have suffered from him. But I would have you consider, Crito, whether you really mean what you are
saying. For this opinion has never been held, and
never will be held, by any considerable number of
persons; and those who are agreed and those who
are not agreed upon this point have no common
ground, and can only despise one another when they
see how widely they differ. Tell me, then, whether
you agree with and assent to my first principle, that
neither injury nor retaliation nor warding off evil
by evil is ever right. And shall that be the premiss of
our argument? Or do you decline and dissent from
this? For so I have ever thought, and continue to
think; but, if you are of another opinion, let me hear
what you have to say. If, however, you remain of the
same mind as formerly, I will proceed to the next step.

CRITO. You may proceed, for I have not changed
my mind.

SOCRATES. Then I will go on to the next point,
which may be put in the form of a question:—
Ought a man to do what he admits to be right, or
ought he to betray the right?

CRITO. He ought to do what he thinks right.

SOCRATES. But if this is true, what is the application? In leaving the prison against the will of the
Athenians, do I wrong any? or rather do I not wrong
those whom I ought least to wrong? Do I not desert
the principles which were acknowledged by us to
be just—what do you say?

CRITO. I cannot tell, Socrates; for I do not know.

SOCRATES. Then consider the matter in this way:
—Imagine that I am about to play truant (you may
call the proceeding by any name which you like),
and the laws and the government come and interrogate me: "Tell us, Socrates," they say; "what are
you about? are you not going by an act of yours to
overturn us—the laws, and the whole State, as far
as in you lies? Do you imagine that a State can subsist and not be overthrown, in which the decisions of
law have no power, but are set aside and trampled
upon by individuals?" What will be our answer,
Crito, to these and the like words? Any one, and
especially a rhetorician, will have a good deal to say
on behalf of the law which requires a sentence to be
carried out. He will argue that this law should not
be set aside; and shall we reply, "Yes; but the State
has injured us and given an unjust sentence." Suppose I say that?

CRITO. Very good, Socrates.

SOCRATES. "And was that our agreement with
you?" the law would answer; "or were you to abide
by the sentence of the State?" And if I were to express my astonishment at their words, the law would
probably add: "Answer, Socrates, instead of opening your eyes—you are in the habit of asking and
answering questions. Tell us,—What complaint have
you to make against us which justifies you in attempting to destroy us and the State? In the first
place did we not bring you into existence? Your
father married your mother by our aid and begat
you. Say whether you have any objection to urge
against those of us who regulate marriage?" None,
I should reply. "Or against those of us who after
birth regulate the nurture and education of children,
in which you also were trained? Were not the laws,
which have the charge of education, right in commanding your father to train you in music and
gymnastic?" Right, I should reply. "Well, then, since
you were brought into the world and nurtured and
educated by us, can you deny in the first place that
you are our child and slave, as your fathers were
before you? And if this is true, you are not on equal
terms with us; nor can you think that you have a
right to do to us what we are doing to you. Would
you have any right to strike or revile or do any other
evil to your father or your master, if you had one,
because you have been struck or reviled by him, or
received some other evil at his hands?—you would
not say this? And because we think right to destroy
you, do you think that you have any right to destroy
us in return, and your country as far as in you lies?
Will you, O professor of true virtue, pretend that
you are justified in this? Has a philosopher like you
failed to discover that our country is more to be
valued and higher and holier far than mother or
father or any ancestor, and more to be regarded in

the eyes of the gods and of men of understanding? also to be soothed, and gently and reverently entreated when angry, even more than a father, and either to be persuaded, or if not persuaded, to be obeyed? And when we are punished by her, whether with imprisonment or stripes, the punishment is to be endured in silence; and if she lead us to wounds or death in battle, thither we follow as is right; neither may any one yield or retreat or leave his rank, but whether in battle or in a court of law, or in any other place, he must do what his city and his country order him; or he must change their view of what is just: and if he may do no violence to his father or mother, much less may he do violence to his country." What answer shall we make to this, Crito? Do the laws speak truly, or do they not?

CRITO. I think that they do.

SOCRATES. Then the laws will say: "Consider, Socrates, if we are speaking truly that in your present attempt you are going to do us an injury. For, having brought you into the world, and nurtured and educated you, and given you and every other citizen a share in every good which we had to give, we further proclaim to any Athenian by the liberty which we allow him, that if he does not like us when he has become of age and has seen the ways of the city, and made our acquaintance, he may go where he pleases and take his goods with him. None of us laws will forbid him or interfere with him. Any one who does not like us and the city, and who wants to emigrate to a colony or to any other city, may go where he likes, retaining his property. But he who has experience of the manner in which we order justice and administer the State, and still remains, has entered into an implied contract that he will do as we command him. And he who disobeys us is, as we maintain, thrice wrong; first, because in disobeying us he is disobeying his parents; secondly, because we are the authors of his education; thirdly, because he has made an agreement with us that he will duly obey our commands; and he neither obeys them nor convinces us that our commands are unjust; and we do not rudely impose them, but give him the alternative of obeying or convincing us;— that is what we offer, and he does neither.

"These are the sort of accusations to which, as we were saying, you, Socrates, will be exposed if you accomplish your intentions; you, above all other Athenians." Suppose now I ask, why I rather than anybody else? they will justly retort upon me that I above all other men have acknowledged the agreement. "There is clear proof," they will say, "Socrates, that we and the city were not displeasing to you. Of all Athenians you have been the most constant resident in the city, which, as you never leave, you may be supposed to love. For you never went out of the city either to see the games, except once when

you went to the Isthmus, or to any other place unless when you were on military service; nor did you travel as other men do. Nor had you any curiosity to know other States or their laws: your affections did not go beyond us and our State; we were your special favourites, and you acquiesced in our government of you; and here in this city you begat your children, which is a proof of your satisfaction. Moreover, you might in the course of the trial, if you had liked, have fixed the penalty at banishment; the State which refuses to let you go now would have let you go then. But you pretended that you preferred death to exile, and that you were not unwilling to die. And now you have forgotten these fine sentiments, and pay no respect to us, the laws, of whom you are the destroyer; and are doing what only a miserable slave would do, running away and turning your back upon the compacts and agreements which you made as a citizen. And, first of all, answer this very question: Are we right in saying that you agreed to be governed according to us in deed, and not in word only? Is that true or not?" How shall we answer, Crito? Must we not assent?

CRITO. We cannot help it, Socrates.

SOCRATES. Then will they not say: "You, Socrates, are breaking the covenants and agreements which you made with us at your leisure, not in any haste or under any compulsion or deception, but after you have had seventy years to think of them, during which time you were at liberty to leave the city, if we were not to your mind, or if our covenants appeared to you to be unfair. You had your choice, and might have gone either to Lacedaemon or Crete, both which States are often praised by you for their good government, or to some other Hellenic or foreign State. Whereas you, above all other Athenians, seemed to be so fond of the State, or, in other words, of us, her laws (and who would care about a State which has no laws?), that you never stirred out of her; the halt, the blind, the maimed were not more stationary in her than you were. And now you run away and forsake your agreements. Not so, Socrates, if you will take our advice; do not make yourself ridiculous by escaping out of the city.

"For just consider, if you transgress and err in this sort of way, what good will you do either to yourself or to your friends? That your friends will be driven into exile and deprived of citizenship, or will lose their property, is tolerably certain; and you yourself, if you fly to one of the neighbouring cities, as, for example, Thebes or Megara, both of which are well governed, will come to them as an enemy, Socrates, and their government will be against you, and all patriotic citizens will cast an evil eye upon you as a subverter of the laws, and you will confirm in the minds of the judges the justice of their own condemnation of you. For he who is a corrupter of the laws is more than likely to be a corrupter of the young and foolish portion of mankind. Will you then flee from well-ordered cities and virtuous men? and is existence worth having on these terms? Or will you go to them without shame, and talk to them, Socrates? And what will you say to them? What you say here about virtue and justice and institutions and laws being the best things among men? Would that be decent of you? Surely not. But if you go away from well-governed States to Crito's friends in Thessaly, where there is great disorder and licence, they will be charmed to hear the tale of your escape from prison, set off with ludicrous particulars of the manner in which you were wrapped in a goatskin or some other disguise, and metamorphosed as the manner is of runaways; but will there be no one to remind you that in your old age you were not ashamed to violate the most sacred laws from a miserable desire of a little more life? Perhaps not, if you keep them in a good temper; but if they are out of temper you will hear many degrading things; you will live, but how?—as the flatterer of all men, and the servant of all men; and doing what?—eating and drinking in Thessaly, having gone abroad in order that you may get a dinner. And where will be your fine sentiments about justice and virtue? Say that you wish to live for the sake of your children—you want to bring them up and educate them—will you take them into Thessaly and deprive them of Athenian citizenship? Is this the benefit which you will confer upon them? Or are you under the impression that they will be better cared for and educated here if you are still alive, although absent from them; for your friends will take care of them? Do you fancy that if you are an inhabitant of Thessaly they will take care of them, and if you are an inhabitant of the other world that they will not take care of them? Nay; but if they who call themselves friends are good for anything, they will—to be sure they will.

"Listen, then, Socrates, to us who have brought you up. Think not of life and children first, and of justice afterwards, but of justice first, that you may be justified before the princes of the world below. For neither will you nor any that belong to you be happier or holier or juster in this life, or happier in another, if you do as Crito bids. Now you depart in innocence, a sufferer and not a doer of evil; a victim, not of the laws but of men. But if you go forth, returning evil for evil, and injury for injury, breaking the covenants and agreements which you have made with us, and wronging those whom you ought least of all to wrong, that is to say, yourself, your friends, your country, and us, we shall be angry with you while you live, and our brethren, the laws in the world below, will receive you as an enemy; for they will know that you have done your best to destroy us. Listen, then, to us and not to Crito."

This, dear Crito, is the voice which I seem to hear murmuring in my ears, like the sound of the flute in the ears of the mystic; that voice, I say, is humming in my ears, and prevents me from hearing any other. And I know that anything more which you may say will be vain. Yet speak, if you have anything to say.

CRITO. I have nothing to say, Socrates.

SOCRATES. Leave me then, Crito, to fulfil the will of God, and to follow whither he leads.

Phaedo

. . . OF THAT upper earth which is under the heaven, I can tell you a charming tale, Simmias, which is well worth hearing.

And we, Socrates, replied Simmias, shall be charmed to listen to you.

The tale, my friend, he said, is as follows:—In the first place, the earth, when looked at from above, is in appearance streaked like one of those balls which have leather coverings in twelve pieces, and is decked with various colours, of which the colours used by painters on earth are in a manner samples. But there the whole earth is made up of them, and they are brighter far and clearer than ours; there is a purple of wonderful lustre, also the radiance of gold, and the white which is in the earth is whiter than any chalk or snow. Of these and other colours the earth is made up, and they are more in number and fairer than the eye of man has ever seen; the very hollows (of which I was speaking) filled with air and water have a colour of their own, and are seen like light gleaming amid the diversity of the other colours, so that the whole presents a single and continuous appearance of variety in unity. And in this fair region everything that grows—trees, and flowers, and fruits—are in a like degree fairer than any here; and there are hills, having stones in them in a like degree smoother, and more transparent, and fairer in colour than our highly valued emeralds and sardonyxes and jaspers, and other gems, which are but minute fragments of them: for there all the stones are like our precious stones, and fairer still. The reason is, that they are pure, and not, like our precious stones, infected or corroded by the corrupt briny elements which coagulate among us, and which breed foulness and disease both in earth and stones, as well as in animals and plants. They are the jewels of the upper earth which also shines with gold and silver and the like, and they are set in the light of day and are large and abundant and in all places, making the earth a sight to gladden the beholder's

*Phaedo.*³ Translated by Benjamin Jowett. Published by The Clarendon Press, Oxford. Phaedo, a disciple of Socrates, tells a friend how Socrates, shortly before he drank the hemlock, discoursed with his disciples on the immortality of the soul and the nature of the other world.

eye. And there are animals and men, some in a middle region, others dwelling about the air as we dwell about the sea; others in islands which the air flows round, near the continent; and, in a word, the air is used by them as the water and the sea are by us, and the ether is to them what the air is to us. Moreover, the temperament of their seasons is such that they have no disease, and live much longer than we do, and have sight and hearing and smell, and all the other senses, in far greater perfection, in the same proportion that air is purer than water or the ether than air. Also they have temples and sacred places in which the gods really dwell, and they hear their voices and receive their answers, and are conscious of them and hold converse with them; and they see the sun, moon, and stars as they truly are, and their other blessedness is of a piece with this.

Such is the nature of the whole earth, and of the things which are around the earth; and there are divers regions in the hollows on the faces of the globe everywhere, some of them deeper and more extended than that which we inhabit, others deeper but with a narrower opening than ours, and some are shallower and also wider. All have numerous perforations, and there are passages broad and narrow in the interior of the earth, connecting them with one another; and there flows out of and into them, as into basins, a vast tide of water, and huge subterranean streams of perennial rivers, and springs hot and cold, and a great fire, and great rivers of fire, and streams of liquid mud, thin or thick (like the rivers of mud in Sicily, and the lava streams which follow them), and the regions about which they happen to flow are filled up with them. And there is a swinging or seesaw in the interior of the earth which moves all this up and down, and is due to the following cause:—There is a chasm which is the vastest of them all, and pierces right through the whole earth; this is that chasm which Homer describes in the words,—

"Far off, where is the inmost depth beneath the
    earth";

and which he in other places, and many other poets, have called Tartarus. And the seesaw is caused by the streams flowing into and out of this chasm, and they each have the nature of the soil through which they flow. And the reason why the streams are always flowing in and out, is that the watery element has no bed or bottom, but is swinging and surging up and down, and the surrounding wind and air do the same; they follow the water up and down, hither and thither, over the earth—just as in the act of respiration the air is always in process of inhalation and exhalation,—and the wind swinging with the water in and out produces fearful and irresistible blasts: when the waters retire with a rush into the lower parts of the earth, as they are called, they flow through the earth in those regions, and fill them up like water raised by a pump, and then when they leave those regions and rush back hither, they again fill the hollows here, and when these are filled, flow through subterranean channels and find their way to their several places, forming seas, and lakes, and rivers, and springs. Thence they again enter the earth, some of them making a long circuit into many lands, others going to a few places and not so distant; and again fall into Tartarus, some at a point a good deal lower than that at which they rose, and others not much lower, but all in some degree lower than the point from which they came. And some burst forth again on the opposite side, and some on the same side, and some wind round the earth with one or many folds like the coils of a serpent, and descend as far as they can, but always return and fall into the chasm. The rivers flowing in either direction can descend only to the centre and no further, for opposite to the rivers is a precipice.

Now these rivers are many, and mighty, and diverse, and there are four principal ones, of which the greatest and outermost is that called Oceanus, which flows round the earth in a circle; and in the opposite direction flows Acheron, which passes under the earth through desert places into the Acherusian lake: this is the lake to the shores of which the souls of the many go when they are dead, and after waiting an appointed time, which is to some a longer and to some a shorter time, they are sent back to be born again as animals. The third river passes out between the two, and near the place of outlet pours into a vast region of fire, and forms a lake larger than the Mediterranean Sea, boiling with water and mud; and proceeding muddy and turbid, and winding about the earth, comes, among other places, to the extremities of the Acherusian lake, but mingles not with the waters of the lake, and after making many coils about the earth plunges into Tartarus at a deeper level. This is that Pyriphlegethon, as the stream is called, which throws up jets of fire in different parts of the earth. The fourth river goes out on the opposite side, and falls first of all into a wild and savage region, which is all of a dark blue colour, like lapis lazuli; and this is that river which is called the Stygian river, and falls into and forms the Lake Styx, and after falling into the lake and receiving strange powers in the waters, passes under the earth, winding round in the opposite direction, and comes near the Acherusian lake from the opposite side to Pyriphlegethon. And the water of this river too mingles with no other, but flows round in a circle and falls into Tartarus over against Pyriphlegethon; and the name of the river, as the poets say, is Cocytus.

Such is the nature of the other world; and when

the dead arrive at the place to which the genius of each severally guides them, first of all, they have sentence passed upon them, as they have lived well and piously or not. And those who appear to have lived neither well nor ill, go to the river Acheron, and embarking in any vessels which they may find, are carried in them to the lake, and there they dwell and are purified of their evil deeds, and having suffered the penalty of the wrongs which they have done to others, they are absolved, and receive the rewards of their good deeds, each of them according to his deserts. But those who appear to be incurable by reason of the greatness of their crimes—who have committed many and terrible deeds of sacrilege, murders foul and violent, or the like—such are hurled into Tartarus which is their suitable destiny, and they never come out. Those again who have committed crimes, which, although great, are not irremediable—who in a moment of anger, for example, have done some violence to a father or a mother, and have repented for the remainder of their lives, or, who have taken the life of another under the like extenuating circumstances—these are plunged into Tartarus, the pains of which they are compelled to undergo for a year, but at the end of the year the wave casts them forth—mere homicides by way of Cocytus, parricides and matricides by Pyriphlegethon—and they are borne to the Acherusian lake, and there they lift up their voices and call upon the victims whom they have slain or wronged, to have pity on them, and to be kind to them, and let them come out into the lake. And if they prevail, then they come forth and cease from their troubles; but if not, they are carried back again into Tartarus and from thence into the rivers unceasingly, until they obtain mercy from those whom they have wronged: for that is the sentence inflicted upon them by their judges. Those too who have been preeminent for holiness of life are released from this earthly prison, and go to their pure home which is above, and dwell in the purer earth; and of these, such as have duly purified themselves with philosophy live henceforth altogether without the body, in mansions fairer still which may not be described, and of which the time would fail me to tell.

Wherefore, Simmias, seeing all these things, what ought not we to do that we may obtain virtue and wisdom in this life? Fair is the prize, and the hope great!

A man of sense ought not to say, nor will I be very confident, that the description which I have given of the soul and her mansions is exactly true. But I do say that, inasmuch as the soul is shown to be immortal, he may venture to think, not improperly or unworthily, that something of the kind is true. The venture is a glorious one, and he ought to comfort himself with words like these, which is the reason why I lengthen out the tale. Wherefore, I say, let a man be of good cheer about his soul, who having cast away the pleasures and ornaments of the body as alien to him and working harm rather than good, has sought after the pleasures of knowledge; and has arrayed the soul, not in some foreign attire, but in her own proper jewels, temperance, and justice, and courage, and nobility, and truth—in these adorned she is ready to go on her journey to the world below, when her hour comes. You, Simmias and Cebes, and all other men, will depart at some time or other. Me already, as a tragic poet would say, the voice of fate calls. Soon I must drink the poison; and I think that I had better repair to the bath first, in order that the women may not have the trouble of washing my body after I am dead.

When he had done speaking, Crito said: And have you any commands for us, Socrates—anything to say about your children, or any other matter in which we can serve you?

Nothing particular, Crito, he replied: only, as I have always told you, take care of yourselves; that is a service which you may be ever rendering to me and mine and to all of us, whether you promise to do so or not. But if you have no thought for yourselves, and care not to walk according to the rule which I have prescribed for you, not now for the first time, however much you may profess or promise at the moment, it will be of no avail.

We will do our best, said Crito: And in what way shall we bury you?

In any way that you like; but you must get hold of me, and take care that I do not run away from you. Then he turned to us, and added with a smile: —I cannot make Crito believe that I am the same Socrates who have been talking and conducting the argument; he fancies that I am the other Socrates whom he will soon see, a dead body—and he asks, How shall he bury me? And though I have spoken many words in the endeavour to show that when I have drunk the poison I shall leave you and go to the joys of the blessed,—these words of mine, with which I was comforting you and myself, have had, as I perceive, no effect upon Crito. And therefore I want you to be surety for me to him now, as at the trial he was surety to the judges for me: but let the promise be of another sort; for he was surety for me to the judges that I would remain, and you must be my surety to him that I shall not remain, but go away and depart; and then he will suffer less at my death, and not be grieved when he sees my body being burned or buried. I would not have him sorrow at my hard lot, or say at the burial, Thus we lay out Socrates, or, Thus we follow him to the grave or bury him; for false words are not only evil in themselves, but they inflict the soul with evil. Be of good cheer then, my dear Crito, and say that you are burying my body only, and do with that whatever is usual, and what you think best.

When he had spoken these words, he arose and went into a chamber to bathe; Crito followed him and told us to wait. So we remained behind, talking and thinking of the subject of discourse, and also of the greatness of our sorrow; he was like a father of whom we were being bereaved, and we were about to pass the rest of our lives as orphans. When he had taken the bath his children were brought to him (he had two young sons and an elder one); and the women of his family also came, and he talked to them and gave them a few directions in the presence of Crito; then he dismissed them and returned to us.

Now the hour of sunset was near, for a good deal of time had passed while he was within. When he came out, he sat down with us again after his bath, but not much was said. Soon the jailer, who was the servant of the Eleven, entered and stood by him, saying:—To you, Socrates, whom I know to be the noblest and gentlest and best of all who ever came to this place, I will not impute the angry feeling of other men, who rage and swear at me, when, in obedience to the authorities, I bid them drink the poison —indeed, I am sure that you will not be angry with me; for others, as you are aware, and not I, are to blame. And so fare you well, and try to bear lightly what must needs be—you know my errand. Then bursting into tears he turned away and went out.

Socrates looked at him and said: I return your good wishes, and will do as you bid. Then turning to us, he said, How charming the man is: since I have been in prison he has always been coming to see me, and at times he would talk to me, and was as good to me as could be, and now see how generously he sorrows on my account. We must do as he says, Crito; and therefore let the cup be brought, if the poison is prepared: if not, let the attendant prepare some.

Yet, said Crito, the sun is still upon the hill-tops, and I know that many a one has taken the draught late, and after the announcement has been made to him, he has eaten and drunk, and enjoyed the society of his beloved: do not hurry—there is time enough.

Socrates said: Yes, Crito, and they of whom you speak are right in so acting, for they think that they will be gainers by the delay; but I am right in not following their example, for I do not think that I should gain anything by drinking the poison a little later; I should only be ridiculous in my own eyes for sparing and saving a life which is already forfeit. Please then to do as I say, and not to refuse me.

Crito made a sign to the servant, who was stand-

ing by; and he went out, and having been absent for some time, returned with the jailer carrying the cup of poison. Socrates said: You, my good friend, who are experienced in these matters, shall give me directions how I am to proceed. The man answered: You have only to walk about until your legs are heavy, and then to lie down, and the poison will act. At the same time he handed the cup to Socrates, who in the easiest and gentlest manner, without the least fear or change of colour or feature, looking at the man with all his eyes, as his manner was, took the cup and said: What do you say about making a libation out of this cup to any god? May I, or not? The man answered: We only prepare, Socrates, just so much as we deem enough. I understand, he said: but I may and must ask the gods to prosper my journey from this to the other world—even so—and so be it according to my prayer. Then raising the cup to his lips, quite readily and cheerfully he drank off the poison. And hitherto most of us had been able to control our sorrow; but now when we saw him drinking, and saw too that he had finished the draught, we could no longer forbear, and in spite of myself my own tears were flowing fast; so that I covered my face and wept, not for him, but at the thought of my own calamity in having to part from such a friend. Nor was I the first; for Crito, when he found himself unable to restrain his tears, had got up, and I followed; and at that moment, Apollodorus, who had been weeping all the time, broke out in a loud and passionate cry which made cowards of us all. Socrates alone retained his calmness: What is this strange outcry? he said. I sent away the women mainly in order that they might not misbehave in this way, for I have been told that a man should die in peace. Be quiet then, and have patience. When we heard his words we were ashamed, and refrained our tears; and he walked about until, as he said, his legs began to fail, and then he lay on his back, according to directions, and the man who gave him the poison now and then looked at his feet and legs; and after a while he pressed his foot hard, and asked him if he could feel; and he said, No; and then his leg, and so upwards and upwards, and showed us that he was cold and stiff. And he felt them himself, and said: When the poison reaches the heart, that will be the end. He was beginning to grow cold about the groin, when he uncovered his face, for he had covered himself up, and said—they were his last words—he said: Crito, I owe a cock to Asclepius; will you remember to pay the debt? The debt shall be paid, said Crito; is there anything else? There was no answer to this question; but in a minute or two a movement was heard, and the attend-

106. **I owe a cock.** . . . A cock was the usual sacrifice to Asclepius, god of healing, for recovery from an illness.

ants uncovered him; his eyes were set, and Crito closed his eyes and mouth.

Such was the end, Echecrates, of our friend; concerning whom I may truly say, that of all men of his time whom I have known, he was the wisest and justest and best.

Republic

BOOK VII

A ND now, I said, let me show in a figure how far our nature is enlightened or unenlightened:—Behold! human beings living in an underground den, which has a mouth open towards the light and reaching all along the den; here they have been from their childhood, and have their legs and necks chained so that they cannot move, and can only see before them, being prevented by the chains from turning round their heads. Above and behind them a fire is blazing at a distance, and between the fire and the prisoners there is a raised way; and you will see, if you look, a low wall built along the way, like the screen which marionette players have in front of them, over which they show the puppets.

I see.

And do you see, I said, men passing along the wall carrying all sorts of vessels, and statues and figures of animals made of wood and stone and various materials, which appear over the wall? Some of them are talking, others silent.

You have shown me a strange image, and they are strange prisoners.

Like ourselves, I replied; and they see only their own shadows, or the shadows of one another, which the fire throws on the opposite wall of the cave.

True, he said; how could they see anything but the shadows if they were never allowed to move their heads?

And of the objects which are being carried in like manner they would only see the shadows?

Yes, he said.

And if they were able to converse with one another, would they not suppose that they were naming what was actually before them?

Very true.

And suppose further that the prison had an echo which came from the other side, would they not be sure to fancy when one of the passers-by spoke that the voice which they heard came from the passing shadow?

No question, he replied.

Republic. Translated by Benjamin Jowett. Published by The Clarendon Press, Oxford.

7. **I said.** . . . Plato has Socrates present the famous apologue of the cave of Glaucon.

To them, I said, the truth would be literally nothing but the shadows of the images.

That is certain.

And now look again, and see what will naturally follow if the prisoners are released and disabused of their error. At first, when any of them is liberated and compelled suddenly to stand up and turn his neck round and walk and look towards the light, he will suffer sharp pains; the glare will distress him, and he will be unable to see the realities of which in his former state he had seen the shadows; and then conceive someone saying to him, that what he saw before was an illusion, but that now, when he is approaching nearer to being and his eye is turned towards more real existence, he has a clearer vision,—what will be his reply? And you may further imagine that his instructor is pointing to the objects as they pass and requiring him to name them,—will he not be perplexed? Will he not fancy that the shadows which he formerly saw are truer than the objects which are now shown to him?

Far truer.

And if he is compelled to look straight at the light, will he not have a pain in his eyes which will make him turn away to take refuge in the objects of vision which he can see, and which he will conceive to be in reality clearer than the things which are now being shown to him?

True, he said.

And suppose once more, that he is reluctantly dragged up a steep and rugged ascent, and held fast until he is forced into the presence of the sun himself, is he not likely to be pained and irritated? When he approaches the light his eyes will be dazzled, and he will not be able to see anything at all of what are now called realities.

Not all in a moment, he said.

He will require to grow accustomed to the sight of the upper world. And first he will see the shadows best, next the reflections of men and other objects in the water, and then the objects themselves; then he will gaze upon the light of the moon and the stars and the spangled heaven; and he will see the sky and the stars by night better than the sun or the light of the sun by day?

Certainly.

Last of all he will be able to see the sun, and not mere reflections of him in the water, but he will see him in his own proper place, and not in another; and he will contemplate him as he is.

Certainly.

He will then proceed to argue that this is he who gives the season and the years, and is the guardian of all that is in the visible world, and in a certain way the cause of all things which he and his fellows have been accustomed to behold?

Clearly, he said, he would first see the sun and then reason about him.

And when he remembered his old habitation, and the wisdom of the den and his fellow-prisoners, do you not suppose that he would felicitate himself on the change, and pity them?

Certainly, he would.

And if they were in the habit of conferring honours among themselves on those who were quickest to observe the passing shadows and to remark which of them went before, and which followed after, and which were together; and who were therefore best able to draw conclusions as to the future, do you think that he would care for such honours and glories, or envy the possessors of them? Would he not say with Homer,

'Better to be the poor servant of a poor master,'

and to endure anything, rather than think as they do and live after their manner?

Yes, he said, I think that he would rather suffer anything than entertain these false notions and live in this miserable manner.

Imagine once more, I said, such an one coming suddenly out of the sun to be replaced in his old situation; would he not be certain to have his eyes full of darkness?

To be sure, he said.

And if there were a contest, and he had to compete in measuring the shadows with the prisoners who had never moved out of the den, while his sight was still weak, and before his eyes had become steady (and the time which would be needed to acquire this new habit of sight might be very considerable), would he not be ridiculous? Men would say of him that up he went and down he came without his eyes; and that it was better not even to think of ascending; and if any one tried to loose another and lead him up to the light, let them only catch the offender, and they would put him to death.

No question, he said.

This entire allegory, I said, you may now append, dear Glaucon, to the previous argument; the prison-house is the world of sight, the light of the fire is the sun, and you will not misapprehend me if you interpret the journey upwards to be the ascent of the soul into the intellectual world according to my poor belief, which, at your desire, I have expressed—whether rightly or wrongly God knows. But, whether true or false, my opinion is that in the world of knowledge the idea of good appears last of all, and is seen only with an effort; and, when seen, is also inferred to be the universal author of all things beautiful and right, parent of light and of the lord of light in this visible world, and the immediate source of reason and truth in the intellectual; and that this is the power upon which he who would act

rationally either in public or private life must have his eye fixed.

I agree, he said, as far as I am able to understand you.

Moreover, I said, you must not wonder that those who attain to this beatific vision are unwilling to descend to human affairs; for their souls are ever hastening into the upper world where they desire to dwell; which desire of theirs is very natural, if our allegory may be trusted.

Yes, very natural.

And is there anything surprising in one who passes from divine contemplations to the evil state of man, misbehaving himself in a ridiculous manner; if, while his eyes are blinking and before he has become accustomed to the surrounding darkness, he is compelled to fight in courts of law, or in other places, about the images or the shadows of images of justice, and is endeavouring to meet the conceptions of those who have never yet seen absolute justice?

Anything but surprising, he replied.

Anyone who has common sense will remember that the bewilderments of the eyes are of two kinds, and arise from two causes, either from coming out of the light or from going into the light, which is true of the mind's eye, quite as much as of the bodily eye; and he who remembers this when he sees anyone whose vision is perplexed and weak, will not be too ready to laugh; he will first ask whether that soul of man has come out of the brighter life, and is unable to see because unaccustomed to the dark, or having turned from darkness to the day is dazzled by excess of light. And he will count the one happy in his condition and state of being, and he will pity the other; or, if he have a mind to laugh at the soul which comes from below into the light, there will be more reason in this than in the laugh which greets him who returns from above out of the light into the den.

That, he said, is a very just distinction.

But then, if I am right, certain professors of education must be wrong when they say that they can put a knowledge into the soul which was not there before, like sight into blind eyes.

They undoubtedly say this, he replied.

Whereas, our argument shows that the power and capacity of learning exists in the soul already; and that just as the eye was unable to turn from darkness to light without the whole body, so too the instrument of knowledge can only by the movement of the whole soul be turned from the world of becoming into that of being, and learn by degrees to endure the sight of being, and of the brightest and best of being, or in other words, of the good.

Very true.

And must there not be some art which will effect

conversion in the easiest and quickest manner; not implanting the faculty of sight, for that exists already, but has been turned in the wrong direction, and is looking away from the truth?

Yes, he said, such an art may be presumed.

And whereas the other so-called virtues of the soul seem to be akin to bodily qualities, for even when they are not originally innate they can be implanted later by habit and exercise, the virtue of wisdom more than anything else contains a divine element which always remains, and by this conversion is rendered useful and profitable; or, on the other hand, hurtful and useless. Did you never observe the narrow intelligence flashing from the keen eye of a clever rogue—how eager he is, how clearly his paltry soul sees the way to his end; he is the reverse of blind, but his keen eye-sight is forced into the service of evil, and he is mischievous in proportion to his cleverness?

Very true, he said.

But what if there had been a circumcision of such natures in the days of their youth; and they had been severed from those sensual pleasures, such as eating and drinking, which, like leaden weights, were attached to them at their birth, and which drag them down and turn the vision of their souls upon the things that are below—if, I say, they had been released from these impediments and turned in the opposite direction, the very same faculty in them would have seen the truth as keenly as they see what their eyes are turned to now. . . .

BOOK III

. . . You are aware, I suppose, that all mythology and poetry is a narration of events, either past, present, or to come?

Certainly, he replied.

And narration may be either simple narration, or imitation, or a union of the two?

That again, he said, I do not quite understand.

I fear that I must be a ridiculous teacher when I have so much difficulty in making myself apprehended. Like a bad speaker, therefore, I will not take the whole of the subject, but will break a piece off in illustration of my meaning. You know the first lines of the Iliad, in which the poet says that Chryses prayed Agamemnon to release his daughter, and that Agamemnon flew into a passion with him; whereupon Chryses, failing of his object, invoked the anger of the God against the Achaeans. Now as far as these lines,

32. **You are aware. . . .** Socrates is supposedly presenting to Adeimantus his (actually Plato's) theory of art and its place in an ideal republic.

'And he prayed all the Greeks, but especially the two sons of Atreus, the chiefs of the people,' the poet is speaking in his own person; he never leads us to suppose that he is any one else. But in what follows he takes the person of Chryses, and then he does all that he can to make us believe that the speaker is not Homer, but the aged priest himself. And in this double form he has cast the entire narrative of the events which occurred at Troy and in Ithaca and throughout the Odyssey.

Yes.

And a narrative it remains both in the speeches which the poet recites from time to time and in the intermediate passages?

Quite true.

But when the poet speaks in the person of another, may we not say that he assimilates his style to that of the person who, as he informs you, is going to speak?

Certainly.

And this assimilation of himself to another, either by the use of voice or gesture, is the imitation of the person whose character he assumes?

Of course.

Then in this case the narrative of the poet may be said to proceed by way of imitation?

Very true.

Or, if the poet everywhere appears and never conceals himself, then again the imitation is dropped, and his poetry becomes simple narration. However, in order that I may make my meaning quite clear, and that you may no more say, 'I don't understand,' I will show how the change might be effected. If Homer had said, 'The priest came, having his daughter's ransom in his hands, supplicating the Achaeans, and above all the kings'; and then if, instead of speaking in the person of Chryses, he had continued in his own person, the words would have been, not imitation, but simple narration. The passage would have run as follows (I am no poet, and therefore I drop the metre), 'The priest came and prayed the gods on behalf of the Greeks that they might capture Troy and return safely home, but begged that they would give him back his daughter, and take the ransom which he brought, and respect the God. Thus he spoke, and the other Greeks revered the priest and assented. But Agamemnon was wroth, and bade him depart and not come again, lest the staff and chaplets of the God should be of no avail to him—the daughter of Chryses should not be released, he said—she should grow old with him in Argos. And then he told him to go away and not to provoke him, if he intended to get home unscathed. And the old man went away in fear and silence, and, when he had left the camp, he called upon Apollo by his many names, reminding him of everything which he had done pleasing to him, whether in building his temples, or in offering sacrifice, and praying that his good deeds might be returned to him, and that the Achaeans might expiate his tears by the arrows of the god,'—and so on. In this way the whole becomes simple narrative.

I understand, he said.

Or you may suppose the opposite case—that the intermediate passages are omitted, and the dialogue only left.

That also, he said, I understand; you mean, for example, as in tragedy.

You have conceived my meaning perfectly; and if I mistake not, what you failed to apprehend before is now made clear to you, that poetry and mythology are, in some cases, wholly imitative—instances of this are supplied by tragedy and comedy; there is likewise the opposite style, in which the poet is the only speaker—of this the dithyramb affords the best example; and the combination of both is found in epic, and in several other styles of poetry. Do I take you with me?

Yes, he said; I see now what you meant.

I will ask you to remember also what I began by saying, that we had done with the subject and might proceed to the style.

Yes, I remember.

In saying this, I intended to imply that we must come to an understanding about the mimetic art,— whether the poets, in narrating their stories, are to be allowed by us to imitate, and if so, whether in whole or in part, and if the latter, in what parts; or should all imitation be prohibited?

You mean, I suspect, to ask whether tragedy and comedy shall be admitted into our State?

Yes, I said; but there may be more than this in question: I really do not know as yet, but whither the argument may blow, thither we go.

And go we will, he said.

Then, Adeimantus, let me ask you whether our guardians ought to be imitators; or rather, has not this question been decided by the rule already laid down that one man can only do one thing well, and not many; and that if he attempt many, he will alto- gether fail of gaining much reputation in any?

Certainly.

And this is equally true of imitation; no one man can imitate many things as well as he would imitate a single one?

He cannot.

Then the same person will hardly be able to play a serious part in life, and at the same time to be an imitator and imitate many other parts as well; for even when two species of imitation are nearly allied, the same persons cannot succeed in both, as, for example, the writers of tragedy and comedy—did you not just now call them imitations?

Yes, I did; and you are right in thinking that the same persons cannot succeed in both.

Any more than they can be rhapsodists and actors at once?

True.

Neither are comic and tragic actors the same; yet all these things are but imitations.

They are so.

And human nature, Adeimantus, appears to have been coined into yet smaller pieces, and to be as incapable of imitating many things well, as of per- forming well the actions of which the imitations are copies.

Quite true, he replied. . . .

And therefore when any one of these pantomimic gentlemen, who are so clever that they can imitate anything, comes to us, and makes a proposal to exhibit himself and his poetry, we will fall down and worship him as a sweet and holy and wonderful being; but we must also inform him that in our State such as he are not permitted to exist; the law will not allow them. And so when we have anointed him with myrrh, and set a garland of wool upon his head, we shall send him away to another city. For we mean to employ for our souls' health the rougher and severer poet or story-teller, who will imitate the style of the virtuous only, and will follow those models which we prescribed at first when we began the education of our soldiers. . . . We would not have our guardians grow up amid images of moral deformity, as in some noxious pasture, and there browse and feed upon many a baneful herb and flower day by day, little by little, until they silently gather a festering mass of corruption in their own soul. Let our artists rather be those who are gifted to discern the true nature of the beautiful and grace- ful; then will our youth dwell in a land of health, amid fair sights and sounds, and receive the good in everything; and beauty, the effluence of fair works, shall flow into the eye and ear, like a health-giving breeze from a purer region, and insensibly draw the soul from earliest years into likeness and sympathy with the beauty of reason. . . .

BOOK X

Can you tell me what imitation is? for I really do not know.

A likely thing, then, that I should know.

Why not? for the duller eye may often see a thing sooner than the keener.

Very true, he said; but in your presence, even if I had any faint notion, I could not muster courage to utter it. Will you enquire yourself?

Well then, shall we begin the enquiry in our usual manner: Whenever a number of individuals have a

101. **Can you tell me.** . . . Plato has Socrates enlarge upon his theory of art to Glaucon.

common name, we assume them to have also a corresponding idea or form:—do you understand me?

I do.

Let us take any common instance; there are beds and tables in the world—plenty of them, are there not?

Yes.

But there are only two ideas or forms of them—one the idea of a bed, the other of a table.

True.

And the maker of either of them makes a bed or he makes a table for our use, in accordance with the idea—that is our way of speaking in this and similar instances—but no artificer makes the ideas themselves: how could he?

Impossible.

And there is another artist,—I should like to know what you would say of him.

Who is he?

One who is the maker of all the works of all other workmen.

What an extraordinary man!

Wait a little, and there will be more reason for your saying so. For this is he who is able to make not only vessels of every kind, but plants and animals, himself and all other things—the earth and heaven, and the things which are in heaven or under the earth; he makes the god also.

He must be a wizard and no mistake.

Oh! you are incredulous, are you? Do you mean that there is no such maker or creator, or that in one sense there might be a maker of all these things but in another not? Do you see that there is a way in which you could make them all yourself?

What way?

An easy way enough; or rather, there are many ways in which the feat might be quickly and easily accomplished, none quicker than that of turning a mirror round and round—you would soon enough make the sun and the heavens, and the earth and yourself, and other animals and plants, and all the other things of which we were just now speaking, in the mirror.

Yes, he said; but they would be appearances only.

Very good, I said, you are coming to the point now. And the painter too is, as I conceive, just such another—a creator of appearances, is he not?

Of course.

But then I suppose you will say that what he creates is untrue. And yet there is a sense in which the painter also creates a bed?

Yes, he said, but not a real bed.

And what of the maker of the bed? were you not saying that he too makes, not the idea which, according to our view, is the essence of the bed, but only a particular bed?

Yes, I did.

Then if he does not make that which exists he cannot make true existence, but only some semblance of existence; and if any one were to say that the work of the maker of the bed, or of any other workman, has real existence, he could hardly be supposed to be speaking the truth.

At any rate, he replied, philosophers would say that he was not speaking the truth.

No wonder, then, that his work too is an indistinct expression of truth.

No wonder.

Suppose now that by the light of the examples just offered we enquire who this imitator is?

If you please.

Well then, here are three beds: one existing in nature, which is made by God, as I think that we may say—for no one else can be the maker?

No.

There is another which is the work of the carpenter?

Yes.

And the work of the painter is a third?

Yes.

Beds, then, are of three kinds, and there are three artists who superintend them: God, the maker of the bed, and the painter?

Yes, there are three of them.

God, whether from choice or from necessity, made one bed in nature and one only; two or more such ideal beds neither ever have been nor ever will be made by God.

Why is that?

Because even if He had made but two, a third would still appear behind them which both of them would have for their idea, and that would be the ideal bed and not the two others.

Very true, he said.

God knew this, and He desired to be the real maker of a real bed, not a particular maker of a particular bed, and therefore He created a bed which is essentially and by nature one only.

So we believe.

Shall we, then, speak of Him as the natural author or maker of the bed?

Yes, he replied; inasmuch as by the natural process of creation He is the author of this and of all other things.

And what shall we say of the carpenter—is not he also the maker of the bed?

Yes.

But would you call the painter a creator and maker?

Certainly not.

Yet if he is not the maker, what is he in relation to the bed?

I think, he said, that we may fairly designate him as the imitator of that which the others make.

Good, I said; then you call him who is third in the descent from nature an imitator?

Certainly, he said.

And the tragic poet is an imitator, and therefore, like all other imitators, he is thrice removed from the king and from the truth?

That appears to be so.

Then about the imitator we are agreed. And what about the painter?—I would like to know whether he may be thought to imitate that which originally exists in nature, or only the creations of artists?

The latter.

As they are or as they appear? you have still to determine this.

What do you mean?

I mean, that you may look at a bed from different points of view, obliquely or directly or from any other point of view, and the bed will appear different, but there is no difference in reality. And the same of all things.

Yes, he said, the difference is only apparent.

Now let me ask you another question: Which is the art of painting designed to be—an imitation of things as they are, or as they appear—of appearance or of reality?

Of appearance.

Then the imitator, I said, is a long way off the truth, and can do all things because he lightly touches on a small part of them, and that part an image. For example: A painter will paint a cobbler, carpenter, or any other artist, though he knows nothing of their arts; and, if he is a good artist, he may deceive children or simple persons, when he shows them his picture of a carpenter from a distance, and they will fancy that they are looking at a real carpenter.

Certainly.

And whenever any one informs us that he has found a man who knows all the arts, and all things else that anybody knows, and every single thing with a higher degree of accuracy than any other man— whoever tells us this, I think that we can only imagine him to be a simple creature who is likely to have been deceived by some wizard or actor whom he met, and whom he thought all-knowing, because he himself was unable to analyze the nature of knowledge and ignorance and imitation.

Most true.

And so, when we hear persons saying that the tragedians, and Homer, who is at their head, know all the arts and all things human, virtue as well as vice, and divine things too, for that the good poet cannot compose well unless he knows his subject, and that he who has not this knowledge can never be a poet, we ought to consider whether here also there may not be a similar illusion. Perhaps they may have come across imitators and been deceived by them; they may not have remembered when they saw their works that these were but imitations thrice removed from the truth, and could easily be made without any knowledge of the truth, because they are appearances only and not realities? Or, after all, they may be in the right, and poets do really know the things about which they seem to the many to speak so well?

The question, he said, should by all means be considered.

Now do you suppose that if a person were able to make the original as well as the image, he would seriously devote himself to the image-making branch? Would he allow imitation to be the ruling principle of his life, as if he had nothing higher in him?

I should say not.

The real artist, who knew what he was imitating, would be interested in realities and not in imitations; and would desire to leave as memorials of himself works many and fair; and, instead of being the author of encomiums, he would prefer to be the theme of them. . . .

But we have not yet brought forward the heaviest count in our accusation:—the power which poetry has of harming even the good (and there are very few who are not harmed), is surely an awful thing?

Yes, certainly, if the effect is what you say.

Hear and judge: The best of us, as I conceive, when we listen to a passage of Homer, or one of the tragedians, in which he represents some pitiful hero who is drawling out his sorrows in a long oration, or weeping, and smiting his breast—the best of us, you know, delight in giving way to sympathy, and are in raptures at the excellence of the poet who stirs our feelings most.

Yes, of course I know.

But when any sorrow of our own happens to us, then you may observe that we pride ourselves on the opposite quality—we would fain be quiet and patient; this is the manly part, and the other which delighted us in the recitation is now deemed to be the part of a woman.

Very true, he said.

Now can we be right in praising and admiring another who is doing that which any one of us would abominate and be ashamed of in his own person?

No, he said, that is certainly not reasonable.

Nay, I said, quite reasonable from one point of view.

What point of view?

If you consider, I said, that when in misfortune we feel a natural hunger and desire to relieve our sorrow by weeping and lamentation, and that this feeling which is kept under control in our own calamities is satisfied and delighted by the poets;—the better nature in each of us, not having been suffi-ciently trained by reason or habit, allows the sym-pathetic element to break loose because the sorrow is another's; and the spectator fancies that there can be no disgrace to himself in praising and pitying any one who comes telling him what a good man he is, and making a fuss about his troubles; he thinks that the pleasure is a gain, and why should he be super-cilious and lose this and the poem too? Few persons ever reflect, as I should imagine, that from the evil of other men something of evil is communicated to themselves. And so the feeling of sorrow which has gathered strength at the sight of the misfortunes of others is with difficulty repressed in our own.

How very true!

And does not the same hold also of the ridiculous? There are jests which you would be ashamed to make yourself, and yet on the comic stage, or in-deed in private, when you hear them, you are greatly amused by them, and are not at all dis-gusted at their unseemliness;—the case of pity is repeated;—there is a principle in human nature which is disposed to raise a laugh, and this which you once restrained by reason, because you were afraid of being thought a buffoon, is now let out again; and having stimulated the risible faculty at the theatre, you are betrayed unconsciously to your-self into playing the comic poet at home.

Quite true, he said.

And the same may be said of lust and anger and all the other affections, of desire and pain and pleas-ure, which are held to be inseparable from every action—in all of them poetry feeds and waters the passions instead of drying them up; she lets them rule, although they ought to be controlled, if man-kind are ever to increase in happiness and virtue.

I cannot deny it.

Therefore, Glaucon, I said, whenever you meet with any of the eulogists of Homer declaring that he has been the educator of Hellas, and that he is profit-able for education and for the ordering of human things, and that you should take him up again and again and get to know him and regulate your whole life according to him, we may love and hon-our those who say these things—they are excellent people, as far as their lights extend; and we are ready to acknowledge that Homer is the greatest of poets and first of tragedy writers (but we must re-main firm in our conviction that hymns to the gods and praises of famous men are the only poetry which ought to be admitted into our State). For if you go beyond this and allow the honeyed muse to enter, either in epic or lyric verse, not law and rea-son of mankind, which by common consent have ever been deemed best, but pleasure and pain will be the rulers in our State. . . .

Aristotle

384–322 B.C.

Little of Aristotle's work belongs to literature, and yet he was the most influential of all ancient philosophers from his day until the seventeenth century of Christian Europe. Only the rise of modern scientific method undermined the prestige of his contributions to knowledge. In ancient times he was known also as a man of letters, on the strength of philosophical dialogues simi-lar to Plato's. But only one of his literary works, *The Con-stitution of Athens,* has been preserved, and it is a minor achievement. His reputation as a thinker and scientist rests on bare lecture notes written for his conferences at the Lyceum in Athens. Though they were long accepted as the very foundation of human knowledge, they have no literary value.

Aristotle was a student and teacher at the Academy during the last twenty years of Plato's life. Unlike his master, he was much less interested in mathematics, meta-physics, and ethics than in biological and physical sci-ence. His father, physician to the king of Macedonia, had fostered his curiosity about science from childhood. Ru-mors of friction between Plato and Aristotle are probably exaggerated, but it is clear that their views diverged sharply. Plato was a poet and idealist, given to specula-tion and even mysticism. Aristotle was a hard-headed, practical man, content to record facts with accuracy and good sense.

After Plato's death Aristotle lived for three years with Hermeias, tyrant of Atarneus, whose niece he married, and later served as tutor to Alexander the Great through the years preceding the youth's accession to the Macedo-nian throne. To his influence may be ascribed Alexander's enthusiastic dissemination of Greek science and culture through his Eastern empire. But Aristotle returned to Athens and, when the headship of the Academy was not offered to him, founded a rival university, the Lyceum, in the grove of Apollo Lyceius. It was an enclosed place with gardens between the buildings, and since much of the instruction was given on walks around the enclosure, Aristotle and his followers came to be called the Peripa-tetics. Here he taught for eighteen years and composed the majority of his works, until the death of Alexander forced him into exile as a Macedonian. He died a year later.

Aristotle was the first Western scholar to attempt an encyclopedic classification of human knowledge. Indeed, he was also the last, because in clarifying the divisions of science and philosophy and indicating the channels that later research would follow, he began the specialization of learning that soon made encyclopedic knowledge im-possible for one man. He was conscious of the highly tentative nature of his pioneer work and would hardly have approved the later elevation of his findings to the sacrosanct position of law. In the Christian era his works were widely known in the Latin translation of Boethius and were gradually grafted with all their errors upon Christian doctrine. Although a source of enlightenment, his works impeded scientific progress because of their hallowed status.

The breadth of Aristotle's interests is reflected in his forty-seven extant treatises, in themselves only a fraction of the hundreds attributed to him. By far the most extensive, if also the least valuable today, are the treatises on various sciences—physics, mechanics, astronomy, meteorology, psychology, and especially biology. But it is his philosophical writings that have endured. His many works on logic are still the conventional authority, though they have been severely challenged in our century by "non-Aristotelian" logicians. His *Metaphysics* presents his familiar distinction between matter and form in opposition to Plato's doctrine of Ideas. In the *Politics* he comes close to Plato's *Republic* in his picture of an ideal city-state founded on aristocratic principles and state education. The lay reader knows Aristotle best through his treatises on ethics (the *Nichomachean Ethics* and *Eudemian Ethics*) and aesthetics (the *Rhetoric* and *Poetics*).

The *Nichomachean Ethics*, named for his son Nichomachus, is the most famous of all books on morals and our best source for the Greek ideal of conduct. According to Aristotle, the good life is the happy life, but happiness does not spring from mere pleasure, health, fame, or money. These important things are only means to an end. Happiness results from acting in harmony with one's nature and one's circumstances, as intelligence dictates. Right action leading to happiness is usually a mean between two extremes of possible action; in other words, the right path of virtue lies between two wrong paths. Intelligence is needed to determine this sensible mean of conduct, but eventually right action becomes a habit with the virtuous man, who is consequently happy. Aristotle illustrates his celebrated doctrine of the Golden Mean with numerous applications to everyday living, but for the best examples we should turn to Roman Horace and our eighteenth-century classicists, who made it their law of life.

The influence of the *Poetics* too was strongest in the Classical Age two thousand years after Aristotle. He intended it as an analysis of Greek tragedy (together with comedy and epic) as practice had molded it, but the authoritarian critics of the later era made it a canon of right composition with which to condemn as heretics any playwrights who violated its laws. The section on comedy is lost, and the allusions to the epic are brief; the *Poetics* is primarily a handbook of tragedy.

Aristotle accepts Plato's view of art as imitation and does not condemn it for being such. Indeed, the whole purpose of tragedy, according to Aristotle, is to call forth the emotions of pity and fear by a spectacle that imitates tragic reality and thus purge the spectator of his accumulation of these upsetting emotions. This is Aristotle's famous doctrine of the *catharsis* (purging effect) of tragedy. The classical doctrine of the dramatic unities of time, place, and action is merely inferred from Aristotle, because he prescribes only unity of action (or a single plot). His definition of the proper hero for tragedy as an essentially good man possessed of a tragic fault that proves his undoing ° is readily applied to Shakespeare's heroes as well as to Oedipus and is still substantially true of tragic characters in modern drama. Indeed, despite the different theater that inspired Aristotle's treatise, it is surprising to observe how much of his advice is still illustrated in the drama of our day, not through conscious imitation but merely as sound practice in reaching an audience. Of course many other ideas in Aristotle's works are outmoded, but his career and his logic and his actual contributions to knowledge are an abiding inspiration to those who seek the truth.

Nicomachéan Ethics

BOOK TWO

Virtue, being of two kinds, intellectual and moral, intellectual virtue in the main owes both its birth and its growth to teaching (for which reason it requires experience and time), while moral virtue comes about as a result of habit, whence also its name *ethike* is one that is formed by a slight variation from the word *ethos* (habit). From this it is also plain that none of the moral virtues arises in us by nature; for nothing that exists by nature can form a habit contrary to its nature. For instance the stone which by nature moves downwards cannot be habituated to move upwards, not even if one tries to train it by throwing it up ten thousand times; nor can fire be habituated to move downwards, nor can anything else that by nature behaves in one way be trained to behave in another. Neither by nature, then, nor contrary to nature do the virtues arise in us; rather we are adapted by nature to receive them, and are made perfect by habit.

Again, of all the things that come to us by nature we first acquire the potentiality and later exhibit the activity (this is plain in the case of the senses; for it was not by often seeing or often hearing that we got these senses, but on the contrary we had them before we used them, and did not come to have them by using them); but the virtues we get by first exercising them, as also happens in the case of the arts as well. For the things we have to learn before we can do them, we learn by doing them, e.g., men become builders by building and lyre-players by playing the lyre; so too we become just by doing just acts, temperate by doing temperate acts, brave by doing brave acts.

* This traditional interpretation of Aristotle's idea has been challenged by some recent scholars, who speak rather of the character's fatal mistake, a wrong decision that leads to tragedy.
Nicomachean Ethics.^A Translated by W. D. Ross. From *The Oxford Student Aristotle*. Reprinted by permission of The Clarendon Press, Oxford.

This is confirmed by what happens in states; for legislators make the citizens good by forming habits in them, and this is the wish of every legislator, and those who do not effect it miss their mark, and it is in this that a good constitution differs from a bad one.

Again, it is from the same causes and by the same means that every virtue is both produced and destroyed, and similarly every art; for it is from playing the lyre that both good and bad lyre-players are produced. And the corresponding statement is true of builders and of all the rest; men will be good or bad builders as a result of building well or badly. For if this were not so, there would have been no need of a teacher, but all men would have been born good or bad at their craft. This, then, is the case with the virtues also; by doing the acts that we do in our transactions with other men we become just or unjust, and by doing the acts that we do in the presence of danger, and being habituated to feel fear or confidence, we become brave or cowardly. The same is true of appetites and feelings of anger; some men become temperate and good-tempered, others self-indulgent and irascible, by behaving in one way or the other in the appropriate circumstances. Thus, in one word, states of character arise out of like activities. This is why the activities we exhibit must be of a certain kind; it is because the states of character correspond to the differences between these. It makes no small difference, then, whether we form habits of one kind or of another from our very youth; it makes a very great difference, or rather *all* the difference. . . .

4. The question might be asked, what we mean by saying that we must become just by doing just acts, and temperate by doing temperate acts; for if men do just and temperate acts, they are already just and temperate, exactly as, if they do what is in accordance with the laws of grammar and of music, they are grammarians and musicians.

Or is this not true even of the arts? It is possible to do something that is in accordance with the laws of grammar, either by chance or at the suggestion of another. A man will be a grammarian, then, only when he has both done something grammatical and done it grammatically; and this means doing it in accordance with the grammatical knowledge in himself.

Again, the case of the arts and that of the virtues are not similar; for the products of the arts have their goodness in themselves, so that it is enough that they should have a certain character, but if the acts that are in accordance with the virtues have themselves a certain character it does not follow that they are done justly or temperately. The agent also must be in a certain condition when he does them; in the first place he must have knowledge, secondly he must choose the acts, and choose them for their own sakes, and thirdly his action must proceed from a firm and unchangeable character. These are not reckoned in as conditions of the possession of the arts, except the bare knowledge; but as a condition of the possession of the virtues knowledge has little or no weight, while the other conditions count not for a little but for everything, i.e. the very conditions which result from often doing just and temperate acts.

Actions, then, are called just and temperate when they are such as the just or the temperate man would do; but it is not the man who does these that is just and temperate, but the man who also does them as just and temperate men do them. It is well said, then, that it is by doing just acts that the just man is produced, and by doing temperate acts the temperate man; without doing these no one would have even a prospect of becoming good.

But most people do not do these, but take refuge in theory and think they are being philosophers and will become good in this way, behaving somewhat like patients who listen attentively to their doctors, but do none of the things they are ordered to do. As the latter will not be made well in body by such a course of treatment, the former will not be made well in soul by such a course of philosophy.

5. Next we must consider what virtue is. Since things that are found in the soul are of three kinds—passions, faculties, states of character, virtue must be one of these. By passions I mean appetite, anger, fear, confidence, envy, joy, friendly feeling, hatred, longing, emulation, pity, and in general the feelings that are accompanied by pleasure or pain; by faculties the things in virtue of which we are said to be capable of feeling these, e.g. of becoming angry or being pained or feeling pity; by states of character the things in virtue of which we stand well or badly with reference to the passions, e.g. with reference to anger we stand badly if we feel it violently or too weakly, and well if we feel it moderately; and similarly with reference to the other passions.

Now neither the virtues nor the vices are *passions*, because we are not called good or bad on the ground of our passions, but are so called on the ground of our virtues and our vices, and because we are neither praised nor blamed for our passions (for the man who feels fear or anger is not praised, nor is the man who simply feels anger blamed, but the man who feels it in a certain way), but for our virtues and our vices we are praised or blamed.

Again, we feel anger and fear without choice, but the virtues are modes of choice or involve choice. Further, in respect of the passions we are said to be moved, but in respect of the virtues and the vices we are said not to be moved but to be disposed in a particular way.

For these reasons also they are not *faculties;* for we are neither called good nor bad, nor praised nor blamed, for the simple capacity of feeling the passions; again, we have the faculties by nature, but we are not made good or bad by nature.

If, then, the virtues are neither passions nor faculties, all that remains is that they should be *states of character.* Thus we have stated what virtue is in respect of its genus.

6. We must, however, not only describe virtue as a state of character, but also say what sort of state it is. We may remark, then, that every virtue or excellence both brings into good condition the thing of which it is the excellence and makes the work of that thing be done well; e.g. the excellence of the eye makes both the eye and its work good; for it is by the excellence of the eye that we see well. Similarly the excellence of the horse makes a horse both good in itself and good at running and at carrying its rider and at awaiting the attack of the enemy. Therefore, if this is true in every case, the virtue of man also will be the state of character which makes a man good and which makes him do his own work well.

How this is to happen we have stated already, but it will be made plain also by the following consideration of the specific nature of virtue. In everything that is continuous and divisible it is possible to take more, less, or an equal amount, and that either in terms of the thing itself or relatively to us; and the equal is an intermediate between excess and defect. By the intermediate in the object I mean that which is equidistant from each of the extremes, which is one and the same for all men; by the intermediate relatively to us that which is neither too much nor too little—and this is not one, nor the same for all. For instance, if ten is many and two is few, six is the intermediate, taken in terms of the object; for it exceeds and is exceeded by an equal amount; this is intermediate according to arithmetical proportion. But the intermediate relatively to us is not to be taken so; if ten pounds are too much for a particular person to eat and two too little, it does not follow that the trainer will order six pounds; for this also is perhaps too much for the person who is to take it, or too little—too little for Milo, too much for the beginner in athletic exercises. The same is true of running and wrestling. Thus a master of any art avoids excess and defect, but seeks the intermediate and chooses this—the intermediate not in the object but relatively to us.

If it is thus, then, that every art does its work well—by looking to the intermediate and judging its works by this standard (so that we often say of good works of art that it is not possible either to

46. Milo, a famous wrestler.

take away or to add anything, implying that excess and defect destroy the goodness of works of art, while the mean preserves it; and good artists, as we say, look to this in their work), and if, further, virtue is more exact and better than any art, as nature also is, then virtue must have the quality of aiming at the intermediate. I mean moral virtue; for it is this that is concerned with passions and actions, and in these there is excess, defect, and the intermediate. For instance, both fear and confidence and appetite and anger and pity and in general pleasure and pain may be felt both too much and too little, and in both cases not well; but to feel them at the right times, with reference to the right objects, towards the right people, with the right motive, and in the right way, is what is both intermediate and best, and this is characteristic of virtue. Similarly with regard to actions also there is excess, defect, and the intermediate. Now virtue is concerned with passions and actions, in which excess is a form of failure, and so is defect, while the intermediate is praised and is a form of success; and being praised and being successful are both characteristics of virtue. Therefore virtue is a kind of mean, since, as we have seen, it aims at what is intermediate.

Again, it is possible to fail in many ways (for evil belongs to the class of the unlimited, as the Pythagoreans conjectured, and good to that of the limited), while to succeed is possible only in one way (for which reason also one is easy and the other difficult—to miss the mark easy, to hit it difficult); for these reasons also, then, excess and defect are characteristic of vice, and the mean of virtue;

For men are good in but one way, but bad in many.

Virtue, then, is a state of character concerned with choice, lying in a mean, i.e. the mean relative to us, this being determined by a rational principle, and by that principle by which the man of practical wisdom would determine it. Now it is a mean between two vices, that which depends on excess and that which depends on defect; and again it is a mean because the vices respectively fall short of or exceed what is right in both passions and actions, while virtue both finds and chooses that which is intermediate. Hence in respect of its substance and the definition which states its essence virtue is a mean, with regard to what is best and right an extreme.

But not every action nor every passion admits of a mean; for some have names that already imply badness, e.g. spite, shamelessness, envy, and in the case of actions adultery, theft, murder; for all of these and suchlike things imply by their names that they are themselves bad, and not the excesses or deficiencies of them. It is not possible, then, ever to be right with regard to them; one must always be wrong. Nor does goodness or badness with regard to such things depend on committing adultery with the right woman, at the right time, and in the right way, but simply to do any of them is to go wrong. It would be equally absurd, then, to expect that in unjust, cowardly, and voluptuous action there should be a mean, an excess, and a deficiency; for at that rate there would be a mean of excess and of deficiency, an excess of excess, and a deficiency of deficiency. But as there is no excess and deficiency of temperance and courage because what is intermediate is in a sense an extreme, so too of the actions we have mentioned there is no mean nor any excess and deficiency, but however they are done they are wrong; for in general there is neither a mean of excess and deficiency, nor excess and deficiency of a mean.

7. We must, however, not only make this general statement, but also apply it to the individual facts. For among statements about conduct those which are general apply more widely, but those which are particular are more genuine, since conduct has to do with individual cases, and our statements must harmonize with the facts in these cases. We may take these cases from our table. With regard to feelings of fear and confidence courage is the mean; of the people who exceed, he who exceeds in fearlessness has no name (many of the states have no name), while the man who exceeds in confidence is rash, and he who exceeds in fear and falls short in confidence is a coward. With regard to pleasures and pains—not all of them, and not so much with regard to the pains—the mean is temperance, the excess self-indulgence. Persons deficient with regard to the pleasures are not often found; hence such persons also have received no name. But let us call them 'insensible.'

With regard to giving and taking of money the mean is liberality, the excess and the defect prodigality and meanness. In these actions people exceed and fall short in contrary ways; the prodigal exceeds in spending and falls short in taking, while the mean man exceeds in taking and falls short in spending. With regard to money there are also other dispositions—a mean, magnificence (for the magnificent man differs from the liberal man; the former deals with large sums, the latter with small ones), and excess, tastelessness and vulgarity, and a deficiency, niggardliness; these differ from the states opposed to liberality.

With regard to honour and dishonour the mean is proper pride, the excess is known as a sort of 'empty vanity' and the deficiency is undue humility; and as liberality was related to magnificence, differing from it by dealing with small sums, so there is a state similarly related to proper pride, being concerned with small honours while that is concerned with great. For it is possible to desire honour as one ought, and more than one ought, and less, and the man who exceeds in his desires is called ambitious, the man who falls short unambitious, while the intermediate person has no name. The dispositions also are nameless, except that that of the ambitious man is called ambition. Hence the people who are at the extremes lay claim to the middle place; and we ourselves sometimes call the intermediate person ambitious and sometimes unambitious, and sometimes praise the ambitious man and sometimes the unambitious.

With regard to anger also there is an excess, a deficiency, and a mean. Although they can scarcely be said to have names, yet since we call the intermediate person good-tempered let us call the mean good temper; of the persons at the extremes let the one who exceeds be called irascible, and his vice irascibility, and the man who falls short an inirascible sort of person, and the deficiency inirascibility.

There are also three other means, which have a certain likeness to one another, but differ from one another: for they are all concerned with intercourse in words and actions, but differ in that one is concerned with truth in this sphere, the other two with pleasantness; and of this one kind is exhibited in giving amusement, the other in all the circumstances of life. We must therefore speak of these too, that we may the better see that in all things the mean is praiseworthy, and the extremes neither praiseworthy nor right, but worthy of blame. Now most of these states also have no names, but we must try, as in the other cases, to invent names ourselves so that we may be clear and easy to follow. With regard to truth, then, the intermediate is a truthful sort of person and the mean may be called truthfulness, while the pretence which exaggerates is boastfulness and the person characterized by it a boaster, and that which understates is mock modesty and the person characterized by it mock-modest. With regard to pleasantness in the giving of amusement the intermediate person is ready-witted and the disposition ready wit, the excess is buffoonery and the person characterized by it a buffoon, while the man who falls short is a sort of boor and his state is boorishness. With regard to the remaining kind of pleasantness, that which is exhibited in life in general, the man who is pleasant in the right way is friendly and the mean is friendliness, while the man who exceeds is an obsequious person if he has no end in view, a flatterer if he is aiming at his own advantage, and the man who falls short and is unpleasant in all circumstances is a quarrelsome and surly sort of person.

There are also means in the passions and concerned with the passions; since shame is not a virtue, and yet praise is extended to the modest man. For even in these matters one man is said to be intermediate, and another to exceed, as for instance the bashful man who is ashamed of everything; while he who falls short or is not ashamed of anything at all is shameless, and the intermediate person is modest. Righteous indignation is a mean between envy and spite, and these states are concerned with the pain and pleasures that are felt at the fortunes of our neighbours; the man who is characterized by righteous indignation is pained at undeserved good fortune, the envious man, going beyond him, is pained at all good fortune, and the spiteful man falls so far short of being pained that he even rejoices.

8. There are three kinds of disposition, then, two of them vices, involving excess and deficiency respectively, and one a virtue, viz. the mean, and all are in a sense opposed to all; for the extreme states are contrary both to the intermediate state and to each other, and the intermediate to the extremes; as the equal is greater relatively to the less, less relatively to the greater, so the middle states are excessive relatively to the deficiencies, deficient relatively to the excesses, both in passions and in actions.

Poetics

A TRAGEDY is the imitation of an action that is serious and also, as having magnitude, complete in itself; in language with pleasurable accessories, each kind brought in separately in the parts of the work; in a dramatic, not in a narrative form; with incidents arousing pity and fear, where-with to accomplish its catharsis of such emotions. Here by 'language with pleasurable accessories' I mean that with rhythm and harmony or song superadded; and by 'the kinds separately' I mean that some portions are worked out with verse only, and others in turn with song.

I. As they act the stories, it follows that in the first place the Spectacle (or stage-appearance of the actors) must be some part of the whole; and in the second Melody and Diction, these two being the means of their imitation. Here by 'Diction' I mean merely this, the composition of the verses; and by 'Melody,' what is too completely understood to require explanation. But further: the subject represented also is an action; and the action involves agents, who must necessarily have their distinctive qualities both of character and thought, since it is

Poetics. (Chapters 6-18.) ⁴ Translated by Ingram Bywater. From *The Oxford Student Aristotle*. Reprinted by permission of The Clarendon Press, Oxford.

from these that we ascribe certain qualities to their actions. There are in the natural order of things, therefore, two causes, Thought and Character, of their actions, and consequently of their success or failure in their lives. Now the action (that which was done) is represented in the play by the Fable or Plot. The Fable, in our present sense of the term, is simply this, the combination of the incidents, or things done in the story; whereas Character is what makes us ascribe certain moral qualities to the agents; and Thought is shown in all they say when proving a particular point or, it may be, enunciating a general truth. There are six parts consequently of every tragedy, as a whole (that is) of such or such quality, viz. a Fable or Plot, Characters, Diction, Thought, Spectacle, and Melody; two of them arising from the means, one from the manner, and three from the objects of the dramatic imitation; and there is nothing else besides these six. Of these, its formative elements, then, not a few of the dramatists have made due use, as every play, one may say, admits of Spectacle, Character, Fable, Diction, Melody, and Thought.

II. The most important of the six is the combination of the incidents of the story. Tragedy is essentially an imitation not of persons but of action and life, of happiness and misery. All human happiness or misery takes the form of action; the end for which we live is a certain kind of activity, not a quality. Character gives us qualities, but it is in our actions —what we do—that we are happy or the reverse. In a play accordingly they do not act in order to portray the Characters; they include the Characters for the sake of the action. So that it is the action in it, i.e. its Fable or Plot, that is the end and purpose of the tragedy; and the end is everywhere the chief thing. Besides this, a tragedy is impossible without action, but there may be one without Character. . . . And again: one may string together a series of characteristic speeches of the utmost finish as regards Diction and Thought, and yet fail to produce the true tragic effect; but one will have much better success with a tragedy which, however inferior in these respects, has a Plot, a combination of incidents, in it. . . . A further proof is in the fact that beginners succeed earlier with the Diction and Characters than with the construction of a story; and the same may be said of nearly all the early dramatists. We maintain, therefore, that the first essential, the life and soul, so to speak, of Tragedy is the Plot; and that the Characters come second—compare the parallel in painting, where the most beautiful colours laid on without order will not give one the same pleasure as a simple black-and-white sketch of a portrait. We maintain that Tragedy is primarily an imitation of action, and that it is mainly for the sake of the action that it imitates the personal agents.

Third comes the element of Thought, i.e. the power of saying whatever can be said, or what is appropriate to the occasion. This is what, in the speeches in Tragedy, falls under the arts of Politics and Rhetoric; for the older poets make their personages discourse like statesmen, and the modern like rhetoricians. One must not confuse it with Character. Character in a play is that which reveals the moral purpose of the agents, i.e. the sort of thing they seek or avoid, where that is not obvious—hence there is no room for Character in a speech on a purely indifferent subject. Thought, on the other hand, is shown in all they say when proving or disproving some particular point, or enunciating some universal proposition. Fourth among the literary elements is the Diction of the personages, the expression of their thoughts in words, which is practically the same thing with verse as with prose. As for the two remaining parts, the Melody is the greatest of the pleasurable accessories of Tragedy. The Spectacle, though an attraction, is the least artistic of all the parts, and has least to do with the art of poetry. The tragic effect is quite possible without a public performance and actors; and besides, the getting-up of the Spectacle is more a matter for the costumier than the poet.

Having thus distinguished the parts, let us now consider the proper construction of the Fable or Plot, as that is at once the first and the most important thing in Tragedy. We have laid it down that a tragedy is an imitation of an action that is complete in itself, as a whole of some magnitude; for a whole is that which has beginning, middle, and end. A beginning is that which is not itself necessarily after anything else, and which has naturally something else after it; an end is that which is naturally after something itself, either as its necessary or usual consequent, and with nothing else after it; and a middle, that which is by nature after one thing and has also another after it. A well-constructed Plot, therefore, cannot either begin or end at any point one likes; beginning and end in it must be of the forms just described. Again: to be beautiful, a living creature, and every whole made up of parts, must not only present a certain order in its arrangement of parts, but also be of a certain definite magnitude. Beauty is a matter of size and order, and therefore impossible either (1) in a very minute creature, since our perception becomes indistinct as it approaches instantaneity; or (2) in a creature of vast size—one, say, 1,000 miles long—as in that case, instead of the object being seen all at once, the unity and wholeness of it is lost to the beholder. Just in the same way, then, as a beautiful whole made up of parts, or a beautiful living creature, must be of some size, but a size to be taken in by the eye, so a story or Plot must be of some length,

but of a length to be taken in by the memory. As for the limit of its length, so far as that is relative to public performances and spectators, it does not fall within the theory of poetry. If they had to perform a hundred tragedies, they would be timed by water-clocks, as they are said to have been at one period. The limit, however, set by the actual nature of the thing is this: the longer the story, consistently with its being comprehensible as a whole, the finer it is by reason of its magnitude. As a rough general formula, 'a length which allows of the hero passing by a series of probable or necessary stages from misfortune to happiness, or from happiness to misfortune,' may suffice as a limit for the magnitude of the story.

The Unity of a Plot does not consist, as some suppose, in its having one man as its subject. An infinity of things befall that one man, some of which it is impossible to reduce to unity; and in like manner there are many actions of one man which cannot be made to form one action. One sees, therefore, the mistake of all the poets who have written a *Heracleid*, a *Theseid*, or similar poems; they suppose that, because Heracles was one man, the story also of Heracles must be one story. Homer, however, evidently understood this point quite well, whether by art or instinct, just in the same way as he excels the rest in every other respect. In writing an *Odyssey*, he did not make the poem cover all that ever befell his hero—it befell him, for instance, to get wounded on Parnassus and also to feign madness at the time of the call to arms, but the two incidents had no necessary or probable connection with one another—instead of doing that, he took as the subject of the *Odyssey*, as also of the *Iliad*, an action with a Unity of the kind we are describing. The truth is that, just as in the other imitative arts one imitation is always of one thing, so in poetry the story, as an imitation of action, must represent one action, a complete whole, with its several incidents so closely connected that the transposal or withdrawal of any one of them will disjoin and dislocate the whole. For that which makes no perceptible difference by its presence or absence is no real part of the whole.

From what we have said it will be seen that the poet's function is to describe, not the thing that has happened, but a kind of thing that might happen, i.e. what is possible as being probable or necessary. The distinction between historian and poet is not in the one writing prose and the other verse—you might put the work of Herodotus into verse, and it would still be a species of history; it consists really in this, that the one describes the thing that has been, and the other a kind of thing that might be.

80. *Heracleid, Theseid;* that is, epics of such heroes as Hercules and Theseus.

Hence poetry is something more philosophic and of graver import than history, since its statements are of the nature rather of universals, whereas those of history are singulars. By a universal statement I mean one as to what such or such a kind of man will probably or necessarily say or do—which is the aim of poetry, though it affixes proper names to the characters; by a singular statement, one as to what, say, Alcibiades did or had done to him. In Comedy this has become clear by this time; it is only when their plot is already made up of probable incidents that they give it a basis of proper names, choosing for the purpose any names that may occur to them, instead of writing like the old iambic poets about particular persons. In Tragedy, however, they still adhere to the historic names; and for this reason: what convinces is the possible; now whereas we are not yet sure as to the possibility of that which has not happened, that which has happened is manifestly possible, else it would not have come to pass. Nevertheless even in Tragedy there are some plays with but one or two known names in them, the rest being inventions; and there are some without a single known name, e.g. Agathon's *Antheus,* in which both incidents and names are of the poet's invention; and it is no less delightful on that account. So that one must not aim at a rigid adherence to the traditional stories on which tragedies are based. It would be absurd, in fact, to do so, as even the known stories are only known to a few, though they are a delight none the less to all.

It is evident from the above that the poet must be more the poet of his stories or Plots than of his verses, inasmuch as he is a poet by virtue of the imitative element in his work, and it is actions that he imitates. And if he should come to take a subject from actual history, he is none the less a poet for that; since some historic occurrences may very well be in the probable and possible order of things; and it is in that aspect of them that he is their poet.

Of simple Plots and actions the episodic are the worst. I call a Plot episodic when there is neither probability nor necessity in the sequence of its episodes. Actions of this sort bad poets construct through their own fault, and good ones on account of the players. His work being for public performance, a good poet often stretches out a Plot beyond its capabilities, and is thus obliged to twist the sequence of incident.

Tragedy, however, is an imitation not only of a complete action, but also of incidents arousing pity and fear. Such incidents have the very greatest effect on the mind when they occur unexpectedly and at the same time in consequence of one another; there is more of the marvellous in them then than if they happened of themselves or by mere chance. Even matters of chance seem most marvellous if there is an appearance of design as it were in them; as for instance the statue of Mitys at Argos killed the author of Mitys' death by falling down on him when a looker-on at a public spectacle; for incidents like that we think to be not without a meaning. A Plot, therefore, of this sort is necessarily finer than others.

Plots are either simple or complex, since the actions they represent are naturally of this twofold description. The action, proceeding in the way defined, as one continuous whole, I call simple, when the change in the hero's fortune takes place without Peripety or Discovery; and complex, when it involves one or the other, or both. These should each of them arise out of the structure of the Plot itself, so as to be the consequence, necessary or probable, of the antecedents. There is a great difference between a thing happening *propter hoc* and *post hoc.*

A Peripety is the change of the kind described from one state of things within the play to its opposite, and that too in the way we are saying, in the probable or necessary sequence of events; as it is for instance in *Oedipus*: here the opposite state of things is produced by the Messenger, who, coming to gladden Oedipus and to remove his fears as to his mother, reveals the secret of his birth. And in *Lynceus*: just as he is being led off for execution, with Danaus at his side to put him to death, the incidents preceding this bring it about that he is saved and Danaus put to death. A Discovery is, as the very word implies, a change from ignorance to knowledge, and thus to either love or hate, in the personages marked for good or evil fortune. The finest form of Discovery is one attended by Peripeties, like that which goes with the Discovery in Oedipus. There are no doubt other forms of it; what we have said may happen in a way in reference to inanimate things, even things of a very casual kind; and it is also possible to discover whether some one has done or not done something. But the form most directly connected with the Plot and the action of the piece is the first-mentioned. This, with a Peripety, will arouse either pity or fear—actions of that nature being what Tragedy is assumed to represent; and it will also serve to bring about the happy or unhappy ending. The Discovery, then, being of persons, it may be that of one party only to the other, the latter being already known; or both the parties may have to discover themselves. Iphigenia, for instance, was discovered to Orestes

24. **Agathon,** Greek tragic poet, friend to Euripides and Plato.

74–75. **There . . .** *post hoc.* That is, the difference between a thing happening *in consequence* of something else and merely *after* something else. 84. *Lynceus,* by Theodectes. 92. **Peripeties,** complete reversals of fortune. 107. **Iphigenia . . .** This occurred in *Iphigenia among the Taurians* by Euripides.

by sending the letter; and another Discovery was required to reveal him to Iphigenia.

Two parts of the Plot, then, Peripety and Discovery, are on matters of this sort. A third part is Suffering; which we may define as an action of a destructive or painful nature, such as murders on the stage, tortures, woundings, and the like. The other two have been already explained. . . .

The next points after what we have said above will be these: (1) What is the poet to aim at, and what is he to avoid, in constructing his Plots? and (2) What are the conditions on which the tragic effect depends?

We assume that, for the finest form of Tragedy, the Plot must be not simple but complex; and further, that it must imitate actions arousing fear and pity, since that is the distinctive function of this kind of imitation. It follows, therefore, that there are three forms of Plot to be avoided. (1) A good man must not be seen passing from happiness to misery, or (2) a bad man from misery to happiness. The first situation is not fear-inspiring or piteous, but simply odious to us. The second is the most untragic that can be; it has no one of the requisites of Tragedy; it does not appeal either to the human feeling in us, or to our fears. Nor, on the other hand, should (3) an extremely bad man be seen falling from happiness into misery. Such a story may arouse the human feeling in us, but it will not move us to either pity or fear; pity is occasioned by undeserved misfortune, and fear by that of one like ourselves; so that there will be nothing either piteous or fear-inspiring in the situation. There remains, then, the intermediate kind of personage, a man not preeminently virtuous and just, whose misfortune, however, is brought upon him not by vice and depravity but by some error of judgement, of the number of those in the enjoyment of great reputation and prosperity; e.g. Oedipus, Thyestes, and the men of note of similar families. The perfect Plot, accordingly, must have a single, and not (as some tell us) a double issue; the change in the hero's fortunes must be not from misery to happiness, but on the contrary from happiness to misery; and the cause of it must lie not in any depravity, but in some great error on his part; the man himself being either such as we have described, or better, not worse, than that.

Fact also confirms our theory. Though the poets began by accepting any tragic story that came to hand, in these days the finest tragedies are always on the story of some few houses, on that of Alcmeon, Oedipus, Orestes, Meleager, Thyestes, Telephus, or any others that may have been involved, as either agents or sufferers, in some deed of horror. The theoretically best tragedy, then, has a Plot of this description. The critics, therefore, are wrong who blame Euripides for taking this line in his tragedies, and giving many of them an unhappy ending. It is, as we have said, the right line to take. The best proof is this: on the stage, and in the public performances, such plays, properly worked out, are seen to be the most truly tragic; and Euripides, even if his execution be faulty in every other point, is seen to be nevertheless the most tragic certainly of the dramatists. After this comes the construction of Plot which some rank first, one with a double story (like the *Odyssey*) and an opposite issue for the good and the bad personages. It is ranked as first only through the weakness of the audiences; the poets merely follow their public, writing as its wishes dictate. But the pleasure here is not that of Tragedy. It belongs rather to Comedy, where the bitterest enemies in the piece (e.g. Orestes and Aegisthus) walk off good friends at the end, with no slaying of any one by any one.

The tragic fear and pity may be aroused by the Spectacle; but they may also be aroused by the very structure and incidents of the play—which is the better way and shows the better poet. The Plot in fact should be so framed that, even without seeing the things take place, he who simply hears the account of them shall be filled with horror and pity at the incidents; which is just the effect that the mere recital of the story in Oedipus would have on one. To produce this same effect by means of the Spectacle is less artistic, and requires extraneous aid. Those, however, who make use of the Spectacle to put before us that which is merely monstrous and not productive of fear, are wholly out of touch with Tragedy; not every kind of pleasure should be required of a tragedy, but only its own proper pleasure.

The tragic pleasure is that of pity and fear, and the poet has to produce it by a work of imitation; it is clear, therefore, that the causes should be included in the incidents of his story. Let us see, then, what kinds of incident strike one as horrible, or rather as piteous. In a deed of this description the parties must necessarily be either friends, or enemies, or indifferent to one another. Now when enemy does it on enemy, there is nothing to move us to pity either in his doing or in his meditating the deed, except so far as the actual pain of the sufferer is concerned; and the same is true when the parties are indifferent to one another. Whenever the tragic deed, however, is done within the family —when murder or the like is done or meditated by brother on brother, by son on father, by mother on son, or son on mother—these are the situations the poet should seek after. The traditional stories, accordingly, must be kept as they are, e.g. the murder of Clytaemnestra by Orestes. At the same time even with these there is something left to the poet himself; it is for him to devise the right way of treating them. Let us explain more clearly what we mean by 'the right way.' The deed of horror may be done by the doer knowingly and consciously, as in the old poets, and in Medea's murder of her children in Euripides. Or he may do it, but in ignorance of his relationship, and discover that afterwards, as does the Oedipus in Sophocles. Here the deed is outside the play; but it may be within it. . . . A third possibility is for one meditating some deadly injury to another, in ignorance of his relationship, to make the discovery in time to draw back. These exhaust the possibilities, since the deed must necessarily be either done or not done, and either knowingly or unknowingly.

The worst situation is when the personage is with full knowledge on the point of doing the deed, and leaves it undone. It is odious and also (through the absence of suffering) untragic; hence it is that no one is made to act thus except in some few instances, e.g. Haemon and Creon in *Antigone*. Next after this comes the actual perpetration of the deed meditated. A better situation than that, however, is for the deed to be done in ignorance, and the relationship discovered afterwards, since there is nothing odious in it, and the Discovery will serve to astound us. But the best of all is the last; what we have in *Cresphontes,* for example, where Merope, on the point of slaying her son, recognizes him in time; in *Iphigenia,* where sister and brother are in a like position; and in *Helle,* where the son recognizes his mother, when on the point of giving her up to her enemy.

This will explain why our tragedies are restricted to such a small number of families. It was accident rather than art that led the poets in quest of subjects to embody this kind of incident in their Plots. They are still obliged, accordingly, to have recourse to the families in which such horrors have occurred.

On the construction of the Plot, and the kind of Plot required for Tragedy, enough has now been said.

In the Characters there are four points to aim at. First and foremost, that they shall be good. There will be an element of character in the play, if (as has been observed) what a personage says or does reveals a certain moral purpose; and a good element of character, if the purpose so revealed is good. Such goodness is possible in every type of personage; even in a woman or a slave, though the one is perhaps an inferior, and the other wholly a worthless being. The second point is to make them appropriate. The Character before us may be, say, manly; but it is not appropriate in a female Character to be manly,

21. *Antigone,* a play by Sophocles. 28, 30, 31. *Cresphontes, Iphigenia, Helle;* the first two plays are by Euripides, the third by an unknown author.

or clever. The third is to make them like the reality, which is not the same as their being good and appropriate, in our sense of the term. The fourth is to make them consistent and the same throughout; even if inconsistency be part of the man before one for imitation as presenting that form of character, he should still be consistently inconsistent. We have an instance of . . . inconsistency in *Iphigenia at Aulis,* where Iphigenia the suppliant is utterly unlike the later Iphigenia. The right thing, however, is in the Characters just as in the incidents of the play to endeavour always after the necessary or the probable; so that whenever such-and-such a personage says or does such-and-such a thing, it shall be the necessary or probable outcome of his character; and whenever this incident follows on that, it shall be either the necessary or the probable consequence of it. From this one sees (to digress for a moment) that the Dénouement also should arise out of the plot itself, and not depend on a stage-artifice. . . . The artifice must be reserved for matters outside the play—for past events beyond human knowledge, or events yet to come, which require to be foretold or announced; since it is the privilege of the Gods to know everything. There should be nothing improbable among the actual incidents. If it be unavoidable, however, it should be outside the tragedy, like the improbability in the *Oedipus* of Sophocles. But to return to the Characters. As Tragedy is an imitation of personages better than the ordinary man, we in our way should follow the example of good portrait-painters, who reproduce the distinctive features of a man, and at the same time, without losing the likeness, make him handsomer than he is. The poet in like manner, in portraying men quick or slow to anger, or with similar infirmities of character, must know how to represent them as such, and at the same time as good men as Agathon and Homer have represented Achilles. . . .

There is a further point to be borne in mind. Every tragedy is in part Complication and in part Dénouement; the incidents before the opening scene, and often certain also of those within the play, forming the Complication; and the rest the Dénouement. By Complication I mean all from the beginning of the story to the point just before the change in the hero's fortunes; by Dénouement, all from the beginning of the change to the end. . . . Now it is right, when one speaks of a tragedy as the same or not the same as another, to do so on the ground before all else of their Plot, i.e. as having the same or not the same Complication and Dénouement. Yet there are many dramatists who, after a good Complication, fail in the Dénouement. But it is necessary for both points of construction to be always duly mastered.

62-63. *Iphigenia at Aulis,* play by Euripides.

Lucian

125–c. 200 A.D.

The last major figure in Greek literature, Lucian of Samosata, is also the wittiest and most entertaining of its prose writers. A product of the so-called Greek Renaissance, which came centuries after the Golden Age, he left some eighty brief works which provide a kind of cynical summary of the Greeks' achievements from Homer down. Lucian is not a creative writer but a critical one, not a constructive thinker but a destructive satirist who reduces the gods and heroes, the statesmen and philosophers of the past to the level of petty but pretentious mortals in order to amuse lesser folk with their foibles and false pride.

By the time of the Greek Renaissance—an artificial revival of Hellenistic culture stimulated by the Roman emperor Hadrian in the second century A.D.—Socrates and Plato were as remote as Chaucer is to us. The traditional religion had been decaying for centuries. All the schools of philosophy, which Lucian passes in contemptuous review in his *Sale of the Philosophers,* had said their say, and the world seemed no better for them. Christianity was growing as a spiritual force underground, but as yet it had barely touched the jaded Graeco-Roman world, and its leaders still suffered martyrdom. Lucian was the cynical spokesman for this age without faith, keenly intellectual, brilliantly artistic, and devoid of serious belief in anything. But underneath his playful irreverence he was a moralist too and satirized humbug and cant out of a healthy respect for truth and right living.

Typical of his cosmopolitan era, Lucian was neither Greek nor Roman, but a Syrian of Samosata on the Euphrates, who was reared in the Roman provinces of Asia Minor and adopted Greek as his literary tongue. Apprenticed to his uncle, a sculptor, he quickly shifted to the professions of law and rhetoric. In maturity he was an itinerant professor, lecturing his way through Greece, Italy, and Gaul. But he eventually settled in Athens around 164 A.D. and probably wrote his major works there. Still the wanderlust was in his blood, and at the time of his death he held a legal position in Egypt. This restless, inquisitive man had covered a good part of the Empire in his quest for knowledge of people and ideas, and if he inclined to the Cynic philosophy of skepticism and asceticism, his wholesome writings suggest that he led a robust life and could laugh at himself as well as at others.

Although Lucian wrote philosophical essays, rhetorical exercises, and comic narratives, his forte was the satiric dialogue, which he developed especially in his later years. Unlike the graceful Platonic dialogues with their long and serious speeches ascribed to the author's friends, the dialogues of Lucian are generally brief fragments of witty conversation between mythical or long-dead characters in short, racy speeches close to the give and take of actual talk. An outgrowth of the ancient *mimes* and reminiscent of the satiric comedies of Aristophanes, they burlesque the hallowed personalities of the past with their rational attack on religion and philosophy. In the *Dialogues of the Gods* the dignitaries of Olympus are politely lampooned as idle aristocrats given to jealous backbiting, catty argument, and free love. The *Dialogues of the Dead* carry underneath their playful picture of Hades the insistent reminder that human ambition and pride are ultimately futile.

Dialogues of the Gods

THE TRICKS OF HERMES

HEPHAESTUS.

HAVE you seen Maia's baby, Apollo? Such a pretty little thing, with a smile for everybody; you can see it is going to be a treasure.

APOLLO. That baby a treasure? Well, in mischief Iapetus is young beside it.

HEPHAESTUS. Why, what harm can it do, only just born?

APOLLO. Ask Posidon; it stole his trident. Ask Ares; he was surprised to find his sword gone out of the scabbard. Not to mention myself, disarmed of bow and arrows.

HEPHAESTUS. Never! That infant? He has hardly found his legs yet; he is not out of his baby-linen.

APOLLO. Ah, you will find out, Hephaestus, if he gets within reach of you.

HEPHAESTUS. He has been.

APOLLO. Well? all your tools safe? None missing?

HEPHAESTUS. Of course not.

APOLLO. I advise you to make sure.

HEPHAESTUS. Zeus! where are my pincers?

APOLLO. Ah, you will find them among the baby-linen.

HEPHAESTUS. So light-fingered? One would swear he had practiced petty larceny in the womb.

APOLLO. Ah, and you don't know what a glib young chatterbox he is; and, if he has his way, he is to be our errand-boy! Yesterday he challenged Eros —tripped up his heels somehow, and had him on his back in a twinkling; before the applause was over,

Dialogues of the Gods. "The Tricks of Hermes" and "Cupid's Exceptions" translated by H. W. Fowler, "The Birth of Athena" and "The Judgement of Paris" translated by F. G. Fowler. From *The Works of Lucian of Samosata* by H. W. and F. G. Fowler. Reprinted by permission of The Clarendon Press, Oxford.
1. **Maia's baby.** Hermes, the precocious and tricky son of Maia by Zeus, was notorious for his thieving in infancy. 5. **Iapetus,** the mischievous Titan, imprisoned in Tartarus.

he had taken the opportunity of a congratulatory hug from Aphrodite to steal her girdle; Zeus had not done laughing before—the sceptre was gone. If the thunderbolt had not been too heavy, and very hot, he would have made away with that too.

HEPHAESTUS. The child has some spirit in him, by your account.

APOLLO. Spirit, yes—and some music, moreover, young as he is.

HEPHAESTUS. How can you tell that?

APOLLO. He picked up a dead tortoise somewhere or other, and contrived an instrument with it. He fitted horns to it, with a cross-bar, stuck in pegs, inserted a bridge, and played a sweet tuneful thing that made an old harper like me quite envious. Even at night, Maia was saying, he does not stay in Heaven; he goes down poking his nose into Hades—on a thieves' errand, no doubt. Then he has a pair of wings, and he has made himself a magic wand, which he uses for marshalling souls—convoying the dead to their place.

HEPHAESTUS. Ah, I gave him that, for a toy.

APOLLO. And by way of payment he stole—

HEPHAESTUS. Well thought on; I must go and get them; you may be right about the baby-linen.

THE BIRTH OF ATHENA

HEPHAESTUS. What are your orders, Zeus? You sent for me, and here I am; with such an edge to my axe as would cleave a stone at one blow.

ZEUS. Ah; that's right, Hephaestus. Just split my head in half, will you?

HEPHAESTUS. You think I am mad, perhaps? . . . Seriously, now, what can I do for you?

ZEUS. What I say: crack my skull. Any insubordination, now, and you shall taste my resentment; it will not be the first time. Come, a good lusty stroke, and quick about it. I am in the pangs of travail; my brain is in a whirl.

HEPHAESTUS. Mind you, the consequences may be

The birth of Athena from the brain of Zeus. Hephaestus at right holds his double axe, with which he clave the skull of Zeus. From an early Greek vase.

serious: the axe is sharp, and will prove but a rough midwife.

ZEUS. Hew away, and fear nothing. I know what I am about.

HEPHAESTUS. H'm. I don't like it: however, one must obey orders. . . . Why, what have we here? A maiden in full armor! This is no joke, Zeus. You might well be waspish, with this great girl growing up beneath your *pia mater;* in armor, too! You have been carrying a regular barracks on your shoulders all this time. So active too! See, she is dancing a war-dance, with shield and spear in full swing. She is like one inspired; and (what is more to the point) she is extremely pretty, and has come to marriageable years in these few minutes; those grey eyes, even, look well beneath a helmet. Zeus, I claim her as the fee for my midwifery.

ZEUS. Impossible! She is determined to remain a maid for ever. Not that *I* have any objection, personally.

HEPHAESTUS. That is all I want. You can leave the rest to me. I'll carry her off this moment.

ZEUS. Well, if you think it so easy. But I am sure it is a hopeless case.

CUPID'S EXCEPTIONS

APHRODITE. Eros, dear, you have your victories over most of the gods—Zeus, Posidon, Rhea, Apollo, nay, your own mother; how is it you make an exception for Athene? Against her your torch has no fire, your quiver no arrows, your right hand no cunning.

EROS. I am afraid of her, mother; those awful flashing eyes! She is like a man, only worse. When I go against her with my arrow on the string, a toss of her plume frightens me; my hand shakes so that it drops the bow.

APHRODITE. I should have thought Ares was more terrible still; but you disarmed and conquered him.

EROS. Ah, he is only too glad to have me; he calls me to him. Athene always eyes me so! Once when I flew close past her, quite by accident, with my torch, 'If you come near me,' she called out, 'I swear by my father, I will run you through with my spear, or take you by the foot and drop you into Tartarus, or tear you in pieces with my own hands'—and more such dreadful things. And she has such a sour look; and then on her breast she wears that horrid face with the snaky hair; that frightens me worst of all; the nasty bogy—I run away directly I see it.

APHRODITE. Well, well, you are afraid of Athene and the Gorgon; at least so you say, though you do not mind Zeus's thunderbolt a bit. But why do you let the Muses go scot free? Do *they* toss their plumes and hold out Gorgons' heads?

87. **the Gorgon,** the terrible Medusa, whose hair was changed to snakes by Athena and whose head Athena placed in the center of her breastplate.

EROS. Ah, mother, they make me bashful; they are so grand, always studying and composing; I love to stand there listening to their music.

APHRODITE. Let them pass too, because they are grand. And why do you never take a shot at Artemis?

EROS. Why, the great thing is that I cannot catch her; she is always over the hills and far away. But besides that, her heart is engaged already.

APHRODITE. Where, child?

EROS. In hunting stags and fawns; she is so fleet, she catches them up, or else shoots them; she can think of nothing else. Her brother, now, though he is an archer too, and draws a good arrow—

APHRODITE. I know, child, you have hit *him* often enough.

THE JUDGEMENT OF PARIS

ZEUS. Hermes, take this apple, and go with it to Phrygia; on the Gargaran peak of Ida you will find Priam's son, the herdsman. Give him this message: "Paris, because you are handsome, and wise in the things of love, Zeus commands you to judge between the Goddesses, and say which is the most beautiful. And the prize shall be this apple."—Now, you three, there is no time to be lost: away with you to your judge. I will have nothing to do with the matter: I love you all exactly alike, and I only wish you could all three win. If I were to give the prize to one of you, the other two would hate me, of course. In these circumstances, I am ill qualified to be your judge. But this young Phrygian to whom you are going is of the royal blood—a relation to Ganymede's, —and at the same time a simple countryman; so that we need have no hesitation in trusting his eyes.

APHRODITE. As far as I am concerned, Zeus, Momus himself might be our judge; *I* should not be afraid to show myself. What fault could he find with *me*? But the others must agree too.

HERA. Oh, we are under no alarm, thank you,— though your admirer Ares should be appointed. But Paris will do; whoever Paris is.

ZEUS. And my little Athene; have we her approval? Nay, never blush, nor hide your face. Well, well, maidens will be coy; 'tis a delicate subject. But there, she nods consent. Now, off with you; and mind, the beaten ones must not be cross with the judge; I will not have the poor lad harmed. The prize of beauty can be but one.

HERMES. Now for Phrygia. I will show the way; keep close behind me, ladies, and don't be nervous. I know Paris well: he is a charming young man; a great gallant, and an admirable judge of beauty. Depend on it, he will make a good award.

14–15. **I know . . . enough.** The handsome Apollo had many affairs. 30. **Ganymede,** the beautiful shepherd boy beloved of Zeus and carried away by him in the guise of an eagle to become cupbearer to the king of the gods. 33–34. **Momus,** the god of censure.

APHRODITE. I am glad to hear that; I ask for nothing better than a just judge.—Has he a wife, Hermes, or is he a bachelor?

HERMES. Not exactly a bachelor.

APHRODITE. What do you mean?

HERMES. I believe there is a wife, as it were; a good enough sort of girl—a native of those parts— but sadly countrified! I fancy he does not care very much about her.—Why do you ask?

APHRODITE. I just wanted to know.

ATHENE. Now, Hermes, that is not fair. No whispering with Aphrodite.

HERMES. It was nothing, Athene; nothing about you. She only asked me whether Paris was a bachelor.

ATHENE. What business is that of hers?

HERMES. None that I know of. She meant nothing by the question; she just wanted to know.

ATHENE. Well, and is he?

HERMES. Why, no.

ATHENE. And does he care for military glory? Has he ambition? Or is he a *mere* neatherd?

HERMES. I couldn't say for certain. But he is a young man, so it is to be presumed that distinction on the field of battle is among his desires.

APHRODITE. There, you see; *I* don't complain; I say nothing when you whisper with *her*. Aphrodite is not so particular as some people.

HERMES. Athene asked me almost exactly the same as you did; so don't be cross. It will do you no harm, my answering a plain question.—Meanwhile, we have left the stars far behind us, and are almost over Phrygia. There is Ida: I can make out the peak of Gargarum quite plainly; and if I am not mistaken, there is Paris himself.

HERA. Where is he? I don't see him.

HERMES. Look over there to the left, Hera: not on the top, but down the side, by that cave where you see the herd.

HERA. But I *don't* see the herd.

HERMES. What, don't you see them coming out from between the rocks,—where I am pointing, look —and the man running down from the crag, and keeping them together with his staff?

HERA. I see him now; if he it is.

HERMES. Oh, that is Paris. But we are getting nearer; it is time to alight and walk. He might be frightened, if we were to descend upon him so suddenly.

HERA. Yes; very well. And now that we are on the earth, you might go on ahead, Aphrodite, and show us the way. You know the country, of course, having been here so often to see Anchises; or so I have heard.

57. **I believe . . . were.** Paris was married to Oenone, the daughter of the river god Cebren.

APHRODITE. Your sneers are thrown away on me, Hera.

HERMES. Come; I'll lead the way myself. I spent some time on Ida, while Zeus was courting Ganymede. Many is the time that I have been sent here to keep watch over the boy; and when at last the eagle came, I flew by his side, and helped him with his lovely burden. This is the very rock, if I remember; yes, Ganymede was piping to his sheep, when down swooped the eagle behind him, and tenderly, oh, so tenderly, caught him up in those talons, and with the turban in his beak bore him off, the frightened boy straining his neck the while to see his captor. I picked up his pipes—he had dropped them in his fright—and—ah! here is our umpire, close at hand. Let us accost him.—Good-morrow, herdsman!

PARIS. Good-morrow, youngster. And who may you be, who come thus far afield? And these dames? They are over comely to be wandering on the mountain-side.

HERMES. "These dames," good Paris, are Hera, Athene, and Aphrodite; and I am Hermes, with a message from Zeus. Why so pale and tremulous? Compose yourself; there is nothing the matter. Zeus appoints you the judge of their beauty. "Because you are handsome, and wise in the things of love" (so runs the message), "I leave the decision to you; and for the prize,—read the inscription on the apple."

PARIS. Let me see what it is about. FOR THE FAIR, it says. But, my lord Hermes, how shall a mortal and a rustic like myself be judge of such unparalleled beauty? This is no sight for a herdsman's eyes; let the fine city folk decide on such matters. As for me, I can tell you which of two goats is the fairer beast; or I can judge betwixt heifer and heifer;—'tis my trade. But here, where all are beautiful alike, I know not how a man may leave looking at one, to look upon another. Where my eyes fall, there they fasten, —for there is beauty: I move them, and what do I find? More loveliness! I am fixed again, yet distracted by neighboring charms. I bathe in beauty: I am enthralled: ah, why am I not *all* eyes like Argus? Methinks it were a fair award, to give the apple to all three. Then again: one is the wife and sister of Zeus; the others are his daughters. Take it where you will, 'tis a hard matter to judge.

HERMES. So it is, Paris. At the same time—Zeus's orders! There is no way out of it.

PARIS. Well, please point out to them, Hermes, that the losers must not be angry with me; the fault will be in my eyes only.

HERMES. That is quite understood. And now to work.

PARIS. I must do what I can; there is no help for it. But first let me ask,—am I just to look at them as they are, or must I go into the matter thoroughly?

HERMES. That is for you to decide, in virtue of your office. You have only to give your orders; it is as you think best.

PARIS. As I think best? Then I will be thorough.

HERMES. Get ready, ladies. Now, Mr. Umpire.— I will look the other way.

HERA. I approve your decision, Paris. I will be the first to submit myself to your inspection. You will see that I have more to boast of than white arms and large eyes: nought of me but is beautiful.

PARIS. Aphrodite, will you also prepare?

ATHENE. Oh, Paris,—make her take off that girdle, first; there is magic in it; she will bewitch you. For that matter, she has no right to come thus tricked out and painted,—just like a courtesan! She ought to show herself unadorned.

PARIS. They are right about the girdle, madam; it must go.

APHRODITE. Oh, very well, Athene: then take off that helmet, and show your head bare, instead of trying to intimidate the judge with that waving plume. I suppose you are afraid the color of your eyes may be noticed, without their formidable surroundings.

ATHENE. Oh, here is my helmet.

APHRODITE. And here is my girdle.

HERA. Now then.

PARIS. God of wonders! What loveliness is here! Oh, rapture! How exquisite these maiden charms! How dazzling the majesty of Heaven's true queen! And oh, how sweet, how enthralling is Aphrodite's smile! 'Tis too much, too much of happiness.—But perhaps it would be well for me to view each in detail; for as yet I doubt, and know not where to look; my eyes are drawn all ways at once.

APHRODITE. Yes, that will be best.

PARIS. Withdraw then, you and Athene; and let Hera remain.

HERA. So be it; and when you have finished your scrutiny, you have next to consider, how you would like the present which I offer you. Paris, give me the prize of beauty, and you shall be lord of all Asia.

PARIS. I will take no presents. Withdraw. I shall judge as I think right. Approach, Athene.

ATHENE. Behold. And, Paris, if you will say that I am the fairest, I will make you a great warrior and conqueror, and you shall always win, in every one of your battles.

PARIS. But I have nothing to do with fighting, Athene. As you see, there is peace throughout all Lydia and Phrygia, and my father's dominion is uncontested. But never mind: I am not going to take your present, but you shall have fair play. You can robe again and put on your helmet; I have seen. And now for Aphrodite.

APHRODITE. Here I am; take your time, and examine carefully; let nothing escape your vigilance. And I have something else to say to you, handsome

Paris. Yes, you handsome boy, I have long had an eye on you; I think you must be the handsomest young fellow in all Phrygia. But it is such a pity that you don't leave these rocks and crags, and live in a town: you will lose all your beauty in this desert. What have you to do with mountains? What satisfaction can your beauty give to a lot of cows? You ought to have been married long ago; not to any of these dowdy women hereabouts, but to some Greek girl; an Argive, perhaps, or a Corinthian, or a Spartan; Helen, now, is a Spartan, and such a pretty girl—quite as pretty as I am—and so susceptible! Why, if she once caught sight of *you*, she would give up everything, I am sure, to go with you, and a most devoted wife she would be. But you have heard of Helen, of course.

PARIS. No, ma'am; but I should like to hear all about her now.

APHRODITE. Well, she is the daughter of Leda, the beautiful woman, you know, whom Zeus visited in the disguise of a swan.

PARIS. And what is she like?

APHRODITE. She is fair, as might be expected from the swan, soft as down (she was hatched from an egg, you know), and such a lithe, graceful figure; and only think, she is so much admired, that there was a war because Theseus ran away with her; and she was a mere child then. And when she grew up, the very first men in Greece were suitors for her hand, and she was given to Menelaus, who is descended from Pelops.—Now, if you like, she shall be your wife.

PARIS. What, when she is married already?

APHRODITE. Tut, child, you are a simpleton: *I* understand these things.

PARIS. I should like to understand them too.

APHRODITE. You will set out for Greece on a tour of inspection: and when you get to Sparta, Helen will see you; and for the rest—her falling in love, and going back with you—that will be my affair.

PARIS. But that is what I cannot believe,—that she will forsake her husband to cross the seas with a stranger, a barbarian.

APHRODITE. Trust me for that. I have two beautiful children, Love and Desire. They shall be your guides. Love will assail her in all his might, and compel her to love you: Desire will encompass you about, and make you desirable and lovely as himself; and I will be there to help. I can get the Graces to come too, and between us we shall prevail.

PARIS. How this will end, I know not. All I do know is, that I am in love with Helen already. I see her before me—I sail for Greece—I am in Sparta—I am on my homeward journey, with her at my side! Ah, why is none of it true?

APHRODITE. Wait. Do not fall in love yet. You have first to secure my interest with the bride, by your award. The union must be graced with my victorious presence: your marriage-feast shall be my feast of victory. Love, beauty, wedlock; all these you may purchase at the price of yonder apple.

PARIS. But perhaps after the award you will forget all about *me*?

APHRODITE. Shall I swear?

PARIS. No; but promise once more.

APHRODITE. I promise that you shall have Helen to wife; that she shall follow you, and make Troy her home; and I will be present with you, and help you in all.

PARIS. And bring Love, and Desire, and the Graces?

APHRODITE. Assuredly; and Passion and Hymen as well.

PARIS. Take the apple: it is yours.

Dialogues of the Dead

HERMES AND CHARON

HERMES.

Ferryman, what do you say to settling up accounts? It will prevent any unpleasantness later on.

CHARON. Very good. It does save trouble to get these things straight.

HERMES. One anchor, to your order, five shillings.

CHARON. That is a lot of money.

HERMES. So help me Pluto, it is what I had to pay. One rowlock-strap, fourpence.

CHARON. Five and four; put that down.

HERMES. Then there was a needle, for mending the sail; ten-pence.

CHARON. Down with it.

HERMES. Caulking-wax; nails; and cord for the brace. Two shillings the lot.

CHARON. They were worth the money.

HERMES. That's all; unless I have forgotten anything. When will you pay it?

CHARON. I can't just now, Hermes; we shall have a war or a plague presently, and then the passengers will come shoaling in, and I shall be able to make a little by jobbing the fares.

HERMES. So for the present I have nothing to do but sit down, and pray for the worst, as my only chance of getting paid?

CHARON. There is nothing else for it;—very little business doing just now, as you see, owing to the peace.

Dialogues of the Dead. Translated by H. W. and F. G. Fowler. From *The Works of Lucian of Samosata*, Vol. I., by H. W. and F. G. Fowler. Reprinted by permission of The Clarendon Press, Oxford.

HERMES. That is just as well, though it does keep me waiting for my money. After all, though, Charon, in old days men were men; you remember the state they used to come down in,—all blood and wounds generally. Nowadays, a man is poisoned by his slave or his wife; or gets dropsy from overfeeding; a pale, spiritless lot, nothing like the men of old. Most of them seem to meet their end in some plot that has money for its object.

CHARON. Ah; money is in great request.

HERMES. Yes; you can't blame me if I am somewhat urgent for payment.

MENIPPUS AND HERMES

MENIPPUS. Where are all the beauties, Hermes? Show me round; I am a new-comer.

HERMES. I am busy, Menippus. But look over there to your right, and you will see Hyacinth, Narcissus, Nireus, Achilles, Tyro, Helen, Leda,—all the beauties of old.

MENIPPUS. I can only see bones, and bare skulls; most of them are exactly alike.

HERMES. Those bones, of which you seem to think so lightly, have been the theme of admiring poets.

MENIPPUS. Well, but show me Helen; I shall never be able to make her out by myself.

HERMES. This skull is Helen.

MENIPPUS. And for this a thousand ships carried warriors from every part of Greece; Greeks and barbarians were slain, and cities made desolate.

HERMES. Ah, Menippus, you never saw the living Helen; or you would have said with Homer,

Well might they suffer grievous years of toil
Who strove for such a prize.

We look at withered flowers, whose dye is gone from them, and what can we call them but unlovely things? Yet in the hour of their bloom these unlovely things were things of beauty.

MENIPPUS. Strange, that the Greeks could not realize what it was for which they laboured; how short-lived, how soon to fade.

HERMES. I have no time for moralizing. Choose your spot, where you will, and lie down. I must go to fetch new dead.

MENIPPUS AND CERBERUS

MENIPPUS. My dear coz—for Cerberus and Cynic are surely related through the dog—I adjure you by the Styx, tell me how Socrates behaved during the descent. A God like you can doubtless articulate instead of barking, if he chooses.

CERBERUS. Well, while he was some way off, he seemed quite unshaken; and I thought he was bent on letting the people outside realize the fact too. Then he passed into the opening and saw the gloom; I at the same time gave him a touch of the hemlock, and a pull by the leg, as he was rather slow. Then he squalled like a baby, whimpered about his children, and, oh, I don't know what he didn't do.

MENIPPUS. So he was one of the theorists, was he? his indifference was a sham?

CERBERUS. Yes; it was only that he accepted the inevitable, and put a bold face on it, pretending to welcome the universal fate, by way of impressing the bystanders. All that sort are the same, I tell you—bold resolute fellows as far as the entrance; it is inside that the real test comes.

MENIPPUS. What did you think of my performance?

CERBERUS. Ah, Menippus, you were the exception; you are a credit to the breed, and so was Diogenes before you. You two came in without any compulsion or pushing, of your own free will, with a laugh for yourselves and a curse for the rest.

MENIPPUS AND CHIRON

MENIPPUS. I have heard that you were a god, Chiron, and that you died of your own choice?

CHIRON. You were rightly informed. I am dead, as you see, and might have been immortal.

MENIPPUS. And what should possess you, to be in love with Death? He has no charm for most people.

CHIRON. You are a sensible fellow; I will tell you. There was no further satisfaction to be had from immortality.

MENIPPUS. Was it not a pleasure merely to live and see the light?

CHIRON. No; it is variety, as I take it, and not monotony, that constitutes pleasure. Living on and on, everything always the same; sun, light, food, spring, summer, autumn, winter, one thing following another in unending sequence,—I sickened of it all. I found that enjoyment lay not in continual possession; that deprivation had its share therein.

MENIPPUS. Very true, Chiron. And how have you got on since you made Hades your home?

CHIRON. Not unpleasantly. I like the truly republican equality that prevails; and as to whether one is in light or darkness, that makes no difference at all. Then again there is no hunger or thirst here; one is independent of such things.

MENIPPUS. Take care, Chiron! You may be caught in the snare of your own reasonings.

CHIRON. How should that be?

MENIPPUS. Why, if the monotony of the other world brought on satiety, the monotony here may do the same. You will have to look about for a further change, and I fancy there is no third life procurable.

CHIRON. Then what is to be done, Menippus?

MENIPPUS. Take things as you find them, I suppose, like a sensible fellow, and make the best of everything.

Sappho

Sixth century B.C.

The Tenth Muse, as Plato ecstatically called Sappho, is a legend of literature built from ancient tradition and a few extant poems into the greatest of all women poets. As late as 1073 a large collection of her verse still existed but in that year it was publicly burned by church dignitaries of Rome and Constantinople. The biographies of Sappho surviving from antiquity were probably derived from her poems and are far from trustworthy.

Sappho belongs to Mitylene, a brilliant city on the Aegean island of Lesbos, and to the sixth century B.C., when a social revolution there was replacing the old landed aristocracy with an upstart bourgeoisie. Along with the poet Alcaeus, she was banished as an aristocrat to Pyrrha, where Alcaeus paid romantic attention to her, at least in verse. But she was indifferent to his proposals, and after further exile to distant Sicily she married a wealthy merchant and probably had a daughter. We know too that she had a younger brother who won his sister's resentment by marrying a courtesan while on a business trip in Egypt.

Sappho's songs, which she herself set to the music of the lyre, are passionate love poems addressed to younger women whom she may have taught in a kind of finishing school. As her disciples left her to marry, she expressed her feelings in sorrowful laments and graceful epithalamia, or wedding songs. The personal note is strong, as in all the Aeolian school, and the simplicity of her style burns her feelings into the reader's mind. Sappho helped to raise her Aeolian dialect to the level of literary expression and perfected several distinctive meters, of which one still bears the name "Sapphic."

Ode
to Aphrodite

DEATHLESS Aphrodite, throned in flowers,
  Daughter of Zeus, O terrible enchantress,
With this sorrow, with this anguish, break my spirit,
    Lady, not longer!

Hear anew the voice! O hear and listen!   5
Come, as in that island dawn thou camest,
Billowing in thy yoked car to Sappho
    Forth from thy father's

Golden house in pity! . . . I remember:
Fleet and fair thy sparrows drew thee, beating   10
Fast their wings above the dusky harvests,
    Down the pale heavens,

Lighting anon! And thou, O blest and brightest,
Smiling with immortal eyelids, asked me:
"Maiden, what betideth thee? Or wherefore   15
    Callest upon me?

"What is here the longing more than other,
Here in this mad heart? And who the lovely
One beloved thou wouldst lure to loving?
    Sappho, who wrongs thee?   20

"See, if now she flies, she soon must follow;
Yes, if spurning gifts, she soon must offer;
Yes, if loving not, she soon must love thee,
    Howso unwilling. . . ."

Come again to me! O now! Release me!   25
End the great pang! And all my heart desireth
Now of fulfillment, fulfill! O Aphrodite,
    Fight by my shoulder!

Ode
to Anactoria

PEER of gods he seemeth to me, the blissful
  Man who sits and gazes at thee before him,
Close beside thee sits, and in silence hears thee
    Silverly speaking,

Laughing love's low laughter. Oh this, this only   5
Stirs the troubled heart in my breast to tremble!
For should I but see thee a little moment,
    Straight is my voice hushed;

Yea, my tongue is broken, and through and through
    me
'Neath the flesh impalpable fire runs tingling;   10
Nothing see mine eyes, and a noise of roaring
    Waves in my ear sounds;

Sweat runs down in rivers, a tremor seizes
All my limbs, and paler than grass in autumn,
Caught by pains of menacing death, I falter,   15
    Lost in the love-trance.

Farewell
To Anactoria

NEVER the tramp of foot or horse,
    Nor lusty cries from ships at sea,
Shall I call loveliest on the dark earth—
    My heart moves lovingly.

I say that what one loves is best—   5
The midnight fastness of the heart. . . .
Helen, you filched the beauty of men
    With unpitying art!

White Paris from Idean hills
For you the Trojan towers razed—   10
Who swiftly plowed the black seas
    Had on your white arms gazed!

Oh, how loving from afar
Led you to grief, for in your mind
The present was too light, as ever   15
    Among fair womankind. . . .

So, Anactoria, you go away
With what calm carelessness of sorrow!
Your gleaming footstep and your grace,
    When comes another morrow,   20

Much would I rather then behold
Than Lydian cars or infantry.
I ask the lot of blessedness,
    Beloved, in memory.

(Fragments)

ROUND about me hum the winds of autumn,
    Cool between the apple boughs: and slumber,
Flowing from the quivering leaves to earthward,
    Spreads as a river.

Love, like a mountain-wind upon an oak,
Falling upon me, shakes me leaf and bough.

The moon and seven Pleiades have set;
It is the midnight now; the hours go by;
And still I'm lying in my bed alone.

Farewell to Anactoria. Translated by Allen Tate. From *Mr. Pope and Other Poems*, by Allen Tate. Copyright 1928 by Minton, Balch & Co. Courtesy of G. P. Putnam's Sons.
Fragments. Translated by William Ellery Leonard. From *A Son of Earth* by William Ellery Leonard. Copyright 1928 by The Viking Press, Inc. Reprinted by permission of The Viking Press, Inc., New York.

Off in the twilight hung the low full moon,
And all the women stood before it grave,
As round an altar. Thus at holy times
The Cretan damsels dance melodiously
With delicate feet about the sacrifice,   5
Trampling the tender bloom of the soft grass.

A Bride

I

LIKE the sweet apple which reddens upon the top-
        most bough,
A-top on the topmost twig,—which the pluckers for-
    got somehow,—
Forgot it not, nay, but got it not, for none could get
    it till now.

II

Like the wild hyacinth flower which on the hills is
    found,
Which the passing feet of the shepherds forever tear
    and wound,   5
Until the purple blossom is trodden in the ground.

Forgotten

DEAD shalt thou lie; and nought
    Be told of thee or thought,
For thou hast plucked not of the Muses' tree:
    And even in Hades' halls
    Amidst thy fellow-thralls   5
No friendly shade thy shade shall company!

A Girl

I HAVE a child; so fair
    As golden flowers is she,
My Cleïs, all my care.
I'd not give her away
For Lydia's wide sway   5
Nor lands men long to see.

A Bride. Translated by Dante Gabriel Rossetti.
Forgotten. Translated by Thomas Hardy. From *Collected Poems* by Thomas Hardy. By permission of The Macmillan Company, publishers. This savage poem was addressed to a wealthy but uneducated woman.
A Girl. Translated by C. M. Bowra. From *The Oxford Book of Greek Verse in Translation*, by T. F. Higham and C. M. Bowra. Reprinted by permission of The Clarendon Press, Oxford.
5. **Lydia,** an ancient kingdom in Asia Minor.

Mother, I Cannot Mind My Wheel

MOTHER, I cannot mind my wheel;
    My fingers ache, my lips are dry;
Oh! if you felt the pain I feel!
    But oh, who ever felt as I!

Hesperus the Bringer

O HESPERUS, thou bringest all good things—
    Home to the weary, to the hungry cheer,
To the young bird the parent's brooding wings,
    The welcome stall to the o'erlabored steer;
Whate'er of peace about our hearthstone clings, 5
    Whate'er our household gods protect of dear,
Are gathered round us by thy look of rest;
Thou bringest the child too to its mother's breast.

The Dust of Timas

THIS dust was Timas; and they say
    That almost on her wedding day
She found her bridal home to be
The dark house of Persephone.

And many maidens, knowing then 5
That she would not come back again,
Unbound their curls; and all in tears,
They cut them off with sharpened shears.

Mother, I Cannot. . . . Translated by Walter Savage Landor.
Hesperus the Bringer. Translated by Lord Byron. "Hesperus the Bringer" is the evening star.
The Dust of Timas. Translated by Edwin Arlington Robinson. From *Captain Craig* by Edwin Arlington Robinson. By permission of The Macmillan Company, publishers.

Women with water jars at the Athenian fountain of Callirrhoe. From a Greek vase.

Anacreon

Sixth century B.C.

Anacreon was an Ionian of Teos in Asia Minor, but his curiosity about the world led him to visit many parts of Hellas—especially Samos and Athens. As individualistic as Sappho, he lacked her seriousness and devoted his long life to an incessant round of pleasure. He detested physical exertion and in his youth threw away his shield on the battlefield and literally ran out of the army. As he grew older, he worked hard at staying young and was still the life of the party in his eighties. Wine and love were his favorite themes, though he was always moderate in both, mixing his wine with two parts water and his love with the common sense that kept him from getting too involved in any affairs of the heart. His language is as simple and his style as delicate as Sappho's, so that the two are complementary spirits of earnest and frivolous in a common lyric tradition. He was beloved after his death as during his life, and his jolly example inspired in the Hellenistic era a host of anonymous imitators whose convivial poems are now lumped together as the "Anacreontic" tradition. Most of the following lyrics belong to this category.

The Wounded Cupid

CUPID, as he lay among
    Roses, by a bee was stung.
Whereupon in anger flying
To his mother, said, thus crying,
Help! O help! your boy's a-dying. 5
And why, my pretty lad? said she.
Then blubbering replièd he,
A wingèd snake has bitten me,
Which country people call a bee.
At which she smiled, then with her hairs 10
And kisses, drying up his tears,
Alas! said she, my wag, if this
Such a pernicious torment is;
Come, tell me then how great's the smart
Of those thou woundest with thy dart! 15

The Cheat of Cupid

OR, THE UNGENTLE GUEST

ONE silent night of late,
    When every creature rested,
Came one unto my gate,
    And knocking, me molested.

The Wounded Cupid. Translated by Robert Herrick.
The Cheat of Cupid. Translated by Robert Herrick.

Who's that, said I, beats there,   5
    And troubles thus the sleepy?
Cast off, said he, all fear,
    And let not locks thus keep ye.

For I am a boy who
    By moonless nights have swervèd,   10
And all with showers wet through,
    And e'en with cold have starvèd.

I pitiful arose,
    And soon a taper lighted,
And did myself disclose   15
    Unto the lad benighted.

I saw he had a bow,
    And wings too, which did shiver;
And looking down below,
    I spied he had a quiver.   20

I to my chimney's shine
    Brought him, as love professes,
And chafed his hands with mine,
    And dried his dropping tresses.

But when he felt him warmed,   25
    Let's try this bow of ours
And string, if they be harmed,
    Said he, with these late showers.

Forthwith his bow he bent,
    And wedded string and arrow,   30
And struck me that it went
    Quite through my heart and marrow.

Then laughing loud, he flew
    Away, and thus said, flying,
Adieu, mine host, adieu,
    I'll leave thy heart a-dying.   35

Love

I'LL sing of heroes and of kings,
    In mighty numbers, mighty things.
Begin, my Muse!—but lo! the strings
To my great song rebellious prove;
The strings will sound of nought but love.   5
—I broke them all, and put on new;
—'Tis this, or nothing, now will do.
"These, sure," said I, "will me obey;
These, sure, heroic notes will play."
Straight I began with thundering Jove   10
And all th' immortal powers; but Love,
Love smiled; and from my enfeebled lyre
Came gentle airs, such as inspire

Love. Translated by Abraham Cowley.

Melting love and soft desire.—
Farewell, then, heroes! farewell, kings!   15
And mighty numbers, mighty things!
Love tunes my heart just to my strings.

The Combat

Now will I a lover be;
    Love himself commanded me.
Full at first of stubborn pride,
To submit my soul denied;
He his quiver takes and bow,   5
Bids defiance, forth I go,
Arm'd with spear and shield, we meet;
On he charges, I retreat:
Till perceiving in the fight
He had wasted every flight,   10
Into me, with fury hot,
Like a dart himself he shot,
And my cold heart melts; my shield
Useless, no defense could yield;
For what boots an outward screen   15
When, alas, the fight's within!

The Epicure

Underneath this myrtle shade,
    On flowery beds supinely laid,
With odorous oils my head o'erflowing,
And around it roses growing,
What should I do but drink away   5
The heat and troubles of the day?
In this more than kingly state,
Love himself shall on me wait.
Fill to me, Love; nay, fill it up;
And mingled cast into the cup   10
Wit, and mirth, and noble fires,
Vigorous health, and gay desires.
The wheel of life no less will stay
In a smooth than rugged way:
Since it equally doth flee,   15
Let the motion pleasant be.
Why do we precious ointments shower,
Nobler wines why do we pour,
Beauteous flowers why do we spread,
Upon the monuments of the dead?   20
Nothing they but dust can show,
Or bones that hasten to be so.
Crown me with roses whilst I live,—
Now your wines and ointments give;
After death I nothing crave,   25
Let me alive my pleasures have!
All are Stoics in the grave.

The Combat. Translated by Thomas Stanley.
The Epicure. Translated by Abraham Cowley.

Beauty

Horns to bulls wise Nature lends;
  Horses she with hoofs defends;
Hares with nimble feet relieves;
Dreadful teeth to lions gives;
Fishes learn through streams to slide;   5
Birds through yielding air to glide;
Men with courage she supplies;
But to women these denies.
What then gives she? Beauty, this
Both their arms and armor is: 10
She that can this weapon use,
Fire and sword with ease subdues.

The Grasshopper

Happy insect! what can be
  In happiness compar'd to thee?
Fed with nourishment divine,
The dewy morning's gentle wine!
Nature waits upon thee still,   5
And thy verdant cup does fill;
'Tis filled wherever thou dost tread,
Nature self's thy Ganymede.
Thou dost drink, and dance, and sing;
Happier than the happiest king!   10
All the fields which thou dost see,
All the plants belong to thee;
All that summer hours produce;
Fertile made with early juice.
Man for thee does sow and plow;   15
Farmer he, and landlord thou!
Thou dost innocently joy;
Nor does thy luxury destroy;
The shepherd gladly heareth thee,
More harmonious than he.   20
Thee country-hinds with gladness hear,
Prophet of the ripen'd year!
Thee Phoebus loves, and does inspire;
Phoebus is himself thy sire.
To thee, of all things upon earth,   25
Life's no longer than thy mirth.
Happy insect, happy, thou
Dost neither age nor winter know;
But, when thou'st drunk and danc'd and sung
Thy fill, the flowery leaves among,   30
(Voluptuous and wise withal,
Epicurean animal!)—
Sated with thy summer feast,
Thou retir'st to endless rest.

Beauty. Translated by Thomas Stanley.
The Grasshopper. Translated by Abraham Cowley.

All Things Drink

Fruitful earth drinks up the rain;
  Trees from earth drink that again;
The sea drinks the air, the sun
Drinks the sea, and him the moon.
Is it reason then, d'ye think,   5
I should thirst when all else drink?

The Cup

Make me a bowl, a mighty bowl,
  Large as my capacious soul,
Vast as my thirst is. Let it have
Depth enough to be my grave.
I mean the grave of all my care,   5
For I intend to bury't there.
Let it of silver fashioned be,
Worthy of wine! worthy of me!
Worthy to adorn the spheres
As that bright Cup among the stars!   10

Yet draw no shapes of armor there,
No casque nor shield nor sword nor spear
Nor wars of Thebes nor wars of Troy,
Nor any other martial toy.
For what do I vain armor prize,   15
Who mind not such rough exercise?
For gentle sieges, softer wars,
Fights that cause no wounds or scars.
I'll have not battles on my plate,
Lest sight of them should brawls create,   20
Lest that provoke to quarrels too,
Which wine itself enough can do.

Old I Am

Old I am, yet can (I think)
  Those that younger are out-drink.
When I dance no staff I take,
But a well-fill'd bottle shake.
He that doth in war delight,   5
Come, and with these arms let's fight.
Fill the cup, let loose a flood
Of the rich grape's luscious blood.
Old I am, and therefore may,
Like Silenus, drink and play.

All Things Drink. Translated by Thomas Stanley.
The Cup. Translated by John Oldham.
Old I Am. Translated by Thomas Stanley. 10. **Silenus,** the jolly
old satyr who spent his life drinking wine and playing the flute.

Youthful Age

YOUNG men dancing, and the old
  Sporting I with joy behold;
But an old man gay and free
Dancing most I love to see.
Age and youth alike he shares,   5
For his heart belies his hairs.

Age

OFT am I by the women told,
  "Poor Anacreon! thou grow'st old.
Look! how thy hairs are falling all;
Poor Anacreon, how they fall!"—
Whether I grow old or no,   5
By the effects I do not know;
But this I know, without being told,
'Tis time to live, if I grow old.
'Tis time short pleasures now to take,
Of little life the best to make,   10
And manage wisely the last stake.

Old Age

SWEET Youth no more will tarry,
  My friend a while ago;
Now white's the head I carry,
  And grey my temples grow,
  My teeth—a ragged row.   5

To taste the joy of living
  But little space have I,
And torn with sick misgiving
  I can but sob and sigh,
  So deep the dead men lie.   10

So deep their place and dismal,
  All means, be sure, they lack
Down in the murk abysmal
  To scale the upward track
  And win their journey back.

Youthful Age. Translated by Thomas Stanley.
Age. Translated by Abraham Cowley.
Old Age. Translated by T. F. Higham. From *The Oxford Book of Greek Verse in Translation*, by T. F. Higham and C. M. Bowra. Reprinted by permission of The Clarendon Press, Oxford.

Theocritus

Flourished 260 B.C.

The best of the Alexandrine poets, Theocritus, was also the founder of the pastoral tradition in world poetry with his ten charming rustic idylls. His total output was slight—twenty-odd idylls and twenty brief epigrams—but its influence on later poetry down to the last century has been prodigious. Theocritus apparently invented the idyll as a little picture of life, usually with some slight dramatic action. Half of his idylls have the beautiful countryside of Sicily for background and turn on the dainty love affairs of poetic shepherds or their contests in wrestling and song for the favor of a ladylove.

Theocritus was born in Sicily, in the fair city of Syracuse, and knew in childhood the charm of its hilly slopes. But ambition took him away to study medicine at Cos and then to seek the favor of the Ptolemies at Alexandria a few years later. His success in this brilliant capital did not satisfy him long, because we hear of him thereafter at Cos again and at Miletus, where he may have died. But wherever he went, he seems to have retained a nostalgia for the simple life of rustic Sicily, and his pastoral idylls are his tribute to his birthplace. Sentimental and unrealistic as they are, these sweet, lively vignettes delighted the sophisticates of Alexandria and other aristocratic societies of later centuries. The sensitive little shepherds with poetic names like Thyrsis, Corydon, and Menalcas, their delicate loves for demure damsels like Amaryllis and Simaetha, and the Arcadian simplicity of a land where there was always sun by day and moon by night hardened into an artificial pastoral tradition. Virgil re-created it in his *Eclogues* for the elegant court of Augustus. It produced Spenser's *Shepheardes Calender* at the English court of Elizabeth. Pope, Ambrose Philips, and John Gay were among the pastoral poets who regaled the aristocratic eighteenth century; and the tradition reached its most insipid depths in the circle of Marie Antoinette, decked out in ribbons with shepherd's crooks. It was applied to the novel in Sidney's *Arcadia* and to the drama in the pastoral plays of Jonson, Fletcher, and Ramsay. And in its loftiest metamorphosis the dirges in Theocritus inspired the great pastoral elegies of Milton, Shelley, and Arnold.

Despite the artificiality of his imitators there is freshness and vivacity in the originals of Theocritus. Moreover, he varied the form of the idyll to include other types of material. The half-pathetic, half-absurd whimpering of Polyphemus, the ugly Cyclops, for love of the nymph Galatea is one of several on mythological subjects. But the most famous and amusing of all is *The Syracusan Ladies*, a realistic dialogue between two housewives on their way to a festival of Adonis in Alexandria. The feminine chatter about fashions and husbands is as modern as today, and nearly every allusion in it can be translated into the terms of our century. This is not the greatest poetry, to be sure, but within his modest limits Theocritus was a true artist.

The Two Workmen

(IDYLL X)

This charming dialogue contrasts the rugged, earthy reaper, Milo, with his melancholy, lovelorn companion, Battus. Their songs reflect their opposite characters.

MILO.

WHAT now, poor o'erworked drudge, is on thy
mind?
No more in even swathe thou layest the corn:
Thy fellow-reapers leave thee far behind,
    As flocks a ewe that's footsore from a thorn.
By noon and midday what will be thy plight   5
If now, so soon, thy sickle fails to bite?
   BATTUS. Hewn from hard rocks, untired at set of
     sun,
Milo, didst ne'er regret some absent one?
   MILO. Not I. What time have workers for regret?
   BATTUS. Hath love ne'er kept thee from thy slum-
     bers yet?   10
   MILO. Nay, heaven forbid! If once the cat taste
     cream!
   BATTUS. Milo, these ten days love hath been my
     dream.
   MILO. You drain your wine, while vinegar's scarce
     with me.
   BATTUS.—Hence since last spring untrimmed my
     borders be.
   MILO. And what lass flouts thee?
   BATTUS.   She whom we heard
     play   15
Amongst Hippocoön's reapers yesterday.
   MILO. Your sins have found you out—you're e'en
     served right:
You'll clasp a corn-crake in your arms all night.
   BATTUS. You laugh: but headstrong Love is blind
     no less
Than Plutus: talking big is foolishness.   20
   MILO. I talk not big. But lay the corn-ears low,
And trill the while some love-song—easier so
Will seem your toil: you used to sing, I know.
   BATTUS. Maids of Pieria, of my slim lass sing!
One touch of yours ennobles everything.   25
                       (Sings)

Fairy Bombyca! thee do men report
   Lean, dusk, a gipsy: I alone nut-brown.
Violets and pencilled hyacinths are swart,
   Yet first of flowers they're chosen for a crown.
As goats pursue the clover, wolves the goat,   30
And cranes the ploughman, upon thee I dote.

The Two Workmen. Translated by C. S. Calverley. **19–20. Love
. . . Plutus.** The god of wealth was thought to be blind, because he
dispensed riches to the undeserving as well as to the deserving. **24.
Maids of Pieria,** the Muses.

Had I but Croesus' wealth, we twain should stand
   Gold-sculptured in Love's temple; thou, thy lyre
(Ay or a rose or apple) in thy hand,
   I in my brave new shoon and dance-attire.   35
Fairy Bombyca! twinkling dice thy feet,
Poppies thy lips, thy ways none knows how sweet!
   MILO. Who dreamed what subtle strains our
     bumpkin wrought?
How shone the artist in each measured verse!
Fie on the beard that I have grown for naught!   40
Mark, lad, these lines by glorious Lytierse.
                       (Sings)

O rich in fruit and cornblade: be this field
Tilled well, Demeter, and fair fruitage yield!

Bind the sheaves, reapers: lest one, passing, say—
'A fig for these; they're never worth their pay.'   45

Let the mown swathes look northward, ye who mow,
Or westward—for the ears grow fattest so.

Avoid a noontide nap, ye threshing men:
The chaff flies thickest from the corn-ears then.

Wake when the lark wakes; when he slumbers,
   close   50
Your work, ye reapers: and at noontide doze.

Boys, the frogs' life for me! They need not him
Who fills the flagon, for in drink they swim.

Better boil herbs, thou toiler after gain,
Than, splitting cummin, split thy hand in twain.   55

Strains such as these, I trow, befit them well
   Who toil and moil when noon is at its height:

Thy meager love-tale, bumpkin, thou shouldst tell
   Thy grandam as she wakes up ere 'tis light.

The Cyclops

(IDYLL XI)

The sweet love-complaint of Polyphemus to the sea-nymph Galatea is charmingly absurd when one recalls him as the cannibal giant of the *Odyssey.*

AND so an easier life our Cyclops drew,
    The Ancient Polyphemus, who in youth
Loved Galatea while the manhood grew
   Adown his cheeks, and darkened round his mouth.
No jot he cared for apples, olives, roses;   5
   Love made him mad; the whole world was neg-
    lected,
The very sheep went backward to their closes

The Cyclops. Translated by Elizabeth Barrett Browning.

From out the fair green pastures, self-directed.
And singing Galatea, thus, he wore
The sunrise down along the weedy shore,　　10
　And pined alone, and felt the cruel wound
Beneath his heart, which Cypris' arrow bore,
　With a deep pang: but, so, the cure was found;
And sitting on a lofty rock, he cast
His eyes upon the sea, and sang at last:　　15
"O whitest Galatea, can it be
　That thou shouldst spurn me off who love thee
　　so?
More white than curds, my girl, thou art to see,
More meek than lambs, more full of leaping glee
　Than kids, and brighter than the early glow　20
On grapes that swell to ripen,—sour like thee!
Thou comest to me with the fragrant sleep,
　And with the fragrant sleep thou goest from me;
Thou fliest . . . fliest as a frightened sheep
　Flies the gray wolf!—yet love did overcome me,
So long!—I loved thee, maiden, first of all,　26
　When down the hills (my mother fast beside
　　thee)
I saw thee stray to pluck the summer-fall
　Of hyacinth-bells, and went myself to guide thee;
And since my eyes have seen thee, they can leave
　　thee　　30
　No more, from that day's light! But thou . . . by
　　Zeus,
Thou wilt not care for *that,* to let it grieve thee!
　I know thee, fair one, why thou springest loose
From my arm round thee. Why? I tell thee, dear!
　One shaggy eyebrow draws its smudging road　35
Straight through my ample front, from ear to ear;
　One eye rolls underneath; and yawning, broad,
Flat nostrils feel the bulging lips too near.
Yet . . . ho, ho!—*I,*—whatever I appear,—
　Do feed a thousand oxen! When I have done,　40
I milk the cows, and drink the milk that's best!
　I lack no cheese, while summer keeps the sun;
And after, in the cold, it's ready prest!
　And then, I know to sing, as there is none
Of all the Cyclops can, . . . a song of thee,　45
Sweet apple of my soul, on love's fair tree,
And of myself who love thee . . . till the West
Forgets the light, and all but I have rest.
I feed for thee, besides, eleven fair does,
　And all in fawn; and four tame whelps of bears.
Come to me, sweet! thou shalt have all of those　51
　In change for love! I will not halve the shares.
Leave the blue sea, with pure white arms extend-
　　ed
　To the dry shore; and, in my cave's recess,
Thou shalt be gladder for the noon-light ended;　55
　For here be laurels, spiral cypresses,
Dark ivy, and a vine whose leaves infold

Most luscious grapes; and here is water cold,
　The wooded Aetna pours down thro the trees
From the white snows, which gods were scarce too
　　bold　　60
　To drink in turn with nectar. Who with these
Would choose the salt wave of the lukewarm
　　seas?
Nay, look on me! If I am hairy and rough,
　I have an oak's heart in me; there's a fire
In these grey ashes which burns hot enough;　65
　And, when I burn for *thee,* I grudge the pyre
No fuel . . . not my soul, nor this one eye,—
Most precious thing I have, because thereby
I see thee, fairest! Out, alas! I wish
My mother had borne me finnèd like a fish,　70
That I might plunge down in the ocean near thee,
　And kiss thy glittering hand beneath the weeds,
If still thy face were turned; and I would bear thee
　Each lily white, and poppy fair that bleeds
Its red heart down its leaves!—one gift, for hours　75
　Of summer,—one for winter; since to cheer
　　thee,
I could not bring at once all kinds of flowers.
Even now, girl, now, I fain would learn to swim,
If stranger in a ship sailed nigh, I wis,
　That I may know how sweet a thing it is　80
To live down with you in the deep and dim!
Come up, O Galatea, from the ocean,
　And, having come, forget again to go!
As I, who sing out here my heart's emotion,
　Could sit forever. Come up from below!　85
Come, keep my flocks beside me, milk my kine;
　Come, press my cheese, distrain my whey and
　　curd!
Ah, mother! she alone . . . that mother of mine . . .
　Did wrong me sore! I blame her! Not a word
Of kindly intercession did she address　90
Thine ear with for my sake; and ne'ertheless
　She saw me wasting, wasting, day by day:
　Both head and feet were aching, I will say,
All sick for grief, as I myself was sick.
　O Cyclops, Cyclops! whither hast thou sent　95
　Thy soul on fluttering wings? If thou wert bent
On turning bowls, or pulling green and thick
　The sprouts to give thy lambkins, thou wouldst
　　make thee
　A wiser Cyclops than for what we take thee.
Milk dry the present! Why pursue too quick　100
That future which is fugitive aright?
Thy Galatea thou shalt haply find,
Or else a maiden fairer and more kind;
For many girls do call me thro the night,
　And, as they call, do laugh out silvery.　105
　I, too, am something in the world, I see!"

While thus the Cyclops love and lambs did fold,
Ease came with song, he could not buy with gold.

The Syracusan Ladies

(IDYLL XV)

Modeled perhaps on an older work by Sophron, this delightful dialogue of two chattering housewives on their way to a festival of Adonis gives a realistic picture of everyday life in Alexandria. Since the festival was given by Arsinoë, sister-queen to Ptolemy Philadelphus, the idyll is dated sometime after their marriage in 266 B.C.

GORGO.

Is Praxinoë at home?

PRAXINOË. Dear Gorgo, how long it is since you have been here! Yes she *is* at home. The wonder is that you have got here at last! Eunoë, see that she has a chair. Throw a cushion on it too.

GORGO. It does most charmingly as it is.

PRAXINOË. Do sit down.

GORGO. Oh, what a thing spirit is! I have scarcely got to you alive, Praxinoë! What a huge crowd, what hosts of four-in-hands! Everywhere cavalry boots, everywhere men in uniform! And the road is endless: yes, you really live *too* far away!

PRAXINOË. It is all the fault of that madman of mine. Here he came to the ends of the earth and took—a hole, not a house, and all that we might not be neighbors. The jealous wretch, always the same, anything for spite!

GORGO. Don't talk of your husband Dinon like that, my dear, before your little boy,—look how he is staring at you! Never mind, Zopyrion, sweet child, she is not speaking about papa.

PRAXINOË. Our Lady! The child does notice.

GORGO. Nice papa!

PRAXINOË. That papa of his the other day went to get soap and rouge at the shop, and came back to me with salt—the great big oaf!

GORGO. Mine is the same—a perfect spendthrift, Diocleides! Yesterday he got what he took for five fleeces, and paid seven drachmas a piece for—what do you suppose?—dog-skins, shreds of old leather wallets, mere trash. But come, take your coat and shawl. Let us be off to the palace of rich Ptolemy the King, to the Adonis. I hear the Queen has provided something splendid!

PRAXINOË. Yes, fine folks do everything finely.

GORGO. What a tale you will have to tell about the things you have seen, to anyone who has not seen them! It is nearly time to go.

PRAXINOË. It's always holiday for idlers, Eunoë, bring the water and put it down in the middle of the room, lazy creature that you are. You cats always like to sleep soft! Come, hurry, bring the water; quicker! I want water first; and how she carries it! Give it to me all the same; don't pour out so much, you extravagant thing. Stupid girl! Why are you wetting my dress? There, stop; I have washed my hands, as heaven would have it. Where is the key to the big chest? Bring it here.

GORGO. Praxinoë, that full dress becomes you wonderfully. Tell me, how much did the stuff cost you off the loom?

PRAXINOË. Don't speak of it, Gorgo! More than eight pounds in good silver money,—and the work on it! I nearly slaved my soul out over it!

GORGO. Well, it is *most* successful, I must say.

PRAXINOË. Thanks for the pretty speech! (*To Eunoë*) Bring my shawl, and set my hat on my head properly.—No, child, I'm not going to take you. Boo! Bogies! There's a horse that bites little boys! You may cry as much as you please, but I am not going to have you lamed.—Let us be moving. Phrygia, take the child, and keep him amused. Call in the dog, and shut the door. (*They go into the street.*) Ye gods, what a crowd! How on earth are we ever to get through this crush? They are like numberless ants. Many a good deed have you done, Ptolemy! Since your father joined the immortals, there's never a thug to maul the pedestrian, creeping up on him in Egyptian fashion. Oh! the tricks those rascals used to play. Birds of a feather, rascals all!—Dear Gorgo, what will become of us? Here come the King's horses!—My dear man, don't trample on me. Look, the bay's rearing; see, what temper!—Eunoë, you foolhardy girl, will you never keep out of the way? The beast will be the death of the man that's leading him. What a good thing it is that I left my brat safe at home.

GORGO. Courage, Praxinoë. We are safe behind them now, and they have got in line.

PRAXINOË. There! I begin to be myself again. Ever since I was a child I have feared nothing so much as horses and slimy snakes. Come along; a huge mob is pouring after us.

GORGO (*to an old woman*). Are you from the court, Mother?

OLD WOMAN. I am, my child.

PRAXINOË. Is it easy to get there?

OLD WOMAN. The Achaeans got into Troy by trying, my pretty. Trying will do everything in the long run.

GORGO. The old wife has spoken her oracles, and off she goes.

The Syracusan Ladies. Translated by Andrew Lang. Reprinted by permission of Macmillan & Co., Ltd. (Revised)

69. Egyptian fashion. The ladies are proud Greeks of Syracuse living in the Greek city of Alexandria established in conquered Egypt. Hence they look with disdain on the native Egyptian population.

PRAXINOË. Women know everything, even how Zeus married Hera!

GORGO. See, Praxinoë, what a crowd there is about the doors.

PRAXINOË. Monstrous, Gorgo! Give me your hand, and you, Eunoë, take hold of Eutychis. Don't lose hold of her, Eutychis, or you will get lost. Let us all go in together; Eunoë, clutch tight to me. Oh dear, Gorgo, my muslin dress is torn in two already!—
10 For heaven's sake, sir, if you wish to be fortunate, look out for my shawl!

STRANGER. I can hardly help myself, but I will be as careful as I can.

PRAXINOË. How close-packed the mob is! They push like a lot of pigs.

STRANGER. Courage, lady, all is well now.

PRAXINOË. Both this year and forever may all be well with you, dear sir, for the care you've taken of us.—What a nice, kind man! We're letting Eunoë
20 get squeezed—come, wretched girl, push your way through. That's the way. Now we are all on the right side of the door, as the bridegroom said when he had shut himself in with his bride.

GORGO. Do come here, Praxinoë. Look at these embroideries. How light and how lovely! You might call them the garments of the gods.

PRAXINOË. Lady Athene! what spinning women wrought them, what painters designed these drawings, so true they are? How naturally they stand and
30 move, like living creatures, not woven patterns. What a clever thing man is! Ah, and himself— Adonis—how beautiful to behold on his silver couch, with the first down on his cheeks, the thrice beloved Adonis—Adonis beloved even among the dead.

A STRANGER. You tiresome women, stop your endless cooing!—They bore one to death with their eternal broad vowels!

GORGO. Indeed! And where may this person come from? What is to you if we are chatter-boxes! Give
40 orders to your own servants, sir. Do you pretend to command ladies of Syracuse? If you must know, we are Corinthians by descent, and we speak Peloponnesian. Dorian women may lawfully speak Doric, I presume?

PRAXINOË. Lady Persephone! never may we have more than one master. I am not afraid of *your* orders.

GORGO. Hush, hush, Praxinoë—the Argive woman's daughter, the great singer, is beginning the
50 *Adonis;* she that won the prize last year for dirge-singing. I am sure she will give us something lovely. See, she is making her bow.

(The idyll ends with the dirge to Adonis, which is omitted here.)

The Greek Anthology

From the days of the Alexandrine scholars, collections of short poems, or epigrams, were made in order to preserve the fugitive Greek verse of older ages. The most famous was compiled by the poet Meleager of Gadara in the first century B.C. and represented forty-six poets ranging in time from Sappho to himself. This collection, which he called the *Stephanos*, or garland, in a charming preface likening his poets to flowers in a wreath, was expanded and reworked by later scholars, until Constantinus Cephalas in the tenth century A.D. prepared what is now known as the Palatine Anthology, containing the verse of 320 poets. With the addition of other poems in recent centuries, it became our *Greek Anthology*, a compilation of over six thousand short poems representing seventeen centuries of Greek and Roman culture and arranged in sixteen books according to subject.

The general tone of this collection of little gems is bright and cynical, with frequent surprises. Although a few major poets are well represented—Simonides, Callimachus, Meleager, and Palladas—most of the authors are minor figures known only through the *Anthology*. It is the poems, not the poets, that are remembered.

Not Such Your Burden

NOT such your burden, happy youths, as
　　ours—
Poor women—children nurtured daintily—
For ye have comrades when ill-fortune lours,
　　To hearten you with talk and company;
And ye have games for solace, and may roam　　5
　　Along the streets and see the painters' shows.
But woe betide us if we stir from home—
　　And there our thoughts are dull enough, God
　　　knows!　　　　　　　　　　——*Agathias*

Undying Thirst

THIS rudely sculptured porter-pot
　　Denotes where sleeps a female sot;
Who passed her life, good easy soul,
In sweetly chirping o'er her bowl.
Not for her friends or children dear　　　　5
She mourns, but only for her beer.
E'en in the very grave, they say,
She thirsts for drink to wet her clay;
And, faith, she thinks it very wrong
This jug should stand unfilled so long.——*Antipater*

Not Such Your Burden. Translated by William H. Hardinge.
Undying Thirst. Translated by Robert Bland.

Sea Dirge

CRUSHED by the waves upon the crag was I,
   Who still must hear these waves among
   the dead,
Breaking and brawling on the promontory,
   Sleepless; and sleepless is my weary head!
For me did strangers bury on the coast   5
   Within the hateful hearing of the deep,
Nor Death, that lulleth all, can lull my ghost,
   One sleepless soul among the souls that sleep!
                    ——*Archias of Byzantium*

To Archinus

IF I did come of set intent
   Then be thy blame my punishment;
But if by love a capture made
Forgive my hasty serenade.
Wine drew me on, Love thrust behind,   5
I was not master of my mind.
And when I came I did not cry
My name aloud, my ancestry;
Only my lips thy lintel pressed;
If this be crime, the crime's confessed.
                    ——*Callimachus*

Saon of Acanthus

HERE lapped in hallowed slumber Saon lies,
   Asleep, not dead; a good man never dies.
                    ——*Callimachus*

Heraclitus

THEY told me, Heraclitus, they told me you
   were dead;
They brought me bitter news to hear and bitter tears
   to shed.
I wept as I remembered how often you and I
Had tired the sun with talking and sent him down
   the sky.
And now that thou art lying, my dear old Carian
   guest,   5
A handful of gray ashes, long, long ago at rest,
Still are thy pleasant voices, thy nightingales, awake;
For Death, he taketh all away, but them he cannot
   take.   ——*Callimachus*

Timon's Epitaph

HERE lie I, Timon; who, alive, all living men
   did hate.
Pass by, and curse thy fill; but pass and stay not here
   thy gait.   ——*Callimachus*

Crethis

FOR Crethis' store of tales and pleasant chat
   Oft sigh the Samian maidens, missing that
Which cheered their tasks, but she, beyond their
   call,
Sleeps here the sleep that must be slept by all.
                    ——*Callimachus*

An Inscription By the Sea

NO dust have I to cover me,
   My grave no man may show;
My tomb is this unending sea,
   And I lie far below.
My fate, O stranger, was to drown;   5
And where it was the ship went down
   Is what the sea-birds know.   ——*Glaucus*

Stay in Town

STAY in town, little wight,
   Safe at home.
   If you roam,
The cranes who delight
Upon pygmies to sup,   5
Will gobble you up.
   Stay at home.   ——*Julianus Antecessor*

A Dinner Gift

THE Muses to Herodotus one day
   Came, nine of them, and dined;
And in return, their host to pay,
   Left each a book behind.   4
                    ——*Leonidas of Alexandria*

Sea Dirge. Translated by Andrew Lang. From *The Poetical Works of Andrew Lang.* Reprinted by permission of Longmans, Green & Co., Ltd. and the representatives of the late Andrew Lang.
To Archinus. Translated by F. A. Wright. From *Poets of the Greek Anthology.* Reprinted by permission of Routledge and Kegan Paul, Ltd.
Saon of Acanthus. Translated by J. A. Symonds.
Heraclitus. Translated by William Cory.

Timon's Epitaph. Translated by William Shakespeare.
Crethis. Translated by Richard Garnett.
An Inscription By the Sea. Translated by Edwin Arlington Robinson. From *Captain Craig* by Edwin Arlington Robinson. By permission of The Macmillan Company, publishers.
Stay in Town. Translated by Henry Wellesley.
A Dinner Gift. Translated by De Teissier.   4. Left . . . behind. The *History* of Herodotus contains nine books.

Old Age

THESE shriveled sinews and this bending frame
The workmanship of Time's strong hand pro-
claim,
Skilled to reverse whate'er the gods create,
And make that crooked which they fashion straight.
Hard choice for man: to die—or else to be   5
That tottering, wretched, wrinkled thing you see.
Age then we all prefer; for age we pray,
And travel on to life's last lingering day;
Then sinking slowly down from worse to worse,
Find heaven's extorted boon our greatest curse.
——*Crates*

The Spinning Woman

MORNING and evening, sleep she drove away,
Old Platthis,—warding hunger from the
door.
And still to wheel and distaff hummed her lay
Hard by the gates of Eld, and bent and hoar;
Plying her loom until the dawn was gray,   5
The long course of Athene did she tread:
With withered hand by withered knee she spun
Sufficient for the loom of goodly thread,
Till all her work and all her days were done.
And in her eightieth year she saw the wave   10
Of Acheron,—old Platthis,—kind and brave.
——*Leonidas of Tarentum*

The Last Journey

WITH courage seek the kingdom of the dead;
The path before you lies.
It is not hard to find, nor tread;
No rocks to climb, no lanes to thread;
But broad, and straight, and even still,   5
And ever gently slopes down-hill;
You cannot miss it, though you shut your eyes.
——*Leonidas of Tarentum*

On An Old Woman

MYCILLA dyes her locks, 'tis said,
But 'tis a foul aspersion.
She buys them black; they therefore need
No subsequent immersion.   ——*Lucilius*

Old Age. Translated by Richard Cumberland.
The Spinning Woman. Translated by Andrew Lang. From *The Poetical Works of Andrew Lang.* Reprinted by permission of Longmans, Green and Co., Ltd. and the representatives of the late Andrew Lang.
The Last Journey. Translated by Charles Merivale.
On An Old Woman. Translated by William Cowper.

Treasure

THEY call thee rich; I deem thee poor;
Since, if thou darest not use thy store,
But savest only for thine heirs,
The treasure is not thine, but theirs.   ——*Lucilius*

A Heavyweight

CHAEREMON, lighter than a wisp of straw,
Sailed once uplifted on a summer's flaw
Sky-high, and might be spinning still through air,
But that his foot caught in a spider's snare.
Five days he downwards dangled there his head,   5
But on the sixth clomb down the spider's thread.
——*Lucilius*

Spring

Now the bright crocus flames, and now
The slim narcissus takes the rain,
And, straying o'er the mountain's brow,
The daffodillies bud again.
The thousand blossoms wax and wane   5
On wold, and heath, and fragrant bough,
But fairer than the flowers art thou,
Than any growth of hill or plain.

Ye gardens, cast your leafy crown,
That my Love's feet may tread it down,   10
Like lilies on the lilies set;
My Love, whose lips are softer far
Than drowsy poppy petals are,
And sweeter than the violet!   ——*Meleager*

Upon a Maid That Died the Day She Was Married

THAT morn which saw me made a bride,
The evening witnessed that I died.
Those holy lights, wherewith they guide
Unto the bed the bashful bride,
Served but as tapers, for to burn,   5
And light my relics to their urn.
This epitaph, which here you see,
Supplied the epithalamy.   ——*Meleager*

Treasure. Translated by William Cowper.
A Heavyweight. Translated by Alexander Lothian. Published by Basil Blackwell & Mott, Ltd., 1920.
Spring. Translated by Andrew Lang. From *The Poetical Works of Andrew Lang.* Reprinted by permission of Longmans, Green & Co., Ltd. and the representatives of the late Andrew Lang.
Upon a Maid That Died. . . . Translated by Robert Herrick.

A Garland for Heliodora

I'LL frame, my Heliodora, a garland for thy hair,
  Which thou, in all thy beauty's pride, mayst
    not disdain to wear;
For I with tender myrtles white violets will twine,
White violets, but not so pure as that pure breast of
    thine.
With laughing lilies I will twine narcissus, and the
    sweet   5
Crocus shall, in its yellow hue, with purple hyacinth
    meet.
And I will twine with all the rest, and all the rest
    above,
Queen of them all, the red red rose, the flower which
    lovers love.   ——*Meleager*

Love at the Door

COLD blows the winter wind: 'tis Love,
  Whose sweet eyes swim with honeyed
    tears,
That bears me to thy doors, my love,
  Tossed by the storm of hopes and fears.
Cold blows the blast of aching Love;   5
  But be thou for my wandering sail,
Adrift upon these waves of love,
  Safe harbor from the whistling gale!
                                          ——*Meleager*

Lost Desire

LOVE brought by night a vision to my bed,
  One that still wore the vesture of a child
But eighteen years of age—who sweetly smiled
Till of the lovely form false hopes were bred
  And keen embraces wild.   5
Ah! for the lost desire that haunts me yet,
Till mine eyes fail in sleep that finds no more
That fleeting ghost! Oh, lovelorn heart, give o'er—
Cease thy vain dreams of beauty's warmth—forget
  The face thou longest for!   ——*Meleager*

The Old Story

LIKE many a one, when you had gold
  Love met you smiling, we are told;
But now that all your gold is gone,
Love leaves you hungry and alone.

And women who have called you more   5
Sweet names than ever were before
Will ask another now to tell
What man you are and where you dwell.

Was ever anyone but you
So long in learning what is true?   10
Must you find only at the end
That who has nothing has no friend?
                              ——*Marcus Argentarius*

Vanity of Vanities

NAKED to earth was I brought—naked to earth
    I descend.
Why should I labor for naught, seeing how naked
    the end?   ——*Palladas*

United

HOW long must we two hide the burning gaze,
  And look by stealth in one another's eyes?
Let us proclaim our love; and whoso stays
The sweet embrace that lulls all miseries—
The sword's our doctor: best that you and I   5
Should live together, or together die.
                              ——*Paul the Silentiary*

An Unknown Grave

MY name, my country, what are they to thee?
  What, whether proud or base my ped-
    igree?
Perhaps I far surpassed all other men;
Perhaps I fell below them all. What then?
Suffice it, stranger, that thou seest a tomb.   5
Thou knowest its use. It hides—no matter whom.
                              ——*Paul the Silentiary*

The Old Story. Translated by Edwin Arlington Robinson. From
Captain Craig by Edwin Arlington Robinson. By permission of The
Macmillan Company, publishers.
Vanity of Vanities. Translated by William M. Hardinge.
United. Translated by W. H. D. Rouse in *An Echo of Greek Song*,
1899. Reprinted by permission of Mr. Philip G. Rouse as represent-
ative of the executors.
An Unknown Grave. Translated by William Cowper.

A Garland for Heliodora. Translated by Christopher North.
Love at the Door. Translated by John Addington Symonds.
Lost Desire. Translated by William M. Hardinge.

Life a Boon

IN every way of life true pleasure flows:
　Immortal fame from public action grows;
Within the doors is found appeasing rest;
In fields the gifts of nature are expressed.
The sea brings gain, the rich abroad provide　5
To blaze their names, the poor their wants to hide.
All households best are governed by a wife;
His cares are light who leads a single life.
Sweet children are delights which marriage bless;
He that hath none disturbs his thoughts the less.　10
Strong youth can triumph in victorious deeds;
Old age the soul with pious motion feeds.
All states are good, and they are falsely led
Who wish to be unborn or quickly dead.
　　　　　　　　　　　——*Metrodorus*

Life a Bane

WHAT course of life should wretched mortals
　　　　take?
In courts hard questions large contention make;
Care dwells in houses, labor in the field;
Tumultuous seas affrighting dangers yield.
In foreign lands thou never canst be blessed:　5
If rich, thou art in fear; if poor, distressed.
In wedlock frequent discontentments swell;
Unmarried persons as in deserts dwell.
How many troubles are with children born;
Yet he that wants them counts himself forlorn.　10
Young men are wanton, and of wisdom void;
Gray hairs are cold, unfit to be employed.
Who would not one of these two offers choose:
Not to be born, or breath with speed to lose?
　　　　　　　　　　——*Posidippus*

The Lover's Posy

I SENT a garland to my love
　Which with my own hands I wove:
Rose and lily here there be
Twined with cool anemone,
White narcissus, dewy wet,　5
And the purple violet.
Take and bind it on your brow,
Nor be proud, as you are now,
As the flowers bloom and fade,
So must you too, haughty maid.　　——*Rufinus*

Life a Boon. Translated by Sir John Beaumont. Compare with the poem of Posidippus that follows.
Life a Bane. Translated by Sir John Beaumont.
The Lover's Posy. Translated by W. H. D. Rouse in *An Echo of Greek Song,* 1899. Reprinted by permission of Mr. Philip G. Rouse as representative of the executors.

On Archaeanassa

TO Archaeanassa, on whose furrow'd brow
　Love sits in triumph, I my service vow.
If her declining graces shine so bright,
What flames felt you who saw her noon of light?
　　　　　　　　　　——*Plato*

A Farewell

VENUS, take my votive glass,
　Since I am not what I was:
What from this day I shall be,
Venus, let me never see.　　　　——*Plato*

Resourcefulness

THE blind man bears the lame, and onward
　　　　hies,
Made right by lending feet and borrowing eyes.
　　　　　　　　　　——*Plato*

To Amyntor

TAKE old Amyntor to thy heart, dear soil,
　In kind remembrance of his former toil;
Who first enriched and ornamented thee
With many a lovely shrub and branching tree,
And lured a stream to fall in artful showers　5
Upon thy thirsting herbs and fainting flowers.
First in the spring he knew the rose to rear,
First in the autumn culled the ripened pear.
His vines were envied all the country round,
And favoring heaven showered plenty on his ground.
Therefore, kind earth, reward him in thy breast　11
With a green covering and an easy rest.
　　　　　　　　——*Simmias of Thebes*

Grapes

WHILE yet the grapes were green, thou didst
　　　　refuse me,
When they were ripe, didst proudly pass me by;
But do not grudge me now a single cluster,
　Now that the grapes are withering and dry.
　　　　　　　　　　——*Anonymous*

On Archaeanassa. Translated by Thomas Stanley.
A Farewell. Translated by Matthew Prior.
Resourcefulness. Translated by Charles Neaves.
To Amyntor. Translated by Robert Bland.
Grapes. Translated by Alma Strettell.

Not of Itself But Thee

I SEND thee myrrh, not that thou mayest be
By it perfumed, but it perfumed by thee.
——*Anonymous*

Dion of Tarsus

DION of Tarsus, here I lie, who sixty years
    have seen.
I was not ever wed, and would my father had not
    been!   ——*Anonymous*

Riches

POOR in my youth, and in life's later scenes
    Rich to no end, I curse my natal hour,
Who nought enjoyed while young, denied the
    means:
And nought when old enjoyed, denied the power.
——*Anonymous*

The Persian Peril

WHEN on a razor's edge all Hellas stood,
    We who lie here preserved her with our
blood.   ——*Anonymous*

Not of Itself But Thee. Translated by Richard Garnett.
Dion of Tarsus. Translated by Alma Strettell.
Riches. Translated by William Cowper.
The Persian Peril. Translated by Charles Neaves.

A Grecian runner in the Olympic games wearing a helmet and carrying a decorated shield. A red-figured vase painting.

This Stone

THIS stone, beloved Sabinus, on thy grave
    Memorial small of our great love shall be.
I still shall seek thee lost; from Lethe's wave,
    Oh, drink not thou forgetfulness of me.
——*Anonymous*

This Stone. Translated by Goldwin Smith. From *Bay Leaves* by
Goldwin Smith. Published by The Macmillan Company.

THE WEST

UNDER

ROMAN SWAY

300 B.C. TO 200 A.D.

analogy

I F Greece was the mother of the West, Rome was its stern and vigorous father. The genius of Greece lay in the warm humanity of its literature, art, and philosophy. The genius of Rome lay in the engineering skill with which it built and equipped an empire and the discipline of law by which it ruled it.

Rome followed Greece by about four hundred years. In the Golden Age of Athens, Rome was a struggling city-state on the Tiber river. During the conquests of Alexander Rome was beginning its own conquest of Italy. Three centuries later it was to add Alexander's eastern domains with their Hellenistic culture to its empire in the West. Rome's own Golden Age is so influenced by Greek culture that the matrimonial metaphor is not far-fetched. The warmth and charm of Greece eventually conquered the matter-of-fact Roman soul * and maintained a continuous tradition from Homer to the Christian overthrow of paganism.

The Romans called the Mediterranean *mare nostrum*—our sea—and it is easy to see in the boot-shaped peninsula of Italy a Roman foot thrust down into the center of this area of many races to claim it all from Gibraltar to Jerusalem. Yet the Romans were not such seafarers as the Greeks. As late as the first Punic War (264 B.C.) Rome had no navy. Italy lacked the many harbors of the Greek peninsula, and her fertile valleys led the Romans to hug the earth and to build their empire first by overland fighting. The sea-loving Greeks, on the other hand, maintained the separate independence of their city-states and their colonies overseas as well.

* As Horace put it in his famous epigram. *Graecia capta ferum victorem cepit*—"Conquered Greece took captive her fierce conqueror" (*Epistles*, II, l.156).

Augustus, the first of the Roman emperors.

Down Italy from the north run the Apennine Mountains, much closer to the east coast than to the west. The thin strip of land along the cold, stormy Adriatic shore did not attract settlers. As the Greeks had faced east, the Romans faced west where their fruitful plains sloped gradually to the sea. It is still a beautiful region of olive groves and vine-clad hills with small rivers like the Tiber, to which Rome was to bring fame. The soft climate and volcanic soil made this west coast the great grain-producer of southern Europe. The upland pastures were ideal for cattle-grazing, and the blue and peaceful Mediterranean attracted fishermen. To the north between the Apennines and the Alps is the vast plain watered by the river Po, but this fertile region, so important to modern Italy, was in ancient times a land apart, Cisalpine Gaul, and was not Romanized until the time of the Punic Wars (222 B.C.).

Into the sunny land of Italy came several races in ancient times to form the mongrel Roman. Mysterious aborigines were absorbed by successive invasions from the north of peoples speaking Indo-European tongues. The Latins and Sabines settled central Italy, and their state of Latium (now Lazio) was to beget Rome and the Latin language that bears their name. Less numerous but more powerful at first were the alien Etruscans, who settled to the north in Etruria (now Toscana, or Tuscany) around 800 B.C. and for a time controlled much of the peninsula.

Greeks had built cities along the central coast in early times, but the chief Greek colonization came in the eighth century B.C., when they converted extreme southern Italy into *Magna Graecia* with its beautiful cities. Finally, there were Celtic barbarians called the Gauls, who swarmed down from their homeland north of the Alps and conquered Rome briefly in 390 B.C. The Latins were far from the strongest of these nations in the centuries of restless settlement, but time held for them the destiny of welding these peoples into the Italians of the empire.

THE REPUBLIC OF ROME

BECAUSE the Gauls destroyed the old records of Rome, only vague and often poetic tradition preserved the ancient past. Virgil was one of many poets to tell how Aeneas, a Trojan prince, supposedly escaped the Greeks at the fall of Troy and found refuge and a wife at Latium. His son Ascanius (or Iulus, the supposed ancestor of Julius Caesar) founded the city of Alba Longa, twenty miles southeast of the site of Rome. Nine generations later, as a usurper tried to exterminate the line of Aeneas, the twins Romulus and Remus were born to the last surviving daughter and the god Mars and suckled by a she-wolf. Grown to manhood, they killed the usurper and seized the women of some Sabine visitors to provide wives for their own settlers. It was Romulus who supposedly founded Rome in 753 B.C. and, killing his brother, named the city for himself.

As myth turns into history at the end of the sixth century B.C., the little state of Latium with its growing city of Rome was fretting under a hundred years of rule by Etruscan kings. The last of these despots, Tarquin the Proud, whose son figures as the villain in Shakespeare's *Rape of Lucrece*, was deposed by the Roman Senate in 510 B.C.

The Romans replaced the monarchy with a "republic," * actually an oligarchy ruled by a Senate of patricians (*patres*) and wealthy businessmen (*equites*), though the executive power was in the hands of two consuls elected for one year by the people of Rome voting by *centuries*, or groups, according to the property they owned. Gradually the plebeians, or *plebs*, came to demand a direct voice in the government alongside the aristocratic classes and twice marched out of the city on strike before their Assembly achieved legislative powers and their two (later ten) tribunes a "veto" power over the Senate's actions. The struggle of the *plebs* against the Senate was long and bloody. For two centuries and more

the commoners fought for a more democratic system and eventually won the right to be ruled by elected officers and to hold the offices of *quaestor, aedile, praetor,* and *consul,* along with such social reforms as limitation of estates and a public dole of grain to the needy. One of the earliest of their victories, important as the beginning of Roman law, was the conversion of the old secret records of the tribal priests into the Twelve Tables of public law (450 B.C.), available for all to see in the Forum of Rome.

Meanwhile, the power of Rome was spreading out over the Italian peninsula. The sack of the city by the Gauls was followed by a century of warfare with her neighbors. The defeat of the powerful Samnites in 290 B.C. gave Rome control of central Italy. Next she forced the Greek cities of the south into an alliance that amounted to annexation. By 272 B.C. Rome controlled all of Italy from the Arno River in the north to the tip of the boot.

This brought Rome into direct conflict with her powerful rival in the western Mediterranean, the Phoenician city of Carthage, in north Africa, associated in Virgil's *Aeneid* with the tragic Queen Dido. Because the Carthaginian threat was the greatest danger that Rome had ever faced, the Roman Senator Cato ended every speech with the famous words, "Also, I move that Carthage must be destroyed." Yet Carthage had great generals—Hamilcar and his son, Hannibal—and instead nearly destroyed Rome until Scipio defeated Hannibal in Africa. The first two Punic Wars (264–201 B.C.) lost Carthage her empire, but the third (150–146 B.C.) led to the utter annihilation of the city and a grim fulfillment of Cato's demand. Sicily, Sardinia, Corsica, and the riches of Spain now belonged to Rome, and imperialism became the settled policy of the republic.

In the same year (146 B.C.), growing impatient after a half century of gentlemanly penetration in Greece, Rome formally annexed the city-states and savagely destroyed Corinth as an ominous lesson to Athens and Sparta. One by one the eastern domains of Alexander fell to the Roman legions, and became

* The term "republic," or *res publica* (the public affairs), meant simply the commonwealth to the Romans, and was applied later to the Imperial government.

A Roman relief depicting a fierce battle between Roman troops and "barbarians," who are being badly defeated.

provinces or protectorates—Egypt in 168 B.C., Macedonia in 146 B.C., "Asia" in 133 B.C. In the last days of the republic, Julius Caesar subdued Gaul (modern France), and Pompey finally pushed Roman rule to the distant Euphrates in the east.

This unique conquest of the western and near-eastern world was carried on from the city of Rome, and largely by a Senate of rugged aristocrats, who thrived on the plunder and tribute that poured in from the provinces. Jealous of their prerogatives and prosperity, they bitterly opposed the extension of political power to lower classes or of citizenship to men outside their little city-state. The whole world was to be exploited for the benefit of one community, which was gradually to lapse into dissipation and cynicism because of the fantastic luxury that these riches provided. The republic tried to govern an empire with the constitution of a city-state. But the republic was dying, and a true empire was to be born out of the personal ambitions of two remarkable men.

Both Pompey and Julius Caesar were first-rate generals supported by personal armies of professional soldiers, and both became contemptuous of the Senate that tried to curb them. The egotistical Pompey began his career with brilliant conquests of Spain and the eastern kingdoms of Alexander, while the no less dashing Caesar thrilled the Roman populace with his nine-year conquest of Gaul. Both realized that the republic had outlived its usefulness, but each wanted to be dictator. At first they worked together (with Crassus) in the First Triumvirate (60 B.C.) to force reforms upon the unwilling Senate. But eventually Pompey took advantage of Caesar's absence in Gaul to become sole dictator in Rome, whereupon Caesar with one of his legions crossed the Rubicon River, part of the northern boundary of Italy (the occasion for his famous "The die is cast") and accumulated a personal army for his march on Rome. In the battles that followed, Pompey showed bad judgment and irresolution and was destroyed by the superior generalship of Caesar at Pharsalia (48 B.C.).

Dictator now, Caesar spent most of the four short years left to him in military campaigns and tarried nine months in Egypt under the spell of the young queen Cleopatra of the Greek Ptolemies. But upon his return to Italy, which he found in chaos after a century of revolution and bad government, he showed generosity toward his enemies and the qualities of great statesmanship. He enlarged the Senate with men from all classes and pursued the land reforms which had been earlier attempted. He stimulated a revival of morality by bolstering the state religion and tried to legislate political corruption away. He relieved unemployment by public works and renovated the dole system. He extended Roman citizenship even to some barbarians in remote provinces and envisioned a united empire functioning for the good of all the far-flung lands that he had seen, rather than for the profit of the city of Rome that bounded the Senators' world. His assassination in 44 B.C. by disgruntled aristocrats and high-minded patriots led by Cassius and Brutus plunged the empire into fourteen years of civil war until the rise of his nephew Octavian to power assured the good government and many reforms that Caesar had projected. These were achieved under a new form of government, an imperial one, in place of the moribund republic.

THE ROMAN POINT OF VIEW

Cf Rome and Sparta

THE world empire of Rome challenges the imagination. We may well ask what traits in the Roman led him to achieve or even to desire a world conquest that the freedom-loving Greeks never dreamed of. We will find the answer in his philosophy and the social pattern of his culture that produced it—perhaps still further back in the geography that influenced his history at every point.

The seafaring Greek felt secure in his sea-girdled homeland and developed without the constant fear of hostile barbarian neighbors, whereas from the start the Roman had to battle enemies on all sides for survival. With war a daily possibility, he organized his society on a military pattern and stood ever ready to lay down the plough for the sword. The bundle of rods, called the *fasces*, that symbolized the judges' authority to punish symbolized also the collective security of the community against threat from outside. The empire grew by successive attempts to insure the safety of the commonwealth from border menace, and in its growth not simply the army but a society built on the military principle of command and obedience carried the day. Such a rule appears not simply in the Roman's public life but in his family career that conditioned him in youth to accept law and discipline outside the home.

In Greece all the forces of the market place and the gymnasium combined to defeat the power of the family in the life of the citizen; in Rome the family was the indestructible nucleus of society, a

Excavation of Pompeii revealed fine examples of Roman buildings. This is the peristyle of the house of the Vettii, partly restored.

microcosm which contained in miniature the structure of the empire itself. The Greek stands forth as an individual, the Roman as a member of a family, a clan, a nation. The family was ruled by the father, the *paterfamilias* in a thoroughly paternalistic society, whose *familia* included not only his children but the servant slaves and the *clientes,* his free dependents, as well. To these must be added the *manes,* or ancestral spirits, and the *lares* and *penates,* the family gods peculiar to each *familia.* In the father were concentrated the traditions of the clan, the laws of his forbears, and the grave responsibilities of family leadership, so that he wielded a traditional and legal power over his household unthinkable today. He owned all the property. He could divorce his wife with a letter or even condemn her to death, though Roman women, unlike the Greek, had a respected social position and shared the government of the family through moral influence, if not legal right. He had a life-and-death power over his dependents and could kill a son for a crime or sell him into slavery, though such drastic uses of authority were uncommon. The Roman son was ever conscious of his father's will and prepared himself seriously for the power that he would someday wield in his father's stead. His very name revealed his absorption in the family—Marcus, his personal name; Tullius, his clan name; Cicero, his family name. The tight, strict organization of the family gave him a stern discipline and unreasoning loyalty quite far from the free individualism of the Greek.

Like the family, the state religion worked to mould a sturdy, practical, unquestioning citizen. Although the Greek pantheon was later identified with Roman deities, Rome had an older and more characteristic religion of its own that persevered with the populace through the coming of Christianity. Primitive fears of nature led to primitive superstitions and taboos and eventually to a myriad of spirits, hardly gods, associated with particular places, seasons, and experiences of men. These deities were not thought to have human form but to dwell as spirits in trees, groves, hills, and rocks—within the Roman earth, not in the sky to which most religions look. Literally thousands of these local divinities peopled the landscape and were a part of the daily life of the Roman. Each family had its spirits for protection—a *lar* to watch over its land and buildings, *penates* to guard the possessions indoors, and the *manes* of male ancestors to guide the new generations. A religion that surrounded the citizen with watchful spirits deprived him of individual freedom and forced upon him a conventional and dutiful behavior. Eventually more universal deities—Jupiter, Juno, Venus, and Mars—emerged and were honored through public ritual and festivals provided by the state. When Greek influence grew

strong in Italy, Zeus, Hera, Aphrodite, and Ares were merged with them to provide an expanded and more attractive theology. Cults from the East continued to find favor in Rome for centuries, though the state frowned on their romantic excesses and did what it could to curb them. Priestly officials, serving under a *pontifex maximus,* superintended the state religion and tended to standardize orthodox belief into law. The stern rigidity of Roman religion is in contrast with the aesthetic variation in the Greek.

Roman religion tended to mould the citizen's behavior according to traditional practice, but did it affect his spiritual life? Certainly on the surface it was like the Greek in emphasizing the legal contract between gods and men implied in ritual and sacrifice. Its *quid-pro-quo* basis suggested that the gods were pleased with gifts rather than morality, and they were themselves as irresponsible and unethical as their Greek counterparts. They did not inspire goodness by their example, nor did they value it in dispensing rewards. For example, Venus exasperates even her son Aeneas by her frivolous deceptions, and when she demands a just reward for Aeneas' *pietas* from Jupiter, she has in mind his faithful performance of sacrifices and other religious rites and his unswerving concern for his mission, not any innate virtue such as we might admire. Yet pious obedience to the gods did promote devotion to duty and the sacrifice of selfish ends to the good of the whole. Religion may not have taught virtue, but it was the part of virtue to care for the gods. They underlay the corporate life of the community and supported the institutions of marriage, family, war, and the state. They inspired piety and justified patriotism, for the real Roman god behind all the gods was Rome itself. In this strictly Roman sense the state religion touched the roots of the Roman's spiritual being—his fanatical love of country and his stoic willingness to sacrifice himself without question for the safety or glory of the state.

Out of such a society and such a religion emerged the peculiarly Roman view of virtue, which is best summarized in the Latin names for the four ideal qualities. *Pietas* was actually a divinity, but an abstraction as well, to which the Roman aspired. Though it gives us the word "piety," it meant for him duty, or dutiful conduct toward his parents, relatives, ancestors, gods, and country. *Pietas* was the supreme virtue, acquired in the family and expressed in action throughout the good Roman's life. *Gravitas* means seriousness, and for the Roman, life was an intensely serious affair. Responsibilities destroy the carefree experimentation so dear to the Greeks, and the Roman had the individual responsibility of family leadership as well as the corporate responsibility of an empire to govern. The Roman's seriousness expressed itself in the formality of his

This small rural sanctuary with a sacrificial altar is from a Roman stucco relief. A garland is being offered here.

being dangerous to order and a status quo in which he had been taught to believe. He was an efficiency expert, concerned with facts rather than theories and demanding of everything that it should be useful first of all. The Latin language that he developed illustrated his practical turn of mind—compact rather than beautiful, elegant rather than noble. Intellectual things are not obviously useful, and consequently played no part in the rapid growth of the empire. The Roman had a serviceable philosophy of life that supplied his needs, but no interest in philosophies. He approved of education so long as it was practical and reverent. He was a masterful engineer but never a creative scientist.

All of these things apply to the Roman in the formative years of the empire before alien influences from his own provinces to the east began to corrupt his soul. The conquest of Greece brought to Roman life a Hellenistic veneer which eventually infected upper-class circles with philosophy. As the unphilosophical Roman surveyed the schools of Greece, he passed over the metaphysical Eleatics, the idealistic Platonists, the scientific Peripatetics to the one school that seemed to give voice to his national point of view. Stoicism originated with the Greek Zeno of Citium (fl. 300 B.C.), who preached that the highest virtue is manhood, which expresses itself in the power to endure hardship and to repress feeling and the demands of the body. He exalted self-denial and impassive reserve as a means of subordinating oneself to the will of the Supreme Deity. This rugged philosophy reached Rome through Panaetius of Rhodes (c. 180–c. 110 B.C.), who taught a modified version to his friend and pupil, Scipio Aemilianus, the Roman general. Man, he said, is part of the physical whole and must function within it, cooperating with his family, his state, and his God. He must act according to his duty without question and with the temperance of the Golden Mean. This gentlemanly code, so completely in harmony with the traditional ideal of Roman conduct, gradually replaced for educated Romans the naïve state religion. Cicero modeled his *De Officiis* on Panaetius' treatise of the same name. Seneca accepted Stoicism as a religion. Epictetus the slave (c. 50–130 A.D.) and Marcus Aurelius the emperor (121–180 A.D.) remind us of the enduring influence of this national philosophy throughout the Silver Age. Aeneas, the Roman hero of Virgil, is a Stoic in his dutiful renunciation of his love for Dido and in his calm resignation to his fate to found Rome. In the English language the word "stoic" still connotes intellectual control of feeling and a resolute indifference to pleasure and pain.

Yet the stoic view of life that built an empire was eventually corrupted by the luxury and cynicism that empire produced. In the last years of the republic, many who thought of themselves as Stoics lived like

life and his intense conservatism. A kind of gloomy earnestness surrounds much of Roman literature, a heaviness that makes the Greeks seem skittish and reckless by comparison. *Simplicitas* comes close to plainness or even bluntness in English. It suggests singleness of purpose and directness in achieving one's ends. At its highest it stands for frankness and honesty, qualities which the Roman esteemed much more than the Greek with his admiration for the cleverness and sly duplicity of an Odysseus. *Virtus* originally meant manliness, but came to suggest physical courage and eventually virtue in our sense, though associated more with the battlefield than with the council chamber. A sober and unimaginative outlook, a strong sense of duty, and courage in performing it—these, then, are the moral qualities in the Roman point of view, and it is not hard to relate them to success in war, efficiency in government, and the stoic acceptance of a god-given destiny to rule the world.

In the intellectual realm the Roman is less satisfactory. Basically he was a prosy, practical man who built an empire without thinking too much about it. He was content to do what had to be done without asking why. The impractical Greek was forever exploring and inquiring into the nature of things. The Roman was suspicious of speculation as

Epicureans, and the opposed philosophy of Epicurus (341–270 B.C.) developed its own school in Rome. Although in modern English "epicurean" suggests a luxurious pursuit of physical pleasure, this debased extension of the term does injustice to the wise and moderate founder of the school and his devoted Roman follower, Lucretius. Outlawing all belief in the supernatural and immortality, the Epicureans were materialists who conceived of the universe in terms of ever-moving atoms. Man is tied to this system by his senses but has also a rational self that chooses a way of life. The sole end of this life is the achievement of pleasure, but not merely physical pleasures; these should only assist us to the supreme pleasure of a peaceful and happy mind. Physical excess produces pain, as does too rigorous self-denial. Prudence shows us how to attain a maximum of enjoyment with a minimum of distress. Virtue, there-

fore, is only a means to an end—happiness. This pleasant doctrine was far removed from the Roman view of life in the robust years of the republic, but it came more and more to explain the practice of many latter-day Romans. Although seemingly opposed to Stoicism, it was actually combined with it in a curiously consistent harmony. Horace illustrates this in his undisguised pursuit of the pleasures of life tempered always by moderation and self-control. In the aesthetic excesses of a Nero, on the other hand, Epicureanism passes into hedonism, and responsible citizens bemoan the decay of the old Roman virtues. A natural stoicism came closest to the Roman point of view. Whether a simple evolution of her community life or an asssimilation of a foreign philosophy, this stern, unimaginative outlook made Rome great and steeled her to resist the barbarian.

LITERATURE OF THE REPUBLIC

LITERATURE came late to Rome, and then as a deliberate importation from the Greeks. Of course there had been folk poetry—hymns and ballads in prehistoric times—but almost none of it has survived and Roman references to it are surprisingly meager. The practical-minded Romans, bent at first upon survival, later upon security through conquest, lacked the warm imagination and sensitivity to beauty that made the Greeks evolve literature and other arts as necessary expressions of their community life. Like many Americans living also in a materialistic culture, the Romans were suspicious of the arts as unmanly and dangerous to the vigor of the state. Only after the Punic Wars, when empire brought wealth and luxury to some classes, did a leisured aristocracy begin to enjoy them without shame and decide that national pride demanded national poets and playwrights. The Greeks had taught them the art of writing; they were now to teach them the art of literature.

So we should not be surprised that the first known Latin poet was a Greek, Livius Andronicus (fl. 240 B.C.), who had been brought as a slave to Rome, or that the first Roman who became a poet, Cnaeus Naevius (fl. 200 B.C.), modeled his Latin verses on Greek meters. These pioneers are now little more than names. Not only were their works to be superseded by later masters, but the early Latin that they used was so uncouth and unliterary in comparison with the melodious Greek that later generations found it unpleasant to recall. The man who refined this coarse speech into a flexible and elegant instrument of expression was the poet Ennius (239–169 B.C.), who prepared the way for Lucretius and

Catullus. This exuberant pathfinder wrote twenty tragedies (all lost) in the manner of Euripides, and an epic history of Rome from Aeneas down, called the *Annales,* which was the Roman national poem till the time of Virgil's *Aeneid.*

To the period of Ennius belong the first two important figures of Roman literature, the comic playwrights Plautus and Terence. Drama of a sort, especially in the form of vulgar mimes, had been popular in Italy from the early days of the republic, but literary drama in the Greek style dates from the first works of Livius Andronicus. Rome had no permanent theater until 55 B.C., largely because of Senate opposition to the drama as a frivolous and immoral entertainment, but the populace crowded around their wooden stages nevertheless to applaud noisily the robust and sometimes obscene plays of their early favorites, which the state did provide. This mob in holiday mood often jeered the tragedies of Ennius and demanded broad farce and obvious satire that they could understand. The man who satisfied them best of all was Plautus (c. 254–184 B.C.), a commoner like themselves, who had lost his earnings in commerce and then wrote plays to keep alive. This robust and jovial fellow had the only sure sense of theater among surviving Roman playwrights.

The comedies of Plautus, totally unlike the satiric Old Comedy of Aristophanes, are derived from the New Comedy of fourth-century Greece and in many instances are frank adaptations of actual plays of Menander and Philemon, though Roman in spirit. Gone is the chorus of birds or frogs and the religious meaning of the occasion. Gone is the satire of famous men and the comment on the politics of the day.

The New Comedy is a harmless comedy of manners involving social types from the Roman scene—an irate father, a spendthrift son, a pompous soldier, a bawdy-house madam, a cunning slave or parasite—in a farcical mix-up that is straightened out in the last scene. As likely as not, the plot is some variation on Terence's *Phormio:* A young Athenian falls in love with a girl of unknown parentage and despite his father's enraged objections maneuvers himself with the aid of the lying parasite Phormio into a legal position where he must marry her. The father is reconciled to the match when the girl turns out to be the long-lost daughter of his brother by a secret early marriage. Everyone is happy except the brother, whose wife berates him for his bigamy. Terence (c. 190–159 B.C.), a freed slave of Carthage who rose to social prominence at Rome in the intellectual coterie of Scipio Africanus, wrote six comedies of this sort. They have a more restrained and finished style than Plautus' but lack the robust humor of the earlier comedian.

The greatest republican literature belongs to the period of Caesar and the revolution that prepared the way for the Augustan empire. We think of it as the Ciceronian era, because the commanding personality of Marcus Tullius Cicero (106–43 B.C.), statesman, orator, and master of prose, gives it stature and continuity. Cicero's long career in the Senate tied his literary work to contemporary politics, and even his philosophical writings, which echo his Greek masters, are most satisfactory when they are prescribing a practical code of conduct for the Roman citizen. His many personal letters reveal the charming, mellow personality of the old Senator of this period, surveying with stoic calm the decline of republican Rome. But perhaps his greatest achievement lies in bringing the Latin language to magnificent maturity as a flexible instrument for expressing thought. The fluent grace and elegant diction of his style first showed the power of Latin as a precise, urbane, and eloquent vehicle for ideas. Down to an age just before our own, Cicero represented an ideal of literary prose for writers in all of western Europe.

To the age of Cicero belong the first great poets of Rome—Lucretius, the superb spokesman for Epicurean philosophy, and Catullus, the greatest of her

Cicero, rugged statesman of the Roman republic.

love poets. The atomic theory of Epicurus does not seem at first sight to be a suitable subject for poetry, but Lucretius expounded it with such an enkindling earnestness and enlivened it with such imaginative illustrations and figures of speech that he created in *Of the Nature of Things* the world's great didactic poem. In our age, when Cicero and Virgil are out of fashion, many critics consider Lucretius Rome's most modern writer, if not her greatest poet as well.

Catullus is the only survivor from a group of Roman lyricists of the Ciceronian era who imitated the graceful Alexandrians in love poems to contemporary ladies. His beloved was the fascinating but dissolute daughter of an old Roman house. To her, Catullus gave a youthful devotion, which he lived to despise, and to us he has left blazing lyric records of both his moods. He is the bridge to Horace and the Augustan Age of Roman poetry.

THE EMPIRE OF ROME

THE dictatorship of Julius Caesar had not established an empire. His assassination left the way open for the Senate to reassert its power under the old Constitution, but by this time the Senate was so weakened by the deaths of old families and the in-flux of the many new ones that it wanted no rule of its own but a new leader who would support its monied interests. Caesar had adopted as his son and heir his nephew Octavian (63 B.C.–14 A.D.), but this stripling of nineteen seemed less fit for command than Caesar's capable general, Mark Antony (83–30 B.C.), who promptly plotted to seize power. His skillful funeral oration over Caesar's body won him popular support against the Senators, some of whom had helped to assassinate Caesar, but he avoided an outright breach with the Senate while using the popular Assembly to sanction his rule.

Meanwhile, Octavian, reverencing the memory of his great-uncle Caesar, was shocked to find that Antony had granted amnesty to his assassins; and with the support in the Senate of the orator Cicero, who had held the favor of Caesar, Octavian led out two legions to defeat Antony and then, as consul, had the conspirators sentenced to death. At once Cicero and the Senate turned against this dictator as they had against Antony, so that Octavian retaliated by inviting Antony and the treacherous general Lepidus to form the Second Triumvirate (43–33). A reign of terror followed as the three leaders coolly sanctioned the murder of all their enemies, including Cicero, and defeated the armies of Caesar's assassins, Cassius and Brutus, at Philippi. Octavian and Antony thereupon divided the empire between themselves, and Antony proceeded to establish his eastern capital at Alexandria, where he fell captive to the charms of that same Cleopatra who had beguiled Caesar. Soon after, he divorced his wife Octavia, the virtuous sister of Octavian, in favor of the Greek-Egyptian siren. While Antony succumbed to Oriental pleasures, Octavian brought order to his western half of the empire, and then set out to avenge his sister's humiliation by depriving Antony of his eastern command. The issue was decided in a naval battle at Actium (31 B.C.), after which Cleopatra followed her devoted Antony to death. Octavian was now sole commander of the Roman world and in a position to carry out the projects of his uncle Caesar.

The servile Senate was delighted to hear that he shunned the title of king as Caesar had done and was content to be called *princeps senatus* (chief in the Senate) and *imperator* (commander of the army, but an army which he bound to himself by oaths of personal loyalty). He had become king and emperor in fact, if not in name, and founded a dynasty that continued for fifty years after his death. In gratitude for his tact, the Senate gave him the title of *Augustus*, which has come to be thought of as his name, and Octavian strove through the forty years of his reign (27 B.C.–14 A.D.) to justify it. Physically weak as he was, his success in war had been a tour de force, but nearly a half century of peace gave his intellectual capacity and strong will the chance to show themselves in wise statesmanship. The Golden Age, predicted by Virgil in his *Fourth Eclogue* ten years before, came to Rome and the empire; and literature was only one phase of life that felt the inspiration of his just and tolerant rule.

Augustus ministered to the needs of all classes with laws favoring each. He encouraged trade by suppressing piracy and maintaining peace throughout the realm. Using the wealth of the Egyptian treasury, he gave employment to the poor by public works, not simply temples, a theater, and a new senate-house, but roads for travel and commerce in the Roman tradition of road building that had been linking the empire overland for two hundred years. His ascetic nature made him attempt to curb the rising immorality of the city with the puritanical Julian Laws, but here he went too far and was ultimately defeated by the cynicism of a populace that had lost the old Roman virtues in luxury and venality. His own daughter and granddaughter shamed him with their flagrant immorality; the one he imprisoned for adultery, the other he exiled, along with the poet Ovid, who was involved in her misconduct. Worn out with disappointment and physical ills, he died at seventy-six, having preserved his frail body by abstemious living for four decades of remarkable service to the empire he created. He had long been worshiped in the east as a god, and his work was to endure in the two centuries of *Pax Romana* that followed.

It is a tribute to the statesmanship of Augustus that the empire functioned prosperously to the end of his dynasty fifty years later, even under the bad rulers who succeeded him. His stepson Tiberius lacked his tact and skill and retired into a morbid seclusion, leaving the government to a treacherous favorite. The notorious psychopaths Caligula and Nero remain in the popular imagination as prototypes of the depraved Roman emperor, cruel, debauched, reckless, and extravagant. The forced suicide of Nero brought the terrible year of the Four Emperors (68–69 A.D.) and civil war. But the Augustan machine of government weathered all these attacks upon its stability, and the empire as a whole continued in peace.

Out of the struggle emerged a new dynasty, the despotic Flavians, who brought sound but unimaginative rule to their vast domain for nearly thirty years. The last of them, Domitian, fostered a revival of art and literature which became the focal point of Rome's Silver Age. The poets Statius and Martial flattered him shamelessly, and the historian Tacitus, the essayist Pliny the Younger, and the satirist Juvenal dissented as immoderately. This glittering galaxy made his reign brilliant with the last great flowering of Roman literary talent. Still the Senate was happy to see the assassination of Domitian in 96 A.D. and the end of the dynastic principle of succession to the throne.

It replaced him with the first of the five Good Emperors who gave the empire its longest period, eighty-four years, of uninterrupted peace and prosperity.

Each of these rulers was chosen by his predecessor to rule, regardless of family connections. They were a varied lot of striking personalities, but all capable and conscientious sovereigns. Hadrian (76–138), the most attractive of them all, was a man of culture, who enthusiastically encouraged the Greek renaissance of literature and philosophy that produced the satires of Lucian and yet found time to reorganize the civil service and supervise the codification of Roman law. The empire reached its greatest extent under Hadrian, and he spent much of his reign in delighted travel from one end of it to the other. Peaceful rule continued under Marcus Aurelius (121–180), the philosopher-king, who did not allow his Stoic asceticism to interfere with a vigorous prosecution of government. His quiet *Meditations* on duty and happiness, written in Greek according to the contemporary fashion, have been a source of inspiration to many of our day.

The Good Emperors made the second century A.D. the most glorious in Roman history. The boundaries of the empire came to include Britain and Dacia (modern Rumania) in the north, Mauretania (Morocco) in the south, and Armenia, Mesopotamia, and northern Arabia to the east. The whole western world and much of the east felt the unifying hand of Roman rule. The *Pax Romana* brought industry and commerce to far-flung provinces, where miniature Romes were built as prosperous outposts of Western civilization. Roman roads provided an easy, safe communication that the world was not to see again until the nineteenth century. Roman architecture flourished in the forums, the triumphal arches, the public baths and aqueducts, the theaters and temples that still dot the Mediterranean world. Portrait sculpture reached new heights of realism and preserved for us the likenesses of many prominent men of the day. Literature declined sharply, but philosophy held its own with Epictetus and Marcus Aurelius, the most famous of the Stoics. The state religion persevered among the lower classes, but the intellectuals merely tolerated it as an instrument of political control. Oriental cults, including Christianity, flourished, and deification and worship of the emperor was encouraged as a bond of political unity throughout the realm. However repugnant to us the imperial system of Rome may be, we should try to judge it at its best by the fruits of prosperity and contentment that it brought to its conquered lands.

From its very founding the empire had within it the seeds of its decay. It evolved as the easiest substitution for an obsolete political system when social unrest fomented civil war. The principate of Augustus gave political stability to the far-flung realm, but it did not eliminate the social inequalities that were destroying the old unity of the nation. For generations Rome had been a place of very

rich and very poor, with a huge slave population to compete with poor citizens as a labor supply. Wars took free farmers away from the land into the army and often laid waste their farms. Service in the army sophisticated the country folk and left them eager for city life and content to live on the grain dole in Rome. Their small farms were added to the large estates of the wealthy, who sought secure investments for their new riches and the power that comes from land ownership. The large estates might be farmed by slaves, but were more often converted to grazing land, since new and cheaper sources of grain in the provinces made cattle-raising more profitable. Wine and olive oil were also produced on a large scale by city capital. The result was to destroy the reliable, hard-working farmer class, the stable backbone of the nation. The evil was not new. Even under the republic, the vested interests had blocked attempts at land reform. Caesar planned to carry out such reforms, and Augustus vainly encouraged a back-to-the-farm movement with land distribution.

Large-scale industry was unknown to the ancient world, and even in the heyday of empire, clothing, furniture, building materials, and household implements were made by artisans, often within the *familia* itself. There were factories for objects that could not readily be produced by individual workers —glassware, metalware, paper, and simple machinery—but these like agriculture enlisted slave labor more often than free. Nearly half the one million population of Rome in the first century A.D. was slave, but the practice of freeing slaves for ability or special services had grown common. Freedmen began to swell the plebeian class of citizens, alongside freeborn artisans, artists, and professional men, and some rose to political power in the imperial palace. A freedman's son, like Horace, had full rights of citizenship; his grandson could become a senator, or even, like Pertinax in the second century A.D., an emperor. Yet in general the freedmen merely augmented the plebeian class and increased the social pressure upon the upper classes. Wealthy men sometimes appeased them with gifts of money to all citizens, and the dole of grain to *clientes*, or parasites, was a common and demoralizing practice which played a major and often sinister role in Roman politics.

Still more vicious were the public games, provided by the state to keep the populace amused and tractable, and multiplied lavishly by demagogues and emperors who sought the favor of the *plebs*. They were presented in connection with religious festivals, military triumphs, political elections, and the like. These were no athletic contests of citizens in friendly rivalry, such as the Greeks had enjoyed at Olympia and Delphi, but bloody struggles of slaves and condemned prisoners. Least objectionable were the

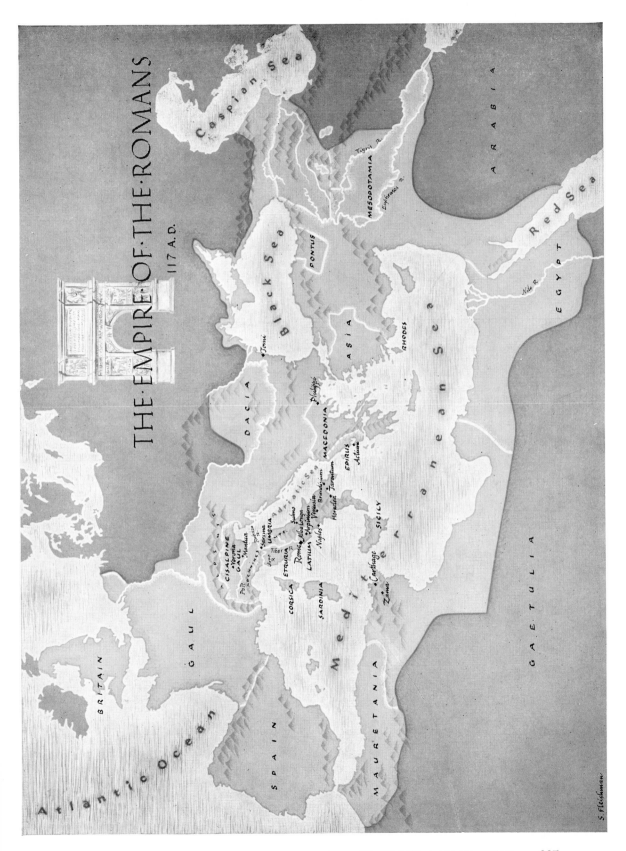

THE·EMPIRE·OF·THE·ROMANS

117 A.D.

Atlantic Ocean

BRITAIN

GAUL

SPAIN

MAURETANIA

GAETULIA

Mediterranean Sea

CORSICA

SARDINIA

SICILY

Carthage

Zama

ALPS

CISALPINE

Verona

GAUL

Mantua

Po R.

ETRURIA

Tiber

Arno R.

UMBRIA

Rome

Alba Longa

LATIUM

Naples

Capua

Caudine Forks

Tarentum

Brundusium

Horace

EPIRUS

Actium

MACEDONIA

Philippi

Adriatic Sea

DACIA

Ioni

Black Sea

PONTUS

ASIA

RHODES

Caspian Sea

MESOPOTAMIA

Tigris R.

Euphrates R.

ARABIA

Red Sea

EGYPT

Nile R.

S. Fleishman

Men wearing tunics and armored vests fight lions in the arena before the spectators of the circus "games." At the bottom of this carved d'ptych one gladiator indicates victory over the beast.

horse races and the chariot races at the Circus Maximus, which combined the functions of our race tracks and professional ball games in the social life of Rome. The competition of rival stables, jockeys, and drivers inspired endless conversation for the populace; gambling ran riot before the races, and the excitement of the events themselves knew no bounds. Most notorious of the entertainments were the fights of the gladiators and of men with wild animals. All classes of Rome turned out in gayest attire to assume their favored places in the Colosseum and watch the shocking spectacle of death. Tigers fought elephants; men hunted lions and panthers; bulls fought men; but worst of all were the contests of men with men to the death. Romans condoned these grisly shows on the ground that most of the gladiators were criminals and war prisoners condemned to death anyway and that they stood the chance of winning freedom by success in combat. A few thoughtful citizens, such as Cicero and Seneca, deplored such brutalizing exhibitions, but most men accepted them as deterrents of crime and examples of stoic courage.

Though the upper classes enjoyed these spectacles with the *plebs*, their special amusement came from private luxuries. When Horace speaks of the modesty of his way of life, we must remember that his Sabine farm was a magnificent affair of twenty-eight rooms with three bathing pools and three slaves to serve him dinner. Yet it seemed humble in comparison with the huge palace of his friend Maecenas on the Esquiline. Maecenas was a middle-class businessman, and to his "equestrian" class the riches of Rome were gravitating in the money-mad era of trade and exploitation of the empire. The laissez-faire economy of Rome put few restrictions on moneymaking.

The *nouveau riche* attitude of the millionaires is reflected in the crude display of wealth in grandiose palaces stocked with legions of slaves, in country estates and villas for vacations at fashionable Baiae, in rare furniture and bric-a-brac imported from eastern provinces, and in gourmet dinners of exotic dishes costing $10,000 or more. With thousands of the *plebs* living on the dole, such sumptuous living among the privileged reflected the cleavage between the classes and the fatal disintegration of Roman society that had come with the decline of Spartan living and stoic thinking. The *familia* was breaking down; celibacy and divorce were common; the suicide of the race was well under way. It appears as an ominous background in the literature of the empire, in the playful cynicism of Horace's satires, in Ovid's decadent absorption in sex, in Juvenal's unpleasant picture of social life in the Imperial City, in the satire of bourgeois splendor and vice in the writings of Petronius.

LITERATURE OF THE EMPIRE

THE enlightened patronage of Augustus and the prosperity of his reign inspired the great period of Roman poetry as a climax to the era of Cicero. Together they form Rome's Golden Age (70 B.C.–14 A.D.). Rich men, of whom the best known was Maecenas, encouraged authors by magnificent gifts, and the writers responded with graceful poetic tributes. It was not a free literature of self-supporting, independently speaking men, but an imperial literature dedicated to Rome and the fashionable society of the city. It glittered with aristocratic sophistication and modeled itself deliberately on the Greeks, who were now extravagantly popular with the intellectuals. Homer reappeared in Virgil's Aeneid, Hesiod in his Georgics, Theocritus in his Eclogues. Anacreon and the Alexandrians inspired the graceful lyrics of Horace and Propertius and the legends of Ovid. Euripides found a stiff reflection in Seneca. But the imitation was not exact, and the Romans substituted for the youthful vigor and nobility of the Greeks their own worldly cynicism and elegant polish.

The great writers who produced this literature were not originally of the city of Rome, but provincials who gravitated to the capital for education, advancement, or a life of urban amusement. Virgil, Horace, Propertius, and Tibullus had all lost their ancestral lands in the civil wars and came to Rome out of necessity to seek their fortunes. But Ovid was a man of means who shocked his middle-class father by sacrificing a promising political career to enjoy the idle pleasures of the town. All disliked war and politics through temperament or rough experience and were embarrassed by the Emperor's insistence on poetry to glorify the Roman military spirit and the ancient institutions of the state. Horace and Propertius occasionally obliged; Ovid celebrated the religious feasts of the Roman calendar in his Fasti; but the gentle, retiring Virgil accepted his duty most cheerfully of them all and assisted the back-to-the-farm movement in his Georgics and the exaltation of the empire and the Caesars in his Aeneid.

All but Ovid lived on the bounty of rich patrons in the luxurious but dignified society of which Augustus approved. Virgil, Horace, and Propertius were of the circle of Maecenas; Tibullus of the circle of Messala; and the historian Livy was only one of many writers befriended by the Emperor himself.

The stamp of patronage is on their work in their fulsome gratitude and their deference to the imperial person and principle. Yet Ovid was the exception. He was the voice for another stratum of Rome's high society, the world of flaming youth and fashionable debauchees who sneered at the seriousness of the inner circle and lived for elegant idleness and cynical lovemaking. The Emperor's stern disapproval of this demimonde eventually forced Ovid into a bitter exile.

Poetry was the special glory of the Augustan Age, and the variety of its themes and types is surprising. Most characteristic of the period and of Rome itself is the stately Aeneid, for Virgil was the national poet of the empire. The majestic role was far from natural to this sensitive, mystical writer, the shyest and least heroic of men. But he loved the soil of Italy and had revealed in his Eclogues and Georgics a nostalgia for the simple country life of his youth. Augustus marked his wholesome devotion to the land and may have remembered the poet's enthusiastic prediction in his Fourth Eclogue, written in the midst of civil war ten years before, that the world was on the eve of a new era of peace and prosperity. The Emperor chose Virgil to glorify this new world of empire in an epic about the founding of the state. The martial poem was a tour de force for the gentle poet, and the middle-aged stoicism of its hero, caught up in a conflict of love and duty, fighting a weary war, reveals the remoteness of Homer's world from Virgil's. But this spirit is also the spirit of Rome, resigned to greatness, obediently accepting the call of history. And despite its sedate quality and intellectual cast, the Aeneid rings with beautiful melody and patriotic devotion. The effect may be studied, the background moralistic, but the perfection of its style and the dramatic interest of its great scenes justify its extraordinary influence in later literature. Because of the general understanding of Latin in the Renaissance, Virgil rather than Homer was the inspiration of later epics from Dante and Camoëns to Pope and Voltaire.

The prolific Ovid was also a master of the long poem, but of a vastly different character. The profligate poet of pleasure fell short of the high seriousness of the epic strain and aspired, not to glorify his race for posterity, but to entertain the smart set of his time with piquant tales and cynical advice to the lovelorn. His *Art of Love* is a systematic guide to flirtation and lechery, and the *Amores* telescope several of his own affairs in an account of his adulterous love for the fanciful Corinna. He even composed a manual of cosmetics in elegant meters.

These racy poems delighted the jaded tastes of his fashionable friends but won him the severe disapproval of Augustus and his circle. Certainly the temperament of Ovid and the spirit of his works are far from the stoicism and *virtus* of Cicero and the Romans who built the empire. He is the soft epicurean, genial, amiable, and light-hearted. His vivacity and downright levity are infectious; he was a man of abundant personality but no character, though we may still admire his unenvious regard for his fellow-poets, his literary ambition, and his persistent devotion to his art. To his contemporaries and many later generations he brought the spirit of romance through his endless inventiveness, his sensitivity to color and life, and his fluent and graceful style. His love poems were to make him the idol of the Wandering Scholars of the Middle Ages as well as a chief source of the courtly love tradition in the age of chivalry. But it is his masterpiece, the *Metamorphoses*, that has had the most lasting influence on world literature. His marvelous retelling of the most picturesque myths of Greece and Rome has delighted young people for generations and inspired such a wide circle of poets as Chaucer, Boccaccio, Spenser, Shakespeare, Milton, and Dryden. The *Metamorphoses* makes Ovid Rome's great storyteller.

Virgil and Ovid excelled in narrative verse; Horace's province was the lyric, of which he was the undisputed master in the Augustan Age. He could command as well the longer poem in his mellow epistles and his *Art of Poetry*, but we meet him at his most engaging in his graceful odes and songs. Horace left the mighty line to Virgil, his friend and literary twin, and, secure on the Sabine farm outside Rome given to him by Maecenas, he lived in happy contempt for ambition and worldly wealth, and casually preached the Golden Mean of Aristotle as the avenue to contentment. His sprightly love lyrics court a galaxy of literary ladies of doubtful virtue. His polished satires poke fun at fools and bores. But no matter where we meet him, Horace is the good companion who enjoyed life as an epicurean and feared death no more than the best of stoics.

His effortless union of the two philosophies makes him the perfect spokesman for the private morality of the imperial Roman. He is cynical but not pessimistic; no passion clouds his realistic eye. He is abundantly aware of the pleasures of life, yet unwilling to wear them out through excess. Horace thought of himself as the laureate of Rome, and in a sense he was. But he has been the laureate as well of a cultured minority in many ages, with a mellow understanding of experience and a sensitivity to his exquisite art. His philosophy put him under a cloud during the Christian Middle Ages, but the Renaissance rediscovered him, and in the Age of Reason he achieved his greatest popularity of all. The modern Augustans of seventeenth-century France and eighteenth-century England found in his common sense and refinement a kinship over nearly twenty centuries.

Although the empire continued strong for two centuries after Augustus, literature began a gradual decline almost immediately. The Silver Age (15–140 A.D.) that followed the Golden had writers of keen intellect and graceful appeal, but the hardness of their outlook and the superficial brilliance of their style betray the corruption of society and the drying up of the Roman soul. Seneca (4 B.C.–65 A.D.) is the most typical and inclusive figure of them all. The tutor and adviser of Nero in some of the most shameful of his crimes, he grew wealthy and tried to retire from the treacherous political scene to a life of study and writing in his handsome villa, but Nero had him pursued and forced him to a stoic suicide. Despite his venality and his complicity in malodorous politics, Seneca thought of himself as a philosopher and wrote voluminously and seriously. His nine closet-dramas, of which the *Medea* is best known, are our only surviving Roman tragedies. But the most readable of his works are the little *Moral Epistles,* or informal essays, which are an urbane and delightful application of Stoicism to everyday life. It is perhaps an indictment of the empire that this brilliant but derivative thinker whose life reflects so little the pious morality of his preaching should have been its greatest philosopher.

Prose flourished in the Silver Age. The patriotic history of Livy (59 B.C.–17 A.D.) in the Augustan era gave way to the savage exposure of the evils of empire in the *Histories* and *Annals* of Tacitus (c. 55–c. 115 A.D.). Our grim impression of the irresponsible brutality of the imperial system stems very largely from this gloomy republican, who had the misfortune to live through the worst years of the Emperor Domitian. But the epigrammatic brilliance of his concentrated style makes Tacitus a master of prose. His condemnation of the Rome of his day is confirmed in the harsh verse satires of Juvenal, who also suffered through the last years of Domitian. Forced to grovel before wealthy patrons, Juvenal became a bitter pessimist and gives an appalling picture of the vices and cruelty of latter-day Rome. He is the undisputed master of verse satire, the one literary invention of Rome, and was widely imitated in our classical eighteenth century. His acquaintance, Martial, chose the neat and witty epigram for his picture of Roman life and presents in delightful snatches an equally cynical appraisal of his times.

Despite the rewards that his obsequious eulogies brought from Domitian, Martial remained discontented, and his impression of his age is no more trustworthy than the jaundiced views of Tacitus and Juvenal.

These were the last major writers of pagan Rome. The decline of her greatness in the chaotic third century is reflected in the decay of her artistic and intellectual life. But the period is one of confused transition to the Christian era of the fourth century, and the first Christian authors of Rome, Tertullian (c. 160–230) and St. Cyprian (c. 200–258), prepare the way for the great St. Augustine a century later. Much of classical Roman literature was to fall quickly into disrepute. St. Jerome in the fourth century scourged himself for his sinful interest in the writers of pagan Rome and dreamed that Christ appeared to deny him heaven because of his fondness for Cicero. Though the energetic Tertullian's mind is surprisingly reminiscent of Cicero, Tacitus, and even Juvenal, he attacked all of Roman literature as idolatrous and eventually rejected even the orthodox Church as insufficiently puritanical. The materialism of Lucretius, the eroticism of Catullus and Ovid, even the moderate epicureanism of Horace were to be eclipsed through many centuries of Christian orthodoxy. But one by one they reappeared in the Middle Ages, the Renaissance, and the Enlightenment to inspire new generations with their vigorous message out of the past.

ROME AND THE WESTERN TRADITION

THE Macedonian conquest did not destroy Greece. It had already grown weary and disillusioned before Alexander arrived, and yet it was to outlive him to Hellenize the Roman world for centuries. Nor was Rome destroyed by the Goths and Vandals who overran the empire in the fifth century. She too had been declining for three hundred years, if not indeed from the last years of the republic. But the Roman accomplishments had already merged with the rising tradition of Christianity, officially with Constantine's edict of 313 A.D., and were to be transmitted in a hundred ways through the Christian era to us.

From the Greeks Christianity absorbed the cult of the martyred and resurrected Dionysus, the mystical ethics of the Platonists, and Aristotle's system of knowledge. But Christian connections with Rome are still more striking. The Latin language became the Church Latin of the Roman Church and remains her universal medium of ritual and communication. The government of the pagan religion is duplicated in the organization of the Church to the very title and vestments of the *pontifex maximus*. Local cults throughout the Mediterranean world were countenanced by the Church in its early years and survive as Christian today. But most important is the continuing symbol of the city of Rome, which lost its political power to the barbarians but conquered their souls in return, and established its spiritual sway over a wider empire than Hadrian had ever dreamed of.

Though the Church may be the only place where Latin itself survives, the ancient tongue was corrupted through the Dark Ages into a half-dozen living languages—Italian, French, Spanish, Portuguese, Rumanian. Even the vocabulary of our Anglo-Saxon English owes a great deal to Latin. And our physicians, scientists, and lawyers find much of their special jargons in Latin phraseology. Throughout the Middle Ages and Renaissance, Latin was the universal speech of educated men in Europe, and when antiquity was rediscovered in its own terms

The Romans constructed aqueducts like this one at Segovia, Spain, throughout the empire.

in the fourteenth century, it was the Roman poets and philosophers who were first read and who first inspired imitation. The Greeks whom they in turn had imitated slumbered still in a language few could read. So we think of Mars, not Ares; Venus, not Aphrodite; Vulcan, not Hephaestus; Cupid, not Eros—reminders that Latin mythology honeycombs our poetry and is as much a part of Western heritage as the stories of the Bible. Imitation of Virgil, Plautus, and Juvenal may not be so common in our time as in the days of Spenser, Ben Jonson, and Pope, but their spirits have found a permanent place in English letters. In literature as in philosophy, architecture, and science, Rome was the carrier from Greece and the East, not the inspired inventor.

But transmitting culture is also a worthy service. In the field of law alone Rome was the great inventor. Through the thousand years from the birth of the republic to the Code of Justinian (529 A.D.) she experimented with democracy and monarchy and evolved a system of checks and balances through legislative and executive branches that survives in our own constitution. Law codes in Italy and France, Spain and Latin America, and our own Louisiana and Puerto Rico are still based on Roman law. Less directly it appears throughout the British Empire and the Mohammedan lands of the East. The law is the greatest glory of Rome, and with it she brought to the world a peace which we have long sought to revive.

Symbolic of the decay of Roman civilization is the ruined interior of the Colosseum at Rome. In the days of Rome's imperial greatness her citizens gathered here to greet their friends and to witness the circus entertainments.

Cicero

106–43 B.C.

The great Stoic philosophers, Epictetus and Marcus Aurelius, belong to the second century A.D., when the empire had begun to decay and Stoicism had become a kind of religion to be merged two centuries later with Christianity. But the stoic moral outlook had grown up with the republic and was well defined as the national ethics long before the Greek founders of Stoicism were known in Rome. Cicero, the perfect philosopher for the unphilosophical republic, thought of himself as the Roman Plato, but was really an eclectic whose moral outlook was chiefly Stoic. He rejected the violent metaphysics of Stoicism, as Romans in general ignored it, but his life and death illustrate the Roman brand of Stoic morality as clearly as his treatise on duty, *De Officiis*, summarizes it.

Marcus Tullius Cicero represents the dignified, able, conscientious Roman senator who built the empire by a stern but practical policy. Yet he was an equestrian, or middle-class man, born in the provincial town of Arpinum, seventy-five miles from Rome, and he won his way to the patrician class only by the force of his talent and integrity. After the military service required of every Roman citizen he studied philosophy with an Epicurean, a Stoic, and a Platonist, but his philosophical interests were always superficial, and his real abilities lay in rhetoric and law, which he mastered under Apollonius Molo of Rhodes. His ambitious wife, Terentia, urged him into public practice, where his oratory and honesty carried him through each step in the round of political offices—quaestor in 76, aedile in 69, praetor in 66, and consul in 63, in which year he reached the height of his career as leader of the state.

But these were troubled times for the republic, and Cicero's effort to unite all that was good in the opposed parties—his "concord of the orders"—was a conservative's dream that ignored the obvious decay of the old order that he idealized. He vacillated between Pompey and Caesar, eventually favored Pompey, but was later pardoned by Caesar. Under the dictatorship he retired from public life to pursue study and writing. His divorce of Terentia for a frivolous young woman, and the death of his beloved daughter, Tullia, clouded his later years and tried his stoic calm. The death of Caesar recalled him to public life as head of the government for one last year, but his fiery opposition to Mark Antony (preserved in fourteen speeches) cost him his life. Antony's soldiers overtook him as slaves were hurrying him to safety on a ship, and true to his stoic code he not only submitted but stretched his head out of his litter so that they might more easily behead him.

The works of Cicero were the best loved of classical prose until our grandfathers' day. Today he is less popular. His 58 surviving orations are admitted to be the greatest of their kind and perfect illustrations of his own treatises on public speaking; but oratory is out of fashion, and the rhetorical tricks and pragmatic insincerity of their rolling periods make them fall short of the greatest literature. His philosophical works are not of the first order. Cicero was, as he readily admitted, an industrious compiler of Greek philosophies rather than a creative thinker, and his great influence on later thought was as transmitter of the teachings of others. Being a typical Roman, he wrote much on political philosophy, but his *Republic* is merely an idealized picture of the Roman state modeled on the dialogue of Plato. His *Laws* applies the Stoic doctrine that reason sanctions law to existing Roman laws and others that Cicero favored. *On the Nature of the Gods* reviews the theology of various schools of philosophy, and the *De Finibus* does the same for their concepts of good and evil. *The Tusculan Disputations* treat superficially death and immortality.

The most readable and characteristic of his philosophical works, *De Officiis*, composed in 44 B.C., a year before his death, was written to strengthen the character of his worthless son. It is a collection of practical rules of conduct based on a lost treatise of the Stoic Panaetius and amounts to a code of behavior for the Roman gentleman. Book I treats duties as virtuous action, Book II considers expedient action, and Book III tries to reconcile the two. The ideal of Roman conduct is brilliantly summarized in this practical work on Stoic ethics, written in Cicero's most elegant style.

But we come closest to the man himself in his informal essays on friendship and old age and, above all, in his 800 surviving letters, carefully collected by his devoted freedman, Tiro. Written to his family, to his brother Quintus, to the conspirators Brutus and Cassius, to the millionaire philosopher Atticus, and other friends, they cover the last twenty-five years of his life but especially the last nine. They treat a wide variety of subjects, from national affairs to troubles in his own household. We get a day-to-day picture of Roman politics tempered with philosophical comments and literary criticism. Although some are formal in tone, the best are surprisingly intimate and reveal the true Cicero as a decent, human sort of man trying to preserve his integrity in a dangerous and chaotic age, a man sometimes cowardly, insufferably vain, yet industrious, honest, and able withal.

The Offices *Portrait of an ideal statesman*

DEAR Son Marcus. . . . Having resolved to write something at present, and a great many others hereafter to you, I thought I could begin on no better argument than that which is fittest for your age, and most becoming my authority as a father; for, of all those useful and important subjects, which philosophers have handled so largely and accurately, the precepts they have delivered about Offices or Duties seem of the largest

*The Offices.*³ Translated by Thomas Cockman.

extent and comprehension; for they take in every part of our lives, so that whatever we go about, whether of public or private affairs, whether at home or abroad, whether considered barely by ourselves, or as we stand in relation to other people, we lie constantly under an obligation to some duties: and as all the virtue and credit of our lives proceed from the due discharge of this, so all the baseness and turpitude of them result from the non-observance of the same. Now, though this be a subject which all philosophers have employed themselves about (for, who ever dared to assume that name without laying down some instructions about duty?), yet have some sects of them given such accounts of man's happiness and misery, as destroy the very being of virtue and honesty: for he that makes any thing his chiefest good, wherein justice or virtue does not bear a part, and sets up profit, not honesty, for the measure of his happiness; as long as he acts in conformity with his own principles, and is not overruled by the mere dictates of reason and humanity, can never do the offices of friendship, justice, or liberality: nor can he ever be a man of courage, who thinks that pain is the greatest evil; or he of temperance, who imagines pleasure to be the sovereign good. Which things are all so obvious and plain, that one would think they could never stand in need of a dispute. . . . These sects, therefore, unless they are resolved to be inconsistent with themselves, ought wholly to abstain from speaking anything about duties; nor indeed can any constant, unalterable, rational rules of them at all be given, unless it be by those who go on this principle—that it is virtue alone, or at least that chiefly, which ought to be desired for its own sake. So that only the Stoics, Academics, and Peripatetics, have a right to lay down any rules on this subject. . . . I shall follow therefore at this time, and on this subject more especially, the Stoics; not as a bare translator of them, but, according to my usual custom, shall take out of their stores so much, and after such a manner, as in my own judgement I shall think most convenient. . . .

III. The whole subject of duties, in its greatest latitude, comprehends under it these two parts: the first is taken up in explaining what is good, and what our greatest good; the second in certain directions and precepts, according to which on all occasions it is our duty to govern our lives and actions. To the first part belong such questions as these, whether all duties are perfect or not? and, whether one can be greater or less than another? with several others to the same purpose. Not but that the duties of this second part, the rules and precepts of which are laid down, have some tendency and relation to our chiefest good; but only it does not so plainly appear, because they seem to concern more immediately the government of our lives and regulation of our manners; and these are they which I design to explain in the following treatise. . . .

IV. The first thing to be taken notice of is this, that every creature doth by nature endeavour to preserve its own self, its life and body; and to shun and avoid those things which appear prejudicial and hurtful to it; but to seek and procure whatever is necessary for the support of its being, and advancement of its happiness, such as food, shelter, and the like. There is likewise common to all sorts of animals a desire for the continuance and propagation of their several species; together with a love and concern for their young ones. Now there is this special difference between men and brutes; that the latter are governed by nothing but their senses, never look any farther than just to what strikes and affects them at present, and have a very little, or hardly any concern, for what is past or to come: but the former are creatures endowed with reason, whch gives them a power to carry their thoughts to the consequences of things, to discover causes before they have yet produced their effects; to see the whole progress, and even the first seeds, as it were, and appearances of them; to compare like occurrences with like, and by joining what is past and what is to come together, to make a just estimate of the one from the other; whereby they are able at once to take a view of their whole lives, and accordingly to make provision for the necessities of them. . . . But of all the properties and inclinations of men, there is none more natural and peculiar to them than an earnest desire and search after truth. Hence it is that our minds are no sooner free from the thoughts and engagements of necessary business, but we presently long to be either seeing, or hearing, or learning of something; and esteem the knowledge of things secret and wonderful as a necessary ingredient of a happy life. Whence it appears that nothing is more agreeable and suited to the nature and minds of men than undisguised openness, truth, and sincerity. Next to this love and affection for truth, there follows in the soul an impatient desire and inclination to pre-eminence; so that whoever has the genuine nature of a man in him, will never endure to be subject to another, unless he be one that instructs or advises, or is invested with a just and lawful authority for the benefit of the public: whence there arises a greatness of soul, which sets it above all the petty concerns and trifling enjoyments of this present world. It is another, and that too no mean prerogative of our reasonable nature, that man alone can discern all the beauties of order and decency, and knows how to govern his words and actions in conformity to them. It is he alone that, of all the creatures, observes and is pleased with the beauty, gracefulness, and symmetry of parts in the objects of sense; which nature and reason observing in them, from thence take occasion

Marginal notes: Typical Roman sentiment; Epicurus; Epicurus; Stoics; Eclecticism; self preservation; stiff between men and animals; Truth; Basis of social justice; Freedom; Beauty; never endure to be subject

honestus — honor, decorum

to apply the same also to those of the mind; and to conclude that beauty, consistency, and regularity, should be much more kept up in our words and actions; and therefore command us, that nothing be done that is effeminate or unbecoming; and that so strict a guard be kept over every thought and action, as that no indecency be either conceived or practised by us. From these inclinations and instincts of nature arises and results that honesty we are seeking for; which, however little valued and esteemed it may be, is nevertheless virtuous and amiable in itself; and which we may justly say, though it were commended by no one, is yet in its own nature truly commendable.

V. Thus, son Marcus, have I given you a rough draught, and just the outlines, as it were, of honesty; which, could she be seen in her full beauty with mortal eye, would make the whole world (as Plato has said) be in love with wisdom. Now whatever is contained under the notion of honesty arises from one of these four heads; first, a sagacious inquiry and observation for the finding out of truth, which may be called by the general name of prudence: secondly, a care to maintain that society and mutual intercourse which is between them; to render to every man what is his due; and to stand to one's words in all promises and bargains; which we call justice: thirdly, the greatness and unshaken resolution of a truly brave and invincible mind, which goes by the name of magnanimity or fortitude: and lastly, a keeping of our words and actions within the due limits of order and decency; under which are comprehended temperance and moderation. . . .

VI. First, of Prudence, which is wholly taken up in the knowledge of truth, and has the nearest affinity of any with the reasonable nature of man. For how are we all of us drawn and enticed with the desire of wisdom! how noble and glorious a thing do we imagine it to excel in knowledge! and how mean and reproachful do we count it, on the other hand, to slip, to be in error, to be ignorant, or to be imposed on? In gratifying this so natural and virtuous inclination in the mind of man, there are two grand faults to be carefully avoided: the first is an over-great hastiness and rashness in giving up our assent, presuming that we know things before we really do so. Whoever desires (as I am sure all ought) to avoid this error, must in all his inquiries allow himself time, and diligently consider the matter with himself, before he proceeds to pass his judgement on it. The second fault is, that a great many men bestow abundance of study, and a world of pains, on very difficult and obscure subjects; and such as, perhaps, when they are found out, are of but very little, or no concernment. Would men but be careful to shun these two mistakes, whatever study or pains they might spend on virtuous, worthy,

or profitable subjects, it would not without reason be highly commended. . . . In a word, the general aim and design of our thought, and application of mind, is either the attainment of such things as are honest, and tend to a virtuous and happy way of life, or else the improvement of our reason and understanding in wisdom and knowledge. And this may suffice for the first of our general heads of duty.

VII. Of the other remaining three, that which consists in upholding society, and keeping up mutual love and good nature amongst mankind, seems of the largest and most diffusive extent. It comprehends under it these two parts: first, justice, which is much the most glorious and splendid of all virtues, and alone entitles us to the name and appellation of good men; and, secondly, beneficence, which may also be called either bounty or liberality. Now the first thing that justice requires of us is this; that no one should do any hurt to another, unless by way of reasonable and just retribution for some injury received from him: and whatever belongs either to all in common, or particular persons as their own property, should not be altered, but made use of accordingly. Now no man can say that he has anything his own by a right of nature; but either by an ancient immemorial seizure, as those who first planted uninhabited countries; or, secondly, by conquest, as those who have got things by the right of the sword; or else by some law compact, agreement, or lot. It is by some of these means that the people inhabiting Arpinum and Tusculum came to have those lands, which are now called theirs; and the same may be said as to private men's estates. However, since at present, by some of these ways, each particular man has his personal possessions, out of that which by nature was common to all, it is but just that each should hold what is now his own; which, if any one endeavour to take away from him, he directly breaks in on common justice, and violates the rights of human society. . . .

Now the great foundation of justice is faithfulness, which consists in being constantly firm to your word, and a conscientious performance of all compacts and bargains. The vice that is opposite to justice is injustice, of which there are two sorts: the first consists in the actual doing an injury to another; the second, in tamely looking on while he is injured, and not helping and defending him though we are able: for he that injuriously falls on another, whether prompted by rage or other violent passion, does as it were leap at the throat of his companion; and he that refuses to help him when injured, and to ward off the wrong if it lies in his power, is as plainly guilty of baseness and injustice as though he had deserted his father, his friends, or his native country. Now that former injustice, which consists in the wilful and actual wronging another, has oftentimes

Requirements of honor

social virtues

Origin of private ownership

fidelity

Injustice by action and omission

Things to be avoided
(a) Presumption of knowledge
(b) Pedantry

no other cause but fear; when he, who designedly does a man an injury, is afraid lest himself should be forced to undergo one, if he does not secure himself by doing it beforehand. But, generally speaking, the great source and fountain of all such injustice is the satisfying some irregular and exorbitant appetite; and in a more especial manner, the desire of riches; of which we shall therefore say something in particular.

10 VIII. Riches then are most commonly desired, either to supply us with the necessaries of life, or furnish us with the pleasures and conveniences of it; or else, as it often is observed to happen in persons of great and aspiring minds, as a means of obtaining an interest in the public, and a power of obliging and gratifying one's friends; to which purpose was that saying of the late Marcus Crassus, that whoever designed to be a leading man in the commonwealth, ought never to think he had estate enough, till he 20 could maintain an army with its yearly revenue. Others take pleasure in splendour and magnificence, in a handsome, noble, and plentiful way of living: all which things have begot an insatiable greediness after money, without which they can never be supported and maintained. Not but that a moderate desire of riches, and bettering a man's estate, so long as it abstains from oppressing of others, is allowable enough; but a very great care ought always to be taken that we be not drawn to any injustice by it. 30 There is another desire that makes men as apt to be forgetful of justice, as that after riches; the thirst, I mean, of empire, glory, honours, etc. For that saying of Ennius, "There is no inviolable faith or friendship in the matter of a kingdom;" though applied by him to that one case only, is yet fully as true in a great many others; for wherever the subject of contention is such, as that only one party can meet with success, and the rest must fall short of what they desire; things are usually carried to so great 40 a height, as that it is very difficult not to break in on faith and friendship. This hath appeared but too manifestly of late, in that rash and most impudent attempt of Caesar's; who has broken through all those ties and obligations, that either by gods or men could be laid on him, for the compassing and getting of that dominion to himself, which he had vainly proposed in his depraved imagination. But in this case, it is one very great unhappiness, that the thirst after honour, empire, power, etc., falls most on men 50 of the greatest souls and most exalted natures; wherefore the greater care ought to be taken that nothing of offence be committed in this kind. Now it makes a great difference in all acts of justice, whether they proceed from some violent passion, which is for the most part of short continuance, or

17. **Marcus Crassus**, the third member of the first Triumvirate, notorious for his love of wealth.

are done with design and previous deliberation: for those that are the effects of a sudden gust of passion ought not to be esteemed of so heinous a nature, as those that proceed from premeditated malice. And this may suffice for the first sort of injustice, which 60 consists in the actual doing of wrong, and the causes of it.

IX. As for the second, which only consists in seeing another injured, and being wanting to our duty, by not defending him; the causes of that are wont to be several: for some are afraid of offending others, or of bringing a trouble and charge on themselves: others are negligent, idle, or mean-spirited: and a third sort there is, who are so taken up with their own concerns, that they have no time left to regard 70 the oppressed, whom yet it is their duty to save and protect. I am therefore of opinion, that Plato's consequence will hardly hold good where, speaking about the philosophers, he says, "They are wholly taken up in the seeking out of truth, and perfectly neglect and make light of those things which the rest of the world are so eager after, and so contend about; and that therefore they are just." This, I say, I am afraid is a bad consequence; for though, it is true, they keep the first sort of justice, inasmuch as 80 they actually do no wrong; yet they run perfectly counter to the other; for being engaged in their learning and studies, they abandon their friends to be injured by others, whom in justice they ought to have protected and defended. So that it is believed they hardly ever trouble themselves so far, as at all to intermeddle with the business of the public, if it was not altogether, as it were, forced on them. But it were a great deal better would they do it voluntarily; for an action, though honest, is not therefore 90 truly virtuous, unless it be done out of choice, and with a good will. There are others yet, who out of a desire of improving their own estates, or else a morose and unsociable sort of temper, cry, they meddle with nobody's business but their own, that so they may seem to be men of strict honesty, and to injure nobody; and they do indeed avoid the one sort of injustice, but directly run themselves into the other; for they desert the common good and society of mankind, while they bestow neither study, pains, 100 nor money toward the preservation of it. . . .

XI. There are certain duties also to be strictly observed, even towards those that have injured us; for we ought not to go beyond certain bounds, in exacting revenge and punishment of another: in which particular it may, perhaps, be enough to make him that has wronged us repent of the wrong done; so that both he himself may abstain from the like, and others may be discouraged from injuring us for the future. There are certain peculiar laws of war 110 also, which are of all things most strictly to be observed in the commonwealth; for there being two

Wars –
1. Self preservation
2. military glory

Keeping faith

Treatment of slaves

Force

Fraud

hypocrisy

Liberality
1. Not injurious to anyone
2. Not beyond means
3. According to desert

sorts of disputing in the world, the one by reason, and the other by open force; and the former of these being that which is agreeable to the nature of man, and the latter to that of brutes; when we cannot obtain what is our right by the one, we must of necessity have recourse to the other. It is allowable therefore to undertake wars, but it must always be with design of obtaining a secure peace: and when we have got the better of our enemies, we should rest content with the victory alone, and show ourselves merciful and kind to them afterwards, unless they are such as have been very cruel, and committed inhuman barbarities in the war. Thus our forefathers took into their city the Aequians, Volscians, Sabines, and others whom they had subdued; whereas Carthage and Numantia they entirely destroyed. I could wish I might not add Corinth too; but I believe they had something in their eye when they did it, and more especially the situation of the place; which, being so very convenient as it was, they were afraid lest it might be at one time or other an encouragement to revolt. In my opinion it is always our duty to do what we can for a fair and safe peace; in which thing, if people would have hearkened unto me, we might at this time have seen the republic, though, it is true, I cannot say in a flourishing condition, yet certainly not as at present we perceive it, entirely subverted and fallen into ruins. As we are bound to be merciful to those whom we have actually conquered; so should those also be received into favour, who have laid down their arms, and thrown themselves wholly on the general's mercy; and that even though the breach be made in their city walls. . . .

XII. We have told you already what previous causes and conditions there should be, before any war can be lawful and just; the same are required even in those wars also, which are undertaken merely for glory and empire; but then all contests of this latter sort should be carried on with less heat and animosities; for as in the differences that happen among citizens, we make a distinction between a violent enemy and a generous rival, in one case nothing but a title of honour, in the other our lives and reputations being concerned; so did our ancestors do in their wars. That which they waged with the Cimbers and Celtibers, was managed as with hateful and implacable enemies; the question then being, not whether of the two should remain a conqueror, but whether should remain a people at all; whereas those with the Latins, Carthaginians, Pyrrhus, etc., were only quarrels about honour and dominion. The Carthaginians were perfidious and treacherous; Hannibal, their great commander, cruel; but all the rest more faithful and merciful. . . .

XIII. It is also the duty of particular persons, if at any time forced by the necessity of their circumstances, they have made any promise or oath to an enemy, afterwards to see that they perform it faithfully. Thus Regulus was taken in the first Punic war by the Carthaginians, and sent by them to Rome about an exchange of prisoners, on solemn oath given that he would return to them again: first, then, as soon as he was come to Rome, he advised the senate against making such an exchange, and when he had done so, though begged on to stay by his friends and relations, rather returned to a certain punishment than his oath should be broken, though made to an enemy. . . . But the greatest example of justice to an enemy was shown by our ancestors towards king Pyrrhus. There came a deserter out of Pyrrhus' camp, and offered the senate to despatch him with poison; which they and Fabricius were so far from accepting of, that they gave him up again as a traitor to his master. Thus we may see, that they would not allow any unjust way of dealing, though for the death of a powerful and invading adversary: and so much for the duties required in war. There is one part of justice remaining behind, and which ought by no means to be forgotten by us; I mean that towards the lowest and meanest sort of people: and these are more especially those we call our slaves; in relation to whom, it is a very good rule that is given by some men, that we should use them no otherwise than we do our day-labourers, make them first do their work, and then pay them honestly what they have earned. In fine, to close up this discourse of justice, there are two ways or methods whereby one man may injure or oppress another; the one is fraud and subtlety, the other open force and violence; the former of which is esteemed the part of a fox, and the latter of a lion; both of them certainly very unworthy of a reasonable creature, though fraud, I think, is the more odious of the two. But of all injustice, theirs is certainly of the deepest die, who make it their business to appear honest men, even whilst they are practising the greatest of villainies.

XIV. We have now gone through with the subject of justice; it remains, in the next place, to go on according to our method proposed, that we say something likewise of bounty and liberality, than which there is nothing more nearly allied to the nature of man. But then we must observe these following cautions—first, that we take care in all acts of bounty, that they be not prejudicial to those we would oblige by them, nor to any other body; secondly, that we do not in our bounty and liberality go beyond our estates; and, thirdly, that we duly proportion our kindness, according to every man's merit and deserts. And first of the former, which is grounded on the great and fundamental principle of all justice, to which this duty in all its particular instances should be referred—for he who, pretending to do one a kindness, does that which is really a prejudice to him, is indeed so far from being kind and obliging, as that he ought to be counted a most pernicious flatterer; and to do any manner of injury to one, that you may show your generosity and bounty to another, is just one and the same sort of roguery and injustice, as to enrich yourself by the spoils of your neighbour. . . . That action therefore of Caesar and Sylla's, in taking away estates from the rightful proprietors, and giving them to others, who had no right to them, ought by no means to be accounted liberal; for nothing can ever be truly such that is not at the same time just and honest. A second caution to be observed was this: that our bounty be not suffered to exceed our abilities; for they who give more than their estates will allow of, are, in the first place, injurious to their own relations, by spending that wealth on other people which should rather have been given or left to them. Beside that this over-great bounty in giving is usually accompanied with an answerable desire and greediness of getting; which often proceeds even to downright oppression, that so men may have wherewithal to supply this extravagant humour. One may also observe in a great many people, that they take a sort of pride in being counted magnificent, and give very plentifully, not from any generous principle in their natures, but only to appear great in the eye of the world; so that all their bounty is resolved into nothing but mere outside pretence, and is nearer of kin to vanity and folly, than it is to either liberality or honesty. The third caution was, that our bounty should be proportioned to the merits of the receiver; in judging of which, we are first to consider the man's honesty or manners; secondly, the good-will he bears towards us; thirdly, the nearness of relation, or society that is between us; and, lastly, the benefits we have formerly received from him. It is desirable that all these inducements might concur in the same person; but when they do not, we should bestow our kindness more especially on him, in whom we find the most and weightiest of them. . . .

Roman politicians. From a painting from Pompeii.

XVI. There is such a thing as a fellowship or society between all men in general: the bond or cement that holds this together is reason and discourse, which, by teaching, learning, communicating one with another, etc., easily make men agree together, and unite them all in one natural sort of conjunction and community: nor does anything set us at a greater distance from the nature of beasts; for we oftentimes talk of the courage of them, such as lions and horses; but never a word of their equity, justice, or goodness: and why is this, but because they are destitute of reason and discourse? This is then the largest and most comprehensive of all societies, being made up of men considered barely as such, and so taking in even the whole race and kind of them one with another; the duties of which are, to let every one have a share in those things which by nature were produced for the common advantage and benefit of all; to let what is already determined by laws and civil constitutions remain as it is, without breaking in on any man's rights; as to which things, however, we should remember a rule, which is now among the Greeks become a usual proverb, "All things in common amongst friends.". . .

XVII. But there are several degrees of society and fellowship amongst mankind; for to take now our leave of that general and universal one already mentioned, there is a nearer among those who are all of the same country, nation, or language, than which nothing more knits and unites men to one another. There is a closer yet among those who are all of the same city; for a great many things are in common to fellow-citizens, such as markets, temples, walks, ways, laws, privileges, courts of justice, freedom of votes, besides common meetings and familiarities, and abundance of business and intercourse with one another. But there is a stricter bond of alliance still between those who belong to the same family, as taking into it but a very small part of that vast and immense one of all mankind. The closest and nearest of all societies is between man and wife; then follows that between them and their children, and afterwards that of the whole family, who inhabit together and have all things in common; which is, as it were, the first beginning of a city, and ground or seed-plot of a whole commonwealth. . . . But when we have gone over all the relations that are in the world, and thoroughly considered the nature of each, we shall find that there is no one of greater obligation, no one that is dearer and nearer to us, than that which we all of us bear to the public. We have a tender concern and regard for our parents, for our children, our kindred, and acquaintance, but the love which we have for our native country swallows up all other loves whatsoever; for which there is no honest man but would die, if by his death he could do it any necessary service. How detestable, then, must the wickedness and barbarity of those people be, who have mangled and rent this their native country by all manner of villanies, and have made it their business (nay, and still do so) to bring it to ruin and utter desolation. Now if there should happen any contest or competition between these relations, which of them should have the greatest share of our duty, we should pay the first regard to our country and parents, from whom we have received the most endearing obligations; the next to our children and family, who all have their eyes on us alone, and have nobody else on whom they can depend; next in order to these come our kindred and relations, whose fortune is generally the same with our own. . . .

XVIII. It is to be observed, that whereas there were laid down four general heads, from which all virtue and honesty is derived, whatever proceeds from a brave and exalted mind, that is raised above fortune and all the little chances and accidents of the world, is usually made most account of amongst men. . . .

XIX. Fortitude is very well defined by the Stoic philosophers, when they call it "a virtue contending for justice and honesty." No man, by baseness and treachery, has ever got the name and reputation of true courage; for nothing can ever be virtuous or creditable that is not just. . . . The first thing therefore I would have in a truly courageous man is, that he be a follower of goodness and fair dealing, of truth and sincerity; which are the principal and constituent parts of justice. But here it is one very unhappy thing, that, most times, these great and exalted minds are naturally ungovernable and desirous of rule: so that what Plato observed of the Spartans, that all their customs had no other aim but to get the superiority, may fitly enough be applied to these persons: for the more any man has of this greatness of soul, the more eager he is of being a sharer in the government, or rather of obtaining it wholly to himself: and it is no easy matter to be fair and equitable in all one's actions, which is the proper and peculiar office of justice, while one is endeavoring to make himself uppermost. Hence it comes to pass, that they never will be conquered in any debates, nor overruled by the laws and constitutions of the public; but make it their business, by factions and bribery, to get a strong party and interest in the republic; and rather choose to be uppermost by force and injustice, than equal to others by fair and upright dealing. But the difficulty of it can only serve to make it more honourable, but never its contrary more excusable: for no sort of case or circumstance whatever can excuse any man for be-

ing guilty of injustice. Those are therefore your truly brave and courageous men, not who rob, plunder, and injure others, but those who secure and protect them from injuries. But that greatness of mind which is truly such, and, under the direction of wisdom and prudence, makes that honour and credit, which we naturally desire, not consist in the outward imaginary applause, but in the real intrinsic goodness of its actions; and is not so eager of appearing to be greater and better than others, as of really being so: for he that is so mean as to depend on the giddy and ignorant multitude, ought never to be accounted of a truly great and exalted spirit; besides that, there is nothing so easily draws men to acts of injustice as a loftiness of mind, when joined with this foolish desire of applause. This is indeed a very dangerous place, and requires our greatest concern and watchfulness; because you shall hardly find any man, who, when he has gone through labours and difficulties, does not expect this honour and applause, as a kind of reward for his courage and achievements.

XX. . . . The desire of glory, robs a man wholly of his freedom and liberty, which generous spirits ought of all things in the world to maintain and contend for. Neither ought places of power to be sought after; but at some times rather to be refused when offered, at others to be laid down if they can conveniently. We should free ourselves, in short, from all vehement passions and disorders of mind, not only those of desire and fear, but also of sorrow, of joy, and anger; that so the state of the mind may be calm and undisturbed; which will make the whole life become graceful and uniform. Now there both are and have been many, who, to gain this repose of which I am speaking, have betaken themselves to a life of retirement, and wholly withdrawn from all business of the public. Among these the noblest and most eminent of the philosophers; and some men of rigid and severe lives, who disliked the manners of the people or their governors; others have withdrawn themselves into the country, being pleased with the management of their own private fortunes. These men proposed the same end to themselves that kings and princes do, viz. the living so as to want for nothing; to be under the power and control of none, but to enjoy a full and perfect freedom; which consists in living so as one's self best pleases.

XXI. . . . One can hardly condemn them, in that they despise, and make little account of glory and applause; but their true reason seems to be rather this, that they do not care to suffer the labour and fatigue of them, and are afraid of encountering with rubs and repulses, as things that are attended with some shame and dishonour: for you shall often find there are a great many men, who are very inconsistent with themselves in things of a contrary nature: as for pleasure, they despise it with all the severity of a

1–5. **those people . . . desolation,** an allusion to Julius Caesar and Marc Antony.

Stoic; but yet are so effeminate, as not to be able to bear the least trouble; are mighty contemners of fame and applause; but extremely concerned at anything of disgrace: which are things that do not very well agree together. Those people then, whom Nature has endowed with abilities for that purpose, should forthwith endeavour to procure themselves places, and manage the business of the commonwealth; otherwise how should the city be well governed, or the greatness of their endowments be made known to the world? But that greatness of soul, and contempt of all human things, which we have often mentioned, together with that calmness and serenity of mind, is requisite in those of a public station, as much, if not more than it is in philosophers, if ever they hope to be free from anxieties, and arrive at any steadiness or uniformity in their lives. Now these things are easier to philosophers than to them; forasmuch as their lives being led in private, require for their support a less number of things, and have fewer within the power and reach of fortune: and if any ill accident should befall them, it is impossible their sufferings can be very considerable. Those men, therefore, that are in public stations, having things of more weight and importance to be taken care of, must in reason be supposed to lie much more open to the assaults of the passions than those who spend their days in privacy and retirement. On which account they should take the more care to fortify themselves with this greatness of spirit. . . .

XXIII. On the whole, that virtue which consists in greatness and elevation of soul, and makes up the subject of our present inquiry, is obtained by the strength of the mind, not the body: however, the body ought not to be neglected, but by exercise brought to such a frame and condition, as that it may be able to obey the prescriptions of the mind, in performing that business, and bearing those fatigues which are required of it. But still the nature of the virtue we are seeking for, consists in due care and application of mind; in which particular, the public receives as much benefit from gownmen, who manage and take care of its civil concerns, as it doth from soldiers, who are generals of its armies: for they by their prudence have often either hindered the breaking out of wars, or else have occasioned their speedy conclusion; and sometimes too have been the cause of their being undertaken, as the third with Carthage was entered into on the advice of Cato, whose credit and authority prevailed in that case even after he was dead. Wisdom, therefore, and skill in determining civil affairs, is more to be desired than courage in fighting: but then we must always be careful in this case that our design be not the avoiding of war, but the being more useful and serviceable to the public. . . .

XXV. Those who design to be partakers in the government should be sure to remember those two precepts of Plato; first, to make the safety and interest of their citizens the great aim and design of all their thoughts and endeavours, without ever considering their own personal advantage; and, secondly, so to take care of the whole collective body of the republic, as not to serve the interest of any one party, to the prejudice or neglect of all the rest: for the government of a state is much like the office of a guardian or trustee; which should always be managed for the good of the pupil, and not of the persons to whom he is entrusted; and those men who, whilst they take care of one, neglect or disregard another part of the citizens, do but occasion sedition and discord, the most destructive things in the world to a state: whence it comes to pass, that while some take part with the popular faction, and others make their court to every great one, there are but very few left who are concerned for the benefit and good of the whole. From this root have sprung many grievous dissensions amongst the Athenians; and not only tumults, but even destructive civil wars in our own republic; things which a worthy and truly brave citizen, and one who deserves to hold the reins of the government, will shun and detest; and will give himself so to the service of the public, as to aim at no riches or power for himself; and will so take care of the whole community, as not to pass over any one part of it. . . .

XXVI. Another great duty of fortitude is, not to be haughty, disdainful, and arrogant when Fortune favours us, and all things go forward according to our wishes: for it shows as much meanness and poorness of spirit to be transported with good, as it does with ill fortune; whereas, on the other hand, nothing is more brave than an evenness of temper in every condition, and (as is reported of Socrates and Laelius) a constant retaining the same air in one's countenance, without ever seeming puffed up or dejected. I find that Philip, the king of Macedonia, was inferior to his son in the outward glory and splendour of his achievements, but very far above him in good nature and condescension: therefore the father kept always the character of a great person, whereas the son often was guilty of base and dishonourable actions. It is a good rule therefore, I think, which is given by some men, that the higher our station in the world is, the more care we should take of our lives and actions, that they be kept within the compass of lowliness and humility. . . . Whoever observes these measures laid down, let his way of life be either public or private, may perform all the duties of magnanimity, constancy, and greatness of soul, as well as of sincerity, fidelity, and doing good to mankind.

XXVII. We are now in the next place to speak of the fourth, and only remaining part of virtue or honesty, under which are comprehended temperance, modesty, government of the passions, and the observing a just order as to time and place in our words and actions; from all which arises a certain engaging kind of beauty and gracefulness, which serves to set off and adorn our lives. Under this head is contained that becomingness, which is in its nature so closely united and riveted to honesty, that there is no way left of pulling them asunder; for whatever is becoming is likewise honest, and whatever is honest is likewise becoming. The difference between them is so very small, that we may better conceive what it is, than explain it; for whatever becomingness there is in any action, it immediately arises from the honesty of it. From hence it appears that becomingness does not peculiarly belong to this one part of honesty, whereof we are now undertaking to discourse, but shows itself also in each of the three former. To reason, for instance, and discourse according to the rules of prudence; to go about nothing but after due consideration, and on every occasion to be quick at espying and defending the truth, are things that are becoming; whereas to be deceived, to be in an error or mistake, and to be imposed on, are very unbecoming, as well as to be mad or beside oneself. So again, all actions of justice are becoming; but those of injustice are both scandalous and unbecoming. The same may be said as to the actions of fortitude: whatever is done with a manly courage and bravery of mind, as it is worthy of, so it becomes a man. . . .

XXVIII. Nature has given every one of us a character, by endowing us with that nobleness and excellence of being, whereby we are set above all other creatures; a character of temperance and modesty, of constancy and moderation. And the same Nature having also taught us that we ought to be careful of our carriage and demeanour towards the rest of men, hence it appears of how large an extent that becomingness is, which belongs to the nature of honesty in general, and also that other, which is seen in the exercise of the several kinds of it: for as the beauty and comeliness of the body draws the eyes to it by the fit composure of all its members, and pleases us only on this account, because all its parts correspond with a kind of proportion and harmony; so this decorum, which gives a sort of lustre and grace to our lives, engages the approbation and esteem of all we live with, by that just and due order, consistency, and regularity, which it keeps up and maintains in our words and actions. . . .

XXIX. Every action therefore should be free, as from precipitancy and rashness on the one hand, so from all carelessness and negligence on the other; nor should anything be done, for which we cannot give a sufficient reason; which is almost the very definition of duty. In order to this the passions must be brought under the power of reason, so as neither through hastiness to run before its orders, nor through coldness and heaviness to disregard them when given; but all their motions must be so quieted and restrained, as to bring no uneasiness or disturbance to the mind: and from this calm and peaceable state of the soul arises that constancy and moderation we have mentioned; for when once the passions grow unruly and extravagant, and refuse to be guided in their desires and aversions by the rules of prudence, they will run without question beyond all bounds and measure; for they abandon and cast off their allegiance to reason, which they ought to obey by the constitution of nature. By this means are all things turned topsy-turvy; and not the mind only, but even the body also, put very much into disorder and confusion. Do but mark those who are inflamed with a vehement anger or desire; who are transported with fear, or an over-great joy; and you will see an alteration in their countenances, voices, gestures, and all their actions; which sufficiently gives us to understand (that we may return again to the duty now before us) how necessary it is to restrain and give check to the movements of the appetite, and to be always watchful and standing on our guard, that so we may neither be careless and inconsiderate, nor do anything rashly and at all adventures: for mankind were never designed by Nature merely to sport and idle away their time, but to follow after grave and serious studies, and business of greater importance than play is. Not but that jesting and diversion are allowable, provided we use them but as we do sleep, and other such necessary refreshments of nature, viz. after the discharge of our serious and more important duties. And even then we must see that our jesting be neither excessive nor immodest, but such as is handsome and becoming a gentleman; for as boys are allowed not all kinds of sports, but only such as have nothing that is vicious or ill in them; so in this jesting we should allow ourselves nothing but what is agreeable to honesty and good manners. We may therefore observe that jesting or merriment is of two sorts: the one clownish, abusive, scandalous, and obscene; the other handsome, genteel, ingenious, and truly pleasant. . . .

XXX. But in all inquiries concerning what becomes us, it is of very great moment to be constantly reflecting how much man's nature excels that of beasts and inferior animals. These have no taste or relish for anything but the pleasures of the body, towards which they are carried with a great deal of eagerness; whereas nothing is more agreeable and nourishing, as it were, to the mind of man, than learning and contemplation. Hence he is always seeking or contriving something that is new, and is greatly delighted with seeing and hearing, for the increase of his knowledge: and if there is any one too much addicted to sensual pleasures, unless he is transformed into a mere brute; (for some such there are, who are men in name, and not in reality) but if, I say, any one is too much addicted, and suffers himself to be conquered by pleasure; yet, for very shame, he will hide and conceal his propensities towards it as much as possible. And what is this now but a plain indication that sensual pleasures are unbecoming the dignity of a reasonable creature, and ought to be despised and rejected by him? and that whoever sets any value on them should be sure to take care that he keep within the limits of reason and moderation? Hence it follows that we should not have any respect to pleasure, but only to the preservation of our health and strength, in our victuals, clothes, and other conveniences belonging to the body. And does not the consideration of the same dignity and excellence of our natures plainly inform us how base and unworthy a thing it is to dissolve in luxury, softness, and effeminacy; and how brave and becoming it is, on the other hand, for a man to lead a life of frugality and temperance, of strictness and sobriety? And here we must observe that Nature has given us, as it were, a double part to be acted in the world: the first is extended to all men in common, forasmuch as we are all of us partakers of reason, and that prerogative of our nature, whereby we are exalted above other animals; it is this that conducts us in the finding out our duty, and from it all honesty and becomingness arises: the second is appropriate to each in particular; for as there is a great deal of difference in bodies, some being nimble and proper for running, others more lusty, and fitter for wrestling; some of a noble and majestic air, others of a sweet and engaging kind of beauty: so there is no less, or rather a far greater variety in humours. . . .

XXXI. The more easily then to arrive at that decorum of which we are speaking, let every one stick to his own peculiar character and humour, provided it has nothing that is vicious in it: I say, provided it has nothing that is vicious in it; for we should always take particular care to do nothing that is contrary to that universal character which Nature has imprinted on every one of us; but, saving the reverence we owe to that, then to live according to our own particular one, so as to follow after that kind of study, and apply ourselves to that course of life which is most suitable and agreeable to our own inclinations, though others perhaps may be more useful and important; for it is in vain to struggle against the bias of your nature, or to engage in that sort of business in which you can never arrive at any perfection. From what has been said it more fully appears what that is which we call becoming; since nothing can be such that is done, as we say, in despite of nature, i.e. contrary to the bent and tendency of a man's genius. Now it is certain, if anything

in the world is becoming, it is a constant uniformity in our whole lives and particular actions; which it is utterly impossible we should ever maintain, so long as we run counter to our own inclinations, and foolishly follow after those of other people: for as we should use our own native language, which all are supposed to understand best, and not lard our talk, as a great many do, with expressions out of Greek, who are therefore deservedly laughed at by others; so we should keep to one constant tenor and regular conduct in our lives and actions, so that nothing may be in them which is not well suited and of a piece with the rest.

Lucretius

c. 99–c. 55 B.C.

Epicurean philosophy was never so popular in Rome as Stoicism, but in the first century B.C. it did produce a modest school, and the greatest of all philosophical poets, Lucretius. Epicurus himself (341–270 B.C.) wrote voluminously, but only three of his philosophical letters, a brief summary of his doctrines, and some fragments have survived. It was his passionate Roman disciple, Lucretius, who converted his matter-of-fact prose into the persuasive form of magnificent poetry.

Titus Lucretius Carus is known to us through only one work. His birth and death dates are doubtful; yet it is clear from his poem that he lived through the chaotic last years of the republic and turned for spiritual peace to nature and philosophy. He apparently came from an obscure branch of an ancient family and addressed his poem as a social inferior to a minor political figure named Memmius. This great work received next to no recognition until centuries later.

It is the metaphysical system of Epicurus that Lucretius sets forth in *Of the Nature of Things*, although his ethical view of pleasure as the end of living can be inferred from the tone and details of the whole. He tells us with a disorderly enthusiasm how epicureanism has enabled him to live happily without religion in the harsh and disillusioning world of men. Although he begins with a beautiful invocation of Venus, he promptly denounces religion as superstition and proposes to show how a philosophical understanding of the universe can free men from fear of the gods and death and make them happy.

His view of things is materialistic, and Books I and II expound the atomic theory of Democritus and Epicurus in terms surprisingly suggestive of modern science. Nothing exists but atoms and space. The atoms are ceaselessly moving, not in straight lines but by "swerves," and are accidentally forming endless combinations that we recognize as the elements of air, fire, earth, and water, and all the things of the universe from the stars to the smallest objects on earth. Since atoms and space alone exist, the disasters of nature that breed fear in men and make them create gods to be placated are mere phenomena of the moving atoms—thunderstorms from clashing clouds, not Jupiter; earthquakes from expanding gases under the earth, not Vulcan.

Book III discusses the place of the soul in such a system. Living things are part of the material system, simply combinations of inert atoms that function for a while as living units. The mind is an organ (situated in the chest), while the soul is spread finely through the body. Both die with the body, though all the atoms of body, mind, and soul move into new combinations with other atoms as indestructible parts of the material system. Therefore we should not fear death, for it cannot come until we have ceased to exist. In Book IV Lucretius applies his materialism to sense-perception, sexual passion, and the mind in general. Book V, the most interesting of the six, gives his theory of the history of the universe and man, discussing sometimes naïvely yet always intelligently, astronomy, biology, and the growth of human institutions. The last book, which is obviously unfinished, applies his theory to a variety of specific phenomena.

Through all of the inaccuracy of Lucretius' speculation shines a courageous attempt to explain the universe and the world of man in rational terms. We need not agree with him to admit the modernity of his outlook and his anticipations of modern science. Nor should we let his cold materialism obscure the vigor of his poem and his Wordsworthian sensitivity to the beauties of the world, however atomic it may be in structure. His whole point is that denying religion and accepting science leads him not to despair but to happiness founded on freedom from fear. In his expression of this satisfaction he proved himself a great artist.

Of the Nature of Things

BOOK I

PROEM

WHILST human kind
    Throughout the lands lay miserably crushed
Before all eyes beneath Religion—who
Would show her head along the region skies,
Glowering on mortals with her hideous face—   5
A Greek it was who first opposing dared — *Epicurus*
Raise mortal eyes that terror to withstand,
Whom nor the fame of Gods nor lightning's stroke
Nor threatening thunder of the ominous sky
Abashed; but rather chafed to angry zest   10

*Of the Nature of Things.*ᴬ Translated by William Ellery Leonard. Taken from *Of the Nature of Things* by Lucretius. Published and copyrighted by E. P. Dutton & Co., Inc., New York, 1922 (Everyman's Lib. Ed.). Reprinted by permission of E. P. Dutton & Co., Inc. and J. M. Dent & Sons, Ltd.
6. A Greek, Epicurus.

His dauntless heart to be the first to rend
The crossbars at the gates of Nature old.
And thus his will and hardy wisdom won;
And forward thus he fared afar, beyond
The flaming ramparts of the world, until   15
He wandered the unmeasurable All.
Whence he to us, a conqueror, reports
What things can rise to being, what cannot,
And by what law to each its scope prescribed,
Its boundary stone that clings so deep in Time.   20
Wherefore religion now is under foot,
And us his victory now exalts to heaven. . . .

I fear perhaps thou deemest that we fare
An impious road to realms of thought profane;
But 'tis that same religion oftener far   25
Hath bred the foul impieties of men:
As once at Aulis, the elected chiefs,
Foremost of heroes, Danaan counsellors,
Defiled Diana's altar, virgin queen,
With Agamemnon's daughter, foully slain.   30
She felt the chaplet round her maiden locks
And fillets, fluttering down on either cheek,
And at the altar marked her grieving sire,
The priests beside him who concealed the knife,
And all the folk in tears at sight of her.   35
With a dumb terror and a sinking knee
She dropped; nor might avail her now that first
'Twas she who gave the king a father's name.
They raised her up, they bore the trembling girl
On to the altar—hither led not now   40
With solemn rites and hymeneal choir,
But sinless woman, sinfully foredone,
A parent felled her on her bridal day,
Making his child a sacrificial beast
To give the ships auspicious winds for Troy: 45
Such are the crimes to which religion leads. . . .
Then be it ours with steady mind to clasp
The purport of the skies—the law behind
The wandering courses of the sun and moon;
To scan the powers that speed all life below;   50
But most to see with reasonable eyes
Of what the mind, of what the soul is made,
And what it is so terrible that breaks
On us asleep, or waking in disease,
Until we seem to mark and hear at hand   55
Dead men whose bones earth bosomed long ago.

SUBSTANCE IS ETERNAL

This terror, then, this darkness of the mind,
Not sunrise with its flaring spokes of light,
Nor glittering arrows of morning can disperse,
But only Nature's aspect and her law,   60
Which, teaching us, hath this exordium:
Nothing from nothing ever yet was born.
Fear holds dominion over mortality

30. Agamemnon's daughter, Iphigenia.

Only because, seeing in land and sky
So much the cause whereof no wise they know, 65
Men think Divinities are working there.
Meantime, when once we know from nothing still
Nothing can be create, we shall divine
More clearly what we seek: those elements
From which alone all things created are, 70
And how accomplished by no tool of Gods. . . .
Confess then, naught from nothing can become,
Since all must have their seeds, wherefrom to grow,
Wherefrom to reach the gentle fields of air.

Hence too it comes that Nature all dissolves 75
Into their primal bodies again, and naught
Perishes ever to annihilation.
For, were aught mortal in its every part,
Before our eyes it might be snatched away
Unto destruction; since no force were needed 80
To sunder its members and undo its bands. . . .
Nothing returns to naught; but all return
At their collapse to primal forms of stuff.
Lo, the rains perish which Ether-father throws
Down to the bosom of Earth-mother; but then 85
Upsprings the shining grain, and boughs are green
Amid the trees, and trees themselves wax big
And lade themselves with fruits; and hence in turn
The race of man and all the wild are fed;
Hence joyful cities thrive with boys and girls; 90
And leafy woodlands echo with new birds. . . .

CHARACTER OF THE ATOMS

Bodies, again,
Are partly primal germs of things, and partly
Unions deriving from the primal germs.
And those which are the primal germs of things 95
No power can quench; for in the end they conquer
By their own solidness; though hard it be
To think that aught in things has solid frame;
For lightnings pass, no less than voice and shout,
Through hedging walls of houses, and the iron 100
White-dazzles in the fire, and rocks will burn
With exhalations fierce and burst asunder.
Totters the rigid gold dissolved in heat;
The ice of bronze melts conquered in the flame;
Warmth and the piercing cold through silver seep,
Since, with the cups held rightly in the hand, 106
We oft feel both, as from above is poured
The dew of waters between their shining sides:
So true it is no solid form is found. . . .
But powerful in old simplicity, 110
Abide the solid, the primeval germs;
And by their combinations more condensed,
All objects can be tightly knit and bound
And made to show unconquerable strength.
Again, since all things kind by kind obtain 115
Fixed bounds of growing and conserving life;
Since nature hath inviolably decreed
What each can do, what each can never do;

Since naught is changed, but all things so abide
That ever the variegated birds reveal 120
The spots or stripes peculiar to their kind,
Spring after spring: thus surely all that is
Must be composed of matter immutable.
For if the primal germs in any wise
Were open to conquest and to change, 'twould be
Uncertain also what could come to birth 126
And what could not, and by what law to each
Its scope prescribed, its boundary stone that clings
So deep in Time. Nor could the generations
Kind after kind so often reproduce 130
The nature, habits, motions, ways of life,
Of their progenitors. . . .

THE INFINITY OF THE UNIVERSE

But since I've taught that bodies of matter, made
Completely solid, hither and thither fly
Forevermore, unconquered through all time, 135
Now come, and whether to the sum of them
There be a limit or be none, for thee
Let us unfold; likewise what has been found
To be the wide inane, or room, or space
Wherein all things soever do go on, 140
Let us examine if it finite be
All and entire, or reach unmeasured round
And downward an illimitable profound.

Thus, then, the All that is is limited
In no one region of its onward paths, 145
For then 'tmust have forever its beyond.
And a beyond 'tis seen can never be
For aught, unless still further on there be
A somewhat somewhere that may bound the same—
So that the thing be seen still on to where 150
The nature of sensation of that thing
Can follow it no longer. Now because
Confess we must there's naught beside the sum,
There's no beyond, and so it lacks all end.
It matters nothing where thou post thyself, 155
In whatsoever regions of the same;
Even any place a man has set him down
Still leaves about him the unbounded all
Outward in all directions; or, supposing
A moment the all of space finite to be, 160
If some one farthest traveller runs forth
Unto the éxtreme coasts and throws ahead
A flying spear, is't then thy wish to think
It goes, hurled off amain, to where 'twas sent
And shoots afar, or that some object there 165
Can thwart and stop it? For the one or other
Thou must admit and take. Either of which
Shuts off escape for thee, and does compel
That thou concede the all spreads everywhere,
Owning no confines. . . . 170
In endless motion everything goes on
Forevermore; out of all regions, even
Out of the pit below, from forth the vast,

[handwritten marginal notes:]
He does not say where the first matter comes from.
Who is the law giver?

Are hurtled bodies evermore supplied.
The nature of room, the space of the abyss   175
Is such that even the flashing thunderbolts
Can neither speed upon their courses through,
Gliding across eternal tracts of time,
Nor, further, bring to pass, as on they run,
That they may bate their journeying one whit: 180
Such huge abundance spreads for things around—
Room off to every quarter, without end.
Lastly, before our very eyes is seen
Thing to bound thing: air hedges hill from hill,
And mountain walls hedge air; land ends the sea,
And sea in turn all lands; but for the All   186
Truly is nothing which outside may bound. . . .

BOOK II
PROEM

'Tis sweet, when, down the mighty main, the winds
Roll up its waste of waters, from the land
To watch another's labouring anguish far,   190
Not that we joyously delight that man
Should thus be smitten, but because 'tis sweet
To mark what evils we ourselves be spared;
'Tis sweet, again, to view the mighty strife
Of armies embattled yonder o'er the plains,   195
Ourselves no sharers in the peril; but naught
There is more goodly than to hold the high
Serene plateaus, well fortressed by the wise,
Whence thou may'st look below on other men
And see them ev'rywhere wand'ring, all dispersed
In their lone seeking for the road of life;   201
Rivals in genius, or emulous in rank,
Pressing through days and nights with hugest toil
For summits of power and mastery of the world.
O wretched minds of men! O blinded hearts!   205
In how great perils, in what darks of life
Are spent the human years, however brief!—
O not to see that nature for herself
Barks after nothing, save that pain keep off,
Disjoined from the body, and that mind enjoy   210
Delightsome feeling, far from care and fear!
Therefore we see that our corporeal life
Needs little, altogether, and only such
As takes the pain away, and can besides
Strew underneath some number of delights.   215
More grateful 'tis at times (for nature craves
No artifice nor luxury), if forsooth
There be no golden images of boys
Along the halls, with right hands holding out
The lamps ablaze, the lights for evening feasts,   220
And if the house doth glitter not with gold
Nor gleam with silver, and to the lyre resound
No fretted and gilded ceilings overhead,
Yet still to lounge with friends in the soft grass
Beside a river of water, underneath   225

A big tree's boughs, and merrily to refresh
Our frames, with no vast outlay—most of all
If the weather is laughing and the times of the year
Besprinkle the green of the grass around with
    flowers.
Nor yet the quicker will hot fevers go,   230
If on a pictured tapestry thou toss,
Or purple robe, than if 'tis thine to lie
Upon the poor man's bedding. Wherefore, since
Treasure, nor rank, nor glory of a reign
Avail us naught for this our body, thus   235
Reckon them likewise nothing for the mind:
Save then perchance, when thou beholdest forth
Thy legions swarming round the Field of Mars,
Rousing a mimic warfare—either side
Strengthened with large auxiliaries and horse,   240
Alike equipped with arms, alike inspired;
Or save when also thou beholdest forth
Thy fleets to swarm, deploying down the sea:
For then, by such bright circumstance abashed,
Religion pales and flees thy mind; O then   245
The fears of death leave heart so free of care.
But if we note how all this pomp at last
Is but a drollery and a mocking sport,
And of a truth man's dread, with cares at heels,
Dreads not these sounds of arms, these savage
    swords,   250
But among kings and lords of all the world
Mingles undaunted, nor is overawed
By gleam of gold nor by the splendour bright
Of purple robe, canst thou then doubt that this
Is aught, but power of thinking?—when, besides   255
The whole of life but labours in the dark.
For just as children tremble and fear all
In the viewless dark, so even we at times
Dread in the light so many things that be
No whit more fearsome than what children feign,
Shuddering, will be upon them in the dark.   261
This terror then, this darkness of the mind,
Not sunrise with its flaring spokes of light,
Nor glittering arrows of morning can disperse,
But only nature's aspect and her law.   265

ATOMIC MOTIONS

Now come: I will untangle for thy steps
Now by what motions the begetting bodies
Of the world-stuff beget the varied world. . . .
For far beneath the ken of senses lies
The nature of those ultimates of the world;   270
And so, since those themselves thou canst not see,
Their motion also must they veil from men—
For mark, indeed, how things we *can* see, oft
Yet hide their motions, when afar from us
Along the distant landscape. Often thus,   275
Upon a hillside will the woolly flocks
Be cropping their goodly food and creeping about
Whither the summons of the grass, begemmed

With the fresh dew, is calling, and the lambs,
Well filled, are frisking, locking horns in sport: 280
Yet all for us seem blurred and blent afar—
A glint of white at rest on a green hill. . . .
　　　When first the dawn is sprinkling with new light
The lands, and all the breed of birds abroad
Flit round the trackless forests, with liquid notes
Filling the regions along the mellow air, 286
We see 'tis forthwith manifest to man
How suddenly the risen sun is wont
At such an hour to overspread and clothe
The whole with its own splendour; but the sun's
Warm exhalations and this sérene light 291
Travel not down an empty void; and thus
They are compelled more slowly to advance,
Whilst, as it were, they cleave the waves of air;
Nor one by one travel these particles 295
Of the warm exhalations, but are all
Entangled and enmassed, whereby at once
Each is restrained by each, and from without
Checked, till compelled more slowly to advance.
But the primordial atoms with their old 300
Simple solidity, when forth they travel
Along the empty void, all undelayed
By aught outside them there, and they, each one
Being one unit from nature of its parts,
Are borne to that one place on which they strive
Still to lay hold, must then, beyond a doubt, 306
Outstrip in speed, and be more swiftly borne
Than light of sun, and over regions rush,
Of space much vaster, in the self-same time 309
The sun's effulgence widens round the sky. . . .
The atoms, as their own weight bears them down
Plumb through the void, at scarce determined times,
In scarce determined places, from their course
Decline a little—call it, so to speak,
Mere changèd trend. For were it not their wont 315
Thuswise to swerve, down would they fall, each one,
Like drops of rain, through the unbottomed void;
And then collisions ne'er could be nor blows
Among the primal elements; and thus
Nature would never have created aught. 320
　　But, if perchance be any that believe
The heavier bodies, as more swiftly borne
Plumb down the void, are able from above
To strike the lighter, thus engendering blows
Able to cause those procreant motions, far 325
From highways of true reason they retire.
For whatsoever through the waters fall,
Or through thin air, must quicken their descent,
Each after its weight—on this account, because
Both bulk of water and the subtle air 330
By no means can retard each thing alike,
But give more quick before the heavier weight;
But contrariwise the empty void cannot,
On any side, at any time, to aught
Oppose resistance, but will ever yield, 335

True to its bent of nature. Wherefore all,
With equal speed, though equal not in weight,
Must rush, borne downward through the still inane.
Thus ne'er at all have heavier from above 339
Been swift to strike the lighter, gendering strokes
Which cause those divers motions, by whose means
Nature transacts her work. And so I say,
The atoms must a little swerve at times—
But only the least, lest we should seem to feign
Motions oblique, and fact refute us there. . . . 345

ATOMIC FORMS
AND THEIR COMBINATIONS

Thus the long war, from everlasting waged,
With equal strife among the elements
Goes on and on. . . . This, too, in these affairs
'Tis fit thou hold well sealed, and keep consigned
With no forgetting brain: nothing there is 350
Whose nature is apparent out of hand
That of one kind of elements consists—
Nothing there is that's not of mixèd seed.
And whatsoe'er possesses in itself
More largely many powers and properties 355
Shows thus that here within itself there are
The largest number of kinds and differing shapes
Of elements. And, chief of all, the earth
Hath in herself first bodies whence the springs,
Rolling chill waters, renew forevermore 360
The unmeasured main; hath whence the fires
　　　arise—
For burns in many a spot her flamèd crust,
Whilst the impetuous Aetna raves indeed
From more profounder fires—and she, again,
Hath in herself the seed whence she can raise 365
The shining grains and gladsome trees for men;
Whence, also, rivers, fronds, and gladsome pastures
Can she supply for mountain-roaming beasts.
Wherefore great mother of gods, and mother of
　　　beasts,
And parent of man hath she alone been named. . . .
So great in any sort of herb thou wilt, 371
So great again in any river of earth
Are the distinct diversities of matter.
Hence, further, every creature—any one
From out them all—compounded is the same 375
Of bones, blood, veins, heat, moisture, flesh, and
　　　thews—
All differing vastly in their forms, and built
Of elements dissimilar in shape. . . .
Thus unlike forms into one mass combine,
And things exist by inter-mixèd seed. . . . 380
　　Now, too: whate'er we see possessing sense
Must yet confessedly be stablished all
From elements insensate. And those signs,
So clear to all and witnessed out of hand,
Do not refute this dictum nor oppose; 385

But rather themselves do lead us by the hand,
Compelling belief that living things are born
Of elements insensate, as I say.
Sooth, we may see from out the stinking dung 389
Live worms spring up, when, after soaking rains,
The drenched earth rots; and all things change the
        same:
Lo, change the rivers, the fronds, the gladsome pas-
        tures
Into the cattle, the cattle their nature change
Into our bodies, and from our body, oft 394
Grow strong the powers and bodies of wild beasts
And mighty-wingèd birds. Thus nature changes
All foods to living frames, and procreates
From *them* the senses of live creatures all,
In manner about as she uncoils in flames
Dry logs of wood and turns them all to fire. 400
And seest not, therefore, how it matters much
After what order are set the primal germs,
And with what other germs they all are mixed,
And what the motions that they give and get?

But now, what is't that strikes thy sceptic mind,
Constraining thee to sundry arguments 406
Against belief that from insensate germs
The sensible is gendered?—Verily,
'Tis this: that liquids, earth, and wood, though
        mixed,
Are yet unable to gender vital sense. 410
And, therefore, 'twill be well in these affairs
This to remember: that I have not said
Senses are born, under conditions all,
From all things absolutely which create
Objects that feel; but much it matters here 415
Firstly, how small the seeds which thus compose
The feeling thing, then, with what shapes endowed,
And lastly what they in *positions* be,
In motions, in arrangements. Of which facts
Naught we perceive in logs of wood and clods; 420
And yet even these, when sodden by the rains,
Give birth to wormy grubs, because the bodies
Of matter, from their old arrangements stirred
By the new factor, then combine anew
In such a way as genders living things. . . . 425

INFINITE WORLDS

Off to all regions round, on either side,
Above, beneath, throughout the universe
End is there none—as I have taught, as too
The very thing of itself declares aloud,
And as from nature of the unbottomed deep 430
Shines clearly forth. . . . Thus, I say,
Again, again, 'tmust be confessed there are
Such congregations of matter otherwhere,
Like this our world which vasty ether holds
In huge embrace. . . . 435
                If store of seeds there is
So great that not whole life-times of the living

Can count the tale . . .
And if their force and nature abide the same,
Able to throw the seeds of things together 440
Into their places, even as here are thrown
The seeds together in this world of ours,
'Tmust be confessed in other realms there are
Still other worlds, still other breeds of men,
And other generations of the wild. 445
Hence too it happens in the sum there is
No one thing single of its kind in birth,
And single and sole in growth, but rather it is
One member of some generated race,
Among full many others of like kind. 450
First, cast thy mind abroad upon the living:
Thou'lt find the race of mountain-ranging wild
Even thus to be, and thus the scions of men
To be begot, and lastly the mute flocks
Of scalèd fish and wingèd frames of birds. 455
Wherefore confess we must on grounds the same
That earth, sun, moon, and ocean, and all else,
Exist not sole and single—rather in number
Exceeding number. Since that deeply set
Old boundary stone of life remains for them 460
No less, and theirs a body of mortal birth
No less, than every kind which here on earth
Is so abundant in its members found.
    Which well perceivèd if thou hold in mind,
Then Nature, delivered from every haughty lord,
And forthwith free, is seen to do all things 466
Herself and through herself of own accord,
Rid of all gods. For—by their holy hearts
Which pass in long tranquillity of peace
Untroubled ages and a sérene life!— 470
Who hath the power (I ask), who hath the power
To rule the sum of the immeasurable,
To hold with steady hand the giant reins
Of the unfathomed deep? Who hath the power
At once to roll a multitude of skies, 475
At once to heat with fires ethereal all
The fruitful lands of multitudes of worlds,
To be at all times in all places near,
To stablish darkness by his clouds, to shake
The sérene spaces of the sky with sound, 480
And hurl his lightnings,—ha, and whelm how oft
In ruins his own temples, and to rave,
Retiring to the wildernesses, there
At practice with that thunderbolt of his,
Which yet how often shoots the guilty by, 485
And slays the honourable blameless ones! . . .

BOOK III
THE SOUL IS MORTAL

Now come: that thou mayst able be to know
That minds and the light souls of all that live
Have mortal birth and death, I will go on
Verses to build meet for thy rule of life, 490

Sought after long, discovered with sweet toil.
But under one name I'd have thee yoke them both;
And when, for instance, I shall speak of soul,
Teaching the same to be but mortal, think
Thereby I'm speaking also of the mind—   495
Since both are one, a substance inter-joined.

First, then, since I have taught how soul exists
A subtle fabric, of particles minute,
Made up from atoms smaller much than those
Of water's liquid damp, or fog, or smoke,   500
So in mobility it far excels,
More prone to move, though strook by lighter cause,
Even moved by images of smoke or fog—
As where we view, when in our sleeps we're lulled,
The altars exhaling steam and smoke aloft—   505
For, beyond doubt, these apparitions come
To us from outward. Now, then, since thou seest,
Their liquids depart, their waters flow away,
When jars are shivered, and since fog and smoke
Depart into the winds away, believe   510
The soul no less is shed abroad and dies
More quickly far, more quickly is dissolved
Back to its primal bodies, when withdrawn
From out man's members it has gone away.
For, sure, if body (container of the same   515 *chias*
Like as a jar), when shivered from some cause,   *m^{us}*
And rarefied by loss of blood from veins,
Cannot for longer hold the soul, how then
Thinkst thou it can be held by any air—
A stuff much rarer than our bodies be?   520

Besides we feel that mind to being comes
Along with body, with body grows and ages.
For just as children totter round about
With frames infirm and tender, so there follows
A weakling wisdom in their minds; and then,   525
Where years have ripened into robust powers,
Counsel is also greater, more increased
The power of mind; thereafter, where already
The body's shattered by master-powers of eld,
And fallen the frame with its enfeebled powers,   530
Thought hobbles, tongue wanders, and the mind
          gives way;
All fails, all's lacking at the selfsame time.
Therefore it suits that even the soul's dissolved,
Like smoke, into the lofty winds of air;
Since we behold the same to being come   535
Along with body and grow, and, as I've taught,
Crumble and crack, therewith outworn by eld.

Then, too, we see, that, just as body takes
Monstrous diseases and the dreadful pain,
So mind its bitter cares, the grief, the fear;   540
Wherefore it tallies that the mind no less
Partaker is of death; for pain and disease
Are both artificers of death,—as well
We've learned by the passing of many a man ere
          now.
Nay, too, in diseases of body, often the mind   545

Wanders afield; for 'tis beside itself,
And crazed it speaks, or many a time it sinks,
With eyelids closing and a drooping nod,
In heavy drowse, on to eternal sleep;
From whence nor hears it any voices more,   550
Nor able is to know the faces here
Of those about him standing with wet cheeks
Who vainly call him back to light and life. . . .

FOLLY OF THE FEAR
OF DEATH

                              Therefore death to us
Is nothing, nor concerns us in the least,   555
Since nature of mind is mortal evermore.
And just as in the ages gone before
We felt no touch of ill, when all sides round
To battle came the Carthaginian host,
And the times, shaken by tumultuous war,   560
Under the aery coasts of arching heaven
Shuddered and trembled, and all humankind
Doubted to which the empery should fall
By land and sea, thus when we are no more,   564
When comes that sundering of our body and soul
Through which we're fashioned to a single state,
Verily naught to us, us then no more,
Can come to pass, naught move our senses then—
No, not if earth confounded were with sea,
And sea with heaven. But if indeed do feel   570
The nature of mind and energy of soul,
After their severance from this body of ours,
Yet nothing 'tis to us who in the bonds
And wedlock of the soul and body live,
Through which we're fashioned to a single state.
And, even if time collected after death   576
The matter of our frames and set it all
Again in place as now, and if again
To us the light of life were given, O yet
That process too would not concern us aught,   580
When once the self-succession of our sense
Has been asunder broken. And now and here,
Little enough we're busied with the selves
We were aforetime, nor, concerning them,
Suffer a sore distress. For shouldst thou gaze   585
Backwards across all yesterdays of time
The immeasurable, thinking how manifold
The motions of matter are, then couldst thou well
Credit this too: often these very seeds
(From which we are to-day) of old were set   590
In the same order as they are to-day—
Yet this we can't to consciousness recall
Through the remembering mind. For there hath
          been
An interposèd pause of life, and wide
Have all the motions wandered everywhere   595
From these our senses. For if woe and ail
Perchance are toward, then the man to whom
The bane can happen must himself be there

At that same time. But death precludeth this,
Forbidding life to him on whom might crowd   600
Such irk and care; and granted 'tis to know:
Nothing for us there is to dread in death,
No wretchedness for him who is no more,
The same estate as if ne'er born before,
When death immortal hath ta'en the mortal
    life. . . .   605
But ask the mourner what's the bitterness
That man should waste in an eternal grief,
If, after all, the thing's but sleep and rest?
For when the soul and frame together are sunk
In slumber, no one then demands his self   610
Or being. Well, this sleep may be forever,
Without desire of any selfhood more,
For all it matters unto us asleep.
Yet not at all do those primordial germs
Roam round our members, at that time, afar   615
From their own motions that produce our senses—
Since, when he's startled from his sleep, a man
Collects his senses. Death is, then, to us
Much less—if there can be a less than that
Which is itself a nothing: for there comes   620
Hard upon death a scattering more great
Of the throng of matter, and no man wakes up
On whom once falls the icy pause of life. . . .

BOOK V

Thus far we've gone; the order of my plan
Hath brought me now unto the point where I   625
Must make report how, too, the universe
Consists of mortal body, born in time,
And in what modes that congregated stuff
Establishèd itself as earth and sky,
Ocean, and stars, and sun, and ball of moon;   630
And then what living creatures rose from out
The old telluric places, and what ones
Were never born at all; and in what mode
The human race began to name its things
And use the varied speech from man to man;   635
And in what modes hath bosomed in their breasts
That awe of gods, which halloweth in all lands
Fanes, altars, groves, lakes, idols of the gods. . . .

FORMATION OF THE WORLD

Cf the Origin   In that long-ago
The wheel of the sun could nowhere be discerned
Flying far up with its abounding blaze,   641
Nor constellations of the mighty world,
Nor ocean, nor heaven, nor even earth nor air,
Nor aught of things like unto things of ours
Could then be seen—but only some strange storm
And a prodigious hurly-burly mass   646
Compounded of all kinds of primal germs,
Whose battling discords in disorder kept
Interstices, and paths, coherencies,

Where did this mass come from?

And weights, and blows, encounterings, and mo-
    tions,   650
Because, by reason of their forms unlike
And varied shapes, they could not all thuswise
Remain conjoinèd nor harmoniously
Have interplay of movements. But from there
Portions began to fly asunder, and like   655
With like to join, and to block out a world,
And to divide its members and dispose
Its mightier parts—that is, to set secure
The lofty heavens from the lands, and cause
The sea to spread with waters separate,   660
And fires of ether separate and pure
Likewise to congregate apart. . . .

ORIGINS OF VEGETABLE
AND ANIMAL LIFE

In the beginning, earth gave forth, around
The hills and over all the length of plains,
The race of grasses and the shining green;   665
The flowery meadows sparkled all aglow
With greening colour, and thereafter, lo,
Unto the divers kinds of trees was given
An emulous impulse mightily to shoot,
With a free rein, aloft into the air.   670
As feathers and hairs and bristles are begot
The first on members of the four-foot breeds
And on the bodies of the strong-y-winged,
Thus then the new Earth first of all put forth
Grasses and shrubs, and afterward begat   675
The mortal generations, there upsprung—
Innumerable in modes innumerable—
After diverging fashions. For from sky
These breathing-creatures never can have dropped,
Nor the land-dwellers ever have come up   680
Out of sea-pools of salt. How true remains,
How merited is that adopted name
Of earth—"The Mother!"—since from out the earth
Are all begotten. And even now arise
From out the loams how many living things—   685
Concreted by the rains and heat of the sun.
Wherefore 'tis less a marvel, if they sprang
In Long Ago more many, and more big,
Matured of those days in the fresh young years
Of earth and ether. First of all, the race   690
Of the wingèd ones and parti-coloured birds,
Hatched out in spring-time, left their eggs behind;
As now-a-days in summer tree-crickets
Do leave their shiny husks of own accord,
Seeking their food and living. Then it was   695
This earth of thine first gave unto the day
The mortal generations; for prevailed
Among the fields abounding hot and wet.
And hence, where any fitting spot was given,
There 'gan to grow womb-cavities, by roots   700
Affixed to earth. And when in ripened time
The age of the young within (that sought the air

And fled earth's damps) had burst these wombs, O
  then
Would Nature thither turn the pores of earth
And make her spurt from open veins a juice   705
Like unto milk; even as a woman now
Is filled, at child-bearing, with the sweet milk,
Because all that swift stream of aliment
Is thither turned unto the mother-breasts.
There earth would furnish to the children food; 710
Warmth was their swaddling cloth, the grass their
  bed
Abounding in soft down. Earth's newness then
Would rouse no dour spells of the bitter cold,
Nor éxtreme heats nor winds of mighty powers—
For all things grow and gather strength through
  time   715
In like proportions; and then earth was young.
  Wherefore, again, again, how merited
Is that adopted name of Earth—the Mother!—
Since she herself begat the human race,
And at one well-nigh fixèd time brought forth 720
Each beast that ranges raving round about
Upon the mighty mountains and all birds
Aerial with many a varied shape.
But, lo, because her bearing years must end,
She ceased, like to a woman worn by eld.   725
For lapsing aeons change the nature of
The whole wide world, and all things needs must
  take
One status after other, nor aught persists
Forever like itself. All things depart;
Nature she changeth all, compelleth all   730
To transformation. Lo, *this* moulders down,
A-slack with weary eld, and *that*, again,
Prospers in glory, issuing from contempt.
In suchwise, then, the lapsing aeons change
The nature of the whole wide world, and earth 735
Taketh one status after other. And what
She bore of old, she now can bear no longer,
And what she never bore, she can to-day. . . .

ORIGINS AND SAVAGE PERIOD
OF MANKIND

                      But mortal man
Was then far hardier in the old champaign, 740
As well he should be, since a hardier earth
Had him begotten; builded too was he
Of bigger and more solid bones within,
And knit with stalwart sinews through the flesh,
Nor easily seized by either heat or cold, 745
Or alien food or any ail or irk.
And whilst so many lustrums of the sun
Rolled on across the sky, men led a life
After the roving habit of wild beasts. 749
Not then were sturdy guiders of curved ploughs,
And none knew then to work the fields with iron,
Or plant young shoots in holes of delvèd loam,

Or lop with hookèd knives from off high trees
The boughs of yester-year. What sun and rains
To them had given, what earth of own accord 755
Created then, was boon enough to glad
Their simple hearts. Mid acorn-laden oaks
Would they refresh their bodies for the nonce;
And the wild berries of the arbute-tree,
Which now thou seest to ripen purple-red 760
In winter time, the old telluric soil
Would bear then more abundant and more big.
And many coarse foods, too, in long ago
The blooming freshness of the rank young world
Produced, enough for those poor wretches there.
And rivers and springs would summon them of old
To slake the thirst, as now from the great hills
The water's down-rush calls aloud and far
The thirsty generations of the wild.   769
So, too, they sought the grottos of the Nymphs—
The woodland haunts discovered as they ranged—
From forth of which they knew that gliding rills
With gush and splash abounding laved the rocks,
The dripping rocks, and trickled from above
Over the verdant moss; and here and there 775
Welled up and burst across the open flats.
As yet they knew not to enkindle fire
Against the cold, nor hairy pelts to use
And clothe their bodies with the spoils of beasts;
But huddled in groves, and mountain-caves, and
  woods,   780
And 'mongst the thickets hid their squalid backs,
When driven to flee the lashings of the winds
And the big rains. Nor could they then regard
The general good, nor did they know to use
In common any customs, any laws: 785
Whatever of booty fortune unto each
Had proffered, each alone would bear away,
By instinct trained for self to thrive and live.
And Venus in the forests then would link
The lovers' bodies; for the woman yielded 790
Either from mutual flame, or from the man's
Impetuous fury and insatiate lust,
Or from a bribe—as acorn-nuts, choice pears,
Or the wild berries of the arbute-tree.
And trusting wondrous strength of hands and legs,
They'd chase the forest-wanderers, the beasts; 796
And many they'd conquer, but some few they fled,
A-skulk into their hiding-places . . .
With the flung stones and with the ponderous heft
Of gnarlèd branch. And by the time of night 800
O'ertaken, they would throw, like bristly boars,
Their wildman's limbs naked upon the earth,
Rolling themselves in leaves and fronded boughs.
Nor would they call with lamentations loud
Around the fields for daylight and the sun, 805
Quaking and wand'ring in shadows of the night;
But, silent and buried in a sleep, they'd wait
Until the sun with rosy flambeau brought

The glory to the sky. From childhood wont
Ever to see the dark and day begot   810
In times alternate, never might they be
Wildered by wild misgiving, lest a night
Eternal should possess the lands, with light
Of sun withdrawn forever. But their care
Was rather that the clans of savage beasts   815
Would often make their sleep-time horrible
For those poor wretches; and, from home y-driven,
They'd flee their rocky shelters at approach
Of boar, the spumy-lipped, or lion strong,
And in the midnight yield with terror up   820
To those fierce guests their beds of out-spread
          leaves.
    And yet in those days not much more than now
Would generations of mortality
Leave the sweet light of fading life behind.
Indeed, in those days here and there a man,   825
More oftener snatched upon, and gulped by fangs,
Afforded the beasts a food that roared alive,
Echoing through groves and hills and forest-trees,
Even as he viewed his living flesh entombed
Within a living grave; whilst those whom flight   830
Had saved, with bone and body bitten, shrieked,
Pressing their quivering palms to loathsome sores,
With horrible voices for eternal death—
Until, forlorn of help, and witless what   834
Might medicine their wounds, the writhing pangs
Took them from life. But not in those far times
Would one lone day give over unto doom
A soldiery in thousands marching on
Beneath the battle-banners, nor would then
The ramping breakers of the main seas dash   840
Whole argosies and crews upon the rocks.
But ocean uprisen would often rave in vain,
Without all end or outcome, and give up
Its empty menacings as lightly too;
Nor soft seductions of a sérene sea   845
Could lure by laughing billows any man
Out to disaster: for the science bold
Of ship-sailing lay dark in those far times.
Again, 'twas *then* that lack of food gave o'er
Men's fainting limbs to dissolution: now   850
'Tis plenty overwhelms. Unwary, they
Oft for themselves themselves would then outpour
The poison; now, with nicer art, themselves
They give the drafts to others.

BEGINNINGS OF CIVILIZATION

                    Afterwards,   855
When huts they had procured and pelts and fire,
And when the woman, joined unto the man,
Withdrew with him into one dwelling place,
    . . . and when they saw an offspring born
From out themselves, then first the human race   860
Began to soften. For 'twas now that fire
Rendered their shivering frames less staunch to bear,

Under the canopy of the sky, the cold;
And Love reduced their shaggy hardiness;
And children, with the prattle and the kiss,   865
Soon broke the parents' haughty temper down.
Then, too, did neighbours 'gin to league as friends,
Eager to wrong no more or suffer wrong,
And urged for children and the womankind
Mercy, of fathers, whilst with cries and gestures
They stammered hints how meet it was that all   871
Should have compassion on the weak. And still,
Though concord not in every wise could then
Begotten be, a good, a goodly part
Kept faith inviolate—or else mankind   875
Long since had been unutterably cut off,
And propagation never could have brought
The species down the ages. . . .
                    And now what cause
Hath spread divinities of gods abroad   880
Through mighty nations, and filled the cities full
Of the high altars, and led to practices
Of solemn rites in season—rites which still
Flourish in midst of great affairs of state
And midst great centres of man's civic life,   885
The rites whence still in poor mortality
Is grafted that quaking awe which rears aloft
Still the new temples of gods from land to land
And drives mankind to visit them in throngs
On holy days—'tis not so hard to give   890
Reason thereof in speech. Because, in sooth,
Even in those days would the race of man
Be seeing excelling visages of gods   893
With mind awake; and in his sleeps, yet more,—
Bodies of wondrous growth. And, thus, to these
Would men attribute sense, because they seemed
To move their limbs and speak pronouncements
          high,
Befitting glorious visage and vast powers.
And men would give them an eternal life,
Because their visages forevermore   900
Were there before them, and their shapes remained,
And chiefly, however, because men would not think
Beings augmented with such mighty powers
Could well by any force o'ermastered be.
And men would think them in their happiness   905
Excelling far, because the fear of death
Vexèd no one of them at all, and since
At same time in men's sleeps men saw them do
So many wonders, and yet feel therefrom
Themselves no weariness. Besides, men marked   910
How in a fixèd order rolled around
The systems of the sky, and changèd times
Of annual seasons, nor were able then
To know thereof the causes. Therefore 'twas
Men would take refuge in consigning all   915
Unto divinities, and in feigning all
Was guided by their nod. And in the sky
They set the seats and vaults of gods, because

Across the sky night and the moon are seen
To roll along—moon, day, and night, and night's
Old awesome constellations evermore,　　921
And the night-wandering fireballs of the sky,
And flying flames, clouds, and the sun, the rains,
Snow and the winds, the lightnings, and the hail,
And the swift rumblings, and the hollow roar　925
Of mighty menacings forevermore.

　　O humankind unhappy!—when it ascribed
Unto divinities such awesome deeds,
And coupled thereto rigours of fierce wrath!
What groans did men on that sad day beget　930
Even for themselves, and O what wounds for us,
What tears for our children's children! Nor, O man,
Is thy true piety in this: with head
Under the veil, still to be seen to turn
Fronting a stone, and ever to approach　　935
Unto all altars; nor so prone on earth
Forward to fall, to spread upturnèd palms
Before the shrines of gods, nor yet to dew
Altars with prófuse blood of four-foot beasts,
Nor vows with vows to link. But rather this:　940
To look on all things with a master eye
And mind at peace. For when we gaze aloft
Upon the skiey vaults of yon great world
And ether, fixèd high o'er twinkling stars,
And into our thought there come the journeyings
Of sun and moon, O then into our breasts,　946
O'erburdened already with their other ills,
Begins forthwith to rear its sudden head
One more misgiving: lest o'er us, percase,
It be the gods' immeasurable power　　950
That rolls, with varied motion, round and round
The far white constellations. For the lack
Of aught of reasons tries the puzzled mind:
Whether was ever a birth-time of the world,
And whether, likewise, any end shall be　　955
How far the ramparts of the world can still
Outstand this strain of ever-rousèd motion,
Or whether, divinely with eternal weal
Endowed, they can through endless tracts of age
Glide on, defying the o'er-mighty powers　960
Of the immeasurable ages. Lo,
What man is there whose mind with dread of gods
Cringes not close, whose limbs with terror-spell
Crouch not together, when the parchèd earth
Quakes with the horrible thunderbolt amain,　965
And across the mighty sky the rumblings run?
Do not the peoples and the nations shake,
And haughty kings do they not hug their limbs,
Strook through with fear of the divinities,
Lest for aught foully done or madly said　970
The heavy time be now at hand to pay?
When, too, fierce force of fury-winds at sea
Sweepeth a navy's admiral down the main
With his stout legions and his elephants,
Doth he not seek the peace of gods with vows,　975

And beg in prayer, a-tremble, lullèd winds
And friendly gales?—in vain, since, often up-caught
In fury-cyclones, is he borne along,
For all his mouthings, to the shoals of doom.
Ah, so irrevocably some hidden power　　980
Betramples forevermore affairs of men,
And visibly grindeth with its heel in mire
The lictors' glorious rods and axes dire,
Having them in derision! Again, when earth
From end to end is rocking under foot,　　985
And shaken cities ruin down, or threaten
Upon the verge, what wonder is it then
That mortal generations abase themselves,
And unto gods in all affairs of earth
Assign as last resort almighty powers　　990
And wondrous energies to govern all? . . .

　　　　　　　　　　　　　In those days
Copper it was that was the thing of price;
And gold lay useless, blunted with dull edge.
Now lies the copper low, and gold hath come　995
Unto the loftiest honours. Thus it is
That rolling ages change the times of things:
What erst was of a price, becomes at last
A discard of no honour; whilst another
Succeeds to glory, issuing from contempt,　1000
And day by day is sought for more and more,
And, when 'tis found, doth flower in men's praise,
Object of wondrous honour. . . .

　　　　　　　　　　　　Nature herself,
Mother of things, was the first seed-sower　1005
And primal grafter; since the berries and acorns,
Dropping from off the trees, would there beneath
Put forth in season swarms of little shoots;
Hence too men's fondness for ingrafting slips
Upon the boughs and setting out in holes　1010
The young shrubs o'er the fields. Then would they
　　try
Ever new modes of tilling their loved crofts,
And mark they would how earth improved the taste
Of the wild fruits by fond and fostering care.
And day by day they'd force the woods to move
Still higher up the mountain, and to yield　1016
The place below for tilth, that there they might,
On plains and uplands, have their meadow-plats,
Cisterns and runnels, crops of standing grain,
And happy vineyards, and that all along　1020
O'er hillocks, intervales, and plains might run
The silvery-green belt of olive-trees,
Marking the plotted landscape; even as now
Thou seest so marked with varied loveliness
All the terrain which men adorn and plant　1025
With rows of goodly fruit-trees and hedge round
With thriving shrubberies sown.

　　　　　　　　　　　　But by the mouth
To imitate the liquid notes of birds
Was earlier far 'mongst men than power to make,
By measured song, melodious verse and give　1030

Delight to ears. And whistlings of the wind
Athrough the hollows of the reeds first taught
The peasantry to blow into the stalks
Of hollow hemlock-herb. Then bit by bit
They learned sweet plainings, such as pipe out-
    pours,   1035
Beaten by finger-tips of singing men,
When heard through unpathed groves and forest
    deeps
And woodsy meadows, through the untrod haunts
Of shepherd folk and spots divinely still.
Thus time draws forward each and everything   1040
Little by little unto the midst of men,
And reason uplifts it to the shores of light.
These tunes would soothe and glad the minds of
    mortals
When sated with food,—for songs are welcome
    then.
And often, lounging with friends in the soft grass
Beside a river of water, underneath   1046
A big tree's branches, merrily they'd refresh
Their frames, with no vast outlay—most of all
If the weather were smiling and the times of the
    year
Were painting the green of the grass around with
    flowers.   1050
Then jokes, then talk, then peals of jollity
Would circle round; for then the rustic muse
Was in her glory; then would antic Mirth
Prompt them to garland head and shoulders about
With chaplets of intertwinèd flowers and leaves,
And to dance onward, out of tune, with limbs   1056
Clownishly swaying, and with clownish foot
To beat our mother earth—from whence arose
Laughter and peals of jollity, for, lo,
Such frolic acts were in their glory then,   1060
Being more new and strange. And wakeful men
Found solaces for their unsleeping hours
In drawing forth variety of notes,
In modulating melodies, in running
With puckered lips along the tunèd reeds,   1065
Whence, even in our day do the watchmen guard
These old traditions, and have learnèd well
To keep true measure. And yet they no whit
Do get a larger fruit of gladsomeness
Than got the woodland aborigines   1070
In olden times. For *what* we have at hand—
If theretofore naught sweeter we have known—
That chiefly pleases and seems best of all;
But then some later, likely better, find
Destroys its worth and changes our desires   1075
Regarding good of yesterday.
                  And thus
Began the loathing of the acorn; thus
Abandoned were those beds with grasses strewn
And with the leaves beladen. Thus, again,

1077. **loathing of the acorn;** as food.

Fell into new contempt the pelts of beasts—   1080
Erstwhile a robe of honour, which, I guess,
Aroused in those days envy so malign
That the first wearer went to woeful death
By ambuscades,—and yet that hairy prize,
Rent into rags by greedy foemen there   1085
And splashed by blood, was ruined utterly
Beyond all use or vantage. Thus of old
'Twas pelts, and of to-day 'tis purple and gold
That cark men's lives with cares and weary with
    war.   1089
Wherefore, methinks, resides the greater blame
With us vain men to-day: for cold would rack,
Without their pelts, the naked sons of earth;
But us it nothing hurts to do without
The purple vestment, broiderèd with gold
And with imposing figures, if we still   1095
Make shift with some mean garment of the Plebs.
So man in vain futilities toils on
Forever and wastes in idle cares his years—
Because, of very truth, he hath not learnt
What the true end of getting is, nor yet   1100
At all how far true pleasure may increase.
And 'tis desire for better and for more
Hath carried by degrees mortality
Out onward to the deep, and rousèd up
From the far bottom mighty waves of war.   1105
    But sun and moon, those watchmen of the world,
With their own lanterns traversing around
The mighty, the revolving vault, have taught
Unto mankind that seasons of the years
Return again, and that the Thing takes place   1110
After a fixèd plan and order fixed.
    Already would they pass their life, hedged round
By the strong towers; and cultivate an earth
All portioned out and boundaried; already
Would the sea flower with sail-wingèd ships;   1115
Already men had, under treaty pacts,
Confederates and allies, when poets began
To hand heroic actions down in verse;
Nor long ere this had letters been devised—
Hence is our age unable to look back   1120
On what has gone before, except where reason
Shows us a footprint.
              Sailings on the seas,
Tillings of fields, walls, laws, and arms, and roads,
Dress and the like, all prizes, all delights
Of finer life, poems, pictures, chiselled shapes   1125
Of polished sculptures—all these arts were learned
By practice and the mind's experience,
As men walked forward step by eager step.
Thus time draws forward each and everything
Little by little into the midst of men,   1130
And reason uplifts it to the shores of light.
For one thing after other did men see
Grow clear by intellect, till with their arts
They've now achieved the súpreme pinnacle.

Plautus

c. 254–184 B.C.

Our best view of Roman society under the republic comes from Plautus, who was inspired by the New Comedy of fourth-century Athens to develop a Roman comedy of manners. He was born into a lower-class family in the Umbrian town of Sarsina and came in his youth to Rome, where he learned the playwright's craft through producing or acting in plays. After he lost his earnings in a trading venture, he is said to have worked as a humble baker's assistant until the success of his first comedies freed him to write. In any case we do know that he began writing late in life and rose to a popularity that continued beyond his death to the time of Cicero.

His business failure and the poverty that resulted made Plautus write with money in mind, and that meant writing to the taste of the motley Roman audiences, who were a rough and rowdy lot with a fondness for broad farce. He followed the Greek Menander in holding up the mirror to his society and amusing the populace with satiric portraits of the social types they knew—the blustering father, the shrewish wife, the romantic son, the mock-innocent damsel, the foolish miser, the pompous soldier, the shifty-eyed parasite, the clever slave. Sometimes, as in *The Pot of Gold*, he gives us a serious study of character, but more often he is content with carefree farce often crudely constructed and full of indecent puns, local allusions, comic surprises, and slapstick humor. His dialogue is racy and exuberant in contrast to the suave elegance of later Roman writers. Particularly in his later plays he interrupts his metrical speech with popular songs in the manner of our musical comedies, but eliminates the Greek chorus entirely. In these and other ways Plautus placed his Roman stamp on Greek originals, for each of his plays began as an adaptation of a Greek comedy of Menander, Philemon, or Apollodorus. Despite this close imitation we feel everywhere the earthy, hearty personality of a distinctly lower-class man.

Tradition credits Plautus with over a hundred comedies, but only twenty survive. These show great variety of mood, subject matter, and worth. *Amphitryon* travesties the myth of Jupiter's amour with Alcmene so wittily that it has inspired endless imitations in later times from Molière to Giraudoux and Behrman.

The Captives is a mild and moral play that unites a family after various vicissitudes. *The Menaechmi Twins*, an absurd farce about mistaken identity, inspired Shakespeare's *Comedy of Errors*. The long play, *The Rope*, is a romantic comedy of shipwreck. But none excels in power or influence the *Aulularia*, or *The Pot of Gold*, which Molière was to adapt into his own comedy of *The Miser*. This brilliant play, probably based on Menander, is built around the subtle character of a miser who loses his treasure because of his own fear that he will do so. With this are interwoven the minor plot of his daughter's seduction and the low-comedy characters of the cooks. Although the last scene is lost, the ending of the play is obvious enough.

The Pot of Gold

CHARACTERS IN THE PLAY

HOUSEHOLD GOD
EUCLIO, *an aged Athenian*
STAPHYLA, *an old woman, slave of* EUCLIO
EUNOMIA, *a lady of Athens*
MEGADORUS, *brother of* EUNOMIA
STROBILUS, *his slave*
CONGRIO, *a cook*
ANTHRAX, *another cook*
PYTHODICUS, *a slave*
LYCONIDES, *a young man, son of* EUNOMIA
SLAVE *of* LYCONIDES
PHAEDRIA, *daughter of* EUCLIO
Music Girls

(SCENE: *A street in Athens on which are the houses of* EUCLIO *and* MEGADORUS *and the temple of Faith.*)

PROLOGUE

HOUSEHOLD GOD.

Lest any wonder who in the world I am,
I'll tell you shortly. I'm the household God
Of this house, which you see me leaving now;
These many years I have it in my care;
Grandfather, father, son who has it now,   5
Have all been friends; the grandfather himself
Intrusted to me secretly a hoard
Of gold, which he within the hearth had buried,
Beseeching me to keep it safe for him.
He died, and was of such a greedy soul   10
He never would reveal it to his son,
But wished to leave him poor and penniless
Rather than show him where the treasure was.
He left him just a bit of ground, on which
With pain and labour he could make his living.   15
And when he died, who gave the trust to me,
I watched with care whether his son would show
More reverence to me than his father had.
But he, it seemed, spent less and less upon me,
And paid me less of honour. So he died;   20
And I revenged myself. And next in line
Is he who has it now, like-mannered too
With those who went before. He has a child,
A daughter, who with incense or with wine
Pays daily worship to me, crowning me   25
With wreaths. And for the sake of her it was
That I to Euclio disclosed the treasure,
That he more easily might marry her;

The Pot of Gold. Translated by Sir Robert Allison. Reprinted by permission of Hatchards, Ltd., London.

A youth of high position had led her
Astray; he knew her who she was, but she   30
Did not know him; nor did the father know
What had taken place. Today I will arrange
That an old man, a neighbour, shall demand
Her for his wife; more gladly will I do it,
That the young man, who was the first to love her
(He met her on the night of Ceres' festival),   36
May marry her more easily. The old man
Who wants to do so is the young man's uncle.
But Euclio's calling out, as is his wont;
He's turned the old woman out of doors, lest she   40
Should know where the treasure is; he wants to see
That the hoard of gold has not been carried off.

(*The* HOUSEHOLD GOD *departs.*)

ACT ONE

(*Enter* EUCLIO *from his house, pushing* STAPHYLA
in front of him.)

EUCLIO. Go out; go out, I say, and get you gone,
You that are looking round with prying eyes!
STAPHYLA. Why beat a miserable wretch like me?
EUCLIO. That you may be more miserable still,
And lead the wretched life you well deserve.   5
STAPHYLA. Pray, why have you thus thrust me
    from the house?
EUCLIO. Am I to argue with a wretch like you,
Whose back is scored with stripes; go from the door,
Be off, I say; how leisurely she goes!
See to yourself, for if I take in hand   10
A stick or goad, I will increase the pace
Of that old tortoise.
STAPHYLA.   Would the gods would bring
Me to the gallows than to serve you thus!
EUCLIO. How the old wretch is murmuring to
    herself!
I'll dig your eyes out that you may not see   15
What I am doing; now away, away,
And further yet; stand there; if from that place
You stir by the width of a finger or the breadth
Of a nail, or if you look back till such time
I give you leave, I'll hand you over straight   20
To torture. (*Aside*) Never surely did I see
A wickeder old woman; much I fear
Lest she may gather from some words of mine
Too rashly said, where the gold is hidden away.
Wretch, she has eyes, too, in the back of her head.   25
Now I will go and see if the gold is there.
Just as I hid it, gold which has become
A constant source of trouble to myself.

(EUCLIO *goes into his house.*)

STAPHYLA (*to herself*). I can't think what has
    happened to my master,
Nor why he is so mad; he beats me so,   30
And thrusts me out of doors ten times a day
I don't know what has put him out of tune;

He wakens all the night, and then by day,
Like a lame cobbler, sits for hours at home.
Nor can I tell how best I can conceal   35
His daughter's state; and nothing more remains
Than to make one long letter of myself—
The letter I—and hang myself full length.

(*Re-enter* EUCLIO *from the house.*)

EUCLIO (*aside*). And now with mind at ease I
    leave the house,
As soon as I have seen all's safe within.   40
(*To* STAPHYLA) Return now to your work.
STAPHYLA.   Why should
    I go?
Is some one going to take the house away?
There is nothing here for thieves; nor aught indeed
But emptiness and spider webs.
EUCLIO.   D'ye think
That for your sake the gods would make me rich,   45
As Philip or Darius, sorceress?
I like to keep those cobwebs; I am poor,
I do admit; and bear it. I'm content
With what the gods may give. Go in and close
The door; I'll come again; let no one enter.   50
If any ask a light, see that the fire
Is quite put out; that none may ask for it;
If it is not, you'll be put out yourself.
Say that the pump is dry, if any seek
For water. If a spade, an axe, a mortar,   55
Or a pestle, things which neighbours always borrow,
Say that the thieves have come and stolen them.
No one's to enter, while I am away.
These are my orders; if Good Fortune comes,
Please say I am not at home.
STAPHYLA.   No fear of that;   60
That never comes, however near it be.
EUCLIO. Be quiet and go within.
STAPHYLA.   I'll go at once.
EUCLIO. Draw both the bolts. I will be back anon.

(*To himself, as* STAPHYLA *goes into the house*)

I'm vexed because I have to leave the house;
I go unwillingly; yet what to do   65
I know not; for the master of our guild
Has said he will divide the funds amongst us.
If I don't go and take my share, they'll think
That I have gold at home; for 'tis not likely
A poor man would despise a dole, though small.   70
For now, although I keep the secret to myself,
All seem to know it, and pay greater court
Than they used to do before; they come, they stay,
They give me their right hands; ask how I am,
And what I'm doing, what my business.   75
Now I'll be off where I was going; and
Return as soon as possible again. (EUCLIO *departs.*)

37–38. **Than . . . The letter I;** because the letter "I" resembles a
hanging body. 46. **Philip or Darius.** Philip of Macedonia and Darius
of Persia were obvious examples of wealthy kings. 59–60. **if Good
Fortune . . . home.** Even good luck may not enter in his absence.

ACT TWO

(*Enter* EUNOMIA *and* MEGADORUS *from the house of the latter.*)

EUNOMIA. I wish, my brother, you would think that I
Am acting in your interest, for your sake,
As well becomes a sister; though I know
We women are not held in much esteem.
We all are told we talk by far too much, 5
And never in the world they say was found
A silent woman. But remember, brother,
How near you are to me, and I to you.
'Tis right that we should one another help.
You should advise and counsel me, I you; 10
Nor keep it secret, nor be afraid to speak,
Make me your confidant, and I the same.
So now I brought you out of doors to speak
In private, as to your and mine concerns.

MEGADORUS. Your hand, my best of women!

EUNOMIA.   Who is she? 15
Where is such woman?

MEGADORUS.   You!

EUNOMIA.   Do you say so?

MEGADORUS. If you deny it, I will do the same.

EUNOMIA. Well, one must speak the truth. There is no best;
For one, I fear, is only worse than other.

MEGADORUS. I think the same; it needs no argument. 20

EUNOMIA. Lend me your ear.

MEGADORUS.   'Tis yours! Do as you like.

EUNOMIA. I come to advise—what is the best for you.

MEGADORUS. You do as you have always done to me.

EUNOMIA. I wish—

MEGADORUS.   What, sister?

EUNOMIA.   What will be to you
An everlasting blessing, that you may 25
Have many children.

MEGADORUS.   May the gods forfend!

EUNOMIA. I would that you should marry.

MEGADORUS.   I'm undone!

EUNOMIA. How so?

MEGADORUS. Your speech nigh splits my head in two!
Poniards you speak, and every word's a stab. 30

EUNOMIA. Do as your sister wishes.

MEGADORUS.   If you wish, I will.

EUNOMIA. It is for your advantage.

MEGADORUS.   May I die
Before I marry, or on this condition,
That she I marry, on the morrow may,

Or the day after that, be carried out 35
To burial. This being settled, get the bride,
Prepare the marriage.

EUNOMIA.   I will get for you
The largest fortune that I can; but she
Is older, of the middle age, and if
You like, I'll ask her hand.

MEGADORUS.   One question first. 40

EUNOMIA. Ask what you will!

MEGADORUS. You see when one has passed
Mid-life, and marries one who's passed it too,
If there should be a child, his name would be,
What could it be but Posthumus? Now I,
Dear sister, will relieve you of this care. 45
I by the goodness of the gods, and our forbears,
Am rich; great family, high spirit, wealth,
Applause, position, splendid equipage,
Dresses and purple, these which oft reduce
A man to slavery, do not appeal 50
At all to me.

EUNOMIA. Then who d'ye wish to marry?

MEGADORUS. Know you poor Euclio who lives next door?

EUNOMIA. I know him; he is quite a decent man.

MEGADORUS. I wish his daughter for my wife. I know
What you are going to say; that she is poor. 55
Don't say a word; I like her poverty.

EUNOMIA. The gods direct things well!

MEGADORUS.   I hope so too.
Farewell. (EUNOMIA *departs.*) I'll see if Euclio is at home.
Ah! There he is! I do not know from whence he comes.

(*Enter* EUCLIO.)

EUCLIO (*to himself*). I thought 'twas all in vain when I went out 60
And so I went unwillingly; for none
Belonging to the guild has ever come;
Nor yet the master, who should give to us
Our share of the funds; so now I hasten home,
For though I'm here myself, my heart is there. 65

MEGADORUS. Good morning, Euclio, good luck to you!

EUCLIO. The blessing of the gods!

MEGADORUS.   And are you well?
And as you wish?

EUCLIO (*aside*). It is not without cause,
When a rich man addresses thus the poor.
He knows I've gold; and hence his kindly words. 70

MEGADORUS. You say you're well?

EUCLIO.   I am, but not too well
In point of money.

MEGADORUS.   If you are content,
You have enough for life and all its needs.

EUCLIO (*aside*). The old woman's told him of the gold; that's clear.

I will cut out her tongue, and gouge out too   75
Her eyes, when I get home.

MEGADORUS.   What say you now,
Thus muttering to yourself?

EUCLIO.   I do bemoan
My poverty; I have a grown-up daughter
Without a dowry whom I cannot wed
Nor give to any.

MEGADORUS. Pray be still. Take courage!   80
I'll help you, you shall have enough and more.
What do you want?

EUCLIO (aside). His promises are fair;
But still there's something that he wants himself.
He gapes for gold to swallow it; he brings
Bread in one hand, a stone within the other.   85
I never trust the man who shows himself
So generous to the poor; he gives his hand
So kindly, but behind there is some hurt.
I know those polyps, with their tentacles,
Clinging to all they touch.

MEGADORUS.   Euclio, a word   90
Respecting what concerns yourself and me.

EUCLIO (aside). Alas! My gold is stolen; he wants,
    I know,
To come to some arrangement. I will have
A look at home.

MEGADORUS. Where are you going, Euclio?

EUCLIO. I will return; there's something that I
    want   95
To see about at home. (Hurries into house.)

MEGADORUS (to himself). I do believe
When I make mention of his daughter that
I wish to marry her, that he will think
I'm laughing at him; nor is any one
More niggardly in poverty than he.   100
        (Re-enter EUCLIO.)

EUCLIO (aside). All, all is safe! Nothing at all is
    gone.
I was too much afraid before I went,
Half mad with fear. (To MEGADORUS) Now, Mega-
    dorus, I
Return to thee, if there is aught you want.

MEGADORUS. Thanks. Now please answer what I
    ask of you.   105

EUCLIO. So be it you ask not what I cannot grant.

MEGADORUS. What think you of my family?

EUCLIO.   'Tis good!

MEGADORUS. My reputation?

EUCLIO.   Good!

MEGADORUS.   My conduct, then?

EUCLIO. Why, that I think is neither bad nor good.

MEGADORUS. You know my age?

EUCLIO.   I know it is advanced,   110
As great as is your fortune.

MEGADORUS.   As to you
I've always thought, and think you are a man
Quite without guile.

Actors wearing masks and performing a comedy.

EUCLIO (aside). Alas! He smells my gold.
(Aloud) What want you now?

MEGADORUS.   Well, as we know each other,
That all may turn out well for me and you,   115
And for your daughter, I do ask for her
In marriage. Promise me her hand.

EUCLIO.   Alas!
That which you do is unworthy of your acts;
To mock at one who's poor, and has never given
Offence to you or yours; in word or deed   120
I have done naught, that you should treat me so.

MEGADORUS. I do not come to mock, nor do I so;
I would not think it fitting.

EUCLIO.   Then why ask
My daughter's hand?

MEGADORUS.   That you, through me,
May be the better off, and I through you.   125

EUCLIO. But I do bear in mind that you are rich.
Eager for power; while I am very poor;
So poor, and if I give my daughter's hand
To you, you are a mighty ox, and I
A humble ass; and when I'm joined with you,   130
Unequal to the load that you can bear,
I, the poor ass, shall founder in the mire;
While you, proud ox, will not acknowledge me.

I'll find you worse than heretofore you were,
While those of my own order will deride;   135
If we should separate, there'll be no stall
Left for me; while the asses with their teeth
Are rending me, the oxen will proceed
To butt me with their horns. This is the danger
Of climbing from one class into another,   140
And being an ass, to try to be an ox.

MEGADORUS. The main thing is still to ally your-
    self
With honest men. Hear me; accept my terms,
And give your daughter to me.

EUCLIO.   But I have
No dowry.

MEGADORUS. Give her none; as long as she   145
Is well conducted, that's enough for me.

EUCLIO. I name it, lest you think I've found a
    treasure.

MEGADORUS. I know; don't tell me; only give her
    hand.

EUCLIO. Well, be it so. But stay, by Jove, I'm
    ruined!

MEGADORUS. What is it?

EUCLIO.   I heard some iron weapon strike.   150
              (*He runs into his house.*)

MEGADORUS. It was my gardener digging. Where's
    the man?
He's gone without an answer; he scorns me,
Because he sees I seek his friendship, just
As men often do; for if a rich man seeks
A favour from a poor one, he's afraid   155
To grant it, and, through fear, misses his chance;
And when the occasion's past, he's sorry for it.
           (*Re-enter* EUCLIO.)

EUCLIO (*to* STAPHYLA *within*): If I don't have
    your tongue taken out by the roots,
You may have me mauled and damaged as you like.

MEGADORUS. I see you think that I'm an old man
    now,   160
Who may be mocked, although I don't deserve it.

EUCLIO. It is not so, nor could I, if I would.

MEGADORUS. Then do you give me your daughter?

EUCLIO.   Yes, I do;
Upon the terms I said, without a dowry.

MEGADORUS. You promise?

EUCLIO.   Yes.

MEGADORUS.   And may the gods
    bless it!   165

EUCLIO. I wish they may. Only remember this:
My daughter brings no dowry.

MEGADORUS.   I remember.

EUCLIO. I know that sometimes men mislike a bar-
    gain;
The bargain's on or off, just as they please.

MEGADORUS. There shall be no dispute. Now, can
    we have   170
The marriage for today?

EUCLIO.   Most certainly.

MEGADORUS. I'll go and get me ready. Want you
    aught?

EUCLIO. No, only that!

MEGADORUS.   'Tis done. Farewell. (*Calling at his door*) Now, slave,
Follow me to the market; now, at once.
              (MEGADORUS *departs.*)

EUCLIO (*to himself*). He's gone. Ye gods immortal,
    what can gold   175
Achieve! He must have heard I think there is
Some treasure here; he's gaping for it now,
And that is the reason he persists in this proposal.

EUCLIO (*calling at his door*). Where are you, who
    has blabbed to all our neighbours,
Gone chitter-chattering to all the town,   180
That I would give a dowry to my daughter?
Hi! Staphyla! I call! D'ye hear? Bring in
The sacred dishes; wash them well. Today
I have betrothed my daughter; she will wed
Today.

STAPHYLA (*as she enters*). The gods direct it well;
    but stay,   185
It cannot be; it is too sudden, sure.

EUCLIO. Begone! Be quiet! See these things are
    done
When I return; shut to the door at once;
I will be here anon.
              (EUCLIO *departs.*)

STAPHYLA (*to herself*).   What must I do?
Destruction waits me and my master's daughter. 190
Her state must now be known; I'll go within
And see my master's orders carried out.
I fear some evil; and of such a kind
That I must drink the poison to the dregs.
        (STAPHYLA *goes into the house.*)

ACT THREE

(*Enter* STROBILUS *bringing the cooks,* ANTHRAX
and CONGRIO, *and music girls; attendants follow
with provisions.*)

STROBILUS. After my master had laid in his stores,
And hired his cooks and flute players at the market,
He bid, that I divide the feast in two.

ANTHRAX. Most certainly you shall not divide me;
But if you wish the whole of me, I'll help.   5

STROBILUS. My master weds today.

ANTHRAX.   Whose daughter
    is it?

STROBILUS. Our neighbour Euclio's here; he bid
    me give
Him half the dinner, and a cook as well,
And one flute player.

ANTHRAX.   Half that is for here,
And half for the other house.

STROBILUS.   Just as you say.   10

ANTHRAX. Could this old man not find his own pro-
visions
To grace his daughter's wedding?
STROBILUS.   Bosh!
ANTHRAX.   What is't?
STROBILUS. What is't you ask? A pumice-stone is
not
So hard and dry as is this old man's heart.
ANTHRAX. Is't so indeed?
STROBILUS.   Why, judge him for your-
self.   15
He's always calling upon gods and men
To witness that he's ruined and undone,
If but a puff of smoke come from his chimney.
Why, when he sleeps, he binds the bellows to his
throat—
ANTHRAX. Why that?
STROBILUS.   For fear in sleep he'll lose
his breath.   20
ANTHRAX. And does he close the lower outlet too,
Lest he lose wind?
STROBILUS.   You might believe my tale,
As I do yours.
ANTHRAX.   I do indeed believe.
STROBILUS. And when he washes, he bewails the
waste
Of water.
ANTHRAX. Do you think there could be begged 25
A good round sum from this man for to buy
Our liberty?
STROBILUS. By Jove! He would not give
Starvation, if you asked him. The other day
The barber cut his nails; he gathered all
The parings up, and carried them away.   30
ANTHRAX. He is indeed a stingy soul you tell of.
STROBILUS. And can you think indeed he lived so
sparely?
A hawk, it seems, once carried off his dinner.
So, full of tears, he goes before the judge;
Howling and plaining there, begins to ask   35
That the hawk should be bound over to appear.
If I had time I'd tell a thousand tales.
But which of you is nimblest?
ANTHRAX.   I, by far.
STROBILUS. A cook I want, and not a thief.
ANTHRAX.   I am one.
STROBILUS. And what say you?
CONGRIO.   I am as you can see. 40
ANTHRAX. He's only fit to cook a funeral feast;
That's all he does.
CONGRIO.   Five letters would describe
What you are; you're a thief.
ANTHRAX.   Trebly a thief.
STROBILUS. Be still! Which is the fatter lamb of
these?
ANTHRAX. This. (*Departs to house of* MEGADORUS
with lamb.)   45

STROBILUS. You, Congrio, take this one straight
within.
(*To some of the attendants*) You follow him; the
rest will come with me.
CONGRIO. It is not fair, they have the fatter lamb.
STROBILUS. But you shall have the fatter music
girl.
Go with him, Phrygia; you, Eleusium,   50
You come with us. (ELEUSIUM *and attendants go into
house of* MEGADORUS.)
CONGRIO.   O clever Strobilus!
You've put me off upon a mean old man,
From whom ev'n if I cried myself all hoarse
I should not get a shilling.
STROBILUS.   You're a fool,
And most ungrateful.
CONGRIO.   How is that?
STROBILUS.   D'ye ask? 55
Why first there'll be no crowd of servants there.
If you want aught, you get it for yourself,
Lest you should waste your time in asking for it;
With us there'll be a large establishment,
A crowd of servants, gold and silver plate,   60
Dresses and furniture; if any one
Should something lose (and you I know could not,
If none were by, prevent yourself from theft),
They say at once: "The cooks have taken it;
Catch him and bind him, put him in the well,   65
And beat him!" None of these will happen there,
For there is naught to steal. Come, follow me.
(*They approach the house of* EUCLIO.)
STROBILUS (*knocking*). Hi! Staphyla, come out,
open the door!
STAPHYLA. (*opening the door cautiously*). Who
calls?
STROBILUS. 'Tis Strobilus.
STAPHYLA.   And what d'ye want?
STROBILUS. Here, take these cooks, this music girl,
the food   70
To serve the wedding. Megadorus sends
All these for Euclio.
STAPHYLA.   I suppose it is
For Ceres' marriage?
STROBILUS.   Why?
STAPHYLA.   Because I see
You bring no wine.
STROBILUS.   That will be brought anon
When he comes from the market.
STAPHYLA.   We've no wood. 75
CONGRIO. Are there no doors?
STAPHYLA.   There are.
CONGRIO.   Then you
have wood.
You need not go outside.

---

74. **You bring no wine.** In the festivals called "the marriage of Ceres,"
the use of wine was forbidden.

STAPHYLA. What, wretch, although
Vulcan you serve, are we, to cook your dinner
That you may get your wage, are we to burn
Our dwelling to the ground?

CONGRIO. I don't ask that. 80

STROBILUS. Then take them in at once. (*Goes into
house of* MEGADORUS.)

STAPHYLA (*opening wide the door*). Come, follow
me! (CONGRIO *and others go inside.*)

(*Enter* PYTHODICUS *from the house of* MEGA-
DORUS.)

PYTHODICUS (*to himself*). Well now, I'll see to
what the cooks are doing;
And that today's a pretty heavy job.
They ought to do it in the cellar; thence
To take it up in baskets; if they eat 85
Below what they have cooked, then those above
Will go without their dinner, those below
Will get it. I am talking just as if
I had no business; when there's in the house
Such a crowd of harpies as is here today. (*Goes into
the house.*) 90

(*Enter* EUCLIO *from the forum with some flowers
and a small package.*)

EUCLIO (*to himself*). I wished today to brace my-
self a little,
To make a show at this my daughter's wedding;
I go to market; ask the price of fish;
They say they're dear, the lamb and beef are dear;
The veal, the dogfish, and the pork are dear; 95
And all the dearer, that I had no money.
Full vexed I come away; there's nought to buy;
To all this unclean herd I said adieu.
Then as I walked I thought thus to myself;
If, on a festal day like this, you spend 100
Your money freely, nothing spare, then you
Will want tomorrow; and this reasoning
My stomach and my heart approved, so I
Intend to celebrate this wedding here
At the smallest possible expense I can. 105
So I have bought a little frankincense,
And a few flowers; these shall now be placed
Around our household god, that he may grant
A happy issue. But do I really see
My house-door open? Such a noise within! 110
What, am I robbed?

CONGRIO (*within*). Go fetch a larger pot
If you can get one; this is far too small.

EUCLIO (*in great alarm*). I am undone; and all my
gold is taken!
The pot is sought; unless I run within
At once I'm good as dead. Oh! Help me now, 115
Apollo! help, and with your arrows slay
These treasure-laden thieves, as you have done
Before. Here must I rush and see what's taking
place.

(EUCLIO *runs into his house.*)

(*Enter* ANTHRAX *from the house of* MEGADORUS.)

ANTHRAX (*to servants within*). Here, Dromo,
clean the fish; Machaerio, you
Bone if you can the lamprey and the eel, 120
That all may be prepared when I return.
I go to seek a bread pan; see that cock
Is plucked e'en smoother than a player's chin.
But what's this noise next door? It is the cooks
At work. I'll go within and try to stop 125
Them making like confusion in this house.

(*He returns to the house of* MEGADORUS.)

(CONGRIO *and his assistants rush in haste from the
house of* EUCLIO.)

CONGRIO. Dear citizens, and fellow-countrymen,
Dwellers or strangers, whosoe'er ye be,
Make room for me to fly; let the whole street
Be open to my path. I never came 130
Before today to cook at such a place;
'Tis like a Bacchic orgy; they have beaten
My pupils and myself with sticks and staves.
I'm sore all over, and indeed quite dead!
That old boy took me for a boxing school; 135
I never saw posts come in handier
Than these; he beat us all and turned us out.
Alas! I am undone! Here comes again
The Bacchanalian orgy; he is here;
He follows. I know what to do; I'll go 140
The way my master went before today.

(*Enter* EUCLIO *from his house, stick in hand.*)

EUCLIO. Hallo! Why fly? Return, return, I say!

CONGRIO. Why are you shouting, fool?

EUCLIO. I'll lay your name
Before the magistrates.

CONGRIO. I pray you why?

EUCLIO. Because you wear a knife.

CONGRIO. As well becomes 145
A cook.

EUCLIO. Ay, and because you threatened me.

CONGRIO. The wrong was that I did not sheath it
in you.

EUCLIO. There's not a man more wicked than you
are,
Nor one I'd rather do an injury to.

CONGRIO. No need to say so; it is clear enough; 150
You've made me supple as a dancer is,
Wretch that I am! Why did you touch me thus,
And for what reason?

EUCLIO. Do you ask me why?
Have I done something less than was your due?

CONGRIO. You'll suffer for it, if my head can feel.

EUCLIO. I don't know what may come; but yours
feels now. 156
But pray what business had you in my house
When I was absent, without my commands?
I wish to know.

CONGRIO. Be quiet, then; we came
To cook your wedding-feast.

EUCLIO.   What matters it   160
To you if I eat meat that's cooked or raw?
Are you my master?

CONGRIO.   Well, I want to know
Whether you wish the dinner cooked or not.

EUCLIO. And I whether my things are safe with
     you
Or not.

CONGRIO. I only hope that I may take   165
The things away, that I have brought with me
All safe and sound. The rest it matters not,
For I want none of yours.

EUCLIO.   I know, I know.

CONGRIO. But why prevent us cook your dinner
     here?
What have we done or said you do not like?   170

EUCLIO. D'ye ask, you wretch, who thus have made
     your way
Through all the corners of my house and rooms?
If you had stopped beside the hearth, which is
Your proper place, your head had not been split.
You well deserved it. Now that you may know   175
My sentiments, if you come nearer to
My door than I shall order, you shall be
The most unhappy man that is. D'ye hear?
          (EUCLIO goes into his house.)

CONGRIO. Art going? Pray come back! And may
     Laverna,
Who watches over thieves, be kind to me!   180
If you don't order all my cooking things
To be returned to me, I'll make a row
Before the house. What am I now to do?
An evil day it was that brought me here;
The money that I got won't pay the doctor.   185
     (Re-enter EUCLIO from the house, with the pot of
gold under his cloak.)

EUCLIO (to himself). Ah! This at all events,
     where'er I go,
I'll carry with me, as my constant friend,
Nor e'er expose it to like perils again.
(To CONGRIO and others) Go now within, cooks and
     flute-players all,
Bring if you like the whole vile venal herd,   190
And cook, and act, and bustle as you please.

CONGRIO. Most timely, after you have split our
     heads.

EUCLIO. Go in! You came to work, and not to talk.

CONGRIO. Old gentleman, for this I'll make you
     pay;
I was engaged to cook, not to be beaten.   195

EUCLIO. Don't bother! Go to law! But first to cook,
Or else go and be hanged.

CONGRIO.   Pray go yourself.
     (CONGRIO and the assistants go into the house of
EUCLIO.)

EUCLIO (to himself). He's gone within. Immortal
     gods, he who,

Though poor, does business with wealthy men
Needs a brave heart to have. Thus Megadorus   200
Tries me in every way, pretends to send
His cooks to do me honour; sent this one
To steal this treasure from me. And to match him
Even my cock, that was the special friend
Of that old woman's, nearly ruined me,   205
And with his claws began to dig a hole
Where this was buried. Further need I say?
My heart was cut to the very quick; I seized
A stick, I kill the cock, in the very act
Of thieving. I believe the cooks themselves   210
Promised that cock a rich reward if he
Disclosed the treasure. Anyhow, I spoiled
Their little game. No more; the cock is dead.
But see, my neighbour Megadorus comes;
I dare not pass him; I must stop and speak.   215
     (Enter MEGADORUS from the forum.)

MEGADORUS (to himself, not seeing EUCLIO). To
     many friends I've told that I propose
To marry Euclio's daughter; they approve;
They think it wise and excellently done.
I would, I think, if others did the same;
If wealthy people married in this way   220
The daughters of the poor, nor asked a dower,
The state would be more happy than it is,
With less of jealousy than now we have;
Our wives would treat us with the more respect,
And we should live at less expense ourselves.   225
'Twould benefit the greater part of men;
A few old misers would object to it,
Whose greedy and insatiable souls
Nor law nor governor can hold in check.
But some may say, if marriage is for the poor,   230
Whom can the wealthy wed? Why, whom they
     choose,
If but their fortune has been left behind.
And in the place of fortune they would bring
A better disposition; I would make
Mules, which are dearer now than any horse,   235
Cheaper by far than any horse can be.

EUCLIO (aside). How gladly here I hearken to
     this man
Who speaks such pleasant things of narrow means!

MEGADORUS. No wife could say: "I brought to you
     a dower
Much larger than your fortune; therefore I   240
Must live in gold and purple, and have maids,
Pages and lackeys, mules and muleteers,
And carriages to ride in."

EUCLIO (aside).   Ah! How well he knows
Fine ladies' ways; I wish he was their tutor.

MEGADORUS. But now where'er you go, at your
     town house   245

233–236. **And in the place of fortune . . . be.** In this attack on the
institution of the dowry Plautus was supporting reforms proposed
at the time by Cato the censor.

You'll find more waggons waiting than you will
Ev'n at your country seat. But that's a trifle
To what it is when they present their bills.
There stands the fuller and embroiderer,
The goldsmith and the man who curls your hair, 250
The tailor and the hosier, and the host
Who dye your bridal veils in red or yellow,
Who sell you muffs, and perfumed slippers too,
Hucksters in linen, showmakers galore,
Clogs, slippers, sandals, all are here to sell, 255
To dye or mend your garments as you wish;
Sellers of stays and girdles swell the train.
You think them all; three hundred go and come.
Outside the duns are watching in the hall,
The weavers and the men who caskets make; 260
They've reckoned up; the money paid; 'tis all,
You fancy; when once more these come in view,
Dyers in something else, some wretched thing
That makes still further levies on your purse.
 EUCLIO (*aside*). I would address him, but I fear
  to stop 265
This nice recital of our ladies' ways.
Let him proceed.
 MEGADORUS. And when at length you've paid
For all this female rubbish, comes in view
The taxgatherer, presents his bill; you go
And reckon with your banker, while he waits 270
Undined, expecting to receive his pay.
When the account is furnished, then you find
You've overdrawn; the tax-man has to wait
Another day. These are the cares that wait,
The inconveniences and vast expense, 275
On these huge dowries; she who's none at all
Is in her husband's power; and dowered wives
Bring loss and trouble to their husband's lives.
But, see, my neighbour comes. Euclio, good day!
 EUCLIO. Most gladly have I listened to your
  words. 280
 MEGADORUS. Didst hear them?
 EUCLIO. Ay. I did from the
  very first.
 MEGADORUS. Methinks it would be better still if
  you
Looked rather sprucer for your daughter's wedding.
 EUCLIO. According to our means and circum-
  stances,
Our wealth and show should still proportioned be.
Let those who have, think of their high estate. 286
But I, and such as me, no more of wealth
Possess than public rumour gives to us.
 MEGADORUS. Surely you have; may the gods make
  it more.
 EUCLIO (*aside*). I do not like his words: "surely
  you have;" 290
He knows as well as I do what I have;
The old woman's told him.
 MEGADORUS. Why d'ye speak apart?

 EUCLIO. I thought of making a complaint to you.
 MEGADORUS. On what?
 EUCLIO. On what, d'ye ask? You
  who have filled
Nigh every corner of my house with thieves; 295
Who've sent into it five hundred cooks at least,
With six hands each, like Geryon of old.
Argus himself who was all eyes, to whom
Jove once entrusted Io, he could not
Keep watch upon them, even if he would. 300
A music girl, who by herself could drink
The famous fountain of Pirene dry,
If bubbling over with wine! And then their food—
 MEGADORUS. I've sent as much as would a legion
  feed;
Aye, and a lamb beside.
 EUCLIO. I've never seen 305
A more curious beast than that.
 MEGADORUS. How curious?
 EUCLIO. All bone and skin; so thin with toil and
  trouble;
You can see right through it in the light of day;
'Tis as transparent as an ivory lamp.
 MEGADORUS. I bought it to be butchered.
 EUCLIO. A splendid bargain,
For 'tis already dead.
 MEGADORUS. Euclio, I wish 311
To drink with you today.
 EUCLIO. I cannot do so.
 MEGADORUS. But I will bid a cask of rich old wine
To be brought from my cellar.
 EUCLIO. I can drink
But water only.
 MEGADORUS. If I live today, 315
I'll send you back as drunk as any lord—
You who drink only water.
 EUCLIO (*aside*). Ah! I see
What is his aim; to get quit of me with wine,
That is his plan, and what I have, annex.
But I'll take care; I'll put it out of doors. 320
And he shall lose his wine and trouble too.
 MEGADORUS. Unless you want me further, I
  shall go
To get me ready for the sacrifice. (*Goes into his
  house.*)
 EUCLIO (*to object under cloak*). Ah, little pot,
  how many foes you have,
You and the gold entrusted to your care. 325
And now the best that I can do is this,
To take you to the temple of Good Faith
And hide you there. Good Faith, you know me well,
And I know you; so take good care to yourself,

297. Geryon, a three-bodied monster in Greek mythology. 298–299.
Argus himself . . . Io. Actually it was Juno who set the many-eyed
Argus to watching her husband's mistress day and night. 302. **foun-
tain of Pirene;** at Corinth in Greece.

And see you do not change the name you bear, 330
If I trust you with this. Relying on
Your honesty, Good Faith, I come to you.

(He goes into the temple of Faith.)

ACT FOUR

(Enter the SLAVE *of* LYCONIDES.*)*

SLAVE *(to himself).* This is the office of a useful
    slave
To do as I do, nor to grumble at
Nor yet oppose a master's bidding. For
The slave who wants to serve his master well,
Does first his master's work and then his own, 5
And if he sleeps, why let him sleep, as if
He were a slave. Who serves a loving master
Like my own, if he should chance to see
That he's in love, that is the slave's concern:
To bring him back to safety, not to drive 10
Him further on the path he wants to go.
Just as to boys who learn to swim is given
A raft of rushes to make less their toil,
That they may use their hands more easily;
In the same way a slave should be a raft, 15
To bear his master up, when he's in love.
His master's will he studies, and his eyes
Note what is on his brow; his last command,
Swifter than courser's flight, he hastes to obey.
Who takes this care, escapes the censuring thong;
Nor keeps his fetters bright by constant wear. 21
My master is in love with Euclio's daughter;
And now we hear that she is to be married
To Megadorus; he has sent me now
To spy about, and learn what is going on. 25
Here by this sacred altar I will stand
All unsuspected, and from hence can judge
What here or there is being carried on.

(Enter EUCLIO *from the temple of faith.)*

EUCLIO *(not seeing* SLAVE). Take care, Good
    Faith, you do not indicate
To a single soul that all my gold is there. 30
I do not fear lest any find the place,
It is so hidden away; still, he would have
A pretty booty who should find the pot
Laden with gold. See to it then, Good Faith.
Now I will wash me for the sacrifice 35
And not delay my neighbour when he comes
To take my daughter home. And so, Good Faith,
Again and yet again, I say, that I
May carry off the pot all sound and safe,
To you I so entrust it. In your shrine 40
And grove it lies securely hidden away.

(He goes into his house.)

SLAVE. Ye gods immortal, what is this I hear
This man to say, that he has hidden away

A heavy pot of gold within this shrine?
Good Faith, see to it that you're not more kind 45
To him than me. This man, methinks, is father
To her my master loves. I will go in
And spy around the temple; if I find
The gold, when this man's back is turned; then if
I do, I'll brew a stoup of wine for you, 50
And, when I do it, drink the same myself.

(He goes into the temple.)

*(*EUCLIO *hurries from his house.)*

EUCLIO *(to himself).* 'Twas not for nothing that
    the raven cried
At my left hand, and flew close to the ground
And croaked anon; my heart began to play
A curious game, and leaped into my throat. 55
I am all shaking; I must run and run.

(He rushes into the temple and drags out the
SLAVE.)

EUCLIO. Out, out of doors, vile worm, that just
    has crept
Out of the ground! But now, you were not here,
And now you are, you die! You wretched cheat,
I'll treat you as you well deserve to be. 60

SLAVE. What demon troubles you? Or what
    have I
To do with you? Why do you trouble me?
Why drag me thus? Why beat me as you do?

EUCLIO. Most worthy of a beating of all men!
Still asking questions, you, who are a thief, 65
Or even more than that, a triple thief.

SLAVE. What have I stolen?

EUCLIO.   Bring it back to me.

SLAVE. What should I bring?

EUCLIO.   D'ye want to know what 'tis?

SLAVE. I've taken nothing.

EUCLIO.   Give it back to me.

SLAVE. What must I do?

EUCLIO.   You shall not take it hence.

SLAVE. What do you want?

EUCLIO.   Now put it down at once.

SLAVE. I think, old gentleman, you're wont to
    jest. 72

EUCLIO. Be done with jesting; put it down, I say.

SLAVE. And put what down? Pray tell me what
    it is
By its own name; I've touched and taken nothing.

EUCLIO. Show me your hands!

SLAVE.   Look there!

EUCLIO.   And yet again!

SLAVE. See there!

EUCLIO.   And show the third hand now, I pray!

SLAVE. Distempered dreams and wild illusions vex
This old man's soul. D'ye want to do mischief?

EUCLIO. Ay, marry, all I can, not hanging you;
And that will come if you do not confess. 81

SLAVE. Confess to what?

EUCLIO.   What you have taken away.

---

1. *Slave of Lyconides.* The manuscripts mistakenly assign the slave's
speeches to Strobilus.

SLAVE. The gods destroy me if I have taken aught,
Or even wished to do so.

EUCLIO.　　　　　　　Shake your cloak.

SLAVE. Yes, as you will.

EUCLIO.　　　　　　　Lest there be something hidden
Between the folds.

SLAVE.　　　　　　Try any way you like.　86

EUCLIO. You wretch, how smooth you speak, that I may not
Detect you in the theft. I know your dodges.
Show me your right hand now.

SLAVE.　　　　　　　Well, there it is.

EUCLIO. And now your left.

SLAVE.　　　　　　You see, I proffer both.

EUCLIO. I do not care to search. Restore the things.　91

SLAVE. And what restore?

EUCLIO.　　　　　You jest, for you must have it.

SLAVE. Have what?

EUCLIO.　　　I need not say, you know full well.
Restore me what you've had of mine.

SLAVE.　　　　　　　You're mad.
You've searched me as you like, and nothing found.　95

EUCLIO. Stay, who is that who was inside with you?
(Aside) I am undone; that other is inside.
If I lose sight of this one, he'll be off.
Yet I have searched him; he has nothing on him.
(Aloud) Go where you like.

SLAVE.　　　　　You be completely damned!

EUCLIO. He is not thankful. I will go inside　101
And wring the neck of your companion.
Are you away? Art off? And out of sight?

SLAVE. I am.

EUCLIO. Take care you never see me more.
　　　　　　　　　(Goes into the temple.)

SLAVE. I'd rather perish by some foul disease　105
Than not contrive to play some nasty trick
On this old man today. He will not dare
To hide away his gold in this place now.
He'll take it out and change the hiding-place.
I hear the door. And see, he brings the gold!　110
I'll stand aside behind the door and watch.

　　(Enter EUCLIO from the temple, with the pot of gold.)

EUCLIO (to himself). I thought Good Faith was fairly to be trusted,
But cruelly she's disappointed me.
But for the raven I had been undone.
I wish to see him once again and make　115
Some small return—a compliment, not meat.
And now I know a solitary place
Where I may hide this pot; it is the grove
Of our god Silvanus, stretching far beyond
The city wall, with willows planted round.　120

There I will choose a spot; for I am sure
I had rather trust Silvanus than Good Faith.
　　　　　　　　　(EUCLIO departs.)

SLAVE. Good luck! The gods are full of kindness to me.
I'll run before and climb into a tree,
And watch from thence where he may hide the gold.　125
For, though my master bid me to stay here,
That gain is worth a blow doth still appear.
　　　　　　　　　(The SLAVE departs.)
　　　　(Enter LYCONIDES and EUNOMIA.)

LYCONIDES. I've told you, mother, and you know the story
Of what has taken place between myself
And Euclio's daughter. Now I pray you tell　130
My uncle all; once more I do beseech you
As I have done before.

EUNOMIA.　　　　　Your wish is mine.
And this I hope my brother will consent
To grant; and, if things be as you assert,
Your cause is just. You say it did take place　135
When you were overcome with use of wine?

LYCONIDES. And think you, mother, I'd impose on you?

PHAEDRIA (inside EUCLIO's house). Help me, dear nurse! Juno Lucina,
Help!

LYCONIDES. The thing is clear enough; she has a child.

EUNOMIA. Then come within with me, and see my brother,　140
That he at my request may grant your prayer.
　　(She goes into the house of MEGADORUS.)

LYCONIDES. I follow you. (To himself) But now I wonder where
My servant Strobilus can be. I bid
Him wait me here. Yet now I think on it,
It were unfair to blame him, as he may　145
Be helping me elsewhere. I'll come within;
The meeting's one of life or death to me.
　　(He goes into the house of MEGADORUS.)
　　(Enter SLAVE of LYCONIDES, with the pot of gold.)

SLAVE (to himself). Myself I do surpass in stores of wealth
The fabled griffins, who are said to dwell
Upon the golden mountains; mighty kings　150
I scarce do notice; they are beggars all.
Philip himself I am. Oh! Blessed day,
On which I went from here, and was the first,
And placed myself in hiding on the tree,
And watched from thence where he would place the gold.　155
When he was gone, I creep along the tree,

138. Juno Lucina. Juno with the attribute of Lucina was goddess of childbirth.　149. fabled griffins. Half eagle and half lion, the griffins guarded gold mines and hidden treasures.

And disinter a pot quite full of gold.
I see the old man go; he sees not me;
I leaned aside a little from the road.
But see, he comes, I'll hide the gold at home. 160
(*Departs.*)
(*Enter* EUCLIO *frantic.*)
EUCLIO (*to himself*). I'm ruined, slaughtered,
    quite undone! Oh, where
Am I to go? Or not to go? Stay! Stop!
But whom? Or what? I cannot see, I'm blind!
I cannot say for certain where I go,
Nor where, nor who I am. (*To audience*) I pray
    your help 165
To point me out the man who stole the gold.
Ay, there they sit in white like honest men.
What say you? I can trust you; and I know
An honest man by sight. What is it now?
Why do you laugh? There are thieves enough, I
    know, 170
And many thieves. What, none of these have it?
You kill me! Don't you know? Say who it is.
Alas, alas, I am undone! I'm killed!
A pretty state of things! So much of woe,
So much of grief has this day brought to me! 175
Hunger and poverty, most wretched man!
What hope of life to one who's lost so much,
So much that I have guarded? I denied
Myself all pleasure; others now will joy,
At my expense, my loss. I cannot bear it! 180
   LYCONIDES (*entering from the house of* MEGADO-
     RUS).
Who is this man who howls before our doors,
Lamenting loudly? Euclio 'tis, I think.
Ah, I am ruined! Everything is known.
He knows what's happened to his daughter now.
What must I do? Stay here, or go away? 185
Approach him, or fly from him? I know not.
   EUCLIO. Who is 't who speaks?
   LYCONIDES.   A most unhappy man!
   EUCLIO. And I not less so, for to me has chanced
Such ills and sorrow.
   LYCONIDES.   Nay, be of good heart.
   EUCLIO. How can I?
   LYCONIDES.   'Cause the deed that troubles you
Is mine. I do admit it.
   EUCLIO.   What is this? 191
   LYCONIDES. The truth.
   EUCLIO.   What have I done, young
    man, to you,
That you should ruin me, and leave forlorn
My children and myself?
   LYCONIDES.   God was my guide;
'Twas he who led me on.
   EUCLIO.   And how was that? 195
   LYCONIDES. I do admit my sin, and know that I
Deserve your blame. Therefore I come to you
And ask your pardon.

   EUCLIO.   But why did you dare
To touch what was not yours?
   LYCONIDES.   What do you want?
It cannot be undone. I think the gods 200
Have willed it, or it never could have been.
   EUCLIO. I think the gods have willed that I should
    kill you.
   LYCONIDES. Nay, say not so.
   EUCLIO.   But why against my will
Have you laid hands on that which was my own?
   LYCONIDES. 'Twas wine and love that made me.
   EUCLIO.   Daring man!
To come to me with such a tale as that! 206
If that is law, then might we just as well
In open daylight take a woman's jewels,
And say when caught that we were drunk, and
    did it
For the sake of love; too vile are wine and love 210
If they excuse whate'er we choose to do.
   LYCONIDES. I come to ask your pardon for my folly.
   EUCLIO. I like not those who first do ill, and then
Excuse themselves. You know it was not yours;
And you should not have touched it.
   LYCONIDES.   Well, I did it.
And now I will not argue more about it. 216
   EUCLIO. Keep mine against my will?
   LYCONIDES.   I do not ask
To have it so, but think it should be mine.
And now, O Euclio, I'm sure you'll realize
It should be mine.
   EUCLIO.   I'll take you to the judge, 220
And serve a writ, until you bring it back.
   LYCONIDES. And bring what back?
   EUCLIO.   Why, what
    you stole from me.
   LYCONIDES. I stole? Whence? And what is it?
   EUCLIO.   May great Jove
Himself so love you in the same degree,
As you are ignorant!
   LYCONIDES.   Unless you tell me 225
What 'tis you seek.
   EUCLIO.   A pot of gold it is
I ask, which you admit that you have stolen.
   LYCONIDES. I never said so, and I never did it.
   EUCLIO. What, you deny?
   LYCONIDES.   Most certainly I do.
I know no gold, nor any pot at all. 230
   EUCLIO. Give me the pot you stole from Silvan's
    grove.
Go, bring it back; I'll give to you a third.
Although a thief, I won't deal hardly with you.
   LYCONIDES. You are not sane, in calling me a
    thief.
I thought that you had spoke of something else, 235
Which close concerns me. If you have the time,
There is a most important thing I want
To speak of to you.

EUCLIO.   Tell me on your word
You have not stolen it.

LYCONIDES.   Upon my honour!

EUCLIO. Nor know who did'st so?

LYCONIDES.   No, upon my word!

EUCLIO. And if you know, you'll tell me.

LYCONIDES.   That I swear.

EUCLIO. And will not ask a share, nor shield the
     thief?   242

LYCONIDES. Most certainly.

EUCLIO.   And what if you play false?

LYCONIDES. May Jupiter do with me what he will.

EUCLIO. Enough! Now tell me what you want
     of me.   245

LYCONIDES. Well, if you do not know my family,
This Megadorus here, he is my uncle;
Antimachus my father was, and I
Lyconides am called; my mother is Eunomia.

EUCLIO. The family I know.   250
But what d'ye want with me?

LYCONIDES.   You have a daughter?

EUCLIO. I have, at home.

LYCONIDES.   Betrothed to my uncle?

EUCLIO. You know it all.

LYCONIDES.   He bid me tell you he
Renounces now her hand.

EUCLIO (angrily).   Renounces now
When all is ready and the wedding furnished? 255
May all the gods and goddesses destroy
This man for whom I've lost so much today.

LYCONIDES. Be of good cheer. May all yet turn
     out well
For you and for your daughter; pray it be so.

EUCLIO. May the gods do it!

LYCONIDES.   And the same to me!
Now listen. There's not a man who's sinned, 261
But is ashamed and sorry, if he's worth
A straw. Now I beseech you, Euclio,
In this misfortune my imprudence caused
You and your daughter, you should pardon me 265
And give her me for wife as the law permits.
I do confess I did her grievous wrong
On Ceres' night, through wine and youthful impulse.

EUCLIO. Alas! Alas! And what is this I hear?

LYCONIDES. Why should you mourn, when at your
     daughter's wedding   270
You will at once as grandfather appear.
She bare a child just ten months after it;
Pray reckon for yourself; and therefore 'tis
My uncle has renounced her hand for me.
Go in, and you will hear that it is so.   275

EUCLIO. Ah me! I am quite ruined! Evils come
One on the top of others, clinging fast.
I'll go within and see if this is so.
                (Goes into his house.)

LYCONIDES. And I will follow. (To himself) My
     affairs appear

To have reached shoal waters, where my safety lies.
But now I cannot find where he should be,   281
My servant Strobilus; I'll wait for him,
And then will follow this man; I will give
Him time to make enquiries from his daughter
And from the nurse; for she at least knows all. 285

ACT FIVE

(Enter SLAVE of LYCONIDES.)

SLAVE (to himself). Ye gods immortal, with what
     joys have you
Presented me; how great the sum of them!
I have a four pound pot that is full of gold!
Who now more rich than me? What man at Athens
To whom the gods are kinder?

LYCONIDES (to himself).   Sure, I thought, 5
I heard the voice of some one speaking here.

SLAVE (aside). Ah! Do I see my master?

LYCONIDES (aside).   And is it
My servant coming here I see?

SLAVE (aside).   It is.

LYCONIDES (aside). And not another.

SLAVE (aside).   I'll advance
     to meet him.

LYCONIDES (aside). And I'll draw nearer. I be-
     lieve that he   10
Has, as I ordered, seen this lady's nurse.

SLAVE (aside). And why not tell him I have found
     this treasure?
I will that he may set me free. I'll go.
(To LYCONIDES) I've found—

LYCONIDES.   What have you found?

SLAVE.   Why, not that which
Boys look for in a bean and shout with joy,   15
When they have found it nestling there inside.

LYCONIDES. You're jesting, as you're wont.

SLAVE.   Stay, master, hear.

LYCONIDES. Speak then.

SLAVE.   Today I found a hoard of wealth,
Too much for me.

LYCONIDES.   And where, I pray, was that?

SLAVE. A four pound pot of gold.

LYCONIDES.   What crime is this?

SLAVE. I stole it from this old man Euclio.   21

LYCONIDES. Where is the gold?

SLAVE.   Why, in a chest at home.
And now I wish my freedom at your hand.

LYCONIDES. I make you free, most scoundrellest
     of knaves?

SLAVE. Off with you, master! I know what you
     want.   25
And cleverly I laid a bait for you.
You were prepared to take it. What if I
Myself had found it?

282. **My servant Strobilus,** that is, his slave, not the Strobilus of Act
Three.

LYCONIDES.   Now we want no trifling.
Bring me the gold.
   SLAVE.   Must I return the gold?
   LYCONIDES. Yes, that it may be given to him.
   SLAVE.   And whence?
   LYCONIDES. Just now you did confess 'twas in
     your chest.   31
   SLAVE. Yes, I was joking, as I'm wont to do.
   LYCONIDES. But how, I pray?
   SLAVE.   Then kill me if you like;
Of this be sure, you shall not take it hence.

(The remainder of the play is lost. Lyconides apparently returned the pot of gold to Euclio and received permission to marry his daughter; Euclio gave the gold to the young couple, saying as he did so, "I never had a minute's peace day or night watching it; now I will sleep.")

Virgil

70–19 B.C.

The arrival of empire with Augustus coincided with a sharp break in Roman literary tradition. The generation of Cicero died out in the forties, and with it that freedom of self-expression characteristic of Lucretius, Catullus, and Cicero himself. In its place came a new school, patronized by Maecenas, Pollio, and the Emperor, which owed its support to the Empire and industriously set about deserving it. Literature took on a new restraint and new brilliance, and authors vied with each other in venerating Augustus, the Julian line, and the empire that it had created. The chief of these new writers was Virgil, the national poet of Rome.

Publius Vergilius Maro of Mantua in Cisalpine Gaul was intended for the law by his ambitious peasant father, but one experience in court convinced the shy and sensitive youth that he should apply his excellent education to philosophy and poetry. Always happiest in peaceful seclusion, he found his studies interrupted by a succession of civil wars. In 41 B.C. his family farm was confiscated in favor of one of Antony's soldiers, but he supposedly applied to Octavian in Rome for redress and thus came to the notice of the future emperor. He had already begun to compose the *Eclogues*, his earliest notable work, and included in the first of them a graceful mention of the incident. The *Eclogues* (39 B.C.), ten little pastorals that the painstaking Virgil took three years to write, seem artificial and cold in comparison with the writings of his model, Theocritus, but they established his reputation and were immensely popular in the centuries to follow. The famous Fourth Eclogue, dedicated to the consul Pollio, passes from the world of playful shepherds to salute the impending birth to a glorious father of a child in whose lifetime the Golden Age of peace and prosperity would be restored to the earth. Though variously interpreted now as referring to a child soon to be born to his patron, Pollio, or Antony, or even Octavian, it was accepted in the Middle Ages as a prophecy of the imminent coming of Christ and accounts for Virgil's inclusion among the Prophets in medieval religious plays.

Securely entrenched in the esteem of Maecenas and Octavian, he next wrote at their request the *Georgics* (30 B.C.), a slender work which occupied him for seven years. It was designed to assist the back-to-the-farm movement of Octavian through painting a fresh and alluring picture of the farmer's occupation. The four books of this magnificent didactic poem treat, in turn, crops and the weather, the culture of grapes and olives, cattle-breeding, and bee-keeping, but the agricultural information is transformed by poetic treatment and enlivened by digressions on the wholesome simplicity of farm-life, myths associated with the earth, and even praise of Augustus. John Dryden called the *Georgics* "the best poem of the best poet."

Modern readers know Virgil largely through his magnum opus, the *Aeneid*. It was begun at the request of Augustus but was left unfinished when Virgil died of a fever at Brundisium in 19 B.C.* Rome had at this time no folk epic comparable to those of Greece and had long since outgrown the crude *Annales* of Ennius. Augustus wanted a literary epic that would do justice to the Empire and emphasize his own part in founding it. Other poets were approached, but only Virgil rose to the task. And although the last eleven years of his life went to the slow composition of its twelve books, this perfectionist was still so dissatisfied with its lack of finish that he requested on his deathbed that it be burned. Augustus prevented this and carried out his alternative wish that two of his friends should edit it. The *Aeneid* was finally published two years later.

Instead of building his epic around the contemporary empire or the personality of Augustus, Virgil showed his good taste in electing to retell and elaborate the traditional legend of the settlement of Aeneas in Latium and the establishment of the Julian line. Superficially, the *Aeneid* imitates the Homeric epics. The meter is once more the hexameter, and the opening "Arms and the man I sing" recalls Homer's beginnings. The epic commonplaces reappear in *pius Aeneas* (dutiful Aeneas) and *fidus Achates* (faithful Achates, his friend). The first six books are reminiscent of the *Odyssey* in telling how the Trojan prince fled from his burning city and, by the spiteful will of the goddess Juno, wandered for years through the Mediterranean. In Books II and III Aeneas tells Dido of his adventures, as Odysseus had told his story at the court of King Alcinoüs. In Book V Aeneas describes the funeral games for his father's memory, comparable to the games in the *Iliad* to honor the dead Patroclus; and in Book VI the descent of Aeneas into Hades recalls the similar experience of Odysseus. But the tragic love of Dido in Book IV is the invention of Virgil and the most famous

---

* Virgil's tomb at Naples became a kind of shrine in the Middle Ages and a Mecca of literary pilgrims down to our day.

and appealing episode in a work not generally distinguished for its warmth.

The last six books recounting the arrival of Aeneas in Italy and his war with the hero Turnus for the hand of Lavinia, daughter of King Latinus of Latium, are intended to suggest Homer's epic of war, the *Iliad*. The struggle for a woman reminds us of the Trojan War for Helen, and the final combat of the heroes in Book XII recalls Achilles and Hector. Again, the roll of the Italian armies in Book VII is modeled on the catalog of the ships in the *Iliad*. Perhaps the weariest Homeric imitation appears in the supernatural machinery, for the struggle of Juno and Venus over the destiny of Aeneas, the son of Venus, is an empty convention without religious conviction or poetic value.

Yet Virgil was in his way a religious man, looking beyond paganism to a mysticism inspired by Greek philosophy and prophetic of Christian teachings. In Hades, Anchises tells his son that all creation is animated by a great spirit, which wars in man against material things that entice him to evil. Hence in the world to come, man's soul must be purified in a kind of Purgatory before it is free to enter the Elysian Fields. If the purification is incomplete the soul is reincarnated in a new body to continue the process. This doctrine made a strong appeal to Dante, who incorporated Virgil's Hades in his *Inferno* and made Virgil himself a leading character in the *Commedia*. Akin to Virgil's mysticism is his romanticism, which appears in the tragic tale of Dido and in the array of fantastic creatures and places in Book VI. The poetic imagination in such episodes as these helps to temper the intellectual cast of the poem as a whole and the weary quality that betrays how inconsistent were the heroic theme and the gory battlefield with the quiet, retiring nature of the poet. The *Aeneid* was written by plan and often with stoic effort, and hence lacks the robustness, simplicity, and spontaneity of Homer. *Pius Aeneas* is a middle-aged man weighed down with stoic duties and denied by his fate and by the gods of any power to act for himself. He is the embodiment of Rome and the prophecy of Augustus, and he must deny his heart, even to abandoning disgracefully the woman he loves, in order to fulfill his high destiny. He is at bottom a Roman senator forced to exchange the toga for the leather tunic of the warrior. Only contrast this reserved and thoughtful man with the passionate youth, Achilles, full of ardor and high spirits and unrestrained in expressing them, and you will sense the difference between the youthful, extravagant Greeks and the stoic, sophisticated Romans.

Virgil's appeal is unlike Homer's, but it is still unmistakable. Though he has lost the refreshing youth of the vigorous Greek, he knows more, and speaks with the wisdom and humanity of a mature mind. He has thought seriously of life and death and feels tenderness for simple people. He is a magnificent poet, with the capacity to express in lovely images his awareness of beauty, and with a sweet and sonorous style—one of the most uniformly polished in all literature. For centuries after his death the *Aeneid* was considered the greatest of all poems, and it has not lost its charm.

The Messiah
(Eclogue IV)

SICILIAN Muse, begin a loftier strain!
Tho' lowly shrubs, and trees that shade the
plain,
Delight not all; Sicilian Muse, prepare
To make the vocal woods deserve a consul's care.
The last great age, foretold by sacred rhymes, 5
Renews its finished course: Saturnian times
Roll round again; and mighty years, begun
From their first orb, in radiant circles run.
The base, degenerate iron offspring ends;
A golden progeny from heaven descends. 10
O chaste Lucina, speed the mother's pains,
And haste the glorious birth! thy own Apollo reigns!
The lovely boy, with his auspicious face,
Shall Pollio's consulship and triumph grace;
Majestic months set out with him to their appointed
race. 15
The father banished virtue shall restore,
And crimes shall threat the guilty world no more.
The son shall lead the life of gods, and be
By gods and heroes seen, and gods and heroes see.
The jarring nations he in peace shall bind, 20
And with paternal virtues rule mankind.
Unbidden Earth shall wreathing ivy bring,
And fragrant herbs (the promises of spring),
As her first offerings to her infant king.
The goats with strutting dugs shall homeward speed,
And lowing herds secure from lions feed. 26
His cradle shall with rising flowers be crowned:
The serpent's brood shall die; the sacred ground
Shall weeds and poisonous plants refuse to bear;
Each common bush shall Syrian roses wear. 30
But when heroic verse his youth shall raise,
And form it to hereditary praise,
Unlabored harvests shall the fields adorn,
And clustered grapes shall blush on every thorn;
The knotted oaks shall showers of honey weep, 35
And thro' the matted grass the liquid gold shall
creep.
Yet of old fraud some footsteps shall remain:
The merchant still shall plow the deep for gain;
Great cities shall with walls be compassed round,
And sharpened shares shall vex the fruitful
ground. . . .

The Messiah. Translated by John Dryden.
1. **Sicilian Muse,** the muse of pastoral verse, associated with Sicily, the birthplace of Theocritus. 4. **consul,** Pollio, apparently the father of the child whose birth is predicted here. 6. **Saturnian times,** the ancient age of gold, when civilization was supposed to have been introduced into Italy by Saturnus, a mythical king identified with the Greek Cronos as the father of Jupiter, Juno, and other gods. 11. **chaste Lucina,** the goddess of childbirth. 18. **The son shall lead the life of gods.** . . . The parallel of this whole passage with the Christian tradition of the life of Christ is striking.

But when to ripened manhood he shall grow,
The greedy sailor shall the seas forego;
No keel shall cut the waves for foreign ware,
For every soil shall every product bear.
The laboring hind his oxen shall disjoin;   45
No plough shall hurt the glebe, no pruning hook the
    vine;
Nor wool shall in dissembled colors shine.
But the luxurious father of the fold,
With native purple, or unborrowed gold,
Beneath his pompous fleece shall proudly sweat;
And under Tyrian robes the lamb shall bleat.   51
The Fates, when they this happy web have spun,
Shall bless the sacred clew, and bid it smoothly run.
Mature in years, to ready honors move,
O of celestial seed! O foster son of Jove!   55
See, laboring Nature calls thee to sustain
The nodding frame of heaven, and earth, and main!
See to their base restored, earth, seas, and air;
And joyful ages, from behind, in crowding ranks ap-
    pear.
To sing thy praise, would Heaven my breath pro-
    long,   60
Infusing spirits worthy such a song. . . .
Begin, auspicious boy, to cast about
Thy infant eyes, and, with a smile, thy mother single
    out:
Thy mother well deserves that short delight,
The nauseous qualms of ten long months and travail
    to requite.   65
Then smile: the frowning infant's doom is read;
No god shall crown the board, nor goddess bless the
    bed.

The Aeneid

BOOK I

the argument

I SING of arms and the man who came of old, a
fated wanderer, from the coasts of Troy to Italy
and the shore of Lavinium; hard driven on land and
on the deep by the violence of heaven, by reason
of cruel Juno's unforgetful anger, and hard bestead
in war also, ere he might found a city and carry his
gods into Latium; from whom is the Latin race, the
lords of Alba, and high-embattled Rome. *Invocation*
    Muse, tell me why, for what attaint of her deity,
or in what vexation, did the Queen of heaven urge
on a man excellent in goodness to circle through all
those afflictions, to face all those toils? Is anger so
fierce in celestial spirits?
    There was a city of ancient days that Tyrian set-
tlers dwelt in, Carthage, over against Italy and the
Tiber mouths afar; plenteous of wealth, and most

10

The Aeneid. A Translated by J.F W. MacKail. Used with the permission of The Macmillan Company.
3. **Lavinium,** a town in Latium, supposedly founded by Aeneas and
named for his wife Lavinia.

grim in the arts of war; wherein, they say, alone
beyond all other lands had Juno her seat, and held   *cause*
Samos itself less dear. Here was her armour, here
her chariot; even now, if fate permit, the goddess   20
strives to nurture it for dominion over the nations.
Nevertheless she had heard that a race was issuing
of the blood of Troy, which sometime should overthrow her Tyrian fortress; from it should come a
people, lord of lands and tyrannous in war, the destroyer of Libya: thus the Fates unrolled their vol-   *idiom*
ume. Fearful of that, the daughter of Saturn . . .
drove all over ocean the Trojan remnant left of the   *idiom*
Greek host and merciless Achilles, and held them
afar from Latium; and many a year were they wan-   30
dering driven of fate around all the seas. Such work
was it to found the Roman people.
    Hardly out of sight of the land of Sicily did they
set their sails joyously to sea, and upturned the salt *metaphor*
foam with brazen prow, when Juno, the undying
wound still deep in her heart, thus broke out alone:
    'Am I then to abandon my baffled purpose, power-
less to keep the Teucrian king from Italy? and because fate forbids me? . . . I, who move queen
among immortals, I sister and wife of Jove, wage   40
warfare all these years with a single people; and is
there any who still adores Juno's divinity, or will lay
sacrifice with prayer on her altars?'
    Such thoughts inly revolving in her fiery heart,
the goddess reaches Aeolia, the home of storm-
clouds, the land teeming with furious southern gales.
Here in a dreary cavern Aeolus keeps under royal
dominion and yokes in dungeon fetters the struggling winds and resounding storms. They with
mighty moan rage indignant round their mountain   50
barriers. In his lofty citadel Aeolus sits sceptred,   *description*
assuages their temper and soothes their rage; else
would they carry with them seas and lands, and the
depth of heaven, and sweep them through space in
their flying course. But, fearful of this, the Lord
omnipotent has hidden them in caverned gloom, and
laid mountains high over them, and appointed them
a ruler, who under a fixed covenant should know to
strain and slacken the reins at command. To him
now Juno spoke thus in suppliant accents: 60
    'Aeolus—for to thee has the father of gods and
king of men given to lull and to lift the wind-blown
waves—the race I hate sails the Tyrrhene sea, carrying Ilium and her conquered household-gods into
Italy. Rouse thy winds to fury, and overwhelm and
sink their hulls, or drive them asunder and strew
ocean with their corpses. Mine are twice seven
nymphs of passing loveliness, and Deïopea is most
excellent in beauty of them all; her will I unite to
thee in wedlock to be thine for ever; that for this

19. **Samos,** where stood one of the most splendid temples of Juno.
38. **Teucrian,** Trojan, after Teucer, first king of Troy.

thy service she may fulfil all her years at thy side, and make thee father of a beautiful race.'

Aeolus thus returned: 'Thine, O queen, the task to search out what thou wilt; for me it is right to do thy bidding. From thee I hold all this my realm, from thee my sceptre and Jove's grace; thou dost grant me to take my seat at the feasts of the gods, and makest me sovereign over clouds and storms.'

Even with these words, turning his spear, he struck the side of the hollow hill, and the winds, as in banded array, pour where passage is given them, and cover earth with eddying blasts. East wind and south wind together, and the gusty south-wester, falling prone on the sea, stir it up from its lowest chambers, and roll vast billows to the shore. Behind rises shouting of men and creaking of cordage. In a moment clouds blot sky and daylight from the Teucrians' eyes; black night broods over the deep. The heavens crash with thunder, and the air quivers with incessant flashes; all menaces them with instant death. Straightway Aeneas' frame grows unnerved and chill, and stretching either hand to heaven, he cries thus aloud: 'Ah, thrice and four times happy they who found their doom in high-embattled Troy before their fathers' faces!'. . .

As the cry leaves his lips, a gust of the shrill north strikes full on the sail and raises the waves up to heaven. The oars are snapped; the prow swings away and gives her side to the waves; down in a heap comes a broken mountain of water. These hang on the wave's ridge; to these the yawning billow shows ground amid the surge, where the tide churns with sand. Three ships the south wind catches and hurls on hidden rocks, rocks amid the waves which Italians call the Altars, a vast reef banking the sea. Three the east forces from the deep into shallows and quicksands, piteous to see, dashes on shoals and girdles with a sandbank. . . .

Meanwhile Neptune discerned with astonishment the loud roaring of the vexed sea, the tempest let loose from prison, and the still water boiling up from its depths, and looking forth over the deep, raised his head serene above the waves. He sees Aeneas' fleet scattered all over ocean, the Trojans overwhelmed by the waves and the tempest of heaven. Juno's guile and wrath lay clear to her brother's eye; East wind and West he calls before him, and . . . quicker than the word he soothes the swollen seas, chases away the gathered clouds, and restores the sunlight. Even as when oft in a throng of people strife has risen, and the base multitude rage in their minds, and now brands and stones are flying; madness lends arms; then if perchance they catch sight of one reverend for goodness and worth, they are silent and stand by with attentive ear; he with speech sways their temper and soothes their breasts; even so has fallen all the thunder of ocean, when

riding with forward gaze beneath a cloudless sky the lord of the sea wheels his coursers and lets his gliding chariot fly with loosened rein.

The outworn Aeneadae hasten to run for the nearest shore, and steer for the coast of Libya. There a place lies deep withdrawn; an island forms a harbour, thrusting forth its sides, whereon all the waves break from the open sea and part into the hollows of the bay. On this side and that enormous cliffs rise threatening heaven, and twin crags beneath whose crest the sheltered water lies wide and calm; above is a background of waving forest, and a woodland overhangs dark with rustling shade. Beneath the seaward brow is a rock-hung cavern, within it fresh springs and seats in the living stone, a haunt of nymphs; here tired ships need no fetters to hold nor anchor to fasten them with crooked fang. Hither with seven sail gathered of all his company Aeneas glides in; and disembarking on the land so sorely desired the Trojans gain the chosen beach, and fling their limbs dripping with brine upon the shore. Forthwith Achates has struck a spark from the flint and caught the fire on leaves, and laying dry fuel round kindled the touchwood into flame. Then, in their weary case, they fetch out sea-soaked corn and weapons of corn-dressing, and set to parch over the fire and bruise with stones the grain that they have rescued.

Meanwhile Aeneas scales the cliff, and scans the whole view wide over ocean. . . . Ship in sight is none; three stags he espies straying on the shore; behind whole herds follow, and graze in long train across the valleys. Stopping short, he snatched up a bow and swift arrows, the arms that trusty Achates was carrying; and first the leaders, their stately heads high with branching antlers, then the common herd he lays low, as he drives them with his shafts in a broken crowd through the leafy woods. Nor stays he till seven great victims are stretched on the sod, and the number of his ships is equalled. Thence he seeks the harbour and parts them among all his company; next the wine-casks that good Acestes had loaded on the Trinacrian beach, the hero's gift at their departure, he shares, and assuages their sorrowing hearts with speech:

'O comrades, for not ere now are we ignorant of ill, O tried by heavier fortunes, to these also God will appoint an end. The fury of Scylla and the roaring recesses of her crags you have come nigh, and known the rocks of the Cyclops. Recall your courage, put sorrow and fear away. This too sometime we shall haply remember with delight. Through chequered fortunes, through many perilous ways, we steer for Latium, where destiny points us a quiet home. There

79. **Achates,** the close friend of Aeneas. 99. **Acestes,** the king of Sicily who had entertained Aeneas hospitably.

the realm of Troy may rise again unforbidden. Keep heart, and endure till prosperous fortune come.'

Such words he utters, and sick with deep distress he feigns hope on his face, and keeps his anguish hidden deep in his breast. . . . when Jupiter looked through the height of air on the sail-winged sea and outspread lands, the shores and broad countries, and looking stood on the cope of heaven, and cast down his eyes on the realm of Libya. To him thus troubled at heart Venus, her bright eyes brimming with tears, sorrowfully speaks:

'O thou who dost sway mortal and immortal things in eternal lordship with the terror of thy thunderbolt, how can my Aeneas have transgressed so grievously against thee? how his Trojans? on whom, after so many deaths borne, all the world is barred for Italy's sake. From them sometime in the rolling years the Romans were to arise indeed; from them were to be rulers who, renewing the blood of Teucer, should hold sea and all lands in dominion. This thou didst promise: why, O father, is thy decree reversed? Is this the reward of goodness? is it thus thou dost restore our throne?'

Smiling on her with that look which clears sky and storms, the parent of men and gods lightly kissed his daughter's lips; then answered thus:

'Spare thy fear, Cytherean; thy people's destiny abides unshaken. Thine eyes shall see the city Lavinium, their promised fortress; thou shalt exalt to the starry heaven thy noble Aeneas; nor is my decree reversed. He whom thou lovest (for I will speak, since this care keeps torturing thee, and will unroll further the secret records of fate) shall wage a great war in Italy, and crush warrior nations; he shall appoint his people a law and a city; till the third summer see him reigning in Latium, and three winters' camps are overpast among the conquered Rutulians. But the boy Ascanius, whose surname is now Iülus—Ilus he was while the Ilian state stood sovereign—thirty great circles of rolling months shall he fulfil in government; he shall carry the kingdom from its seat in Lavinium, and make a strong fortress of Alba the Long. Here the full space of thrice an hundred years shall the kingdom endure under the race of Hector's kin, till the royal priestess Ilia from Mars' embrace shall give birth to a twin progeny. Thence shall Romulus, gay in the tawny hide of the she-wolf that nursed him, take up their line, and name them Romans after his own name. To these I ordain neither period nor boundary of empire: I have given them dominion without end. Nay, harsh Juno, who in her fear now troubles earth and sea and sky, shall change to better counsels, and with me shall cherish the lords of the world, the gowned race of Rome. Thus is it willed. A day

will come in the lapse of cycles, when the house of Assaracus shall lay Phthia and famed Mycenae in bondage, and reign over conquered Argos. From the fair line of Troy a Caesar shall arise, who shall limit his empire with ocean, his glory with the firmament, Julius, inheritor of great Iülus' name. Him one day, thy care done, thou shalt welcome to heaven loaded with Eastern spoils; to him too shall vows be addressed. Then shall war cease, and the iron ages soften. Hoar Faith and Vesta, Quirinus and Remus brothers again, shall deliver statutes. The dreadful steel-clenched gates of War shall be shut fast; inhuman Fury, his hands bound behind him with an hundred rivets of brass, shall sit within on murderous weapons, shrieking with ghastly blood-stained lips.'

So speaking, he sends Maia's son down from above, that the lands and towers of Carthage, the new town, may receive the Trojans with open welcome; lest Dido, ignorant of doom, might debar them her land. Flying through the depth of air on winged oarage, the fleet messenger alights on the Libyan coasts. At once he does his bidding; at once, for a god willed it, the Phoenicians allay their haughty temper; the queen above all takes to herself grace and compassion towards the Teucrians.

But good Aeneas, nightlong revolving many and many a thing, issues forth, so soon as bountiful light is given, to explore the strange country; to what coasts the wind has borne him, who are their habitants, men or wild beasts, for all he sees is wilderness, this he resolves to search, and bring back the certainty to his comrades. The fleet he hides close in embosoming groves beneath a caverned rock, amid rustling shadow of the woodland; himself, Achates alone following, he strides forward, clenching in his hand two broad-headed spears. And amid the forest his mother crossed his way, wearing the face and raiment of a maiden, the arms of a maiden of Sparta. . . . For in huntress fashion had she slung the ready bow from her shoulder, and left her blown tresses free, bared her knee, and knotted together her garments' flowing folds. 'Ho, gallants,' she begins, 'shew me if haply you have seen a sister of mine straying here girt with quiver and dappled lynx-pelt, or pressing with shouts on the track of a foaming boar.'

Thus Venus, and Venus' son answering thus began:

'Sound nor sight have I had of sister of thine, O maiden, how may I name thee? for thy face is not mortal, nor thy voice of human tone; O goddess assuredly! sister of Phoebus perchance, or one of the nymphs' blood? Be thou gracious, whoso thou art, and lighten our distress; deign to instruct us beneath

---

38. **Ascanius,** the son of Aeneas by his wife Creusa, who was lost at the fall of Troy.

57. **Assaracus,** a king of Troy, great-grandfather of Aeneas. **Phthia,** the Greek city of Achilles. 65. **Quirinus,** Romulus, legendary founder of Rome. 72. **Maia's son,** Mercury.

what skies, on what coast of the world, we are thrown. Driven hither by wind and desolate waves, we wander in a strange land among unknown men. Many a sacrifice shall fall by our hand before thine altars.'

Then Venus: 'Nay, to no such offerings do I aspire. Tyrian maidens are wont ever to wear the quiver, to tie the purple buskin high above their ankle. Punic is the realm thou seest, Tyrian the people, and the city of Agenor's kin; but their borders are Libyan, a race untameable in war. Dido sways the sceptre, who flying her brother set sail from the Tyrian town. Long is the tale of crime, long and intricate; but I will follow its argument in brief. Her husband was Sychaeus, wealthiest in lands of the Phoenicians, and loved of her with all-fated passion; to whom with virgin rites her father had given her maidenhood in wedlock. But the kingdom of Tyre was in her brother Pygmalion's hands, a monster of guilt unparalleled. Between these madness came; the unnatural brother, blind with lust of gold, and reckless of his sister's love, lays Sychaeus low before the altars with stealthy unsuspected weapon; and for long he hid the deed, and by many a crafty pretence cheated her love-sickness with hollow hope. But in slumber came the very ghost of her unburied husband, lifting up a face pale in wonderful wise; he exposed the cruel altars and his breast stabbed through with steel, and unwove all the blind web of household guilt. Then he counsels hasty flight and abandonment of her country, and to aid her passage discloses treasures long hidden underground, an untold mass of silver and gold. Stirred thereby, Dido gathered a company for flight. All assemble in whom hatred of the tyrant was relentless or terror keen; they seize on ships that chanced to lie ready, and load them with the gold. Pygmalion's hoarded wealth is borne overseas; a woman guides the enterprise. They came at last to the land where thou wilt descry a city now great, New Carthage, and her rising citadel, and bought ground, called thence Byrsa, as much as a bull's hide would encircle. But who, I pray, are you, or from what coasts come, or whither hold you your way?'

At her question he, sighing and drawing speech deep from his breast, thus replied:

'Ah goddess, should I go on retracing from the fountain head, were time free to hear the history of our woes, sooner will the evening star lay day asleep in the closed gates of heaven. Us, as from ancient Troy (if the name of Troy has haply passed through your ears) we sailed over distant seas, the tempest at his own wild will has driven on the Libyan coast. I am Aeneas the good, who carry in my fleet the household gods I rescued from the enemy; my fame

10. **Agenor's kin.** Dido was descended from Agenor, a king of Phoenicia.

is known high in heaven. I seek Italy my country, and my kin of Jove's supreme blood. With twenty sail did I climb the Phrygian sea; oracular tokens led me on; my goddess mother pointed the way; scarce seven survive the shattering of wave and wind. Myself unknown, destitute, driven from Europe and Asia, I wander over the Libyan wilderness.'

But staying longer complaint, Venus thus broke in on his half-told sorrows:

'Whoso thou art, not hated I think of the immortals dost thou draw the breath of life, who hast reached the Tyrian city. Only go on, and betake thee hence to the courts of the queen. For I declare to thee thy comrades are restored, thy fleet driven back into safety by the shifted northern gales.'. . .

Speaking she turned away, and her neck shone roseate, the immortal tresses on her head breathed the fragrance of deity; her raiment fell flowing down to her feet, and a very goddess was manifest in her tread. He knew her for his mother, and with this cry pursued her flight: 'Thou also merciless! why mockest thou thy son so often in feigned likeness? Why is it forbidden to clasp hand in hand, to hear and to reply in true speech?' Thus reproaching her he bends his steps towards the city. But Venus girt them in their going with dim mist, and her deity wrapped them deep in clothing of cloud, that none might descry them, none touch them, or work delay, or ask wherefore they came. . . .

They meantime have hasted along where the pathway points, and now were climbing the hill which hangs enormous over the city, and looks down on its facing towers. Aeneas marvels at the mass of building, pastoral huts once of old, marvels at the gateways and hum of the paved streets. . . . 'Happy they whose city already rises!' cries Aeneas, looking on the town roofs below. Girt in the cloud he passes amid them, wonderful to tell, and mingling with the throng is descried of none.

In the mid town was a grove deep with luxuriant shade, wherein first the Phoenicians, buffeted by wave and whirlwind, dug up the token Queen Juno had appointed, the head of a war-horse: thereby was their race to be through all ages illustrious in war and at ease in living. Here to Juno was Sidonian Dido founding a vast temple, rich with offerings and her godhead's presence: brazen steps rose on the threshold, the beams were clamped with brass, doors of brass grated on the hinge. First in this grove did a strange chance meet his steps and allay his fears; first here did Aeneas dare to hope for safety and have fairer trust in his shattered fortunes. For while he closely scans the temple that towers above him, while, awaiting the queen, he inly marvels at the

101. **Sidonian;** after Sidon, the wealthy city of Phoenicia from which she came.

fortune of the city, at her craftsmen's handiwork and labouring toil, he sees ranged in order the battles of Ilium, that war whose fame was already rumoured through all the world, the sons of Atreus, and Priam, and Achilles whom both found pitiless. He stopped and cried weeping, 'What land is left, Achates, what tract on earth that is not full of our agony? Behold Priam! Here too is the meed of honour, here are tears over fortune and mortal estate touches the soul. Dismiss thy fears; the fame of this will somehow, I deem, bring salvation.' So speaks he, and feeds his soul with the painted show, sighing often the while, and his face wet with an abundant flood. . . .

While these marvels meet Dardanian Aeneas' eyes, while he hangs rapt in one long breathless gaze, Dido the queen entered the precinct, beautiful exceedingly, a youthful train thronging round her. . . . She joyously advanced amid the throng, urging on the toils of her rising empire. Then in the gates of the goddess, beneath the central vaulting of the temple, she took her seat girt with arms and high enthroned. And now she gave justice and laws to her people, and adjusted or allotted their taskwork in due portion; when suddenly Aeneas sees advancing with a great crowd about them Antheus and Sergestus and brave Cloanthus, and other of his Trojans, whom the black squall had sundered at sea and borne far away on the coast. Dizzy with the shock of joy and fear he and Achates together were on fire with eagerness to clasp their hands; but in confused uncertainty they keep hidden, and clothed in the sheltering cloud wait to espy what fortune befalls them, where they are leaving their fleet ashore, why they now come; for they advanced, chosen men from all the ships, praying for grace, and clamorously sought the temple.

After they entered in, and public speech was granted, aged Ilioneus with placid mien thus began: 'Queen, to whom Jupiter has given to found this new city, and lay the yoke of justice upon haughty tribes, we beseech thee, we wretched Trojans storm-driven over all the seas, stay the dreadful flames from our ships; spare a guiltless race, and bend a gracious regard on our fortunes. . . . Aeneas was our king, foremost of men in righteousness, incomparable in goodness as in warlike arms; whom if fate still preserves, if he draws the breath of heaven and lies not yet low in dispiteous gloom, fear we have none; nor mayest thou repent of challenging the contest of service.'

Thus Ilioneus, and all the Dardanian company murmured assent. . . . Then Dido, lowering her eyes upon them, briefly speaks:

'Cheer your anxious hearts, O Teucrians; put by your care. Hard fortune in a strange realm forces me to this task, to keep watch and ward on my wide frontiers. Who can be ignorant of the race of Aeneas' people, who of Troy town and her men and deeds, or of the great war's consuming fire? My escort shall speed you in safety, my arsenals supply your need. Or will you even find rest here with me and share my kingdom? The city I establish is yours; draw your ships ashore; Trojan and Tyrian shall be held by me in even balance. And would that he your king, that Aeneas were here, storm-driven to this same haven! But I will send messengers along the coast, and bid them trace Libya to its limits, if haply he strays shipwrecked in forest or town.'

Stirred by these words, . . . Aeneas stood discovered in sheen of brilliant light, like a god in face and shoulders; for his mother's self had shed on her son the grace of clustered locks, the radiant light of youth, and the lustre of joyous eyes; as when ivory takes beauty under the artist's hand, or when silver or Parian stone is inlaid in gold. Then breaking in on all with unexpected speech he thus addresses the queen:

'I whom you seek am here before you, Aeneas of Troy, snatched from the Libyan waves. O thou who alone hast pitied Troy's untold agonies, thou who with us, a remnant of the Grecian foe, the cup of misfortune drained on land and sea, with us in our utter want dost share thy city and home! to render meet recompense is not possible for us, O Dido, nor for all who scattered over the wide world are left of our Dardanian race. The gods grant thee worthy reward, if their deity turn any regard on goodness, if aught avails justice and conscious purity of soul. What happy ages bore thee? what mighty parents

Virgil writing the Aeneid. *From a Roman mosaic of c. 100* A.D. *restored.*

gave birth to a soul like thine? While rivers run into the sea, while the mountain shadows move across their slopes, while the stars feed in the fields of heaven, ever shall thine honour, thy name and praises endure in whatsoever lands may summon me.' With these words he advances his right hand to dear Ilioneus, his left to Serestus; then to the rest, brave Gyas and brave Cloanthus.

Dido the Sidonian stood astonished, first at the sight of him, then at his strange fortunes, and thus broke into speech:

'What fate follows thee, goddess-born, through perilous ways? what violence throws thee on this evil coast? Art thou that Aeneas whom Venus the bountiful bore to Dardanian Anchises by the wave of Phrygian Simoïs? . . .

'Enter our house. Me too has a like fortune driven through many a woe, and willed at last to find my rest in this land. Not ignorant of ill I learn to succour the afflicted.'

With such tale she leads Aeneas into the royal house, and orders sacrifice in the gods' temples. Therewith she sends to his crews on the shore twenty bulls, an hundred great bristly-backed swine, an hundred fat lambs and their mothers with them, gifts of the day's gladness. . . . But the palace within is decked with splendour of royal state, and a banquet made ready amid the halls. The coverings are curiously wrought in splendid purple; on the tables is massy silver and deeds of ancestral valour graven in gold, all the long course of history drawn through many a heroic name from the nation's primal antiquity.

Aeneas—for a father's affection let not his spirit rest—sends Achates speeding to his ships, to carry this news to Ascanius, and lead him to the town: in Ascanius is fixed all the parent's loving care. Presents likewise he bids him bring saved from the wreck of Ilium, a mantle stiff with gold embroidery, and a veil with woven border of yellow acanthus-flower, that once decked Helen of Argos, her mother Leda's wondrous gift; Helen had borne them from Mycenae, when she sought Troy towers and a lawless bridal; the sceptre too that Ilione, Priam's eldest daughter, once had worn, a beaded necklace, and a double circlet of jewelled gold. Achates, hasting on his message, bent his way towards the ships.

But in the Cytherean's breast new arts, new schemes revolve; that Cupid, changed in form and feature, may come in sweet Ascanius' room, and his gifts kindle the queen to madness and set her inmost sense aflame. Verily she fears the uncertain house, the double-tongued race of Tyre; cruel Juno frets her, and at nightfall her care floods back. Therefore to winged Love she speaks these words:

'Son, who art my strength and sovereignty, son, who alone scornest the mighty father's Typhon-quelling shafts, to thee I fly for succour, and sue humbly to thy deity. How Aeneas thy brother is driven about all the sea-coasts by bitter Juno's malignity, thou knowest, and hast often grieved in our grief. Now Dido the Phoenician holds him stayed with soft words, and I tremble to think how the welcome of Juno's house may issue; she will not be idle where all hinges on the event. Wherefore I counsel to prevent her wiles and circle the queen with flame, that, unalterable by any deity, she may be held on my side by passionate love for Aeneas. Take now my thought how to do this. The boy prince, my chiefest care, makes ready at his dear father's summons to go to the Sidonian city, carrying gifts that survive the sea and the flames of Troy. Him will I hide deep asleep in my holy habitation, high on Cythera's hills or in Idalium, that he may not know nor cross our wiles. Do thou but for one night feign his form, and, boy as thou art, put on the familiar face of a boy; so when in festal cheer, amid royal dainties and streaming wine, Dido shall take thee to her lap, shall fold thee in her clasp and kiss thee close and sweet, thou mayest imbreathe a hidden fire and unsuspected poison.'

Love obeys his dear mother's words, lays by his wings, and walks rejoicingly with Iülus' tread. But Venus pours gentle dew of slumber on Ascanius' limbs, and lifts him lulled in her lap to the tall Idalian groves of her deity, where soft amaracus folds him round with the shadowed sweetness of its odorous blossoms. And now, obedient to her words, Cupid went merrily in Achates' guiding, with the royal gifts for the Tyrians. Already at his coming the queen has taken her seat in the midmost on her golden throne under the splendid tapestries; now lord Aeneas, now too the men of Troy gather, and all recline on the strewn purple. Servants pour water on their hands, deal corn from baskets, and bring napkins with close-cut pile. Fifty handmaids are within, whose task is in their course to keep unfailing store and kindle the household fire. An hundred others, and as many pages all of like age, are charged to load the board with food and array the cups. Therewithal the Tyrians are gathered full in the wide feasting chamber, and take their appointed places on the broidered cushions. They marvel at Aeneas' gifts, marvel at Iülus, at the god's burning face and feigned speech, at the mantle and veil broidered with yellow acanthus-flower. Above all the hapless Phoenician, victim to coming doom, cannot satiate her soul, but, stirred alike by the boy and the gifts, she gazes and takes fire. He, when hanging clasped on Aeneas' neck he had satisfied all the deluded parent's love, makes his way to the queen; the queen clings to him with her eyes and all her soul, and ever and anon fondles him in her lap, ah, poor Dido! witless how mighty a deity sinks into her breast; but he, mindful of his mother the Acidalian, begins touch by touch to efface Sychaeus, and sows the surprise of a living love in the long-since-unstirred spirit and disaccustomed heart.

Soon as the noise of banquet ceased and the board was cleared, they set down great bowls and enwreathe the wine. The house is filled with hum of voices eddying through the spacious chambers; blazing cressets hang from netted gold, and torches rout the night with flame. . . .

Therewithal luckless Dido wore the night in changing talk, and drank long draughts of love, asking many a thing of Priam, many a thing of Hector; now in what armour the son of the Morning came; now of what breed were Diomede's horses; now of the stature of Achilles. 'Nay, come,' she cries, 'tell to us, O guest, from their first beginning the stratagems of the Grecians, thy people's woes, and thine own wanderings; for this is now the seventh summer that bears thee a wanderer over all lands and seas.' . . . Thus lord Aeneas with all attent retold alone the divine doom and the history of his goings.

BOOK II *cf. Odyssey - IX*

All were hushed, and sate with steadfast countenance; thereon, from his cushioned high seat, lord Aeneas thus began: '. . . If thy desire be such to know our calamities, and briefly to hear Troy's last agony, though my spirit shudders at the remembrance and recoils in pain, I will essay.

'Broken in war, beaten back by fate, and so many years now slid away, the Grecian captains build by Pallas' divine craft a horse of mountain bulk, and frame its ribs with sawn fir; they feign it vowed for their return, and this rumour goes about. Within the blind sides they stealthily imprison chosen men picked out one by one, and fill the vast cavern of its womb full with armed soldiery.

'There lies in sight an island well known in fame, Tenedos, rich of store while the realm of Priam endured, now but a bay and roadstead treacherous to ships. Hither they launch forth, and hide on the solitary shore: we fancied they were gone, and had run down the wind for Mycenae. So all the Teucrian land put her long grief away. The gates are flung open; men go rejoicingly to see the Doric camp, the deserted stations and abandoned shore. Here the Dolopian troops were tented, here cruel Achilles; here their squadrons lay; here they were wont to meet in battle-line. Some gaze astonished at the deadly gift of Minerva the Virgin, and wonder at the horse's bulk; and Thymoetes begins to advise that it be drawn within our walls and set in the citadel, whether in guile, or that the doom of Troy was even now setting thus. But Capys, and they whose mind was of better counsel, bid us either hurl sheer into the sea the guileful and sinister gift of Greece, and heap flames beneath to consume it, or pierce and explore the hollow hiding-place of its womb. The wavering crowd is torn apart in eager dispute.

'At that, foremost of all and with a great throng about him, Laocoön afire runs down from the fortress height, and cries from far: "Ah, wretched citizens, what height of madness is this? Believe you the foe is gone? or think you any Grecian gift is free of treachery? is it thus we know Ulysses? Either Achaeans are hid in this cage of wood, or the engine is fashioned against our walls to overlook the houses and descend upon the city; or some delusion lurks in it: trust not the horse, O Trojans. Be it what it may, I fear the Grecians even when they offer gifts." Thus speaking, he hurled his huge spear with mighty strength at the creature's side and the curved framework of the belly: the spear stood quivering, and the jarred cavern of the womb sounded hollow and uttered a groan. And had divine ordinance been thus and our soul not infatuate he had moved us to lay violent steel on the Argolic hiding place; and Troy would now stand, and you, tall towers of Priam, yet abide.

'Lo, Dardanian shepherds meanwhile dragged clamourously before the King a man with hands tied behind his back, who to compass this very thing, to lay Troy open to the Achaeans, had gone to meet their ignorant approach, confident of his courage, and doubly prepared to spin his snares or to meet assured death. From all sides, in eagerness to see, the people of Troy run streaming in, and vie in jeers at their prisoner. Know now the treachery of the Grecians, and from a single crime learn them all. . . . For as he stood amid our gaze confounded, disarmed, and cast his eyes around the Phrygian columns, "Alas!" he cried, "what land now, what seas may receive me? or what is the last doom that yet awaits a wretch like me? who have neither any place among the Grecians, and likewise the Dardanians clamour in wrath for the forfeit of my blood." At that lament our spirit was changed, and all assault stayed: we encourage him to speak, and tell of what blood he is sprung, or what assurance he brings his captors.

' "In all things assuredly," says he, "O King, befall what may, I will confess to thee the truth; nor will I deny myself of Argolic birth—this first—nor, if Fortune has made Sinon unhappy, shall her malice mould him to a cheat and a liar. . . . Often would the Grecians have taken to flight, leaving Troy behind, and disbanded in weariness of the long war; and would God they had! as often the fierce sea-tempest barred their way, and the south wind frightened them from going. Most of all when this horse already stood framed with beams of maple, storm-

103. **Argolic,** Greek.

clouds roared over all the sky. In perplexity we send Eurypylus to inquire of Phoebus' oracle; and he brings back from the sanctuary these words of terror: *With blood of a slain maiden, O Grecians, you appeased the winds when first you came to the Ilian coasts; with blood must you seek your return, and an Argive life be the accepted sacrifice.* When that utterance reached the ears of the crowd, their hearts stood still, and a cold shudder ran through their inmost sense: for whom is doom purposed? whom does Apollo demand? At this the Ithacan with loud clamour drags Calchas the soothsayer forth amidst them, and demands of him what is this the gods signify. And now many an one foretold me the villain's craft and cruelty, and silently saw what was to come. Twice five days he is speechless in his tent, and will not have any one denounced by his lips, or given up to death. Scarcely at last, at the loud urgence of the Ithacan, he breaks into speech as was planned, and appoints me for the altar. All consented; and each one's particular fear was turned, ah me! to my single destruction. And now the dreadful day was at hand; the rites were being ordered for me, the salted corn, and the chaplets to wreathe my temples. I broke away, I confess it, from death; I burst my bonds, and lurked all night darkling in the sedge of the marshy pool, till they might set their sails, if haply they should set them. Nor have I any hope more of seeing my old home nor my darling children and the father whom I desire. Of them will they even haply claim vengeance for my flight, and wash away this crime in their wretched death. By the heavenly powers I beseech thee, the deities to whom truth is known, by all the faith yet unsullied that is anywhere left among mortals, pity woes so great, pity a soul that bears intolerable wrong."

'At these his tears we grant him life, and accord our pity. Priam himself at once commands his shackles and strait bonds to be undone, and thus speaks with kindly words: "Whoso thou art, now and henceforth dismiss and forget the Greeks: thou shalt be ours. And unfold the truth to this my question: wherefore have they reared the bulk of this monstrous steed? who is their counsellor? or what their aim? what propitiation, or what engine of war is this?" He ended; the other, stored with the treacherous craft of Pelasgia, lifts to heaven his freed hands.

' "All the hope of Greece, and the confidence in which the war began, ever centred in Pallas' aid. But since the wicked son of Tydeus, and Ulysses, forger of crime, made bold to tear the fated Palladium from her sanctuary, and cut down the sentries on the towered height; since they grasped the holy image, and dared with bloody hands to touch the maiden chaplets of the goddess; since then the hope of Greece ebbed and slid away backwards, their strength was broken, and the mind of the goddess estranged. Whereof the Tritonian gave token by no uncertain signs. Scarcely was the image set in the camp; flame shot sparkling from its lifted eyes, and salt sweat started over its body; thrice, wonderful to tell, it leapt from the ground with shield and spear quivering. Immediately Calchas prophesies that the seas must be explored in flight, nor may Troy towers be overthrown by Argive weapons, except they repeat their auspices at Argos, and bring back that divine presence they have borne away with them in the curved ships overseas. And now they have run down the wind for their native Mycenae, to gather arms and gods to attend them; they will remeasure ocean and be on you unawares. So Calchas expounds the omens. This image at his warning they reared in recompense for the Palladium and the injured deity, to expiate the horror of sacrilege. Yet Calchas bade them raise it to this vast size with oaken crossbeams, and build it up to heaven, that it might not find entry at the gates nor be drawn within the city, nor protect your people beneath the consecration of old. For if hand of yours should violate Minerva's offering, then utter destruction (the gods turn rather on himself his augury!) should be upon Priam's empire and the Phrygian people. But if under your hands it climbed into your city, Asia should advance in mighty war to the walls of Pelops, and a like fate awaited our children's children."

'So by Sinon's wiles and craft and perjury the thing gained belief; and we were ensnared by treachery and forced tears, we whom neither the son of Tydeus nor Achilles of Larissa, whom not ten years nor a thousand ships brought down.

'Hereon another sight, greater, alas! and far more terrible meets us, and alarms our thoughtless senses. Laocoön, allotted priest for Neptune, was slaying a great bull at the accustomed altars. And lo! from Tenedos, over the placid depths (I shudder as I recall) two snakes in enormous coils press down the sea and advance together to the shore; their breasts rise through the surge, and their blood-red crests overtop the waves; the rest trails through the main behind and wreathes back in voluminous curves; the brine gurgles and foams. And now they gained the fields, while their bloodshot eyes blazed with fire, and their tongues lapped and flickered in their hissing mouths. We scatter, blanched at the sight. They in unfaltering train make towards Laocoön.

---

48. Pelasgia, Greece, after the name of its early inhabitants, the Pelasgians. 53–54. to tear the fated Palladium from her sanctuary. . . . Diomedes and Ulysses had stolen the ancient effigy of Pallas Athena at Troy, which was essential to the safety of the city.

60. **Tritonian,** Athena, born on Lake Tritonis.

And first the serpents twine in their double embrace his two little children, and bite deep in their wretched limbs; then him likewise, as he comes up to help with arms in his hand, they seize and fasten in their enormous coils; and now twice clasping his waist, twice encircling his neck with their scaly bodies, they tower head and neck above him. He at once strains his hands to tear their knots apart, his fillets spattered with foul black venom; at once raises to heaven awful cries; as when, bellowing, a bull shakes the wavering axe from his neck and rushes wounded from the altar. But the two snakes glide away to the high sanctuary and seek the fierce Tritonian's citadel, and take shelter under the goddess' feet beneath the circle of her shield. Then indeed a strange terror thrills in all our amazed breasts; and Laocoön, men say, has fulfilled his crime's desert, in piercing the consecrated wood and hurling his guilty spear into its body. All cry out that the image must be drawn to its home and supplication made to her deity. . . . We breach the walls, and lay open the ramparts of the city. All set to the work; they fix sliding rollers under its feet, and tie hempen bands on its neck. The fated engine climbs our walls, big with arms. Around it boys and unwedded girls chant hymns and joyfully lay their hand on the rope. It moves up, and glides menacing into the middle of the town. O native land! O Ilium, house of gods, and Dardanian ramparts renowned in war! four times in the very gateway did it come to a stand, and four times armour rang in its womb. Yet we urge it on, mindless and infatuate, and plant the ill-omened portent in our hallowed citadel. Even then Cassandra opens her lips to the coming doom, lips at a god's bidding never believed by the Trojans. We, the wretched people to whom that day was our last, hang the shrines of the gods with festal boughs throughout the city. Meanwhile the heavens wheel on, and night rises from the sea, wrapping in her vast shadow earth and sky and the wiles of the Myrmidons; about the town the Teucrians are stretched in silence; slumber laps their tired limbs.

'And now the Argive squadron was sailing in order from Tenedos, and in the favouring stillness of the quiet moon sought the shores it knew; when the royal galley ran out a flame, and, protected by the gods' malign decrees, Sinon stealthily lets loose the imprisoned Grecians from their barriers of pine; the horse opens and restores them to the air; and joyfully issuing from the hollow wood, Thessander and Sthenelus the captains, and terrible Ulysses, slide down the dangling rope, with Acamas and Thoas and Neoptolemus son of Peleus, and Machaon first of all, and Menelaus, and Epeüs himself the artificer of the snare. They rush upon a city buried in

35. lips at a god's bidding . . . Trojans. Apollo condemned her for spurning his love.

drunken sleep; the watchmen are cut down, and at the open gates they welcome all their comrades, and unite their confederate bands.

'It was the time when by the gift of God rest comes stealing first and sweetest on unhappy men. In slumber, lo! before mine eyes Hector seemed to stand by, deep in grief and shedding abundant tears; torn by the chariot, as once of old, and black with gory dust, his swoln feet pierced with the thongs. . . . "Ah, fly, goddess-born," he says, "and rescue thyself from these flames. The foe holds our walls; from her high ridges Troy is toppling down. Thy country and Priam ask no more. If our towers might be defended by strength of hand, this hand too had been their defence. Troy commends to thee her holy things and household gods; take them to accompany thy fate; seek for them a city, which, after all the seas have known thy wanderings, thou shalt at last establish in might." So speaks he, and carries forth in his hands from their inner shrine the chaplets and strength of Vesta, and the everlasting fire.

'Meanwhile the city is stirred with mingled agony; and more and more, though my father Anchises' house lay deep withdrawn and screened by trees, the noises grew clearer and the clash of armour swells. I shake myself from sleep and mount over the sloping roof, and stand there with ears attent: even as when flame catches a corn-field while south winds are furious, or the racing torrent of a mountain stream sweeps the fields, sweeps the smiling crops and labours of the oxen, and hurls the forest with it headlong; the shepherd in ignorant amaze hears the roar from the cliff-top. Then indeed proof is clear, and the treachery of the Grecians opens out. . . . Cries of men and blare of trumpets rise up. Madly I seize my arms, nor is there much purpose in arms; but my spirit is on fire to gather a band for fighting and charge for the citadel with my comrades. Fury and wrath drive me headlong, and I think how noble is death in arms. . . . Who may unfold in speech that night's horror and death-agony, or measure its woes in weeping? The ancient city falls with her long years of sovereignty; corpses lie stretched stiff all about the streets and houses and awful courts of the gods. Nor do Teucrians alone pay forfeit of their blood; once and again valour returns even in conquered hearts, and the victorious Grecians fall. Everywhere is cruel agony, everywhere terror, and the multiplied sight of death. . . . We tear ourselves away, I and Iphitus and Pelias, Iphitus now stricken in age, Pelias halting too under the wound of Ulysses, called forward by the clamour to Priam's house.

'Here indeed the fight is fiercest, as if all the rest of the warfare were nowhere, and no slaughter but here throughout the city, so do we descry the battle in full fury, the Grecians rushing on the building,

and their shielded column driving up against the beleaguered threshold. Ladders cling to the walls; and hard by the doors and planted on the rungs they hold up their shields in the left hand to ward off our weapons, and with their right clutch the battlements. The Dardanians tear down turrets and whole pinnacles of the palace against them; with these for weapons, since they see the end is come, they prepare to defend themselves even in death's extremity:
10 and hurl down gilded beams, the stately decorations of their fathers of old. Others with drawn swords have beset the doorway below and keep it in crowded column. We renew our courage, to aid the royal dwelling, to support them with our succour, and swell the force of the conquered.

'There was a blind doorway giving passage through the range of Priam's halls by a solitary postern, whereby, while our realm endured, hapless Andromache would often and often glide unattended to her
20 father-in-law's house, and carry the boy Astyanax to his grandsire. I issue out on the sloping height of the ridge, whence wretched Teucrian hands were hurling their ineffectual weapons. A tower stood on the sheer brink, its roof ascending high into heaven, whence was wont to be seen all Troy and the Grecian ships and Achaean camp: attacking it with iron round about, where the joints of the lofty flooring yielded, we wrench it from its high foundations and shake it free; it gives way, and suddenly falls thun-
30 dering in ruin, crashing wide over the Grecian ranks. But others swarm up; nor meanwhile do stones nor any sort of missile slacken. . . . Right before the vestibule and in the front doorway Pyrrhus moves rejoicingly in the sparkle of arms and gleaming brass: like as when a snake fed on poisonous herbs, whom chill winter kept hid and swollen underground, now fresh from his weeds outworn and shining in youth wreathes his slippery body into the daylight, his upreared breast meets the sun, and his
40 triple-cloven tongue flickers in his mouth. . . . Himself among the foremost he grasps a poleaxe, bursts through the hard doorway, and wrenches the brazen-plated doors from the hinge; and now he has cut out a plank from the solid oak and pierced a vast gaping hole. The house within is open to sight, and the long halls lie plain; open to sight are the secret chambers of Priam and the kings of old, and they see armed men standing in front of the doorway.

'But the inner house is stirred with shrieks and
50 misery and confusion, and the court echoes deep with women's wailing; the din strikes up to the golden stars. Affrighted mothers stray about the vast house, and cling fast to the doors and print them with kisses. With his father's might Pyrrhus presses on; nor guards nor barriers can hold out. The gate

33. **Pyrrhus**, son of Achilles, also called Neoptolemus.

totters under the hard-driven ram, and the doors fall flat, rent from the hinge. The passage is forced; the Greeks burst through the entrance and pour in, slaughtering the foremost, and filling the space with a wide stream of soldiers. Not so furiously when a 60 foaming river bursts his banks and overflows, beating down the opposing dykes with whirling water, is he borne mounded over the fields, and sweeps herds and pens all about the plains. Myself I saw in the gateway Neoptolemus mad with carnage, and the two sons of Atreus, saw Hecuba and the hundred daughters of her house, and Priam polluting with his blood the altar fires of his own consecration. The fifty bridal chambers, the abundant hope of his children's children, their doors magnificent with spoils 70 of barbaric gold, have sunk in ruin; where the fire fails the Greeks are in possession.

'Perchance too thou mayest inquire what was Priam's fate. When he saw the ruin of his captured city, the gates of his house burst open, and the enemy amid his innermost chambers, the old man idly fastens round his aged trembling shoulders his long disused armour, girds on the unavailing sword, and advances on his death among the thronging foe.

'Within the palace and under the bare cope of sky 80 was a massive altar, and hard on the altar an ancient bay tree leaned clasping the household gods in its shadow. Here Hecuba and her daughters crowded vainly about the altar-stones, like doves driven headlong by a black tempest, and crouched clasping the gods' images. And when she saw Priam her lord with the armour of youth on him, "What spirit of madness, my poor husband," she cries, "has moved thee to gird on these weapons? or whither dost thou run? Not such the succour nor these the defenders the 90 time requires; no, were mine own Hector now beside us. Retire, I beseech thee, hither; this altar will protect us all, or thou wilt share our death." With these words on her lips she drew the aged man to her, and set him on the holy seat.

'And lo, escaped from slaughtering Pyrrhus through the weapons of the enemy, Polites, one of Priam's children, flies wounded down the long colonnades and circles the empty halls. Pyrrhus pursues him fiercely with aimed wound, just catching at him, 100 and follows hard on him with his spear. As at last he issued before his parents' eyes and faces, he fell, and shed his life in a pool of blood. At this Priam, although even now fast in the toils of death, yet withheld not nor spared a wrathful cry: "Ah, for thy crime, for this thy hardihood, may the gods, if there is goodness in heaven to care for aught such, pay thee in full thy worthy meed, and return thee the reward that is due! who hast made me look face to face on my child's murder, and polluted a father's counte- 110 nance with death. Ah, not such to a foe was the Achilles whose parentage thou beliest; but he revered a suppliant's right and trust, restored to the tomb Hector's blood-drained corpse, and sent me back to my own realm." Thus the old man spoke, and launched his weak and unwounding spear, which, recoiling straight from the jarring brass, hung idly from his shield above the boss. Thereat Pyrrhus: "Thou then shalt tell this, and go with the message to my sire the son of Peleus: remember to tell him of my baleful deeds, and the degeneracy of Neoptolemus. Now die." So saying, he drew him quivering to the very altar, slipping in the pool of his child's blood, and wound his hair in the left hand, while in the right the sword flashed out and plunged to the hilt in his side. This was the end of Priam's fortunes; thus did allotted fate find him, with burning Troy and her sunken towers before his eyes, once magnificent lord over so many peoples and lands of Asia. The great corpse lies along the shore, a head severed from the shoulders and a body without a name.

'But then an awful terror began to encircle me; I stood in amaze; there rose before me the sight of my loved father, as I saw the king, old as he, sobbing out his life under the ghastly wound; there rose Creüsa forlorn, my plundered house, and little Iülus' peril. I look back and survey what force is around me. All, outwearied, have given up and leapt headlong to the ground, or flung themselves wretchedly into the fire.

'Yes, and now I only was left; when I espy the daughter of Tyndarus close in the courts of Vesta, crouching silently in the fane's recesses; the bright glow of the fires lights my wandering, as my eyes stray all about. Fearing Teucrian anger for the overthrown towers of Troy, and the Grecians' vengeance and the wrath of the husband she had abandoned, she, the common Fury of Troy and her native country, had hidden herself and cowered unseen by the altars. My spirit kindles to fire, and rises in wrath to avenge my dying land and take repayment for her crimes. Shall she verily see Sparta and her native Mycenae unscathed, and depart a queen and triumphant? Shall she see her spousal and her father's house and children, attended by a crowd of Trojan women and Phrygians to serve her? and Priam have fallen under the sword? Troy blazed in fire? the shore of Dardania so often soaked with blood? Not so. For though there is no name or fame in a woman's punishment, nor honour in the victory, yet shall I have praise in quenching a guilty life and exacting a just recompense; and it will be good to fill my soul with the flame of vengeance, and satisfy the ashes of my people. Thus broke I forth, and advanced infuriate; when my mother came visibly before me, clear to sight as never till then, and shone forth

31. **daughter of Tyndarus,** Helen.

in pure radiance through the night, gracious, evident in godhead, in shape and stature such as she is wont to appear to the heavenly people; she caught me by the hand and stayed me, and pursued thus with roseate lips:

'"Son, what overmastering pain thus wakes thy wrath? Why ravest thou? or whither is thy care for us fled? Wilt thou not first look to it, where thou hast left Anchises, thine aged worn father; or if Creüsa thy wife and the child Ascanius survive? round about whom all the Greek battalions range; and without my preventing care, the flames ere this had consumed them, and the hostile sword drunk their blood. Not the hated face of the Laconian woman, Tyndarus' daughter; not Paris is to blame; the gods, the gods in anger overturn this magnificence, and make Troy topple down. Look, for all the cloud that now veils thy gaze and dulls mortal vision with damp encircling mist, I will rend from before thee. Fear thou no commands of thy mother, nor refuse to obey her counsels. Here, where thou seest sundered piles of masonry and rocks violently torn from rocks, and smoke eddying mixed with dust, Neptune with his great trident shakes wall and foundation out of their places, and upturns all the city from her base. Here Juno in all her terror holds the Scaean gates at the entry, and, girt with steel, calls her allied army furiously from their ships. . . . Even now on the citadel's height, look back! Tritonian Pallas is planted with glittering bordure and awful Gorgon head. Their lord himself pours courage and prosperous strength on the Grecians, himself stirs the gods against the arms of Dardania. Haste away, O son, and put an end to the struggle. Nowhere will I desert thee; I will set thee safe in the courts of thy father's house."

'She ended, and plunged in the dense blackness of the night. Awful faces shine forth, and, set against Troy, divine majesties. . . .

'Then indeed I saw all Ilium sinking in flame, and Neptunian Troy uprooted from her base: even as an ancient ash on the mountain heights, hacked all about with steel and fast-glancing axes, when husbandmen emulously strain to cut it down: it nods to the fall, with shaken top and quivering tresses asway; till gradually overmastered with wounds, it utters one last groan, and rending itself away, falls in ruin along the ridge. I descend, and under a god's guidance clear my way between foe and flame; weapons give ground before me, and flames retire.

'And now, when I have reached the courts of my ancestral dwelling, our home of old, my father, whom it was my first desire to carry high into the hills, and whom first I sought, refuses wholly, now Troy is rooted out, to prolong his life through the pains of exile.

'"Ah, you," he cries, "whose blood is at the prime,

whose strength stands firm in native vigour, do you take your flight. . . . Had the lords of heaven willed to prolong life for me, they should have preserved this my home. Enough and more is the one desolation we have seen, survivors of a captured city. Thus, oh thus salute me and depart, as a body laid out for burial. Mine own hand shall find me death: the foe will be merciful and seek my spoils: light is the loss of a tomb. This long time hated of heaven, I uselessly delay the years, since the father of gods and king of men blasted me with wind of thunder and scathe of flame.". . .

'Thereat I again gird on my sword, and fitting my left arm into the clasps of the shield, strode forth of the palace. But lo! my wife clung round my feet on the threshold, and held little Iülus up to his father's sight. "If thou goest to die, let us too hurry with thee to the end. But if thou knowest any hope to place in arms, be this household thy first defence. To what is little Iülus and thy father, to what am I left who once was called thy wife?"

'So she shrieked, and filled all the house with her weeping; when a sign arises sudden and marvellous to tell. For, between the hands and before the faces of his sorrowing parents, lo! above Iülus' head there seemed to stream a light luminous cone, and a flame whose touch hurt not to flicker in his soft hair and play round his brows. We in hurrying affright shook out the blazing hair and quenched the holy fires with spring water. But lord Anchises joyfully upraised his eyes; and stretching his hands to heaven: "Jupiter omnipotent," he cries, "if thou dost relent at any prayers, look on us this once alone; and if our goodness deserve it, give a sign hereafter, O lord, and confirm this thine omen."

'Scarcely had the aged man spoken thus, when with sudden crash it thundered on the left, and a star gliding through the dusk shot from heaven drawing a bright trail of light. We watch it slide over the palace roof, leaving the mark of its pathway, and bury its brilliance in the wood of Ida; the long-drawn track shines, and the region all about reeks with sulphur. Then conquered indeed my father rises to address the gods and worship the holy star. "Now, now delay is done with: I follow, and where you lead, I come, gods of my fathers; save my house, save my grandchild. Yours is this omen, and in your deity Troy stands. I yield, O my son, and refuse not to pass forth beside thee."

'He ended; and now more loudly the fire roars along the city, and nearer roll the burning tides. "Up then, beloved father, and place thyself on my neck; these shoulders of mine will sustain thee, nor will a burden so dear weigh me down. Howsoever fortune fall, one and undivided shall be our peril, one the escape of us twain. Little Iülus shall go along with me, and my wife follow our steps afar.

You of my household, give heed to what I say. On a mound as you leave the city an ancient temple of Ceres stands lonely, and hard by an aged cypress, guarded many years in ancestral observance: to this gathering-place we will come from diverse quarters. Thou, O father, take the sacred things and the household gods of our ancestors in thine hand. For me, just parted from the desperate battle, with slaughter fresh upon me, to handle them were guilt, until I have washed me in a living stream. . . ." So spoke I, and spread over my neck and broad shoulders a tawny lion-skin for covering, and stoop to my burden. Little Iülus, with his hand fast in mine, keeps uneven pace after his father. Behind my wife follows. We pass on in the shadows. And I, lately moved by no weapons launched against me, nor by the thronging bands of my Grecian foes, am now terrified at every breath, startled by every noise, thrilling with fear alike for my companion and my burden.

'And now I was nearing the gates, and thought I had outsped all the way; when suddenly the crowded trampling of feet came to our ears, and my father, looking forth into the darkness, cries: "My son, my son, fly; they draw near. I espy gleaming shields and the flicker of brass." At this, in my flurry and confusion, some hostile god bereft me of my senses. For while I plunge down byways, and swerve from where the familiar streets ran, Creüsa, alas! whether, torn by fate from her unhappy husband, she stood still, or did she mistake the way, or sink down outwearied? I know not; and never again was she given back to our eyes; nor did I turn to look for my lost one, or cast back a thought, ere we were come to ancient Ceres' mound and hallowed seat; here at last, when all gathered, one was missing, vanished from her child's and her husband's company. What man or god did I spare in frantic reproaches? or what crueller sight did I see in our city's overthrow? I charge my comrades with Ascanius and lord Anchises, and the gods of Teucria, hiding them in the winding vale. Myself I regain the city, girding on my shining armour; fixed to renew every danger, to retrace my way throughout Troy, and fling myself again on its perils. First of all I regain the walls and the dim gateway whence my steps had issued; I scan and follow back my footprints with searching gaze in the night. Everywhere my spirit shudders, dismayed at the very silence. Thence I pass on home, if haply her feet (if haply!) had led her thither. The Grecians had poured in, and filled the palace. The devouring fire goes rolling before the wind high as the roof; the flames tower over it, and the heat surges up into the air. I move on, and revisit the citadel and Priam's dwelling; where now in the spacious porticoes of Juno's sanctuary Phoenix and accursed Ulysses, chosen sentries, were guarding the spoil. Hither from all quarters is flung in masses the treasure of Troy torn from burning shrines, tables of the gods, bowls of solid gold, and captive raiment. Boys and cowering mothers in long file stand round. . . . Yes, and I dared to cry abroad through the darkness; I filled the streets with calling, and again and yet again with vain reiterance cried piteously on Creüsa. As I sought her and rushed endlessly among the houses of the town, there rose before mine eyes a melancholy phantom, the ghost of very Creüsa, in likeness larger than her wont. I was motionless; my hair stood up, and the voice choked in my throat. Then she thus addressed me, and with this speech allayed my distresses: "What help is there in this mad passion of grief, sweet my husband? not without divine influence does this come to pass: nor may it be, nor does the high lord of Olympus allow, that thou shouldest carry Creüsa hence in thy company. Long shall be thine exile, and weary spaces of sea must thou plough; yet thou shalt come to the land Hesperia, where Lydian Tiber flows with soft current through rich and populous fields. There prosperity awaits thee, and a kingdom, and a king's daughter for thy wife. Dispel these tears for thy beloved Creüsa. Never will I look on the proud homes of the Myrmidons or Dolopians, or go to be the slave of Greek matrons, I a daughter of Dardania, a daughter-in-law of Venus the goddess. . . . But the mighty mother of the gods keeps me in these her borders. And now farewell, and still love thy child and mine." This speech uttered, while I wept and would have said many a thing, she left me and retreated into thin air. Thrice there was I fain to lay mine arms round her neck; thrice the vision I vainly clasped fled out of my hands, even as the light breezes, or most like to fluttering sleep. So at last, when night is spent, I revisit my comrades.

'And here I find a marvellous great company, newly flocked in, mothers and men, a people gathered for exile, a pitiable crowd. From all quarters they are assembled, ready in heart and fortune, to whatsoever land I will conduct them overseas. And now the morning star rose over the high ridges of Ida, and led on the day; and the Grecians held the gateways in leaguer, nor was any hope of help given. I withdrew, and raising my father up, I sought the mountains.'

[Book III, describing the seven years' wandering of Aeneas, is omitted.]

BOOK IV

But the Queen, long ere now pierced sore with passion, feeds the wound with her life-blood, and wastes in a hidden fire. Again and again his own valiance and his line's renown flood back upon her spirit; look and accent cling fast in her bosom, and the pain allows not her limbs rest or calm. The morrow's dawn bore the torch of Phoebus across the earth, and had rolled away the dewy darkness from the sky, when, scarce herself, she thus addresses the sister of her heart:

'Anna, my sister, such dreams of terror thrill me through! What guest unknown is this who has entered our dwelling? How high his mien! how great in heart as in arms! I believe it well, with no vain assurance, his blood is divine. Fear proves the vulgar spirit. Alas, by what destinies is he driven! of what wars fought out he told! Were my mind not planted, fixed and immovable, to ally myself to none in wedlock since my first love of old played me false in death; were I not sick to the heart of bridal torch and chamber, to this temptation alone I might haply yield. Anna, I will confess it; since Sychaeus mine husband met his piteous doom, and our household was shattered by a brother's murder, he only has touched mine heart and shaken my soul from its balance. I know the prints of the ancient flame. But rather, I pray, may earth first yawn deep for me, or the Lord omnipotent hurl me with his thunderbolt into gloom, the pallid gloom and profound night of Erebus, ere I soil thee, mine honour, or undo thy laws. He took my love away who made me one with him at first; he shall keep it with him, and guard it in the tomb.' She spoke, and filled her bosom with welling tears.

Anna replies: 'O dearer than the daylight to thy sister, wilt thou waste, sad and alone, all thy length of youth, and know not the sweetness of motherhood, nor love's bounty? Deemest thou the ashes care for that, or the ghost within the tomb? Be it so: in days gone by no wooers bent thy sorrow, not in Libya, not ere then in Tyre; Iarbas was slighted, and other princes nurtured by the triumphal land of Africa; wilt thou contend even with a love to thy liking? . . . Under gods' control to my thinking, and with Juno's favour, has the Ilian fleet held on hither before the gale. What a city wilt thou discern here, O sister! what a realm will rise on such a union! the arms of Troy ranged with ours, what glory will exalt the Punic state!' . . . With these words she fired her spirit with resolved love, put hope in her wavering soul, and undid her shame.

First they visit the shrines, and desire grace from altar to altar; they sacrifice sheep fitly chosen to Ceres the Lawgiver, to Phoebus and lord Lyaeus, to Juno before all, guardian of the marriage bond. Dido herself, excellent in beauty, holds the cup in her hand, and pours libation between the horns of a milk-white cow, or moves in state to the rich altars before the gods' presences, day by day renewing her

89. **Iarbas,** king of the Getulians, whose attentions Dido had spurned.

gifts, and plunges her gaze into the breasts of cattle laid open to take counsel from the throbbing entrails. Ah, witless souls of soothsayers! how may vows or shrines help her madness? all the while the subtle flame consumes her inly, and deep in her breast the wound is silent and alive. Stung to misery, Dido wanders in frenzy all down the city, even as an arrow-stricken deer, whom, far and heedless amid the Cretan woodland, a shepherd archer has pierced and left the flying steel in her unaware; she ranges in flight the Dictaean forest lawns; fast in her side clings the deadly reed. Now she leads Aeneas with her through the town, and displays her Sidonian treasure and ordered city; she essays to speak, and breaks off half-way in utterance. Now, as day wanes, she seeks the repeated banquet, and again in her madness pleads to hear the agonies of Ilium, and again hangs on the teller's lips. Thereafter, when all are gone their ways, and the dim moon in turn quenches her light, and the setting stars counsel to sleep, alone in the empty house she mourns, and flings herself on the couch he left: distant she hears and sees him in the distance; or enthralled by some look of his father, she holds Ascanius on her lap, if so she may steal her love unuttered. No more do the unfinished towers rise, no more do the people exercise in arms, nor work for safety in war on harbour or bastion; the works hang broken off, vast looming walls and engines towering into the sky.

So soon as she perceives her thus fast in the toils, and madly careless of her name, Jove's beloved wife, daughter of Saturn, accosts Venus thus:

'Noble indeed is the fame and splendid the spoils you win, thou and that boy of thine, and mighty the renown of your deity, if two gods have vanquished one woman by treachery. Nor am I so blind to thy terror of our town, thine old jealousy of the high house of Carthage. But what shall be the end? or why all this contest now? Nay, rather let us work an enduring peace and a bridal compact. Thou hast what all thy soul desired; Dido is on fire with love, and has caught the madness through and through. Then rule we this people jointly in equal lordship; allow her to be a Phrygian husband's slave, and to lay her Tyrians for dowry in thine hand.'

To her—for she knew the dissembled purpose in her words, to turn the kingdom of Italy away to the coasts of Libya—Venus thus began in answer: 'Who so mad as to reject these terms, or choose rather to try the fortune of war with thee? if only when done, as thou sayest, fortune follow. But I move uncertain of Jove's ordinance, whether he will that Tyrians and wanderers from Troy be one city, or approve the mingling of peoples or the treaty of union. Thou art his wife, and thy prayers may put his mind to proof. Go on; I will follow.'

Then Queen Juno thus rejoined: 'That task shall be mine. Now, by what means the present need may be fulfilled, attend and I will explain in brief. Aeneas and lovelorn Dido are to go hunting together in the woodland when to-morrow's rising sun goes forth and his rays unveil the world. On them, while the beaters run up and down, and encircle the lawns with toils, will I pour down a blackening rain-cloud mingled with hail, and wake all the sky with thunder. Their company will scatter for shelter in the dim darkness; Dido and the Trojan captain will take covert in the same cavern. I will be there, and if thy goodwill is assured me, I will unite them in wedlock, and make her wholly his; here shall Hymen be present.' The Cytherean gave ready assent to her request, and laughed at the guileful device.

Meanwhile Dawn has arisen forth of ocean. A chosen company issue from the gates while the morning star is high; they pour forth with meshed nets, toils, broad-headed hunting spears, Massylian horsemen and hounds of scent. At her doorway the Punic princes await their queen, who yet lingers in her chamber, and her horse stands splendid in gold and purple with clattering feet and jaws champing on the foamy bit. At last she comes forth amid a great thronging train, girt in a Sidonian mantle, broidered with needlework; her quiver is of gold, her tresses gathered into gold, a golden buckle clasps up her crimson gown. Therewithal the Phrygian train advances with joyous Iülus. Himself first and foremost of all, Aeneas joins her company and mingles his train with hers. . . . When they are come to the mountain heights and pathless coverts, lo, wild goats driven from the cliff-tops run down the ridge; in another quarter stags speed over the open plain and gather their flying column in a cloud of dust as they leave the hills. But the boy Ascanius is in the valleys, exultant on his fiery horse, and gallops past one and another, praying that among the unwarlike herds a foaming boar may issue or a tawny lion descend the hill.

Meanwhile the sky begins to thicken and roar aloud. A rain-cloud comes down mingled with hail; the Tyrian train and the men of Troy, and Venus' Dardanian grandchild, scatter in fear and seek shelter far over the fields. Streams pour from the hills. Dido and the Trojan captain take covert in the same cavern. Primeval Earth and Juno the bridesmaid give the sign; fires flash out high in air, witnessing the union, and Nymphs cry aloud on the mountain-top. That day opened the gate of death and the springs of ill. For now Dido recks not of eye or tongue, nor sets her heart on love in secret: she calls it marriage, and with this word shrouds her blame.

Straightway Rumour runs through the great cities of Libya,—Rumour, than whom none other is more swift to mischief; she thrives on restlessness and gains strength by going: at first small and timorous;

soon she lifts herself on high and paces the ground with head hidden among the clouds. Her, as they tell, Mother Earth, when stung by wrath against the gods, bore last sister to Coeus and Enceladus, fleet-footed and swift of wing, ominous, awful, vast; for every feather on her body is a waking eye beneath, wonderful to tell, and a tongue, and as many loud lips and straining ears. By night she flits between sky and land, shrilling through the dusk, and droops not her lids in sweet slumber; in daylight she sits on guard upon tall towers or the ridge of the house-roof, and makes great cities afraid; obstinate in perverseness and forgery no less than messenger of truth. She then exultingly filled the countries with manifold talk, and blazoned alike what was done and undone: one Aeneas is come, born of Trojan blood; on him beautiful Dido thinks no shame to fling herself; now they pass the long winter-tide together in revelry, regardless of their realms and enthralled by dishonouring passion. This the pestilent goddess spreads abroad in the mouths of men, and bends her course right on to King Iarbas, and with her words fires his spirit and swells his wrath.

He, the seed of Ammon by a ravished Garamantian Nymph, had built to Jove in his wide realms an hundred great temples, an hundred altars, and consecrated the wakeful fire that keeps watch by night before the gods perpetually, where the soil is fat with blood of beasts and the courts blossom with pied garlands. And he, distraught at heart and on fire at the bitter tidings, before his altars, amid the divine presences often, it is said, bowed in prayer to Jove with uplifted hands:

'Jupiter omnipotent, to whom from the broidered cushions of their banqueting halls the Maurusian people now pour offering of the wine-vat, lookest thou on this? or do we shudder vainly when our father hurls the thunderbolt, and do blind fires in the clouds and idle rumblings appal our soul? The woman wanderer who in our coasts planted a small town on purchased ground, to whom we gave fields by the shore and laws of settlement, has spurned our alliance and taken Aeneas for lord of her realm. And now that Paris, with his effeminate crew, his chin and oozy hair swathed in the turban of Maeonia, takes and keeps her; since to thy temples we bear oblation, and hallow an empty name.'

In such words he pleaded, clasping the altars; the Lord omnipotent heard, and cast his eye on the royal city and the lovers forgetful of their fairer fame. Then he addresses this charge to Mercury:

'Up and away, O son! call the breezes and slide down them on thy wings: accost the Dardanian captain who now loiters in Tyrian Carthage and casts not a look on the cities destined for him; carry down my words through the fleet air. Not such an one did his mother most beautiful vouch him to us, nor for this twice rescue him from Grecian arms; but he was to rule an Italy teeming with empire and loud with war, to transmit the line of Teucer's royal blood, and lay all the world beneath his law. If such glories kindle him in no wise, and he take no trouble for his own honour, does a father grudge his Ascanius the towers of Rome? with what device or in what hope loiters he among a hostile race, and casts not a glance on his Ausonian children and the fields of Lavinium? Let him set sail: this is the sum: thereof be thou our messenger.'

He ended: the other made ready to obey his father's high command. And first he laces to his feet the shoes of gold that bear him winging high over seas or land as fleet as the blast; then takes the rod wherewith he calls wan souls forth of Orcus, or sends them again to the sad depth of hell, gives sleep and takes it away and unseals dead eyes; in whose strength he courses the winds and swims through the tossing clouds. . . . So soon as his winged feet touched at the hut-villages, he espies Aeneas founding towers and ordering new dwellings; his sword twinkled with yellow jasper, and a cloak hung from his shoulders ablaze with Tyrian sea-purple, a gift that Dido had made costly and shot the warp with threads of gold. Straightway he breaks in: 'Layest thou now the foundations of high Carthage, and buildest up a fair city in dalliance? ah, forgetful of thine own kingdom and state! From bright Olympus I descend to thee at express command of heaven's sovereign, whose deity sways sky and earth; expressly he bids me carry this charge through the fleet air: with what device or in what hope dost thou loiter idly on Libyan lands? if such glories kindle thee in no wise, yet cast an eye on growing Ascanius, on Iülus thine hope and heir, to whom the kingdom of Italy and the Roman land is due.' As these words left his lips the Cyllenian, yet speaking, quitted mortal sight and vanished into thin air away out of his eyes.

But Aeneas in truth gazed in dumb amazement, his hair thrilled up, and the voice choked in his throat. He burns to flee away and leave the pleasant land, aghast at the high warning and divine ordinance. Alas, what shall he do? how venture now to smooth the tale to the frenzied queen? what prologue shall he find? and this way and that he rapidly throws his mind, and turns it on all hands in swift change of thought. In his perplexity this seemed the better counsel; he calls Mnestheus and Sergestus, and brave Serestus, and bids them silently equip the fleet, gather their crews to the shore, and prepare their armament, keeping the cause of the commotion hid; himself meanwhile, since Dido in her kindness knows not and looks not for severance to so strong a love, will essay to approach her when she may be told most gently, and the way for it be fair. All at once gladly do as bidden, and obey his command.

But the Queen—who may delude a lover?—foreknew his devices, and at once caught the presaging stir, fearing even where no fear was. To her likewise had evil Rumour borne the maddening news of the fleet in equipment and the voyage prepared. Helpless at heart, she reels aflame with rage throughout the city. . . . Thus at last she breaks out upon
10 Aeneas:

'And thou didst hope, traitor, to mask such infamy, and slip away silently from my land? Our love holds thee not, nor the hand thou once gavest, nor the bitter death that is left for Dido's portion? Nay, even in winter weather thou labourest on thy fleet, and hastenest to launch into the deep amid northern gales; ah, cruel! Why, were thy quest not of alien fields and unknown dwellings, did thine ancient Troy remain, should Troy be sought in voyages
20 over tempestuous seas? Fliest thou from me? me who by these tears and thine own hand beseech thee, since naught else, alas! have I kept mine own —by our union and the marriage rites begun; if I have done thee any grace, or aught of mine was once sweet to thee,—pity our sinking house, and if there yet be room for prayers, put off this purpose of thine. For thy sake Libyan tribes and Nomad kings are hostile; my Tyrians are estranged; for thy sake, thine, is mine honour perished, and the former
30 fame, my one title to the skies. How leavest thou me to die, O my guest? since of the name of husband all that is left is this. For what do I wait? till Pygmalion overthrow his sister's city, or Gaetulian Iarbas lead me to captivity? At least if before thy flight a child of thine had been clasped in my arms, if a tiny Aeneas were playing in my hall, whose face might yet image thine, I would not think myself ensnared and deserted utterly.'

She ended; he by counsel of Jove held his gaze
40 unstirred, and kept his anguish hard down in his heart. At last he briefly answers:

'Never, O Queen, will I deny that thy goodness has gone high as thy words can swell the reckoning; nor will I grudge a memory to Elissa while I remember myself, and breath sways this body. Little will I say where little is to be said. I never hoped to slip away in stealthy flight; fancy not that; nor did I ever hold out the marriage torch or enter thus into alliance. Did fate allow me to guide my life by mine
50 own government, and calm my sorrows as I would, my first duty were to the Trojan city and the dear remnant of my kindred; the high house of Priam should abide, and my hand had set up Troy towers anew for a conquered people. But now for broad Italy has Apollo of Grynos bidden me steer, for Italy

44. **Elissa,** Dido.

the oracles of Lycia. Here is my desire; this is my native country. If thy Phoenician eyes are stayed on the fortress of Carthage and thy Libyan city, what wrong is it, I pray, that we Trojans should find rest on Ausonian land? We too may seek a foreign realm 60 unforbidden. In my sleep, often as the dank shades of night veil the earth, often as the stars lift their fires, the troubled phantom of my father Anchises comes in warning and dread; my boy Ascanius comes and the wrong done to one so dear in cheating him of an Hesperian kingdom and destined fields. Now even the gods' interpreter, sent straight from Jove—I call both to witness—has borne down his commands through the fleet air. Myself in broad daylight I saw the deity passing within the walls, 70 and these ears drank his utterance. Cease to madden me and thyself alike with plaints. Not of my will do I follow Italy.' . . .

Long ere he ended she gazes on him askance, turning her eyes from side to side and perusing him with silent glances; then thus wrathfully speaks:

'No goddess was thy mother, nor Dardanus founder of thy line, traitor! but rough Caucasus bore thee on his iron crags, and Hyrcanian tigresses gave thee suck. For why do I conceal it? For what further 80 outrage do I wait? Has our weeping cost him a sigh, or a lowered glance? Has he broken into tears, or had pity on his lover? Where, where shall I begin? Now neither doth Queen Juno nor our Saturnian lord regard us with righteous eyes. Nowhere is trust safe. Cast ashore and destitute I welcomed him, and madly gave him place and portion in my kingdom; I found him his lost fleet and drew his comrades from death. Alas, the fire of madness speeds me on. Now prophetic Apollo, now oracles of Lycia, now 90 the very gods' interpreter sent straight from Jove through the air carries these rude commands! Truly that is work for the gods, that a care to vex their peace! I detain thee not, nor gainsay thy words: go, follow thine Italy down the wind; seek thy realm overseas. Yet midway my hope is, if righteous gods can do aught at all, thou wilt drain the cup of vengeance on the rocks, and re-echo calls on Dido's name. In murky fires I will follow far away, and when chill death has severed body from soul, my 100 ghost will haunt thee in every region. Wretch, thou shalt repay! I will hear; and the rumour of it shall reach me deep in the under world.'

Even on these words she breaks off her speech unfinished, and, sick at heart, escapes out of the air and sweeps round and away out of sight, leaving him in fear and much hesitance, and with much on his mind to say. Her women catch her in their arms, and carry her swooning limbs to her marble chamber and lay her on her bed. 110

But good Aeneas, though he would fain soothe and comfort her grief, and quell her passion by speech, with many a sigh, and melted in soul by his great love, yet fulfills the divine commands and returns to his fleet. Then indeed the Teucrians set to work, and haul down their tall ships all along the shore. The hulls are oiled and afloat; they carry from the woodland green boughs for oars and massy logs unhewn, in hot haste to go. . . . One might descry them shifting their quarters and pouring out of all the town: even as ants, mindful of winter, plunder a great heap of wheat and store it in their house; a black column advances on the plain as they carry home their spoil on a narrow track through the grass. Some shove and strain with their shoulders at big grains, some marshal the ranks and chastise delay; all the path is aswarm with work. What then were thy thoughts, O Dido, as thou sawest it? What sighs didst thou utter, viewing from the fortress roof the broad beach aswarm, and seeing before thine eyes the whole sea stirred with their noisy din? Injurious Love, to what dost thou not compel mortal hearts! Again she must needs break into tears, again essay entreaty, and bow her spirit down to love, not to leave aught untried and go to death in vain.

'Anna, thou seest the bustle that fills the circle of the shore. They have gathered from every quarter; already their canvas woos the breezes, and the joyous sailors have garlanded the sterns. This great pain, my sister, I shall have strength to bear, as I have had strength to foresee. Yet this one thing, Anna, for love and pity's sake—for of thee alone was the traitor fain, to thee even his secret thoughts were confided, alone thou knewest his moods and tender fits—go, my sister, and humbly accost the haughty stranger: I did not take the Grecian oath in Aulis to root out the race of Troy; I sent no fleet against her fortresses, neither have I disentombed his father Anchises' ashes and ghost. Why does he refuse my words entrance to his stubborn ears? Whither does he run? let him grant this grace—alas, the last!—to his lover, and await fair winds and an easy passage. No more do I pray for the old delusive marriage, nor that he give up fair Latium and abandon a kingdom. A breathing-space I ask, to give my madness rest and room, till my very fortune teach my grief submission. This last grace I implore—sister, be pitiful—let him but grant me this and I will repay it weighted with my death.'

So she pleaded, and so her sister carries and recarries the piteous tale of weeping. But by no weeping is he stirred, and no words that he hears may bend him. Fate withstands, and lays divine bars on unmoved mortal ears. Even as when the eddying blasts of northern Alpine winds are emulous to uproot the secular strength of a mighty oak, it wails on, and the trunk quivers and the high foliage strews the ground; the tree clings fast on the rocks, and

high as her top soars into the aëry sky, so deep strike her roots to hell; even thus is the hero buffeted with changeful perpetual accents, and distress thrills his mighty breast, while his purpose stays unstirred, and her tears are shed in vain.

Then indeed, hapless and dismayed by doom, Dido prays for death, and is weary of looking on the arch of heaven. The more to make her fulfil her purpose and quit the light, she saw, when she laid her gifts on the altars alight with incense, awful to tell, the holy streams blacken, and the wine turn as it poured into ghastly blood. Of this sight she spoke to none—no, not to her sister. Likewise there was within the house a marble temple of her ancient lord, kept of her in marvellous honour, and fastened with snowy fleeces and festal boughs. Forth of it she seemed to hear her husband's voice crying and calling when night was dim upon earth, and alone on the house-tops the screech-owl often made moan with funeral note and long-drawn sobbing cry. Therewithal many a warning of wizards of old terrifies her with appalling presage. In her sleep fierce Aeneas drives her wildly, and ever she seems being left by herself alone, ever going uncompanioned on a weary way, and seeking her Tyrians in a solitary land. . . .

So when, overcome by her pangs, she has caught the madness and resolved to die, she works out secretly the time and fashion, and accosts her sorrowing sister with mien hiding her design and hope calm on her brow.

'I have found a way, mine own—wish me joy, sisterlike—to restore him to me or release me of my love for him. Hard by the ocean limit and the set of sun is the extreme Aethiopian land, where ancient Atlas turns on his shoulders the starred burning axletree of heaven. Out of it has been shown to me a priestess of Massylian race, warder of the temple of the Hesperides, even she who gave the dragon his food, and kept the holy boughs on the tree, sprinkling clammy honey and slumberous poppy-seed. She vouches with her spells to relax the purposes of whom she will, but on others to bring passion and pain; to stay the river-waters and turn the stars backward: she calls up ghosts by night; thou shalt see earth moaning under foot and mountain-ashes descending from the hills. I take heaven, sweet, to witness, and thee, mine own darling sister, I do not willingly arm myself with the arts of magic. Do thou secretly raise a pyre in the inner court, and lay upon it the arms of the man that he cruelly left hanging in our chamber, and all the dress he wore, and the bridal bed where I fell. It is good to wipe out all traces of the accursed one, and the priestess orders thus.' So speaks she, and is silent, while pallor overruns her face. Yet Anna deems not her sister drapes death in these strange rites, and grasps not her wild purpose, nor fears aught deeper than at Sychaeus' death. So she makes ready as bidden. . . .

But the Queen, when the pyre is built up of piled faggots and cleft ilex in the inmost of her dwelling, hangs the room with chaplets and garlands it with funeral boughs: on the pillow she lays the dress he wore, the sword he left, and an image of him, knowing what was to come. Altars are reared around, and the priestess, with hair undone, thrice peals from her lips the hundred gods of Erebus and Chaos, and the triform Hecate, the triple-faced maidenhood of Diana. Likewise she had sprinkled pretended waters of Avernus' spring, and rank herbs are sought mown by moonlight with brazen sickles, dark with milky venom, and sought is the tailsman torn from a horse's forehead at birth ere the dam could snatch it. . . . Herself, the holy cake in her pure hands, hard by the altars, with one foot unshod and garments flowing loose, she invokes the gods ere she die, and the stars that know of doom; then prays to whatsoever deity looks in righteousness and remembrance on lovers ill allied.

Night fell; weary creatures took quiet slumber all over earth, and woodland and wild waters had sunk to rest; now the stars wheel midway on their gliding path, now all the country is silent, and beasts and gay birds that haunt liquid levels of lake or thorny rustic thicket lay couched asleep under the still night. But not so the distressed Phoenician, nor does she ever sink asleep or take the night upon eyes or breast; her pain redoubles, and her love swells to renewed madness, as she tosses on the strong tide of wrath. Even so she begins, and thus revolves with her heart alone:

'Lo, what do I? Shall I again make trial of mine old wooers that will scorn me? and stoop to sue for a Numidian marriage among those whom already over and over I have disdained for husbands? Then shall I follow the Ilian fleets and the uttermost bidding of the Teucrians? because they are glad to have been once raised up by my succour, or the grace of mine old kindness is fresh in their remembrance? And who will permit me, if I would? or take a hated woman on their proud fleet? art thou ignorant, ah me, even in ruin, and knowest not yet the forsworn race of Laomedon? And then? shall I accompany the triumphant sailors, a lonely fugitive? or plunge forth girt with all my Tyrian train? so hardly severed from Sidon city, shall I again drive them seaward, and bid them spread their sails to the tempest? Nay die thou, as thou deservest, and let the steel end thy pain. With thee it began; overborne by my tears, thou, O my sister, dost load me with this madness and agony, and cast me to the enemy. It was not mine to spend a wild life without stain, far from a bridal chamber, and untouched by this passion. O

46. **Laomedon,** king of Troy and father to Priam.

faith ill kept, that was plighted to Sychaeus' ashes!' Thus her heart broke in long lamentation.

Now Aeneas was fixed to go, and now, with all set duly in order, was taking hasty sleep on his high quarterdeck. To him as he slept the god appeared once again in the same fashion of countenance, and thus seemed to renew his warning, in all points like to Mercury, voice and hue and golden hair and limbs gracious in youth. 'Goddess-born, canst thou sleep on in such danger? and seest not the coming perils that hem thee in, madman! nor hearest the breezes blowing fair? She, fixed on death, is revolving craft and crime grimly in her bosom, and swells the changing surge of wrath. Fliest thou not hence headlong, while headlong flight is yet possible? Even now wilt thou see ocean weltering with broken timbers, see the fierce glare of torches and the beach in a riot of flame, if dawn break on thee yet dallying in this land. Up ho! linger no more! Woman is ever a fickle and changing thing.' So spoke he, and melted in the black night.

Then indeed Aeneas, startled by the sudden phantom, leaps out of slumber and bestirs his crew to headlong haste. 'Awake, O men, and sit down to the thwarts; shake out sail speedily. A god sent from high heaven, lo! again spurs us to speed our flight and cut the twisted cables. We follow thee, holy one ot heaven, whoso thou art, and again joyfully obey thy command. O be favourable; give gracious aid and bring fair sky and weather.' He spoke, and snatching his sword like lightning from the sheath, strikes at the hawser with the drawn steel. The same zeal catches all at once; rushing and tearing they quit the shore; the sea is hidden under their fleets; strongly they toss up the foam and sweep the blue water.

And now Dawn broke, and, leaving the saffron bed of Tithonus, shed her radiance anew over the world; when the Queen saw from her watch-tower the first light whitening, and the fleet standing out under squared sail, and discerned shore and haven empty of all their oarsmen. Thrice and four times she struck her hand on her lovely breast and rent her yellow hair: 'God!' she cries, 'shall he go? shall an alien make mock of our realm? Will they not issue in armed pursuit from all the city, and some launch ships from the dockyards? Go; bring fire in haste, serve out weapons, ply the oars! What do I talk? or where am I? what mad change is on my purpose? Alas, Dido! now evil deeds touch thee; that had been fitting once, when thou gavest away thy crown. Behold the faith and hand of him! who, they say, carries his household's ancestral gods about with him! who stooped his shoulders to a father outworn with age! Could I not have riven his body in sunder and strewn it on the waves? and slain with the sword his comrades and his dear Ascanius, and served him for the banquet at his father's table? But the chance of battle had been dubious. If it had! whom did I fear in the death-agony? I should have borne firebrands into his camp and filled his decks with flame, blotted out father and son and race together, and flung myself atop of all. Sun, whose fires lighten all the works of the world, and thou, Juno, mediatress and witness of these my distresses, and Hecate, cried on by night in crossways of cities, and you, fatal avenging sisters and gods of dying Elissa, hear me now; bend your just deity to my woes, and listen to our prayers. If it must needs be that the accursed one touch his haven and float up to land, if thus Jove's decrees demand, and this is the appointed term,—yet, distressed in war by an armed and gallant nation, driven homeless from his borders, rent from Iülus' embrace, let him sue for succour and see death on death untimely on his people; nor when he has yielded him to the terms of a harsh peace, may he have joy of his kingdom or the pleasant light; but let him fall before his day and without burial amid its soil. This I pray; this and my blood with it I pour for the last utterance. Then do you, O Tyrians, pursue his seed with your hatred for all ages to come; send this guerdon to our ashes. Let no kindness nor truce be between the nations. Arise, some avenger, out of our dust, to follow the Dardanian settlers with firebrand and steel. Now, then, whensoever strength shall be given, I invoke the enmity of shore to shore, wave to water, sword to sword; let their battles go down to their children's children.'

So speaks she as she kept turning her mind round about, seeking how soonest to break away from the hateful light. Thereon she speaks briefly to Barce, nurse of Sychaeus; for a heap of dusky ashes held her own, in her country of long ago:

'Sweet nurse, bring Anna my sister hither to me. Bid her haste and sprinkle river water over her body, and bring with her the beasts ordained for expiation: so let her come: and thou likewise veil thy brows with a pure chaplet. I would fulfil the rites of Stygian Jove that I have fitly ordered and begun, so to set the limit to my distresses and give over to flame the pyre of the Dardanian chief.'

So speaks she; the old woman went eagerly with quickened pace. But Dido, panting and fierce in her awful purpose, with bloodshot restless gaze, and spots on her quivering cheeks burning through the pallor of imminent death, bursts into the inner courts of the house, and mounts in madness the lofty stairs, and unsheathes the sword of Dardania, a gift sought for other use than this. Then after her eyes fell on the Ilian raiment and the bed she knew, dallying a little with her purpose through her tears, she sank on the pillow and spoke the last words of all:

'Dress he wore, sweet while doom and deity allowed! receive my spirit now, and release me from my distresses. I have lived and fulfilled Fortune's allotted course; and now shall I go a queenly phantom under the earth. I have built a renowned city; I have seen my ramparts rise; by my brother's punishment I have avenged my husband of his enemy; happy, ah me! and over happy, had but the keels of Dardania never touched our shores!' She spoke; and burying her face in the pillow, 'Death it will be,' she cries, 'and unavenged; but death be it. Thus, thus is it good to pass into the dark. Let the pitiless Dardanian's gaze drink in this fire out at sea, and my death be the omen he carries on his way.'

She ceased; and even as she spoke her people see her sunk on the steel, and blood reeking on the sword and spattered on her hands. A cry rises in the high halls; Rumour riots down the quaking city. The house resounds with lamentation and sobbing and bitter crying of women; heaven echoes their loud wails; even as though all Carthage or ancient Tyre went down as the foe poured in, and the flames rolled furious over the roofs of house and temple. Death-stricken her sister heard, and in swift hurrying dismay, with torn face and smitten bosom, darts through them all, and calls the dying woman by her name. 'Was it this, mine own? Was my summons a snare? Was it this thy pyre, ah me, this thine altar fires meant? How shall I begin my desolate moan? Didst thou disdain a sister's company in death? Thou shouldest have called me to share thy doom; in the self-same hour, the self-same pang of steel had been our portion. Did these very hands build it, did my voice call on our father's gods, that with thee lying thus I should be away, O merciless? Thou hast destroyed thyself and me together, O my sister, and the Sidonian lords and people, and this thy city. Give her wounds water: I will bathe them and catch on my lips the last breath that haply yet lingers.' So speaking she had climbed the high steps, and, wailing, clasped and caressed her half-lifeless sister in her bosom, and stanched the dark streams of blood with her gown. She, essaying to lift her heavy eyes, swoons back; the deep-driven wound gurgles in her breast. Thrice she rose, and strained to lift herself on her elbow; thrice she rolled back on the pillow and with wandering eyes sought the light of high heaven, and moaned as she found it.

Then Juno omnipotent, pitying her long pain and difficult decease, sent Iris down from heaven to unloose the struggling life from the body where it clung. For since neither by fate did she perish, nor as one who had earned her death, but woefully before her day, and fired by sudden madness, not yet had Proserpine taken her tress from the golden head, nor sentenced her to the nether Stygian world. So Iris on dewy saffron pinions flits down through the sky athwart the sun in a trail of a thousand changing dyes, and stopping over her head: 'This lock, sacred to Dis, I take as bidden, and release thee from that body of thine.' So speaks she, and cuts it with her hand. And therewith all the warmth ebbed forth from her, and the life passed away upon the winds.

BOOK VI

. . . So [Aeneas] gives his fleet the rein, and at last glides in to Euboïc Cumae's coast. They turn the prows seaward; the ships grounded fast on the
10 anchor-flukes, and the curving sterns line the beach. The warrior band leaps forth eagerly on the Hesperian shore; some seek the seeds of flame hidden in veins of flint, some scour the woods, the thick coverts of wild beasts, and find and shew the streams. But good Aeneas seeks the fortress where Apollo sits high enthroned, and the lone mystery of the awful Sibyl's cavern depth, over whose mind and soul the prophetic Delian breathes high inspiration and reveals futurity. . . .

20 A vast cavern is scooped in the side of the Euboïc cliff, whither lead an hundred wide passages by an hundred gates, whence peal forth as manifold the responses of the Sibyl. They had reached the threshold. . . . A cold shiver ran through the Teucrians' iron frames, and the king pours heart-deep supplication: '. . . O prophetess most holy, foreknower of the future, grant (for no unearned realm does my destiny claim) a resting-place in Latium to the Teucrians, to their wandering gods and the storm-
30 tossed deities of Troy. Then will I ordain to Phoebus and Trivia a temple of solid marble, and festal days in Phoebus' name. Thee likewise a mighty sanctuary awaits in our realm. . . . One thing I pray; since here is the gate named of the infernal king, and the darkling marsh of Acheron's overflow, be it given me to go to my beloved father, to see him face to face; teach thou the way, and open the consecrated portals. Him on these shoulders I rescued from encircling flames and a thousand pursuing weapons,
40 and brought him safe from amid the enemy; he shared my journey over all the seas, and bore with me all the threats of ocean and sky, in weakness, beyond his age's strength and due. Nay, he it was who besought and enjoined me to seek thy grace and draw nigh the courts. Have pity, I beseech thee, on son and father, O gracious one! for thou art all-powerful, nor in vain has Hecate given thee rule in the groves of Avernus.' . . .

In such words he pleaded and clasped the altars;
50 when the soothsayer thus began to speak:

'O sprung of gods' blood, child of Anchises of Troy, easy is the descent into hell; all night and day the gate of dark Dis stands open; but to recall thy steps and issue to upper air, this is the task, this the burden. Some few of gods' lineage have availed, such as Jupiter's gracious favour or virtue's ardour has upborne to heaven. Midway all is muffled in forest, and the black sliding coils of Cocytus circle it round. Yet if thy soul is so passionate and so desirous twice to float across the Stygian lake, twice to
60 see dark Tartarus, and thy pleasure is to plunge into the mad task, learn what must first be accomplished. Hidden in a shady tree is a bough with leafage and pliant shoot all of gold, consecrate to nether Juno, wrapped in the depth of woodland and shut in by dim dusky vales. But to him only who first has plucked the golden-tressed fruitage from the tree is it given to enter the hidden places of the earth. This has beautiful Proserpine ordained to be borne to her for her proper gift. The first torn away, a second fills
70 the place in gold, and the spray burgeons with even such ore again. So let thine eyes trace it home, and thine hand pluck it duly when found; for lightly and unreluctant will it follow if thine is fate's summons; else will no strength of thine avail to conquer it nor hard steel to cut it away. Yet again, a friend of thine lies a lifeless corpse, alas! thou knowest it not, and defiles all the fleet with death, while thou seekest our counsel and lingerest in our courts. First lay him
80 in his resting-place and hide him in the tomb; lead thither black cattle; be this first thine expiation; so at last shalt thou behold the Stygian groves and the realm untrodden of the living.' She spoke, and her lips shut to silence.

Aeneas goes forth, and leaves the cavern with lowered eyes and sad countenance, his soul revolving inly the unseen issues. By his side goes faithful Achates, and plants his footsteps in equal perplexity. Long they ran on in mutual change of talk; of what lifeless comrade spoke the soothsayer, of what body
90 for burial? And even as they came, they see on the dry beach Misenus cut off by untimely death, Misenus the Aeolid, excelled of none other in stirring men with brazen breath and kindling battle with his trumpet-note. He had been attendant on mighty Hector; in Hector's train he waged battle, renowned alike for bugle and spear: after victorious Achilles robbed him of life the valiant hero had joined Dardanian Aeneas' company, and followed no meaner leader. But now, while he makes his hollow shell
100 echo over the seas, ah fool! and calls the gods to rival his blast, jealous Triton, if belief is due, had caught him among the rocks and sunk him in the foaming waves. So all surrounded him with loud murmur and cries, good Aeneas the foremost. Then weeping they quickly hasten on the Sibyl's orders, and work hard to pile trees for the altar of burial, and heap it up into the sky. They pass into the

8. **Euboïc Cumae's coast**; in central Italy. 18. **prophetic Delian**, Apollo. 53. **Dis**, the underworld.

58. **Cocytus**, the "river of wailing," a tributary of Acheron. 61. **Tartarus**, the underworld. 69. **Proserpine**, queen of the underworld.

ancient forest, the deep coverts of game; pitch-pines fall flat, ilex rings to the stroke of axes, and ashen beams and oak are split in clefts with wedges; they roll in huge mountain-ashes from the hills. Aeneas likewise is first in the work, and cheers on his crew and arms himself with their weapons. And alone with his sad heart he ponders it all, gazing on the endless forest, and thus idly prays: 'If but now that bough of gold would shew itself to us on the tree in this depth of woodland! since all the soothsayer's tale of thee, Misenus, was, alas! too truly spoken.' Scarcely has he said thus, when twin doves haply came flying down the sky, and lit on the green sod right under his eyes. Then the kingly hero knows them for his mother's birds, and joyfully prays: 'Ah, be my guides, if way there be, and direct your aëry passage into the groves where the rich bough overshadows the fertile ground! and thou, O goddess mother, fail not our wavering fortune!' So spoke he and stayed his steps, marking what they signify, whither they urge their way. Feeding and flying they advance at such distance as following eyes could keep them in view; then, when they came to Avernus' pestilent gorge, they tower swiftly, and sliding down through the liquid air, choose their seat and light side by side on a tree, through whose boughs shone out the contrasting sheen of gold. As in chill mid-winter the woodland is wont to blossom with the strange leafage of the mistletoe, sown on an alien tree and wreathing the smooth stems with burgeoning saffron; so on the shadowy ilex seemed that leafy gold, so the foil tinkled in the light breeze. Immediately Aeneas seizes it and eagerly breaks off its resistance, and carries it beneath the Sibyl's roof.

And therewithal the Teucrians on the beach wept Misenus, and bore the last rites to the thankless ashes. . . .

This done, he hastens to fulfil the Sibyl's ordinance. A deep cave yawned dreary and vast, shingle-strewn, sheltered by the black lake and the gloom of the forests; over it no flying things could wing their way scathless, such a vapour streamed from the dark gorge and rose into the overarching sky. Here the priestess first arrays four black-bodied bullocks and pours wine upon their forehead; and plucking the topmost hairs from between the horns, lays them on the sacred fire for first-offering, calling aloud on Hecate, mistress of heaven and hell. Others lay knives to their throats, and catch the warm blood in cups. Aeneas himself smites with the sword a black-fleeced she-lamb to the mother of the Eumenides and her mighty sister, and a barren heifer to thee, O Proserpine. Then he uprears darkling altars to the Stygian king, and lays whole carcases of bulls upon the flames, pouring fat oil over the blazing entrails. And lo! about the first rays of sunrise the ground moaned underfoot, and the woodland ridges began to stir, and dogs seemed to howl through the dusk as the goddess came. 'Apart, ah keep apart, O ye unsanctified!' cries the soothsayer; 'retire from all the grove; and thou, stride on and unsheath thy steel; now is need of courage, O Aeneas, now of strong resolve.' So much she spoke, and plunged in ecstasy into the cavern's opening; he with unflinching steps keeps pace with his advancing guide.

Gods who are sovereign over souls! silent ghosts, and Chaos and Phlegethon, the wide dumb realm of night! as I have heard, so let me tell, and according to your will unfold things sunken deep under earth in gloom.

They went darkling through the dusk beneath the solitary night, through the empty dwellings and bodiless realm of Dis; even as one walks in the forest beneath the jealous light of a doubtful moon, when Jupiter shrouds the sky in shadow and black night blots out the world. Right in front of the doorway, in the entry of the jaws of hell, Grief and avenging Cares have made their bed; there dwell wan Sickness and gloomy Eld, and Fear, and ill-counselling Hunger, and loathly Penury, shapes terrible to see; and Death and Travail, and thereby Sleep, Death's kinsman, and the Soul's guilty Joys, and death-dealing War full in the gateway, and the Furies in their iron cells, and mad Discord with blood-stained fillets enwreathing her serpent locks. . . .

Hence a road leads to Tartarus and Acheron's wave. Here the dreary pool swirls thick in muddy eddies and disgorges into Cocytus all its load of sand. Charon, the dread ferryman, guards these flowing streams, ragged and awful, his chin covered with untrimmed masses of hoary hair, and his eyes a steady flame; his soiled raiment hangs knotted from his shoulders. Himself he plies the pole and trims the sails of his vessel, the steel-blue galley with freight of dead; stricken now in years, but a god's old age is lusty and green. Hither all crowded, and rushed streaming to the bank, matrons and men and high-hearted heroes dead and done with life, boys and unwedded girls, and children laid young on the bier before their parents' eyes, multitudinous as leaves fall dropping in the forests at autumn's earliest frost, or birds swarm landward from the deep gulf, when the chill of the year routs them overseas and drives them to sunny lands. They stood pleading for the first passage across, and stretched forth passionate hands to the farther shore. But the grim mariner admits now one and now another, while some he pushes back far apart on the strand. Moved with marvel at the confused throng: 'Say, O maiden,' cries Aeneas, 'what means this flocking to the river? of what are the souls so fain? or what difference makes these retire from the banks, those go with sweeping oars over the leaden waterways?'

To him the ancient priestess thus briefly returned: 'Seed of Anchises, most sure progeny of gods, thou seest the deep pools of Cocytus and the Stygian marsh, by whose divinity the gods fear to swear falsely. All this crowd thou discernest is helpless and unsepultured; Charon is the ferryman; they who ride on the wave found a tomb. Nor is it given to cross the awful banks and hoarse streams ere the dust has found a resting-place. An hundred years they wander here flitting about the shore; then at last they gain entrance, and revisit the pools so sorely desired.' . . .

Lo, there went by Palinurus the steersman, who of late, while he watched the stars in their Libyan passage, had slipped from the stern and fallen amid the waves. To him, soon as he barely knew the melancholy form in that depth of shade, he thus opens speech: 'What god, O Palinurus, reft thee from us and sank thee amid the seas? forth and tell. For in this single answer Apollo deceived me, never found false before, when he prophesied thee safety on ocean and arrival on the Ausonian coasts. Lo, is this his promise-keeping?'

And he: 'Neither did Phoebus on his oracular seat delude thee, O prince, Anchises' son, nor did any god plunge me in the sea. For while I clung to my appointed charge and governed our course, I pulled the tiller with me in my fall, and the shock as I slipped wrenched it away. By the rough seas I swear, fear for myself never wrung me so sore as for thy ship, lest, the rudder lost and the pilot struck away, those gathering waves might master it. Three wintry nights in the water the blustering south drove me over the endless sea; scarcely on the fourth dawn I descried Italy as I rose on the climbing wave. Little by little I swam shoreward; already I clung safe; but while, encumbered with my dripping raiment, I caught with crooked fingers at the jagged mountain-headlands, the barbarous people attacked me in arms and ignorantly deemed me a prize. Now the wave holds me, and the winds toss me on the shore. By heaven's pleasant light and breezes I beseech thee, by thy father, by Iülus thy rising hope, rescue me from these distresses, O unconquered one! Either do thou, for thou canst, cast earth over me and again seek the haven of Velia; or do thou, if any wise that may be, if in any wise the goddess who bore thee shews a way,—for not without divine will do I deem thou wilt float across these vast rivers and the Stygian pool,—lend me a pitying hand, and bear me over the waves in thy company, that at least in death I may find a quiet resting-place.'

Thus he ended, and the soothsayer thus began: 'Whence, O Palinurus, this fierce longing of thine? Shalt thou without burial behold the Stygian waters and the awful river of the Furies, or draw nigh the bank unbidden? Cease to hope prayers may bend the decrees of heaven. But take my words to thy memory, for comfort in thy woeful case: far and wide shall the bordering cities be driven by celestial portents to appease thy dust; they shall rear a tomb, and pay the tomb a yearly offering, and for ever-more shall the place keep Palinurus' name.' The words soothed away his distress, and for a while drove grief away from his sorrowing heart; the land is glad in his name.

So they complete their journey's beginning, and draw nigh the river: and now the waterman de-scried them from the Stygian wave advancing through the silent woodland and turning their feet towards the bank, and open on them in these words of challenge and chiding: 'Whoso thou art who marchest in arms towards our river, forth and say, there as thou art, why thou comest, and stay thine advance. This is the land of Shadows, of Sleep, and slumberous Night; no living body may pass in the Stygian ferry-boat.' . . .

Thereto the Amphrysian soothsayer made brief reply: 'No such plot is here; be not moved; nor do our weapons offer violence. . . . Aeneas of Troy, renowned in goodness as in arms, goes down to meet his father in the deep shades of Erebus. If the sight of such affection stirs thee in nowise, yet this bough' (she discovers the bough hidden in her rai-ment) 'thou must know.' Then his heaving breast allays its anger, and he says no more; but marvel-ling at the awful gift, the fated rod so long unseen, he steers in his dusky vessel and draws to shore. Next he routs out the souls that sate on the long benches, and clears the thwarts, while he takes mighty Aeneas on board. The galley groaned under the weight in all her seams, and the marsh-water leaked fast in. At length prophetess and prince are landed unscathed on the ugly ooze and livid sedge.

This realm rings with the triple-throated baying of vast Cerberus, couched huge in the cavern oppo-site; to whom the prophetess, seeing the serpents al-ready bristling up on his neck, throws a cake made slumberous with honey and drugged grain. He, with threefold jaws gaping in ravenous hunger, catches it when thrown, and sinks to earth with monstrous body outstretched, and sprawling huge over all his den. The warder overwhelmed, Aeneas makes en-trance, and quickly overstrides the bank of the ir-remeable wave.

Immediately wailing voices are loud in their ears, the souls of babies crying, whom, taken from sweet life at the doorway and torn from the breast, a dark day cut off and drowned in bitter death. Hard by them are those condemned to death on false accusa-tion. Neither indeed are these dwellings assigned without lot and judgment; Minos presides and shakes the urn; he summons a council of the silent people, and inquires of their lives and impeachments. Next in order have these mourners their place whose own innocent hands dealt them death, who flung away their souls in hatred of the day. How fain were they now in upper air to endure their poverty and sore travail! It may not be; the gloomy pool of that unlovely wave confines them, and Styx pours her ninefold barrier between. And not far from here are shewn stretching on every side the Wailing Fields; so they call them by name. Here they whom pitiless love has wasted in cruel decay hide among untrodden ways, shrouded in embosoming myrtle thickets; not death itself ends their distresses. . . . Among whom Dido the Phoenician, fresh from her death-wound, wandered into the vast forest; by her the Trojan hero stood, and knew the dim form through the darkness, even as the moon at the month's beginning to him who sees or thinks he sees her rising through the vapours; he let tears fall, and spoke to her lovingly and sweet:

'Alas, Dido! so the news was true that reached me; thou didst perish, and the sword sealed thy doom! Ah me, was I cause of thy death? By the stars I swear, by the heavenly powers and all that is sacred beneath the earth, unwillingly, O queen, I left thy shore. But the gods' commands, which now compel me to pass through this shadowy place, this land of mouldering overgrowth and deep night, drove me imperiously forth; nor could I deem my departure would bring thee pain so great. Stay thy footstep, and withdraw not from our gaze. From whom fliest thou? the last speech of thee fate ordains me is this.'

In such words and with starting tears Aeneas soothed the burning and fierce-eyed spirit. She turned away with looks fixed fast on the ground, stirred no more in countenance by the speech he essays than if she stood in iron flint or Marpesian stone. At length she started, and fled wrathfully into the shadowy woodland, where Sychaeus, in responsive passion and equal love, is her husband as long ago. Yet Aeneas, dismayed by her cruel doom, follows her far on her way with pitying tears.

Thence he pursues his appointed path. And now they trod those utmost fields where the renowned in war have their haunt apart. . . . The souls throng round him to right and left; nor is one look enough; it delights them to linger on, to pace by his side and learn wherefore he is come. But the princes of the Grecians and Agamemnon's armies, when they see him glittering in arms through the gloom, hurry terror-stricken away; some turn backward, as when of old they fled to the ships; some raise their voice faintly, and gasp out a broken ineffectual cry.

Dawn had already crossed heaven's mid axle on her rose-charioted way; and haply had they thus drawn out all the allotted time; but the Sibyl made brief warning speech to her companion: 'Night falls, Aeneas; we waste the hours in weeping. Here is the place where the road disparts; by this that runs to the right under the city of great Dis is our path to Elysium; but the leftward wreaks vengeance on the wicked and sends them to unrelenting hell.' . . .

Aeneas looks back on a sudden, and sees beneath the cliff on the left hand a wide city, girt with a triple wall and encircled by a swift river of boiling flame, Tartarean Phlegethon, rolling its loud boulders down. In front is the gate, huge and pillared with solid adamant, that no warring force of men nor the very habitants of heaven may avail to overthrow; the iron tower uprears itself, and Tisiphone sitting girt in blood-stained pall keeps sleepless watch at the entry by night and day. Hence moans are heard and fierce lashes resound, with the clank of iron and dragging chains. Aeneas stopped and drank in the tumult dismayed. 'What shapes of crime are here? declare, O maiden; or what the punishment that pursues them, and all this clashing in mine ears?' Then the soothsayer thus began to speak: 'Illustrious chief of Troy, no pure foot may tread these guilty courts; but me Hecate herself, when she gave me rule over the groves of Avernus, taught how the gods punish, and guided through all her realm. Gnosian Rhadamanthus here holds unrelaxing sway, chastises secret crime revealed, and exacts confession, wheresoever in the upper world one vainly exultant in stolen guilt has put off, till death makes it too late, the expiation of his crimes. Straightway avenging Tisiphone, girt with her scourge, tramples down the shivering sinners, menaces them with the grim snakes in her left hand, and summons forth her sisters in merciless train. Then at last the sacred gates are flung open and grate on jarring hinge. Markest thou what sentry is seated in the doorway? what shape guards the threshold? More grim within sits the monstrous Hydra with her fifty black yawning throats: and Tartarus' self gapes sheer and strikes into the gloom through twice the space that one looks upward to Olympus and the skyey heaven. Here Earth's ancient children, the Titans' brood, hurled down by the thunderbolt, lie wallowing in the abyss. . . . Here are they who hated their brethren while life endured, or struck a parent or entangled a client in wrong, or who brooded alone over found treasure and shared it not with their fellows, this the greatest multitude of all; and they who were slain for adultery, and who followed unrighteous arms, and feared not to betray their masters' plighted hand. Imprisoned they await their doom. Seek not to be told what doom, or in what guise fortune has overwhelmed them. Some roll a vast stone, or hang out-

70. **Tisiphone,** one of the Furies. 83. **Gnosian Rhadamanthus,** a judge in Hades because of his reputation for justice while on earth.

stretched on the spokes of wheels; hapless Theseus sits and shall sit for ever, and Phlegyas in his misery gives counsel to all and witnesses aloud through the gloom. *Learn by this warning to do justly and not to slight the gods.* This man sold his country for gold, and laid her under a tyrant's sway; he set up and pulled down laws at a price; this other forced his daughter's bridal chamber and a forbidden marriage; all ventured some monstrous wickedness, and gained their venture. Not had I an hundred tongues, an hundred mouths, and a voice of iron, could I sum up all the shapes of crime or name over all their punishments.'

Thus spoke Phoebus' ancient priestess; then 'But come now,' she cries; 'hasten on the way and perfect the service begun; let us go faster; I descry the ramparts cast in Cyclopean furnaces, and in front the arched gateway where they bid us lay the gifts foreordained.' She ended, and advancing side by side along the shadowy ways, they overtake the space between, and draw nigh the gates. Aeneas makes entrance, and sprinkling his body with fresh water, plants the bough in front of the gateway.

Now at length, this fully done, and the service of the goddess perfected, they came to the happy place, the green pleasances and blissful seats of the Fortunate Woodlands. Here an ampler air clothes the meadows in lustrous sheen, and they know their own sun and a starlight of their own. Some exercise their limbs in tournament on the greensward, contend in games, and wrestle on the yellow sand. Some dance with beating footfall and lips that sing. . . . Others, lo! he beholds feasting on the sward to right and left, and singing in chorus the glad Paean-cry, within a scented laurel-grove whence Eridanus river surges upward full-volumed through the wood. Here is the band of them who bore wounds in fighting for their country, and they who were pure in priesthood while life endured, and the good poets whose speech abased not Apollo; and they who made life beautiful by the arts of their invention, and who won by service a memory among others, the brows of all girt with the snow-white fillet. . . .

But lord Anchises, deep in the green valley, was musing in earnest survey over the imprisoned souls destined to the daylight above, and haply reviewing his beloved children and all the tale of his people, them and their fates and fortunes, their works and ways. And he, when he saw Aeneas advancing to meet him over the greensward, stretched forth both hands eagerly, while tears rolled over his cheeks, and his lips parted in a cry: 'Art thou come at last, and has thy love, child of my desire, conquered the difficult road? Is it granted, O my son, to gaze on thy face, to hear and to answer in the speech we

1. **Theseus**, who assisted in a plot to carry off Proserpine from the underworld.   2. **Phlegyas**, who burned a temple of Apollo.

know? Thus indeed did I forecast in spirit, counting the days between; nor has my care misled me. What lands, what space of seas hast thou traversed to reach me, through what surge of perils, O my son! How I dreaded lest the realm of Libya might work thee harm!'

And he: 'Thy melancholy phantom, thine, O my father, came before me often and often, and moved me to steer to these portals. My fleet is anchored on the Tyrrhenian brine. Give thine hand to clasp, O my father, give it, and withdraw not from our embrace.'

So spoke he, his face wet the while with abundant weeping. Thrice there did he essay to fling his arms about his neck; thrice the phantom vainly grasped fled out of his hands even as light wind, and most like to fluttering sleep.

Meanwhile Aeneas sees deep withdrawn in the covert of the vale a woodland and rustling forest thickets, and the river of Lethe that floats past the peaceful dwellings. Around it flittered nations and peoples innumerable; even as in the meadows when in clear summer weather bees settle on the variegated flowers and stream round the snow-white lilies, all the plain is murmurous with their humming. Aeneas starts at the sudden view, and asks the reason he knows not; what are those spreading streams, or who are they whose endless train fills the banks? Then lord Anchises: 'Souls, for whom second bodies are destined and due, drink at the wave of the Lethean stream the heedless water of long forgetfulness. These of a truth have I long desired to tell thee and shew thee face to face, and number all the generation of thy children, that so thou mayest the more rejoice with me in finding Italy.'—'O father, must we think that any souls travel hence into upper air, and return again to bodily fetters? why this strange sad longing for the light?' 'I will tell,' rejoins Anchises, 'nor will I hold thee in suspense, O my son.' And he unfolds all things in order one by one.

'First of all, heaven and earth and the liquid fields, the shining orb of the moon and the Titanian star, doth a spirit sustain inly, and a soul shed abroad in them sways all their members and mingles in the mighty frame. Thence is the generation of man and beast, the life of winged things, and the monstrous forms that ocean breeds under his glittering floor. Those seeds have fiery force and divine birth, so far as they are not clogged by sinful bodies and dulled by earthy frames and limbs ready to die. From these is it that they fear and desire, sorrow and rejoice; nor do their eyes pierce the air while barred in the blind darkness of their prison-house. Nay, even when the last ray of life is gone, nor yet, alas! does all their woe, nor do all the plagues of the body wholly leave them free; and needs must be that many a long hardened evil should take root marvellously deep. Therefore they are schooled in punishment, and pay all the forfeit of a lifelong ill; some are hung stretched to the viewless winds; some have the taint of guilt washed away beneath the dreary deep, or burned out in fire. We suffer, each in his own ghost; thereafter we are sent to the broad spaces of Elysium, some few of us to possess the happy fields; till length of days completing time's circle takes out the clotted soilure and leaves untainted the ethereal sense and pure spiritual flame. All these before thee, when the wheel of a thousand years has come fully round, a God summons in vast train to the river of Lethe, that so they may regain in forgetfulness the slopes of upper earth again, and begin to desire to return into the body.'

Anchises ceased, and leads his son and the Sibyl likewise amid the assembled murmurous throng, and mounts a hillock whence he might scan all the long ranks and learn their countenances as they came.

'Now come, the glory hereafter to follow our Dardanian progeny, the posterity to abide in our Italian people, illustrious souls and inheritors of our name to be, these will I rehearse, and instruct thee of thy destinies. He yonder, seest thou? the warrior who leans on his pointless spear, holds the place allotted nearest to daylight, and shall rise first into the air of heaven from the mingling blood of Italy, Silvius of Alban name, the child of thine age, whom late in thy length of days thy wife Lavinia shall nurture in the woodland, king and father of kings; from him in Alba the Long shall our house have dominion. . . . Nay, Romulus likewise shall join his grandsire's company. Seest thou how the twin plumes stand upright on his crest, and his father's own emblazonment already marks him for upper air? Behold, O son! in his auspices shall Rome the renowned fill earth with her empire and heaven with her pride, and gird about seven fortresses with her single wall, prosperous mother of men. . . . Hither now bend thy twin-eyed gaze; behold this people, the Romans that are thine. Here is Caesar and all Iülus' posterity that shall arise under the mighty cope of heaven. Here is he, he of whose promise thou hearest so often, Caesar Augustus, a god's son, who shall again establish the ages of gold in Latium over the fields that once were the realm of Saturn, and carry his empire afar to Garamant and Indian, to the land that lies beyond our stars, beyond the sun's year-long ways, where Atlas the sky-bearer wheels on his shoulder the glittering star-spangled pole. Before his coming even now the kingdoms of the Caspian shudder at oracular answers, and the Maeotic land and the mouths of sevenfold Nile shudder in alarm. . . . Others shall beat out the breathing bronze to softer lines, I believe it well; shall draw living lineaments from the marble; the cause shall be more eloquent

on their lips; their pencil shall portray the pathways of heaven, and tell the stars in their arising: be thy charge, O Roman, to rule the nations in thine empire; this shall be thine art, to ordain the law of peace, to be merciful to the conquered and beat the haughty down.' . . .

Thus they wander up and down over the whole region of broad vaporous plains, and scan all the scene. And when Anchises had led his son over it, each point by each, and kindled his spirit with passion for the glories on their way, he tells him thereafter of the war he next must wage, and instructs him of the Laurentine peoples and the city of Latinus, and in what wise he may avoid or endure every burden.

There are twin portals of Sleep, whereof the one is fabled of horn, and by it real shadows are given easy outlet; the other shining white of polished ivory, but false visions issue upward from the ghostly world. With these words then Anchises follows forth his son and the Sibyl together there, and dismisses them by the ivory gate. He pursues his way to the ships and revisits his comrades; then bears on to Caieta's haven straight along the shore. The anchor is cast from the prow; the sterns lie aground on the beach.

BOOK VII

. . . And now the sea reddened with shafts of light, and high in heaven yellow Dawn shone in her rosy car; when the winds fell, and every breath sank suddenly, and the oar-blades toil through the heavy ocean-floor. And on this Aeneas descries from sea a mighty forest. Midway in it the pleasant Tiber stream breaks to sea in swirling eddies, laden with yellow sand. Around and above fowl many in sort, that haunt his banks and the channel of his flood, solaced heaven with song and flew about the forest. He orders his crew to bend their course and turn their prows to land, and glides joyfully into the shady river.

Forth now, Erato! and I will unfold who were the kings, what the times, how it was with the state of ancient Latium when first that foreign army drew their fleet ashore on the Ausonian coast, and will recall the preluding of battle. . . . Latinus the King, now growing old, ruled in a long peace over quiet tilth and town. . . . Son of his, by divine ordinance, and male descent was none, cut off in the early spring of youth. One alone kept the household and its august home, a daughter now ripe for a husband and of full years for marriage. Many wooed her from wide Latium and all Ausonia. Fairest and foremost of all is Turnus, of long and lordly ancestry, whose union to her daughter the queen-consort urged with

46. **Garamant,** the southernmost land in Africa known in antiquity.

78. **Caieta,** a town in Latium.

wondrous desire; but boding signs from heaven, many and terrible, bar the way. . . . While maiden Lavinia stands beside her father feeding the altars with holy fuel, she seemed, O horror! to catch fire in her long tresses, and burn with flickering flame in all her array, her queenly hair lit up, lit up her jewelled circlet; till, enwreathed in smoke and ruddy light, she scattered fire over all the palace. That sight was rumoured wonderful and terrible; herself, they
10 prophesied, she should be glorious in fame and fortune; but a great war was foreshadowed for her people. But the King, troubled by the omen, visits the oracle of his father Faunus the soothsayer, and the groves deep under Albunea, and . . . paid fit sacrifice of an hundred woolly ewes, and lay couched on the strewn fleeces they had worn. Out of the lofty grove a sudden voice was uttered: 'Seek not, O my child, to unite thy daughter in Latin espousals, nor trust her to the bridal chambers ready to thine hand;
20 foreigners shall come to be thy sons, whose blood shall raise our name to heaven, and the children of whose race shall see, where the circling sun looks on either ocean, all the rolling world swayed beneath their feet.' This his father Faunus' answer and counsel given in the silent night Latinus keeps not within locked lips; but wide-flitting Rumour had already borne it round among the Ausonian cities, when the seed of Laomedon moored their fleet to the grassy slope of the river bank. . . .
30 And lo! the fierce consort of Jove was returning from Inachian Argos, and held her way along the air, when out of the distant sky, far as from Sicilian Pachynus, she espied the rejoicing of Aeneas and the Dardanian fleet. She sees them already building homes, already trusting in the land, their ships left empty. She stops, shot with sharp pain; then shaking her head, . . . she descends to earth in all her terrors, and calls dolorous Allecto from the home of the awful goddesses in nether gloom, whose delight
40 is in woeful wars, in wrath and treachery and evil feuds: hateful to lord Pluto himself, hateful and horrible to her hell-born sisters; into so many faces does she turn, so savage the guise of each, so thick her black viper-growth. With these words Juno spurs her on, saying thus:

'Grant me, virgin born of Night, this thy proper task and service, that our renown may not be broken or our fame dwindle, nor the Aeneadae have power to win Latinus by marriage or beset the borders of
50 Italy. Thou canst set in armed conflict brothers once united, and overturn families with hatreds; thou canst launch into houses thy whips and deadly brands; thine are a thousand names, a thousand devices of injury. Stir up thy teeming breast, sunder the peace they have joined, and sow seeds of quar-

rel; let their warriors at once desire and demand and fly to arms.'

Thereon Allecto, steeped in Gorgonian venom, first seeks Latium and the high house of the Laurentine monarch, and silently sits down before Amata's 60 doors, whom a woman's distress and anger heated to frenzy over the Teucrians' coming and the marriage of Turnus. At her the goddess flings a snake out of her dusky tresses, and slips it into her bosom to her very inmost heart, that she may embroil all her house under its maddening magic. Sliding between her raiment and smooth breasts, it coils without touch, and instils its viperous breath unseen; the great serpent turns into the twisted gold about her neck, turns into the long ribbon of her chaplet, in- 70 weaves her hair, and winds slippery over her body. And while the gliding infection of the clammy poison begins to penetrate her sense and run in fire through her frame, nor as yet has all her breast caught the fire, softly she spoke and in mothers' wonted wise, with many a tear over her daughter's Phrygian bridal:

'Is it to exiles, to Teucrians, that Lavinia is proffered in marriage, O father? and hast thou no compassion on thy daughter and on thyself? no compas- 80 sion on her mother, whom with the first northern wind the treacherous rover will abandon, steering to sea with his maiden prize? . . . What of thy plighted faith? What of thine ancient care for thy people, and the hand Turnus thy kinsman has clasped so often?' . . . .

When in this vain essay of words she sees Latinus fixed against her, and the serpent's maddening poison is sunk deep in her vitals and runs through and through her, then indeed, stung by infinite horrors, 90 hapless and frenzied, she rages wildly through the endless city. . . .

The dolorous goddess next flies onward, soaring on dusky wing, to the walls of the gallant Rutulian. . . . Here in his high house Turnus now took rest in the black midnight. Allecto puts off her grim feature and the body of a Fury; she transforms her face to an aged woman's, and furrows her brow with ugly wrinkles; she puts on white tresses fillet-bound, and entwines them with an olive spray; she becomes aged 100 Calybe, priestess of Juno's temple, and presents herself before his eyes, uttering thus:

'Turnus, wilt thou brook all these toils poured out in vain, and the conveyance of thy crown to Dardanian settlers? The King denies thee thy bride and the dower thy blood had earned; and a foreigner is sought for heir to the kingdom. Forth now, dupe, and face thankless perils; forth, mow down the Tyrrhenian lines; give the Latins peace in thy protection. This Saturn's omnipotent daughter in very pres- 110 ence commanded me to pronounce to thee, as thou wert lying in the still night. Wherefore arise, and

---

38. **Allecto,** one of the Furies.

make ready with good cheer to arm thy people and march through thy gates to battle; consume those Phrygian captains that lie with their painted hulls in the beautiful river. All the force of heaven orders thee on. Let King Latinus himself, unless he consents to give thee thy bridal, and abide by his words, be aware and at last make proof of Turnus' arms.'

But he, deriding her inspiration, with the words of his mouth thus answers her again:

10 'The fleets ride on the Tiber wave; that news has not, as thou deemest, escaped mine ears. Frame not such terrors before me. Neither is Queen Juno forgetful of us. . . . But thee, O mother, overworn old age, exhausted and untrue, frets with vain distress, and amid embattled kings mocks thy presage with false dismay. Thy charge it is to keep the divine images and temples; war and peace shall be in the hands of men whose task is warfare.'

At such words Allecto's wrath blazed out. But 20 amid his utterance a quick shudder overruns his limbs; his eyes are fixed in horror; so thickly hiss the snakes of the Fury, so vast her form expands. Then rolling her fiery eyes, she thrust him back as he would stammer out more, raised two serpents in her hair, and, sounding her whip, resumed with furious tone:

'Behold me the overworn! me whom old age, exhausted and untrue, mocks with false dismay amid embattled kings! Look on this! I am come from the 30 home of the Dread Sisters: war and death are in my hand. . . .'

So speaking, she hurled her torch at him, and pierced his breast with the lurid smoking brand. He breaks from sleep in overpowering fear, his limbs and frame bathed in sweat that starts out all over his body; he shrieks madly for arms, searches for arms on his bed and in his palace. The passion of the sword rages high, the accursed fury of war, and wrath over all: even as when flaming sticks are 40 heaped roaring loud under the sides of a seething caldron, and the boiling tides leap up; the river of water within smokes furiously and swells high in overflowing foam, and now the wave contains itself no longer; the dark steam flies aloft. So, in breach of peace, he orders his chief warriors to march on King Latinus, and bids prepare for battle, to defend Italy and drive the foe from their borders; himself will suffice for Trojans and Latins together. When he uttered these words and called the gods to hear 50 his vows, the Rutulians stir one another up to arms. One the splendour of his youthful beauty, one his royal ancestry fires, another the noble deeds of his hand.

BOOK VIII

When Turnus ran up the flag of war on the towers of Laurentum, and the trumpets blared with harsh music, when he spurred his fiery steeds and clashed his armour, straightway men's hearts are in tumult; all Latium at once bands together in stir of uprisal, and youthful rage maddens her warriors. . . . And the hero of Laomedon's blood, seeing it all, tosses 60 on a heavy surge of care, and throws his mind rapidly this way and that, and turns it on all hands in swift change of thought. . . . Night fell, and over all lands weary creatures were fast in deep slumber, the race of fowl and of cattle; when lord Aeneas, vexed at heart by the dismal warfare, stretched him on the river bank under the cope of the cold sky, and let sleep, though late, overspread his limbs. To him the very god of the ground, the pleasant Tiber stream, seemed to raise his aged form 70 among the poplar boughs; thin lawn veiled him with its grey covering, and shadowy reeds hid his hair. Thereon he addressed him thus, and with these words allayed his distresses:

'O born of the family of the gods, thou who bearest back our Trojan city from hostile hands, and keepest Troy towers in eternal life; O long looked for on Laurentine ground and Latin fields! here is thine assured home, thine home's assured gods. Now hearken, and I will briefly instruct thee how thou 80 mayest unravel and overcome thy present task. An Arcadian people sprung of Pallas, following in their king Evander's company beneath his banners, have chosen a place in these coasts, and set a city on the hills, called Pallanteum after Pallas their forefather. These wage perpetual war with the Latin race; these do thou take to thy camp as allies, and join with them in league. Myself I will lead thee by my banks and straight along my stream, that thou mayest oar thy way upward against the river.' . . . 90

All that night long Tiber assuaged his swelling stream, and silently stayed his refluent wave, smoothing the surface of his waters to the fashion of still pool and quiet mere, to spare labour to the oar. So they set out and speed on their way; with prosperous cries the painted fir slides along the water-way; the waves and unwonted woods marvel at their fargleaming shields, and the gay hulls afloat on the river. They outwear a night and a day in rowing, ascend the long reaches, and pass under the cheq- 100 uered shadows of the trees, and cut through the green woodland in the calm water. The fiery sun had climbed midway in the circle of the sky when they see afar fortress walls and scattered house roofs, where now the might of Rome has risen high as heaven; then Evander held a slender state. Quickening their pace, they turn their prows to land and draw near the town.

It chanced on that day the Arcadian king paid his accustomed sacrifice to the great son of Amphit-

60. hero . . . blood, Aeneas. 110. son of Amphitryon, Hercules.

ryon and all the gods in a grove before the city. With him his son Pallas, with him all the chief of his people and his poor senate were offering incense, and the blood steamed warm at their altars. When they saw the high ships gliding up between the shady woodlands and resting on their silent oars, the sudden sight appals them, and all at once they rise and stop the banquet. Pallas courageously forbids them to break off the rites; snatching up a spear, he flies forward, and from a hillock cries afar: 'O men, what cause has driven you to explore these unknown ways? or whither do you steer? What is your kin, whence your habitation? Is it peace or arms you carry hither?' Then from the lofty stern lord Aeneas thus speaks, stretching forth in his hand a peace-bearing olive bough:

'Thou seest men born of Troy and arms hostile to the Latins, who have driven us to flight in insolent warfare. We seek Evander; carry this message, and tell him that chosen men of the Dardanian captains are come pleading for an armed alliance.'

Pallas stood amazed at the august name. 'Descend,' he cries, 'whoso thou art, and speak with my father face to face, and enter our home and hospitality.' And giving him the grasp of welcome, he caught and clung to his hand. Advancing, they enter the grove and leave the river. Then Aeneas in courteous words addresses the King:

'Best of the Grecian race, thou whom by fortune's decree I supplicate, holding before me boughs dressed in fillets, no fear stayed me because thou wert a Grecian chief and an Arcadian, or allied by descent to the twin sons of Atreus. Nay, mine own prowess and the sanctity of divine oracles, our ancestral kinship, and the fame of thee that is spread abroad over the earth, have allied me to thee and led me willingly on the path of fate. . . . In this confidence I sent no embassy, I framed no crafty overtures; myself I have presented mine own person, and come a suppliant to thy courts. The same Daunian race pursues us and thee in merciless warfare; we once expelled, they trust nothing will withhold them from laying all Hesperia wholly beneath their yoke, and holding the two seas that wash it above and below. Accept and return our friendship. We can give brave hearts in war, high souls and men approved in deeds.'

Aeneas ended. The other ere now scanned in a long gaze the face and eyes and all the form of the speaker; then thus briefly returns:

'How gladly, bravest of the Teucrians, do I hail and own thee! how I recall thy father's words and the very tone and glance of great Anchises! For I remember how Priam son of Laomedon, when he sought Salamis on his way to the realm of his sister Hesione, went on to visit the cold borders of Arcadia. Then early youth clad my cheeks with bloom:

I admired the Teucrian captains, admired their lord, the son of Laomedon; but Anchises moved high above them all. My heart burned with youthful passion to accost him and clasp hand in hand; I made my way to him, and led him eagerly to Pheneus' high town. Departing he gave me an adorned quiver and Lycian arrows, a scarf interwoven with gold, and a pair of golden bits that now my Pallas possesses. Therefore my hand is already joined in the alliance you seek, and soon as to-morrow's dawn rises again over earth, I will send you away rejoicing in mine aid, and supply you from my store. Meanwhile, since you are come hither in friendship, solemnise with us these yearly rites which we may not defer, and even now learn to be familiar at your comrades' board.'

This said, he commands the feast and the winecups to be replaced whence they were taken, and with his own hand ranges them on the grassy seat, and welcomes Aeneas to the place of honour, with a lion's shaggy fell for cushion and a hospitable chair of maple. Then chosen men with the priest of the altar in emulous haste bring roasted flesh of bulls, and pile baskets with the gift of dressed corn, and serve the wine. Aeneas and the men of Troy with him feed on the long chines of oxen and the entrails of the sacrifice.

After hunger is driven away and the desire of food stayed, King Evander speaks: 'Princely chief of the Teucrians, in whose lifetime I will never allow the state or realm of Troy vanquished, our strength is scant to succour in war for so great a name. On this side the Tuscan river shuts us in; on that the Rutulian drives us hard, and thunders in arms about our walls. But I purpose to unite to thee mighty peoples and the camp of a wealthy realm; an unforeseen chance offers this for thy salvation. Thou comest at Fate's call. Not far from here stands fast Agylla city, an ancient pile of stone, where of old the Lydian race, eminent in war, settled on the Etruscan ridges. For many years it flourished, till King Mezentius ruled it with insolent sway and armed terror. Why should I relate the horrible murders, the savage deeds of the monarch? May the gods keep them in store for himself and his line! Nay, he would even link dead bodies to living, fitting hand to hand and face to face (the torture!), and in the oozy foulness and corruption of the dreadful embrace so slay them by a lingering death. But at last his citizens, outwearied by his mad excesses, surround him and his house in arms, cut down his comrades, and hurl fire in his roof. Amid the massacre he escaped to the refuge of Rutulian land and the armed defence of Turnus' friendship. So all Etruria has risen in righteous fury, and in immediate battle claim their king for punishment. Over these thousands will I make thee chief, O Aeneas. . . . Mine own Pallas likewise, our hope and comfort, I will send with thee; let him grow used to endure warfare and the stern work of battle under thy teaching, to regard thine actions, and from his earliest years look up to thee. To him will I give two hundred Arcadian cavalry, the choice of our warlike strength, and Pallas as many more to thee in his own name.'

Scarce had he ended; Aeneas, son of Anchises, and trusty Achates gazed with steadfast face, and, sad at heart, were revolving inly many a labour, had not the Cytherean sent a sign from the clear sky. For suddenly a flash and peal come quivering from heaven, and all seemed in a moment to totter, and the Tyrrhene trumpet-blast to roar along the sky. They look up; again and yet again the heavy crash re-echoes. They see in a serene space of sky armour gleam red through a cloud in the clear air, and ring clashing out. The others stood in amaze; but the Trojan hero knew the sound and the promise of his goddess mother; then he speaks: 'Ask not, O friend, ask not in any wise what fortune this presage announces; it is I who am summoned. This sign the goddess who bore me foretold she would send from heaven if war were gathering, and would bring through the air to my succour armour from Vulcan's hands. . . . Ah, what slaughter awaits the wretched Laurentines! what a price, O Turnus, wilt thou pay me! how many shields and helmets and brave bodies of men shalt thou, Lord Tiber, roll under thy waves! Let them call for armed array and break the treaty!'

These words uttered, he rises from the high seat, and first wakes with fresh fire the slumbering altars of Hercules, and gladly draws nigh his tutelar god of yesternight and the small deities of the household. . . .

And now the cavalry had issued from the open gates, Aeneas and trusty Achates among the foremost, then other of the Trojan princes, Pallas conspicuous amid the column in scarf and inlaid armour, even as when the Morning Star, newly washed in the ocean wave, whom Venus cherishes before the other starry fires, shews his holy face in heaven, and melts the darkness away. Fearful mothers stand on the walls and follow with their eyes the cloud of dust and the squadrons gleaming in brass.

[Fierce battles ensue.]

BOOK X

. . . The armies close, matched in strength and in captains; the rear ranks crowd in; weapons and hands are locked in the press. Here Pallas strains and pushes on, here Lausus opposite, nearly matched in age, excellent in beauty; but fortune had denied both return to their own land. Yet that they should meet face to face the sovereign of high Olympus allowed

not; an early fate awaits them beneath a mightier foe.

Meanwhile Turnus' gracious sister bids him come to Lausus' aid, and his fleet chariot parts the ranks. When he saw his comrades, 'It is time,' he cried, 'to stay from battle. I alone must assail Pallas; to me and none other Pallas is due; I would his father himself were here to see.' So speaks he, and his Rutulians draw back from a level space at his bidding. But then as they withdrew, he, wondering at the haughty command, stands in amaze at Turnus, his eyes scanning the vast frame, and his fierce glance perusing him from afar. And with these words he returns the words of the monarch: 'For me, my praise shall even now be in the lordly spoils I win, or in illustrious death: my father will bear calmly either lot: away with menaces.' He speaks, and advances into the level ring. The Arcadians' blood gathers chill about their hearts. Turnus leaps from his chariot and prepares to close with him. And as a lion sees from some lofty outlook a bull stand far off on the plain revolving battle, and flies at him, even such to see is Turnus' coming. When Pallas deemed him within reach of a spear-throw, he advances, if so chance may assist the daring of his overmatched strength, and thus cries into the depth of sky: 'By my father's hospitality and the board whereto thou camest a wanderer, on thee I call, Alcides; be favourable to my high emprise; let Turnus even in death discern me stripping his blood-stained armour, and his swooning eyes endure the sight of his conqueror.' Alcides heard him, and deep in his heart he stifled a heavy sigh, and let idle tears fall. Then with kindly words the father accosts his son: 'Each has his own appointed day; short and irrecoverable is the span of life for all: but to spread renown by deeds is the task of valour. Turnus too his own fate summons, and his allotted period has reached the goal.' So speaks he, and turns his eyes away from the Rutulian fields.

But Pallas hurls his spear with all his strength, and pulls his sword flashing out of the hollow scabbard. The flying spear lights where the armour rises high above the shoulder, and, forcing a way through the shield's rim, stayed not till it drew blood from mighty Turnus. At this Turnus long poises the spear-shaft with its sharp steel head, and hurls it on Pallas with these words: 'See thou if our weapon have not a keener point.' He ended; but for all the shield's plating of iron and brass, for all the bull-hide that covers it round about, the quivering spear-head smashes it fair through and through, passes the guard of the corslet, and pierces the breast with a gaping hole. He tears the warm weapon from the wound; in vain; together and at once lifeblood and

49. **Lausus,** an Etruscan prince in the army of Turnus.

55. **Turnus' . . . sister,** Juturna, a nymph.   81. **Alcides,** Hercules.

sense follow it. He falls heavily on the ground, his armour clashes over him, and his bloodstained face sinks in death on the hostile soil. And Turnus standing over him . . . : 'Arcadians,' he cries, "remember these my words, and bear them to Evander. I send him back his Pallas as was due. All the meed of the tomb, all the solace of sepulture, I give freely. Dearly must he pay his welcome to Aeneas.' And with these words, planting his left foot on the dead, he tore away the broad heavy sword-belt . . . wrought richly in gold. Now Turnus exults in spoiling him of it, and rejoices at his prize. Ah spirit of man, ignorant of fate and the allotted future, or to keep bounds when elate with prosperity!—the day will come when Turnus shall desire to have bought Pallas' safety at a great ransom, and curse the spoils of this fatal day. But with many moans and tears Pallas' comrades lay him on his shield and bear him away amid their ranks. O grief and glory and grace of the father to whom thou shalt return! This one day sent the first to war, this one day takes thee away, while yet thou leavest heaped high thy Rutulian dead. . . .

BOOK XI

Pallas' lifeless body is laid out for burial. . . . Around is the whole train of servants, with a crowd of Trojans, and the Ilian women with hair unbound in mourning after their fashion. When Aeneas entered at the high doorway they beat their breasts and raise a loud wail aloft, and the palace moans to their grievous lamentation. Himself, when he saw the pillowed head and fair face of Pallas, and on his smooth breast the gaping wound of the Ausonian spear-head, speaks thus with welling tears:

'Did Fortune in her joyous coming,' he cries, 'O luckless boy, grudge thee to see our realm, and ride victorious to thy father's dwelling? Not this promise of thee had I given to Evander thy sire at my departure, when he embraced me as I went and bade me speed to a wide empire, and yet warned me in fear that the men were valiant, the people obstinate in battle. And now he, fast ensnared by empty hope, perchance offers vows and heaps gifts on his altars; we, a mourning train, go in hollow honour by his corpse, who now owes no more to aught in heaven. Unhappy! thou wilt see thy son cruelly slain; is this the triumphal return we awaited? is this my strong assurance? Yet thou shalt not see him, Evander, with the shameful wounds of flight, nor shall death's terrors be welcome to the father because the son lives. Ah me, what a shield is lost, Iülus, to Ausonia and to thee!'

This lament done, he bids raise the piteous body, and sends a thousand men chosen from all his army for the last honour of escort, to mingle in the father's tears; a small comfort in a great sorrow, yet the unhappy parent's due. Others quickly plait a soft wicker bier of arbutus rods and oak shoots, and shadow the heaped pillows with a leafy covering. Here they lay him, high on their rustic strewing; even as some tender violet or drooping hyacinth-blossom plucked by a maiden's finger, whose sheen and whose grace is not yet departed, but no more does Earth the mother feed it or lend it strength. Then Aeneas bore forth two purple garments stiff with gold, that Sidonian Dido's own hands, happy over their work, had once wrought for him, and shot the warp with thread of gold. One of these he sadly folds round him, a last honour, and veils in its covering the tresses destined to the fire; and heaps up besides many a Laurentine battle-prize, and bids his spoils be led forth in long train; with them the horses and arms whereof he had stripped the enemy, and those, with hands tied behind their back, whom he would send as nether offering to his ghost, and sprinkle the blood of their slaying on the flame, and bids his captains carry stems dressed in the armour of the foe, with the hostile names fixed on them. . . . Then follow in mourning array the Teucrians and all the Tyrrhenians, and the Arcadians with arms reversed. When the whole long escorting file had advanced, Aeneas stopped, and sighing deep, pursued thus: 'Once again war's dreadful destiny calls us hence to other tears: hail thou for evermore, O princely Pallas, and for evermore farewell.' And without more words he bent his way to the high walls and advanced towards his camp. . . .

And now flying Rumour, harbinger of the heavy woe, fills Evander and Evander's house and city with the same voice that but now told of Pallas victorious over Latium. The Arcadians stream to the gates, snatching funeral torches after their ancient use; the road gleams with the long line of flame, and parts the fields with a broad pathway of light; the arriving crowd of Phrygians meets them and mingles in mourning array. When the matrons saw all the train approach their dwellings they kindle the town with loud wailing. But no force may withhold Evander; he comes amid them; the bier is set down; he flings himself on Pallas, and clasps him with tears and sighs, and scarcely at last does grief let loose his utterance. 'Not this, O Pallas! was the promise that thou hadst given thy father. Hadst thou been content to plunge less recklessly into the fury of battle! I knew well how strong was the fresh pride of arms and the sweetness of honour in a first battle. Ah, unhappy first-fruits of his youth and bitter prelude of the war upon our borders! ah, vows and prayers of mine that no god heard! and thou, holiest of wives, happy that thou art dead and not spared for this sorrow! But I have outgone my destiny in living, to stay here the survivor of my child. Would I had followed the allied arms of Troy, to be overwhelmed by Rutulian weapons! Would my life had been given, and I and not my Pallas were borne home in this procession! I would not blame you, O Teucrians, nor our treaty and the friendly hands we clasped: our old age had that appointed debt to pay. Yet if untimely death awaited my son, we will be glad that he perished leading the Teucrians into Latium, and slew his Volscian thousands before he fell. Nay, no other funeral would I deem thy due, my Pallas, than good Aeneas does, than the mighty Phrygians, than the Tyrrhene captains and all the army of Tyrrhenia. Great are the trophies they bring on whom thine hand deals death; thou also, Turnus, wert standing now a great trunk dressed in arms, had his age and his strength of years equalled thine. But why does my misery keep back the Trojans from arms? Go, and forget not to carry this message to your king: Thine hand keeps me lingering in a life that is hateful since Pallas fell, and Turnus is the debt thou seest son and father claim: for thy virtue and thy fortune this scope alone is left. I ask not joy in life; I may not; but to carry this to my son deep in the under world.' . . .

BOOK XII

. . . At this Aeneas' mother most beautiful inspired him to advance on the walls, directing his columns on the town and dismaying the Latins with sudden and swift disaster. As in search for Turnus he bent his glance this way and that round the separate ranks, he descries the city free from all this warfare, unpunished and unstirred. Straightway he kindles at the view of a greater battle; he summons Mnestheus and Sergestus and brave Serestus his captains, and mounts a hillock; there the rest of the Teucrian army gathers thickly, still grasping shield and spear. Standing on the high mound amid them, he speaks: 'Be there no delay to my words; Jupiter is with us; neither let any be slower to move that the design is sudden. This city to-day, the source of war, the royal seat of Latinus, unless they yield them to receive our yoke and obey their conquerors, will I raze to ground, and lay her smoking roofs level with the dust. Must I wait forsooth till Turnus please to stoop to combat, and choose again to face his conqueror? This, O citizens, is the head and sum of the accursed war. Bring firebrands speedily, and reclaim the treaty in flame.' He ended; all with spirit alike emulous form a wedge and advance in serried mass to the walls. Ladders are run up, and fire leaps sudden to sight. Some rush to the several gates, and cut down the guards of the entry, others hurl their steel and darken the sky with weapons. Aeneas himself among the foremost, upstretching his hand to the city walls, loudly reproaches Latinus, and takes the gods to witness that he is again forced into battle, that twice now do the Italians choose warfare and

break a second treaty. Discord rises among the shaken citizens: some bid unbar the town and fling wide their gates to the Dardanians, and pull the king himself towards the ramparts; others bring arms and hasten to defend the walls: as when a shepherd tracks bees to their retreat in a sheltering rock, and fills it with stinging smoke, they within run uneasily up and down their waxen fortress, and hum louder in rising wrath; the black pungent cloud rolls through their dwelling, and a blind murmur echoes within the rock as the smoke issues to the empty air.

This fortune likewise befell the despairing Latins, this woe shook the whole city to her base. The queen espies from her roof the enemy's approach, the walls scaled and firebrands flying on the houses; and nowhere Rutulian ranks, none of Turnus' columns to meet them; alas! she deems him destroyed in the shock of battle, and, distracted by sudden anguish, shrieks that she is the source of guilt, the spring of ill, and with many a mad utterance of frenzied grief rends her purple attire with dying hand, and ties from a lofty beam the ghastly noose of death. And when the unhappy Latin women knew this calamity, first her daughter Lavinia tears her flower-like tresses and roseate cheeks, and the frenzy spreads from her to the whole train around; the wide palace echoes to their wailing, and from it the sorrowful rumour spreads abroad throughout the town. All hearts sink; Latinus goes with torn raiment, in dismay at his wife's doom and his city's downfall, defiling his hoary hair with soilure of sprinkled dust. . . .

As the scene shifted before him Turnus froze in horror and stood in dumb gaze; together in his heart sweep the vast mingling tides of shame and maddened grief, and love stung to frenzy and resolved valour. So soon as the darkness cleared and light returned to his soul, he fiercely turned his blazing eyeballs towards the ramparts, and gazed back from his wheels on the great city. And lo! a spire of flame wreathing through the floors wavered up skyward and held a turret fast, a turret that he himself had reared of mortised planks and set on rollers and laid with high gangways. 'Now, fate prevails: let us follow where deity and stern fortune call. I am resolved to face Aeneas, resolved to bear what bitterness there is in death; nor shalt thou longer see me shamed, sister of mine. Let me be mad, I pray thee, with this madness before the end.' He spoke, and leapt swiftly from his chariot to the field, and darting through weapons and through enemies, leaves his sorrowing sister, and bursts in rapid course amid their columns. And as when a rock rushes headlong from some mountain peak, torn away by the blast, or if the rushing rain washes it away, or the stealing years loosen its ancient hold; the reckless mountain mass goes sheer and impetuous, and leaps along the ground, hurling with it forests and herds and men;

thus through the scattering columns Turnus rushes to the city walls, where the earth is wettest with bloodshed and the air sings with spears; and beckons with his hand, and thus begins aloud: 'Forbear now, O Rutulians, and you, Latins, stay your weapons. Whatsoever fortune is left is mine: I singly must expiate the treaty for you all, and make decision with the sword.' All drew aside and left him room.

But lord Aeneas, hearing Turnus' name, abandons the walls, abandons the fortress height, and in exultant joy flings aside all hindrance, breaks off all work, and clashes his armour terribly. Now indeed Rutulians and Trojans and all Italy turned in emulous gaze, both they who held the high city, and they whose ram was battering the wall below, and took off the armour from their shoulders. Latinus himself stands in amaze at the mighty men, born in distant quarters of the world, met and making decision with the sword. . . .

Meanwhile the King of Heaven's omnipotence accosts Juno as she gazes on the battle from a sunlit cloud. 'What yet shall be the end, O wife? what remains at the last? Aeneas is claimed by Heaven as his country's god, thou thyself knowest and avowest to know, and is lifted by fate to the stars. With what device or in what hope hangest thou chill in cloudland? . . . The end is come. Thou hast had power to hunt the Trojans on land or wave, to kindle accursed war, to put the house in mourning, and plunge the bridal in grief: further attempt I forbid thee.' Thus Jupiter began: thus the goddess, daughter of Saturn, returned with humbled aspect:

'Even because this thy will, great Jupiter, is known to me for thine, have I left, though loth, Turnus and earth; nor else wouldst thou see me now, alone on this skyey seat, enduring even past endurance; but girt in flame I were standing by their very lines, and dragging the Teucrians into the deadly battle. I counselled Juturna, I confess it, to succour her hapless brother, and for his life's sake favoured a greater daring; yet not the arrow-shot, not the bending of the bow, I swear by the merciless well-head of the Stygian spring, the single ordained dread of the gods in heaven. And now I retire, and leave the battle in loathing. This thing I beseech thee, that is bound by no fatal law, for Latium and for the majesty of thy kindred. When now they shall plight peace with prosperous marriages (be it so!), when now they shall join in laws and treaties, bid thou not the native Latins change their name of old, nor become Trojans and take the Teucrian name, or change their language, or alter their attire: let Latium be, let Alban kings endure through ages, let Italian valour be potent in the race of Rome. Troy is fallen; let her and her name lie where they fell.'

To her smilingly the designer of men and things:

'Jove's own sister thou art, and second offspring of Saturn, such surge of wrath tosses within thy breast! But come, allay this madness so vainly stirred. I give thee thy will, and yield thee ungrudged victory. Ausonia shall keep her native speech and usage, and as her name is, it shall be. The Trojans shall sink incorporate with them; I will add their sacred law and ritual, and make all Latins and of a single speech. Hence shall spring a race of tempered Ausonian blood, whom thou shalt see outdo men and gods in duty; nor shall any nation so observe thy worship.' To this Juno assented, and in gladness withdrew her purpose; meanwhile she quits her cloud, and retires out of the sky. . . .

But Aeneas presses on, brandishing his vast treelike spear, and fiercely speaks thus: 'What more delay is there now? or why, Turnus, dost thou yet shrink away? Not in speed of foot, in grim arms, hand to hand, must be the conflict. Transform thyself as thou wilt, and collect what strength of courage or skill is thine; pray that thou mayest wing thy flight to the stars on high, or that sheltering earth may shut thee in.' The other, shaking his head: 'Thy fierce words dismay me not, insolent! the gods dismay me, and Jupiter's enmity.' And no more said, his eyes light on a vast stone, a stone ancient and vast that haply lay upon the plain, set for a landmark to divide contested fields: scarcely might twelve chosen men lift it on their shoulders, of such frame as now earth breeds mankind: then the hero caught it up with shaking hand and whirled it at the enemy, rising higher and quickening his speed. But he knows not his own self running nor going nor lifting his hands or moving the mighty stone; his knees totter, his blood freezes cold; the very stone he hurls, spinning through the empty void, neither wholly reached its distance nor carried its blow home. And as in sleep, when rest at night weighs down our tired eyes, we seem vainly to will to run eagerly on, and sink faint amidst our struggles; the tongue is powerless, the familiar strength fails the body, nor do words or utterance follow: so the awful goddess brings to naught all the valour of Turnus where he seeks a way. Shifting thoughts pass through his breast; he gazes on his Rutulians and on the city, and falters in terror, and shudders at the imminent death; neither sees he whither he may escape nor what force is his to meet the foe, and nowhere his chariot, nowhere his sister at the reins. As he wavers Aeneas poises the deadly weapon, and, marking his chance, hurls it in from afar with all his strength of body. Never with such a roar are stones hurled from some engine on ramparts, nor does the thunder burst in so loud a peal. Carrying grim death with it, the spear flies in fashion of some dark whirlwind, and opens the rim of the corslet and the utmost circles of the sevenfold shield. Right through the thigh it passes hurtling on; under the blow Turnus

falls huge to earth with his leg doubled under him. The Rutulians start up with a groan, and all the hill echoes round about, and the width of high woodland returns their cry. Lifting up beseechingly his humbled eyes and suppliant hand: 'I have deserved it,' he says, 'nor do I ask for mercy; use thy fortune. If an unhappy parent's distress may at all touch thee, this I pray; even such a father was Anchises to thee; pity Daunus' old age, and restore to my kindred
10 which thou wilt, me or my body bereft of day. Thou art conqueror, and the Ausonians have seen me stretch conquered hands. Lavinia is thine in marriage; press not hatred farther.'

Aeneas stood wrathful in arms, with rolling eyes, and lowered his hand; and now and now yet more the speech began to bend him to waver: when high on his shoulder appeared the sword-belt with the shining bosses that he knew, the luckless belt of the boy Pallas, whom Turnus had struck down with
20 mastering wound, and wore on his shoulders the fatal ornament. The other, as his eyes drank in the plundered record of his fierce grief, kindles to fury, and cries terrible in anger: 'Mayest thou, clad in the spoils of my dearest, be snatched from me now? Pallas it is, Pallas who strikes the deathblow, and exacts vengeance in thy guilty blood.' So saying, he fiercely plunges the steel full in his breast. But his limbs grow slack and chill, and the life with a moan flies indignant into the dark.

Horace

65–8 B.C.

Horace too could sing the patriotic strain, and he vied with Virgil in respectful praise of Augustus and Maecenas, his patrons. But national propaganda was not to his taste, and he produced it only because his security depended on it. Close friend to Virgil, he was quite unlike that shy, rustic spirit in being a man of the world, equally at home in the court circles of Rome or on his Sabine farm some forty miles away. His philosophy of life was a practical rationalism, lacking totally the melancholy mysticism of Virgil, and he avoided the long verse forms of Virgil to compose lyrics and brief satires that are among the most finished and exquisite in all literature. He resembled his friend only in being a thoroughly genial and generous man, who, indeed, excelled Virgil as a jovial companion and witty conversationalist.

Quintus Horatius Flaccus was the son of an ambitious freedman who had retired to a small farm at Venusia in the south and devoted his life to educating his son for an important career. At Rome young Horace studied under the grammarian Orbilius, whom the poet later nicknamed "plagosus" (flogging) because of his generous application of the rod. His father, whom Horace revered all his life, taught him the stoic morality that was to mature into the mellow philosophy of his later years. Toward twenty Horace went to Athens to complete his education and there became embroiled in civil war on the side of Brutus. But when Octavian's army routed Brutus' forces at Philippi in 42, Horace fled from the field and returned to Rome with the general amnesty, there to find his father dead and their farm confiscated. In poverty he took a small government post and began writing poetry as an avenue to patronage and security. The satires and epodes of this early period betray a bitterness that was to disappear with his later success.

Virgil was the first to recognize the talent of young Horace and introduced him to Maecenas. In time his work and his friendly personality won him a secure place in the circle. For thirty years he was the close intimate of Maecenas, who gave him his Sabine farm around 34 B.C. and on his deathbed asked Augustus to "be mindful of Horatius Flaccus as of myself." With Maecenas and Virgil he made a diplomatic jaunt by boat, coach, and foot across Italy to Brundisium in 37, which he immortalized amusingly in the fifth satire of Book I. Together they spent many evenings over gourmet dinners and the intellectual conversation that they loved—"the feasts of the gods," as he called them. But in his later years, having learned the evils as well as the pleasures of the capital, he retired more frequently to his Sabine farm, where Maecenas insured him the modest comforts and the leisure that he needed to pursue his writing at his own speed. Here his philosophy ripened, and his works are full of gratitude to Maecenas and the Empire that had given his life stability and peace. He devoutly predicted that he would not long outlive Maecenas, and this prediction proved true, for he died a few months after his patron.

Although in youth Horace had been a dark-haired, attractive fellow who philandered a good deal with the courtesans of the town, we think of him especially as the roly-poly little man turned forty who had grown prematurely gray and middle-aged. The romantic Catullus was at his best in his passionate twenties; the classical Horace reached his zenith in his mellow forties. His life was a long experiment in the art of living, for which he was equipped with a singularly detached, tolerant, and serene mind. He had a natural love for the simple things of life —a mountain stream and the sky at night, a winter fire and a jug of peasant wine beside him, his little farm, which was at least little for his day—but he could enjoy also the pleasures of luxury—the boulevards and rich men's houses, the conversation of statesmen and the companionship of courtesans, the feasts of a Lucullus and the feel of fine clothes. He was a true epicurean; experience had sharpened his taste, but had made him independent of luxury. His pleasures entailed no hangover or heartache. He never drank to excess and thought of love as only one kind of enjoyment, to be abandoned when it threatened to become tragic. His ladies entertained him with their charms, as he entertained them with his wit and good nature, but if we can trust his verses, he passed quickly from one to another—Phyllis, Cinara, Lydia, and Chloe, to mention a few.

As his shrewd common sense interpreted his experience, he evolved a philosophy that is half Stoic, half Epicurean. All men, he decided, are ruled by two opposing drives—emotion and reason. Many fluctuate violently from one of these extremes to the other, now expend themselves in passion, now regret it with reason. The secret of happiness is to preserve the balance between them, to indulge one's emotions up to a point for pleasurable experience, but to keep a rational check on them always to ward off failure and despair. So the golden mean of Aristotle becomes the "Golden Mediocrity" of Horace, as it is often called. One's ambition should be to possess enough for happiness; more brings only responsibility and pain. Desire should be kept under rational control, for happiness lies in our response to what fate brings us, not in the things themselves. Hence, we should, like Lucretius, rise above hope and fear to a perfect equanimity, appreciative of life but indifferent to death. So Horace became the preacher of moderation.

Such a detached attitude does not make for emotional or highly imaginative poetry, and Horace is as aware of that as he is sure of his lasting fame. He is the spokesman for hard work, not mystical inspiration, in poetry, and he polished every line of his verse to a perfection that defies translation. Tearing up far more than he published, he strove for the inevitable word and the perfect technique. The result is one thin volume of poems, the perfect essence and no more, of what he had to say. These are thought of in groups according to literary type. The eighteen *Sermones,* or "little talks," usually called his *Satires,* are the earliest and most uneven of his works and betray the bitterness of his outlook during his years of poverty in Rome. The best are charming discussions of many subjects—the foibles and vices of mankind, or incidents in the poet's own life. The fifth relates his Brundisium jaunt with Virgil and Maecenas. The sixth extolls his father and his patron. The ninth is the amusing satire of a bore. The sixteenth contrasts town life and country life and contains the fable of the town mouse and the country mouse. The seventeen *Epodes,* so-named from a Greek meter of Archilochus which they imitated, were culled from ten years of writing in this form, but they are still the least satisfactory of all his work.

He reached his peak in his *Carmina,* or "songs," usually called his *Odes,* which imitate a number of Greek meters with consummate success. These are his true lyrics, 103 gems issued in four books and covering a wide variety of themes—politics and patriotism (especially the famous "Ship of State"), hymns and prayers, his friends and their journeys (especially his address to Virgil's ship to Greece), their love affairs and his, the joys of wine and the brevity of life (especially *Carpe diem,* "snatch the day"), and of course his doctrine of the Golden Mean. His final works were his twenty-three *Epistles,* a forbidding title for a collection of delightful literary letters to his friends, discoursing familiarly on subjects that interested him—the joys of his farm, the state of Latin literature, the

value of personal freedom. The last of these, now called *The Art of Poetry,* is his charming advice to authors on the pursuit of their craft, by no means intended as the writer's bible that it became in the classical seventeenth century. Yet it is studded with famous literary concepts and phrases, such as "Homer nods," "in medias res" to signify Homer's beginning his tales in the middle, and "purple patches." Horace exerted little influence on the Middle Ages or early Renaissance, but with the sixteenth century he came into his own again, and his perfection of style, his urbane humor, and his common sense had an unparalleled appeal for the intellectual age of reason.

To the Ship in Which Virgil Sailed to Athens

So may the auspicious Queen of Love,
  And the twin Stars (the seed of Jove),
And he who rules the raging wind,
To thee, O sacred ship, be kind,
And gentle breezes fill thy sails,   5
Supplying soft Etesian gales,
As thou, to whom the Muse commends
The best of poets and of friends,
Dost thy committed pledge restore,
And land him safely on the shore;   10
And save the better part of me
From perishing with him at sea.

Sure he who first the passage tried,
In harden'd oak his heart did hide,
And ribs of iron arm'd his side!   15
Or his at least, in hollow wood
Who tempted first the briny flood;
Nor fear'd the winds' contending roar,
Nor billows beating on the shore;
Nor Hyades portending rain;   20
Nor all the tyrants of the main.
What form of death could him affright
Who, unconcern'd, with steadfast sight,
Could view the surges mounting steep,
And monsters rolling in the deep?   25
Could through the ranks of ruin go,
With storms above and rocks below?
In vain did Nature's wise command
Divide the waters from the land,
If daring ships and men profane   30
Invade the inviolable main,
The eternal fences overleap,

To the Ship in Which Virgil Sailed to Athens. Translated by John Dryden.
2. **the seed of Jove,** Castor and Pollux, the Dioscuri. 20. **Hyades portending rain.** The Hyades, or Rainers, were sea-nymphs forming a constellation.

And pass at will the boundless deep.
No toil, no hardship can restrain
Ambitious man inured to pain;   35
The more confin'd, the more he tries,
And at forbidden quarry flies.
Thus bold Prometheus did aspire,
And stole from heaven the reed of fire:
A train of ills, a ghastly crew,   40
The robber's blazing track pursue;
Fierce Famine, with her meager face,
And fevers of the fiery race,
In swarms the offending wretch surround,
All brooding on the blasted ground;   45
And limping Death, lash'd on by Fate,
Comes up to shorten half our date.
This made not Dedalus beware,
With borrow'd wings to sail in air:
To hell Alcides forced his way,   50
Plunged through the lake, and snatch'd the prey.
Nay, scarce the gods or heavenly climes
Are safe from our audacious crimes:
We reach at Jove's imperial crown,
And pull the unwilling thunder down.

The Love-Sick Athlete

WHY, Lydia, why,
       I pray, by all the gods above,
Art so resolved that Sybaris should die,
And all for love?

    Why doth he shun   5
The Campus Martius' sultry glare,
    He that once recked of neither dust nor sun?
Why rides he there,

    First of the brave,
Taming the Gallic steed no more?   10
    Why doth he shrink from Tiber's yellow wave?
Why thus abhor

    The wrestler's oil
As 't were from viper's tongue distilled?
    Why do his arms no livid bruises soil,   15
He, once so skilled

    The disk or dart
Far, far beyond the mark to hurl?
    And tell me, tell me, in what nook apart
Like baby-girl,   20

50. **Alcides,** Hercules, grandson of Alcaeus.   51. **prey,** Cerberus, the three-headed dog guarding the entrance to Hades, whom Hercules had to bring to the upper world as the last of his twelve labors.
The Love-Sick Athlete. From *Horace,* translated by Sir Theodore Martin. Reprinted by permission of J. B. Lippincott Company and Wm. Blackwood & Sons Ltd.

Lurks the poor boy,
Veiling his manhood, as did Thetis' son
    To 'scape war's bloody clang, while fated Troy
Was yet undone.

To Pyrrha, a Flirt

WHAT slender youth, with perfumed locks,
        In some sweet nook beneath the rocks,
Pyrrha, where clustering roses grow,
Bends to thy fatal beauty now?
For whom is now that golden hair   5
Wreathed in a bank so simply fair?
How often will he weep to find
Thy pledges frail, Love's power unkind?
And start to see the tempest sweep
With angry blast the darkening deep;   10
Though sunned by thy entrancing smile,
He fears no change, suspects no guile.
A sailor on bright summer seas,
He wots not of the fickle breeze.
For me—yon votive tablet scan;   15
It tells that I, a shipwrecked man,
Hung my dank weeds in Neptune's fane
And ne'er will tempt those seas again.

"Fair and Colder"

How snowy white Soracte stands!
    How still the streams with cold!
Pile the logs higher upon the fire!
Decant that four-year old!

Leave to the gods the other things!   5
The ash and cypress trees
Shall fall asleep when on the deep
Blows not the battling breeze.

Ask not about the morrow morn;
Take what the gods may give,   10
Nor scorn the dance and sweet romance—
Life is not long to live.

Come seek the Campus and the squares,
As fall the shades of night
Where many a maid, all unafraid,   15
Laughs absolute delight.

22. **Thetis' son,** Achilles.
To Pyrrha, a Flirt. Translated by Goldwin Smith. From *Bay Leaves,* by Goldwin Smith. Published by The Macmillan Company, 1893.
"Fair and Colder." Translated by Franklin P. Adams. From *The Melancholy Lute* by Franklin P. Adams, copyright 1936 by Franklin P. Adams. Reprinted by permission of The Viking Press, Inc.
1. **Soracte,** a snow-capped peak in Etruria, visible in Rome.

Ad Leuconoen

IT is not right for you to know, so do not ask,
  Leuconoë,
How long a life the gods may give or ever we are
  gone away;
Try not to read the Final Page, the ending colo-
  phonian,
Trust not the gypsy's tea-leaves, nor the prophets
  Babylonian.
Better to have what is to come enshrouded in ob-
  scurity   5
Than to be certain of the sort and length of our
  futurity.
Why, even as I monologue on wisdom and longevity
How Time has flown! Spear some of it!
  The longest life is brevity.

The Ship of State

SHIP of State, beware!
  Hold fast the port. Cling to the friendly
  shore
Lest sudden storms and whirling eddies bear
Thy shattered hull to faithless seas once more.

See how the rower faints upon his oar!   5
  Hark to the groaning of the mast,
  Sore stricken by the Libyan blast!
  Thy shrouds are burst; thy sails are torn;
  And through thy gaping ribs forlorn
  The floods remorseless pour.   10

Dare not to call for aid on powers divine;
  Dishonored once, they hear no more:
  Nor boast, majestic pine,
Daughter of Pontic forests, thy great name,
  Old lineage, well-earned fame,   15
  The honors of this sculptured prow—
Sport of the mocking winds, nor feared nor trusted
  now.

Alas! my country, long my anxious care,
Source now of bitter pain and fond regret!
  Thy stars obscured, thy course beset   20
  By rocks unseen, beware!
Trust not soft winds and treacherous seas
Or the false glitter of the Cyclades.

Ad Leuconoen (*Carpe Diem*). Translated by Franklin P. Adams.
From *Tobogganing on Parnassus* by Franklin P. Adams, copyright
1911 by Doubleday & Company, Inc.
The Ship of State. Translated by Stephen Edward De Vere. Horace
may have borrowed his famous figure of the Roman state as a hard-
pressed ship from a speech of Maecenas urging Augustus not to
resign his leadership of the government. He uses the figure to warn
his countrymen against reviving the civil war.
23. **Cyclades,** a group of islands in the Aegean Sea.

Lalage

THAT happy man whose virtuous heart
  Is free from guilt and conscious fear
Needs not the poisoned Moorish dart,
  Nor bow, nor sword, nor deadly spear.

Whether on shores that Ganges laves,   5
  Or Syrtes' quivering sands among,
Or where the Hydaspes' fabled waves
  In strange meanders wind along.

When free from care I dared to rove,
  And Lalage inspired my lay,   10
A wolf within the Sabine grove
  Fled wild from his defenceless prey.

Such prodigy the Daunian bands
  In their drear haunts shall never trace,
Nor barren Libya's arid sands,   15
  Rough parent of the lion race.

O place where no verdure smiles,
  No vernal zephyrs fan the ground,
No varied scene the eye beguiles,
  Nor murmuring rivulets glide around.   20

Place me on Thracia's frozen lands,
  Uncheered by genial light of day!
Place me on Afric's burning sands,
  Scorched by the sun's inclement ray!

Love in my heart shall pain beguile,   25
  Sweet Lalage shall be my song,
The gentle beauties of her smile,
  The gentle music of her tongue.

To Chloë

YOU shun me, Chloë, wild and shy,
  As some stray fawn that seeks its mother
Through trackless woods. If spring winds sigh
  It vainly strives its fears to smother.

Its trembling knees assail each other   5
  When lizards stir the brambles dry;—
You shun me, Chloë, wild and shy,
  As some stray fawn that seeks its mother.

Lalage. Translated by W. Herbert.
6. **Syrtes' quivering sands.** The Syrtes was a great gulf on the
northern coast of Africa, notoriously dangerous because of its quicksands.   7. **Hydaspes,** one of the great tributaries of the Indus River
in India, remote and mysterious.   13. **Daunian bands,** the people of
southeastern Italy.
To Chloë. Translated by Austin Dobson. Reprinted by permission
of Oxford University Press, London, and Mr. A. T. A. Dobson as
representative of the Executors.

And yet no Libyan lion I,—
    No ravening thing to rend another; 10
Lay by your tears, your tremors dry,
    A husband's better than a brother;
Nor shun me, Chloë, wild and shy,
    As some stray fawn that seeks its mother.

Past Her Prime

SWAINS in numbers
    Break your slumbers,
Saucy Lydia, now but seldom,
Ay, though at your casement nightly,
Tapping loudly, tapping lightly, 5
By the dozen once you held them.

    Ever turning,
    Night and morning
Swung your door upon its hinges;
Now, from dawn till evening's closing, 10
Lone and desolate reposing,
Not a soul its rest infringes.

    Serenaders,
    Sweet invaders,
Scanter grow, and daily scanter, 15
Singing, "Lydia, art thou sleeping?
Lonely watch thy love is keeping!
Wake, O wake, thou dear enchanter!"

    Lone and faded,
    You, as they did, 20
Woo, and in your turn are slighted,
Worn and torn by passion's fret.
You, the pitiless coquette,
Waste by fires yourself have lighted,

    Late relenting, 25
    Left lamenting,—
"Withered leaves strew wintry brooks!
Ivy garlands greenly darkling,
Myrtles brown with dew-drops sparkling,
Best beseem youth's glowing looks!"

Faith Renewed

WISE in the love of philosophic fools
    I strayed perplexed amid conflicting
      schools:
O worshipped not, believed not, hoped not! Now
To long-neglected gods perforce must bow,
Reverse my shattered sail, and turn once more, 5
Repentant, to the course I steered of yore;

Past Her Prime. From *Horace,* translated by Sir Theodore Martin. Reprinted by permission of J. B. Lippincott Company and Wm. Blackwood & Sons Ltd.
Faith Renewed. Translated by Stephen Edward De Vere.

For Jove, whose lightnings from Olympus hurled
Erewhile through rifted storm-clouds smote the
    world,
Through cloudless skies and azure depths afar
Drove now his fiery steeds and thunder-winged car.
Trembled the solid earth, the ocean floor, 11
The wandering rivers, and the Stygian shore,
Dark Taenarus accurst and Atlas hoar.

There is a god: his justice and his might
Adjust the balance of the world aright; 15
Abase the proud; exalt and glorify
The lowly grace of true humility.
Fortune at his command plucks monarchs down,
And on the humble outcast lays the crown.

Persian Fopperies

BOY, I hate their empty shows,
    Persian garlands I detest,
Bring me not the late-blown rose
    Lingering after all the rest:

Plainer myrtle pleases me 5
    Thus outstretched beneath my vine,
Myrtle more becoming thee,
    Waiting with thy master's wine.

Ad Xanthiam
Phoceum

NAY, Xanthias, feel unashamed
    That she you love is but a servant.
Remember, lovers far more famed
    Were just as fervent.

Achilles loved the pretty slave 5
    Brisëis for her fair complexion;
And to Tecmessa Ajax gave
    His young affection.

Why, Agamemnon at the height
    Of feasting, triumph, and anointment, 10
Left everything to keep, one night,
    A small appointment.

And are you sure the girl you love—
    This maid on whom you have your heart set—
Is lowly—that she is not of 15
    The Roman smart set?

13. **Dark Taenarus accurst,** a cave-entrance to the underworld.
Persian Fopperies. Translated by William Cowper.
Ad Xanthiam Phoceum (*Xanthias Jollied*). Translated by Franklin P. Adams. From *Tobogganing on Parnassus* by Franklin P. Adams, copyright 1911 by Doubleday & Company, Inc.

A maiden modest as is she,
    So full of sweetness and forbearance,
Must be all right; her folks must be
    Delightful parents.   20

Her arms and face I can commend,
    And, as the writer of a poem,
I fain would compliment, old friend,
    The limbs below 'em.

Nay, be not jealous. Stop your fears.   25
    My tendencies are far from sporty.
Besides, the number of my years
    Is over forty.

To Licinius

RECEIVE, dear friend, the truths I teach;
    So shalt thou live beyond the reach
        Of adverse Fortune's power;
Not always tempt the distant deep,
Nor always timorously creep   5
    Along the treacherous shore.

He that holds fast the golden mean
And lives contentedly between
    The little and the great,
Feels not the wants that pinch the poor, 10
Nor plagues that haunt the rich man's door,
    Embittering all his state.

The tallest pines feel most the power
Of wintry blasts; the loftiest tower
    Comes heaviest to the ground;   15
The bolts that spare the mountain's side,
His cloud-capt eminence divide,
    And spread the ruin round.

The well-inform'd philosopher
Rejoices with a wholesome fear,   20
    And hopes, in spite of pain;
If winter bellow from the north,
Soon the sweet spring comes dancing forth,
    And Nature laughs again.

What if thine heaven be overcast?   25
The dark appearance will not last;
    Expect a brighter sky.
The god that strings the silver bow
Awakes sometimes the Muses too,
    And lays his arrows by.   30

If hindrances obstruct thy way,
Thy magnanimity display,
    And let thy strength be seen;
But oh! if Fortune fill thy sail
With more than a propitious gale,   35
    Take half thy canvas in.

To Licinius. Translated by William Cowper.

To Postumus

SWIFTLY fly the rolling years, my friend!
    Nor can your anxious prayers extend
        The fleeting joys of youth.
The trembling hand, the wrinkled cheek,
Too plainly life's decay bespeak,   5
    With sad but silent truth.

What though your daily offerings rise
In fragrant clouds of sacrifice
    To Jove's immortal seat;
You cannot fly death's cold embrace,   10
Where peasants—chiefs of kingly race
    An equal welcome meet.

In vain, from battlefields afar
You gently dream of waging war,
    Secure in peace and wealth: 15
In vain you shun the stormy wave,
The scorching breeze that others brave,
    Profuse of vigorous health.

Though zealous friends your portals throng,
They cannot still your life prolong   20
    By one short lingering hour;
Whate'er our plans, whate'er our state,
We mortals own one common fate,
    One stern, unbending power.

When your parched lips shall faintly press 25
On your fond wife their faint caress,
    And farewell murmurs breathe,
Your wandering eyes shall feebly rove
O'er each loved wood and well-trained grove,
    To seek a funeral wreath.   30

The purple vineyard's luscious stores,
Secured by trebly bolted doors,
    Excite, in vain, your care;
Soon shall the rich and sparkling hoard
Flow largely o'er the festive board   35
    Of your unsparing heir.

To Postumus. Translated by Ralph Bernal.
32. **trebly bolted doors,** the doors of his wine cellar.

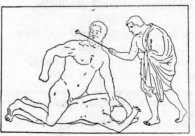

Wrestlers and referee. From a Roman painting.

Extremum Tanain

Before thy door too long of late,
  O Lyce, I bewail my fate;
    Not Don's barbarian maids, I trow,
    Would treat their luckless lovers so;
Thou,—thou alone art obstinate.   5
Hast thou nor eyes nor ears, Ingrate!
Hark! how the NORTH WIND shakes thy gate!
    Look! how the laurels bend with snow
      Before thy doors!

Lay by thy pride,—nor hesitate,   10
Lest Love and I grow desperate;
    If prayers, if gifts for naught must go,
    If naught my frozen pallor show,—
Beware! . . . I shall not always wait
      Before thy doors!

To the Fountain of Bandusia

O Fountain of Bandusia!
    Whence crystal waters flow,
With garlands gay and wine I'll pay
    The sacrifice I owe;
A sportive kid with budding horns   5
    I have, whose crimson blood
Anon shall dye and sanctify
    Thy cool and babbling flood.

O fountain of Bandusia!
    The Dog-star's hateful spell   10
No evil brings into the springs
    That from thy bosom well;
Here oxen, wearied by the plow,
    The roving cattle here
Hasten in quest of certain rest,   15
    And quaff thy gracious cheer.

O fountain of Bandusia!
    Ennobled shalt thou be,
For I shall sing the joys that spring
    Beneath yon ilex-tree.   20
Yes, fountain of Bandusia,
    Posterity shall know
The cooling brooks that from thy nooks
    Singing and dancing go.

Extremum Tanain. Translated by Austin Dobson. Reprinted by permission of Oxford University Press, London, and Mr. A. T. A. Dobson as representative of the Executors.
To the Fountain of Bandusia. Translated by Eugene Field. From *Echoes from the Sabine Farm,* by Eugene and R. M. Field, copyright 1893 by Eugene Field, 1921 by Julia Sutherland Field; used by permission of the publishers, Charles Scribner's Sons.

Holiday

What celebration should there be? . . .
    Quick, Lyde, bring a jar!
Against a dull sobriety
    We'll wage a lusty war.

The festive sun is setting low,   5
    The dusk is almost there;
And yet you scarcely move, as though
    We both had time to spare!

Let's pour the wine and sing in turns
    Of Neptune in his lair,   10
Of mermaids in the water-ferns,
    And of their sea-green hair.

And you, upon your curving lyre,
    Shall spend a tuneful hour,
Singing Diana's darts of fire   15
    And her benignant power.

Hymns shall arise to Her who sends
    Fresh laughter and delight,
Until our weary singing ends
    In lullabies tonight.

The Immortality of Verse

Lest you should think that verse shall die,
    Which sounds the silver Thames along,
Taught on the wings of truth to fly
    Above the reach of vulgar song;

Though daring Milton sits sublime,   5
    In Spenser native Muses play;
Nor yet shall Waller yield to time,
    Nor pensive Cowley's Mortal lay.

Sages and chiefs long since had birth
    Ere Caesar was, or Newton named;   10
These raised new empires o'er the earth,
    And those, new heavens and systems framed.

Vain was the chief's, the sage's pride!
    They had no poet, and they died.
In vain they schemed, in vain they bled!   15
    They had no poet, and are dead.

Holiday. Translated by Louis Untermeyer. From *Including Horace* by Louis Untermeyer, copyright 1919 by Harcourt, Brace and Company, Inc.
The Immortality of Verse. Translated by Alexander Pope.
2. silver Thames. Pope has replaced Horace's Roman allusions with English counterparts.

The Noble Soul

THE man of firm and noble soul
  No factious clamors can control;
No threat'ning tyrant's darkling brow
  Can swerve him from his just intent.
Gales the warring waves which plough   5
  By Auster on the billows spent,
  To curb the Adriatic main,
Would awe his fix'd, determin'd mind in vain.

Ay, and the red right arm of Jove,
  Hurtling his lightnings from above,   10
With all his terrors then unfurl'd,
  He would unmoved, unawed behold.
The flames of an expiring world
  Again in crashing chaos roll'd,
  In vast promiscuous ruin hurl'd,   15
Might light his glorious funeral pile:
Still dauntless mid the wreck of earth he'd smile.

Rain Tomorrow

UNLESS yon old soothsaying crow
  Deceive me, from the East shall blow
  Tomorrow such a blast
As will with leaves the forest strew,
And heaps of useless sea-weed, too,   5
  Upon the sea-beach cast.

Dry faggots, then, house while you may;
Give all your household holiday
  Tomorrow, and with wine
Your spirits cheer; be blithe and bold,   10
And on a pigling two moons old
  Most delicately dine!

To a Jar of Wine

O PRECIOUS crock, whose summers date,
  Like mine, from Manlius' consulate,
I wot not whether in your breast
Lie maudlin wail or merry jest,
Or sudden choler, or the fire   5
Of tipsy Love's insane desire,
Or fumes of soft caressing sleep,
Or what more potent charms you keep;
But this I know, your ripened power
Befits some choicely festive hour!   10

The Noble Soul. Translated by Lord Byron.
6. **Auster,** the sultry south wind, called *sirocco* in modern Italy.
Rain Tomorrow and *To a Jar of Wine.* From *Horace,* translated by
Sir Theodore Martin. Reprinted by permission of J. B. Lippincott
Company and Wm. Blackwood & Sons Ltd.

A cup peculiarly mellow
Corvinus asks; so come, old fellow,
From your time-honored bin descend,
And let me gratify my friend!
No churl is he, your charms to slight,   15
Though most intensely erudite:
And even old Cato's worth, we know,
Took from good wine a nobler glow.

  Your magic power of wit can spread
The halo round a dullard's head   20
Can make the sage forget his care,
His bosom's inmost thoughts unbare,
And drown his solemn-faced pretense
Beneath your blithesome influence.
Bright hope you bring and vigor back   25
To minds outworn upon the rack,
And put such courage in the brain
As makes the poor be men again
Whom neither tyrants' wrath affrights,
Nor all their bristling satellites.   30

  Bacchus and Venus, so that she
Bring only frank festivity,
With sister Graces in her train,
Twining close in lovely chain,
And gladsome tapers' living light,   35
Shall spread your treasures o'er the night,
Till Phoebus the red East unbars,
And puts to rout the trembling stars.

Renouncing Love

FOR ladies' love I late was fit,
  And good success my warfare blest;
But now my arms, my lyre I quit,
  And hang them up to rust or rest.
Here, where arising from the sea   5
  Stands Venus, lay the load at last,
Links, crowbars, and artillery,
  Threatening all doors that dared be fast.
O goddess! Cyprus owns thy sway,
  And Memphis, far from Thracian snow: 10
Raise high thy lash, and deal me, pray,
  That haughty Chloë just one blow!

To Venus

VENUS, again thou mov'st a war
  Long intermitted, pray thee, pray thee,
    spare!
I am not such as in the reign
  Of the good Cynara I was; refrain,

Renouncing Love. Translated by John Conington.
To Venus. Translated by Ben Jonson.

Sour mother of sweet Loves, forbear   5
   To bend a man, now at his fiftieth year.
Too stubborn for commands so slack:
   Go where youth's soft entreaties call thee back.
More timely hie thee to the house
   (With thy bright swans) of Paulus Maximus: 10
There jest and feast, make him thine host
   If a fit liver thou dost seek to toast.
For he's both noble, lovely, young,
   And for the troubled client files his tongue:
Child of a hundred arts, and far   15
   Will he display the ensigns of thy war.
And when he, smiling, finds his grace
   With thee 'bove all his rivals' gifts take place,
He'll thee a marble statue make,
   Beneath a sweet-wood roof, near Alba lake;   20
There shall thy dainty nostril take
   In many a gum, and for thy soft ear's sake
Shall verse be set to harp and lute,
   And Phrygian hau'boy, not without the flute.
There twice a day in sacred lays,   25
   The youths and tender maids shall sing thy
     praise!
And in the Salian manner meet
   Thrice 'bout thy altar, with their ivory feet.
Me now, nor girl, nor wanton boy
   Delights, nor credulous hope of mutual joy;   30
Nor care I now health to propound
   Or with fresh flowers to gird my temples round.
But why, oh why, my Ligurine,
   Flow my thin tears down these pale cheeks of
     mine?
Or why my well-graced words among,   35
   With an uncomely silence, fails my tongue?
Hard-hearted, I dream every night
   I hold thee fast! but fled hence with the light,
Whether in Mars his field thou be,
   Or Tiber's winding streams, I follow thee.

Revenge!

THE gods have heard me, Lyce,
   The gods have heard my prayer.
Now you, who were so icy,
   Observe with cold despair
   Your thin and snowy hair.   5

Your cheeks are lined and sunken;
   Your smiles have turned to leers;
But still you sing, a drunken
   Appeal to Love, who hears
   With inattentive ears.   10

Young Chia, with her fluty
   Caressing voice compels.
Love lives upon her beauty;
   Her cheeks, in which He dwells,
   Are His fresh citadels.   15

He saw the battered ruin,
   This old and twisted tree;
He marked the scars, and flew in
   Haste that He might not see
   Your torn senility.   20

No silks, no purple gauzes
   Can hide the lines that last.
Time, with his iron laws, is
   Implacable and fast.
   You cannot cheat the past.   25

Where now are all your subtle
   Disguises and your fair
Smile like a gleaming shuttle?
   Your shining skin, your rare
   Beauty half-breathless—where?   30

Only excelled by Cinara,
   Your loveliness ranked high.
You even seemed the winner, a
   Victor as years went by,
   And she was first to die.   35

But now—the young men lightly
   Laugh at your wrinkled brow.
The torch that burned so brightly
   Is only ashes now;
   A charred and blackened bough.

To His Book

YOU vain, self-conscious little book,
   Companion of my happy days,
How eagerly you seem to look
For wider fields to spread your lays;
   My desk and locks cannot contain you,   5
   Nor blush of modesty restrain you.

Well, then, begone, fool that thou art!
But do not come to me and cry,
   When critics strike you to the heart:
"Oh, wretched little book am I!"
   You know I tried to educate you
   To shun the fate that must await you.

27. **Salian manner.** The Salii, or "jumpers," were priests of Mars.
Revenge! Translated by Louis Untermeyer. From *Including Horace* by Louis Untermeyer, copyright 1919 by Harcourt, Brace and Company, Inc.

To His Book (Epistle XX). Translated by R. M. Field. Reprinted from *Echoes from the Sabine Farm* by Eugene and R. M. Field; copyright 1893 by Eugene Field, 1921 by Julia Sutherland Field; used by permission of the publishers, Charles Scribner's Sons.

In youth you may encounter friends
(Pray this prediction be not wrong),
  But wait until old age descends   15
And thumbs have smeared your gentlest song;
  Then will the moths connive to eat you
  And rural libraries secrete you.

However, should a friend some word
Of my obscure career request,   20
  Tell him how deeply I was stirred
To spread my wings beyond the nest;
  Take from my years, which are before you,
  To boom my merits, I implore you.

Tell him that I am short and fat,   25
Quick in my temper, soon appeased,
  With locks of gray,—but what of that?
Loving the sun, with nature pleased.
  I'm more than four and forty, hark you,—
  But ready for a night off, mark you!

Satires

CONTENTMENT

How comes it, say, Maecenas, if you can,
    That none will live like a contented man
Where choice or chance directs, but each must praise
The folk who pass through life by other ways?
'Those lucky merchants!' cries the soldier stout, 5
When years of toil have well-nigh worn him out:
What says the merchant, tossing o'er the brine?
'Yon soldier's lot is happier, sure, than mine:
One short, sharp shock, and presto! all is done:
Death in an instant comes, or victory's won.' 10
The lawyer lauds the farmer, when a knock
Disturbs his sleep at crowing of the cock:
The farmer, dragged to town on business, swears
That only citizens are free from cares.
I need not run through all: so long the list, 15
Fabius himself would weary and desist:
So take in brief my meaning: just suppose
Some God should come, and with their wishes close:
'See, here am I, come down of my mere grace
To right you: soldier, take the merchant's place! 20
You, counsellor, the farmer's! go your way,
One here, one there! None stirring? all say nay?
How now? you won't be happy when you may.'
Now, after this, would Jove be aught to blame
If with both cheeks he burst into a flame, 25
And vowed, when next they pray, they shall not find
His temper easy, or his ear inclined?
  Well, not to treat things lightly (though, for me,

Satires: "Contentment." Translated by John Conington.
16. Fabius . . . desist. The patient Fabius, known for his delay and
caution in prosecuting the war against Hannibal, is here meant.

Roman painting
of a
city merchant.

Why truth may not be gay, I cannot see:
Just as, we know, judicious teachers coax   30
With sugar-plum or cake their little folks
To learn their alphabet):—still, we will try
A graver tone, and lay our joking by.
The man that with his plough subdues the land,
The soldier stout, the vintner sly and bland,   35
The venturous sons of ocean, all declare
That with one view the toils of life they bear,
When age has come, and labour has amassed
Enough to live on, to retire at last:
E'en so the ant (for no bad pattern she),   40
That tiny type of giant industry,
Drags grain by grain, and adds it to the sum
Of her full heap, foreseeing cold to come:
Yet she, when winter turns the year to chill,
Stirs not an inch beyond her mounded hill,   45
But lives upon her savings: you, more bold,
Ne'er quit your gain for fiercest heat or cold:
Fire, ocean, sword, defying all, you strive
To make yourself the richest man alive.
Yet where's the profit, if you hide by stealth   50
In pit or cavern your enormous wealth?
'Why, once break in upon it, friend, you know,
And, dwindling piece by piece, the whole will go.
But, if 'tis still unbroken, what delight
Can all that treasure give to mortal wight?'   55
Say, you've a million quarters on your floor:
Your stomach is like mine: it holds no more:
Just as the slave who 'neath the bread-bag sweats
No larger ration than his fellows gets.
What matters it to reasonable men   60
Whether they plough a hundred fields or ten?
'But there's a pleasure, spite of all you say,
In a large heap from which to take away.'
If both contain the modicum we lack,
Why should your barn be better than my sack?   65
You want a draught of water: a mere urn,
Perchance a goblet, well would serve your turn:
You say, 'The stream looks scanty at its head;
I'll take my quantum where 'tis broad instead.'
But what befalls the wight who yearns for more   70

Than Nature bids him? down the waters pour,
And whelm him, bank and all; while he whose greed
Is kept in check, proportioned to his need,
He neither draws his water mixed with mud,
Nor leaves his life behind him in the flood.   75

But there's a class of persons, led astray
By false desires, and this is what they say:
'You cannot have enough: what you possess,
That makes your value, be it more or less.'
What answer would you make to such as these?   80
Why, let them hug their misery if they please,
Like the Athenian miser, who was wont
To meet men's curses with a hero's front:
'Folks hiss me,' said he, 'but myself I clap
When I tell o'er my treasures on my lap.'   85
So Tantalus catches at the waves that fly
His thirsty palate—Laughing, are you? why?
Change but the name, of you the tale is told:
You sleep, mouth open, on your hoarded gold;
Gold that you treat as sacred, dare not use,   90
In fact, that charms you as a picture does.
Come, will you hear what wealth can fairly do?
'Twill buy you bread, and vegetables too,
And wine, a good pint measure: add to this
Such needful things as flesh and blood would miss.
But to go mad with watching, nights and days   96
To stand in dread of thieves, fires, runaways
Who filch and fly,—in these if wealth consist,
Let me rank lowest on the paupers' list.

'But if you suffer from a chill attack,   100
Or other chance should lay you on your back,
You then have one who'll sit by your bed-side,
Will see the needful remedies applied,
And call in a physician, to restore
Your health, and give you to your friends once more.'
Nor wife nor son desires your welfare: all   106
Detest you, neighbours, gossips, great and small.
What marvel if, when wealth's your one concern,
None offers you the love you never earn?
Nay, would you win the kinsmen Nature sends   110
Made ready to your hand, and keep them friends,
'Twere but lost labour, as if one should train
A donkey for the course by bit and rein.

Make then an end of getting: know, the more
Your wealth, the less the risk of being poor;   115
And, having gained the object of your quest,
Begin to slack your efforts and take rest;
Nor act like one Ummidius (never fear,
The tale is short, and 'tis the last you'll hear).
So rich, his gold he by the peck would tell,   120
So mean, the slave that served him dressed as well;
E'en to his dying day he went in dread
Of perishing for simple want of bread,
Till a brave damsel, of Tyndarid line
The true descendant, clove him down the chine.   125

86–87. So Tantalus . . . palate. This was his punishment in Hades
for divulging the secrets of Jupiter.

'What? would you have me live like some we
      know,
Maenius or Nomentanus?' There you go!
Still in extremes! in bidding you forsake
A miser's ways, I say not, Be a rake.
'Twixt Tanais and Visellius' sire-in-law   130
A step there is, and broader than a straw.
Yes, there's a mean in morals: life has lines,
To north or south of which all virtue pines.

Now to resume our subject: why, I say,
Should each man act the miser in his way,   135
Still discontented with his natural lot,
Still praising those who have what he has not?
Why should he waste with very spite, to see
His neighbour has a milkier cow than he,
Ne'er think how much he's richer than the mass,   140
But always strive this man or that to pass?
In such a contest, speed we as we may,
There's some one wealthier ever in the way.
So from their base when vying chariots pour,
Each driver presses on the car before,   145
Wastes not a thought on rivals overpast,
But leaves them to lay on among the last.
Hence comes it that the man is rarely seen
Who owns that his a happy life has been,
And, thankful for past blessings, with good will 150
Retires, like one who has enjoyed his fill.
Enough: you'll think I've rifled the scrutore
Of blind Crispinus, if I prose on more.

ABOUT MYSELF

Now on myself, the freedman's son, I touch,
      The freedman's son, by all condemned as
      such,
Once, when a legion followed my command,
Now, when Maecenas takes me by the hand.
But this and that are different: some stern judge   5
My military rank with cause might grudge,
But not your friendship, studious as you've been
To choose good men, not pushing, base, or mean.
In truth, to luck I care not to pretend,
For 'twas not luck that mark'd me for your friend: 10
Virgil at first, that faithful heart and true,
And Varius after, named my name to you.
Brought to your presence, stammeringly I told
(For modesty forbade me to be bold)
No vaunting tale of ancestry of pride,   15
Of good broad acres and sleek nags to ride,
But simple truth: a few brief words you say,
As is your wont, and wish me a good day.
Then, nine months after, graciously you send,
Desire my company, and hail me friend.   20
O, 'tis no common fortune, when one earns

130. Tanais, unidentified.
"About Myself." Translated by John Conington.
12. Varius, Lucius Varius Rufus, epic poet and friend to Horace
and Virgil.

A friend's regard, who man from man discerns,
Not by mere accident of lofty birth
But by unsullied life, and inborn worth!
    Yet, if my nature, otherwise correct, 25
But with some few and trifling faults is flecked,
Just as a spot or mole might be to blame
Upon somebody else of comely frame,
If none can call me miserly and mean
Or tax my life with practices unclean, 30
If I have lived unstained and unreproved
(Forgive self-praise), if loving and beloved,
I owe it to my father, who, though poor,
Passed by the village school at his own door,
The school where great tall urchins in a row, 35
Sons of great tall centurions, used to go,
With slate and satchel on their backs, to pay
Their monthly quota punctual to the day,
And took his boy to Rome, to learn the arts
Which knight or senator to *his* imparts. 40
Whoe'er had seen me, neat and more than neat,
With slaves behind me, in the crowded street,
Had surely thought a fortune fair and large,
Two generations old, sustained the charge.
Himself the true tried guardian of his son, 45
Whene'er I went to class, he still made one.
Why lengthen out the tale? he kept me chaste,
Which is the crown of virtue, undisgraced
In deed and name: he feared not lest one day
The world should talk of money thrown away, 50
If after all I plied some trade for hire,
Like him, a tax-collector, or a crier:
Nor had I murmured: as it is, the score
Of gratitude and praise is all the more.
No: while my head's unturned, I ne'er shall need 55
To blush for that dear father, or to plead
As men oft plead, 'tis Nature's fault, not mine,
I came not of a better, worthier line.
Not thus I speak, not thus I feel: the plea
Might serve another, but 'twere base in me. 60
Should Fate this moment bid me to go back
O'er all my length of years, my life retrack
To its first hour, and pick out such descent
As man might wish for e'en to pride's content,
I should rest satisfied with mine, nor choose 65
New parents, decked with senatorial shoes.
Mad, most would think me, sane, as you'll allow,
To waive a load ne'er thrust on me till now.
More gear 'twould make me get without delay,
More bows there'd be to make, more calls to pay, 70
A friend or two must still be at my side,
That all alone I might not drive or ride,
More nags would want their corn, more grooms their
    meat,
And waggons must be bought, to save their feet.
Now on my bobtailed mule I jog at ease, 75
As far as e'en Tarentum, if I please,
A wallet for my things behind me tied,

Which galls his crupper, as I gall his side,
And no one rates my meanness, as they rate
Yours, noble Tillius, when you ride in state 80
On the Tiburtine road, five slaves *en suite*,
Wineholder and et-ceteras all complete.
    'Tis thus my life is happier, man of pride,
Than yours and that of half the world beside.
When the whim leads, I saunter forth alone, 85
Ask how are herbs, and what is flour a stone,
Lounge through the Circus with its crowd of liars,
Or in the Forum, when the sun retires,
Talk to a soothsayer, then go home to seek
My frugal meal of fritter, vetch, and leek: 90
Three youngsters serve the food: a slab of white
Contains two cups, one ladle, clean and bright:
Next, a cheap basin ranges on the shelf,
With jug and saucer of Campanian delf:
Then off to bed, where I can close my eyes 95
Not thinking how with morning I must rise
And face grim Marsyas, who is known to swear
Young Novius' looks are what he cannot bear.
I lie a-bed till ten: then stroll a bit,
Or read or write, if in a silent fit, 100
And rub myself with oil, not taken whence
Natta takes his, at some poor lamp's expense.
So to the field and ball; but when the sun
Bids me go bathe, the field and ball I shun:
Then eat a temperate luncheon, just to stay 105
A sinking stomach till the close of day,
Kill time in-doors, and so forth. Here you see
A careless life, from stir and striving free,
Happier (O be that flattering unction mine!)
Than if three quaestors figured in my line.

CITY LIFE
AND COUNTRY LIFE

THIS used to be my wish: a bit of land,
    A house and garden with a spring at hand,
And just a little wood. The gods have crowned
My humble vows; I prosper and abound:
Nor ask I more, kind Mercury, save that thou 5
Wouldst give me still the goods thou giv'st me now:
If crime has ne'er increased them, nor excess
And want of thrift are like to make them less;
If I ne'er pray like this, 'O might that nook
Which spoils my field be mine by hook or crook! 10
O for a stroke of luck like his, who found
A crock of silver, turning up the ground,
And, thanks to good Alcides, farmed as buyer
The very land where he had slaved for hire!'
If what I have contents me, hear my prayer: 15
Still let me feel thy tutelary care,
And let my sheep, my pastures, this and that,
My all, in fact, (except my brains), be fat.

86. stone, fourteen pounds, English weight.
"City Life and Country Life." Translated by John Conington.
13. Alcides, Hercules.

*From
a Roman
painting.*

Now, lodged in my hill-castle, can I choose
Companion fitter than my homely Muse?   20
Here no town duties vex, no plague-winds blow,
Nor Autumn, friend to graveyards, works me woe.
Sire of the morning (do I call thee right,
Or hear'st thou Janus' name with more delight?)
Who introducest, so the gods ordain,   25
Life's various tasks, inaugurate my stain.
At Rome to bail I'm summoned. 'Do your part,'
Thou bidd'st me; 'Quick, lest others get the start.'
So, whether Boreas roars, or winter's snow
Clips short the day, to court I needs must go.   30
I give the fatal pledge, distinct and loud,
Then pushing, struggling, battle with the crowd.
'Now, madman!' clamours some one, not without
A threat or two, 'just mind what you're about:
What? you must knock down all that's in your way,
Because you're posting to Maecenas, eh?'   36
This pleases me, I own; but when I get
To black Esquiliae, trouble waits me yet:
For other people's matters in a swarm
Buzz round my head and take my ears by storm.   40
'Sir, Roscius would be glad if you'd arrange
By eight a.m. to be with him on 'Change.'
'Quintus, the scribes entreat you to attend
A meeting of importance, as their friend.'
'Just get Maecenas' seal attached to these.'   45
'I'll try.' 'O, you can do it, if you please.'
Seven years, or rather eight, have well-nigh passed
Since with Maecenas' friends I first was classed,
To this extent, that, driving through the street,
He'd stop his car and offer me a seat,   50
Or make such chance remarks as 'What's o'clock?'
'Will Syria's champion beat the Thracian cock?'
'These morning frosts are apt to be severe';
Just chit-chat, suited to a leaky ear.
Since that auspicious date, each day and hour   55
Has placed me more and more in envy's power:
'He joined his play, sat next him at the games:
A child of Fortune!' all the world exclaims.
From the high rostra a report comes down,

And like a chilly fog, pervades the town: 60
Each man I meet accosts me 'Is it so?
You live so near the gods, you're sure to know:
What news about Dacians? have you heard
No secret tidings?' 'Not a single word.'
'O yes! you love to banter us poor folk.'   65
'Nay, if I've heard a tittle, may I choke!'
'Will Caesar grant his veterans their estates
In Italy, or t'other side of the straits?'
I swear that I know nothing, and am dumb:
They think me deep, miraculously mum.   70
And so my day between my fingers slips,
While fond regrets keep rising to my lips:
O my dear homestead in the country! when
Shall I behold your pleasant face again;
And, studying now, now dozing and at ease,   75
Imbibe forgetfulness of all this tease?
O when, Pythagoras, shall thy brother bean,
With pork and cabbage, on my board be seen?
O happy nights and suppers half divine,
When, at the home-gods' altar, I and mine   80
Enjoy a frugal meal, and leave the treat
Unfinished for my merry slaves to eat!
Not bound by mad-cap rules, but free to choose
Big cups or small, each follows his own views:
You toss your wine off boldly, if you please,   85
Or gently sip, and mellow by degrees.
We talk of—not our neighbour's house or field,
Nor the last feat of Lepos, the light-heeled—
But matters which to know concerns us more,
Which none but at his peril can ignore: 90
Whether 'tis wealth or virtue makes men blest,
What leads to friendship, worth or interest,
In what the good consists, and what the end
And chief of goods, on which the rest depend:
While neighbour Cervius, with his rustic wit,   95
Tells old wives' tales, this case or that to hit.
Should some one be unwise enough to praise
Arellius' toilsome wealth, he straightway says:
'One day a country mouse in his poor home

63. **Dacians,** the troublesome people of Dacia, a Roman province
north of the lower Danube. 77. **brother bean,** the humble bean
named for the philosopher Pythagoras, whose ascetic followers forbade the eating of beans.

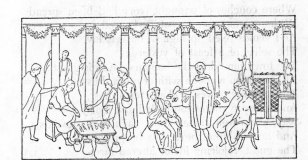

Merchants and clients. From a Roman painting.

Country scene. From a Roman mosaic.

Received an ancient friend, a mouse from Rome: 100
The host, though close and careful, to a guest
Could open still: so now he did his best.
He spares not oaks or vetches: in his chaps
Raisins he brings and nibbled bacon-scraps,
Hoping by varied dainties to entice 105
His town-bred guest, so delicate and nice,
Who condescended graciously to touch
Thing after thing, but never would take much,
While he, the owner of the mansion, sate
On threshed-out straw, and spelt and darnels ate. 110
At length the townsman cries: "I wonder how
You can live here, friend, on this hill's rough brow:
Take my advice, and leave these ups and downs,
This hill and dale, for humankind and towns.
Come now, go home with me: remember, all 115
Who live on earth are mortal, great and small;
Then take, good sir, your pleasure while you may;
With life so short, 'twere wrong to lose a day."
This reasoning made the rustic's head turn round;
Forth from his hole he issues with a bound, 120
And they two make together for their mark,
In hopes to reach the city during dark.
The midnight sky was bending over all,
When they set foot within a stately hall,
Where couches of wrought ivory had been spread
With gorgeous coverlets of Tyrian red, 126
And viands piled up high in baskets lay,
The relics of a feast of yesterday.
The townsman does the honours, lays his guest
At ease upon a couch with crimson dressed, 130
Then nimbly moves in character of host,
And offers in succession boiled and roast;
Nay, like a well-trained slave, each wish prevents,
And tastes before the tit-bits he presents.
The guest, rejoicing in his altered fare, 135
Assumes in turn a genial diner's air,
When hark! a sudden banging of the door:

Each from his couch is tumbled on the floor;
Half dead, they scurry round the room, poor things,
While the whole house with barking mastiffs rings.
Then says the rustic: "It may do for you, 141
This life, but I don't like it; so adieu:
Give me my hole, secure from all alarms,
I'll prove that tares and vetches still have charms." '

The Art
of Poetry

Good authors, take a brother bard's advice:
Ponder your subject o'er not once nor twice,
And oft and oft consider, if the weight
You hope to lift be or be not too great.
Let but our theme be equal to our powers, 5
Choice language, clear arrangement, both are ours.
Would you be told how best your pearls to thread?
Why, say just now what should just now be said,
But put off other matter for to-day,
To introduce it later by the way. 10
In words again be cautious and select,
And duly pick out this, and that reject.
High praise and honour to the bard is due
Whose dexterous setting makes an old word new.
Nay more, should some recondite subject need 15
Fresh signs to make it clear to those who read,
A power of issuing terms till now unused,
If claimed with modesty, is ne'er refused.
New words will find acceptance, if they flow
Forth from the Greek, with just a twist or so. 20
But why should Rome capriciously forbid
Our bards from doing what their fathers did? . . .
To utter words stamped current by the mill
Has always been thought right and always will. . . .
Why hail me poet, if I fail to seize 25
The shades of style, its fixed proprieties?
Why should false shame compel me to endure
An ignorance which common pains would cure?
A comic subject steadily declines
To be related in high tragic lines. 30
The Thyestean feast no less disdains
The vulgar vehicle of comic strains.
Each has its place allotted; each is bound
To keep it, nor invade its neighbour's ground. . . .
Mere grace is not enough: a play should thrill 35
The hearer's soul, and move it at its will.
Smiles are contagious; so are tears; to see
Another sobbing, brings a sob from me.
No, no, good Peleus; set the example, pray,
And weep yourself; then weep perhaps I may: 40

The Art of Poetry. Translated by John Conington.
31. **Thyestean feast,** the feast at which Atreus served his brother
Thyestes the flesh of Thyestes' own murdered sons.

But if no sorrow in your speech appear,
I nod or laugh; I cannot squeeze a tear.
Words follow looks: wry faces are expressed
By wailing, scowls by bluster, smiles by jest,
Grave airs by saws, and so of all the rest.   45
For nature forms our spirits to receive
Each bent that outward circumstance can give:
She kindles pleasure, bids resentment glow,
Or bows the soul to earth in hopeless woe;
Then, as the tide of feeling waxes strong,   50
She vents it through her conduit-pipe, the
            tongue. . . .

   In painting characters, adhere to fame,
Or study keeping in the type you frame:
If great Achilles figure in the scene,
Make him impatient, fiery, ruthless, keen;   55
All laws, all covenants let him still disown,
And test his quarrel by the sword alone. . . .

   If you would be original still, and seek
To frame some character ne'er seen in Greek,
See it be wrought on one consistent plan,   60
And end the same creation it began.
'Tis hard, I grant, to treat a subject known
And hackneyed so that it may look one's own;
Far better turn the Iliad to a play
And carve out acts and scenes the readiest way,   65
Than alter facts and characters, and tell
In a strange form the tale men know so well.
But with some few precautions, you may set
Your private mark on public chattels yet:
Avoid careering and careering still   70
In the old round, like carthorse in a mill;
Nor, bound too closely to the Grecian Muse,
Translate the words whose soul you should transfuse,
Nor act the copyist's part, and work in chains
Which, once put on by rashness, shame retains. . . .

   Now listen, dramatists, and I will tell   76
What I expect, and all the world as well.
If you would have your auditors to stay
Till curtain-rise and plaudit end the play,
Observe each age's temper, and impart   80
To each the grace and finish of your art.
   Note first the boy who just knows how to talk
And feels his feet beneath him in his walk:
He likes his young companions, loves a game,
Soon vexed, soon soothed, and not two hours the
            same.   85
   The beardless youth, at last from tutor freed,
Loves playing-field and tennis, dog and steed:
Pliant as wax to those who lead him wrong,
But all impatience with a faithful tongue;
Imprudent, lavish, hankering for the moon,   90
He takes things up and lays them down as soon.
   His nature revolutionized, the man
Makes friends and money when and how he can:
Keen-eyed and cool, though on ambition bent,
He shuns all acts of which he may repent.   95

Grey hairs have many evils: without end
The old man gathers what he dares not spend,
While, as for action, do he what he will,
'Tis all half-hearted, spiritless, and chill:
Inert, irresolute, his neck he cranes   100
Into the future, grumbles, and complains,
Extols his own young years with peevish praise,
But rates and censures these degenerate days.
   Years, as they come, bring blessings in their train;
Years, as they go, take blessings back again: 105
Yet haste or chance may blink the obvious truth,
Make youth discourse like age, and age like youth:
Attention fixed on life alone can teach
The traits and adjuncts which pertain to each.
   Sometimes 'tis done elsewhere, and there made
            known.   110
A thing when heard, remember, strikes less keen
On the spectator's mind than when 'tis seen.
Yet 'twere not well in public to display
A business best transacted far away,
And much may be secluded from the eye   115
For well-graced tongues to tell of by and by.
Medea must not shed her children's blood,
Nor savage Atreus cook man's flesh for food,
Nor Philomel turn bird or Cadmus snake,
With people looking on and wide awake.   120
If scenes like these before my eyes be thrust,
They shock belief and generate disgust.
   Would you your play should prosper and endure?
Then let it have five acts, nor more nor fewer.
Bring in no god save as a last resource,   125
Nor make four speakers join in the discourse.
   An actor's part the chorus should sustain
And do their best to get the plot in train:
And whatsoe'er between the acts they chant
Should all be apt, appropriate, relevant.   130
Still let them give sage counsel, back the good,
Attemper wrath, and cool impetuous blood,
Praise the spare meal that pleases but not sates,
Justice, and law, and peace with unbarred gates,
Conceal all secrets, and the gods implore   135
To crush the proud and elevate the poor. . . .
   My friends, make Greece your model when you
            write,
And turn her volumes over day and night.
'But Plautus pleased our sires, the good old folks;
They praised his numbers, and they praised his
            jokes.'   140
They did: 'twas mighty tolerant in them
To praise where wisdom would perhaps condemn;
That is, if you and I and our compeers
Can trust our tastes, our fingers, and our ears,
Know polished wit from horse-play, and can tell   145
What verses do, and what do not, run well.
   Thespis began the drama: rumour says
In travelling carts he carried round his plays,
Where actors, smeared with lees, before the throng

Performed their parts with gesture and with song. 150
Then Aeschylus brought in the mask and pall,
Put buskins on his men to make them tall,
Turned boards into a platform, not too great,
And taught high monologue and grand debate.
The elder Comedy had next its turn, 155
Nor small the glory it contrived to earn:
But freedom passed into unbridled spite,
And law was soon invoked to set things right;
And (shame to say) thenceforth refused to sing.
    Our poets have tried all things; nor do they 160
Deserve least praise, who follow their own way,
And tell in comedy or history-piece
Some story of home growth, not drawn from Greece.
Nor would the land we love be now more strong
In warrior's prowess than in poet's song, 165
Did not her bards with one consent decline
The tedious task, to alter and refine.
Dear Pisos! as you prize old Numa's blood,
Set down that work, and that alone, as good,
Which, blurred and blotted, checked and counter-
        checked, 170
Has stood all tests, and issued forth correct. . . .
    Of writing well, be sure, the secret lies
In wisdom: therefore study to be wise.
The page of Plato may suggest the thought,
Which found, the words will come as soon as sought.
The man who once has learned to comprehend 176
His duty to his country and his friend,
The love that parent, brother, guest may claim,
The judge's, senator's, or general's aim,
That man, when need occurs, will soon invent 180
For every part its proper sentiment.
Look too to life and manners, as they lie

168. **Dear Pisos,** the father and two sons to whom this Epistle was
addressed. **Numa,** the legendary second king of Rome.

City workers in Rome.

Before you: these will living words supply.
A play, devoid of beauty, strength, and art,
So but the thought and morals suit each part, 185
Will catch men's minds and rivet them when caught
More than the clink of verses without thought. . . .
    Some faults may claim forgiveness: for the lyre
Not always gives the note that we desire;
We ask a flat; a sharp is its reply; 190
And the best bow will sometimes shoot awry.
But when I meet with beauties thickly sown,
A blot or two I readily condone,
Such as may trickle from a careless pen,
Or pass unwatched: for authors are but men. 195
What then? the copyist who keeps stumbling still
At the same word had best lay down his quill:
The harp-player, who for ever wounds the ear
With the same discord, makes the audience jeer:
So the poor dolt who's often in the wrong 200
I rank with Choerilus, that dunce of song,
Who, should he ever deviate into sense,
Moves but fresh laughter at his own expense:
While e'en good Homer may deserve a tap,
If, as he does, he drop his head and nap. 205
Yet, when a work is long, 'twere somewhat hard
To blame a drowsy moment in a bard. . . .
    But here occurs a question some men start,
If good verse comes from nature or from art.
For me, I cannot see how native wit 210
Can e'er dispense with art, or art with it.
Set them to pull together, they're agreed,
And each supplies what each is found to need.
    The youth who runs for prizes wisely trains,
Bears cold and heat, is patient and abstains: 215
The flute-player at a festival, before
He plays in public, has to learn his lore.
Not so our bardlings: they come bouncing in—
'I'm your true poet: let them laugh that win:
Plague take the last! although I ne'er was taught, 220
Is that a cause for owning I know nought?' . . .
    Read verses to Quintilius, he would say,
'I don't like this and that: improve it, pray':
Tell him you found it hopeless to correct;
You'd tried it twice or thrice without effect: 225
He'd calmly bid you make the three times four,
And take the unlicked cub in hand once more.
But if you chose to vindicate the crime,
Not mend it, he would waste no further time,
But let you live, untroubled by advice, 230
Sole tenant of your own fool's paradise.
    A wise and faithful counsellor will blame
Weak verses, note the rough, condemn the lame,
Retrench luxuriance, make obscureness plain,

201. **Choerilus, that dunce of song,** a mediocre epic poet, friend to
Alexander the Great. 204–205. **While e'en good Homer . . . nap.**
This is another translation of the familiar "Homer nods." 222.
Quintilius, Quintilius Varus, the poet and critic, a friend of Virgil.

Cross-question this, bid that be writ again: 235
A second Aristarch, he will not ask,
'Why for such trifles take my friend to task?'
Such trifles bring to serious grief ere long
A hapless bard, once flattered and led wrong. . . .

Catullus

87–54 B.C.

Romantic love was a subject of little interest to Greeks of the Golden Age because of the inferior social position of women and a system of education and marriage that discouraged it. In Rome women enjoyed almost complete emancipation, but the formality of marital arrangements and a stoic training that subjected the emotions to reason and duty discouraged romantic love here as well. The love poetry of Horace and Ovid is *vers de societé*, celebrating casual affairs with a variety of rather dubious ladies. Tibullus (54?–19 B.C.) with his Delia, and Propertius (50?–15 B.C.) with his Cynthia are more convincing, but the only great love poetry of Rome is that of Catullus, inspired by an authentic devotion to a worthless woman. It too was a blighted product of the fashionable, reckless circles of the capital in the days of its sophistication.

Gaius Valerius Catullus came of a distinguished family in the northern city of Verona and was probably of warm Celtic blood. His father's wealth provided him a gentleman's education and took him to Rome in his early twenties. Here he was caught up in the youthful smart set which was emulating the cultured society of Alexandria with its free love and idle living, and the poets of Alexandria with their gay love ditties. He adopted the fashionable policy of lampooning Caesar but otherwise took no part in politics. He spent his time in his town house with its fine library or at one of his two country estates, where his extravagance led him to complain of an empty purse. In a misguided effort to recoup his finances, he accompanied Memmius, the governor of Bithynia, to that province and visited Greece en route. Debonair and dissipated, he squandered his life in a decade and died the Romantic's early death at thirty.

Lovemaking was a favorite pastime of the young blades of the capital, but Catullus was unconventional in devoting himself to a depraved and heartless woman. She was Clodia, the sister of Cicero's enemy, Publius Clodius, and the wife of Metellus Celer, who was away governing Cisalpine Gaul in the year 62, when Catullus probably arrived in Rome and began his attachment to her. Cicero has left us a blistering account of this bold and libidinous siren in defending another of her lovers, Caelius Rufus, from her charge that he tried to poison her. She was older than Catullus and saw in this naïve youth from the provinces a refreshing interlude in her

236. **Aristarch**, Aristarchus (fl. 150 B.C.), considered the greatest critic of antiquity.

round of amours. For him it was love at first sight, and he wooed her with exquisite verses of passionate and innocent devotion. All the stages of an ill-fated love are there: his first attraction, his jealousy of her pet bird and tender grief at its death, the frenzy of passion in which he abandoned all reserves, his final recoil from her infidelities in bitter revenge. He stoops to obscenity in his last revulsion, and eventually turns to other poetic themes.

The trembling lyrics that preserve the anguished love of this great poet are partially in the contemporary tradition of the polished Alexandrians, partially in the old Greek tradition of Sappho of Lesbos, whose memory Catullus recalled in the poetic name Lesbia, with which he addressed Clodia. The meters of his 116 poems are varied, and their subjects go beyond his love affair to shocking obscenities, charming wedding songs, myths retold, poems of tender friendship, and the salute to his brother's grave with its *ave atque vale* (Hail and farewell!). Nearly all are brief and fervent, and their light grace, warm color, and frenzied abandonment to joy and despair stamp them as more modern than Roman. Catullus in his untrammeled moods has been variously compared to Sappho, Shelley, and Robert Burns. His poems were completely forgotten in the Middle Ages, but returned in the fourteenth century with the accidental discovery of the one surviving manuscript. They have had a profound effect on modern poets from Petrarch down.

To Lesbia's Sparrow

SPARROW, the plaything of my fair,
 Whom in her lap she loves to bear,
Or with raised finger-tip excites
Till wickedly he pecks and bites;
When the bright lady of my yearning   5
To some dear dainty play is turning,
Sweet solace for love's pain, I trow,
Or in the lull of passion's glow,—
Oh! might I play with you as she,
And my heart's burden lighter be.

On the Death of Lesbia's Sparrow

MOURN Loves and Graces all, and you
 Of men the lovelier chosen few.
The sparrow of my love is dead,
The playmate of my love is sped,
Her sparrow, prized beyond her eyes,   5
So honey-sweet was he, and wise

To Lesbia's Sparrow; On the Death of Lesbia's Sparrow. Translated by Hugh MacNaghton. From *The Poems of Catullus* by Hugh MacNaghton. Reprinted by permission of The University Press, Cambridge, England.

To know her as a girl her mother.
He would not leave her for another,
Would on her lap be still astir
And chirping still for none but her.   10
And now he journeys whence they say
No steps retrace the darkling way.
Cursed shades, I curse you, swallowing
In Orcus every dainty thing:
The dainty pet ye ravished here!   15
Fie, fie for shame! ah, birdie dear!
Flushed, heavy eyelids are the due
My love is paying, all for you.

Catullus Contrasts Quintia with Lesbia (86)

MANY say Quintia is "lovely." I
    Say "fair" and "straight" and "tall."
Each single claim
I grant, but not the sum of "lovely." Why?
    Sparkles nor wit nor grace in all her frame.   5
But Lesbia is lovely, cap-à-pie,
And from all others takes all charm away.

On Lesbia

LESBIA forever on me rails.
    To talk of me she never fails.
Now, hang me, but for all her art,
I find that I have gained her heart.
My proof is this: I plainly see   5
The case is just the same with me;
I curse her every hour sincerely,
Yet, hang me, but I love her dearly.

"Love Is Best" (5)

O! LET us love and have our day,
    All that the bitter greybeards say
Appraising at a single mite.
My Lesbia, suns can set and rise:
For us the brief light dawns and dies   5
Once only, and the rest is night.
A thousand kisses, then five score,
A thousand and a hundred more,
Then one for each you gave before.
Then, as the many thousands grow,   10
We'll wreck the counting lest we know,
Or lest an evil eye prevail
Through knowledge of the kisses' tale.

14. In Orcus; that is, in the abode of Orcus or Pluto, god of the underworld. Roman poets called him either Dis or Orcus.
Catullus Contrasts Quintia . . . ; "Love Is Best." Translated by Hugh MacNaghton. From *The Poems of Catullus* by Hugh MacNaghton. Reprinted by permission of The University Press, Cambridge, England.
On Lesbia. Translated by Jonathan Swift.

Of Metellus, Husband of Clodia

LESBIA reviles me when her husband's by.
    This throws the booby into ecstasy.
You senseless ass! Were I unnamed, forgot,
She were heart-whole: who snarls, forgets me not;
Who rails is angry. Sure, the wound is sore;   5
'Tis "The heart flames, the mouth proclaims" once
    more.

After a Quarrel

IF that which is the heart's desire be told
    Unhoped for, it is joy beyond the rest;
Therefore I count it joy more dear than gold
That, love, you turn again and make me blest;
You turn, my heart's desire so long denied,   5
Unasked, unhoped for. Oh! the white, bright day!
What happiness in all the world beside
Is like to mine? The rapture who shall say?

Doubt

THOUGH Jupiter himself should court her,
    My lady vows she'd marry only me.
She vows—but what a lady vows her lover
    Write on the wind and in the shifting sea.

True or False

NONE could ever say that she,
    Lesbia! was so loved by me.
Never all the world around
Faith so true as mine was found.
If no longer it endures   5
(Would it did!) the fault is yours.
I can never think again
Well of you: I try in vain.
But . . . be false . . . do what you will.—
Lesbia! I must love you still.

Odi et Amo

I LOVE and hate. Ah! never ask why so!
    I hate and love . . . and that is all I know.
I see 'tis folly; but I feel 'tis woe.

Of Metellus, Husband of Clodia; After a Quarrel. Translated by Hugh MacNaghton. From *The Poems of Catullus* by Hugh MacNaghton. Reprinted by permission of The University Press, Cambridge, England.
Doubt. Translated by Robert Warnock.
True or False. Translated by Walter Savage Landor.
Odi et Amo. Translated by Walter Savage Landor.

The Undying Fire (72)

ONCE you would say to me: 'Your heart has
found me
And yours alone.
I would not have the arms of Jove around me
More than your own.'
Saying it, you became no more the fashion   5
Of cheap desire,
But wife and child and home, loved with the pas-
sion
Of life-long fire.

I know you now. Yet my soul goes on burning,
As burn it must,   10
When you and all I gave to you are turning
To death and dust.
Strange, do you say? How strange that love should
cherish
Light that is gone!
That every kindly thought of you should perish, 15
Yet love last on.

Journey's End

THEY say that benefits to others rendered
Win in our memories their late reward.
They say that love, once it is loyally tendered,
Stays sweet and keeps the lover's heart unscarred.

If it is true that faith promised and given   5
Is profit, and a guileless heart is gain,
How surely shall I profit, who hath striven
So long with pain.

The gentle word, the generous intent,
The decent things that men can do or say,   10
All these to gladden her I freely spent
But could not touch her when she turned away.

Why then, you fool, cherish your long affliction?
Why fight against the thing that must prevail?
Put her away from you. Need resolution   15
Forever fail?

"It is impossible to lay aside forever
In one brief point of time the love of years."
Then do th' impossible. Steel yourself. Sever
This knot, and wring relief from bitter tears.   20

The Undying Fire. Translated by E. A. Havelock. From The Lyric
Genius of Catullus by E. A. Havelock. Reprinted by permission of
Basil Blackwell & Mott, Ltd.
Journey's End; The Office of My Heart. Translated by E. A. Have-
lock. From The Lyric Genius of Catullus by E. A. Havelock. Reprinted
by permission of Basil Blackwell & Mott, Ltd.

O gods, if yours be pity, yours compassion
Given to failing men even on the road
Leading to death, dispel this black obsession,
Rescue my soul from hell. Support its load—

How like a stupor every sense pervading   25
My sorrow steals! How faint I grow with grief!
How swift the sunlight of my life is fading,
My bliss how brief!

I look no more for her to be my lover
As I love her. That thing could never be.   30
Nor pray I for her purity—that's over.
Only this much I pray, that I be free,

Free from insane desire myself, and guarded
In peace at last. O heaven, grant that yet
The faith by which I've lived may be rewarded.   35
Let me forget.

Catullus Struggles to Be Free

CATULLUS, hapless one, be sane at last,
Believe your eyes, confess the past is past.
So bright, so white the suns that shone before!
Then where your lady led you followed fain,
And loved her as none else shall love again.   5
Ah! then the glad surprises and the play—
You wished it so, nor said your lady nay.
So white, so bright the suns that shine no more!
Now she says nay: ah! weakling, say it too,
Nor live to grieve, nor one who flies pursue,   10
But stubborn stand and bear the purpose through.
Lady, good-bye! now stands Catullus fast,
Nor woos against your will nor mourns the past:
But surely you shall mourn when wooed no more.
Poor culprit! ah, the days for you in store!   15
Who will now heed your beauty, take your hand?
Whom will you fondle? who will call you his?
Whose lips will you devour with kiss on kiss?
But thou, Catullus, stubborn, steadfast stand.

The Office of My Heart

THE office of my heart is still to love
When I would hate.
Time and again your faithlessness I prove
Proven too late.
Your ways might mend, yet my contempt could
never   5
Be now undone.
Yet crimes repeated cannot stop this fever
From burning on.

Catullus Struggles to Be Free. Translated by Hugh MacNaghton.
From The Poems of Catullus by Hugh MacNaghton. Reprinted by
permission of The University Press, Cambridge, England.

She That I Loved

SHE that I loved, that face,
  Those hands, that hair,
Dearer than all my race,
  As dear as fair—
See her where throngs parade   5
  Th' imperial route,
Plying her skill unpaid—
  Rome's prostitute.

At the Grave of His Brother

BY ways remote and distant waters sped,
  Brother, to thy sad graveside am I come,
That I may give the last gifts to the dead,
  And vainly parley with thine ashes dumb;
Since She who now bestows and now denies   5
  Have ta'en thee, hapless brother, from mine
    eyes.
But lo! These gifts, the heirlooms of past years,
  Are made sad things to grace thy coffin-shell;
Take them, all drenchèd with a brother's tears,
  And, brother, for all time, hail and farewell.

Sirmio (31)

GEM of all isthmuses and isles that lie
  Fresh or salt water's children, in clear lake
Or ampler ocean: with what joy do I
Approach thee, Sirmio! Oh! am I awake,
Or dream that once again my eye beholds   5
Thee, and has looked its last on Thynian wolds?
Sweetest of sweets to me that pastime seems,
When the mind drops her burden: when—the pain
Of travel past—our own cot we regain,
And nestle on the pillow of our dreams!   10
'Tis this one thought that cheers us as we roam.
Hail, O fair Sirmio! Joy, thy lord is here!
Joy too, ye waters of the Garda Mere!
And ring out, all ye laughter-peals of home.

She That I Loved. Translated by E. A. Havelock. From *The Lyric Genius of Catullus* by E. A. Havelock. Reprinted by permission of Basil Blackwell & Mott, Ltd.
At the Grave of His Brother. Translated by Aubrey Beardsley. The grave was at Rhoetum, which Catullus visited on his journey to Bithynia in Asia Minor in 57 B.C.
5. **She**, the goddess Fortuna. 10. **hail and farewell**, *Ave atque vale*, a common grave inscription.
Sirmio. Translated by Charles Stuart Calverley. Catullus's "all-but-island," since it was connected to the mainland by a narrow strip of land which was at times covered by water. In 56 B.C. Catullus was returning to his villa there from his journey to Bithynia. This fourteen-line poem has been called the first sonnet, though its resemblance to the later form is purely accidental.
13. **Garda Mere**, the lake of Garda, into which Sirmio stretched.

To Varus (22)

SUFFENUS, whom so well you know,
  My Varus, as a wit and beau,
Of smart address and smirking smile,
Will write you verses by the mile.
You cannot meet with daintier fare   5
Than title-page and binding are;
But when you once begin to read
You find it sorry stuff indeed,
And you are ready to cry out
Upon this beau—"O what a lout!"   10
No man on earth so proud as he
Of his own precious poetry,
Or knows such perfect bliss as when
He takes in hand that nibbled pen.
Have we not all some faults like these?   15
Are we not all Suffenuses?
In others the defect we find,
But cannot see our sack behind.

Ovid

43 B.C.–17 A.D.

The most scandalous of Roman love poets was Ovid, another playboy of the city smart set, who lacked entirely the emotional depths of Catullus and converted his many love affairs into fashionable erotic verse. Coming more than a generation after Catullus, he belonged to the empire in the glorious days of Augustus, but turned from the intellectual circles of Horace and Propertius to the demimonde that carried on the traditions of Clodia's salon. Publius Ovidius Naso (or Ovid, as we call him) was intended by his ambitious equestrian father for a career in the government and was sent from his provincial birthplace at Sulmo to schools in Rome and Athens. But when he settled in the capital, his attentions quickly shifted from law to poetry, for which he had shown a natural talent since childhood. Most of all, he enjoyed idleness and play and was to become Rome's poet of pleasure, especially amorous pleasure. These interests endeared him to the jaded fast set, whose poet laureate he was for thirty years.

Despite the questionable taste of much of his work and the frivolous insincerity of his mind, Ovid is a thoroughly charming writer of endless facility and bright grace. Unlike the studied verses of Virgil and Horace, his bubble on delightfully without effort or strain on the intellect. Even his most decadent love poems have an insidious effervescence that makes them highly entertaining. His *Amores*, 49 short lyrics, pretend to record an affair of his

To Varus. Translated by Walter Savage Landor.

own with a certain Corinna, who has eluded identification. Probably she is a composite figure made out of numerous mistresses; certainly the passion is feigned, as the sprightly mood and dainty style betray. Alexandrian influence is strong here as in the *Heroides*, a series of imaginary letters from mythical heroines like Penelope and Dido condemning their husbands or lovers for deserting them. The most notorious of his love poems is the *Art of Love*, a lively treatise giving instruction in the first two books to men, in the last one to women. But the "love" alluded to is mere physical conquest inspired by Ovid's own liaisons with Roman courtesans. A sequel provided instructions for falling out of love and into marriage; but whether it is love or marriage that he is discussing, his attitude is as amoral as it is amusing. However much it may entertain us, we must agree with Augustus that it does not conduce to sincere and lofty sentiment, a substantial family life, or even good citizenship.

As Ovid turned forty, his interests shifted to a larger sphere and a more serious theme, though he knew that he had not the seriousness of mind to attempt an epic. The fifteen books of the *Metamorphoses* display his endless ingenuity and great narrative skill in a kind of poetic summary of ancient myths. The old tales were of course familiar to his audience and in his time considered no more religious than we consider them. But he arranged them by a clever chronology according to the four ages of man—gold, silver, bronze, and iron—and built almost every one around a transformation of some kind, as the title indicates—the changing of Pygmalion's statue into a beautiful woman, the metamorphosis of the weeping Niobe into a column of stone and a spring. But it is the brilliant style and fanciful beauty of his world of fable that make the *Metamorphoses*, not simply our best compendium of classical myths, but a source of endless entertainment.

In 8 A.D. Ovid's career in Rome ended abruptly with his exile by Augustus to the barbarous town of Tomi on the Black Sea coast for reasons that are still obscure— "a poem and an error," he tells us: probably the *Art of Love*, written ten years before, and his complicity in an immoral affair of Augustus' granddaughter. The sentence was abrupt and cruel, for the gay poet of fashionable society was now lost in an uncultured wilderness; but his unmanly response to his misfortune does not inspire our pity. His work declined, and the *Tristia* in five books are wearisome complaints of his desolation. His whimpering betrays his fatal lack of character. It is best to remember Ovid in the gay and cynical capital of his youthful success.

The Art of Love

BOOK I

IF any here be ignorant of love,
  Let him read this, he shall a lover prove.
To sail swift ships, in chariots to ride,
Require an art; no less is art love's guide. . . .
Love raging is, he struggles oft with me,   5

*The Art of Love.*ᴬ Translated by Francis Wolferston.

But he's a boy and must directed be. . . .
So I can Love subdue, my heart though he
Wound with his bow, and dart his flames at me;
The more he doth vindictive torments make,
Greater shall be the vengeance that I take. . . .   10
Experience is my muse; the truths I know,
I sing; Venus, grace my beginnings now. . . .
  You who a soldier in this war would prove
Must labour first to find out whom to love,
And next, the girl that pleases you to gain,   15
And last that constant may her love remain.
This way, this manner to our course assign,
Nor must our chariot-wheel this goal decline.
  With out-cast lures, go round about, choose one
Of whom to say, 'She pleaseth me alone.'   20
Heaven will not drop one down; then look about
Until you find a pleasing beauty out.
The huntsman knows where best his toils to lay,
And in what dale the foaming boar to slay;
The fowler knows the trees, the angler's taught   25
To know the places where most fish are caught;
So you that would a lover be must walk
In groves where maidens love to meet and talk.
To find these out I would not bid you go
Afar, nor plough the ocean to and fro. . . .   30
But Rome so many beauties offers you—
None better though you search the wide world
      through.
As corn on Ida, grapes on Lesbos found,
As seas with fish, as trees with birds abound,
As heaven with stars, of maids so full is Rome: 35
The city of her son is Venus' home.
If that a tender growing age you prize,
Unstained virgins are before your eyes.
If one mature you seek, here thousands are;
You cannot choose one than the rest more fair.   40
If a grave matron do delight you much,
No trouble will you have in finding such.
  You in the theatre must a-hunting go—
Choice beauties there will best repay your vow.
There you will find with whom you may make bold
In dalliance, or perhaps for longer hold.   46
As busy ants in troops march to and fro—
With mouths full-stored with wonted food they go—
Or as the bee from grove to meadow hies,
There from one flower to another flies;   50
So thick the ladies to the stage repair:
Oft have I wondered at their numbers there.
Hither they come to see and to be seen—
Here modesty hath oft neglected been. . . .
And at the horse-race in the Circus too   55
Here opportunity will wait on you.
With look and nod you need not here beseech
Your mistress, nor with finger's silent speech,
But go straight to her, here by none denied,

36. her son, Aeneas.

The god Eros.

It often will young men with love inspire—
Love joined with wine is putting fire to fire.
Choose not in wine nor do so when 'tis night; 105
One injures judgment, and the other sight.
Paris by day the goddesses did see
When Venus was the fairest judged to be.
Night imperfection hides, will no fault show,
Makes them that are not fair seem to be so. 110
Rich gems and purple cloth by day peruse,
And in the sun a good complexion choose. . . .
   The several places where choice beauties be—
Thus far hath my Thalia sung to thee.
The fair one which thou most dost fancy, how 115
To obtain—the top of art—I'll teach thee now. . . .
Doubt not to gain what beauty e'er you choose;
'Mongst many you'll not find one to refuse.
They grant or they deny, yet love to be
Entreated; so no harm is done if she 120
Refuses. But why should she? Your love's new;
What's new is welcome—to the old adieu.
The corn is riper in adjacent fields;
Your neighbour's cow a larger udder yields.
   Before the mistress you must win the maid, 125
For she will help you in your escapade.
It is the handmaid that all secrets knows,
To whom the mistress will her thoughts disclose.
With gifts and promises corrupt her: she
Will bring you to her mistress willingly. 130
Like a physician, she a time will choose
When she you love is least apt to refuse.
At times of joy she won't from love recoil:
So standing corn thrives best in fatting soil.
When mirth she entertains, no griefs molest, 135
Venus is soon admitted to her breast.
Ilion, when sad, with arms defended sits;
When glad, the foe-containing horse admits.
Try when some rival steals her husband, too;
For her revenge on him she'll pleasure you. 140
The handmaid while she combs her mistress' hair
May further this, your faithfulness declare,
Suggest the husband should be made to rue:
'He takes elsewhere his pleasure; why not you?'
Your name she'll mention then and urge your praise,
Swear, if you have her not you'll end your days. 146
Make haste then and go to her lest she may
Be angry, and grow cold through your delay. . . .
   Times are appointed when to sow and reap,
And times when sailors venture on the deep: 150
So in your courting be not overlong;
For love there is a right time and a wrong.
When she her birthday keeps, or when the Queen
Of Love with Mars is in conjunction seen,
Or at those times when costly merchandise 155
Is in the Circus spread before your eyes,
Desist: when storms come with the Pleiades
And when the Goat is swallowed in the seas,
'Tis best leave off; then they which trust the deep

And gently join yourself unto her side. 60
If she refuse that you should sit so near,
The custom of the place allows it here.
Here you must ask (for 'tis the readiest way
To gain discourse) things in the present play:
Whose horse is this comes up? And then must you,
Whatever she commends, commend it too. . . . 66
Or if the dust raised high fall on her, then
You with your hand must brush it off again.
If none light on her, yet brush off that none;
Action in such a case becometh one. 70
If her loose mantle's trailing down, you must
Catch up the hem and keep it from the dust,
And when you stoop, observe with nimble eye
If you can there a dainty leg espy.
Take care lest they that sit behind should push, 75
Or with their knees her tender back should crush.
'Tis profitable—slight things please her oft—
With ready hand to make her cushions soft.
Some fanning cool air do their mistress move,
Or with a foot eased give a birth to love. 80
The Circus yields such opportunities;
The Forum too whereon the grim sand lies.
Cupid has oft in the arena fought,
And the spectator then has worse wounds caught
Than those he looks on; while he lays his bet 85
And asks his mistress who she thinks will get
The prize that day, himself is struck to the heart
And cries out, wounded with Love's cruel dart. . . .
Then if your mistress ask a prince's name,
O lover, or from where the captives came, 90
Her questions answer—whether she ask or not;
Pretend to knowledge which thou hast not got—
Name him Euphrates with his reedy crown;
That one is Tigris whose dark hair hangs down!
Call these Armenians, those Persians are, 95
Say 'tis a city in Achaemenia.
Some were once chieftains; these by right name call
If well you can; if not, feign names for all.
   Chance waits on you whene'er the banquet's spread
And something besides wine is to be had. . . . 100
Wine often will our private thoughts declare,
And by its means concealments banished are.

Scarce any part of their torn sails can keep. 160
Begin such time as Allia heretofore
Ran red, its waters stained with Roman gore;
Or on that feast begin to court again,
Which Syrians of Palestine ordain.
But let her birthday solemnly be spent; 165
A black day when you must a gift present:
Women for gifts will always find excuses
And put their lover's wealth to many uses.
The milliner will to your mistress go—
While you look on, to her his wares will show; 170
She'll your opinion ask and something try,
Then with a kiss solicit you to buy.
She'll say it will for long her uses fit—
'Tis very cheap and she hath need of it.
Then if you say you can't so much expend, 175
She'll bid you write for money from a friend.
Give her upon her birthday what you will—
Whate'er she wants, it is her birthday still;
Perhaps her jewelled ear-ring's dropped, she'll feign,
And then you must buy one for her again. 180
She'll borrow many things, yet none restore,
Nor shall your loss of them gain favour more.
Ten mouths, as many tongues, too little are
For me the arts of women to declare.

First must a letter sealed an entrance find; 185
Let your wax bear the impress of your mind.
And let your letter love-expressions bear,
To which you must add an imploring prayer.
Achilles at the king's request did send
Back Hector; Heaven will to prayers bend. 190
A promise hurts you not; then promise much;
It makes those that are not rich seem to be such.
Your letter wins her, if she credit it;
Hope's a false goddess, yet for you most fit.
Give her not much, for fear that you should part;
She only gains then; thou the loser art. 196
Be always giving, yet let nothing go:
Swains are with barren soil deluded so.
Thus gamblers fear to lose, yet losing more
Clutch at the dice that was their loss before. 200
You may her favour without gifts procure;
If she loves gratis, it will long endure.
With handsome words you must prepare her mind;
First try if those will entertainment find. . . .

I'd have young men to learn to plead a cause:
For them, not for their clients, is th' applause. 206
Women to him their pleasing glances send
Whom the grave judge and senators commend.
But wear your learning gracefully and well;
Let not your lips on tedious stories dwell. 210
Whoever to his mistress would declaim?
Lengthy epistles only bring you blame.
Use smooth and taking words, a handsome style,
That she may on your pleading language smile.

161–162. **Begin such time . . . gore**; that is, July 16, when the Gauls defeated the Romans on the Allia in 390 B.C.

Should she your letter back unopened send, 215
Proceed and hope she'll read it in the end. . . .
The softest drops by constant falling on
Will make impression on the hardest stone.
Persist; were she Penelope you'd gain;
Troy's towers late, but yet at last were ta'en. 220
Ere you ask her to write I bid you pause:
'Tis grace enough if she but look on yours.
If once she read she will write back, but these
Great favours she bestoweth by degrees.
Perhaps no pleasure her first letter brings— 225
Bids you not trouble her with such fond things;
But yet she hopes that you may fixed remain:
Pursue and fear not but you will obtain.

If you should see your mistress in the street
On litter borne, be wary when you meet; 230
Be sure that none o'erhear lest they defame
And add a scandal to your mistress' name.
If in the porch you chance to see her loiter,
Walk at a distance while you reconnoitre;
Sometimes before, sometimes behind her go, 235
Now you may walk apace, and then walk slow.
When you shall overtake her, don't divide,
But go as close as may be to her side.
Perchance if to the theatre she has gone,
There follow her, observe what she hath on; 240
There you may boldly look on her attire,
Commend her eyes and every part admire.
Applaud the woman in the mummer's art,
And favour him who acts a lover's part.
When she stands, stand; when she sits, do not stir,
And gladly spend your time observing her. 246

Do not use instruments to curl your hair,
Nor make your legs with pumice smooth and
    bare. . . .
Neatness delights; the fields won't tan too much;
Be sure your clothes are handsome, without smutch.
Keep shoe-straps smooth and let your teeth be fair;
And see they're not too big, the shoes you wear; 252
And then your hair in order neatly put,
And let your beard by skillful hands be cut.
Look that your nails be clean and keep them low,
Nor let the hairs within your nostrils grow. 256
Lest your presence should be known by other sense
Than sight, let your breath be without offence.
Leave other things for shameless maids to use,
And men that basely their own sex abuse. . . . 260

When Bacchus has presented gifts to you,
And should a lady share your banquet too,
The gods nocturnal you must beg to lend
Their aid, that wine may not your head offend.
You in a covert way may speak things so 265
That she, 'tis only she you mean, may know.
Let sweet discourse wait on your wine, that she
May mistress of your table choose to be;
And that your flame may be acknowledged, you
Must teach your looks as well as lips to woo. 270

First take the cup and kiss the very place
Which with her lips she did in drinking grace.
The food her fair hand touches, ask for, and
As you receive it, gently touch her hand.
Take care to please her husband also; such   275
A friend will expedite your business much.
When you drink, first to him your cup direct;
In keeping your head bare, show him respect.
Whether he be your equal or below,
Yet still a like respect unto him show.   280
Through friendship to deceive is saf'st of all;
Yet he that so deceives is criminal.
If friendship does some liberty permit,
You may take more as you've a mind to it.

    Observe to keep a mean in drinking, so   285
Your tongue and feet their office best will know.
Chiefly beware of quarrelling in wine,
For then your hands too much to blows incline. . . .
Have you a voice, then sing; if nimble, dance;
What pleasing part soe'er you have, advance.   290
Real drunkenness is harm, but so to feign
I think is good; pretend you can't speak plain,
Then if you speak or do what is unfit
The wine is judged to be the cause of it.
Say the man she'll sleep with shall most happy be,
But pray not for him if she means not thee.   296
The banquet ended and the table moved,
Then is your chance to show her she is loved.
The crowd itself allows that you should press
Her close; foot touches foot, fingers caress.   300
Now is the time to speak; what fears you have,
Banish: Venus and Fortune aid the brave.
Art cannot eloquence on you bestow:
Only begin, and you shall find it so.
You must act love, and feeling wounds must feign;
By all means try a promise to obtain.   306
Say she is lovely, and she will believe:
No woman thinks her looks are cause to grieve.
Oft a dissembler I have seen in love;
What first he feigned, at length did real prove.   310
Then, ladies, use men kindly; in the end
Their love proves true, which they at first pretend.
With praises you may captivate her mind,
So banks are with soft water undermined.
Her face admire, her lovely hair commend,   315
Her little slender foot, her dainty hand:
The chastest maids with praise delighted are,
A virgin's beauty is her love and care. . . .

    Fear not to promise—promises will move—
And call the gods as witness to your love.   320
Jove from above laughs at love's perjuries,—
Bidding Aeolus blow away such tricks,
For he himself to Juno swore by Styx
Falsely, and he our great exemplar is.
'Tis fit there should be gods; then gods there be;
In wine and incense let us pay their fee.   326
Be sure they do not bind themselves in sleep,

All seeing they; your life then harmless keep.
Restore what you have borrowed, none delude,
Nor have your hand in human blood imbrued.   330
Only to maids does falsehood go unblamed;
Break faith with women and be not ashamed.
Only deceive those who deceivers are,
And let them fall into their self-made snare. . . .
So perjury its own reward must earn,   335
And women who wrong us are wronged in turn.

    Shed tears, for they a stony heart will move;
By your wet eyes let her perceive your love.
If tears are lacking (for men cannot cry
At need), with a wet finger rub your eye.   340
Wise men mix kisses with the words they speak;
If they're not given, those ungiven take;
But she'll perhaps refuse and anger feign,
Yet wishes her resistance be in vain.
Take heed that when upon her lips you seize,   345
You press them not too hard lest it displease.
Who gains a kiss and other sweets get not,
Deserves to lose that kiss which he hath got.
If after kisses further pleasures were
Forgone, 'twas clownishness, not bashful fear.   350
She who is forced will find that forcing sweet:
Unwilling, willingly she will it meet.
She that's of Venus will no rape forsake,
But let her wantonness full pleasure take.   354
And she who might, yet doth untouched depart,
Although she may seem pleased, is sad at heart. . . .
They're bashful till the first time's over; then
Having once tried, they must be tried again.

    Too confident is he who doth expect
His mistress to ask first and him select.   360
First let the man approach her, and beseech;
A woman hearkens to a handsome speech.
Speak if you would obtain, she would be asked;
And your desire with words shall be unmasked.
Jove suppliant went unto the maids of old,   365
Deny his suit no maiden ever could.
If you perceive her scorn at and disdain
Your prayers, forbear; from her a while abstain.
They love what's not, at what is theirs they scoff,
Take their disdain away by keeping off.   370
Be always wooing and she'll never bend,
Sometimes a simple friendliness pretend.
I have known one this strategy display,
Come an adviser, and a lover stay.

    Sailors should not pale faces have, but be   375
Made swarthy by the sun and storms at sea. . . .
But lovers with a pining look excel;
Though some say not, yet it becomes them well. . . .
Thin looks a lover argue; sometimes wear
A hood and cover up your gleaming hair.   380
Sorrows and griefs immense with watchings late—
The effects of love—young men attenuate.
By looking melancholy, you will prove
Successful; all will say, 'This man's in love.'

And must I warn you now that wrong and right
Mean nothing? Truth and friendship turn to spite;
And if you praise your mistress to a friend,   387
His love for her begins and yours will end. . . .
Men nowadays are selfish, lost to shame;
To hurt another is their favourite game.   390
Ah, wicked times! Fear not an open foe;
Shun whom you trust and you may safely go.
Nor brother, nor a friend confide in; just
Occasion they will give you to mistrust.

I'd almost done; but women are diverse,   395
And each one's heart doth take a different course.
One kind of produce suits each piece of ground,
Here vines, there olives, elsewhere corn is found.
Hearts are so various, alike are none,
That a wise man prepares for every one. . . .   400
Some fish with darts are caught, others with hook,
And some within a hollow net are took.
With various ages various ways agree:
The older a woman grows, more wary she.
If learned to the rude you seem, or wanton to   405
The chaste, she will mistrust herself and you.
Hence timid women honest husbands lose;
Instead, a man of meaner sort they choose.

Part of my work remains, part now is made,
And here my ship is by her anchor stayed.

Metamorphoses

NARCISSUS

Thus did the nymphs in vain caress the boy,
He still was lovely, but he still was coy;
When one fair virgin of the slighted train   ?
Thus pray'd the gods, provok'd by his disdain,
"Oh may he love like me, and love like me in vain!"
Rhamnusia pity'd the neglected fair,   6
And with just vengeance answer'd to her pray'r.

There stands a fountain in a darksome wood,
Nor stain'd with falling leaves nor rising mud;
Untroubled by the breath of winds it rests,   10
Unsully'd by the touch of men or beasts;
High bow'rs of shady trees above it grow,
And rising grass and cheerful greens below.
Pleas'd with the form and coolness of the place,
And over-heated by the morning chase,   15
Narcissus on the grassy verdure lies:
But whilst within the crystal fount he tries
To quench his heat, he feels new heats arise.
For as his own bright image he survey'd,
He fell in love with the fantastic shade;   20

Metamorphoses. "Narcissus," translated by Joseph Addison;
"Pyramus and Thisbe," translated by Laurence Eusden; "Daedalus
and Icarus," translated by Samuel Croxall; "Baucis and Philemon,"
translated by John Dryden; "Orpheus and Eurydice," translated by
William Congreve.
1. **boy**, Narcissus. 6. **Rhamnusia**, Nemesis, goddess of divine vengeance.

And o'er the fair resemblance hung unmov'd,
Nor knew, fond youth! it was himself he lov'd.
The well-turn'd neck and shoulders he descries,
The spacious forehead, and the sparkling eyes;
The hands that Bacchus might not scorn to show,
And hair that round Apollo's head might flow;   26
With all the purple youthfulness of face,
That gently blushes in the wat'ry glass;
By his own flames consum'd the lover lies,
And gives himself the wound by which he dies.   30
To the cold water oft he joins his lips,
Oft catching at the beauteous shade he dips
His arms, as often from himself he slips.
Nor knows he who it is his arms pursue
With eager clasps, but loves he knows not who.   35
    What could, fond youth, this helpless passion
        move?
What kindle in thee this unpity'd love?
Thy own warm blush within the water glows,
With thee the colour'd shadow comes and goes,
Its empty being on thy self relies;   40
Step thou aside, and the frail charmer dies.

    Still o'er the fountain's wat'ry gleam he stood,
Mindless of sleep, and negligent of food.
Still view'd his face, and languish'd as he view'd.
At length he rais'd his head, and thus began   45
To vent his griefs, and tell the woods his pain.
"You trees," says he, "and thou surrounding grove,
Who oft have been the kindly scenes of love,
Tell me, if e'er within your shades did lie
A youth so tortur'd, so perplex'd as I?   50
I, who before me see the charming fair,
Whilst there he stands, and yet he stands not there:
In such a maze of love my thoughts are lost;
And yet no bulwark'd town, nor distant coast,
Preserves the beauteous youth from being seen,   55
No mountains rise, nor oceans flow between,
A shallow water hinders my embrace;
And yet the lovely mimic wears a face
That kindly smiles, and when I bend to join
My lips to his, he fondly bends to mine.   60
Hear, gentle youth, and pity my complaint,
Come from thy well, thou fair inhabitant.
My charms an easy conquest have obtain'd
O'er other hearts, by thee alone disdain'd.
But why should I despair? I'm sure he burns   65
With equal flames, and languishes by turns.
Whene'er I stoop he offers at a kiss,
And when my arms I stretch, he stretches his.
His eye with pleasure on my face he keeps,
He smiles my smiles, and when I weep he weeps.
Whene'er I speak, his moving lips appear   71
To utter something, which I cannot hear.
"Ah wretched me! I now begin too late
To find out all the long-perplex'd deceit:
It is myself I love, myself I see;   75
The gay delusion is a part of me.

I kindle up the fires by which I burn,
And my own beauties from the well return.
Whom should I court? how utter my complaint!
Enjoyment but produces my restraint,   80
And too much plenty makes me die for want.
How gladly would I from myself remove!
And at a distance set the thing I love.
My breast is warm'd with such unusual fire,
I wish him absent whom I most desire.   85
And now I faint with grief; my fate draws nigh;
In all the pride of blooming youth I die.
Death will the sorrows of my heart relieve:
Oh might the visionary youth survive,
I should with joy my latest breath resign!   90
But oh! I see his fate involv'd in mine."
This said, the weeping youth again return'd
To the clear fountain, where again he burn'd;
His tears defac'd the surface of the well,
With circle after circle, as they fell: 95
And now the lovely face but half appears,
O'er-run with wrinkles, and deform'd with tears.
"Ah whither," cries Narcissus, "dost thou fly?
Let me still feed the flame by which I die;
Let me still see, tho' I'm no further blest."   100
Then rends his garment off, and beats his breast:
His naked bosom redden'd with the blow,
In such a blush as purple clusters show,
Ere yet the sun's autumnal heats refine
Their sprightly juice, and mellow it to wine.   105
The glowing beauties of his breast he spies,
And with a new redoubled passion dies.
As wax dissolves, as ice begins to run,
And trickle into drops before the sun;
So melts the youth, and languishes away,   110
His beauty withers, and his limbs decay;
And none of those attractive charms remain,
To which the slighted Echo su'd in vain.
    She saw him in his present misery,
Whom, spight of all her wrongs, she griev'd to see.
She answer'd sadly to the lover's moan,   116
Sigh'd back his sighs, and groan'd to ev'ry groan:
"Ah youth! belov'd in vain," Narcissus cries;

*Narcissus
watching
his image
with Eros
in the background.
From a
Roman painting.*

"Ah youth! belov'd in vain," the nymph replies.
"Farewell," says he; the parting sound scarce fell
From his faint lips, but she reply'd, "Farewell."   121
Then on th' unwholesome earth he gasping lies,
Till death shuts up those self-admiring eyes.
To the cold shades his flitting ghost retires,
And in the Stygian waves itself admires.   125
    For him the Naiads and the Dryads mourn,
Whom the sad Echo answers in her turn,
And now the sister-nymphs prepare his urn:
When, looking for his corpse, they only found
A rising stalk, with yellow blossoms crown'd.   130

PYRAMUS AND THISBE

In Babylon, where first her queen, for state
    Rais'd walls of brick magnificently great,
Liv'd Pyramus and Thisbe, lovely pair!
He found no eastern youth his equal there,
And she beyond the fairest nymph was fair.   5
A closer neighbourhood was never known:
Tho' two the houses, yet the roof was one.
Acquaintance grew, th' acquaintance they improve
To friendship, friendship ripen'd into love:
Love had been crown'd, but impotently mad,   10
What parents could not hinder, they forbade.
For with fierce flames young Pyramus still burn'd,
And grateful Thisbe's flames as fierce return'd.
Aloud in words their thoughts they dare not break
But silent stand, and silent looks can speak.   15
The fire of love the more it is supprest,
The more it glows, and rages in the breast.
    When the division-wall was built, a chink
Was left, the cement unobserv'd to shrink.
So slight the cranny, that it still had been   20
For centuries unclos'd, because unseen.
But oh! what thing so small, so secret lies,
Which 'scapes, if form'd for love, a lover's eyes?
Ev'n in this narrow chink they quickly found
A friendly passage for a trackless sound.   25
Safely they told their sorrows and their joys,
In whisper'd murmurs, and a dying noise.
By turns to catch each other's breath they strove,
And suck'd in all the balmy breeze of love.
Oft as on diff'rent sides they stood, they cry'd,   30
"Malicious wall, thus lovers to divide!
Suppose, thou should'st awhile to us give place
To lock, and fasten in a close embrace:
But if too much to grant so sweet a bliss,
Indulge at least the pleasure of a kiss.   35
We scorn ingratitude: To thee, we know,
This safe conveyance of our minds we owe."
    Thus they their vain petition did renew
Till night, and then they softly sigh'd adieu.
But first they strove to kiss, and that was all;   40
Their kisses dy'd untasted on the wall.

130. **A rising stalk . . . crown'd,** the narcissus flower.

Soon as the morn had o'er the stars prevail'd,
And warn'd by Phoebus, flow'rs their dews exhal'd,
The lovers to their well-known place return,
Alike they suffer, and alike they mourn.   45
At last their parents they resolve to cheat,
(If to deceive in love be call'd deceit)
To steal by night from home, and thence unknown
To seek the fields, and quit th' unfaithful town.
But to prevent their wand'ring in the dark,   50
They both agree to fix upon a mark;
A mark that could not their designs expose:
The tomb of Ninus was the mark they chose;
There they might rest secure beneath the shade,
Which boughs, with snowy fruit encumber'd, made:
A wide-spread mulberry its rise had took   56
Just on the margin of a gurgling brook.
Impatient for the friendly dusk they stay;
And chide the slowness of departing day;
In western seas down sank at last the light,   60
From western seas up-rose the shades of night.
The loving Thisbe ev'n prevents the hour,
With cautious silence she unlocks the door,
And veils her face, and marching thro' the gloom
Swiftly arrives at th' assignation tomb.   65
For still the fearful sex can fearless prove;
Boldly they act, if spirited by love.
When lo! a lioness rush'd o'er the plain,
Grimly besmear'd with blood of oxen slain:
And what to the dire sight new horrors brought,   70
To slake her thirst the neighb'ring spring she sought.
Which, by the moon, when trembling Thisbe spies,
Wing'd with her fear, swift as the wind, she flies;
And in a cave recovers from her fright,
But dropp'd her veil, confounded in her flight.   75
When sated with repeated draughts, again
The queen of beasts scour'd back along the plain.
She found the veil, and mouthing it all o'er
With bloody jaws the lifeless prey she tore.
   The youth, who could not cheat his guards so soon,   80
Late came, and noted by the glimm'ring moon
Some savage feet, new printed on the ground,
His cheeks turn'd pale, his limbs no vigour found:
But, when advancing on, the veil he spied
Distain'd with blood, and ghastly torn, he cried, 85
"One night shall death to two young lovers give,
But she deserv'd unnumber'd years to live!
'Tis I am guilty, I have thee betray'd,
Who came not early, as my charming maid.
Whatever slew thee, I the cause remain,   90
I nam'd, and fix'd the place, where thou wast slain.
Ye lions from your neighb'ring dens repair,
Pity the wretch, this impious body tear!
But cowards thus for death can idly cry;
The brave still have it in their pow'r to die."   95
Then to th' appointed tree he hastes away,
The veil first gather'd, tho' all rent it lay:

The veil all rent, yet still itself endears,
He kist, and kissing, wash'd it with his tears.
"Tho' rich," he cry'd, "with many a precious stain,
Still from my blood a deeper tincture gain."   101
Then in his breast his shining sword he drown'd,
And fell supine, extended on the ground.
As out again the blade he dying drew,
Out spun the blood, and streaming upwards flew.
So if a conduit pipe e'er burst you saw,   106
Swift spring the gushing waters through the flaw:
Then spouting in a bow, they rise on high,
And a new fountain plays amid the sky.
The berries, stain'd with blood, began to show   110
A dark complexion, and forgot their snow;
While fatten'd with the flowing gore, the root
Was doom'd forever to a purple fruit.
   Meantime poor Thisbe fear'd, so long she stay'd,
Her lover might suspect a perjur'd maid.   115
Her fright scarce o'er, she strove the youth to find
With ardent eyes, which spoke an ardent mind.
Already in his arms, she hears him sigh
At her destruction, which was once so nigh.
The tomb, the tree, but not the fruit she knew,   120
The fruit she doubted for its alter'd hue.
Still as she doubts, her eyes a body found
Quiv'ring in death, and gasping on the ground.
She started back, the red her cheeks forsook,
And ev'ry nerve with thrilling horrors shook.   125
So trembles the smooth surface of the seas,
If brush'd o'er gently with a rising breeze.
But when her view her bleeding love confest,
She shriek'd, she tore her hair, she beat her breast;
She rais'd the body, and embrac'd it round,   130
And bath'd with tears unfeign'd the gaping wound.
Then her warm lips to the cold face apply'd.
"And is it thus, ah! thus we meet!" she cry'd.
"My Pyramus! whence sprung thy cruel fate?
My Pyramus!—ah! speak, e'er 'tis too late.   135
I, thy own Thisbe, but one word implore,
One word thy Thisbe never ask'd before."
At Thisbe's name, awak'd, he open'd wide
His dying eyes; with dying eyes he try'd
On her to dwell, but clos'd them slow, and dy'd.
   The fatal cause was now at last explor'd;   141
Her veil she knew, and saw his sheathless sword:
"From thy own hand thy ruin thou hast found,"
She said, "but love first taught that hand to wound
Ev'n I for thee as bold a hand can show,   145
And love, which shall as true direct the blow.
I will against the woman's weakness strive,
And never thee, lamented youth, survive.
The world may say, I caus'd, alas! thy death,
But saw thee breathless, and resign'd my breath.
Fate, tho' it conquers, shall no triumph gain,   151
Fate, that divides us, still divides in vain.
   "Now, both our cruel parents, hear my pray'r,
My pray'r to offer for us both I dare;

Oh! see our ashes in one urn confin'd,   155
Whom love at first, and fate at last has join'd.
The bliss you envy'd is not our request;
Lovers, when dead, may sure together rest.
Thou, tree, where now one lifeless lump is laid,
Ere long o'er two shalt cast a friendly shade.   160
Still let our loves from thee be understood,
Still witness in thy purple fruit our blood."
She spoke, and in her bosom plung'd the sword,
All warm and reeking from its slaughter'd lord.

The pray'r, which dying Thisbe had preferr'd,
Both gods and parents with compassion heard.   166
The whiteness of the mulberry soon fled,
And rip'ning sadden'd in a dusky red:
While both their parents their lost children mourn,
And mix their ashes in one golden urn.   170

DAEDALUS AND ICARUS

IN tedious exile now too long detain'd,
Daedalus languish'd for his native land:
The sea foreclos'd his flight; yet thus he said:
"Tho' earth and water in subjection laid,
O cruel Minos, thy dominion be,   5
We'll go thro' air; for sure the air is free."
Then to new arts his cunning thought applies,
And to improve the work of nature tries.
A row of quills in gradual order plac'd,
Rise by degrees in length from first to last;   10
As on a cliff th' ascending thicket grows,
Or different reeds the rural pipe compose.
Along the middle runs a twine of flax,
The bottom stems are join'd by pliant wax.
Thus, well compact, a hollow bending brings   15
The fine composure into real wings.
His boy, young Icarus, that near him stood,
Unthinking of his fate, with smiles pursu'd
The floating feathers, which the moving air
Bore loosely from the ground, and wafted here and
    there.   20
Or with the wax impertinently play'd,
And with his childish tricks the great design delay'd.
The final master-stroke at last impos'd,
And now, the neat machine completely clos'd;
Fitting his pinions on, a flight he tries,   25
And hung self-balanc'd in the beaten skies.
Then thus instructs his child: "My boy, take care
To wing your course along the middle air;
If low, the surges wet your flagging plumes,
If high, the sun the melting wax consumes: 30
Steer between both: nor to the northern skies,
Nor south Orion turn your giddy eyes;
But follow me: Let me before you lay
Rules for the flight, and mark the pathless way."
Then teaching, with a fond concern, his son,   35
He took the untry'd wings, and fix'd 'em on,
But fix'd with trembling hands; and, as he speaks,
The tears roll gently down his aged cheeks.

The fall of Icarus.
From a Roman painting.

Then kiss'd, and in his arms embrac'd him fast,
But knew not this embrace must be the last.   40
And mounting upward, as he wings his flight,
Back on his charge he turns his aching sight,
As parent birds, when first their callow care
Leave the high nest to tempt the liquid air;
Then cheers him on, and oft, with fatal art,   45
Reminds the stripling to perform his part.
These, as the angler at the silent brook,
Or mountain-shepherd leaning on his crook,
Or gaping ploughman from the vale descries,
They stare, and view 'em with religious eyes,   50
And straight conclude 'em gods; since none, but
    they,
Thro' their own azure skies could find a way.
Now Delos, Paros, on the left are seen,
And Samos, favour'd by Jove's haughty queen;
Upon the right, the isle Lebynthos nam'd,   55
And fair Calymne for its honey fam'd.
When now the boy, whose childish thoughts aspire
To loftier aims, and make him ramble high'r,
Grown wild, and wanton, more embolden'd flies
Far from his guide, and soars among the skies.   60
The soft'ning wax, that felt a nearer sun,
Dissolv'd apace, and soon began to run.
The youth in vain his melting pinions shakes,
His feathers gone, no longer care he takes:
"Oh! father, father," as he strove to cry,   65
Down to the sea he tumbled from on high,
And found his fate; yet still subsists by fame,
Among those waters that retain his name.
The father, now no more a father, cries,
"Ho, Icarus! where are you?" as he flies;   70
"Where shall I seek my boy?" he cries again,
And saw his feathers scatter'd on the main.
Then curs'd his art; and fun'ral rites conferr'd,
Naming the country from the youth interr'd.
A partridge, from a neighb'ring stump, beheld

The sire his monumental marble build;   76
Who, with peculiar call, and flutt'ring wing,
Chirpt joyful, and malicious seem'd to sing:
The only bird of all its kind, and late
Transform'd in pity to a feather'd state: 80
From whence, O Daedalus, thy guilt we date.

BAUCIS AND PHILEMON

HEAV'N's pow'r is infinite: earth, air, and sea,
    The manufactur'd mass, the making pow'r
    obey
By proof to clear your doubt: in Phrygian ground
Two neighb'ring trees, with walls encompass'd
    round,
Stand on a mod'rate rise, with wonder shown,   5
One a hard oak, a softer linden one. . . .
Not far from thence is seen a lake, the haunt
Of coots, and of the fishing cormorant:
Here Jove with Hermes came; but in disguise
Of mortal men conceal'd their deities;   10
One laid aside his thunder, one his rod;
And many toilsome steps together trod:
For harbour at a thousand doors they knock'd,
Not one of all the thousand but was lock'd.
At last an hospitable house they found,   15
A homely shed; the roof, not far from ground,
Was thatch'd with reeds, and straw together bound.
There Baucis and Philemon liv'd, and there
Had liv'd long marry'd, and a happy pair:
Now old in love, though little was their store,   20
Inur'd to want, their poverty they bore,
Nor aim'd at wealth, professing to be poor.
For master or for servant here to call,
Was all alike, where only two were all.
Command was none, where equal love was paid,
Or rather both commanded, both obey'd.   26
   From lofty roofs the gods repuls'd before,
Now stooping, enter'd through the little door:
The man (their hearty welcome first express'd)
A common settle drew for either guest,   30
Inviting each his weary limbs to rest.
But ere they sat, officious Baucis lays
Two cushions stuff'd with straw, the seat to raise;
Coarse, but the best she had; then rakes the load
Of ashes from the hearth, and spreads abroad   35
The living coals; and, lest they should expire,
With leaves, and bark she feeds her infant fire:
It smokes; and then with trembling breath she
    blows,
Till in a cheerful blaze the flames arose.
With brush-wood and with chips she strengthens
    these,   40
And adds at last the boughs of rotten trees.
The fire thus form'd, she sets the kettle on,
(Like burnish'd gold the little seether shone)
Next took the coleworts which her husband got   44
From his own ground (a small well-water'd spot);

She stripp'd the stalks of all their leaves; the best
She cull'd, and them with handy care she drest.
High o'er the hearth a chine of bacon hung;
Good old Philemon seiz't it with a prong,
And from the sooty rafter drew it down,   50
Then cut a slice, but scarce enough for one;
Yet a large portion of a little store,
Which for their sakes alone he wish'd were more.
This in the pot he plung'd without delay,
To tame the flesh, and drain the salt away.   55
The time between, before the fire they sat,
And shorten'd the delay by pleasing chat.
   A beam there was, on which a beechen pail
Hung by the handle, on a driven nail:
This fill'd with water, gently warm'd, they set   60
Before their guests; in this they bath'd their feet,
And after with clean towels dry'd their sweat.
This done, the host produc'd the genial bed,
Sallow the feet, the borders, and the sted,
Which with no costly coverlet they spread,   65
But coarse old garments; yet such robes as these
They laid alone, at feasts or holidays.
The good old housewife, tucking up her gown,
The table sets; th' invited gods lie down.
The trivet-table of a foot was lame,   70
A blot which prudent Baucis overcame,
Who thrusts beneath the limping leg a sherd,
So was the mended board exactly rear'd:
Then rubb'd it o'er with newly gather'd mint,
A wholesome herb, that breath'd a grateful scent.
Pallas began the feast, where first was seen   76
The party-colour'd olive, black, and green:
Autumnal cornels next in order serv'd,
In lees of wine well pickled and preserv'd.
A garden salad was the third supply,   80
Of endive, radishes, and succory:
Then curds, and cream, the flow'r of country fare,
And new-laid eggs, which Baucis' busy care
Turn'd by a gentle fire, and roasted rare.
All these in earthen ware were serv'd to board;   85
And next in place, an earthen pitcher stor'd,
With liquor of the best the cottage could afford.
This was the table's ornament, and pride,
With figures wrought: like pages at his side
Stood beechen bowls; and these were shining clean,
Varnish'd with wax without, and lin'd within.   91
By this the boiling kettle had prepar'd,
And to the table sent the smoking lard;
On which with eager appetite they dine,
A sav'ry bit, that serv'd to relish wine: 95
The wine itself was suiting to the rest,
Still working in the must, and lately press'd.
The second course succeeds like that before,
Plums, apples, nuts, and of their wintry store
Dry figs, and grapes, and wrinkled dates were set
In canisters, t' enlarge the little treat: 101
All these a milk-white honey-comb surround,

Which in the midst the country banquet crown'd:
But the kind hosts their entertainment grace
With hearty welcome, and an open face: 105
In all they did, you might discern with ease,
A willing mind, and a desire to please.

 Meantime the beechen bowls went round, and
  still,
Though often empty'd, were observ'd to fill;
Fill'd without hands, and of their own accord   110
Ran without feet, and danc'd about the board.
Devotion seiz'd the pair, to see the feast
With wine, and of no common grape, increas'd;
And up they held their hands, and fell to pray'r,
Excusing, as they could, their country fare,   115

 One goose they had ('twas all they could allow),
A wakeful sentry, and on duty now,
Whom to the gods for sacrifice they vow:
Her with malicious zeal the couple view'd;
She ran for life, and limping they pursu'd: 120
Full well the fowl perceiv'd their bad intent,
And would not make her master's compliment;
But persecuted, to the pow'rs she flies,
And close between the legs of Jove she lies:
He with a gracious ear the suppliant heard,   125
And sav'd her life; then what he was declar'd,
And own'd the god. "The neighbourhood," said he,
"Shall justly perish for impiety:
You stand alone exempted; but obey   129
With speed, and follow where we lead the way:
Leave these accurs'd; and to the mountain's height
Ascend; nor once look backward in your flight."

 They haste, and what their tardy feet deny'd,
The trusty staff (their better leg) supply'd.
An arrow's flight they wanted to the top,   135
And there secure, but spent with travel, stop;
Then turn their now no more forbidden eyes;
Lost in a lake the floated level lies:
A wat'ry desert covers all the plains,
Their cot alone, as in an isle, remains.   140
Wond'ring with weeping eyes, while they deplore
Their neighbours' fate, and country now no more,
Their little shed, scarce large enough for two,
Seems, from the ground increas'd, in height and bulk
  to grow.
A stately temple shoots within the skies,   145
The crotchets of their cot in columns rise:
The pavement polish'd marble they behold,
The gates with sculpture grac'd, the spires and tiles
  of gold.

 Then thus the sire of gods, with looks serene:
"Speak thy desire, thou only just of men;   150
And thou, O woman, only worthy found
To be with such a man in marriage bound."

 Awhile they whisper; then, to Jove address'd,
Philemon thus prefers their joint request:
"We crave to serve before your sacred shrine,   155
And offer at your altars rites divine:

And since not any action of our life
Has been polluted with domestic strife;
We beg one hour of death, that neither she
With widow's tears may live to bury me,   160
Nor weeping I, with wither'd arms may bear
My breathless Baucis to the sepulchre."

 The godheads sign their suit. They run their race
In the same tenour all th' appointed space:
Then, when their hour was come, while they relate
These past adventures at the temple gate,   166
Old Baucis is by old Philemon seen
Sprouting with sudden leaves of spritely green:
Old Baucis look'd where old Philemon stood,
And saw his lengthen'd arms a sprouting wood;   170
New roots their fasten'd feet begin to bind,
Their bodies stiffen in a rising rind:
Then, ere the bark above their shoulders grew,
They give, and take at once their last adieu.   174
At once, "Farewell, O faithful spouse," they said;
At once th' incroaching rinds their closing lips in-
  vade.
Ev'n yet, an ancient Tyanaean shows
A spreading oak, that near a linden grows;
The neighbourhood confirm the prodigy,
Grave men, not vain of tongue, or like to lie.   180
I saw myself the garlands on their boughs,
And tablets hung for gifts of granted vows;
And off'ring fresher up, with pious pray'r,
The good, said I, are God's peculiar care,
And such as honour heav'n, shall heav'nly honour
  share.

ORPHEUS AND EURYDICE

Thence, in his saffron robe, for distant Thrace,
Hymen departs, thro' air's unmeasur'd space;
By Orpheus call'd, the nuptial pow'r attends,
But with ill-omen'd augury descends;   4
Nor cheerful look'd the god, nor prosp'rous spoke,
Nor blaz'd his torch, but wept in hissing smoke.
In vain they whirl it round, in vain they shake,
No rapid motion can its flames awake.

 With dread these inauspicious signs were view'd,
And soon a more disastrous end ensu'd;   10
For as the bride, amid the Naiad train,
Ran joyful, sporting o'er the flow'ry plain,
A venom'd viper bit her as she pass'd;
Instant she fell, and sudden breath'd her last.

 When long his loss the Thracian had deplor'd,   15
Not by superior pow'rs to be restor'd;
Inflam'd by love, and urg'd by deep despair,
He leaves the realms of light, and upper air;
Daring to tread the dark Tenarian road,
And tempt the shades in their obscure abode;   20
Thro' gliding spectres of th' interr'd to go,
And phantom people of the world below:
Persephone he seeks, and him who reigns
O'er ghosts, and hell's uncomfortable plains.

Arriv'd, he, tuning to his voice his strings, 25
Thus to the king and queen of shadows sings:
"Ye pow'rs, who under earth your realms extend,
To whom all mortals must one day descend:
If here 'tis granted sacred truth to tell;
I come not curious to explore your hell; 30
Nor come to boast (by vain ambition fir'd)
How Cerberus at my approach retir'd.
My wife alone I seek; for her lov'd sake
These terrors I support, this journey take.
She, luckless wand'ring, or by fate misled, 35
Chanc'd on a lurking viper's crest to tread;
The vengeful beast, enflam'd with fury, starts,
And thro' her heel his deathful venom darts.
Thus was she snatch'd untimely to her tomb;
Her growing years cut short, and springing bloom.
Long I my loss endeavour'd to sustain, 41
And strongly strove, but strove, alas, in vain:
At length I yielded, won by mighty love;
Well known is that omnipotence above!
But here, I doubt, his unfelt influence fails; 45
And yet a hope within my heart prevails,
That here, ev'n here, he has been known of old;
At least, if truth be by tradition told;
If fame of former rapes belief may find,
You both by love, and love alone were join'd. 50
Now, by the horrors which these realms surround,
By the vast chaos of these depths profound;
By the sad silence which eternal reigns
O'er all the waste of these wide-stretching plains;
Let me again Eurydice receive, 55
Let fate her quick-spun thread of life re-weave.
All our possessions are but loans from you,
And soon, or late, you must be paid your due;
Hither we haste to human-kind's last seat,
Your endless empire, and our sure retreat. 60
She too, when ripen'd years she shall attain,
Must, of avoidless right, be yours again:
I but the transient use of that require,
Which soon, too soon, I must resign entire.
But if the destines refuse my vow, 65
And no remission of her doom allow;
Know, I'm determin'd to return no more;
So both retain, or both to life restore."
Thus, while the bard melodiously complains,
And to his lyre accords his vocal strains, 70
The very bloodless shades attention keep,
And silent, seem compassionate to weep;
Ev'n Tantalus his flood unthirsty views,
Nor flies the stream, nor he the stream pursues;
Ixion's wond'ring wheel its whirl suspends, 75
And the voracious vulture, charm'd, attends . . .
Then first ('tis said) by sacred verse subdu'd,
The Furies felt their cheeks with tears bedew'd:
Nor could the rigid king, or queen of hell,
Th' impulse of pity in their hearts repel. 80
Now, from a troop of shades that last arriv'd,

Eurydice was call'd, and stood reviv'd.
Slow she advanc'd, and halting seem'd to feel
The fatal wound, yet painful in her heel.
Thus he obtains the suit so much desir'd, 85
On strict observance of the terms requir'd:
For if, before he reach the realms of air,
He backward cast his eyes to view the fair,
The forfeit grant, that instant, void is made,
And she forever left a lifeless shade. 90
Now thro' the noiseless throng their way they
bend,
And both with pain the rugged road ascend;
Dark was the path, and difficult, and steep,
And thick with vapours from the smoky deep.
They well-nigh now had pass'd the bounds of night,
And just approach'd the margin of the light, 96
When he, mistrusting lest her steps might stray,
And gladsome of the glimpse of dawning day,
His longing eyes, impatient, backward cast
To catch a lover's look, but look'd his last; 100
For, instant dying, she again descends,
While he to empty air his arms extends.
Again she dy'd, nor yet her lord reprov'd;
What could she say, but that too well he lov'd?
One last farewell she spoke, which scarce he heard;
So soon she dropp'd, so sudden disappear'd. 106
All stunn'd he stood, when thus his wife he
view'd
By second fate, and double death subdu'd . . .
Now to repass the Styx in vain he tries,
Charon averse, his pressing suit denies. 110
Sev'n days entire, along th' infernal shores,
Disconsolate, the bard Eurydice deplores;
Defil'd with filth his robe, with tears his cheeks,
No sustenance but grief, and cares he seeks;
Of rigid fate incessant he complains, 115
And hell's inexorable gods arraigns.
This ended, to high Rhodope he hastes,
And Haemus' mountain, bleak with northern blasts.
And now his yearly race the circling sun
Had thrice compleat thro' wat'ry Pisces run, 120
Since Orpheus fled the face of womankind,
And all soft union with the sex declin'd. . . .
A hill there was, and on that hill a mead,
With verdure thick, but destitute of shade.
Where, now, the Muses' son no sooner sings, 125
No sooner strikes his sweet resounding strings,
But distant groves the flying sounds receive,
And list'ning trees their rooted stations leave;
Themselves transplanting, all around they grow,
And various shades their various kinds bestow. 130
Here, tall Chaonian oaks their branches spread,
While weeping poplars there erect their head. . . .
Here, brittle hazels, laurels here advance,
And there tough ash to form the hero's lance;
Here silver first with knotless trunks ascend, 135
There, scarlet oaks beneath their acorns bend.

That spot admits the hospitable plain,
On this, the maple grows with clouded grain;
Here wat'ry willows are with lotus seen,
There, tamarisk, and box forever green.   140
With double hue here myrtles grace the ground,
And laurestines, with purple berries crown'd.
With pliant feet, now, ivies this way wind,
Vines yonder rise, and elms with vines entwin'd.
Wild Ornus now, the pitch-tree next takes root,   145
And arbutus adorn'd with blushing fruit.
Then easy bending palms, the victor's prize,
And pines erect with bristly tops arise.
To Rhea grateful still the pine remains,
For Atys still some favour she retains;   150
He once in human shape her breast had warm'd,
And now is cherish'd to a tree transform'd.

Juvenal

60–140 A.D.

In the Silver Age the stoic intellectualism of the
Romans hardened into a cold and cynical aloofness and produced the formal satire as the one literary invention of Rome. The first Roman satirist, Lucilius (180–
102 B.C.), survives only in fragments. Horace wrote playful satires on men and manners, and Persius (34–62 A.D.)
used the satire to dispense Stoic morality. It remained for
Juvenal, Rome's master of the form, to apply it to the social evils of his day and to show how a vitriolic pen can
annihilate one's enemies. Certainly Rome in its decline
offered abundant material for attack, but the savage in-
vective of Juvenal springs from a personal pessimism close
to misanthropy.

Decimus Junius Juvenalis, to give him his full name,
is known chiefly through his works; the many medieval
biographies of the man are largely fictitious. Born in
Aquinum in central Italy he became a rhetorician in
Rome. There he attached himself to several wealthy
patrons, but the humiliation of such a situation and his
persistent poverty soured his nature, and he vented his
spleen against the rich and successful in a series of
moralistic satires. A doubtful tradition adds that his
lampoon of the actor Paris was later misunderstood as
an attack on an actor close to the throne and that Juvenal
was consequently exiled to a military post in distant
Egypt or possibly Britain.

His sixteen satires, written between 100 and 128 A.D.,
are the venomous outpourings of a middle-aged man,
grown disgruntled with failure and self-righteous in his
stoic morality. His hatred of vice and love of simple living
sound genuine, but the shocking picture of conditions in
Rome in the Third Satire is certainly exaggerated. Yet it
has contributed heavily to our grim impression of the city
in its decline and inspired Dr. Johnson's satire of another
city, *London*, many centuries later. The Sixth Satire is the

bitterest diatribe against woman ever penned, and the
Tenth is the source of Johnson's *Vanity of Human Wishes*
with its noble pessimism about human hopes and ambitions. Everywhere in Juvenal we meet the same indignant
censure of a world lost to the vilest corruption; no hopeful
rays illuminate the sordid picture. Granted the unfairness
of his jaundiced eye, we can still enjoy the incessant lash of
his attack and the stately rhetoric in which he phrased it.

Third Satire

Umbritius, a friend of the author, disgusted at the
prevalence of vice and the disregard of unassuming virtue, is on the point of quitting Rome; and when a little
way from the city, stops short to acquaint the poet, who
has accompanied him, with the causes of his retirement.
These may be arranged under the following heads: that
flattery and vice are the only thriving arts at Rome; in
these, especially the first, foreigners have a manifest superiority over the natives, and consequently engross all
favor; that the poor are universally exposed to scorn and
insult; that the general habits of extravagance render it
difficult for them to subsist; that the want of a well-
regulated police subjects them to numberless miseries and
inconveniences, aggravated by the crowded state of the
capital, from all which a country life is happily free: on
the tranquillity and security of which he dilates with
great beauty.

GRIEVED though I am to see the man depart,
Who long has shared, and still must share,
          my heart,
Yet (when I call my better judgment home)
I praise his purpose: to retire from Rome
And give, on Cumae's solitary coast,   5
The Sibyl one inhabitant to boast!
  Full on the road to Baiae, Cumae lies,
And many a sweet retreat her shore supplies—
Though I prefer ev'n Prochyta's bare strand
To the Suburra; for what desert land,   10
What wild, uncultured spot, can more affright
Than fires wide blazing through the gloom of night,
Houses, with ceaseless ruin, thundering down,
And all the horrors of this hateful town?
Where poets, while the dog-star glows, rehearse   15
To gasping multitudes their barbarous verse!
  Now had my friend, impatient to depart,
Consigned his little all to one poor cart:
For this, without the town he chose to wait;   19
But stopped a moment at the Conduit-gate. . . .

Third Satire. Translated by William Gifford.
7. **Baiae**, a fashionable watering-place. 9–10. **Prochyta's bare
strand . . . Suburra.** Prochyta was a desolate volcanic island; the
Suburra, the busiest and most questionable section of Rome.

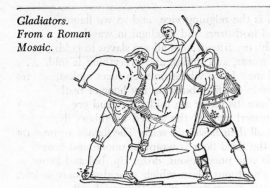

*Gladiators.
From a Roman
Mosaic.*

Umbritius here his sullen silence broke,
And turned on Rome, indignant, as he spoke.
Since virtue droops, he cried, without regard,
And honest toil scarce hopes a poor reward;
Since every morrow sees my means decay, 25
And still makes less the little of today;
I go where Daedalus, as poets sing,
First checked his flight and closed his weary wing:
While something yet of health and strength remains,
And yet no staff my faltering step sustains; 30
While few grey hairs upon my head are seen,
And my old age is vigorous still and green.
Here, then, I bid my much-loved home farewell—
Ah, mine no more!—there let Arturius dwell,
And Catullus, knaves who, in truth's despite, 35
Can white to black transform, and black to white,
Build temples, furnish funerals, auctions hold,
Farm rivers, ports, and scour the drains for gold!
    Once they were trumpeters, and always found
With strolling fencers in their annual round, 40
While their puffed cheeks, which every village knew,
Called to "high feats of arms" the rustic crew.
Now they give shows themselves, and, at the will
Of the base rabble, raise the sign—to kill,
Ambitious of their voice; then turn once more 45
To their vile gains, and farm the common shore!
And why not everything?—since Fortune throws
Her more peculiar smiles on such as those
Whene'er, to wanton merriment inclined,
She lifts to thrones the dregs of humankind! 50
    But why, my friend, should I at Rome remain?
I cannot teach my stubborn lips to feign;
Nor, when I hear a great man's verses, smile,
And beg a copy, if I think them vile.
A sublunary wight, I have no skill 55
To read the stars. I neither can nor will
Presage a father's death. I never pried
In toads for poison, nor—in aught beside.
Others may aid the adulterer's vile design,
And bear the insidious gift and melting line, 60
Seduction's agents! I such deeds detest;

And, honest, let no thief partake my breast.
For this, without a friend, the world I quit;
A palsied limb, for every use unfit. 64
    Who now is loved, but he whose conscious breast
Swells with dark deeds, still, still to be supprest?
He pays, he owes, thee nothing (strictly just),
Who gives an honest secret to thy trust.
But a dishonest!—there he feels thy power,
And buys thy friendship high from hour to hour. 70
But let not all the wealth which Tagus pours
In Ocean's lap, not all his glittering stores,
Be deemed a bribe sufficient to requite
The loss of peace by day, of sleep by night.
O take not, take not, what thy soul rejects, 75
Nor sell the faith which he who buys suspects!
    The nation, by the great admired, carest,
And hated, shunned by me above the rest,
No longer now restrained by wounded pride,
I haste to show (nor thou my warmth deride), 80
I cannot rule my spleen and calmly see
A Grecian capital in Italy!
Grecian? O no! With this vast sewer compared,
The dregs of Greece are scarcely worth regard.
Long since, the stream that wanton Syria laves 85
Has disembogued its filth in Tiber's waves,
Its language, arts; o'erwhelmed us with the scum
Of Antioch's streets, its minstrel, harp, and drum.
Hie to the Circus! There in crowds they stand, 89
Tires on their head and timbrels in their hand. . . .
    For lo! where versed in every soothing art,
The wily Greek assails his patron's heart,
Finds in each dull harangue an air, a grace,
And all Adonis in a Gorgon face;
Admires the voice that grates upon the ear 95
Like the shrill scream of amorous chanticleer;
And equals the crane neck and narrow chest
To Hercules, when, straining to his breast
The giant son of Earth, his every vein
Swells with the toil and more than mortal pain. 100
    We too can cringe as low and praise as warm,
But flattery from the Greeks alone can charm.
See! They step forth and figure to the life
The naked nymph, the mistress, or the wife,
So just, you view the very woman there, 105
And fancy all beneath the girdle bare!
No longer now the favourites of the stage
Boast their exclusive power to charm the age;
The happy art with them a nation shares:
Greece is a theatre, where all are players. 110
For lo! their patron smiles—they burst with mirth;

27. **Daedalus.** Escaping from the labyrinth of Crete, Daedalus flew on wings of wax and descended to earth at Cumae, where he built a temple to Apollo.

71. **Tagus,** a river in central Spain, renowned as a bearer of gold. 83. **Grecian? O no!** The Greeks had long since been conquered by the Romans and were now despised at Rome for their Oriental ways. 85. **the stream . . . laves,** the Orontes, largest river in Syria. 88. **minstrel, harp, and drum.** Greek and Oriental street-musicians were hired to play at Roman banquets. 99. **giant son of Earth,** Antaeus. 104. **The naked nymph . . . wife.** So the debased Greek can play the woman's role offstage.

He weeps—they droop, the saddest souls on earth;
He calls for fire—they court the mantle's heat;
'Tis warm, he cries—and they dissolve in sweat.
Ill-matched!—secure of victory they start,   115
Who, taught from youth to play a borrowed part,
Can with a glance the rising passion trace
And mould with their own to suit their patron's
      face;
At deeds of shame their hands admiring raise,
And mad debauchery's worst excesses praise.   120

Besides, no mound their raging lust restrains;
All ties it breaks, all sanctity profanes;
Wife, virgin-daughter, son unstained before—
And where these fail, they tempt the grandam hoar.
They notice every word, haunt every ear,   125
Your secrets learn, and fix you theirs from fear. . . .

Produce at Rome your witness: let him boast
The sanctity of Berecynthia's host,
To search his rent-roll first the bench prepares;
His honesty employs their latest cares.   130
What table does he keep, what slaves maintain,
And what, they ask, and where, is his domain?
These weighty matters known, his faith they rate,
And square his probity to his estate.
The poor may swear by all the immortal powers,
By the great gods of Samothrace and ours;   136
His oaths are false, they cry; he scoffs at heaven
And all its thunders; scoffs—and is forgiven!
Add that the wretch is still the theme of scorn
If the soiled cloak be patched, the gown o'erworn;
If through the bursting shoe the foot be seen,   141
Or the coarse seam tell where the rent has been.
O Poverty, thy thousand ills combined
Sink not so deep into the generous mind
As the contempt and laughter of mankind! . . .

There's many a part of Italy, 'tis said,   146
Where none assumes the toga but the dead.
There, when the toil foregone and annual play
Mark from the rest some high and solemn day,
To theatres of turf the rustics throng,   150
Charmed with the farce that charmed their sires so
      long;
While the pale infant, of the mask in dread,
Hides in his mother's breast his little head.
No modes of dress high birth distinguish there:
All ranks, all orders, the same habit wear,   155
And the dread aedile's dignity is known,
O sacred badge! by his white vest alone.
But here, beyond our power arrayed we go,
In all the gay varieties of show;
And when our purse supplies the charge no more,
Borrow, unblushing, from our neighbor's store.   161

128. **Berecynthia's host.** Berecynthia was a surname of Cybele, the
Great Mother. Hence, an unquestionable proof of the honesty of the
witness.   147. **Where none assumes . . . dead.** This is an indication of the simplicity of country life in contrast to the city of Rome,
where a gentleman had to buy several new togas each year.

Such is the reigning vice, and so we flaunt,
Proud in distress and prodigal in want!
Briefly, my friend, here all are slaves to gold;
And words, and smiles, and everything is sold. . . .

O! may I live where no such fears molest,   166
No midnight fires burst on my hour of rest!
For here 'tis terror all; midst the loud cry
Of "water! water!" the scared neighbors fly,
With all their haste can seize. The flames aspire,   170
And the third floor is wrapt in smoke and fire
While you, unconscious, doze. Up, ho! and know,
The impetuous blaze which spreads dismay below,
By swift degrees will reach the aerial cell   174
Where, crouching, underneath the tiles you dwell,
Where your tame doves their golden couplets rear,
"And you could no mischance but drowning fear!"
"Codrus had but one bed, and that too short
For his short wife;" his goods of every sort
Were else but few: six little pipkins graced   180
His cupboard head; a little can was placed
On a snug shelf beneath, and near it lay
A Chiron, of the same cheap marble—clay.
And was this all? O no: he yet possest
A few Greek books, shrined in an ancient chest,   185
Where barbarous mice through many an inlet crept
And fed on heavenly numbers while he slept.
"Codrus, in short, had nothing." You say true;
And yet poor Codrus lost that nothing too!
One curse alone was wanting to complete   190
His woes: that, cold and hungry, through the street
The wretch should beg, and in the hour of need
Find none to lodge, to clothe him, or to feed!
But should the raging flames on grandeur prey,
And low in dust Asturius' palace lay,   195
The squalid matron sighs, the senate mourns,
The pleaders cease, the judge the court adjourns;

*A mother
and daughter
before the
Roman judges.*

All join to wail the city's hapless fate
And rail at fire with more than common hate.   199
Lo! while it burns, the obsequious courtiers haste,
With rich materials to repair the waste.
This brings him marble, that a finished piece,
The far-famed boast of Polyclete and Greece;
This, ornaments which graced of old the fane

183. **A Chiron.** A clay statue of Chiron, the noble Centaur, was one
of the few possessions of humble Codrus.   203. **Polyclete,** the great
Greek sculptor.

Of Asia's gods; that, figured plate and plain; 205
This, cases, books, and busts the shelves to grace,
And piles of coin his specie to replace.
So much the childless Persian swells his store
(Though deemed the richest of the rich before)
That all ascribe the flames to thirst of pelf 210
And swear, Asturius fired his house himself.

O, had you, from the Circus, power to fly,
In many a halcyon village might you buy
Some elegant retreat for what will here
Scarce hire a gloomy dungeon through the year! 215
There wells, by nature formed, which need no rope,
No laboring arm, to crane their waters up,
Around your lawn their facile streams shall shower
And cheer the springing plant and opening flower.
There live, delighted with the rustic's lot, 220
And till with your own hands the little spot;
The little spot shall yield you large amends
And glad with many a feast your Samian friends.
And sure—in any corner we can get,
To call one lizard ours, is something yet. 225

Flushed with a mass of indigested food,
Which clogs the stomach and inflames the blood,
What crowds, with watching wearied and o'erprest,
Curse the slow hours and died for want of rest!
For who can hope his languid lids to close 230
Where brawling taverns banish all repose?
Sleep, to the rich alone, "his visits pays:"
And hence the seeds of many a dire disease.
The carts loud rumbling through the narrow way,
The drivers' clamors at each casual stay, 235
From drowsy Drusus would his slumber take,
And keep the calves of Proteus broad awake!

If business calls, obsequious crowds divide,
While o'er their heads the rich securely ride,
By tall Illyrians borne, and read or write, 240
Or (should the early hour to rest invite)
Close the soft litter and enjoy the night.
Yet reach they first the goal; while, by the throng
Elbowed and jostled, scarce we creep along;
Sharp strokes from poles, tubs, rafters, doomed to feel, 245
And plastered o'er with mud from head to heel;
While the rude soldier gores us as he goes,
Or marks in blood his progress on our toes!

See, from the Dole a vast tumultuous throng,
Each followed by his kitchen, pours along! 250
Huge pans, which Corbulo could scarce uprear,

With steady neck a puny slave must bear,
And, lest amid the way the flames expire,
Glide nimbly on and, gliding, fan the fire; 254
Through the close press with sinuous efforts wind,
And piece by piece leave his botched rags behind.

Hark! groaning on, the unwieldy wagon spreads
Its cumbrous load, tremendous! o'er our heads,
Projecting elm or pine, that nods on high
And threatens death to every passerby. 260
Heavens! should the axle crack, which bears a weight
Of huge Ligurian stone, and pour the freight
On the pale crowd beneath, what would remain,
What joint, what bone, what atom of the slain?
The body, with the soul, would vanish quite, 265
Invisible as air to mortal sight!—
Meanwhile, unconscious of their fellow's fate,
At home they heat the water, scour the plate,
Arrange the strigils, fill the cruse with oil,
And ply their several tasks with fruitless toil. 270
For he who bore the dole, poor mangled ghost,
Sits pale and trembling on the Stygian coast,
Scared at the horrors of the novel scene,
At Charon's threatening voice and scowling mien;
Nor hopes a passage, thus abruptly hurled 275
Without his farthing to the nether world

Pass we these fearful dangers, and survey
What other evils threat our nightly way.
And first, behold the mansion's towering size,
Where floors on floors to the tenth story rise; 280
Whence heedless garretteers their potsherds throw,
And crush the unwary wretch that walks below!
Clattering, the storm descends from heights unknown,
Ploughs up the street, and wounds the flinty stone!
'Tis madness, dire improvidence of ill, 285
To sup abroad before you sign your will,
Since fate in ambush lies and marks his prey
From every wakeful window in the way.
Pray, then—and count your humble prayer well sped
If pots be only—emptied on your head. 290

The drunken bully, ere his man be slain,
Frets through the night and courts repose in vain,
And while the thirst of blood his bosom burns,
From side to side in restless anguish turns, 294
Like Peleus' son when, quelled by Hector's hand,
His loved Patroclus pressed the Phrygian strand.

There are, who murder as an opiate take,
And only when no brawls await them wake.
Yet even these heroes, flushed with youth and wine,
All contest with the purple robe decline; 300
Securely give the lengthened train to pass,
The sun-bright flambeaux and the lamps of brass.
Me, whom the moon or candle's paler gleam,

223. **Samian friends,** followers of Pythagoras of Samos, who ate nothing but vegetables. 225. **To call one lizard ours.** According to Dr. Johnson, this means to own "as much ground as one may have a chance to find a lizard upon." 236–237. **From drowsy Drusus . . . awake!** Both the Emperor Tiberius (Drusus) and seals in the sea (the calves of Proteus) were thought to sleep soundly. 249–250. **See, from the Dole . . . pours along!** The Roman dole, a feature of Roman life throughout the empire, often consisted of food rather than money, in which case the needy citizens might have their slaves bring along portable kitchens to cook the food in the street. 251. **Corbulo,** a famous strong man.

262. **Ligurian stone,** marble. 299–302. **Yet even these heroes . . . lamps of brass.** The impudent street-bully still is wise enough not to attack the rich man, with his large retinue of attendants.

Whose wick I husband to the last extreme,
Guides through the gloom, he braves, devoid of
    fear.   305
The prelude to our doughty quarrel, hear—
If that be deemed a quarrel where, heaven knows,
He only gives, and I receive, the blows!
Across my path he strides, and bids me stand!
I bow, obsequious to the dread command;   310
What else remains where madness, rage combine
With youth and strength superior far to mine?
    "Whence come you, rogue?" he cries; "whose
      beans tonight
Have stuffed you thus? What cobbler clubbed his
    mite
For leeks and sheep's-head porridge? Dumb! quite
    dumb!   315
Speak, or be kicked. —Yet once again! Your home?
Where shall I find you? At what beggar's stand
(Temple or bridge) whimp'ring with outstretched
    hand?"
    Whether I strive some humble plea to frame
Or steal in silence by, 'tis just the same: 320
I'm beaten first, then dragged in rage away;
Bound to the peace or punished for the fray!
    Mark here the boasted freedom of the poor!
Beaten and bruised, that goodness to adore,
Which, at their humble prayer, suspends its ire   325
And sends them home with yet a bone entire.
    Nor this the worst; for when deep midnight reigns,
And bolts secure our doors, and massy chains,
When noisy inns a transient silence keep,
And harassed nature woos the balm of sleep,   330
Then thieves and murderers ply their dreadful trade,
With stealthy steps our secret couch invade.
Roused from the treacherous calm, aghast we start,
And the fleshed sword—is buried in our heart!
    Hither from bogs, from rocks, and caves pursued
(The Pontine marsh and Gallinarian wood),   336
The dark assassins flock, as to their home,
And fill with dire alarm the streets of Rome.
Such countless multitudes our peace annoy
That bolts and shackles every forge employ,   340
And cause so wide a waste, the country fears
A want of ore for mattocks, rakes, and shares.
    O! happy were our sires, estranged from crimes;
And happy, happy, were the good old times,
Which saw, beneath their kings', their tribunes' reign,
One cell the nation's criminals contain!   346
    Much could I add, more reasons could I cite,
If time were ours, to justify my flight;
But see! the impatient team is moving on,
The sun declining; and I must be gone.   350
Long since, the driver murmured at my stay
And jerked his whip to beckon me away.

Farewell, my friend! with this embrace we part;
Cherish my memory ever in your heart.
And when from crowds and business you repair   355
To breathe at your Aquinum freer air,
Fail not to draw me from my loved retreat
To Elvine Ceres and Diana's seat.
For your bleak hills my Cumae I'll resign,
And (if you blush not at such aid as mine)   360
Come well equipped to wage in angry rhymes
Fierce war with you on follies and on crimes.

Martial

c. 40–c. 104 A.D.

Though considerably older than Juvenal, Martial was apparently his close friend and saluted him in three of his epigrams. Their friendship seems appropriate, for both were caustic, dissatisfied men who have left equally sinister impressions of their age. Marcus Valerius Martialis was born and educated in Roman Spain, but gravitated to the capital in 64 A.D. to seek his fortune. His first patrons, Seneca and Lucan, were also Spaniards, but their fall from power under Nero cast a shadow over Martial's career. His later success was modest at best, but in his search for it he accumulated many acquaintances and a cynical understanding of city people.

Martial specialized in the tiniest of literary forms, the epigram. Each of his 1561 epigrams (arranged in fifteen books) is a brief, pithy poem with its own unity and a sting or surprise at the end. Imported from Greece, the type became completely Roman in Martial through the force of his mordant wit and spicy humor.

At bottom, Martial is a keen social critic who brings Imperial Rome to life with less exaggeration than Juvenal. He has an ever-watchful eye for meaningful details, and from his many little observations we can build a fairly accurate picture of the city. His approach is straightforward and free from Juvenal's rhetoric. Friends appear for direct tribute, but his enemies are disguised, since his satiric purpose is to attack vices, not persons. We must overlook the cringing sycophancy of his poems to patrons and his gross vulgarity in many places. What remains is the ironic or sportive jests of a highly original talent that seems ever fresh and vigorous.

Post-Obits and the Poets

He unto whom thou art so partial
    Oh, reader! is the well-known Martial,
The Epigrammatist: while living,
Give him the fame thou wouldst be giving;
So shall he hear, and feel, and know it—   5
    Post-obits rarely reach a poet.

---

336. **Pontine marsh and Gallinarian wood,** two notorious haunts of bandits. 346. **One cell . . . contain!** This refers to the Mamertine prison, for many years the only one in Rome.

356–358. **Aquinum . . . Diana's seat.** Juvenal was probably born in Aquinum near the shrine of Ceres and Diana.
Post-Obits and the Poets. Translated by Lord Byron.

To His Book

To read my book, the virgin shy
   May blush, while Brutus standeth by;
But when he's gone, read through what's writ,
And never stain a cheek for it.

"'Tis Wise to Forget"

I may have asked you here to dine,
   But that was late at night,
And none of us had spared the wine
   If I remember right.
You thought the invitation meant,   5
   Though wine obscured my wit!
And—O most parlous precedent—
   You made a note of it!
The maxim that in Greece was true
   Is true in Rome to-day—   10
"I hate a fellow-toper who
   Remembers what I say."

On Acerra

He reeks, you might think, of his yesterday's
   drink;
   But knowing his customs and ways,
You are wrong, I'll be sworn, for he drank till the
   morn,
   So the savor is truly to-day's.

To Diaulus

A surgeon once, you now begin
   As undertaker's man,
To earn a bedside practice in
   The only way you can.

Moderation

You bid me say what kind of maid
   Can draw me or repel?
My friend, I hate a forward jade
   But loathe a prude as well.
I love the mean: extremes are vain   5
   And never bring me joy;
Love long denied is grief and pain,
   While easy favors cloy.

To His Book. Translated by Robert Herrick.
"'Tis Wise to Forget"; On Acerra; To Diaulus; Moderation. Translated by J. A. Pott. From *The Epigrams* of *Martial* by J. A. Pott and F. A. Wright. Reprinted by permission of Routledge and Kegan Paul, Ltd.

Non Amo Te

I do not love thee, Doctor Fell,
   The reason why I cannot tell;
But this alone I know full well,
I do not love thee, Doctor Fell.

On Charinus

His health is good, yet he is always pale;
   He drinks but little, 'tis of no avail,
So wan his face no sun can darken it,
And good digestion aids him not a whit,
Not even rouge that pallid cheek can flush—   5
And e'en his vices do not make him blush!

To Bithynicus

Though you hope that her cough will soon
   carry her off,
   For gasping and swooning is she,
Do not flatter yourself that you'll finger her pelf;
   For her faint is a feint with an "e."

To Naevia

You would not carve the hare: it was not
   basted,
So you declared: the mullet went untasted:
The boar was more than high—our senses proved
   it—
You called it "over-fresh," and then removed it.
"Uneatable and raw," you kept repeating;   5
In proof whereof you gave your cook a beating.
A vain excuse; we're safe beyond all question.
A meal of nothing gives no indigestion.

To Apicius

You had spent sixty thousand on gorging your
   fill,
And there only remained a poor ten thousand still.
That to you was starvation; so into your cup
You poured deadly poison and drank the lot up.
You were always a gourmet, of that I am sure;   5
But by death you were proved the complete epicure.

Non Amo Te. Translated by Tom Brown.
On Charinus; To Bithynicus; To Naevia; To Apicius. Translated by J. A. Pott. From *The Epigrams of Martial* by J. A. Pott and F. A. Wright. Reprinted by permission of Routledge and Kegan Paul, Ltd.

On a Bas-Relief

THEY'RE Pheidias' fish, engraved by him,
Add water—and behold they swim.

To Ligurinus

YOU never your friends, sir, to dinner invite
Except when you have some bad verse to
recite.
We have scarcely sat down when on our weary ears
Comes the sound of "Book One," ere the *hors-
d'oeuvre* appears.
You read through Book Two while the entrée we
wait;   5
Book Three makes dessert and the savory late.
Then comes Number Four and at last Number Five:
Even dainties so frequent a surfeit would give.
If you won't to the waste-paper merchant consign
Your poems, in future alone you must dine.

To Chloë

I COULD resign that eye of blue
Howe'er its splendor used to thrill me;
And even that cheek of roseate hue,—
To lose it, Chloë, scarce would kill me.
That snowy neck I ne'er should miss,   5
However much I've raved about it;
And sweetly as that lip can kiss,
I *think* I could exist without it.
In short, so well I've learned to fast,
That, sooth my love, I know not whether   10
I might not bring myself at last,
To—do without you altogether.

To Polla

LEAVE off thy paint, perfumes, and youthful
dress,
And nature's failing honestly confess;
Double we see those faults which art would mend,
Plain downright ugliness would less offend.

On a Bas-Relief. Translated by J. A. Pott. From *The Epigrams of
Martial* by J. A. Pott and F. A. Wright. Reprinted by permission of
Routledge and Kegan Paul, Ltd.
1. **Pheidias,** the great Greek sculptor.
To Ligurinus. Translated by F. A. Wright. From *The Epigrams of
Martial* by J. A. Pott and F. A. Wright. Reprinted by permission
of Routledge and Kegan Paul, Ltd.
To Chloë. Translated by Thomas Moore.
To Polla. Translated by Sir Charles Sedley.

A Total Abstainer

THOUGH you serve richest wines,
Paulus, Rumor opines
That they poisoned your four wives, I think.
It's of course all a lie;
None believes less than I—   5
No, I really don't care for a drink.

The Author's Reward

'TIS my fifth book of merry verse,
Yet no man has protested,
Or said he is one whit the worse,
So gently I have jested.
But many a reader finds his name   5
Is honored in my pages,
And these rejoice to know their fame
Will last throughout the ages.
"Such tributes all are profitless,
For no one will requite them"—   10
They bring no money, I confess,
And yet I love to write them.

Procrastination

TO-MORROW you will live, you always cry;
In what far country does this morrow lie,
That 'tis so mighty long ere it arrive?
Beyond the Indies does this morrow live?
'Tis so far fetched, this morrow, that I fear   5
'Twill be both very old and very dear.
To-morrow I will live, the fool does say;
To-day itself's too late: the wise lived yesterday.

To Maximus

SYRISCUS a full hundred thousand received
From his patron, and though it will scarce be
believed,
He managed at taverns to squander the lot
About the four baths, drinking pot after pot.
What a thirst he must have such a fortune to drown,
And to do it too standing, without sitting down.   6

A Total Abstainer. Translated by Paul Nixon. From *A Roman Wit*
by Paul Nixon. Reprinted by permission of Houghton Mifflin Company.
The Author's Reward. Translated by J. A. Pott. **To Maximus.** Translated by F. A. Wright. From *The Epigrams of Martial* by J. A. Pott
and F. A. Wright. Reprinted by permission of Routledge and Kegan
Paul, Ltd.
Procrastination. Translated by Abraham Cowley.

Return Favors

WHY don't I send my book to you
    Although you often urge me to?
The reason's good, for if I did
You'd send me yours—which God forbid!

Galla's Hair

THE golden hair that Galla wears
    Is hers: who would have thought it?
She swears 'tis hers, and true she swears,
    For I know where she bought it.

On an Ant
in Amber

THE amber dripped from Phaethon's fair tree
    And whelmed a petty ant that wandered there,
And, though of little worth in life was she,
    Now in her death she is a treasure rare.

Respectability

NOW, a suspected past to cover,
    You make a husband of your lover,
Lest law should visit your transgression;
This is not marriage but confession!

A Promising Youth

AT sixty years of age is he
    A man of promise still:
Methinks he needs eternity
    That promise to fulfill.

To Quintus

YOUR birthday I wished to observe with a gift;
    You forbade, and your firmness is known.
    Every man to his taste:
    I remark with some haste,
May the third is the date of my own.

Return Favors; On an Ant in Amber; Respectability; A Promising Youth. Translated by J. A. Pott. From *The Epigrams of Martial,* by Pott and Wright. Reprinted by permission of Routledge and Kegan Paul, Ltd.
Galla's Hair. Translated by Sir John Harington.
To Quintus; Union Labor. Translated by Paul Nixon. From *A Roman Wit* by Paul Nixon. Reprinted by permission of Houghton Mifflin Company.

To a Rival Poet

YOUR verses are full of a sugary grace,
    As spotless and pure as a well-powdered
      face,
Not an atom of salt or suspicion of gall,
So how can they but on an audience pall!
Even food does not please if the cooking's too
      simple,   5
And cheeks lack in charm when they haven't a dim-
      ple.
A child may like apples and figs without savor;
But give me the sort that have got a sharp flavor.

Presentation Copies

PRESENT you with my books? Not I indeed.
    I know you want to sell them, not to read.

Union Labor

BY the time the Barber Eurus
    Had circled Lupo's face,
A second beard had sprouted
    In the first one's place.

False Appearances

HE makes parade of poverty—a plot
    To make us think him rich when he is not.

The Cook

BECAUSE I beat my cook who spoilt the dinner
    You say, "Oh cruel wretch, oh greedy sinner,
Such penalties for greater faults are fit."
What greater crime, I ask, can cooks commit?

On Picentinus' Marriage
with Galla

SEVEN husbands she got,
    Made away with the lot
    And has buried them all—but I know
That as you're number eight,
She has not long to wait   5
    Before she rejoins them—below.

To a Rival Poet. Translated by F. A. Wright. *Presentation Copies; False Appearances; The Cook; On Picentinus' Marriage with Galla.* Translated by J. A. Pott. From *The Epigrams of Martial* by Pott and Wright. Reprinted by permission of Routledge and Kegan Paul, Ltd.

A Productive Estate

SEVEN wives you've had and all of them lie
    buried in your field;
I don't suppose that any land could boast more rich
    a yield.

What Makes
a Happy Life

WHAT makes a happy life, dear friend,
    If thou wouldst briefly learn, attend—
An income left, not earned by toil;
Some acres of a kindly soil;
The pot unfailing on the fire;   5
No lawsuits, seldom town attire;
Health, strength with grace; a peaceful mind;
Shrewdness with honesty combined;
Plain living; equal friends and free;
Evenings of temperate gayety;   10
A wife discreet yet blithe and bright;
Sound slumber that lends wings to night.
With all thy heart embrace thy lot,
Wish not for death, and fear it not.

To Lupus

YOU gave me a farm—so you called it, at least,
    In a sort of rhetorical turn—
But I'm forced to relate that the total estate
    Doesn't hold as much dirt as an urn.

A grove of Diana, you told me, I think,   5
    Was a notable sight on the place:
But beyond one poor beet, overcome by the heat,
    Of grove I deny there's a trace.

The wing of a cricket would cover that farm,
    And an overfed ant with the gout   10
Couldn't find enough crops to tickle his chops
    To last till the sun flickered out.

Moreover that garden you bragged so about
    Proves a worm-eaten rose with one leaf,
And the lawn's yield of grass doesn't greatly sur-
        pass   15
    Its produce of gravy and beef.

A cucumber hasn't got room to lie straight,
    And a snake's bound to live there in pieces.
A grasshopper hopped just one day and then
    stopped—
    Starved to death, with its stomach in creases.   20

A mole is the sole agriculturist there,
    And he's hardly got room to turn around.
Why, a mushroom can't spread, or a flower wave its
    head
    Sans trespass on my neighbor's ground.

An undergrown mouse when he gets at that farm
    Makes it look as though hit by the plague,   26
And my whole crop of hay was carried away
    By a thrush hardly out of the egg.

A statue of Pan—minus head, legs, and trunk—
    Casts its shade over all the domain: 30
And the shell of a clam, without sign of a jam,
    My harvest complete can contain.

Now pardon, my friend, if my praise has been
    faint—
    We can seldom express what we feel:
So I merely will add that I'd be mighty glad   35
    To swap farm for a thirty-cent meal.

To Fabullus

OF all the guests you ask to dine
    I know not one, so I decline;
Why should you grumble? 'Tis not rude
To hate a crowded solitude.

A Hinted Wish

YOU told me, Maro, whilst you live
    You'd not a single penny give,
But that, whene'er you chanct to die,
You'd leave a handsome legacy:
You must be mad beyond redress,   5
If my next wish you cannot guess!

A Pretty Pair

SAYS your wife with a sneer, "You're the lady-
    maid's dear,"
    And she mocks at your conduct as shady;
But well-matched you must be; 'tis notorious that
    she
    Is the gentleman's gentleman's lady!

A Productive Estate. Translated by J. A. Pott. From *The Epigrams of Martial* by Pott and Wright. Reprinted by permission of Routledge and Kegan Paul, Ltd.
What Makes a Happy Life. Translated by Goldwin Smith. From *Bay Leaves*, by Goldwin Smith. Published by The Macmillan Company, 1893.
To Lupus. Translated by Paul Nixon. From *A Roman Wit* by Paul Nixon. Reprinted by permission of Houghton Mifflin Company.

To Fabullus; A Pretty Pair. Translated by J. A. Pott. From *The Epigrams of Martial* by Pott and Wright. Reprinted by permission of Routledge and Kegan Paul, Ltd.
A Hinted Wish. Translated by Samuel Johnson.

GENERAL INDEX

The name of an author represented by selections appears in capitals and small capitals (Aelus); the number in boldface after the name is the page on which his biographical sketch begi
Selections that are reprinted in this book are listed in boldface italic; the number in bold
after the title is the page on which the selection begins; the other numbers are pages on whic
is mentioned.

Epic, defined, 97–98; in Greece, 98
Epic Period of Greek literature, 97
Epictetus, 322, 333
Epicure, The, **304**
Epicureanism, in Rome, 323
Epicurus, and influence on Lucretius, 342; philosophy of, 323
Epidaurus, Theater of, 99; *pictured,* 100
Epigram, use by Martial, 436
Epistles, of Horace, 402
Eratosthenes, 106
Eros, 88
Etruscans, 318
Euclid, 106
Eudemian Ethics, 286
Eumenides, The, 93; *see Furies, The.*
EURIPIDES, 99, 101, **212**; influence on Seneca, 329; satirized by Aristophanes, 228
Excursion, The, **26**
Extremum Tanain, 407

"Fair and Colder," **403**
Faith Renewed, **405**
False Appearances, **439**
Farewell, A, **314**
Farewell to Anactoria, **302**
Fasces, 320
Fate, in Greek tragedy, 195
Five Classics, 17
Forgotten, **302**
Fourth Eclogue, 329. *See Eclogue IV (The Messiah).*
Fragments, **302**
Frogs, The, 102, 194, 212, 228
Funeral Speech of Pericles, **251**, **252**
Furies, in Greek mythology, 88, 89
Furies, The, 172

Galla's Hair, **439**
Garland for Heliodora, A, **313**
Gaul, subdued by Caesar, 319
Gauls, early conquest of Rome, 318
Gautama Buddha. *See* Buddha.
Georgic, invention of, 98
Georgics, 329, 367
Ghettos, 16
Girl, A, **302**
Gita, The, **30**
Gladiators, Roman, 328
GLAUCUS, **311**
Gold, Age of, 89
Golden Age, of Athens, 91; and Greek literature, 97; of Rome, 329
Grapes, **314**
Grasshopper, The, **305**
Gravitas, as Roman ideal, 321
Greece, annexed by Rome, 318–319; geography of, 85–86; Macedonian conquest of, 105; *see* Greeks.

Greek Anthology, The, **310**
Greeks, art of, 96–97; attitude toward women, 94–95; and athletics, 95; compared to Romans, 320–321; drama of, 98–102; government of, 91–92; and Hellenistic culture, 106–108; historians of, 102–104; history, 87–93, 105–108; influence on Christianity, 331; influence on Rome, 108; language of, 88; literary Renaissance of, 295; and lyric, 98; periods of literature, 97–98; philosophers of, 104–105; point of view of, 93–97; and public life, 95; religion of, 88–89, 93, 94; and slavery, 94

Hades, 88; Greek concept of, 94
Hadrian, and Greek Renaissance, 295; as Roman Emperor, 326
Hamilcar, 318
Hannibal, assisted by Macedonia, 108; in Punic Wars, 318
Hard Road, The, **24**
Heavyweight, A, **312**
Hebrews, agricultural life, 72; cultural characteristics, 3; Diaspora of, 15–16; effect on Christianity, 3–4; history, 12–16; music of, 72; prophets of, 13–14; and rabbinical law, 16; settling of Canaan, 12; and Zionism, 16
Hector, 109
Helen, 109
Hellas. *See* Greece.
Hellenes. *See* Greeks.
Hellenica, 102
Hellenistic culture, 106–108, 295
Hellenistic period of Greek literature, 97–98
Hephaestos, 88
Hera, 88
Heracles, and Age of Bronze, 89
Heraclitus, **311**
Herodotus, 97, 102; compared to Thucydides, 251
Heroes, Age of, 89
Heroides, 421
Hesiod, 98; and ages of man, 89; and Greek religion, 88; influence on Virgil, 329
Hesperus The Bringer, **303**
Himalayas, influence on Hindus, 9
Hindu, caste system, 3, 9
Hinduism, 9–10; influence on West, 7–8
Hinted Wish, A, **440**
Hippolytus, **213**, **214**
Historians, Greek, 102–104; Roman, 330
History, origin of, 102
History, of Herodotus, 97, 102
History of the Peloponnesian War, 102, 251; *see Funeral Speech of Pericles* and *Melian Dialogue*
Holiday, 407
Holy Land. *See* Israel.
HOMER, 95, **109**; and Age of Heroes, 89; importance to Greeks, 94; influence on Virgil, 329, 367

HORACE (QUINTUS HORATIUS FLACCUS), 328, 329, 330, **401**

Idyll, invention of the form, 106
Idylls, of Theocritus, 306
Iliad, The, 109, 111
Immortality of Verse, The, **407**
In the Quiet Night, 24
India, cultural characteristics, 3, 7–9; geography, 8–9; literature, 9, 10–12; *see* Hinduism.
Inscription By the Sea, An, 311
Ionians, characteristics of, 90–91
Iphigenia, sacrifice of, 109, 172
Iphigenia at Aulis, 101, 212
Iron, Age of, 89
Israel, as Promised Land, 12
Israelites. *See* Hebrews.
Italy, geography of, 317–318

Jason, 89
Jeremiah, 13–14
Jerome, 331
Jerusalem, capture of, 13; rebuilding of, 15; siege by Titus, 15
Jesus, as Messiah of Jews, 15
Jews. *See* Hebrews.
Johanan ben Zakkai, 15
Jonah, 73, **80**
Journey's End, **419**
Judah, two tribes of, 13
Judah Halevi, 16
Judaism, becomes monotheism, 15; effect on Christianity, 3–4; spread of, 15
JULIANUS ANTECESSOR, **311**
Juno, 321
Jupiter, 321
Justinian, and Roman law, 332
JUVENAL (DECIMUS JUNIUS JUVENALIS), 325, 329, 330, **432**

KALIDASA, 11, **40**
Kena-Upanishad, **28**
Kings, Greek, 89
Knights, The, 102, 228
"Know thyself," as Greek motto, 94
Krishna, 30
Kronos, 88

Lalage, **404**
Lao-Tzŭ, founding of Taoism, 5
Lares, 321
Last Journey, The, **312**
Latin, influence on languages, 331–332; origin of, 318
Latins, 318
Law, The, in Hebrew Bible, 72
Laws, 259, 333
LEONIDAS, of Alexandria, **311**

LEONIDAS, of Tarentum, **312**
Lesbos, 98, 301
Li, and Confucius, 17
LI PO, **22**
Libation-Bearers, The, 93, 172
Life a Bane, **314**
Life a Boon, **314**
Livy, 329, 330
Lost Desire, **313**
Love, **304**
Love at the Door, **313**
"Love Is Best," **418**
Love-Sick Athlete, The, **403**
Lover's Posy, The, **314**
LUCIAN, **295**
LUCILIUS, **312**, 432
LUCRETIUS (TITUS LUCRETIUS CARUS), 323, 324, **342**
Lyceum, of Aristotle, 104, 285
Lyric, origin in Greece, 98
Lyric Period of Greek literature, 97, 98
Lysistrata, 228

Maccabeus, Judas, 15
Macedonia, Alexander of, 105–106; annexed by Rome, 319; and conquest of Greece, 105; Philip of, 105; and spread of Greek culture, 106
Maecenas, 328, 401; as patron of literature, 329
Magna Graecia, 318
Mahâbhârata, 11, **30**
Marathon, Battle of, 92
Marcus Aurelius. *See* Antoninus.
Mars, 321
MARTIAL (MARCUS VALERIUS MARTIALIS), 325, 330, 331, **436**
Masks, in Greek theater, 99
Maya, 10
Medea, of Seneca, 330
Meditations, 326
MELEAGER, 310, **312**, **313**
Melian Dialogue, 251, **255**
Memorabilia, 258
Menaechmi Twins, The, 354
Menander, influence on Plautus, 354; and New Comedy, 228
Mencius, and Confucianism, 6
Menelaus, 109
Messiah, The (Eclogue IV), 329, **368**
Metamorphoses, 330, 421, **425**
Metaphysics, of Aristotle, 286
METRODORUS, **314**
Mishna, 16
Moderation, **437**
Moral Epistles, 330
Moses, 12
Mother, I Cannot Mind My Wheel, **303**
Muses, in Greek mythology, 88
Museum, of Alexandria, 106

10 11 12 13 14 15 16 17 18 19 20 21 22 23 24 25 K 65 64 63 62

Design (Eddie Fischer)

Unity - dominant motif
Variety - repetition with
              difference
Harmony - fitness
Balance - formal, informal

symmetrical   assymetrical

Area of golden mean between
½ and ⅓ and ⅓ and ⅔
mathematical center, visual
center and aesthetic (center?)

Unity, theme
like with like
Harmony, intro-
duction appro-
priate to theme.
Tail grows out
of animal

Life not absurd & chaotic
Everything must have design
or the human mind re-
jects it.